ALL GLORY TO ŚRĪ GURU AND GAURĀṄGA

ŚRĪMAD BHĀGAVATAM

of

KṚṢṆA - DVAIPĀYANA VYĀSA

कृष्णे स्वधामोपगते धर्मज्ञानादिभिः सह।
कलौ नष्टदृशामेष पुराणार्कोऽधुनोदितः ॥४३॥

kṛṣṇe sva-dhāmopagate
dharma-jñānādibhiḥ saha
kalau naṣṭa-dṛśām eṣa
purāṇārko 'dhunoditaḥ
(*Śrīmad-Bhāgavatam* 1.3.43)

Books by His Divine Grace
A. C. Bhaktivedanta Swami Prabhupāda:

Bhagavad-gītā As It Is
Śrīmad-Bhāgavatam (1st to 10th Cantos)
Śrī Caitanya-Caritāmṛta (9 vols.)
Kṛṣṇa, The Supreme Personality of Godhead
Teachings of Lord Caitanya
The Nectar of Devotion
The Nectar of Instruction
Śrī Īśopaniṣad
Light of the Bhāgavata
Easy Journey to Other Planets
The Science of Self-Realization
Kṛṣṇa Consciousness: The Topmost Yoga System
Perfect Questions, Perfect Answers
Teachings of Lord Kapila, the Son of Devahuti
Transcendental Teachings of Prahlāda Mahārāja
Teachings of Queen Kuntī
Kṛṣṇa, the Reservoir of Pleasure
The Path of Perfection
Life Comes from Life
Message of Godhead
The Perfection of Yoga
Beyond Birth and Death
On the Way to Kṛṣṇa
Rāja-vidyā: The King of Knowledge
Elevation to Kṛṣṇa Consciousness
Kṛṣṇa Consciousness: The Matchless Gift
Selected Verses from the Vedic Scriptures
Back to Godhead magazine (founder)

A complete catalogue is available upon request.
The Bhaktivedanta Book Trust, ISKCON Temple,
Hare Krishna Land, Juhu, Mumbai 400 049. India.
The above books are also available at ISKCON centers.
Please contact a center near to your place.

ŚRĪMAD BHĀGAVATAM

First Canto

"Creation"

With the Original Sanskrit Text,
Its Roman Transliteration, Synonyms,
Translation and Elaborate Purports

by

His Divine Grace
A.C.Bhaktivedanta Swami Prabhupāda
Founder - *Ācārya* of the International Society for Krishna Consciousness

THE BHAKTIVEDANTA BOOK TRUST

Readers interested in the subject matter of this book are invited by The Bhaktivedanta Book Trust to correspond with its secretary at the following address:

The Bhaktivedanta Book Trust
Hare Krishna Land,
Juhu, Mumbai 400 049, India.

Website / E-mail :
www.indiabbt.com
admin@indiabbt.com

Śrīmad Bhāgavatam First Canto (English)

First printing in India : 2,000 copies
Second to Eighteenth printings : 64,900 copies
Ninteenth printing, November 2018 : 7,000 copies

ISBN : 978-93-84564-01-8 (v. 1)
ISBN : 978-93-84564-00-1 (18-volume set)

Published and Printed by
The Bhaktivedanta Book Trust.

SJ1K

To

Śrīla Prabhupāda

Bhaktisiddhānta Sarasvatī

Gosvāmī Mahārāja

MY SPIRITUAL MASTER

On the 26th Annual Ceremony of His Disappearance Day

He lives forever by his divine instructions
and
the follower lives with him.

Table of Contents

CHAPTER TWO

Divinity and Divine Service   79

CHAPTER THREE

Kṛṣṇa Is the Source of All Incarnations   129

CHAPTER FOUR

Appearance of Śrī Nārada   183

CHAPTER FIVE

Nārada's Instructions on Śrīmad-Bhāgavatam for Vyāsadeva   213

CHAPTER SIX

Conversation Between Nārada and Vyāsadeva   269

CHAPTER SEVEN

The Son of Droṇa Punished 305

CHAPTER EIGHT

Prayers by Queen Kuntī and Parīkṣit Saved 363

CHAPTER NINE

The Passing Away of Bhīṣmadeva in the Presence of Lord Kṛṣṇa   **425**

CHAPTER TEN

Departure of Lord Kṛṣṇa for Dvārakā   **495**

CHAPTER ELEVEN

Lord Kṛṣṇa's Entrance into Dvārakā   **539**

CHAPTER TWELVE

Birth of Emperor Parīkṣit   591

CHAPTER THIRTEEN

Dhṛtarāṣṭra Quits Home   645

CHAPTER SEVENTEEN
Punishment and Reward of Kali   859

CHAPTER EIGHTEEN
Mahārāja Parīkṣit Cursed by a Brāhmaṇa Boy   909

Preface

We must know the present need of human society. And what is that need? Human society is no longer bounded by geographical limits to particular countries or communities. Human society is broader than in the Middle Ages, and the world tendency is toward one state or one human society. The ideals of spiritual communism, according to *Śrīmad-Bhāgavatam,* are based more or less on the oneness of the entire human society, nay, of the entire energy of living beings. The need is felt by great thinkers to make this a successful ideology. *Śrīmad-Bhāgavatam* will fill this need in human society. It begins, therefore, with an aphorism of Vedānta philosophy, *janmādy asya yataḥ,* to establish the ideal of a common cause.

Human society, at the present moment, is not in the darkness of oblivion. It has made rapid progress in the fields of material comforts, education and economic development throughout the entire world. But there is a pinprick somewhere in the social body at large, and therefore there are large-scale quarrels, even over less important issues. There is need of a clue as to how humanity can become one in peace, friendship and prosperity with a common cause. *Śrīmad-Bhāgavatam* will fill this need, for it is a cultural presentation for the respiritualization of the entire human society.

Śrīmad-Bhāgavatam should be introduced also in the schools and colleges, for it is recommended by the great student-devotee Prahlāda Mahārāja in order to change the demoniac face of society.

kaumāra ācaret prājño
dharmān bhāgavatān iha
durlabhaṁ mānuṣaṁ janma
tad apy adhruvam artha-dam
(Bhāg. 7.6.1)

Disparity in human society is due to lack of principles in a godless civilization. There is God, or the Almighty One, from whom everything emanates, by whom everything is maintained and in whom everything is merged to rest. Material science has tried to find the ultimate source of creation very insufficiently, but it is a fact that there is one ultimate source of everything that be. This ultimate source is explained rationally and authoritatively in the beautiful *Bhāgavatam,* or *Śrīmad-Bhāgavatam.*

Śrīmad-Bhāgavatam is the transcendental science not only for knowing the ultimate source of everything but also for knowing our relation with Him and our duty toward perfection of the human society on the basis of this perfect knowledge. It is powerful reading matter in the Sanskrit language, and it is now rendered into English elaborately so that simply by a careful reading one will know God perfectly well, so much so that the reader will be sufficiently educated to defend himself from the onslaught of atheists. Over and above this, the reader will be able to convert others to accepting God as a concrete principle.

Śrīmad-Bhāgavatam begins with the definition of the ultimate source. It is a bona fide commentary on the *Vedānta-sūtra* by the same author, Śrīla Vyāsadeva, and gradually it develops into nine cantos up to the highest state of God realization. The only qualification one needs to study this great book of transcendental knowledge is to proceed step by step cautiously and not jump forward haphazardly as with an ordinary book. It should be gone through chapter by chapter, one after another. The reading matter is so arranged with the original Sanskrit text, its English transliteration, synonyms, translation and purports so that one is sure to become a God-realized soul at the end of finishing the first nine cantos.

The Tenth Canto is distinct from the first nine cantos because it deals directly with the transcendental activities of the Personality of Godhead, Śrī Kṛṣṇa. One will be unable to capture the effects of the Tenth Canto without going through the first nine cantos. The book is complete in twelve cantos, each independent, but it is good for all to read them in small installments one after another.

I must admit my frailties in presenting *Śrīmad-Bhāgavatam,* but still I am hopeful of its good reception by the thinkers and leaders of society on the strength of the following statement of *Śrīmad-Bhāgavatam* (1.5.11):

tad-vāg-visargo janatāgha-viplavo
yasmin prati-ślokam abaddhavaty api
nāmāny anantasya yaśo 'ṅkitāni yac
chṛṇvanti gāyanti gṛṇanti sādhavaḥ

"On the other hand, that literature which is full of descriptions of the transcendental glories of the name, fame, form and pastimes of the unlimited Supreme Lord is a transcendental creation meant for bringing about a revolution in the impious life of a misdirected civilization. Such transcendental literature, even though irregularly composed, is heard, sung and accepted by purified men who are thoroughly honest."

Oṁ tat sat

A. C. Bhaktivedanta Swami

Foreword

"This *Bhāgavata Purāṇa* is as brilliant as the sun, and it has arisen just after the departure of Lord Kṛṣṇa to His own abode, accompanied by religion, knowledge, etc. Persons who have lost their vision due to the dense darkness of ignorance in the age of Kali shall get light from this *Purāṇa*." (*Śrīmad-Bhāgavatam* 1.3.43)

The timeless wisdom of India is expressed in the *Vedas*, ancient Sanskrit texts that touch upon all fields of human knowledge. Originally preserved through oral tradition, the *Vedas* were first put into writing five thousand years ago by Śrīla Vyāsadeva, the "literary incarnation of God." After compiling the *Vedas*, Vyāsadeva set forth their essence in the aphorisms known as *Vedānta-sūtras*. *Śrīmad-Bhāgavatam* (*Bhāgavata Purāṇa*) is Vyāsadeva's commentary on his own *Vedānta-sūtras*. It was written in the maturity of his spiritual life under the direction of Nārada Muni, his spiritual master. Referred to as "the ripened fruit of the tree of Vedic literature," *Śrīmad-Bhāgavatam* is the most complete and authoritative exposition of Vedic knowledge.

After compiling the *Bhāgavatam*, Vyāsa imparted the synopsis of it to his son, the sage Śukadeva Gosvāmī. Śukadeva Gosvāmī subsequently recited the entire *Bhāgavatam* to Mahārāja Parīkṣit in an assembly of learned saints on the bank of the Ganges at Hastināpura (now Delhi). Mahārāja Parīkṣit was the emperor of the world and was a great *rājarṣi* (saintly king). Having received a warning that he would die within a week, he renounced his entire kingdom and retired to the bank of the Ganges to fast until death and receive spiritual enlightenment. The *Bhāgavatam* begins with Emperor Parīkṣit's sober inquiry to Śukadeva Gosvāmī: "You are the spiritual master of great saints and devotees. I am therefore begging you to show the way of perfection for all persons, and especially for one who is about to die. Please let me know what a man should hear, chant, remember and worship, and also what he should not do. Please explain all this to me."

Śukadeva Gosvāmī's answer to this question, and numerous other questions posed by Mahārāja Parīkṣit, concerning everything from the nature of the self to the origin of the universe, held the assembled sages in rapt attention continuously for the seven days leading up to the king's death. The sage Sūta Gosvāmī, who was present in that assembly when Śukadeva Gosvāmī first recited *Śrīmad-Bhāgavatam*, later repeated the *Bhāgavatam* before a gathering of sages in the forest of Naimiṣāraṇya. Those sages, concerned about the spiritual welfare of the people in general, had gathered to perform a long, continuous chain of sacrifices to counteract the degrading influence of the incipient age of Kali. In response to the sages' request that he speak the essence of Vedic wisdom, Sūta Gosvāmī repeated from memory the entire eighteen thousand verses of *Śrīmad-Bhāgavatam*, as spoken by Śukadeva Gosvāmī to Mahārāja Parīkṣit.

The reader of *Śrīmad-Bhāgavatam* hears Sūta Gosvāmī relate the questions of Mahārāja Parīkṣit and the answers of Śukadeva Gosvāmī. Also, Sūta Gosvāmī sometimes responds directly to questions put by Śaunaka Ṛṣi, the spokesman for the sages gathered at Naimiṣāraṇya. One therefore simultaneously hears two dialogues: one between Mahārāja Parīkṣit and Śukadeva Gosvāmī on the bank of the Ganges, and another at Naimiṣāraṇya between Sūta Gosvāmī and the sages at Naimiṣāraṇya forest, headed by Śaunaka Ṛṣi. Futhermore, while instructing King Parīkṣit, Śukadeva Gosvāmī often relates historical episodes and gives accounts of lengthy philosophical discussions between such great souls as Nārada Muni and Vasudeva. With this understanding of the history of the *Bhāgavatam*, the reader will easily be able to follow its intermingling of dialogues and events from various sources. Since philosophical wisdom, not chronological order, is most important in the text, one need only be attentive to the subject matter of *Śrīmad-Bhāgavatam* to appreciate fully its profound message.

The translators of this edition compare the *Bhāgavatam* to sugar candy—wherever you taste it, you will find it equally sweet and relishable. Therefore, to taste the sweetness of the *Bhāgavatam*, one may begin by reading any of its volumes. After such an introductory taste, however, the serious reader is best advised to go back to the First Canto and then proceed through the *Bhāgavatam*, canto after canto, in its natural order.

This edition of the *Bhāgavatam* is the first complete English translation of this important text with an elaborate commentary, and it is the first widely available to the English-speaking public. The first twelve volumes (Canto One through Canto Ten, Part One) are the product of the scholarly and devotional effort of His Divine Grace A. C. Bhaktivedanta Swami Prabhupāda, the founder-*ācārya* of the International Society for Krishna Consciousness and the world's most distinguished teacher of Indian religious and Philosophical thought. His consummate Sanskrit scholarship and intimate familiarity with Vedic culture and thought as well as the modern way of life combine to reveal to the West a magnificent exposition of this important classic. After the departure of Śrīla Prabhupāda from this world in 1977, his monumental work of translating and annotating *Śrīmad-Bhāgavatam* has been continued by his disciples Hridayananda dāsa Goswami and Gopīparāṇadhana dāsa.

Readers will find this work of value for many reasons. For those interested in the classical roots of Indian civilization, it serves as a vast reservoir of detailed information on virtually every one of its aspects. For students of comparative philosophy and religion, the *Bhāgavatam* offers a penetrating view into the meaning of India's profound spiritual heritage. To sociologists and anthropologists, the *Bhāgavatam* reveals the practical workings of a peaceful and scientifically organized Vedic culture, whose institutions were integrated on the basis of a highly developed spiritual world view. Students of literature will discover the *Bhāgavatam* to be a masterpiece of majestic poetry. For students of psychology, the text provides important perspectives on the nature of consciousness, human behavior and the philosophical study of identity. Finally, to those seeking spiritual insight, the *Bhāgavatam* offers simple and practical guidance for attainment of the highest self-knowledge and realization of the Absolute Truth. The entire multivolume text, presented by the Bhaktivedanta Book Trust, promises to occupy a significant place in the intellectual, cultural and spiritual life of modern man for a long time to come.

—The Publishers

Introduction

The conception of God and the conception of Absolute Truth are not on the same level. The *Śrīmad-Bhāgavatam* hits on the target of the Absolute Truth. The conception of God indicates the controller, whereas the conception of the Absolute Truth indicates the *summum bonum* or the ultimate source of all energies. There is no difference of opinion about the personal feature of God as the controller because a controller cannot be impersonal. Of course modern government, especially democratic government, is impersonal to some extent, but ultimately the chief executive head is a person, and the impersonal feature of government is subordinate to the personal feature. So without a doubt whenever we refer to control over others we must admit the existence of a personal feature. Because there are different controllers for different managerial positions, there may be many small gods. According to the *Bhagavad-gītā* any controller who has some specific extraordinary power is called a *vibhūtimat sattva,* or controller empowered by the Lord. There are many *vibhūtimat sattvas,* controllers or gods with various specific powers, but the Absolute Truth is one without a second. This *Śrīmad-Bhāgavatam* designates the Absolute Truth or the *summum bonum* as the *paraṁ satyam.*

The author of *Śrīmad-Bhāgavatam,* Śrīla Vyāsadeva, first offers his respectful obeisances unto the *paraṁ satyam* (Absolute Truth), and because the *paraṁ satyam* is the ultimate source of all energies, the *paraṁ satyam* is the Supreme Person. The gods or the controllers are undoubtedly persons, but the *paraṁ satyam* from whom the gods derive powers of control is the Supreme Person. The Sanskrit word *īśvara* (controller) conveys the import of God, but the Supreme Person is called the *parameśvara,* or the supreme *īśvara.* The Supreme Person, or *parameśvara,* is the supreme conscious personality, and because He does not derive any power from any other source, He is supremely independent. In the Vedic literatures Brahmā is described as the supreme god or the head of all other gods like Indra, Candra and Varuṇa, but the *Śrīmad-Bhāgavatam* confirms that even Brahmā is not independent as far as his power and knowledge are concerned. He received knowledge in the form of the *Vedas* from the Supreme Person who resides within the heart of every living being. That Supreme Personality knows everything directly and indirectly. Individual infinitesimal persons, who are parts and parcels of the Supreme Personality, may know directly and indirectly everything about their bodies or external features, but the Supreme Personality knows everything about both His external and internal features.

The words *janmādy asya* suggest that the source of all production, maintenance or destruction is the same supreme conscious person. Even in our present experience we can know that nothing is generated from inert matter, but inert matter can be generated from the living entity. For instance, by contact with the living entity, the material body develops into a working machine. Men with a poor fund of knowledge mistake the bodily machinery to be the living being, but the fact is that the living being is the basis of the bodily machine. The bodily machine is useless as soon as the living spark is away from it. Similarly, the original source of all material energy is the Supreme Person. This fact is expressed in all the Vedic literatures, and all the exponents of spiritual science have accepted this truth. The living force is called Brahman, and one of the greatest *ācāryas* (teachers), namely Śrīpāda Śaṅkarācārya, has preached that Brahman is substance whereas the cosmic world is category. The original source of all energies is the living force, and He is logically accepted as the Supreme Person. He is therefore conscious of everything past, present and future, and also of each and every corner of His manifestations, both material and spiritual. An imperfect living being does not even know what is happening within his own personal body. He eats his food but does not know how this food is transformed into energy or how it sustains his body. When a living being is perfect, he is aware of everything that happens, and since the Supreme Person is all-perfect, it is quite natural that He knows everything in all detail. Consequently the perfect personality is addressed in the *Śrīmad-Bhāgavatam* as Vāsudeva, or one who lives everywhere in full consciousness and in full possession of His complete energy. All of this is clearly explained in the *Śrīmad-Bhāgavatam,* and the reader has ample opportunity to study this critically.

In the modern age Lord Śrī Caitanya Mahāprabhu preached the *Śrīmad-Bhāgavatam* by practical demonstration. It is easier to penetrate into the topics of the *Śrīmad-Bhāgavatam* through the medium of Śrī Caitanya's causeless mercy. Therefore a short sketch of His life and precepts is inserted herein to help the reader understand the real merit of *Śrīmad-Bhāgavatam.*

It is imperative that one learn the *Śrīmad-Bhāgavatam* from the person *Bhāgavatam.* The person *Bhāgavatam* is one whose very life is *Śrīmad-Bhāgavatam* in practice. Since Śrī Caitanya Mahāprabhu is the Absolute Personality of Godhead, He is both Bhagavān and *Bhāgavatam* in person and in sound. Therefore His process of approaching the *Śrīmad-Bhāgavatam* is practical for all people of the world. It was His wish that the *Śrīmad-Bhāgavatam* be preached in every nook and corner of the world by those who happened to take their birth in India.

The *Śrīmad-Bhāgavatam* is the science of Kṛṣṇa, the Absolute Personality of Godhead of whom we have preliminary information from the text of the *Bhagavad-gītā.* Śrī Caitanya Mahāprabhu has said that anyone, regardless of what he is, who is well versed in the science of Kṛṣṇa (*Śrīmad-Bhāgavatam* and *Bhagavad-gītā*) can become an authorized preacher or preceptor in the science of Kṛṣṇa.

There is a need for the science of Kṛṣṇa in human society for the good of all suffering humanity of the world, and we simply request the leaders of all nations to pick up this science of Kṛṣṇa for their own good, for the good of society and for the good of all the world's people.

A SHORT SKETCH OF THE LIFE AND TEACHINGS OF LORD CAITANYA, THE PREACHER OF ŚRĪMAD-BHĀGAVATAM

Lord Śrī Caitanya Mahāprabhu, the great apostle of love of God and the father of the congregational chanting of the holy name of the Lord, advented Himself at Śrīdhāma Māyāpura, a quarter in the city of Navadvīpa in Bengal, on the Phālgunī Pūrṇimā evening in the year 1407 Śakābda (corresponding to February 1486 by the Christian calendar).

His father, Śrī Jagannātha Miśra, a learned *brāhmaṇa* from the district of Sylhet, came to Navadvīpa as a student because at that time Navadvīpa was considered to be the center of education and culture. He domiciled on the banks of the Ganges after marrying Śrīmatī Śacīdevī, a daughter of Śrīla Nīlāmbara Cakravartī, the great learned scholar of Navadvīpa.

Jagannātha Miśra had a number of daughters by his wife, Śrīmatī Śacīdevī, and most of them expired at an early age. Two surviving sons, Śrī Viśvarūpa and Viśvambhara, became at last the object of their parental affection. The tenth and youngest son, who was named Viśvambhara, later became known as Nimāi Paṇḍita and then, after accepting the renounced order of life, Lord Śrī Caitanya Mahāprabhu.

Lord Śrī Caitanya Mahāprabhu exhibited His transcendental activities for forty-eight years and then disappeared in the year 1455 Śakābda at Purī.

For His first twenty-four years He remained at Navadvīpa as a student and householder. His first wife was Śrīmatī Lakṣmīpriyā, who died at an early age when the Lord was away from home. When He returned from East Bengal He was requested by His mother to accept a second wife, and He agreed. His second wife was Śrīmatī Viṣṇupriyā Devī, who bore the separation of the Lord throughout her life because the Lord took the order of *sannyāsa* at the age of twenty-four, when Śrīmatī Viṣṇupriyā was barely sixteen years old.

After taking *sannyāsa,* the Lord made His headquarters at Jagannātha Purī due to the request of His mother, Śrīmatī Śacīdevī. The Lord remained for twenty-four years at Purī. For six years of this time He traveled continuously all over India (and especially throughout southern India) preaching the *Śrīmad-Bhāgavatam.*

Lord Caitanya not only preached the *Śrīmad-Bhāgavatam* but propagated the teachings of the *Bhagavad-gītā* as well in the most practical way. In the *Bhagavad-gītā* Lord Śrī Kṛṣṇa is depicted as the Absolute Personality of Godhead, and His last teachings in that great book of transcendental knowledge instruct that one should give up all the modes of religious activities and accept Him (Lord Śrī Kṛṣṇa) as the *only* worshipable Lord. The Lord then assured that all His devotees would be protected from all sorts of sinful acts and that for them there would be no cause for anxiety.

Unfortunately, despite Lord Śrī Kṛṣṇa's direct order and the teachings of the *Bhagavad-gītā,* less intelligent people misunderstand Him to be nothing but a great historical personality, and thus they cannot accept Him as the original Personality of Godhead. Such men with a poor fund of knowledge are misled by many nondevotees. Thus the teachings of the *Bhagavad-gītā* were misinterpreted even by great scholars. After the disappearance of Lord Śrī Kṛṣṇa there were hundreds of commentaries on the *Bhagavad-gītā* by many erudite scholars, and almost every one of them was motivated by self-interest.

Lord Śrī Caitanya Mahāprabhu is the selfsame Lord Śrī Kṛṣṇa. This time, however, He appeared as a great devotee of the Lord in order to preach to the people in general, as well as to religionists and philosophers, about the transcendental position of Śrī Kṛṣṇa, the primeval Lord and the cause of all causes. The essence of His preaching is that Lord Śrī Kṛṣṇa, who appeared at Vrajabhūmi (Vṛndāvana) as the son of the King of Vraja (Nanda Mahārāja), is the Supreme Personality of Godhead and is therefore worshipable by all. Vṛndāvana-dhāma is nondifferent from the Lord because the name, fame, form and place where the Lord manifests Himself are all identical with the Lord as absolute knowledge. Therefore Vṛndāvana-dhāma is as worshipable as the Lord. The highest form of transcendental worship of the Lord was exhibited by the damsels of Vrajabhūmi in the form of pure affection for the Lord, and Lord Śrī Caitanya Mahāprabhu recommends this process as the most excellent mode of worship. He accepts the *Śrīmad-Bhāgavata Purāṇa* as the spotless literature for understanding the Lord, and He preaches that the ultimate goal of life for all human beings is to attain the stage of *premā,* or love of God.

Many devotees of Lord Caitanya like Śrīla Vṛndāvana dāsa Ṭhākura, Śrī Locana dāsa Ṭhākura, Śrīla Kṛṣṇadāsa Kavirāja Gosvāmī, Śrī Kavikarṇapūra, Śrī Prabodhānanda Sarasvatī, Śrī Rūpa Gosvāmī, Śrī Sanātana Gosvāmī, Śrī Raghunātha Bhaṭṭa Gosvāmī, Śrī Jīva Gosvāmī, Śrī Gopāla Bhaṭṭa Gosvāmī, Śrī Raghunātha dāsa Gosvāmī and in this latter age, within two hundred years, Śrī Viśvanātha Cakravartī, Śrī Baladeva Vidyābhūṣaṇa, Śrī Śyāmānanda Gosvāmī, Śrī Narottama dāsa Ṭhākura, Śrī Bhaktivinoda Ṭhākura and at last Śrī Bhaktisiddhānta Sarasvatī Ṭhākura (our spiritual master) and many other great and renowned scholars and devotees of the Lord have prepared voluminous books and literatures on the life and precepts of the Lord. Such literatures are all based on the *śāstras* like the *Vedas, Purāṇas, Upaniṣads, Rāmāyaṇa, Mahābhārata* and other histories and authentic literatures approved by the recognized *ācāryas.* They are unique in composition and unrivaled in presentation, and they are full of transcendental knowledge. Unfortunately the people of the world are still ignorant of them, but when these literatures, which are mostly in Sanskrit and Bengali, come to light the world and when they are presented before thinking people, then India's glory and the message of love will overflood this morbid world, which is vainly searching after peace and prosperity by various illusory methods not approved by the *ācāryas* in the chain of disciplic succession.

The readers of this small description of the life and precepts of Lord Caitanya will profit much to go through the books of Śrīla Vṛndāvana dāsa Ṭhākura (*Śrī Caitanya-bhāgavata*) and Śrīla Kṛṣṇadāsa Kavirāja Gosvāmī (*Śrī Caitanya-caritāmṛta*). The early life of the Lord is most fascinatingly expressed by the author of *Caitanya-bhāgavata,* and as far as the teachings are concerned, they are more vividly explained in the *Caitanya-caritāmṛta.* Now they are available to the English-speaking public in our *Teachings of Lord Caitanya.*

The Lord's early life was recorded by one of His chief devotees and contemporaries, namely Śrīla Murāri Gupta, a medical practitioner of that time, and the latter part of the life of Śrī Caitanya Mahāprabhu was recorded by His private secretary Śrī Dāmodara Gosvāmī, or Śrīla Svarūpa Dāmodara, who was practically a constant companion of the Lord at Purī. These two devotees recorded practically all the incidents of the Lord's activities, and later on all the books dealing with the Lord, which are above mentioned, were composed on the basis of *kaḍacās* (notebooks) by Śrīla Dāmodara Gosvāmī and Murāri Gupta.

So the Lord advented Himself on the Phālgunī Pūrṇimā evening of 1407 Śakābda, and it was by the will of the Lord that there was a lunar eclipse on that evening. During the hours of eclipse it was the custom of the Hindu public to take bath in the Ganges or any other sacred river and chant the Vedic *mantras* for purification. When Lord Caitanya was born during the lunar eclipse, all India was roaring with the holy sound of Hare Kṛṣṇa, Hare Kṛṣṇa, Kṛṣṇa Kṛṣṇa, Hare Hare/ Hare Rāma, Hare Rāma, Rāma Rāma, Hare Hare. These sixteen names of the Lord are mentioned in many *Purāṇas* and *Upaniṣads,* and they are described as the *Tāraka-brahma nāma* of this age. It is recommended in the *śāstras* that offenseless chanting of these holy names of the Lord can deliver a fallen soul from material bondage. There are innumerable names of the Lord both in India and outside, and all of them are equally good because all of them indicate the Supreme Personality of Godhead. But because these sixteen are especially recommended for this age, people should take advantage of them and follow the path of the great *ācāryas* who attained success by practicing the rules of the *śāstras* (revealed scriptures).

The simultaneous occurrence of the Lord's appearance and the lunar eclipse indicated the distinctive mission of the Lord. This mission was to preach the importance of chanting the holy names of the Lord in this age of Kali (quarrel). In this present age quarrels take place even over trifles, and therefore the *śāstras* have recommended for this age a common platform for realization, namely chanting the holy names of the Lord. People can hold meetings to glorify the Lord in their respective languages and with melodious songs, and if such performances are executed in an offenseless manner, it is certain that the participants will gradually attain spiritual perfection without having to undergo more rigorous methods. At such meetings everyone, the learned and the foolish, the rich and the poor, the Hindus and the Muslims, the Englishmen and the Indians, and the *caṇḍālas* and the *brāhmaṇas,* can all hear the transcendental sounds and thus cleanse the dust of material association from the mirror of the heart. To confirm the Lord's mission, all the people of the world will accept the holy name of the Lord as the common platform for the universal religion of mankind. In other words, the advent of the holy name took place along with the advent of Lord Śrī Caitanya Mahāprabhu.

When the Lord was on the lap of His mother, He would at once stop crying as soon as the ladies surrounding Him chanted the holy names and clapped their hands. This peculiar incident was observed by the neighbors with awe and veneration. Sometimes the young girls took pleasure in making the Lord cry and then stopping Him by chanting the holy name. So from His very childhood the Lord began to preach the importance of the holy name. In His early age Lord Śrī Caitanya was known as Nimāi. This name was given by His beloved mother because the Lord took His birth beneath a *nimba* tree in the courtyard of His paternal house.

When the Lord was offered solid food at the age of six months in the *anna-prāśana* ceremony, the Lord indicated His future activities. At this time it was customary to offer the child both coins and books in order to get some indication of the future tendencies of the child. The Lord was offered on one side coins and on the other the *Śrīmad-Bhāgavatam.* The Lord accepted the *Bhāgavatam* instead of the coins.

When He was a mere baby crawling in the yard, one day a snake appeared before Him, and the Lord began to play with it. All the members of the house were struck with fear and awe, but after a little while the snake went away, and the baby was taken away by His mother. Once He was stolen by a thief who intended to steal His ornaments, but the Lord took a pleasure trip on the shoulder of the bewildered thief, who was searching for a solitary place in order to rob the baby. It so happened that the thief, wandering hither and thither, finally arrived just before the house of Jagannātha Miśra and, being afraid of being caught, dropped the baby at once. Of course the anxious parents and relatives were glad to see the lost child.

Once a pilgrim *brāhmaṇa* was received at the house of Jagannātha Miśra, and when he was offering food to the Godhead, the Lord appeared before him and partook of the prepared food. The eatables had to be rejected because the child touched them, and so the *brāhmaṇa* had to make another preparation. The next time the same thing happened, and when this happened repeatedly for the third time, the baby was finally put to bed. At about twelve at night when all the members of the house were fast asleep within their closed rooms, the pilgrim *brāhmaṇa* offered his specially prepared foods to the Deity, and, in the same way, the baby Lord appeared before the pilgrim and spoiled his offerings. The *brāhmaṇa* then began to cry, but since everyone was fast asleep, no one could hear him. At that time the baby Lord appeared before the fortunate *brāhmaṇa* and disclosed His identity as Kṛṣṇa Himself. The *brāhmaṇa* was forbidden to disclose this incident, and the baby returned to the lap of His mother.

There are many similar incidents in His childhood. As a naughty boy He sometimes used to tease the orthodox *brāhmaṇas* who used to bathe in the

Ganges. When the *brāhmaṇas* complained to His father that He was splashing them with water instead of attending school, the Lord suddenly appeared before His father as though just coming from school with all His school clothes and books. At the bathing *ghāṭa* He also used to play jokes on the neighboring girls who engaged in worshiping Śiva in hopes of getting good husbands. This is a common practice amongst unmarried girls in Hindu families. While they were engaged in such worship, the Lord naughtily appeared before them and said, "My dear sisters, please give Me all the offerings you have just brought for Lord Śiva. Lord Śiva is My devotee, and Pārvatī is My maidservant. If you worship Me, then Lord Śiva and all the other demigods will be more satisfied." Some of them refused to obey the naughty Lord, and He would curse them that due to their refusal they would be married to old men who had seven children by their previous wives. Out of fear and sometimes out of love the girls would also offer Him various goods, and then the Lord would bless them and assure them that they would have very good young husbands and that they would be mothers of dozens of children. The blessings would enliven the girls, but they used often to complain of these incidents to their mothers.

In this way the Lord passed His early childhood. When He was just sixteen years old He started His own *catuṣpāṭhī* (village school conducted by a learned *brāhmaṇa*). In this school He would simply explain Kṛṣṇa, even in readings of grammar. Śrīla Jīva Gosvāmī, in order to please the Lord, later composed a grammar in Sanskrit, in which all the rules of grammar were explained with examples that used the holy names of the Lord. This grammar is still current. It is known as *Hari-nāmāmṛta-vyākaraṇa* and is prescribed in the syllabus of schools in Bengal.

During this time a great Kashmir scholar named Keśava Kāśmīri came to Navadvīpa to hold discussions on the *śāstras.* The Kashmir *paṇḍita* was a champion scholar, and he had traveled to all places of learning in India. Finally he came to Navadvīpa to contest the learned *paṇḍitas* there. The *paṇḍitas* of Navadvīpa decided to match Nimāi Paṇḍita (Lord Caitanya) with the Kashmir *paṇḍita,* thinking that if Nimāi Paṇḍita were defeated, they would have another chance to debate with the scholar, for Nimāi Paṇḍita was only a boy. And if the Kashmir *paṇḍita* were defeated, then they would even be more glorified because people would proclaim that a mere boy of Navadvīpa had defeated a champion scholar who was famous throughout India. It so happened that Nimāi Paṇḍita met Keśava Kāśmīri while strolling on the banks of the Ganges. The Lord requested him to compose a Sanskrit verse in praise of the Ganges, and the *paṇḍita* within a short time composed a hundred *ślokas,* reciting the verses like

His Divine Grace
A. C. Bhaktivedanta Swami Prabhupāda
Founder-Ācārya of ISKCON and greatest exponent of Kṛṣṇa consciousness in the modern world

Śrīla Jagannātha dāsa Bābājī Mahārāja

The instructing spiritual master of Śrīla Bhaktivinoda Ṭhākura

Śrīla Bhaktivinoda Ṭhākura

The pioneer of the program to inundate the entire world with Kṛṣṇa consciousness

Śrīla Bhaktisiddhānta Sarasvatī Gosvāmī Mahārāja

The spiritual master of His Divine Grace A. C. Bhaktivedanta Swami Prabhupāda and foremost scholar and devotee in the recent age

Śrīla Gaurakiśora dāsa Bābājī Mahārāja

The spiritual master of Śrīla Bhaktisiddhānta Sarasvatī Gosvāmī and intimate student of Śrīla Bhaktivinoda Ṭhākura

Śrī Pañca-tattva
Lord Śri Kṛṣṇa Caitanya,
the ideal preacher of Śrīmad-Bhāgavatam, surrounded by His principal associates.

O my Lord, Śrī Kṛṣṇa, son of Vasudeva, O all-pervading Personality of Godhead, I offer my respectful obeisances unto You. I meditate upon Lord Śrī Kṛṣṇa because He is the Absolute Truth and the primeval cause of all causes of the creation, sustenance and destruction of the manifested universes.(1.1.1)

The transcendental Personality of Godhead is indirectly associated with the three modes of material nature, namely passion, goodness and ignorance, and just for the material world's creation, maintenance and destruction He accepts the three qualitative forms of Brahmā, Viṣṇu and Śiva. Of these three, all human beings can derive ultimate benefit from Viṣṇu, the form of the quality of goodness. (1.2.23)

In the nineteenth and twentieth incarnations, the Lord advented Himself as Lord Balarāma and Lord Kṛṣṇa in the family of Vṛṣṇi [the Yadu dynasty], and by so doing He removed the burden of the world. (1.3.23)

The sunlike *Śrīmad-Bhāgavatam* can bring enlightenment to those who are immersed in the darkness of ignorance produced by the Age of Kali. (1.3.43)

Nārada reached the cottage of Kṛṣṇa-dvaipāyana Vyāsa on the banks of the Sarasvatī just as Vyāsadeva was regretting his defects. (1.4.32)

Nārada Muni, a liberated spaceman, travels throughout the material and spiritual worlds singing the glories of the Lord and delivering the fallen souls. (1.6.31–32)

Lord Śrī Kṛṣṇa, who resides within everyone's heart as the Paramātmā, could at once understand that Aśvatthāmā had thrown the brahmāstra to finish the last life in the Pāṇḍava family. As such, just to protect the progeny of the Kuru dynasty, He covered the embryo of Uttarā by His personal energy. (1.8.11–15)

As Queen Kuntī offered her heartfelt prayers to Lord Kṛṣṇa just before His departure for Dvārakā, the Lord mildly smiled out of compassion. (1.8.44)

Fulfilling my desire and sacrificing His own promise, He got down from the chariot, took up its wheel, and ran towards me hurriedly, just as a lion goes to kill an elephant. He even dropped His outer garment on the way. (1.9.37)

As Yudhiṣṭhira and Bhīma waited for Arjuna to return from Dvārakā, they witnessed many evil omens, which indicated the disappearance of Lord Kṛṣṇa and the advent of the Age of Kali.(1.14.2–5)

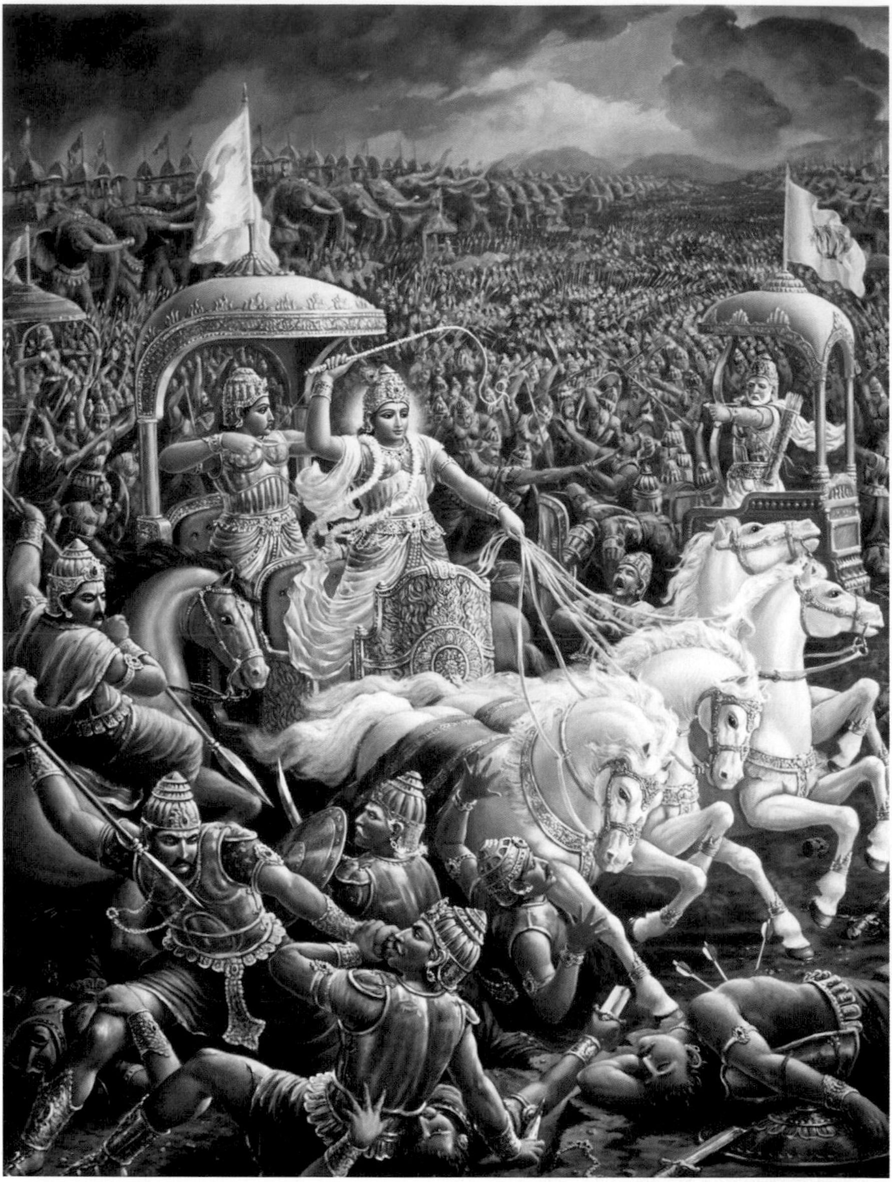

On the Battlefield of Kurukṣetra, the invincible military strength of the Kauravas was like a great ocean. But because of Kṛṣṇa's friendship, Arjuna, seated on his chariot, was able to cross over it. (1.15.14)

Mahārāja Yudhiṣṭhira was intelligent enough to understand the influence of the age of Kali, characterized by increasing avarice, falsehood, cheating and violence throughout the capital, state, home and among individuals. So he wisely prepared himself to leave home, and he dressed accordingly. (1.15.37)

While leaving, the King, being so insulted, picked up a lifeless snake with his bow and angrily placed it on the shoulder of the sage. Then he returned to his palace. (1.18.30)

a storm and showing the strength of his vast learning. Nimāi Paṇḍita at once memorized all the *ślokas* without an error. He quoted the sixty-fourth *śloka* and pointed out certain rhetorical and literary irregularities. He particularly questioned the *paṇḍita's* use of the word *bhavānī-bhartuḥ.* He pointed out that the use of this word was redundant. *Bhavānī* means the wife of Śiva, and who else can be her *bhartā,* or husband? He also pointed out several other discrepancies, and the Kashmir *paṇḍita* was struck with wonder. He was astonished that a mere student of grammar could point out the literary mistakes of an erudite scholar. Although this matter was ended prior to any public meeting, the news spread like wildfire all over Navadvīpa. But finally Keśava Kāśmīri was ordered in a dream by Sarasvatī, the goddess of learning, to submit to the Lord, and thus the Kashmir *paṇḍita* became a follower of the Lord.

The Lord was then married with great pomp and gaiety, and at this time He began to preach the congregational chanting of the holy name of the Lord at Navadvīpa. Some of the *brāhmaṇas* became envious of His popularity, and they put many hindrances on His path. They were so jealous that they finally took the matter before the Muslim magistrate at Navadvīpa. Bengal was then governed by Pathans, and the governor of the province was Nawab Hussain Shah. The Muslim magistrate of Navadvīpa took up the complaints of the *brāhmaṇas* seriously, and at first he warned the followers of Nimāi Paṇḍita not to chant loudly the name of Hari. But Lord Caitanya asked His followers to disobey the orders of the Kazi, and they went on with their *saṅkīrtana* (chanting) party as usual. The magistrate then sent constables who interrupted a *saṅkīrtana* and broke some of the *mṛdaṅgas* (drums). When Nimāi Paṇḍita heard of this incident He organized a party for civil disobedience. He is the pioneer of the civil disobedience movement in India for the right cause. He organized a procession of one hundred thousand men with thousands of *mṛdaṅgas* and *karatālas* (hand cymbals), and this procession passed over the roads of Navadvīpa in defiance of the Kazi who had issued the order. Finally the procession reached the house of the Kazi, who went upstairs out of fear of the masses. The great crowds assembled at the Kazi's house displayed a violent temper, but the Lord asked them to be peaceful. At this time the Kazi came down and tried to pacify the Lord by addressing Him as nephew. He pointed out that he referred to Nīlāmbara Cakravartī as uncle, and thus Śrīmatī Śacīdevī, Nimāi Paṇḍita's mother, was his cousin-sister. He asked the Lord whether his sister's son could be angry at His maternal uncle, and the Lord replied that since the Kazi was His maternal uncle he should receive his nephew well at his home. In this way the issue was mitigated, and the two learned scholars began a long discussion on the Koran and Hindu *śāstras.* The Lord raised the question of cow-killing, and the Kazi properly answered Him by referring to the Koran. In turn the Kazi also questioned the Lord about cow sacrifice in the *Vedas,* and the Lord replied that such sacrifice as mentioned in the *Vedas* is not actually cow-killing. In that sacrifice an old bull or cow was sacrificed for the sake of receiving a fresh younger life by the power of Vedic *mantras.* But in the Kali-yuga such cow sacrifices are forbidden because there are no qualified *brāhmaṇas* capable of conducting such a sacrifice. In fact, in Kali-yuga all *yajñas* (sacrifices) are forbidden because they are useless attempts by foolish men. In Kali-yuga only the *saṅkīrtana-yajña* is recommended for all practical purposes. Speaking in this way, the Lord finally convinced the Kazi, who became the Lord's follower. The Kazi thenceforth declared that no one should hinder the *saṅkīrtana* movement which was started by the Lord, and the Kazi left this order in his will for the sake of progeny. The Kazi's tomb still exists in the area of Navadvīpa, and Hindu pilgrims go there to show their respects. The Kazi's descendants are residents, and they never objected to *saṅkīrtana,* even during the Hindu-Muslim riot days.

This incident shows clearly that the Lord was not a so-called timid Vaiṣṇava. A Vaiṣṇava is a fearless devotee of the Lord, and for the right cause he can take any step suitable for the purpose. Arjuna was also a Vaiṣṇava devotee of Lord Kṛṣṇa, and he fought valiantly for the satisfaction of the Lord. Similarly, Vajrāṅgajī, or Hanumān, was also a devotee of Lord Rāma, and he gave lessons to the nondevotee party of Rāvaṇa. The principles of Vaiṣṇavism are to satisfy the Lord by all means. A Vaiṣṇava is by nature a nonviolent, peaceful living being, and he has all the good qualities of God, but when the nondevotee blasphemes the Lord or His devotee, the Vaiṣṇava never tolerates such impudency.

After this incident the Lord began to preach and propagate His *Bhāgavata-dharma,* or *saṅkīrtana* movement, more vigorously, and whoever stood against this propagation of the *yuga-dharma,* or duty of the age, was properly punished by various types of chastisement. Two *brāhmaṇa* gentlemen named Cāpala and Gopāla, who also happened to be maternal uncles of the Lord, were inflicted with leprosy by way of chastisement, and later, when they were repentant, they were accepted by the Lord. In the course of His preaching work, He used to send daily all His followers, including Śrīla Nityānanda Prabhu and Ṭhākura Haridāsa, two chief whips of His party, from door to door to preach the *Śrīmad-Bhāgavatam.* All of Navadvīpa was surcharged with His *saṅkīrtana* movement, and His headquarters were situated at the house of Śrīvāsa Ṭhākura and Śrī Advaita Prabhu, two of His chief householder disciples. These two learned heads of the *brāhmaṇa* community were the most ardent supporters of Lord Caitanya's movement. Śrī Advaita Prabhu was the chief cause for the advent of the Lord. When Advaita Prabhu saw that the total human society was full of materialistic activities and devoid of devotional service, which alone could save mankind from the threefold miseries of material existence, He, out of His causeless compassion for the age-worn human society, prayed fervently for the incarnation of the Lord and continually worshiped the Lord with water of the Ganges and leaves of the holy *tulasī* tree. As far as preaching work in the *saṅkīrtana* movement was concerned, everyone was expected to do his daily share according to the order of the Lord.

Once Nityānanda Prabhu and Śrīla Haridāsa Ṭhākura were walking down a main road, and on the way they saw a roaring crowd assembled. Upon inquiring from passers-by, they understood that two brothers, named Jagāi and Mādhāi, were creating a public disturbance in a drunken state. They also heard that these two brothers were born in a respectable *brāhmaṇa* family, but because of low association they had turned into debauchees of the worst type. They were not only drunkards but also meat-eaters, woman-hunters, dacoits and sinners of all description. Śrīla Nityānanda Prabhu heard all of these stories and decided that these two fallen souls must be the first to be delivered. If they were delivered from their sinful life, then the good name of Lord Caitanya would be even still more glorified. Thinking in this way, Nityānanda Prabhu and Haridāsa pushed their way through the crowd and asked the two brothers to chant the holy name of Lord Hari. The drunken brothers became enraged upon this request and attacked Nityānanda Prabhu with filthy language. Both brothers chased them a considerable distance. In the evening the report of the preaching work was submitted to the Lord, and He was glad to learn that Nityānanda and Haridāsa had attempted to deliver such a stupid pair of fellows.

The next day Nityānanda Prabhu went to see the brothers, and as soon as He approached them one of them threw a piece of earthen pot at Him. This struck Him on the forehead, and immediately blood began to flow. But Nityānanda Prabhu was so kind that instead of protesting this heinous act, He said, "It does not matter that you have thrown this stone at Me. I still request you to chant the holy name of Lord Hari."

One of the brothers, Jagāi, was astonished to see this behavior of Nityānanda Prabhu, and he at once fell down at His feet and asked Him to pardon his sinful brother. When Mādhāi again attempted to hurt Nityānanda Prabhu, Jagāi stopped him and implored him to fall down at His feet. In the meantime the news of Nityānanda's injury reached the Lord, who at once hurried to the spot in a fiery and angry mood. The Lord immediately invoked His Sudarśana *cakra* (the Lord's ultimate weapon, shaped like a wheel) to kill the sinners, but Nityānanda Prabhu reminded Him of His mission. The mission of the Lord was to deliver the hopelessly fallen souls of Kali-yuga, and the brothers Jagāi and Mādhāi were typical examples of these fallen souls. Ninety percent of the population of this age resembles these brothers, despite high birth and mundane respectability. According to the verdict of the revealed scriptures, the total population of the world in this age will be of the lowest *śūdra* quality, or even lower. It should be noted that Śrī Caitanya Mahāprabhu never acknowledged the stereotyped caste system by birthright; rather, He strictly followed the verdict of the *śāstras* in the matter of one's *svarūpa,* or real identity.

When the Lord was invoking His Sudarśana *cakra* and Śrīla Nityānanda Prabhu was imploring Him to forgive the two brothers, both the brothers fell down at the lotus feet of the Lord and begged His pardon for their gross behavior. The Lord was also asked by Nityānanda Prabhu to accept these repenting souls, and the Lord agreed to accept them on one condition, that they henceforward completely give up all their sinful activities and habits of debauchery. Both the brothers agreed and promised to give up all their sinful habits, and the kind Lord accepted them and did not again refer to their past misdeeds.

This is the specific kindness of Lord Caitanya. In this age no one can say that he is free from sin. It is impossible for anyone to say this. But Lord Caitanya accepts all kinds of sinful persons on the one condition that they promise not to indulge in sinful habits after being spiritually initiated by the bona fide spiritual master.

There are a number of instructive points to be observed in this incident of the two brothers. In this Kali-yuga practically all people are of the quality of Jagāi and Mādhāi. If they want to be relieved from the reactions of their misdeeds, they must take shelter of Lord Caitanya Mahāprabhu and after spiritual initiation thus refrain from those things which are prohibited in the *śāstras.* The prohibitory rules are dealt with in the Lord's teachings to Śrīla Rūpa Gosvāmī.

During His householder life, the Lord did not display many of the miracles which are generally expected from such personalities, but He did once perform a wonderful miracle in the house of Śrīnivāsa Ṭhākura while *saṅkīrtana* was in full swing. He asked the devotees what they wanted to eat, and when He was informed that they wanted to eat mangoes, He asked for a seed of a mango, although this fruit was out of season. When the seed was brought to Him He sowed it in the yard of Śrīnivāsa, and at once a creeper began to grow out of the seed. Within no time this creeper became a full-grown mango tree heavy with more ripened fruits than the devotees could eat. The tree remained in Śrīnivāsa's yard, and from then on the devotees used to take as many mangoes from the tree as they wanted.

The Lord had a very high estimation of the affections of the damsels of Vrajabhūmi (Vṛndāvana) for Kṛṣṇa, and in appreciation of their unalloyed service to the Lord, once Śrī Caitanya Mahāprabhu chanted the holy names of the *gopīs* (cowherd girls) instead of the names of the Lord. At this time some of His students, who were also disciples, came to see Him, and when they saw that the Lord was chanting the names of the *gopīs,* they were astonished. Out of sheer foolishness they asked the Lord why He was chanting the names of the *gopīs* and advised Him to chant the name of Kṛṣṇa. The Lord, who was in ecstasy, was thus disturbed by these foolish students. He chastised them and chased them away. The students were almost the same age as the Lord, and thus they wrongly thought of the Lord as one of their peers. They held a meeting and resolved that they would attack the Lord if He dared to punish them again in such a manner. This incident provoked some malicious talks about the Lord on the part of the general public.

When the Lord became aware of this, He began to consider the various types of men found in society. He noted that especially the students, professors, fruitive workers, *yogīs,* nondevotees, and different types of atheists were all opposed to the devotional service of the Lord. "My mission is to deliver all the fallen souls of this age," He thought, "but if they commit offenses against Me, thinking Me to be an ordinary man, they will not benefit. If they are to begin their life of spiritual realization, they must some way or another offer obeisances unto Me." Thus the Lord decided to accept the renounced order of life (*sannyāsa*) because people in general were inclined to offer respects to a *sannyāsī.*

Five hundred years ago the condition of society was not as degraded as it is today. At that time people would show respects to a *sannyāsī,* and the *sannyāsī* was rigid in following the rules and regulations of the renounced order of life. Śrī Caitanya Mahāprabhu was not very much in favor of the renounced order of life in this age of Kali, but that was only for the reason that very few *sannyāsīs* in this age are able to observe the rules and regulations of *sannyāsa* life. Śrī Caitanya Mahāprabhu decided to accept the order and become an ideal *sannyāsī* so that the general populace would show Him respect. One is duty-bound to show respect to a *sannyāsī,* for a *sannyāsī* is considered to be the master of all *varṇas* and *āśramas.*

While He was contemplating accepting the *sannyāsa* order, it so happened that Keśava Bhāratī, a *sannyāsī* of the Māyāvādī school and resident of Katwa (in Bengal), visited Navadvīpa and was invited to dine with the Lord. When Keśava Bhāratī came to His house, the Lord asked him to award Him the *sannyāsa* order of life. This was a matter of formality. The *sannyāsa* order is to be accepted from another *sannyāsī.* Although the Lord was independent in all respects, still, to keep up the formalities of the *śāstras,* He accepted the *sannyāsa* order from Keśava Bhāratī, although Keśava Bhāratī was not in the Vaiṣṇava *sampradāya* (school).

After consulting with Keśava Bhāratī, the Lord left Navadvīpa for Katwa to formally accept the *sannyāsa* order of life. He was accompanied by Śrīla Nityānanda Prabhu, Candraśekhara Ācārya and Mukunda Datta. These three assisted Him in the details of the ceremony. The incident of the Lord's accepting the *sannyāsa* order is very elaborately described in the *Caitanya-bhāgavata* by Śrīla Vṛndāvana dāsa Ṭhākura.

Thus at the end of His twenty-fourth year the Lord accepted the *sannyāsa* order of life in the month of Māgha. After accepting this order He became a full-fledged preacher of the *Bhāgavata-dharma.* Although He was doing the same preaching work in His householder life, when He experienced some obstacles to His preaching He sacrificed even the comfort of His home life for the sake of the fallen souls. In His householder life His chief assistants were Śrīla Advaita Prabhu and Śrīla Śrīvāsa Ṭhākura, but after He accepted the *sannyāsa* order His chief assistants became Śrīla Nityānanda Prabhu, who was deputed to preach specifically in Bengal, and the six Gosvāmīs (Rūpa Gosvāmī, Sanātana Gosvāmī, Jīva Gosvāmī, Gopāla Bhaṭṭa Gosvāmī, Raghunātha dāsa Gosvāmī and Raghunātha Bhaṭṭa Gosvāmī), headed by Śrīla Rūpa and Sanātana, who were deputed to go to Vṛndāvana to excavate the present places of pilgrimage. The present city of Vṛndāvana and the importance of Vrajabhūmi were thus disclosed by the will of Lord Śrī Caitanya Mahāprabhu.

The Lord, after accepting the *sannyāsa* order, at once wanted to start for Vṛndāvana. For three continuous days He traveled in the Rāḍha-deśa (places where the Ganges does not flow). He was in full ecstasy over the idea of going to Vṛndāvana. However, Śrīla Nityānanda diverted His path and brought Him instead to the house of Advaita Prabhu in Śāntipura. The Lord stayed at Śrī

Advaita Prabhu's house for a few days, and knowing well that the Lord was leaving His hearth and home for good, Śrī Advaita Prabhu sent His men to Navadvīpa to bring Mother Śacī to have a last meeting with her son. Some unscrupulous people say that Lord Caitanya met His wife also after taking *sannyāsa* and offered her His wooden slipper for worship, but the authentic sources give no information about such a meeting. His mother met Him at the house of Advaita Prabhu, and when she saw her son in *sannyāsa,* she lamented. By way of compromise, she requested her son to make His headquarters in Purī so that she would easily be able to get information about Him. The Lord granted this last desire of His beloved mother. After this incident the Lord started for Purī, leaving all the residents of Navadvīpa in an ocean of lamentation over His separation.

The Lord visited many important places on the way to Purī. He visited the temple of Gopīnāthajī, who had stolen condensed milk for His devotee Śrīla Mādhavendra Purī. Since then Deity Gopīnāthajī is well known as Kṣīra-corā-gopīnātha. The Lord relished this story with great pleasure. The propensity of stealing is there even in the absolute consciousness, but because this propensity is exhibited by the Absolute, it loses its perverted nature and thus becomes worshipable even by Lord Caitanya on the basis of the absolute consideration that the Lord and His stealing propensity are one and identical. This interesting story of Gopīnāthajī is vividly explained in the *Caitanya-caritāmṛta* by Kṛṣṇadāsa Kavirāja Gosvāmī.

After visiting the temple of Kṣīra-corā-gopīnātha of Remuṇā at Balasore in Orissa, the Lord proceeded towards Purī and on the way visited the temple of Sākṣi-gopāla, who appeared as a witness in the matter of two *brāhmaṇa* devotees' family quarrel. The Lord heard the story of Sākṣi-gopāla with great pleasure because He wanted to impress upon the atheists that the worshipable Deities in the temples approved by the great *ācāryas* are not idols, as alleged by men with a poor fund of knowledge. The Deity in the temple is the *arcā* incarnation of the Personality of Godhead, and thus the Deity is identical with the Lord in all respects. He responds to the proportion of the devotee's affection for Him. In the story of Sākṣi-gopāla, in which there was a family misunderstanding by two devotees of the Lord, the Lord, in order to mitigate the turmoil as well as to show specific favor to His servitors, traveled from Vṛndāvana to Vidyānagara, a village in Orissa, in the form of His *arcā* incarnation. From there the Deity was brought to Cuttack, and thus the temple of Sākṣi-gopāla is even today visited by thousands of pilgrims on the way to Jagannātha Purī. The Lord stayed overnight there and began to proceed toward Purī. On the way, His *sannyāsa* rod was broken by Nityānanda Prabhu. The Lord became apparently angry with Him about this and went alone to Purī, leaving His companions behind.

At Purī, when He entered the temple of Jagannātha, He became at once saturated with transcendental ecstasy and fell down on the floor of the temple unconscious. The custodians of the temple could not understand the transcendental feats of the Lord, but there was a great learned *paṇḍita* named Sārvabhauma Bhaṭṭācārya, who was present, and he could understand that the Lord's losing His consciousness upon entering the Jagannātha temple was not an ordinary thing. Sārvabhauma Bhaṭṭācārya, who was the chief appointed *paṇḍita* in the court of the King of Orissa, Mahārāja Pratāparudra, was attracted by the youthful luster of Lord Śrī Caitanya Mahāprabhu and could understand that such a transcendental trance was only rarely exhibited and only then by the topmost devotees who are already on the transcendental plane in complete forgetfulness of material existence. Only a liberated soul could show such a transcendental feat, and the Bhaṭṭācārya, who was vastly learned, could understand this in the light of the transcendental literature with which he was familiar. He therefore asked the custodians of the temple not to disturb the unknown *sannyāsī.* He asked them to take the Lord to his home so He could be further observed in His unconscious state. The Lord was at once carried to the home of Sārvabhauma Bhaṭṭācārya, who at that time had sufficient power of authority due to his being the *sabhā-paṇḍita,* or the state dean of faculty in Sanskrit literatures. The learned *paṇḍita* wanted to scrutinizingly test the transcendental feats of Lord Caitanya because often unscrupulous devotees imitate physical feats in order to flaunt transcendental achievements just to attract innocent people and take advantage of them. A learned scholar like the Bhaṭṭācārya can detect such imposters, and when he finds them out he at once rejects them.

In the case of Lord Caitanya Mahāprabhu, the Bhaṭṭācārya tested all the symptoms in the light of the *śāstras.* He tested as a scientist, not as a foolish sentimentalist. He observed the movement of the stomach, the beating of the heart and the breathing of the nostrils. He also felt the pulse of the Lord and saw that all His bodily activities were in complete suspension. When he put a small cotton swab before the nostrils, he found that there was a slight breathing as the fine fibers of cotton moved slightly. Thus he came to know that the Lord's unconscious trance was genuine, and he began to treat Him in the prescribed fashion. But Lord Caitanya Mahāprabhu could only be treated in a special way. He would respond only to the resounding of the holy names of the Lord by His devotees. This special treatment was unknown to Sārvabhauma Bhaṭṭācārya because the Lord was still unknown to him. When the Bhaṭṭācārya saw Him for the first time in the temple, he simply took Him to be one of many pilgrims.

In the meantime the companions of the Lord, who reached the temple a little after Him, heard of the Lord's transcendental feats and of His being carried away by the Bhaṭṭācārya. The pilgrims at the temple were still gossiping about the incident. But by chance, one of these pilgrims had met Gopīnātha Ācārya, who was known to Gadādhara Paṇḍita, and from him it was learned that the Lord was lying in an unconscious state at the residence of Sārvabhauma Bhaṭṭācārya, who happened to be the brother-in-law of Gopīnātha Ācārya. All the members of the party were introduced by Gadādhara Paṇḍita to Gopīnātha Ācārya, who took them all to the house of Bhaṭṭācārya, where the Lord was lying unconscious in a spiritual trance. All the members then chanted loudly the holy name of the Lord Hari as usual, and the Lord regained His consciousness. After this, Bhaṭṭācārya received all the members of the party, including Lord Nityānanda Prabhu, and asked them to become his guests of honor. The party, including the Lord, went for a bath in the sea, and the Bhaṭṭācārya arranged for their residence and meals at the house of Kāśī Miśra. Gopīnātha Ācārya, his brother-in-law, also assisted. There were some friendly talks about the Lord's divinity between the two brothers-in-law, and in this argument Gopīnātha Ācārya, who knew the Lord before, now tried to establish the Lord as the Personality of Godhead, and the Bhaṭṭācārya tried to establish Him as one of the great devotees. Both of them argued from the angle of vision of authentic *śāstras* and not on the strength of sentimental *vox populi.* The incarnations of God are determined by authentic *śāstras* and not by popular votes of foolish fanatics. Because Lord Caitanya was an incarnation of God in fact, foolish fanatics have proclaimed so many so-called incarnations of God in this age without referring to authentic scriptures. But Sārvabhauma Bhaṭṭācārya or Gopīnātha Ācārya did not indulge in such foolish sentimentalism; on the contrary, both of them tried to establish or reject His divinity on the strength of authentic *śāstras.*

Later it was disclosed that Bhaṭṭācārya also came from the Navadvīpa area, and it was understood from him that Nīlāmbara Cakravartī, the maternal grandfather of Lord Caitanya, happened to be a class fellow of the father of Sārvabhauma Bhaṭṭācārya. In that sense, the young *sannyāsī* Lord Caitanya evoked paternal affection from Bhaṭṭācārya. Bhaṭṭācārya was the professor of many *sannyāsīs* in the order of the Śaṅkarācārya-sampradāya, and he himself also belonged to that cult. As such, the Bhaṭṭācārya desired that the young *sannyāsī* Lord Caitanya also hear from him about the teachings of Vedānta.

Those who are followers of the Śaṅkara cult are generally known as Vedāntists. This does not, however, mean that Vedānta is a monopoly study of the Śaṅkara *sampradāya.* Vedānta is studied by all the bona fide *sampradāyas,* but they have their own interpretations. But those in the Śaṅkara *sampradāya* are generally known to be ignorant of the knowledge of the Vedāntist Vaiṣṇavas. For this reason the Bhaktivedanta title was first offered to the author by the Vaiṣṇavas.

The Lord agreed to take lessons from Bhaṭṭācārya on the Vedānta, and they sat together in the temple of Lord Jagannātha. The Bhaṭṭācārya went on speaking continually for seven days, and the Lord heard him with all attention and did not interrupt. The Lord's silence raised some doubts in Bhaṭṭācārya's heart, and he asked the Lord how it was that He did not ask anything or comment on his explanations of Vedānta.

The Lord posed Himself before the Bhaṭṭācārya as a foolish student and pretended that He heard the Vedānta from him because the Bhaṭṭācārya felt that this was the duty of a *sannyāsī.* But the Lord did not agree with his lectures. By this the Lord indicated that the so-called Vedāntists amongst the Śaṅkara *sampradāya,* or any other *sampradāya* who do not follow the instructions of Śrīla Vyāsadeva, are mechanical students of the Vedānta. They are not fully aware of that great knowledge. The explanation of the *Vedānta-sūtra* is given by the author himself in the text of *Śrīmad-Bhāgavatam.* One who has no knowledge of the *Bhāgavatam* will hardly be able to know what the Vedānta says.

The Bhaṭṭācārya, being a vastly learned man, could follow the Lord's sarcastic remarks on the popular Vedāntist. He therefore asked Him why He did not ask about any point which He could not follow. The Bhaṭṭācārya could understand the purpose of His dead silence for the days He heard him. This showed clearly that the Lord had something else in mind; thus the Bhaṭṭācārya requested Him to disclose His mind.

Upon this, the Lord spoke as follows: "My dear sir, I can understand the meaning of the *sūtras* like *janmādy asya yataḥ, śāstra-yonitvāt,* and *athāto brahma-jijñāsā* of the *Vedānta-sūtra,* but when you explain them in your own way it becomes difficult for Me to follow them. The purpose of the *sūtras* is already explained in them, but your explanations are covering them with something else. You do not purposely take the direct meaning of the *sūtras* but indirectly give your own interpretations."

The Lord thus attacked all Vedāntists who interpret the *Vedānta-sūtra* fashionably, according to their limited power of thinking, to serve their own purpose. Such indirect interpretations of the authentic literatures like the *Vedānta-sūtra* are hereby condemned by the Lord.

The Lord continued: "Śrīla Vyāsadeva has summarized the direct meanings of the *mantras* in the *Upaniṣads* in the *Vedānta-sūtra.* Unfortunately you do not take their direct meaning. You indirectly interpret them in a different way."

"The authority of the *Vedas* is unchallengeable and stands without any question of doubt. And whatever is stated in the *Vedas* must be accepted completely, otherwise one challenges the authority of the *Vedas.*"

"The conchshell and cow dung are bone and stool of two living beings. But because they have been recommended by the *Vedas* as pure, people accept them as such because of the authority of the *Vedas.*"

The idea is that one cannot set his imperfect reason above the authority of the *Vedas.* The orders of the *Vedas* must be obeyed as they stand, without any mundane reasoning. The so-called followers of the Vedic injunctions make their own interpretations of the Vedic injunctions, and thus they establish different parties and sects of the Vedic religion. Lord Buddha directly denied the authority of the *Vedas,* and he established his own religion. Only for this reason, the Buddhist religion was not accepted by the strict followers of the *Vedas.* But those who are so-called followers of the *Vedas* are more harmful than the Buddhists. The Buddhists have the courage to deny the *Vedas* directly, but the so-called followers of the *Vedas* have no courage to deny the *Vedas,* although indirectly they disobey all the injunctions of the *Vedas.* Lord Caitanya condemned this.

The examples given by the Lord of the conchshell and the cow dung are very much appropriate in this connection. If one argues that since cow dung is pure, the stool of a learned *brāhmaṇa* is still more pure, his argument will not be accepted. Cow dung is accepted, and the stool of a highly posted *brāhmaṇa* is rejected. The Lord continued:

"The Vedic injunctions are self-authorized, and if some mundane creature adjusts the interpretations of the *Vedas,* he defies their authority. It is foolish to think of oneself as more intelligent than Śrīla Vyāsadeva. He has already expressed himself in his *sūtras,* and there is no need of help from personalities of lesser importance. His work, the *Vedānta-sūtra,* is as dazzling as the midday sun, and when someone tries to give his own interpretations on the self-effulgent sunlike *Vedānta-sūtra,* he attempts to cover this sun with the cloud of his imagination."

"The *Vedas* and *Purāṇas* are one and the same in purpose. They ascertain the Absolute Truth, which is greater than everything else. The Absolute Truth is ultimately realized as the Absolute Personality of Godhead with absolute controlling power. As such, the Absolute Personality of Godhead must be completely full of opulence, strength, fame, beauty, knowledge and renunciation. Yet the transcendental Personality of Godhead is astonishingly ascertained as impersonal."

"The impersonal description of the Absolute Truth in the *Vedas* is given to nullify the mundane conception of the absolute whole. Personal features of the Lord are completely different from all kinds of mundane features. The living entities are all individual persons, and they are all parts and parcels of the supreme whole. If the parts and parcels are individual persons, the source of their emanation must not be impersonal. He is the Supreme Person amongst all the relative persons."

"The *Vedas* inform us that from Him [Brahman] everything emanates, and on Him everything rests. And after annihilation, everything merges in Him only. Therefore, He is the ultimate dative, causative and accommodating cause of all causes. And these causes cannot be attributed to an impersonal object."

"The *Vedas* inform us that He alone became many, and when He so desires He glances over material nature. Before He glanced over material nature there was no material cosmic creation. Therefore, His glance is not material. Material mind or senses were unborn when the Lord glanced over material nature. Thus evidence in the *Vedas* proves that beyond a doubt the Lord has transcendental eyes and a transcendental mind. They are not material. His impersonality therefore is a negation of His materiality, but not a denial of His transcendental personality."

"Brahman ultimately refers to the Personality of Godhead. Impersonal Brahman realization is just the negative conception of the mundane creations. Paramātmā is the localized aspect of Brahman within all kinds of material bodies. Ultimately the Supreme Brahman realization is the realization of the Personality of Godhead according to all evidence of the revealed scriptures. He is the ultimate source of *viṣṇu-tattvas*."

"The *Purāṇas* are also supplementary to the *Vedas*. The Vedic *mantras* are too difficult for an ordinary man. Women, *śūdras* and the so-called twice-born higher castes are unable to penetrate into the sense of the *Vedas*. And thus the *Mahābhārata* and the *Purāṇas* are made easy to explain the truths of the *Vedas*. In his prayers before the boy Śrī Kṛṣṇa, Brahmā said that there is no limit to the fortune of the residents of Vrajabhūmi headed by Śrī Nanda

Mahārāja and Yaśodāmayī, because the eternal Absolute Truth has become their intimate relative."

"The Vedic *mantra* maintains that the Absolute Truth has no legs and no hands and yet goes faster than all and accepts everything that is offered to Him in devotion. The latter statements definitely suggest the personal features of the Lord, although His hands and legs are distinguished from mundane hands and legs or other senses."

"Brahman, therefore, is never impersonal, but when such *mantras* are indirectly interpreted, it is wrongly thought that the Absolute Truth is impersonal. The Absolute Truth Personality of Godhead is full of all opulences, and therefore He has a transcendental form of full existence, knowledge and bliss. How then can one establish that the Absolute Truth is impersonal?"

"Brahman, being full of opulences, is understood to have manifold energies, and all these energies are classified under three headings under the authority of *Viṣṇu Purāṇa,* [6.7.60] which says that the transcendental energies of Lord Viṣṇu are primarily three. His spiritual energy and the energy of the living entities are classified as superior energy, whereas the material energy is an inferior one, which is sprouted out of ignorance."

"The energy of the living entities is technically called *kṣetrajña* energy. This *kṣetrajña-śakti,* although equal in quality with the Lord, becomes overpowered by material energy out of ignorance and thus suffers all sorts of material miseries. In other words, the living entities are located in the marginal energy between the superior (spiritual) and inferior (material) energies, and in proportion to the living being's contact with either the material or spiritual energies, the living entity is situated in proportionately higher and lower levels of existence."

"The Lord is beyond the inferior and marginal energies as above mentioned, and His spiritual energy is manifested in three different phases: as eternal existence, eternal bliss and eternal knowledge. As far as eternal existence is concerned, it is conducted by the *sandhinī* potency; similarly, bliss and knowledge are conducted by the *hlādinī* and *saṁvit* potencies respectively. As the supreme energetic Lord, He is the supreme controller of the spiritual, marginal and material energies. And all these different types of energies are connected with the Lord in eternal devotional service."

"The Supreme Personality of Godhead is thus enjoying in His transcendental eternal form. Is it not astounding that one dares to call the Supreme Lord nonenergetic? The Lord is the controller of all energies, and the living entities are parts and parcels of one of the energies. Therefore there is a gulf of difference between the Lord and the living entities. How then can one say that the Lord and the living entities are one and the same? In the *Bhagavad-gītā* also the living entities are described as belonging to the superior energy of the Lord. According to the principles of intimate correlation between the energy and the energetic, both of them are nondifferent also. Therefore, the Lord and the living entities are nondifferent as the energy and the energetic."

"Earth, water, fire, air, ether, mind, intelligence and ego are all inferior energies of the Lord, but the living entities are different from all as superior energy. This is the version of *Bhagavad-gītā* [7.4]."

"The transcendental form of the Lord is eternally existent and full of transcendental bliss. How then can such a form be a product of the material mode of goodness? Anyone, therefore, who does not believe in the form of the Lord is certainly a faithless demon and as such is untouchable, a not to be seen *persona non grata* fit to be punished by the Plutonic king."

"The Buddhists are called atheists because they have no respect for the *Vedas,* but those who defy the Vedic conclusions, as above mentioned, under the pretense of being followers of the *Vedas* are verily more dangerous than the Buddhists."

"Śrī Vyāsadeva very kindly compiled the Vedic knowledge in his *Vedānta-sūtra,* but if one hears the commentation of the Māyāvāda school (as represented by the Śaṅkara-sampradāya) certainly he will be misled on the path of spiritual realization."

"The theory of emanations is the beginning subject of the *Vedānta-sūtra.* All the cosmic manifestations are emanations from the Absolute Personality of Godhead by His inconceivable different energies. The example of the touchstone is applicable to the theory of emanation. The touchstone can convert an unlimited quantity of iron into gold, and still the touchstone remains as it is. Similarly, the Supreme Lord can produce all manifested worlds by His inconceivable energies, and yet He is full and unchanged. He is *pūrṇa* [complete], and although an unlimited number of *pūrṇas* emanate from Him, He is still *pūrṇa.*"

"The theory of illusion of the Māyāvāda school is advocated on the ground that the theory of emanation will cause a transformation of the Absolute Truth. If that is the case, Vyāsadeva is wrong. To avoid this, they have skillfully brought in the theory of illusion. But the world or the cosmic creation is not false, as maintained by the Māyāvāda school. It simply has no permanent existence. A nonpermanent thing cannot be called false altogether. But the conception that the material body is the self is certainly wrong."

"*Praṇava* [oṁ], or the *oṁkāra* in the *Vedas,* is the primeval hymn. This transcendental sound is identical with the form of the Lord. All the Vedic hymns are based on this *praṇava oṁkāra. Tat tvam asi* is but a side word in the Vedic literatures, and therefore this word cannot be the primeval hymn of the *Vedas.* Śrīpāda Śaṅkarācārya has given more stress on the side word *tat tvam asi* than on the primeval principle *oṁkāra."*

The Lord thus spoke on the *Vedānta-sūtra* and defied all the propaganda of the Māyāvāda school *. The Bhaṭṭācārya tried to defend himself and his Māyāvāda school by jugglery of logic and grammar, but the Lord defeated him by His forceful arguments. He affirmed that we are all related with the Personality of Godhead eternally and that devotional service is our eternal function in exchanging the dealings of our relations. The result of such exchanges is to attain *premā,* or love of Godhead. When love of Godhead is attained, love for all other beings automatically follows because the Lord is the sum total of all living beings.

The Lord said that but for these three items—namely, eternal relation with God, exchange of dealings with Him and the attainment of love for Him—all that is instructed in the *Vedas* is superfluous and concocted.

The Lord further added that the Māyāvāda philosophy taught by Śrīpāda Śaṅkarācārya is an imaginary explanation of the *Vedas,* but it had to be taught by him (Śaṅkarācārya) because he was ordered to teach it by the Personality of Godhead. In the *Padma Purāṇa* it is stated that the Personality of Godhead ordered His Lordship Śiva to deviate the human race from Him (the Personality of Godhead). The Personality of Godhead was to be so covered so that people would be encouraged to generate more and more population. His Lordship Śiva said to Devī: "In the Kali-yuga, I shall preach the Māyāvāda philosophy, which is nothing but clouded Buddhism, in the garb of a *brāhmaṇa."*

After hearing all these speeches of the Lord Śrī Caitanya Mahāprabhu, the Bhaṭṭācārya was struck with wonder and awe and regarded Him in dead silence. The Lord then encouraged him with assurance that there was no cause to wonder. "I say that *devotional service unto the Personality of Godhead is the highest goal of human life."* He then quoted a *śloka* from the *Bhāgavatam,* and assured him that even the liberated souls who are absorbed in the spirit and spiritual realization also take to the devotional service of the Lord Hari because the Personality of Godhead has such transcendental qualities that He attracts the heart of the liberated soul too.

* In our *Teachings of Lord Caitanya* we have more elaborately explained all these philosophical intricacies. *Śrīmad-Bhāgavatam* clarifies them all.

Then the Bhaṭṭācārya desired to listen to the explanation of the "*ātmārāma*" *śloka* from the *Bhāgavatam* (1.7.10). The Lord first of all asked Bhaṭṭācārya to explain it, and after that He would explain it. The Bhaṭṭācārya then explained the *śloka* in a scholarly way with special reference to logic. He explained the *śloka* in nine different ways chiefly based on logic because he was the most renowned scholar of logic of the time.

The Lord, after hearing the Bhaṭṭācārya, thanked him for the scholarly presentation of the *śloka,* and then, at the request of the Bhaṭṭācārya, the Lord explained the *śloka* in sixty-four different ways without touching the nine explanations given by the Bhaṭṭācārya.

Thus after hearing the explanation of the *ātmārāma śloka* from the Lord, the Bhaṭṭācārya was convinced that such a scholarly presentation is impossible for an earthly creature *. Before this, Śrī Gopīnātha Ācārya had tried to convince him of the divinity of the Lord, but at the time he could not so accept Him. But the Bhaṭṭācārya was astounded by the Lord's exposition of the *Vedānta-sūtra* and explanations of the *ātmārāma śloka,* and thus he began to think that he had committed a great offense at the lotus feet of the Lord by not recognizing Him to be Kṛṣṇa Himself. He then surrendered unto Him, repenting for his past dealings with Him, and the Lord was kind enough to accept the Bhaṭṭācārya. Out of His causeless mercy, the Lord manifested before him first as four-handed Nārāyaṇa and then again as two-handed Lord Kṛṣṇa with a flute in His hand.

The Bhaṭṭācārya at once fell down at the lotus feet of the Lord and composed many suitable *ślokas* in praise of the Lord by His grace. He composed one hundred *ślokas* in praise of the Lord. The Lord then embraced him, and out of transcendental ecstasy the Bhaṭṭācārya lost consciousness of the physical state of life. Tears, trembling, throbbing of the heart, perspiration, emotional waves, dancing, singing, crying and all the eight symptoms of trance were manifested in the body of the Bhaṭṭācārya. Śrī Gopīnātha Ācārya became very glad and astonished by this marvelous conversion of his brother-in-law by the grace of the Lord.

Out of the hundred celebrated *ślokas* composed by the Bhaṭṭācārya in praise of the Lord, the following two are most important, and these two *ślokas* explain the mission of the Lord in gist.

1. Let me surrender unto the Personality of Godhead who has appeared now as Lord Śrī Caitanya Mahāprabhu. He is the ocean of all mercy and has now come down to teach us material detachment, learning and devotional service to Himself.

---

* The complete text of the explanation given by the Lord will form a booklet itself, and therefore we have presented it in a chapter in our *Teachings of Lord Caitanya.*

2. Since pure devotional service of the Lord has been lost in the oblivion of time, the Lord has appeared to renovate the principles, and therefore I offer my obeisances unto His lotus feet.

The Lord explained the word *mukti* to be equivalent to the word Viṣṇu, or the Personality of Godhead. To attain *mukti,* or liberation from the bondage of material existence, is to attain to the service of the Lord.

The Lord then proceeded towards South India for some time and converted all He met on the way to become devotees of Lord Śrī Kṛṣṇa. Such devotees also converted many others to the cult of devotional service, or to the *Bhāgavata-dharma* of the Lord, and thus He reached the bank of the Godāvarī, where He met Śrīla Rāmānanda Rāya, the governor of Madras on behalf of Mahārāja Pratāparudra, the King of Orissa. His talks with Rāmānanda Rāya are very important for higher realization of transcendental knowledge, and the conversation itself forms a small booklet. We shall, however, give herewith a summary of the conversation.

Śrī Rāmānanda Rāya was a self-realized soul, although outwardly he belonged to a caste lower than the *brāhmaṇa* in social status. He was not in the renounced order of life, and besides that he was a high government servant in the state. Still, Śrī Caitanya Mahāprabhu accepted him as a liberated soul on the strength of the high order of his realization of transcendental knowledge. Similarly, the Lord accepted Śrīla Haridāsa Ṭhākura, a veteran devotee of the Lord coming from a Mohammedan family. And there are many other great devotees of the Lord who came from different communities, sects and castes. The Lord's only criterion was the standard of devotional service of the particular person. He was not concerned with the outward dress of a man; He was concerned only with the inner soul and its activities. Therefore all the missionary activities of the Lord are to be understood to be on the spiritual plane, and as such the cult of Śrī Caitanya Mahāprabhu, or the cult of *Bhāgavata-dharma,* has nothing to do with mundane affairs, sociology, politics, economic development or any such sphere of life. *Śrīmad-Bhāgavatam* is the purely transcendental urge of the soul.

When He met Śrī Rāmānanda Rāya on the bank of the Godāvarī, the *varṇāśrama-dharma* followed by the Hindus was mentioned by the Lord. Śrīla Rāmānanda Rāya said that by following the principles of *varṇāśrama-dharma,* the system of four castes and four orders of human life, everyone could realize Transcendence. In the opinion of the Lord, the system of *varṇāśrama-dharma* is superficial only, and it has very little to do with the highest realization of spiritual values. The highest perfection of life is to get detached from the material attachment and proportionately realize the transcendental loving service of the Lord. The Personality of Godhead recognizes a living being who is progressing in that line. Devotional service, therefore, is the culmination of the culture of all knowledge. When Śrī Kṛṣṇa, the Supreme Personality of Godhead, appeared for the deliverance of all fallen souls, He advised the deliverance of all living entities as follows. The Supreme Absolute Personality of Godhead, from whom all living entities have emanated, must be worshiped by all their respective engagements, because everything that we see is also the expansion of His energy. That is the way of real perfection, and it is approved by all bona fide *ācāryas* past and present. The system of *varṇāśrama* is more or less based on moral and ethical principles. There is very little realization of the Transcendence as such, and Lord Śrī Caitanya Mahāprabhu rejected it as superficial and asked Rāmānanda Rāya to go further into the matter.

Śrī Rāmānanda Rāya then suggested renunciation of fruitive actions unto the Lord. The *Bhagavad-gītā* (9.27) advises in this connection: "Whatever you do, whatever you eat and whatever you give, as well as whatever you perform in penance, offer to Me alone." This dedication on the part of the worker suggests that the Personality of Godhead is a step higher than the impersonal conception of the *varṇāśrama* system, but still the relation of the living being and the Lord is not distinct in that way. The Lord therefore rejected this proposition and asked Rāmānanda Rāya to go further.

Rāya then suggested renunciation of the *varṇāśrama-dharma* and acceptance of devotional service. The Lord did not approve of this suggestion also for the reason that all of a sudden one should not renounce his position, for that may not bring in the desired result.

It was further suggested by Rāya that attainment of spiritual realization freed from the material conception of life is the topmost achievement for a living being. The Lord rejected this suggestion also because on the plea of such spiritual realization much havoc has been wrought by unscrupulous persons; therefore all of a sudden this is not possible. The Rāya then suggested sincere association of self-realized souls and hearing submissively the transcendental message of the pastimes of the Personality of Godhead. This suggestion was welcomed by the Lord. This suggestion was made following in the footsteps of Brahmājī, who said that the Personality of Godhead is known as *ajita,* or the one who cannot be conquered or approached by anyone. But such *ajita* also becomes *jita* (conquered) by one method, which is very simple and easy. The simple method is that one has to give up the arrogant attitude of declaring oneself to be God Himself. One must be very meek and submissive and try to live peacefully by lending the ear to the speeches of the transcendentally self-realized soul who speaks on the message of *Bhāgavata-dharma,* or the religion of glorifying the Supreme Lord and His devotees. To glorify a great man is a natural instinct for living beings, but they have not learned to glorify the Lord. Perfection of life is attained simply by glorifying the Lord in association with a self-realized devotee of the Lord *. The self-realized devotee is he who surrenders unto the Lord fully and who does not have attachment for material prosperity. Material prosperity and sense enjoyment and their advancement are all activities of ignorance in human society. Peace and friendship are impossible for a society detached from the association of God and His devotees. It is imperative, therefore, that one sincerely seek the association of pure devotees and hear them patiently and submissively from any position of life. The position of a person in the higher or lower status of life does not hamper one in the path of self-realization. The only thing one has to do is to hear from a self-realized soul with a routine program. The teacher may also deliver lectures from the Vedic literatures, following in the footsteps of the bygone *ācāryas* who realized the Absolute Truth. Lord Śrī Caitanya Mahāprabhu recommended this simple method of self-realization generally known as *Bhāgavata-dharma. Śrīmad-Bhāgavatam* is the perfect guide for this purpose.

Above these topics discussed by the Lord and Śrī Rāmānanda Rāya, there were still more elevated spiritual talks between the two great personalities, and we purposely withhold those topics for the present because one has to come to the spiritual plane before further talks with Rāmānanda Rāya can be heard. We have presented further talks of Śrīla Rāmānanda Rāya with the Lord in another book (*Teachings of Lord Caitanya*).

At the conclusion of this meeting, Śrī Rāmānanda Rāya was advised by the Lord to retire from service and come to Purī so that they could live together and relish a transcendental relationship. Some time later, Śrī Rāmānanda Rāya retired from the government service and took a pension from the King. He returned to his residence in Purī, where he was one of the most confidential devotees of the Lord. There was another gentleman at Purī of the name Śikhi Māhiti, who was also a confidant like Rāmānanda Rāya. The Lord used to hold confidential talks on spiritual values with three or four companions at Purī, and He passed eighteen years in that way in spiritual trance. His talks were

*The International Society for Krishna Consciousness has been formed for this purpose.

recorded by His private secretary Śrī Dāmodara Gosvāmī, one of the four most intimate devotees.

The Lord extensively traveled all over the southern part of India. The great saint of Mahārāṣṭra known as Saint Tukārāma was also initiated by the Lord. Saint Tukārāma, after initiation by the Lord, overflooded the whole of the Mahārāṣṭra Province with the *saṅkīrtana* movement, and the transcendental flow is still rolling on in the southwestern part of the great Indian peninsula.

The Lord excavated from South India two very important old literatures, namely the *Brahma-saṁhitā** and *Kṛṣṇa-karṇāmṛta,* and these two valuable books are authorized studies for the person in the devotional line. The Lord then returned to Purī after His South Indian tour.

On His return to Purī, all the anxious devotees of the Lord got back their life, and the Lord remained there with continued pastimes of His transcendental realizations. The most important incident during that time was His granting audience to King Pratāparudra. King Pratāparudra was a great devotee of the Lord, and he considered himself to be one of the servants of the Lord entrusted with sweeping the temple. This submissive attitude of the King was very much appreciated by Śrī Caitanya Mahāprabhu. The King requested both Bhaṭṭācārya and Rāya to arrange his meeting with the Lord. When, however, the Lord was petitioned by His two stalwart devotees, He flatly refused to grant the request, even though it was put forward by personal associates like Rāmānanda Rāya and Sārvabhauma Bhaṭṭācārya. The Lord maintained that it is dangerous for a *sannyāsī* to be in intimate touch with worldly money-conscious men and with women. The Lord was an ideal *sannyāsī.* No woman could approach the Lord even to offer respects. Women's seats were accommodated far away from the Lord. As an ideal teacher and *ācārya,* He was very strict in the routine work of a *sannyāsī.* Apart from being a divine incarnation, the Lord was an ideal character as a human being. His behavior with other persons was also above suspicion. In His dealing as *ācārya,* He was harder than the thunderbolt and softer than the rose. One of His associates, Junior Haridāsa, committed a great mistake by lustfully glancing at a young woman. The Lord as Supersoul could detect this lust in the mind of Junior Haridāsa, who was at once banished from the Lord's association and was never accepted again, even though the Lord was implored to excuse Haridāsa for the mistake. Junior Haridāsa afterwards committed suicide due to being disassociated from the company of the Lord, and the news of suicide was duly related to the Lord. Even at that time the Lord was not

---

*Summary of *Śrīmad-Bhāgavatam*

forgetful of the offense, and He said that Haridāsa had rightly met with the proper punishment.

On the principles of the renounced order of life and discipline, the Lord knew no compromise, and therefore even though He knew that the King was a great devotee, He refused to see the King, only because the King was a dollar-and-cent man. By this example the Lord wanted to emphasize the proper behavior for a transcendentalist. A transcendentalist has nothing to do with women and money. He must always refrain from such intimate relations. The King was, however, favored by the Lord by the expert arrangement of the devotees. This means that the beloved devotee of the Lord can favor a neophyte more liberally than the Lord. Pure devotees, therefore, never commit an offense at the feet of another pure devotee. An offense at the lotus feet of the Lord is sometimes excused by the merciful Lord, but an offense at the feet of a devotee is very dangerous for one who actually wants to make progress in devotional service.

As long as the Lord remained at Purī, thousands of His devotees used to come to see Him during the Ratha-yātrā car festival of Lord Jagannātha. And during the car festival, the washing of the Guṇḍicā temple under the direct supervision of the Lord was an important function. The Lord's congregational *saṅkīrtana* movement at Purī was a unique exhibition for the mass of people. That is the way to turn the mass mind towards spiritual realization. The Lord inaugurated this system of mass *saṅkīrtana,* and leaders of all countries can take advantage of this spiritual movement in order to keep the mass of people in a pure state of peace and friendship with one another. This is now the demand of the present human society all over the world.

After some time the Lord again started on His tour towards northern India, and He decided to visit Vṛndāvana and its neighboring places. He passed through the jungles of Jharikhaṇḍa (Madhya Bhārata), and all the wild animals also joined His *saṅkīrtana* movement. The wild tigers, elephants, bears and deer all together accompanied the Lord, and the Lord accompanied them in *saṅkīrtana.* By this He proved that by the propagation of the *saṅkīrtana* movement (congregational chanting and glorifying of the name of the Lord) even the wild animals can live in peace and friendship, and what to speak of men who are supposed to be civilized. No man in the world will refuse to join the *saṅkīrtana* movement. Nor is the Lord's *saṅkīrtana* movement restricted to any caste, creed, color or species. Here is direct evidence of His great mission: He allowed even the wild animals to partake in His great movement.

On His way back from Vṛndāvana He first came to Prayāga, where He met

Rūpa Gosvāmī along with his younger brother, Anupama. Then He came down to Benares (Varanasi). For two months, He instructed Śrī Sanātana Gosvāmī in the transcendental science. The instruction to Sanātana Gosvāmī is in itself a long narration, and full presentation of the instruction will not be possible here. The main ideas are given as follows.

Sanātana Gosvāmī (formerly known as Sākara Mallika) was in the cabinet service of the Bengal government under the regime of Nawab Hussain Shah. He decided to join with the Lord and thus retired from the service. On His way back from Vṛndāvana, when He reached Vārāṇasī, the Lord became the guest of Śrī Tapana Miśra and Candraśekhara, assisted by a Mahārāṣṭra *brāhmaṇa.* At that time Vārāṇasī was headed by a great *sannyāsī* of the Māyāvāda school named Śrīpāda Prakāśānanda Sarasvatī. When the Lord was at Vārāṇasī, the people in general became more attracted to Lord Caitanya Mahāprabhu on account of His mass *saṅkīrtana* movement. Wherever He visited, especially the Viśvanātha temple, thousands of pilgrims would follow Him. Some were attracted by His bodily features, and others were attracted by His melodious songs glorifying the Lord.

The Māyāvādī *sannyāsīs* designate themselves as Nārāyaṇa. Vārāṇasī is still overflooded with many Māyāvādī *sannyāsīs.* Some people who saw the Lord in His *saṅkīrtana* party considered Him to be actually Nārāyaṇa, and this report reached the camp of the great *sannyāsī* Prakāśānanda.

In India there is always a kind of spiritual rivalry between the Māyāvāda and *Bhāgavata* schools, and thus when the news of the Lord reached Prakāśānanda he knew that the Lord was a Vaiṣṇava *sannyāsī,* and therefore he minimized the value of the Lord before those who brought him the news. He deprecated the activities of the Lord because of His preaching the *saṅkīrtana* movement, which was in his opinion nothing but religious sentiment. Prakāśānanda was a profound student of the Vedānta, and he advised his followers to give attention to the Vedānta and not to indulge in *saṅkīrtana.*

One devotee *brāhmaṇa,* who became a devotee of the Lord, did not like the criticism of Prakāśānanda, and he went to the Lord to express his regrets. He told the Lord that when he uttered the Lord's name before the *sannyāsī* Prakāśānanda, the latter strongly criticized the Lord, although the *brāhmaṇa* heard Prakāśānanda uttering several times the name Caitanya. The *brāhmaṇa* was astonished to see that the *sannyāsī* Prakāśānanda could not vibrate the sound Kṛṣṇa even once, although he uttered the name Caitanya several times.

The Lord smilingly explained to the devotee *brāhmaṇa* why the Māyāvādī cannot utter the holy name of Kṛṣṇa. "The Māyāvādīs are offenders at the lotus feet of Kṛṣṇa, although they utter always *brahma, ātmā* or *caitanya,* etc. And because they are offenders at the lotus feet of Kṛṣṇa, they are actually unable to utter the holy name of Kṛṣṇa. The name Kṛṣṇa and the Personality of Godhead Kṛṣṇa are identical. There is no difference in the absolute realm between the name, form or person of the Absolute Truth because in the absolute realm everything is transcendental bliss. There is no difference between the body and the soul for the Personality of Godhead, Kṛṣṇa. Thus He is different from the living entity, who is always different from his outward body. Because of Kṛṣṇa's transcendental position, it is very difficult for a layman to actually know the Personality of Godhead Kṛṣṇa, His holy name and fame, etc. His name, fame, form and pastimes all are one and the same transcendental identity, and they are not knowable by the exercise of the material senses.

"The transcendental relationship of the pastimes of the Lord is the source of still more bliss than one can experience by realization of Brahman or by becoming one with the Supreme. Had it not been so, then those who are already situated in the transcendental bliss of Brahman would not have been attracted by the transcendental bliss of the pastimes of the Lord."

After this, a great meeting was arranged by the devotees of the Lord in which all the *sannyāsīs* were invited, including the Lord and Prakāśānanda Sarasvatī. In this meeting both the scholars (the Lord and Prakāśānanda) had a long discourse on the spiritual values of the *saṅkīrtana* movement, and a summary is given below.

The great Māyāvādī *sannyāsī* Prakāśānanda inquired from the Lord as to the reason for His preferring the *saṅkīrtana* movement to the study of the *Vedānta-sūtra.* Prakāśānanda said that it is the duty of a *sannyāsī* to read the *Vedānta-sūtra.* What caused the Lord to indulge in *saṅkīrtana*?

After this inquiry, the Lord submissively replied: "I have taken to the *saṅkīrtana* movement instead of the study of Vedānta because I am a great fool." The Lord thus represented Himself as one of the numberless fools of this age who are absolutely incapable of studying the Vedānta philosophy. The fools' indulgence in the study of Vedānta has caused so much havoc in society. The Lord thus continued: "And because I am a great fool, My spiritual master forbade Me to play with Vedānta philosophy. He said that it is better that I chant the holy name of the Lord, for that would deliver Me from material bondage."

"In this age of Kali there is no other religion but the glorification of the Lord by utterance of His holy name, and that is the injunction of all the revealed scriptures. And My spiritual master has taught Me one *śloka* [from the *Bṛhan-nāradīya Purāṇa*]:

harer nāma harer nāma harer nāmaiva kevalam
kalau nāsty eva nāsty eva nāsty eva gatir anyathā

"So on the order of My spiritual master, I chant the holy name of Hari, and I am now mad after this holy name. Whenever I utter the holy name I forget Myself completely, and sometimes I laugh, cry and dance like a madman. I thought that I had actually gone mad by this process of chanting, and therefore I asked My spiritual master about it. He informed Me that this was the real effect of chanting the holy name, which produces a transcendental emotion that is a rare manifestation. It is the sign of love of God, which is the ultimate end of life. Love of God is transcendental to liberation [*mukti*], and thus it is called the fifth stage of spiritual realization, above the stage of liberation. By chanting the holy name of Kṛṣṇa one attains the stage of love of God, and it was good that fortunately I was favored with the blessing."

On hearing this statement from the Lord, the Māyāvādī *sannyāsī* asked the Lord what was the harm in studying the Vedānta along with chanting the holy name. Prakāśānanda Sarasvatī knew well that the Lord was formerly known as Nimāi Paṇḍita, a very learned scholar of Navadvīpa, and His posing as a great fool was certainly to some purpose. Hearing this inquiry by the *sannyāsī,* the Lord smiled and said, "My dear sir, if you do not mind, I will answer your inquiry."

All the *sannyāsīs* there were very much pleased with the Lord for His honest dealings, and they unanimously replied that they would not be offended by whatever He replied. The Lord then spoke as follows:

"*Vedānta-sūtra* consists of transcendental words or sounds uttered by the transcendental Personality of Godhead. As such, in the Vedānta there cannot be any human deficiencies like mistake, illusion, cheating or inefficiency. The message of the *Upaniṣads* is expressed in the *Vedānta-sūtra,* and what is said there directly is certainly glorified. Whatever interpretations have been given by Śaṅkarācārya have no direct bearing on the *sūtra,* and therefore such commentation spoils everything."

"The word Brahman indicates the greatest of all, which is full with transcendental opulences, superior to all. Brahman is ultimately the Personality of Godhead, and He is covered by indirect interpretations and established as impersonal. Everything that is in the spiritual world is full of transcendental bliss, including the form, body, place and paraphernalia of the Lord. All are eternally cognizant and blissful. It is not the fault of the Ācārya Śaṅkara that he has so interpreted Vedānta, but if someone accepts it, then certainly he is doomed. Anyone who accepts the transcendental body of the Personality of Godhead as something mundane certainly commits the greatest blasphemy."

The Lord thus spoke to the *sannyāsī* almost in the same way that He spoke to the Bhaṭṭācārya of Purī, and by forceful arguments He nullified the Māyāvāda interpretations of the *Vedānta-sūtra.* All the *sannyāsīs* there claimed that the Lord was the personified *Vedas* and the Personality of Godhead. All the *sannyāsīs* were converted to the cult of *bhakti,* all of them accepted the holy name of the Lord Śrī Kṛṣṇa, and they dined together with the Lord in the midst of them. After this conversion of the *sannyāsīs,* the popularity of the Lord increased at Vārāṇasī, and thousands of people assembled to see the Lord in person. The Lord thus established the primary importance of *Śrīmad-Bhāgavata-dharma,* and He defeated all other systems of spiritual realization. After that everyone at Vārāṇasī was overwhelmed with the transcendental *saṅkīrtana* movement.

While the Lord was camping at Vārāṇasī, Sanātana Gosvāmī also arrived after retiring from office. He was formerly one of the state ministers in the government of Bengal, then under the regime of Nawab Hussain Shah. He had some difficulty in getting relief from the state service, for the Nawab was reluctant to let him leave. Nonetheless he came to Vārāṇasī, and the Lord taught him the principles of devotional service. He taught him about the constitutional position of the living being, the cause of his bondage under material conditions, his eternal relation with the Personality of Godhead, the transcendental position of the Supreme Personality of Godhead, His expansions in different plenary portions of incarnations, His control of different parts of the universe, the nature of His transcendental abode, devotional activities, their different stages of development, the rules and regulations for achieving the gradual stages of spiritual perfection, the symptoms of different incarnations in different ages, and how to detect them with reference to the context of revealed scriptures.

The Lord's teachings to Sanātana Gosvāmī form a big chapter in the text of *Śrī Caitanya-caritāmṛta,* and to explain the whole teachings in minute details will require a volume in itself. These are treated in detail in our book *Teachings of Lord Caitanya.*

At Mathurā, the Lord visited all the important places; then He reached Vṛndāvana. Lord Caitanya appeared in the family of a high-caste *brāhmaṇa,* and over and above that,as *sannyāsī* He was the preceptor for all the *varṇas* and *āśramas.* But He used to accept meals from all classes of Vaiṣṇavas. At

Mathurā the Sanoḍiyā *brāhmaṇas* are considered to be in the lower status of society, but the Lord accepted meals in the family of such a *brāhmaṇa* also because His host happened to be a disciple of the Mādhavendra Purī family.

At Vṛndāvana the Lord took bath in twenty-four important bathing places and ghats. He traveled to all the twelve important *vanas* (forests). In these forests all the cows and birds welcomed Him, as if He were their very old friend. The Lord also began to embrace all the trees of those forests, and by doing so He felt the symptoms of transcendental ecstasy. Sometimes He fell unconscious, but He was made to regain consciousness by the chanting of the holy name of Kṛṣṇa. The transcendental symptoms that were visible on the body of the Lord during His travel within the forest of Vṛndāvana were all unique and inexplicable, and we have just given a synopsis only.

Some of the important places that were visited by the Lord in Vṛndāvana were Kāmyavana, Ādīśvara, Pāvana-sarovara, Khadiravana, Śeṣaśāyī, Khela-tīrtha, Bhāṇḍīravana, Bhadravana, Śrīvana, Lauhavana, Mahāvana, Gokula, Kāliya-hrada, Dvādaśāditya, Keśī-tīrtha, etc. When He saw the place where the *rāsa* dance took place, He at once fell down in trance. As long as He remained at Vṛndāvana, He made His headquarters at Akrūra-ghāṭa.

From Vṛndāvana His personal servitor Kṛṣṇadāsa Vipra induced Him to go back to Prayāga to take bath during the Māgha Mela. The Lord acceded to this proposal, and they started for Prayāga. On the way they met with some Pathans, amongst whom there was a learned Moulana. The Lord had some talks with the Moulana and his companions, and the Lord convinced the Moulana that in the Koran also there are descriptions of *Bhāgavata-dharma* and Kṛṣṇa. All the Pathans were converted to His cult of devotional service.

When He returned to Prayāga, Śrīla Rūpa Gosvāmī and his youngest brother met Him near Bindu-mādhava temple. This time the Lord was welcomed by the people of Prayāga more respectfully. Vallabha Bhaṭṭa, who resided on the other bank of Prayāga in the village of Āḍāila, was to receive Him at his place, but while going there the Lord jumped in the River Yamunā. With great difficulty He was picked up in an unconscious state. Finally He visited the headquarters of Vallabha Bhaṭṭa. This Vallabha Bhaṭṭa was one of His chief admirers, but later on he inaugurated his own party, the Vallabha *sampradāya.*

On the bank of the Daśāśvamedha-ghāṭa at Prayāga for ten days continually the Lord instructed Rūpa Gosvāmī in the science of devotional service to the Lord. He taught the Gosvāmī the divisions of the living creatures in the 8,400,000 species of life. Then He taught him about the human species. Out of them He discussed the followers of the Vedic principles, out of them the fruitive workers, out of them the empiric philosophers, and out of them the liberated souls. He said that there are only a few who are actually pure devotees of Lord Śrī Kṛṣṇa.

Śrīla Rūpa Gosvāmī was the younger brother of Sanātana Gosvāmī, and when he retired from service he brought with him two boatfuls of gold coins. This means that he brought with him some hundreds of thousands of rupees accumulated by the labor of his service. And before leaving home for Lord Caitanya Mahāprabhu, he divided the wealth as follows: fifty percent for the service of the Lord and His devotees, twenty-five percent for relatives and twenty-five percent for his personal needs in case of emergency. In that way he set an example for all householders.

The Lord taught the Gosvāmī about devotional service, comparing it to a creeper, and advised him to protect the *bhakti* creeper most carefully against the mad elephant offense against the pure devotees. In addition, the creeper has to be protected from the desires of sense enjoyment, monistic liberation and perfection of the *haṭha-yoga* system. They are all detrimental on the path of devotional service. Similarly, violence against living beings, and desire for worldly gain, worldly reception and worldly fame are all detrimental to the progress of *bhakti,* or *Bhāgavata-dharma.*

Pure devotional service must be freed from all desires for sense gratification, fruitive aspirations and culture of monistic knowledge. One must be freed from all kinds of designations, and when one is thus converted to transcendental purity, one can then serve the Lord by purified senses.

As long as there is the desire to enjoy sensually or to become one with the Supreme or to possess the mystic powers, there is no question of attaining the stage of pure devotional service.

Devotional service is conducted under two categories, namely primary practice and spontaneous emotion. When one can rise to the platform of spontaneous emotion, he can make further progress by spiritual attachment, feeling, love, and many higher stages of devotional life for which there are no English words. We have tried to explain the science of devotional service in our book *The Nectar of Devotion,* based on the authority of *Bhakti-rasāmṛta-sindhu* by Śrīla Rūpa Gosvāmī.

Transcendental devotional service has five stages of reciprocation:

1. The self-realization stage just after liberation from material bondage is called the *śānta,* or neutral stage.

2. After that, when there is development of transcendental knowledge of the Lord's internal opulences, the devotee engages himself in the *dāsya* stage.

3. By further development of the *dāsya* stage, a respectful fraternity with the Lord develops, and above that a feeling of friendship on equal terms becomes manifest. Both these stages are called *sākhya* stage, or devotional service in friendship.

4. Above this is the stage of parental affection toward the Lord, and this is called the *vātsalya* stage.

5. And above this is the stage of conjugal love, and this stage is called the highest stage of love of God, although there is no difference in quality in any of the above stages. The last stage of conjugal love of God is called the *mādhurya* stage.

Thus He instructed Rūpa Gosvāmī in devotional science and deputed him to Vṛndāvana to excavate the lost sites of the transcendental pastimes of the Lord. After this, the Lord returned to Vārāṇasī and delivered the *sannyāsīs* and instructed the elder brother of Rūpa Gosvāmī. We have already discussed this.

The Lord left only eight *ślokas* of His instructions in writing, and they are known as the *Śikṣāṣṭaka.* All other literatures of His divine cult were extensively written by the Lord's principal followers, the six Gosvāmīs of Vṛndāvana, and their followers. The cult of Caitanya philosophy is richer than any other, and it is admitted to be the living religion of the day with the potency for spreading as *viśva-dharma,* or universal religion. We are glad that the matter has been taken up by some enthusiastic sages like Bhaktisiddhānta Sarasvatī Gosvāmī Mahārāja and his disciples. We shall eagerly wait for the happy days of *Bhāgavata-dharma,* or *prema-dharma,* inaugurated by the Lord Śrī Caitanya Mahāprabhu.

The eight *ślokas* completed by the Lord are:

1

Glory to the Śrī Kṛṣṇa saṅkīrtana, which cleanses the heart of all the dust accumulated for years and extinguishes the fire of conditional life, of repeated birth and death. This saṅkīrtana movement is the prime benediction for humanity at large because it spreads the rays of the benediction moon. It is the life of all transcendental knowledge. It increases the ocean of transcendental bliss, and it enables us to fully taste the nectar for which we are always anxious.

2

O my Lord, Your holy name alone can render all benediction to living beings, and thus You have hundreds and millions of names like Kṛṣṇa and Govinda. In these transcendental names You have invested all Your transcendental energies. There are not even hard and fast rules for chanting these names. O my Lord, out of kindness You enable us to easily approach You by chanting Your holy names, but I am so unfortunate that I have no attraction for them.

3

One should chant the holy name of the Lord in a humble state of mind, thinking oneself lower than the straw in the street; one should be more tolerant than a tree, devoid of all sense of false prestige, and ready to offer all respect to others. In such a state of mind one can chant the holy name of the Lord constantly.

4

O almighty Lord, I have no desire to accumulate wealth, nor do I desire beautiful women, nor do I want any number of followers. I only want Your causeless devotional service birth after birth.

5

O son of Mahārāja Nanda [Kṛṣṇa], I am Your eternal servitor, yet somehow or other I have fallen into the ocean of birth and death. Please pick me up from this ocean of death and place me as one of the atoms of Your lotus feet.

6

O my Lord, when will my eyes be decorated with tears of love flowing constantly when I chant Your holy name? When will my voice choke up, and when will the hairs of my body stand on end at the recitation of Your name?

7

O Govinda! Feeling Your separation, I am considering a moment to be like twelve years or more. Tears are flowing from my eyes like torrents of rain, and I am feeling all vacant in the world in Your absence.

8

I know no one but Kṛṣṇa as my Lord, and He shall remain so even if He handles me roughly in His embrace or makes me brokenhearted by not being present before me. He is completely free to do anything and everything, for He is always my worshipful Lord unconditionally.

CHAPTER ONE

Questions by the Sages

TEXT 1

ॐ नमो भगवते वासुदेवाय
जन्माद्यस्य यतोऽन्वयादितरतश्चार्थेष्वभिज्ञः स्वराट्
तेने ब्रह्म हृदा य आदिकवये मुह्यन्ति यत्सूरयः ।
तेजोवारिमृदां यथा विनिमयो यत्र त्रिसर्गोऽमृषा
धाम्ना स्वेन सदा निरस्तकुहकं सत्यं परं धीमहि ॥१॥

oṁ namo bhagavate vāsudevāya
janmādy asya yato 'nvayād itarataś cārtheṣv abhijñaḥ svarāṭ
tene brahma hṛdā ya ādi-kavaye muhyanti yat sūrayaḥ
tejo-vāri-mṛdāṁ yathā vinimayo yatra tri-sargo 'mṛṣā
dhāmnā svena sadā nirasta-kuhakaṁ satyaṁ paraṁ dhīmahi

om—O my Lord; *namaḥ*—offering my obeisances; *bhagavate*—unto the Personality of Godhead; *vāsudevāya*—unto Vāsudeva (the son of Vasudeva), or Lord Śrī Kṛṣṇa, the primeval Lord; *janma-ādi*—creation, sustenance and destruction; *asya*—of the manifested universes; *yataḥ*—from whom; *anvayāt*—directly; *itarataḥ*—indirectly; *ca*—and; *artheṣu*—purposes; *abhijñaḥ*—fully cognizant; *sva-rāṭ*—fully independent; *tene*—imparted; *brahma*—the Vedic knowledge; *hṛdā*—consciousness of the heart; *yaḥ*—one who; *ādi-kavaye*—unto the original created being; *muhyanti*—are illusioned; *yat*—about whom; *sūrayaḥ*—great sages and demigods; *tejaḥ*—fire; *vāri*—water; *mṛdām*—earth; *yathā*—as much as; *vinimayaḥ*—action and reaction; *yatra*—whereupon; *tri-sargaḥ*—three modes of creation, creative faculties; *amṛṣā*—almost factual; *dhāmnā*—along with all transcendental paraphernalia; *svena*—self-sufficiently; *sadā*—always; *nirasta*—negation by absence; *kuhakam*—illusion; *satyam*—truth; *param*—absolute; *dhīmahi*—I do meditate upon.

TRANSLATION

O my Lord, Śrī Kṛṣṇa, son of Vasudeva, O all-pervading Personality of Godhead, I offer my respectful obeisances unto You. I meditate upon Lord

Śrī Kṛṣṇa because He is the Absolute Truth and the primeval cause of all causes of the creation, sustenance and destruction of the manifested universes. He is directly and indirectly conscious of all manifestations, and He is independent because there is no other cause beyond Him. It is He only who first imparted the Vedic knowledge unto the heart of Brahmājī, the original living being. By Him even the great sages and demigods are placed into illusion, as one is bewildered by the illusory representations of water seen in fire, or land seen on water. Only because of Him do the material universes, temporarily manifested by the reactions of the three modes of nature, appear factual, although they are unreal. I therefore meditate upon Him, Lord Śrī Kṛṣṇa, who is eternally existent in the transcendental abode, which is forever free from the illusory representations of the material world. I meditate upon Him, for He is the Absolute Truth.

PURPORT

Obeisances unto the Personality of Godhead, Vāsudeva, directly indicate Lord Śrī Kṛṣṇa, who is the divine son of Vasudeva and Devakī. This fact will be more explicitly explained in the text of this work.Śrī Vyāsadeva asserts herein that Śrī Kṛṣṇa is the original Personality of Godhead, and all others are His direct or indirect plenary portions or portions of the portion. Śrīla Jīva Gosvāmī has even more explicitly explained the subject matter in his *Kṛṣṇa-sandarbha.* And Brahmā, the original living being, has explained the subject of Śrī Kṛṣṇa substantially in his treatise named *Brahma-saṁhitā. In the Sāma-veda Upaniṣad ,* it is also stated that Lord Śrī Kṛṣṇa is the divine son of Devakī. Therefore, in this prayer, the first proposition holds that Lord Śrī Kṛṣṇa is the primeval Lord, and if any transcendental nomenclature is to be understood as belonging to the Absolute Personality of Godhead, it must be the name indicated by the word Kṛṣṇa, which means the all-attractive. In *Bhagavad-gītā,* in many places, the Lord asserts Himself to be the original Personality of Godhead, and this is confirmed by Arjuna, and also by great sages like Nārada, Vyāsa, and many others. In the *Padma Purāṇa,* it is also stated that out of the innumerable names of the Lord, the name of Kṛṣṇa is the principal one. Vāsudeva indicates the plenary portion of the Personality of Godhead, and all the different forms of the Lord, being identical with Vāsudeva, are indicated in this text. The name Vāsudeva particularly indicates the divine son of Vasudeva and Devakī. Śrī Kṛṣṇa is always meditated upon by the *paramahaṁsas,* who are the perfected ones among those in the renounced order of life.

Vāsudeva, or Lord Śrī Kṛṣṇa, is the cause of all causes. Everything that exists emanates from the Lord. How this is so is explained in later chapters of this work. This work is described by Mahāprabhu Śrī Caitanya as the spotless *Purāṇa* because it contains the transcendental narration of the Personality of Godhead Śrī Kṛṣṇa. The history of the *Śrīmad-Bhāgavatam* is also very glorious. It was compiled by Śrī Vyāsadeva after he had attained maturity in transcendental knowledge. He wrote this under the instructions of Śrī Nāradajī, his spiritual master. Vyāsadeva compiled all Vedic literatures, containing the four divisions of the *Vedas,* the *Vedānta-sūtras* (or the *Brahma-sūtras*), the *Purāṇas,* the *Mahābhārata,* and so on. But nevertheless he was not satisfied. His dissatisfaction was observed by his spiritual master, and thus Nārada advised him to write on the transcendental activities of Lord Śrī Kṛṣṇa. These transcendental activities are described specifically in theTenth Canto of this work. But, in order to reach to the very substance, one must proceed gradually by developing knowledge of the categories.

It is natural that a philosophical mind wants to know about the origin of the creation. At night he sees the stars in the sky, and he naturally speculates about their inhabitants. Such inquiries are natural for man because man has a developed consciousness which is higher than that of the animals. The author of *Śrīmad-Bhāgavatam* gives a direct answer to such inquiries. He says that the Lord Śrī Kṛṣṇa is the origin of all creations. He is not only the creator of the universe, but the destroyer as well. The manifested cosmic nature is created at a certain period by the will of the Lord. It is maintained for some time, and then it is annihilated by His will. Therefore, the supreme will is behind all cosmic activities. Of course, there are atheists of various categories who do not believe in a creator, but that is due to a poor fund of knowledge. The modern scientist, for example, has created space satellites, and by some arrangement or other, these satellites are thrown into outer space to fly for some time at the control of the scientist who is far away. Similarly, all the universes with innumerable stars and planets are controlled by the intelligence of the Personality of Godhead.

In Vedic literatures, it is said that the Absolute Truth, Personality of Godhead, is the chief amongst all living personalities. All living beings, beginning from the first created being, Brahmā, down to the smallest ant, are individual living beings. And above Brahmā, there are even other living beings with individual capacities, and the Personality of Godhead is also a similar living being. And He is an individual as are the other living beings. But the Supreme Lord, or the supreme living being, has the greatest intelligence, and He possesses supermost inconceivable energies of all different varieties. If a man's brain can produce a space satellite, one can very easily imagine how brains higher than man can produce similarly wonderful things which are far superior. The reasonable person will easily accept this argument, but there are stubborn atheists who would never agree. Śrīla Vyāsadeva, however, at once accepts the supreme intelligence as the *parameśvara.* He offers his respectful obeisances unto the supreme intelligence addressed as the *para* or the *parameśvara* or the Supreme Personality of Godhead. And that *parameśvara* is Śrī Kṛṣṇa, as admitted in *Bhagavad-gītā* and other scriptures delivered by Śrī Vyāsadeva and specifically in this *Śrīmad-Bhāgavatam.* In *Bhagavad-gītā,* the Lord says that there is no other *para-tattva* (*summum bonum*) than Himself. Therefore, Śrī Vyāsadeva at once worships the *para-tattva,* Śrī Kṛṣṇa, whose transcendental activities are described in the Tenth Canto.

Unscrupulous persons go immediately to the Tenth Canto and especially to the five chapters which describe the Lord's *rāsa* dance. This portion of the *Śrīmad-Bhāgavatam* is the most confidential part of this great literature. Unless one is thoroughly accomplished in the transcendental knowledge of the Lord, one is sure to misunderstand the Lord's worshipable transcendental pastimes called *rāsa* dance and His love affairs with the *gopīs.* This subject matter is highly spiritual, and only the liberated persons who have gradually attained to the stage of *paramahaṁsa* can transcendentally relish this *rāsa* dance. Śrīla Vyāsadeva therefore gives the reader the chance to gradually develop spiritual realization before actually relishing the essence of the pastimes of the Lord. Therefore, he purposely invokes a Gāyatrī *mantra, dhīmahi.* This Gāyatrī *mantra* is meant for spiritually advanced people. When one is successful in chanting the Gāyatrī *mantra,* he can enter into the transcendental position of the Lord. One must therefore acquire brahminical qualities or be perfectly situated in the quality of goodness in order to chant the Gāyatrī *mantra* successfully and then attain to the stage of transcendentally realizing the Lord, His name, His fame, His qualities and so on.

Śrīmad-Bhāgavatam is the narration of the *svarūpa* of the Lord manifested by His internal potency, and this potency is distinguished from the external potency which has manifested the cosmic world, which is within our experience. Śrīla Vyāsadeva makes a clear distinction between the two in this *śloka.* Śrī Vyāsadeva says herein that the manifested internal potency is real, whereas the external manifested energy in the form of material existence is only temporary and illusory like the mirage in the desert. In the desert mirage there is no actual water. There is only the appearance of water.

Real water is somewhere else. The manifested cosmic creation appears as reality. But reality, of which this is but a shadow, is in the spiritual world. Absolute Truth is in the spiritual sky, not the material sky. In the material sky everything is relative truth. That is to say, one truth depends on something else. This cosmic creation results from interaction of the three modes of nature, and the temporary manifestations are so created as to present an illusion of reality to the bewildered mind of the conditioned soul, who appears in so many species of life, including the higher demigods, like Brahmā, Indra, Candra, and so on. In actuality, there is no reality in the manifested world. There appears to be reality, however, because of the true reality which exists in the spiritual world, where the Personality of Godhead eternally exists with His transcendental paraphernalia.

The chief engineer of a complicated construction does not personally take part in the construction, but he knows every nook and corner because everything is done under his direction. He knows everything about the construction, both directly and indirectly. Similarly, the Personality of Godhead, who is the supreme engineer of this cosmic creation, knows every nook and corner, although affairs are being carried out by demigods. Beginning from Brahmā down to the insignificant ant, no one is independent in the material creation. The hand of the Lord is seen everywhere. All material elements as well as all spiritual sparks emanate from Him only. And whatever is created in this material world is but the interaction of two energies, the material and the spiritual, which emanate from the Absolute Truth, the Personality of Godhead, Śrī Kṛṣṇa. A chemist can manufacture water in the chemical laboratory by mixing hydrogen and oxygen. But, in reality, the living entity works in the laboratory under the direction of the Supreme Lord. And the materials with which he works are also supplied by the Lord. The Lord knows everything directly and indirectly, and He is cognizant of all minute details, and He is fully independent. He is compared to a mine of gold, and the cosmic creations in so many different forms are compared to objects made from the gold, such as gold rings, necklaces and so on. The gold ring and the gold necklace are qualitatively one with the gold in the mine, but quantitatively the gold in the mine is different. Therefore, the Absolute Truth is simultaneously one and different. Nothing is absolutely equal with the Absolute Truth, but at the same time, nothing is independent of the Absolute Truth.

Conditioned souls, beginning from Brahmā, who engineers the entire universe, down to the insignificant ant, are all creating, but none of them are independent of the Supreme Lord. The materialist wrongly thinks that there is no creator other than his own self. This is called *māyā,* or illusion. Because of his poor fund of knowledge, the materialist cannot see beyond the purview of his imperfect senses, and thus he thinks that matter automatically takes its own shape without the aid of a superior intelligence. This is refuted in this *śloka* by Śrīla Vyāsadeva: "Since the complete whole or the Absolute Truth is the source of everything, nothing can be independent of the body of the Absolute Truth." Whatever happens to the body quickly becomes known to the embodied. Similarly, the creation is the body of the absolute whole. Therefore, the Absolute knows everything directly and indirectly that happens in the creation.

In the *śruti-mantra,* it is also stated that the absolute whole or Brahman is the ultimate source of everything. Everything emanates from Him, and everything is maintained by Him. And at the end, everything enters into Him. That is the law of nature. In the *smṛti-mantra,* the same is confirmed. It is said that the source from which everything emanates at the beginning of Brahmā's millennium, and the reservoir to which everything ultimately enters, is the Absolute Truth, or Brahman. Material scientists take it for granted that the ultimate source of the planetary system is the sun, but they are unable to explain the source of the sun. Herein, the ultimate source is explained. According to the Vedic literatures, Brahmā, who may be compared to the sun, is not the ultimate creator. It is stated in this *śloka* that Brahmā was taught Vedic knowledge by the Personality of Godhead. One may argue that Brahmā, being the original living being, could not be inspired because there was no other being living at that time. Herein it is stated that the Supreme Lord inspired the secondary creator, Brahmā, in order that Brahmā could carry out his creative functions. So, the supreme intelligence behind all creations is the Absolute Godhead, Śrī Kṛṣṇa. In *Bhagavad-gītā,* Lord Śrī Kṛṣṇa states that it is He only who superintends the creative energy, *prakṛti,* which constitutes the totality of matter. Therefore, Śrī Vyāsadeva does not worship Brahmā, but the Supreme Lord, who guides Brahmā in his creative activities. In this *śloka,* the particular words *abhijñaḥ* and *svarāṭ* are significant. These two words distinguish the Supreme Lord from all the other living entities. No other living entity is either *abhijñaḥ* or *svarāṭ.* That is, no one is either fully cognizant or fully independent. Even Brahmā has to meditate upon the Supreme Lord in order to create. Then what to speak of great scientists like Einstein! The brains of such a scientist are certainly not the products of any human being. Scientists cannot manufacture such a brain, and what to speak of foolish atheists who defy the authority of the

Lord? Even Māyāvādī impersonalists who flatter themselves that they can become one with the Lord are neither *abhijñaḥ* nor *svarāṭ.* Such impersonalists undergo severe austerities to acquire knowledge to become one with the Lord. But ultimately they become dependent on some rich disciple who supplies them with money to build monasteries and temples. Atheists like Rāvaṇa or Hiraṇyakaśipu had to undergo severe penances before they could flout the authority of the Lord. But ultimately, they were rendered helpless and could not save themselves when the Lord appeared before them as cruel death. This is also the case with the modern atheists who also dare to flout the authority of the Lord. Such atheists will be dealt with similarly, for history repeats itself. Whenever men neglect the authority of the Lord, nature and her laws are there to penalize them. This is confirmed in *Bhagavad-gītā* in the well-known verse *yadā yadā hi dharmasya glāniḥ.* "Whenever there is a decline of *dharma* and a rise of *adharma,* O Arjuna, then I incarnate Myself."(Bg.4.7)

That the Supreme Lord is all-perfect is confirmed in all *śruti-mantras.* It is said in the *śruti-mantras* that the all-perfect Lord threw a glance over matter and thus created all living beings. The living beings are parts and parcels of the Lord, and He impregnates the vast material creation with seeds of spiritual sparks, and thus the creative energies are set in motion to enact so many wonderful creations. An atheist may argue that God is no more expert than a watchmaker, but of course God is greater because He can create machines in duplicate male and female forms. The male and female forms of different types of machineries go on producing innumerable similar machines without God's further attention. If a man could manufacture such a set of machines that could produce other machines without his attention, then he could approach the intelligence of God. But that is not possible, for each machine has to be handled individually. Therefore, no one can create as well as God. Another name for God is *asamaurdhva,* which means that no one is equal to or greater than Him. *Paraṁ satyam,* or the Supreme Truth, is He who has no equal or superior. This is confirmed in the *śruti-mantras.* It is said that before the creation of the material universe there existed the Lord only, who is master of everyone. That Lord instructed Brahmā in Vedic knowledge. That Lord has to be obeyed in all respects. Anyone who wants to get rid of the material entanglement must surrender unto Him. This is also confirmed in *Bhagavad-gītā.*

Unless one surrenders unto the lotus feet of the Supreme Lord, it is certain that he will be bewildered. When an intelligent man surrenders unto the lotus feet of Kṛṣṇa and knows completely that Kṛṣṇa is the cause of all causes, as confirmed in *Bhagavad-gītā,* then only can such an intelligent man become a *mahātmā,* or great soul. But such a great soul is rarely seen. Only the *mahātmās* can understand that the Supreme Lord is the primeval cause of all creations. He is *parama* or ultimate truth because all other truths are relative to Him. He is omniscient. For Him, there is no illusion.

Some Māyāvādī scholars argue that *Śrīmad-Bhāgavatam* was not compiled by Śrī Vyāsadeva. And some of them suggest that this book is a modern creation written by someone named Vopadeva. In order to refute such meaningless arguments, Śrī Śrīdhara Svāmī points out that there is reference to the *Bhāgavatam* in many of the oldest *Purāṇas.* This first *śloka* of the *Bhāgavatam* begins with the Gāyatrī *mantra.* There is reference to this in the *Matsya Purāṇa,* which is the oldest *Purāṇa.* In that *Purāṇa,* it is said with reference to the Gāyatrī mantra in the *Bhāgavatam* that there are many narrations of spiritual instructions begining with the Gāyatrī *mantra. And there is* the history of Vṛtrāsura. Anyone who makes a gift of this great work on a full-moon day attains to the highest perfection of life by returning to Godhead. There is reference to the *Bhāgavatam* in other *Purāṇas* also, where it is clearly stated that this work was finished in twelve cantos, which include eighteen thousand *ślokas.* In the *Padma Purāṇa* also there is reference to the *Bhāgavatam* in a conversation between Gautama and Mahārāja Ambarīṣa. The king was advised therein to read regularly *Śrīmad-Bhāgavatam* if he desired liberation from material bondage. Under the circumstances, there is no doubt about the authority of the *Bhāgavatam.* Within the past five hundred years, many erudite scholars and *ācāryas* like Jīva Gosvāmī, Sanātana Gosvāmī, Viśvanātha Cakravartī, Vallabhācārya, and many other distinguished scholars even after the time of Lord Caitanya made elaborate commentaries on the *Bhāgavatam.* And the serious student would do well to attempt to go through them to better relish the transcendental messages.

Śrīla Viśvanātha Cakravartī Ṭhākura specifically deals with the original and pure sex psychology (*ādi-rasa*), devoid of all mundane inebriety. *The whole material creation is moving under the principle of sex life.* In modern civilization, sex life is the focal point for all activities. Wherever one turns his face, he sees sex life predominant. Therefore, sex life is not unreal. Its reality is experienced in the spiritual world. The material sex life is but a perverted reflection of the original fact. The original fact is in the Absolute Truth, and thus the Absolute Truth cannot be impersonal. It is not possible to be impersonal and contain pure sex life. Consequently, the impersonalist philosophers have given indirect impetus to the abominable mundane sex life because they have overstressed the impersonality of the ultimate truth.

Consequently, man without information of the actual spiritual form of sex has accepted perverted material sex life as the all in all. There is a distinction between sex life in the diseased material condition and spiritual sex life.

This *Śrīmad-Bhāgavatam* will gradually elevate the unbiased reader to the highest perfectional stage of transcendence. It will enable him to transcend the three modes of material activities: fruitive actions, speculative philosophy, and worship of functional deities as inculcated in Vedic verses.

TEXT 2

धर्मः प्रोज्झितकैतवोऽत्र परमो निर्मत्सराणां सतां
वेद्यं वास्तवमत्र वस्तु शिवदं तापत्रयोन्मूलनम् ।
श्रीमद्भागवते महामुनिकृते किं वा परैरीश्वरः
सद्यो हृद्यवरुध्यतेऽत्र कृतिभिः शुश्रूषुभिस्तत्क्षणात् ॥२॥

dharmaḥ projjhita-kaitavo 'tra paramo nirmatsarāṇāṁ satāṁ
vedyaṁ vāstavam atra vastu śivadaṁ tāpa-trayonmūlanam
śrīmad-bhāgavate mahā-muni-kṛte kiṁ vā parair īśvaraḥ
sadyo hṛdy avarudhyate 'tra kṛtibhiḥ śuśrūṣubhis tat-kṣaṇāt

dharmaḥ—religiosity; *projjhita*—completely rejected; *kaitavaḥ*—covered by fruitive intention; *atra*—herein; *paramaḥ*—the highest; *nirmatsarāṇām*—of the one-hundred-percent pure in heart; *satām*—devotees; *vedyam*—understandable; *vāstavam*—factual; *atra*—herein; *vastu*—substance; *śivadam*—well-being; *tāpa-traya*—threefold miseries; *unmūlanam*—causing uprooting of; *śrīmat*—beautiful; *bhāgavate*—the *Bhāgavata Purāṇa; mahā-muni*—the great sage (Vyāsadeva); *kṛte*—having compiled; *kim*—what is; *vā*—the need; *paraiḥ*—others; *īśvaraḥ*—the Supreme Lord; *sadyaḥ*—at once; *hṛdi*—within the heart; *avarudhyate*—become compact; *atra*—herein; *kṛtibhiḥ*—by the pious men; *śuśrūṣubhiḥ*—by culture; *tat-kṣaṇāt*—without delay.

TRANSLATION

Completely rejecting all religious activities which are materially motivated, this Bhāgavata Purāṇa propounds the highest truth, which is understandable by those devotees who are fully pure in heart. The highest truth is reality distinguished from illusion for the welfare of all. Such truth uproots the threefold miseries. This beautiful Bhāgavatam, compiled by

the great sage Vyāsadeva [in his maturity], is sufficient in itself for God realization. What is the need of any other scripture? As soon as one attentively and submissively hears the message of Bhāgavatam, by this culture of knowledge the Supreme Lord is established within his heart.

PURPORT

Religion includes four primary subjects, namely pious activities, economic development, satisfaction of the senses, and finally liberation from material bondage. Irreligious life is a barbarous condition. Indeed, human life begins when religion begins. Eating, sleeping, fearing, and mating are the four principles of animal life. These are common both to animals and to human beings. But religion is the extra function of the human being. Without religion, human life is no better than animal life. Therefore, in human societies there is some form of religion which aims at self-realization and which makes reference to man's eternal relationship with God.

In the lower stages of human civilization, there is always competition to lord it over the material nature or, in other words, there is a continuous rivalry to satisfy the senses. Driven by such consciousness, man turns to religion. He thus performs pious activities or religious functions in order to gain something material. But if such material gains are obtainable in other ways, then so-called religion is neglected. This is the situation in modern civilization. Man is thriving economically, so at present he is not very interested in religion. Churches, mosques or temples are now practically vacant. Men are more interested in factories, shops, and cinemas than in religious places which were erected by their forefathers. This practically proves that religion is performed for some economic gains. Economic gains are needed for sense gratification. Often when one is baffled in the pursuit of sense gratification, he takes to salvation and tries to become one with the Supreme Lord. Consequently, all these states are simply different types of sense gratification.

In the *Vedas,* the above-mentioned four activities are prescribed in the regulative way so that there will not be any undue competition for sense gratification. But *Śrīmad-Bhāgavatam* is transcendental to all these sense gratificatory activities. It is purely transcendental literature which can be understood only by the pure devotees of the Lord who are transcendental to competitive sense gratification. In the material world there is keen competition between animal and animal, man and man, community and community, nation and nation. But the devotees of the Lord rise above such competitions. They do not compete with the materialist because they are on the path back to Godhead where life is eternal and blissful. Such transcendentalists are nonenvious and pure in heart. In the material world, everyone is envious of everyone else, and therefore there is competition. But the transcendental devotees of the Lord are not only free from material envy, but are well-wishers to everyone, and they strive to establish a competitionless society with God in the center. The contemporary socialist's conception of a competitionless society is artificial because in the socialist state there is competition for the post of dictator. From the point of view of the *Vedas* or from the point of view of common human activities, sense gratification is the basis of material life. There are three paths mentioned in the *Vedas.* One involves fruitive activities to gain promotion to better planets. Another involves worshiping different demigods for promotion to the planets of the demigods, and another involves realizing the Absolute Truth and His impersonal feature and becoming one with Him.

The impersonal aspect of the Absolute Truth is not the highest. Above the impersonal feature is the Paramātmā feature, and above this is the personal feature of the Absolute Truth, or Bhagavān. *Śrīmad-Bhāgavatam* gives information about the Absolute Truth in His personal feature. It is higher than impersonalist literatures and higher than the *jñāna-kāṇḍa* division of the *Vedas.* It is even higher than the *karma-kāṇḍa* division, and even higher than the *upāsanā-kāṇḍa* division, because it recommends the worship of the Supreme Personality of Godhead, Lord Śrī Kṛṣṇa. In the *karma-kāṇḍa,* there is competition to reach heavenly planets for better sense gratification, and there is similar competition in the *jñāna-kāṇḍa* and the *upāsanā-kāṇḍa.* The *Śrīmad-Bhāgavatam* is superior to all of these because it aims at the Supreme Truth which is the substance or the root of all categories. From *Śrīmad-Bhāgavatam* one can come to know the substance as well as the categories. The substance is the Absolute Truth, the Supreme Lord, and all emanations are relative forms of energy.

Nothing is apart from the substance, but at the same time the energies are different from the substance. This conception is not contradictory. *Śrīmad-Bhāgavatam* explicitly promulgates this simultaneously-one-and-different philosophy of the *Vedānta-sūtra,* which begins with the "*janmādy asya*" *sūtra.*

This knowledge that the energy of the Lord is simultaneously one with and different from the Lord is an answer to the mental speculators' attempt to establish the energy as the Absolute. When this knowledge is factually understood, one sees the conceptions of monism and dualism to be imperfect. Development of this transcendental consciousness grounded in the conception of simultaneously-one-and-different leads one immediately to the stage of freedom from the threefold miseries. The threefold miseries are (1) those miseries which arise from the mind and body, (2) those miseries inflicted by other living beings, and (3) those miseries arising from natural catastrophes over which one has no control. *Śrīmad-Bhāgavatam* begins with the surrender of the devotee unto the Absolute Person. The devotee is fully aware that he is one with the Absolute and at the same time in the eternal position of servant to the Absolute. In the material conception, one falsely thinks himself the lord of all he surveys, and therefore he is always troubled by the threefold miseries of life. But as soon as one comes to know his real position as transcendental servant, he at once becomes free from all miseries. As long as the living entity is trying to master material nature, there is no possibility of his becoming servant of the Supreme. Service to the Lord is rendered in pure consciousness of one's spiritual identity; by service one is immediately freed from material encumbrances.

Over and above this, *Śrīmad-Bhāgavatam* is a personal commentation on the *Vedānta-sūtra* by Śrī Vyāsadeva. It was written in the maturity of his spiritual life through the mercy of Nārada. Śrī Vyāsadeva is the authorized incarnation of Nārāyaṇa, the Personality of Godhead. Therefore, there is no question as to his authority. He is the author of all other Vedic literatures, yet he recommends the study of *Śrīmad-Bhāgavatam* above all others. In other *Purāṇas* there are different methods set forth by which one can worship the demigods. But in the *Bhāgavatam* only the Supreme Lord is mentioned. The Supreme Lord is the total body, and the demigods are the different parts of that body. Consequently, by worshiping the Supreme Lord, one does not need to worship the demigods. The Supreme Lord becomes fixed in the heart of the devotee immediately. Lord Caitanya Mahāprabhu has recommended the *Śrīmad-Bhāgavatam* as the spotless *Purāṇa* and distinguishes it from all other *Purāṇas.*

The proper method for receiving this transcendental message is to hear it submissively. A challenging attitude cannot help one realize this transcendental message. One particular word is used herein for proper guidance. This word is *śuśrūṣu.* One must be anxious to hear this transcendental message. The desire to sincerely hear is the first qualification.

Less fortunate persons are not at all interested in hearing this *Śrīmad-Bhāgavatam.* The process is simple, but the application is difficult. Unfortunate people find enough time to hear idle social and political conversations, but when invited to attend a meeting of devotees to hear *Śrīmad-Bhāgavatam* they suddenly become reluctant. Sometimes professional readers of the

Bhāgavatam immediately plunge into the confidential topics of the pastimes of the Supreme Lord, which they seemingly interpret as sex literature. *Śrīmad-Bhāgavatam* is meant to be heard from the beginning. Those who are fit to assimilate this work are mentioned in this *śloka:* "One becomes qualified to hear *Śrīmad-Bhāgavatam* after many pious deeds." The intelligent person, with thoughtful discretion, can be assured by the great sage Vyāsadeva that he can realize the Supreme Personality directly by hearing *Śrīmad-Bhāgavatam.* Without undergoing the different stages of realization set forth in the *Vedas,* one can be lifted immediately to the position of *paramahaṁsa* simply by agreeing to receive this message.

TEXT 3

निगमकल्पतरोर्गलितं फलं
शुकमुखादमृतद्रवसंयुतम् ।
पिबत भागवतं रसमालयं
मुहुरहो रसिका भुवि भावुकाः ॥ ३ ॥

nigama-kalpa-taror galitaṁ phalaṁ
śuka-mukhād amṛta-drava-saṁyutam
pibata bhāgavataṁ rasam ālayam
muhur aho rasikā bhuvi bhāvukāḥ

nigama—the Vedic literatures; *kalpa-taroḥ*—the desire tree; *galitam*—fully matured; *phalam*—fruit; *śuka*—Śrīla Śukadeva Gosvāmī, the original speaker of *Śrīmad-Bhāgavatam; mukhāt*—from the lips of; *amṛta*—nectar; *drava*—semisolid and soft and therefore easily swallowable; *saṁyutam*—perfect in all respects; *pibata*—do relish it; *bhāgavatam*—the book dealing in the science of the eternal relation with the Lord; *rasam*—juice (that which is relishable); *ālayam*—until liberation, or even in a liberated condition; *muhuḥ*—always; *aho*—O; *rasikāḥ*—those who are full in the knowledge of mellows; *bhuvi*—on the earth; *bhāvukāḥ*—expert and thoughtful.

TRANSLATION

O expert and thoughtful men, relish Śrīmad-Bhāgavatam, the mature fruit of the desire tree of Vedic literatures. It emanated from the lips of Śrī Śukadeva Gosvāmī. Therefore this fruit has become even more tasteful, although its nectarean juice was already relishable for all, including liberated souls.

PURPORT

In the two previous *ślokas* it has been definitely proved that the *Śrīmad-Bhāgavatam* is the sublime literature which surpasses all other Vedic scriptures due to its transcendental qualities. It is transcendental to all mundane activities and mundane knowledge. In this *śloka* it is stated that *Śrīmad-Bhāgavatam* is not only a superior literature but is the ripened fruit of all Vedic literatures. In other words, it is the cream of all Vedic knowledge. Considering all this, patient and submissive hearing is definitely essential. With great respect and attention, one should receive the message and lessons imparted by the *Śrīmad-Bhāgavatam.*

The *Vedas* are compared to the desire tree because they contain all things knowable by man. They deal with mundane necessities as well as spiritual realization. The *Vedas* contain regulated principles of knowledge covering social, political, religious, economic, military, medicinal, chemical, physical and metaphysical subject matter and all that may be necessary to keep the body and soul together. Above and beyond all this are specific directions for spiritual realization. Regulated knowledge involves a gradual raising of the living entity to the spiritual platform, and the highest spiritual realization is knowledge that the Personality of Godhead is the reservoir of all spiritual tastes, or *rasas.*

Every living entity, beginning from Brahmā, the first-born living being within the material world, down to the insignificant ant, desires to relish some sort of taste derived from sense perceptions. These sensual pleasures are technically called *rasas.* Such *rasas* are of different varieties. In the revealed scriptures the following twelve varieties of *rasas* are enumerated: (1) *raudra* (anger), (2) *adbhuta* (wonder), (3) *śṛṅgāra* (conjugal love), (4) *hāsya* (comedy), (5) *vīra* (chivalry), (6) *dayā* (mercy), (7) *dāsya* (servitorship), (8) *sakhya* (fraternity), (9) *bhayānaka* (horror), (10) *bībhatsa* (shock), (11) *śānta* (neutrality), (12) *vātsalya* (parenthood).

The sum total of all these *rasas* is called affection or love. Primarily, such signs of love are manifested in adoration, service, friendship, parental affection, and conjugal love. And when these five are absent, love is present indirectly in anger, wonder, comedy, chivalry, fear, shock and so on. For example, when a man is in love with a woman, the *rasa* is called conjugal love. But when such love affairs are disturbed there may be wonder, anger, shock, or even horror. Sometimes love affairs between two persons culminate in ghastly murder scenes. Such *rasas* are displayed between man and man and between animal and animal. There is no possibility of an exchange or *rasa* between a man and an animal or between a man and any other species of living beings within the material world. The *rasas* are exchanged between members of the same species. But as far as the spirit souls are concerned, they are one qualitatively with the Supreme Lord. Therefore, the *rasas* were originally exchanged between the spiritual living being and the spiritual whole, the Supreme Personality of Godhead. The spiritual exchange or *rasa* is fully exhibited in spiritual existence between living beings and the Supreme Lord.

The Supreme Personality of Godhead is therefore described in the *śruti-mantras,* Vedic hymns, as "the fountainhead of all *rasas.*" When one associates with the Supreme Lord and exchanges one's constitutional *rasa* with the Lord, then the living being is actually happy.

These *śruti-mantras* indicate that every living being has its constitutional position, which is endowed with a particular type of *rasa* to be exchanged with the Personality of Godhead. In the liberated condition only, this primary *rasa* is experienced in full. In the material existence, the *rasa* is experienced in the perverted form, which is temporary. And thus the *rasas* of the material world are exhibited in the material form of *raudra* (anger) and so on.

Therefore, one who attains full knowledge of these different *rasas,* which are the basic principles of activities, can understand the false representations of the original *rasas* which are reflected in the material world. The learned scholar seeks to relish the real *rasa* in the spiritual form. In the beginning he desires to become one with the Supreme. Thus, less intelligent transcendentalists cannot go beyond this conception of becoming one with the spirit whole, without knowing of the different *rasas.*

In this *śloka,* it is definitely stated that spiritual *rasa,* which is relished even in the liberated stage, can be experienced in the literature of the *Śrīmad-Bhāgavatam* due to its being the ripened fruit of all Vedic knowledge. By submissively hearing this transcendental literature, one can attain the full pleasure of his heart's desire. But one must be very careful to hear the message from the right source. *Śrīmad-Bhāgavatam* is exactly received from the right source. It was brought by Nārada Muni from the spiritual world and given to his disciple Śrī Vyāsadeva. The latter in turn delivered the message to his son Śrīla Śukadeva Gosvāmī, and Śrīla Śukadeva Gosvāmī delivered the message to Mahārāja Parīkṣit just seven days before the King's death. Śrīla Śukadeva Gosvāmī was a liberated soul from his very birth. He was liberated even in the womb of his mother, and he did not undergo any sort of spiritual training after his birth. At birth no one is qualified, neither in the mundane nor in the spiritual sense. But Śrī Śukadeva Gosvāmī, due to his being a perfectly liberated soul, did not have to undergo an evolutionary process for spiritual realization. Yet despite his being a completely liberated person situated in the transcendental position above the three material modes, he was attracted to this transcendental *rasa* of the Supreme Personality of Godhead, who is adored by liberated souls who sing Vedic hymns. The Supreme Lord's pastimes are more attractive to liberated souls than to mundane people. He is of necessity not impersonal because it is only possible to carry on transcendental *rasa* with a person.

In the *Śrīmad-Bhāgavatam* the transcendental pastimes of the Lord are narrated, and the narration is systematically depicted by Śrīla Śukadeva Gosvāmī. Thus the subject matter is appealing to all classes of persons, including those who seek liberation and those who seek to become one with the supreme whole.

In Sanskrit the parrot is also known as *śuka.* When a ripened fruit is cut by the red beaks of such birds, its sweet flavor is enhanced. The Vedic fruit which is mature and ripe in knowledge is spoken through the lips of Śrīla Śukadeva Gosvāmī, who is compared to the parrot not for his ability to recite the *Bhāgavatam* exactly as he heard it from his learned father, but for his ability to present the work in a manner that would appeal to all classes of men.

The subject matter is so presented through the lips of Śrīla Śukadeva Gosvāmī that any sincere listener that hears submissively can at once relish transcendental tastes which are distinct from the perverted tastes of the material world. The ripened fruit is not dropped all of a sudden from the highest planet of Kṛṣṇaloka. Rather, it has come down carefully through the chain of disciplic succession without change or disturbance. Foolish people who are not in the transcendental disciplic succession commit great blunders by trying to understand the highest transcendental *rasa* known as the *rāsa* dance without following in the footsteps of Śukadeva Gosvāmī, who presents this fruit very carefully by stages of transcendental realization. One should be intelligent enough to know the position of *Śrīmad-Bhāgavatam* by considering personalities like Śukadeva Gosvāmī, who deals with the subject so carefully. This process of disciplic succession of the *Bhāgavata* school suggests that in the future also *Śrīmad-Bhāgavatam* has to be understood from a person who is factually a representative of Śrīla Śukadeva Gosvāmī. A professional man who makes a business out of reciting the *Bhāgavatam* illegally is certainly not a representative of Śukadeva Gosvāmī. Such a man's business is only to earn his livelihood. Therefore one should refrain from hearing the lectures of such professional men. Such men usually go to the most confidential part of the literature without undergoing the gradual process of understanding this grave subject. They usually plunge into the subject matter of the *rāsa* dance, which is misunderstood by the foolish class of men. Some of them take this to be immoral, while others try to cover it up by their own stupid interpretations. They have no desire to follow in the footsteps of Śrīla Śukadeva Gosvāmī.

One should conclude, therefore, that the serious student of the *rasa* should receive the message of *Bhāgavatam* in the chain of disciplic succession from Śrīla Śukadeva Gosvāmī, who describes the *Bhāgavatam* from its very beginning and not whimsically to satisfy the mundaner who has very little knowledge in transcendental science. *Śrīmad-Bhāgavatam* is so carefully presented that a sincere and serious person can at once enjoy the ripened fruit of Vedic knowledge simply by drinking the nectarean juice through the mouth of Śukadeva Gosvāmī or his bona fide representative.

TEXT 4

नैमिषेऽनिमिषक्षेत्रे ऋषयः शौनकादयः ।
सत्रं स्वर्गायलोकाय सहस्रसममासत ॥४॥

naimiṣe 'nimiṣa-kṣetre
ṛṣayaḥ śaunakādayaḥ
satraṁ svargāya lokāya
sahasra-samam āsata

naimiṣe—in the forest known as Naimiṣāraṇya; *animiṣa-kṣetre*—the spot which is especially a favorite of Viṣṇu (who does not close His eyelids); *ṛṣayaḥ*—sages; *śaunaka-ādayaḥ*—headed by the sage Śaunaka; *satram*—sacrifice; *svargāya*—the Lord who is glorified in heaven; *lokāya*—and for the devotees who are always in touch with the Lord; *sahasra*—one thousand; *samam*—years; *āsata*—performed.

TRANSLATION

Once, in a holy place in the forest of Naimiṣāraṇya, great sages headed by the sage Śaunaka assembled to perform a great thousand-year sacrifice for the satisfaction of the Lord and His devotees.

PURPORT

The prelude of the *Śrīmad-Bhāgavatam* was spoken in the previous three *ślokas.* Now the main topic of this great literature is being presented. *Śrīmad-*

Bhāgavatam, after its first recitation by Śrīla Śukadeva Gosvāmī, was repeated for the second time at Naimiṣāraṇya.

In the *Vāyavīya Tantra,* it is said that Brahmā, the engineer of this particular universe, contemplated a great wheel which could enclose the universe. The hub of this great circle was fixed at a particular place known as Naimiṣāraṇya. Similarly, there is another reference to the forest of Naimiṣāraṇya in the *Varāha Purāṇa,* where it is stated that by performance of sacrifice at this place, the strength of demoniac people is curtailed. Thus *brāhmaṇas* prefer Naimiṣāraṇya for such sacrificial performances.

The devotees of Lord Viṣṇu offer all kinds of sacrifices for His pleasure. The devotees are always attached to the service of the Lord, whereas fallen souls are attached to the pleasures of material existence. In *Bhagavad-gītā,* it is said that anything performed in the material world for any reason other than for the pleasure of Lord Viṣṇu causes further bondage for the performer. It is enjoined therefore that all acts must be performed sacrificially for the satisfaction of Viṣṇu and His devotees. This will bring everyone peace and prosperity.

The great sages are always anxious to do good to the people in general, and as such the sages headed by Śaunaka and others assembled at this holy place of Naimiṣāraṇya with a program of performing a great and continuous chain of sacrificial ceremonies. Forgetful men do not know the right path for peace and prosperity. However, the sages know it well, and therefore for the good of all men they are always anxious to perform acts which may bring about peace in the world. They are sincere friends to all living entities, and at the risk of great personal inconvenience they are always engaged in the service of the Lord for the good of all people. Lord Viṣṇu is just like a great tree, and all others, including the demigods, men, Siddhas, Cāraṇas, Vidyādharas and other living entities, are like branches, twigs and leaves of that tree. By pouring water on the root of the tree, all the parts of the tree are automatically nourished. Only those branches and leaves which are detached cannot be so satisfied. Detached branches and leaves dry up gradually despite all watering attempts. Similarly, human society, when it is detached from the Personality of Godhead like detached branches and leaves, is not capable of being watered, and one attempting to do so is simply wasting his energy and resources.

The modern materialistic society is detached from its relation to the Supreme Lord. And all its plans which are being made by atheistic leaders are sure to be baffled at every step. Yet they do not wake up to this.

In this age, the congregational chanting of the holy names of the Lord is the prescribed method for waking up. The ways and means are most scientifically presented by Lord Śrī Caitanya Mahāprabhu, and intelligent persons may take advantage of His teachings in order to bring about real peace and prosperity. *Śrīmad-Bhāgavatam* is also presented for the same purpose, and this will be explained more specifically later in the text.

TEXT 5

त एकदा तु मुनयः प्रातर्हुतहुताग्नयः ।
सत्कृतं सूतमासीनं पप्रच्छुरिदमादरात् ॥५॥

ta ekadā tu munayaḥ
prātar huta-hutāgnayaḥ
sat-kṛtaṁ sūtam āsīnaṁ
papracchur idam ādarāt

te—the sages; *ekadā*—one day; *tu*—but; *munayaḥ*—sages; *prātaḥ*—morning; *huta*—burning; *huta-agnayaḥ*—the sacrificial fire; *sat-kṛtam*—due respects; *sūtam*—Śrī Sūta Gosvāmī; *āsīnam*—seated on; *papracchuḥ*—made inquiries; *idam*—on this (as follows); *ādarāt*—with due regards.

TRANSLATION

One day, after finishing their morning duties by burning a sacrificial fire and offering a seat of esteem to Śrīla Sūta Gosvāmī, the great sages made inquiries, with great respect, about the following matters.

PURPORT

Morning is the best time to hold spiritual services. The great sages offered the speaker of the *Bhāgavatam* an elevated seat of respect called the *vyāsāsana,* or the seat of Śrī Vyāsadeva. Śrī Vyāsadeva is the original spiritual preceptor for all men. And all other preceptors are considered to be his representatives. A representative is one who can exactly present the viewpoint of Śrī Vyāsadeva. Śrī Vyāsadeva impregnated the message of *Bhāgavatam* unto Śrīla Śukadeva Gosvāmī, and Śrī Sūta Gosvāmī heard it from him (Śrī Śukadeva Gosvāmī). All bona fide representatives of Śrī Vyāsadeva in the chain of disciplic succession are to be understood to be *gosvāmīs.* These *gosvāmīs* restrain all their senses, and they stick to the path made by the previous *ācāryas.* The *gosvāmīs* do not deliver lectures on the *Bhāgavatam* capriciously. Rather, they execute their services most carefully, following their predecessors who delivered the spiritual message unbroken to them.

Those who listen to the *Bhāgavatam* may put questions to the speaker in order to elicit the clear meaning, but this should not be done in a challenging spirit. One must submit questions with a great regard for the speaker and the subject matter. This is also the way recommended in *Bhagavad-gītā.* One must learn the transcendental subject by submissive aural reception from the right sources. Therefore these sages addressed the speaker Sūta Gosvāmī with great respect.

TEXT 6

ऋषय ऊचुः
त्वया खलु पुराणानि सेतिहासानि चानघ।
आख्यातान्यप्यधीतानि धर्मशास्त्राणि यान्युत ॥६॥

ṛṣaya ūcuḥ
tvayā khalu purāṇāni
setihāsāni cānagha
ākhyātāny apy adhītāni
dharma-śāstrāṇi yāny uta

ṛṣayaḥ—the sages; *ūcuḥ*—said; *tvayā*—by you; *khalu*—undoubtedly; *purāṇāni*—the supplements to the *Vedas* with illustrative narrations; *sa-itihāsāni*—along with the histories; *ca*—and; *anagha*—freed from all vices; *ākhyātāni*—explained; *api*—although; *adhītāni*—well read; *dharma-śāstrāṇi*—scriptures giving right directions to progressive life; *yāni*—all these; *uta*—said.

TRANSLATION

The sages said: Respected Sūta Gosvāmī, you are completely free from all vice. You are well versed in all the scriptures famous for religious life, and in the Purāṇas and the histories as well, for you have gone through them under proper guidance and have also explained them.

PURPORT

A *gosvāmī,* or the bona fide representative of Śrī Vyāsadeva, must be free from all kinds of vices. The four major vices of Kali-yuga are (1) illicit connection with women, (2) animal slaughter, (3) intoxication, (4) speculative gambling of all sorts. A *gosvāmī* must be free from all these vices before he can dare sit on the *vyāsāsana.* No one should be allowed to sit on the *vyāsāsana* who is not spotless in character and who is not freed from the above-mentioned vices. He not only should be freed from all such vices, but must also be well versed in all revealed scriptures or in the *Vedas.* The *Purāṇas* are also parts of the *Vedas.* And histories like the *Mahābhārata* or *Rāmāyaṇa* are also parts of the *Vedas.* The *ācārya* or the *gosvāmī* must be well acquainted with all these literatures. To hear and explain them is more important than reading them. One can assimilate the knowledge of the revealed scriptures only by hearing and explaining. Hearing is called *śravaṇa,* and explaining is called *kīrtana.* The two processes of *śravaṇa* and *kīrtana* are of primary importance to progressive spiritual life. Only one who has properly grasped the transcendental knowledge from the right source by submissive hearing can properly explain the subject.

TEXT 7

यानि वेदविदां श्रेष्ठो भगवान् बादरायणः।
अन्ये च मुनयः सूत परावरविदो विदुः ॥७॥

yāni veda-vidāṁ śreṣṭho
bhagavān bādarāyaṇaḥ
anye ca munayaḥ sūta
parāvara-vido viduḥ

yāni—all that; *veda-vidām*—scholars of the *Vedas; śreṣṭhaḥ*—seniormost; *bhagavān*—incarnation of Godhead; *bādarāyaṇaḥ*—Vyāsadeva; *anye*—others; *ca*—and; *munayaḥ*—the sages; *sūta*—O Sūta Gosvāmī; *parāvara-vidaḥ*—amongst the learned scholars, one who is conversant with physical and metaphysical knowledge; *viduḥ*—one who knows.

TRANSLATION

Being the eldest learned Vedāntist, O Sūta Gosvāmī, you are acquainted with the knowledge of Vyāsadeva, who is the incarnation of Godhead, and you also know other sages who are fully versed in all kinds of physical and metaphysical knowledge.

PURPORT

Śrīmad-Bhāgavatam is a natural commentation on the *Brahma-sūtra,* or the *Bādarāyaṇi Vedānta-sūtras.* It is called natural because Vyāsadeva is author of both the *Vedānta-sūtras* and *Śrīmad-Bhāgavatam,* or the essence of all Vedic literatures. Besides Vyāsadeva, there are other sages who are the authors of six different philosophical systems, namely Gautama, Kaṇāda, Kapila, Patañjali, Jaimini and Aṣṭāvakra. Theism is explained completely in the *Vedānta-sūtra,* whereas in other systems of philosophical speculations, practically no mention is given to the ultimate cause of all causes. One can sit on the *vyāsāsana* only after being conversant in all systems of philosophy so that one can present fully the theistic views of the *Bhāgavatam* in defiance of all other systems. Śrīla Sūta Gosvāmī was the proper teacher, and therefore the sages at Naimiṣāraṇya elevated him to the *vyāsāsana.* Śrīla Vyāsadeva is designated herein as the Personality of Godhead because he is the authorized empowered incarnation.

TEXT 8

वेत्थ त्वं सौम्य तत्सर्वं तत्त्वतस्तदनुग्रहात् ।
ब्रूयुः स्निग्धस्य शिष्यस्य गुरवो गुह्यमप्युत ॥८॥

vettha tvaṁ saumya tat sarvaṁ
tattvatas tad-anugrahāt
brūyuḥ snigdhasya śiṣyasya
guravo guhyam apy uta

vettha—you are well conversant; *tvam*—Your Honor; *saumya*—one who is pure and simple; *tat*—those; *sarvam*—all; *tattvataḥ*—in fact; *tat*—their; *anugrahāt*—by the favor of; *brūyuḥ*—will tell; *snigdhasya*—of the one who is submissive; *śiṣyasya*—of the disciple; *guravaḥ*—the spiritual masters; *guhyam*—secret; *api uta*—endowed with.

TRANSLATION

And because you are submissive, your spiritual masters have endowed you with all the favors bestowed upon a gentle disciple. Therefore you can tell us all that you have scientifically learned from them.

PURPORT

The secret of success in spiritual life is in satisfying the spiritual master and thereby getting his sincere blessings. Śrīla Viśvanātha Cakravartī Ṭhākura has sung in his famous eight stanzas on the spiritual master as follows: "I offer my respectful obeisances unto the lotus feet of my spiritual master. Only by his satisfaction can one please the Personality of Godhead, and when he is dissatisfied there is only havoc on the path of spiritual realization." It is essential, therefore, that a disciple be very much obedient and submissive to the bona fide spiritual master. Śrīla Sūta Gosvāmī fulfilled all these qualifications as a disciple, and therefore he was endowed with all favors by his learned and self-realized spiritual masters such as Śrīla Vyāsadeva and others. The sages of Naimiṣāraṇya were confident that Śrīla Sūta Gosvāmī was bona fide. Therefore they were anxious to hear from him.

TEXT 9

तत्र तत्राञ्जसायुष्मन् भवता यद्विनिश्चितम् ।
पुंसामेकान्ततः श्रेयस्तन्नः शंसितुमर्हसि ॥९॥

tatra tatrāñjasāyuṣman
bhavatā yad viniścitam
puṁsām ekāntataḥ śreyas
tan naḥ śaṁsitum arhasi

tatra—thereof; *tatra*—thereof; *añjasā*—made easy; *āyuṣman*—blessed with a long duration of life; *bhavatā*—by your good self; *yat*—whatever; *viniścitam*—ascertained; *puṁsām*—for the people in general; *ekāntataḥ*—absolutely; *śreyaḥ*—ultimate good; *tat*—that; *naḥ*—to us; *śaṁsitum*—to explain; *arhasi*—deserve.

TRANSLATION

Please, therefore, being blessed with many years, explain to us, in an easily understandable way, what you have ascertained to be the absolute and ultimate good for the people in general.

PURPORT

In *Bhagavad-gītā,* worship of the *ācārya* is recommended. The *ācāryas* and *gosvāmīs* are always absorbed in thought of the well-being of the general public, especially their spiritual well-being. Spiritual well-being is automatically followed by material well-being. The *ācāryas* therefore give directions in spiritual well-being for people in general. Foreseeing the incompetencies of the people in this age of Kali, or the iron age of quarrel, the sages requested that Sūta Gosvāmī give a summary of all revealed scriptures because the people of this age are condemned in every respect. The sages, therefore, inquired of the absolute good, which is the ultimate good for the people. The condemned state of affairs of the people of this age is described as follows.

TEXT 10

प्रायेणाल्पायुषः सभ्य कलावस्मिन् युगे जनाः ।
मन्दाः सुमन्दमतयो मन्दभाग्या ह्युपद्रुताः ॥१०॥

prāyeṇālpāyuṣaḥ sabhya
kalāv asmin yuge janāḥ
mandāḥ sumanda-matayo
manda-bhāgyā hy upadrutāḥ

prāyeṇa—almost always; *alpa*—meager; *āyuṣaḥ*—duration of life; *sabhya*—member of a learned society; *kalau*—in this age of Kali (quarrel); *asmin*—herein; *yuge*—age; *janāḥ*—the public; *mandāḥ*—lazy; *sumanda-matayaḥ*—misguided; *manda-bhāgyāḥ*—unlucky; *hi*—and above all; *upadrutāḥ*—disturbed.

TRANSLATION

O learned one, in this iron age of Kali men have but short lives. They are quarrelsome, lazy, misguided, unlucky and, above all, always disturbed.

PURPORT

The devotees of the Lord are always anxious for the spiritual improvement of the general public. When the sages of Naimiṣāraṇya analyzed the state of affairs of the people in this age of Kali, they foresaw that men would live short lives. In Kali-yuga, the duration of life is shortened not so much because of insufficient food but because of irregular habits. By keeping regular habits and eating simple food, any man can maintain his health. Overeating, over-sense gratification, overdependence on another's mercy, and artificial standards of living sap the very vitality of human energy. Therefore the duration of life is shortened.

The people of this age are also very lazy, not only materially but in the matter of self-realization. The human life is especially meant for self-realization. That is to say, man should come to know what he is, what the world is, and what the supreme truth is. Human life is a means by which the living entity can end all the miseries of the hard struggle for life in material existence and by which he can return to Godhead, his eternal home. But, due to a bad system of education, men have no desire for self-realization. Even if they come to know about it, they unfortunately become victims of misguided teachers.

In this age, men are victims not only of different political creeds and parties, but also of many different types of sense gratificatory diversions, such as cinemas, sports, gambling, clubs, mundane libraries, bad association, smoking, drinking, cheating, pilfering, bickerings and so on. Their minds are always disturbed and full of anxieties due to so many different engagements. In this age, many unscrupulous men manufacture their own religious faiths which are not based on any revealed scriptures, and very often people who are addicted to sense gratification are attracted by such institutions. Consequently, in the name of religion so many sinful acts are being carried on that the people in general have neither peace of mind nor health of body. The student (*brahmacārī*) communities are no longer being maintained, and householders do not observe the rules and regulations of the *gṛhastha-āśrama.* Consequently, the so-called *vānaprasthas* and *sannyāsīs* who come out of such *gṛhastha-āśramas* are easily deviated from the rigid path. In the Kali-yuga the whole atmosphere is surcharged with faithlessness. Men are no longer interested in spiritual values. Material sense gratification is now the standard of civilization. For the maintenance of such material civilizations, man has formed complex nations and communities, and there is a constant strain of hot and cold wars between these different groups. It has become very difficult, therefore, to raise the spiritual standard due to the present distorted values of human society. The sages of Naimiṣāraṇya are anxious to disentangle all fallen souls, and here they are seeking the remedy from Śrīla Sūta Gosvāmī.

TEXT 11

भूरीणि भूरिकर्माणि श्रोतव्यानि विभागशः ।
अतः साधोऽत्र यत्सारं समुद्धृत्य मनीषया ।
ब्रूहि भद्राय भूतानां येनात्मा सुप्रसीदति ॥११॥

bhūrīṇi bhūri-karmāṇi
śrotavyāni vibhāgaśaḥ
ataḥ sādho 'tra yat sāraṁ
samuddhṛtya manīṣayā

brūhi bhadrāya bhūtānām
yenātmā suprasīdati

bhūrīṇi—multifarious; *bhūri*—many; *karmāṇi*—duties; *śrotavyāni*—to be learned; *vibhāgaśaḥ*—by divisions of subject matter; *ataḥ*—therefore; *sādho*—O sage; *atra*—herein; *yat*—whatever; *sāram*—essence; *samuddhṛtya*—by selection; *manīṣayā*—best to your knowledge; *brūhi*—please tell us; *bhadrāya*—for the good of; *bhūtānām*—the living beings; *yena*—by which; *ātmā*—the self; *suprasīdati*—becomes fully satisfied.

TRANSLATION

There are many varieties of scriptures, and in all of them there are many prescribed duties, which can be learned only after many years of study in their various divisions. Therefore, O sage, please select the essence of all these scriptures and explain it for the good of all living beings, that by such instruction their hearts may be fully satisfied.

PURPORT

Ātmā, or self, is distinguished from matter and material elements. It is spiritual in constitution, and thus it is never satisfied by any amount of material planning. All scriptures and spiritual instructions are meant for the satisfaction of this self, or *ātmā.* There are many varieties of approaches which are recommended for different types of living beings in different times and at different places. Consequently, the numbers of revealed scriptures are innumerable. There are different methods and prescribed duties recommended in these various scriptures. Taking into consideration the fallen condition of the people in general in this age of Kali, the sages of Naimiṣāraṇya suggested that Śrī Sūta Gosvāmī relate the essence of all such scriptures because in this age it is not possible for the fallen souls to understand and undergo all the lessons of all these various scriptures in a *varṇa* and *āśrama* system.

The *varṇa* and *āśrama* society was considered to be the best institution for lifting the human being to the spiritual platform, but due to Kali-yuga it is not possible to execute the rules and regulations of these institutions. Nor is it possible for the people in general to completely sever relations with their families as the *varṇāśrama* institution prescribes. The whole atmosphere is surcharged with opposition. And considering this, one can see that spiritual emancipation for the common man in this age is very difficult. The reason the sages presented this matter to Śrī Sūta Gosvāmī is explained in the following verses.

TEXT 12

सूत जानासि भद्रं ते भगवान् सात्वतां पतिः ।
देवक्यां वसुदेवस्य जातो यस्य चिकीर्षया ॥१२॥

sūta jānāsi bhadraṁ te
bhagavān sātvatāṁ patiḥ
devakyāṁ vasudevasya
jāto yasya cikīrṣayā

sūta—O Sūta Gosvāmī; *jānāsi*—you know; *bhadram te*—all blessings upon you; *bhagavān*—the Personality of Godhead; *sātvatām*—of the pure devotees; *patiḥ*—the protector; *devakyām*—in the womb of Devakī; *vasudevasya*—by Vasudeva; *jātaḥ*—born of; *yasya*—for the purpose of; *cikīrṣayā*—executing.

TRANSLATION

All blessings upon you, O Sūta Gosvāmī. You know for what purpose the Personality of Godhead appeared in the womb of Devakī as the son of Vasudeva.

PURPORT

Bhagavān means the almighty God who is the controller of all opulence, power, fame, beauty, knowledge and renunciation. He is the protector of His pure devotees. Although God is equally disposed to everyone, He is especially inclined to His devotees. *Sat* means the Absolute Truth. And persons who are servitors of the Absolute Truth are called *sātvatas.* And the Personality of Godhead who protects such pure devotees is known as the protector of the *sātvatas. Bhadraṁ te,* or "blessings upon you," indicates the sages' anxiety to know the Absolute Truth from the speaker. Lord Śrī Kṛṣṇa, the Supreme Personality of Godhead, appeared to Devakī, the wife of Vasudeva. Vasudeva is the symbol of the transcendental position wherein the appearance of the Supreme Lord takes place.

TEXT 13

तन्नः शुश्रूषमाणानामर्हस्यङ्गानुवर्णितुम् ।
यस्यावतारो भूतानां क्षेमाय च भवाय च ॥१३॥

tan naḥ śuśrūṣamāṇānām
arhasy aṅgānuvarṇitum
yasyāvatāro bhūtānāṁ
kṣemāya ca bhavāya ca

tat—those; *naḥ*—unto us; *śuśrūṣamāṇānām*—those who are endeavoring for; *arhasi*—ought to do it; *aṅga*—O Sūta Gosvāmī; *anuvarṇitum*—to explain by following in the footsteps of previous *ācāryas; yasya*—whose; *avatāraḥ*—incarnation; *bhūtānām*—of the living beings; *kṣemāya*—for good; *ca*—and; *bhavāya*—upliftment; *ca*—and.

TRANSLATION

O Sūta Gosvāmī, we are eager to learn about the Personality of Godhead and His incarnations. Please explain to us those teachings imparted by previous masters [ācāryas], for one is uplifted both by speaking them and by hearing them.

PURPORT

The conditions for hearing the transcendental message of the Absolute Truth are set forth herein. The first condition is that the audience must be very sincere and eager to hear. And the speaker must be in the line of disciplic succession from the recognized *ācārya.* The transcendental message of the Absolute is not understandable by those who are materially absorbed. Under the direction of a bona fide spiritual master, one becomes gradually purified. Therefore, one must be in the chain of disciplic succession and learn the spiritual art of submissive hearing. In the case of Sūta Gosvāmī and the sages of Naimiṣāraṇya, all these conditions are fulfilled because Śrīla Sūta Gosvāmī is in the line of Śrīla Vyāsadeva, and the sages of Naimiṣāraṇya are all sincere souls who are anxious to learn the truth. Thus the transcendental topics of Lord Śrī Kṛṣṇa's superhuman activities, His incarnation, His birth, appearance or disappearance, His forms, His names and so on are all easily understandable because all requirements are fulfilled. Such discourses help all men on the path of spiritual realization.

TEXT 14

आपन्नः संसृतिं घोरां यन्नाम विवशो गृणन्।
ततः सद्यो विमुच्येत यद्बिभेति स्वयं भयम् ॥१४॥

āpannaḥ saṁsṛtiṁ ghorāṁ
yan-nāma vivaśo gṛṇan
tataḥ sadyo vimucyeta
yad bibheti svayaṁ bhayam

āpannaḥ—being entangled; *saṁsṛtim*—in the hurdle of birth and death; *ghorām*—too complicated; *yat*—what; *nāma*—the absolute name; *vivaśaḥ*—unconsciously; *gṛṇan*—chanting; *tataḥ*—from that; *sadyaḥ*—at once; *vimucyeta*—gets freedom; *yat*—that which; *bibheti*—fears; *svayam*—personally; *bhayam*—fear itself.

TRANSLATION

Living beings who are entangled in the complicated meshes of birth and death can be freed immediately by even unconsciously chanting the holy name of Kṛṣṇa, which is feared by fear personified.

PURPORT

Vāsudeva, or Lord Kṛṣṇa, the Absolute Personality of Godhead, is the supreme controller of everything. There is no one in creation who is not afraid of the rage of the Almighty. Great *asuras* like Rāvaṇa, Hiraṇyakaśipu, Kaṁsa, and others who were very powerful living entities were all killed by the Personality of Godhead. And the almighty Vāsudeva has empowered His name with the powers of His personal Self. Everything is related to Him, and everything has its identity in Him. It is stated herein that the name of Kṛṣṇa is feared even by fear personified. This indicates that the name of Kṛṣṇa is nondifferent from Kṛṣṇa. Therefore, the name of Kṛṣṇa is as powerful as Lord Kṛṣṇa Himself. There is no difference at all. Anyone, therefore, can take advantage of the holy names of Lord Śrī Kṛṣṇa even in the midst of greatest dangers. The transcendental name of Kṛṣṇa, even though uttered unconsciously or by force of circumstances, can help one obtain freedom from the hurdle of birth and death.

TEXT 15

यत्पादसंश्रयाः सूत मुनयः प्रशमायनाः ।
सद्यः पुनन्त्युपस्पृष्टाः स्वर्धुन्यापोऽनुसेवया ॥१५॥

yat-pāda-saṁśrayāḥ sūta
munayaḥ praśamāyanāḥ

sadyaḥ punanty upaspṛṣṭāḥ
svardhuny-āpo 'nusevayā

yat—whose; *pāda*—lotus feet; *saṁśrayāḥ*—those who have taken shelter of; *sūta*—O Sūta Gosvāmī; *munayaḥ*—great sages; *praśamāyanāḥ*—absorbed in devotion to the Supreme; *sadyaḥ*—at once; *punanti*—sanctify; *upaspṛṣṭāḥ*—simply by association; *svardhunī*—of the sacred Ganges; *āpaḥ*—water; *anusevayā*—bringing into use.

TRANSLATION

O Sūta, those great sages who have completely taken shelter of the lotus feet of the Lord can at once sanctify those who come in touch with them, whereas the waters of the Ganges can sanctify only after prolonged use.

PURPORT

Pure devotees of the Lord are more powerful than the waters of the sacred river Ganges. One can derive spiritual benefit out of prolonged use of the Ganges waters. But one can be sanctified at once by the mercy of a pure devotee of the Lord. In *Bhagavad-gītā* it is said that any person, regardless of birth as *śūdra,* woman, or merchant, can take shelter of the lotus feet of the Lord and by so doing can return to Godhead. To take shelter of the lotus feet of the Lord means to take shelter of the pure devotees. The pure devotees whose only business is serving are honored by the names Prabhupāda and Viṣṇupāda, which indicate such devotees to be representatives of the lotus feet of the Lord. Anyone, therefore, who takes shelter of the lotus feet of a pure devotee by accepting the pure devotee as his spiritual master can be at once purified. Such devotees of the Lord are honored equally with the Lord because they are engaged in the most confidential service of the Lord, for they deliver out of the material world the fallen souls whom the Lord wants to return home, back to Godhead. Such pure devotees are better known as vice-lords according to revealed scriptures. The sincere disciple of the pure devotee considers the spiritual master equal to the Lord, but always considers himself to be a humble servant of the servant of the Lord. This is the pure devotional path.

TEXT 16

को वा भगवतस्तस्य पुण्यश्लोकेड्यकर्मणः ।
शुद्धिकामो न शृणुयाद्यशः कलिमलापहम् ॥१६॥

ko vā bhagavatas tasya
puṇya-ślokeḍya-karmaṇaḥ
śuddhi-kāmo na śṛṇuyād
yaśaḥ kali-malāpaham

kaḥ—who; *vā*—rather; *bhagavataḥ*—of the Lord; *tasya*—His; *puṇya*—virtuous; *śloka-īḍya*—worshipable by prayers; *karmaṇaḥ*—deeds; *śuddhi-kāmaḥ*—desiring deliverance from all sins; *na*—not; *śṛṇuyāt*—does hear; *yaśaḥ*—glories; *kali*—of the age of quarrel; *mala-apaham*—the agent for sanctification.

TRANSLATION

Who is there, desiring deliverance from the vices of the age of quarrel, who is not willing to hear the virtuous glories of the Lord?

PURPORT

The age of Kali is the most condemned age due to its quarrelsome features. Kali-yuga is so saturated with vicious habits that there is a great fight at the slightest misunderstanding. Those who are engaged in the pure devotional service of the Lord, who are without any desire for self-aggrandizement and who are freed from the effects of fruitive actions and dry philosophical speculations are capable of getting out of the estrangements of this complicated age. The leaders of the people are very much anxious to live in peace and friendship, but they have no information of the simple method of hearing the glories of the Lord. On the contrary, such leaders are opposed to the propagation of the glories of the Lord. In other words, the foolish leaders want to completely deny the existence of the Lord. In the name of secular state, such leaders are enacting various plans every year. But by the insurmountable intricacies of the material nature of the Lord, all these plans for progress are being constantly frustrated. They have no eyes to see that their attempts at peace and friendship are failing. But here is the hint to get over the hurdle. If we want actual peace, we must open the road to understanding of the Supreme Lord Kṛṣṇa and glorify Him for His virtuous activities as they are depicted in the pages of *Śrīmad-Bhāgavatam.*

TEXT 17

तस्य कर्माण्युदाराणि परिगीतानि सूरिभिः।
ब्रूहि नः श्रद्दधानानां लीलया दधतः कलाः ॥१७॥

tasya karmāṇy udārāṇi
parigītāni sūribhiḥ
brūhi naḥ śraddadhānānāṁ
līlayā dadhataḥ kalāḥ

tasya—His; *karmāṇi*—transcendental acts; *udārāṇi*—magnanimous; *parigītāni*—broadcast; *sūribhiḥ*—by the great souls; *brūhi*—please speak; *naḥ*—unto us; *śraddadhānānām*—ready to receive with respect; *līlayā*—pastimes; *dadhataḥ*—advented; *kalāḥ*—incarnations.

TRANSLATION

His transcendental acts are magnificent and gracious, and great learned sages like Nārada sing of them. Please, therefore, speak to us, who are eager to hear about the adventures He performs in His various incarnations.

PURPORT

The Personality of Godhead is never inactive as some less intelligent persons suggest. His works are magnificent and magnanimous. His creations both material and spiritual are all wonderful and contain all variegatedness. They are described nicely by such liberated souls as Śrīla Nārada, Vyāsa, Vālmīki, Devala, Asita, Madhva, Śrī Caitanya, Rāmānuja, Viṣṇusvāmī, Nimbārka, Śrīdhara, Viśvanātha, Baladeva, Bhaktivinoda, Siddhānta Sarasvatī and many other learned and self-realized souls. These creations, both material and spiritual, are full of opulence, beauty and knowledge, but the spiritual realm is more magnificent due to its being full of knowledge, bliss and eternity. The material creations are manifested for some time as perverted shadows of the spiritual kingdom and can be likened to cinemas. They attract people of less intelligent caliber who are attracted by false things. Such foolish men have no information of the reality, and they take it for granted that the false material manifestation is the all in all. But more intelligent men guided by sages like Vyāsa and Nārada know that the eternal kingdom of God is more delightful, larger, and eternally full of bliss and knowledge. Those who are not conversant with the activities of the Lord and His transcendental realm are sometimes favored by the Lord in His adventures as incarnations wherein He displays the eternal bliss of His association in the transcendental realm. By such activities He attracts the conditioned souls of the material world. Some of these conditioned souls are engaged in the false enjoyment of material senses and others in simply negating their real life in the spiritual world. These less intelligent persons are known as karmīs, or fruitive workers, and *jñānīs,* or dry mental speculators. But above these two classes of men is the transcendentalist known as *sātvata,* or the devotee, who is busy neither with rampant material activity nor with material speculation. He is engaged in the positive service of the Lord, and thereby he derives the highest spiritual benefit unknown to the *karmīs* and *jñānīs.*

As the supreme controller of both the material and spiritual worlds, the Lord has different incarnations of unlimited categories. Incarnations like Brahmā, Rudra, Manu, Pṛthu and Vyāsa are His material qualitative incarnations, but His incarnations like Rāma, Narasiṁha, Varāha and Vāmana are His transcendental incarnations. Lord Śrī Kṛṣṇa is the fountainhead of all incarnations, and He is therefore the cause of all causes.

TEXT 18

अथाख्याहि हरेर्धीमन्नवतारकथाः शुभाः।
लीला विदधतः स्वैरमीश्वरस्यात्ममायया ॥१८॥

athākhyāhi harer dhīmann
avatāra-kathāḥ śubhāḥ
līlā vidadhataḥ svairam
īśvarasyātma-māyayā

atha—therefore; *ākhyāhi*—describe; *hareḥ*—of the Lord; *dhīman*—O sagacious one; *avatāra*—incarnations; *kathāḥ*—narratives; *śubhāḥ*—auspicious; *līlā*—adventures; *vidadhataḥ*—performed; *svairam*—pastimes; *īśvarasya*—of the supreme controller; *ātma*—personal; *māyayā*—energies.

TRANSLATION

O wise Sūta, please narrate to us the transcendental pastimes of the Supreme Godhead's multi-incarnations. Such auspicious adventures and pastimes of the Lord, the supreme controller, are performed by His internal powers.

PURPORT

For the creation, maintenance and destruction of the material worlds, the Supreme Lord Personality of Godhead Himself appears in many thousands of forms of incarnations, and the specific adventures found in those transcendental forms are all auspicious. Both those who are present during such activities and those who hear the transcendental narrations of such activities are benefited.

TEXT 19

वयं तु न वितृप्याम उत्तमश्लोकविक्रमे।
यच्छृण्वतां रसज्ञानां स्वादु स्वादु पदे पदे ॥१९॥

vayaṁ tu na vitṛpyāma
uttama-śloka-vikrame
yac-chṛṇvatāṁ rasa-jñānāṁ
svādu svādu pade pade

vayam—we; *tu*—but; *na*—not; *vitṛpyāmaḥ*—shall be at rest; *uttama-śloka*—the Personality of Godhead, who is glorified by transcendental prayers; *vikrame*—adventures; *yat*—which; *śṛṇvatām*—by continuous hearing; *rasa*—humor; *jñānām*—those who are conversant with; *svādu*—relishing; *svādu*—palatable; *pade pade*—at every step.

TRANSLATION

We never tire of hearing the transcendental pastimes of the Personality of Godhead, who is glorified by hymns and prayers. Those who have developed a taste for transcendental relationships with Him relish hearing of His pastimes at every moment.

PURPORT

There is a great difference between mundane stories, fiction, or history and the transcendental pastimes of the Lord. The histories of the whole universe contain references to the pastimes of the incarnations of the Lord. The *Rāmāyaṇa,* the *Mahābhārata,* and the *Purāṇas* are histories of bygone ages recorded in connection with the pastimes of the incarnations of the Lord and therefore remain fresh even after repeated readings. For example, anyone may read *Bhagavad-gītā* or the *Śrīmad-Bhāgavatam* repeatedly throughout his whole life and yet find in them new light of information. Mundane news is static whereas transcendental news is dynamic, inasmuch as the spirit is dynamic and matter is static. Those who have developed a taste for understanding the transcendental subject matter are never tired of hearing such narrations. One is quickly satiated by mundane activities, but no one is satiated by transcendental or devotional activities. *Uttama-śloka* indicates that literature which is not meant for nescience. Mundane literature is in the mode of darkness or ignorance, whereas transcendental literature is quite different. Transcendental literature is above the mode of darkness, and its light becomes more luminous with progressive reading and realization of the transcendental subject matter. The so-called liberated persons are never satisfied by the repetition of the words *ahaṁ brahmāsmi.* Such artificial realization of Brahman becomes hackneyed, and so to relish real pleasure they turn to the narrations of the *Śrīmad-Bhāgavatam.* Those who are not so fortunate turn to altruism and worldly philanthropy. This means the Māyāvāda philosophy is mundane, whereas the philosophy of *Bhagavad-gītā* and *Śrīmad-Bhāgavatam* is transcendental.

TEXT 20

कृतवान् किल कर्माणि सह रामेण केशवः ।
अतिमर्त्यानि भगवान् गूढः कपटमानुषः ॥२०॥

kṛtavān kila karmāṇi
saha rāmeṇa keśavaḥ
atimartyāni bhagavān
gūḍhaḥ kapaṭa-mānuṣaḥ

kṛtavān—done by; *kila*—what; *karmāṇi*—acts; *saha*—along with; *rāmeṇa*—Balarāma; *keśavaḥ*—Śrī Kṛṣṇa; *atimartyāni*—superhuman; *bhagavān*—the Personality of Godhead; *gūḍhaḥ*—masked as; *kapaṭa*—apparently; *mānuṣaḥ*—human being.

TRANSLATION

Lord Śrī Kṛṣṇa, the Personality of Godhead, along with Balarāma, played like a human being, and so masked He performed many superhuman acts.

PURPORT

The doctrines of anthropomorphism and zoomorphism are never applicable to Śrī Kṛṣṇa, or the Personality of Godhead. The theory that a man becomes God by dint of penance and austerities is very much rampant nowadays, especially in India. Since Lord Rāma, Lord Kṛṣṇa and Lord Caitanya Mahāprabhu were detected by the sages and saints to be the Personality of

Godhead as indicated in revealed scriptures, many unscrupulous men have created their own incarnations. This process of concocting an incarnation of God has become an ordinary business, especially in Bengal. Any popular personality with a few traits of mystic powers will display some feat of jugglery and easily become an incarnation of Godhead by popular vote. Lord Śrī Kṛṣṇa was not that type of incarnation. He was actually the Personality of Godhead from the very beginning of His appearance. He appeared before His so-called mother as four-armed Viṣṇu. Then, at the request of the mother, He became like a human child and at once left her for another devotee at Gokula, where He was accepted as the son of Nanda Mahārāja and Yaśodā Mātā. Similarly, Śrī Baladeva, the counterpart of Lord Śrī Kṛṣṇa, was also considered a human child born of another wife of Śrī Vasudeva. In *Bhagavad-gītā,* the Lord says that His birth and deeds are transcendental and that anyone who is so fortunate as to know the transcendental nature of His birth and deeds will at once become liberated and eligible to return to the kingdom of God. So knowledge of the transcendental nature of the birth and deeds of Lord Śrī Kṛṣṇa is sufficient for liberation. In the *Bhāgavatam,* the transcendental nature of the Lord is described in nine cantos, and in the Tenth Canto His specific pastimes are taken up. All this becomes known as one's reading of this literature progresses. It is important to note here, however, that the Lord exhibited His divinity even from the lap of His mother, that His deeds are all superhuman (He lifted Govardhana Hill at the age of seven), and that all these acts definitely prove Him to be actually the Supreme Personality of Godhead. Yet, due to His mystic covering, He was always accepted as an ordinary human child by His so-called father and mother and other relatives. Whenever some herculean task was performed by Him, the father and mother took it otherwise. And they remained satisfied with unflinching filial love for their son. As such, the sages of Naimiṣāraṇya describe Him as apparently resembling a human being, but actually He is the supreme almighty Personality of Godhead.

TEXT 21

कलिमागतमाज्ञाय क्षेत्रेऽस्मिन् वैष्णवे वयम्।
आसीना दीर्घसत्रेण कथायां सक्षणा हरेः ॥२१॥

kalim āgatam ājñāya
kṣetre 'smin vaiṣṇave vayam

āsīnā dīrgha-satreṇa
kathāyāṁ sakṣaṇā hareḥ

kalim—the age of Kali (iron age of quarrel); *āgatam*—having arrived; *ājñāya*—knowing this; *kṣetre*—in this tract of land; *asmin*—in this; *vaiṣṇave*—specially meant for the devotee of the Lord; *vayam*—we; *āsīnāḥ*—seated; *dīrgha*—prolonged; *satreṇa*—for performance of sacrifices; *kathāyām*—in the words of; *sa-kṣaṇāḥ*—with time at our disposal; *hareḥ*—of the Personality of Godhead.

TRANSLATION

Knowing well that the age of Kali has already begun, we are assembled here in this holy place to hear at great length the transcendental message of Godhead and in this way perform sacrifice.

PURPORT

This age of Kali is not at all suitable for self-realization as was Satya-yuga, the golden age, or Tretā- or Dvāpara-yugas, the silver and copper ages. For self-realization, the people in Satya-yuga, living a lifetime of a hundred thousand years, were able to perform prolonged meditation. And in Tretā-yuga, when the duration of life was ten thousand years, self-realization was attained by performance of great sacrifice. And in the Dvāpara-yuga, when the duration of life was one thousand years, self-realization was attained by worship of the Lord. But in the Kali-yuga, the maximum duration of life being one hundred years only and that combined with various difficulties, the recommended process of self-realization is that of hearing and chanting of the holy name, fame, and pastimes of the Lord. The sages of Naimiṣāraṇya began this process in a place meant specifically for the devotees of the Lord. They prepared themselves to hear the pastimes of the Lord over a period of one thousand years. By the example of these sages one should learn that regular hearing and recitation of the *Bhāgavatam* is the only way for self-realization. Other attempts are simply a waste of time, for they do not give any tangible results. Lord Śrī Caitanya Mahāprabhu preached this system of *Bhāgavata-dharma,* and He recommended that all those who were born in India should take the responsibility of broadcasting the messages of Lord Śrī Kṛṣṇa, primarily the message of *Bhagavad-gītā.* And when one is well established in the teachings of *Bhagavad-gītā,* he can take up the study of *Śrīmad-Bhāgavatam* for further enlightenment in self-realization.

TEXT 22

त्वं नः सन्दर्शितो धात्रा दुस्तरं निस्तितीर्षताम्।
कलिं सत्त्वहरं पुंसां कर्णधार इवार्णवम् ॥२२॥

tvaṁ naḥ sandarśito dhātrā
dustaraṁ nistitīrṣatām
kaliṁ sattva-haraṁ puṁsāṁ
karṇa-dhāra ivārṇavam

tvam—Your Goodness; *naḥ*—unto us; *sandarśitaḥ*—meeting; *dhātrā*—by providence; *dustaram*—insurmountable; *nistitīrṣatām*—for those desiring to cross over; *kalim*—the age of Kali; *sattva-haram*—that which deteriorates the good qualities; *puṁsām*—of a man; *karṇa-dhāraḥ*—captain; *iva*—as; *arṇavam*—the ocean.

TRANSLATION

We think that we have met Your Goodness by the will of providence, just so that we may accept you as captain of the ship for those who desire to cross the difficult ocean of Kali, which deteriorates all the good qualities of a human being.

PURPORT

The age of Kali is very dangerous for the human being. Human life is simply meant for self-realization, but due to this dangerous age, men have completely forgotten the aim of life. In this age, the life span will gradually decrease. People will gradually lose their memory, finer sentiments, strength, and better qualities. A list of the anomalies for this age is given in the Twelfth Canto of this work. And so this age is very difficult for those who want to utilize this life for self-realization. The people are so busy with sense gratification that they completely forget about self-realization. Out of madness they frankly say that there is no need for self-realization because they do not realize that this brief life is but a moment on our great journey towards self-realization. The whole system of education is geared to sense gratification, and if a learned man thinks it over, he sees that the children of this age are being intentionally sent to the slaughterhouses of so-called education. Learned men, therefore, must be cautious of this age, and if they at all want to cross over the dangerous ocean of Kali, they must follow the footsteps of the sages of Naimiṣāraṇya and accept Śrī Sūta Gosvāmī or his bona fide representative as the captain of the ship. The ship is the message of Lord Śrī Kṛṣṇa in the shape of *Bhagavad-gītā* or the *Śrīmad-Bhāgavatam.*

TEXT 23

ब्रूहि योगेश्वरे कृष्णे ब्रह्मण्ये धर्मवर्मणि।
स्वां काष्ठामधुनोपेते धर्मः कं शरणं गतः ॥२३॥

brūhi yogeśvare kṛṣṇe
brahmaṇye dharma-varmaṇi
svāṁ kāṣṭhām adhunopete
dharmaḥ kaṁ śaraṇaṁ gataḥ

brūhi—please tell; *yoga-īśvare*—the Lord of all mystic powers; *kṛṣṇe*—Lord Kṛṣṇa; *brahmaṇye*—the Absolute Truth; *dharma*—religion; *varmaṇi*—protector; *svām*—own; *kāṣṭhām*—abode; *adhunā*—nowadays; *upete*—having gone away; *dharmaḥ*—religion; *kam*—unto whom; *śaraṇam*—shelter; *gataḥ*—gone.

TRANSLATION

Since Śrī Kṛṣṇa, the Absolute Truth, the master of all mystic powers, has departed for His own abode, please tell us to whom the religious principles have now gone for shelter.

PURPORT

Essentially religion is the prescribed codes enunciated by the Personality of Godhead Himself. Whenever there is gross misuse or neglect of the principles of religion, the Supreme Lord appears Himself to restore religious principles. This is stated in *Bhagavad-gītā.* Here the sages of Naimiṣāraṇya are inquiring about these principles. The reply to this question is given later. The *Śrīmad-Bhāgavatam* is the transcendental sound representation of the Personality of Godhead, and thus it is the full representation of transcendental knowledge and religious principles.

Thus end the Bhaktivedanta purports of the First Canto, First Chapter, of the Śrīmad-Bhāgavatam, *entitled "Questions by the Sages."*

CHAPTER TWO

Divinity and Divine Service

TEXT 1

व्यास उवाच

इति सम्प्रश्नसंहृष्टो विप्राणां रौमहर्षणिः ।
प्रतिपूज्य वचस्तेषां प्रवक्तुमुपचक्रमे ॥१॥

vyāsa uvāca
iti sampraśna-saṁhṛṣṭo
viprāṇāṁ raumaharṣaṇiḥ
pratipūjya vacas teṣāṁ
pravaktum upacakrame

vyāsaḥ uvāca—Vyāsa said; *iti*—thus; *sampraśna*—perfect inquiries; *saṁhṛṣṭaḥ*—perfectly satisfied; *viprāṇām*—of the sages there; *raumaharṣaṇiḥ*—the son of Romaharṣaṇa, namely Ugraśravā; *pratipūjya*—after thanking them; *vacaḥ*—words; *teṣām*—their; *pravaktum*—to reply to them; *upacakrame*—attempted.

TRANSLATION

Ugraśravā [Sūta Gosvāmī], the son of Romaharṣaṇa, being fully satisfied by the perfect questions of the brāhmaṇas, thanked them and thus attempted to reply.

PURPORT

The sages of Naimiṣāraṇya asked Sūta Gosvāmī six questions, and so he is answering them one by one.

TEXT 2

सूत उवाच

यं प्रव्रजन्तमनुपेतमपेतकृत्यं
द्वैपायनो विरहकातर आजुहाव ।
पुत्रेति तन्मयतया तरवोऽभिनेदु-
स्तं सर्वभूतहृदयं मुनिमानतोऽस्मि ॥२॥

sūta uvāca
yaṁ pravrajantam anupetam apeta-kṛtyaṁ
dvaipāyano viraha-kātara ājuhāva
putreti tan-mayatayā taravo 'bhinedus
taṁ sarva-bhūta-hṛdayaṁ munim ānato 'smi

sūtaḥ—Sūta Gosvāmī; *uvāca*—said; *yam*—whom; *pravrajantam*—while going away for the renounced order of life; *anupetam*—without being reformed by the sacred thread; *apeta*—not undergoing ceremonies; *kṛtyam*—prescribed duties; *dvaipāyanaḥ*—Vyāsadeva; *viraha*—separation; *kātaraḥ*—being afraid of; *ājuhāva*—exclaimed; *putra iti*—O my son; *tat-mayatayā*—being absorbed in that way; *taravaḥ*—all the trees; *abhineduḥ*—responded; *tam*—unto him; *sarva*—all; *bhūta*—living entities; *hṛdayam*—heart; *munim*—sage; *ānataḥ asmi*—offer obeisances.

TRANSLATION

Śrīla Sūta Gosvāmī said: Let me offer my respectful obeisances unto that great sage [Śukadeva Gosvāmī] who can enter the hearts of all. When he went away to take up the renounced order of life [sannyāsa], leaving home without undergoing reformation by the sacred thread or the ceremonies observed by the higher castes, his father, Vyāsadeva, fearing separation from him, cried out, "O my son!" Indeed, only the trees, which were absorbed in the same feelings of separation, echoed in response to the begrieved father.

PURPORT

The institution of *varṇa* and *āśrama* prescribes many regulative duties to be observed by its followers. Such duties enjoin that a candidate willing to study the *Vedas* must approach a bona fide spiritual master and request acceptance as his disciple. The sacred thread is the sign of those who are competent to study the *Vedas* from the *ācārya,* or the bona fide spiritual master. Śrī Śukadeva Gosvāmī did not undergo such purificatory ceremonies because he was a liberated soul from his very birth.

Generally, a man is born as an ordinary being, and by the purificatory processes he is born for the second time. When he sees a new light and seeks direction for spiritual progress, he approaches a spiritual master for instruction in the *Vedas.* The spiritual master accepts only the sincere inquirer as his disciple and gives him the sacred thread. In this way a man becomes twice-born, or a *dvija.* After qualifying as a *dvija* one may study the *Vedas,* and after becoming well versed in the *Vedas* one becomes a *vipra.* A *vipra,* or a qualified *brāhmaṇa,* thus realizes the Absolute and makes further progress in spiritual life until he reaches the Vaiṣṇava stage. The Vaiṣṇava stage is the postgraduate status of a *brāhmaṇa.* A progressive *brāhmaṇa* must necessarily become a Vaiṣṇava, for a Vaiṣṇava is a self-realized, learned *brāhmaṇa.*

Śrīla Śukadeva Gosvāmī was a Vaiṣṇava from the beginning; therefore, there was no need for him to undergo all the processes of the *varṇāśrama* institution. Ultimately the aim of *varṇāśrama-dharma* is to turn a crude man into a pure devotee of the Lord, or a Vaiṣṇava. Anyone, therefore, who becomes a Vaiṣṇava accepted by the first-class Vaiṣṇava, or *uttama-adhikārī* Vaiṣṇava, is already considered a *brāhmaṇa,* regardless of his birth or past deeds. Śrī Caitanya Mahāprabhu accepted this principle and recognized Śrīla Haridāsa Ṭhākura as the *ācārya* of the holy name, although Ṭhākura Haridāsa appeared in a Mohammedan family. In conclusion, Śrīla Śukadeva Gosvāmī was born a Vaiṣṇava, and, therefore, brahminism was included in him. He did not have to undergo any ceremonies. Any lowborn person—be he a Kirāta, Hūṇa, Āndhra, Pulinda, Pulkaśa, Ābhīra, Śumbha, Yavana, Khasa or even lower—can be delivered to the highest transcendental position by the mercy of Vaiṣṇavas. Śrīla Śukadeva Gosvāmī was the spiritual master of Śrī Sūta Gosvāmī, who therefore offers his respectful obeisances unto Śrīla Śukadeva Gosvāmī before he begins his answers to the questions of the sages at Naimiṣāraṇya.

TEXT 3

यः स्वानुभावमखिलश्रुतिसारमेक-
मध्यात्मदीपमतितितीर्षतां तमोऽन्धम् ।
संसारिणां करुणयाह पुराणगुह्यं
तं व्याससूनुमुपयामि गुरुं मुनीनाम् ॥३॥

yaḥ svānubhāvam akhila-śruti-sāram ekam
adhyātma-dīpam atititīrṣatāṁ tamo 'ndham
saṁsāriṇāṁ karuṇayāha purāṇa-guhyaṁ
taṁ vyāsa-sūnum upayāmi guruṁ munīnām

yaḥ—he who; *sva-anubhāvam*—self-assimilated (experienced); *akhila*—all around; *śruti*—the *Vedas; sāram*—cream; *ekam*—the only one;

adhyātma—transcendental; *dīpam*—torchlight; *atititīrṣatām*—desiring to overcome; *tamaḥ andham*—deeply dark material existence; *saṁsāriṇām*—of the materialistic men; *karuṇayā*—out of causeless mercy; *āha*—said; *purāṇa*—supplement to the *Vedas; guhyam*—very confidential; *tam*—unto him; *vyāsa-sūnum*—the son of Vyāsadeva; *upayāmi*—let me offer my obeisances; *gurum*—the spiritual master; *munīnām*—of the great sages.

TRANSLATION

Let me offer my respectful obeisances unto him [Śuka], the spiritual master of all sages, the son of Vyāsadeva, who, out of his great compassion for those gross materialists who struggle to cross over the darkest regions of material existence, spoke this most confidential supplement to the cream of Vedic knowledge, after having personally assimilated it by experience.

PURPORT

In this prayer, Śrīla Sūta Gosvāmī practically summarizes the complete introduction of *Śrīmad-Bhāgavatam. Śrīmad-Bhāgavatam* is the natural supplementary commentary on the *Vedānta-sūtras.* The *Vedānta-sūtras,* or the *Brahma-sūtras,* were compiled by Vyāsadeva with a view to presenting just the cream of Vedic knowledge. *Śrīmad-Bhāgavatam* is the natural commentary on this cream. Śrīla Śukadeva Gosvāmī was a thoroughly realized master on the *Vedānta-sūtra,* and consequently he also personally realized the commentary, *Śrīmad-Bhāgavatam.* And just to show his boundless mercy upon bewildered materialistic men who want to cross completely over nescience, he recited for the first time this confidential knowledge.

There is no point in arguing that a materialistic man can be happy. No materialistic creature—be he the great Brahmā or an insignificant ant—can be happy. Everyone tries to make a permanent plan for happiness, but everyone is baffled by the laws of material nature. Therefore the materialistic world is called the darkest region of God's creation. Yet the unhappy materialists can get out of it simply by desiring to get out. Unfortunately they are so foolish that they do not want to escape. Therefore they are compared to the camel who relishes thorny twigs because he likes the taste of the twigs mixed with blood. He does not realize that it is his own blood and that his tongue is being cut by the thorns. Similarly, to the materialist his own blood is as sweet as honey, and although he is always harassed by his own material creations, he does not wish to escape. Such materialists are called *karmīs.* Out of hundreds of thousands of *karmīs,* only a few may feel tired of material engagement and desire to get out of the labyrinth. Such intelligent persons are called *jñānīs.* The *Vedānta-sūtra* is directed to such *jñānīs.* But Śrīla Vyāsadeva, being the incarnation of the Supreme Lord, could foresee the misuse of the *Vedānta-sūtra* by unscrupulous men, and, therefore, he personally supplemented the *Vedānta-sūtra* with the *Bhāgavata Purāṇa.* It is clearly said that this *Bhāgavatam* is the original commentary on the *Brahma-sūtras.* Śrīla Vyāsadeva also instructed the *Bhāgavatam* to his own son, Śrīla Śukadeva Gosvāmī, who was already at the liberated stage of transcendence. Śrīla Śukadeva realized it personally and then explained it. By the mercy of Śrīla Śukadeva, the *Bhāgavata-vedānta-sūtra* is available for all those sincere souls who want to get out of material existence.

Śrīmad-Bhāgavatam is the one unrivaled commentary on *Vedānta-sūtra.* Śrīpāda Śaṅkarācārya intentionally did not touch it because he knew that the natural commentary would be difficult for him to surpass. He wrote his *Śārīraka-bhāṣya,* and his so-called followers deprecated the *Bhāgavatam* as some "new" presentation. One should not be misled by such propaganda directed against the *Bhāgavatam* by the Māyāvāda school. From this introductory *śloka,* the beginning student should know that *Śrīmad-Bhāgavatam* is the only transcendental literature meant for those who are *paramahaṁsas* and completely freed from the material disease called malice. The Māyāvādīs are envious of the Personality of Godhead despite Śrīpāda Śaṅkarācārya's admission that Nārāyaṇa, the Personality of Godhead, is above the material creation. The envious Māyāvādī cannot have access to the *Bhāgavatam,* but those who are really anxious to get out of this material existence may take shelter of this *Bhāgavatam* because it is uttered by the liberated Śrīla Śukadeva Gosvāmī. It is the transcendental torchlight by which one can see perfectly the transcendental Absolute Truth realized as Brahman, Paramātmā and Bhagavān.

TEXT 4

नारायणं नमस्कृत्य नरं चैव नरोत्तमम् ।
देवीं सरस्वतीं व्यासं ततो जयमुदीरयेत् ॥४॥

nārāyaṇaṁ namaskṛtya
naraṁ caiva narottamam

devīṁ sarasvatīṁ vyāsaṁ
tato jayam udīrayet

nārāyaṇam—the Personality of Godhead; *namaḥ-kṛtya*—after offering respectful obeisances; *naram ca eva*—and Nārāyaṇa Ṛṣi; *nara-uttamam*—the supermost human being; *devīm*—the goddess; *sarasvatīm*—the mistress of learning; *vyāsam*—Vyāsadeva; *tataḥ*—thereafter; *jayam*—all that is meant for conquering; *udīrayet*—be announced.

TRANSLATION

Before reciting this Śrīmad-Bhāgavatam, which is the very means of conquest, one should offer respectful obeisances unto the Personality of Godhead, Nārāyaṇa, unto Nara-nārāyaṇa Ṛṣi, the supermost human being, unto Mother Sarasvatī, the goddess of learning, and unto Śrīla Vyāsadeva, the author.

PURPORT

All the Vedic literatures and the *Purāṇas* are meant for conquering the darkest region of material existence. The living being is in the state of forgetfulness of his relation with God due to his being overly attracted to material sense gratification from time immemorial. His struggle for existence in the material world is perpetual, and it is not possible for him to get out of it by making plans. If he at all wants to conquer this perpetual struggle for existence, he must reestablish his eternal relation with God. And one who wants to adopt such remedial measures must take shelter of literatures such as the *Vedas* and the *Purāṇas.* Foolish people say that the *Purāṇas* have no connection with the *Vedas.* However, the *Purāṇas* are supplementary explanations of the *Vedas* intended for different types of men. All men are not equal. There are men who are conducted by the mode of goodness, others who are under the mode of passion and others who are under the mode of ignorance. The *Purāṇas* are so divided that any class of men can take advantage of them and gradually regain their lost position and get out of the hard struggle for existence. Śrīla Sūta Gosvāmī shows the way of chanting the *Purāṇas.* This may be followed by persons who aspire to be preachers of the Vedic literatures and the *Purāṇas. Śrīmad-Bhāgavatam* is the spotless *Purāṇa,* and it is especially meant for them who desire to get out of the material entanglement permanently.

TEXT 5

मुनयः साधु पृष्टोऽहं भवद्भिर्लोकमङ्गलम्।
यत्कृतः कृष्णसम्प्रश्नो येनात्मा सुप्रसीदति ॥५॥

munayaḥ sādhu pṛṣṭo 'haṁ
bhavadbhir loka-maṅgalam
yat kṛtaḥ kṛṣṇa-sampraśno
yenātmā suprasīdati

munayaḥ—O sages; *sādhu*—devotee; *pṛṣṭaḥ*—questioned; *aham*—myself; *bhavadbhiḥ*—by all of you; *loka*—the world; *maṅgalam*—welfare; *yat*—because; *kṛtaḥ*—made; *kṛṣṇa*—the Personality of Godhead; *sampraśnaḥ*—relevant question; *yena*—by which; *ātmā*—self; *suprasīdati*—completely pleased.

TRANSLATION

O sages, I have been justly questioned by you. Your questions are worthy because they relate to Lord Kṛṣṇa and so are of relevance to the world's welfare. Only questions of this sort are capable of completely satisfying the self.

PURPORT

Since it has been stated hereinbefore that in the *Bhāgavatam* the Absolute Truth is to be known, the questions of the sages of Naimiṣāraṇya are proper and just, because they pertain to Kṛṣṇa, who is the Supreme Personality of Godhead, the Absolute Truth. In *Bhagavad-gītā* (15.15) the Personality of Godhead says that in all the *Vedas* there is nothing but the urge for searching after Him, Lord Kṛṣṇa. Thus the questions that pertain to Kṛṣṇa are the sum and substance of all the Vedic inquiries.

The whole world is full of questions and answers. The birds, beasts and men are all busy in the matter of perpetual questions and answers. In the morning the birds in the nest become busy with questions and answers, and in the evening also the same birds come back and again become busy with questions and answers. The human being, unless he is fast asleep at night, is busy with questions and answers. The businessmen in the market are busy with questions and answers, and so also the lawyers in the court and the students in the schools and colleges. The legislators in the parliament are also busy with questions and answers, and the politicians and the press representatives are all busy with questions and answers. Although they go on making such questions and answers for their whole lives, they are not at all satisfied. Satisfaction of the soul can only be obtained by questions and answers on the subject of Kṛṣṇa.

Kṛṣṇa is our most intimate master, friend, father or son and object of conjugal love. Forgetting Kṛṣṇa, we have created so many objects of questions and answers, but none of them are able to give us complete satisfaction. All things—but Kṛṣṇa—give temporary satisfaction only, so if we are to have complete satisfaction we must take to the questions and answers about Kṛṣṇa. We cannot live for a moment without being questioned or without giving answers. Because the *Śrīmad-Bhāgavatam* deals with questions and answers that are related to Kṛṣṇa, we can derive the highest satisfaction only by reading and hearing this transcendental literature. One should learn the *Śrīmad-Bhāgavatam* and make an all-around solution to all problems pertaining to social, political or religious matters. *Śrīmad-Bhāgavatam* and Kṛṣṇa are the sum total of all things.

TEXT 6

स वै पुंसां परो धर्मो यतो भक्तिरधोक्षजे।
अहैतुक्यप्रतिहता ययात्मा सुप्रसीदति ॥६॥

sa vai puṁsāṁ paro dharmo
yato bhaktir adhokṣaje
ahaituky apratihatā
yayātmā suprasīdati

saḥ—that; *vai*—certainly; *puṁsām*—for mankind; *paraḥ*—sublime; *dharmaḥ*—occupation; *yataḥ*—by which; *bhaktiḥ*—devotional service; *adhokṣaje*—unto the Transcendence; *ahaitukī*—causeless; *apratihatā*—unbroken; *yayā*—by which; *ātmā*—the self; *suprasīdati*—completely satisfied.

TRANSLATION

The supreme occupation [dharma] for all humanity is that by which men can attain to loving devotional service unto the transcendent Lord. Such devotional service must be unmotivated and uninterrupted to completely satisfy the self.

PURPORT

In this statement, Śrī Sūta Gosvāmī answers the first question of the sages of Naimiṣāraṇya. The sages asked him to summarize the whole range of revealed scriptures and present the most essential part so that fallen people or the people in general might easily take it up. The *Vedas* prescribe two different types of occupation for the human being. One is called the *pravṛtti-mārga,* or the path of sense enjoyment, and the other is called the *nivṛtti-mārga,* or the path of renunciation. The path of enjoyment is inferior, and the path of sacrifice for the supreme cause is superior. The material existence of the living being is a diseased condition of actual life. Actual life is spiritual existence, or *brahma-bhūta* existence, where life is eternal, blissful and full of knowledge. Material existence is temporary, illusory and full of miseries. There is no happiness at all. There is just the futile attempt to get rid of the miseries, and temporary cessation of misery is falsely called happiness. Therefore, the path of progressive material enjoyment, which is temporary, miserable and illusory, is inferior. But devotional service to the Supreme Lord, which leads one to eternal, blissful and all-cognizant life, is called the superior quality of occupation. This is sometimes polluted when mixed with the inferior quality. For example, adoption of devotional service for material gain is certainly an obstruction to the progressive path of renunciation. Renunciation or abnegation for ultimate good is certainly a better occupation than enjoyment in the diseased condition of life. Such enjoyment only aggravates the symptoms of disease and increases its duration. Therefore devotional service to the Lord must be pure in quality, i.e., without the least desire for material enjoyment. One should, therefore, accept the superior quality of occupation in the form of the devotional service of the Lord without any tinge of unnecessary desire, fruitive action and philosophical speculation. This alone can lead one to perpetual solace in His service.

We have purposely denoted *dharma* as occupation because the root meaning of the word *dharma* is "that which sustains one's existence." A living being's sustenance of existence is to coordinate his activities with his eternal relation with the Supreme Lord Kṛṣṇa. Kṛṣṇa is the central pivot of living beings, and He is the all-attractive living entity or eternal form amongst all other living beings or eternal forms. Each and every living being has his eternal form in the spiritual existence, and Kṛṣṇa is the eternal attraction for all of them. Kṛṣṇa is the complete whole, and everything else is His part and parcel. The relation is one of the servant and the served. It is transcendental and is completely distinct from our experience in material existence. This relation of servant and the served is the most congenial form of intimacy. One can realize it as devotional service progresses. Everyone should engage himself in that transcendental loving service of the Lord, even in the present conditional state of material existence. That will gradually give one the clue to actual life and please him to complete satisfaction.

TEXT 7

वासुदेवे भगवति भक्तियोगः प्रयोजितः ।
जनयत्याशु वैराग्यं ज्ञानं च यदहैतुकम् ॥७॥

vāsudeve bhagavati
bhakti-yogaḥ prayojitaḥ
janayaty āśu vairāgyaṁ
jñānaṁ ca yad ahaitukam

vāsudeve—unto Kṛṣṇa; *bhagavati*—unto the Personality of Godhead; *bhakti-yogaḥ*—contact of devotional service; *prayojitaḥ*—being applied; *janayati*—does produce; *āśu*—very soon; *vairāgyam*—detachment; *jñānam*—knowledge; *ca*—and; *yat*—that which; *ahaitukam*—causeless.

TRANSLATION

By rendering devotional service unto the Personality of Godhead, Śrī Kṛṣṇa, one immediately acquires causeless knowledge and detachment from the world.

PURPORT

Those who consider devotional service to the Supreme Lord Śrī Kṛṣṇa to be something like material emotional affairs may argue that in the revealed scriptures, sacrifice, charity, austerity, knowledge, mystic powers and similar other processes of transcendental realization are recommended. According to them, *bhakti,* or the devotional service of the Lord, is meant for those who cannot perform the high-grade activities. Generally it is said that the *bhakti* cult is meant for the *śūdras, vaiśyas* and the less intelligent woman class. But that is not the actual fact. The *bhakti* cult is the topmost of all transcendental activities, and therefore it is simultaneously sublime and easy. It is sublime for the pure devotees who are serious about getting in contact with the Supreme Lord, and it is easy for the neophytes who are just on the threshold of the house of *bhakti.* To achieve the contact of the Supreme Personality of Godhead, Śrī Kṛṣṇa, is a great science, and it is open for all living beings, including the *śūdras, vaiśyas,* women and even those lower than the lowborn *śūdras,* so what to speak of the high-class men like the qualified *brāhmaṇas* and the great self-realized kings. The other high-grade activities designated as sacrifice, charity, austerity, etc., are all corollary factors following the pure and scientific *bhakti* cult.

The principles of knowledge and detachment are two important factors on the path of transcendental realization. The whole spiritual process leads to perfect knowledge of everything material and spiritual, and the results of such perfect knowledge are that one becomes detached from material affection and becomes attached to spiritual activities. Becoming detached from material things does not mean becoming inert altogether, as men with a poor fund of knowledge think. *Naiṣkarma* means not undertaking activities that will produce good or bad effects. Negation does not mean negation of the positive. Negation of the nonessentials does not mean negation of the essential. Similarly, detachment from material forms does not mean nullifying the positive form. The *bhakti* cult is meant for realization of the positive form. When the positive form is realized, the negative forms are automatically eliminated. Therefore, with the development of the *bhakti* cult, with the application of positive service to the positive form, one naturally becomes detached from inferior things, and he becomes attached to superior things. Similarly, the *bhakti* cult, being the supermost occupation of the living being, leads him out of material sense enjoyment. That is the sign of a pure devotee. He is not a fool, nor is he engaged in the inferior energies, nor does he have material values. This is not possible by dry reasoning. It actually happens by the grace of the Almighty. In conclusion, one who is a pure devotee has all other good qualities, namely knowledge, detachment, etc., but one who has only knowledge or detachment is not necessarily well acquainted with the principles of the *bhakti* cult. *Bhakti* is the supermost occupation of the human being.

TEXT 8

धर्मः स्वनुष्ठितः पुंसां विष्वक्सेनकथासु यः ।
नोत्पादयेद्यदि रतिं श्रम एव हि केवलम् ॥८॥

dharmaḥ svanuṣṭhitaḥ puṁsāṁ
viṣvaksena-kathāsu yaḥ

notpādayed yadi ratiṁ
śrama eva hi kevalam

dharmaḥ—occupation; *svanuṣṭhitaḥ*—executed in terms of one's own position; *puṁsām*—of humankind; *viṣvaksena*—the Personality of Godhead (plenary portion); *kathāsu*—in the message of; *yaḥ*—what is; *na*—not; *utpādayet*—does produce; *yadi*—if; *ratim*—attraction; *śramaḥ*—useless labor; *eva*—only; *hi*—certainly; *kevalam*—entirely.

TRANSLATION

The occupational activities a man performs according to his own position are only so much useless labor if they do not provoke attraction for the message of the Personality of Godhead.

PURPORT

There are different occupational activities in terms of man's different conceptions of life. To the gross materialist who cannot see anything beyond the gross material body, there is nothing beyond the senses. Therefore his occupational activities are limited to concentrated and extended selfishness. Concentrated selfishness centers around the personal body—this is generally seen amongst the lower animals. Extended selfishness is manifested in human society and centers around the family, society, community, nation and world with a view to gross bodily comfort. Above these gross materialists are the mental speculators who hover aloft in the mental spheres, and their occupational duties involve making poetry and philosophy or propagating some *ism* with the same aim of selfishness limited to the body and the mind. But above the body and mind is the dormant spirit soul whose absence from the body makes the whole range of bodily and mental selfishness completely null and void. But less intelligent people have no information of the needs of the spirit soul.

Because foolish people have no information of the soul and how it is beyond the purview of the body and mind, they are not satisfied in the performance of their occupational duties. The question of the satisfaction of the self is raised herein. The self is beyond the gross body and subtle mind. He is the potent active principle of the body and mind. Without knowing the need of the dormant soul, one cannot be happy simply with emolument of the body and mind. The body and the mind are but superfluous outer coverings of the spirit soul. The spirit soul's needs must be fulfilled. Simply by cleansing the cage of the bird, one does not satisfy the bird. One must actually know the needs of the bird himself.

The need of the spirit soul is that he wants to get out of the limited sphere of material bondage and fulfill his desire for complete freedom. He wants to get out of the covered walls of the greater universe. He wants to see the free light and the spirit. That complete freedom is achieved when he meets the complete spirit, the Personality of Godhead. There is a dormant affection for God within everyone; spiritual existence is manifested through the gross body and mind in the form of perverted affection for gross and subtle matter. Therefore we have to engage ourselves in occupational engagements that will evoke our divine consciousness. This is possible only by hearing and chanting the divine activities of the Supreme Lord, and any occupational activity which does not help one to achieve attachment for hearing and chanting the transcendental message of Godhead is said herein to be simply a waste of time. This is because other occupational duties (whatever *ism* they may belong to) cannot give liberation to the soul. Even the activities of the salvationists are considered to be useless because of their failure to pick up the fountainhead of all liberties. The gross materialist can practically see that his material gain is limited only to time and space, either in this world or in the other. Even if he goes up to the Svargaloka, he will find no permanent abode for his hankering soul. The hankering soul must be satisfied by the perfect scientific process of perfect devotional service.

TEXT 9

धर्मस्य ह्यापवर्ग्यस्य नार्थोऽर्थायोपकल्पते ।
नार्थस्य धर्मैकान्तस्य कामो लाभाय हि स्मृतः ॥९॥

dharmasya hy āpavargyasya
nārtho 'rthāyopakalpate
nārthasya dharmaikāntasya
kāmo lābhāya hi smṛtaḥ

dharmasya—occupational engagement; *hi*—certainly; *āpavargyasya*—ultimate liberation; *na*—not; *arthaḥ*—end; *arthāya*—for material gain; *upakalpate*—is meant for; *na*—neither; *arthasya*—of material gain; *dharma-eka-antasya*—for one who is engaged in the ultimate occupational service; *kāmaḥ*—sense gratification; *lābhāya*—attainment of; *hi*—exactly; *smṛtaḥ*—is described by the great sages.

TRANSLATION

All occupational engagements are certainly meant for ultimate liberation. They should never be performed for material gain. Furthermore, according to sages, one who is engaged in the ultimate occupational service should never use material gain to cultivate sense gratification.

PURPORT

We have already discussed that pure devotional service to the Lord is automatically followed by perfect knowledge and detachment from material existence. But there are others who consider that all kinds of different occupational engagements, including those of religion, are meant for material gain. The general tendency of any ordinary man in any part of the world is to gain some material profit in exchange for religious or any other occupational service. Even in the Vedic literatures, for all sorts of religious performances an allurement of material gain is offered, and most people are attracted by such allurements or blessings of religiosity. Why are such so-called men of religion allured by material gain? Because material gain can enable one to fulfill desires, which in turn satisfy sense gratification. This cycle of occupational engagements includes so-called religiosity followed by material gain and material gain followed by fulfillment of desires. Sense gratification is the general way for all sorts of fully occupied men. But in the statement of Sūta Gosvāmī, as per the verdict of the *Śrīmad-Bhāgavatam,* this is nullified by the present *śloka.*

One should not engage himself in any sort of occupational service for material gain only. Nor should material gain be utilized for sense gratification. How material gain should be utilized is described as follows.

TEXT 10

कामस्य नेन्द्रियप्रीतिर्लाभो जीवेत यावता।
जीवस्य तत्त्वजिज्ञासा नार्थो यश्चेह कर्मभिः ॥१०॥

kāmasya nendriya-prītir
lābho jīveta yāvatā
jīvasya tattva-jijñāsā
nārtho yaś ceha karmabhiḥ

kāmasya—of desires; *na*—not; *indriya*—senses; *prītiḥ*—satisfaction; *lābhaḥ*—gain; *jīveta*—self-preservation; *yāvatā*—so much so; *jīvasya*—of the living being; *tattva*—the Absolute Truth; *jijñāsā*—inquiries; *na*—not; *arthaḥ*—end; *yaḥ ca iha*—whatsoever else; *karmabhiḥ*—by occupational activities.

TRANSLATION

Life's desires should never be directed toward sense gratification. One should desire only a healthy life, or self-preservation, since a human being is meant for inquiry about the Absolute Truth. Nothing else should be the goal of one's works.

PURPORT

The completely bewildered material civilization is wrongly directed towards the fulfillment of desires in sense gratification. In such civilization, in all spheres of life, the ultimate end is sense gratification. In politics, social service, altruism, philanthropy and ultimately in religion or even in salvation, the very same tint of sense gratification is ever-increasingly predominant. In the political field the leaders of men fight with one another to fulfill their personal sense gratification. The voters adore the so-called leaders only when they promise sense gratification. As soon as the voters are dissatisfied in their own sense satisfaction, they dethrone the leaders. The leaders must always disappoint the voters by not satisfying their senses. The same is applicable in all other fields; no one is serious about the problems of life. Even those who are on the path of salvation desire to become one with the Absolute Truth and desire to commit spiritual suicide for sense gratification. But the *Bhāgavatam* says that one should not live for sense gratification. One should satisfy the senses only insomuch as required for self-preservation, and not for sense gratification. Because the body is made of senses, which also require a certain amount of satisfaction, there are regulative directions for satisfaction of such senses. But the senses are not meant for unrestricted enjoyment. For example, marriage or the combination of a man with a woman is necessary for progeny, but it is not meant for sense enjoyment. In the absence of voluntary restraint, there is propaganda for family planning, but foolish men do not know that family planning is automatically executed as soon as there is search after the Absolute Truth. Seekers of the Absolute Truth are never allured by unnecessary engagements in sense gratification because the serious students seeking the

Absolute Truth are always overwhelmed with the work of researching the Truth. In every sphere of life, therefore, the ultimate end must be seeking after the Absolute Truth, and that sort of engagement will make one happy because he will be less engaged in varieties of sense gratification. And what that Absolute Truth is is explained as follows.

TEXT 11

वदन्ति तत्तत्त्वविदस्तत्त्वं यज्ज्ञानमद्वयम्।
ब्रह्मेति परमात्मेति भगवानिति शब्द्यते ॥११॥

vadanti tat tattva-vidas
tattvaṁ yaj jñānam advayam
brahmeti paramātmeti
bhagavān iti śabdyate

vadanti—they say; *tat*—that; *tattva-vidaḥ*—the learned souls; *tattvam*—the Absolute Truth; *yat*—which; *jñānam*—knowledge; *advayam*—nondual; *brahma iti*—known as Brahman; *paramātmā iti*—known as Paramātmā; *bhagavān iti*—known as Bhagavān; *śabdyate*—it' so sounded.

TRANSLATION

Learned transcendentalists who know the Absolute Truth call this nondual substance Brahman, Paramātmā or Bhagavān.

PURPORT

The Absolute Truth is both subject and object, and there is no qualitative difference there. Therefore, Brahman, Paramātmā and Bhagavān are qualitatively one and the same. The same substance is realized as impersonal Brahman by the students of the *Upaniṣads,* as localized Paramātmā by the Hiraṇyagarbhas or the *yogīs,* and as Bhagavān by the devotees. In other words, Bhagavān, or the Personality of Godhead, is the last word of the Absolute Truth. Paramātmā is the partial representation of the Personality of Godhead, and impersonal Brahman is the glowing effulgence of the Personality of Godhead, as the sun rays are to the sun-god. Less intelligent students of either of the above schools sometimes argue in favor of their own respective realization, but those who are perfect seers of the Absolute Truth know well that the above three features of the one Absolute Truth are different perspective views seen from different angles of vision.

As it is explained in the first *śloka* of the First Chapter of the *Bhāgavatam,* the Supreme Truth is self-sufficient, cognizant and free from the illusion of relativity. In the relative world the knower is different from the known, but in the Absolute Truth both the knower and the known are one and the same thing. In the relative world the knower is the living spirit or superior energy, whereas the known is inert matter or inferior energy. Therefore, there is a duality of inferior and superior energy, whereas in the absolute realm both the knower and the known are of the same superior energy. There are three kinds of energies of the supreme energetic. There is no difference between the energy and energetic, but there is a difference of quality of energies. The absolute realm and the living entities are of the same superior energy, but the material world is inferior energy. The living being in contact with the inferior energy is illusioned, thinking he belongs to the inferior energy. Therefore there is the sense of relativity in the material world. In the Absolute there is no such sense of difference between the knower and the known, and therefore everything there is absolute.

TEXT 12

तच्छ्रद्दधाना मुनयो ज्ञानवैराग्ययुक्तया।
पश्यन्त्यात्मनि चात्मानं भक्त्या श्रुतगृहीतया ॥१२॥

tac chraddadhānā munayo
jñāna-vairāgya-yuktayā
paśyanty ātmani cātmānaṁ
bhaktyā śruta-gṛhītayā

tat—that; *śraddadhānāḥ*—seriously inquisitive; *munayaḥ*—sages; *jñāna*—knowledge; *vairāgya*—detachment; *yuktayā*—well equipped with; *paśyanti*—see; *ātmani*—within himself; *ca*—and; *ātmānam*—the Paramātmā; *bhaktyā*—in devotional service; *śruta*—the *Vedas; gṛhītayā*—well received.

TRANSLATION

The seriously inquisitive student or sage, well equipped with knowledge and detachment, realizes that Absolute Truth by rendering devotional service in terms of what he has heard from the Vedānta-śruti.

PURPORT

The Absolute Truth is realized in full by the process of devotional service to the Lord, Vāsudeva, or the Personality of Godhead, who is the full-fledged Absolute Truth. Brahman is His transcendental bodily effulgence, and Paramātmā is His partial representation. As such, Brahman or Paramātmā realization of the Absolute Truth is but a partial realization. There are four different types of human beings—the *karmīs,* the *jñānīs,* the *yogīs* and the devotees. The *karmīs* are materialistic, whereas the other three are transcendental. The first-class transcendentalists are the devotees who have realized the Supreme Person. The second-class transcendentalists are those who have partially realized the plenary portion of the Absolute Person. And the third-class transcendentalists are those who have barely realized the spiritual focus of the Absolute Person. As stated in the *Bhagavad-gītā* and other Vedic literatures, the Supreme Person is realized by devotional service, which is backed by full knowledge and detachment from material association. We have already discussed the point that devotional service is followed by knowledge and detachment from material association. As Brahman and Paramātmā realization are imperfect realizations of the Absolute Truth, so the means of realizing Brahman and Paramātmā, i.e., the paths of *jñāna* and *yoga,* are also imperfect means of realizing the Absolute Truth. Devotional service, which is based on the foreground of full knowledge combined with detachment from material association and which is fixed by the aural reception of the *Vedānta-śruti,* is the only perfect method by which the seriously inquisitive student can realize the Absolute Truth. Devotional service is not, therefore, meant for the less intelligent class of transcendentalist. There are three classes of devotees, namely first, second, and third class. The third-class devotees, or the neophytes, who have no knowledge and are not detached from material association, but who are simply attracted by the preliminary process of worshiping the Deity in the temple, are called material devotees. Material devotees are more attached to material benefit than transcendental profit. Therefore, one has to make definite progress from the position of material devotional service to the second-class devotional position. In the second-class position, the devotee can see four principles in the devotional line, namely the Personality of Godhead, His devotees, the ignorant and the envious. One has to raise himself at least to the stage of a second-class devotee and thus become eligible to know the Absolute Truth.

A third-class devotee, therefore, has to receive the instructions of devotional service from the authoritative sources of *Bhāgavata.* The number one *Bhāgavata* is the established personality of devotee, and the other *Bhāgavatam* is the message of Godhead. The third-class devotee therefore has to go to the personality of devotee in order to learn the instructions of devotional service. Such a personality of devotee is not a professional man who earns his livelihood by the business of *Bhāgavatam.* Such a devotee must be a representative of Śukadeva Gosvāmī, like Sūta Gosvāmī, and must preach the cult of devotional service for the all-around benefit of all people. A neophyte devotee has very little taste for hearing from the authorities. Such a neophyte devotee makes a show of hearing from the professional man to satisfy his senses. This sort of hearing and chanting has spoiled the whole thing, so one should be very careful about the faulty process. The holy messages of Godhead, as inculcated in the *Bhagavad-gītā* or in the *Śrīmad-Bhāgavatam,* are undoubtedly transcendental subjects, but even though they are so, such transcendental matters are not to be received from the professional man, who spoils them as the serpent spoils milk simply by the touch of his tongue.

A sincere devotee must, therefore, be prepared to hear the Vedic literature like the *Upaniṣads, Vedānta* and other literatures left by the previous authorities or Gosvāmīs, for the benefit of his progress. Without hearing such literatures, one cannot make actual progress. And without hearing and following the instructions, the show of devotional service becomes worthless and therefore a sort of disturbance in the path of devotional service. Unless, therefore, devotional service is established on the principles of *śruti, smṛti, purāṇa* or *pañcarātra* authorities, the make-show of devotional service should at once be rejected. An unauthorized devotee should never be recognized as a pure devotee. By assimilation of such messages from the Vedic literatures, one can see the all-pervading localized aspect of the Personality of Godhead within his own self constantly. This is called *samādhi.*

TEXT 13

अतः पुम्भिर्द्विजश्रेष्ठा वर्णाश्रमविभागशः ।
स्वनुष्ठितस्य धर्मस्य संसिद्धिर्हरितोषणम् ॥१३॥

ataḥ pumbhir dvija-śreṣṭhā
varṇāśrama-vibhāgaśaḥ

svanuṣṭhitasya dharmasya
saṁsiddhir hari-toṣaṇam

ataḥ—so; *pumbhiḥ*—by the human being; *dvija-śreṣṭhāḥ*—O best among the twice-born; *varṇa-āśrama*—the institution of four castes and four orders of life; *vibhāgaśaḥ*—by the division of; *svanuṣṭhitasya*—of one's own prescribed duties; *dharmasya*—occupational; *saṁsiddhiḥ*—the highest perfection; *hari*—the Personality of Godhead; *toṣaṇam*—pleasing.

TRANSLATION

O best among the twice-born, it is therefore concluded that the highest perfection one can achieve by discharging the duties prescribed for one's own occupation according to caste divisions and orders of life is to please the Personality of Godhead.

PURPORT

Human society all over the world is divided into four castes and four orders of life. The four castes are the intelligent caste, the martial caste, the productive caste and the laborer caste. These castes are classified in terms of one's work and qualification and not by birth. Then again there are four orders of life, namely the student life, the householder's life, the retired and the devotional life. In the best interest of human society there must be such divisions of life, otherwise no social institution can grow in a healthy state. And in each and every one of the above-mentioned divisions of life, *the aim must be to please the supreme authority of the Personality of Godhead.* This institutional function of human society is known as the system of *varṇāśrama-dharma,* which is quite natural for the civilized life. The *varṇāśrama* institution is constructed to enable one to realize the Absolute Truth. It is not for artificial domination of one division over another. When the aim of life, i.e., realization of the Absolute Truth, is missed by too much attachment for *indriya-prīti,* or sense gratification, as already discussed hereinbefore, the institution of the *varṇāśrama* is utilized by selfish men to pose an artificial predominance over the weaker section. In the Kali-yuga, or in the age of quarrel, this artificial predominance is already current, but the saner section of the people know it well that the divisions of castes and orders of life are meant for smooth social intercourse and high-thinking self-realization and not for any other purpose.

Herein the statement of *Bhāgavatam* is that the highest aim of life or the highest perfection of the institution of the *varṇāśrama-dharma* is to cooperate jointly for the satisfaction of the Supreme Lord. This is also confirmed in the *Bhagavad-gītā* (4.13).

TEXT 14

तस्मादेकेन मनसा भगवान् सात्वतां पतिः ।
श्रोतव्यः कीर्तितव्यश्च ध्येयः पूज्यश्च नित्यदा ॥१४॥

tasmād ekena manasā
bhagavān sātvatāṁ patiḥ
śrotavyaḥ kīrtitavyaś ca
dhyeyaḥ pūjyaś ca nityadā

tasmāt—therefore; *ekena*—by one; *manasā*—attention of the mind; *bhagavān*—the Personality of Godhead; *sātvatām*—of the devotees; *patiḥ*—protector; *śrotavyaḥ*—is to be heard; *kīrtitavyaḥ*—to be glorified; *ca*—and; *dhyeyaḥ*—to be remembered; *pūjyaḥ*—to be worshiped; *ca*—and; *nityadā*—constantly.

TRANSLATION

Therefore, with one-pointed attention, one should constantly hear about, glorify, remember and worship the Personality of Godhead, who is the protector of the devotees.

PURPORT

If realization of the Absolute Truth is the ultimate aim of life, it must be carried out by all means. In any one of the above-mentioned castes and orders of life, the four processes, namely glorifying, hearing, remembering and worshiping, are general occupations. Without these principles of life, no one can exist. Activities of the living being involve engagements in these four different principles of life. Especially in modern society, all activities are more or less dependent on hearing and glorifying. Any man from any social status becomes a well-known man in human society within a very short time if he is simply glorified truly or falsely in the daily newspapers. Sometimes political leaders of a particular party are also advertised by newspaper propaganda, and by such a method of glorification an insignificant man becomes an important man—within no time. But such propaganda by false glorification of an unqualified person cannot bring about any good, either for the particular man or for the society. There may be some temporary reactions to such propaganda, but there are no permanent effects. Therefore such activities are a waste of time. The actual object of glorification is the Supreme Personality of Godhead, who has created everything manifested before us. We have broadly discussed this fact from the beginning of the "*janmādy asya*" *śloka* of this *Bhāgavatam.* The tendency to glorify others or hear others must be turned to the real object of glorification—the Supreme Being. And that will bring happiness.

TEXT 15

यदनुध्यासिना युक्ताः कर्मग्रन्थिनिबन्धनम् ।
छिन्दन्ति कोविदास्तस्य को न कुर्यात्कथारतिम् ॥१५॥

yad-anudhyāsinā yuktāḥ
karma-granthi-nibandhanam
chindanti kovidās tasya
ko na kuryāt kathā-ratim

yat—which; *anudhyā*—remembrance; *asinā*—sword; *yuktāḥ*—being equipped with; *karma*—reactionary work; *granthi*—knot; *nibandhanam*—interknit; *chindanti*—cut; *kovidāḥ*—intelligent; *tasya*—His; *kaḥ*—who; *na*—not; *kuryāt*—shall do; *kathā*—messages; *ratim*—attention.

TRANSLATION

With sword in hand, intelligent men cut through the binding knots of reactionary work [karma] by remembering the Personality of Godhead. Therefore, who will not pay attention to His message?

PURPORT

The contact of the spiritual spark with material elements creates a knot which must be cut if one wants to be liberated from the actions and reactions of fruitive work. Liberation means freedom from the cycle of reactionary work. This liberation automatically follows for one who constantly remembers the transcendental pastimes of the Personality of Godhead. This is because all the activities of the Supreme Lord (His *līlā*) are transcendental to the modes of the material energy. They are all-attractive spiritual activities, and therefore constant association with the spiritual activities of the Supreme

Lord gradually spiritualizes the conditioned soul and ultimately severs the knot of material bondage.

Liberation from material bondage is, therefore, a by-product of devotional service. Attainment of spiritual knowledge is not sufficient to insure liberation. Such knowledge must be overcoated with devotional service so that ultimately the devotional service alone predominates. Then liberation is made possible. Even the reactionary work of the fruitive workers can lead one to liberation when it is overcoated with devotional service. *Karma* overcoated with devotional service is called *karma-yoga.* Similarly, empirical knowledge overcoated with devotional service is called *jñāna-yoga.* But pure *bhakti-yoga* is independent of such *karma* and *jñāna* because it alone can not only endow one with liberation from conditional life but also award one the transcendental loving service of the Lord.

Therefore, any sensible man who is above the average man with a poor fund of knowledge must constantly remember the Personality of Godhead by hearing about Him, by glorifying Him, by remembering Him and by worshiping Him always, without cessation. That is the perfect way of devotional service. The Gosvāmīs of Vṛndāvana, who were authorized by Śrī Caitanya Mahāprabhu to preach the *bhakti* cult, rigidly followed this rule and made immense literatures of transcendental science for our benefit. They have chalked out ways for all classes of men in terms of the different castes and orders of life in pursuance of the teachings of *Śrīmad-Bhāgavatam* and similar other authoritative scriptures.

TEXT 16

शुश्रूषोः श्रद्दधानस्य वासुदेवकथारुचिः ।
स्यान्महत्सेवया विप्राः पुण्यतीर्थनिषेवणात् ॥१६॥

śuśrūṣoḥ śraddadhānasya
vāsudeva-kathā-ruciḥ
syān mahat-sevayā viprāḥ
puṇya-tīrtha-niṣevaṇāt

śuśrūṣoḥ—one who is engaged in hearing; *śraddadhānasya*—with care and attention; *vāsudeva*—in respect to Vāsudeva; *kathā*—the message; *ruciḥ*—affinity; *syāt*—is made possible; *mahat-sevayā*—by service rendered to pure devotees; *viprāḥ*—O twice-born; *puṇya-tīrtha*—those who are cleansed of all vice; *niṣevaṇāt*—by service.

TRANSLATION

O twice-born sages, by serving those devotees who are completely freed from all vice, great service is done. By such service, one gains affinity for hearing the messages of Vāsudeva.

PURPORT

The conditioned life of a living being is caused by his revolting against the Lord. There are men called *deva,* or godly living beings, and there are men called *asuras,* or demons, who are against the authority of the Supreme Lord. In the *Bhagavad-gītā* (Sixteenth Chapter) a vivid description of the *asuras* is given in which it is said that the *asuras* are put into lower and lower states of ignorance life after life and so sink to the lower animal forms and have no information of the Absolute Truth, the Personality of Godhead. These *asuras* are gradually rectified to God consciousness by the mercy of the Lord's liberated servitors in different countries according to the supreme will. Such devotees of God are very confidential associates of the Lord, and when they come to save human society from the dangers of godlessness, they are known as the powerful incarnations of the Lord, as sons of the Lord, as servants of the Lord or as associates of the Lord. But none of them falsely claim to be God themselves. This is a blasphemy declared by the *asuras,* and the demoniac followers of such *asuras* also accept pretenders as God or His incarnation. In the revealed scriptures there is definite information of the incarnation of God. No one should be accepted as God or an incarnation of God unless he is confirmed by the revealed scriptures.

The servants of God are to be respected as God by the devotees who actually want to go back to Godhead. Such servants of God are called *mahātmās,* or *tīrthas,* and they preach according to particular time and place. The servants of God urge people to become devotees of the Lord. They never tolerate being called God. Śrī Caitanya Mahāprabhu was God Himself according to the indication of the revealed scriptures, but He played the part of a devotee. People who knew Him to be God addressed Him as God, but He used to block His ears with His hands and chant the name of Lord Viṣṇu. He strongly protested against being called God, although undoubtedly He was God Himself. The Lord behaves so to warn us against unscrupulous men who take pleasure in being addressed as God.

The servants of God come to propagate God consciousness, and intelligent people should cooperate with them in every respect. By serving the servant of God, one can please God more than by directly serving the Lord. The Lord is more pleased when He sees that His servants are properly respected because such servants risk everything for the service of the Lord and so are very dear to the Lord. The Lord declares in the *Bhagavad-gītā* (18.69) that no one is dearer to Him than one who risks everything to preach His glory. By serving the servants of the Lord, one gradually gets the quality of such servants, and thus one becomes qualified to hear the glories of God. The eagerness to hear about God is the first qualification of a devotee eligible for entering the kingdom of God.

TEXT 17

शृण्वतां स्वकथाः कृष्णः पुण्यश्रवणकीर्तनः ।
हृद्यन्तःस्थो ह्यभद्राणि विधुनोति सुहृत्सताम् ॥१७॥

śṛṇvatāṁ sva-kathāḥ kṛṣṇaḥ
puṇya-śravaṇa-kīrtanaḥ
hṛdy antaḥ stho hy abhadrāṇi
vidhunoti suhṛt satām

śṛṇvatām—those who have developed the urge to hear the message of; *sva-kathāḥ*—His own words; *kṛṣṇaḥ*—the Personality of Godhead; *puṇya*—virtues; *śravaṇa*—hearing; *kīrtanaḥ*—chanting; *hṛdi antaḥ sthaḥ*—within one's heart; *hi*—certainly; *abhadrāṇi*—desire to enjoy matter; *vidhunoti*—cleanses; *suhṛt*—benefactor; *satām*—of the truthful.

TRANSLATION

Śrī Kṛṣṇa, the Personality of Godhead, who is the Paramātmā [Supersoul] in everyone's heart and the benefactor of the truthful devotee, cleanses desire for material enjoyment from the heart of the devotee who has developed the urge to hear His messages, which are in themselves virtuous when properly heard and chanted.

PURPORT

Messages of the Personality of Godhead, Śrī Kṛṣṇa, are nondifferent from Him. Whenever, therefore, offenseless hearing and glorification of God are undertaken, it is to be understood that Lord Kṛṣṇa is present there in the form of transcendental sound, which is as powerful as the Lord personally. Śrī Caitanya Mahāprabhu, in His *Śikṣāṣṭaka,* declares clearly that the holy name of the Lord has all the potencies of the Lord and that He has endowed His innumerable names with the same potency. There is no rigid fixture of time, and anyone can chant the holy name with attention and reverence at his convenience. The Lord is so kind to us that He can be present before us personally in the form of transcendental sound, but unfortunately we have no taste for hearing and glorifying the Lord's name and activities. We have already discussed developing a taste for hearing and chanting the holy sound. It is done through the medium of service to the pure devotee of the Lord.

The Lord is reciprocally respondent to His devotees. When He sees that a devotee is completely sincere in getting admittance to the transcendental service of the Lord and has thus become eager to hear about Him, the Lord acts from within the devotee in such a way that the devotee may easily go back to Him. The Lord is more anxious to take us back into His kingdom than we can desire. Most of us do not desire at all to go back to Godhead. Only a very few men want to go back to Godhead. But anyone who desires to go back to Godhead, Śrī Kṛṣṇa helps in all respects.

One cannot enter into the kingdom of God unless one is perfectly cleared of all sins. The material sins are products of our desires to lord it over material nature. It is very difficult to get rid of such desires. Women and wealth are very difficult problems for the devotee making progress on the path back to Godhead. Many stalwarts in the devotional line fell victim to these allurements and thus retreated from the path of liberation. But when one is helped by the Lord Himself, the whole process becomes as easy as anything by the divine grace of the Lord.

To become restless in the contact of women and wealth is not an astonishment, because every living being is associated with such things from remote time, practically immemorial, and it takes time to recover from this foreign nature. But if one is engaged in hearing the glories of the Lord, gradually he realizes his real position. By the grace of God such a devotee gets sufficient strength to defend himself from the state of disturbances, and gradually all disturbing elements are eliminated from his mind.

TEXT 18

नष्टप्रायेष्वभद्रेषु नित्यं भागवतसेवया।
भगवत्युत्तमश्लोके भक्तिर्भवति नैष्ठिकी ॥१८॥

naṣṭa-prāyeṣv abhadreṣu
nityaṁ bhāgavata-sevayā
bhagavaty uttama-śloke
bhaktir bhavati naiṣṭhikī

naṣṭa—destroyed; *prāyeṣu*—almost to nil; *abhadreṣu*—all that is inauspicious; *nityam*—regularly; *bhāgavata*—*Śrīmad-Bhāgavatam,* or the pure devotee; *sevayā*—by serving; *bhagavati*—unto the Personality of Godhead; *uttama*—transcendental; *śloke*—prayers; *bhaktiḥ*—loving service; *bhavati*—comes into being; *naiṣṭhikī*—irrevocable.

TRANSLATION

By regular attendance in classes on the Bhāgavatam and by rendering of service to the pure devotee, all that is troublesome to the heart is almost completely destroyed, and loving service unto the Personality of Godhead, who is praised with transcendental songs, is established as an irrevocable fact.

PURPORT

Here is the remedy for eliminating all inauspicious things within the heart, which are considered to be obstacles in the path of self-realization. The remedy is the association of the *Bhāgavatas.* There are two types of *Bhāgavatas,* namely the book *Bhāgavata* and the devotee *Bhāgavata.* Both the *Bhāgavatas* are competent remedies, and both of them or either of them can be good enough to eliminate the obstacles. A devotee *Bhāgavata* is as good as the book *Bhāgavata* because the devotee *Bhāgavata* leads his life in terms of the book *Bhāgavata* and the book *Bhāgavata* is full of information about the Personality of Godhead and His pure devotees, who are also *Bhāgavatas. Bhāgavata* book and person are identical.

The devotee *Bhāgavata* is a direct representative of Bhagavān, the Personality of Godhead. So by pleasing the devotee *Bhāgavata* one can receive the benefit of the book *Bhāgavata.* Human reason fails to understand how by serving the devotee *Bhāgavata* or the book *Bhāgavata* one gets gradual promotion on the path of devotion. But actually these are facts explained by Śrīla Nāradadeva, who happened to be a maidservant's son in his previous life. The maidservant was engaged in the menial service of the sages, and thus he also came into contact with them. And simply by associating with them and accepting the remnants of foodstuff left by the sages, the son of the maidservant got the chance to become the great devotee and personality Śrīla Nāradadeva. These are the miraculous effects of the association of *Bhāgavatas.* And to understand these effects practically, it should be noted that by such sincere association of the *Bhāgavatas* one is sure to receive transcendental knowledge very easily, with the result that he becomes fixed in the devotional service of the Lord. The more progress is made in devotional service under the guidance of the *Bhāgavatas,* the more one becomes fixed in the transcendental loving service of the Lord. The messages of the book *Bhāgavata,* therefore, have to be received from the devotee *Bhāgavata,* and the combination of these two *Bhāgavatas* will help the neophyte devotee to make progress on and on.

TEXT 19

तदा रजस्तमोभावाः कामलोभादयश्च ये।
चेत एतैरनाविद्धं स्थितं सत्त्वे प्रसीदति ॥१९॥

tadā rajas-tamo-bhāvāḥ
kāma-lobhādayaś ca ye
ceta etair anāviddhaṁ
sthitaṁ sattve prasīdati

tadā—at that time; *rajaḥ*—in the mode of passion; *tamaḥ*—the mode of ignorance; *bhāvāḥ*—the situation; *kāma*—lust and desire; *lobha*—hankering; *ādayaḥ*—others; *ca*—and; *ye*—whatever they are; *cetaḥ*—the mind; *etaiḥ*—by these; *anāviddham*—without being affected; *sthitam*—being fixed; *sattve*—in the mode of goodness; *prasīdati*—thus becomes fully satisfied.

TRANSLATION

As soon as irrevocable loving service is established in the heart, the effects of nature's modes of passion and ignorance, such as lust, desire and hankering, disappear from the heart. Then the devotee is established in goodness, and he becomes completely happy.

PURPORT

A living being in his normal constitutional position is fully satisfied in spiritual bliss. This state of existence is called *brahma-bhūta or ātmānandi,* or the state of self-satisfaction. This self-satisfaction is not like the satisfaction of the inactive fool. The inactive fool is in the state of foolish ignorance, whereas the self-satisfied *ātmānandī* is transcendental to the material state of existence. This stage of perfection is attained as soon as one is fixed in irrevocable devotional service. Devotional service is not inactivity, but the unalloyed activity of the soul.

The soul's activity becomes adulterated in contact with matter, and as such the diseased activities are expressed in the form of lust, desire, hankering, inactivity, foolishness and sleep. The effect of devotional service becomes manifest by complete elimination of these effects of passion and ignorance. The devotee is fixed at once in the mode of goodness, and he makes further progress to rise to the position of *vasudeva*, or the state of unmixed *sattva*, or *śuddha-sattva*. Only in this *śuddha-sattva* state can one always see Kṛṣṇa eye to eye by dint of pure affection for the Lord.

A devotee is always in the mode of unalloyed goodness; therefore he harms no one. But the nondevotee, however educated he may be, is always harmful. A devotee is neither foolish nor passionate. The harmful, foolish and passionate cannot be devotees of the Lord, however they may advertise themselves as devotees by outward dress. A devotee is always qualified with all the good qualities of God. Quantitatively such qualifications may be different, but qualitatively both the Lord and His devotee are one and the same.

TEXT 20

एवं प्रसन्नमनसो भगवद्भक्तियोगतः ।
भगवत्तत्त्वविज्ञानं मुक्तसङ्गस्य जायते ॥२०॥

evaṁ prasanna-manaso
bhagavad-bhakti-yogataḥ
bhagavat-tattva-vijñānaṁ
mukta-saṅgasya jāyate

evam—thus; *prasanna*—enlivened; *manasaḥ*—of the mind; *bhagavat-bhakti*—the devotional service of the Lord; *yogataḥ*—by contact of; *bhagavat*—regarding the Personality of Godhead; *tattva*—knowledge; *vijñānam*—scientific; *mukta*—liberated; *saṅgasya*—of the association; *jāyate*—becomes effective.

TRANSLATION

Thus established in the mode of unalloyed goodness, the man whose mind has been enlivened by contact with devotional service to the Lord

gains positive scientific knowledge of the Personality of Godhead in the stage of liberation from all material association.

PURPORT

In the *Bhagavad-gītā* (7.3) it is said that out of many thousands of ordinary men, one fortunate man endeavors for perfection in life. Mostly men are conducted by the modes of passion and ignorance, and thus they are engaged always in lust, desire, hankerings, ignorance and sleep. Out of many such manlike animals, there is actually a man who knows the responsibility of human life and thus tries to make life perfect by following the prescribed duties. And out of many thousands of such persons who have thus attained success in human life, one may know scientifically about the Personality of Godhead, Śrī Kṛṣṇa. In the same *Bhagavad-gītā* (18.55) it is also said that scientific knowledge of Śrī Kṛṣṇa is understood only by the process of devotional service *(bhakti-yoga).*

The very same thing is confirmed herein in the above words. No ordinary man, or even one who has attained success in human life, can know scientifically or perfectly the Personality of Godhead. Perfection of human life is attained when one can understand that he is not the product of matter but is in fact spirit. And as soon as one understands that he has nothing to do with matter, he at once ceases his material hankerings and becomes enlivened as a spiritual being. This attainment of success is possible when one is above the modes of passion and ignorance, or, in other words, when one is actually a *brāhmaṇa* by qualification. A *brāhmaṇa* is the symbol of *sattva-guṇa,* or the mode of goodness. And others, who are not in the mode of goodness, are either *kṣatriyas, vaiśyas, śūdras* or less than the *śūdras.* The brahminical stage is the highest stage of human life because of its good qualities. So one cannot be a devotee unless one at least qualifies as a *brāhmaṇa.* The devotee is already a *brāhmaṇa* by action. But that is not the end of it. As referred to above, such a *brāhmaṇa* has to become a Vaiṣṇava in fact to be actually in the transcendental stage. A pure Vaiṣṇava is a liberated soul and is transcendental even to the position of a *brāhmaṇa.* In the material stage even a *brāhmaṇa* is also a conditioned soul because although in the brahminical stage the conception of Brahman or transcendence is realized, scientific knowledge of the Supreme Lord is lacking. One has to surpass the brahminical stage and reach the *vasudeva* stage to understand the Personality of Godhead, Kṛṣṇa. The science of the Personality of Godhead is the subject matter for study by the postgraduate students in the spiritual line. Foolish men, or men with a poor fund of knowledge, do not understand the Supreme Lord, and they interpret Kṛṣṇa according to their respective whims. The fact is, however, that one cannot understand the science of the Personality of Godhead unless one is freed from the contamination of the material modes, even up to the stage of a *brāhmaṇa.* When a qualified *brāhmaṇa* factually becomes a Vaiṣṇava, in the enlivened state of liberation he can know what is actually the Personality of Godhead.

TEXT 21

भिद्यते हृदयग्रन्थिश्छिद्यन्ते सर्वसंशयाः ।
क्षीयन्ते चास्य कर्माणि दृष्ट एवात्मनीश्वरे ॥२१॥

bhidyate hṛdaya-granthiś
chidyante sarva-saṁśayāḥ
kṣīyante cāsya karmāṇi
dṛṣṭa evātmanīśvare

bhidyate—pierced; *hṛdaya*—heart; *granthiḥ*—knots; *chidyante*—cut to pieces; *sarva*—all; *saṁśayāḥ*—misgivings; *kṣīyante*—terminated; *ca*—and; *asya*—his; *karmāṇi*—chain of fruitive actions; *dṛṣṭe*—having seen; *eva*—certainly; *ātmani*—unto the self; *īśvare*—dominating.

TRANSLATION

Thus the knot in the heart is pierced, and all misgivings are cut to pieces. The chain of fruitive actions is terminated when one sees the self as master.

PURPORT

Attaining scientific knowledge of the Personality of Godhead means seeing one's own self simultaneously. As far as the identity of the living being as spirit self is concerned, there are a number of speculations and misgivings. The materialist does not believe in the existence of the spirit self, and empiric philosophers believe in the impersonal feature of the whole spirit without individuality of the living beings. But the transcendentalists affirm that the soul and the Supersoul are two different identities, qualitatively one but quantitatively different. There are many other theories, but all these different speculations are at once cleared off as soon as Śrī Kṛṣṇa is realized in truth by the process of *bhakti-yoga.* Śrī Kṛṣṇa is like the sun, and the materialistic speculations about the Absolute Truth are like the darkest midnight. As soon as the Kṛṣṇa sun is arisen within one's heart, the darkness of materialistic speculations about the Absolute Truth and the living beings is at once cleared off. In the presence of the sun, the darkness cannot stand, and the relative truths that were hidden within the dense darkness of ignorance become clearly manifested by the mercy of Kṛṣṇa, who is residing in everyone's heart as the Supersoul.

In the *Bhagavad-gītā* (10.11) the Lord says that in order to show special favor to His pure devotees, He personally eradicates the dense darkness of all misgivings by switching on the light of pure knowledge within the heart of a devotee. Therefore, because of the Personality of Godhead's taking charge of illuminating the heart of His devotee, certainly a devotee, engaged in His service in transcendental love, cannot remain in darkness. He comes to know everything of the absolute and the relative truths. The devotee cannot remain in darkness, and because a devotee is enlightened by the Personality of Godhead, his knowledge is certainly perfect. This is not the case for those who speculate on the Absolute Truth by dint of their own limited power of approach. Perfect knowledge is called *paramparā,* or deductive knowledge coming down from the authority to the submissive aural receiver who is bona fide by service and surrender. One cannot challenge the authority of the Supreme and know Him also at the same time. He reserves the right of not being exposed to such a challenging spirit of an insignificant spark of the whole, a spark subjected to the control of illusory energy. The devotees are submissive, and therefore the transcendental knowledge descends from the Personality of Godhead to Brahmā and from Brahmā to his sons and disciples in succession. This process is helped by the Supersoul within such devotees. That is the perfect way of learning transcendental knowledge.

This enlightenment perfectly enables the devotee to distinguish spirit from matter because the knot of spirit and matter is untied by the Lord. This knot is called *ahaṅkāra,* and it falsely obliges a living being to become identified with matter. As soon as this knot is loosened, therefore, all the clouds of doubt are at once cleared off. One sees his master and fully engages himself in the transcendental loving service of the Lord, making a full termination of the chain of fruitive action. In material existence, a living being creates his own chain of fruitive work and enjoys the good and bad effects of those actions life after life. But as soon as he engages himself in the loving service of the Lord, he at once becomes free from the chain of *karma.* His actions no longer create any reaction.

TEXT 22

अतो वै कवयो नित्यं भक्तिं परमया मुदा।
वासुदेवे भगवति कुर्वन्त्यात्मप्रसादनीम् ॥२२॥

ato vai kavayo nityaṁ
bhaktiṁ paramayā mudā
vāsudeve bhagavati
kurvanty ātma-prasādanīm

ataḥ—therefore; *vai*—certainly; *kavayaḥ*—all transcendentalists; *nityam*—from time immemorial; *bhaktim*—service unto the Lord; *paramayā*—supreme; *mudā*—with great delight; *vāsudeve*—Śrī Kṛṣṇa; *bhagavati*—the Personality of Godhead; *kurvanti*—do render; *ātma*—self; *prasādanīm*—that which enlivens.

TRANSLATION

Certainly, therefore, since time immemorial, all transcendentalists have been rendering devotional service to Lord Kṛṣṇa, the Personality of Godhead, with great delight, because such devotional service is enlivening to the self.

PURPORT

The speciality of devotional service unto the Personality of Godhead Lord Śrī Kṛṣṇa is specifically mentioned herein. Lord Śrī Kṛṣṇa is the *svayaṁ-rūpa* Personality of Godhead, and all other forms of Godhead, beginning from Śrī Baladeva, Saṅkarṣaṇa, Vāsudeva, Aniruddha, Pradyumna and Nārāyaṇa and extending to the *puruṣa-avatāras, guṇa-avatāras, līlā-avatāras, yuga-āvatāras* and many other thousands of manifestations of the Personality of Godhead, are Lord Śrī Kṛṣṇa's plenary portions and integrated parts. The living entities are separated parts and parcels of the Personality of Godhead. Therefore Lord Śrī Kṛṣṇa is the original form of Godhead, and He is the last word in the Transcendence. Thus He is more attractive to the higher transcendentalists who participate in the eternal pastimes of the Lord. In forms of the Personality of Godhead other than Śrī Kṛṣṇa and Baladeva, there is no facility for intimate personal contact as in the transcendental pastimes of the Lord at Vrajabhūmi. The transcendental pastimes of Lord Śrī Kṛṣṇa are not newly accepted, as argued by some less intelligent persons; His pastimes are eternal and are manifested in due course once in a day of Brahmājī, as the sun rises on the eastern horizon at the end of every twenty-four hours.

TEXT 23

सत्त्वं रजस्तम इति प्रकृतेर्गुणास्तै-
र्युक्तः परः पुरुष एक इहास्य धत्ते ।
स्थित्यादये हरिविरिञ्चिहरेति संज्ञाः
श्रेयांसि तत्र खलु सत्त्वतनोर्नृणां स्युः ॥२३॥

sattvaṁ rajas tama iti prakṛter guṇās tair
yuktaḥ paraḥ puruṣa eka ihāsya dhatte
sthity-ādaye hari-viriñci-hareti saṁjñāḥ
śreyāṁsi tatra khalu sattva-tanor nṛṇāṁ syuḥ

sattvam—goodness; *rajaḥ*—passion; *tamaḥ*—the darkness of ignorance; *iti*—thus; *prakṛteḥ*—of the material nature; *guṇāḥ*—qualities; *taiḥ*—by them; *yuktaḥ*—associated with; *paraḥ*—transcendental; *puruṣaḥ*—the personality; *ekaḥ*—one; *iha asya*—of this material world; *dhatte*—accepts; *sthiti-ādaye*—for the matter of creation, maintenance and destruction, etc.; *hari*—Viṣṇu, the Personality of Godhead; *viriñci*—Brahmā; *hara*—Lord Śiva; *iti*—thus; *saṁjñāḥ*—different features; *śreyāṁsi*—ultimate benefit; *tatra*—therein; *khalu*—of course; *sattva*—goodness; *tanoḥ*—form; *nṛṇām*—of the human being; *syuḥ*—derived.

TRANSLATION

The transcendental Personality of Godhead is indirectly associated with the three modes of material nature, namely passion, goodness and ignorance, and just for the material world's creation, maintenance and destruction He accepts the three qualitative forms of Brahmā, Viṣṇu and Śiva. Of these three, all human beings can derive ultimate benefit from Viṣṇu, the form of the quality of goodness.

PURPORT

That Lord Śrī Kṛṣṇa, by His plenary parts, should be rendered devotional service, as explained above, is confirmed by this statement. Lord Śrī Kṛṣṇa and all His plenary parts are *viṣṇu-tattva,* or the Lordship of Godhead. From Śrī Kṛṣṇa, the next manifestation is Baladeva. From Baladeva is Saṅkarṣaṇa, from

Saṅkarṣaṇa is Nārāyaṇa, from Nārāyaṇa there is the second Saṅkarṣaṇa, and from this Saṅkarṣaṇa the Viṣṇu *puruṣa-avatāras.* The Viṣṇu or the Deity of the quality of goodness in the material world is the *puruṣa-avatāra* known as Kṣīrodakaśāyī Viṣṇu or Paramātmā. Brahmā is the deity of *rajas* (passion), and Śiva of ignorance. They are the three departmental heads of the three qualities of this material world. Creation is made possible by the goodness of Viṣṇu, and when it requires to be destroyed, Lord Śiva does it by the *tāṇḍava-nṛtya.* The materialists and the foolish human beings worship Brahmā and Śiva respectively. But the pure transcendentalists worship the form of goodness, Viṣṇu, in His various forms. Viṣṇu is manifested by His millions and billions of integrated forms and separated forms. The integrated forms are called Godhead, and the separated forms are called the living entities or the *jīvas.* Both the *jīvas* and Godhead have their original spiritual forms. *Jīvas* are sometimes subjected to the control of material energy, but the Viṣṇu forms are always controllers of this energy. When Viṣṇu, the Personality of Godhead, appears in the material world, He comes to deliver the conditioned living beings who are under the material energy. Such living beings appear in the material world with intentions of being lords, and thus they become entrapped by the three modes of nature. As such, the living entities have to change their material coverings for undergoing different terms of imprisonment. The prison house of the material world is created by Brahmā under instruction of the Personality of Godhead, and at the conclusion of a *kalpa* the whole thing is destroyed by Śiva. But as far as maintenance of the prison house is concerned, it is done by Viṣṇu, as much as the state prison house is maintained by the state. Anyone, therefore, who wishes to get out of this prison house of material existence, which is full of miseries like repetition of birth, death, disease and old age, must please Lord Viṣṇu for such liberation. Lord Viṣṇu is worshiped by devotional service only, and if anyone has to continue prison life in the material world, he may ask for relative facilities for temporary relief from the different demigods like Śiva, Brahmā, Indra and Varuṇa. No demigod, however, can release the imprisoned living being from the conditioned life of material existence. This can be done only by Viṣṇu. Therefore, the ultimate benefit may be derived from Viṣṇu, the Personality of Godhead.

TEXT 24

पार्थिवाद्दारुणो धूमस्तस्मादग्निस्त्रयीमयः ।
तमसस्तु रजस्तस्मात्सत्त्वं यद्ब्रह्मदर्शनम् ॥२४॥

pārthivād dāruṇo dhūmas
tasmād agnis trayīmayaḥ
tamasas tu rajas tasmāt
sattvaṁ yad brahma-darśanam

pārthivāt—from earth; *dāruṇaḥ*—firewood; *dhūmaḥ*—smoke; *tasmāt*—from that; *agniḥ*—fire; *trayī*—Vedic sacrifices; *mayaḥ*—made of; *tamasaḥ*—in the mode of ignorance; *tu*—but; *rajaḥ*—the mode of passion; *tasmāt*—from that; *sattvam*—the mode of goodness; *yat*—which; *brahma*—the Absolute Truth; *darśanam*—realization.

TRANSLATION

Firewood is a transformation of earth, but smoke is better than the raw wood. And fire is still better, for by fire we can derive the benefits of superior knowledge [through Vedic sacrifices]. Similarly, passion [rajas] is better than ignorance [tamas], but goodness [sattva] is best because by goodness one can come to realize the Absolute Truth.

PURPORT

As explained above, one can get release from the conditioned life of material existence by devotional service to the Personality of Godhead. It is further comprehended herein that one has to rise to the platform of the mode of goodness *(sattva)* so that one can be eligible for the devotional service of the Lord. But if there are impediments on the progressive path, anyone, even from the platform of *tamas,* can gradually rise to the *sattva* platform by the expert direction of the spiritual master. Sincere candidates must, therefore, approach an expert spiritual master for such a progressive march, and the bona fide, expert spiritual master is competent to direct a disciple from any stage of life: *tamas, rajas* or *sattva.*

It is a mistake, therefore, to consider that worship of any quality or any form of the Supreme Personality of Godhead is equally beneficial. Except Viṣṇu, all separated froms are manifested under the conditions of material energy, and therefore the forms of material energy cannot help anyone to rise to the platform of *sattva,* which alone can liberate a person from material bondage.

The uncivilized state of life, or the life of the lower animals, is controlled by the mode of *tamas.* The civilized life of man, with a passion for various types of material benefits, is the stage of *rajas.* The *rajas* stage of life gives a slight clue to the realization of the Absolute Truth in the forms of fine sentiments in philosophy, art and culture with moral and ethical principles, but the mode of *sattva* is a still higher stage of material quality, which actually helps one in realizing the Absolute Truth. In other words, there is a qualitative difference between the different kinds of worshiping methods as well as the respective results derived from the predominating deities, namely Brahmā, Viṣṇu and Hara.

TEXT 25

भेजिरे मुनयोऽथाग्रे भगवन्तमधोक्षजम् ।
सत्त्वं विशुद्धं क्षेमाय कल्पन्ते येऽनु तानिह ॥२५॥

bhejire munayo 'thāgre
bhagavantam adhokṣajam
sattvaṁ viśuddhaṁ kṣemāya
kalpante ye 'nu tān iha

bhejire—rendered service unto; *munayaḥ*—the sages; *atha*—thus; *agre*—previously; *bhagavantam*—unto the Personality of Godhead; *adhokṣajam*—the Transcendence; *sattvam*—existence; *viśuddham*—above the three modes of nature; *kṣemāya*—to derive the ultimate benefit; *kalpante*—deserve; *ye*—those; *anu*—follow; *tān*—those; *iha*—in this material world.

TRANSLATION

Previously all the great sages rendered service unto the Personality of Godhead due to His existence above the three modes of material nature. They worshiped Him to become free from material conditions and thus derive the ultimate benefit. Whoever follows such great authorities is also eligible for liberation from the material world.

PURPORT

The purpose of performing religion is neither to profit by material gain nor to get the simple knowledge of discerning matter from spirit. The ultimate aim of religious performances is to release oneself from material bondage and regain the life of freedom in the transcendental world, where the Personality of Godhead is the Supreme Person. Laws of religion, therefore, are directly enacted by the Personality of Godhead, and except for the *mahājanas,* or the authorized agents of the Lord, no one knows the purpose of religion. There are twelve particular agents of the Lord who know the purpose of religion, and all of them render transcendental service unto Him. Persons who desire their own good may follow these *mahājanas* and thus attain the supreme benefit.

TEXT 26

मुमुक्षवो घोररूपान् हित्वा भूतपतीनथ।
नारायणकलाः शान्ता भजन्ति ह्यनसूयवः ॥२६॥

mumukṣavo ghora-rūpān
hitvā bhūta-patīn atha
nārāyaṇa-kalāḥ śāntā
bhajanti hy anasūyavaḥ

mumukṣavaḥ—persons desiring liberation; *ghora*—horrible, ghastly; *rūpān*—forms like that; *hitvā*—rejecting; *bhūta-patīn*—demigods; *atha*—for this reason; *nārāyaṇa*—the Personality of Godhead; *kalāḥ*—plenary portions; *śāntāḥ*—all-blissful; *bhajanti*—do worship; *hi*—certainly; *anasūyavaḥ*—nonenvious.

TRANSLATION

Those who are serious about liberation are certainly nonenvious, and they respect all. Yet they reject the horrible and ghastly forms of the demigods and worship only the all-blissful forms of Lord Viṣṇu and His plenary portions.

PURPORT

The Supreme Personality of Godhead Śrī Kṛṣṇa, who is the original person of the Viṣṇu categories, expands Himself in two different categories, namely integrated plenary portions and separated parts and parcels. The separated parts and parcels are the servitors, and the integrated plenary portions of *viṣṇu-tattvas* are the worshipful objects of service.

All demigods who are empowered by the Supreme Lord are also separated parts and parcels. They do not belong to the categories of *viṣṇu-tattva.* The *viṣṇu-tattvas* are living beings equally as powerful as the original form of the Personality of Godhead, and They display different categories of power in consideration of different times and circumstances. The separated parts and parcels are powerful by limitation. They do not have unlimited power like the *viṣṇu-tattvas.* Therefore, one should never classify the *viṣṇu-tattvas,* or the plenary portions of Nārāyaṇa, the Personality of Godhead, in the same categories with the parts and parcels. If anyone does so he becomes at once an offender by the name *pāṣaṇḍī.* In the age of Kali many foolish persons commit such unlawful offenses and equalize the two categories.

The separated parts and parcels have different positions in the estimation of material powers, and some of them are like Kāla-bhairava, Śmaśāna-bhairava, Śani, Mahākālī and Caṇḍikā. These demigods are worshiped mostly by those who are in the lowest categories of the mode of darkness or ignorance. Other demigods, like Brahmā, Śiva, Sūrya, Gaṇeśa and many similar deities, are worshiped by men in the mode of passion, urged on by the desire for material enjoyment. But those who are actually situated in the mode of goodness (*sattva-guṇa*) of material nature worship only *viṣṇu-tattvas. Viṣṇu-tattvas* are represented by various names and forms, such as Nārāyaṇa, Dāmodara, Vāmana, Govinda and Adhokṣaja.

The qualified *brāhmaṇas* worship the *viṣṇu-tattvas* represented by the *śālagrāma-śilā,* and some of the higher castes like the *kṣatriyas* and *vaiśyas* also generally worship the *viṣṇu-tattvas.*

Highly qualified *brāhmaṇas* situated in the mode of goodness have no grudges against the mode of worship of others. They have all respect for other demigods, even though they may look ghastly, like Kāla-bhairava or Mahākālī. They know very well that these horrible features of the Supreme Lord are all different servitors of the Lord under different conditions, yet they reject the worship of both horrible and attractive features of the demigods, and they concentrate only on the forms of Viṣṇu because they are serious about liberation from the material conditions. The demigods, even to the stage of Brahmā, the supreme of all the demigods, cannot offer liberation to anyone. Hiraṇyakaśipu underwent a severe type of penance to become eternal in life, but his worshipful deity, Brahmā, could not satisfy him with such blessings. Therefore Viṣṇu, and none else, is called *mukti-pāda,* or the Personality of Godhead who can bestow upon us mukti, liberation. The demigods, being like other living entities in the material world, are all liquidated at the time of the annihilation of the material structure. They are themselves unable to get liberation, and what to speak of giving liberation to their devotees. The demigods can award the worshipers some temporary benefit only, and not the ultimate one.

It is for this reason only that candidates for liberation deliberately reject the worship of the demigods, although they have no disrespect for any one of them.

TEXT 27

रजस्तमःप्रकृतयः समशीला भजन्ति वै।
पितृभूतप्रजेशादीन्श्रियैश्वर्यप्रजेप्सवः ॥२७॥

rajas-tamaḥ-prakṛtayaḥ
sama-śīlā bhajanti vai
pitṛ-bhūta-prajeśādīn
śriyaiśvarya-prajepsavaḥ

rajaḥ—the mode of passion; *tamaḥ*—the mode of ignorance; *prakṛtayaḥ*—of that mentality; *sama-śīlāḥ*—of the same categories; *bhajanti*—do worship; *vai*—actually; *pitṛ*—the forefathers; *bhūta*—other living beings; *prajeśa-ādīn*—controllers of cosmic administration; *śriyā*—enrichment; *aiśvarya*—wealth and power; *prajā*—progeny; *īpsavaḥ*—so desiring.

TRANSLATION

Those who are in the modes of passion and ignorance worship the forefathers, other living beings and the demigods who are in charge of cosmic activities, for they are urged by a desire to be materially benefited with women, wealth, power and progeny.

PURPORT

There is no need to worship demigods of whatsoever category if one is serious about going back to Godhead. In the *Bhagavad-gītā* (7.20, 23) it is clearly said that those who are mad after material enjoyment approach the different demigods for temporary benefits, which are meant for men with a poor fund of knowledge. We should never desire to increase the depth of material enjoyment. Material enjoyment should be accepted only up to the point of the bare necessities of life and not more or less than that. To accept more material enjoyment means to bind oneself more and more to the miseries of material existence. More wealth, more women and false aristocracy are some of the demands of the materially disposed man because he has no information of the benefit derived from Viṣṇu worship. By Viṣṇu worship one can derive benefit in this life as well as in life after death. Forgetting these principles, foolish people who are after more wealth, more wives and more children worship various demigods. The aim of life is to end the miseries of life and not to increase them.

For material enjoyment there is no need to approach the demigods. The demigods are but servants of the Lord. As such, they are duty-bound to supply necessities of life in the form of water, light, air, etc. *One should work hard and worship the Supreme Lord by the fruits of one's hard labor for existence, and that should be the motto of life.* One should be careful to execute occupational service with faith in God in the proper way, and that will lead one gradually on the progressive march back to Godhead.

Lord Śrī Kṛṣṇa, when He was personally present at Vrajadhāma, stopped the worship of the demigod Indra and advised the residents of Vraja to worship by their business and to have faith in God. Worshiping the multidemigods for material gain is practically a perversity of religion. This sort of religious activity has been condemned in the very beginning of the *Bhāgavatam* as *kaitava-dharma.* There is only one religion in the world to be followed by one and all, and that is the *Bhāgavata-dharma,* or the religion which teaches one to worship the Supreme Personality of Godhead and no one else.

TEXTS 28–29

वासुदेवपरा वेदा वासुदेवपरा मखाः ।
वासुदेवपरा योगा वासुदेवपराः क्रियाः ॥२८॥
वासुदेवपरं ज्ञानं वासुदेवपरं तपः ।
वासुदेवपरो धर्मो वासुदेवपरा गतिः ॥२९॥

vāsudeva-parā vedā
vāsudeva-parā makhāḥ
vāsudeva-parā yogā
vāsudeva-parāḥ kriyāḥ

vāsudeva-paraṁ jñānaṁ
vāsudeva-paraṁ tapaḥ
vāsudeva-paro dharmo
vāsudeva-parā gatiḥ

vāsudeva—the Personality of Godhead; *parāḥ*—the ultimate goal; *vedāḥ*—revealed scriptures; *vāsudeva*—the Personality of Godhead; *parāḥ*—for worshiping; *makhāḥ*—sacrifices; *vāsudeva*—the Personality of Godhead; *parāḥ*—the means of attaining; *yogāḥ*—mystic paraphernalia; *vāsudeva*—the Personality of Godhead; *parāḥ*—under His control; *kriyāḥ*—fruitive activities; *vāsudeva*—the Personality of Godhead; *param*—the supreme;

jñānam—knowledge; *vāsudeva*—the Personality of Godhead; *param*—best; *tapaḥ*—austerity; *vāsudeva*—the Personality of Godhead; *paraḥ*—superior quality; *dharmaḥ*—religion; *vāsudeva*—the Personality of Godhead; *parāḥ*—ultimate; *gatiḥ*—goal of life.

TRANSLATION

In the revealed scriptures, the ultimate object of knowledge is Śrī Kṛṣṇa, the Personality of Godhead. The purpose of performing sacrifice is to please Him. Yoga is for realizing Him. All fruitive activities are ultimately rewarded by Him only. He is supreme knowledge, and all severe austerities are performed to know Him. Religion [dharma] is rendering loving service unto Him. He is the supreme goal of life.

PURPORT

That Śrī Kṛṣṇa, the Personality of Godhead, is the only object of worship is confirmed in these two *ślokas.* In the Vedic literature there is the same objective: establishing one's relationship and ultimately reviving our lost loving service unto Him. That is the sum and substance of the *Vedas.* In the *Bhagavad-gītā* the same theory is confirmed by the Lord in His own words: the ultimate purpose of the *Vedas* is to know Him only. All the revealed scriptures are prepared by the Lord through His incarnation in the body of Śrīla Vyāsadeva just to remind the fallen souls, conditioned by material nature, of Śrī Kṛṣṇa, the Personality of Godhead. No demigod can award freedom from material bondage. That is the verdict of all the Vedic literatures. Impersonalists who have no information of the Personality of Godhead minimize the omnipotency of the Supreme Lord and put Him on equal footing with all other living beings, and for this act such impersonalists get freedom from material bondage only with great difficulty. They can surrender unto Him only after many, many births in the culture of transcendental knowledge.

One may argue that the Vedic activities are based on sacrificial ceremonies. That is true. But all such sacrifices are also meant for realizing the truth about Vāsudeva. Another name of Vāsudeva is Yajña (sacrifice), and in the *Bhagavad-gītā* it is clearly stated that all sacrifices and all activities are to be conducted for the satisfaction of Yajña, or Viṣṇu, the Personality of Godhead. This is the case also with the *yoga* systems. *Yoga* means to get into touch with the Supreme Lord. The process, however, includes several bodily features such as *āsana, dhyāna, prāṇāyāma* and meditation, and all of them are meant for concentrating upon the localized aspect of Vāsudeva represented as Paramātmā. Paramātmā realization is but partial realization of Vāsudeva, and if one is successful in that attempt, one realizes Vāsudeva in full. But by ill luck most *yogīs* are stranded by the powers of mysticism achieved through the bodily process. Ill-fated *yogīs* are given a chance in the next birth by being placed in the families of good learned *brāhmaṇas* or in the families of rich merchants in order to execute the unfinished task of Vāsudeva realization. If such fortunate *brāhmaṇas* and sons of rich men properly utilize the chance, they can easily realize Vāsudeva by good association with saintly persons. Unfortunately, such preferred persons are captivated again by material wealth and honor, and thus they practically forget the aim of life.

This is also so for the culture of knowledge. According to *Bhagavad-gītā* there are eighteen items in culturing knowledge. By such culture of knowledge one becomes gradually prideless, devoid of vanity, nonviolent, forbearing, simple, devoted to the great spiritual master, and self-controlled. By culture of knowledge one becomes unattached to hearth and home and becomes conscious of the miseries due to death, birth, old age and disease. And all culture of knowledge culminates in devotional service to the Personality of Godhead, Vāsudeva. Therefore, Vāsudeva is the ultimate aim in culturing all different branches of knowledge. Culture of knowledge leading one to the transcendental plane of meeting Vāsudeva is real knowledge. Physical knowledge in its various branches is condemned in the *Bhagavad-gītā* as *ajñāna,* or the opposite of real knowledge. The ultimate aim of physical knowledge is to satisfy the senses, which means prolongation of the term of material existence and thereby continuance of the threefold miseries. So prolonging the miserable life of material existence is nescience. But the same physical knowledge leading to the way of spiritual understanding helps one to end the miserable life of physical existence and to begin the life of spiritual existence on the plane of Vāsudeva.

The same applies to all kinds of austerities. *Tapasya* means voluntary acceptance of bodily pains to achieve some higher end of life. Rāvaṇa and Hiraṇyakaśipu underwent a severe type of bodily torture to achieve the end of sense gratification. Sometimes modern politicians also undergo severe types of austerities to achieve some political end. This is not actually *tapasya.* One should accept voluntary bodily inconvenience for the sake of knowing Vāsudeva because that is the way of real austerities. Otherwise all forms of austerities are classified as modes of passion and ignorance. Passion and ignorance cannot end the miseries of life. Only the mode of goodness can mitigate the threefold miseries of life. Vasudeva and Devakī, the so-called father and mother of Lord Kṛṣṇa, underwent penances to get Vāsudeva as their son. Lord Śrī Kṛṣṇa is the father of all living beings (Bg. 14.4). Therefore He is the original living being of all other living beings. He is the original eternal enjoyer amongst all other enjoyers. Therefore no one can be His begetting father, as the ignorant may think. Lord Śrī Kṛṣṇa agreed to become the son of Vasudeva and Devakī upon being pleased with their severe austerities. Therefore if any austerities have to be done, they must be done to achieve the end of knowledge, Vāsudeva.

Vāsudeva is the original Personality of Godhead, Lord Śrī Kṛṣṇa. As explained before, the original Personality of Godhead expands Himself by innumerable forms. Such expansion of forms is made possible by His various energies. His energies are also multifarious, and His internal energies are superior and external energies inferior in quality. They are explained in the *Bhagavad-gītā* (7.4–6) as the *parā* and the *aparā prakṛtis.* So His expansions of various forms which take place via the internal energies are superior forms, whereas the expansions which take place via the external energies are inferior forms. The living entities are also His expansions. The living entities who are expanded by His internal potency are eternally liberated persons, whereas those who are expanded in terms of the material energies are eternally conditioned souls. Therefore, all culture of knowledge, austerities, sacrifice and activities should be aimed at changing the quality of the influence that is acting upon us. For the present, we are all being controlled by the external energy of the Lord, and just to change the quality of the influence, we must endeavor to cultivate spiritual energy. In the *Bhagavad-gītā* it is said that those who are *mahātmās,* or those whose minds have been so broadened as to be engaged in the service of Lord Kṛṣṇa, are under the influence of the internal potency, and the effect is that such broad-minded living beings are constantly engaged in the service of the Lord without deviation. That should be the aim of life. And that is the verdict of all the Vedic literatures. No one should bother himself with fruitive activities or dry speculation about transcendental knowledge. Everyone should at once engage himself in the transcendental loving service of the Lord. Nor should one worship different demigods who work as different hands of the Lord for creation, maintenance or destruction of the material world. There are innumerable powerful demigods who look over the external management of the material world. They are all different assisting hands of Lord Vāsudeva. Even Lord Śiva and Lord Brahmā are included in the list of demigods, but Lord Viṣṇu, or Vāsudeva, is always transcendentally situated. Even though He accepts the quality of goodness of the material world, He is still transcendental to all the material modes. The following example will clear that matter more explicitly. In the prison house there are the prisoners and the managers of the prison house. Both the managers and the prisoners are bound by the laws of the king. But even though the king sometimes comes in the prison, he is not bound by the laws of the prison house. The king is therefore always transcendental to the laws of the prison house, as the Lord is always transcendental to the laws of the material world.

TEXT 30

स एवेदं ससर्जाग्रे भगवानात्ममायया।
सदसद्रूपया चासौ गुणमयागुणो विभुः ॥३०॥

sa evedaṁ sasarjāgre
bhagavān ātma-māyayā
sad-asad-rūpayā cāsau
guṇamayāguṇo vibhuḥ

saḥ—that; *eva*—certainly; *idam*—this; *sasarja*—created; *agre*—before; *bhagavān*—the Personality of Godhead; *ātma-māyayā*—by His personal potency; *sat*—the cause; *asat*—the effect; *rūpayā*—by forms; *ca*—and; *asau*—the same Lord; *guṇa-maya*—in the modes of material nature; *aguṇaḥ*—transcendental; *vibhuḥ*—the Absolute.

TRANSLATION

In the beginning of the material creation, that Absolute Personality of Godhead [Vāsudeva], in His transcendental position, created the energies of cause and effect by His own internal energy.

PURPORT

The position of the Lord is always transcendental because the causal and effectual energies required for the creation of the material world were also created by Him. He is unaffected, therefore, by the qualities of the material modes. His existence, form, activities and paraphernalia all existed before the material creation.* *He is all-spiritual* and has nothing to do with the qualities

*Śrīpāda Śaṅkarācārya, the head of the Māyāvāda school, accepts this transcendental position of Lord Kṛṣṇa in his commentation on *Bhagavad-gītā*.

of the material world, which are qualitatively distinct from the spiritual qualities of the Lord.

TEXT 31

तया विलसितेष्वेषु गुणेषु गुणवानिव।
अन्तःप्रविष्ट आभाति विज्ञानेन विजृम्भितः ॥३१॥

tayā vilasiteṣv eṣu
guṇeṣu guṇavān iva
antaḥ-praviṣṭa ābhāti
vijñānena vijṛmbhitaḥ

tayā—by them; *vilasiteṣu*—although in the function; *eṣu*—these; *guṇeṣu*—the modes of material nature; *guṇavān*—affected by the modes; *iva*—as if; *antaḥ*—within; *praviṣṭaḥ*—entered into; *ābhāti*—appears to be; *vijñānena*—by transcendental consciousness; *vijṛmbhitaḥ*—fully enlightened.

TRANSLATION

After creating the material substance, the Lord [Vāsudeva] expands Himself and enters into it. And although He is within the material modes of nature and appears to be one of the created beings, He is always fully enlightened in His transcendental position.

PURPORT

The living entities are separated parts and parcels of the Lord, and the conditioned living entities, who are unfit for the spiritual kingdom, are strewn within the material world to enjoy matter to the fullest extent. As Paramātmā and eternal friend of the living entities, the Lord, by one of His plenary portions, accompanies the living entities to guide them in their material enjoyment and to become witness to all activities. While the living entities enjoy the material conditions, the Lord maintains His transcendental position without being affected by the material atmosphere. In the Vedic literatures (*śruti*) it is said that there are two birds in one tree.* One of them is eating the fruit of the tree, while the other is witnessing the actions. The witness is the Lord, and the fruit-eater is the living entity. The fruit-eater (living entity) has forgotten his real

---

**dvā suparnā sayujā sakhāyā samānaṁ vṛkṣaṁ pariṣasvajāte*
taayor anyaū pappalaṁ svādv atty anaśnann anyo 'bhicākaśīti
(Muṇḍaka Upaniṣad 3.1.1)

identity and is overwhelmed in the fruitive activities of the material conditions, but the Lord (Paramātmā) is always full in transcendental knowledge. That is the difference between the Supersoul and the conditioned soul. The conditioned soul, the living entity, is controlled by the laws of nature, while the Paramātmā, or the Supersoul, is the controller of the material energy.

TEXT 32

यथा ह्यवहितो वह्निर्दारुष्वेकः स्वयोनिषु।
नानेव भाति विश्वात्मा भूतेषु च तथा पुमान् ॥३२॥

yathā hy avahito vahnir
dāruṣv ekaḥ sva-yoniṣu
nāneva bhāti viśvātmā
bhūteṣu ca tathā pumān

yathā—as much as; *hi*—exactly like; *avahitaḥ*—surcharged with; *vahniḥ*—fire; *dāruṣu*—in wood; *ekaḥ*—one; *sva-yoniṣu*—the source of manifestation; *nānā iva*—like different entities; *bhāti*—illuminates; *viśva-ātmā*—the Lord as Paramātmā; *bhūteṣu*—in the living entities; *ca*—and; *tathā*—in the same way; *pumān*—the Absolute Person.

TRANSLATION

The Lord, as Supersoul, pervades all things, just as fire permeates wood, and so He appears to be of many varieties, though He is the absolute one without a second.

PURPORT

Lord Vāsudeva, the Supreme Personality of Godhead, by one of His plenary parts expands Himself all over the material world, and His existence can be perceived even within the atomic energy. Matter, antimatter, proton, neutron, etc., are all different effects of the Paramātmā feature of the Lord. As from wood, fire can be manifested, or as butter can be churned out of milk, so also the presence of the Lord as Paramātmā can be felt by the process of legitimate hearing and chanting of the transcendental subjects which are especially treated in the Vedic literatures like the *Upaniṣads* and *Vedānta. Śrīmad-Bhāgavatam* is the bona fide explanation of these Vedic literatures. The Lord can be realized through the aural reception of the transcendental message, and that is the only way to experience the transcendental subject. As fire is kindled from wood by another fire, the divine consciousness of man can similarly be kindled by another divine grace. His Divine Grace the spiritual master can kindle the spiritual fire from the woodlike living entity by imparting proper spiritual messages injected through the receptive ear. Therefore one is required to approach the proper spiritual master with receptive ears only, and thus divine existence is gradually realized. The difference between animality and humanity lies in this process only. A human being can hear properly, whereas an animal cannot.

TEXT 33

असौ गुणमयैर्भावैर्भूतसूक्ष्मेन्द्रियात्मभिः ।
स्वनिर्मितेषु निर्विष्टो भुङ्क्ते भूतेषु तद्गुणान् ॥३३॥

asau guṇamayair bhāvair
bhūta-sūkṣmendriyātmabhiḥ
sva-nirmiteṣu nirviṣṭo
bhuṅkte bhūteṣu tad-guṇān

asau—that Paramātmā; *guṇa-mayaiḥ*—influenced by the modes of nature; *bhāvaiḥ*—naturally; *bhūta*—created; *sūkṣma*—subtle; *indriya*—senses; *ātmabhiḥ*—by the living beings; *sva-nirmiteṣu*—in His own creation; *nirviṣṭaḥ*—entering; *bhuṅkte*—causes to enjoy; *bhūteṣu*—in the living entities; *tat-guṇān*—those modes of nature.

TRANSLATION

The Supersoul enters into the bodies of the created beings who are influenced by the modes of material nature and causes them to enjoy the effects of these modes by the subtle mind.

PURPORT

There are 8,400,000 species of living beings beginning from the highest intellectual being, Brahmā, down to the insignificant ant, and all of them are enjoying the material world according to the desires of the subtle mind and gross material body. The gross material body is based on the conditions of the subtle mind, and the senses are created according to the desire of the living being. The Lord as Paramātmā helps the living being to get material happiness because the living being is helpless in all respects in obtaining what he desires. He proposes, and the Lord disposes. In another sense, the living beings are parts and parcels of the Lord. They are therefore one with the Lord. In the *Bhagavad-gītā* the living beings in all varieties of bodies have been claimed by the Lord as His sons. The sufferings and enjoyments of the sons are indirectly the sufferings and enjoyments of the father. Still the father is not in any way affected directly by the suffering and enjoyment of the sons. He is so kind that He constantly remains with the living being as Paramātmā and always tries to convert the living being towards the real happiness.

TEXT 34

भावयत्येष सत्त्वेन लोकान् वै लोकभावनः ।
लीलावतारानुरतो देवतिर्यङ्नरादिषु ॥३४॥

bhāvayaty eṣa sattvena
lokān vai loka-bhāvanaḥ
līlāvatārānurato
deva-tiryaṅ-narādiṣu

bhāvayati—maintains; *eṣaḥ*—all these; *sattvena*—in the mode of goodness; *lokān*—all over the universe; *vai*—generally; *loka-bhāvanaḥ*—the master of all the universes; *līlā*—pastimes; *avatāra*—incarnation; *anurataḥ*—assuming the role; *deva*—the demigods; *tiryak*—lower animals; *nara-ādiṣu*—in the midst of human beings.

TRANSLATION

Thus the Lord of the universes maintains all planets inhabited by demigods, men and lower animals. Assuming the roles of incarnations, He performs pastimes to reclaim those in the mode of pure goodness.

PURPORT

There are innumerable material universes, and in each and every universe there are innumerable planets inhabited by different grades of living entities in different modes of nature. The Lord (Viṣṇu) incarnates Himself in each and every one of them and in each and every type of living society. He manifests His transcendental pastimes amongst them just to create the desire to go back to Godhead. The Lord does not change His original transcendental position, but He appears to be differently manifested according to the particular time, circumstances and society.

Sometimes He incarnates Himself or empowers a suitable living being to act for Him, but in either case the purpose is the same: the Lord wants the suffering living being to go back home, back to Godhead. The happiness which the living beings are hankering for is not to be found within any corner of the innumerable universes and material planets. The eternal happiness which the living being wants is obtainable in the kingdom of God, but the forgetful living beings under the influence of the material modes have no information of the kingdom of God. The Lord, therefore, comes to propagate the message of the kingdom of God, either personally as an incarnation or through His bona fide representative as the good son of God. Such incarnations or sons of God are not making propaganda for going back to Godhead only within the human society. Their work is also going on in all types of societies, amongst demigods and those other than human beings.

Thus end the Bhaktivedanta purports of the First Canto, Second Chapter, of the Śrīmad-Bhāgavatam, *entitled "Divinity and Divine Service."*

CHAPTER THREE

Kṛṣṇa Is the Source of All Incarnations

TEXT 1

सूत उवाच
जगृहे पौरुषं रूपं भगवान्महदादिभिः ।
सम्भूतं षोडशकलमादौ लोकसिसृक्षया ॥१॥

sūta uvāca
jagṛhe pauruṣaṁ rūpaṁ
bhagavān mahad-ādibhiḥ
sambhūtaṁ ṣoḍaśa-kalam
ādau loka-sisṛkṣayā

sūtaḥ uvāca—Sūta said; *jagṛhe*—accepted; *pauruṣam*—plenary portion as the *puruṣa* incarnation; *rūpam*—form; *bhagavān*—the Personality of Godhead; *mahat-ādibhiḥ*—with the ingredients of the material world; *sambhūtam*—thus there was the creation of; *ṣoḍaśa-kalam*—sixteen primary principles; *ādau*—in the beginning; *loka*—the universes; *sisṛkṣayā*—on the intention of creating.

TRANSLATION

Sūta said: In the beginning of the creation, the Lord first expanded Himself in the universal form of the puruṣa incarnation and manifested all the ingredients for the material creation. And thus at first there was the creation of the sixteen principles of material action. This was for the purpose of creating the material universe.

PURPORT

The *Bhagavad-gītā* states that the Personality of Godhead, Śrī Kṛṣṇa, maintains these material universes by extending His plenary expansions. So this *puruṣa* form is the confirmation of the same principle. The original Personality of Godhead Vāsudeva, or Lord Kṛṣṇa, who is famous as the son of King Vasudeva or King Nanda, is full with all opulences, all potencies, all fame, all beauty, all knowledge and all renunciation. Part of His opulences are manifested as impersonal Brahman, and part of His opulences are manifested as Paramātmā. This *puruṣa* feature of the same Personality of Godhead, Śrī Kṛṣṇa, is the original Paramātmā manifestation of the Lord. There are three *puruṣa* features in the material creation, and this form, who is known as the Kāraṇodakaśāyī Viṣṇu, is the first of the three. The others are known as the Garbhodakaśāyī Viṣṇu and the Kṣīrodakaśāyī Viṣṇu, which we shall know one after another. The innumerable universes are generated from the skin holes of this Kāraṇodakaśāyī Viṣṇu, and in each one of the universes the Lord enters as Garbhodakaśāyī Viṣṇu.

In the *Bhagavad-gītā* it is also mentioned that the material world is created at certain intervals and then again destroyed. This creation and destruction is done by the supreme will because of the conditioned souls, or the *nitya-baddha* living beings. The *nitya-baddha,* or the eternally conditioned souls, have the sense of individuality or *ahaṅkāra,* which dictates them sense enjoyment, which they are unable to have constitutionally. The Lord is the only enjoyer, and all others are enjoyed. The living beings are predominated enjoyers. But the eternally conditioned souls, forgetful of this constitutional position, have strong aspirations to enjoy. The chance to enjoy matter is given to the conditioned souls in the material world, and side by side they are given the chance to understand their real constitutional position. Those fortunate living entities who catch the truth and surrender unto the lotus feet of Vāsudeva after many, many births in the material world join the eternally liberated souls and thus are allowed to enter into the kingdom of Godhead. After this, such fortunate living entities need not come again within the occasional material creation. But those who cannot catch the constitutional truth are again merged into the *mahat-tattva* at the time of the annihilation of the material creation. When the creation is again set up, this *mahat-tattva* is again let loose. This *mahat-tattva* contains all the ingredients of the material manifestations, including the conditioned souls. Primarily this *mahat-tattva* is divided into sixteen parts, namely the five gross material elements and the eleven working instruments or senses. It is like the cloud in the clear sky. In the spiritual sky, the effulgence of Brahman is spread all around, and the whole system is dazzling in spiritual light. The *mahat-tattva* is assembled in some corner of the vast, unlimited spiritual sky, and the part which is thus covered by the *mahat-tattva* is called the material sky. This part of the spiritual sky, called the *mahat-tattva,* is only an insignificant portion of the whole spiritual sky, and within this *mahat-tattva* there are innumerable universes. All these universes are collectively produced by the Kāraṇodakaśāyī Viṣṇu, called also the Mahā-Viṣṇu, who simply throws His glance to impregnate the material sky.

TEXT 2

यस्याम्भसि शयानस्य योगनिद्रां वितन्वतः ।
नाभिह्रदाम्बुजादासीद्ब्रह्मा विश्वसृजां पतिः ॥२॥

yasyāmbhasi śayānasya
yoga-nidrāṁ vitanvataḥ
nābhi-hradāmbujād āsīd
brahmā viśva-sṛjāṁ patiḥ

yasya—whose; *ambhasi*—in the water; *śayānasya*—lying down; *yoga-nidrām*—sleeping in meditation; *vitanvataḥ*—ministering; *nābhi*—navel; *hrada*—out of the lake; *ambujāt*—from the lotus; *āsīt*—was manifested; *brahmā*—the grandfather of the living beings; *viśva*—the universe; *sṛjām*—the engineers; *patiḥ*—master.

TRANSLATION

A part of the puruṣa lies down within the water of the universe, from the navel lake of His body sprouts a lotus stem, and from the lotus flower atop this stem, Brahmā, the master of all engineers in the universe, becomes manifest.

PURPORT

The first *puruṣa* is the Kāraṇodakaśāyī Viṣṇu. From His skin holes innumerable universes have sprung up. In each and every universe, the *puruṣa* enters as the Garbhodakaśāyī Viṣṇu. He is lying within the half of the universe which is full with the water of His body. And from the navel of Garbhodakaśāyī Viṣṇu has sprung the stem of the lotus flower, the birthplace of Brahmā, who is the father of all living beings and the master of all the demigod engineers engaged in the perfect design and working of the universal order. Within the stem of the lotus there are fourteen divisions of planetary systems, and the earthly planets are situated in the middle. Upwards there are other, better planetary systems, and the topmost system is called Brahmaloka or Satyaloka. Downwards from the earthly planetary system there are seven lower planetary systems inhabited by the *asuras* and similar other materialistic living beings.

From Garbhodakaśāyī Viṣṇu there is expansion of the Kṣīrodakaśāyī Viṣṇu, who is the collective Paramātmā of all living beings. He is called Hari, and from Him all incarnations within the universe are expanded.

Therefore, the conclusion is that the *puruṣa-avatāra* is manifested in three features—first the Kāraṇodakaśāyī who creates aggregate material ingredients in the *mahat-tattva,* second the Garbhodakaśāyī who enters in each and every universe, and third the Kṣīrodakaśāyī Viṣṇu who is the Paramātmā of every material object, organic or inorganic. One who knows these plenary features of the Personality of Godhead knows Godhead properly, and thus the knower becomes freed from the material conditions of birth, death, old age and disease, as it is confirmed in *Bhagavad-gītā.* In this *śloka* the subject matter of Mahā-Viṣṇu is summarized. The Mahā-Viṣṇu lies down in some part of the spiritual sky by His own free will. Thus He lies on the ocean of *kāraṇa,* from where He glances over His material nature, and the *mahat*-tattva is at once created. Thus electrified by the power of the Lord, the material nature at once creates innumerable universes, just as in due course a tree decorates itself with innumerable grown fruits. The seed of the tree is sown by the cultivator, and the tree or creeper in due course becomes manifested with so many fruits. Nothing can take place without a cause. The Kāraṇa Ocean is therefore called the Causal Ocean. *Kāraṇa* means "causal." We should not foolishly accept the atheistic theory of creation. The description of the atheists is given in the *Bhagavad-gītā.* The atheist does not believe in the creator, but he cannot give a good theory to explain the creation. Material nature has no power to create without the power of the *puruṣa,* just as a *prakṛti,* or woman, cannot produce a child without the connection of a *puruṣa,* or man. The *puruṣa* impregnates, and the *prakṛti* delivers. We should not expect milk from the fleshy bags on the neck of a goat, although they look like breastly nipples. Similarly, we should not expect any creative power from the material ingredients; we must believe in the power of the *puruṣa,* who impregnates *prakṛti,* or nature. Because the Lord wished to lie down in meditation, the material energy created innumerable universes at once, in each of them the Lord lay down, and thus all the planets and the different paraphernalia were created at once by the will of the Lord. The Lord has unlimited potencies, and thus He can act as He likes by perfect planning, although personally He has nothing to do. No one is greater than or equal to Him. That is the verdict of the *Vedas.*

TEXT 3

यस्यावयवसंस्थानैः कल्पितो लोकविस्तरः।
तद्वै भगवतो रूपं विशुद्धं सत्त्वमूर्जितम् ॥३॥

yasyāvayava-saṁsthānaiḥ
kalpito loka-vistaraḥ
tad vai bhagavato rūpaṁ
viśuddhaṁ sattvam ūrjitam

yasya—whose; *avayava*—bodily expansion; *saṁsthānaiḥ*—situated in; *kalpitaḥ*—is imagined; *loka*—planets of inhabitants; *vistaraḥ*—various; *tat vai*—but that is; *bhagavataḥ*—of the Personality of Godhead; *rūpam*—form; *viśuddham*—purely; *sattvam*—existence; *ūrjitam*—excellence.

TRANSLATION

It is believed that all the universal planetary systems are situated on the extensive body of the puruṣa, but He has nothing to do with the created material ingredients. His body is eternally in spiritual existence par excellence.

PURPORT

The conception of the *virāṭ-rūpa* or *viśva-rūpa* of the Supreme Absolute Truth is especially meant for the neophyte who can hardly think of the transcendental form of the Personality of Godhead. To him a form means something of this material world, and therefore an opposite conception of the Absolute is necessary in the beginning to concentrate the mind on the power extension of the Lord. As stated above, the Lord extends His potency in the form of the *mahat-tattva,* which includes all material ingredients. The extension of power by the Lord and the Lord Himself personally are one in one sense, but at the same time the *mahat-tattva* is different from the Lord. Therefore the potency of the Lord and the Lord are simultaneously different and nondifferent. The conception of the *virāṭ-rūpa,* especially for the impersonalist, is thus nondifferent from the eternal form of the Lord. This eternal form of the Lord exists prior to the creation of the *mahat-tattva,* and it is stressed here that the eternal form of the Lord is par excellence spiritual or transcendental to the modes of material nature. The very same transcendental form of the Lord is manifested by His internal potency, and the formation of

His multifarious manifestations of incarnations is always of the same transcendental quality, without any touch of the *mahat-tattva.*

TEXT 4

पश्यन्त्यदो रूपमदभ्रचक्षुषा
सहस्रपादोरुभुजाननाद्भुतम् ।
सहस्रमूर्धश्रवणाक्षिनासिकं
सहस्रमौल्यम्बरकुण्डलोल्लसत् ॥४॥

paśyanty ado rūpam adabhra-cakṣuṣā
sahasra-pādoru-bhujānanādbhutam
sahasra-mūrdha-śravaṇākṣi-nāsikaṁ
sahasra-mauly-ambara-kuṇḍalollasat

paśyanti—see; *adaḥ*—the form of the *puruṣa; rūpam*—form; *adabhra*—perfect; *cakṣuṣā*—by the eyes; *sahasra-pāda*—thousands of legs; *ūru*—thighs; *bhuja-ānana*—hands and faces; *adbhutam*—wonderful; *sahasra*—thousands of; *mūrdha*—heads; *śravaṇa*—ears; *akṣi*—eyes; *nāsikam*—noses; *sahasra*—thousands; *mauli*—garlands; *ambara*—dresses; *kuṇḍala*—earrings; *ullasat*—all glowing.

TRANSLATION

The devotees, with their perfect eyes, see the transcendental form of the puruṣa who has thousands of legs, thighs, arms and faces—all extraordinary. In that body there are thousands of heads, ears, eyes and noses. They are decorated with thousands of helmets and glowing earrings and are adorned with garlands.

PURPORT

With our present materialized senses we cannot perceive anything of the transcendental Lord. Our present senses are to be rectified by the process of devotional service, and then the Lord Himself becomes revealed to us. In the *Bhagavad-gītā* it is confirmed that the transcendental Lord can be perceived only by pure devotional service. So it is confirmed in the *Vedas* that only devotional service can lead one to the side of the Lord and that only devotional service can reveal Him. In the *Brahma-saṁhitā* also it is said that the Lord is always visible to the devotees whose eyes have been anointed with the tinge of devotional service. So we have to take information of the transcendental form of the Lord from persons who have actually seen Him with perfect eyes smeared with devotional service. In the material world also we do not always see things with our own eyes; we sometimes see through the experience of those who have actually seen or done things. If that is the process for experiencing a mundane object, it is more perfectly applicable in matters transcendental. So only with patience and perseverance can we realize the transcendental subject matter regarding the Absolute Truth and His different forms. He is formless to the neophytes, but He is in transcendental form to the expert servitor.

TEXT 5

एतन्नानावताराणां निधानं बीजमव्ययम्।
यस्यांशांशेन सृज्यन्ते देवतिर्यङ्नरादयः ॥५॥

etan nānāvatārāṇāṁ
nidhānaṁ bījam avyayam
yasyāṁśāṁśena sṛjyante
deva-tiryaṅ-narādayaḥ

etat—this (form); *nānā*—multifarious; *avatārāṇām*—of the incarnations; *nidhānam*—source; *bījam*—seed; *avyayam*—indestructible; *yasya*—whose; *aṁśa*—plenary portion; *aṁśena*—part of the plenary portion; *sṛjyante*—create; *deva*—demigods; *tiryak*—animals; *nara-ādayaḥ*—human beings and others.

TRANSLATION

This form [the second manifestation of the puruṣa] is the source and indestructible seed of multifarious incarnations within the universe. From the particles and portions of this form, different living entities, like demigods, men and others, are created.

PURPORT

The *puruṣa,* after creating innumerable universes in the *mahat-tattva,* entered in each of them as the second *puruṣa,* Garbhodakaśāyī Viṣṇu. When He saw that within the universe there was only darkness and space, without a resting place, He filled half of the universe with water from His own perspiration and laid Himself down on the same water. This water is called

Garbhodaka. Then from His navel the stem of the lotus flower sprouted, and on the flower petals the birth of Brahmā, or the master engineer of the universal plan, took place. Brahmā became the engineer of the universe, and the Lord Himself took charge of the maintenance of the universe as Viṣṇu. Brahmā was generated from *rajo-guṇa* of *prakṛti,* or the mode of passion in nature, and Viṣṇu became the Lord of the mode of goodness. Viṣṇu, being transcendental to all the modes, is always aloof from materialistic affection. This has already been explained. From Brahmā there is Rudra (Śiva), who is in charge of the mode of ignorance or darkness. He destroys the whole creation by the will of the Lord. Therefore all three, namely Brahmā, Viṣṇu and Śiva, are incarnations of the Garbhodakaśāyī Viṣṇu. From Brahmā the other demigods like Dakṣa, Marīci, Manu and many others become incarnated to generate living entities within the universe. This Garbhodakaśāyī Viṣṇu is glorified in the *Vedas* in the hymns of *Garbha-stuti,* which begin with the description of the Lord as having thousands of heads, etc. The Garbhodakaśāyī Viṣṇu is the Lord of the universe, and although He appears to be lying within the universe, He is always transcendental. This also has already been explained. The Viṣṇu who is the plenary portion of the Garbhodakaśāyī Viṣṇu is the Supersoul of the universal life, and He is known as the maintainer of the universe or Kṣīrodakaśāyī Viṣṇu. So the three features of the original *puruṣa* are thus understood. And all the incarnations within the universe are emanations from this Kṣīrodakaśāyī Viṣṇu.

In different millennia there are different incarnations, and they are innumerable, although some of them are very prominent, such as Matsya, Kūrma, Varāha, Rāma, Nṛsiṁha, Vāmana and many others. These incarnations are called *līlā* incarnations. Then there are qualitative incarnations such as Brahmā, Viṣṇu, and Śiva (or Rudra), who take charge of the different modes of material nature.

Lord Viṣṇu is nondifferent from the Personality of Godhead. Lord Śiva is in the marginal position between the Personality of Godhead and the living entities, or *jīvas.* Brahmā is always a *jīva-tattva.* The highest pious living being, or the greatest devotee of the Lord, is empowered with the potency of the Lord for creation, and he is called Brahmā. His power is like the power of the sun reflected in valuable stones and jewels. When there is no such living being to take charge of the post of Brahmā, the Lord Himself becomes a Brahmā and takes charge of the post.

Lord Śiva is not an ordinary living being. He is the plenary portion of the Lord, but because Lord Śiva is in direct touch with material nature, he is not exactly in the same transcendental position as Lord Viṣṇu. The difference is like that between milk and curd. Curd is nothing but milk, and yet it cannot be used in place of milk.

The next incarnations are the Manus. Within one day's duration of the life of Brahmā (which is calculated by our solar year as 4,300,000 x 1,000 years) there are fourteen Manus. Therefore there are 420 Manus in one month of Brahmā and 5,040 Manus in one year of Brahmā. Brahmā lives for one hundred years of his age, and therefore there are 5,040 x 100 or 504,000 Manus in the duration of Brahmā's life. There are innumerable universes, with one Brahmā in each of them, and all of them are created and annihilated during the breathing time of the *puruṣa.* Therefore one can simply imagine how many millions of Manus there are during one breath of the *puruṣa.*

The Manus who are prominent within this universe are as follows: Yajña as Svāyambhuva Manu, Vibhu as Svārociṣa Manu, Satyasena as Uttama Manu, Hari as Tāmasa Manu, Vaikuṇṭha as Raivata Manu, Ajita as Cākṣuṣa Manu, Vāmana as Vaivasvata Manu (the present age is under the Vaivasvata Manu), Sārvabhauma as Sāvarṇi Manu, Ṛṣabha as Dakṣa-sāvarṇi Manu, Viṣvaksena as Brahma-sāvarṇi Manu, Dharmasetu as Dharma-sāvarṇi Manu, Sudhāmā as Rudra-sāvarṇi Manu, Yogeśvara as Deva-sāvarṇi Manu, and Bṛhadbhānu as Indra-sāvarṇi Manu. These are the names of one set of fourteen Manus covering 4,300,000,000 solar years as described above.

Then there are the *yugāvatāras,* or the incarnations of the millennia. The *yugas* are known as Satya-yuga, Tretā-yuga, Dvāpara-yuga and Kali-yuga. The incarnations of each *yuga* are of different color. The colors are white, red, black and yellow. In the Dvāpara-yuga, Lord Kṛṣṇa in black color appeared, and in the Kali-yuga Lord Caitanya in yellow color appeared.

So all the incarnations of the Lord are mentioned in the revealed scriptures. There is no scope for an imposter to become an incarnation, for an incarnation must be mentioned in the *śāstras.* An incarnation does not declare Himself to be an incarnation of the Lord, but great sages agree by the symptoms mentioned in the revealed scriptures. The features of the incarnation and the particular type of mission which He has to execute are mentioned in the revealed scriptures.

Apart from the direct incarnations, there are innumerable empowered incarnations. They are also mentioned in the revealed scriptures. Such incarnations are directly as well as indirectly empowered. When they are directly empowered they are called incarnations, but when they are indirectly empowered they are called *vibhūtis.* Directly empowered incarnations are the

Kumāras, Nārada, Pṛthu, Śeṣa, Ananta, etc. As far as *vibhūtis* are concerned, they are very explicitly described in the *Bhagavad-gītā* in the *Vibhūti-yoga* chapter. And for all these different types of incarnations, the fountainhead is the Garbhodakaśāyī Viṣṇu.

TEXT 6

स एव प्रथमं देवः कौमारं सर्गमाश्रितः ।
चचार दुश्चरं ब्रह्मा ब्रह्मचर्यमखण्डितम् ॥६॥

sa eva prathamaṁ devaḥ
kaumāraṁ sargam āśritaḥ
cacāra duścaraṁ brahmā
brahmacaryam akhaṇḍitam

saḥ—that; *eva*—certainly; *prathamam*—first; *devaḥ*—Supreme Lord; *kaumāram*—named the Kumāras (unmarried); *sargam*—creation; *āśritaḥ*—under; *cacāra*—performed; *duścaram*—very difficult to do; *brahmā*—in the order of Brahman; *brahmacaryam*—under discipline to realize the Absolute (Brahman); *akhaṇḍitam*—unbroken.

TRANSLATION

First of all, in the beginning of creation, there were the four unmarried sons of Brahmā [the Kumāras], who, being situated in a vow of celibacy, underwent severe austerities for realization of the Absolute Truth.

PURPORT

The creation of the material world is effected, maintained and then again annihilated at certain intervals. So there are different names of the creations in terms of the particular types of Brahmā, the father of the living beings in the creation. The Kumāras, as above mentioned, appeared in the Kaumāra creation of the material world, and to teach us the process of Brahman realization, they underwent a severe type of disciplinary action as bachelors. These Kumāras are empowered incarnations. And before executing the severe type of disciplinary actions, all of them became qualified *brāhmaṇas.* This example suggests that one must first acquire the qualifications of a *brāhmaṇa,* not simply by birth but also by quality, and then one can undergo the process of Brahman realization.

TEXT 7

द्वितीयं तु भवायास्य रसातलगतां महीम्।
उद्धरिष्यन्नुपादत्त यज्ञेशः सौकरं वपुः ॥७॥

dvitīyaṁ tu bhavāyāsya
rasātala-gatāṁ mahīm
uddhariṣyann upādatta
yajñeśaḥ saukaraṁ vapuḥ

dvitīyam—the second; *tu*—but; *bhavāya*—for the welfare; *asya*—of this earth; *rasātala*—of the lowest region; *gatām*—having gone; *mahīm*—the earth; *uddhariṣyan*—lifting; *upādatta*—established; *yajñeśaḥ*—the proprietor or the supreme enjoyer; *saukaram*—hoggish; *vapuḥ*—incarnation.

TRANSLATION

The supreme enjoyer of all sacrifices accepted the incarnation of a boar [the second incarnation], and for the welfare of the earth He lifted the earth from the nether regions of the universe.

PURPORT

The indication is that for each and every incarnation of the Personality of Godhead, the particular function executed is also mentioned. There cannot be any incarnation without a particular function, and such functions are always extraordinary. They are impossible for any living being to perform. The incarnation of the boar was to take the earth out of Pluto's region of filthy matter. Picking up something from a filthy place is done by a boar, and the all-powerful Personality of Godhead displayed this wonder to the *asuras,* who had hidden the earth in such a filthy place. There is nothing impossible for the Personality of Godhead, and although He played the part of a boar, by the devotees He is worshiped, staying always in transcendence.

TEXT 8

तृतीयमृषिसर्गं वै देवर्षित्वमुपेत्य सः।
तन्त्रं सात्वतमाचष्ट नैष्कर्म्यं कर्मणां यतः ॥८॥

tṛtīyam ṛṣi-sargaṁ vai
devarṣitvam upetya saḥ

tantraṁ sātvatam ācaṣṭa
naiṣkarmyaṁ karmaṇāṁ yataḥ

tṛtīyam—the third one; *ṛṣi-sargam*—the millennium of the *ṛṣis; vai*—certainly; *devarṣitvam*—incarnation of the *ṛṣi* amongst the demigods; *upetya*—having accepted; *saḥ*—he; *tantram*—exposition of the *Vedas; sātvatam*—which is especially meant for devotional service; *ācaṣṭa*—collected; *naiṣkarmyam*—nonfruitive; *karmaṇām*—of work; *yataḥ*—from which.

TRANSLATION

In the millennium of the ṛṣis, the Personality of Godhead accepted the third empowered incarnation in the form of Devarṣi Nārada, who is a great sage among the demigods. He collected expositions of the Vedas which deal with devotional service and which inspire nonfruitive action.

PURPORT

The great Ṛṣi Nārada, who is an empowered incarnation of the Personality of Godhead, propagates devotional service all over the universe. All great devotees of the Lord all over the universe and in different planets and species of life are his disciples. Śrīla Vyāsadeva, the compiler of the *Śrīmad-Bhāgavatam,* is also one of his disciples. Nārada is the author of *Nārada-pañcarātra,* which is the exposition of the *Vedas* particularly for the devotional service of the Lord. This *Nārada-pañcarātra* trains the *karmīs,* or the fruitive workers, to achieve liberation from the bondage of fruitive work. The conditioned souls are mostly attracted by fruitive work because they want to enjoy life by the sweat of their own brows. The whole universe is full of fruitive workers in all species of life. The fruitive works include all kinds of economic development plans. But the law of nature provides that every action has its resultant reaction, and the performer of the work is bound up by such reactions, good or bad. The reaction of good work is comparative material prosperity, whereas the reaction of bad work is comparative material distress. But material conditions, either in so-called happiness or in so-called distress, are all meant ultimately for distress only. Foolish materialists have no information of how to obtain eternal happiness in the unconditional state. Śrī Nārada informs these foolish fruitive workers how to realize the reality of happiness. He gives direction to the diseased men of the world how one's present engagement can lead one to the path of spiritual emancipation. The physician directs the patient to take treated milk in the form of curd for his sufferings from indigestion due to his taking another milk preparation. So the cause of the disease and the remedy of the disease may be the same, but it must be treated by an expert physician like Nārada. The *Bhagavad-gītā* also gives the same solution of serving the Lord by the fruits of one's labor. That will lead one to the path of *naiṣkarmya*, or liberation.

TEXT 9

तुर्ये धर्मकलासर्गे नरनारायणावृषी।
भूत्वात्मोपशमोपेतमकरोत् दुश्चरं तपः ॥९॥

turye dharma-kalā-sarge
nara-nārāyaṇāv ṛṣī
bhūtvātmopaśamopetam
akarot duścaraṁ tapaḥ

turye—in the fourth of the line; *dharma-kalā*—wife of Dharmarāja; *sarge*—being born of; *nara-nārāyaṇau*—named Nara and Nārāyaṇa; *ṛṣī*—sages; *bhūtvā*—becoming; *ātma-upaśama*—controlling the senses; *upetam*—for achievement of; *akarot*—undertook; *duścaram*—very strenuous; *tapaḥ*—penance.

TRANSLATION

In the fourth incarnation, the Lord became Nara and Nārāyaṇa, the twin sons of the wife of King Dharma. Thus He undertook severe and exemplary penances to control the senses.

PURPORT

As King Ṛṣabha advised His sons, *tapasya,* or voluntary acceptance of penance for realization of the Transcendence, is the only duty of the human being; it was so done by the Lord Himself in an exemplary manner to teach us. The Lord is very kind to the forgetful souls. He therefore comes Himself and leaves behind necessary instructions and also sends His good sons as representatives to call all the conditioned souls back to Godhead. Recently, within the memory of everyone, Lord Caitanya also appeared for the same purpose: to show special favor to fallen souls of this age of iron industry. The incarnation of Nārāyaṇa is worshiped still at Badarī-nārāyaṇa, on the range of the Himalayas.

TEXT 10

पञ्चमः कपिलो नाम सिद्धेशः कालविप्लुतम् ।
प्रोवाचासुरये साङ्ख्यं तत्त्वग्रामविनिर्णयम् ॥१०॥

pañcamaḥ kapilo nāma
siddheśaḥ kāla-viplutam
provācāsuraye sāṅkhyaṁ
tattva-grāma-vinirṇayam

pañcamaḥ—the fifth one; *kapilaḥ*—Kapila; *nāma*—of the name; *siddheśaḥ*—the foremost amongst the perfect; *kāla*—time; *viplutam*—lost; *provāca*—said; *āsuraye*—unto the *brāhmaṇa* named Āsuri; *sāṅkhyam*—metaphysics; *tattva-grāma*—the sum total of the creative elements; *vinirṇayam*—exposition.

TRANSLATION

The fifth incarnation, named Lord Kapila, is foremost among perfected beings. He gave an exposition of the creative elements and metaphysics to Āsuri Brāhmaṇa, for in course of time this knowledge had been lost.

PURPORT

The sum total of the creative elements is twenty-four in all. Each and every one of them is explicitly explained in the system of Sāṅkhya philosophy. Sāṅkhya philosophy is generally called metaphysics by the European scholars. The etymological meaning of *sāṅkhya* is "that which explains very lucidly by analysis of the material elements." This was done for the first time by Lord Kapila, who is said herein to be the fifth in the line of incarnations.

TEXT 11

षष्ठमत्रेरपत्यत्वं वृतः प्राप्तोऽनसूयया ।
आन्वीक्षिकीमलर्काय प्रह्लादादिभ्य ऊचिवान् ॥११॥

ṣaṣṭham atrer apatyatvaṁ
vṛtaḥ prāpto 'nasūyayā
ānvīkṣikīm alarkāya
prahlādādibhya ūcivān

ṣaṣṭham—the sixth one; *atreḥ*—of Atri; *apatyatvam*—sonship; *vṛtaḥ*—being prayed for; *prāptaḥ*—obtained; *anasūyayā*—by Anasūyā; *ānvīkṣikīm*

—on the subject of transcendence; *alarkāya*—unto Alarka; *prahlāda-ādibhyaḥ* —unto Prahlāda and others; *ūcivān*—spoke.

TRANSLATION

The sixth incarnation of the puruṣa was the son of the sage Atri. He was born from the womb of Anasūyā, who prayed for an incarnation. He spoke on the subject of transcendence to Alarka, Prahlāda and others [Yadu, Haihaya, etc.].

PURPORT

The Lord incarnated Himself as Dattātreya, the son of Ṛṣi Atri and Anasūyā. The history of the birth of Dattātreya as an incarnation of the Lord is mentioned in the *Brahmāṇḍa Purāṇa* in connection with the story of the devoted wife. It is said there that Anasūyā, the wife of Ṛṣi Atri, prayed before the lords Brahmā, Viṣṇu and Śiva as follows: "My lords, if you are pleased with me, and if you desire me to ask from you some sort of blessings, then I pray that you combine together to become my son." This was accepted by the lords, and as Dattātreya the Lord expounded the philosophy of the spirit soul and especially instructed Alarka, Prahlāda, Yadu, Haihaya, etc.

TEXT 12

ततः सप्तम आकूत्यां रुचेर्यज्ञोऽभ्यजायत।
स यामाद्यैः सुरगणैरपात्स्वायम्भुवान्तरम् ॥१२॥

tataḥ saptama ākūtyāṁ
rucer yajño 'bhyajāyata
sa yāmādyaiḥ sura-gaṇair
apāt svāyambhuvāntaram

tataḥ—after that; *saptame*—the seventh in the line; *ākūtyām*—in the womb of Ākūti; *ruceḥ*—by Prajāpati Ruci; *yajñaḥ*—the Lord's incarnation as Yajña; *abhyajāyata*—advented; *saḥ*—He; *yāma-ādyaiḥ*—with Yāma and others; *sura-gaṇaiḥ*—with demigods; *apāt*—ruled; *svāyambhuva-antaram* —the change of the period of Svāyambhuva Manu.

TRANSLATION

The seventh incarnation was Yajña, the son of Prajāpati Ruci and his wife Ākūti. He controlled the period during the change of Svāyambhuva Manu and was assisted by demigods such as His son Yama.

PURPORT

The administrative posts occupied by the demigods for maintaining the regulations of the material world are offered to the highly elevated pious living beings. When there is a scarcity of such pious living beings, the Lord incarnates Himself as Brahmā, Prajāpati, Indra, etc., and takes up the charge. During the period of Svāyambhuva Manu (the present period is of Vaivasvata Manu) there was no suitable living being who could occupy the post of Indra, the King of the Indraloka (heaven) planet. The Lord Himself at that time became Indra. Assisted by His own sons like Yama and other demigods, Lord Yajña ruled the administration of the universal affairs.

TEXT 13

अष्टमे मेरुदेव्यां तु नाभेर्जात उरुक्रमः ।
दर्शयन् वर्त्म धीराणां सर्वाश्रमनमस्कृतम् ॥१३॥

aṣṭame merudevyāṁ tu
nābher jāta urukramaḥ
darśayan vartma dhīrāṇāṁ
sarvāśrama-namaskṛtam

aṣṭame—the eighth of the incarnations; *merudevyām tu*—in the womb of Merudevī, the wife of; *nābheḥ*—King Nābhi; *jātaḥ*—took birth; *urukramaḥ*—the all-powerful Lord; *darśayan*—by showing; *vartma*—the way; *dhīrāṇām*—of the perfect beings; *sarva*—all; *āśrama*—orders of life; *namaskṛtam*—honored by.

TRANSLATION

The eighth incarnation was King Ṛṣabha, son of King Nābhi and his wife Merudevī. In this incarnation the Lord showed the path of perfection, which is followed by those who have fully controlled their senses and who are honored by all orders of life.

PURPORT

The society of human beings is naturally divided into eight by orders and statuses of life—the four divisions of occupation and four divisions of cultural advancement. The intelligent class, the administrative class, the productive class and the laborer class are the four divisions of occupation. And the student life, the householder's life, retired life and renounced life are the four statuses of cultural advancement towards the path of spiritual realization. Out of these, the renounced order of life, or the order of *sannyāsa,* is considered the highest of all, and a *sannyāsī* is constitutionally the spiritual master for all the orders and divisions. In the *sannyāsa* order also there are four stages of upliftment toward perfection. These stages are called *kuṭīcaka, bahūdaka, parivrājakācārya,* and *paramahaṁsa.* The *paramahaṁsa* stage of life is the highest stage of perfection. This order of life is respected by all others. Mahārāja Ṛṣabha, the son of King Nābhi and Merudevī, was an incarnation of the Lord, and He instructed His sons to follow the path of perfection by *tapasya,* which sanctifies one's existence and enables one to attain the stage of spiritual happiness which is eternal and ever increasing. Every living being is searching after happiness, but no one knows where eternal and unlimited happiness is obtainable. Foolish men seek after material sense pleasure as a substitute for real happiness, but such foolish men forget that temporary so-called happiness derived from sense pleasures is also enjoyed by the dogs and hogs. No animal, bird or beast is bereft of this sense pleasure. In every species of life, including the human form of life, such happiness is immensely obtainable. The human form of life, however, is not meant for such cheap happiness. The human life is meant for attaining eternal and unlimited happiness by spiritual realization. This spiritual realization is obtained by *tapasya,* or undergoing voluntarily the path of penance and abstinence from material pleasure. Those who have been trained for abstinence in material pleasures are called *dhīra,* or men undisturbed by the senses. Only these *dhīras* can accept the orders of *sannyāsa,* and they can gradually rise to the status of the *paramahaṁsa,* which is adored by all members of society. King Ṛṣabha propagated this mission, and at the last stage He became completely aloof from the material bodily needs, which is a rare stage not to be imitated by foolish men, but to be worshiped by all.

TEXT 14

ऋषिभिर्याचितो भेजे नवमं पार्थिवं वपुः।
दुग्धेमामोषधीर्विप्रास्तेनायं स उशत्तमः ॥१४॥

ṛṣibhir yācito bheje
navamaṁ pārthivaṁ vapuḥ
dugdhemām oṣadhīr viprās
tenāyaṁ sa uśattamaḥ

ṛṣibhiḥ—by the sages; *yācitaḥ*—being prayed for; *bheje*—accepted; *navamam*—the ninth one; *pārthivam*—the ruler of the earth; *vapuḥ*—body; *dugdha*—milking; *imām*—all these; *oṣadhīḥ*—products of the earth; *viprāḥ*—O *brāhmaṇas; tena*—by; *ayam*—this; *saḥ*—he; *uśattamaḥ*—beautifully attractive.

TRANSLATION

O brāhmaṇas, in the ninth incarnation, the Lord, prayed for by sages, accepted the body of a king [Pṛthu] who cultivated the land to yield various produces, and for that reason the earth was beautiful and attractive.

PURPORT

Before the advent of King Pṛthu, there was great havoc of maladministration due to the vicious life of the previous king, the father of Mahārāja Pṛthu. The intelligent class of men (namely the sages and the *brāhmaṇas*) not only prayed for the Lord to come down, but also dethroned the previous king. It is the duty of the king to be pious and thus look after the all-around welfare of the citizens. Whenever there is some negligence on the part of the king in discharging his duty, the intelligent class of men must dethrone him. The intelligent class of men, however, do not occupy the royal throne, because they have much more important duties for the welfare of the public. Instead of occupying the royal throne, they prayed for the incarnation of the Lord, and the Lord came as Mahārāja Pṛthu. Real intelligent men, or qualified *brāhmaṇas,* never aspire for political posts. Mahārāja Pṛthu excavated many produces from the earth, and thus not only did the citizens become happy to have such a good king, but the complete sight of the earth also became beautiful and attractive.

TEXT 15

रूपं स जगृहे मात्स्यं चाक्षुषोदधिसम्प्लवे ।
नाव्यारोप्य महीमय्यामपाद्वैवस्वतं मनुम् ॥१५॥

rūpaṁ sa jagṛhe mātsyaṁ
cākṣuṣodadhi-samplave
nāvy āropya mahī-mayyām
apād vaivasvataṁ manum

rūpam—form; *saḥ*—He; *jagṛhe*—accepted; *mātsyam*—of a fish; *cākṣuṣa*—Cākṣuṣa; *udadhi*—water; *samplave*—inundation; *nāvi*—on the boat;

āropya—keeping on; *mahī*—the earth; *mayyām*—drowned in; *apāt*—protected; *vaivasvatam*—Vaivasvata; *manum*—Manu, the father of man.

TRANSLATION

When there was a complete inundation after the period of the Cākṣuṣa Manu and the whole world was deep within water, the Lord accepted the form of a fish and protected Vaivasvata Manu, keeping him up on a boat.

PURPORT

According to Śrīpāda Śrīdhara Svāmī, the original commentator on the *Bhāgavatam,* there is not always a devastation after the change of every Manu. And yet this inundation after the period of Cākṣuṣa Manu took place in order to show some wonders to Satyavrata. But Śrī Jīva Gosvāmī has given definite proofs from authoritative scriptures (like *Viṣṇu-dharmottara, Mārkaṇḍeya Purāṇa, Harivaṁśa,* etc.) that there is always a devastation after the end of each and every Manu. Śrīla Viśvanātha Cakravartī has also supported Śrīla Jīva Gosvāmī, and he (Śrī Cakravartī) has also quoted from *Bhāgavatāmṛta* about this inundation after each Manu. Apart from this, the Lord, in order to show special favor to Satyavrata, a devotee of the Lord, in this particular period, incarnated Himself.

TEXT 16

सुरासुराणामुदधिं मथ्नतां मन्दराचलम् ।
दध्रे कमठरूपेण पृष्ठ एकादशे विभुः ॥१६॥

surāsurāṇām udadhiṁ
mathnatāṁ mandarācalam
dadhre kamaṭha-rūpeṇa
pṛṣṭha ekādaśe vibhuḥ

sura—the theists; *asurāṇām*—of the atheists; *udadhim*—in the ocean; *mathnatām*—churning; *mandarācalam*—the Mandarācala Hill; *dadhre*—sustained; *kamaṭha*—tortoise; *rūpeṇa*—in the form of; *pṛṣṭhe*—shell; *ekādaśe*—the eleventh in the line; *vibhuḥ*—the great.

TRANSLATION

The eleventh incarnation of the Lord took the form of a tortoise whose shell served as a pivot for the Mandarācala Hill, which was being used as a churning rod by the theists and atheists of the universe.

PURPORT

Once both the atheists and the theists were engaged in producing nectar from the sea so that all of them could become deathless by drinking it. At that time the Mandarācala Hill was used as the churning rod, and the shell of Lord Tortoise, the incarnation of Godhead, became the resting place (pivot) of the hill in the seawater.

TEXT 17

धान्वन्तरं द्वादशमं त्रयोदशममेव च।
अपाययत्सुरानन्यान्मोहिन्या मोहयन् स्त्रिया ॥१७॥

dhānvantaraṁ dvādaśamaṁ
trayodaśamam eva ca
apāyayat surān anyān
mohinyā mohayan striyā

dhānvantaram—the incarnation of Godhead named Dhanvantari; *dvādaśamam*—the twelfth in the line; *trayodaśamam*—the thirteenth in the line; *eva*—certainly; *ca*—and; *apāyayat*—gave to drink; *surān*—the demigods; *anyān*—others; *mohinyā*—by charming beauty; *mohayan*—alluring; *striyā*—in the form of a woman.

TRANSLATION

In the twelfth incarnation, the Lord appeared as Dhanvantari, and in the thirteenth He allured the atheists by the charming beauty of a woman and gave nectar to the demigods to drink.

TEXT 18

चतुर्दशं नारसिंहं बिभ्रद्दैत्येन्द्रमूर्जितम्।
ददार करजैरूरावेरकां कटकृद्यथा ॥१८॥

caturdaśaṁ nārasiṁhaṁ
bibhrad daityendram ūrjitam
dadāra karajair ūrāv
erakāṁ kaṭa-kṛd yathā

caturdaśam—the fourteenth in the line; *nāra-siṁham*—the incarnation of the Lord as half-man and half-lion; *bibhrat*—advented; *daitya-indram*—

the king of the atheists; *ūrjitam*—strongly built; *dadāra*—bifurcated; *karajaiḥ*—by the nails; *ūrau*—on the lap; *erakām*—canes; *kaṭa-kṛt*—carpenter; *yathā*—just like.

TRANSLATION

In the fourteenth incarnation, the Lord appeared as Nṛsiṁha and bifurcated the strong body of the atheist Hiraṇyakaśipu with His nails, just as a carpenter pierces cane.

TEXT 19

पञ्चदशं वामनकं कृत्वागादध्वरं बलेः ।
पदत्रयं याचमानः प्रत्यादित्सुस्त्रिपिष्टपम् ॥१९॥

pañcadaśaṁ vāmanakaṁ
kṛtvāgād adhvaraṁ baleḥ
pada-trayaṁ yācamānaḥ
pratyāditsus tri-piṣṭapam

pañcadaśam—the fifteenth in the line; *vāmanakam*—the dwarf-*brāhmaṇa; kṛtvā*—by assumption of; *agāt*—went; *adhvaram*—arena of sacrifice; *baleḥ*—of King Bali; *pada-trayam*—three steps only; *yācamānaḥ*—begging; *pratyāditsuḥ*—willing at heart to return; *tri-piṣṭapam*—the kingdom of the three planetary systems.

TRANSLATION

In the fifteenth incarnation, the Lord assumed the form of a dwarf-brāhmaṇa [Vāmana] and visited the arena of sacrifice arranged by Mahārāja Bali. Although at heart He was willing to regain the kingdom of the three planetary systems, He simply asked for a donation of three steps of land.

PURPORT

The almighty God can bestow upon anyone the kingdom of the universe from a very small beginning, and similarly He can take away the kingdom of the universe on the plea of begging a small piece of land.

TEXT 20

अवतारे षोडशमे पश्यन् ब्रह्मद्रुहो नृपान् ।
त्रिःसप्तकृत्वः कुपितो निःक्षत्रामकरोन्महीम् ॥२०॥

avatāre ṣoḍaśame
paśyan brahma-druho nṛpān
triḥ-sapta-kṛtvaḥ kupito
niḥ-kṣatrām akaron mahīm

avatāre—in the incarnation of the Lord; *ṣoḍaśame*—the sixteenth; *paśyan*—seeing; *brahma-druhaḥ*—disobedient to the orders of the *brāhmaṇas; nṛpān*—the kingly order; *triḥ-sapta*—thrice seven times; *kṛtvaḥ*—had done; *kupitaḥ*—being engaged; *niḥ*—negation; *kṣatrām*—the administrative class; *akarot*—did perform; *mahīm*—the earth.

TRANSLATION

In the sixteenth incarnation of the Godhead, the Lord [as Bhṛgupati] annihilated the administrative class [kṣatriyas] twenty-one times, being angry with them because of their rebellion against the brāhmaṇas [the intelligent class].

PURPORT

The *kṣatriyas,* or the administrative class of men, are expected to rule the planet by the direction of the intelligent class of men, who give direction to the rulers in terms of the standard *śāstras,* or the books of revealed knowledge. The rulers carry on the administration according to that direction. Whenever there is disobedience on the part of the *kṣatriyas,* or the administrative class, against the orders of the learned and intelligent *brāhmaṇas,* the administrators are removed by force from the posts, and arrangement is made for better administration.

TEXT 21

ततः सप्तदशे जातः सत्यवत्यां पराशरात्।
चक्रे वेदतरोः शाखा दृष्ट्वा पुंसोऽल्पमेधसः ॥२१॥

tataḥ saptadaśe jātaḥ
satyavatyāṁ parāśarāt
cakre veda-taroḥ śākhā
dṛṣṭvā puṁso 'lpa-medhasaḥ

tataḥ—thereafter; *saptadaśe*—in the seventeenth incarnation; *jātaḥ*—advented; *satyavatyām*—in the womb of Satyavatī; *parāśarāt*—by Parāśara

Muni; *cakre*—prepared; *veda-taroḥ*—of the desire tree of the *Vedas; śākhāḥ* —branches; *dṛṣṭvā*—be seeing; *puṁsaḥ*—the people in general; *alpa-medhasaḥ*—less intelligent.

TRANSLATION

Thereafter, in the seventeenth incarnation of Godhead, Śrī Vyāsadeva appeared in the womb of Satyavatī through Parāśara Muni, and he divided the one Veda into several branches and subbranches, seeing that the people in general were less intelligent.

PURPORT

Originally the *Veda* is one. But Śrīla Vyāsadeva divided the original *Veda* into four, namely *Sāma, Yajur, Ṛg, Atharva,* and then again they were explained in different branches like the *Purāṇas* and the *Mahābhārata.* Vedic language and the subject matter are very difficult for ordinary men. They are understood by the highly intelligent and self-realized *brāhmaṇas.* But the present age of Kali is full of ignorant men. Even those who are born by a *brāhmaṇa* father are, in the present age, no better than the *śūdras* or the women. The twice-born men, namely the *brāhmaṇas, kṣatriyas* and *vaiśyas,* are expected to undergo a cultural purificatory process known as *saṁskāras,* but because of the bad influence of the present age the so-called members of the *brāhmaṇa* and other high-order families are no longer highly cultured. They are called the *dvija-bandhus,* or the friends and family members of the twice-born. But these *dvija-bandhus* are classified amongst the *śūdras* and the women. Śrīla Vyāsadeva divided the *Vedas* into various branches and subbranches for the sake of the less intelligent classes like the *dvija-bandhus, śūdras* and women.

TEXT 22

नरदेवत्वमापन्नः सुरकार्यचिकीर्षया ।
समुद्रनिग्रहादीनि चक्रे वीर्याण्यतः परम् ॥२२॥

nara-devatvam āpannaḥ
sura-kārya-cikīrṣayā
samudra-nigrahādīni
cakre vīryāṇy ataḥ param

nara—human being; *devatvam*—divinity; *āpannaḥ*—having assumed the form of; *sura*—the demigods; *kārya*—activities; *cikīrṣayā*—for the purpose of performing; *samudra*—the Indian Ocean; *nigraha-ādīni*—controlling, etc.; *cakre*—did perform; *vīryāṇi*—superhuman prowess; *ataḥ param*—thereafter.

TRANSLATION

In the eighteenth incarnation, the Lord appeared as King Rāma. In order to perform some pleasing work for the demigods, He exhibited superhuman powers by controlling the Indian Ocean and then killing the atheist King Rāvaṇa, who was on the other side of the sea.

PURPORT

The Personality of Godhead Śrī Rāma assumed the form of a human being and appeared on the earth for the purpose of doing some pleasing work for the demigods or the administrative personalities to maintain the order of the universe. Sometimes great demons and atheists like Rāvaṇa and Hiraṇyakaśipu and many others become very famous due to advancing material civilization by the help of material science and other activities with a spirit of challenging the established order of the Lord. For example, the attempt to fly to other planets by material means is a challenge to the established order. The conditions of each and every planet are different, and different classes of human beings are accommodated there for particular purposes mentioned in the codes of the Lord. But, puffed up by tiny success in material advancement, sometimes the godless materialists challenge the existence of God. Rāvaṇa was one of them, and he wanted to deport ordinary men to the planet of Indra (heaven) by material means without consideration of the necessary qualifications. He wanted a staircase to be built up directly reaching the heavenly planet so that people might not be required to undergo the routine of pious work necessary to enter that planet. He also wanted to perform other acts against the established rule of the Lord. He even challenged the authority of Śrī Rāma, the Personality of Godhead, and kidnapped His wife, Sītā. Of course Lord Rama came to chastise this atheist, answering the prayer and desire of the demigods. He therefore took up the challenge of Rāvaṇa, and the complete activity is the subject matter of the *Rāmāyaṇa*. Because Lord Rāmacandra was the Personality of Godhead, He exhibited superhuman activities which no human being, including the materially advanced Rāvaṇa, could perform. Lord Rāmacandra prepared a royal road on the Indian Ocean with stones that floated on the water. The modern scientists have done research in the area of weightlessness, but it is not possible to bring in weightlessness anywhere and everywhere. But because weightlessness is the creation of the Lord by which He can make the gigantic planets fly and float in the air, He made the stones even within this earth to be weightless and prepared a stone bridge on the sea without any supporting pillar. That is the display of the power of God.

TEXT 23

एकोनविंशे विंशतिमे वृष्णिषु प्राप्य जन्मनी ।
रामकृष्णाविति भुवो भगवानहरद्भरम् ॥२३॥

ekonaviṁśe viṁśatime
vṛṣṇiṣu prāpya janmanī
rāma-kṛṣṇāv iti bhuvo
bhagavān aharad bharam

ekonaviṁśe—in the nineteenth; *viṁśatime*—in the twentieth also; *vṛṣṇiṣu*—in the Vṛṣṇi dynasty; *prāpya*—having obtained; *janmanī*—births; *rāma*—Balarāma; *kṛṣṇau*—Śrī Kṛṣṇa; *iti*—thus; *bhuvaḥ*—of the world; *bhagavān*—the Personality of Godhead; *aharat*—removed; *bharam*—burden.

TRANSLATION

In the nineteenth and twentieth incarnations, the Lord advented Himself as Lord Balarāma and Lord Kṛṣṇa in the family of Vṛṣṇi [the Yadu dynasty], and by so doing He removed the burden of the world.

PURPORT

The specific mention of the word *bhagavān* in this text indicates that Balarāma and Kṛṣṇa are original forms of the Lord. This will be further explained later. Lord Kṛṣṇa is not an incarnation of the *puruṣa,* as we learned from the beginning of this chapter. He is directly the original Personality of Godhead, and Balarāma is the first plenary manifestation of the Lord. From Baladeva the first phalanx of plenary expansions, Vāsudeva, Saṅkarṣaṇa, Aniruddha and Pradyumna, expands. Lord Śrī Kṛṣṇa is Vāsudeva, and Baladeva is Saṅkarṣaṇa.

TEXT 24

ततः कलौ सम्प्रवृत्ते सम्मोहाय सुरद्विषाम् ।
बुद्धो नाम्नाञ्जनसुतः कीकटेषु भविष्यति ॥२४॥

tataḥ kalau sampravṛtte
sammohāya sura-dviṣām
buddho nāmnāñjana-sutaḥ
kīkaṭeṣu bhaviṣyati

tataḥ—thereafter; *kalau*—the age of Kali; *sampravṛtte*—having ensued; *sammohāya*—for the purpose of deluding; *sura*—the theists; *dviṣām*—those who are envious; *buddhaḥ*—Lord Buddha; *nāmnā*—of the name; *añjana-sutaḥ*—whose mother was Añjanā; *kīkaṭeṣu*—in the province of Gayā (Bihar); *bhaviṣyati*—will take place.

TRANSLATION

Then, in the beginning of Kali-yuga, the Lord will appear as Lord Buddha, the son of Añjanā, in the province of Gayā, just for the purpose of deluding those who are envious of the faithful theist.

PURPORT

Lord Buddha, a powerful incarnation of the Personality of Godhead, appeared in the province of Gayā (Bihar) as the son of Añjanā, and he preached his own conception of nonviolence and deprecated even the animal sacrifices sanctioned in the *Vedas.* At the time when Lord Buddha appeared, the people in general were atheistic and preferred animal flesh to anything else. On the plea of Vedic sacrifice, every place was practically turned into a slaughterhouse, and animal-killing was indulged in unrestrictedly. Lord Buddha preached nonviolence, taking pity on the poor animals. He preached that he did not believe in the tenets of the *Vedas* and stressed the adverse psychological effects incurred by animal-killing. Less intelligent men of the age of Kali, who had no faith in God, followed his principle, and for the time being they were trained in moral discipline and nonviolence, the preliminary steps for proceeding further on the path of God realization. He deluded the atheists because such atheists who followed his principles did not believe in God, but they kept their absolute faith in Lord Buddha, who himself was the incarnation of God. Thus the faithless people were made to believe in God in the form of Lord Buddha. That was the mercy of Lord Buddha: he made the faithless faithful to him.

Killing of animals before the advent of Lord Buddha was the most prominent feature of the society. People claimed that these were Vedic sacrifices. When the *Vedas* are not accepted through the authoritative disciplic succession, the casual readers of the *Vedas* are misled by the flowery language of that system of knowledge. In the *Bhagavad-gītā* a comment has been made on such foolish scholars (*avipaścitaḥ*). The foolish scholars of Vedic literature who do not care to receive the transcendental message through the transcendental realized sources of disciplic succession are sure to be bewildered. To them, the ritualistic ceremonies are considered to be all in all. They have no depth of knowledge. According to the *Bhagavad-gītā* (15.15), *vedaiś ca sarvair aham eva vedyaḥ:* the whole system of the *Vedas* is to lead one gradually to the path of the Supreme Lord. The whole theme of Vedic literature is to know the Supreme Lord, the individual soul, the cosmic situation and the relation between all these items. When the relation is known, the relative function begins, and as a result of such a function the ultimate goal of life or going back to Godhead takes place in the easiest manner. Unfortunately, unauthorized scholars of the *Vedas* become captivated by the purificatory ceremonies only, and natural progress is thereby checked.

To such bewildered persons of atheistic propensity, Lord Buddha is the emblem of theism. He therefore first of all wanted to check the habit of animal-killing. The animal-killers are dangerous elements on the path going back to Godhead. There are two types of animal-killers. The soul is also sometimes called the "animal" or the living being. Therefore, both the slaughterer of animals and those who have lost their identity of soul are animal-killers.

Mahārāja Parīkṣit said that only the animal-killer cannot relish the transcendental message of the Supreme Lord. Therefore if people are to be educated to the path of Godhead, they must be taught first and foremost to *stop the process of animal-killing* as above mentioned. *It is nonsensical to say that animal-killing has nothing to do with spiritual realization.* By this dangerous theory many so-called *sannyāsīs* have sprung up by the grace of Kali-yuga who preach animal-killing under the garb of the *Vedas.* The subject matter has already been discussed in the conversation between Lord Caitanya and Maulana Chand Kazi Shaheb. The animal sacrifice as stated in the *Vedas* is different from the unrestricted animal-killing in the slaughterhouse. Because the *asuras* or the so-called scholars of Vedic literatures put forward the evidence of animal-killing in the *Vedas,* Lord Buddha superficially denied the authority of the *Vedas.* This rejection of the *Vedas* by Lord Buddha was adopted in order to save people from the vice of animal-killing as well as to save the poor animals from the slaughtering process of their big brothers who clamor for universal brotherhood, peace, justice and equity. There is no justice when there is animal-killing. Lord Buddha wanted to stop it completely, and therefore his cult of *ahiṁsā* was propagated not only in India but also outside the country.

Technically Lord Buddha's philosophy is called atheistic because there is no acceptance of the Supreme Lord and because that system of philosophy denied the authority of the *Vedas.* But that is an act of camouflage by the Lord. Lord Buddha is the incarnation of Godhead. As such, he is the original propounder of Vedic knowledge. He therefore cannot reject Vedic philosophy. But he rejected it outwardly because the *sura-dviṣa,* or the demons who are always envious of the devotees of Godhead, try to support cow-killing or animal-killing from the pages of the *Vedas,* and this is now being done by the modernized *sannyāsīs.* Lord Buddha had to reject the authority of the *Vedas* altogether. This is simply technical, and had it not been so he would not have been so accepted as the incarnation of Godhead. Nor would he have been worshiped in the transcendental songs of the poet Jayadeva, who is a Vaiṣṇava *ācārya.* Lord Buddha preached the preliminary principles of the *Vedas* in a manner suitable for the time being (and so also did Śaṅkarācārya) to establish the authority of the *Vedas.* Therefore both Lord Buddha and Ācārya Śaṅkara paved the path of theism, and Vaiṣṇava *ācāryas,* specifically Lord Śrī Caitanya Mahāprabhu, led the people on the path towards a realization of going back to Godhead.

We are glad that people are taking interest in the nonviolent movement of Lord Buddha. But will they take the matter very seriously and close the animal slaughterhouses altogether? *If not, there is no meaning to the ahiṁsā cult.*

Śrīmad-Bhāgavatam was composed just prior to the beginning of the age of Kali (about five thousand years ago), and Lord Buddha appeared about twenty-six hundred years ago. Therefore in the *Śrīmad-Bhāgavatam* Lord Buddha is foretold. Such is the authority of this clear scripture. There are many such prophecies, and they are being fulfilled one after another. They will indicate the positive standing of *Śrīmad-Bhāgavatam,* which is without *trace of mistake, illusion, cheating and imperfection,* which are the four flaws of all conditioned souls. The liberated souls are above these flaws; therefore they can see and foretell things which are to take place on distant future dates.

TEXT 25

अथासौ युगसन्ध्यायां दस्युप्रायेषु राजसु ।
जनिता विष्णुयशसो नाम्ना कल्किर्जगत्पतिः ॥२५॥

athāsau yuga-sandhyāyāṁ
dasyu-prāyeṣu rājasu
janitā viṣṇu-yaśaso
nāmnā kalkir jagat-patiḥ

atha—thereafter; *asau*—the same Lord; *yuga-sandhyāyām*—at the conjunction of the *yugas; dasyu*—plunderers; *prāyeṣu*—almost all; *rājasu*—the governing personalities; *janitā*—will take His birth; *viṣṇu*—named Viṣṇu; *yaśasaḥ*—surnamed Yaśā; *nāmnā*—in the name of; *kalkiḥ*—the incarnation of the Lord; *jagat-patiḥ*—the Lord of the creation.

TRANSLATION

Thereafter, at the conjunction of two yugas, the Lord of the creation will take His birth as the Kalki incarnation and become the son of Viṣṇu Yaśā. At this time the rulers of the earth will have degenerated into plunderers.

PURPORT

Here is another foretelling of the advent of Lord Kalki, the incarnation of Godhead. He is to appear at the conjunction of the two *yugas,* namely at the end of Kali-yuga and the beginning of Satya-yuga. The cycle of the four *yugas,* namely Satya, Tretā, Dvāpara and Kali, rotates like the calendar months. The present Kali-yuga lasts 432,000 years, out of which we have passed only 5,000 years after the Battle of Kurukṣetra and the end of the regime of King Parīkṣit. So there are 427,000 years balance yet to be finished. Therefore at the end of this period, the incarnation of Kalki will take place, as foretold in the *Śrīmad-Bhāgavatam.* The name of His father, Viṣṇu Yaśā, a learned *brāhmaṇa,* and the village Śambhala are also mentioned. As above mentioned, all these foretellings will prove to be factual in chronological order. That is the authority of *Śrīmad-Bhāgavatam.*

TEXT 26

अवतारा ह्यसङ्ख्येया हरेः सत्त्वनिधेर्द्विजाः ।
यथाविदासिनः कुल्याः सरसः स्युः सहस्रशः ॥२६॥

avatārā hy asaṅkhyeyā
hareḥ sattva-nidher dvijāḥ

yathāvidāsinaḥ kulyāḥ
sarasaḥ syuḥ sahasraśaḥ

avatārāḥ—incarnations; *hi*—certainly; *asaṅkhyeyāḥ*—innumerable; *hareḥ*—of Hari, the Lord; *sattva-nidheḥ*—of the ocean of goodness; *dvijāḥ*—the *brāhmaṇas; yathā*—as it is; *avidāsinaḥ*—inexhaustible; *kulyāḥ*—rivulets; *sarasaḥ*—of vast lakes; *syuḥ*—are; *sahasraśaḥ*—thousands of.

TRANSLATION

O brāhmaṇas, the incarnations of the Lord are innumerable, like rivulets flowing from inexhaustible sources of water.

PURPORT

The list of incarnations of the Personality of Godhead given herein is not complete. It is only a partial view of all the incarnations. There are many others, such as Śrī Hayagrīva, Hari, Haṁsa, Pṛśnigarbha, Vibhu, Satyasena, Vaikuṇṭha, Sārvabhauma, Viṣvaksena, Dharmasetu, Sudhāmā, Yogeśvara, Bṛhadbhānu and others of the bygone ages. Śrī Prahlāda Mahārāja said in his prayer, "My Lord, You manifest as many incarnations as there are species of life, namely the aquatics, the vegetables, the reptiles, the birds, the beasts, the men, the demigods, etc., just for the maintenance of the faithful and the annihilation of the unfaithful. You advent Yourself in this way in accordance with the necessity of the different *yugas.* In the Kali-yuga You have incarnated garbed as a devotee." This incarnation of the Lord in the Kali-yuga is Lord Caitanya Mahāprabhu. There are many other places, both in the *Bhāgavatam* and in other scriptures, in which the incarnation of the Lord as Śrī Caitanya Mahāprabhu is explicitly mentioned. In the *Brahma-saṁhitā* also it is said indirectly that although there are many incarnations of the Lord, such as Rāma, Nṛsiṁha, Varāha, Matsya, Kūrma and many others, the Lord Himself sometimes incarnates in person. Lord Kṛṣṇa and Lord Śrī Caitanya Mahāprabhu are not, therefore, incarnations, but the original source of all other incarnations. This will be clearly explained in the next *śloka.* So the Lord is the inexhaustible source for innumerable incarnations which are not always mentioned. But such incarnations are distinguished by specific extraordinary feats which are impossible to be performed by any living being. That is the general test to identify an incarnation of the Lord, directly and indirectly empowered. Some incarnations mentioned above are almost plenary portions. For instance, the Kumāras are empowered with transcendental knowledge. Śrī Nārada is empowered with devotional service. Mahārāja Pṛthu is an empowered incarnation with executive function. The Matsya incarnation is directly a plenary portion. So the innumerable incarnations of the Lord are manifested all over the universes constantly, without cessation, as water flows constantly from waterfalls.

TEXT 27

ऋषयो मनवो देवा मनुपुत्रा महौजसः।
कलाः सर्वे हरेरेव सप्रजापतयः स्मृताः ॥२७॥

ṛṣayo manavo devā
manu-putrā mahaujasaḥ
kalāḥ sarve harer eva
saprajāpatayaḥ smṛtāḥ

ṛṣayaḥ—all the sages; *manavaḥ*—all the Manus; *devāḥ*—all the demigods; *manu-putrāḥ*—all the descendants of Manu; *mahā-ojasaḥ*—very powerful; *kalāḥ*—portion of the plenary portion; *sarve*—all collectively; *hareḥ*—of the Lord; *eva*—certainly; *sa-prajāpatayaḥ*—along with the Prajāpatis; *smṛtāḥ*—are known.

TRANSLATION

All the ṛṣis, Manus, demigods and descendants of Manu, who are especially powerful, are plenary portions or portions of the plenary portions of the Lord. This also includes the Prajāpatis.

PURPORT

Those who are comparatively less powerful are called *vibhūti,* and those who are comparatively more powerful are called *āveśa* incarnations.

TEXT 28

एते चांशकलाः पुंसः कृष्णस्तु भगवान् स्वयम्।
इन्द्रारिव्याकुलं लोकं मृडयन्ति युगे युगे ॥२८॥

ete cāṁśa-kalāḥ puṁsaḥ
kṛṣṇas tu bhagavān svayam

indrāri-vyākulaṁ lokaṁ
mṛḍayanti yuge yuge

ete—all these; *ca*—and; *aṁśa*—plenary portions; *kalāḥ*—portions of the plenary portions; *puṁsaḥ*—of the Supreme; *kṛṣṇaḥ*—Lord Kṛṣṇa; *tu*—but; *bhagavān*—the Personality of Godhead; *svayam*—in person; *indra-ari*—the enemies of Indra; *vyākulam*—disturbed; *lokam*—all the planets; *mṛḍayanti*—gives protection; *yuge yuge*—in different ages.

TRANSLATION

All of the above-mentioned incarnations are either plenary portions or portions of the plenary portions of the Lord, but Lord Śrī Kṛṣṇa is the original Personality of Godhead. All of them appear on planets whenever there is a disturbance created by the atheists. The Lord incarnates to protect the theists.

PURPORT

In this particular stanza Lord Śrī Kṛṣṇa, the Personality of Godhead, is distinguished from other incarnations. He is counted amongst the *avatāras* (incarnations) because out of His causeless mercy the Lord descends from His transcendental abode. *Avatāra* means "one who descends." All the incarnations of the Lord, including the Lord Himself, descend on the different planets of the material world as also in different species of life to fulfill particular missions. Sometimes He comes Himself, and sometimes His different plenary portions or parts of the plenary portions, or His differentiated portions directly or indirectly empowered by Him, descend on this material world to execute certain specific functions. Originally the Lord is full of all opulences, all prowess, all fame, all beauty, all knowledge and all renunciation. When they are partly manifested through the plenary portions or parts of the plenary portions, it should be noted that certain manifestations of His different powers are required for those particular functions. When in the room small electric bulbs are displayed, it does not mean that the electric powerhouse is limited by the small bulbs. The same powerhouse can supply power to operate large-scale industrial dynamos with greater volts. Similarly, the incarnations of the Lord display limited powers because so much power is needed at that particular time.

For example, Lord Paraśurāma and Lord Nṛsiṁha displayed unusual opulence by killing the disobedient *kṣatriyas* twenty-one times and killing the greatly powerful atheist Hiraṇyakaśipu. Hiraṇyakaśipu was so powerful that even the demigods in other planets would tremble simply by the unfavorable raising of his eyebrow. The demigods in the higher level of material existence many, many times excel the most well-to-do human beings, in duration of life, beauty, wealth, paraphernalia, and in all other respects. Still they were afraid of Hiraṇyakaśipu. Thus we can simply imagine how powerful Hiraṇyakaśipu was in this material world. But even Hiraṇyakaśipu was cut into small pieces by the nails of Lord Nṛsiṁha. This means that anyone materially powerful cannot stand the strength of the Lord's nails. Similarly, Jāmadagnya displayed the Lord's power to kill all the disobedient kings powerfully situated in their respective states. The Lord's empowered incarnation Nārada and plenary incarnation Varāha, as well as indirectly empowered Lord Buddha, created faith in the mass of people. The incarnations of Rāma and Dhanvantari displayed His fame, and Balarāma, Mohinī and Vāmana exhibited His beauty. Dattātreya, Matsya, Kumāra and Kapila exhibited His transcendental knowledge. Nara and Nārāyaṇa Ṛṣis exhibited His renunciation. So all the different incarnations of the Lord indirectly or directly manifested different features, but Lord Kṛṣṇa, the primeval Lord, exhibited the complete features of Godhead, and thus it is confirmed that He is the source of all other incarnations. And the most extraordinary feature exhibited by Lord Śrī Kṛṣṇa was His internal energetic manifestation of His pastimes with the cowherd girls. His pastimes with the *gopīs* are all displays of transcendental existence, bliss and knowledge, although these are manifested apparently as sex love. The specific attraction of His pastimes with the *gopīs* should never be misunderstood. The *Bhāgavatam* relates these transcendental pastimes in the Tenth Canto. And in order to reach the position to understand the transcendental nature of Lord Kṛṣṇa's pastimes with the *gopīs,* the *Bhāgavatam* promotes the student gradually in nine other cantos.

According to Śrīla Jīva Gosvāmī's statement, in accordance with authoritative sources, Lord Kṛṣṇa is the source of all other incarnations. It is not that Lord Kṛṣṇa has any source of incarnation. All the symptoms of the Supreme Truth in full are present in the person of Lord Śrī Kṛṣṇa, and in the *Bhagavad-gītā* the Lord emphatically declares that there is no truth greater than or equal to Himself. In this stanza the word *svayam* is particularly mentioned to confirm that Lord Kṛṣṇa has no other source than Himself. Although in other places the incarnations are described as *bhagavān* because of their specific functions, nowhere are they declared to be the Supreme Personality. In this stanza the word *svayam* signifies the supremacy as the *summum bonum.*

The *summum bonum* Kṛṣṇa is one without a second. He Himself has expanded Himself in various parts, portions and particles as *svayaṁ-rūpa, svayam-prakāśa, tad-ekātmā, prābhava, vaibhava, vilāsa, avatāra, āveśa,* and *jīvas,* all provided with innumerable energies just suitable to the respective persons and personalities. Learned scholars in transcendental subjects have carefully analyzed the *summum bonum* Kṛṣṇa to have sixty-four principal attributes. All the expansions or categories of the Lord possess only some percentages of these attributes. But Śrī Kṛṣṇa is the possessor of the attributes cent percent. And His personal expansions such as *svayam-prakāśa and tad-ekātmā,* up to the categories of the *avatāras* who are all *viṣṇu-tattva,* possess up to ninety-three percent of these transcendental attributes. Lord Śiva, who is neither *avatāra* nor *āveśa* nor in between them, possesses almost eighty-four percent of the attributes. But the *jīvas,* or the individual living beings in different statuses of life, possess up to the limit of seventy-eight percent of the attributes. In the conditioned state of material existence, the living being possesses these attributes in very minute quantity, varying in terms of the pious life of the living being. The most perfect of living beings is Brahmā, the supreme administrator of one universe. He possesses seventy-eight percent of the attributes in full. All other demigods have the same attributes in less quantity, whereas human beings possess the attributes in very minute quantity. The standard of perfection for a human being is to develop the attributes up to seventy-eight percent in full. The living being can never possess attributes like Śiva, Viṣṇu or Lord Kṛṣṇa. A living being can become godly by developing the seventy-eight-percent transcendental attributes in fullness, but he can never become a God like Śiva, Viṣṇu or Kṛṣṇa. He can become a Brahmā in due course. The godly living beings who are all residents of the planets in the spiritual sky are eternal associates of God in different spiritual planets called Hari-dhāma and Maheśa-dhāma. The abode of Lord Kṛṣṇa above all spiritual planets is called Kṛṣṇaloka or Goloka Vṛndāvana, and the perfected living being, by developing seventy-eight percent of the above attributes in fullness, can enter the planet of Kṛṣṇaloka after leaving the present material body.

TEXT 29

जन्म गुह्यं भगवतो य एतत्प्रयतो नरः ।
सायं प्रातर्गृणन् भक्त्या दुःखग्रामाद्विमुच्यते ॥२९॥

janma guhyaṁ bhagavato
ya etat prayato naraḥ

sāyaṁ prātar gṛṇan bhaktyā
duḥkha-grāmād vimucyate

janma—birth; *guhyam*—mysterious; *bhagavataḥ*—of the Lord; *yaḥ*—one; *etat*—all these; *prayataḥ*—carefully; *naraḥ*—man; *sāyam*—evening; *prātaḥ*—morning; *gṛṇan*—recites; *bhaktyā*—with devotion; *duḥkha-grāmāt*—from all miseries; *vimucyate*—gets relief from.

TRANSLATION

Whoever carefully recites the mysterious appearances of the Lord, with devotion in the morning and in the evening, gets relief from all miseries of life.

PURPORT

In the *Bhagavad-gītā* the Personality of Godhead has declared that anyone who knows the principles of the transcendental birth and activities of the Lord will go back to Godhead after being relieved from this material tabernacle. So simply knowing factually the mysterious way of the Lord's incarnation in this material world can liberate one from material bondage. Therefore the birth and activities of the Lord, as manifested by Him for the welfare of the people in general, are not ordinary. They are mysterious, and only by those who carefully try to go deep into the matter by spiritual devotion is the mystery discovered. Thus one gets liberation from material bondage. It is advised therefore that one who simply recites this chapter of *Bhāgavatam,* describing the appearance of the Lord in different incarnations, in sincerity and devotion, can have insight into the birth and activities of the Lord. The very word *vimukti,* or liberation, indicates that the Lord's birth and activities are all transcendental; otherwise simply by reciting them one could not attain liberation. They are therefore mysterious, and those who do not follow the prescribed regulations of devotional service are not entitled to enter into the mysteries of His births and activities.

TEXT 30

एतद्रूपं भगवतो ह्यरूपस्य चिदात्मनः ।
मायागुणैर्विरचितं महदादिभिरात्मनि ॥३०॥

etad rūpaṁ bhagavato
hy arūpasya cid-ātmanaḥ

māyā-guṇair viracitaṁ
mahadādibhir ātmani

etat—all these; *rūpam*—forms; *bhagavataḥ*—of the Lord; *hi*—certainly; *arūpasya*—of one who has no material form; *cit-ātmanaḥ*—of the Transcendence; *māyā*—material energy; *guṇaiḥ*—by the qualities; *viracitam*—manufactured; *mahat-ādibhiḥ*—with the ingredients of matter; *ātmani*—in the self.

TRANSLATION

The conception of the virāṭ universal form of the Lord, as appearing in the material world, is imaginary. It is to enable the less intelligent [and neophytes] to adjust to the idea of the Lord's having form. But factually the Lord has no material form.

PURPORT

The conception of the Lord known as the *viśva-rūpa* or the *virāṭ-rūpa* is particularly not mentioned along with the various incarnations of the Lord because all the incarnations of the Lord mentioned above are transcendental and there is not a tinge of materialism in their bodies. There is no difference between the body and self as there is in the conditioned soul. The *virāṭ-rūpa* is conceived for those who are just neophyte worshipers. For them the material *virāṭ-rūpa* is presented, and it will be explained in the Second Canto. In the *virāṭ-rūpa* the material manifestations of different planets have been conceived as His legs, hands, etc. Actually all such descriptions are for the neophytes. The neophytes cannot conceive of anything beyond matter. The material conception of the Lord is not counted in the list of His factual forms. As Paramātmā, or Supersoul, the Lord is within each and every material form, even within the atoms, but the outward material form is but an imagination, both for the Lord and for the living being. The present forms of the conditioned souls are also not factual. The conclusion is that the material conception of the body of the Lord as *virāṭ* is imaginary. Both the Lord and the living beings are living spirits and have original spiritual bodies.

TEXT 31

यथा नभसि मेघौघो रेणुर्वा पार्थिवोऽनिले।
एवं द्रष्टरि दृश्यत्वमारोपितमबुद्धिभिः ॥३१॥

yathā nabhasi meghaugho
reṇur vā pārthivo 'nile
evaṁ draṣṭari dṛśyatvam
āropitam abuddhibhiḥ

yathā—as it is; *nabhasi*—in the sky; *megha-oghaḥ*—a mass of clouds; *reṇuḥ*—dust; *vā*—as well as; *pārthivaḥ*—muddiness; *anile*—in the air; *evam*—thus; *draṣṭari*—to the seer; *dṛśyatvam*—for the purpose of seeing; *āropitam*—is implied; *abuddhibhiḥ*—by the less intelligent persons.

TRANSLATION

Clouds and dust are carried by the air, but less intelligent persons say that the sky is cloudy and the air is dirty. Similarly, they also implant material bodily conceptions on the spirit self.

PURPORT

It is further confirmed herein that with our material eyes and senses we cannot see the Lord, who is all spirit. We cannot even detect the spiritual spark which exists within the material body of the living being. We look to the outward covering of the body or subtle mind of the living being, but we cannot see the spiritual spark within the body. So we have to accept the living being's presence by the presence of his gross body. Similarly, those who want to see the Lord with their present material eyes or with the material senses are advised to meditate on the gigantic external feature called the *virāṭ-rūpa.* For instance, when a particular gentleman goes in his car, which can be seen very easily, we identify the car with the man within the car. When the President goes out in his particular car, we say, "There is the President." For the time being we identify the car with the President. Similarly, less intelligent men who want to see God immediately without necessary qualification are shown first the gigantic material cosmos as the form of the Lord, although the Lord is within and without. The clouds in the sky and the blue of the sky are better appreciated in this connection. Although the bluish tint of the sky and the sky itself are different, we conceive of the color of the sky as blue. But that is a general conception for the laymen only.

TEXT 32

अतः परं यदव्यक्तमव्यूढगुणबृंहितम् ।
अदृष्टाश्रुतवस्तुत्वात्स जीवो यत्पुनर्भवः ॥३२॥

ataḥ paraṁ yad avyaktam
avyūḍha-guṇa-bṛṁhitam
adṛṣṭāśruta-vastutvāt
sa jīvo yat punar-bhavaḥ

ataḥ—this; *param*—beyond; *yat*—which; *avyaktam*—unmanifested; *avyūḍha*—without formal shape; *guṇa-bṛṁhitam*—affected by the qualities; *adṛṣṭa*—unseen; *aśruta*—unheard; *vastutvāt*—being like that; *saḥ*—that; *jīvaḥ*—living being; *yat*—that which; *punaḥ-bhavaḥ*—takes birth repeatedly.

TRANSLATION

Beyond this gross conception of form is another, subtle conception of form which is without formal shape and is unseen, unheard and unmanifest. The living being has his form beyond this subtlety, otherwise he could not have repeated births.

PURPORT

As the gross cosmic manifestation is conceived as the gigantic body of the Lord, so also there is the conception of His subtle form, which is simply realized without being seen, heard or manifested. But in fact all these gross or subtle conceptions of the body are in relation with the living beings. The living being has his spiritual form beyond this gross material or subtle psychic existence. The gross body and psychic functions cease to act as soon as the living being leaves the visible gross body. In fact, we say that the living being has gone away because he is unseen and unheard. Even when the gross body is not acting when the living being is in sound sleep, we know that he is within the body by his breathing. So the living being's passing away from the body does not mean that there is no existence of the living soul. It is there, otherwise how can he repeat his births again and again?

The conclusion is that the Lord is eternally existent in His transcendental form, which is neither gross nor subtle like that of the living being; His body is never to be compared to the gross and subtle bodies of the living being. All such conceptions of God's body are imaginary. The living being has his eternal spiritual form, which is conditioned only by his material contamination.

TEXT 33

यत्रेमे सदसद्रूपे प्रतिषिद्धे स्वसंविदा।
अविद्ययात्मनि कृते इति तद्ब्रह्मदर्शनम् ॥३३॥

yatreme sad-asad-rūpe
pratiṣiddhe sva-saṁvidā
avidyayātmani kṛte
iti tad brahma-darśanam

yatra—whenever; *ime*—in all these; *sat-asat*—gross and subtle; *rūpe*—in the forms of; *pratiṣiddhe*—on being nullified; *sva-saṁvidā*—by self-realization; *avidyayā*—by ignorance; *ātmani*—in the self; *kṛte*—having been imposed; *iti*—thus; *tat*—that is; *brahma-darśanam*—the process of seeing the Absolute.

TRANSLATION

Whenever a person experiences, by self-realization, that both the gross and subtle bodies have nothing to do with the pure self, at that time he sees himself as well as the Lord.

PURPORT

The difference between self-realization and material illusion is to know that the temporary or illusory impositions of material energy in the shape of gross and subtle bodies are superficial coverings of the self. The coverings take place due to ignorance. Such coverings are never effective in the person of the Personality of Godhead. Knowing this convincingly is called liberation, or seeing the Absolute. This means that perfect self-realization is made possible by adoption of godly or spiritual life. Self-realization means becoming indifferent to the needs of the gross and subtle bodies and becoming serious about the activities of the self. The impetus for activities is generated from the self, but such activities become illusory due to ignorance of the real position of the self. By ignorance, self-interest is calculated in terms of the gross and subtle bodies, and therefore a whole set of activities is spoiled, life after life. When, however, one meets the self by proper culture, the activities of the self begin. Therefore a man who is engaged in the activities of the self is called *jīvan-mukta,* or a liberated person even in the conditional existence.

This perfect stage of self-realization is attained not by artificial means, but under the lotus feet of the Lord, who is always transcendental. In the *Bhagavad-gītā* the Lord says that He is present in everyone's heart, and from Him only all knowledge, remembrance or forgetfulness take place. When the living being desires to be an enjoyer of material energy (illusory phenomena), the Lord covers the living being in the mystery of forgetfulness, and thus the living being misinterprets the gross body and subtle mind to be his own self. And by culture of transcendental knowledge, when the living being prays to the Lord for deliverance from the clutches of forgetfulness, the Lord, by His causeless mercy, removes the living being's illusory curtain, and thus he realizes his own self. He then engages himself in the service of the Lord in his eternal constitutional position, becoming liberated from the conditioned life. All this is executed by the Lord either through His external potency or directly by the internal potency.

TEXT 34

यद्येषोपरता देवी माया वैशारदी मतिः ।
सम्पन्न एवेति विदुर्महिम्नि स्वे महीयते ॥३४॥

yady eṣoparatā devī
māyā vaiśāradī matiḥ
sampanna eveti vidur
mahimni sve mahīyate

yadi—if, however; *eṣā*—they; *uparatā*—subsided; *devī māyā*—illusory energy; *vaiśāradī*—full of knowledge; *matiḥ*—enlightenment; *sampannaḥ*—enriched with; *eva*—certainly; *iti*—thus; *viduḥ*—being cognizant of; *mahimni*—in the glories; *sve*—of the self; *mahīyate*—being situated in.

TRANSLATION

If the illusory energy subsides and the living entity becomes fully enriched with knowledge by the grace of the Lord, then he becomes at once enlightened with self-realization and thus becomes situated in his own glory.

PURPORT

Because the Lord is the Absolute Transcendence, all of His forms, names, pastimes, attributes, associates and energies are identical with Him. His transcendental energy acts according to His omnipotency. The same energy acts as His external, internal and marginal energies, and by His omnipotency He can perform anything and everything through the agency of any of the above energies. He can turn the external energy into internal by His will.

Therefore by His grace the external energy, which is employed in illusioning those living beings who want to have it, subsides by the will of the Lord in terms of repentance and penance for the conditioned soul. And the very same energy then acts to help the purified living being make progress on the path of self-realization. The example of electrical energy is very appropriate in this connection. The expert electrician can utilize the electrical energy for both heating and cooling by adjustment only. Similarly, the external energy, which now bewilders the living being into continuation of birth and death, is turned into internal potency by the will of the Lord to lead the living being to eternal life. When a living being is thus graced by the Lord, he is placed in his proper constitutional position to enjoy eternal spiritual life.

TEXT 35

एवं जन्मानि कर्माणि ह्यकर्तुरजनस्य च।
वर्णयन्ति स्म कवयो वेदगुह्यानि हृत्पतेः ॥३५॥

evaṁ janmāni karmāṇi
hy akartur ajanasya ca
varṇayanti sma kavayo
veda-guhyāni hṛt-pateḥ

evam—thus; *janmāni*—birth; *karmāṇi*—activities; *hi*—certainly; *akartuḥ*—of the inactive; *ajanasya*—of the unborn; *ca*—and; *varṇayanti*—describe; *sma*—in the past; *kavayaḥ*—the learned; *veda-guhyāni*—undiscoverable by the *Vedas; hṛt-pateḥ*—of the Lord of the heart.

TRANSLATION

Thus learned men describe the births and activities of the unborn and inactive, which is undiscoverable even in the Vedic literatures. He is the Lord of the heart.

PURPORT

Both the Lord and the living entities are essentially all spiritual. Therefore both of them are eternal, and neither of them has birth and death. The difference is that the so-called births and disappearances of the Lord are unlike those of the living beings. The living beings who take birth and then again accept death are bound by the laws of material nature. But the so-called appearance and disappearance of the Lord are not actions of material nature, but are demonstrations of the internal potency of the Lord. They are described by the great sages for the purpose of self-realization. It is stated in the *Bhagavad-gītā* by the Lord that His so-called birth in the material world and His activities are all transcendental. And simply by meditation on such activities one can attain realization of Brahman and thus become liberated from material bondage. In the *śrutis* it is said that the birthless appears to take birth. The Supreme has nothing to do, but because He is omnipotent, everything is performed by Him naturally, as if done automatically. As a matter of fact, the appearance and disappearance of the Supreme Personality of Godhead and His different activities are all confidential, even to the Vedic literatures. Yet they are displayed by the Lord to bestow mercy upon the conditioned souls. We should always take advantage of the narrations of the activities of the Lord, which are meditations on Brahman in the most convenient and palatable form.

TEXT 36

स वा इदं विश्वममोघलीलः
सृजत्यवत्यत्ति न सज्जतेऽस्मिन् ।
भूतेषु चान्तर्हित आत्मतन्त्रः
षाड्वर्गिकं जिघ्रति षड्गुणेशः ॥३६॥

sa vā idaṁ viśvam amogha-līlaḥ
sṛjaty avaty atti na sajjate 'smin
bhūteṣu cāntarhita ātma-tantraḥ
ṣāḍ-vargikaṁ jighrati ṣaḍ-guṇeśaḥ

saḥ—the Supreme Lord; *vā*—alternately; *idam*—this; *viśvam*—manifested universes; *amogha-līlaḥ*—one whose activities are spotless; *sṛjati*—creates; *avati atti*—maintains and annihilates; *na*—not; *sajjate*—is affected by; *asmin*—in them; *bhūteṣu*—in all living beings; *ca*—also; *antarhitaḥ*—living within; *ātma-tantraḥ*—self-independent; *ṣāṭ-vargikam*—endowed with all the potencies of His opulences; *jighrati*—superficially attached, like smelling the fragrance; *ṣaṭ-guṇa-īśaḥ*—master of the six senses.

TRANSLATION

The Lord, whose activities are always spotless, is the master of the six senses and is fully omnipotent with six opulences. He creates

the manifested universes, maintains them and annihilates them without being in the least affected. He is within every living being and is always independent.

PURPORT

The prime difference between the Lord and the living entities is that the Lord is the creator and the living entities are the created. Here He is called the *amogha-līlaḥ,* which indicates that there is nothing lamentable in His creation. Those who create disturbance in His creation are themselves disturbed. He is transcendental to all material afflictions because He is full with all six opulences, namely wealth, power, fame, beauty, knowledge and renunciation, and thus He is the master of the senses. He creates these manifested universes in order to reclaim the living beings who are within them suffering threefold miseries, maintains them, and in due course annihilates them without being the least affected by such actions. He is connected with this material creation very superficially, as one smells odor without being connected with the odorous article. Nongodly elements, therefore, can never approach Him, despite all endeavors.

TEXT 37

न चास्य कश्चिन्निपुणेन धातु-
रवैति जन्तुः कुमनीष ऊतीः ।
नामानि रूपाणि मनोवचोभिः
सन्तन्वतो नटचर्यामिवाज्ञः ॥३७॥

na cāsya kaścin nipuṇena dhātur
avaiti jantuḥ kumanīṣa ūtīḥ
nāmāni rūpāṇi mano-vacobhiḥ
santanvato naṭa-caryām ivājñaḥ

na—not; *ca*—and; *asya*—of Him; *kaścit*—anyone; *nipuṇena*—by dexterity; *dhātuḥ*—of the creator; *avaiti*—can know; *jantuḥ*—the living being; *kumanīṣaḥ*—with a poor fund of knowledge; *ūtīḥ*—activities of the Lord; *nāmāni*—His names; *rūpāṇi*—His forms; *manaḥ-vacobhiḥ*—by dint of mental speculation or deliverance of speeches; *santanvataḥ*—displaying; *naṭa-caryām*—a dramatic action; *iva*—like; *ajñaḥ*—the foolish.

TRANSLATION

The foolish with a poor fund of knowledge cannot know the transcendental nature of the forms, names and activities of the Lord, who is playing like an actor in a drama. Nor can they express such things, neither in their speculations nor in their words.

PURPORT

No one can properly describe the transcendental nature of the Absolute Truth. Therefore it is said that He is beyond the expression of mind and speech. And yet there are some men, with a poor fund of knowledge, who desire to understand the Absolute Truth by imperfect mental speculation and faulty description of His activities. To the layman His activities, appearance and disappearance, His names, His forms, His paraphernalia, His personalities and all things in relation with Him are mysterious. There are two classes of materialists, namely the fruitive workers and the empiric philosophers. The fruitive workers have practically no information of the Absolute Truth, and the mental speculators, after being frustrated in fruitive activities, turn their faces towards the Absolute Truth and try to know Him by mental speculation. And for all these men, the Absolute Truth is a mystery, as the jugglery of the magician is a mystery to children. Being deceived by the jugglery of the Supreme Being, the nondevotees, who may be very dexterous in fruitive work and mental speculation, are always in ignorance. With such limited knowledge, they are unable to penetrate into the mysterious region of transcendence. The mental speculators are a little more progressive than the gross materialists or the fruitive workers, but because they are also within the grip of illusion, they take it for granted that anything which has form, a name and activities is but a product of material energy. For them the Supreme Spirit is formless, nameless and inactive. And because such mental speculators equalize the transcendental name and form of the Lord with mundane names and form, they are in fact in ignorance. With such a poor fund of knowledge, there is no access to the real nature of the Supreme Being. As stated in *Bhagavad-gītā,* the Lord is always in a transcendental position, even when He is within the material world. But ignorant men consider the Lord one of the great personalities of the world, and thus they are misled by the illusory energy.

TEXT 38

स वेद धातुः पदवीं परस्य
दुरन्तवीर्यस्य रथाङ्गपाणेः ।

योऽमायया सन्ततयानुवृत्त्या
भजेत तत्पादसरोजगन्धम् ॥३८॥

sa veda dhātuḥ padavīṁ parasya
duranta-vīryasya rathāṅga-pāṇeḥ
yo 'māyayā santatayānuvṛttyā
bhajeta t at-pāda-saroja-gandham

saḥ—He alone; *veda*—can know; *dhātuḥ*—of the creator; *padavīm*—glories; *parasya*—of the transcendence; *duranta-vīryasya*—of the greatly powerful; *ratha-aṅga-pāṇeḥ*—of Lord Kṛṣṇa, who bears in His hand the wheel of a chariot; *yaḥ*—one who; *amāyayā*—without reservation; *santatayā*—without any gap; *anuvṛttyā*—favorably; *bhajeta*—renders service; *tat-pāda*—of His feet; *saroja-gandham*—fragrance of the lotus.

TRANSLATION

Only those who render unreserved, uninterrupted, favorable service unto the lotus feet of Lord Kṛṣṇa, who carries the wheel of the chariot in His hand, can know the creator of the universe in His full glory, power and transcendence.

PURPORT

Only the pure devotees can know the transcendental name, form and activities of Lord Kṛṣṇa due to their being completely freed from the reactions of fruitive work and mental speculation. The pure devotees have nothing to derive as personal profit from their unalloyed service to the Lord. They render incessant service to the Lord spontaneously, without any reservation. Everyone within the creation of the Lord is rendering service to the Lord indirectly or directly. No one is an exception to this law of the Lord. Those who are rendering service indirectly, being forced by the illusory agent of the Lord, are rendering service unto Him unfavorably. But those who are rendering service unto Him directly under the direction of His beloved agent are rendering service unto Him favorably. Such favorable servitors are devotees of the Lord, and by the grace of the Lord they can enter into the mysterious region of transcendence by the mercy of the Lord. But the mental speculators remain in darkness all the time. As stated in *Bhagavad-gītā,* the Lord Himself guides the pure devotees toward the path of realization due to their constant engagement in the loving service of the Lord in spontaneous affection. That is the secret of entering into the kingdom of God. Fruitive activities and speculation are no qualifications for entering.

TEXT 39

अथेह धन्या भगवन्त इत्थं
यद्वासुदेवेऽखिललोकनाथे ।
कुर्वन्ति सर्वात्मकमात्मभावं
न यत्र भूयः परिवर्त उग्रः ॥३९॥

atheha dhanyā bhagavanta itthaṁ
yad vāsudeve 'khila-loka-nāthe
kurvanti sarvātmakam ātma-bhāvaṁ
na yatra bhūyaḥ parivarta ugraḥ

atha—thus; *iha*—in this world; *dhanyāḥ*—successful; *bhagavantaḥ*—perfectly cognizant; *ittham*—such; *yat*—what; *vāsudeve*—unto the Personality of Godhead; *akhila*—all-embracing; *loka-nāthe*—unto the proprietor of all the universes; *kurvanti*—inspires; *sarva-ātmakam*—one-hundred-percent; *ātma*—spirit; *bhāvam*—ecstasy; *na*—never; *yatra*—wherein; *bhūyaḥ*—again; *parivartaḥ*—repetition; *ugraḥ*—dreadful.

TRANSLATION

Only by making such inquiries in this world can one be successful and perfectly cognizant, for such inquiries invoke transcendental ecstatic love unto the Personality of Godhead, who is the proprietor of all the universes, and guarantee cent-percent immunity from the dreadful repetition of birth and death.

PURPORT

The inquiries of the sages headed by Śaunaka are herewith praised by Sūta Gosvāmī on the merit of their transcendental nature. As already concluded, only the devotees of the Lord can know Him to a considerable extent, and no one else can know Him at all, so the devotees are perfectly cognizant of all spiritual knowledge. The Personality of Godhead is the last word in Absolute Truth. Impersonal Brahman and localized Paramātmā (Supersoul) are included in the knowledge of the Personality of Godhead. So one who knows the Personality of Godhead can automatically know all about Him, His multipotencies and His expansions. So the devotees are congratulated as being all-successful. A cent-percent devotee of the Lord is immune to the dreadful material miseries of repeated birth and death.

TEXT 40

इदं भागवतं नाम पुराणं ब्रह्मसम्मितम् ।
उत्तमश्लोकचरितं चकार भगवानृषिः ।
निःश्रेयसाय लोकस्य धन्यं स्वस्त्ययनं महत् ॥४०॥

idaṁ bhāgavataṁ nāma
purāṇaṁ brahma-sammitam
uttama-śloka-caritaṁ
cakāra bhagavān ṛṣiḥ
niḥśreyasāya lokasya
dhanyaṁ svasty-ayanaṁ mahat

idam—this; *bhāgavatam*—book containing the narration of the Personality of Godhead and His pure devotees; *nāma*—of the name; *purāṇam*—supplementary to the *Vedas; brahma-sammitam*—incarnation of Lord Śrī Kṛṣṇa; *uttama-śloka*—of the Personality of Godhead; *caritam*—activities; *cakāra*—compiled; *bhagavān*—incarnation of the Personality of Godhead; *ṛṣiḥ*—Śrī Vyāsadeva; *niḥśreyasāya*—for the ultimate good; *lokasya*—of all people; *dhanyam*—fully successful; *svasti-ayanam*—all-blissful; *mahat*—all-perfect.

TRANSLATION

This Śrīmad-Bhāgavatam is the literary incarnation of God, and it is compiled by Śrīla Vyāsadeva, the incarnation of God. It is meant for the ultimate good of all people, and it is all-successful, all-blissful and all-perfect.

PURPORT

Lord Śrī Caitanya Mahāprabhu declared that *Śrīmad-Bhāgavatam* is the spotless sound representation of all Vedic knowledge and history. There are selected histories of great devotees who are in direct contact with the Personality of Godhead. *Śrīmad-Bhāgavatam* is the literary incarnation of Lord Śrī Kṛṣṇa and is therefore nondifferent from Him. *Śrīmad-Bhāgavatam* should be worshiped as respectfully as we worship the Lord. Thereby we can derive the ultimate blessings of the Lord through its careful and patient study. As God is all light, all bliss and all perfection, so also is *Śrīmad-Bhāgavatam.* We can have all the transcendental light of the Supreme Brahman, Śrī Kṛṣṇa, from the recitation of *Śrīmad-Bhāgavatam,* provided it is received through the medium of the transparent spiritual master. Lord Caitanya's private secretary Śrīla Svarūpa Dāmodara Gosvāmī advised all intending visitors who came to see the Lord at Purī to make a study of the *Bhāgavatam* from the person *Bhāgavatam.* Person *Bhāgavatam* is the self-realized bona fide spiritual master, and through him only can one understand the lessons of *Bhāgavatam* in order to receive the desired result. One can derive from the study of the *Bhāgavatam* all benefits that are possible to be derived from the personal presence of the Lord. It carries with it all the transcendental blessings of Lord Śrī Kṛṣṇa that we can expect from His personal contact.

TEXT 41

तदिदं ग्राहयामास सुतमात्मवतां वरम् ।
सर्ववेदेतिहासानां सारं सारं समुद्धृतम् ॥४१॥

tad idaṁ grāhayām āsa
sutam ātmavatāṁ varam
sarva-vedetihāsānāṁ
sāraṁ sāraṁ samuddhṛtam

tat—that; *idam*—this; *grāhayām āsa*—made to accept; *sutam*—unto his son; *ātmavatām*—of the self-realized; *varam*—most respectful; *sarva*—all; *veda*—Vedic literatures (books of knowledge); *itihāsānām*—of all the histories; *sāram*—cream; *sāram*—cream; *samuddhṛtam*—taken out.

TRANSLATION

Śrī Vyāsadeva delivered it to his son, who is the most respected among the self-realized, after extracting the cream of all Vedic literatures and histories of the universe.

PURPORT

Men with a poor fund of knowledge only accept the history of the world from the time of Buddha, or since 600 B.C., and prior to this period all histories mentioned in the scriptures are calculated by them to be only imaginary stories. That is not a fact. All the stories mentioned in the *Purāṇas* and *Mahābhārata,* etc., are actual histories, not only of this planet but also of millions of other planets within the universe. Sometimes the history of planets beyond this world appears to such men to be unbelievable. But they do not know that different planets are not equal in all respects and that therefore some of the historical facts derived from other planets do not correspond with the experience of this planet. Considering the different situation of different planets and also time and circumstances, there is nothing wonderful in the stories of the *Purāṇas,* nor are they imaginary. We should always remember the maxim that one man's food is another man's poison. We should not, therefore, reject the stories and histories of the *Purāṇas* as imaginary. The great *ṛṣis* like Vyāsa had no business putting some imaginary stories in their literatures.

In the *Śrīmad-Bhāgavatam* historical facts selected from the histories of different planets have been depicted. It is therefore accepted by all the spiritual authorities as the *Mahā-purāṇa.* The special significance of these histories is that they are all connected with activities of the Lord in a different time and atmosphere. Śrīla Śukadeva Gosvāmī is the topmost personality of all the self-realized souls, and he accepted this as the subject of studies from his father, Vyāsadeva. Śrīla Vyāsadeva is the great authority, and the subject matter of *Śrīmad-Bhāgavatam* being so important, he delivered the message first to his great son Śrīla Śukadeva Gosvāmī. It is compared to the cream of the milk. Vedic literature is like the milk ocean of knowledge. Cream or butter is the most palatable essence of milk, and so also is *Śrīmad-Bhāgavatam,* for it contains all palatable, instructive and authentic versions of different activities of the Lord and His devotees. There is no gain, however, in accepting the message of *Bhāgavatam* from the unbelievers, atheists and professional reciters who make a trade of *Bhāgavatam* for the laymen. It was delivered to Śrīla Śukadeva Gosvāmī, and he had nothing to do with the *Bhāgavata* business. He did not have to maintain family expenses by such trade. *Śrīmad-Bhāgavatam* should therefore be received from the representative of Śukadeva, who must be in the renounced order of life without family encumbrance. Milk is undoubtedly very good and nourishing, but when it is touched by the mouth of a snake it is no longer nourishing; rather, it becomes a source of death. Similarly, those who are not strictly in the Vaiṣṇava discipline should not make a business of this *Bhāgavatam* and become a cause of spiritual death for so many hearers. In the *Bhagavad-gītā* the Lord says that the purpose of all the *Vedas* is to know Him (Lord Kṛṣṇa), and *Śrīmad-Bhāgavatam* is Lord Śrī Kṛṣṇa Himself in the form of recorded knowledge. Therefore, it is the cream of all the *Vedas,* and it contains all historical facts of all times in relation with Śrī Kṛṣṇa. It is factually the essence of all histories.

TEXT 42

स तु संश्रावयामास महाराजं परीक्षितम् ।
प्रायोपविष्टं गङ्गायां परीतं परमर्षिभिः ॥४२॥

sa tu saṁśrāvayām āsa
mahārājaṁ parīkṣitam
prāyopaviṣṭaṁ gaṅgāyāṁ
parītaṁ paramarṣibhiḥ

saḥ—the son of Vyāsadeva; *tu*—again; *saṁśrāvayām āsa*—make them audible; *mahā-rājam*—unto the emperor; *parīkṣitam*—of the name Parīkṣit; *prāya-upaviṣṭam*—who sat until death without food or drink; *gaṅgāyām*—on the bank of the Ganges; *parītam*—being surrounded; *parama-ṛṣibhiḥ*—by great sages.

TRANSLATION

Śukadeva Gosvāmī, the son of Vyāsadeva, in his turn delivered the Bhāgavatam to the great Emperor Parīkṣit, who sat surrounded by sages on the bank of the Ganges, awaiting death without taking food or drink.

PURPORT

All transcendental messages are received properly in the chain of disciplic succession. This disciplic succession is called *paramparā.* Unless therefore *Bhāgavatam* or any other Vedic literatures are received through the *paramparā* system, the reception of knowledge is not bona fide. Vyāsadeva delivered the message to Śukadeva Gosvāmī, and from Śukadeva Gosvāmī, Sūta Gosvāmī received the message. One should therefore receive the message of *Bhāgavatam* from Sūta Gosvāmī or from his representative and not from any irrelevant interpreter.

Emperor Parīkṣit received the information of his death in time, and he at once left his kingdom and family and sat down on the bank of the Ganges to fast till death. All great sages, *ṛṣis,* philosophers, mystics, etc., went there due to his imperial position. They offered many suggestions about his immediate duty, and at last it was settled that he would hear from Śukadeva Gosvāmī about Lord Kṛṣṇa. Thus the *Bhāgavatam* was spoken to him.

Śrīpāda Śaṅkarācārya, who preached Māyāvāda philosophy and stressed the impersonal feature of the Absolute, also recommended that one must take shelter at the lotus feet of Lord Śrī Kṛṣṇa, for there is no hope of gain from debating. Indirectly Śrīpāda Śaṅkarācārya admitted that what he had preached in the flowery grammatical interpretations of the *Vedānta-sūtra* cannot help one at the time of death. At the critical hour of death one must recite the name of Govinda. This is the recommendation of all great transcendentalists. Śukadeva Gosvāmī had long ago stated the same truth, that at the end one must remember Nārāyaṇa. That is the essence of all spiritual activities. In pursuance of this eternal truth, *Śrīmad-Bhāgavatam* was heard by Emperor Parīkṣit, and it was recited by the able Śukadeva Gosvāmī. And both the speaker and the receiver of the messages of *Bhāgavatam* were duly delivered by the same medium.

TEXT 43

कृष्णे स्वधामोपगते धर्मज्ञानादिभिः सह।
कलौ नष्टदृशामेष पुराणार्कोऽधुनोदितः ॥४३॥

kṛṣṇe sva-dhāmopagate
dharma-jñānādibhiḥ saha
kalau naṣṭa-dṛśām eṣa
purāṇārko 'dhunoditaḥ

kṛṣṇe—in Kṛṣṇa's; *sva-dhāma*—own abode; *upagate*—having returned; *dharma*—religion; *jñāna*—knowledge; *ādibhiḥ*—combined together; *saha*—along with; *kalau*—in the Kali-yuga; *naṣṭa-dṛśām*—of persons who have lost their sight; *eṣaḥ*—all these; *purāṇa-arkaḥ*—the *Purāṇa* which is brilliant like the sun; *adhunā*—just now; *uditaḥ*—has arisen.

TRANSLATION

This Bhāgavata Purāṇa is as brilliant as the sun, and it has arisen just after the departure of Lord Kṛṣṇa to His own abode, accompanied by religion, knowledge, etc. Persons who have lost their vision due to the dense darkness of ignorance in the age of Kali shall get light from this Purāṇa.

PURPORT

Lord Śrī Kṛṣṇa has His eternal *dhāma,* or abode, where He eternally enjoys Himself with His eternal associates and paraphernalia. And His eternal abode is a manifestation of His internal energy, whereas the material world is a manifestation of His external energy. When He descends on the material world, He displays Himself with all paraphernalia in His internal potency, which is called *ātma-māyā.* In the *Bhagavad-gītā* the Lord says that He descends by His own potency (*ātma-māyā*). His form, name, fame, paraphernalia, abode, etc., are not, therefore, creations of matter. He descends to reclaim the fallen souls and to reestablish codes of religion which are directly enacted by Him. Except for God, no one can establish the principles of religion. Either He or a suitable person empowered by Him can dictate the codes of religion. Real religion means to know God, our relation with Him and our duties in relation with Him and to know ultimately our destination after leaving this material body. The conditioned souls, who are entrapped by the material energy, hardly know all these principles of life. Most of them are like animals engaged in eating, sleeping, fearing and mating. They are mostly engaged in sense enjoyment under the pretension of religiosity, knowledge or salvation. They are still more blind in the present age of quarrel, or Kali-yuga. In the Kali-yuga the population is just a royal edition of the animals. They have nothing to do with spiritual knowledge or godly religious life. They are so blind that they cannot see anything beyond the jurisdiction of the subtle mind, intelligence or ego, but they are very much proud of their advancement in knowledge, science and material prosperity. They can risk their lives to become a dog or hog just after leaving the present body, for they have completely lost sight of the ultimate aim of life. The Personality of Godhead, Śrī Kṛṣṇa, appeared before us just a little prior to the beginning of Kali-yuga, and He returned to His eternal home practically at the commencement of Kali-yuga. While He was present, He exhibited everything by His different activities. He spoke the *Bhagavad-gītā* specifically and eradicated all pretentious principles of religiosity. And prior to His departure from this material world, He empowered Śrī Vyāsadeva through Nārada to compile the messages of the *Śrīmad-Bhāgavatam,* and thus both the *Bhagavad-gītā* and the *Śrīmad-Bhāgavatam* are like torchbearers for the blind people of this age. In other words, if men in this age of Kali want to see the real light of life, they must take to these two books only, and their aim of life will be fulfilled. *Bhagavad-gītā* is the preliminary study of the *Bhāgavatam.* And *Śrīmad-Bhāgavatam* is the *summum bonum* of life, Lord Śrī Kṛṣṇa personified. We must therefore accept *Śrīmad-Bhāgavatam* as the direct representation of Lord Kṛṣṇa. One who can see *Śrīmad-Bhāgavatam* can see also Lord Śrī Kṛṣṇa in person. They are identical.

TEXT 44

तत्र कीर्तयतो विप्रा विप्रर्षेर्भूरितेजसः ।
अहं चाध्यगमं तत्र निविष्टस्तदनुग्रहात् ।
सोऽहं वः श्रावयिष्यामि यथाधीतं यथामति ॥४४॥

tatra kīrtayato viprā
viprarṣer bhūri-tejasaḥ
ahaṁ cādhyagamaṁ tatra
niviṣṭas tad-anugrahāt
so 'haṁ vaḥ śrāvayiṣyāmi
yathādhītaṁ yathā-mati

tatra—there; *kīrtayataḥ*—while reciting; *viprāḥ*—O *brāhmaṇas; vipra-ṛṣeḥ*—from the great *brāhmaṇa-ṛṣi; bhūri*—greatly; *tejasaḥ*—powerful; *aham*—I; *ca*—also; *adhyagamam*—could understand; *tatra*—in that meeting; *niviṣṭaḥ*—being perfectly attentive; *tat-anugrahāt*—by his mercy; *saḥ*—that very thing; *aham*—I; *vaḥ*—unto you; *śrāvayiṣyāmi*—shall let you hear; *yathā-adhītam yathā-mati*—as far as my realization.

TRANSLATION

O learned brāhmaṇas, when Śukadeva Gosvāmī recited Bhāgavatam there [in the presence of Emperor Parīkṣit], I heard him with rapt attention, and thus, by his mercy, I learned the Bhāgavatam from that great and powerful sage. Now I shall try to make you hear the very same thing as I learned it from him and as I have realized it.

PURPORT

One can certainly see directly the presence of Lord Śrī Kṛṣṇa in the pages of *Bhāgavatam* if one has heard it from a self-realized great soul like Śukadeva Gosvāmī. One cannot, however, learn *Bhāgavatam* from a bogus hired reciter whose aim of life is to earn some money out of such recitation and employ the earning in sex indulgence. No one can learn *Śrīmad-Bhāgavatam* who is associated with persons engaged in sex life. That is the secret of learning *Bhāgavatam.* Nor can one learn *Bhāgavatam* from one who interprets the text by his mundane scholarship. One has to learn *Bhāgavatam* from the representative of Śukadeva Gosvāmī, and no one else, if one at all wants to see Lord Śrī Kṛṣṇa in the pages. That is the process, and there is no alternative. Sūta Gosvāmī is a bona fide representative of Śukadeva Gosvāmī because he wants to present the message which he received from the great learned *brāhmaṇa.* Śukadeva Gosvāmī presented *Bhāgavatam* as he heard it from his great father, and so also Sūta Gosvāmī is presenting *Bhāgavatam* as he had heard it from Śukadeva Gosvāmī. Simple hearing is not all; one must realize the text with proper attention. The word *niviṣṭa* means that Sūta Gosvāmī drank the juice of *Bhāgavatam* through his ears. That is the real process of receiving *Bhāgavatam.* One should hear with rapt attention from the real person, and then he can at once realize the presence of Lord Kṛṣṇa in every page. The secret of knowing *Bhāgavatam* is mentioned here. No one can give rapt attention who is not pure in mind. No one can be pure in mind who is not pure in action. No one can be pure in action who is not pure in eating, sleeping, fearing and mating. But somehow or other if someone hears with rapt attention from the right person, at the very beginning one can assuredly see Lord Śrī Kṛṣṇa in person in the pages of *Bhāgavatam.*

Thus end the Bhaktivedanta purports of the First Canto, Third Chapter, of the Śrīmad-Bhāgavatam, *entitled "Kṛṣṇa Is the Source of All Incarnations."*

CHAPTER FOUR

The Appearance of Śrī Nārada

TEXT 1

व्यास उवाच

इति ब्रुवाणं संस्तूय मुनीनां दीर्घसत्रिणाम्।
वृद्धः कुलपतिः सूतं बह्वृचः शौनकोऽब्रवीत् ॥१॥

vyāsa uvāca
iti bruvāṇaṁ saṁstūya
munīnāṁ dīrgha-satriṇām
vṛddhaḥ kula-patiḥ sūtaṁ
bahvṛcaḥ śaunako 'bravīt

vyāsaḥ—Vyāsadeva; *uvāca*—said; *iti*—thus; *bruvāṇam*—speaking; *saṁstūya*—congratulating; *munīnām*—of the great sages; *dīrgha*—prolonged; *satriṇām*—of those engaged in the performance of sacrifice; *vṛddhaḥ*—elderly; *kula-patiḥ*—head of the assembly; *sūtam*—unto Sūta Gosvāmī; *bahu-ṛcaḥ*—learned; *śaunakaḥ*—of the name Śaunaka; *abravīt*—addressed.

TRANSLATION

On hearing Sūta Gosvāmī speak thus, Śaunaka Muni, who was the elderly, learned leader of all the ṛṣis engaged in that prolonged sacrificial ceremony, congratulated Sūta Gosvāmī by addressing him as follows.

PURPORT

In a meeting of learned men, when there are congratulations or addresses for the speaker, the qualifications of the congratulator should be as follows. He must be the leader of the house and an elderly man. He must be vastly learned also. Śrī Śaunaka Ṛṣi had all these qualifications, and thus he stood up to congratulate Śrī Sūta Gosvāmī when he expressed his desire to present *Śrīmad-Bhāgavatam* exactly as he heard it from Śukadeva Gosvāmī and also realized it personally. Personal realization does not mean that one should, out of vanity, attempt to show one's own learning by trying to surpass the previous *ācārya.* He must have full confidence in the previous *ācārya,* and at the same time he must realize the subject matter so nicely that he can present the matter for the particular circumstances in a suitable manner. *The original purpose of the text must be maintained.* No obscure meaning should be screwed out of it, yet it should be presented in an interesting manner for the understanding of the audience. This is called realization. The leader of the assembly, Śaunaka, could estimate the value of the speaker, Śrī Sūta Gosvāmī, simply by his uttering *yathādhītam* and *yathā-mati,* and therefore he was very glad to congratulate him in ecstasy. No learned man should be willing to hear a person who does not represent the original *ācārya.* So the speaker and the audience were bona fide in this meeting where *Bhāgavatam* was being recited for the second time. That should be the standard of recitation of *Bhāgavatam,* so that the real purpose can be served without difficulty. Unless this situation is created, *Bhagavatam* recitation for extraneous purposes is useless labor both for the speaker and for the audience.

TEXT 2

शौनक उवाच
सूत सूत महाभाग वद नो वदतां वर।
कथां भागवतीं पुण्यां यदाह भगवाञ्छुकः ॥२॥

śaunaka uvāca
sūta sūta mahā-bhāga
vada no vadatāṁ vara
kathāṁ bhāgavatīṁ puṇyāṁ
yad āha bhagavāñ chukaḥ

śaunakaḥ—Śaunaka; *uvāca*—said; *sūta sūta*—O Sūta Gosvāmī; *mahā-bhāga*—the most fortunate; *vada*—please speak; *naḥ*—unto us; *vadatām*—of those who can speak; *vara*—respected; *kathām*—message; *bhāgavatīm*—of the *Bhāgavatam; puṇyām*—pious; *yat*—which; *āha*—said; *bhagavān*—greatly powerful; *śukaḥ*—Śrī Śukadeva Gosvāmī.

TRANSLATION

Śaunaka said: O Sūta Gosvāmī, you are the most fortunate and respected of all those who can speak and recite. Please relate the pious message of Śrīmad-Bhāgavatam, which was spoken by the great and powerful sage Śukadeva Gosvāmī.

PURPORT

Sūta Gosvāmī is twice addressed herein by Śaunaka Gosvāmī out of great joy because he and the members of the assembly were eager to hear the text of *Bhāgavatam* uttered by Śukadeva Gosvāmī. They were not interested in hearing it from a bogus person who would interpret in his own way to suit his own purpose. Generally the so-called *Bhāgavatam* reciters are either professional readers or so-called learned impersonalists who cannot enter into the transcendental personal activities of the Supreme Person. Such impersonalists twist some meanings out of *Bhāgavatam* to suit and support impersonalist views, and the professional readers at once go to the Tenth Canto to misexplain the most confidential part of the Lord's pastimes. Neither of these reciters are bona fide persons to recite *Bhāgavatam.* Only one who is prepared to present *Bhāgavatam* in the light of Śukadeva Gosvāmī and only those who are prepared to hear Śukadeva Gosvāmī and his representative are bona fide participants in the transcendental discussion of *Śrīmad-Bhāgavatam.*

TEXT 3

कस्मिन् युगे प्रवृत्तेयं स्थाने वा केन हेतुना।
कुतः सञ्चोदितः कृष्णः कृतवान् संहितां मुनिः ॥३॥

kasmin yuge pravṛtteyaṁ
sthāne vā kena hetunā
kutaḥ sañcoditaḥ kṛṣṇaḥ
kṛtavān saṁhitāṁ muniḥ

kasmin—in which; *yuge*—period; *pravṛttā*—was begun; *iyam*—this; *sthāne*—in the place; *vā*—or; *kena*—on what; *hetunā*—ground; *kutaḥ*—wherefrom; *sañcoditaḥ*—inspired by; *kṛṣṇaḥ*—Kṛṣṇa-dvaipāyana Vyāsa; *kṛtavān*—compiled; *saṁhitām*—Vedic literature; *muniḥ*—the learned.

TRANSLATION

In what period and at what place was this first begun, and why was this taken up? From where did Kṛṣṇa-dvaipāyana Vyāsa, the great sage, get the inspiration to compile this literature?

PURPORT

Because *Śrīmad-Bhāgavatam* is the special contribution of Śrīla Vyāsadeva, there are so many inquiries by the learned Śaunaka Muni. It was known to them that Śrīla Vyāsadeva had already explained the text of the *Vedas* in various ways up to the *Mahābhārata* for the understanding of less intelligent women, *śūdras* and fallen members of the family of twice-born men. *Śrīmad-Bhāgavatam* is transcendental to all of them because it has nothing to do with anything mundane. So the inquiries are very intelligent and relevant.

TEXT 4

तस्य पुत्रो महायोगी समदृङ्निर्विकल्पकः।
एकान्तमतिरुन्निद्रो गूढो मूढ इवेयते ॥४॥

tasya putro mahā-yogī
sama-dṛṅ nirvikalpakaḥ
ekānta-matir unnidro
gūḍho mūḍha iveyate

tasya—his; *putraḥ*—son; *mahā-yogī*—a great devotee; *sama-dṛk*—equibalanced; *nirvikalpakaḥ*—absolute monist; *ekānta-matiḥ*—fixed in monism or oneness of mind; *unnidraḥ*—surpassed nescience; *gūḍhaḥ*—not exposed; *mūḍhaḥ*—stunted; *iva*—like; iyate—appears like.

TRANSLATION

His [Vyāsadeva's] son was a great devotee, an equibalanced monist, whose mind was always concentrated in monism. He was transcendental to mundane activities, but being unexposed, he appeared like an ignorant person.

PURPORT

Śrīla Śukadeva Gosvāmī was a liberated soul, and thus he remained always alert not to be trapped by the illusory energy. In the *Bhagavad-gītā* this alertness is very lucidly explained. The liberated soul and the conditioned soul have different engagements. The liberated soul is always engaged in the progressive path of spiritual attainment, which is something like a dream for the conditioned soul. The conditioned soul cannot imagine the actual engagements of the liberated soul. While the conditioned soul thus dreams about spiritual engagements, the liberated soul is awake. Similarly, the engagement of a conditioned soul appears to be a dream for the liberated soul. A conditioned soul and a liberated soul may apparently be on the same platform, but factually they are differently engaged, and their attention is always alert, either in sense enjoyment or in self-realization. The conditioned soul is absorbed in matter, whereas the liberated soul is completely indifferent to matter. This indifference is explained as follows.

TEXT 5

दृष्ट्वानुयान्तमृषिमात्मजमप्यनग्नं
देव्यो ह्रिया परिदधुर्न सुतस्य चित्रम् ।
तद्वीक्ष्य पृच्छति मुनौ जगदुस्तवास्ति
स्त्रीपुम्भिदा न तु सुतस्य विविक्तदृष्टेः ॥५॥

dṛṣṭvānuyāntam ṛṣim ātmajam apy anagnaṁ
devyo hriyā paridadhur na sutasya citram
tad vīkṣya pṛcchati munau jagadus tavāsti
strī-pum-bhidā na tu sutasya vivikta-dṛṣṭeḥ

dṛṣṭvā—by seeing; *anuyāntam*—following; *ṛṣim*—the sage; *ātmajam*—his son; *api*—in spite of; *anagnam*—not naked; *devyaḥ*—beautiful damsels; *hriyā*—out of shyness; *paridadhuḥ*—covered the body; *na*—not; *sutasya*—of the son; *citram*—astonishing; *tat vīkṣya*—by seeing that; *pṛcchati*—asking; *munau*—unto the *muni* (Vyāsa); *jagaduḥ*—replied; *tava*—your; *asti*—there are; *strī-pum*—male and female; *bhidā*—differences; *na*—not; *tu*—but; *sutasya*—of the son; *vivikta*—purified; *dṛṣṭeḥ*—of one who looks.

TRANSLATION

While Śrī Vyāsadeva was following his son, beautiful young damsels who were bathing naked covered their bodies with cloth, although Śrī Vyāsadeva himself was not naked. But they had not done so when his son had passed. The sage inquired about this, and the young ladies replied that his son was purified and when looking at them made no distinction between male and female. But the sage made such distinctions.

PURPORT

In the *Bhagavad-gītā* (5.18) it is said that a learned sage looks equally on a learned and gentle *brāhmaṇa,* a *caṇḍāla* (dog-eater), a dog or a cow due to his spiritual vision. Śrīla Śukadeva Gosvāmī attained that stage. Thus he did not see a male or female; he saw all living entities in different dress. The ladies who were bathing could understand the mind of a man simply by studying his demeanor, just as by looking at a child one can understand how innocent he is. Śukadeva Gosvāmī was a young boy sixteen years old, and therefore all the parts of his body were developed. He was naked also, and so were the ladies. But because Śukadeva Gosvāmī was transcendental to sex relations, he appeared very innocent. The ladies, by their special qualifications, could sense this at once, and therefore they were not very concerned about him. But when his father passed, the ladies quickly dressed. The ladies were exactly like his children or grandchildren, yet they reacted to the presence of Vyāsadeva according to the social custom because Śrīla Vyāsadeva played the part of a householder. A householder has to distinguish between a male and female; otherwise he cannot be a householder. One should, therefore, attempt to know the distinction between body and soul without any attachment for male and female. As long as such distinction is there, one should not try to become a *sannyāsī* like Śukadeva Gosvāmī. At least theoretically one must be convinced that a living entity is neither male nor female. The outward dress is made of matter by material nature to attract the opposite sex and thus keep one entangled in material existence. A liberated soul is above this perverted distinction. He does not distinguish between one living being and another. For him they are all one and the same spirit. The perfection of this spiritual vision is the liberated stage, and Śrīla Śukadeva Gosvāmī attained that stage. Śrīla Vyāsadeva was also in the transcendental stage, but because he was in the householder's life, he did not pretend to be a liberated soul, as a matter of custom.

TEXT 6

कथमालक्षितः पौरैः सम्प्राप्तः कुरुजाङ्गलान् ।
उन्मत्तमूकजडवद्विचरन् गजसाह्वये ॥६॥

katham ālakṣitaḥ pauraiḥ
samprāptaḥ kuru-jāṅgalān
unmatta-mūka-jaḍavad
vicaran gaja-sāhvaye

katham—how; *ālakṣitaḥ*—recognized; *pauraiḥ*—by the citizens; *samprāptaḥ*—reaching; *kuru-jāṅgalān*—the Kuru-jāṅgala provinces; *unmatta*—mad; *mūka*—dumb; *jaḍavat*—stunted; *vicaran*—wandering; *gaja-sāhvaye*—Hastināpura.

TRANSLATION

How was he [Śrīla Śukadeva, the son of Vyāsa] recognized by the citizens when he entered the city of Hastināpura [now Delhi], after wandering in the provinces of Kuru and Jāṅgala, appearing like a madman, dumb and retarded?

PURPORT

The present city of Delhi was formerly known as Hastināpura because it was first established by King Hastī. Gosvāmī Śukadeva, after leaving his paternal home, was roaming like a madman, and therefore it was very difficult for the citizens to recognize him in his exalted position. A sage is not, therefore, recognized by sight, but by hearing. One should approach a *sādhu* or great sage not to see but to hear him. If one is not prepared to hear the words of a *sādhu,* there is no profit. Śukadeva Gosvāmī was a *sādhu* who could speak on the transcendental activities of the Lord. He did not satisfy the whims of ordinary citizens. He was recognized when he spoke on the subject of *Bhāgavatam,* and he never attempted jugglery like a magician. Outwardly he appeared to be a retarded, dumb madman, but in fact he was the most elevated transcendental personality.

TEXT 7

कथं वा पाण्डवेयस्य राजर्षेर्मुनिना सह।
संवादः समभूत्तात यत्रैषा सात्वती श्रुतिः ॥७॥

kathaṁ vā pāṇḍaveyasya
rājarṣer muninā saha
saṁvādaḥ samabhūt tāta
yatraiṣā sātvatī śrutiḥ

katham—how is it; *vā*—also; *pāṇḍaveyasya*—of the descendant of Pāṇḍu (Parīkṣit); *rājarṣeḥ*—of the king who was a sage; *muninā*—with the *muni;* *saha*—with; *saṁvādaḥ*—discussion; *samabhūt*—took place; *tāta*—O darling; *yatra*—whereupon; *eṣā*—like this; *sātvatī*—transcendental; *śrutiḥ*—essence of the *Vedas.*

TRANSLATION

How did it so happen that King Parīkṣit met this great sage, making it possible for this great transcendental essence of the Vedas [Bhāgavatam] to be sung to him?

PURPORT

Śrīmad-Bhāgavatam is stated here as the essence of the *Vedas.* It is not an imaginary story as it is sometimes considered by unauthorized men. It is also called *Śuka-saṁhitā*, or the Vedic hymn spoken by Śrī Śukadeva Gosvāmī, the great liberated sage.

TEXT 8

स गोदोहनमात्रं हि गृहेषु गृहमेधिनाम्।
अवेक्षते महाभागस्तीर्थीकुर्वंस्तदाश्रमम् ॥८॥

sa go-dohana-mātraṁ hi
gṛheṣu gṛha-medhinām
avekṣate mahā-bhāgas
tīrthī-kurvaṁs tad āśramam

saḥ—he (Śukadeva Gosvāmī); *go-dohana-mātram*—only for the time of milking the cow; *hi*—certainly; *gṛheṣu*—in the house; *gṛha-medhinām*—of the householders; *avekṣate*—waits; *mahā-bhāgaḥ*—the most fortunate; *tīrthī*—pilgrimage; *kurvan*—transforming; *tat āśramam*—the residence.

TRANSLATION

He [Śukadeva Gosvāmī] was accustomed to stay at the door of a householder only long enough for a cow to be milked. And he did this just to sanctify the residence.

PURPORT

Śukadeva Gosvāmī met Emperor Parīkṣit and explained the text of *Śrīmad-Bhāgavatam.* He was not accustomed to stay at any householder's residence for more than half an hour (at the time of milking the cow), and he would just take alms from the fortunate householder. That was to sanctify the residence by his auspicious presence. Therefore Śukadeva Gosvāmī is an ideal preacher established in the transcendental position. From his activities, those who are in the renounced order of life and dedicated to the mission of preaching the message of Godhead should learn that they have no business with householders save and except to enlighten them in transcendental knowledge. Such asking for alms from the householder should be for the purpose of sanctifying his home. One who is in the renounced order of life should not be allured by the glamor of the householder's worldly possessions and thus become subservient to worldly men. For one who is in the renounced order of life, this is much more dangerous than drinking poison and committing suicide.

TEXT 9

अभिमन्युसुतं सूत प्राहुर्भागवतोत्तमम् ।
तस्य जन्म महाश्चर्यं कर्माणि च गृणीहि नः ॥९॥

abhimanyu-sutaṁ sūta
prāhur bhāgavatottamam
tasya janma mahāścaryaṁ
karmāṇi ca gṛṇīhi naḥ

abhimanyu-sutam—the son of Abhimanyu; *sūta*—O Sūta; *prāhuḥ*—is said to be; *bhāgavata-uttamam*—the first-class devotee of the Lord; *tasya*—his; *janma*—birth; *mahā-āścaryam*—very wonderful; *karmāṇi*—activities; *ca*—and; *gṛṇīhi*—please speak to; *naḥ*—us.

TRANSLATION

It is said that Mahārāja Parīkṣit is a great first-class devotee of the Lord and that his birth and activities are all wonderful. Please tell us about him.

PURPORT

The birth of Mahārāja Parīkṣit is wonderful because in the womb of his mother he was protected by the Personality of Godhead, Śrī Kṛṣṇa. His activities are also wonderful because he chastised Kali, who was attempting to kill a cow. To kill cows means to end human civilization. He wanted to protect the cow from being killed by the great representative of sin. His death is also wonderful because he got previous notice of his death, which is wonderful for any mortal being, and thus he prepared himself for passing away by sitting down on the bank of the Ganges and hearing the transcendental activities of the Lord. During all the days he heard *Bhāgavatam,* he did not take food or drink, nor did he sleep a moment. So everything about him is wonderful, and his activities are worth hearing attentively. Desire is expressed herein to hear about him in detail.

TEXT 10

स सम्राट् कस्य वा हेतोः पाण्डूनां मानवर्धनः ।
प्रायोपविष्टो गङ्गायामनादृत्याधिराट्श्रियम् ॥१०॥

sa samrāṭ kasya vā hetoḥ
pāṇḍūnāṁ māna-vardhanaḥ
prāyopaviṣṭo gaṅgāyām
anādṛtyādhirāṭ-śriyam

saḥ—he; *samrāṭ*—the Emperor; *kasya*—for what; *vā*—or; *hetoḥ*—reason; *pāṇḍūnām*—of the sons of Pāṇḍu; *māna-vardhanaḥ*—one who enriches the family; *prāya-upaviṣṭaḥ*—sitting and fasting; *gaṅgāyām*—on the bank of the Ganges; *anādṛtya*—neglecting; *adhirāṭ*—acquired kingdom; *śriyam*—opulences.

TRANSLATION

He was a great emperor and possessed all the opulences of his acquired kingdom. He was so exalted that he was increasing the prestige of the Pāṇḍu dynasty. Why did he give up everything to sit down on the bank of the Ganges and fast until death?

PURPORT

Mahārāja Parīkṣit was the Emperor of the world and all the seas and oceans, and he did not have to take the trouble to acquire such a kingdom by his own effort. He inherited it from his grandfathers Mahārāja Yudhiṣṭhira and brothers. Besides that, he was doing well in the administration and was worthy of the good names of his forefathers. Consequently there was nothing undesirable in his opulence and administration. Then why should he give up all these favorable circumstances and sit down on the bank of the Ganges, fasting till death? This is astonishing, and therefore all were eager to know the cause.

TEXT 11

नमन्ति यत्पादनिकेतमात्मनः
शिवाय हानीय धनानि शत्रवः ।
कथं स वीरः श्रियमङ्ग दुस्त्यजां
युवैषतोत्स्रष्टुमहो सहासुभिः ॥११॥

namanti yat-pāda-niketam ātmanaḥ
śivāya hānīya dhanāni śatravaḥ
kathaṁ sa vīraḥ śriyam aṅga dustyajāṁ
yuvaiṣatotsraṣṭum aho sahāsubhiḥ

namanti—bow down; *yat-pāda*—whose feet; *niketam*—under; *ātmanaḥ*—own; *śivāya*—welfare; *hānīya*—used to bring about; *dhanāni*—wealth; *śatravaḥ*—enemies; *katham*—for what reason; *saḥ*—he; *vīraḥ*—the chivalrous; *śriyam*—opulences; *aṅga*—O ; *dustya-jām*—insuperable; *yuvā*—in full youth; *aiṣata*—desired; *utsraṣṭum*—to give up; *aho*—exclamation; *saha*—with; *asubhiḥ*—life.

TRANSLATION

He was such a great emperor that all his enemies would come and bow down at his feet and surrender all their wealth for their own benefit. He was full of youth and strength, and he possessed insuperable kingly opulences. Why did he want to give up everything, including his life?

PURPORT

There was nothing undesirable in his life. He was quite a young man and could enjoy life with power and opulence. So there was no question of retiring from active life. There was no difficulty in collecting the state taxes because he was so powerful and chivalrous that even his enemies would come to him and bow down at his feet and surrender all wealth for their own benefit. Mahārāja Parīkṣit was a pious king. He conquered his enemies, and therefore the kingdom was full of prosperity. There was enough milk, grains and metals, and all the rivers and mountains were full of potency. So materially everything was satisfactory. Therefore, there was no question of untimely giving up his kingdom and life. The sages were eager to hear about all this.

TEXT 12

शिवाय लोकस्य भवाय भूतये
य उत्तमश्लोकपरायणा जनाः ।
जीवन्ति नात्मार्थमसौ पराश्रयं
मुमोच निर्विद्य कुतः कलेवरम् ॥१२॥

śivāya lokasya bhavāya bhūtaye
ya uttama-śloka-parāyaṇā janāḥ
jīvanti nātmārtham asau parāśrayaṁ
mumoca nirvidya kutaḥ kalevaram

śivāya—welfare; *lokasya*—of all living beings; *bhavāya*—for flourishing; *bhūtaye*—for economic development; *ye*—one who is; *uttama-śloka-*

parāyaṇāḥ—devoted to the cause of the Personality of Godhead; *janāḥ*—men; *jīvanti*—do live; *na*—but not; *ātma-artham*—selfish interest; *asau*—that; *para-āśrayam*—shelter for others; *mumoca*—gave up; *nirvidya*—being freed from all attachment; *kutaḥ*—for what reason; *kalevaram*—mortal body.

TRANSLATION

Those who are devoted to the cause of the Personality of Godhead live only for the welfare, development and happiness of others. They do not live for any selfish interest. So even though the Emperor [Parīkṣit] was free from all attachment to worldly possessions, how could he give up his mortal body, which was shelter for others?

PURPORT

Parīkṣit Mahārāja was an ideal king and householder because he was a devotee of the Personality of Godhead. A devotee of the Lord automatically has all good qualifications. And the Emperor was a typical example of this. Personally he had no attachment for all the worldly opulences in his possession. But since he was king for the all-around welfare of his citizens, he was always busy in the welfare work of the public, not only for this life, but also for the next. He would not allow slaughterhouses or killing of cows. He was not a foolish and partial administrator who would arrange for the protection of one living being and allow another to be killed. Because he was a devotee of the Lord, he knew perfectly well how to conduct his administration for everyone's happiness—men, animals, plants and all living creatures. He was not selfishly interested. Selfishness is either self-centered or self-extended. He was neither. His interest was to please the Supreme Truth, Personality of Godhead. The king is the representative of the Supreme Lord, and therefore the king's interest must be identical with that of the Supreme Lord. The Supreme Lord wants all living beings to be obedient to Him and thereby become happy. Therefore the king's interest is to guide all subjects back to the kingdom of God. Hence the activities of the citizens should be so coordinated that they can at the end go back home, back to Godhead. Under the administration of a representative king, the kingdom is full of opulence. At that time, human beings need not eat animals. There are ample food grains, milk, fruit and vegetables so that the human beings as well as the animals can eat sumptuously and to their heart's content. If all living beings are satisfied with food and shelter and obey the prescribed rules, there cannot be any disturbance between one living being and another. Emperor Parīkṣit was a worthy king, and therefore all were happy during his reign.

TEXT 13

तत्सर्वं नः समाचक्ष्व पृष्टो यदिह किञ्चन।
मन्ये त्वां विषये वाचां स्नातमन्यत्र छान्दसात् ॥१३॥

tat sarvaṁ naḥ samācakṣva
pṛṣṭo yad iha kiñcana
manye tvāṁ viṣaye vācāṁ
snātam anyatra chāndasāt

tat—that; *sarvam*—all; *naḥ*—unto us; *samācakṣva*—clearly explain; *pṛṣṭaḥ*—questioned; *yat iha*—herein; *kiñcana*—all that; *manye*—we think; *tvām*—you; *viṣaye*—in all subjects; *vācām*—meanings of words; *snātam*—fully acquainted; *anyatra*—except; *chāndasāt*—portion of the *Vedas.*

TRANSLATION

We know that you are expert in the meaning of all subjects, except some portions of the Vedas, and thus you can clearly explain the answers to all the questions we have just put to you.

PURPORT

The difference between the *Vedas* and the *Purāṇas* is like that between the *brāhmaṇas* and the *parivrājakas.* The *brāhmaṇas* are meant to administer some fruitive sacrifices mentioned in the *Vedas,* but the *parivrājakācāryas,* or learned preachers, are meant to disseminate transcendental knowledge to one and all. As such, the *parivrājakācāryas* are not always expert in pronouncing the Vedic *mantras,* which are practiced systematically by accent and meter by the *brāhmaṇas* who are meant for administering Vedic rites. Yet it should not be considered that the *brāhmaṇas* are more important than the itinerant preachers. They are one and different simultaneously because they are meant for the same end, in different ways.

There is no difference also between the Vedic *mantras* and what is explained in the *Purāṇas* and *Itihāsa.* According to Śrīla Jīva Gosvāmī, it is mentioned in the *Mādhyandina-śruti* that all the *Vedas,* namely the *Sāma, Atharva, Ṛg, Yajur, Purāṇas, Itihāsas, Upaniṣads,* etc., are emanations from the breathing of the Supreme Being. The only difference is that the Vedic *mantras* are mostly begun with *praṇava oṁkāra,* and it requires some training to practice the metric pronunciation of the Vedic *mantras.* But that does not mean that *Śrīmad-Bhāgavatam* is of less importance than the Vedic *mantras.* On the contrary, it is the ripened fruit of all the *Vedas,* as stated before. Besides that, the most perfectly liberated soul, Śrīla Śukadeva Gosvāmī, is absorbed in the studies of the *Bhāgavatam,* although he is already self-realized. Śrīla Sūta Gosvāmī is following his footsteps, and therefore his position is not the least less important because he was not expert in chanting Vedic *mantras* with metric pronunciation, which depends more on practice than actual realization. Realization is more important than parrotlike chanting.

TEXT 14

सूत उवाच
द्वापरे समनुप्राप्ते तृतीये युगपर्यये ।
जातः पराशराद्योगी वासव्यां कलया हरेः ॥१४॥

sūta uvāca
dvāpare samanuprāpte
tṛtīye yuga-paryaye
jātaḥ parāśarād yogī
vāsavyāṁ kalayā hareḥ

sūtaḥ—Sūta Gosvāmī; *uvāca*—said; *dvāpare*—in the second millennium; *samanuprāpte*—on the advent of; *tṛtīye*—third; *yuga*—millennium; *paryaye*—in the place of; *jātaḥ*—was begotten; *parāśarāt*—by Parāśara; *yogī*—the great sage; *vāsavyām*—in the womb of the daughter of Vasu; *kalayā*—in the plenary portion; *hareḥ*—of the Personality of Godhead.

TRANSLATION

Sūta Gosvāmī said: When the second millennium overlapped the third, the great sage [Vyāsadeva] was born to Parāśara in the womb of Satyavatī, the daughter of Vasu.

PURPORT

There is a chronological order of the four millenniums, namely Satya, Dvāpara, Tretā and Kali. But sometimes there is overlapping. During the regime of Vaivasvata Manu, there was an overlapping of the twenty-eighth round of the four millenniums, and the third millennium appeared prior to the second. In that particular millennium, Lord Śrī Kṛṣṇa also descends, and because of this there was some particular alteration. The mother of the great sage was Satyavatī, the daughter of the Vasu (fisherman), and the father was the great Parāśara Muni. That is the history of Vyāsadeva's birth. Every millennium is divided into three periods, and each period is called a *sandhyā*. Vyāsadeva appeared in the third *sandhyā* of that particular age.

TEXT 15

स कदाचित्सरस्वत्या उपस्पृश्य जलं शुचिः ।
विविक्त एक आसीन उदिते रविमण्डले ॥१५॥

sa kadācit sarasvatyā
upaspṛśya jalaṁ śuciḥ
vivikta eka āsīna
udite ravi-maṇḍale

saḥ—he; *kadācit*—once; *sarasvatyāḥ*—on the bank of the Sarasvatī; *upaspṛśya*—after finishing morning ablutions; *jalam*—water; *śuciḥ*—being purified; *vivikte*—concentration; *ekaḥ*—alone; *āsīnaḥ*—being thus seated; *udite*—on the rise; *ravi-maṇḍale*—of the sun disc.

TRANSLATION

Once upon a time he [Vyāsadeva], as the sun rose, took his morning ablution in the waters of the Sarasvatī and sat alone to concentrate.

PURPORT

The river Sarasvatī is flowing in the Badarikāśrama area of the Himalayas. So the place indicated here is Śamyāprāsa in Badarikāśrama, where Śrī Vyāsadeva is residing.

TEXT 16

परावरज्ञः स ऋषिः कालेनाव्यक्तरंहसा ।
युगधर्मव्यतिकरं प्राप्तं भुवि युगे युगे ॥१६॥

parāvara-jñaḥ sa ṛṣiḥ
kālenāvyakta-raṁhasā

yuga-dharma-vyatikaraṁ
prāptaṁ bhuvi yuge yuge

para-avara—past and future; *jñaḥ*—one who knows; *saḥ*—he; *ṛṣiḥ*—Vyāsadeva; *kālena*—in the course of time; *avyakta*—unmanifested; *raṁhasā*—by great force; *yuga-dharma*—acts in terms of the millennium; *vyatikaram*—anomalies; *prāptam*—having accrued; *bhuvi*—on the earth; *yuge yuge*—different ages.

TRANSLATION

The great sage Vyāsadeva saw anomalies in the duties of the millennium. This happens on the earth in different ages, due to unseen forces in the course of time.

PURPORT

The great sages like Vyāsadeva are liberated souls, and therefore they can see clearly past and future. Thus he could see the future anomalies in the Kali age, and accordingly he made arrangement for the people in general so that they can execute a progressive life in this age, which is full of darkness. The people in general in this age of Kali are too much interested in matter, which is temporary. Because of ignorance they are unable to evaluate the assets of life and be enlightened in spiritual knowledge.

TEXTS 17–18

भौतिकानां च भावानां शक्तिह्रासं च तत्कृतम् ।
अश्रद्दधानान्निःसत्त्वान्दुर्मेधान् ह्रसितायुषः ॥१७॥
दुर्भगांश्च जनान् वीक्ष्य मुनिर्दिव्येन चक्षुषा ।
सर्ववर्णाश्रमाणां यद्दध्यौ हितममोघदृक् ॥१८॥

bhautikānāṁ ca bhāvānāṁ
śakti-hrāsaṁ ca tat-kṛtam
aśraddadhānān niḥsattvān
durmedhān hrasitāyuṣaḥ

durbhagāṁś ca janān vīkṣya
munir divyena cakṣuṣā
sarva-varṇāśramāṇāṁ yad
dadhyau hitam amogha-dṛk

bhautikānām ca—also of everything that is made of matter; *bhāvānām*—actions; *śakti-hrāsam ca*—and deterioration of natural power; *tat-kṛtam*—rendered by that; *aśraddadhānān*—of the faithless; *niḥsattvān*—impatient due to want of the mode of goodness; *durmedhān*—dull-witted; *hrasita*—reduced; *āyuṣaḥ*—of duration of life; *durbhagān ca*—also the unlucky; *janān*—people in general; *vīkṣya*—by seeing; *muniḥ*—the *muni; divyena*—by transcendental; *cakṣuṣā*—vision; *sarva*—all; *varṇa-āśramāṇām*—of all the statuses and orders of life; *yat*—what; *dadhyau*—contemplated; *hitam*—welfare; *amogha-dṛk*—one who is fully equipped in knowledge.

TRANSLATION

The great sage, who was fully equipped in knowledge, could see, through his transcendental vision, the deterioration of everything material, due to the influence of the age. He could also see that the faithless people in general would be reduced in duration of life and would be impatient due to lack of goodness. Thus he contemplated for the welfare of men in all statuses and orders of life.

PURPORT

The unmanifested forces of time are so powerful that they reduce all matter to oblivion in due course. In Kali-yuga, the last millennium of a round of four millenniums, the power of all material objects deteriorates by the influence of time. In this age the duration of the material body of the people in general is much reduced, and so is the memory. The action of matter has also not so much incentive. The land does not produce food grains in the same proportions as it did in other ages. The cow does not give as much milk as it used to give formerly. The production of vegetables and fruits is less than before. As such, all living beings, both men and animals, do not have sumptuous, nourishing food. Due to want of so many necessities of life, naturally the duration of life is reduced, the memory is short, intelligence is meager, mutual dealings are full of hypocrisy and so on.

The great sage Vyāsadeva could see this by his transcendental vision. As an astrologer can see the future fate of a man, or an astronomer can foretell the solar and lunar eclipses, those liberated souls who can see through the scriptures can foretell the future of all mankind. They can see this due to their sharp vision of spiritual attainment.

And all such transcendentalists, who are naturally devotees of the Lord, are always eager to render welfare service to the people in general. They are the real friends of the people in general, not the so-called public leaders who are unable to see what is going to happen five minutes ahead. In this age the people in general as well as their so-called leaders are all unlucky fellows, faithless in spiritual knowledge and influenced by the age of Kali. They are always disturbed by various diseases. For example, in the present age there are so many TB patients and TB hospitals, but formerly this was not so because the time was not so unfavorable. The unfortunate men of this age are always reluctant to give a reception to the transcendentalists who are representatives of Śrīla Vyāsadeva and selfless workers always busy in planning something which may help everyone in all statuses and orders of life. The greatest philanthropists are those transcendentalists who represent the mission of Vyāsa, Nārada, Madhva, Caitanya, Rūpa, Sarasvatī, etc. They are all one and the same. The personalities may be different, but the aim of the mission is one and the same, namely, to deliver the fallen souls back home, back to Godhead.

TEXT 19

चातुर्होत्रं कर्म शुद्धं प्रजानां वीक्ष्य वैदिकम् ।
व्यदधाद्यज्ञसन्तत्यै वेदमेकं चतुर्विधम् ॥१९॥

cātur-hotraṁ karma śuddhaṁ
prajānāṁ vīkṣya vaidikam
vyadadhād yajña-santatyai
vedam ekaṁ catur-vidham

cātuḥ—four; *hotram*—sacrificial fires; *karma śuddham*—purification of work; *prajānām*—of the people in general; *vīkṣya*—after seeing; *vaidikam*—according to Vedic rites; *vyadadhāt*—made into; *yajña*—sacrifice; *santatyai*—to expand; *vedam ekam*—only one *Veda; catuḥ-vidham*—in four divisions.

TRANSLATION

He saw that the sacrifices mentioned in the Vedas were means by which the people's occupations could be purified. And to simplify the process he divided the one Veda into four, in order to expand them among men.

PURPORT

Formerly there was only the *Veda* of the name *Yajur,* and the four divisions of sacrifices were there specifically mentioned. But to make them more easily performable, the *Veda* was divided into four divisions of sacrifice, just to purify the occupational service of the four orders. Above the four *Vedas,* namely *Ṛg, Yajur, Sāma,* and *Atharva,* there are the *Purāṇas,* the *Mahābhārata, Saṁhitās,* etc., which are known as the fifth *Veda.* Śrī Vyāsadeva and his many disciples were all historical personalities, and they were very kind and sympathetic toward the fallen souls of this age of Kali. As such, the *Purāṇas* and *Mahābhārata* were made from related historical facts which explained the teaching of the four *Vedas.* There is no point in doubting the authority of the *Purāṇas* and *Mahābhārata* as parts and parcels of the *Vedas.* In the *Chāndogya Upaniṣad* (7.1.4), the *Purāṇas* and *Mahābhārata,* generally known as histories, are mentioned as the fifth *Veda.* According to Śrīla Jīva Gosvāmī, that is the way of ascertaining the respective values of the revealed scriptures.

TEXT 20

ऋग्यजुःसामाथर्वाख्या वेदाश्चत्वार उद्धृताः ।
इतिहासपुराणं च पञ्चमो वेद उच्यते ॥२०॥

ṛg-yajuḥ-sāmātharvākhyā
vedāś catvāra uddhṛtāḥ
itihāsa-purāṇaṁ ca
pañcamo veda ucyate

ṛg-yajuḥ-sāma-atharva-ākhyāḥ—the names of the four *Vedas; vedāḥ*—the *Vedas; catvāraḥ*—four; *uddhṛtāḥ*—made into separate parts; *itihāsa*—historical records (*Mahābhārata*); *purāṇam ca*—and the *Purāṇas; pañcamaḥ*—the fifth; *vedaḥ*—the original source of knowledge; *ucyate*—is said to be.

TRANSLATION

The four divisions of the original sources of knowledge [the Vedas] were made separately. But the historical facts and authentic stories mentioned in the Purāṇas are called the fifth Veda.

TEXT 21

तत्रर्ग्वेदधरः पैलः सामगो जैमिनिः कविः ।
वैशम्पायन एवैको निष्णातो यजुषामुत ॥२१॥

tatrarg-veda-dharaḥ pailaḥ
sāmago jaiminiḥ kaviḥ

vaiśampāyana evaiko
niṣṇāto yajuṣām uta

tatra—thereupon; *ṛg-veda-dharaḥ*—the professor of the *Ṛg Veda; pailaḥ* —the *ṛṣi* named Paila; *sāma-gaḥ*—that of the *Sāma Veda; jaiminiḥ*—the *ṛṣi* named Jaimini; *kaviḥ*—highly qualified; *vaiśampāyanaḥ*—the *ṛṣi* named Vaiśampāyana; *eva*—only; *ekaḥ*—alone; *niṣṇātaḥ*—well versed; *yajuṣām*—of the *Yajur Veda; uta*—glorified.

TRANSLATION

After the Vedas were divided into four divisions, Paila Ṛṣi became the professor of the Ṛg Veda, Jaimini the professor of the Sāma Veda, and Vaiśampāyana alone became glorified by the Yajur Veda.

PURPORT

The different *Vedas* were entrusted to different learned scholars for development in various ways.

TEXT 22

अथर्वाङ्गिरसामासीत्सुमन्तुर्दारुणो मुनिः ।
इतिहासपुराणानां पिता मे रोमहर्षणः ॥२२॥

atharvāṅgirasām āsīt
sumantur dāruṇo muniḥ
itihāsa-purāṇānāṁ
pitā me romaharṣaṇaḥ

atharva—the *Atharva Veda; aṅgirasām*—unto the *ṛṣi* Aṅgirā; *āsīt*—was entrusted; *sumantuḥ*—also known as Sumantu Muni; *dāruṇaḥ*—seriously devoted to the *Atharva Veda; muniḥ*—the sage; *itihāsa-purāṇānām*—of the historical records and the *Purāṇas; pitā*—father; *me*—mine; *romaharṣaṇaḥ*—the *ṛṣi* Romaharṣaṇa.

TRANSLATION

The Sumantu Muni Aṅgirā, who was very devotedly engaged, was entrusted with the Atharva Veda. And my father, Romaharṣaṇa, was entrusted with the Purāṇas and historical records.

PURPORT

In the *śruti-mantras* also it is stated that Aṅgirā Muni, who strictly followed the rigid principles of the *Atharva Veda,* was the leader of the followers of the *Atharva Veda.*

TEXT 23

त एत ऋषयो वेदं स्वं स्वं व्यस्यन्ननेकधा।
शिष्यैः प्रशिष्यैस्तच्छिष्यैर्वेदास्ते शाखिनोऽभवन् ॥२३॥

ta eta ṛṣayo vedaṁ
svaṁ svaṁ vyasyann anekadhā
śiṣyaiḥ praśiṣyais tac-chiṣyair
vedās te śākhino 'bhavan

te—they; *ete*—all these; *ṛṣayaḥ*—learned scholars; *vedam*—the respective *Vedas; svam svam*—in their own entrusted matters; *vyasyan*—rendered; *anekadhā*—many; *śiṣyaiḥ*—disciples; *praśiṣyaiḥ*—granddisciples; *tat-śiṣyaiḥ*—great-granddisciples; *vedāḥ te*—followers of the respective *Vedas; śākhinaḥ*—different branches; *abhavan*—thus became.

TRANSLATION

All these learned scholars, in their turn, rendered their entrusted Vedas unto their many disciples, granddisciples and great-granddisciples, and thus the respective branches of the followers of the Vedas came into being.

PURPORT

The original source of knowledge is the *Vedas.* There are no branches of knowledge, either mundane or transcendental, which do not belong to the original text of the *Vedas.* They have simply been developed into different branches. They were originally rendered by great, respectable and learned professors. In other words, the Vedic knowledge, broken into different branches by different disciplic successions, has been distributed all over the world. No one, therefore, can claim independent knowledge beyond the *Vedas.*

TEXT 24

त एव वेदा दुर्मेधैर्धार्यन्ते पुरुषैर्यथा।
एवं चकार भगवान् व्यासः कृपणवत्सलः ॥२४॥

ta eva vedā durmedhair
dhāryante puruṣair yathā
evaṁ cakāra bhagavān
vyāsaḥ kṛpaṇa-vatsalaḥ

te—that; *eva*—certainly; *vedāḥ*—the book of knowledge; *durmedhaiḥ*—by the less intellectual; *dhāryante*—can assimilate; *puruṣaiḥ*—by the man; *yathā*—as much as; *evam*—thus; *cakāra*—edited; *bhagavān*—the powerful; *vyāsaḥ*—the great sage Vyāsa; *kṛpaṇa-vatsalaḥ*—very kind to the ignorant mass.

TRANSLATION

Thus the great sage Vyāsadeva, who is very kind to the ignorant masses, edited the Vedas so they might be assimilated by less intellectual men.

PURPORT

The *Veda* is one, and the reasons for its divisions in many parts are explained herewith. The seed of all knowledge, or the *Veda,* is not a subject matter which can easily be understood by any ordinary man. There is a stricture that no one should try to learn the *Vedas* who is not a qualified *brāhmaṇa.* This stricture has been wrongly interpreted in so many ways. A class of men, who claim brahminical qualification simply by their birthright in the family of a *brāhmaṇa,* claim that the study of the *Vedas* is a monopoly of the *brāhmaṇa* caste only. Another section of the people take this as an injustice to members of other castes, who do not happen to take birth in a *brāhmaṇa* family. But both of them are misguided. The *Vedas* are subjects which had to be explained even to Brahmājī by the Supreme Lord. Therefore the subject matter is understood by persons with exceptional qualities of goodness. Persons who are in the modes of passion and ignorance are unable to understand the subject matter of the *Vedas.* The ultimate goal of Vedic knowledge is Śrī Kṛṣṇa, the Personality of Godhead. This Personality is very rarely understood by those who are in the modes of passion and ignorance. In the Satya-yuga everyone was situated in the mode of goodness. Gradually the mode of goodness declined during the Tretā and Dvāpara-yugas, and the general mass of people became corrupt. In the present age the mode of goodness is almost nil, and so for the general mass of people, the kindhearted, powerful sage Śrīla Vyāsadeva divided the *Vedas* in various ways so that they may be practically followed by less intelligent persons in the modes of passion and ignorance. It is explained in the next *śloka* as follows.

TEXT 25

स्त्रीशूद्रद्विजबन्धूनां त्रयी न श्रुतिगोचरा।
कर्मश्रेयसि मूढानां श्रेय एवं भवेदिह।
इति भारतमाख्यानं कृपया मुनिना कृतम् ॥२५॥

strī-śūdra-dvijabandhūnāṁ
trayī na śruti-gocarā
karma-śreyasi mūḍhānāṁ
śreya evaṁ bhaved iha
iti bhāratam ākhyānaṁ
kṛpayā muninā kṛtam

strī—the woman class; *śūdra*—the laboring class; *dvija-bandhūnām*—of the friends of the twice-born; *trayī*—three; *na*—not; *śruti-gocarā*—for understanding; *karma*—in activities; *śreyasi*—in welfare; *mūḍhānām*—of the fools; *śreyaḥ*—supreme benefit; *evam*—thus; *bhavet*—achieved; *iha*—by this; *iti*—thus thinking; *bhāratam*—the great *Mahābhārata; ākhyānam*—historical facts; *kṛpayā*—out of great mercy; *muninā*—by the *muni; kṛtam*—is completed.

TRANSLATION

Out of compassion, the great sage thought it wise that this would enable men to achieve the ultimate goal of life. Thus he compiled the great historical narration called the Mahābhārata for women, laborers and friends of the twice-born.

PURPORT

The friends of the twice-born families are those who are born in the families of *brāhmaṇas, kṣatriyas* and *vaiśyas,* or the spiritually cultured families, but who themselves are not equal to their forefathers. Such descendants are not recognized as such, for want of purificatory achievements. The purificatory activities begin even before the birth of a child, and the seed-giving reformatory process is called *Garbhādhāna-saṁskāra.* One who has not undergone such *Garbhādhāna-saṁskāra,* or spiritual family planning, is not accepted as being of an actual twice-born family. The *Garbhādhāna-saṁskāra* is followed by other purificatory processes, out of which the sacred thread ceremony is one. This is performed at the time of spiritual initiation. After this particular *saṁskāra,* one is rightly called twice-born. One birth is calculated during the seed-giving *saṁskāra,* and the second birth is calculated at the time of spiritual initiation. One who has been able to undergo such important *saṁskāras* can be called a bona fide twice-born.

If the father and the mother do not undertake the process of spiritual family planning and simply beget children out of passion only, their children are called *dvija-bandhus.* These *dvija-bandhus* are certainly not as intelligent as the children of the regular twice-born families. The *dvija-bandhus* are classified with the *śūdras* and the woman class, who are by nature less intelligent. The *śūdras* and the woman class do not have to undergo any *saṁskāra* save and except the ceremony of marriage.

The less intelligent classes of men, namely women, *śūdras* and unqualified sons of the higher castes, are devoid of necessary qualifications to understand the purpose of the transcendental *Vedas.* For them the *Mahābhārata* was prepared. The purpose of the *Mahābhārata* is to administer the purpose of the *Vedas,* and therefore within this *Mahābhārata* the summary *Veda* of *Bhagavad-gītā* is placed. The less intelligent are more interested in stories than in philosophy, and therefore the philosophy of the *Vedas* in the form of the *Bhagavad-gītā* is spoken by the Lord Śrī Kṛṣṇa. Vyāsadeva and Lord Kṛṣṇa are both on the transcendental plane, and therefore they collaborated in doing good to the fallen souls of this age. The *Bhagavad-gītā* is the essence of all Vedic knowledge. It is the first book of spiritual values, as the *Upaniṣads* are. The Vedānta philosophy is the subject matter for study by the spiritual graduates. Only the postgraduate spiritual student can enter into the spiritual or devotional service of the Lord. It is a great science, and the great professor is the Lord Himself in the form of Lord Śrī Caitanya Mahāprabhu. And persons who are empowered by Him can initiate others in the transcendental loving service of the Lord.

TEXT 26

एवं प्रवृत्तस्य सदा भूतानां श्रेयसि द्विजाः ।
सर्वात्मकेनापि यदा नातुष्यद्धृदयं ततः ॥२६॥

evaṁ pravṛttasya sadā
bhūtānāṁ śreyasi dvijāḥ
sarvātmakenāpi yadā
nātuṣyad dhṛdayaṁ tataḥ

evam—thus; *pravṛttasya*—one who is engaged in; *sadā*—always; *bhūtānām*—of the living beings; *śreyasi*—in the ultimate good; *dvijāḥ*—O twice-born; *sarvātmakena api*—by all means; *yadā*—when; *na*—not; *atuṣyat*—become satisfied; *hṛdayam*—mind; *tataḥ*—at that time.

TRANSLATION

O twice-born brāhmaṇas, still his mind was not satisfied, although he engaged himself in working for the total welfare of all people.

PURPORT

Śrī Vyāsadeva was not satisfied with himself, although he had prepared literatures of Vedic value for the all-around welfare of the general mass of people. It was expected that he would be satisfied by all such activities, but ultimately he was not satisfied.

TEXT 27

नातिप्रसीदद्धृदयः सरस्वत्यास्तटे शुचौ ।
वितर्कयन् विविक्तस्थ इदं चोवाच धर्मवित् ॥२७॥

nātiprasīdad dhṛdayaḥ
sarasvatyās taṭe śucau
vitarkayan vivikta-stha
idaṁ covāca dharma-vit

na—not; *atiprasīdat*—very much satisfied; *hṛdayaḥ*—at heart; *sarasvatyāḥ*—of the river Sarasvatī; *taṭe*—on the bank of; *śucau*—being purified; *vitarkayan*—having considered; *vivikta-sthaḥ*—situated in a lonely place; *idam ca*—also this; *uvāca*—said; *dharma-vit*—one who knows what religion is.

TRANSLATION

Thus the sage, being dissatisfied at heart, at once began to reflect, because he knew the essence of religion, and he said within himself:

PURPORT

The sage began to search out the cause of not being satisfied at heart. Perfection is never attained until one is satisfied at heart. This satisfaction of heart has to be searched out beyond matter.

TEXTS 28–29

धृतव्रतेन हि मया छन्दांसि गुरवोऽग्नयः ।
मानिता निर्व्यलीकेन गृहीतं चानुशासनम् ॥२८॥
भारतव्यपदेशेन ह्याम्नायार्थश्च प्रदर्शितः ।
दृश्यते यत्र धर्मादि स्त्रीशूद्रादिभिरप्युत ॥२९॥

dhṛta-vratena hi mayā
chandāṁsi guravo 'gnayaḥ
mānitā nirvyalīkena
gṛhītaṁ cānuśāsanam

bhārata-vyapadeśena
hy āmnāyārthaś ca pradarśitaḥ
dṛśyate yatra dharmādi
strī-śūdrādibhir apy uta

dhṛta-vratena—under a strict disciplinary vow; *hi*—certainly; *mayā*—by me; *chandāṁsi*—the Vedic hymns; *guravaḥ*—the spiritual masters; *agnayaḥ*—the sacrificial fire; *mānitāḥ*—properly worshiped; *nirvyalīkena*—without pretense; *gṛhītam ca*—also accepted; *anuśāsanam*—traditional discipline; *bhārata*—the *Mahābhārata; vyapadeśena*—by compilation of; *hi*—certainly; *āmnāya-arthaḥ*—import of disciplic succession; *ca*—and; *pradarśitaḥ*—properly explained; *dṛśyate*—by what is necessary; *yatra*—where; *dharma-ādiḥ*—the path of religion; *strī-śūdra-ādibhiḥ api*—even by women, *śūdras,* etc.; *uta*—spoken.

TRANSLATION

I have, under strict disciplinary vows, unpretentiously worshiped the Vedas, the spiritual master and the altar of sacrifice. I have also abided by the rulings and have shown the import of disciplic succession through the explanation of the Mahābhārata, by which even women, śūdras and others [friends of the twice-born] can see the path of religion.

PURPORT

No one can understand the import of the *Vedas* without having undergone a strict disciplinary vow and disciplic succession. The *Vedas,* spiritual masters and sacrificial fire must be worshiped by the desiring candidate. All these intricacies of Vedic knowledge are systematically presented in the *Mahābhārata* for the understanding of the woman class, the laborer class and the unqualified members of *brāhmaṇa, kṣatriya* or *vaiśya* families. In this age, the *Mahābhārata* is more essential than the original *Vedas.*

TEXT 30

तथापि बत मे दैह्यो ह्यात्मा चैवात्मना विभुः ।
असम्पन्न इवाभाति ब्रह्मवर्चस्य सत्तमः ॥३०॥

tathāpi bata me daihyo
hy ātmā caivātmanā vibhuḥ
asampanna ivābhāti
brahma-varcasya sattamaḥ

tathāpi—although; *bata*—defect; *me*—mine; *daihyaḥ*—situated in the body; *hi*—certainly; *ātmā*—living being; *ca*—and; *eva*—even; *ātmanā*—myself; *vibhuḥ*—sufficient; *asampannaḥ*—wanting in; *iva ābhāti*—it appears to be; *brahma-varcasya*—of the Vedāntists; *sattamaḥ*—the supreme.

TRANSLATION

I am feeling incomplete, though I myself am fully equipped with everything required by the Vedas.

PURPORT

Undoubtedly Śrīla Vyāsadeva was complete in all the details of Vedic achievements. Purification of the living being submerged in matter is made possible by the prescribed activities in the *Vedas,* but the ultimate achievement is different. Unless it is attained, the living being, even though fully equipped, cannot be situated in the transcendentally normal stage. Śrīla Vyāsadeva appeared to have lost the clue and therefore felt dissatisfaction.

TEXT 31

किं वा भागवता धर्मा न प्रायेण निरूपिताः ।
प्रियाः परमहंसानां त एव ह्यच्युतप्रियाः ॥३१॥

kiṁ vā bhāgavatā dharmā
na prāyeṇa nirūpitāḥ

priyāḥ paramahaṁsānāṁ
ta eva hy acyuta-priyāḥ

kiṁ vā—or; *bhāgavatāḥ dharmāḥ*—devotional activities of the living beings; *na*—not; *prāyeṇa*—almost; *nirūpitāḥ*—directed; *priyāḥ*—dear; *paramahaṁsānām*—of the perfect beings; *te eva*—that also; *hi*—certainly; *acyuta*—the infallible; *priyāḥ*—attractive.

TRANSLATION

This may be because I did not specifically point out the devotional service of the Lord, which is dear both to perfect beings and to the infallible Lord.

PURPORT

The dissatisfaction which was being felt by Śrīla Vyāsadeva is expressed herein in his own words. This was felt for the normal condition of the living being in the devotional service of the Lord. Unless one is fixed in the normal condition of service, neither the Lord nor the living being can become fully satisfied. This defect was felt by him when Nārada Muni, his spiritual master, reached him. It is described as follows.

TEXT 32

तस्यैवं खिलमात्मानं मन्यमानस्य खिद्यतः ।
कृष्णस्य नारदोऽभ्यागादाश्रमं प्रागुदाहृतम् ॥३२॥

tasyaivaṁ khilam ātmānaṁ
manyamānasya khidyataḥ
kṛṣṇasya nārado 'bhyāgād
āśramaṁ prāg udāhṛtam

tasya—his; *evam*—thus; *khilam*—inferior; *ātmānam*—soul; *manyamānasya*—thinking within the mind; *khidyataḥ*—regretting; *kṛṣṇasya*—of Kṛṣṇa-dvaipāyana Vyāsa; *nāradaḥ abhyāgāt*—Nārada came there; *āśramam*—the cottage; *prāk*—before; *udāhṛtam*—said.

TRANSLATION

As mentioned before, Nārada reached the cottage of Kṛṣṇa-dvaipāyana Vyāsa on the banks of the Sarasvatī just as Vyāsadeva was regretting his defects.

PURPORT

The vacuum felt by Vyāsadeva was not due to his lack of knowledge. *Bhāgavata-dharma* is purely devotional service of the Lord to which the monist has no access. The monist is not counted amongst the *paramahaṁsas* (the most perfect of the renounced order of life). *Śrīmad-Bhāgavatam* is full of narrations of the transcendental activities of the Personality of Godhead. Although Vyāsadeva was an empowered divinity, he still felt dissatisfaction because in none of his works were the transcendental activities of the Lord properly explained. The inspiration was infused by Śrī Kṛṣṇa directly in the heart of Vyāsadeva, and thus he felt the vacuum as explained above. It is definitely expressed herewith that without the transcendental loving service of the Lord, everything is void; but in the transcendental service of the Lord, everything is tangible without any separate attempt at fruitive work or empiric philosophical speculation.

TEXT 33

तमभिज्ञाय सहसा प्रत्युत्थायागतं मुनिः ।
पूजयामास विधिवन्नारदं सुरपूजितम् ॥३३॥

tam abhijñāya sahasā
pratyutthāyāgataṁ muniḥ
pūjayām āsa vidhivan
nāradaṁ sura-pūjitam

tam abhijñāya—seeing the good fortune of his (Nārada's) arrival; *sahasā*—all of a sudden; *pratyutthāya*—getting up; *āgatam*—arrived at; *muniḥ*—Vyāsadeva; *pūjayām āsa*—worship; *vidhi-vat*—with the same respect as offered to Vidhi (Brahmā); *nāradam*—to Nārada; *sura-pūjitam*—worshiped by the demigods.

TRANSLATION

At the auspicious arrival of Śrī Nārada, Śrī Vyāsadeva got up respectfully and worshiped him, giving him veneration equal to that given to Brahmājī, the creator.

PURPORT

Vidhi means Brahmā, the first created living being. He is the original student as well as professor of the *Vedas.* He learned it from Śrī Kṛṣṇa and taught Nārada first. So Nārada is the second *ācārya* in the line of spiritual disciplic succession. He is the representative of Brahmā, and therefore he is respected exactly like Brahmā, the father of all *vidhis* (regulations); similarly all other successive disciples in the chain are also equally respected as representatives of the original spiritual master.

Thus end the Bhaktivedanta purports of the First Canto, Fourth Chapter, of the Śrīmad-Bhāgavatam, *entitled "The Appearance of Śrī Nārada."*

CHAPTER FIVE

Nārada's Instructions on Śrīmad-Bhāgavatam for Vyāsadeva

TEXT 1

सूत उवाच
अथ तं सुखमासीन उपासीनं बृहच्छ्रवाः ।
देवर्षिः प्राह विप्रर्षिं वीणापाणिः स्मयन्निव ॥१॥

sūta uvāca
atha taṁ sukham āsīna
upāsīnaṁ bṛhac-chravāḥ
devarṣiḥ prāha viprarṣiṁ
vīṇā-pāṇiḥ smayann iva

sūtaḥ—Sūta; *uvāca*—said; *atha*—therefore; *tam*—him; *sukham āsīnaḥ*—comfortably seated; *upāsīnam*—unto one sitting nearby; *bṛhat-śravāḥ*—greatly respected; *devarṣiḥ*—the great *ṛṣi* among the gods; *prāha*—said; *viprarṣim*—unto the *ṛṣi* among the *brāhmaṇas; vīṇā-pāṇiḥ*—one who carries a *vīṇā* in his hand; *smayan iva*—apparently smiling.

TRANSLATION

Sūta Gosvāmī said: Thus the sage amongst the gods [Nārada], comfortably seated and apparently smiling, addressed the ṛṣi amongst the brāhmaṇas [Vedavyāsa].

PURPORT

Nārada was smiling because he well knew the great sage Vedavyāsa and the cause of his disappointment. As he will explain gradually, Vyāsadeva's disappointment was due to insufficiency in presenting the science of devotional service. Nārada knew the defect, and it was confirmed by the position of Vyāsa.

TEXT 2

नारद उवाच
पाराशर्य महाभाग भवतः कच्चिदात्मना।
परितुष्यति शारीर आत्मा मानस एव वा ॥२॥

nārada uvāca
pārāśarya mahā-bhāga
bhavataḥ kaccid ātmanā
parituṣyati śārīra
ātmā mānasa eva vā

nāradaḥ—Nārada; *uvāca*—said; *pārāśarya*—O son of Parāśara; *mahā-bhāga*—the greatly fortunate; *bhavataḥ*—your; *kaccit*—if it is; *ātmanā*—by the self-realization of; *parituṣyati*—does it satisfy; *śārīraḥ*—identifying the body; *ātmā*—self; *mānasaḥ*—identifying the mind; *eva*—certainly; *vā*—and.

TRANSLATION

Addressing Vyāsadeva, the son of Parāśara, Nārada inquired: Are you satisfied by identifying with the body or the mind as objects of self-realization?

PURPORT

This was a hint by Nārada to Vyāsadeva regarding the cause of his despondency. Vyāsadeva, as the descendant of Parāśara, a greatly powerful sage, had the privilege of having a great parentage which should not have given Vyāsadeva cause for despondency. Being a great son of a great father, he should not have identified the self with the body or the mind. Ordinary men with a poor fund of knowledge can identify the body as self or the mind as self, but Vyāsadeva should not have done so. One cannot be cheerful by nature unless one is factually seated in self-realization, which is transcendental to the material body and mind.

TEXT 3

जिज्ञासितं सुसम्पन्नमपि ते महदद्भुतम्।
कृतवान् भारतं यस्त्वं सर्वार्थपरिबृंहितम् ॥३॥

jijñāsitaṁ susampannam
api te mahad-adbhutam

kṛtavān bhāratam yas tvaṁ
sarvārtha-paribṛṁhitam

jijñāsitam—fully inquired; *susampannam*—well versed; *api*—in spite of; *te*—your; *mahat-adbhutam*—great and wonderful; *kṛtavān*—prepared; *bhāratam*—the *Mahābhārata; yaḥ tvam*—what you have done; *sarva-artha*—including all sequences; *paribṛṁhitam*—elaborately explained.

TRANSLATION

Your inquiries were full and your studies were also well fulfilled, and there is no doubt that you have prepared a great and wonderful work, the Mahābhārata, which is full of all kinds of Vedic sequences elaborately explained.

PURPORT

The despondency of Vyāsadeva was certainly not due to his lack of sufficient knowledge because as a student he had fully inquired about the Vedic literatures, as a result of which the *Mahābhārata* is compiled with full explanation of the *Vedas.*

TEXT 4

जिज्ञासितमधीतं च ब्रह्मयत्तत् सनातनम् ।
तथापि शोचस्यात्मानमकृतार्थ इव प्रभो ॥४॥

jijñāsitam adhītaṁ ca
brahma yat tat sanātanam
tathāpi śocasy ātmānam
akṛtārtha iva prabho

jijñāsitam—deliberated fully well; *adhītam*—the knowledge obtained; *ca*—and; *brahma*—the Absolute; *yat*—what; *tat*—that; *sanātanam*—eternal; *tathāpi*—in spite of that; *śocasi*—lamenting; *ātmānam*—unto the self; *akṛta-arthaḥ*—undone; *iva*—like; *prabho*—my dear sir.

TRANSLATION

You have fully delineated the subject of impersonal Brahman as well as the knowledge derived therefrom. Why should you be despondent in spite of all this, thinking that you are undone, my dear prabhu?

PURPORT

The *Vedānta-sūtra,* or *Brahma-sūtra,* compiled by Śrī Vyāsadeva is the full deliberation of the impersonal absolute feature, and it is accepted as the most exalted philosophical exposition in the world. It covers the subject of eternity, and the methods are scholarly. So there cannot be any doubt about the transcendental scholarship of Vyāsadeva. So why should he lament?

TEXT 5

व्यास उवाच
अस्त्येव मे सर्वमिदं त्वयोक्तं
तथापि नात्मा परितुष्यते मे ।
तन्मूलमव्यक्तमगाधबोधं
पृच्छामहे त्वात्मभवात्मभूतम् ॥५॥

vyāsa uvāca
asty eva me sarvam idaṁ tvayoktaṁ
tathāpi nātmā parituṣyate me
tan-mūlam avyaktam agādha-bodhaṁ
pṛcchāmahe tvātma-bhavātma-bhūtam

vyāsaḥ—Vyāsa; *uvāca*—said; *asti*—there is; *eva*—certainly; *me*—mine; *sarvam*—all; *idam*—this; *tvayā*—by you; *uktam*—uttered; *tathāpi*—and yet; *na*—not; *ātmā*—self; *parituṣyate*—does pacify; *me*—unto me; *tat*—of which; *mūlam*—root; *avyaktam*—undetected; *agādha-bodham*—the man of unlimited knowledge; *pṛcchāmahe*—do inquire; *tvā*—unto you; *ātma-bhava*—self-born; *ātma-bhūtam*—offspring.

TRANSLATION

Śrī Vyāsadeva said: All you have said about me is perfectly correct. Despite all this, I am not pacified. I therefore question you about the root cause of my dissatisfaction, for you are a man of unlimited knowledge due to your being the offspring of one [Brahmā] who is self-born [without mundane father and mother].

PURPORT

In the material world everyone is engrossed with the idea of identifying the body or the mind with the self. As such, all knowledge disseminated in the material world is related either with the body or with the mind, and that is the root cause of all despondencies. This is not always detected, even though one may be the greatest erudite scholar in materialistic knowledge. It is good, therefore, to approach a personality like Nārada to solve the root cause of all despondencies. Why Nārada should be approached is explained below.

TEXT 6

स वै भवान् वेद समस्तगुह्य-
मुपासितो यत्पुरुषः पुराणः ।
परावरेशो मनसैव विश्वं
सृजत्यवत्यत्ति गुणैरसङ्गः ॥६॥

sa vai bhavān veda samasta-guhyam
upāsito yat puruṣaḥ purāṇaḥ
parāvareśo manasaiva viśvaṁ
sṛjaty avaty atti guṇair asaṅgaḥ

saḥ—thus; *vai*—certainly; *bhavān*—yourself; *veda*—know; *samasta*—all-inclusive; *guhyam*—confidential; *upāsitaḥ*—devotee of; *yat*—because; *puruṣaḥ*—the Personality of Godhead; *purāṇaḥ*—the oldest; *parāvareśaḥ*—the controller of the material and spiritual worlds; *manasā*—mind; *eva*—only; *viśvam*—the universe; *sṛjati*—creates; *avati atti*—annihilates; *guṇaiḥ*—by the qualitative matter; *asaṅgaḥ*—unattached.

TRANSLATION

My lord! Everything that is mysterious is known to you because you worship the creator and destroyer of the material world and the maintainer of the spiritual world, the original Personality of Godhead, who is transcendental to the three modes of material nature.

PURPORT

A person who is cent-percent engaged in the service of the Lord is the emblem of all knowledge. Such a devotee of the Lord in full perfection of devotional service is also perfect by the qualification of the Personality of Godhead. As such, the eightfold perfections of mystic power (*aṣṭa-siddhi*) constitute very little of his godly opulence. A devotee like Nārada can act wonderfully by his spiritual perfection, which every individual is trying to attain. Śrīla Nārada is a cent-percent perfect living being, although not equal to the Personality of Godhead.

TEXT 7

त्वं पर्यटन्नर्क इव त्रिलोकी-
मन्तश्चरो वायुरिवात्मसाक्षी ।
परावरे ब्रह्मणि धर्मतो व्रतैः
स्नातस्य मे न्यूनमलं विचक्ष्व ॥ ७ ॥

tvaṁ paryaṭann arka iva tri-lokīm
antaś-caro vāyur ivātma-sākṣī
parāvare brahmaṇi dharmato vrataiḥ
snātasya me nyūnam alaṁ vicakṣva

tvam—Your Goodness; *paryaṭan*—traveling; *arkaḥ*—the sun; *iva*—like; *tri-lokīm*—the three worlds; *antaḥ-caraḥ*—can penetrate into everyone's heart; *vāyuḥ iva*—as good as the all-pervading air; *ātma*—self-realized; *sākṣī*—witness; *parāvare*—in the matter of cause and effect; *brahmaṇi*—in the Absolute; *dharmataḥ*—under disciplinary regulations; *vrataiḥ*—in vow; *snātasya*—having been absorbed in; *me*—mine; *nyūnam*—deficiency; *alam*—clearly; *vicakṣva*—search out.

TRANSLATION

Like the sun, Your Goodness can travel everywhere in the three worlds, and like the air you can penetrate the internal region of everyone. As such, you are as good as the all-pervasive Supersoul. Please, therefore, find out the deficiency in me, despite my being absorbed in transcendence under disciplinary regulations and vows.

PURPORT

Transcendental realization, pious activities, worshiping the Deities, charity, mercifulness, nonviolence and studying the scriptures under strict disciplinary regulations are always helpful.

TEXT 8

श्रीनारद उवाच

भवतानुदितप्रायं यशो भगवतोऽमलम् ।
येनैवासौ न तुष्येत मन्ये तद्दर्शनं खिलम् ॥८॥

śrī-nārada uvāca
bhavatānudita-prāyaṁ
yaśo bhagavato 'malam
yenaivāsau na tuṣyeta
manye tad darśanaṁ khilam

śrī-nāradaḥ—Śrī Nārada; *uvāca*—said; *bhavatā*—by you; *anudita-prāyam*—almost not praised; *yaśaḥ*—glories; *bhagavataḥ*—of the Personality of Godhead; *amalam*—spotless; *yena*—by which; *eva*—certainly; *asau*—He (the Personality of Godhead); *na*—does not; *tuṣyeta*—be pleased; *manye*—I think; *tat*—that; *darśanam*—philosophy; *khilam*—inferior.

TRANSLATION

Śrī Nārada said: You have not actually broadcast the sublime and spotless glories of the Personality of Godhead. That philosophy which does not satisfy the transcendental senses of the Lord is considered worthless.

PURPORT

The eternal relation of an individual soul with the Supreme Soul Personality of Godhead is constitutionally one of being the eternal servitor of the eternal master. The Lord has expanded Himself as living beings in order to accept loving service from them, and this alone can satisfy both the Lord and the living beings. Such a scholar as Vyāsadeva has completed many expansions of the Vedic literatures, ending with the Vedānta philosophy, but none of them have been written directly glorifying the Personality of Godhead. Dry philosophical speculations even on the transcendental subject of the Absolute have very little attraction without directly dealing with the glorification of the Lord. The Personality of Godhead is the last word in transcendental realization. The Absolute realized as impersonal Brahman or localized Supersoul, Paramātmā, is less productive of transcendental bliss than the supreme personal realization of His glories.

The compiler of the *Vedānta-darśana* is Vyāsadeva himself. Yet he is troubled, although he is the author. So what sort of transcendental bliss can be derived by the readers and listeners of Vedānta which is not explained directly by Vyāsadeva, the author? Herein arises the necessity of explaining *Vedānta-sūtra* in the form of *Śrīmad-Bhāgavatam* by the self-same author.

TEXT 9

यथा धर्मादयश्चार्था मुनिवर्यानुकीर्तिताः ।
न तथा वासुदेवस्य महिमा ह्यनुवर्णितः ॥९॥

yathā dharmādayaś cārthā
muni-varyānukīrtitāḥ
na tathā vāsudevasya
mahimā hy anuvarṇitaḥ

yathā—as much as; *dharma-ādayaḥ*—all four principles of religious behavior; *ca*—and; *arthāḥ*—purposes; *muni-varya*—by yourself, the great sage; *anukīrtitāḥ*—repeatedly described; *na*—not; *tathā*—in that way; *vāsudevasya*—of the Personality of Godhead, Śrī Kṛṣṇa; *mahimā*—glories; *hi*—certainly; *anuvarṇitaḥ*—so constantly described.

TRANSLATION

Although, great sage, you have very broadly described the four principles beginning with religious performances, you have not described the glories of the Supreme Personality, Vāsudeva.

PURPORT

The prompt diagnosis of Śrī Nārada is at once declared. The root cause of the despondency of Vyāsadeva was his deliberate avoidance of glorifying the Lord in his various editions of the *Purāṇas.* He has certainly, as a matter of course, given descriptions of the glories of the Lord (Śrī Kṛṣṇa), but not as many as given to religiosity, economic development, sense gratification and salvation. These four items are by far inferior to engagement in the devotional service of the Lord. Śrī Vyāsadeva, as the authorized scholar, knew very well this difference. And still instead of giving more importance to the better type of engagement, namely, devotional service to the Lord, he had more or less improperly used his valuable time, and thus he was despondent. From this it is clearly indicated that no one can be pleased substantially without being engaged in the devotional service of the Lord. In the *Bhagavad-gītā* this fact is clearly mentioned.

After liberation, which is the last item in the line of performing religiosity, etc., one is engaged in pure devotional service. This is called the stage of self-realization, or the *brahma-bhūta* stage. After attainment of this *brahma-bhūta* stage, one is satisfied. But satisfaction is the beginning of transcendental bliss. One should progress by attaining neutrality and equality in the relative world. And passing this stage of equanimity, one is fixed in the transcendental loving service of the Lord. This is the instruction of the Personality of Godhead in the *Bhagavad-gītā.* The conclusion is that in order to maintain the status quo of the *brahma-bhūta* stage, as also to increase the degree of transcendental realization, Nārada recommended to Vyāsadeva that he (Vyāsadeva) should now eagerly and repeatedly describe the path of devotional service. This would cure him from gross despondency.

TEXT 10

न यद्वचश्चित्रपदं हरेर्यशो
जगत्पवित्रं प्रगृणीत कर्हिचित् ।
तद्वायसं तीर्थमुशन्ति मानसा
न यत्र हंसा निरमन्त्युशिक्क्षयाः ॥१०॥

na yad vacaś citra-padaṁ harer yaśo
jagat-pavitraṁ pragṛṇīta karhicit
tad vāyasaṁ tīrtham uśanti mānasā
na yatra haṁsā niramanty uśik-kṣayāḥ

na—not; *yat*—that; *vacaḥ*—vocabulary; *citra-padam*—decorative; *hareḥ*—of the Lord; *yaśaḥ*—glories; *jagat*—universe; *pavitram*—sanctified; *pragṛṇīta*—described; *karhicit*—hardly; *tat*—that; *vāyasam*—crows; *tīrtham*—place of pilgrimage; *uśanti*—think; *mānasāḥ*—saintly persons; *na*—not; *yatra*—where; *haṁsāḥ*—all-perfect beings; *niramanti*—take pleasure; *uśik-kṣayāḥ*—those who reside in the transcendental abode.

TRANSLATION

Those words which do not describe the glories of the Lord, who alone can sanctify the atmosphere of the whole universe, are considered by saintly persons to be like unto a place of pilgrimage for crows. Since the all-perfect persons are inhabitants of the transcendental abode, they do not derive any pleasure there.

PURPORT

Crows and swans are not birds of the same feather because of their different mental attitudes. The fruitive workers or passionate men are compared to the crows, whereas the all-perfect saintly persons are compared to the swans. The crows take pleasure in a place where garbage is thrown out, just as the passionate fruitive workers take pleasure in wine and woman and places for gross sense pleasure. The swans do not take pleasure in the places where crows are assembled for conferences and meetings. They are instead seen in the atmosphere of natural scenic beauty where there are transparent reservoirs of water nicely decorated with stems of lotus flowers in variegated colors of natural beauty. That is the difference between the two classes of birds.

Nature has influenced different species of life with different mentalities, and it is not possible to bring them up into the same rank and file.

Similarly, there are different kinds of literature for different types of men of different mentality. Mostly the market literatures which attract men of the crow's categories are literatures containing refused remnants of sensuous topics. They are generally known as mundane talks in relation with the gross body and subtle mind. They are full of subject matter described in decorative language full of mundane similes and metaphorical arrangements. Yet with all that, they do not glorify the Lord. Such poetry and prose, on any subject matter, is considered decoration of a dead body. Spiritually advanced men who are compared to the swans do not take pleasure in such dead literatures, which are sources of pleasure for men who are spiritually dead. These literatures in the modes of passion and ignorance are distributed under different labels, but they can hardly help the spiritual urge of the human being, and thus the swanlike spiritually advanced men have nothing to do with them. Such spiritually advanced men are called also *mānasa* because they always keep up the standard of transcendental voluntary service to the Lord on the spiritual plane. This completely forbids fruitive activities for gross bodily sense satisfaction or subtle speculation of the material egoistic mind.

Social literary men, scientists, mundane poets, theoretical philosophers and politicians who are completely absorbed in the material advancement of sense pleasure are all dolls of the material energy. They take pleasure in a place where rejected subject matters are thrown. According to Svāmī Śrīdhara, this is the pleasure of the prostitute-hunters.

But literatures which describe the glories of the Lord are enjoyed by the *paramahaṁsas* who have grasped the essence of human activities.

TEXT 11

तद्वाग्विसर्गो जनताघविप्लवो
यस्मिन् प्रतिश्लोकमबद्धवत्यपि ।

नामान्यनन्तस्य यशोऽङ्कितानि यत्
श्रृण्वन्ति गायन्ति गृणन्ति साधवः ॥११॥

tad-vāg-visargo janatāgha-viplavo
yasmin prati-ślokam abaddhavaty api
nāmāny anantasya yaśo 'ṅkitāni yat
śṛṇvanti gāyanti gṛṇanti sādhavaḥ

tat—that; *vāk*—vocabulary; *visargaḥ*—creation; *janatā*—the people in general; *agha*—sins; *viplavaḥ*—revolutionary; *yasmin*—in which; *prati-ślokam*—each and every stanza; *abaddhavati*—irregularly composed; *api*—in spite of; *nāmāni*—transcendental names, etc.; *anantasya*—of the unlimited Lord; *yaśaḥ*—glories; *aṅkitāni*—depicted; *yat*—what; *śṛṇvanti*—do hear; *gāyanti*—do sing; *gṛṇanti*—do accept; *sādhavaḥ*—the purified men who are honest.

TRANSLATION

On the other hand, that literature which is full of descriptions of the transcendental glories of the name, fame, forms, pastimes, etc., of the unlimited Supreme Lord is a different creation, full of transcendental words directed toward bringing about a revolution in the impious lives of this world's misdirected civilization. Such transcendental literatures, even though imperfectly composed, are heard, sung and accepted by purified men who are thoroughly honest.

PURPORT

It is a qualification of the great thinkers to pick up the best even from the worst. It is said that the intelligent man should pick up nectar from a stock of poison, should accept gold even from a filthy place, should accept a good and qualified wife even from an obscure family and should accept a good lesson even from a man or from a teacher who comes from the untouchables. These are some of the ethical instructions for everyone in every place without exception. But a saint is far above the level of an ordinary man. He is always absorbed in glorifying the Supreme Lord because by broadcasting the holy name and fame of the Supreme Lord, the polluted atmosphere of the world will change, and as a result of propagating the transcendental literatures like *Śrīmad-Bhāgavatam,* people will become sane in their transactions. While preparing this commentation on this particular stanza of *Śrīmad-Bhāgavatam* we have a crisis before us. Our neighboring friend China has attacked the border of India with a militaristic spirit. We have practically no business in the political field, yet we see that previously there were both China and India, and they both lived peacefully for centuries without ill feeling. The reason is that they lived those days in an atmosphere of God consciousness, and every country, over the surface of the world, was God-fearing, purehearted and simple, and there was no question of political diplomacy. There is no cause of quarrel between the two countries China and India over land which is not very suitable for habitation, and certainly there is no cause for fighting on this issue. But due to the age of quarrel, Kali, which we have discussed, there is always a chance of quarrel on slight provocation. This is due not to the issue in question, but to the polluted atmosphere of this age: systematically there is propaganda by a section of people *to stop glorification of the name and fame of the Supreme Lord.* Therefore, there is a great need for disseminating the *message of Śrīmad-Bhāgavatam* all over the world. It is the duty of every responsible Indian to broadcast the transcendental message of *Śrīmad-Bhāgavatam* throughout the world to do all the supermost good as well as to bring about the desired peace in the world. Because India has failed in her duty by neglecting this responsible work, there is so much quarrel and trouble all over the world. We are confident that if the transcendental message of *Śrīmad-Bhāgavatam* is received only by the leading men of the world, certainly there will be a change of heart, and naturally the people in general will follow them. The mass of people in general are tools in the hands of the modern politicians and leaders of the people. If there is a change of heart of the leaders only, certainly there will be a radical change in the atmosphere of the world. We know that our honest attempt to present this great literature conveying transcendental messages for reviving the God consciousness of the people in general and respiritualizing the world atmosphere is fraught with many difficulties. Our presenting this matter in adequate language, especially a foreign language, will certainly fail, and there will be so many literary discrepancies despite our honest attempt to present it in the proper way. But we are sure that with all our faults in this connection the seriousness of the subject matter will be taken into consideration, and the leaders of society will still accept this due to its being an honest attempt to glorify the almighty God. When there is fire in a house, the inmates of the house go out to get help from the neighbors who may be foreigners, and yet without knowing the language the victims of the fire express themselves, and the neighbors understand the need, even though not expressed in the same language. The same spirit of cooperation is needed to broadcast this transcendental message of the *Śrīmad-Bhāgavatam* throughout the polluted atmosphere of the world. After all, it is a technical science of spiritual values, and thus we are concerned with the techniques and not with the language. If the techniques of this great literature are understood by the people of the world, there will be success.

When there are too many materialistic activities by the people in general all over the world, there is no wonder that a person or a nation attacks another person or nation on slight provocation. That is the rule of this age of Kali or quarrel. The atmosphere is already polluted with corruption of all description, and everyone knows it well. There are so many unwanted literatures full of materialistic ideas of sense gratification. In many countries there are bodies appointed by the state to detect and censor obscene literature. This means that neither the government nor the responsible leaders of the public want such literature, yet it is in the marketplace because the people want it for sense gratification. The people in general want to read (that is a natural instinct), but because their minds are polluted they want such literatures. Under the circumstances, transcendental literature like *Śrīmad-Bhāgavatam* will not only diminish the activities of the corrupt mind of the people in general, but also it will supply food for their hankering after reading some interesting literature. In the beginning they may not like it because one suffering from jaundice is reluctant to take sugar candy, but we should know that sugar candy is the only remedy for jaundice. Similarly, let there be systematic propaganda for popularizing reading of the *Bhagavad-gītā* and the *Śrīmad-Bhāgavatam,* which will act like sugar candy for the jaundicelike condition of sense gratification. When men have a taste for this literature, the other literatures, which are catering poison to society, will then automatically cease.

We are sure, therefore, that everyone in human society will welcome *Śrīmad-Bhāgavatam,* even though it is now presented with so many faults, for it is recommended by Śrī Nārada, who has very kindly appeared in this chapter.

TEXT 12

नैष्कर्म्यमप्यच्युतभाववर्जितं
न शोभते ज्ञानमलं निरञ्जनम् ।
कुतः पुनः शश्वदभद्रमीश्वरे
न चार्पितं कर्म यदप्यकारणम् ॥१२॥

naiṣkarmyam apy acyuta-bhāva-varjitaṁ
na śobhate jñānam alaṁ nirañjanam

kutaḥ punaḥ śaśvad abhadram īśvare
na cārpitaṁ karma yad apy akāraṇam

naiṣkarmyam—self-realization, being freed from the reactions of fruitive work; *api*—in spite of; *acyuta*—the infallible Lord; *bhāva*—conception; *varjitam*—devoid of; *na*—does not; *śobhate*—look well; *jñānam*—transcendental knowledge; *alam*—by and by; *nirañjanam*—free from designations; *kutaḥ*—where is; *punaḥ*—again; *śaśvat*—always; *abhadram*—uncongenial; *īśvare*—unto the Lord; *na*—not; *ca*—and; *arpitam*—offered; *karma*—fruitive work; *yat api*—what is; *akāraṇam*—not fruitive.

TRANSLATION

Knowledge of self-realization, even though free from all material affinity, does not look well if devoid of a conception of the Infallible [God]. What, then, is the use of fruitive activities, which are naturally painful from the very beginning and transient by nature, if they are not utilized for the devotional service of the Lord?

PURPORT

As referred to above, not only ordinary literatures devoid of the transcendental glorification of the Lord are condemned, but also Vedic literatures and speculation on the subject of impersonal Brahman when they are devoid of devotional service. When speculation on the impersonal Brahman is condemned on the above ground, then what to speak of ordinary fruitive work, which is not meant to fulfill the aim of devotional service. Such speculative knowledge and fruitive work cannot lead one to the goal of perfection. Fruitive work, in which almost all people in general are engaged, is always painful either in the beginning or at the end. It can be fruitful only when made subservient to the devotional service of the Lord. In the *Bhagavad-gītā* also it is confirmed that the result of such fruitive work may be offered for the service of the Lord, otherwise it leads to material bondage. The bona fide enjoyer of the fruitive work is the Personality of Godhead, and thus when it is engaged for the sense gratification of the living beings, it becomes an acute source of trouble.

TEXT 13

अथो महाभाग भवानमोघदृक्
शुचिश्रवाः सत्यरतो धृतव्रतः ।

उरुक्रमस्याखिलबन्धमुक्तये
समाधिनानुस्मर तद्विचेष्टितम् ॥१३॥

atho mahā-bhāga bhavān amogha-dṛk
śuci-śravāḥ satya-rato dhṛta-vrataḥ
urukramasyākhila-bandha-muktaye
samādhinānusmara tad-viceṣṭitam

atho—therefore; *mahā-bhāga*—highly fortunate; *bhavān*—yourself; *amogha-dṛk*—the perfect seer; *śuci*—spotless; *śravāḥ*—famous; *satya-rataḥ*—having taken the vow of truthfulness; *dhṛta-vrataḥ*—fixed in spiritual qualities; *urukramasya*—of the one who performs supernatural activities (God); *akhila*—universal; *bandha*—bondage; *muktaye*—for liberation from; *samādhinā*—by trance; *anusmara*—think repeatedly and then describe them; *tat-viceṣṭitam*—various pastimes of the Lord.

TRANSLATION

O Vyāsadeva, your vision is completely perfect. Your good fame is spotless. You are firm in vow and situated in truthfulness. And thus you can think of the pastimes of the Lord in trance for the liberation of the people in general from all material bondage.

PURPORT

People in general have a taste for literatures by instinct. They want to hear and read from the authorities something about the unknown, but their taste is exploited by unfortunate literatures which are full of subject matter for satisfaction of the material senses. Such literatures contain different kinds of mundane poems and philosophical speculations, more or less under the influence of *māyā,* ending in sense gratification. These literatures, although worthless in the true sense of the term, are variously decorated to attract the attention of the less intelligent men. Thus the attracted living entities are more and more entangled in material bondage without hope of liberation for thousands and thousands of generations. Śrī Nārada Ṛṣi, being the best amongst the Vaiṣṇavas, is compassionate toward such unfortunate victims of worthless literatures, and thus he advises Śrī Vyāsadeva to compose transcendental literature which is not only attractive but can also actually bring liberation from all kinds of bondage. Śrīla Vyāsadeva or his representatives are qualified because they are rightly trained to see things in true perspective. Śrīla Vyāsadeva and his representatives are pure in thought due to their spiritual enlightenment, fixed in their vows due to their devotional service, and determined to deliver the fallen souls rotting in material activities. The fallen souls are very eager to receive novel informations every day, and the transcendentalists like Vyāsadeva or Nārada can supply such eager people in general with unlimited news from the spiritual world. In the *Bhagavad-gītā* it is said that the material world is only a part of the whole creation and that this earth is only a fragment of the whole material world.

There are thousands and thousands of literary men all over the world, and they have created many, many thousands of literary works for the information of the people in general for thousands and thousands of years. Unfortunately none of them have brought peace and tranquillity on the earth. This is due to a spiritual vacuum in those literatures; therefore the Vedic literatures, especially the *Bhagavad-gītā* and the *Śrīmad-Bhāgavatam,* are specifically recommended to suffering humanity to bring about the desired effect of liberation from the pangs of material civilization, which is eating the vital part of human energy. The *Bhagavad-gītā* is the spoken message of the Lord Himself recorded by Vyāsadeva, and the *Śrīmad-Bhāgavatam* is the transcendental narration of the activities of the same Lord Kṛṣṇa, which alone can satisfy the hankering desires of the living being for eternal peace and liberation from miseries. *Śrīmad-Bhāgavatam,* therefore, is meant for all the living beings all over the universe for total liberation from all kinds of material bondage. Such transcendental narrations of the pastimes of the Lord can be described only by liberated souls like Vyāsadeva and his bona fide representatives who are completely merged in the transcendental loving service of the Lord. Only to such devotees do the pastimes of the Lord and their transcendental nature become automatically manifest by dint of devotional service. No one else can either know or describe the acts of the Lord, even if they speculate on the subject for many, many years. The descriptions of the *Bhāgavatam* are so precise and accurate that whatever has been predicted in this great literature about five thousand years ago is now exactly happening. Therefore, the vision of the author comprehends past, present and future. Such liberated persons as Vyāsadeva are perfect not only by the power of vision and wisdom, but also in aural reception, in thinking, feeling and all other sense activities. A liberated person possesses perfect senses, and with perfect senses only can one serve the sense proprietor, Hṛṣīkeśa, Śrī Kṛṣṇa the Personality of Godhead. *Śrīmad-Bhāgavatam,* therefore, is the perfect description of the all-perfect Personality of Godhead by the all-perfect personality Śrīla Vyāsadeva, the compiler of the *Vedas.*

TEXT 14

ततोऽन्यथा किञ्चन यद्विवक्षतः
पृथग्दृशस्तत्कृतरूपनामभिः ।
न कर्हिचित्क्वापि च दुःस्थिता मति-
र्लभेत वाताहतनौरिवास्पदम् ॥१४॥

tato 'nyathā kiñcana yad vivakṣataḥ
pṛthag dṛśas tat-kṛta-rūpa-nāmabhiḥ
na karhicit kvāpi ca duḥsthitā matir
labheta vātāhata-naur ivāspadam

tataḥ—from that; *anyathā*—apart; *kiñcana*—something; *yat*—whatsoever; *vivakṣataḥ*—desiring to describe; *pṛthak*—separately; *dṛśaḥ*—vision; *tat-kṛta*—reactionary to that; *rūpa*—form; *nāmabhiḥ*—by names; *na karhicit*—never; *kvāpi*—any; *ca*—and; *duḥsthitā matiḥ*—oscillating mind; *labheta*—gains; *vāta-āhata*—troubled by the wind; *nauḥ*—boat; *iva*—like; *āspadam*—place.

TRANSLATION

Whatever you desire to describe that is separate in vision from the Lord simply reacts, with different forms, names and results, to agitate the mind as the wind agitates a boat which has no resting place.

PURPORT

Śrī Vyāsadeva is the editor of all descriptions of the Vedic literatures, and thus he has described transcendental realization in different ways, namely by fruitive activities, speculative knowledge, mystic power and devotional service. Besides that, in his various *Purāṇas* he has recommended the worship of so many demigods in different forms and names. The result is that people in general are puzzled how to fix their minds in the service of the Lord; they are always disturbed about finding the real path of self-realization. Śrīla Nāradadeva is stressing this particular defect in the Vedic literatures compiled by Vyāsadeva, and thus he is trying to emphasize describing everything in relation with the Supreme Lord, and no one else. In fact, there is nothing existent except the Lord. The Lord is manifested in different expansions. He is the root of the complete tree. He is the stomach of the complete body. Pouring water on the root is the right process to water the tree, as much as feeding the stomach supplies energy to all parts of the body. Therefore, Śrīla Vyāsadeva should not have compiled any *Purāṇas* other than the *Bhāgavata Purāṇa* because a slight deviation from that may create havoc for self-realization. If a slight deviation can create such havoc, then what to speak of deliberate expansion of the ideas separate from the Absolute Truth Personality of Godhead. The most defective part of worshiping demigods is that it creates a definite conception of pantheism, ending disastrously in many religious sects detrimental to the progress of the principles of the *Bhāgavatam,* which alone can give the accurate direction for self-realization in eternal relation with the Personality of Godhead by devotional service in transcendental love. The example of the boat disturbed by whirling wind is suitable in this respect. The diverted mind of the pantheist can never reach the perfection of self-realization, due to the disturbed condition of the selection of object.

TEXT 15

जुगुप्सितं धर्मकृतेऽनुशासतः
स्वभावरक्तस्य महान् व्यतिक्रमः ।
यद्वाक्यतो धर्म इतीतरः स्थितो
न मन्यते तस्य निवारणं जनः ॥१५॥

jugupsitaṁ dharma-kṛte 'nuśāsataḥ
svabhāva-raktasya mahān vyatikramaḥ
yad-vākyato dharma itītaraḥ sthito
na manyate tasya nivāraṇaṁ janaḥ

jugupsitam—verily condemned; *dharma-kṛte*—for the matter of religion; *anuśāsataḥ*—instruction; *svabhāva-raktasya*—naturally inclined; *mahān*—great; *vyatikramaḥ*—unreasonable; *yat-vākyataḥ*—under whose instruction; *dharmaḥ*—religion; *iti*—it is thus; *itaraḥ*—the people in general; *sthitaḥ*—fixed; *na*—do not; *manyate*—think; *tasya*—of that; *nivāraṇam*—prohibition; *janaḥ*—they.

TRANSLATION

The people in general are naturally inclined to enjoy, and you have encouraged them in that way in the name of religion. This is verily

condemned and is quite unreasonable. Because they are guided under your instructions, they will accept such activities in the name of religion and will hardly care for prohibitions.

PURPORT

Śrīla Vyāsadeva's compilation of different Vedic literatures on the basis of regulated performances of fruitive activities as depicted in the *Mahābhārata* and other literature is condemned herewith by Śrīla Nārada. The human beings, by long material association, life after life, have a natural inclination, by practice, to endeavor to lord it over material energy. They have no sense of the responsibility of human life. This human form of life is a chance to get out of the clutches of illusory matter. The *Vedas* are meant for going back to Godhead, going back home. To revolve in the cycle of transmigration in a series of lives numbering 8,400,000 is an imprisoned life for the condemned conditioned souls. The human form of life is a chance to get out of this imprisoned life, and as such the only occupation of the human being is to reestablish his lost relationship with God. Under the circumstances, one should never be encouraged in making a plan for sense enjoyment in the name of religious functions. Such diversion of the human energy results in a misguided civilization. Śrīla Vyāsadeva is the authority in Vedic explanations in the *Mahābhārata,* etc., and his encouragement in sense enjoyment in some form or other is a great barrier for spiritual advancement because the people in general will not agree to renounce material activities which hold them in material bondage. At a certain stage of human civilization when such material activities in the name of religion (as sacrificing animals in the name of *yajña*) were too much rampant, the Lord incarnated Himself as Buddha and decried the authority of the *Vedas* in order to stop animal sacrifice in the name of religion. This was foreseen by Nārada, and therefore he condemned such literatures. The flesh-eaters still continue to perform animal sacrifice before some demigod or goddess in the name of religion because in some of the Vedic literatures such regulated sacrifices are recommended. They are so recommended to discourage flesh-eating, but gradually the purpose of such religious activities is forgotten, and the slaughterhouse becomes prominent. This is because foolish materialistic men do not care to listen to others who are actually in a position to explain the Vedic rites.

In the *Vedas* it is distinctly said that the perfection of life is never to be attained either by voluminous work, or by accumulation of wealth or even by increasing the population. But it is so attained only by renunciation. The materialistic men do not care to listen to such injunctions. According to them, the so-called renounced order of life is meant for those who are unable to earn their livelihood because of some corporeal defects, or for persons who have failed to achieve prosperity in family life.

In histories like the *Mahābhārata,* of course, there are topics on transcendental subjects along with material topics. The *Bhagavad-gītā* is there in the *Mahābhārata.* The whole idea of the *Mahābhārata* culminates in the ultimate instructions of the *Bhagavad-gītā,* that one should relinquish all other engagements and should engage oneself solely and fully in surrendering unto the lotus feet of Lord Śrī Kṛṣṇa. But men with materialistic tendencies are more attracted to the politics, economics and philanthropic activities mentioned in the *Mahābhārata* than to the principal topic, namely the *Bhagavad-gītā.* This compromising spirit of Vyāsadeva is directly condemned by Nārada, who advises him to directly proclaim that the prime necessity of human life is to realize one's eternal relation with the Lord and thus surrender unto Him without delay.

A patient suffering from a particular type of malady is almost always inclined to accept eatables which are forbidden for him. The expert physician does not make any compromise with the patient by allowing him to take partially what he should not at all take. In the *Bhagavad-gītā* it is also said that a man attached to fruitive work should not be discouraged from his occupation, for gradually he may be elevated to the position of self-realization. This is sometimes applicable for those who are only dry empiric philosophers without spiritual realization. But those who are in the devotional line need not be always so advised.

TEXT 16

विचक्षणोऽस्यार्हति वेदितुं विभो-
रनन्तपारस्य निवृत्तितः सुखम् ।
प्रवर्तमानस्य गुणैरनात्मन-
स्ततो भवान्दर्शय चेष्टितं विभोः ॥१६॥

vicakṣaṇo 'syārhati veditum̐ vibhor
ananta-pārasya nivṛttitaḥ sukham
pravartamānasya guṇair anātmanas
tato bhavān darśaya ceṣṭitam̐ vibhoḥ

vicakṣaṇaḥ—very expert; *asya*—of him; *arhati*—deserves; *veditum*—to understand; *vibhoḥ*—of the Lord; *ananta-pārasya*—of the unlimited; *nivṛttitaḥ*—retired from; *sukham*—material happiness; *pravartamānasya*—those who are attached to; *guṇaiḥ*—by the material qualities; *anātmanaḥ*—devoid of knowledge in spiritual value; *tataḥ*—therefore; *bhavān*—Your Goodness; *darśaya*—show the ways; *ceṣṭitam*—activities; *vibhoḥ*—of the Lord.

TRANSLATION

The Supreme Lord is unlimited. Only a very expert personality, retired from the activities of material happiness, deserves to understand this knowledge of spiritual values. Therefore those who are not so well situated, due to material attachment, should be shown the ways of transcendental realization, by Your Goodness, through descriptions of the transcendental activities of the Supreme Lord.

PURPORT

Theological science is a difficult subject, especially when it deals with the transcendental nature of God. It is not a subject matter to be understood by persons who are too much attached to material activities. Only the very expert, who have almost retired from materialistic activities by culture of spiritual knowledge, can be admitted to the study of this great science. In the *Bhagavad-gītā* it is clearly stated that out of many hundreds and thousands of men only one person deserves to enter into transcendental realization. And out of many thousands of such transcendentally realized persons, only a few can understand the theological science specifically dealing with God as a person. Śrī Vyāsadeva is therefore advised by Nārada to describe the science of God directly by relating His transcendental activities. Vyāsadeva is himself a personality expert in this science, and he is unattached to material enjoyment. Therefore he is the right person to describe it, and Śukadeva Gosvāmī, the son of Vyāsadeva, is the right person to receive it.

Śrīmad-Bhāgavatam is the topmost theological science, and therefore it can react on the laymen as medicinal doses. Because it contains the transcendental activities of the Lord, there is no difference between the Lord and the literature. The literature is the factual literary incarnation of the Lord. So the laymen can hear the narration of the activities of the Lord. Thereby they are able to associate with the Lord and thus gradually become purified from material diseases. The expert devotees also can discover novel ways and means to convert the nondevotees in terms of particular time and circumstance. Devotional service is dynamic activity, and the expert devotees can find out competent means to inject it into the dull brains of the materialistic population. Such transcendental activities of the devotees for the service of the Lord can bring a new order of life to the foolish society of materialistic men. Lord Śrī Caitanya Mahāprabhu and His subsequent followers exhibited expert dexterity in this connection. By following the same method, one can bring the materialistic men of this age of quarrel into order for peaceful life and transcendental realization.

TEXT 17

त्यक्त्वा स्वधर्मं चरणाम्बुजं हरे-
भर्जन्नपक्वोऽथ पतेत्ततो यदि ।
यत्र क्व वाभद्रमभूदमुष्य किं
को वार्थ आप्तोऽभजतां स्वधर्मतः ॥१७॥

tyaktvā sva-dharmaṁ caraṇāmbujaṁ harer
bhajann apakvo 'tha patet tato yadi
yatra kva vābhadram abhūd amuṣya kiṁ
ko vārtha āpto 'bhajatāṁ sva-dharmataḥ

tyaktvā—having forsaken; *sva-dharmam*—one's own occupational engagement; *caraṇa-ambujam*—the lotus feet; *hareḥ*—of Hari (the Lord); *bhajan*—in the course of devotional service; *apakvaḥ*—immature; *atha*—for the matter of; *patet*—falls down; *tataḥ*—from that place; *yadi*—if; *yatra*—whereupon; *kva*—what sort of; *vā*—or (used sarcastically); *abhadram*—unfavorable; *abhūt*—shall happen; *amuṣya*—of him; *kim*—nothing; *kaḥ vā arthaḥ*—what interest; *āptaḥ*—obtained; *abhajatām*—of the nondevotee; *sva-dharmataḥ*—being engaged in occupational service.

TRANSLATION

One who has forsaken his material occupations to engage in the devotional service of the Lord may sometimes fall down while in an immature stage, yet there is no danger of his being unsuccessful. On the other hand, a nondevotee, though fully engaged in occupational duties, does not gain anything.

PURPORT

As far as the duties of mankind are concerned, there are innumerable duties. Every man is duty-bound not only to his parents, family members, society, country, humanity, other living beings, the demigods, etc., but also to the great philosophers, poets, scientists, etc. It is enjoined in the scriptures that one can relinquish all such duties and surrender unto the service of the Lord. So if one does so and becomes successful in the discharge of his devotional service unto the Lord, it is well and good. But it so happens sometimes that one surrenders himself unto the service of the Lord by some temporary sentiment, and in the long run, due to so many other reasons, he falls down from the path of service by undesirable association. There are so many instances of this in the histories. Bharata Mahārāja was obliged to take his birth as a stag due to his intimate attachment to a stag. He thought of this stag when he died. As such, in the next birth he became a stag, although he did not forget the incident of his previous birth. Similarly, Citraketu also fell down due to his offenses at the feet of Śiva. But in spite of all this, the stress is given here to surrendering unto the lotus feet of the Lord, even if there is a chance of falling down, because even though one falls down from the prescribed duties of devotional service, he will never forget the lotus feet of the Lord. Once engaged in the devotional service of the Lord, one will continue the service in all circumstances. In the *Bhagavad-gītā* it is said that even a small quantity of devotional service can save one from the most dangerous position. There are many instances of such examples in history. Ajāmila is one of them. Ajāmila in his early life was a devotee, but in his youth he fell down. Still he was saved by the Lord at the end.

TEXT 18

तस्यैव हेतोः प्रयतेत कोविदो
न लभ्यते यद्भ्रमतामुपर्यधः ।
तल्लभ्यते दुःखवदन्यतः सुखं
कालेन सर्वत्र गभीररंहसा ॥१८॥

tasyaiva hetoḥ prayateta kovido
na labhyate yad bhramatām upary adhaḥ
tal labhyate duḥkhavad anyataḥ sukhaṁ
kālena sarvatra gabhīra-raṁhasā

tasya—for that purpose; *eva*—only; *hetoḥ*—reason; *prayateta*—should endeavor; *kovidaḥ*—one who is philosophically inclined; *na*—*not*; *labhyate*—is not obtained; *yat*—what; *bhramatām*—wandering; *upari adhaḥ*—from top to bottom; *tat*—that; *labhyate*—can be obtained; *duḥkhavat*—like the miseries; *anyataḥ*—as a result of previous work; *sukham*—sense enjoyment; *kālena*—in course of time; *sarvatra*—everywhere; *gabhīra*—subtle; *raṁhasā*—progress.

TRANSLATION

Persons who are actually intelligent and philosophically inclined should endeavor only for that purposeful end which is not obtainable even by wandering from the topmost planet [Brahmaloka] down to the lowest planet [Pātāla]. As far as happiness derived from sense enjoyment is concerned, it can be obtained automatically in course of time, just as in course of time we obtain miseries even though we do not desire them.

PURPORT

Every man everywhere is trying to obtain the greatest amount of sense enjoyment by various endeavors. Some men are busy engaged in trade, industry, economic development, political supremacy, etc., and some of them are engaged in fruitive work to become happy in the next life by attaining higher planets. It is said that on the moon the inhabitants are fit for greater sense enjoyment by drinking *soma-rasa*, and the Pitṛloka is obtained by good charitable work. So there are various programs for sense enjoyment, either during this life or in the life after death. Some are trying to reach the moon or other planets by some mechanical arrangement, for they are very anxious to get into such planets without doing good work. But it is not to happen. By the law of the Supreme, different places are meant for different grades of living beings according to the work they have performed. By good work only, as prescribed in the scriptures, can one obtain birth in a good family, opulence, good education and good bodily features. We see also that even in this life one obtains a good education or money by good work. Similarly, in our next birth we get such desirable positions only by good work. Otherwise, it would not so happen that two persons born in the same place at the same time are seen differently placed according to previous work. But all such material positions are impermanent. The positions in the topmost Brahmaloka and in the lowest Pātāla are also changeable according to our own work. The philosophically inclined person must not be tempted by such changeable positions. He should try to get into the permanent life of bliss and knowledge where he will not be forced to come back again to the miserable material world, either in this or that planet. Miseries and mixed happiness are two features of material life, and they are obtained in Brahmaloka and in other *lokas* also. They are obtained in the life of the demigods and also in the life of the dogs and hogs. The miseries and mixed happiness of all living beings are only of different degree and quality, but no one is free from the miseries of birth, death, old age and disease. Similarly, everyone has his destined happiness also. No one can get more or less of these things simply by personal endeavors. Even if they are obtained, they can be lost again. One should not, therefore, waste time with these flimsy things; one should only endeavor to go back to Godhead. That should be the mission of everyone's life.

TEXT 19

न वै जनो जातु कथंचनाव्रजे-
न्मुकुन्दसेव्यन्यवदङ्ग संसृतिम् ।
स्मरन्मुकुन्दाङ्घ्र्युपगूहनं पुन-
र्विहातुमिच्छेन्न रसग्रहो जनः ॥१९॥

na vai jano jātu kathañcanāvrajen
mukunda-sevy anyavad aṅga saṁsṛtim
smaran mukundāṅghry-upagūhanaṁ punar
vihātum icchen na rasa-graho janaḥ

na—never; *vai*—certainly; *janaḥ*—a person; *jātu*—at any time; *kathañcana*—somehow or other; *āvrajet*—does not undergo; *mukunda-sevī*—the devotee of the Lord; *anyavat*—like others; *aṅga*—O my dear; *saṁsṛtim*—material existence; *smaran*—remembering; *mukunda-aṅghri*—the lotus feet of the Lord; *upagūhanam*—embracing; *punaḥ*—again; *vihātum*—willing to give up; *icchet*—desire; *na*—never; *rasa-grahaḥ*—one who has relished the mellow; *janaḥ*—person.

TRANSLATION

My dear Vyāsa, even though a devotee of Lord Kṛṣṇa sometimes falls down somehow or other, he certainly does not undergo material existence like others [fruitive workers, etc.] because a person who has once relished the taste of the lotus feet of the Lord can do nothing but remember that ecstasy again and again.

PURPORT

A devotee of the Lord automatically becomes uninterested in the enchantment of material existence because he is *rasa-graha,* or one who has tasted the sweetness of the lotus feet of Lord Kṛṣṇa. There are certainly many instances where devotees of the Lord have fallen down due to uncongenial association, just like fruitive workers, who are always prone to degradation. But even though he falls down, a devotee is never to be considered the same as a fallen *karmī.* A *karmī* suffers the result of his own fruitive reactions, whereas a devotee is reformed by chastisement directed by the Lord Himself. The sufferings of an orphan and the sufferings of a beloved child of a king are not one and the same. An orphan is really poor because he has no one to take care of him, but a beloved son of a rich man, although he appears to be on the same level as the orphan, is always under the vigilance of his capable father. A devotee of the Lord, due to wrong association, sometimes imitates the fruitive workers. The fruitive workers want to lord it over the material world. Similarly, a neophyte devotee foolishly thinks of accumulating some material power in exchange for devotional service. Such foolish devotees are sometimes put into difficulty by the Lord Himself. As a special favor, He may remove all material paraphernalia. By such action, the bewildered devotee is forsaken by all friends and relatives, and so he comes to his senses again by the mercy of the Lord and is set right to execute his devotional service.

In the *Bhagavad-gītā* it is also said that such fallen devotees are given a chance to take birth in a family of highly qualified *brāhmaṇas* or in a rich mercantile family. A devotee in such a position is not as fortunate as one who is chastised by the Lord and put into a position seemingly of helplessness. The devotee who becomes helpless by the will of the Lord is more fortunate than those who are born in good families. The fallen devotees born in a good family may forget the lotus feet of the Lord because they are less fortunate, but the devotee who is put into a forlorn condition is more fortunate because he swiftly returns to the lotus feet of the Lord, thinking himself helpless all around.

Pure devotional service is so spiritually relishable that a devotee becomes automatically uninterested in material enjoyment. That is the sign of perfection in progressive devotional service. A pure devotee continuously remembers the lotus feet of Lord Śrī Kṛṣṇa and does not forget Him even for a moment, not even in exchange for all the opulence of the three worlds.

TEXT 20

इदं हि विश्वं भगवानिवेतरो
यतो जगत्स्थाननिरोधसम्भवाः ।
तद्धि स्वयं वेद भवांस्तथापि ते
प्रादेशमात्रं भवतः प्रदर्शितम् ॥२०॥

idaṁ hi viśvaṁ bhagavān ivetaro
yato jagat-sthāna-nirodha-sambhavāḥ
tad dhi svayaṁ veda bhavāṁs tathāpi te
prādeśa-mātraṁ bhavataḥ pradarśitam

idam—this; *hi*—all; *viśvam*—cosmos; *bhagavān*—the Supreme Lord; *iva*—almost the same; *itaraḥ*—different from; *yataḥ*—from whom; *jagat*—the worlds; *sthāna*—exist; *nirodha*—annihilation; *sambhavāḥ*—creation; *tat hi*—all about; *svayam*—personally; *veda*—know; *bhavān*—your good self; *tathā api*—still; *te*—unto you; *prādeśa-mātram*—a synopsis only; *bhavataḥ*—unto you; *pradarśitam*—explained.

TRANSLATION

The Supreme Lord Personality of Godhead is Himself this cosmos, and still He is aloof from it. From Him only has this cosmic manifestation emanated, in Him it rests, and unto Him it enters after annihilation. Your good self knows all about this. I have given only a synopsis.

PURPORT

For a pure devotee, the conception of Mukunda, Lord Śrī Kṛṣṇa, is both personal and impersonal. The impersonal cosmic situation is also Mukunda because it is the emanation of the energy of Mukunda. For example, a tree is a complete unit, whereas the leaves and the branches of the tree are emanated parts and parcels of the tree. The leaves and branches of the tree are also the tree, but the tree itself is neither the leaves nor the branches. The Vedic version that the whole cosmic creation is nothing but Brahman means that since everything is emanating from the Supreme Brahman, nothing is apart from Him. Similarly, the part-and-parcel hands and legs are called the body, but the body as the whole unit is neither the hands nor the legs. The Lord is the transcendental form of eternity, cognition and beauty. And thus the creation of the energy of the Lord appears to be partially eternal, full of knowledge and beautiful also. The captivated conditioned souls under the influence of the external energy, *māyā,* are therefore entrapped in the network of the material nature. They accept this as all in all, for they have no information of the Lord who is the primeval cause. Nor have they information that the parts and parcels of the body, being detached from the whole body, are no longer the same hand or leg as when attached to the body. Similarly, a godless civilization detached from the transcendental loving service of the Supreme Personality of Godhead is just like a detached hand or leg. Such parts and parcels may appear like hands and legs, but they have no efficiency. The devotee of the Lord, Śrīla Vyāsadeva, knows this very well. He is further advised by Śrīla Nārada to expand the idea so that the entrapped conditioned souls may take lessons from him to understand the Supreme Lord as the primeval cause.

According to the Vedic version, the Lord is naturally fully powerful, and thus His supreme energies are always perfect and identical with Him. Both the spiritual and the material skies and their paraphernalia are emanations of the internal and external energies of the Lord. External energy is comparatively inferior, whereas the internal potency is superior. The superior energy is living force, and therefore she is completely identical, but the external energy, being inert, is partially identical. But both the energies are neither equal to nor greater than the Lord, who is the generator of all energies; such energies are always under His control, exactly as electrical energy, however powerful it may be, is always under the control of the engineer.

The human being and all other living beings are products of His internal energies. Thus the living being is also identical with the Lord. But he is never equal or superior to the Personality of Godhead. The Lord and living beings are all individual persons. With the help of the material energies the living beings are also creating something, but none of their creations are equal or superior to the creations of the Lord. The human being may create a small playful sputnik and may throw it into outer space, but that does not mean that he can create a planet like the earth or moon and float it in the air as the Lord does. Men with a poor fund of knowledge claim to be equal to the Lord. They are never equal to the Lord. This is never to be. The human being, after attaining complete perfection, may achieve a large percentage of the qualities of the Lord (say up to seventy-eight percent), but it is never possible to surpass the Lord or to become equal with Him. In a diseased condition only, the foolish being claims to be one with the Lord and thus becomes misled by the illusory energy. The misguided living beings, therefore, must accept the supremacy of the Lord and agree to render loving service to Him. For this they have been created. Without this, there cannot be any peace or tranquillity in the world. Śrīla Vyāsadeva is advised by Śrīla Nārada to expand this idea in the *Bhāgavatam.* In the *Bhagavad-gītā* also the same idea is explained: surrender fully unto the lotus feet of the Lord. That is the only business of the perfect human being.

TEXT 21

त्वमात्मनात्मानमवेह्यमोघदृक्
परस्य पुंसः परमात्मनः कलाम् ।
अजं प्रजातं जगतः शिवाय त-
न्महानुभावाभ्युदयोऽधिगण्यताम् ॥२१॥

tvam ātmanātmānam avehy amogha-dṛk
parasya puṁsaḥ paramātmanaḥ kalām
ajaṁ prajātaṁ jagataḥ śivāya tan
mahānubhāvābhyudayo 'dhigaṇyatām

tvam—yourself; *ātmanā*—by your own self; *ātmānam*—the Supersoul; *avehi*—search out; *amogha-dṛk*—one who has perfect vision; *parasya*—of the Transcendence; *puṁsaḥ*—the Personality of Godhead; *paramātmanaḥ*—of the Supreme Lord; *kalām*—plenary part; *ajam*—birthless; *prajātam*—have taken birth; *jagataḥ*—of the world; *śivāya*—for the well-being; *tat*—that; *mahā-anubhāva*—of the Supreme Personality of Godhead, Śrī Kṛṣṇa; *abhyudayaḥ*—pastimes; *adhigaṇya-tām*—describe most vividly.

TRANSLATION

Your Goodness has perfect vision. You yourself can know the Supersoul Personality of Godhead because you are present as the plenary portion of the Lord. Although you are birthless, you have appeared on this earth for the well-being of all people. Please, therefore, describe the transcendental pastimes of the Supreme Personality of Godhead, Śrī Kṛṣṇa, more vividly.

PURPORT

Śrīla Vyāsadeva is the empowered plenary portion incarnation of the Personality of Godhead, Śrī Kṛṣṇa. He descended by his causeless mercy to deliver the fallen souls in the material world. The fallen and forgotten souls are detached from the transcendental loving service of the Lord. The living entities are parts and parcels of the Lord, and they are eternally servitors of the Lord. All the Vedic literatures, therefore, are put into systematic order for the benefit of the fallen souls, and it is the duty of the fallen souls to take advantage of such literatures and be freed from the bondage of material existence. Although formally Śrīla Nārada Ṛṣi is his spiritual master, Śrīla Vyāsadeva is not at all dependent on a spiritual master because in essence he is the spiritual master of everyone else. But because he is doing the work of an *ācārya,* he has taught us by his own conduct that one must have a spiritual master, even though he be God Himself. Lord Śrī Kṛṣṇa, Lord Śrī Rāma and Lord Śrī Caitanya Mahāprabhu, all incarnations of Godhead, accepted formal spiritual masters, although by Their transcendental nature They were cognizant of all knowledge. In order to direct people in general to the lotus feet of Lord Śrī Kṛṣṇa, He Himself in the incarnation of Vyāsadeva is delineating the transcendental pastimes of the Lord.

TEXT 22

इदं हि पुंसस्तपसः श्रुतस्य वा
स्विष्टस्य सूक्तस्य च बुद्धिदत्तयोः ।
अविच्युतोऽर्थः कविभिर्निरूपितो
यदुत्तमश्लोकगुणानुवर्णनम् ॥२२॥

idaṁ hi puṁsas tapasaḥ śrutasya vā
sviṣṭasya sūktasya ca buddhi-dattayoḥ
avicyuto 'rthaḥ kavibhir nirūpito
yad-uttamaśloka-guṇānuvarṇanam

idam—this; *hi*—certainly; *puṁsaḥ*—of everyone; *tapasaḥ*—by dint of austerities; *śrutasya*—by dint of study of the *Vedas; vā*—or; *sviṣṭasya*—sacrifice; *sūktasya*—spiritual education; *ca*—and; *buddhi*—culture of knowledge; *dattayoḥ*—charity; *avicyutaḥ*—infallible; *arthaḥ*—interest; *kavibhiḥ*—by the recognized learned person; *nirūpitaḥ*—concluded; *yat*—what; *uttamaśloka*—the Lord, who is described by choice poetry; *guṇa-anuvarṇanam*—description of the transcendental qualities of.

TRANSLATION

Learned circles have positively concluded that the infallible purpose of the advancement of knowledge, namely austerities, study of the Vedas,

sacrifice, chanting of hymns and charity, culminates in the transcendental descriptions of the Lord, who is defined in choice poetry.

PURPORT

Human intellect is developed for advancement of learning in art, science, philosophy, physics, chemistry, psychology, economics, politics, etc. By culture of such knowledge the human society can attain perfection of life. This perfection of life culminates in the realization of the Supreme Being, Viṣṇu. The *śruti* therefore directs that those who are actually advanced in learning should aspire for the service of Lord Viṣṇu. Unfortunately persons who are enamored by the external beauty of *viṣṇu-māyā* do not understand that culmination of perfection or self-realization depends on Viṣṇu. *Viṣṇu-māyā* means sense enjoyment, which is transient and miserable. Those who are entrapped by *viṣṇu-māyā* utilize advancement of knowledge for sense enjoyment. Śrī Nārada Muni has explained that all paraphernalia of the cosmic universe is but an emanation from the Lord out of His different energies because the Lord has set in motion, by His inconceivable energy, the actions and reactions of the created manifestation. They have come to be out of His energy, they rest on His energy, and after annihilation they merge into Him. Nothing is, therefore, different from Him, but at the same time the Lord is always different from them.

When advancement of knowledge is applied in the service of the Lord, the whole process becomes absolute. The Personality of Godhead and His transcendental name, fame, glory, etc., are all nondifferent from Him. Therefore, all the sages and devotees of the Lord have recommended that the subject matter of art, science, philosophy, physics, chemistry, psychology and all other branches of knowledge should be wholly and solely applied in the service of the Lord. Art, literature, poetry, painting, etc., may be used in glorifying the Lord. The fiction writers, poets and celebrated litterateurs are generally engaged in writing of sensuous subjects, but if they turn towards the service of the Lord they can describe the transcendental pastimes of the Lord. Vālmīki was a great poet, and similarly Vyāsadeva is a great writer, and both of them have absolutely engaged themselves in delineating the transcendental activities of the Lord and by doing so have become immortal. Similarly, science and philosophy also should be applied in the service of the Lord. There is no use presenting dry speculative theories for sense gratification. Philosophy and science should be engaged to establish the glory of the Lord. Advanced people are eager to understand the Absolute Truth through the medium of science, and therefore a great scientist should endeavor to prove the existence of the Lord on a scientific basis. Similarly, philosophical speculations should be utilized to establish the Supreme Truth as sentient and all-powerful. Similarly, all other branches of knowledge should always be engaged in the service of the Lord. In the *Bhagavad-gītā* also the same is affirmed. All "knowledge" not engaged in the service of the Lord is but nescience. Real utilization of advanced knowledge is to establish the glories of the Lord, and that is the real import. Scientific knowledge engaged in the service of the Lord and all similar activities are all factually *hari-kīrtana,* or glorification of the Lord.

TEXT 23

अहं पुरातीतभवेऽभवं मुने
दास्यास्तु कस्याश्चन वेदवादिनाम्।
निरूपितो बालक एव योगिनां
शुश्रूषणे प्रावृषि निर्विविक्षताम् ॥२३॥

ahaṁ purātīta-bhave 'bhavaṁ mune
dāsyās tu kasyāścana veda-vādinām
nirūpito bālaka eva yogināṁ
śuśrūṣaṇe prāvṛṣi nirvivikṣatām

aham—I; *purā*—formerly; *atīta-bhave*—in the previous millennium; *abhavam*—became; *mune*—O *muni; dāsyāḥ*—of the maidservant; *tu*—but; *kasyāścana*—certain; *veda-vādinām*—of the followers of Vedānta; *nirūpitaḥ*—engaged; *bālakaḥ*—boy servant; *eva*—only; *yoginām*—of the devotees; *śuśrūṣaṇe*—in the service of; *prāvṛṣi*—during the four months of the rainy season; *nirvivikṣatām*—living together.

TRANSLATION

O Muni, in the last millennium I was born as the son of a certain maidservant engaged in the service of brāhmaṇas who were following the principles of Vedānta. When they were living together during the four months of the rainy season, I was engaged in their personal service.

PURPORT

The wonder of an atmosphere surcharged with devotional service to the Lord is briefly described herein by Śrī Nārada Muni. He was the son of the most insignificant parentage. He was not properly educated. Still, because his complete energy was engaged in the service of the Lord, he became an immortal sage. Such is the powerful action of devotional service. The living entities are the marginal energy of the Lord, and therefore they are meant for being properly utilized in the transcendental loving service of the Lord. When this is not done, one's situation is called *māyā.* Therefore the illusion of *māyā* is at once dissipated as soon as one's full energy is converted in the service of the Lord instead of in sense enjoyment. From the personal example of Śrī Nārada Muni in his previous birth, it is clear that the service of the Lord begins with the service of the Lord's bona fide servants. The Lord says that the service of His servants is greater than His personal service. Service of the devotee is more valuable than the service of the Lord. One should therefore choose a bona fide servant of the Lord constantly engaged in His service, accept such a servant as the spiritual master and engage himself in his (the spiritual master's) service. Such a spiritual master is the transparent medium by which to visualize the Lord, who is beyond the conception of the material senses. By service of the bona fide spiritual master, the Lord consents to reveal Himself in proportion to the service rendered. Utilization of the human energy in the service of the Lord is the progressive path of salvation. The whole cosmic creation becomes at once identical with the Lord as soon as service in relation with the Lord is rendered under the guidance of a bona fide spiritual master. The expert spiritual master knows the art of utilizing everything to glorify the Lord, and therefore under his guidance the whole world can be turned into the spiritual abode by the divine grace of the Lord's servant.

TEXT 24

ते मय्यपेताखिलचापलेऽर्भके
दान्तेऽधृतक्रीडनकेऽनुवर्तिनि ।
चक्रुः कृपां यद्यपि तुल्यदर्शनाः
शुश्रूषमाणे मुनयोऽल्पभाषिणि ॥२४॥

te mayy apetākhila-cāpale 'rbhake
dānte 'dhṛta-krīḍanake 'nuvartini
cakruḥ kṛpāṁ yadyapi tulya-darśanāḥ
śuśrūṣamāṇe munayo 'lpa-bhāṣiṇi

te—they; *mayi*—unto me; *apeta*—not having undergone; *akhila*—all kinds of; *cāpale*—proclivities; *arbhake*—unto a boy; *dānte*—having controlled the senses; *adhṛta-krīḍanake*—without being accustomed to sporting habits; *anuvartini*—obedient; *cakruḥ*—did bestow; *kṛpām*—causeless mercy; *yadyapi*—although; *tulya-darśanāḥ*—impartial by nature; *śuśrūṣamāṇe*—unto the faithful; *munayaḥ*—the *muni* followers of the Vedānta; *alpa-bhāṣiṇi*—one who does not speak more than required.

TRANSLATION

Although they were impartial by nature, those followers of the Vedānta blessed me with their causeless mercy. As far as I was concerned, I was self-controlled and had no attachment for sports, even though I was a boy. In addition, I was not naughty, and I did not speak more than required.

PURPORT

In the *Bhagavad-gītā* the Lord says, "All the *Vedas* are searching after Me." Lord Śrī Caitanya says that in the *Vedas* the subject matters are only three, namely to establish the relation of the living entities with the Personality of Godhead, perform the relative duties in devotional service and thus achieve the ultimate goal, back to Godhead. As such, *vedānta-vādīs,* or the followers of the Vedānta, indicate the pure devotees of the Personality of Godhead. Such *vedānta-vādīs,* or the *bhakti-vedāntas,* are impartial in distributing the transcendental knowledge of devotional service. To them no one is enemy or friend; no one is educated or uneducated. No one is especially favorable, and no one is unfavorable. The *bhakti-vedāntas* see that the people in general are wasting time in false sensuous things. Their business is to get the ignorant mass of people to reestablish the lost relationship with the Personality of Godhead. By such endeavor, even the most forgotten soul is roused up to the sense of spiritual life, and thus being initiated by the *bhakti-vedāntas,* the people in general gradually progress on the path of transcendental realization. So the *vedānta-vādīs* initiated the boy even before he became self-controlled and was detached from childish sporting, etc. But before the initiation, he (the boy) became more and more advanced in discipline, which is very essential for one who wishes to make progress in the line. In the system of *varṇāśrama-dharma,* which is the beginning of actual human life, small boys after five years of age are sent to become *brahmacārī* at the *guru's āśrama,* where these things are systematically taught to boys, be they kings' sons or sons of ordinary citizens. The training was compulsory not only to create good citizens of the state, but also to prepare each boy's future life for spiritual realization. The irresponsible life of sense enjoyment was unknown to the children of the followers of the *varṇāśrama* system. The boy was even injected with spiritual acumen before being placed by the father in the womb of the mother. Both the father and the mother were responsible for the boy's success in being liberated from the material bondage. That is the process of successful family planning. It is to beget children for complete perfection. Without being self-controlled, without being disciplined and without being fully obedient, no one can become successful in following the instructions of the spiritual master, and without doing so, no one is able to go back to Godhead.

TEXT 25

उच्छिष्टलेपाननुमोदितो द्विजैः
सकृत्स्म भुञ्जे तदपास्तकिल्बिषः ।
एवं प्रवृत्तस्य विशुद्धचेतस-
स्तद्धर्म एवात्मरुचिः प्रजायते ॥२५॥

ucchiṣṭa-lepān anumodito dvijaiḥ
sakṛt sma bhuñje tad-apāsta-kilbiṣaḥ
evaṁ pravṛttasya viśuddha-cetasas
tad-dharma evātma-ruciḥ prajāyate

ucchiṣṭa-lepān—the remnants of foodstuff; *anumoditaḥ*—being permitted; *dvijaiḥ*—by the Vedāntist *brāhmaṇas; sakṛt*—once upon a time; *sma*—in the past; *bhuñje*—took; *tat*—by that action; *apāsta*—eliminated; *kilbiṣaḥ*—all sins; *evam*—thus; *pravṛttasya*—being engaged; *viśuddha-cetasaḥ*—of one whose mind is purified; *tat*—that particular; *dharmaḥ*—nature; *eva*—certainly; *ātma-ruciḥ*—transcendental attraction; *prajāyate*—was manifested.

TRANSLATION

Once only, by their permission, I took the remnants of their food, and by so doing all my sins were at once eradicated. Thus being engaged, I became purified in heart, and at that time the very nature of the transcendentalist became attractive to me.

PURPORT

Pure devotion is as much infectious, in a good sense, as infectious diseases. A pure devotee is cleared from all kinds of sins. The Personality of

Godhead is the purest entity, and unless one is equally pure from the infection of material qualities, one cannot become a pure devotee of the Lord. The *bhakti-vedāntas* as above mentioned were pure devotees, and the boy became infected with their qualities of purity by their association and by eating once the remnants of the foodstuff taken by them. Such remnants may be taken even without permission of the pure devotees. There are sometimes pseudodevotees, and one should be very much cautious about them. There are many things which hinder one from entering devotional service. But by the association of pure devotees all these obstacles are removed. The neophyte devotee becomes practically enriched with the transcendental qualities of the pure devotee, which means attraction for the Personality of Godhead's name, fame, qualities, pastimes, etc. Infection of the qualities of the pure devotee means to imbibe the taste of pure devotion always in the transcendental activities of the Personality of Godhead. This transcendental taste at once makes all material things distasteful. Therefore a pure devotee is not at all attracted by material activities. After the elimination of all sins or obstacles on the path of devotional service, one can become attracted, one can have steadiness, one can have perfect taste, one can have transcendental emotions, and at last one can be situated on the plane of loving service of the Lord. All these stages develop by the association of pure devotees, and that is the purport of this stanza.

TEXT 26

तत्रान्वहं कृष्णकथाः प्रगायता-
मनुग्रहेणाश्रृणवं मनोहराः ।
ताः श्रद्धया मेऽनुपदं विश्रृण्वतः
प्रियश्रवस्यङ्ग ममाभवद्रुचिः ॥२६॥

tatrānvahaṁ kṛṣṇa-kathāḥ pragāyatām
anugraheṇāśṛṇavaṁ manoharāḥ
tāḥ śraddhayā me 'nupadaṁ viśṛṇvataḥ
priyaśravasy aṅga mamābhavad ruciḥ

tatra—thereupon; *anu*—every day; *aham*—I; *kṛṣṇa-kathāḥ*—narration of Lord Kṛṣṇa's activities; *pragāyatām*—describing; *anugraheṇa*—by causeless mercy; *aśṛṇavam*—giving aural reception; *manaḥ-harāḥ*—attractive; *tāḥ*—those; *śraddhayā*—respectfully; *me*—unto me; *anupadam*

—every step; *viśṛṇvataḥ*—hearing attentively; *priyaśravasi*—of the Personality of Godhead; *aṅga*—O Vyāsadeva; *mama*—mine; *abhavat*—it so became; *ruciḥ*—taste.

TRANSLATION

O Vyāsadeva, in that association and by the mercy of those great Vedāntists, I could hear them describe the attractive activities of Lord Kṛṣṇa. And thus listening attentively, my taste for hearing of the Personality of Godhead increased at every step.

PURPORT

Lord Śrī Kṛṣṇa, the Absolute Personality of Godhead, is attractive not only in His personal features, but also in His transcendental activities. It is so because the Absolute is absolute by His name, fame, form, pastimes, entourage, paraphernalia, etc. The Lord descends on this material world out of His causeless mercy and displays His various transcendental pastimes as a human being so that human beings attracted towards Him become able to go back to Godhead. Men are naturally apt to hear histories and narrations of various personalities performing mundane activities, without knowing that by such association one simply wastes valuable time and also becomes addicted to the three qualities of mundane nature. Instead of wasting time, one can get spiritual success by turning his attention to the transcendental pastimes of the Lord. By hearing the narration of the pastimes of the Lord, one contacts directly the Personality of Godhead, and, as explained before, by hearing about the Personality of Godhead, from within, all accumulated sins of the mundane creature are cleared. Thus being cleared of all sins, the hearer gradually becomes liberated from mundane association and becomes attracted to the features of the Lord. Nārada Muni has just explained this by his personal experience. The whole idea is that simply by hearing about the Lord's pastimes one can become one of the associates of the Lord. Nārada Muni has eternal life, unlimited knowledge and unfathomed bliss, and he can travel all over the material and spiritual worlds without restriction. One can attain to the highest perfection of life simply by attentive hearing of the transcendental pastimes of the Lord from the right sources, as Śrī Nārada heard them from the pure devotees (*bhakti-vedāntas*) in his previous life. This process of hearing in the association of the devotees is especially recommended in this age of quarrel (Kali).

TEXT 27

तस्मिंस्तदा लब्धरुचेर्महामते
प्रियश्रवस्यस्खलिता मतिर्मम ।
ययाहमेतत्सदसत्स्वमायया
पश्ये मयि ब्रह्मणि कल्पितं परे ॥२७॥

tasmiṁs tadā labdha-rucer mahā-mate
priyaśravasy askhalitā matir mama
yayāham etat sad-asat sva-māyayā
paśye mayi brahmaṇi kalpitaṁ pare

tasmin—it being so; *tadā*—at that time; *labdha*—achieved; *ruceḥ*—taste; *mahā-mate*—O great sage; *priyaśravasi*—upon the Lord; *askhalitā matiḥ*—uninterrupted attention; *mama*—mine; *yayā*—by which; *aham*—I; *etat*—all these; *sat-asat*—gross and subtle; *sva-māyayā*—one's own ignorance; *paśye*—see; *mayi*—in me; *brahmaṇi*—the Supreme; *kalpitam*—is accepted; *pare*—in the Transcendence.

TRANSLATION

O great sage, as soon as I got a taste of the Personality of Godhead, my attention to hear of the Lord was unflinching. And as my taste developed, I could realize that it was only in my ignorance that I had accepted gross and subtle coverings, for both the Lord and I are transcendental.

PURPORT

Ignorance in material existence is compared to darkness, and in all Vedic literatures the Personality of Godhead is compared to the sun. Wherever there is light there cannot be darkness. Hearing of the Lord's pastimes is itself transcendental association with the Lord because there is no difference between the Lord and His transcendental pastimes. To become associated with the supreme light is to dissipate all ignorance. By ignorance only, the conditioned soul wrongly thinks that both he and the Lord are products of material nature. But in fact the Personality of Godhead and the living beings are transcendental, and they have nothing to do with the material nature. When ignorance is removed and it is perfectly realized that there is nothing existing without the Personality of Godhead, then nescience is removed. Since the gross and subtle bodies are emanations from the Personality of Godhead, the knowledge of light permits one to engage both of them in the service of the Lord. The gross body should be engaged in acts of rendering service to the Lord (as in bringing water, cleansing the temple or making obeisances, etc.). The path of *arcanā,* or worshiping the Lord in the temple, involves engaging one's gross body in the service of the Lord. Similarly, the subtle mind should be engaged in hearing the transcendental pastimes of the Lord, thinking about them, chanting His name, etc. All such activities are transcendental. None of the gross or subtle senses should otherwise be engaged. Such realization of transcendental activities is made possible by many, many years of apprenticeship in the devotional service, but simply attraction of love for the Personality of Godhead, as it was developed in Nārada Muni, by hearing, is highly effective.

TEXT 28

इत्थं शरत्प्रावृषिकावृतू हरे-
र्विशृण्वतो मेऽनुसवं यशोऽमलम्।
संकीर्त्यमानं मुनिभिर्महात्मभि-
र्भक्तिः प्रवृत्तात्मरजस्तमोपहा ॥२८॥

ittham̐ śarat-prāvṛṣikāv ṛtū harer
viśṛṇvato me 'nusavam̐ yaśo 'malam
saṅkīrtyamānam̐ munibhir mahātmabhir
bhaktiḥ pravṛttātma-rajas-tamopahā

ittham—thus; *śarat*—autumn; *prāvṛṣikau*—rainy season; *ṛtū*—two seasons; *hareḥ*—of the Lord; *viśṛṇvataḥ*—continuously hearing; *me*—myself; *anusavam*—constantly; *yaśaḥ amalam*—unadulterated glories; *saṅkīrtyamānam*—chanted by; *munibhiḥ*—the great sages; *mahā-ātmabhiḥ*—great souls; *bhaktiḥ*—devotional service; *pravṛttā*—began to flow; *ātma*—living being; *rajaḥ*—mode of passion; *tama*—mode of ignorance; *upahā*—vanishing.

TRANSLATION

Thus during two seasons—the rainy season and autumn—I had the opportunity to hear these great-souled sages constantly chant the unadulterated glories of the Lord Hari. As the flow of my devotional service began, the coverings of the modes of passion and ignorance vanished.

PURPORT

Transcendental loving service for the Supreme Lord is the natural inclination of every living being. The instinct is dormant in everyone, but due to the association of material nature the modes of passion and ignorance cover this from time immemorial. If, by the grace of the Lord and the great-souled devotees of the Lord, a living being becomes fortunate enough to associate with the unadulterated devotees of the Lord and gets a chance to hear the unadulterated glories of the Lord, certainly the flow of devotional service takes place like the flow of a river. As the river flows on till she reaches the sea, similarly pure devotional service flows by the association of pure devotees till it reaches the ultimate goal, namely, transcendental love of God. Such a flow of devotional service cannot stop. On the contrary, it increases more and more without limitation. The flow of devotional service is so potent that any onlooker also becomes liberated from the influence of the modes of passion and ignorance. These two qualities of nature are thus removed, and the living being is liberated, being situated in his original position.

TEXT 29

तस्यैवं मेऽनुरक्तस्य प्रश्रितस्य हतैनसः।
श्रद्दधानस्य बालस्य दान्तस्यानुचरस्य च ॥२९॥

tasyaivaṁ me 'nuraktasya
praśritasya hatainasaḥ
śraddadhānasya bālasya
dāntasyānucarasya ca

tasya—his; *evam*—thus; *me*—mine; *anuraktasya*—attached to them; *praśritasya*—obediently; *hata*—freed from; *enasaḥ*—sins; *śraddadhānasya*—of the faithful; *bālasya*—of the boy; *dāntasya*—subjugated; *anucarasya*—strictly following the instructions; *ca*—and.

TRANSLATION

I was very much attached to those sages. I was gentle in behavior, and all my sins were eradicated in their service. In my heart I had strong faith in them. I had subjugated the senses, and I was strictly following them with body and mind.

PURPORT

These are the necessary qualifications of a prospective candidate who can expect to be elevated to the position of a pure unadulterated devotee. Such a candidate must always seek the association of pure devotees. One should not be misled by a pseudodevotee. He himself must be plain and gentle to receive the instructions of such a pure devotee. A pure devotee is a completely surrendered soul unto the Personality of Godhead. He knows the Personality of Godhead as the supreme proprietor and all others as His servitors. And by the association of pure devotees only, one can get rid of all sins accumulated by mundane association. A neophyte devotee must faithfully serve the pure devotee, and he should be very much obedient and strictly follow the instructions. These are the signs of a devotee who is determined to achieve success even in the existing duration of life.

TEXT 30

ज्ञानं गुह्यतमं यत्तत्साक्षाद्भगवतोदितम् ।
अन्ववोचन् गमिष्यन्तः कृपया दीनवत्सलाः ॥३०॥

jñānaṁ guhyatamaṁ yat tat
sākṣād bhagavatoditam
anvavocan gamiṣyantaḥ
kṛpayā dīna-vatsalāḥ

jñānam—knowledge; *guhyatamam*—most confidential; *yat*—what is; *tat*—that; *sākṣāt*—directly; *bhagavatā uditam*—propounded by the Lord Himself; *anvavocan*—gave instruction; *gamiṣyantaḥ*—while departing from; *kṛpayā*—by causeless mercy; *dīna-vatsalāḥ*—those who are very kind to the poor and meek.

TRANSLATION

As they were leaving, those bhakti-vedāntas, who are very kind to poor-hearted souls, instructed me in that most confidential subject which is instructed by the Personality of Godhead Himself.

PURPORT

A pure Vedāntist, or a *bhakti-vedānta,* instructs followers exactly according to the instructions of the Lord Himself. The Personality of Godhead, both in the *Bhagavad-gītā* and in all other scriptures, has definitely instructed men to follow the Lord only. The Lord is the creator, maintainer and annihilator of everything. The whole manifested creation is existing by His will, and by His will when the whole show is finished He will remain in His eternal abode with all His paraphernalia. Before the creation He was there in the eternal abode, and after the annihilation He will continue to remain. He is not, therefore, one of the created beings. He is transcendental. In the *Bhagavad-gītā* the Lord says that long, long before the instruction was imparted to Arjuna, the same was instructed to the sun god, and in course of time, the same instruction, being wrongly handled and being broken, was again instructed to Arjuna because he was His perfect devotee and friend. Therefore, the instruction of the Lord can be understood by the devotees only and no one else. The impersonalist, who has no idea of the transcendental form of the Lord, cannot understand this most confidential message of the Lord. The expression "most confidential" is significant here because knowledge of devotional service is far, far above knowledge of impersonal Brahman. *Jñānam* means ordinary knowledge or any branch of knowledge. This knowledge develops up to the knowledge of impersonal Brahman. Above this, when it is partially mixed with devotion, such knowledge develops to knowledge of Paramātmā, or the all-pervading Godhead. This is more confidential. But when such knowledge is turned into pure devotional service and the confidential part of transcendental knowledge is attained, it is called the most confidential knowledge. This most confidential knowledge was imparted by the Lord to Brahmā, Arjuna, Uddhava, etc.

TEXT 31

येनैवाहं भगवतो वासुदेवस्य वेधसः ।
मायानुभावमविदं येन गच्छन्ति तत्पदम् ॥३१॥

yenaivāhaṁ bhagavato
vāsudevasya vedhasaḥ
māyānubhāvam avidaṁ
yena gacchanti tat-padam

yena—by which; *eva*—certainly; *aham*—I; *bhagavataḥ*—of the Personality of Godhead; *vāsudevasya*—of Lord Śrī Kṛṣṇa; *vedhasaḥ*—of the supreme creator; *māyā*—energy; *anubhāvam*—influence; *avidam*—easily understood; *yena*—by which; *gacchanti*—they go; *tat-padam*—at the lotus feet of the Lord.

TRANSLATION

By that confidential knowledge, I could understand clearly the influence of the energy of Lord Śrī Kṛṣṇa, the creator, maintainer and annihilator of everything. By knowing that, one can return to Him and personally meet Him.

PURPORT

By devotional service or by the most confidential knowledge, one can understand very easily how the different energies of the Lord are working. One part of energy is manifesting the material world; the other (superior) part of His energy is manifesting the spiritual world. And the via medium energy is manifesting the living entities who are serving either of the above-mentioned energies. The living entities serving material energy are struggling hard for existence and happiness, which is presented to them as illusion. But those in the spiritual energy are placed under the direct service of the Lord in eternal life, complete knowledge and perpetual bliss. The Lord desires, as He has directly said in the *Bhagavad-gītā,* that all conditioned souls, rotting in the kingdom of material energy, come back to Him by giving up all engagements in the material world. This is the most confidential part of knowledge. But this can be understood only by the pure devotees, and only such devotees enter the kingdom of God to see Him personally and serve Him personally. The concrete example is Nārada himself, who attained this stage of eternal knowledge and eternal bliss. And the ways and means are open to all, provided one agrees to follow in the footsteps of Śrī Nārada Muni. According to *śruti,* the Supreme Lord has unlimited energies (without effort by Him), and these are described under three principal headings, as above mentioned.

TEXT 32

एतत्संसूचितं ब्रह्मंस्तापत्रयचिकित्सितम् ।
यदीश्वरे भगवति कर्म ब्रह्मणि भावितम् ॥३२॥

etat saṁsūcitaṁ brahmaṁs
tāpa-traya-cikitsitam
yad īśvare bhagavati
karma brahmaṇi bhāvitam

etat—this much; *saṁsūcitam*—decided by the learned; *brahman*—O *brāhmaṇa* Vyāsa; *tāpa-traya*—three kinds of miseries; *cikitsitam*—remedial measures; *yat*—what; *īśvare*—the supreme controller; *bhagavati*—unto the Personality of Godhead; *karma*—one's prescribed activities; *brahmaṇi*—unto the great; *bhāvitam*—dedicated.

TRANSLATION

O Brāhmaṇa Vyāsadeva, it is decided by the learned that the best remedial measure for removing all troubles and miseries is to dedicate one's activities to the service of the Supreme Lord Personality of Godhead [Śrī Kṛṣṇa].

PURPORT

Śrī Nārada Muni personally experienced that the most feasible and practical way to open the path of salvation or get relief from all miseries of life is to hear submissively the transcendental activities of the Lord from the right and bona fide sources. This is the only remedial process. The entire material existence is full of miseries. Foolish people have manufactured, out of their tiny brains, many remedial measures for removing the threefold miseries pertaining to the body and mind, pertaining to the natural disturbances and in relation with other living beings. The whole world is struggling very hard to exist out of these miseries, but men do not know that without the sanction of the Lord no plan or no remedial measure can actually bring about the desired peace and tranquillity. The remedial measure to cure a patient by medical treatment is useless if it is not sanctioned by the Lord. To cross the river or the ocean by a suitable boat is no remedial measure if it is not sanctioned by the Lord. We should know for certain that the Lord is the ultimate sanctioning officer, and we must therefore dedicate our attempts to the mercy of the Lord for ultimate success or to get rid of the obstacles on the path of success. The Lord is all-pervading, all-powerful, omniscient and omnipresent. He is the ultimate sanctioning agent of all good or bad effects. We should, therefore, learn to dedicate our activities unto the mercy of the Lord and accept Him either as impersonal Brahman, localized Paramātmā or the Supreme Personality of Godhead. It does not matter what one is. One must dedicate everything in the service of the Lord. If one is a learned scholar, scientist, philosopher, poet, etc., then he should employ his learning to establish the supremacy of the Lord. Try to study the energy of the Lord in every sphere of life. Do not decry Him and try to become like Him or take His position simply by fragmental accumulation of knowledge. If one is an administrator, statesman, warrior, politician, etc., then one should try to establish the Lord's supremacy in statesmanship. Fight for the cause of the Lord as Śrī Arjuna did. In the beginning, Śrī Arjuna, the great fighter, declined to fight, but when he was convinced by the Lord that the fighting was necessary, Śrī Arjuna changed his decision and fought for His cause. Similarly, if one is a businessman, an industrialist, an agriculturist, etc., then one should spend his hard-earned money for the cause of the Lord. Think always that the money which is accumulated is the wealth of the Lord. Wealth is considered to be the goddess of fortune (Lakṣmī), and the Lord is Nārāyaṇa, or the husband of Lakṣmī. Try to engage Lakṣmī in the service of Lord Nārāyaṇa and be happy. That is the way to realize the Lord in every sphere of life. The best thing is, after all, to get relief from all material activities and engage oneself completely in hearing the transcendental pastimes of the Lord. But in case of the absence of such an opportunity, one should try to engage in the service of the Lord everything for which one has specific attraction, and that is the way of peace and prosperity.The word *saṁsūcitam* in this stanza is also significant. One should not think for a moment that the realization of Nārada was childish imagination only. It is not like that. It is so realized by the expert and erudite scholars, and that is the real import of the word *saṁsūcitam.*

TEXT 33

आमयो यश्च भूतानां जायते येन सुव्रत।
तदेव ह्यामयं द्रव्यं न पुनाति चिकित्सितम् ॥३३॥

āmayo yaś ca bhūtānāṁ
jāyate yena suvrata
tad eva hy āmayaṁ dravyaṁ
na punāti cikitsitam

āmayaḥ—diseases; *yaḥ ca*—whatever; *bhūtānām*—of the living being; *jāyate*—become possible; *yena*—by the agency; *suvrata*—O good soul; *tat*—that; *eva*—very; *hi*—certainly; *āmayam*—disease; *dravyam*—thing; *na*—does it not; *punāti*—cure; *cikitsitam*—treated with.

TRANSLATION

O good soul, does not a thing, applied therapeutically, cure a disease which was caused by that very same thing?

PURPORT

An expert physician treats his patient with a therapeutic diet. For example, milk preparations sometimes cause disorder of the bowels, but the very same milk converted into curd and mixed with some other remedial ingredients cures such disorders. Similarly, the threefold miseries of material existence cannot be mitigated simply by material activities. Such activities have to be spiritualized, just as by fire iron is made red-hot, and thereby the action of fire begins. Similarly, the material conception of a thing is at once changed as soon as it is put into the service of the Lord. That is the secret of spiritual success. We should not try to lord it over the material nature, nor should we reject material things. The best way to make the best use of a bad bargain is to use everything in relation with the supreme spiritual being. Everything is an emanation from the Supreme Spirit, and by His inconceivable power He can convert spirit into matter and matter into spirit. Therefore a material thing (so-called) is at once turned into a spiritual force by the great will of the Lord. The necessary condition for such a change is to employ so-called matter in the service of the spirit. That is the way to treat our material diseases and elevate ourselves to the spiritual plane where there is no misery, no lamentation and no fear. When everything is thus employed in the service of the Lord, we can experience that there is nothing except the Supreme Brahman. The Vedic *mantra* that "everything is Brahman" is thus realized by us.

TEXT 34

एवं नृणां क्रियायोगाः सर्वे संसृतिहेतवः ।
त एवात्मविनाशाय कल्पन्ते कल्पिताः परे ॥३४॥

evaṁ nṛṇāṁ kriyā-yogāḥ
sarve saṁsṛti-hetavaḥ
ta evātma-vināśāya
kalpante kalpitāḥ pare

evam—thus; *nṛṇām*—of the human being; *kriyā-yogāḥ*—all activities; *sarve*—everything; *saṁsṛti*—material existence; *hetavaḥ*—causes; *te*—that; *eva*—certainly; *ātma*—the tree of work; *vināśāya*—killing; *kalpante*—become competent; *kalpitāḥ*—dedicated; *pare*—unto the Transcendence.

TRANSLATION

Thus when all a man's activities are dedicated to the service of the Lord, those very activities which caused his perpetual bondage become the destroyer of the tree of work.

PURPORT

Fruitive work which has perpetually engaged the living being is compared to the banyan tree in the *Bhagavad-gītā,* for it is certainly very deeply rooted. As long as the propensity for enjoying the fruit of work is there, one has to continue the transmigration of the soul from one body or place to another, according to one's nature of work. The propensity for enjoyment may be turned into the desire for serving the mission of the Lord. By doing so, one's activity is changed into *karma-yoga,* or the way by which one can attain spiritual perfection while engaging in the work for which he has a natural tendency. Here the word *ātmā* indicates the categories of all fruitive work. The conclusion is that when the result of all fruitive and other work is dovetailed with the service of the Lord, it will cease to generate further *karma* and will gradually develop into transcendental devotional service, which will not only cut off completely the root of the banyan tree of work but will also carry the performer to the lotus feet of the Lord.

The summary is that one has to, first of all, seek the association of pure devotees who not only are learned in the Vedānta but are self-realized souls and unalloyed devotees of Lord Śrī Kṛṣṇa, the Personality of Godhead. In that association, the neophyte devotees must render loving service physically and mentally without reservation. This service attitude will induce the great souls to be more favorable in bestowing their mercy, which injects the neophyte with all the transcendental qualities of the pure devotees. Gradually this is developed into a strong attachment to hearing the transcendental pastimes of the Lord, which makes him able to catch up the constitutional position of the gross and subtle bodies and beyond them the knowledge of pure soul and his eternal relation with the Supreme Soul, the Personality of Godhead. After the relation is ascertained by establishment of the eternal relation, pure devotional service to the Lord begins gradually developing into perfect knowledge of the Personality of Godhead beyond the purview of impersonal Brahman and localized Paramātmā. By such *puruṣottama-yoga,* as it is stated in the *Bhagavad-gītā,* one is made perfect even during the present corporeal existence, and one exhibits all the good qualities of the Lord to the highest percentage. Such is the gradual development by association of pure devotees.

TEXT 35

यदत्र क्रियते कर्म भगवत्परितोषणम् ।
ज्ञानं यत्तदधीनं हि भक्तियोगसमन्वितम् ॥३५॥

yad atra kriyate karma
bhagavat-paritoṣaṇam
jñānaṁ yat tad adhīnaṁ hi
bhakti-yoga-samanvitam

yat—whatever; *atra*—in this life or world; *kriyate*—does perform; *karma*—work; *bhagavat*—unto the Personality of Godhead; *paritoṣaṇam*—satisfaction of; *jñānam*—knowledge; *yat tat*—what is so called; *adhīnam*—dependent; *hi*—certainly; *bhakti-yoga*—devotional; *samanvitam*—dovetailed with *bhakti-yoga.*

TRANSLATION

Whatever work is done here in this life for the satisfaction of the mission of the Lord is called bhakti-yoga, or transcendental loving service to the Lord, and what is called knowledge becomes a concomitant factor.

PURPORT

The general and popular notion is that by discharging fruitive work in terms of the direction of the scriptures one becomes perfectly able to acquire transcendental knowledge for spiritual realization. *Bhakti-yoga* is considered by some to be another form of *karma.* But factually *bhakti-yoga* is above both *karma* and *jñāna. Bhakti-yoga* is independent of *jñāna* or *karma;* on the other hand, *jñāna* and *karma* are dependent on *bhakti-yoga.* This *kriyā-yoga* or *karma-yoga,* as recommended by Śrī Nārada to Vyāsa, is specifically recommended because the principle is to satisfy the Lord. The Lord does not want His sons, the living beings, to suffer the threefold miseries of life. He desires that all of them come to Him and live with Him, but going back to Godhead means that one must purify himself from material infections. When work is performed, therefore, to satisfy the Lord, the performer becomes gradually purified from the material affection. This purification means attainment of spiritual knowledge. Therefore knowledge is dependent on *karma,* or work, done on behalf of the Lord. Other knowledge, being devoid of *bhakti-yoga* or satisfaction of the Lord, cannot lead one back to the kingdom of God, which means that it cannot even offer salvation, as already explained in connection with the stanza *naiṣkarmyam apy acyuta-bhāva-varjitam.* The conclusion is that a devotee engaged in the unalloyed service of the Lord, specifically in hearing and chanting of His transcendental glories, becomes simultaneously spiritually enlightened by the divine grace, as confirmed in the *Bhagavad-gītā.*

TEXT 36

कुर्वाणा यत्र कर्माणि भगवच्छिक्षयासकृत्।
गृणन्ति गुणनामानि कृष्णस्यानुस्मरन्ति च ॥३६॥

kurvāṇā yatra karmāṇi
bhagavac-chikṣayāsakṛt
gṛṇanti guṇa-nāmāni
kṛṣṇasyānusmaranti ca

kurvāṇāḥ—while performing; *yatra*—thereupon; *karmāṇi*—duties; *bhagavat*—the Personality of Godhead; *śikṣayā*—by the will of; *asakṛt*—constantly; *gṛṇanti*—takes on; *guṇa*—qualities; *nāmāni*—names; *kṛṣṇasya*—of Kṛṣṇa; *anusmaranti*—constantly remembers; *ca*—and.

TRANSLATION

While performing duties according to the order of Śrī Kṛṣṇa, the Supreme Personality of Godhead, one constantly remembers Him, His names and His qualities.

PURPORT

An expert devotee of the Lord can mold his life in such a way that while performing all kinds of duties either for this or the next life, he can constantly remember the Lord's name, fame, qualities, etc. The order of the Lord is distinctly there in the *Bhagavad-gītā:* one should work only for the Lord in all spheres of life. In every sphere of life the Lord should be situated as the proprietor. According to the Vedic rites, even in the worship of some demigods like Indra, Brahmā, Sarasvatī and Gaṇeśa, the system is that in all circumstances the representation of Viṣṇu must be there as *yajñeśvara,* or the controlling power of such sacrifices. It is recommended that a particular demigod be worshiped for a particular purpose, but still the presence of Viṣṇu is compulsory in order to make the function proper.

Apart from such Vedic duties, even in our ordinary dealings (for example, in our household affairs or in our business or profession) we must consider that the result of all activities must be given over to the supreme enjoyer, Lord Kṛṣṇa.

In the *Bhagavad-gītā* the Lord has declared Himself to be the supreme enjoyer of everything, the supreme proprietor of every planet and the supreme friend of all beings. No one else but Lord Śrī Kṛṣṇa can claim to be the proprietor of everything within His creation. A pure devotee remembers this constantly, and in doing so he repeats the transcendental name, fame and qualities of the Lord, which means that he is constantly in touch with the Lord. The Lord is identical with His name, fame, etc., and therefore to be associated with His name, fame, etc., constantly, means actually to associate with the Lord.

The major portion of our monetary income, not less than fifty percent, must be spent to carry out the order of Lord Kṛṣṇa. Not only should we give the profit of our earning to this cause, but we must also arrange to preach this cult of devotion to others because that is also one of the orders of the Lord. The Lord definitely says that no one is more dear to Him than one who is always engaged in the preaching work of the Lord's name and fame all over the world. The scientific discoveries of the material world can also be equally engaged in carrying out His order. He wants the message of the *Bhagavad-gītā* to be preached amongst His devotees. It may not be so done amongst those who have no credit of austerities, charity, education, etc. Therefore, the attempt must go on to convert unwilling men to become His devotees. Lord Caitanya has taught a very simple method in this connection. He has taught the lesson for preaching the transcendental message through singing, dancing and refreshment. As such, fifty percent of our income may be spent for this purpose. In this fallen age of quarrel and dissension, if only the leading and wealthy persons of society agree to spend fifty percent of their income in the service of the Lord, as it is taught by Lord Śrī Caitanya Mahāprabhu, there is absolute certainty of converting this hell of pandemonium to the transcendental abode of the Lord. No one will disagree to partake in a function where good singing, dancing and refreshment are administered. Everyone will attend such a function, and everyone is sure to feel individually the transcendental presence of the Lord. This alone will help the attendant associate with the Lord and thereby purify himself in spiritual realization. The only condition for successfully executing such spiritual activities is that they must be conducted under the guidance of a pure devotee who is completely free from all mundane desires, fruitive activities and dry speculations about the nature of the Lord. No one has to discover the nature of the Lord. It is already spoken by the Lord Himself in the *Bhagavad-gītā* especially and in all other Vedic literatures generally. We have simply to accept them *in toto* and abide by the orders of the Lord. That will guide us to the path of perfection.

One can remain in his own position. No one has to change his position, especially in this age of variegated difficulties. The only condition is that one must give up the habit of dry speculation aimed at becoming one with the Lord. And after giving up such lofty puffed-up vanities, one may very submissively receive the orders of the Lord in the *Bhagavad-gītā* or *Bhāgavatam* from the lips of a bona fide devotee whose qualification is mentioned above. That will make everything successful, without a doubt.

TEXT 37

ॐ नमो भगवते तुभ्यं वासुदेवाय धीमहि ।
प्रद्युम्नायानिरुद्धाय नमः सङ्कर्षणाय च ॥३७॥

oṁ namo bhagavate tubhyaṁ
vāsudevāya dhīmahi
pradyumnāyāniruddhāya
namaḥ saṅkarṣaṇāya ca

oṁ—the sign of chanting the transcendental glory of the Lord; *namaḥ*—offering obeisances unto the Lord; *bhagavate*—unto the Personality of Godhead; *tubhyam*—unto You; *vāsudevāya*—unto the Lord, the son of Vasudeva; *dhīmahi*—let us chant; *pradyumnāya, aniruddhāya* and *saṅkarṣaṇāya*—all plenary expansions of Vāsudeva; *namaḥ*—respectful obeisances; *ca*—and.

TRANSLATION

Let us all chant the glories of Vāsudeva along with His plenary expansions Pradyumna, Aniruddha and Saṅkarṣaṇa.

PURPORT

According to *Pañcarātra,* Nārāyaṇa is the primeval cause of all expansions of Godhead. These are Vāsudeva, Saṅkarṣaṇa, Pradyumna and Aniruddha. Vāsudeva and Saṅkarṣaṇa are on the middle left and right, Pradyumna is on the right of Saṅkarṣaṇa, and Aniruddha is on the left of Vāsudeva, and thus the four Deities are situated. They are known as the four aides-de-camp of Lord Śrī Kṛṣṇa.

This is a Vedic hymn or *mantra* beginning with *oṁkāra praṇava,* and thus the *mantra* is established by the transcendental chanting process, namely, *oṁ namo dhīmahi,* etc.

The purport is that any transaction, either in the field of fruitive work or in empiric philosophy, which is not ultimately aimed at transcendental realization of the Supreme Lord, is considered to be useless. Nāradajī has therefore explained the nature of unalloyed devotional service by his personal experience in the development of intimacy between the Lord and the living entity by a gradual process of progressive devotional activities. Such a progressive march of transcendental devotion for the Lord culminates in the attainment of loving service of the Lord, which is called *premā* in different transcendental variegatedness called *rasas* (tastes). Such devotional service is also executed in mixed forms, namely mixed with fruitive work or empiric philosophical speculations.

Now the question which was raised by the great *ṛṣis* headed by Śaunaka regarding the confidential part of Sūta's achievement through the spiritual master is explained herein by the chanting of this hymn consisting of thirty-three letters. And this *mantra* is addressed to the four Deities, or the Lord with His plenary expansions. The central figure is Lord Śrī Kṛṣṇa because the plenary portions are His aides-de-camp. The most confidential part of the instruction is that one should always chant and remember the glories of the Lord Śrī Kṛṣṇa, the Supreme Personality of Godhead, along with His different plenary portions expanded as Vāsudeva, Saṅkarṣaṇa, Pradyumna and Aniruddha. These expansions are the original Deities for all other truths, namely either *viṣṇu-tattva* or *śakti-tattvas.*

TEXT 38

इति मूर्त्यभिधानेन मन्त्रमूर्तिममूर्तिकम् ।
यजते यज्ञपुरुषं स सम्यग्दर्शनः पुमान् ॥३८॥

iti mūrty-abhidhānena
mantra-mūrtim amūrtikam
yajate yajña-puruṣaṁ
sa samyag-darśanaḥ pumān

iti—thus; *mūrti*—representation; *abhidhānena*—in sound; *mantra-mūrtim*—form representation of transcendental sound; *amūrtikam*—the Lord, who has no material form; *yajate*—worship; *yajña*—Viṣṇu; *puruṣam*—the Personality of Godhead; *saḥ*—he alone; *samyak*—perfectly; *darśanaḥ*—one who has seen; *pumān*—person.

TRANSLATION

Thus he is the actual seer who worships, in the form of transcendental sound representation, the Supreme Personality of Godhead, Viṣṇu, who has no material form.

PURPORT

Our present senses are all made of material elements, and therefore they are imperfect in realizing the transcendental form of Lord Viṣṇu. He is therefore worshiped by sound representation via the transcendental method of chanting. Anything which is beyond the scope of experience by our imperfect senses can be realized fully by the sound representation. A person transmitting sound from a far distant place can be factually experienced. If this is materially possible, why not spiritually? This experience is not a vague impersonal experience. It is actually an experience of the transcendental Personality of Godhead, who possesses the pure form of eternity, bliss and knowledge.

In the *Amarakośa* Sanskrit dictionary the word *mūrti* carries import in twofold meanings, namely, form and difficulty. Therefore *amūrtikam* is explained by Ācārya Śrī Viśvanātha Cakravartī Ṭhākura as meaning "without difficulty." The transcendental form of eternal bliss and knowledge can be experienced by our original spiritual senses, which can be revived by chanting of the holy *mantras,* or transcendental sound representations. Such sound should be received from the transparent agency of the bona fide spiritual master, and the chanting may be practiced by the direction of the spiritual master. That will gradually lead us nearer to the Lord. This method of worship is recommended in the *pāñcarātrika* system, which is both recognized and authorized. The *pāñcarātrika* system has the most authorized codes for transcendental devotional service. Without the help of such codes, one cannot approach the Lord, certainly not by dry philosophical speculation. The *pāñcarātrika* system is both practical and suitable for this age of quarrel. The *Pañcarātra* is more important than the *Vedānta* for this modern age.

TEXT 39

इमं स्वनिगमं ब्रह्मन्नवेत्य मदनुष्ठितम् ।
अदान्मे ज्ञानमैश्वर्यं स्वस्मिन् भावं च केशवः ॥३९॥

imaṁ sva-nigamaṁ brahmann
avetya mad-anuṣṭhitam

adān me jñānam aiśvaryaṁ
svasmin bhāvaṁ ca keśavaḥ

imam—thus; *sva-nigamam*—confidential knowledge of the *Vedas* in respect to the Supreme Personality of Godhead; *brahman*—O *brāhmaṇa* (Vyāsadeva); *avetya*—knowing it well; *mat*—by me; *anuṣṭhitam*—executed; *adāt*—bestowed upon me; *me*—me; *jñānam*—transcendental knowledge; *aiśvaryam*—opulence; *svasmin*—personal; *bhāvam*—intimate affection and love; *ca*—and; *keśavaḥ*—Lord Kṛṣṇa.

TRANSLATION

O brāhmaṇa, thus by the Supreme Lord Kṛṣṇa I was endowed first with the transcendental knowledge of the Lord as inculcated in the confidential parts of the Vedas, then with the spiritual opulences, and then with His intimate loving service.

PURPORT

Communion with the Lord by transmission of the transcendental sound is nondifferent from the whole spirit Lord Śrī Kṛṣṇa. It is a completely perfect method for approaching the Lord. By such pure contact with the Lord, without offense of material conceptions (numbering ten), the devotee can rise above the material plane to understand the inner meaning of the Vedic literatures, including the Lord's existence in the transcendental realm. The Lord reveals His identity gradually to one who has unflinching faith, both in the spiritual master and in the Lord. After this, the devotee is endowed with mystic opulences, which are eight in number. And above all, the devotee is accepted in the confidential entourage of the Lord and is entrusted with specific service of the Lord through the agency of the spiritual master. A pure devotee is more interested in serving the Lord than in showing an exhibition of the mystic powers dormant in him. Śrī Nārada has explained all these from his personal experience, and one can obtain all the facilities which Śrī Nārada obtained by perfecting the chanting process of the sound representation of the Lord. There is no bar for chanting this transcendental sound by anyone, provided it is received through Nārada's representative, coming down by the chain of disciplic succession, or the *paramparā* system.

TEXT 40

त्वमप्यदभ्रश्रुत विश्रुतं विभोः
समाप्यते येन विदां बुभुत्सितम् ।

प्राख्याहि दुःखैर्मुहुरर्दितात्मनां
सङ्क्लेशनिर्वाणमुशन्ति नान्यथा ॥४०॥

tvam apy adabhra-śruta viśrutaṁ vibhoḥ
samāpyate yena vidāṁ bubhutsitam
prākhyāhi duḥkhair muhur arditātmanāṁ
saṅkleśa-nirvāṇam uśanti nānyathā

tvam—your good soul; *api*—also; *adabhra*—vast; *śruta*—Vedic literatures; *viśrutam*—have heard also; *vibhoḥ*—of the Almighty; *samāpyate*—satisfied; *yena*—by which; *vidām*—of the learned; *bubhutsitam*—who always desire to learn transcendental knowledge; *prākhyāhi*—describe; *duḥkhaiḥ*—by miseries; *muhuḥ*—always; *ardita-ātmanām*—suffering mass of people; *saṅkleśa*—sufferings; *nirvāṇam*—mitigation; *uśanti na*—do not get out of; *anyathā*—by other means.

TRANSLATION

Please, therefore, describe the almighty Lord's activities which you have learned by your vast knowledge of the Vedas, for that will satisfy the hankerings of great learned men and at the same time mitigate the miseries of the masses of common people who are always suffering from material pangs. Indeed, there is no other way to get out of such miseries.

PURPORT

Śrī Nārada Muni from practical experience definitely asserts that the prime solution of all problems of material work is to broadcast very widely the transcendental glories of the Supreme Lord. There are four classes of good men, and there are four classes of bad men also. The four classes of good men acknowledge the authority of the almighty God, and therefore such good men (1) when they are in difficulty, (2) when they are in need of money, (3) when they are advanced in knowledge and (4) when they are inquisitive to know more and more about God, intuitively take shelter of the Lord. As such, Nāradajī advises Vyāsadeva to broadcast the transcendental knowledge of God in terms of the vast Vedic knowledge which he had already attained.

As far as the bad men are concerned, they are also four in number: (1) those who are simply addicted to the mode of progressive fruitive work and thus are subjected to the accompanying miseries, (2) those who are simply addicted to vicious work for sense satisfaction and so suffer the consequence,

(3) those who are materially very much advanced in knowledge, but who suffer because they do not have the sense to acknowledge the authority of the almighty Lord, and (4) the class of men who are known as atheists and who therefore purposely hate the very name of God, although they are always in difficulty.

Śrī Nāradajī advised Vyāsadeva to describe the glories of the Lord just to do good to all eight classes of men, both good and bad. *Śrīmad-Bhāgavatam* is therefore not meant for any particular class of men or sect. It is for the sincere soul who actually wants his own welfare and peace of mind.

Thus end the Bhaktivedanta purports of the First Canto, Fifth Chapter, of the Śrīmad-Bhāgavatam, *entitled "Nārada's Instructions on* Śrīmad-Bhāgavatam *for Vyāsadeva."*

CHAPTER SIX

Conversation Between Nārada and Vyāsadeva

TEXT 1

सूत उवाच
एवं निशम्य भगवान्देवर्षेर्जन्म कर्म च।
भूयः पप्रच्छ तं ब्रह्मन् व्यासः सत्यवतीसुतः ॥१॥

sūta uvāca
evaṁ niśamya bhagavān
devarṣer janma karma ca
bhūyaḥ papraccha taṁ brahman
vyāsaḥ satyavatī-sutaḥ

sūtaḥ uvāca—Sūta said; *evam*—thus; *niśamya*—hearing; *bhagavān*—the powerful incarnation of God; *devarṣeḥ*—of the great sage among the gods; *janma*—birth; *karma*—work; *ca*—and; *bhūyaḥ*—again; *papraccha*—asked; *tam*—him; *brahman*—O *brāhmaṇas; vyāsaḥ*—Vyāsadeva; *satyavatī-sutaḥ*—the son of Satyavatī.

TRANSLATION

Sūta said: O brāhmaṇas, thus hearing all about Śrī Nārada's birth and activities, Vyāsadeva, the incarnation of God and son of Satyavatī, inquired as follows.

PURPORT

Vyāsadeva was further inquisitive to know about the perfection of Nāradajī, and therefore he wanted to know about him more and more. In this chapter Nāradajī will describe how he was able to have a brief audience with the Lord while he was absorbed in the transcendental thought of separation from the Lord and when it was very painful for him.

TEXT 2

व्यास उवाच
भिक्षुभिर्विप्रवसिते विज्ञानादेष्टृभिस्तव ।
वर्तमानो वयस्याद्ये ततः किमकरोद्भवान् ॥२॥

vyāsa uvāca
bhikṣubhir vipravasite
vijñānādeṣṭṛbhis tava
vartamāno vayasy ādye
tataḥ kim akarod bhavān

vyāsaḥ uvāca—Śrī Vyāsadeva said; *bhikṣubhiḥ*—by the great mendicants; *vipravasite*—having departed for other places; *vijñāna*—scientific knowledge in transcendence; *ādeṣṭṛbhiḥ*—those who had instructed; *tava*—of your; *vartamānaḥ*—present; *vayasi*—of the duration of life; *ādye*—before the beginning of; *tataḥ*—after that; *kim*—what; *akarot*—did; *bhavān*—your good self.

TRANSLATION

Śrī Vyāsadeva said: What did you [Nārada] do after the departure of the great sages who had instructed you in scientific transcendental knowledge before the beginning of your present birth?

PURPORT

Vyāsadeva himself was the disciple of Nāradajī, and therefore it was natural to be anxious to hear what Nārada did after initiation from the spiritual masters. He wanted to follow in Nārada's footsteps in order to attain to the same perfect stage of life. This desire to inquire from the spiritual master is an essential factor to the progressive path. This process is technically known as *sad-dharma-pṛcchā.*

TEXT 3

स्वायम्भुव कया वृत्त्या वर्तितं ते परं वयः ।
कथं चेदमुदस्राक्षीः काले प्राप्ते कलेवरम् ॥३॥

svāyambhuva kayā vṛttyā
vartitaṁ te paraṁ vayaḥ

kathaṁ cedam udasrākṣīḥ
kāle prāpte kalevaram

svāyambhuva—O son of Brahmā; *kayā*—under what condition; *vṛttyā*—occupation; *vartitam*—was spent; *te*—you; *param*—after the initiation; *vayaḥ*—duration of life; *katham*—how; *ca*—and; *idam*—this; *udasrākṣīḥ*—did you quit; *kāle*—in due course; *prāpte*—having attained; *kalevaram*—body.

TRANSLATION

O son of Brahmā, how did you pass your life after initiation, and how did you attain this body, having quit your old one in due course?

PURPORT

Śrī Nārada Muni in his previous life was just an ordinary maidservant's son, so how he became so perfectly transformed into the spiritual body of eternal life, bliss and knowledge is certainly important. Śrī Vyāsadeva desired him to disclose the facts for everyone's satisfaction.

TEXT 4

प्राक्कल्पविषयामेतां स्मृतिं ते मुनिसत्तम ।
न ह्येष व्यवधात्काल एष सर्वनिराकृतिः ॥४॥

prāk-kalpa-viṣayām etāṁ
smṛtiṁ te muni-sattama
na hy eṣa vyavadhāt kāla
eṣa sarva-nirākṛtiḥ

prāk—prior; *kalpa*—the duration of Brahmā's day; *viṣayām*—subject matter; *etām*—all these; *smṛtim*—remembrance; *te*—your; *muni-sattama*—O great sage; *na*—not; *hi*—certainly; *eṣaḥ*—all these; *vyavadhāt*—made any difference; *kālaḥ*—course of time; *eṣaḥ*—all these; *sarva*—all; *nirākṛtiḥ*—annihilation.

TRANSLATION

O great sage, time annihilates everything in due course, so how is it that this subject matter, which happened prior to this day of Brahmā, is still fresh in your memory, undisturbed by time?

PURPORT

As spirit is not annihilated even after the annihilation of the material body, so also spiritual consciousness is not annihilated. Śrī Nārada developed this spiritual consciousness even when he had his material body in the previous *kalpa.* Consciousness of the material body means spiritual consciousness expressed through the medium of a material body. This consciousness is inferior, destructible and perverted. But superconsciousness of the supramind in the spiritual plane is as good as the spirit soul and is never annihilated.

TEXT 5

नारद उवाच
भिक्षुभिर्विप्रवसिते विज्ञानादेष्टृभिर्मम ।
वर्तमानो वयस्याद्ये तत एतदकारषम् ॥५॥

nārada uvāca
bhikṣubhir vipravasite
vijñānādeṣṭṛbhir mama
vartamāno vayasy ādye
tata etad akārasam

nāradaḥ uvāca—Śrī Nārada said; *bhikṣubhiḥ*—by the great sages; *vipravasite*—having departed for other places; *vijñāna*—scientific spiritual knowledge; *ādeṣṭṛbhiḥ*—those who imparted unto me; *mama*—mine; *vartamānaḥ*—present; *vayasi ādye*—before this life; *tataḥ*—thereafter; *etat*—this much; *akāraṣam*—performed.

TRANSLATION

Śrī Nārada said: The great sages, who had imparted scientific knowledge of transcendence to me, departed for other places, and I had to pass my life in this way.

PURPORT

In his previous life, when Nāradajī was impregnated with spiritual knowledge by the grace of the great sages, there was a tangible change in his life, although he was only a boy of five years. That is an important symptom visible after initiation by the bona fide spiritual master. Actual association of devotees brings about a quick change in life for spiritual realization. How it so acted upon the previous life of Śrī Nārada Muni is described by and by in this chapter.

TEXT 6

एकात्मजा मे जननी योषिन्मूढा च किङ्करी।
मय्यात्मजेऽनन्यगतौ चक्रे स्नेहानुबन्धनम् ॥६॥

ekātmajā me jananī
yoṣin mūḍhā ca kiṅkarī
mayy ātmaje 'nanya-gatau
cakre snehānubandhanam

eka-ātmajā—having only one son; *me*—my; *jananī*—mother; *yoṣit*—woman by class; *mūḍhā*—foolish; *ca*—and; *kiṅkarī*—maidservant; *mayi*—unto me; *ātmaje*—being her offspring; *ananya-gatau*—one who has no alternative for protection; *cakre*—did it; *sneha-anubandhanam*—tied by affectionate bondage.

TRANSLATION

I was the only son of my mother, who was not only a simple woman but a maidservant as well. Since I was her only offspring, she had no other alternative for protection: she bound me with the tie of affection.

TEXT 7

सास्वतन्त्रा न कल्पासीद्योगक्षेमं ममेच्छती।
ईशस्य हि वशे लोको योषा दारुमयी यथा ॥७॥

sāsvatantrā na kalpāsīd
yoga-kṣemaṁ mamecchatī
īśasya hi vaśe loko
yoṣā dārumayī yathā

sā—she; *asvatantrā*—was dependent; *na*—not; *kalpā*—able; *āsīt*—was; *yoga-kṣemam*—maintenance; *mama*—my; *icchatī*—although desirous; *īśasya*—of providence; *hi*—for; *vaśe*—under the control of; *lokaḥ*—everyone; *yoṣā*—doll; *dāru-mayī*—made of wood; *yathā*—as much as.

TRANSLATION

She wanted to look after my maintenance properly, but because she was not independent, she was not able to do anything for me. The world

is under the full control of the Supreme Lord; therefore everyone is like a wooden doll in the hands of a puppet master.

TEXT 8

अहं च तद्ब्रह्मकुले ऊषिवांस्तदुपेक्षया।
दिग्देशकालाव्युत्पन्नो बालकः पञ्चहायनः ॥८॥

ahaṁ ca tad-brahma-kule
ūṣivāṁs tad-upekṣayā
dig-deśa-kālāvyutpanno
bālakaḥ pañca-hāyanaḥ

aham—I; *ca*—also; *tat*—that; *brahma-kule*—in the school of the *brāhmaṇas; ūṣivān*—lived; *tat*—her; *upekṣayā*—being dependent on; *dik-deśa*—direction and country; *kāla*—time; *avyutpannaḥ*—having no experience; *bālakaḥ*—a mere child; *pañca*—five; *hāyanaḥ*—years old.

TRANSLATION

When I was a mere child of five years, I lived in a brāhmaṇa school. I was dependent on my mother's affection and had no experience of different lands.

TEXT 9

एकदा निर्गतां गेहाद्दुहन्तीं निशि गां पथि ।
सर्पोऽदशत्पदा स्पृष्टः कृपणां कालचोदितः ॥९॥

ekadā nirgatāṁ gehād
duhantīṁ niśi gāṁ pathi
sarpo 'daśat padā spṛṣṭaḥ
kṛpaṇāṁ kāla-coditaḥ

ekadā—once upon a time; *nirgatām*—having gone away; *gehāt*—from home; *duhantīm*—for milking; *niśi*—at night; *gām*—the cow; *pathi*—on the path; *sarpaḥ*—snake; *adaśat*—bitten; *padā*—on the leg; *spṛṣṭaḥ*—thus struck; *kṛpaṇām*—the poor woman; *kāla-coditaḥ*—influenced by supreme time.

TRANSLATION

Once upon a time, my poor mother, when going out one night to milk a cow, was bitten on the leg by a serpent, influenced by supreme time.

PURPORT

That is the way of dragging a sincere soul nearer to God. The poor boy was being looked after only by his affectionate mother, and yet the mother was taken from the world by the supreme will in order to put him completely at the mercy of the Lord.

TEXT 10

तदा तदहमीशस्य भक्तानां शमभीप्सतः।
अनुग्रहं मन्यमानः प्रातिष्ठं दिशमुत्तराम् ॥१०॥

tadā tad aham īśasya
bhaktānāṁ śam abhīpsataḥ
anugrahaṁ manyamānaḥ
prātiṣṭhaṁ diśam uttarām

tadā—at that time; *tat*—that; *aham*—I; *īśasya*—of the Lord; *bhaktānām*—of the devotees; *śam*—mercy; *abhīpsataḥ*—desiring; *anugraham*—special benediction; *manyamānaḥ*—thinking in that way; *prātiṣṭham*—departed; *diśam uttarām*—in the northern direction.

TRANSLATION

I took this as the special mercy of the Lord, who always desires benediction for His devotees, and so thinking, I started for the north.

PURPORT

Confidential devotees of the Lord see in every step a benedictory direction of the Lord. What is considered to be an odd or difficult moment in the mundane sense is accepted as special mercy of the Lord. Mundane prosperity is a kind of material fever, and by the grace of the Lord the temperature of this material fever is gradually diminished, and spiritual health is obtained step by step. Mundane people misunderstand it.

TEXT 11

स्फीताञ्जनपदांस्तत्र पुरग्रामव्रजाकरान्।
खेटखर्वटवाटीश्च वनान्युपवनानि च ॥११॥

sphītāñ janapadāṁs tatra
pura-grāma-vrajākarān

kheṭa-kharvaṭa-vāṭīś ca
vanāny upavanāni ca

sphītān—very flourishing; *jana-padān*—metropolises; *tatra*—there; *pura*—towns; *grāma*—villages; *vraja*—big farms; *ākarān*—mineral fields (mines); *kheṭa*—agricultural lands; *kharvaṭa*—valleys; *vāṭīḥ*—flower gardens; *ca*—and; *vanāni*—forests; *upavanāni*—nursery gardens; *ca*—and.

TRANSLATION

After my departure, I passed through many flourishing metropolises, towns, villages, animal farms, mines, agricultural lands, valleys, flower gardens, nursery gardens and natural forests.

PURPORT

Man's activities in agriculture, mining, farming, industries, gardening, etc., were all on the same scale as they are now, even previous to the present creation, and the same activities will remain as they are, even in the next creation. After many hundreds of millions of years, one creation is started by the law of nature, and the history of the universe repeats itself practically in the same way. The mundane wranglers waste time with archaeological excavations without searching into the vital necessities of life. After getting an impetus in spiritual life, Śrī Nārada Muni, even though a mere child, did not waste time for a single moment with economic development, although he passed towns and villages, mines and industries. He continually went on to progressive spiritual emancipation. *Śrīmad-Bhāgavatam* is the repetition of history which happened some hundreds of millions of years ago. As it is said herein, only the most important factors of history are picked up to be recorded in this transcendental literature.

TEXT 12

चित्रधातुविचित्राद्रीनिभभग्नभुजद्रुमान् ।
जलाशयाञ्छिवजलान्नलिनीः सुरसेविताः ।
चित्रस्वनैः पत्ररथैर्विभ्रमद्भ्रमरश्रियः ॥१२॥

citra-dhātu-viciträdrīn
ibha-bhagna-bhuja-drumān
jalāśayāñ chiva-jalān
nalinīḥ sura-sevitāḥ

citra-svanaiḥ patra-rathair
vibhramad bhramara-śriyaḥ

citra-dhātu—valuable minerals like gold, silver and copper; *vicitra*—full of variegatedness; *adrīn*—hills and mountains; *ibha-bhagna*—broken by the giant elephants; *bhuja*—branches; *drumān*—trees; *jalāśayān śiva*—health-giving; *jalān*—reservoirs of water; *nalinīḥ*—lotus flowers; *sura-sevitāḥ* —aspired to by the denizens of heaven; *citra-svanaiḥ*—pleasing to the heart; *patra-rathaiḥ*—by the birds; *vibhramat*—bewildering; *bhramara-śriyaḥ*—decorated by drones.

TRANSLATION

I passed through hills and mountains full of reservoirs of various minerals like gold, silver and copper, and through tracts of land with reservoirs of water filled with beautiful lotus flowers, fit for the denizens of heaven, decorated with bewildered bees and singing birds.

TEXT 13

नलवेणुशरस्तन्बकुशकीचकगह्वरम् ।
एक एवातियातोऽहमद्राक्षं विपिनं महत् ।
घोरं प्रतिभयाकारं व्यालोलूकशिवाजिरम् ॥१३॥

nala-veṇu-śaras-tanba-
kuśa-kīcaka-gahvaram
eka evātiyāto 'ham
adrākṣaṁ vipinaṁ mahat
ghoraṁ pratibhayākāraṁ
vyālolūka-śivājiram

nala—pipes; *veṇu*—bamboo; *śaraḥ*—pens; *tanba*—full of; *kuśa*—sharp grass; *kīcaka*—weeds; *gahvaram*—caves; *ekaḥ*—alone; *eva*—only; *atiyātaḥ* —difficult to go through; *aham*—I; *adrākṣam*—visited; *vipinam*—deep forests; *mahat*—great; *ghoram*—fearful; *pratibhaya-ākāram*—dangerously; *vyāla*—snakes; *ulūka*—owls; *śiva*—jackals; *ajiram*—playgrounds.

TRANSLATION

I then passed alone through many forests of rushes, bamboo, reeds, sharp grass, weeds and caves, which were very difficult to go through

alone. I visited deep, dark and dangerously fearful forests, which were the play yards of snakes, owls and jackals.

PURPORT

It is the duty of a mendicant (*parivrājakācārya*) to experience all varieties of God's creation by traveling alone through all forests, hills, towns, villages, etc., to gain faith in God and strength of mind as well as to enlighten the inhabitants with the message of God. A *sannyāsī* is duty-bound to take all these risks without fear, and the most typical *sannyāsī* of the present age is Lord Caitanya, who traveled in the same manner through the central Indian jungles, enlightening even the tigers, bears, snakes, deer, elephants and many other jungle animals. In this age of Kali, *sannyāsa* is forbidden for ordinary men. One who changes his dress to make propaganda is a different man from the original ideal *sannyāsī.* One should, however, take the vow to stop social intercourse completely and devote life exclusively to the service of the Lord. The change of dress is only a formality. Lord Caitanya did not accept the name of a *sannyāsī,* and in this age of Kali the so-called *sannyāsīs* should not change their former names, following in the footsteps of Lord Caitanya. In this age, devotional service of hearing and repeating the holy glories of the Lord is strongly recommended, and one who takes the vow of renunciation of family life need not imitate the *parivrājakācārya* like Nārada or Lord Caitanya, but may sit down at some holy place and devote his whole time and energy to hear and repeatedly chant the holy scriptures left by the great *ācāryas* like the six Gosvāmīs of Vṛndāvana.

TEXT 14

परिश्रान्तेन्द्रियात्माहं तृट्परीतो बुभुक्षितः ।
स्नात्वा पीत्वा ह्रदे नद्या उपस्पृष्टो गतश्रमः ॥१४॥

pariśrāntendriyātmāhaṁ
tṛṭ-parīto bubhukṣitaḥ
snātvā pītvā hrade nadyā
upaspṛṣṭo gata-śramaḥ

pariśrānta—being tired; *indriya*—bodily; *ātmā*—mentally; *aham*—I; *tṛṭ-parītaḥ*—being thirsty; *bubhukṣitaḥ*—and hungry; *snātvā*—taking a bath; *pītvā*—and drinking water also; *hrade*—in the lake; *nadyāḥ*—of a river; *upaspṛṣṭaḥ*—being in contact with; *gata*—got relief from; *śramaḥ*—tiredness.

TRANSLATION

Thus traveling, I felt tired, both bodily and mentally, and I was both thirsty and hungry. So I took a bath in a river lake and also drank water. By contacting water, I got relief from my exhaustion.

PURPORT

A traveling mendicant can meet the needs of the body, namely thirst and hunger, by the gifts of nature without being a beggar at the doors of the householders. The mendicant therefore does not go to the house of a householder to beg but to enlighten him spiritually.

TEXT 15

तस्मिन्निर्मनुजेऽरण्ये पिप्पलोपस्थ आश्रितः ।
आत्मनात्मानमात्मस्थं यथाश्रुतमचिन्तयम् ॥१५॥

tasmin nirmanuje 'raṇye
pippalopastha āśritaḥ
ātmanātmānam ātmasthaṁ
yathā-śrutam acintayam

tasmin—in that; *nirmanuje*—without human habitation; *araṇye*—in the forest; *pippala*—banyan tree; *upasthe*—sitting under it; *āśritaḥ*—taking shelter of; *ātmanā*—by intelligence; *ātmānam*—the Supersoul; *ātma-stham*—situated within myself; *yathā-śrutam*—as I had heard it from the liberated souls; *acintayam*—thought over.

TRANSLATION

After that, under the shadow of a banyan tree in an uninhabited forest I began to meditate upon the Supersoul situated within, using my intelligence, as I had learned from liberated souls.

PURPORT

One should not meditate according to one's personal whims. One should know perfectly well from the authoritative sources of scriptures through the transparent medium of a bona fide spiritual master and by proper use of one's trained intelligence for meditating upon the Supersoul dwelling within every living being. This consciousness is firmly developed by a devotee who has rendered loving service unto the Lord by carrying out the orders of the spiritual master. Śrī Nāradajī contacted bona fide spiritual masters, served them sincerely and got enlightenment rightly. Thus he began to meditate.

TEXT 16

ध्यायतश्चरणाम्भोजं भावनिर्जितचेतसा ।
औत्कण्ठ्याश्रुकलाक्षस्य हृद्यासीन्मे शनैर्हरिः ॥१६॥

dhyāyataś caraṇāmbhojaṁ
bhāva-nirjita-cetasā
autkaṇṭhyāśru-kalākṣasya
hṛdy āsīn me śanair hariḥ

dhyāyataḥ—thus meditating upon; *caraṇa-ambhojam*—the lotus feet of the localized Personality of Godhead; *bhāva-nirjita*—mind transformed in transcendental love for the Lord; *cetasā*—all mental activities (thinking, feeling and willing); *autkaṇṭhya*—eagerness; *aśru-kala*—tears rolled down; *akṣasya*—of the eyes; *hṛdi*—within my heart; *āsīt*—appeared; *me*—my; *śanaiḥ*—without delay; *hariḥ*—the Personality of Godhead.

TRANSLATION

As soon as I began to meditate upon the lotus feet of the Personality of Godhead with my mind transformed in transcendental love, tears rolled down my eyes, and without delay the Personality of Godhead, Śrī Kṛṣṇa, appeared on the lotus of my heart.

PURPORT

The word *bhāva* is significant here. This *bhāva* stage is attained after one has transcendental affection for the Lord. The first initial stage is called *śraddhā,* or a liking for the Supreme Lord, and in order to increase that liking one has to associate with pure devotees of the Lord. The third stage is to practice the prescribed rules and regulations of devotional service. This will dissipate all sorts of misgivings and remove all personal deficiencies that hamper progress in devotional service.

When all misgivings and personal deficiencies are removed, there is a standard faith in transcendental matter, and the taste for it increases in greater proportion. This stage leads to attraction, and after this there is *bhāva,* or the prior stage of unalloyed love for God. All the above different stages are but different stages of development of transcendental love. Being so surcharged with transcendental love, there comes a strong feeling of separation which leads to eight different kinds of ecstasies. Tears from the eyes of a devotee is an automatic reaction, and because Śrī Nārada Muni in his previous birth attained that stage very quickly after his departure from home, it was quite possible for him to perceive the actual presence of the Lord, which he tangibly experienced by his developed spiritual senses without material tinge.

TEXT 17

प्रेमातिभरनिर्भिन्नपुलकाङ्गोऽतिनिर्वृतः ।
आनन्दसम्प्लवे लीनो नापश्यमुभयं मुने ॥१७॥

premātibhara-nirbhinna-
pulakāṅgo 'tinirvṛtaḥ
ānanda-samplave līno
nāpaśyam ubhayaṁ mune

premā—love; *atibhara*—excessive; *nirbhinna*—especially distinguished; *pulaka*—feelings of happiness; *aṅgaḥ*—different bodily parts; *ati-nirvṛtaḥ*—being fully overwhelmed; *ānanda*—ecstasy; *samplave*—in the ocean of; *līnaḥ*—absorbed in; *na*—not; *apaśyam*—could see; *ubhayam*—both; *mune*—O Vyāsadeva.

TRANSLATION

O Vyāsadeva, at that time, being exceedingly overpowered by feelings of happiness, every part of my body became separately enlivened. Being absorbed in an ocean of ecstasy, I could not see both myself and the Lord.

PURPORT

Spiritual feelings of happiness and intense ecstasies have no mundane comparison. Therefore it is very difficult to give expression to such feelings. We can just have a glimpse of such ecstasy in the words of Śrī Nārada Muni. Each and every part of the body or senses has its particular function. After seeing the Lord, all the senses become fully awakened to render service unto the Lord because in the liberated state the senses are fully efficient in serving the Lord. As such, in that transcendental ecstasy it so happened that the senses became separately enlivened to serve the Lord. This being so, Nārada Muni lost himself in seeing both himself and the Lord simultaneously.

TEXT 18

रूपं भगवतो यत्तन्मनःकान्तं शुचापहम् ।
अपश्यन् सहसोत्तस्थे वैक्लव्याद्दुर्मना इव ॥१८॥

rūpaṁ bhagavato yat tan
manaḥ-kāntaṁ śucāpaham
apaśyan sahasottasthe
vaiklavyād durmanā iva

rūpam—form; *bhagavataḥ*—of the Personality of Godhead; *yat*—as it is; *tat*—that; *manaḥ*—of the mind; *kāntam*—as it desires; *śucā-apaham*—vanishing all disparity; *apaśyan*—without seeing; *sahasā*—all of a sudden; *uttasthe*—got up; *vaiklavyāt*—being perturbed; *durmanāḥ*—having lost the desirable; *iva*—as it were.

TRANSLATION

The transcendental form of the Lord, as it is, satisfies the mind's desire and at once erases all mental incongruities. Upon losing that form, I suddenly got up, being perturbed, as is usual when one loses that which is desirable.

PURPORT

That the Lord is not formless is experienced by Nārada Muni. But His form is completely different from all forms of our material experience. For the whole duration of our life we go see different forms in the material world, but none of them is just apt to satisfy the mind, nor can any one of them vanish all perturbance of the mind. These are the special features of the transcendental form of the Lord, and one who has once seen that form is not satisfied with anything else; no form in the material world can any longer satisfy the seer. That the Lord is formless or impersonal means that He has nothing like a material form and is not like any material personality.

As spiritual beings, having eternal relations with that transcendental form of the Lord, we are, life after life, searching after that form of the Lord, and we are not satisfied by any other form of material appeasement. Nārada Muni got a glimpse of this, but having not seen it again he became perturbed and stood up all of a sudden to search it out. What we desire life after life was obtained by Nārada Muni, and losing sight of Him again was certainly a great shock for him.

TEXT 19

दिदृक्षुस्तदहं भूयः प्रणिधाय मनो हृदि।
वीक्षमाणोऽपि नापश्यमवितृप्त इवातुरः ॥१९॥

didṛkṣus tad ahaṁ bhūyaḥ
praṇidhāya mano hṛdi
vīkṣamāṇo 'pi nāpaśyam
avitṛpta ivāturaḥ

didṛkṣuḥ—desiring to see; *tat*—that; *aham*—I; *bhūyaḥ*—again; *praṇidhāya*—having concentrated the mind; *manaḥ*—mind; *hṛdi*—upon the heart; *vīkṣamāṇaḥ*—waiting to see; *api*—in spite of; *na*—never; *apaśyam*—saw Him; *avitṛptaḥ*—without being satisfied; *iva*—like; *āturaḥ*—aggrieved.

TRANSLATION

I desired to see again that transcendental form of the Lord, but despite my attempts to concentrate upon the heart with eagerness to view the form again, I could not see Him any more, and thus dissatisfied, I was very much aggrieved.

PURPORT

There is no mechanical process to see the form of the Lord. It completely depends on the causeless mercy of the Lord. We cannot demand the Lord to be present before our vision, just as we cannot demand the sun to rise whenever we like. The sun rises out of his own accord; so also the Lord is pleased to be present out of His causeless mercy. One should simply await the opportune moment and go on discharging his prescribed duty in devotional service of the Lord. Nārada Muni thought that the Lord could be seen again by the same mechanical process which was successful in the first attempt, but in spite of his utmost endeavor he could not make the second attempt successful. The Lord is completely independent of all obligations. He can simply be bound up by the tie of unalloyed devotion. Nor is He visible or perceivable by our material senses. When He pleases, being satisfied with the sincere attempt of devotional service depending completely on the mercy of the Lord, then He may be seen out of His own accord.

TEXT 20

एवं यतन्तं विजने मामाहागोचरो गिराम्।
गम्भीरश्लक्ष्णया वाचा शुचः प्रशमयन्निव ॥२०॥

evaṁ yatantaṁ vijane
mām āhāgocaro girām
gambhīra-ślakṣṇayā vācā
śucaḥ praśamayann iva

evam—thus; *yatantam*—one who is engaged in attempting; *vijane*—in that lonely place; *mām*—unto me; *āha*—said; *agocaraḥ*—beyond the range of physical sound; *girām*—utterances; *gambhīra*—grave; *ślakṣṇayā*—pleasing to hear; *vācā*—words; *śucaḥ*—grief; *praśamayan*—mitigating; *iva*—like.

TRANSLATION

Seeing my attempts in that lonely place, the Personality of Godhead, who is transcendental to all mundane description, spoke to me with gravity and pleasing words, just to mitigate my grief.

PURPORT

In the *Vedas* it is said that God is beyond the approach of mundane words and intelligence. And yet by His causeless mercy one can have suitable senses to hear Him or to speak to Him. This is the Lord's inconceivable energy. One upon whom His mercy is bestowed can hear Him. The Lord was much pleased with Nārada Muni, and therefore the necessary strength was invested in him so that he could hear the Lord. It is not, however, possible for others to perceive directly the touch of the Lord during the probationary stage of regulative devotional service. It was a special gift for Nārada. When he heard the pleasing words of the Lord, the feelings of separation were to some extent mitigated. A devotee in love with God feels always the pangs of separation and is therefore always enwrapped in transcendental ecstasy.

TEXT 21

हन्तास्मिञ्जन्मनि भवान्मा मां द्रष्टुमिहार्हति ।
अविपक्वकषायाणां दुर्दर्शोऽहं कुयोगिनाम् ॥२१॥

hantāsmiñ janmani bhavān
mā māṁ draṣṭum ihārhati
avipakva-kaṣāyāṇāṁ
durdarśo 'haṁ kuyoginām

hanta—O Nārada; *asmin*—this; *janmani*—duration of life; *bhavān*—yourself; *mā*—not; *mām*—Me; *draṣṭum*—to see; *iha*—here; *arhati*—deserve; *avipakva*—immature; *kaṣāyāṇām*—material dirt; *durdarśaḥ*—difficult to be seen; *aham*—I; *kuyoginām*—incomplete in service.

TRANSLATION

O Nārada [the Lord spoke], I regret that during this lifetime you will not be able to see Me anymore. Those who are incomplete in service and who are not completely free from all material taints can hardly see Me.

PURPORT

The Personality of Godhead is described in the *Bhagavad-gītā* as the most pure, the Supreme and the Absolute Truth. There is no trace of a tinge of materiality in His person, and thus one who has the slightest tinge of material affection cannot approach Him. The beginning of devotional service starts from the point when one is freed from at least two forms of material modes, namely the mode of passion and the mode of ignorance. The result is exhibited by the signs of being freed from kāma (lust) and *lobha* (covetousness). That is to say, one must be freed from the desires for sense satisfaction and avarice for sense gratification. The balanced mode of nature is goodness. And to be completely freed from all material tinges is to become free from the mode of goodness also. To search the audience of God in a lonely forest is considered to be in the mode of goodness. One can go out into the forest to attain spiritual perfection, but that does not mean that one can see the Lord personally there. One must be completely freed from all material attachment and be situated on the plane of transcendence, which alone will help the devotee get in personal touch with the Personality of Godhead. The best method is that one should live at a place where the transcendental form of the Lord is worshiped. The temple of the Lord is a transcendental place, whereas the forest is a materially good habitation. A neophyte devotee is always recommended to worship the Deity of the Lord (*arcanā*) rather than go into the forest to search out the Lord. Devotional service begins from the process of *arcanā,* which is better than going out in the forest. In his present life, which is completely freed from all material hankerings, Śrī Nārada Muni does not go into the forest, although he can turn every place into Vaikuṇṭha by his presence only. He travels from one planet to another to convert men, gods, Kinnaras, Gandharvas, *ṛṣis, munis* and all others to become devotees of the Lord. By his activities he has engaged many devotees like Prahlāda Mahārāja, Dhruva Mahārāja and many others in the transcendental service of the Lord. A pure devotee of the Lord, therefore, follows in the footsteps of the great devotees like Nārada and Prahlāda and engages his whole time in glorifying the Lord by the process of *kīrtana*. Such a preaching process is transcendental to all material qualities.

TEXT 22

सकृद् यद्दर्शितं रूपमेतत्कामाय तेऽनघ ।
मत्कामः शनकैः साधु सर्वान्मुञ्चति हृच्छयान् ॥२२॥

sakṛd yad darśitaṁ rūpam
etat kāmāya te 'nagha
mat-kāmaḥ śanakaiḥ sādhu
sarvān muñcati hṛc-chayān

sakṛt—once only; *yat*—that; *darśitam*—shown; *rūpam*—form; *etat*—this is; *kāmāya*—for hankerings; *te*—your; *anagha*—O virtuous one; *mat*—Mine; *kāmaḥ*—desire; *śanakaiḥ*—by increasing; *sādhuḥ*—devotee; *sarvān*—all; *muñcati*—gives away; *hṛt-śayān*—material desires.

TRANSLATION

O virtuous one, you have only once seen My person, and this is just to increase your desire for Me, because the more you hanker for Me, the more you will be freed from all material desires.

PURPORT

A living being cannot be vacant of desires. He is not a dead stone. He must be working, thinking, feeling and willing. But when he thinks, feels and wills materially, he becomes entangled, and conversely when he thinks, feels and wills for the service of the Lord, he becomes gradually freed from all entanglement. The more a person is engaged in the transcendental loving service of the Lord, the more he acquires a hankering for it. That is the transcendental nature of godly service. Material service has satiation, whereas spiritual service of the Lord has neither satiation nor end. One can go on increasing his hankerings for the loving transcendental service of the Lord, and yet he will not find satiation or end. By intense service of the Lord, one can experience the presence of the Lord transcendentally. Therefore seeing the Lord means being engaged in His service because His service and His person are identical. The sincere devotee should go on with sincere service of the Lord.

The Lord will give proper direction as to how and where it has to be done. There was no material desire in Nārada, and yet just to increase his intense desire for the Lord, he was so advised.

TEXT 23

सत्सेवयादीर्घयापि जाता मयि दृढा मतिः ।
हित्वावद्यमिमं लोकं गन्ता मज्जनतामसि ॥२३॥

sat-sevayādīrghayāpi
jātā mayi dṛḍhā matiḥ
hitvāvadyam imaṁ lokaṁ
gantā maj-janatām asi

sat-sevayā—by service of the Absolute Truth; *adīrghayā*—for some days; *api*—even; *jātā*—having attained; *mayi*—unto Me; *dṛḍhā*—firm; *matiḥ*—intelligence; *hitvā*—having given up; *avadyam*—deplorable; *imam*—this; *lokam*—material worlds; *gantā*—going to; *mat-janatām*—My associates; *asi*—become.

TRANSLATION

By service of the Absolute Truth, even for a few days, a devotee attains firm and fixed intelligence in Me. Consequently he goes on to become My associate in the transcendental world after giving up the present deplorable material worlds.

PURPORT

Serving the Absolute Truth means rendering service unto the Absolute Personality of Godhead under the direction of the bona fide spiritual master, who is a transparent via medium between the Lord and the neophyte devotee. The neophyte devotee has no ability to approach the Absolute Personality of Godhead by the strength of his present imperfect material senses, and therefore under the direction of the spiritual master he is trained in transcendental service of the Lord. And by such training, even for some days, the neophyte devotee gets intelligence in such transcendental service, which leads him ultimately to get free from perpetual inhabitation in the material worlds and to be promoted to the transcendental world to become one of the liberated associates of the Lord in the kingdom of God.

TEXT 24

मतिर्मयि निबद्धेयं न विपद्येत कर्हिचित्।
प्रजासर्गनिरोधेऽपि स्मृतिश्च मदनुग्रहात् ॥२४॥

matir mayi nibaddheyaṁ
na vipadyeta karhicit
prajā-sarga-nirodhe 'pi
smṛtiś ca mad-anugrahāt

matiḥ—intelligence; *mayi*—devoted to Me; *nibaddhā*—engaged; *iyam*—this; *na*—never; *vipadyeta*—separate; *karhicit*—at any time; *prajā*—living beings; *sarga*—at the time of creation; *nirodhe*—also at the time of annihilation; *api*—even; *smṛtiḥ*—remembrance; *ca*—and; *mat*—Mine; *anugrahāt*—by the mercy of.

TRANSLATION

Intelligence engaged in My devotion cannot be thwarted at any time. Even at the time of creation, as well as at the time of annihilation, your remembrance will continue by My mercy.

PURPORT

Devotional service rendered to the Personality of Godhead never goes in vain. Since the Personality of Godhead is eternal, intelligence applied in His service or anything done in His relation is also permanent. In the *Bhagavad-gītā* it is said that such transcendental service rendered unto the Personality of Godhead accumulates birth after birth, and when the devotee is fully matured, the total service counted together makes him eligible to enter into the association of the Personality of Godhead. Such accumulation of God's service is never vanquished, but increases till fully matured.

TEXT 25

एतावदुक्त्वोपरराम तन्महद्
भूतं नभोलिङ्गमलिङ्गमीश्वरम् ।
अहं च तस्मै महतां महीयसे
शीर्ष्णावनामं विदधेऽनुकम्पितः ॥२५॥

etāvad uktvopararāma tan mahad
bhūtaṁ nabho-liṅgam aliṅgam īśvaram

ahaṁ ca tasmai mahatāṁ mahīyase
śīrṣṇāvanāmaṁ vidadhe 'nukampitaḥ

etāvat—thus; *uktvā*—spoken; *upararāma*—stopped; *tat*—that; *mahat*—great; *bhūtam*—wonderful; *nabhaḥ-liṅgam*—personified by sound; *aliṅgam*—unseen by the eyes; *īśvaram*—the supreme authority; *aham*—I; *ca*—also; *tasmai*—unto Him; *mahatām*—the great; *mahīyase*—unto the glorified; *śīrṣṇā*—by the head; *avanāmam*—obeisances; *vidadhe*—executed; *anukampitaḥ*—being favored by Him.

TRANSLATION

Then that supreme authority, personified by sound and unseen by eyes, but most wonderful, stopped speaking. Feeling a sense of gratitude, I offered my obeisances unto Him, bowing my head.

PURPORT

That the Personality of Godhead was not seen but only heard does not make any difference. The Personality of Godhead produced the four *Vedas* by His breathing, and He is seen and realized through the transcendental sound of the *Vedas.* Similarly, the *Bhagavad-gītā* is the sound representation of the Lord, and there is no difference in identity. The conclusion is that the Lord can be seen and heard by persistent chanting of the transcendental sound.

TEXT 26

नामान्यनन्तस्य हतत्रपः पठन्
गुह्यानि भद्राणि कृतानि च स्मरन्।
गां पर्यटंस्तुष्टमना गतस्पृहः
कालं प्रतीक्षन् विमदो विमत्सरः ॥२६॥

nāmāny anantasya hata-trapaḥ paṭhan
guhyāni bhadrāṇi kṛtāni ca smaran
gāṁ paryaṭaṁs tuṣṭa-manā gata-spṛhaḥ
kālaṁ pratīkṣan vimado vimatsaraḥ

nāmāni—the holy name, fame, etc.; *anantasya*—of the unlimited; *hata-trapaḥ*—being freed from all formalities of the material world; *paṭhan*—by recitation, repeated reading, etc.; *guhyāni*—mysterious; *bhadrāṇi*—all benedictory; *kṛtāni*—activities; *ca*—and; *smaran*—constantly remembering; *gām*—on the earth; *paryaṭan*—traveling all through; *tuṣṭa-manāḥ*—fully satisfied; *gata-spṛhaḥ*—completely freed from all material desires; *kālam*—time; *pratīkṣan*—awaiting; *vimadaḥ*—without being proud; *vimatsaraḥ*—without being envious.

TRANSLATION

Thus I began chanting the holy name and fame of the Lord by repeated recitation, ignoring all the formalities of the material world. Such chanting and remembering of the transcendental pastimes of the Lord are benedictory. So doing, I traveled all over the earth, fully satisfied, humble and unenvious.

PURPORT

The life of a sincere devotee of the Lord is thus explained in a nutshell by Nārada Muni by his personal example. Such a devotee, after his initiation by the Lord or His bona fide representative, takes very seriously chanting of the glories of the Lord and traveling all over the world so that others may also hear the glories of the Lord. Such devotees have no desire for material gain. They are conducted by one single desire: to go back to Godhead. This awaits them in due course on quitting the material body. Because they have the highest aim of life, going back to Godhead, they are never envious of anyone, nor are they proud of being eligible to go back to Godhead. Their only business is to chant and remember the holy name, fame and pastimes of the Lord and, according to personal capacity, to distribute the message for others' welfare without motive of material gain.

TEXT 27

एवं कृष्णमतेर्ब्रह्मन्नासक्तस्यामलात्मनः ।
कालः प्रादुरभूत्काले तडित्सौदामनी यथा ॥२७॥

evaṁ kṛṣṇa-mater brahman
nāsaktasyāmalātmanaḥ
kālaḥ prādurabhūt kāle
taḍit saudāmanī yathā

evam—thus; *kṛṣṇa-mateḥ*—one who is fully absorbed in thinking of Kṛṣṇa; *brahman*—O Vyāsadeva; *na*—not; *āsaktasya*—of one who is attached;

amala-ātmanaḥ—of one who is completely free from all material dirt; *kālaḥ* —death; *prādurabhūt*—become visible; *kāle*—in the course of time; *taḍit*—lightning; *saudāmanī*—illuminating; *yathā*—as it is.

TRANSLATION

And so, O Brāhmaṇa Vyāsadeva, in due course of time I, who was fully absorbed in thinking of Kṛṣṇa and who therefore had no attachments, being completely freed from all material taints, met with death, as lightning and illumination occur simultaneously.

PURPORT

To be fully absorbed in the thought of Kṛṣṇa means clearance of material dirts or hankerings. As a very rich man has no hankerings for small petty things, so also a devotee of Lord Kṛṣṇa, who is guaranteed to pass on to the kingdom of God, where life is eternal, fully cognizant and blissful, naturally has no hankerings for petty material things, which are like dolls or shadows of the reality and are without permanent value. That is the sign of spiritually enriched persons. And in due course of time, when a pure devotee is completely prepared, all of a sudden the change of body occurs which is commonly called death. And for the pure devotee such a change takes place exactly like lightning, and illumination follows simultaneously. That is to say a devotee simultaneously changes his material body and develops a spiritual body by the will of the Supreme. Even before death, a pure devotee has no material affection, due to his body's being spiritualized like a red-hot iron in contact with fire.

TEXT 28

प्रयुज्यमाने मयि तां शुद्धां भागवतीं तनुम्।
आरब्धकर्मनिर्वाणो न्यपतत् पाञ्चभौतिकः ॥२८॥

prayujyamāne mayi tāṁ
śuddhāṁ bhāgavatīṁ tanum
ārabdha-karma-nirvāṇo
nyapatat pāñca-bhautikaḥ

prayujyamāne—having been awarded; *mayi*—on me; *tām*—that; *śuddhām*—transcendental; *bhāgavatīm*—fit for associating with the Personality of Godhead; *tanum*—body; *arabdha*—acquired; *karma*—fruitive work; *nirvāṇaḥ*—prohibitive; *nyapatat*—quit; *pāñca-bhautikaḥ*—body made of five material elements.

TRANSLATION

Having been awarded a transcendental body befitting an associate of the Personality of Godhead, I quit the body made of five material elements, and thus all acquired fruitive results of work [karma] stopped.

PURPORT

Informed by the Personality of Godhead that he would be awarded a transcendental body befitting the Lord's association, Nārada got his spiritual body as soon as he quitted his material body. This transcendental body is free from material affinity and invested with three primary transcendental qualities, namely eternity, freedom from material modes, and freedom from reactions of fruitive activities. The material body is always afflicted with the lack of these three qualities. A devotee's body becomes at once surcharged with the transcendental qualities as soon as he is engaged in the devotional service of the Lord. It acts like the magnetic influence of a touchstone upon iron. The influence of transcendental devotional service is like that. Therefore change of the body means stoppage of the reaction of three qualitative modes of material nature upon the pure devotee. There are many instances of this in the revealed scriptures. Dhruva Mahārāja and Prahlāda Mahārāja and many other devotees were able to see the Personality of Godhead face to face apparently in the same body. This means that the quality of a devotee's body changes from material to transcendence. That is the opinion of the authorized Gosvāmīs via the authentic scriptures. In the *Brahma-saṁhitā* it is said that beginning from the *indra-gopa* germ up to the great Indra, King of heaven, all living beings are subjected to the law of *karma* and are bound to suffer and enjoy the fruitive results of their own work. Only the devotee is exempt from such reactions, by the causeless mercy of the supreme authority, the Personality of Godhead.

TEXT 29

कल्पान्त इदमादाय शयानेऽम्भस्युदन्वतः ।
शिशयिषोरनुप्राणं विविशेऽन्तरहं विभोः ॥२९॥

kalpānta idam ādāya
śayāne 'mbhasy udanvataḥ

śiśayiṣor anuprāṇaṁ
viviśe 'ntar ahaṁ vibhoḥ

kalpa-ante—at the end of Brahmā's day; *idam*—this; *ādāya*—taking together; *śayāne*—having gone to lie down; *ambhasi*—in the causal water; *udanvataḥ*—devastation; *śiśayiṣoḥ*—lying of the Personality of Godhead (Nārāyaṇa); *anuprāṇam*—breathing; *viviśe*—entered into; *antaḥ*—within; *aham*—I; *vibhoḥ*—of Lord Brahmā.

TRANSLATION

At the end of the millennium, when the Personality of Godhead, Lord Nārāyaṇa, lay down within the water of devastation, Brahmā began to enter into Him along with all creative elements, and I also entered through His breathing.

PURPORT

Nārada is known as the son of Brahmā, as Lord Kṛṣṇa is known as the son of Vasudeva. The Personality of Godhead and His liberated devotees like Nārada appear in the material world by the same process. As it is said in the *Bhagavad-gītā,* the birth and activities of the Lord are all transcendental. Therefore, according to authorized opinion, the birth of Nārada as the son of Brahmā is also a transcendental pastime. His appearance and disappearance are practically on the same level as that of the Lord. The Lord and His devotees are therefore simultaneously one and different as spiritual entities. They belong to the same category of transcendence.

TEXT 30

सहस्त्रयुगपर्यन्ते उत्थायेदं सिसृक्षतः ।
मरीचिमिश्रा ऋषयः प्राणेभ्योऽहं च जज्ञिरे ॥३०॥

sahasra-yuga-paryante
utthāyedaṁ sisṛkṣataḥ
marīci-miśrā ṛṣayaḥ
prāṇebhyo 'haṁ ca jajñire

sahasra—one thousand; *yuga*—4,300,000 years; *paryante*—at the end of the duration; *utthāya*—having expired; *idam*—this; *sisṛkṣataḥ*—desired to create again; *marīci-miśrāḥ*—*ṛṣis* like Marīci; *ṛṣayaḥ*—all the *ṛṣis;* *prāṇebhyaḥ*—out of His senses; *aham*—I; *ca*—also; *jajñire*—appeared.

TRANSLATION

After 4,300,000,000 solar years, when Brahmā awoke to create again by the will of the Lord, all the ṛṣis like Marīci, Aṅgirā, Atri and so on were created from the transcendental body of the Lord, and I also appeared along with them.

PURPORT

The duration of a day in the life of Brahmā is 4,320,000,000 solar years. This is stated also in the *Bhagavad-gītā.* So for this period Brahmājī rests in *yoga-nidrā* within the body of the Garbhodakaśāyī Viṣṇu, the generator of Brahmā. Thus after the sleeping period of Brahmā, when there is again creation by the will of the Lord through the agency of Brahmā, all the great *ṛṣis* again appear from different parts of the transcendental body, and Nārada also appears. This means that Nārada appears in the same transcendental body, just as a man awakes from sleep in the same body. Śrī Nārada is eternally free to move in all parts of the transcendental and material creations of the Almighty. He appears and disappears in his own transcendental body, which is without distinction of body and soul, unlike conditioned beings.

TEXT 31

अन्तर्बहिश्च लोकांस्त्रीन् पर्येम्यस्कन्दितव्रतः ।
अनुग्रहान्महाविष्णोरविघातगतिः क्वचित् ॥३१॥

antar bahiś ca lokāṁs trīn
paryemy askandita-vrataḥ
anugrahān mahā-viṣṇor
avighāta-gatiḥ kvacit

antaḥ—in the transcendental world; *bahiḥ*—in the material world; *ca*—and; *lokān*—planets; *trīn*—three (divisions); *paryemi*—travel; *askandita*—unbroken; *vrataḥ*—vow; *anugrahāt*—by the causeless mercy; *mahā-viṣṇoḥ*—of the Mahā-Viṣṇu (Kāraṇodakaśāyī Viṣṇu); *avighāta*—without restriction; *gatiḥ*—entrance; *kvacit*—at any time.

TRANSLATION

Since then, by the grace of the almighty Viṣṇu, I travel everywhere without restriction both in the transcendental world and in the three

divisions of the material world. This is because I am fixed in unbroken devotional service of the Lord.

PURPORT

As stated in the *Bhagavad-gītā,* there are three divisions of the material spheres, namely the *ūrdhva-loka* (topmost planets), *madhya-loka* (midway planets) and *adho-loka* (downward planets). Beyond the *ūrdhva-loka* planets, that is to say above the Brahmaloka, are the material coverings of the universes, and above that is the spiritual sky, which is unlimited in expansion, containing unlimited self-illuminated Vaikuṇṭha planets inhabited by God Himself along with His associates, who are all eternally liberated living entities. Śrī Nārada Muni could enter all these planets in both the material and spiritual spheres without restriction, as much as the almighty Lord is free to move personally in any part of His creation. In the material world the living beings are influenced by the three material modes of nature, namely goodness, passion and ignorance. But Śrī Nārada Muni is transcendental to all these material modes, and thus he can travel everywhere unrestricted. He is a liberated spaceman. The causeless mercy of Lord Viṣṇu is unparalleled, and such mercy is perceived by the devotees only by the grace of the Lord. Therefore, the devotees never fall down, but the materialists, i.e., the fruitive workers and the speculative philosophers, do fall down, being forced by their respective modes of nature. The *ṛṣis,* as above mentioned, cannot enter into the transcendental world like Nārada. This fact is disclosed in *the Narasiṁha Purāṇa. Ṛṣis* like Marīci are authorities in fruitive work, and *ṛṣis* like Sanaka and Sanātana are authorities in philosophical speculations. But Śrī Nārada Muni is the prime authority for transcendental devotional service of the Lord. All the great authorities in the devotional service of the Lord follow in the footsteps of Nārada Muni in the order of the *Nārada-bhakti-sūtra,* and therefore all the devotees of the Lord are unhesitatingly qualified to enter into the kingdom of God, Vaikuṇṭha.

TEXT 32

देवदत्तामिमां वीणां स्वरब्रह्मविभूषिताम् ।
मूर्च्छयित्वा हरिकथां गायमानश्चराम्यहम् ॥३२॥

deva-dattām imāṁ vīṇāṁ
svara-brahma-vibhūṣitām

mūrcchayitvā hari-kathāṁ
gāyamānaś carāmy aham

deva—the Supreme Personality of Godhead (Śrī Kṛṣṇa); *dattām*—gifted by; *imām*—this; *vīṇām*—a musical stringed instrument; *svara*—singing meter; *brahma*—transcendental; *vibhūṣitām*—decorated with; *mūrcchayitvā*—vibrating; *hari-kathām*—transcendental message; *gāyamānaḥ*—singing constantly; *carāmi*—do move; *aham*—I.

TRANSLATION

And thus I travel, constantly singing the transcendental message of the glories of the Lord, vibrating this instrument called a vīṇā, which is charged with transcendental sound and which was given to me by Lord Kṛṣṇa.

PURPORT

The musical stringed instrument called the *vīṇā,* which was handed to Nārada by Lord Śrī Kṛṣṇa, is described in the *Liṅga Purāṇa,* and this is confirmed by Śrīla Jīva Gosvāmī. This transcendental instrument is identical with Lord Śrī Kṛṣṇa and Nārada because all of them are of the same transcendental category. Sound vibrated by the instrument cannot be material, and therefore the glories and pastimes which are broadcast by the instrument of Nārada are also transcendental, without a tinge of material inebriety. The seven singing meters, namely *ṣa* (*ṣaḍja*), *ṛ* (*ṛṣabha*), *gā* (*gāndhāra*), *ma* (*madhyama*), *pa* (*pañcama*), *dha* (*dhaivata*) and *ni* (*niṣāda*), are also transcendental and specifically meant for transcendental songs. As a pure devotee of the Lord, Śrī Nāradadeva is always fulfilling his obligation to the Lord for His gift of the instrument, and thus he is always engaged in singing His transcendental glories and is therefore infallible in his exalted position. Following in the footsteps of Śrīla Nārada Muni, a self-realized soul in the material world should also properly use the sound meters, namely *ṣa, ṛ, gā, ma,* etc., in the service of the Lord by constantly singing the glories of the Lord, as confirmed in the *Bhagavad-gītā.*

TEXT 33

प्रगायतः स्ववीर्याणि तीर्थपादः प्रियश्रवाः ।
आहूत इव मे शीघ्रं दर्शनं याति चेतसि ॥३३॥

pragāyataḥ sva-vīryāṇi
tīrtha-pādaḥ priya-śravāḥ
āhūta iva me śīghraṁ
darśanaṁ yāti cetasi

pragāyataḥ—thus singing; *sva-vīryāṇi*—own activities; *tīrtha-pādaḥ*—the Lord, whose lotus feet are the source of all virtues or holiness; *priya-śravāḥ*—pleasing to hear; *āhūtaḥ*—called for; *iva*—just like; *me*—to me; *śīghram*—very soon; *darśanam*—sight; *yāti*—appears; *cetasi*—on the seat of the heart.

TRANSLATION

The Supreme Lord Śrī Kṛṣṇa, whose glories and activities are pleasing to hear, at once appears on the seat of my heart, as if called for, as soon as I begin to chant His holy activities.

PURPORT

The Absolute Personality of Godhead is not different from His transcendental name, form, pastimes and the sound vibrations thereof. As soon as a pure devotee engages himself in the pure devotional service of hearing, chanting and remembering the name, fame and activities of the Lord, at once He becomes visible to the transcendental eyes of the pure devotee by reflecting Himself on the mirror of the heart by spiritual television. Therefore a pure devotee who is related with the Lord in loving transcendental service can experience the presence of the Lord at every moment. It is a natural psychology in every individual case that a person likes to hear and enjoy his personal glories enumerated by others. That is a natural instinct, and the Lord, being also an individual personality like others, is not an exception to this psychology because psychological characteristics visible in the individual souls are but reflections of the same psychology in the Absolute Lord. The only difference is that the Lord is the greatest personality of all and absolute in all His affairs. If, therefore, the Lord is attracted by the pure devotee's chanting of His glories, there is nothing astonishing. Since He is absolute, He can appear Himself in the picture of His glorification, the two things being identical. Śrīla Nārada chants the glorification of the Lord not for his personal benefit but because the glorifications are identical with the Lord. Nārada Muni penetrates into the presence of the Lord by the transcendental chanting.

TEXT 34

एतद्ध्यातुरचित्तानां मात्रास्पर्शेच्छया मुहुः ।
भवसिन्धुप्लवो दृष्टो हरिचर्यानुवर्णनम् ॥३४॥

etad dhy ātura-cittānāṁ
mātrā-sparśecchayā muhuḥ
bhava-sindhu-plavo dṛṣṭo
hari-caryānuvarṇanam

etat—this; *hi*—certainly; *ātura-cittānām*—of those whose minds are always full of cares and anxieties; *mātrā*—objects of sense enjoyment; *sparśa*—senses; *icchayā*—by desires; *muhuḥ*—always; *bhava-sindhu*—the ocean of nescience; *plavaḥ*—boat; *dṛṣṭaḥ*—experienced; *hari-carya*—activities of Hari, the Personality of Godhead; *anuvarṇanam*—constant recitation.

TRANSLATION

It is personally experienced by me that those who are always full of cares and anxieties due to desiring contact of the senses with their objects can cross the ocean of nescience on a most suitable boat—the constant chanting of the transcendental activities of the Personality of Godhead.

PURPORT

The symptom of a living being is that he cannot remain silent even for some time. He must be doing something, thinking of something or talking about something. Generally the materialistic men think and discuss about subjects which satisfy their senses. But as these things are exercised under the influence of the external, illusory energy, such sensual activities do not actually give them any satisfaction. On the contrary, they become full with cares and anxieties. This is called *māyā,* or what is not. That which cannot give them satisfaction is accepted as an object for satisfaction. So Nārada Muni, by his personal experience, says that satisfaction for such frustrated beings engaged in sense gratification is to chant always the activities of the Lord. The point is that the subject matter only should be changed. No one can check the thinking activities of a living being, nor the feeling, willing or working processes. But if one wants actual happiness, one must change the subject matter only. Instead of talking of the politics of a dying man, one might discuss the politics administered by the Lord Himself. Instead of relishing activities of the cinema artists, one can turn his attention to the activities of the Lord with His eternal associates like the *gopīs* and Lakṣmīs. The almighty Personality of Godhead, by His causeless mercy, descends to the earth and manifests activities almost on the line of the worldly men, but at the same time extraordinarily, because He is almighty. He does so for the benefit of all conditioned souls so that they can turn their attention to transcendence. By doing so, the conditioned soul will gradually be promoted to the transcendental position and easily cross the ocean of nescience, the source of all miseries. This is stated from personal experience by such an authority as Śrī Nārada Muni. And we can have the same experience also if we begin to follow in the footsteps of the great sage, the dearmost devotee of the Lord.

TEXT 35

यमादिभिर्योगपथैः कामलोभहतो मुहुः ।
मुकुन्दसेवया यद्वत्तथात्माद्धा न शाम्यति ॥३५॥

yamādibhir yoga-pathaiḥ
kāma-lobha-hato muhuḥ
mukunda-sevayā yadvat
tathātmāddhā na śāmyati

yama-ādibhiḥ—by the process of practicing self-restraint; *yoga-pathaiḥ*—by the system of *yoga* (mystic bodily power to attain the godly stage); *kāma*—desires for sense satisfaction; *lobha*—lust for satisfaction of the senses; *hataḥ*—curbed; *muhuḥ*—always; *mukunda*—the Personality of Godhead; *sevayā*—by the service of; *yadvat*—as it is; *tathā*—like that; *ātmā*—the soul; *addhā*—for all practical purposes; *na*—does not; *śāmyati*—be satisfied.

TRANSLATION

It is true that by practicing restraint of the senses by the yoga system one can get relief from the disturbances of desire and lust, but this is not sufficient to give satisfaction to the soul, for this [satisfaction] is derived from devotional service to the Personality of Godhead.

PURPORT

Yoga aims at controlling the senses. By practice of the mystic process of bodily exercise in sitting, thinking, feeling, willing, concentrating, meditating and at last being merged into transcendence, one can control the senses. The senses are considered like venomous serpents, and the *yoga* system is just to control them. On the other hand, Nārada Muni recommends another method for controlling the senses in the transcendental loving service of Mukunda, the Personality of Godhead. By his experience he says that devotional service to the Lord is more effective and practical than the system of artificially controlling the senses. In the service of the Lord Mukunda, the senses are transcendentally engaged. Thus there is no chance of their being engaged in sense satisfaction. The senses want some engagement. To check them artificially is no check at all because as soon as there is some opportunity for enjoyment, the serpentlike senses will certainly take advantage of it. There are many such instances in history, just like Viśvāmitra Muni's falling a victim to the beauty of Menakā. But Ṭhākura Haridāsa was allured at midnight by the well-dressed Māyā, and still she could not induce that great devotee into her trap.

The whole idea is that without devotional service of the Lord, neither the *yoga* system nor dry philosophical speculation can ever become successful. Pure devotional service of the Lord, without being tinged with fruitive work, mystic *yoga* or speculative philosophy, is the foremost procedure to attain self-realization. Such pure devotional service is transcendental in nature, and the systems of *yoga* and *jñāna* are subordinate to such a process. When the transcendental devotional service is mixed with a subordinate process, it is no longer transcendental but is called mixed devotional service. Śrīla Vyāsadeva, the author of *Śrīmad-Bhāgavatam,* will gradually develop all these different systems of transcendental realization in the text.

TEXT 36

सर्वं तदिदमाख्यातं यत्पृष्टोऽहं त्वयानघ।
जन्मकर्मरहस्यं मे भवतश्चात्मतोषणम् ॥३६॥

sarvaṁ tad idam ākhyātaṁ
yat pṛṣṭo 'haṁ tvayānagha
janma-karma-rahasyaṁ me
bhavataś cātma-toṣaṇam

sarvam—all; *tat*—that; *idam*—this; *ākhyātam*—described; *yat*—whatever; *pṛṣṭaḥ*—asked by; *aham*—me; *tvayā*—by you; *anagha*—without any sins; *janma*—birth; *karma*—activities; *rahasyam*—mysteries; *me*—mine; *bhavataḥ*—your; *ca*—and; *ātma*—self; *toṣaṇam*—satisfaction.

TRANSLATION

O Vyāsadeva, you are freed from all sins. Thus I have explained my birth and activities for self-realization, as you asked. All this will be conducive for your personal satisfaction also.

PURPORT

The process of devotional activities from the beginning to the stage of transcendence is all duly explained to satisfy the inquiries of Vyāsadeva. He has explained how the seeds of devotional service were sown by transcendental association and how they gradually developed by hearing the sages. The result of such hearing is detachment from worldliness, so much so that even a small boy could receive the death news of his mother, who was his only caretaker, as the blessing of God. And at once he took the opportunity to search out the Lord. A sincere urge for having an interview with the Lord was also granted to him, although it is not possible for anyone to see the Lord with mundane eyes. He also explained how by execution of pure transcendental service one can get rid of the fruitive action of accumulated work and how he transformed his material body into a spiritual one. The spiritual body is alone able to enter into the spiritual realm of the Lord, and no one but a pure devotee is eligible to enter into the kingdom of God. All the mysteries of transcendental realization are duly experienced by Nārada Muni himself, and therefore by hearing such an authority one can have some idea of the results of devotional life, which are hardly delineated even in the original texts of the *Vedas.* In the *Vedas* and *Upaniṣads* there are only indirect hints to all this. Nothing is directly explained there, and therefore *Śrīmad-Bhāgavatam* is the mature fruit of all the Vedic trees of literatures.

TEXT 37

सूत उवाच
एवं सम्भाष्य भगवान्नारदो वासवीसुतम्।
आमन्त्र्य वीणां रणयन् ययौ यादृच्छिको मुनिः ॥३७॥

sūta uvāca
evaṁ sambhāṣya bhagavān
nārado vāsavī-sutam
āmantrya vīṇāṁ raṇayan
yayau yādṛcchiko muniḥ

sūtaḥ—Sūta Gosvāmī; *uvāca*—said; *evam*—thus; *sambhāṣya*—addressing; *bhagavān*—transcendentally powerful; *nāradaḥ*—Nārada Muni; *vāsavī*—named Vāsavī (Satyavatī); *sutam*—son; *āmantrya*—inviting; *vīṇām*—instrument; *raṇayan*—vibrating; *yayau*—went; *yādṛcchikaḥ*—wherever willing; *muniḥ*—the sage.

TRANSLATION

Sūta Gosvāmī said: Thus addressing Vyāsadeva, Śrīla Nārada Muni took leave of him, and vibrating on his vīṇā instrument, he left to wander at his free will.

PURPORT

Every living being is anxious for full freedom because that is his transcendental nature. And this freedom is obtained only through the transcendental service of the Lord. Illusioned by the external energy, everyone thinks that he is free, but actually he is bound up by the laws of nature. A conditioned soul cannot freely move from one place to another even on this earth, and what to speak of one planet to another. But a full-fledged free soul like Nārada, always engaged in chanting the Lord's glory, is free to move not only on earth but also in any part of the universe, as well as in any part of the spiritual sky. We can just imagine the extent and unlimitedness of his freedom, which is as good as that of the Supreme Lord. There is no reason or obligation for his traveling, and no one can stop him from his free movement. Similarly, the transcendental system of devotional service is also free. It may or may not develop in a particular person even after he undergoes all the detailed formulas. Similarly, the association of the devotee is also free. One may be fortunate to have it, or one may not have it even after thousands of endeavors. Therefore, in all spheres of devotional service, freedom is the main pivot. Without freedom there is no execution of devotional service. The freedom surrendered to the Lord does not mean that the devotee becomes dependent in every respect. To surrender unto the Lord through the transparent medium of the spiritual master is to attain complete freedom of life.

TEXT 38

अहो देवर्षिर्धन्योऽयं यत्कीर्तिं शार्ङ्गधन्वनः ।
गायन्माद्यन्निदं तन्त्र्या रमयत्यातुरं जगत् ॥३८॥

aho devarṣir dhanyo 'yaṁ
yat-kīrtiṁ śārṅgadhanvanaḥ
gāyan mādyann idaṁ tantryā
ramayaty āturaṁ jagat

aho—all glory to; *devarṣiḥ*—the sage of the gods; *dhanyaḥ*—all success; *ayam yat*—one who; *kīrtim*—glories; *śārṅga-dhanvanaḥ*—of the Personality of Godhead; *gāyan*—singing; *mādyan*—taking pleasure in; *idam*—this; *tantryā*—by means of the instrument; *ramayati*—enlivens; *āturam*—distressed; *jagat*—world.

TRANSLATION

All glory and success to Śrīla Nārada Muni because he glorifies the activities of the Personality of Godhead, and so doing he himself takes pleasure and also enlivens all the distressed souls of the universe.

PURPORT

Śrī Nārada Muni plays on his instrument to glorify the transcendental activities of the Lord and to give relief to all miserable living entities of the universe. No one is happy here within the universe, and what is felt as happiness is *māyā's* illusion. The illusory energy of the Lord is so strong that even the hog who lives on filthy stool feels happy. No one can be truly happy within the material world. Śrīla Nārada Muni, in order to enlighten the miserable inhabitants, wanders everywhere. His mission is to get them back home, back to Godhead. That is the mission of all genuine devotees of the Lord following the footsteps of that great sage.

Thus end the Bhaktivedanta purports of the First Canto, Sixth Chapter, of the Śrīmad-Bhāgavatam, *entitled "Conversation Between Nārada and Vyāsadeva."*

CHAPTER SEVEN

The Son of Droṇa Punished

TEXT 1

शौनक उवाच
निर्गते नारदे सूत भगवान् बादरायणः ।
श्रुतवांस्तदभिप्रेतं ततः किमकरोद्विभुः ॥१॥

śaunaka uvāca
nirgate nārade sūta
bhagavān bādarāyaṇaḥ
śrutavāṁs tad-abhipretaṁ
tataḥ kim akarod vibhuḥ

śaunakaḥ—Śrī Śaunaka; *uvāca*—said; *nirgate*—having gone; *nārade*—Nārada Muni; *sūta*—O Sūta; *bhagavān*—the transcendentally powerful; *bādarāyaṇaḥ*—Vedavyāsa; *śrutavān*—who heard; *tat*—his; *abhipretam*—desire of the mind; *tataḥ*—thereafter; *kim*—what; *akarot*—did he do; *vibhuḥ*—the great.

TRANSLATION

Ṛṣi Śaunaka asked: O Sūta, the great and transcendentally powerful Vyāsadeva heard everything from Śrī Nārada Muni. So after Nārada's departure, what did Vyāsadeva do?

PURPORT

In this chapter the clue for describing *Śrīmad-Bhāgavatam* is picked up as Mahārāja Parīkṣit is miraculously saved in the womb of his mother. This was caused by Drauṇi (Aśvatthāmā), Ācārya Droṇa's son, who killed the five sons of Draupadī while they were asleep, for which he was punished by Arjuna. Before commencing the great epic *Śrīmad-Bhāgavatam,* Śrī Vyāsadeva realized the whole truth by trance in devotion.

TEXT 2

सूत उवाच
ब्रह्मनद्यां सरस्वत्यामाश्रमः पश्चिमे तटे।
शम्याप्रास इति प्रोक्त ऋषीणां सत्रवर्धनः ॥२॥

sūta uvāca
brahma-nadyāṁ sarasvatyām
āśramaḥ paścime taṭe
śamyāprāsa iti prokta
ṛṣīṇāṁ satra-vardhanaḥ

sūtaḥ—Śrī Sūta; *uvāca*—said; *brahma-nadyām*—on the bank of the river intimately related with *Vedas, brāhmaṇas,* saints, and the Lord; *sarasvatyām*—Sarasvatī; *āśramaḥ*—cottage for meditation; *paścime*—on the west; *taṭe*—bank; *śamyāprāsaḥ*—the place named Śamyāprāsa; *iti*—thus; *proktaḥ*—said to be; *ṛṣīṇām*—of the sages; *satra-vardhanaḥ*—that which enlivens activities.

TRANSLATION

Śrī Sūta said: On the western bank of the river Sarasvatī, which is intimately related with the Vedas, there is a cottage for meditation at Śamyāprāsa which enlivens the transcendental activities of the sages.

PURPORT

For spiritual advancement of knowledge a suitable place and atmosphere are definitely required. The place on the western bank of the Sarasvatī is especially suitable for this purpose. And there is the *āśrama* of Vyāsadeva at Śamyāprāsa. Śrīla Vyāsadeva was a householder, yet his residential place is called an *āśrama.* An *āśrama* is a place where spiritual culture is always foremost. It does not matter whether the place belongs to a householder or a mendicant. The whole *varṇāśrama* system is so designed that each and every status of life is called an *āśrama.* This means that spiritual culture is the common factor for all. The *brahmacārīs,* the *gṛhasthas,* the *vānaprasthas* and the *sannyāsīs* all belong to the same mission of life, namely, realization of the Supreme. Therefore none of them are less important as far as spiritual culture is concerned. The difference is a matter of formality on the strength of renunciation. The *sannyāsīs* are held in high estimation on the strength of practical renunciation.

TEXT 3

तस्मिन् स्व आश्रमे व्यासो बदरीषण्डमण्डिते।
आसीनोऽप उपस्पृश्य प्रणिदध्यौ मनः स्वयम् ॥३॥

tasmin sva āśrame vyāso
badarī-ṣaṇḍa-maṇḍite
āsīno 'pa upaspṛśya
praṇidadhyau manaḥ svayam

tasmin—in that (*āśrama*); *sve*—own; *āśrame*—in the cottage; *vyāsaḥ*—Vyāsadeva; *badarī*—berry; *ṣaṇḍa*—trees; *maṇḍite*—surrounded by; *āsīnaḥ*—sitting; *apaḥ upaspṛśya*—touching water; *praṇidadhyau*—concentrated; *manaḥ*—the mind; *svayam*—himself.

TRANSLATION

In that place, Śrīla Vyāsadeva, in his own āśrama, which was surrounded by berry trees, sat down to meditate after touching water for purification.

PURPORT

Under instructions of his spiritual master Śrīla Nārada Muni, Vyāsadeva concentrated his mind in that transcendental place of meditation.

TEXT 4

भक्तियोगेन मनसि सम्यक् प्रणिहितेऽमले।
अपश्यत्पुरुषं पूर्णं मायां च तदपाश्रयम् ॥४॥

bhakti-yogena manasi
samyak praṇihite 'male
apaśyat puruṣaṁ pūrṇaṁ
māyāṁ ca tad-apāśrayam

bhakti—devotional service; *yogena*—by the process of linking up; *manasi*—upon the mind; *samyak*—perfectly; *praṇihite*—engaged in and fixed upon; *amale*—without any matter; *apaśyat*—saw; *puruṣam*—the Personality of Godhead; *pūrṇam*—absolute; *māyām*—energy; *ca*—also; *tat*—His; *apāśrayam*—under full control.

TRANSLATION

Thus he fixed his mind, perfectly engaging it by linking it in devotional service [bhakti-yoga] without any tinge of materialism, and thus he saw the Absolute Personality of Godhead along with His external energy, which was under full control.

PURPORT

Perfect vision of the Absolute Truth is possible only by the linking process of devotional service. This is also confirmed in the *Bhagavad-gītā.* One can perfectly realize the Absolute Truth Personality of Godhead only by the process of devotional service, and one can enter into the kingdom of God by such perfect knowledge. Imperfect realization of the Absolute by the partial approach of the impersonal Brahman or localized Paramātmā does not permit anyone to enter into the kingdom of God. Śrī Nārada advised Śrīla Vyāsadeva to become absorbed in transcendental meditation on the Personality of Godhead and His activities. Śrīla Vyāsadeva did not take notice of the effulgence of Brahman because that is not absolute vision. The absolute vision is the Personality of Godhead, as it is confirmed in the *Bhagavad-gītā* (7.19): *vāsudevaḥ sarvam iti.* In the *Upaniṣads* also it is confirmed that Vāsudeva, the Personality of Godhead, is covered by the golden glowing *hiraṇmayena pātreṇa* veil of impersonal Brahman, and when that curtain is removed by the mercy of the Lord the real face of the Absolute is seen. The Absolute is mentioned here as the *puruṣa,* or person. The Absolute Personality of Godhead is mentioned in so many Vedic literatures, and in the *Bhagavad-gītā,* the *puruṣa* is confirmed as the eternal and original person. The Absolute Personality of Godhead is the perfect person. The Supreme Person has manifold energies, out of which the internal, external and marginal energies are specifically important. The energy mentioned here is the external energy, as will be clear from the statements of her activities. The internal energy is there along with the Absolute Person as the moonlight is there with the moon. The external energy is compared to darkness because it keeps the living entities in the darkness of ignorance. The word *apāśrayam* suggests that this energy of the Lord is under full control. The internal potency or superior energy is also called *māyā,* but it is spiritual *māyā,* or energy exhibited in the absolute realm. When one is under the shelter of this internal potency, the darkness of material ignorance is at once dissipated. And even those who are *ātmārāma,* or fixed in trance, take shelter of this *māyā,* or internal energy. Devotional service, or *bhakti-yoga,* is the function of the internal energy; thus there is no place for the inferior energy, or material energy, just as there is no place for darkness in the effulgence of spiritual light. Such internal energy is even superior to the spiritual bliss attainable in the conception of impersonal Brahman. It is stated in the *Bhagavad-gītā* that the impersonal Brahman effulgence is also an emanation from the Absolute Personality of Godhead, Śrī Kṛṣṇa. The *parama-puruṣa* cannot be anyone except Śrī Kṛṣṇa Himself, as will be explained in the later *ślokas.*

TEXT 5

यया सम्मोहितो जीव आत्मानं त्रिगुणात्मकम्।
परोऽपि मनुतेऽनर्थं तत्कृतं चाभिपद्यते ॥५॥

yayā sammohito jīva
ātmānaṁ tri-guṇātmakam
paro 'pi manute 'narthaṁ
tat-kṛtaṁ cābhipadyate

yayā—by whom; *sammohitaḥ*—illusioned; *jīvaḥ*—the living entities; *ātmānam*—self; *tri-guṇa-ātmakam*—conditioned by the three modes of nature, or a product of matter; *paraḥ*—transcendental; *api*—in spite of; *manute*—takes it for granted; *anartham*—things not wanted; *tat*—by that; *kṛtam ca*—reaction; *abhipadyate*—undergoes thereof.

TRANSLATION

Due to this external energy, the living entity, although transcendental to the three modes of material nature, thinks of himself as a material product and thus undergoes the reactions of material miseries.

PURPORT

The root cause of suffering by the materialistic living beings is pointed out with remedial measures which are to be undertaken and also the ultimate perfection to be gained. All this is mentioned in this particular verse. The living being is by constitution transcendental to material encagement, but he is now imprisoned by the external energy, and therefore he thinks himself one of the material products. And due to this unholy contact, the pure spiritual entity suffers material miseries under the modes of material nature. The living entity misunderstands himself to be a material product. This means that the present perverted way of thinking, feeling and willing, under material conditions, is not natural for him. But he has his normal way of thinking, feeling and willing. The living being in his original state is not without thinking, willing and feeling power. It is also confirmed in the *Bhagavad-gītā* that the actual knowledge of the conditioned soul is now covered by nescience. Thus the theory that a living being is absolute impersonal Brahman is refuted herein. This cannot be, because the living entity has his own way of thinking in his original unconditional state also. The present conditional state is due to the influence of the external energy, which means that the illusory energy takes the initiative while the Supreme Lord is aloof. The Lord does not desire that a living being be illusioned by external energy. The external energy is aware of this fact, but still she accepts a thankless task of keeping the forgotten soul under illusion by her bewildering influence. The Lord does not interfere with the task of the illusory energy because such performances of the illusory energy are also necessary for reformation of the conditioned soul. An affectionate father does not like his children to be chastised by another agent, yet he puts his disobedient children under the custody of a severe man just to bring them to order. But the all-affectionate Almighty Father at the same time desires relief for the conditioned soul, relief from the clutches of the illusory energy. The king puts the disobedient citizens within the walls of the jail, but sometimes the king, desiring the prisoners' relief, personally goes there and pleads for reformation, and on his doing so the prisoners are set free. Similarly, the Supreme Lord descends from His kingdom upon the kingdom of illusory energy and personally gives relief in the form of the *Bhagavad-gītā,* wherein He personally suggests that although the ways of illusory energy are very stiff to overcome, one who surrenders unto the lotus feet of the Lord is set free by the order of the Supreme. This surrendering process is the remedial measure for getting relief from the bewildering ways of the illusory energy. The surrendering process is completed by the influence of association. The Lord has suggested, therefore, that by the influence of the speeches of saintly persons who have actually realized the Supreme, men are engaged in His transcendental loving service. The conditioned soul gets a taste for hearing about the Lord, and by such hearing only he is gradually elevated to the platform of respect, devotion and attachment for the Lord. The whole thing is completed by the surrendering process. Herein also the same suggestion is made by the Lord in His incarnation of Vyāsadeva. This means that the conditioned souls are being reclaimed by the Lord both ways, namely by the process of punishment by the external energy of the Lord, and by Himself as the spiritual master within and without. Within the heart of every living being the Lord Himself as the Supersoul (Paramātmā) becomes the spiritual master, and from without He becomes the spiritual master in the shape of scriptures, saints and the initiator spiritual master. This is still more explicitly explained in the next *śloka.*

Personal superintendence of the illusory energy is confirmed in the *Vedas* (the *Kena Upaniṣad*) in relation to the demigods' controlling power. Herein also it is clearly stated that the living entity is controlled by the external energy in a personal capacity. The living being thus subject to the control of external energy is differently situated. It is clear, however, from the present statement of *Bhāgavatam* that the same external energy is situated in the inferior position before the Personality of Godhead, or the perfect being. The perfect being, or the Lord, cannot be approached even by the illusory energy, who can only work on the living entities. Therefore it is sheer imagination that the Supreme Lord is illusioned by the illusory energy and thus becomes a living being. If the living being and the Lord were in the same category, then it would have been quite possible for Vyāsadeva to see it, and there would have been no question of material distress on the part of the illusioned being, for the Supreme Being is fully cognizant. So there are so many unscrupulous imaginations on the part of the monists to endeavor to put both the Lord and the living being in the same category. Had the Lord and the living beings been the same, then Śrīla Śukadeva Gosvāmī would not have taken the trouble to describe the transcendental pastimes of the Lord, for they would all be manifestations of illusory energy.

Śrīmad-Bhāgavatam is the *summum bonum* remedy for suffering humanity in the clutches of *māyā.* Śrīla Vyāsadeva therefore first of all diagnosed the actual disease of the conditioned souls, i.e., their being illusioned by the external energy. He also saw the perfect Supreme Being, from whom illusory energy is far removed, though He saw both the diseased conditioned souls and also the cause of the disease. And the remedial measures are suggested in the next verse. Both the Supreme Personality of Godhead and the living beings are undoubtedly qualitatively one, but the Lord is the controller of the illusory energy, whereas the living entity is controlled by the illusory energy. Thus the Lord and the living beings are simultaneously one and different. Another point is distinct herein: that eternal relation between the Lord and the living being is transcendental, otherwise the Lord would not have taken the trouble to reclaim the conditioned souls from the clutches of *māyā.* In the same way, the living entity is also required to revive his natural love and affection for the Lord, and that is the highest perfection of the living entity. *Śrīmad-Bhāgavatam* treats the conditioned soul with an aim to that goal of life.

TEXT 6

अनर्थोपशमं साक्षाद्भक्तियोगमधोक्षजे ।
लोकस्याजानतो विद्वांश्चक्रे सात्वतसंहिताम् ॥६॥

anarthopaśamaṁ sākṣād
bhakti-yogam adhokṣaje
lokasyājānato vidvāṁś
cakre sātvata-saṁhitām

anartha—things which are superfluous; *upaśamam*—mitigation; *sākṣāt*—directly; *bhakti-yogam*—the linking process of devotional service; *adhokṣaje*—unto the Transcendence; *lokasya*—of the general mass of men; *ajānataḥ*—those who are unaware of; *vidvān*—the supremely learned; *cakre*—compiled; *sātvata*—in relation with the Supreme Truth; *saṁhitām*—Vedic literature.

TRANSLATION

The material miseries of the living entity, which are superfluous to him, can be directly mitigated by the linking process of devotional service. But the mass of people do not know this, and therefore the learned Vyāsadeva compiled this Vedic literature, which is in relation to the Supreme Truth.

PURPORT

Śrīla Vyāsadeva saw the all-perfect Personality of Godhead. This statement suggests that the complete unit of the Personality of Godhead includes His parts and parcels also. He saw, therefore, His different energies, namely the internal energy, the marginal energy and the external energy. He also saw His different plenary portions and parts of the plenary portions, namely His different incarnations also, and he specifically observed the unwanted miseries of the conditioned souls, who are bewildered by the external energy. And at last he saw the remedial measure for the conditioned souls, namely, the process of devotional service. It is a great transcendental science and begins with the process of hearing and chanting the name, fame, glory, etc., of the Supreme Personality of Godhead. Revival of the dormant affection or love of Godhead does not depend on the mechanical system of hearing and chanting, but it solely and wholly depends on the causeless mercy of the Lord. When the Lord is fully satisfied with the sincere efforts of the devotee, He may endow him with His loving transcendental service. But even with the prescribed forms of hearing and chanting, there is at once mitigation of the superfluous and unwanted miseries of material existence. Such mitigation of material affection does not wait for development of transcendental knowledge. Rather, knowledge is dependent on devotional service for the ultimate realization of the Supreme Truth.

TEXT 7

यस्यां वै श्रूयमाणायां कृष्णे परमपूरुषे।
भक्तिरुत्पद्यते पुंसः शोकमोहभयापहा ॥७॥

yasyāṁ vai śrūyamāṇāyāṁ
kṛṣṇe parama-pūruṣe
bhaktir utpadyate puṁsaḥ
śoka-moha-bhayāpahā

yasyām—this Vedic literature; *vai*—certainly; *śrūyamāṇāyām*—simply by giving aural reception; *kṛṣṇe*—unto Lord Kṛṣṇa; *parama*—supreme; *pūruṣe*—unto the Personality of Godhead; *bhaktiḥ*—feelings of devotional service; *utpadyate*—sprout up; *puṁsaḥ*—of the living being; *śoka*—lamentation; *moha*—illusion; *bhaya*—fearfulness; *apahā*—that which extinguishes.

TRANSLATION

Simply by giving aural reception to this Vedic literature, the feeling for loving devotional service to Lord Kṛṣṇa, the Supreme Personality of Godhead, sprouts up at once to extinguish the fire of lamentation, illusion and fearfulness.

PURPORT

There are various senses, of which the ear is the most effective. This sense works even when a man is deep asleep. One can protect himself from the hands of an enemy while awake, but while asleep one is protected by the ear only. The importance of hearing is mentioned here in connection with attaining the highest perfection of life, namely getting free from three material pangs. Everyone is full of lamentation at every moment, he is after the mirage of illusory things, and he is always afraid of his supposed enemy. These are the primary symptoms of material disease. And it is definitely suggested herein that simply by hearing the message of *Śrīmad-Bhāgavatam* one gets attachment for the Supreme Personality of Godhead, Śrī Kṛṣṇa, and as soon as this is effected the symptoms of the material diseases disappear. Śrīla Vyāsadeva saw the all-perfect Personality of Godhead, and in this statement the all-perfect Personality of Godhead, Śrī Kṛṣṇa, is clearly confirmed.

The ultimate result of devotional service is to develop genuine love for the Supreme Personality. Love is a word which is often used in relation with man and woman. And love is the only word that can be properly used to indicate the relation between Lord Kṛṣṇa and the living entities. The living entities are mentioned as *prakṛti* in the *Bhagavad-gītā,* and in Sanskrit *prakṛti* is a feminine object. The Lord is always described as the *parama-puruṣa,* or the supreme male personality. Thus the affection between the Lord and the living entities is something like that between the male and the female. Therefore the term love of Godhead is quite appropriate.

Loving devotional service to the Lord begins with hearing about the Lord. There is no difference between the Lord and the subject matter heard about Him. The Lord is absolute in all respects, and thus there is no difference between Him and the subject matter heard about Him. Therefore, hearing about Him means immediate contact with Him by the process of vibration of the transcendental sound. And the transcendental sound is so effective that it acts at once by removing all material affections mentioned above. As mentioned before, a living entity develops a sort of complexity by material association, and the illusory encagement of the material body is accepted as an actual fact. Under such false complexity, the living beings under different categories of life become illusioned in different ways. Even in the most developed stage of human life, the same illusion prevails in the form of many *isms* and divides the loving relation with the Lord and thereby divides the loving relation between man and man. By hearing the subject matter of *Śrīmad-Bhāgavatam* this false complexity of materialism is removed, and real peace in society begins, which politicians aspire for so eagerly in so many political situations. The politicians want a peaceful situation between man and man, and nation and nation, but at the same time, because of too much attachment for material domination, there is illusion and fearfulness.

Therefore the politicians' peace conferences cannot bring about peace in society. It can only be done by hearing the subject matter described in the *Śrīmad-Bhāgavatam* about the Supreme Personality of Godhead, Śrī Kṛṣṇa. The foolish politicians may go on holding peace and summit conferences for hundreds of years, but they will fail to achieve success. Until we reach the stage of reestablishing our lost relation with Kṛṣṇa, the illusion of accepting the body as the self will prevail, and thus fearfulness will also prevail. As for the validity of Śrī Kṛṣṇa as the Supreme Personality of Godhead, there are hundreds and thousands of evidences from revealed scriptures, and there are hundreds and thousands of evidences from personal experiences of devotees in various places like Vṛndāvana, Navadvīpa and Purī. Even in the *Kaumudī* dictionary the synonyms of Kṛṣṇa are given as "the son of Yaśodā" and "the Supreme Personality of Godhead, Parabrahman." The conclusion is that simply by hearing the Vedic literature *Śrīmad-Bhāgavatam,* one can have direct connection with the Supreme Personality of Godhead, Śrī Kṛṣṇa, and thereby one can attain the highest perfection of life by transcending worldly miseries, illusion and fearfulness. These are practical tests for one who has actually given a submissive hearing to the readings of the *Śrīmad-Bhāgavatam.*

TEXT 8

स संहितां भागवतीं कृत्वानुक्रम्य चात्मजम्।
शुकमध्यापयामास निवृत्तिनिरतं मुनिः ॥८॥

sa saṁhitāṁ bhāgavatīṁ
kṛtvānukramya cātma-jam
śukam adhyāpayām āsa
nivṛtti-nirataṁ muniḥ

saḥ—that; *saṁhitām*—Vedic literature; *bhāgavatīm*—in relation with the Personality of Godhead; *kṛtvā*—having done; *anukramya*—by correction and repetition; *ca*—and; *ātma-jam*—his own son; *śukam*—Śukadeva Gosvāmī; *adhyāpayām āsa*—taught; *nivṛtti*—path of self- realization; *niratam*—engaged; *muniḥ*—the sage.

TRANSLATION

The great sage Vyāsadeva, after compiling the Śrīmad-Bhāgavatam and revising it, taught it to his own son, Śrī Śukadeva Gosvāmī, who was already engaged in self-realization.

PURPORT

Śrīmad-Bhāgavatam is the natural commentation on the *Brahma-sūtras* compiled by the same author. This *Brahma-sūtra,* or *Vedānta-sūtra,* is meant for those who are already engaged in self-realization. *Śrīmad-Bhāgavatam* is so made that one becomes at once engaged in the path of self-realization simply by hearing the topics. Although it is especially meant for the *paramahaṁsas,* or those who are totally engaged in self-realization, it works into the depths of the hearts of those who may be worldly men. Worldly men are all engaged in sense gratification. But even such men will find in this Vedic literature a remedial measure for their material diseases. Śukadeva Gosvāmī was a liberated soul from the very beginning of his birth, and his father taught him *Śrīmad-Bhāgavatam.* Amongst mundane scholars, there is some diversity of opinion as to the date of compilation of *Śrīmad-Bhāgavatam.* It is, however, certain from the text of the *Bhāgavatam* that it was compiled before the disappearance of King Parīkṣit and after the departure of Lord Kṛṣṇa. When Mahārāja Parīkṣit was ruling the world as the King of Bhārata-varṣa, he chastised the personality of Kali. According to revealed scriptures and astrological calculation, the age of Kali is in its five thousandth year. Therefore, *Śrīmad-Bhāgavatam* was compiled not less than five thousand years ago. *Mahābhārata* was compiled before *Śrīmad-Bhāgavatam,* and the *Purāṇas* were compiled before *Mahābhārata.* That is an estimation of the date of compilation of the different Vedic literatures. The synopsis of *Śrīmad-Bhāgavatam* was given before the detailed description under instruction of Nārada. *Śrīmad-Bhāgavatam* is the science for following the path of *nivṛtti-mārga.* The path of *pravṛtti-mārga* was condemned by Nārada. That path is the natural inclination for all conditioned souls. The theme of *Śrīmad-Bhāgavatam* is the cure of the materialistic disease of the human being, or stopping completely the pangs of material existence.

TEXT 9

शौनक उवाच
स वै निवृत्तिनिरतः सर्वत्रोपेक्षको मुनिः ।
कस्य वा बृहतीमेतामात्मारामः समभ्यसत् ॥९॥

śaunaka uvāca
sa vai nivṛtti-nirataḥ
sarvatropekṣako muniḥ

kasya vā bṛhatīm etām
ātmārāmaḥ samabhyasat

śaunakaḥ uvāca—Śrī Śaunaka asked; *saḥ*—he; *vai*—of course; *nivṛtti*—on the path of self-realization; *nirataḥ*—always engaged; *sarvatra*—in every respect; *upekṣakaḥ*—indifferent; *muniḥ*—sage; *kasya*—for what reason; *vā*—or; *bṛhatīm*—vast; *etām*—this; *ātma-ārāmaḥ*—one who is pleased in himself; *samabhyasat*—undergo the studies.

TRANSLATION

Śrī Śaunaka asked Sūta Gosvāmī: Śrī Śukadeva Gosvāmī was already on the path of self-realization, and thus he was pleased with his own self. So why did he take the trouble to undergo the study of such a vast literature?

PURPORT

For the people in general the highest perfection of life is to cease from material activities and be fixed on the path of self-realization. Those who take pleasure in sense enjoyment, or those who are fixed in material bodily welfare work, are called *karmīs.* Out of thousands and millions of such karmīs, one may become an *ātmārāma* by self-realization. *Ātmā* means self, and *ārāma* means to take pleasure. Everyone is searching after the highest pleasure, but the standard of pleasure of one may be different from the standard of another. Therefore, the standard of pleasure enjoyed by the *karmīs* is different from that of the *ātmārāmas.* The *ātmārāmas* are completely indifferent to material enjoyment in every respect. Śrīla Śukadeva Gosvāmī had already attained that stage, and still he was attracted to undergo the trouble of studying the great *Bhāgavatam* literature. This means that *Śrīmad-Bhāgavatam* is a postgraduate study even for the *ātmārāmas,* who have surpassed all the studies of Vedic knowledge.

TEXT 10

सूत उवाच
आत्मारामाश्च मुनयो निर्ग्रन्था अप्युरुक्रमे।
कुर्वन्त्यहैतुकीं भक्तिमित्थम्भूतगुणो हरिः ॥१०॥

sūta uvāca
ātmārāmāś ca munayo
nirgranthā apy urukrame

kurvanty ahaitukīṁ bhaktim
ittham-bhūta-guṇo hariḥ

sūtaḥ uvāca—Sūta Gosvāmī said; *ātmārāmāḥ*—those who take pleasure in *ātmā* (generally, spirit self); *ca*—also; *munayaḥ*—sages; *nirgranthāḥ*—freed from all bondage; *api*—in spite of; *urukrame*—unto the great adventurer; *kurvanti*—do; *ahaitukīm*—unalloyed; *bhaktim*—devotional service; *ittham-bhūta*—such wonderful; *guṇaḥ*—qualities; *hariḥ*—of the Lord.

TRANSLATION

All different varieties of ātmārāmas [those who take pleasure in ātmā, or spirit self], especially those established on the path of self-realization, though freed from all kinds of material bondage, desire to render unalloyed devotional service unto the Personality of Godhead. This means that the Lord possesses transcendental qualities and therefore can attract everyone, including liberated souls.

PURPORT

Lord Śrī Caitanya Mahāprabhu explained this *ātmārāma śloka* very vividly before His chief devotee Śrīla Sanātana Gosvāmī. He points out eleven factors in the *śloka,* namely (1) *ātmārāma,* (2) *munayaḥ,* (3) *nirgrantha,* (4) *api,* (5) *ca,* (6) *urukrama,* (7) *kurvanti,* (8) *ahaitukīm,* (9) *bhaktim,* (10) *ittham-bhūta-guṇaḥ* and (11) *hariḥ.* According to the *Viśva-prakāśa* Sanskrit dictionary, there are seven synonyms for the word *ātmārāma,* which are as follows: (1) Brahman (the Absolute Truth), (2) body, (3) mind, (4) endeavor, (5) endurance, (6) intelligence and (7) personal habits.

The word *munayaḥ* refers to (1) those who are thoughtful, (2) those who are grave and silent, (3) ascetics, (4) the persistent, (5) mendicants, (6) sages and (7) saints.

The word *nirgrantha* conveys these ideas: (1) one who is liberated from nescience, (2) one who has no connection with scriptural injunction, i.e., who is freed from the obligation of the rules and regulations mentioned in the revealed scriptures like ethics, *Vedas,* philosophy, psychology and metaphysics (in other words the fools, illiterate, urchins, etc., who have no connection with regulative principles), (3) a capitalist, and also (4) one who is penniless.

According to the *Śabda-kośa* dictionary, the affix *ni* is used in the sense of

(1) certainty, (2) counting, (3) building, and (4) forbiddance, and the word *grantha* is used in the sense of wealth, thesis, vocabulary, etc.

The word *urukrama* means "the one whose activities are glorious." *Krama* means "step." This word *urukrama* specifically indicates the Lord's incarnation as Vāmana, who covered the whole universe by immeasurable steps. Lord Viṣṇu is powerful, and His activities are so glorious that He has created the spiritual world by His internal potency and the material world by His external potency. By His all-pervading features He is everywhere present as the Supreme Truth, and in His personal feature He is always present in His transcendental abode of Goloka Vṛndāvana, where He displays His transcendental pastimes in all variegatedness. His activities cannot be compared to anyone else's, and therefore the word *urukrama* is just applicable to Him only.

According to Sanskrit verbal arrangement, *kurvanti* refers to doing things for someone else. Therefore, it means that the *ātmārāmas* render devotional service unto the Lord not for personal interest but for the pleasure of the Lord, Urukrama.

Hetu means "causal." There are many causes for one's sense satisfaction, and they can be chiefly classified as material enjoyment, mystic powers and liberation, which are generally desired by progressive persons. As far as material enjoyments are concerned, they are innumerable, and the materialists are eager to increase them more and more because they are under the illusory energy. There is no end to the list of material enjoyments, nor can anyone in the material universe have all of them. As far as the mystic powers are concerned, they are eight in all (such as to become the minutest in form, to become weightless, to have anything one desires, to lord it over the material nature, to control other living beings, to throw earthly globes in outer space, etc.). These mystic powers are mentioned in the *Bhāgavatam.* The forms of liberation are five in number.

Therefore, unalloyed devotion means service to the Lord without desire for the above-mentioned personal benefits. And the powerful Personality of Godhead, Śrī Kṛṣṇa, can be fully satisfied by such unalloyed devotees free from all sorts of desires for personal benefit.

Unalloyed devotional service of the Lord progresses in different stages. Practice of devotional service in the material field is of eighty-one different qualities, and above such activities is the transcendental practice of devotional service, which is one and is called *sādhana-bhakti.* When unalloyed practice of *sādhana-bhakti* is matured into transcendental love for the Lord, the transcendental loving service of the Lord begins gradually developing into nine progressive stages of loving service under the headings of attachment, love, affection, feelings, affinity, adherence, following, ecstasy, and intense feelings of separation.

The attachment of an inactive devotee develops up to the stage of transcendental love of God. Attachment of an active servitor develops up to the stage of adherence, and that for a friendly devotee develops up to the stage of following, and the same is also the case for the parental devotees. Devotees in conjugal love develop ecstasy up to the stage of intense feelings of separation. These are some of the features of unalloyed devotional service of the Lord.

According to *Hari-bhakti-sudhodaya,* the import of the word *ittham-bhūta* is "complete bliss." Transcendental bliss in the realization of impersonal Brahman becomes comparable to the scanty water contained in the pit made by a cow's hoof. It is nothing compared with the ocean of bliss of the vision of the Personality of Godhead. The personal form of Lord Śrī Kṛṣṇa is so attractive that it comprehends all attraction, all bliss and all tastes (*rasas*). These attractions are so strong that *no one wants to exchange them for material enjoyment, mystic powers and liberation.* There is no need of logical arguments in support of this statement, but out of one's own nature one becomes attracted by the qualities of Lord Śrī Kṛṣṇa. We must know for certain that the qualities of the Lord have nothing to do with mundane qualities. All of them are full of bliss, knowledge and eternity. There are innumerable qualities of the Lord, and one is attracted by one quality while another is attracted by another.

Great sages, such as the four bachelor-devotees Sanaka, Sanātana, Sananda and Sanat-kumāra, were attracted by the fragrance of flowers and *tulasī* leaves anointed with the pulp of sandalwood offered at the lotus feet of the Lord. Similarly, Śukadeva Gosvāmī was attracted by the transcendental pastimes of the Lord. Śukadeva Gosvāmī was already situated in the liberated stage, yet he was attracted by the pastimes of the Lord. This proves that the quality of His pastimes has nothing to do with material affinity. Similarly, the young cowherd damsels were attracted by the bodily features of the Lord, and Rukmiṇī was attracted by hearing about the glories of the Lord. Lord Kṛṣṇa attracts even the mind of the goddess of fortune. He attracts, in special cases, the minds of all young girls. He attracts the minds of the elderly ladies by parental affection. He attracts the minds of the males in the humors of servitude and friendship.

The word *hari* conveys various meanings, but the chief import of the word is that He (the Lord) vanquishes everything inauspicious and takes away the mind of the devotee by awarding pure transcendental love. By remembering the Lord in acute distress one can be free from all varieties of miseries and anxieties. Gradually the Lord vanquishes all obstacles on the path of devotional service of a pure devotee, and the result of nine devotional activities, such as hearing and chanting, becomes manifested.

By His personal features and transcendental attributes, the Lord attracts all psychological activities of a pure devotee. Such is the attractive power of Lord Kṛṣṇa. The attraction is so powerful that a pure devotee never hankers for any one of the four principles of religion. These are the attractive features of the transcendental attributes of the Lord. And adding to this the words *api* and *ca,* one can increase the imports unlimitedly. According to Sanskrit grammar there are seven synonyms for the word *api.*

So by interpreting each and every word of this *śloka,* one can see unlimited numbers of transcendental qualities of Lord Kṛṣṇa that attract the mind of a pure devotee.

TEXT 11

हरेर्गुणाक्षिप्तमतिर्भगवान् बादरायणिः ।
अध्यगान्महदाख्यानं नित्यं विष्णुजनप्रियः ॥११॥

harer guṇākṣipta-matir
bhagavān bādarāyaṇiḥ
adhyagān mahad ākhyānaṁ
nityaṁ viṣṇu-jana-priyaḥ

hareḥ—of Hari, the Personality of Godhead; *guṇa*—transcendental attribute; *ākṣipta*—being absorbed in; *matiḥ*—mind; *bhagavān*—powerful; *bādarāyaṇiḥ*—the son of Vyāsadeva; *adhyagāt*—underwent studies; *mahat*—great; *ākhyānam*—narration; *nityam*—regularly; *viṣṇu-jana*—devotees of the Lord; *priyaḥ*—beloved.

TRANSLATION

Śrīla Śukadeva Gosvāmī, son of Śrīla Vyāsadeva, was not only transcendentally powerful. He was also very dear to the devotees of the Lord. Thus he underwent the study of this great narration [Śrīmad-Bhāgavatam].

PURPORT

According to *Brahma-vaivarta Purāṇa,* Śrīla Śukadeva Gosvāmī was a liberated soul even within the womb of his mother. Śrīla Vyāsadeva knew that the child, after his birth, would not stay at home. Therefore he (Vyāsadeva) impressed upon him the synopsis of the *Bhāgavatam* so that the child could be made attached to the transcendental activities of the Lord. After his birth, the child was still more educated in the subject of the *Bhāgavatam* by recitation of the actual poems.

The idea is that generally the liberated souls are attached to the feature of impersonal Brahman with a monistic view of becoming one with the supreme whole. But by the association of pure devotees like Vyāsadeva, even the liberated soul becomes attracted to the transcendental qualities of the Lord. By the mercy of Śrī Nārada, Śrīla Vyāsadeva was able to narrate the great epic of *Śrīmad-Bhāgavatam,* and by the mercy of Vyāsadeva, Śrīla Śukadeva Gosvāmī was able to grasp the import. The transcendental qualities of the Lord are so attractive that Śrīla Śukadeva Gosvāmī became detached from being completely absorbed in impersonal Brahman and positively took up the personal activity of the Lord.

Practically he was thrown from the impersonal conception of the Absolute, thinking within himself that he had simply wasted so much time in devoting himself to the impersonal feature of the Supreme, or in other words, he realized more transcendental bliss with the personal feature than the impersonal. And from that time, not only did he himself become very dear to the *viṣṇu-janas,* or the devotees of the Lord, but also the *viṣṇu-janas* became very dear to him. The devotees of the Lord, who do not wish to kill the individuality of the living entities and who desire to become personal servitors of the Lord, do not very much like the impersonalists, and similarly the impersonalists, who desire to become one with the Supreme, are unable to evaluate the devotees of the Lord. Thus from time immemorial these two transcendental pilgrims have sometimes been competitors. In other words, each of them likes to keep separate from the other because of the ultimate personal and impersonal realizations. Therefore it appears that Śrīla Śukadeva Gosvāmī also had no liking for the devotees. But since he himself became a saturated devotee, he desired always the transcendental association of the *viṣṇu-janas,* and the *viṣṇu-janas* also liked his association, since he became a personal *Bhāgavata.* Thus both the son and the father were completely cognizant of transcendental knowledge in Brahman, and afterwards both of them became absorbed in the personal features of the Supreme Lord. The question as to how Śukadeva Gosvāmī was attracted by the narration of the *Bhāgavatam* is thus completely answered by this *śloka.*

TEXT 12

परीक्षितोऽथ राजर्षेर्जन्मकर्मविलापनम् ।
संस्थां च पाण्डुपुत्राणां वक्ष्ये कृष्णकथोदयम् ॥१२॥

parīkṣito 'tha rājarṣer
janma-karma-vilāpanam
saṁsthāṁ ca pāṇḍu-putrāṇāṁ
vakṣye kṛṣṇa-kathodayam

parīkṣitaḥ—of King Parīkṣit; *atha*—thus; *rājarṣeḥ*—of the King who was the *ṛṣi* among the kings; *janma*—birth; *karma*—activities; *vilāpanam*—deliverance; *saṁsthām*—renunciation of the world; *ca*—and; *pāṇḍu-putrāṇām*—of the sons of Pāṇḍu; *vakṣye*—I shall speak; *kṛṣṇa-kathā-udayam*—that which gives rise to the transcendental narration of Kṛṣṇa, the Supreme Personality of Godhead.

TRANSLATION

Sūta Gosvāmī thus addressed the ṛṣis headed by Śaunaka: Now I shall begin the transcendental narration of the Lord Śrī Kṛṣṇa and topics of the birth, activities and deliverance of King Parīkṣit, the sage amongst kings, as well as topics of the renunciation of the worldly order by the sons of Pāṇḍu.

PURPORT

Lord Kṛṣṇa is so kind to the fallen souls that He personally incarnates Himself amongst the different kinds of living entities and takes part with them in daily activities. Any historical fact old or new which has a connection with the activities of the Lord is to be understood as a transcendental narration of the Lord. Without Kṛṣṇa, all the supplementary literatures like the *Purāṇas* and *Mahābhārata* are simply stories or historical facts. But with Kṛṣṇa they become transcendental, and when we hear of them we at once become transcendentally related with the Lord. *Śrīmad-Bhāgavatam* is also a *Purāṇa*, but the special significance of this *Purāṇa* is that the activities of the Lord are central and not just supplementary historical facts. *Śrīmad-Bhāgavatam* is thus recommended by Lord Śrī Caitanya Mahāprabhu as the spotless *Purāṇa.* There is a class of less intelligent devotees of the *Bhāgavata Purāṇa* who desire to relish at once the activities of the Lord narrated in the Tenth Canto without first understanding the primary cantos. They are under the false impression that the other cantos are not concerned with Kṛṣṇa, and thus more foolishly than intelligently they take to the reading of the Tenth Canto. These readers are specifically told herein that the other cantos of the *Bhāgavatam* are as important as the Tenth Canto. No one should try to go into the matters of the Tenth Canto without having thoroughly understood the purport of the other nine cantos. Kṛṣṇa and His pure devotees like the Pāṇḍavas are on the same plane. Kṛṣṇa is not without His devotees of all the *rasas,* and the pure devotees like the Pāṇḍavas are not without Kṛṣṇa. The devotees and the Lord are interlinked, and they cannot be separated. Therefore talks about them are all *kṛṣṇa-kathā,* or topics of the Lord.

TEXTS 13–14

यदा मृधे कौरवसृञ्जयानां
वीरेष्वथो वीरगतिं गतेषु ।
वृकोदराविद्धगदाभिमर्श-
भग्नोरुदण्डे धृतराष्ट्रपुत्रे ॥१३॥
भर्तुः प्रियं द्रौणिरिति स्म पश्यन्
कृष्णासुतानां स्वपतां शिरांसि ।
उपाहरद्विप्रियमेव तस्य
जुगुप्सितं कर्म विगर्हयन्ति ॥१४॥

yadā mṛdhe kaurava-sṛñjayānāṁ
vīreṣv atho vīra-gatiṁ gateṣu
vṛkodarāviddha-gadābhimarśa-
bhagnoru-daṇḍe dhṛtarāṣṭra-putre

bhartuḥ priyaṁ drauṇir iti sma paśyan
kṛṣṇā-sutānāṁ svapatāṁ śirāṁsi
upāharad vipriyam eva tasya
jugupsitaṁ karma vigarhayanti

yadā—when; *mṛdhe*—in the battlefield; *kaurava*—the party of Dhṛtarāṣṭra; *sṛñjayānām*—of the party of the Pāṇḍavas; *vīreṣu*—of the warriors; *atho*—thus; *vīra-gatim*—the destination deserved by the warriors; *gateṣu*—being obtained; *vṛkodara*—Bhīma (the second Pāṇḍava); *āviddha*—beaten; *gadā*—by the club; *abhimarśa*—lamenting; *bhagna*—broken; *uru-daṇḍe*—spinal cord; *dhṛtarāṣṭra-putre*—the son of King Dhṛtarāṣṭra; *bhartuḥ*—of the master; *priyam*—pleasing; *drauṇiḥ*—the son of Droṇācārya; *iti*—thus; *sma*—shall be; *paśyan*—seeing; *kṛṣṇā*—Draupadī; *sutānām*—of the sons; *svapatām*—while sleeping; *śirāṁsi*—heads; *upāharat*—delivered as a prize; *vipriyam*—pleasing; *eva*—like; *tasya*—his; *jugupsitam*—most heinous; *karma*—act; *vigarhayanti*—disapproving.

TRANSLATION

When the respective warriors of both camps, namely the Kauravas and the Pāṇḍavas, were killed on the Battlefield of Kurukṣetra and the dead warriors obtained their deserved destinations, and when the son of Dhṛtarāṣṭra fell down lamenting, his spine broken, being beaten by the club of Bhīmasena, the son of Droṇācārya [Aśvatthāmā] beheaded the five sleeping sons of Draupadī and delivered them as a prize to his master, foolishly thinking that he would be pleased. Duryodhana, however, disapproved of the heinous act, and he was not pleased in the least.

PURPORT

Transcendental topics of the activities of Lord Śrī Kṛṣṇa in the *Śrīmad-Bhāgavatam* begin from the end of the battle at Kurukṣetra, where the Lord Himself spoke about Himself in the *Bhagavad-gītā.* Therefore, both the *Bhagavad-gītā* and *Śrīmad-Bhāgavatam* are transcendental topics of Lord Kṛṣṇa. The *Gītā* is *kṛṣṇa-kathā,* or topics of Kṛṣṇa, because it is spoken by the Lord, and the *Bhāgavatam* is also *kṛṣṇa-kathā* because it is spoken about the Lord. Lord Śrī Caitanya Mahāprabhu wanted everyone to be informed of both *kṛṣṇa-kathās* by His order. Lord Kṛṣṇa Caitanya is Kṛṣṇa Himself in the garb of a devotee of Kṛṣṇa, and therefore the versions of both Lord Kṛṣṇa and Śrī Kṛṣṇa Caitanya Mahāprabhu are identical. *Lord Caitanya desired that all who are born in India seriously understand such kṛṣṇa-kathās* and then after full realization preach the transcendental message to everyone in all parts of the world. That will bring about the desired peace and prosperity of the stricken world.

TEXT 15

माता शिशूनां निधनं सुतानां
निशम्य घोरं परितप्यमाना ।

तदारुदद्वाष्पकलाकुलाक्षी
तां सान्त्वयन्नाह किरीटमाली ॥१५॥

mātā śiśūnāṁ nidhanaṁ sutānāṁ
niśamya ghoraṁ paritapyamānā
tadārudad vāṣpa-kalākulākṣī
tāṁ sāntvayann āha kirīṭamālī

mātā—the mother; *śiśūnām*—of the children; *nidhanam*—massacre; *sutānām*—of the sons; *niśamya*—after hearing; *ghoram*—ghastly; *paritapyamānā*—lamenting; *tadā*—at that time; *arudat*—began to cry; *vāṣpa-kala-ākula-akṣī*—with tears in the eyes; *tām*—her; *sāntvayan*—pacifying; *āha*—said; *kirīṭamālī*—Arjuna.

TRANSLATION

Draupadī, the mother of the five children of the Pāṇḍavas, after hearing of the massacre of her sons, began to cry in distress with eyes full of tears. Trying to pacify her in her great loss, Arjuna spoke to her thus:

TEXT 16

तदा शुचस्ते प्रमृजामि भद्रे
यद्ब्रह्मबन्धोः शिर आततायिनः ।
गाण्डीवमुक्तैर्विशिखैरुपाहरे
त्वाक्रम्य यत्स्नास्यसि दग्धपुत्रा ॥१६॥

tadā śucas te pramṛjāmi bhadre
yad brahma-bandhoḥ śira ātatāyinaḥ
gāṇḍīva-muktair viśikhair upāhare
tvākramya yat snāsyasi dagdha-putrā

tadā—at that time only; *śucaḥ*—tears in grief; *te*—your; *pramṛjāmi*—shall wipe away; *bhadre*—O gentle lady; *yat*—when; *brahma-bandhoḥ*—of a degraded *brāhmaṇa; śiraḥ*—head; *ātatāyinaḥ*—of the aggressor; *gāṇḍīva-muktaiḥ*—shot by the bow named Gāṇḍīva; *viśikhaiḥ*—by the arrows; *upāhare*—shall present to you; *tvā*—yourself; *ākramya*—riding on it; *yat*—which; *snāsyasi*—take your bath; *dagdha-putrā*—after burning the sons.

TRANSLATION

O gentle lady, when I present you with the head of that brāhmaṇa, after beheading him with arrows from my Gāṇḍīva bow, I shall then wipe the

tears from your eyes and pacify you. Then, after burning your sons' bodies, you can take your bath standing on his head.

PURPORT

An enemy who sets fire to the house, administers poison, attacks all of a sudden with deadly weapons, plunders wealth or usurps agricultural fields, or entices one's wife is called an aggressor. Such an aggressor, though he be a *brāhmaṇa* or a so-called son of a *brāhmaṇa,* has to be punished in all circumstances. When Arjuna promised to behead the aggressor named Aśvatthāmā, he knew well that Aśvatthāmā was the son of a *brāhmaṇa,* but because the so-called *brāhmaṇa* acted like a butcher, he was taken as such, and there was no question of sin in killing such a *brāhmaṇa's* son who proved to be a villain.

TEXT 17

इति प्रियां वल्गुविचित्रजल्पैः
स सान्त्वयित्वाच्युतमित्रसूतः ।
अन्वाद्रवद्दंशित उग्रधन्वा
कपिध्वजो गुरुपुत्रं रथेन ॥१७॥

iti priyāṁ valgu-vicitra-jalpaiḥ
sa sāntvayitvācyuta-mitra-sūtaḥ
anvādravad daṁśita ugra-dhanvā
kapi-dhvajo guru-putraṁ rathena

iti—thus; *priyām*—unto the dear; *valgu*—sweet; *vicitra*—variegated; *jalpaiḥ*—by statements; *saḥ*—he; *sāntvayitvā*—satisfying; *acyuta-mitra-sūtaḥ*—Arjuna, who is guided by the infallible Lord as a friend and driver; *anvādravat*—followed; *daṁśitaḥ*—being protected by *kavaca; ugra-dhanvā*—equipped with furious weapons; *kapi-dhvajaḥ*—Arjuna; *guru-putram*—the son of the martial teacher; *rathena*—getting on the chariot.

TRANSLATION

Arjuna, who is guided by the infallible Lord as friend and driver, thus satisfied the dear lady by such statements. Then he dressed in armor and armed himself with furious weapons, and getting into his chariot, he set out to follow Aśvatthāmā, the son of his martial teacher.

TEXT 18

तमापतन्तं स विलक्ष्य दूरात्
कुमारहोद्विग्नमना रथेन।
पराद्रवत्प्राणपरीप्सुरुर्व्यां
यावद्गमं रुद्रभयाद्यथा कः ॥१८॥

tam āpatantaṁ sa vilakṣya dūrāt
kumāra-hodvigna-manā rathena
parādravat prāṇa-parīpsur urvyāṁ
yāvad-gamaṁ rudra-bhayād yathā kaḥ

tam—him; *āpatantam*—coming over furiously; *saḥ*—he; *vilakṣya*—seeing; *dūrāt*—from a distance; *kumāra-hā*—the murderer of the princes; *udvigna-manāḥ*—disturbed in mind; *rathena*—on the chariot; *parādravat*—fled; *prāṇa*—life; *parīpsuḥ*—for protecting; *urvyām*—with great speed; *yāvat-gamam*—as he fled; *rudra-bhayāt*—by fear of Śiva; *yathā*—as; *kaḥ*—Brahmā (or *arkaḥ*—Sūrya).

TRANSLATION

Aśvatthāmā, the murderer of the princes, seeing from a great distance Arjuna coming at him with great speed, fled in his chariot, panic stricken, just to save his life, as Brahmā fled in fear from Śiva.

PURPORT

According to the reading matter, either *kaḥ* or *arkaḥ,* there are two references in the *Purāṇas. Kaḥ* means Brahmā, who once became allured by his daughter and began to follow her, which infuriated Śiva, who attacked Brahmā with his trident. Brahmājī fled in fear of his life. As far as *arkaḥ* is concerned, there is a reference in the *Vāmana Purāṇa.* There was a demon by the name Vidyunmālī who was gifted with a glowing golden airplane which traveled to the back of the sun, and night disappeared because of the glowing effulgence of this plane. Thus the sun god became angry, and with his virulent rays he melted the plane. This enraged Lord Śiva. Lord Śiva then attacked the sun god, who fled away and at last fell down at Kāśī (Vārāṇasī), and the place became famous as Lolārka.

TEXT 19

यदाशरणमात्मानमैक्षत श्रान्तवाजिनम्।
अस्त्रं ब्रह्मशिरो मेने आत्मत्राणं द्विजात्मजः ॥१९॥

yadāśaraṇam ātmānam
aikṣata śrānta-vājinam
astraṁ brahma-śiro mene
ātma-trāṇaṁ dvijātmajaḥ

yadā—when; *aśaraṇam*—without being alternatively protected; *ātmānam*—his own self; *aikṣata*—saw; *śrānta-vājinam*—the horses being tired; *astram*—weapon; *brahma-śiraḥ*—the topmost or ultimate (nuclear); *mene*—applied; *ātma-trāṇam*—just to save himself; *dvija-ātma-jaḥ*—the son of a *brāhmaṇa.*

TRANSLATION

When the son of the brāhmaṇa [Aśvatthāmā] saw that his horses were tired, he considered that there was no alternative for protection outside of his using the ultimate weapon, the brahmāstra [nuclear weapon].

PURPORT

In the ultimate issue only, when there is no alternative, the nuclear weapon called the *brahmāstra* is applied. The word *dvijātmajaḥ* is significant here because Aśvatthāmā, although the son of Droṇācārya, was not exactly a qualified *brāhmaṇa.* The most intelligent man is called a *brāhmaṇa,* and it is not a hereditary title. Aśvatthāmā was also formerly called the *brahma-bandhu,* or the friend of a *brāhmaṇa.* Being a friend of a *brāhmaṇa* does not mean that one is a *brāhmaṇa* by qualification. A friend or son of a *brāhmaṇa,* when fully qualified, can be called a *brāhmaṇa* and not otherwise. Since Aśvatthāmā's decision is immature, he is purposely called herein the son of a *brāhmaṇa.*

TEXT 20

अथोपस्पृश्य सलिलं सन्दधे तत्समाहितः ।
अजानन्नपि संहारं प्राणकृच्छ्र उपस्थिते ॥२०॥

athopaspṛśya salilaṁ
sandadhe tat samāhitaḥ
ajānann api saṁhāraṁ
prāṇa-kṛcchra upasthite

atha—thus; *upaspṛśya*—touching in sanctity; *salilam*—water; *sandadhe*—chanted the hymns; *tat*—that; *samāhitaḥ*—being in concentration; *ajānan*

—without knowing; *api*—although; *saṁhāram*—withdrawal; *prāṇa-kṛcchre* —life being put in danger; *upasthite*—being placed in such a position.

TRANSLATION

Since his life was in danger, he touched water in sanctity and concentrated upon the chanting of the hymns for throwing nuclear weapons, although he did not know how to withdraw such weapons.

PURPORT

The subtle forms of material activities are finer than grosser methods of material manipulation. Such subtle forms of material activities are effected through purification of sound. The same method is adopted here by chanting hymns to act as nuclear weapons.

TEXT 21

ततः प्रादुष्कृतं तेजः प्रचण्डं सर्वतोदिशम्।
प्राणापदमभिप्रेक्ष्य विष्णुं जिष्णुरुवाच ह ॥२१॥

tataḥ prāduṣkṛtaṁ tejaḥ
pracaṇḍaṁ sarvato diśam
prāṇāpadam abhiprekṣya
viṣṇuṁ jiṣṇur uvāca ha

tataḥ—thereafter; *prāduṣkṛtam*—disseminated; *tejaḥ*—glare; *pracaṇḍam*—fierce; *sarvataḥ*—all around; *diśam*—directions; *prāṇa-āpadam* —affecting life; *abhiprekṣya*—having observed it; *viṣṇum*—unto the Lord; *jiṣṇuḥ*—Arjuna; *uvāca*—said; *ha*—in the past.

TRANSLATION

Thereupon a glaring light spread in all directions. It was so fierce that Arjuna thought his own life in danger, and so he began to address Lord Śrī Kṛṣṇa.

TEXT 22

अर्जुन उवाच

कृष्ण कृष्ण महाबाहो भक्तानामभयङ्कर।
त्वमेको दह्यमानानामपवर्गोऽसि संसृतेः ॥२२॥

arjuna uvāca
kṛṣṇa kṛṣṇa mahā-bāho
bhaktānām abhayaṅkara
tvam eko dahyamānānām
apavargo 'si saṁsṛteḥ

arjunaḥ uvāca—Arjuna said; *kṛṣṇa*—O Lord Kṛṣṇa; *kṛṣṇa*—O Lord Kṛṣṇa; *mahā-bāho*—He who is the Almighty; *bhaktānām*—of the devotees; *abhayaṅkara*—eradicating the fears of; *tvam*—You; *ekaḥ*—alone; *dahyamānānām*—those who are suffering from; *apavargaḥ*—the path of liberation; *asi*—are; *saṁsṛteḥ*—in the midst of material miseries.

TRANSLATION

Arjuna said: O my Lord Śrī Kṛṣṇa, You are the almighty Personality of Godhead. There is no limit to Your different energies. Therefore only You are competent to instill fearlessness in the hearts of Your devotees. Everyone in the flames of material miseries can find the path of liberation in You only.

PURPORT

Arjuna was aware of the transcendental qualities of Lord Śrī Kṛṣṇa, as he had already experienced them during the Kurukṣetra War, in which both of them were present. Therefore, Arjuna's version of Lord Kṛṣṇa is authoritative. Kṛṣṇa is almighty and is especially the cause of fearlessness for the devotees. A devotee of the Lord is always fearless because of the protection given by the Lord. Material existence is something like a blazing fire in the forest, which can be extinguished by the mercy of the Lord Śrī Kṛṣṇa. The spiritual master is the mercy representative of the Lord. Therefore, a person burning in the flames of material existence may receive the rains of mercy of the Lord through the transparent medium of the self-realized spiritual master. The spiritual master, by his words, can penetrate into the heart of the suffering person and inject knowledge transcendental, which alone can extinguish the fire of material existence.

TEXT 23

त्वमाद्यः पुरुषः साक्षादीश्वरः प्रकृतेः परः ।
मायां व्युदस्य चिच्छक्त्या कैवल्ये स्थित आत्मनि ॥२३॥

tvam ādyaḥ puruṣaḥ sākṣād
īśvaraḥ prakṛteḥ paraḥ
māyāṁ vyudasya cic-chaktyā
kaivalye sthita ātmani

tvam ādyaḥ—You are the original; *puruṣaḥ*—the enjoying personality; *sākṣāt*—directly; *īśvaraḥ*—the controller; *prakṛteḥ*—of material nature; *paraḥ*—transcendental; *māyām*—the material energy; *vyudasya*—one who has thrown aside; *cit-śaktyā*—by dint of internal potency; *kaivalye*—in pure eternal knowledge and bliss; *sthitaḥ*—placed; *ātmani*—own self.

TRANSLATION

You are the original Personality of Godhead who expands Himself all over the creations and is transcendental to material energy. You have cast away the effects of the material energy by dint of Your spiritual potency. You are always situated in eternal bliss and transcendental knowledge.

PURPORT

The Lord states in the *Bhagavad-gītā* that one who surrenders unto the lotus feet of the Lord can get release from the clutches of nescience. Kṛṣṇa is just like the sun, and *māyā* or material existence is just like darkness. Wherever there is the light of the sun, darkness or ignorance at once vanishes. The best means to get out of the world of ignorance is suggested here. The Lord is addressed herein as the original Personality of Godhead. From Him all other Personalities of Godhead expand. The all-pervasive Lord Viṣṇu is Lord Kṛṣṇa's plenary portion or expansion. The Lord expands Himself in innumerable forms of Godhead and living beings, along with His different energies. But Śrī Kṛṣṇa is the original primeval Lord from whom everything emanates. The all-pervasive feature of the Lord experienced within the manifested world is also a partial representation of the Lord. Paramātmā, therefore, is included within Him. He is the Absolute Personality of Godhead. He has nothing to do with the actions and reactions of the material manifestation because He is far above the material creation. Darkness is a perverse representation of the sun, and therefore the existence of darkness depends on the existence of the sun, but in the sun proper there is no trace of darkness. As the sun is full of light only, similarly the Absolute Personality of Godhead, beyond the material existence, is full of bliss. He is not only full of bliss, but also full of transcendental variegatedness. Transcendence is not at all static, but full of dynamic variegatedness. He is distinct from the material nature, which is complicated by the three modes of material nature. He is *parama,* or the chief. Therefore He is absolute. He has manifold energies, and through His diverse energies He creates, manifests, maintains and destroys the material world. In His own abode, however, everything is eternal and absolute. The world is not conducted by the energies or powerful agents by themselves, but by the potent all-powerful with all energies.

TEXT 24

स एव जीवलोकस्य मायामोहितचेतसः ।
विधत्से स्वेन वीर्येण श्रेयो धर्मादिलक्षणम् ॥२४॥

sa eva jīva-lokasya
māyā-mohita-cetasaḥ
vidhatse svena vīryeṇa
śreyo dharmādi-lakṣaṇam

saḥ—that Transcendence; *eva*—certainly; *jīva-lokasya*—of the conditioned living beings; *māyā-mohita*—captivated by the illusory energy; *cetasaḥ*—by the heart; *vidhatse*—execute; *svena*—by Your own; *vīryeṇa*—influence; *śreyaḥ*—ultimate good; *dharma-ādi*—four principles of liberation; *lakṣaṇam*—characterized by.

TRANSLATION

And yet, though You are beyond the purview of the material energy, You execute the four principles of liberation characterized by religion and so on for the ultimate good of the conditioned souls.

PURPORT

The Personality of Godhead, Śrī Kṛṣṇa, out of His causeless mercy, descends on the manifested world without being influenced by the material modes of nature. He is eternally beyond the material manifestations. He descends out of His causeless mercy only to reclaim the fallen souls who are captivated by the illusory energy. They are attacked by the material energy, and they want to enjoy her under false pretexts, although in essence the living entity is unable to enjoy. One is eternally the servitor of the Lord, and when he forgets this position he thinks of enjoying the material world, but factually he is in illusion.

The Lord descends to eradicate this false sense of enjoyment and thus reclaim conditioned souls back to Godhead. That is the all-merciful nature of the Lord for the fallen souls.

TEXT 25

तथायं चावतारस्ते भुवो भारजिहीर्षया।
स्वानां चानन्यभावानामनुध्यानाय चासकृत् ॥२५॥

tathāyaṁ cāvatāras te
bhuvo bhāra-jihīrṣayā
svānāṁ cānanya-bhāvānām
anudhyānāya cāsakṛt

tathā—thus; *ayam*—this; *ca*—and; *avatāraḥ*—incarnation; *te*—Your; *bhuvaḥ*—of the material world; *bhāra*—burden; *jihīrṣayā*—for removing; *svānām*—of the friends; *ca ananya-bhāvānām*—and of the exclusive devotees; *anudhyānāya*—for remembering repeatedly; *ca*—and; *asakṛt*—fully satisfied.

TRANSLATION

Thus You descend as an incarnation to remove the burden of the world and to benefit Your friends, especially those who are Your exclusive devotees and are rapt in meditation upon You.

PURPORT

It appears that the Lord is partial to His devotees. Everyone is related with the Lord. He is equal to everyone, and yet He is more inclined to His own men and devotees. The Lord is everyone's father. No one can be His father, and yet no one can be His son. His devotees are His kinsmen, and His devotees are His relations. This is His transcendental pastime. It has nothing to do with mundane ideas of relations, fatherhood or anything like that. As mentioned above, the Lord is above the modes of material nature, and thus there is nothing mundane about His kinsmen and relations in devotional service.

TEXT 26

किमिदं स्वित्कुतो वेति देवदेव न वेद्म्यहम्।
सर्वतोमुखमायाति तेजः परमदारुणम् ॥२६॥

kim idaṁ svit kuto veti
deva-deva na vedmy aham
sarvato mukham āyāti
tejaḥ parama-dāruṇam

kim—what is; *idam*—this; *svit*—does it come; *kutaḥ*—wherefrom; *vā iti*—be either; *deva-deva*—O Lord of lords; *na*—not; *vedmi*—do I know; *aham*—I; *sarvataḥ*—all around; *mukham*—directions; *āyāti*—coming from; *tejaḥ*—effulgence; *parama*—very much; *dāruṇam*—dangerous.

TRANSLATION

O Lord of lords, how is it that this dangerous effulgence is spreading all around? Where does it come from? I do not understand it.

PURPORT

Anything that is presented before the Personality of Godhead should be so done after due presentation of respectful prayers. That is the standard procedure, and Śrī Arjuna, although an intimate friend of the Lord, is observing this method for general information.

TEXT 27

श्रीभगवानुवाच
वेत्थेदं द्रोणपुत्रस्य ब्राह्ममस्त्रं प्रदर्शितम्।
नैवासौ वेद संहारं प्राणबाध उपस्थिते ॥२७॥

śrī-bhagavān uvāca
vetthedaṁ droṇa-putrasya
brāhmam astraṁ pradarśitam
naivāsau veda saṁhāraṁ
prāṇa-bādha upasthite

śrī-bhagavān—the Supreme Personality of Godhead; *uvāca*—said; *vettha*—just know from Me; *idam*—this; *droṇa-putrasya*—of the son of Droṇa; *brāhmam astram*—hymns of the *brāhma* (nuclear) weapon; *pradarśitam*—exhibited; *na*—not; *eva*—even; *asau*—he; *veda*—know it; *saṁhāram*—retraction; *prāṇa-bādhe*—extinction of life; *upasthite*—being imminent.

TRANSLATION

The Supreme Personality of Godhead said: Know from Me that this is the act of the son of Droṇa. He has thrown the hymns of nuclear energy [brahmāstra], and he does not know how to retract the glare. He has helplessly done this, being afraid of imminent death.

PURPORT

The *brahmāstra* is similar to the modern nuclear weapon manipulated by atomic energy. The atomic energy works wholly on total combustibility, and so the *brahmāstra* also acts. It creates an intolerable heat similar to atomic radiation, but the difference is that the atomic bomb is a gross type of nuclear weapon, whereas the *brahmāstra* is a subtle type of weapon produced by chanting hymns. It is a different science, and in the days gone by such science was cultivated in the land of Bhārata-varṣa. The subtle *science of chanting hymns* is also *material,* but it has yet to be known by the modern material scientists. Subtle material science *is not spiritual,* but it has a direct relationship with the spiritual method, which is still subtler. A chanter of hymns knew how to apply the weapon as well as how to retract it. That was perfect knowledge. But the son of Droṇācārya, who made use of this subtle science, did not know how to retract. He applied it, being afraid of his imminent death, and thus the practice was not only improper but also irreligious. As the son of a *brāhmaṇa,* he should not have made so many mistakes, and for such gross negligence of duty he was to be punished by the Lord Himself.

TEXT 28

न ह्यस्यान्यतमं किञ्चिदस्त्रं प्रत्यवकर्शनम्।
जह्यस्त्रतेज उन्नद्धमस्त्रज्ञो ह्यस्त्रतेजसा ॥२८॥

na hy asyānyatamaṁ kiñcid
astraṁ pratyavakarśanam
jahy astra-teja unnaddham
astra-jño hy astra-tejasā

na—not; *hi*—certainly; *asya*—of it; *anyatamam*—other; *kiñcit*—anything; *astram*—weapon; *prati*—counter; *avakarśanam*—reactionary; *jahi*—subdue it; *astra-tejaḥ*—the glare of this weapon; *unnaddham*—very powerful; *astra-jñaḥ*—expert in military science; *hi*—as a matter of fact; *astra-tejasā*—by the influence of your weapon.

TRANSLATION

O Arjuna, only another brahmāstra can counteract this weapon. Since you are expert in the military science, subdue this weapon's glare with the power of your own weapon.

PURPORT

For the atomic bombs there is no counterweapon to neutralize the effects. But by subtle science the action of a *brahmāstra* can be counteracted, and those who were expert in the military science in those days could counteract the *brahmāstra.* The son of Droṇācārya did not know the art of counteracting the weapon, and therefore Arjuna was asked to counteract it by the power of his own weapon.

TEXT 29

सूत उवाच

श्रुत्वा भगवता प्रोक्तं फाल्गुनः परवीरहा।
स्पृष्ट्वापस्तं परिक्रम्य ब्राह्मं ब्राह्मास्त्रं सन्दधे ॥२९॥

sūta uvāca
śrutvā bhagavatā proktaṁ
phālgunaḥ para-vīra-hā
spṛṣṭvāpas taṁ parikramya
brāhmaṁ brāhmāstraṁ sandadhe

sūtaḥ—Sūta Gosvāmī; *uvāca*—said; *śrutvā*—after hearing; *bhagavatā*—by the Personality of Godhead; *proktam*—what was said; *phālgunaḥ*—another name of Śrī Arjuna; *para-vīra-hā*—the killer of the opposing warrior; *spṛṣṭvā*—after touching; *āpaḥ*—water; *tam*—Him; *parikramya*—circumambulating; *brāhmam*—the Supreme Lord; *brāhma-astram*—the supreme weapon; *sandadhe*—acted on.

TRANSLATION

Śrī Sūta Gosvāmī said: Hearing this from the Personality of Godhead, Arjuna touched water for purification, and after circumambulating Lord Śrī Kṛṣṇa, he cast his brahmāstra weapon to counteract the other one.

TEXT 30

संहत्यान्योन्यमुभयोस्तेजसी शरसंवृते।
आवृत्य रोदसी खं च ववृधातेऽर्कवह्निवत् ॥३०॥

saṁhatyānyonyam ubhayos
tejasī śara-saṁvṛte
āvṛtya rodasī khaṁ ca
vavṛdhāte 'rka-vahnivat

saṁhatya—by combination of; *anyonyam*—one another; *ubhayoḥ*—of both; *tejasī*—the glares; *śara*—weapons; *saṁvṛte*—covering; *āvṛtya*—covering; *rodasī*—the complete firmament; *kham ca*—outer space also; *vavṛdhāte*—increasing; *arka*—the sun globe; *vahni-vat*—like fire.

TRANSLATION

When the rays of the two brahmāstras combined, a great circle of fire, like the disc of the sun, covered all outer space and the whole firmament of planets.

PURPORT

The heat created by the flash of a *brahmāstra* resembles the fire exhibited in the sun globe at the time of cosmic annihilation. The radiation of atomic energy is very insignificant in comparison to the heat produced by a *brahmāstra.* The atomic bomb explosion can at utmost blow up one globe, but the heat produced by the *brahmāstra* can destroy the whole cosmic situation. The comparison is therefore made to the heat at the time of annihilation.

TEXT 31

दृष्ट्वास्त्रतेजस्तु तयोस्त्रील्लोकान् प्रदहन्महत्।
दह्यमानाः प्रजाः सर्वाः सांवर्तकममंसत ॥३१॥

dṛṣṭvāstra-tejas tu tayos
trīl lokān pradahan mahat
dahyamānāḥ prajāḥ sarvāḥ
sāṁvartakam amaṁsata

dṛṣṭvā—thus seeing; *astra*—weapon; *tejaḥ*—heat; *tu*—but; *tayoḥ*—of both; *trīn*—three; *lokān*—planets; *pradahat*—blazing; *mahat*—severely; *dahyamānāḥ*—burning; *prajāḥ*—population; *sarvāḥ*—all over; *sāṁvartakam*—the name of the fire which devastates during the annihilation of the universe; *amaṁsata*—began to think.

TRANSLATION

All the population of the three worlds was scorched by the combined heat of the weapons. Everyone was reminded of the sāṁvartaka fire which takes place at the time of annihilation.

PURPORT

The three worlds are the upper, lower and intermediate planets of the universe. Although the *brahmāstra* was released on this earth, the heat produced by the combination of both weapons covered all the universe, and all the populations on all the different planets began to feel the heat excessively and compared it to that of the *sāṁvartaka* fire. No planet, therefore, is without living beings, as less intelligent materialistic men think.

TEXT 32

प्रजोपद्रवमालक्ष्य लोकव्यतिकरं च तम्।
मतं च वासुदेवस्य संजहारार्जुनो द्वयम् ॥३२॥

prajopadravam ālakṣya
loka-vyatikaraṁ ca tam
mataṁ ca vāsudevasya
sañjahārārjuno dvayam

prajā—the people in general; *upadravam*—disturbance; *ālakṣya*—having seen it; *loka*—the planets; *vyatikaram*—destruction; *ca*—also; *tam*—that; *matam ca*—and the opinion; *vāsudevasya*—of Vāsudeva, Śrī Kṛṣṇa; *sañjahāra*—retracted; *arjunaḥ*—Arjuna; *dvayam*—both the weapons.

TRANSLATION

Thus seeing the disturbance of the general populace and the imminent destruction of the planets, Arjuna at once retracted both brahmāstra weapons, as Lord Śrī Kṛṣṇa desired.

PURPORT

The theory that the modern atomic bomb explosions can annihilate the world is a childish imagination. First of all, the atomic energy is not powerful enough to destroy the world. And secondly, ultimately it all rests on the supreme will of the Supreme Lord because without His will or sanction nothing can be built up or destroyed. It is foolish also to think that natural laws are ultimately powerful. Material nature's law works under the direction of the Lord, as confirmed in the *Bhagavad-gītā.* The Lord says there that natural laws work under His supervision. The world can be destroyed only by the will of the Lord and not by the whims of tiny politicians. Lord Śrī Kṛṣṇa desired that the weapons released by both Drauṇi and Arjuna be withdrawn, and it was carried out by Arjuna at once. Similarly, there are many agents of the all-powerful Lord, and by His will only can one execute what He desires.

TEXT 33

तत आसाद्य तरसा दारुणं गौतमीसुतम्।
बबन्धामर्षताम्राक्षः पशुं रशनया यथा ॥३३॥

tata āsādya tarasā
dāruṇaṁ gautamī-sutam
babandhāmarṣa-tāmrākṣaḥ
paśuṁ raśanayā yathā

tataḥ—thereupon; *āsādya*—arrested; *tarasā*—dexterously; *dāruṇam*—dangerous; *gautamī-sutam*—the son of Gautamī; *babandha*—bound up; *amarṣa*—angry; *tāmra-akṣaḥ*—with copper-red eyes; *paśum*—animal; *raśanayā*—by ropes; *yathā*—as it were.

TRANSLATION

Arjuna, his eyes blazing in anger like two red balls of copper, dexterously arrested the son of Gautamī and bound him with ropes like an animal.

PURPORT

Aśvatthāmā's mother, Kṛpī, was born in the family of Gautama. The significant point in this *śloka* is that Aśvatthāmā was caught and bound up with ropes like an animal. According to Śrīdhara Svāmī, Arjuna was obliged to catch this son of a *brāhmaṇa* like an animal as a part of his duty (*dharma*). This suggestion by Śrīdhara Svāmī is also confirmed in the later statement of Śrī Kṛṣṇa. Aśvatthāmā was a bona fide son of Droṇācārya and Kṛpī, but because he had degraded himself to a lower status of life, it was proper to treat him as an animal and not as a *brāhmaṇa.*

TEXT 34

शिबिराय निनीषन्तं रज्ज्वाबद्ध्वा रिपुं बलात्।
प्राहार्जुनं प्रकुपितो भगवानम्बुजेक्षणः ॥३४॥

śibirāya ninīṣantaṁ
rajjvā baddhvā ripuṁ balāt
prāhārjunaṁ prakupito
bhagavān ambujekṣaṇaḥ

śibirāya—on the way to the military camp; *ninīṣantam*—while bringing him; *rajjvā*—by the ropes; *baddhvā*—bound up; *ripum*—the enemy; *balāt*—by force; *prāha*—said; *arjunam*—unto Arjuna; *prakupitaḥ*—in an angry mood; *bhagavān*—the Personality of Godhead; *ambuja-īkṣaṇaḥ*—who looks with His lotus eyes.

TRANSLATION

After binding Aśvatthāmā, Arjuna wanted to take him to the military camp. The Personality of Godhead Śrī Kṛṣṇa, looking on with His lotus eyes, spoke to angry Arjuna .

PURPORT

Both Arjuna and Lord Śrī Kṛṣṇa are described here in an angry mood, but Arjuna's eyes were like balls of red copper whereas the eyes of the Lord were like lotuses. This means that the angry mood of Arjuna and that of the Lord are not on the same level. The Lord is Transcendence, and thus He is absolute in any stage. His anger is not like the anger of a conditioned living being within the modes of qualitative material nature. Because He is absolute, both His anger and pleasure are the same. His anger is not exhibited in the three modes of material nature. It is only a sign of His bent of mind towards the cause of His devotee because that is His transcendental nature. Therefore, even if He is angry, the object of anger is blessed. He is unchanged in all circumstances.

TEXT 35

मैनं पार्थार्हसि त्रातुं ब्रह्मबन्धुमिमं जहि।
योऽसावनागसः सुप्तानवधीन्निशि बालकान् ॥३५॥

mainaṁ pārthārhasi trātuṁ
brahma-bandhum imaṁ jahi
yo 'sāv anāgasaḥ suptān
avadhīn niśi bālakān

mā enam—never unto him; *pārtha*—O Arjuna; *arhasi*—ought to; *trātum*—give release; *brahma-bandhum*—a relative of a *brāhmaṇa; imam*—him; *jahi*—kill; *yaḥ*—he (who has); *asau*—those; *anāgasaḥ*—faultless; *suptān*—while sleeping; *avadhīt*—killed; *niśi*—at night; *bālakān*—the boys.

TRANSLATION

Lord Śrī Kṛṣṇa said: O Arjuna, you should not show mercy by releasing this relative of a brāhmaṇa [brahma-bandhu], for he has killed innocent boys in their sleep.

PURPORT

The word *brahma-bandhu* is significant. A person who happens to take birth in the family of a *brāhmaṇa* but is not qualified to be called a *brāhmaṇa* is addressed as the relative of a *brāhmaṇa,* and not as a *brāhmaṇa.* The son of a high-court judge is not virtually a high-court judge, but there is no harm in addressing a high-court judge's son as a relative of the honorable justice. Therefore, as by birth only one does not become a high-court judge, so also one does not become a *brāhmaṇa* simply by birthright but by acquiring the necessary qualifications of a *brāhmaṇa.* As the high-court judgeship is a post for the qualified man, so also the post of a *brāhmaṇa* is attainable by qualification only. The *śāstra* enjoins that even if good qualifications are seen in a person born in a family other than that of a *brāhmaṇa,* the qualified man has to be accepted as a *brāhmaṇa,* and similarly if a person born in the family of a *brāhmaṇa* is void of brahminical qualification, then he must be treated as a non-*brāhmaṇa* or, in better terms, a relative of a *brāhmaṇa.* Lord Śrī Kṛṣṇa, the supreme authority of all religious principles, the *Vedas,* has personally pointed out these differences, and He is about to explain the reason for this in the following *ślokas.*

TEXT 36

मत्तं प्रमत्तमुन्मत्तं सुप्तं बालं स्त्रियं जडम्।
प्रपन्नं विरथं भीतं न रिपुं हन्ति धर्मवित् ॥३६॥

mattaṁ pramattam unmattaṁ
suptaṁ bālaṁ striyaṁ jaḍam
prapannaṁ virathaṁ bhītaṁ
na ripuṁ hanti dharma-vit

mattam—careless; *pramattam*—intoxicated; *unmattam*—insane; *suptam*—asleep; *bālam*—boy; *striyam*—woman; *jaḍam*—foolish; *prapannam*—surrendered; *viratham*—one who has lost his chariot; *bhītam*—afraid; *na*—not; *ripum*—enemy; *hanti*—kill; *dharma-vit*—one who knows the principles of religion.

TRANSLATION

A person who knows the principles of religion does not kill an enemy who is careless, intoxicated, insane, asleep, afraid or devoid of his chariot. Nor does he kill a boy, a woman, a foolish creature or a surrendered soul.

PURPORT

An enemy who does not resist is never killed by a warrior who knows the principles of religion. Formerly battles were fought on the *principles of religion* and not for the sake of sense gratification. If the enemy happened to be intoxicated, asleep, etc., as above mentioned, he was never to be killed. These are some of the codes of religious war. Formerly war was never declared by the whims of selfish political leaders; it was carried out on religious principles free from all vices. Violence carried out on religious principles is far superior to so-called nonviolence.

TEXT 37

स्वप्राणान् यः परप्राणैः प्रपुष्णात्यघृणः खलः ।
तद्वधस्तस्य हि श्रेयो यद्दोषाद्यात्यधः पुमान् ॥३७॥

sva-prāṇān yaḥ para-prāṇaiḥ
prapuṣṇāty aghṛṇaḥ khalaḥ
tad-vadhas tasya hi śreyo
yad-doṣād yāty adhaḥ pumān

sva-prāṇān—one's own life; *yaḥ*—one who; *para-prāṇaiḥ*—at the cost of others' lives; *prapuṣṇāti*—maintains properly; *aghṛṇaḥ*—shameless;

khalaḥ—wretched; *tat-vadhaḥ*—killing of him; *tasya*—his; *hi*—certainly; *śreyaḥ*—well-being; *yat*—by which; *doṣāt*—by the fault; *yāti*—goes; *adhaḥ* —downwards; *pumān*—a person.

TRANSLATION

A cruel and wretched person who maintains his existence at the cost of others' lives deserves to be killed for his own well-being, otherwise he will go down by his own actions.

PURPORT

A life for a life is just punishment for a person who cruelly and shamelessly lives at the cost of another's life. Political morality is to punish a person by a death sentence in order to save a cruel person from going to hell. That a murderer is condemned to a death sentence by the state is good for the culprit because in his next life he will not have to suffer for his act of murder. Such a death sentence for the murderer is the lowest possible punishment offered to him, and it is said in the *smṛti-śāstras* that men who are punished by the king on the principle of a life for a life are purified of all their sins, so much so that they may be eligible for being promoted to the planets of heaven. According to Manu, the great author of civic codes and religious principles, even the killer of an animal is to be considered a murderer because animal food is never meant for the civilized man, whose prime duty is to prepare himself for going back to Godhead. He says that in the act of killing an animal, there is a regular conspiracy by the party of sinners, and all of them are liable to be punished as murderers exactly like a party of conspirators who kill a human being combinedly. *He who gives permission, he who kills the animal, he who sells the slaughtered animal, he who cooks the animal, he who administers distribution of the foodstuff, and at last he who eats such cooked animal food are all murderers, and all of them are liable to be punished by the laws of nature.* No one can create a living being despite all advancement of material science, and therefore no one has the right to kill a living being by one's independent whims. For the animal-eaters, the scriptures have sanctioned restricted animal sacrifices only, and such sanctions are there just to restrict the opening of slaughterhouses and not to encourage animal-killing. The procedure under which animal sacrifice is allowed in the scriptures is good both for the animal sacrificed and the animal-eaters. It is good for the animal in the sense that the sacrificed animal is at once promoted to the human form of life after being sacrificed at the altar, and the animal-eater is saved from grosser types of sins (eating meats supplied by organized slaughterhouses which are ghastly places for breeding all kinds of material afflictions to society, country and the people in general). The material world is itself a place always full of anxieties, and by encouraging animal slaughter the whole atmosphere becomes polluted more and more by war, pestilence, famine and many other unwanted calamities.

TEXT 38

प्रतिश्रुतं च भवता पाञ्चाल्यै शृण्वतो मम।
आहरिष्ये शिरस्तस्य यस्ते मानिनि पुत्रहा ॥३८॥

pratiśrutaṁ ca bhavatā
pāñcālyai śṛṇvato mama
āhariṣye śiras tasya
yas te mānini putra-hā

pratiśrutam—it is promised; *ca*—and; *bhavatā*—by you; *pāñcālyai*—unto the daughter of the King of Pāñcāla (Draupadī); *śṛṇvataḥ*—which was heard; *mama*—by Me personally; *āhariṣye*—must I bring; *śiraḥ*—the head; *tasya*—of him; *yaḥ*—whom; *te*—your; *mānini*—consider; *putra-hā*—the killer of your sons.

TRANSLATION

Furthermore, I have personally heard you promise Draupadī that you would bring forth the head of the killer of her sons.

TEXT 39

तदसौ वध्यतां पाप आततायात्मबन्धुहा।
भर्तुश्च विप्रियं वीर कृतवान् कुलपांसनः ॥३९॥

tad asau vadhyatāṁ pāpa
ātatāyy ātma-bandhu-hā
bhartuś ca vipriyaṁ vīra
kṛtavān kula-pāṁsanaḥ

tat—therefore; *asau*—this man; *vadhyatām*—will be killed; *pāpaḥ*—the sinner; *ātatāyī*—assaulter; *ātma*—own; *bandhu-hā*—killer of sons; *bhartuḥ*—of the master; *ca*—also; *vipriyam*—having not satisfied; *vīra*—O warrior; *kṛtavān*—one who has done it; *kula-pāṁsanaḥ*—the burnt remnants of the family.

TRANSLATION

This man is an assassin and murderer of your own family members. Not only that, but he has also dissatisfied his master. He is but the burnt remnants of his family. Kill him immediately.

PURPORT

The son of Droṇācārya is condemned here as the burnt remnants of his family. The good name of Droṇācārya was very much respected. Although he joined the enemy camp, the Pāṇḍavas held him always in respect, and Arjuna saluted him before beginning the fight. There was nothing wrong in that way. But the son of Droṇācārya degraded himself by committing acts which are never done by the *dvijas,* or the twice-born higher castes. Aśvatthāmā, the son of Droṇācārya, committed murder by killing the five sleeping sons of Draupadī, by which he dissatisfied his master Duryodhana, who never approved of the heinous act of killing the five sleeping sons of the Pāṇḍavas. This means that Aśvatthāmā became an assaulter of Arjuna's own family members, and thus he was liable to be punished by him. In the *śāstras,* he who attacks without notice or kills from behind or sets fire to another's house or kidnaps one's wife is condemned to death. Kṛṣṇa reminded Arjuna of these facts so that he might take notice of them and do the needful.

TEXT 40

सूत उवाच
एवं परीक्षता धर्मं पार्थः कृष्णेन चोदितः ।
नैच्छद्धन्तुं गुरुसुतं यद्यप्यात्महनं महान् ॥४०॥

sūta uvāca
evaṁ parīkṣatā dharmaṁ
pārthaḥ kṛṣṇena coditaḥ
naicchad dhantuṁ guru-sutaṁ
yadyapy ātma-hanaṁ mahān

sūtaḥ—Sūta Gosvāmī; *uvāca*—said; *evam*—this; *parīkṣatā*—being examined; *dharmam*—in the matter of duty; *pārthaḥ*—Śrī Arjuna; *kṛṣṇena*—by Lord Kṛṣṇa; *coditaḥ*—being encouraged; *na aicchat*—did not like;

hantum—to kill; *guru-sutam*—the son of his teacher; *yadyapi*—although; *ātma-hanam*—murderer of sons; *mahān*—very great.

TRANSLATION

Sūta Gosvāmī said: Although Kṛṣṇa, who was examining Arjuna in religion, encouraged Arjuna to kill the son of Droṇācārya, Arjuna, a great soul, did not like the idea of killing him, although Aśvatthāmā was a heinous murderer of Arjuna's family members.

PURPORT

Arjuna was a great soul undoubtedly, which is proved here also. He is encouraged herein personally by the Lord to kill the son of Droṇa, but Arjuna considers that the son of his great teacher should be spared, for he happens to be the son of Droṇācārya, even though he is an unworthy son, having done all sorts of heinous acts whimsically for no one's benefit.

Lord Śrī Kṛṣṇa encouraged Arjuna outwardly just to test Arjuna's sense of duty. It is not that Arjuna was incomplete in the sense of his duty, nor was Lord Śrī Kṛṣṇa unaware of Arjuna's sense of duty. But Lord Śrī Kṛṣṇa put to test many of His pure devotees just to magnify the sense of duty. The *gopīs* were put to such tests as well. Prahlāda Mahārāja also was put to such a test. All pure devotees come out successful in the respective tests by the Lord.

TEXT 41

अथोपेत्य स्वशिबिरं गोविन्दप्रियसारथिः ।
न्यवेदयत्तं प्रियायै शोचन्त्या आत्मजान् हतान् ॥४१॥

athopetya sva-śibiraṁ
govinda-priya-sārathiḥ
nyavedayat taṁ priyāyai
śocantyā ātma-jān hatān

atha—thereafter; *upetya*—having reached; *sva*—own; *śibiram*—camp; *govinda*—one who enlivens the senses (Lord Śrī Kṛṣṇa); *priya*—dear; *sārathiḥ*—the charioteer; *nyavedayat*—entrusted to; *tam*—him; *priyāyai*—unto the dear; *śocantyai*—lamenting for; *ātma-jān*—own sons; *hatān*—murdered.

TRANSLATION

After reaching his own camp, Arjuna, along with his dear friend and charioteer [Śrī Kṛṣṇa], entrusted the murderer unto his dear wife, who was lamenting for her murdered sons.

PURPORT

The transcendental relation of Arjuna with Kṛṣṇa is of the dearmost friendship. In the *Bhagavad-gītā* the Lord Himself has claimed Arjuna as His dearmost friend. Every living being is thus related with the Supreme Lord by some sort of affectionate relation, either as servant or as friend or as parent or as an object of conjugal love. Everyone thus can enjoy the company of the Lord in the spiritual realm if he at all desires and sincerely tries for it by the process of *bhakti-yoga.*

TEXT 42

तथाहृतं पशुवत् पाशबद्ध-
मवाङ्मुखं कर्मजुगुप्सितेन ।
निरीक्ष्य कृष्णापकृतं गुरोः सुतं
वामस्वभावा कृपया ननाम च ॥४२॥

tathāhṛtaṁ paśuvat pāśa-baddham
avāṅ-mukhaṁ karma-jugupsitena
nirīkṣya kṛṣṇāpakṛtaṁ guroḥ sutaṁ
vāma-svabhāvā kṛpayā nanāma ca

tathā—thus; *āhṛtam*—brought in; *paśu-vat*—like an animal; *pāśa-baddham*—tied with ropes; *avāk-mukham*—without a word in his mouth; *karma*—activities; *jugupsitena*—being heinous; *nirīkṣya*—by seeing; *kṛṣṇā*—Draupadī; *apakṛtam*—the doer of the degrading; *guroḥ*—the teacher; *sutam*—son; *vāma*—beautiful; *svabhāvā*—nature; *kṛpayā*—out of compassion; *nanāma*—offered obeisances; *ca*—and.

TRANSLATION

Śrī Sūta Gosvāmī said: Draupadī then saw Aśvatthāmā, who was bound with ropes like an animal and silent for having enacted the most inglorious murder. Due to her female nature, and due to her being naturally good and well-behaved, she showed him due respects as a brāhmaṇa.

PURPORT

Aśvatthāmā was condemned by the Lord Himself, and he was treated by Arjuna just like a culprit, not like the son of a *brāhmaṇa* or teacher. But when he was brought before Śrīmatī Draupadī, she, although begrieved for the murder of her sons, and although the murderer was present before her, could not withdraw the due respect generally offered to a *brāhmaṇa* or to the son of a *brāhmaṇa.* This is due to her mild nature as a woman. Women as a class are no better than boys, and therefore they have no discriminatory power like that of a man. Aśvatthāmā proved himself to be an unworthy son of Droṇācārya or of a *brāhmaṇa,* and for this reason he was condemned by the greatest authority, Lord Śrī Kṛṣṇa, and yet a mild woman could not withdraw her natural courtesy for a *brāhmaṇa.*

Even to date, in a Hindu family a woman shows proper respect to the *brāhmaṇa* caste, however fallen and heinous a *brahma-bandhu* may be. But the men have begun to protest against *brahma-bandhus* who are born in families of good *brāhmaṇas* but by action are less than *śūdras.*

The specific words used in this *śloka* are *vāma-svabhāvā,* "mild and gentle by nature." A good man or woman accepts anything very easily, but a man of average intelligence does not do so. But, anyway, we should not give up our reason and discriminatory power just to be gentle. One must have good discriminatory power to judge a thing on its merit. We should not follow the mild nature of a woman and thereby accept that which is not genuine. Aśvatthāmā may be respected by a good-natured woman, but that does not mean that he is as good as a genuine *brāhmaṇa.*

TEXT 43

उवाच चासहन्त्यस्य बन्धनानयनं सती।
मुच्यतां मुच्यतामेष ब्राह्मणो नितरां गुरुः ॥४३॥

uvāca cāsahanty asya
bandhanānayanaṁ satī
mucyatāṁ mucyatām eṣa
brāhmaṇo nitarāṁ guruḥ

uvāca—said; *ca*—and; *asahantī*—being unbearable for her; *asya*—his; *bandhana*—being bound; *ānayanam*—bringing him; *satī*—the devoted; *mucyatām mucyatām*—just get him released; *eṣaḥ*—this; *brāhmaṇaḥ*—a *brāhmaṇa; nitarām*—our; *guruḥ*—teacher.

TRANSLATION

She could not tolerate Aśvatthāmā's being bound by ropes, and being a devoted lady, she said: Release him, for he is a brāhmaṇa, our spiritual master.

PURPORT

As soon as Aśvatthāmā was brought before Draupadī, she thought it intolerable that a *brāhmaṇa* should be arrested like a culprit and brought before her in that condition, especially when the *brāhmaṇa* happened to be a teacher's son.

Arjuna arrested Aśvatthāmā knowing perfectly well that he was the son of Droṇācārya. Kṛṣṇa also knew him to be so, but both of them condemned the murderer without consideration of his being the son of a *brāhmaṇa.* According to revealed scriptures, a teacher or spiritual master is liable to be rejected if he proves himself unworthy of the position of a *guru* or spiritual master. A *guru* is called also an *ācārya,* or a person who has personally assimilated all the essence of *śāstras* and has helped his disciples to adopt the ways. Aśvatthāmā failed to discharge the duties of a *brāhmaṇa* or teacher, and therefore he was liable to be rejected from the exalted position of a *brāhmaṇa.* On this consideration, both Lord Śrī Kṛṣṇa and Arjuna were right in condemning Aśvatthāmā. But to a good lady like Draupadī, the matter was considered not from the angle of *śāstric* vision, but as a matter of custom. By custom, Aśvatthāmā was offered the same respect as offered to his father. It was so because generally the people accept the son of a *brāhmaṇa* as a real brāhmaṇa, by sentiment only. Factually the matter is different. A *brāhmaṇa* is accepted on the merit of qualification and not on the merit of simply being the son of a *brāhmaṇa.*

But in spite of all this, Draupadī desired that Aśvatthāmā be at once released, and it was all the same a good sentiment for her. This means that a devotee of the Lord can tolerate all sorts of tribulation personally, but still such devotees are never unkind to others, even to the enemy. These are the characteristics of one who is a pure devotee of the Lord.

TEXT 44

सरहस्यो धनुर्वेदः सविसर्गोपसंयमः ।
अस्त्रग्रामश्च भवता शिक्षितो यदनुग्रहात् ॥४४॥

sarahasyo dhanur-vedaḥ
savisargopasaṁyamaḥ
astra-grāmaś ca bhavatā
śikṣito yad-anugrahāt

sa-rahasyaḥ—confidential; *dhanuḥ-vedaḥ*—knowledge in the art of manipulating bows and arrows; *sa-visarga*—releasing; *upasaṁyamaḥ*—controlling; *astra*—weapons; *grāmaḥ*—all kinds of; *ca*—and; *bhavatā*—by yourself; *śikṣitaḥ*—learned; *yat*—by whose; *anugrahāt*—mercy of.

TRANSLATION

It was by Droṇācārya's mercy that you learned the military art of throwing arrows and the confidential art of controlling weapons.

PURPORT

Dhanur-veda, or military science, was taught by Droṇācārya with all its confidential secrets of throwing and controlling by Vedic hymns. Gross military science is dependent on material weapons, but finer than that is the art of throwing the arrows saturated with Vedic hymns, which act more effectively than gross material weapons like machine guns or atomic bombs. The control is by Vedic *mantras,* or the transcendental science of sound. It is said in the *Rāmāyaṇa* that Mahārāja Daśaratha, the father of Lord Śrī Rāma, used to control arrows by sound only. He could pierce his target with his arrow by only hearing the sound, without seeing the object. So this is a finer military science than that of the gross material military weapons used nowadays. Arjuna was taught all this, and therefore Draupadī wished that Arjuna feel obliged to Ācārya Droṇa for all these benefits. And in the absence of Droṇācārya, his son was his representative. That was the opinion of the good lady Draupadī. It may be argued why Droṇācārya, a rigid *brāhmaṇa,* should be a teacher in military science. But the reply is that a *brāhmaṇa* should become a teacher, regardless of what his department of knowledge is. A learned *brāhmaṇa* should become a teacher, a priest and a recipient of charity. A bona fide *brāhmaṇa* is authorized to accept such professions.

TEXT 45

स एष भगवान्द्रोणः प्रजारूपेण वर्तते।
तस्यात्मनोऽर्धं पत्न्यास्ते नान्वगाद्वीरसूः कृपी ॥४५॥

sa eṣa bhagavān droṇaḥ
prajā-rūpeṇa vartate
tasyātmano 'rdhaṁ patny āste
nānvagād vīrasūḥ kṛpī

saḥ—he; *eṣaḥ*—certainly; *bhagavān*—lord; *droṇaḥ*—Droṇācārya; *prajā-rūpeṇa*—in the form of his son Aśvatthāmā; *vartate*—is existing; *tasya*—his; *ātmanaḥ*—of the body; *ardham*—half; *patnī*—wife; *āste*—living; *na*—not; *anvagāt*—undertook; *vīrasūḥ*—having the son present; *kṛpī*—the sister of Kṛpācārya.

TRANSLATION

He [Droṇācārya] is certainly still existing, being represented by his son. His wife Kṛpī did not undergo a satī with him because she had a son.

PURPORT

The wife of Droṇācārya, Kṛpī, is the sister of Kṛpācārya. A devoted wife, who is according to revealed scripture the better half of her husband, is justified in embracing voluntary death along with her husband if she is without issue. But in the case of the wife of Droṇācārya, she did not undergo such a trial because she had her son, the representative of her husband. A widow is a widow only in name if there is a son of her husband existing. So in either case Aśvatthāmā was the representative of Droṇācārya, and therefore killing Aśvatthāmā would be like killing Droṇācārya. That was the argument of Draupadī against the killing of Aśvatthāmā.

TEXT 46

तद् धर्मज्ञ महाभाग भवद्भिर्गौरवं कुलम् ।
वृजिनं नार्हति प्राप्तुं पूज्यं वन्द्यमभीक्ष्णशः ॥४६॥

tad dharmajña mahā-bhāga
bhavadbhir gauravaṁ kulam
vṛjinaṁ nārhati prāptuṁ
pūjyaṁ vandyam abhīkṣṇaśaḥ

tat—therefore; *dharma-jña*—one who is aware of the principles of religion; *mahā-bhāga*—the most fortunate; *bhavadbhiḥ*—by your good self; *gauravam*—glorified; *kulam*—the family; *vṛjinam*—that which is painful; *na*—not; *arhati*—does deserve; *prāptum*—for obtaining; *pūjyam*—the worshipable; *vandyam*—respectable; *abhīkṣṇaśaḥ*—constantly.

TRANSLATION

O most fortunate one who knows the principles of religion, it is not good for you to cause grief to glorious family members who are always respectable and worshipful.

PURPORT

A slight insult for a respectable family is sufficient to invoke grief. Therefore, a cultured man should always be careful in dealing with worshipful family members.

TEXT 47

मा रोदीदस्य जननी गौतमी पतिदेवता।
यथाहं मृतवत्सार्ता रोदिम्यश्रुमुखी मुहुः ॥४७॥

mā rodīd asya jananī
gautamī pati-devatā
yathāhaṁ mṛta-vatsārtā
rodimy aśru-mukhī muhuḥ

mā—do not; *rodīt*—make cry; *asya*—his; *jananī*—mother; *gautamī*—the wife of Droṇa; *pati-devatā*—chaste; *yathā*—as has; *aham*—myself; *mṛta-vatsā*—one whose child is dead; *ārtā*—distressed; *rodimi*—crying; *aśru-mukhī*—tears in the eyes; *muhuḥ*—constantly.

TRANSLATION

My lord, do not make the wife of Droṇācārya cry like me. I am aggrieved for the death of my sons. She need not cry constantly like me.

PURPORT

Sympathetic good lady as she was, Śrīmatī Draupadī did not want to put the wife of Droṇācārya in the same position of childlessness, both from the point of motherly feelings and from the respectable position held by the wife of Droṇācārya.

TEXT 48

यैः कोपितं ब्रह्मकुलं राजन्यैरजितात्मभिः।
तत् कुलं प्रदहत्याशु सानुबन्धं शुचार्पितम् ॥४८॥

yaiḥ kopitaṁ brahma-kulaṁ
rājanyair ajitātmabhiḥ
tat kulaṁ pradahaty āśu
sānubandhaṁ śucārpitam

yaiḥ—by those; *kopitam*—enraged; *brahma-kulam*—the order of the *brāhmaṇas; rājanyaiḥ*—by the administrative order; *ajita*—unrestricted; *ātmabhiḥ*—by oneself; *tat*—that; *kulam*—family; *pradahati*—is burnt up; *āśu*—within no time; *sa-anubandham*—together with family members; *śucā-arpitam*—being put into grief.

TRANSLATION

If the kingly administrative order, being unrestricted in sense control, offends the brāhmaṇa order and enrages them, then the fire of that rage burns up the whole body of the royal family and brings grief upon all.

PURPORT

The *brāhmaṇa* order of society, or the spiritually advanced caste or community, and the members of such highly elevated families, were always held in great esteem by the other, subordinate castes, namely the administrative kingly order, the mercantile order and the laborers.

TEXT 49

सूत उवाच
धर्म्यं न्याय्यं सकरुणं निर्व्यलीकं समं महत्।
राजा धर्मसुतो राज्ञ्याः प्रत्यनन्दद्वचो द्विजाः ॥४९॥

sūta uvāca
dharmyaṁ nyāyyaṁ sakaruṇaṁ
nirvyalīkaṁ samaṁ mahat
rājā dharma-suto rājñyāḥ
pratyanandad vaco dvijāḥ

sūtaḥ uvāca—Sūta Gosvāmī said; *dharmyam*—in accordance with the principles of religion; *nyāyyam*—justice; *sa-karuṇam*—full of mercy; *nirvyalīkam*—without duplicity in *dharma; samam*—equity; *mahat*—glorious; *rājā*—the King; *dharma-sutaḥ*—son; *rājñyāḥ*—by the Queen; *pratyanandat*—supported; *vacaḥ*—statements; *dvijāḥ*—O *brāhmaṇas.*

TRANSLATION

Sūta Gosvāmī said: O brāhmaṇas, King Yudhiṣṭhira fully supported the statements of the Queen, which were in accordance with the principles of

religion and were justified, glorious, full of mercy and equity, and without duplicity.

PURPORT

Mahārāja Yudhiṣṭhira, who was the son of Dharmarāja, or Yamarāja, fully supported the words of Queen Draupadī in asking Arjuna to release Aśvatthāmā. One should not tolerate the humiliation of a member of a great family. Arjuna and his family were indebted to the family of Droṇācārya because of Arjuna's learning the military science from him. If ingratitude were shown to such a benevolent family, it would not be at all justified from the moral standpoint. The wife of Droṇācārya, who was the half body of the great soul, must be treated with compassion, and she should not be put into grief because of her son's death. That is compassion. Such statements by Draupadī are without duplicity because actions should be taken with full knowledge. The feeling of equality was there because Draupadī spoke out of her personal experience. A barren woman cannot understand the grief of a mother. Draupadī was herself a mother, and therefore her calculation of the depth of Kṛpī's grief was quite to the point. And it was glorious because she wanted to show proper respect to a great family.

TEXT 50

नकुलः सहदेवश्च युयुधानो धनंजयः।
भगवान् देवकीपुत्रो ये चान्ये याश्च योषितः ॥५०॥

nakulaḥ sahadevaś ca
yuyudhāno dhanañjayaḥ
bhagavān devakī-putro
ye cānye yāś ca yoṣitaḥ

nakulaḥ—Nakula; *sahadevaḥ*—Sahadeva; *ca*—and; *yuyudhānaḥ*—Sātyaki; *dhanañjayaḥ*—Arjuna; *bhagavān*—the Personality of Godhead; *devakī-putraḥ*—the son of Devakī, Lord Śrī Kṛṣṇa; *ye*—those; *ca*—and; *anye*—others; *yāḥ*—those; *ca*—and; *yoṣitaḥ*—ladies.

TRANSLATION

Nakula and Sahadeva [the younger brothers of the King] and also Sātyaki, Arjuna, the Personality of Godhead Lord Sri Kṛṣṇa, son of Devakī, and the ladies and others all unanimously agreed with the King.

TEXT 51

तत्राहामर्षितो भीमस्तस्य श्रेयान् वधः स्मृतः।
न भर्तुर्नात्मनश्चार्थे योऽहन् सुप्तान् शिशून् वृथा ॥५१॥

tatrāhāmarṣito bhīmas
tasya śreyān vadhaḥ smṛtaḥ
na bhartur nātmanaś cārthe
yo 'han suptān śiśūn vṛthā

tatra—thereupon; *āha*—said; *amarṣitaḥ*—in an angry mood; *bhīmaḥ*—Bhīma; *tasya*—his; *śreyān*—ultimate good; *vadhaḥ*—killing; *smṛtaḥ*—recorded; *na*—not; *bhartuḥ*—of the master; *na*—nor; *ātmanaḥ*—of his own self; *ca*—and; *arthe*—for the sake of; *yaḥ*—one who; *ahan*—killed; *suptān*—sleeping; *śiśūn*—children; *vṛthā*—without purpose.

TRANSLATION

Bhīma, however, disagreed with them and recommended killing this culprit who, in an angry mood, had murdered sleeping children for no purpose and for neither his nor his master's interest.

TEXT 52

निशम्य भीमगदितं द्रौपद्याश्च चतुर्भुजः।
आलोक्य वदनं सख्युरिदमाह हसन्निव ॥५२॥

niśamya bhīma-gaditaṁ
draupadyāś ca catur-bhujaḥ
ālokya vadanaṁ sakhyur
idam āha hasann iva

niśamya—just after hearing; *bhīma*—Bhīma; *gaditam*—spoken by; *draupadyāḥ*—of Draupadī; *ca*—and; *catuḥ-bhujaḥ*—the four-handed (Personality of Godhead); *ālokya*—having seen; *vadanam*—the face; *sakhyuḥ*—of His friend; *idam*—this; *āha*—said; *hasan*—smiling; *iva*—as it.

TRANSLATION

Caturbhuja [the four-armed one], or the Personality of Godhead, after hearing the words of Bhīma, Draupadī and others, saw the face of His dear friend Arjuna, and He began to speak as if smiling.

PURPORT

Lord Śrī Kṛṣṇa had two arms, and why He is designated as four-armed is explained by Śrīdhara Svāmī. Both Bhīma and Draupadī held opposite views about killing Aśvatthāmā. Bhīma wanted him to be immediately killed, whereas Draupadī wanted to save him. We can imagine Bhīma ready to kill while Draupadī is obstructing him. And in order to prevent both of them, the Lord discovered another two arms. Originally, the primeval Lord Śrī Kṛṣṇa displays only two arms, but in His Nārāyaṇa feature He exhibits four. In His Nārāyaṇa feature He resides with His devotees in the Vaikuṇṭha planets, while in His original Śrī Kṛṣṇa feature He resides in the Kṛṣṇaloka planet far, far above the Vaikuṇṭha planets in the spiritual sky. Therefore, if Śrī Kṛṣṇa is called *caturbhujaḥ,* there is no contradiction. If need be He can display hundreds of arms, as He exhibited in His *viśva-rūpa* shown to Arjuna. Therefore, one who can display hundreds and thousands of arms can also manifest four whenever needed.

When Arjuna was perplexed about what to do with Aśvatthāmā, Lord Śrī Kṛṣṇa, as the very dear friend of Arjuna, voluntarily took up the matter just to make a solution. And He was smiling also.

TEXTS 53–54

श्रीभगवानुवाच

ब्रह्मबन्धुर्न हन्तव्य आततायी वधार्हणः ।
मयैवोभयमाम्नातं परिपाह्यनुशासनम् ॥५३॥
कुरु प्रतिश्रुतं सत्यं यत्तत्सान्त्वयता प्रियाम् ।
प्रियं च भीमसेनस्य पाञ्चाल्या मह्यमेव च ॥५४॥

śrī-bhagavān uvāca
brahma-bandhur na hantavya
ātatāyī vadhārhaṇaḥ
mayaivobhayam āmnātaṁ
paripāhy anuśāsanam

kuru pratiśrutaṁ satyaṁ
yat tat sāntvayatā priyām
priyaṁ ca bhīmasenasya
pāñcālyā mahyam eva ca

śrī-bhagavān—the Personality of Godhead; *uvāca*—said; *brahma-bandhuḥ*—the relative of a *brāhmaṇa; na*—not; *hantavyaḥ*—to be killed;

ātatāyī—the aggressor; *vadha-arhaṇaḥ*—is due to be killed; *mayā*—by Me; *eva*—certainly; *ubhayam*—both; *āmnātam*—described according to rulings of the authority; *paripāhi*—carry out; *anuśāsanam*—rulings; *kuru*—abide by; *pratiśrutam*—as promised by; *satyam*—truth; *yat tat*—that which; *sāntvayatā*—while pacifying; *priyām*—dear wife; *priyam*—satisfaction; *ca*—also; *bhīmasenasya*—of Śrī Bhīmasena; *pāñcālyāḥ*—of Draupadī; *mahyam*—unto Me also; *eva*—certainly; *ca*—and.

TRANSLATION

The Personality of Godhead, Śrī Kṛṣṇa said: A friend of a brāhmaṇa is not to be killed, but if he is an aggressor he must be killed. All these rulings are in the scriptures, and you should act accordingly. You have to fulfill your promise to your wife, and you must also act to the satisfaction of Bhīmasena and Me.

PURPORT

Arjuna was perplexed because Aśvatthāmā was to be killed as well as spared according to different scriptures cited by different persons. As a *brahma-bandhu,* or a worthless son of a *brāhmaṇa,* Aśvatthāmā was not to be killed, but he was at the same time an aggressor also. And according to the rulings of Manu, an aggressor, even though he be a *brāhmaṇa* (and what to speak of an unworthy son of a *brāhmaṇa*), is to be killed. Droṇācārya was certainly a *brāhmaṇa* in the true sense of the term, but because he stood in the battlefield he was killed. But although Aśvatthāmā was an aggressor, he stood without any fighting weapons. The ruling is that an aggressor, when he is without weapon or chariot, cannot be killed. All these were certainly perplexities. Besides that, Arjuna had to keep the promise he had made before Draupadī just to pacify her. And he also had to satisfy both Bhīma and Kṛṣṇa, who advised killing him. This dilemma was present before Arjuna, and the solution was awarded by Kṛṣṇa.

TEXT 55

सूत उवाच
अर्जुनः सहसाज्ञाय हरेर्हार्दमथासिना ।
मणिं जहार मूर्धन्यं द्विजस्य सहमूर्धजम् ॥५५॥

sūta uvāca
arjunaḥ sahasājñāya
harer hārdam athāsinā

maṇiṁ jahāra mūrdhanyaṁ
dvijasya saha-mūrdhajam

sūtaḥ—Sūta Gosvāmī; *uvāca*—said; *arjunaḥ*—Arjuna; *sahasā*—just at that time; *ājñāya*—knowing it; *hareḥ*—of the Lord; *hārdam*—motive; *atha*—thus; *asinā*—by the sword; *maṇim*—the jewel; *jahāra*—separated; *mūrdhanyam*—on the head; *dvijasya*—of the twice-born; *saha*—with; *mūrdhajam*—hairs.

TRANSLATION

Just then Arjuna could understand the motive of the Lord by His equivocal orders, and thus with his sword he severed both hair and jewel from the head of Aśvatthāmā.

PURPORT

Contradictory orders of different persons are impossible to carry out. Therefore a compromise was selected by Arjuna by his sharp intelligence, and he separated the jewel from the head of Aśvatthāmā. This was as good as cutting off his head, and yet his life was saved for all practical purposes. Here Aśvatthāmā is indicated as twice-born. Certainly he was twice-born, but he fell down from his position, and therefore he was properly punished.

TEXT 56

विमुच्य रशनाबद्धं बालहत्याहतप्रभम् ।
तेजसा मणिना हीनं शिबिरान्निरयापयत् ॥५६॥

vimucya raśanā-baddhaṁ
bāla-hatyā-hata-prabham
tejasā maṇinā hīnaṁ
śibirān nirayāpayat

vimucya—after releasing him; *raśanā-baddham*—from the bondage of ropes; *bāla-hatyā*—infanticide; *hata-prabham*—loss of bodily luster; *tejasā*—of the strength of; *maṇinā*—by the jewel; *hīnam*—being deprived of; *śibirāt*—from the camp; *nirayāpayat*—drove him out.

TRANSLATION

He [Aśvatthāmā] had already lost his bodily luster due to infanticide, and now, moreover, having lost the jewel from his head, he lost even more strength. Thus he was unbound and driven out of the camp.

PURPORT

Thus being insulted, the humiliated Aśvatthāmā was simultaneously killed and not killed by the intelligence of Lord Kṛṣṇa and Arjuna.

TEXT 57

वपनं द्रविणादानं स्थानान्निर्यापणं तथा।
एष हि ब्रह्मबन्धूनां वधो नान्योऽस्ति दैहिकः ॥५७॥

vapanaṁ draviṇādānaṁ
sthānān niryāpaṇaṁ tathā
eṣa hi brahma-bandhūnāṁ
vadho nānyo 'sti daihikaḥ

vapanam—cleaving the hairs from the head; *draviṇa*—wealth; *adānam*—forfeiting; *sthānāt*—from the residence; *niryāpaṇam*—driving away; *tathā*—also; *eṣaḥ*—all these; *hi*—certainly; *brahma-bandhūnām*—of the relatives of a *brāhmaṇa; vadhaḥ*—killing; *na*—not; *anyaḥ*—any other method; *asti*—there is; *daihikaḥ*—in the matter of the body.

TRANSLATION

Cutting the hair from his head, depriving him of his wealth and driving him from his residence are the prescribed punishments for the relative of a brāhmaṇa. There is no injunction for killing the body.

TEXT 58

पुत्रशोकातुराः सर्वे पाण्डवाः सह कृष्णया।
स्वानां मृतानां यत्कृत्यं चक्रुर्निर्हरणादिकम् ॥५८॥

putra-śokāturāḥ sarve
pāṇḍavāḥ saha kṛṣṇayā
svānāṁ mṛtānāṁ yat kṛtyaṁ
cakrur nirharaṇādikam

putra—son; *śoka*—bereavement; *āturāḥ*—overwhelmed with; *sarve*—all of them; *pāṇḍavāḥ*—the sons of Pāṇḍu; *saha*—along with; *kṛṣṇayā*—with Draupadī; *svānām*—of the kinsmen; *mṛtānām*—of the dead; *yat*—what; *kṛtyam*—ought to be done; *cakruḥ*—did perform; *nirharaṇa-ādikam*—undertakable.

TRANSLATION

Thereafter, the sons of Pāṇḍu and Draupadī, overwhelmed with grief, performed the proper rituals for the dead bodies of their relatives.

Thus end the Bhaktivedanta purports of the First Canto, Seventh Chapter, of the Śrīmad-Bhāgavatam, *entitled "The Son of Droṇa Punished."*

CHAPTER EIGHT

Prayers by Queen Kuntī and Parīkṣit Saved

TEXT 1

सूत उवाच
अथ ते सम्परेतानां स्वानामुदकमिच्छताम्।
दातुं सकृष्णा गङ्गायां पुरस्कृत्य ययुः स्त्रियः ॥१॥

sūta uvāca
atha te samparetānāṁ
svānām udakam icchatām
dātuṁ sakṛṣṇā gaṅgāyāṁ
puraskṛtya yayuḥ striyaḥ

sūtaḥ uvāca—Sūta said; *atha*—thus; *te*—the Pāṇḍavas; *samparetānām*—of the dead; *svānām*—of the relatives; *udakam*—water; *icchatām*—willing to have; *dātum*—to deliver; *sa-kṛṣṇāḥ*—along with Draupadī; *gaṅgāyām*—on the Ganges; *puraskṛtya*—putting in the front; *yayuḥ*—went; *striyaḥ*—the women.

TRANSLATION

Sūta Gosvāmī said: Thereafter the Pāṇḍavas, desiring to deliver water to the dead relatives who had desired it, went to the Ganges with Draupadī. The ladies walked in front.

PURPORT

To date it is the custom in Hindu society to go to the Ganges or any other sacred river to take bath when death occurs in the family. Each of the family members pours out a potful of the Ganges water for the departed soul and walks in a procession, with the ladies in the front. The Pāṇḍavas also followed the rules more than five thousand years ago. Lord Kṛṣṇa, being a cousin of the Pāṇḍavas, was also amongst the family members.

TEXT 2

ते निनीयोदकं सर्वे विलप्य च भृशं पुनः ।
आप्लुता हरिपादाब्जरजःपूतसरिज्जले ॥२॥

te ninīyodakaṁ sarve
vilapya ca bhṛśaṁ punaḥ
āplutā hari-pādābja-
rajaḥ-pūta-sarij-jale

te—all of them; *ninīya*—having offered; *udakam*—water; *sarve*—every one of them; *vilapya*—having lamented; *ca*—and; *bhṛśam*—sufficiently; *punaḥ*—again; *āplutāḥ*—took bath; *hari-pādābja*—the lotus feet of the Lord; *rajaḥ*—dust; *pūta*—purified; *sarit*—of the Ganges; *jale*—in the water.

TRANSLATION

Having lamented over them and sufficiently offered Ganges water, they bathed in the Ganges, whose water is sanctified due to being mixed with the dust of the lotus feet of the Lord.

TEXT 3

तत्रासीनं कुरुपतिं धृतराष्ट्रं सहानुजम् ।
गान्धारीं पुत्रशोकार्तां पृथां कृष्णां च माधवः ॥३॥

tatrāsīnaṁ kuru-patiṁ
dhṛtarāṣṭraṁ sahānujam
gāndhārīṁ putra-śokārtāṁ
pṛthāṁ kṛṣṇāṁ ca mādhavaḥ

tatra—there; *āsīnam*—sitting; *kuru-patim*—the King of the Kurus; *dhṛtarāṣṭram*—Dhṛtarāṣṭra; *saha-anujam*—with his younger brothers; *gāndhārīm*—Gāndhārī; *putra*—son; *śoka-artām*—overtaken by bereavement; *pṛthām*—Kuntī; *kṛṣṇām*—Draupadī; *ca*—also; *mādhavaḥ*—Lord Śrī Kṛṣṇa.

TRANSLATION

There sat the King of the Kurus, Mahārāja Yudhiṣṭhira, along with his younger brothers and Dhṛtarāṣṭra, Gāndhārī, Kuntī and Draupadī, all overwhelmed with grief. Lord Kṛṣṇa was also there.

PURPORT

The Battle of Kurukṣetra was fought between family members, and thus all affected persons were also family members like Mahārāja Yudhiṣṭhira and brothers, Kuntī, Draupadī, Subhadrā, Dhṛtarāṣṭra, Gāndhārī and her daughters-in-law, etc. All the principal dead bodies were in some way or other related with each other, and therefore the family grief was combined. Lord Kṛṣṇa was also one of them as a cousin of the Pāṇḍavas and nephew of Kuntī, as well as brother of Subhadrā, etc. The Lord, therefore, was equally sympathetic toward all of them, and therefore he began to pacify them befittingly.

TEXT 4

सान्त्वयामास मुनिभिर्हतबन्धूञ्शुचार्पितान् ।
भूतेषु कालस्य गतिं दर्शयन्न प्रतिक्रियाम् ॥४॥

sāntvayām āsa munibhir
hata-bandhūñ śucārpitān
bhūteṣu kālasya gatiṁ
darśayan na pratikriyām

sāntvayām āsa—pacified; *munibhiḥ*—along with the *munis* present there; *hata-bandhūn*—those who lost their friends and relatives; *śucārpitān*—all shocked and affected; *bhūteṣu*—unto the living beings; *kālasya*—of the supreme law of the Almighty; *gatim*—reactions; *darśayan*—demonstrated; *na*—no; *pratikriyām*—remedial measures.

TRANSLATION

Citing the stringent laws of the Almighty and their reactions upon living beings, Lord Śrī Kṛṣṇa and the munis began to pacify those who were shocked and affected.

PURPORT

The stringent laws of nature, under the order of the Supreme Personality of Godhead, cannot be altered by any living entity. The living entities are eternally under the subjugation of the almighty Lord. The Lord makes all the laws and orders, and these laws and orders are generally called *dharma* or religion. No one can create any religious formula. Bona fide religion is to abide by the orders of the Lord. The Lord's orders are clearly declared in the

Bhagavad-gītā. Everyone should follow Him only or His orders, and that will make all happy, both materially and spiritually. As long as we are in the material world, our duty is to follow the orders of the Lord, and if by the grace of the Lord we are liberated from the clutches of the material world, then in our liberated stage also we can render transcendental loving service unto the Lord. In our material stage we can see neither ourselves nor the Lord for want of spiritual vision. But when we are liberated from material affection and are situated in our original spiritual form we can see both ourselves and the Lord face to face. *Mukti* means to be reinstated in one's original spiritual status after giving up the material conception of life. Therefore, human life is specifically meant for qualifying ourselves for this spiritual liberty. Unfortunately, under the influence of illusory material energy, we accept this spot-life of only a few years as our permanent existence and thus become illusioned by possessing so-called country, home, land, children, wife, community, wealth, etc., which are false representations created by *māyā* (illusion). And under the dictation of *māyā*, we fight with one another to protect these false possessions. By cultivating spiritual knowledge, we can realize that we have nothing to do with all this material paraphernalia. Then at once we become free from material attachment. This clearance of the misgivings of material existence at once takes place by association with the Lord's devotees, who are able to inject the transcendental sound into the depths of the bewildered heart and thus make one practically liberated from all lamentation and illusion. That is a summary of the pacifying measures for those affected by the reaction of stringent material laws, exhibited in the forms of birth, death, old age and disease, which are insoluble factors of material existence. The victims of war, namely, the family members of the Kurus, were lamenting the problems of death, and the Lord pacified them on the basis of knowledge.

TEXT 5

साधयित्वाजातशत्रोः स्वं राज्यं कितवैर्हृतम् ।
घातयित्वासतो राज्ञः कचस्पर्शक्षतायुषः ॥५॥

sādhayitvājāta-śatroḥ
svaṁ rājyaṁ kitavair hṛtam
ghātayitvāsato rājñaḥ
kaca-sparśa-kṣatāyuṣaḥ

sādhayitvā—having executed; *ajāta-śatroḥ*—of one who has no enemy; *svam rājyam*—own kingdom; *kitavaiḥ*—by the clever (Duryodhana and party); *hṛtam*—usurped; *ghātayitvā*—having killed; *asataḥ*—the unscrupulous; *rājñaḥ*—of the queen's; *kaca*—bunch of hair; *sparśa*—roughly handled; *kṣata*—decreased; *āyuṣaḥ*—by the duration of life.

TRANSLATION

The clever Duryodhana and his party cunningly usurped the kingdom of Yudhiṣṭhira, who had no enemy. By the grace of the Lord, the recovery was executed, and the unscrupulous kings who joined with Duryodhana were killed by Him. Others also died, their duration of life having decreased for their rough handling of the hair of Queen Draupadī.

PURPORT

In the glorious days, or before the advent of the age of Kali, the *brāhmaṇas,* the cows, the women, the children and the old men were properly given protection.

1. The protection of the *brāhmaṇas* maintains the institution of *varṇa* and *āśrama,* the most scientific culture for attainment of spiritual life.

2. The protection of cows maintains the most miraculous form of food, i.e., milk, for maintaining the finer tissues of the brain for understanding higher aims of life.

3. The protection of women maintains the chastity of society, by which we can get a good generation for peace, tranquillity and progress of life.

4. The protection of children gives the human form of life its best chance to prepare the way of liberty from material bondage. Such protection of children begins from the very day of begetting a child by the purificatory process of *garbhādhāna-saṁskāra,* the beginning of pure life.

5. The protection of the old men gives them a chance to prepare themselves for better life after death.

This complete outlook is based on factors leading to successful humanity as against the civilization of polished cats and dogs. The killing of the above-mentioned innocent creatures is totally forbidden because even by insulting them one loses one's duration of life. In the age of Kali they are not properly protected, and therefore the duration of life of the present generation has shortened considerably. In the *Bhagavad-gītā* it is stated that when the women become unchaste for want of proper protection, there are unwanted children called *varṇa-saṅkara.* To insult a chaste woman means to bring about disaster in the duration of life. Duḥśāsana, a brother of Duryodhana, insulted Draupadī, an ideal chaste lady, and therefore the miscreants died untimely. These are some of the stringent laws of the Lord mentioned above.

TEXT 6

याजयित्वाश्वमेधैस्तं त्रिभिरुत्तमकल्पकैः ।
तद्यशः पावनं दिक्षु शतमन्योरिवातनोत् ॥६॥

yājayitvāśvamedhais taṁ
tribhir uttama-kalpakaiḥ
tad-yaśaḥ pāvanaṁ dikṣu
śata-manyor ivātanot

yājayitvā—by performing; *aśvamedhaiḥ*—*yajña* in which a horse is sacrificed; *tam*—him (King Yudhiṣṭhira); *tribhiḥ*—three; *uttama*—best; *kalpakaiḥ*—supplied with proper ingredients and performed by able priests; *tat*—that; *yaśaḥ*—fame; *pāvanam*—virtuous; *dikṣu*—all directions; *śata-manyoḥ*—Indra, who performed one hundred such sacrifices; *iva*—like; *atanot*—spread.

TRANSLATION

Lord Śrī Kṛṣṇa caused three well-performed aśvamedha-yajñas [horse sacrifices] to be conducted by Mahārāja Yudhiṣṭhira and thus caused his virtuous fame to be glorified in all directions, like that of Indra, who had performed one hundred such sacrifices.

PURPORT

This is something like the preface to the performances of *aśvamedha-yajña* by Mahārāja Yudhiṣṭhira. The comparison of Mahārāja Yudhiṣṭhira to the King of heaven is significant. The King of heaven is thousands and thousands of times greater than Mahārāja Yudhiṣṭhira in opulence, yet the fame of Mahārāja Yudhiṣṭhira was not less. The reason is that Mahārāja Yudhiṣṭhira was a pure devotee of the Lord, and by His grace only was King Yudhiṣṭhira on the level of the King of heaven, even though he performed only three *yajñas* whereas the King of heaven performed hundreds. That is the prerogative of the devotee of the Lord. The Lord is equal to everyone, but a devotee of the Lord is more glorified because he is always in touch with the all-great. The sun rays are equally distributed, but still there are some places which are always dark. This is not due to the sun but to the receptive power. Similarly, those who are cent-percent devotees of the Lord get the full-fledged mercy of the Lord, which is always equally distributed everywhere.

TEXT 7

आमन्त्र्य पाण्डुपुत्रांश्च शैनेयोद्धवसंयुतः ।
द्वैपायनादिभिर्विप्रैः पूजितैः प्रतिपूजितः ॥७॥

āmantrya pāṇḍu-putrāṁś ca
śaineyoddhava-saṁyutaḥ
dvaipāyanādibhir vipraiḥ
pūjitaiḥ pratipūjitaḥ

āmantrya—inviting; *pāṇḍu-putrān*—all the sons of Pāṇḍu; *ca*—also; *śaineya*—Sātyaki; *uddhava*—Uddhava; *saṁyutaḥ*—accompanied; *dvaipāyana-ādibhiḥ*—by the *ṛṣis* like Vedavyāsa; *vipraiḥ*—by the *brāhmaṇas; pūjitaiḥ*—being worshiped; *pratipūjitaḥ*—the Lord also reciprocated equally.

TRANSLATION

Lord Śrī Kṛṣṇa then prepared for His departure. He invited the sons of Pāṇḍu, after having been worshiped by the brāhmaṇas, headed by Śrīla Vyāsadeva. The Lord also reciprocated greetings.

PURPORT

Apparently Lord Śrī Kṛṣṇa was a *kṣatriya* and was not worshipable by the *brāhmaṇas.* But the *brāhmaṇas* present there, headed by Śrīla Vyāsadeva, all knew Him to be the Personality of Godhead, and therefore they worshiped Him. The Lord reciprocated the greetings just to honor the social order that a *kṣatriya* is obedient to the orders of the *brāhmaṇas.* Although Lord Śrī Kṛṣṇa was always offered the respects due the Supreme Lord from all responsible quarters, the Lord never deviated from the customary usages between the four orders of society. The Lord purposely observed all these social customs so that others would follow Him in the future.

TEXT 8

गन्तुं कृतमतिर्ब्रह्मन् द्वारकां रथमास्थितः ।
उपलेभेऽभिधावन्तीमुत्तरां भयविह्वलाम् ॥८॥

gantuṁ kṛtamatir brahman
dvārakāṁ ratham āsthitaḥ
upalebhe 'bhidhāvantīm
uttarāṁ bhaya-vihvalām

gantum—just desiring to start; *kṛtamatiḥ*—having decided; *brahman*—O *brāhmaṇa; dvārakām*—towards Dvārakā; *ratham*—on the chariot; *āsthitaḥ*—seated; *upalebhe*—saw; *abhidhāvantīm*—coming hurriedly; *uttarām*—Uttarā; *bhaya-vihvalām*—being afraid.

TRANSLATION

As soon as He seated Himself on the chariot to start for Dvārakā, He saw Uttarā hurrying toward Him in fear.

PURPORT

All the members of the family of the Pāṇḍavas were completely dependent on the protection of the Lord, and therefore the Lord protected all of them in all circumstances. The Lord protects everyone, but one who depends completely upon Him is especially looked after by the Lord. The father is more attentive to the little son who is exclusively dependent on the father.

TEXT 9

उत्तरोवाच
पाहि पाहि महायोगिन् देवदेव जगत्पते।
नान्यं त्वदभयं पश्ये यत्र मृत्युः परस्परम् ॥९॥

uttarovāca
pāhi pāhi mahā-yogin
deva-deva jagat-pate
nānyaṁ tvad abhayaṁ paśye
yatra mṛtyuḥ parasparam

uttarā uvāca—Uttarā said; *pāhi pāhi*—protect, protect; *mahā-yogin*—the greatest mystic; *deva-deva*—the worshipable of the worshiped; *jagat-pate*—O Lord of the universe; *na*—not; *anyam*—anyone else; *tvat*—than You; *abhayam*—fearlessness; *paśye*—do I see; *yatra*—where there is; *mṛtyuḥ*—death; *parasparam*—in the world of duality.

TRANSLATION

Uttarā said: O Lord of lords, Lord of the universe! You are the greatest of mystics. Please protect me, for there is no one else who can save me from the clutches of death in this world of duality.

PURPORT

This material world is the world of duality, in contrast with the oneness of the absolute realm. The world of duality is composed of matter and spirit, whereas the absolute world is complete spirit without any tinge of the material qualities. In the dual world everyone is falsely trying to become the master of the world, whereas in the absolute world the Lord is the absolute Lord, and all others are His absolute servitors. In the world of duality everyone is *envious* of all others, and death is inevitable due to the dual existence of matter and spirit. The Lord is the only shelter of fearlessness for the surrendered soul. One cannot save himself from the cruel hands of death in the material world without having surrendered himself at the lotus feet of the Lord.

TEXT 10

अभिद्रवति मामीश शरस्तप्तायसो विभो।
कामं दहतु मां नाथ मा मे गर्भो निपात्यताम् ॥१०॥

abhidravati mām īśa
śaras taptāyaso vibho
kāmaṁ dahatu māṁ nātha
mā me garbho nipātyatām

abhidravati—coming towards; *mām*—me; *īśa*—O Lord; *śaraḥ*—the arrow; *tapta*—fiery; *ayasaḥ*—iron; *vibho*—O great one; *kāmam*—desire; *dahatu*—let it burn; *mām*—me; *nātha*—O protector; *mā*—not; *me*—my; *garbhaḥ*—embryo; *nipātyatām*—be aborted.

TRANSLATION

O my Lord, You are all-powerful. A fiery iron arrow is coming towards me fast. My Lord, let it burn me personally, if You so desire, but please do not let it burn and abort my embryo. Please do me this favor, my Lord.

PURPORT

This incident took place after the death of Abhimanyu, the husband of Uttarā. Abhimanyu's widow, Uttarā, should have followed the path of her husband, but because she was pregnant, and Mahārāja Parīkṣit, a great devotee of the Lord, was lying in embryo, she was responsible for his protection. The mother of a child has a great responsibility in giving all protection to the child, and therefore Uttarā was not ashamed to express this frankly before Lord Kṛṣṇa. Uttarā was the daughter of a great king, the wife of a great hero, and student of a great devotee, and later she was the mother of a good king also. She was fortunate in every respect.

TEXT 11

सूत उवाच

उपधार्य वचस्तस्या भगवान् भक्तवत्सलः।
अपाण्डवमिदं कर्तुं द्रौणेरस्त्रमबुध्यत ॥११॥

sūta uvāca
upadhārya vacas tasyā
bhagavān bhakta-vatsalaḥ
apāṇḍavam idaṁ kartuṁ
drauṇer astram abudhyata

sūtaḥ uvāca—Sūta Gosvāmī said; *upadhārya*—by hearing her patiently; *vacaḥ*—words; *tasyāḥ*—her; *bhagavān*—the Personality of Godhead; *bhakta-vatsalaḥ*—He who is very much affectionate towards His devotees; *apāṇḍavam*—without the existence of the Pāṇḍavas' descendants; *idam*—this; *kartum*—to do it; *drauṇeḥ*—of the son of Droṇācārya; *astram*—weapon; *abudhyata*—understood.

TRANSLATION

Sūta Gosvāmī said: Having patiently heard her words, Lord Śrī Kṛṣṇa, who is always very affectionate to His devotees, could at once understand that Aśvatthāmā, the son of Droṇācārya, had thrown the brahmāstra to finish the last life in the Pāṇḍava family.

PURPORT

The Lord is impartial in every respect, but still He is inclined towards His devotees because there is a great necessity of this for everyone's well-being. The Pāṇḍava family was a family of devotees, and therefore the Lord wanted them to rule the world. That was the reason He vanquished the rule of the company of Duryodhana and established the rule of Mahārāja Yudhiṣṭhira.

Therefore, He also wanted to protect Mahārāja Parīkṣit, who was lying in embryo. He did not like the idea that the world should be without the Pāṇḍavas, the ideal family of devotees.

TEXT 12

तर्ह्येवाथ मुनिश्रेष्ठ पाण्डवाः पञ्च सायकान्।
आत्मनोऽभिमुखान्दीप्तानालक्ष्यास्त्राण्युपाददुः ॥१२॥

tarhy evātha muni-śreṣṭha
pāṇḍavāḥ pañca sāyakān
ātmano 'bhimukhān dīptān
ālakṣyāstrāṇy upādaduḥ

tarhi—then; *eva*—also; *atha*—therefore; *muni-śreṣṭha*—O chief amongst the *munis; pāṇḍavāḥ*—all the sons of Pāṇḍu; *pañca*—five; *sāyakān*—weapons; *ātmanaḥ*—own selves; *abhimukhān*—towards; *dīptān*—glaring; *ālakṣya*—seeing it; *astrāṇi*—weapons; *upādaduḥ*—took up.

TRANSLATION

O foremost among the great thinkers [munis] [Śaunaka], seeing the glaring brahmāstra proceeding towards them, the Pāṇḍavas took up their five respective weapons.

PURPORT

The *brahmāstras* are finer than the nuclear weapons. Aśvatthāmā discharged the *brahmāstra* simply to kill the Pāṇḍavas, namely the five brothers headed by Mahārāja Yudhiṣṭhira and their only grandson, who was lying within the womb of Uttarā. Therefore the *brahmāstra,* more effective and finer than the atomic weapons, was not as blind as the atomic bombs. When the atomic bombs are discharged they do not discriminate between the target and others. Mainly the atomic bombs do harm to the innocent because there is no control. The *brahmāstra* is not like that. It marks out the target and proceeds accordingly without harming the innocent.

TEXT 13

व्यसनं वीक्ष्य तत्तेषामनन्यविषयात्मनाम्।
सुदर्शनेन स्वास्त्रेण स्वानां रक्षां व्यधाद्विभुः ॥१३॥

vyasanaṁ vīkṣya tat teṣām
ananya-viṣayātmanām
sudarśanena svāstreṇa
svānāṁ rakṣāṁ vyadhād vibhuḥ

vyasanam—great danger; *vīkṣya*—having observed; *tat*—that; *teṣām*—their; *ananya*—no other; *viṣaya*—means; *ātmanām*—thus inclined; *sudarśanena*—by the wheel of Śrī Kṛṣṇa; *sva-astreṇa*—by the weapon; *svānām*—of His own devotees; *rakṣām*—protection; *vyadhāt*—did it; *vibhuḥ*—the Almighty.

TRANSLATION

The almighty Personality of Godhead, Śrī Kṛṣṇa, having observed that a great danger was befalling His unalloyed devotees, who were fully surrendered souls, at once took up His Sudarśana disc to protect them.

PURPORT

The *brahmāstra,* the supreme weapon released by Aśvatthāmā, was something similar to the nuclear weapon but with more radiation and heat. This *brahmāstra* is the product of a more subtle science, being the product of a finer sound, a *mantra* recorded in the *Vedas.* Another advantage of this weapon is that it is not blind like the nuclear weapon because it can be directed only to the target and nothing else. Aśvatthāmā released the weapon just to finish all the male members of Pāṇḍu's family; therefore in one sense it was more dangerous than the atomic bombs because it could penetrate even the most protected place and would never miss the target. Knowing all this, Lord Śrī Kṛṣṇa at once took up His personal weapon to protect His devotees, who did not know anyone other than Kṛṣṇa. In the *Bhagavad-gītā* the Lord has clearly promised that His devotees are never to be vanquished. And He behaves according to the quality or degree of the devotional service rendered by the devotees. Here the word *ananya-viṣayātmanām* is significant. The Pāṇḍavas were cent-percent dependent on the protection of the Lord, although they were all great warriors themselves. But the Lord neglects even the greatest warriors and also vanquishes them in no time. When the Lord saw that there was no time for the Pāṇḍavas to counteract the *brahmāstra* of Aśvatthāmā, He took up His weapon even at the risk of breaking His own vow. Although the Battle of Kurukṣetra was almost finished, still, according to His vow, He should not have taken up His own weapon. But the emergency was more important than the vow. He is better known as the *bhakta-vatsala,* or the lover of His devotee, and thus He preferred to continue as *bhakta-vatsala* than to be a worldly moralist who never breaks his solemn vow.

TEXT 14

अन्तःस्थः सर्वभूतानामात्मा योगेश्वरो हरिः ।
स्वमाययावृणोद्गर्भं वैराट्याः कुरुतन्तवे ॥१४॥

antaḥsthaḥ sarva-bhūtānām
ātmā yogeśvaro hariḥ
sva-māyayāvṛṇod garbhaṁ
vairāṭyāḥ kuru-tantave

antaḥsthaḥ—being within; *sarva*—all; *bhūtānām*—of the living beings; *ātmā*—soul; *yoga-īśvaraḥ*—the Lord of all mysticism; *hariḥ*—the Supreme Lord; *sva-māyayā*—by the personal energy; *āvṛṇot*—covered; *garbham*—embryo; *vairāṭyāḥ*—of Uttarā; *kuru-tantave*—for the progeny of Mahārāja Kuru.

TRANSLATION

The Lord of supreme mysticism, Śrī Kṛṣṇa, resides within everyone's heart as the Paramātmā. As such, just to protect the progeny of the Kuru dynasty, He covered the embryo of Uttarā by His personal energy.

PURPORT

The Lord of supreme mysticism can simultaneously reside within everyone's heart, or even within the atoms, by His Paramātmā feature, His plenary portion. Therefore, from within the body of Uttarā He covered the embryo to save Mahārāja Parīkṣit and protect the progeny of Mahārāja Kuru, of whom King Pāṇḍu was also a descendant. Both the sons of Dhṛtarāṣṭra and those of Pāṇḍu belonged to the same dynasty of Mahārāja Kuru; therefore both of them were generally known as Kurus. But when there were differences between the two families, the sons of Dhṛtarāṣṭra were known as Kurus whereas the sons of Pāṇḍu were known as Pāṇḍavas. Since the sons and grandsons of Dhṛtarāṣṭra were all killed in the Battle of Kurukṣetra, the last son of the dynasty is designated as the son of the Kurus.

TEXT 15

यद्यप्यस्त्रं ब्रह्मशिरस्त्वमोघं चाप्रतिक्रियम्।
वैष्णवं तेज आसाद्य समशाम्यद् भृगूद्वह ॥१५॥

yadyapy astraṁ brahma-śiras
tv amoghaṁ cāpratikriyam
vaiṣṇavaṁ teja āsādya
samaśāmyad bhṛgūdvaha

yadyapi—although; *astram*—weapon; *brahma-śiraḥ*—supreme; *tu*—but; *amogham*—without check; *ca*—and; *apratikriyam*—not to be counteracted; *vaiṣṇavam*—in relation with Viṣṇu; *tejaḥ*—strength; *āsādya*—being confronted with; *samaśāmyat*—was neutralized; *bhṛgu-udvaha*—O glory of the family of Bhṛgu.

TRANSLATION

O Śaunaka, although the supreme brahmāstra weapon released by Aśvatthāmā was irresistible and without check or counteraction, it was neutralized and foiled when confronted by the strength of Viṣṇu [Lord Kṛṣṇa].

PURPORT

In the *Bhagavad-gītā* it is said that the *brahmajyoti,* or the glowing transcendental effulgence, is resting on Lord Śrī Kṛṣṇa. In other words, the glowing effulgence known as *brahma-tejas* is nothing but the rays of the Lord, just as the sun rays are rays of the sun disc. So this Brahma weapon also, although materially irresistible, could not surpass the supreme strength of the Lord. The weapon called *brahmāstra,* released by Aśvatthāmā, was neutralized and foiled by Lord Śrī Kṛṣṇa by His own energy; that is to say, He did not wait for any other's help because He is absolute.

TEXT 16

मा मंस्था ह्येतदाश्चर्यं सर्वाश्चर्यमयेऽच्युते।
य इदं मायया देव्या सृजत्यवति हन्त्यजः ॥१६॥

mā maṁsthā hy etad āścaryaṁ
sarvāścaryamaye 'cyute

ya idaṁ māyayā devyā
sṛjaty avati hanty ajaḥ

mā—do not; *maṁsthāḥ*—think; *hi*—certainly; *etat*—all these; *āścaryam*—wonderful; *sarva*—all; *āścarya-maye*—in the all-mysterious; *acyute*—the infallible; *yaḥ*—one who; *idam*—this (creation); *māyayā*—by His energy; *devyā*—transcendental; *sṛjati*—creates; *avati*—maintains; *hanti*—annihilates; *ajaḥ*—unborn.

TRANSLATION

O brāhmaṇas, do not think this to be especially wonderful in the activities of the mysterious and infallible Personality of Godhead. By His own transcendental energy, He maintains and annihilates all material things, although He Himself is unborn.

PURPORT

The activities of the Lord are always inconceivable to the tiny brain of the living entities. Nothing is impossible for the Supreme Lord, but all His actions are wonderful for us, and thus He is always beyond the range of our conceivable limits. The Lord is the all-powerful, all-perfect Personality of Godhead. The Lord is cent-percent perfect, whereas others, namely Nārāyaṇa, Brahmā, Śiva, the demigods and all other living beings, possess only different percentages of such perfection. No one is equal to or greater than Him. He is unrivaled.

TEXT 17

ब्रह्मतेजोविनिर्मुक्तैरात्मजैः सह कृष्णया ।
प्रयाणाभिमुखं कृष्णमिदमाह पृथा सती ॥१७॥

brahma-tejo-vinirmuktair
ātmajaiḥ saha kṛṣṇayā
prayāṇābhimukhaṁ kṛṣṇam
idam āha pṛthā satī

brahma-tejaḥ—the radiation of the *brahmāstra; vinirmuktaiḥ*—being saved from; *ātma-jaiḥ*—along with her sons; *saha*—with; *kṛṣṇayā*—Draupadī; *prayāṇa*—outgoing; *abhimukham*—towards; *kṛṣṇam*—unto Lord Kṛṣṇa; *idam*—this; *āha*—said; *pṛthā*—Kuntī; *satī*—chaste, devoted to the Lord.

TRANSLATION

Thus saved from the radiation of the brahmāstra, Kuntī, the chaste devotee of the Lord, and her five sons and Draupadī addressed Lord Kṛṣṇa as He started for home.

PURPORT

Kuntī is described herein as *satī,* or chaste, due to her unalloyed devotion to Lord Śrī Kṛṣṇa. Her mind will now be expressed in the following prayers for Lord Kṛṣṇa. A chaste devotee of the Lord does not look to others, namely any other living being or demigod, even for deliverance from danger. That was all along the characteristic of the whole family of the Pāṇḍavas. They knew nothing except Kṛṣṇa, and therefore the Lord was also always ready to help them in all respects and in all circumstances. That is the transcendental nature of the Lord. He reciprocates the dependence of the devotee. One should not, therefore, look for help from imperfect living beings or demigods, but one should look for all help from Lord Kṛṣṇa, who is competent to save His devotees. Such a chaste devotee also never asks the Lord for help, but the Lord, out of His own accord, is always anxious to render it.

TEXT 18

कुन्त्युवाच
नमस्ये पुरुषं त्वाद्यमीश्वरं प्रकृतेः परम्।
अलक्ष्यं सर्वभूतानामन्तर्बहिरवस्थितम् ॥१८॥

kunty uvāca
namasye puruṣaṁ tvādyam
īśvaraṁ prakṛteḥ param
alakṣyaṁ sarva-bhūtānām
antar bahir avasthitam

kuntī uvāca—Śrīmatī Kuntī said; *namasye*—let me bow down; *puruṣam*—the Supreme Person; *tvā*—You; *ādyam*—the original; *īśvaram*—the controller; *prakṛteḥ*—of the material cosmos; *param*—beyond; *alakṣyam*—the invisible; *sarva*—all; *bhūtānām*—of living beings; *antaḥ*—within; *bahiḥ*—without; *avasthitam*—existing.

TRANSLATION

Śrīmatī Kuntī said: O Kṛṣṇa, I offer my obeisances unto You because You are the original personality and are unaffected by the qualities of the

material world. You are existing both within and without everything, yet You are invisible to all.

PURPORT

Śrīmatī Kuntīdevī was quite aware that Kṛṣṇa is the original Personality of Godhead, although He was playing the part of her nephew. Such an enlightened lady could not commit a mistake by offering obeisances unto her nephew. Therefore, she addressed Him as the original *puruṣa* beyond the material cosmos. Although all living entities are also transcendental, they are neither original nor infallible. The living entities are apt to fall down under the clutches of material nature, but the Lord is never like that. In the *Vedas,* therefore, He is described as the chief among all living entities (*nityo nityānāṁ cetanaś cetanānām*). Then again He is addressed as *īśvara,* or the controller. The living entities or the demigods like Candra and Sūrya are also to some extent *īśvara,* but none of them is the supreme *īśvara,* or the ultimate controller. He is the *parameśvara,* or the Supersoul. He is both within and without. Although He was present before Śrīmatī Kuntī as her nephew, He was also within her and everyone else. In the *Bhagavad-gītā* (15.15) the Lord says, "I am situated in everyone's heart, and only due to Me one remembers, forgets and is cognizant, etc. Through all the *Vedas* I am to be known because I am the compiler of the *Vedas,* and I am the teacher of the *Vedānta.*" Queen Kuntī affirms that the Lord, although both within and without all living beings, is still invisible. The Lord is, so to speak, a puzzle for the common man. Queen Kuntī experienced personally that Lord Kṛṣṇa was present before her, yet He entered within the womb of Uttarā to save her embryo from the attack of Aśvatthāmā's *brahmāstra.* Kuntī herself was puzzled about whether Śrī Kṛṣṇa is all-pervasive or localized. In fact, He is both, but He reserves the right of not being exposed to persons who are not surrendered souls. This checking curtain is called the *māyā* energy of the Supreme Lord, and it controls the limited vision of the rebellious soul. It is explained as follows.

TEXT 19

मायाजवनिकाच्छन्नमज्ञाधोक्षजमव्ययम् ।
न लक्ष्यसे मूढदृशा नटो नाट्यधरो यथा ॥१९॥

māyā-javanikācchannam
ajñādhokṣajam avyayam

na lakṣyase mūḍha-dṛśā
naṭo nāṭyadharo yathā

māyā—deluding; *javanikā*—curtain; *ācchannam*—covered by; *ajñā*—ignorant; *adhokṣajam*—beyond the range of material conception (transcendental); *avyayam*—irreproachable; *na*—not; *lakṣyase*—observed; *mūḍha-dṛśā*—by the foolish observer; *naṭaḥ*—artist; *nāṭya-dharaḥ*—dressed as a player; *yathā*—as.

TRANSLATION

Being beyond the range of limited sense perception, You are the eternally irreproachable factor covered by the curtain of deluding energy. You are invisible to the foolish observer, exactly as an actor dressed as a player is not recognized.

PURPORT

In the *Bhagavad-gītā* Lord Śrī Kṛṣṇa affirms that less intelligent persons mistake Him to be an ordinary man like us, and thus they deride Him. The same is confirmed herein by Queen Kuntī. The less intelligent persons are those who rebel against the authority of the Lord. Such persons are known as *asuras.* The *asuras* cannot recognize the Lord's authority. When the Lord Himself appears amongst us, as Rāma, Nṛsiṁha, Varāha or in His original form as Kṛṣṇa, He performs many wonderful acts which are humanly impossible. As we shall find in the Tenth Canto of this great literature, Lord Śrī Kṛṣṇa exhibited His humanly impossible activities even from the days of His lying on the lap of His mother. He killed the Pūtanā witch, although she smeared her breast with poison just to kill the Lord. The Lord sucked her breast like a natural baby, and He sucked out her very life also. Similarly, He lifted the Govardhana Hill, just as a boy picks up a frog's umbrella, and stood several days continuously just to give protection to the residents of Vṛndāvana. These are some of the superhuman activities of the Lord described in the authoritative Vedic literatures like the *Purāṇas, Itihāsas* (histories) and *Upaniṣads.* He has delivered wonderful instructions in the shape of the *Bhagavad-gītā.* He has shown marvelous capacities as a hero, as a householder, as a teacher and as a renouncer. He is accepted as the Supreme Personality of Godhead by such authoritative personalities as Vyāsa, Devala, Asita, Nārada, Madhva, Śaṅkara, Rāmānuja, Śrī Caitanya Mahāprabhu, Jīva

Gosvāmī, Viśvanātha Cakravartī, Bhaktisiddhānta Sarasvatī and all other authorities of the line. He Himself has declared as much in many places of the authentic literatures. And yet there is a class of men with demoniac mentality who are always reluctant to accept the Lord as the Supreme Absolute Truth. This is partially due to their poor fund of knowledge and partially due to their stubborn obstinacy, which results from various misdeeds in the past and present. Such persons could not recognize Lord Śrī Kṛṣṇa even when He was present before them. Another difficulty is that those who depend more on their imperfect senses cannot realize Him as the Supreme Lord. Such persons are like the modern scientist. They want to know everything by their experimental knowledge. But it is not possible to know the Supreme Person by imperfect experimental knowledge. He is described herein as *adhokṣaja,* or beyond the range of experimental knowledge. All our senses are imperfect. We claim to observe everything and anything, but we must admit that we can observe things under certain material conditions only, which are also beyond our control. The Lord is beyond the observation of sense perception. Queen Kuntī accepts this deficiency of the conditioned soul, especially of the woman class, who are less intelligent. For less intelligent men there must be such things as temples, mosques or churches so that they may begin to recognize the authority of the Lord and hear about Him from authorities in such holy places. For less intelligent men, this beginning of spiritual life is essential, and only foolish men decry the establishment of such places of worship, which are required to raise the standard of spiritual attributes for the mass of people. For less intelligent persons, bowing down before the authority of the Lord, as generally done in the temples, mosques or churches, is as beneficial as it is for the advanced devotees to meditate upon Him by active service.

TEXT 20

तथा परमहंसानां मुनीनाममलात्मनाम् ।
भक्तियोगविधानार्थं कथं पश्येम हि स्त्रियः ॥२०॥

tathā paramahaṁsānāṁ
munīnām amalātmanām
bhakti-yoga-vidhānārthaṁ
kathaṁ paśyema hi striyaḥ

tathā—besides that; *paramahaṁsānām*—of the advanced transcendentalists; *munīnām*—of the great philosophers or mental speculators; *amala-ātmanām*—those whose minds are competent to discern between spirit and matter; *bhakti-yoga*—the science of devotional service; *vidhāna-artham*—for executing; *katham*—how; *paśyema*—can observe; *hi*—certainly; *striyaḥ*—women.

TRANSLATION

You Yourself descend to propagate the transcendental science of devotional service unto the hearts of the advanced transcendentalists and mental speculators, who are purified by being able to discriminate between matter and spirit. How, then, can we women know You perfectly?

PURPORT

Even the greatest philosophical speculators cannot have access to the region of the Lord. It is said in the *Upaniṣads* that the Supreme Truth, the Absolute Personality of Godhead, is beyond the range of the thinking power of the greatest philosopher. He is unknowable by great learning or by the greatest brain. He is knowable only by one who has His mercy. Others may go on thinking about Him for years together, yet He is unknowable. This very fact is corroborated by the Queen, who is playing the part of an innocent woman. Women in general are unable to speculate like philosophers, but they are blessed by the Lord because they believe at once in the superiority and almightiness of the Lord, and thus they offer obeisances without reservation. The Lord is so kind that He does not show special favor only to one who is a great philosopher. He knows the sincerity of purpose. For this reason only, women generally assemble in great number in any sort of religious function. In every country and in every sect of religion it appears that the women are more interested than the men. This simplicity of acceptance of the Lord's authority is more effective than showy insincere religious fervor.

TEXT 21

कृष्णाय वासुदेवाय देवकीनन्दनाय च।
नन्दगोपकुमाराय गोविन्दाय नमो नमः ॥२१॥

kṛṣṇāya vāsudevāya
devakī-nandanāya ca
nanda-gopa-kumārāya
govindāya namo namaḥ

kṛṣṇāya—the Supreme Lord; *vāsudevāya*—unto the son of Vasudeva; *devakī-nandanāya*—unto the son of Devakī; *ca*—and; *nanda-gopa*—Nanda and the cowherd men; *kumārāya*—unto their son; *govindāya*—unto the Personality of Godhead, who enlivens the cows and the senses; *namaḥ*—respectful obeisances; *namaḥ*—obeisances.

TRANSLATION

Let me therefore offer my respectful obeisances unto the Lord, who has become the son of Vasudeva, the pleasure of Devakī, the boy of Nanda and the other cowherd men of Vṛndāvana, and the enlivener of the cows and the senses.

PURPORT

The Lord, being thus unapproachable by any material assets, out of unbounded and causeless mercy descends on the earth as He is in order to show His special mercy upon His unalloyed devotees and to diminish the upsurges of the demoniac persons. Queen Kuntī specifically adores the incarnation or descent of Lord Kṛṣṇa above all other incarnations because in this particular incarnation He is more approachable. In the Rāma incarnation He remained a king's son from His very childhood, but in the incarnation of Kṛṣṇa, although He was the son of a king, He at once left the shelter of His real father and mother (King Vasudeva and Queen Devakī) just after His appearance and went to the lap of Yaśodāmayī to play the part of an ordinary cowherd boy in the blessed Vrajabhūmi, which is very sanctified because of His childhood pastimes. Therefore Lord Kṛṣṇa is more merciful than Lord Rāma. He was undoubtedly very kind to Kuntī's brother Vasudeva and the family. Had He not become the son of Vasudeva and Devakī, Queen Kuntī could not claim Him to be her nephew and thus address Kṛṣṇa in parental affection. But Nanda and Yaśodā are more fortunate because they could relish the Lord's childhood pastimes, which are more attractive than all other pastimes. There is no parallel to His childhood pastimes as exhibited at Vrajabhūmi, which are the prototypes of His eternal affairs in the original Kṛṣṇaloka described as the *cintāmaṇi-dhāma* in the *Brahma-saṁhitā.* Lord Śrī Kṛṣṇa descended Himself at Vrajabhūmi with all His transcendental entourage and paraphernalia. Śrī Caitanya Mahāprabhu therefore confirmed that no one is as fortunate as the residents of Vrajabhūmi, and specifically the cowherd girls, who dedicated their everything for the satisfaction of the Lord. His pastimes with Nanda and Yaśodā and His pastimes with the cowherd men and especially with the cowherd boys and the cows have caused Him to be known as Govinda. Lord Kṛṣṇa as Govinda is more inclined to the *brāhmaṇas* and the cows, indicating thereby that human prosperity depends more on these two items, namely brahminical culture and cow protection. Lord Kṛṣṇa is never satisfied where these are lacking.

TEXT 22

नमः पङ्कजनाभाय नमः पङ्कजमालिने ।
नमः पङ्कजनेत्राय नमस्ते पङ्कजाङ्घ्रये ॥२२॥

namaḥ paṅkaja-nābhāya
namaḥ paṅkaja-māline
namaḥ paṅkaja-netrāya
namas te paṅkajāṅghraye

namaḥ—all respectful obeisances; *paṅkaja-nābhāya*—unto the Lord who has a specific depression resembling a lotus flower in the center of His abdomen; *namaḥ*—obeisances; *paṅkaja-māline*—one who is always decorated with a garland of lotus flowers; *namaḥ*—obeisances; *paṅkaja-netrāya*—one whose glance is as cooling as a lotus flower; *namaḥ te*—respectful obeisances unto You; *paṅkaja-aṅghraye*—unto You, the soles of whose feet are engraved with lotus flowers (and who are therefore said to possess lotus feet).

TRANSLATION

My respectful obeisances are unto You, O Lord, whose abdomen is marked with a depression like a lotus flower, who are always decorated with garlands of lotus flowers, whose glance is as cool as the lotus and whose feet are engraved with lotuses.

PURPORT

Here are some of the specific symbolical marks on the spiritual body of the Personality of Godhead which distinguish His body from the bodies of all others. They are all special features of the body of the Lord. The Lord may appear as one of us, but He is always distinct by His specific bodily features. Śrīmatī Kuntī claims herself unfit to see the Lord because of her being a woman. This is claimed because women, *śūdras* (the laborer class) and the *dvija-bandhus,* or the wretched descendants of the higher three classes, are unfit by intelligence to understand transcendental subject matter concerning the spiritual name, fame, attributes, forms, etc., of the Supreme Absolute Truth. Such persons, although they are unfit to enter into the spiritual affairs of the Lord, can see Him as the *arcā-vigraha,* who descends to the material world just to distribute favors to the fallen souls, including the above-mentioned women, *śūdras* and *dvija-bandhus.* Because such fallen souls cannot see anything beyond matter, the Lord condescends to enter into each and every one of the innumerable universes as the Garbhodakaśāyī Viṣṇu, who grows a lotus stem from the lotuslike depression in the center of His transcendental abdomen, and thus Brahmā, the first living being in the universe, is born. Therefore, the Lord is known as the Paṅkajanābhi. The Paṅkajanābhi Lord accepts the *arcā-vigraha* (His transcendental form) in different elements, namely a form within the mind, a form made of wood, a form made of earth, a form made of metal, a form made of jewel, a form made of paint, a form drawn on sand, etc. All such forms of the Lord are always decorated with garlands of lotus flowers, and there should be a soothing atmosphere in the temple of worship to attract the burning attention of the nondevotees always engaged in material wranglings. The meditators worship a form within the mind. Therefore, the Lord is merciful even to the women, *śūdras* and *dvija-bandhus,* provided they agree to visit the temple of worship in different forms made for them. Such temple visitors are not idolaters, as alleged by some men with a poor fund of knowledge. All the great *ācāryas* established such temples of worship in all places just to favor the less intelligent, and one should not pose himself as transcending the stage of temple worship while one is actually in the category of the *śūdras* and the women or less. One should begin to see the Lord from His lotus feet, gradually rising to the thighs, waist, chest and face. One should not try to look at the face of the Lord without being accustomed to seeing the lotus feet of the Lord. Śrīmatī Kuntī, because of her being the aunt of the Lord, did not begin to see the Lord from the lotus feet because the Lord might feel ashamed, and thus Kuntīdevī, just to save a painful situation for the Lord, began to see the Lord just above His lotus feet, i.e., from the waist of the Lord, gradually rising to the face, and then down to the lotus feet. In the round, everything there is in order.

TEXT 23

यथा हृषीकेश खलेन देवकी
कंसेन रुद्धातिचिरं शुचार्पिता ।

विमोचिताहं च सहात्मजा विभो
त्वयैव नाथेन मुहुर्विपद्गणात् ॥२३॥

yathā hṛṣīkeśa khalena devakī
kaṁsena ruddhāticiraṁ śucārpitā
vimocitāhaṁ ca sahātmajā vibho
tvayaiva nāthena muhur vipad-gaṇāt

yathā—as it were; *hṛṣīkeśa*—the master of the senses; *khalena*—by the envious; *devakī*—Devakī (the mother of Śrī Kṛṣṇa); *kaṁsena*—by King Kaṁsa; *ruddhā*—imprisoned; *ati-ciram*—for a long time; *śuca-arpitā*—distressed; *vimocitā*—released; *aham ca*—also myself; *saha-ātma-jā*—along with my children; *vibho*—O great one; *tvayā eva*—by Your Lordship; *nāthena*—as the protector; *muhuḥ*—constantly; *vipat-gaṇāt*—from a series of dangers.

TRANSLATION

O Hṛṣīkeśa, master of the senses and Lord of lords, You have released Your mother, Devakī, who was long imprisoned and distressed by the envious King Kaṁsa, and me and my children from a series of constant dangers.

PURPORT

Devakī, the mother of Kṛṣṇa and sister of King Kaṁsa, was put into prison along with her husband, Vasudeva, because the envious King was afraid of being killed by Devakī's eighth son (Kṛṣṇa). He killed all the sons of Devakī who were born before Kṛṣṇa, but Kṛṣṇa escaped the danger of child-slaughter because He was transferred to the house of Nanda Mahārāja, Lord Kṛṣṇa's foster father. Kuntīdevī, along with her children, was also saved from a series of dangers. But Kuntīdevī was shown far more favor because Lord Kṛṣṇa did not save the other children of Devakī, whereas He saved the children of Kuntīdevī. This was done because Devakī's husband, Vasudeva, was living, whereas Kuntīdevī was a widow, and there was none to help her except Kṛṣṇa. The conclusion is that Kṛṣṇa endows more favor to a devotee who is in greater dangers. Sometimes He puts His pure devotees in such dangers because in that condition of helplessness the devotee becomes more attached to the Lord. The more the attachment is there for the Lord, the more success is there for the devotee.

TEXT 24

विषान्महाग्नेः पुरुषाददर्शना-
दसत्सभाया वनवासकृच्छ्रतः ।
मृधे मृधेऽनेकमहारथास्त्रतो
द्रौण्यस्त्रतश्चास्म हरेऽभिरक्षिताः ॥२४॥

viṣān mahāgneḥ puruṣāda-darśanād
asat-sabhāyā vana-vāsa-kṛcchrataḥ
mṛdhe mṛdhe 'neka-mahārathāstrato
drauṇy-astrataś cāsma hare 'bhirakṣitāḥ

viṣāt—from poison; *mahā-agneḥ*—from the great fire; *puruṣa-ada*—the man-eaters; *darśanāt*—by combating; *asat*—vicious; *sabhāyāḥ*—assembly; *vana-vāsa*—exiled to the forest; *kṛcchrataḥ*—sufferings; *mṛdhe mṛdhe*—again and again in battle; *aneka*—many; *mahā-ratha*—great generals; *astrataḥ*—weapons; *drauṇi*—the son of Droṇācārya; *astrataḥ*—from the weapon of; *ca*—and; *āsma*—indicating past tense; *hare*—O my Lord; *abhirakṣitāḥ*—protected completely.

TRANSLATION

My dear Kṛṣṇa, Your Lordship has protected us from a poisoned cake, from a great fire, from cannibals, from the vicious assembly, from sufferings during our exile in the forest and from the battle where great generals fought. And now You have saved us from the weapon of Aśvatthāmā.

PURPORT

The list of dangerous encounters is submitted herein. Devakī was once put into difficulty by her envious brother, otherwise she was well. But Kuntīdevī and her sons were put into one difficulty after another for years and years together. They were put into trouble by Duryodhana and his party due to the kingdom, and each and every time the sons of Kuntī were saved by the Lord. Once Bhīma was administered poison in a cake, once they were put into the house made of shellac and set afire, and once Draupadī was dragged out, and attempts were made to insult her by stripping her naked in the vicious assembly of the Kurus. The Lord saved Draupadī by supplying an immeasurable length of cloth, and Duryodhana's party failed to see her naked. Similarly, when they were exiled in the forest, Bhīma had to fight with the man-eater demon Hiḍimba Rākṣasa, but the Lord saved him. So it was not finished there. After all these tribulations, there was the great Battle of Kurukṣetra, and Arjuna had to meet such great generals as Droṇa, Bhīṣma and Karṇa, all powerful fighters. And at last, even when everything was done away with, there was the *brahmāstra* released by the son of Droṇācārya to kill the child within the womb of Uttarā, and so the Lord saved the only surviving descendant of the Kurus, Mahārāja Parīkṣit.

TEXT 25

विपदः सन्तु ताः शश्वत्तत्र तत्र जगद्गुरो ।
भवतो दर्शनं यत्स्यादपुनर्भवदर्शनम् ॥२५॥

vipadaḥ santu tāḥ śaśvat
tatra tatra jagad-guro
bhavato darśanaṁ yat syād
apunar bhava-darśanam

vipadaḥ—calamities; *santu*—let there be; *tāḥ*—all; *śaśvat*—again and again; *tatra*—there; *tatra*—and there; *jagat-guro*—O Lord of the universe; *bhavataḥ*—Your; *darśanam*—meeting; *yat*—that which; *syāt*—is; *apunaḥ*—not again; *bhava-darśanam*—seeing repetition of birth and death.

TRANSLATION

I wish that all those calamities would happen again and again so that we could see You again and again, for seeing You means that we will no longer see repeated births and deaths.

PURPORT

Generally the distressed, the needy, the intelligent and the inquisitive, who have performed some pious activities, worship or begin to worship the Lord. Others, who are thriving on misdeeds only, regardless of status, cannot approach the Supreme due to being misled by the illusory energy. Therefore, for a pious person, if there is some calamity there is no other alternative than to take shelter of the lotus feet of the Lord. Constantly remembering the lotus feet of the Lord means preparing for liberation from birth and death. Therefore, even though there are so-called calamities, they are welcome because they give us an opportunity to remember the Lord, which means liberation.

One who has taken shelter of the lotus feet of the Lord, which are accepted as the most suitable boat for crossing the ocean of nescience, can achieve liberation as easily as one leaps over the holes made by the hoofs of a calf. Such persons are meant to reside in the abode of the Lord, and they have nothing to do with a place where there is danger in every step.

This material world is certified by the Lord in the *Bhagavad-gītā* as a dangerous place full of calamities. Less intelligent persons prepare plans to adjust to those calamities without knowing that the nature of this place is itself full of calamities. They have no information of the abode of the Lord, which is full of bliss and without trace of calamity. The duty of the sane person, therefore, is to be undisturbed by worldly calamities, which are sure to happen in all circumstances. Suffering all sorts of unavoidable misfortunes, one should make progress in spiritual realization because that is the mission of human life. The spirit soul is transcendental to all material calamities; therefore, the so-called calamities are called false. A man may see a tiger swallowing him in a dream, and he may cry for this calamity. Actually there is no tiger and there is no suffering; it is simply a case of dreams. In the same way, all calamities of life are said to be dreams. If someone is lucky enough to get in contact with the Lord by devotional service, it is all gain. Contact with the Lord by any one of the nine devotional services is always a forward step on the path going back to Godhead.

TEXT 26

जन्मैश्वर्यश्रुतश्रीभिरेधमानमदः पुमान्।
नैवार्हत्यभिधातुं वै त्वामकिञ्चनगोचरम् ॥२६॥

janmaiśvarya-śruta-śrībhir
edhamāna-madaḥ pumān
naivārhaty abhidhātuṁ vai
tvām akiñcana-gocaram

janma—birth; *aiśvarya*—opulence; *śruta*—education; *śrībhiḥ*—by the possession of beauty; *edhamāna*—progressively increasing; *madaḥ*—intoxication; *pumān*—the human being; *na*—never; *eva*—ever; *arhati*—deserves; *abhidhātum*—to address in feeling; *vai*—certainly; *tvām*—You; *akiñcana gocaram*—one who is approached easily by the materially exhausted man.

TRANSLATION

My Lord, Your Lordship can easily be approached, but only by those who are materially exhausted. One who is on the path of [material] progress, trying to improve himself with respectable parentage, great opulence, high education and bodily beauty, cannot approach You with sincere feeling.

PURPORT

Being materially advanced means taking birth in an aristocratic family and possessing great wealth, an education and attractive personal beauty. All materialistic men are mad after possessing all these material opulences, and this is known as the advancement of material civilization. But the result is that by possessing all these material assets one becomes artificially puffed up, intoxicated by such temporary possessions. Consequently, such materially puffed up persons are incapable of uttering the holy name of the Lord by addressing Him feelingly, "O Govinda, O Kṛṣṇa." It is said in the *śāstras* that by once uttering the holy name of the Lord, the sinner gets rid of a quantity of sins that he is unable to commit. Such is the power of uttering the holy name of the Lord. There is not the least exaggeration in this statement. Actually the Lord's holy name has such powerful potency. But there is a quality to such utterances also. It depends on the quality of feeling. A helpless man can feelingly utter the holy name of the Lord, whereas a man who utters the same holy name in great material satisfaction cannot be so sincere. A materially puffed up person may utter the holy name of the Lord occasionally, but he is incapable of uttering the name in quality. Therefore, the four principles of material advancement, namely (1) high parentage, (2) good wealth, (3) high education and (4) attractive beauty, are, so to speak, disqualifications for progress on the path of spiritual advancement. The material covering of the pure spirit soul is an external feature, as much as fever is an external feature of the unhealthy body. The general process is to decrease the degree of the fever and not to aggravate it by maltreatment. Sometimes it is seen that spiritually advanced persons become materially impoverished. This is no discouragement. On the other hand, such impoverishment is a good sign as much as the falling of temperature is a good sign. The principle of life should be to decrease the degree of material intoxication which leads one to be more and more illusioned about the aim of life. Grossly illusioned persons are quite unfit for entrance into the kingdom of God.

TEXT 27

नमोऽकिंचनवित्ताय निवृत्तगुणवृत्तये।
आत्मारामाय शान्ताय कैवल्यपतये नमः ॥२७॥

namo 'kiñcana-vittāya
nivṛtta-guṇa-vṛttaye
ātmārāmāya śāntāya
kaivalya-pataye namaḥ

namaḥ—all obeisances unto You; *akiñcana-vittāya*—unto the property of the materially impoverished; *nivṛtta*—completely transcendental to the actions of the material modes; *guṇa*—material modes; *vṛttaye*—affection; *ātma-ārāmāya*—one who is self-satisfied; *śāntāya*—the most gentle; *kaivalya-pataye*—unto the master of the monists; *namaḥ*—bowing down.

TRANSLATION

My obeisances are unto You, who are the property of the materially impoverished. You have nothing to do with the actions and reactions of the material modes of nature. You are self-satisfied, and therefore You are the most gentle and are master of the monists.

PURPORT

A living being is finished as soon as there is nothing to possess. Therefore a living being cannot be, in the real sense of the term, a renouncer. A living being renounces something for gaining something more valuable. A student sacrifices his childish proclivities to gain better education. A servant gives up his job for a better job. Similarly, a devotee renounces the material world not for nothing but for something tangible in spiritual value. Śrīla Rūpa Gosvāmī, Sanātana Gosvāmī and Śrīla Raghunātha dāsa Gosvāmī and others gave up their worldly pomp and prosperity for the sake of the service of the Lord. They were big men in the worldly sense. The Gosvāmīs were ministers in the government service of Bengal, and Śrīla Raghunātha dāsa Gosvāmī was the son of a big *zamindar* of his time. But they left everything to gain something superior to what they previously possessed. The devotees are generally without material prosperity, but they have a very secret treasure-house in the lotus feet of the Lord. There is a nice story about Śrīla Sanātana Gosvāmī. He had a touchstone, and this stone was left in a pile of refuse. A needy man took it, but later on wondered why the valuable stone was kept in such a neglected place. He therefore asked Sanātana for the most valuable thing, and then he was given the holy name of the Lord. *Akiñcana* means one who has nothing to give materially. A factual devotee, or *mahātmā,* does not give anything material to anyone because he has already left all material assets. He can, however, deliver the supreme asset, namely the Personality of Godhead, because He is the only property of a factual devotee. The touchstone of Sanātana Gosvāmī, which was thrown in the rubbish, was not the property of the Gosvāmī, otherwise it would not have been kept in such a place. This specific example is given for the neophyte devotees just to convince them that material hankerings and spiritual advancement go ill together. Unless one is able to see everything as spiritual in relation with the Supreme Lord, one must always distinguish between spirit and matter. A spiritual master like Śrīla Sanātana Gosvāmī, although personally able to see everything as spiritual, set this example for us only because we have no such spiritual vision.

Advancement of material vision or material civilization is a great stumbling block for spiritual advancement. Such material advancement entangles the living being in the bondage of a material body followed by all sorts of material miseries. Such material advancement is called *anartha,* or things not wanted. Actually this is so. In the present context of material advancement one uses lipstick at a cost of fifty cents, and there are so many unwanted things which are all products of the material conception of life. By diverting attention to so many unwanted things, human energy is spoiled without achievement of spiritual realization, the prime necessity of human life. The attempt to reach the moon is another example of spoiling energy because even if the moon is reached, the problems of life will not be solved. The devotees of the Lord are called *akiñcanas* because they have practically no material assets. Such material assets are all products of the three modes of material nature. They foil spiritual energy, and thus the less we possess such products of material nature, the more we have a good chance for spiritual progress.

The Supreme Personality of Godhead has no direct connection with material activities. All His acts and deeds, which are exhibited even in this material world, are spiritual and without affection for the modes of material nature. In the *Bhagavad-gītā* the Lord says that all His acts, even His appearance and disappearance in and out of the material world, are transcendental, and one who knows this perfectly shall not take his birth again in this material world, but will go back to Godhead.

The material disease is due to hankering after and lording it over material nature. This hankering is due to an interaction of the three modes of nature, and neither the Lord nor the devotees have attachment for such false enjoyment. Therefore, the Lord and the devotees are called *nivṛtta-guṇa-vṛtti.* The perfect *nivṛtta-guṇa-vṛtti* is the Supreme Lord because He never becomes attracted by the modes of material nature, whereas the living beings have such a tendency. Some of them are entrapped by the illusory attraction of material nature.

Because the Lord is the property of the devotees, and the devotees are the property of the Lord reciprocally, the devotees are certainly transcendental to the modes of material nature. That is a natural conclusion. Such unalloyed devotees are distinct from the mixed devotees who approach the Lord for mitigation of miseries and poverty or because of inquisitiveness and speculation. The unalloyed devotees and the Lord are transcendentally attached to one another. For others, the Lord has nothing to reciprocate, and therefore He is called *ātmārāma,* self-satisfied. Self-satisfied as He is, He is the master of all monists who seek to merge into the existence of the Lord. Such monists merge within the personal effulgence of the Lord called the *brahmajyoti,* but the devotees enter into the transcendental pastimes of the Lord, which are never to be misunderstood as material.

TEXT 28

मन्ये त्वां कालमीशानमनादिनिधनं विभुम् ।
समं चरन्तं सर्वत्र भूतानां यन्मिथः कलिः ॥२८॥

manye tvāṁ kālam īśānam
anādi-nidhanaṁ vibhum
samaṁ carantaṁ sarvatra
bhūtānāṁ yan mithaḥ kaliḥ

manye—I consider; *tvām*—Your Lordship; *kālam*—the eternal time; *īśānam*—the Supreme Lord; *anādi-nidhanam*—without beginning and end; *vibhum*—all-pervading; *samam*—equally merciful; *carantam*—distributing; *sarvatra*—everywhere; *bhūtānām*—of the living beings; *yat mithaḥ*—by intercourse; *kaliḥ*—dissension.

TRANSLATION

My Lord, I consider Your Lordship to be eternal time, the supreme controller, without beginning and end, the all-pervasive one. In

distributing Your mercy, You are equal to everyone. The dissensions between living beings are due to social intercourse.

PURPORT

Kuntīdevī knew that Kṛṣṇa was neither her nephew nor an ordinary family member of her paternal house. She knew perfectly well that Kṛṣṇa is the primeval Lord who lives in everyone's heart as the Supersoul, Paramātmā. Another name of the Paramātmā feature of the Lord is *kāla,* or eternal time. Eternal time is the witness of all our actions, good and bad, and thus resultant reactions are destined by Him. It is no use saying that we do not know why and for what we are suffering. We may forget the misdeed for which we may suffer at this present moment, but we must remember that Paramātmā is our constant companion, and therefore He knows everything, past, present and future. And because the Paramātmā feature of Lord Kṛṣṇa destines all actions and reactions, He is the supreme controller also. Without His sanction not a blade of grass can move. The living beings are given as much freedom as they deserve, and misuse of that freedom is the cause of suffering. The devotees of the Lord do not misuse their freedom, and therefore they are the good sons of the Lord. Others, who misuse freedom, are put into miseries destined by the eternal *kāla.* The *kāla* offers the conditioned souls both happiness and miseries. It is all predestined by eternal time. As we have miseries uncalled-for, so we may have happiness also without being asked, for they are all predestined by *kāla.* No one is therefore either an enemy or friend of the Lord. Everyone is suffering and enjoying the result of his own destiny. This destiny is made by the living beings in course of social intercourse. Everyone here wants to lord it over the material nature, and thus everyone creates his own destiny under the supervision of the Supreme Lord. He is all-pervading and therefore He can see everyone's activities. And because the Lord has no beginning or end, He is known also as the eternal time, *kāla.*

TEXT 29

न वेद कश्चिद्भगवंश्चिकीर्षितं
तवेहमानस्य नृणां विडम्बनम्।
न यस्य कश्चिद्दयितोऽस्ति कर्हिचिद्
द्वेष्यश्च यस्मिन् विषमा मतिर्नृणाम् ॥२९॥

na veda kaścid bhagavaṁś cikīrṣitaṁ
tavehamānasya nṛṇāṁ viḍambanam

na yasya kaścid dayito 'sti karhicid
dveṣyaś ca yasmin viṣamā matir nṛṇām

na—does not; *veda*—know; *kaścit*—anyone; *bhagavan*—O Lord; *cikīrṣitam*—pastimes; *tava*—Your; *īhamānasya*—like the worldly men; *nṛṇām*—of the people in general; *viḍambanam*—misleading; *na*—never; *yasya*—His; *kaścit*—anyone; *dayitaḥ*—object of specific favor; *asti*—there is; *karhicit*—anywhere; *dveṣyaḥ*—object of envy; *ca*—and; *yasmin*—unto Him; *viṣamā*—partiality; *matiḥ*—conception; *nṛṇām*—of the people.

TRANSLATION

O Lord, no one can understand Your transcendental pastimes, which appear to be human and so are misleading. You have no specific object of favor, nor do You have any object of envy. People only imagine that You are partial.

PURPORT

The Lord's mercy upon the fallen souls is equally distributed. He has no one as the specific object of hostility. The very conception of the Personality of Godhead as a human being is misleading. His pastimes *appear* to be exactly like a human being's, but actually they are transcendental and without any tinge of material contamination. He is undoubtedly known as partial to His pure devotees, but in fact He is never partial, as much as the sun is never partial to anyone. By utilizing the sun rays, sometimes even the stones become valuable, whereas a blind man cannot see the sun, although there are enough sun rays before him. Darkness and light are two opposite conceptions, but this does not mean that the sun is partial in distributing its rays. The sun rays are open to everyone, but the capacities of the receptacles differ. Foolish people think that devotional service is flattering the Lord to get special mercy. Factually the pure devotees who are engaged in the transcendental loving service of the Lord are not a mercantile community. A mercantile house renders service to someone in exchange for values. The pure devotee does not render service unto the Lord for such exchange, and therefore the full mercy of the Lord is open for him. Suffering men, needy men, inquisitive persons, or philosophers make temporary connections with the Lord to serve a particular purpose. When the purpose is served, there is no more relation with the Lord. A suffering man, if he is pious at all, prays to the Lord for his recovery. But as soon as the recovery is over, in most cases the suffering man no longer cares to keep any connection with the Lord. The mercy of the Lord is open for him, but he is reluctant to receive it. That is the difference between a pure devotee and a mixed devotee. Those who are completely against the service of the Lord are considered to be in abject darkness, those who ask for the Lord's favor only at the time of necessity are partial recipients of the mercy of the Lord, and those who are cent-percent engaged in the service of the Lord are full recipients of the mercy of the Lord. Such partiality in receiving the Lord's mercy is relative to the recipient, and it is not due to the partiality of the all-merciful Lord.

When the Lord descends on this material world by His all-merciful energy, He plays like a human being, and therefore it appears that the Lord is partial to His devotees only, but that is not a fact. Despite such apparent manifestation of partiality, His mercy is equally distributed. In the Battlefield of Kurukṣetra all persons who died in the fight before the presence of the Lord got salvation without the necessary qualifications because death before the presence of the Lord purifies the passing soul from the effects of all sins, and therefore the dying man gets a place somewhere in the transcendental abode. Somehow or other if someone puts himself open in the sun rays, he is sure to get the requisite benefit both by heat and by ultraviolet rays. Therefore, the conclusion is that the Lord is never partial. It is wrong for the people in general to think of Him as partial.

TEXT 30

जन्म कर्म च विश्वात्मन्नजस्याकर्तुरात्मनः ।
तिर्यङ्नृषिषु यादःसु तदत्यन्तविडम्बनम् ॥३०॥

janma karma ca viśvātmann
ajasyākartur ātmanaḥ
tiryaṅ-nṝṣiṣu yādaḥsu
tad atyanta-viḍambanam

janma—birth; *karma*—activity; *ca*—and; *viśva-ātman*—O soul of the universe; *ajasya*—of the unborn; *akartuḥ*—of the inactive; *ātmanaḥ*—of the vital energy; *tiryak*—animal; *nṛ*—human being; *ṛṣiṣu*—in the sages; *yādaḥsu*—in the water; *tat*—that; *atyanta*—veritable; *viḍambanam*—bewildering.

TRANSLATION

Of course it is bewildering, O soul of the universe, that You work, though You are inactive, and that You take birth, though You are the vital

force and the unborn. You Yourself descend amongst animals, men, sages and aquatics. Verily, this is bewildering.

PURPORT

The transcendental pastimes of the Lord are not only bewildering but also apparently contradictory. In other words, they are all inconceivable to the limited thinking power of the human being. The Lord is the all-prevailing Supersoul of all existence, and yet He appears in the form of a boar amongst the animals, in the form of a human being as Rāma, Kṛṣṇa, etc., in the form of a *ṛṣi* like Nārāyaṇa, and in the form of an aquatic like a fish. Yet it is said that He is unborn, and He has nothing to do. In the *śruti mantra* it is said that the Supreme Brahman has nothing to do. No one is equal to or greater than Him. He has manifold energies, and everything is performed by Him perfectly by automatic knowledge, strength and activity. All these statements prove without any question that the Lord's activities, forms and deeds are all inconceivable to our limited thinking power, and because He is inconceivably powerful, everything is possible in Him. Therefore no one can calculate Him exactly; every action of the Lord is bewildering to the common man. He cannot be understood by the Vedic knowledge, but He can be easily understood by the pure devotees because they are intimately related with Him. The devotees therefore know that although He appears amongst the animals, He is not an animal, nor a man, nor a *ṛṣi,* nor a fish. He is eternally the Supreme Lord, in all circumstances.

TEXT 31

गोप्याददे त्वयि कृतागसि दाम तावद्
या ते दशाश्रुकलिलाञ्जनसम्भ्रमाक्षम्।
वक्त्रं निनीय भयभावनया स्थितस्य
सा मां विमोहयति भीरपि यद्बिभेति ॥३१॥

gopy ādade tvayi kṛtāgasi dāma tāvad
yā te daśāśru-kalilāñjana-sambhramākṣam
vaktraṁ ninīya bhaya-bhāvanayā sthitasya
sā māṁ vimohayati bhīr api yad bibheti

gopī—the cowherd lady (Yaśodā); *ādade*—took up; *tvayi*—on Your; *kṛtāgasi*—creating disturbances (by breaking the butter pot); *dāma*—rope;

tāvat—at that time; *yā*—that which; *te*—Your; *daśā*—situation; *aśru-kalila*—overflooded with tears; *añjana*—ointment; *sambhrama*—perturbed; *akṣam*—eyes; *vaktram*—face; *ninīya*—downwards; *bhaya-bhāvanayā*—by thoughts of fear; *sthitasya*—of the situation; *sā*—that; *mām*—me; *vimohayati*—bewilders; *bhīḥ api*—even fear personified; *yat*—whom; *bibheti*—is afraid.

TRANSLATION

My dear Kṛṣṇa, Yaśodā took up a rope to bind You when You committed an offense, and Your perturbed eyes overflooded with tears, which washed the mascara from Your eyes. And You were afraid, though fear personified is afraid of You. This sight is bewildering to me.

PURPORT

Here is another explanation of the bewilderment created by the pastimes of the Supreme Lord. The Supreme Lord is the Supreme in all circumstances, as already explained. Here is a specific example of the Lord's being the Supreme and at the same time a plaything in the presence of His pure devotee. The Lord's pure devotee renders service unto the Lord out of unalloyed love only, and while discharging such devotional service the pure devotee forgets the position of the Supreme Lord. The Supreme Lord also accepts the loving service of His devotees more relishably when the service is rendered spontaneously out of pure affection, without anything of reverential admiration. Generally the Lord is worshiped by the devotees in a reverential attitude, but the Lord is meticulously pleased when the devotee, out of pure affection and love, considers the Lord to be less important than himself. The Lord's pastimes in the original abode of Goloka Vṛndāvana are exchanged in that spirit. The friends of Kṛṣṇa consider Him one of them. They do not consider Him to be of reverential importance. The parents of the Lord (who are all pure devotees) consider Him a child only. The Lord accepts the chastisements of the parents more cheerfully than the prayers of the Vedic hymns. Similarly, He accepts the reproaches of His fiancees more palatably than the Vedic hymns. When Lord Kṛṣṇa was present in this material world to manifest His eternal pastimes of the transcendental realm of Goloka Vṛndāvana as an attraction for the people in general, He displayed a unique picture of subordination before His foster mother, Yaśodā. The Lord, in His naturally childish playful activities, used to spoil the stocked butter of Mother Yaśodā by breaking the pots and distributing the contents to His friends and playmates, including the celebrated monkeys of Vṛndāvana, who took advantage of the Lord's munificence. Mother Yaśodā saw this, and out of her pure love she wanted to make a show of punishment for her transcendental child. She took a rope and threatened the Lord that she would tie Him up, as is generally done in the ordinary household. Seeing the rope in the hands of Mother Yaśodā, the Lord bowed down His head and began to weep just like a child, and tears rolled down His cheeks, washing off the black ointment smeared about His beautiful eyes. This picture of the Lord is adored by Kuntīdevī because she is conscious of the Lord's supreme position. He is feared often by fear personified, yet He is afraid of His mother, who wanted to punish Him just in an ordinary manner. Kuntī was conscious of the exalted position of Kṛṣṇa, whereas Yaśodā was not. Therefore Yaśodā's position was more exalted than Kuntī's. Mother Yaśodā got the Lord as her child, and the Lord made her forget altogether that her child was the Lord Himself. If Mother Yaśodā had been conscious of the exalted position of the Lord, she would certainly have hesitated to punish the Lord. But she was made to forget this situation because the Lord wanted to make a complete gesture of childishness before the affectionate Yaśodā. This exchange of love between the mother and the son was performed in a natural way, and Kuntī, remembering the scene, was bewildered, and she could do nothing but praise the transcendental filial love. Indirectly Mother Yaśodā is praised for her unique position of love, for she could control even the all-powerful Lord as her beloved child.

TEXT 32

केचिदाहुरजं जातं पुण्यश्लोकस्य कीर्तये।
यदोः प्रियस्यान्ववाये मलयस्येव चन्दनम् ॥३२॥

kecid āhur ajaṁ jātaṁ
puṇya-ślokasya kīrtaye
yadoḥ priyasyānvavāye
malayasyeva candanam

kecit—someone; *āhuḥ*—says; *ajam*—the unborn; *jātam*—being born; *puṇya-ślokasya*—of the great pious king; *kīrtaye*—for glorifying; *yadoḥ*—of King Yadu; *priyasya*—of the dear; *anvavāye*—in the family of; *malayasya*—Malaya hills; *iva*—as; *candanam*—sandalwood.

TRANSLATION

Some say that the Unborn is born for the glorification of pious kings, and others say that He is born to please King Yadu, one of Your dearest devotees. You appear in his family as sandalwood appears in the Malaya hills.

PURPORT

Because the Lord's appearance in this material world is bewildering, there are different opinions about the birth of the Unborn. In the *Bhagavad-gītā* the Lord says that He takes His birth in the material world, although He is the Lord of all creations and He is unborn. So there cannot be any denial of the birth of the Unborn because He Himself establishes the truth. But still there are different opinions as to why He takes His birth. That is also declared in the *Bhagavad-gītā.* He appears by His own internal potency to reestablish the principles of religion and to protect the pious and to annihilate the impious. That is the mission of the appearance of the Unborn. Still, it is said that the Lord is there to glorify the pious King Yudhiṣṭhira. Lord Śrī Kṛṣṇa certainly wanted to establish the kingdom of the Pāṇḍavas for the good of all in the world. When there is a pious king ruling over the world, the people are happy. When the ruler is impious, the people are unhappy. In the age of Kali in most cases the rulers are impious, and therefore the citizens are also continuously unhappy. But in the case of democracy, the impious citizens themselves elect their representative to rule over them, and therefore they cannot blame anyone for their unhappiness. Mahārāja Nala was also celebrated as a great pious king, but he had no connection with Lord Kṛṣṇa. Therefore Mahārāja Yudhiṣṭhira is meant here to be glorified by Lord Kṛṣṇa. The Lord had already glorified King Yadu, having taken birth in his family. Although He is known as Yādava, Yaduvīra, Yadunandana, etc., He is always independent of such obligation. He is just like the sandalwood that grows in the Malaya hills. Trees can grow anywhere and everywhere, yet because the sandalwood trees grow mostly in the area of the Malaya hills, the name sandalwood and the Malaya hills are interrelated. Therefore, the conclusion is that the Lord is ever unborn like the sun, and yet He appears as the sun rises on the eastern horizon. As the sun is never the sun of the eastern horizon, so the Lord is no one's son, but He is the father of everything that be.

TEXT 33

अपरे वसुदेवस्य देवक्यां याचितोऽभ्यगात् ।
अजस्त्वमस्य क्षेमाय वधाय च सुरद्विषाम् ॥३३॥

apare vasudevasya
devakyāṁ yācito 'bhyagāt
ajas tvam asya kṣemāya
vadhāya ca sura-dviṣām

apare—others; *vasudevasya*—of Vasudeva; *devakyām*—of Devakī; *yācitaḥ*—being prayed for; *abhyagāt*—took birth; *ajaḥ*—unborn; *tvam*—You are; *asya*—of him; *kṣemāya*—for the good; *vadhāya*—for the purpose of killing; *ca*—and; *sura-dviṣām*—of those who are envious of the demigods.

TRANSLATION

Others say that since both Vasudeva and Devakī prayed for You, You have taken Your birth as their son. Undoubtedly You are unborn, yet You take Your birth for their welfare and to kill those who are envious of the demigods.

PURPORT

It is also said that Vasudeva and Devakī, in their previous birth as Sutapā and Pṛśni, underwent a severe type of penance to get the Lord as their son, and as a result of such austerities the Lord appeared as their son. It is already declared in the *Bhagavad-gītā* that the Lord appears for the welfare of all people of the world and to vanquish the *asuras,* or the materialistic atheists.

TEXT 34

भारावतारणायान्ये भुवो नाव इवोदधौ।
सीदन्त्या भूरिभारेण जातो ह्यात्मभुवार्थितः ॥३४॥

bhārāvatāraṇāyānye
bhuvo nāva ivodadhau
sīdantyā bhūri-bhāreṇa
jāto hy ātma-bhuvārthitaḥ

bhāra-avatāraṇāya—just to reduce the burden to the world; *anye*—others; *bhuvaḥ*—of the world; *nāvaḥ*—boat; *iva*—like; *udadhau*—on the sea; *sīdantyāḥ*—aggrieved; *bhūri*—extremely; *bhāreṇa*—by the burden; *jātaḥ*—You were born; *hi*—certainly; *ātma-bhuvā*—by Brahmā; *arthitaḥ*—being prayed for.

TRANSLATION

Others say that the world, being overburdened like a boat at sea, is much aggrieved, and that Brahmā, who is Your son, prayed for You, and so You have appeared to diminish the trouble.

PURPORT

Brahmā, or the first living being born just after the creation, is the direct son of Nārāyaṇa. Nārāyaṇa, as Garbhodakaśāyī Viṣṇu, first of all entered the material universe. Without spiritual contact, matter cannot create. This principle was followed from the very beginning of the creation. The Supreme Spirit entered the universe, and the first living being, Brahmā, was born on a lotus flower grown out of the transcendental abdomen of Viṣṇu. Viṣṇu is therefore known as Padmanābha. Brahmā is known as *ātma-bhū* because he was begotten directly from the father without any contact of Mother Lakṣmījī. Lakṣmījī was present near Nārāyaṇa, engaged in the service of the Lord, and still, without contact with Lakṣmījī, Nārāyaṇa begot Brahmā. That is the omnipotency of the Lord. One who foolishly considers Nārāyaṇa like other living beings should take a lesson from this. Nārāyaṇa is not an ordinary living being. He is the Personality of Godhead Himself, and He has all the potencies of all the senses in all parts of His transcendental body. An ordinary living being begets a child by sexual intercourse, and he has no other means to beget a child other than the one designed for him. But Nārāyaṇa, being omnipotent, is not bound to any condition of energy. He is complete and independent to do anything and everything by His various potencies, very easily and perfectly. Brahmā is therefore directly the son of the father and was not put into the womb of a mother. Therefore he is known as *ātma-bhū.* This Brahmā is in charge of further creations in the universe, secondarily reflected by the potency of the Omnipotent. Within the halo of the universe there is a transcendental planet known as Śvetadvīpa, which is the abode of the Kṣīrodakaśāyī Viṣṇu, the Paramātmā feature of the Supreme Lord. Whenever there is trouble in the universe that cannot be solved by the administrative demigods, they approach Brahmājī for a solution, and if it is not to be solved even by Brahmājī, then Brahmājī consults and prays to the Kṣīrodakaśāyī Viṣṇu for an incarnation and solution to the problems. Such a problem arose when Kaṁsa and others were ruling over the earth and the earth became too much overburdened by the misdeeds of the *asuras.* Brahmājī, along with other demigods, prayed at the shore of the Kṣīrodaka Ocean, and they were advised of the descent of Kṛṣṇa as the son of Vasudeva and Devakī. So some people say that the Lord appeared because of the prayers of Brahmājī.

TEXT 35

भवेऽस्मिन् क्लिश्यमानानामविद्याकामकर्मभिः ।
श्रवणस्मरणार्हाणि करिष्यन्निति केचन ॥३५॥

bhave 'smin kliśyamānānām
avidyā-kāma-karmabhiḥ
śravaṇa-smaraṇārhāṇi
kariṣyann iti kecana

bhave—in the material creation; *asmin*—this; *kliśyamānānām*—of those who are suffering from; *avidyā*—nescience; *kāma*—desire; *karmabhiḥ*—by execution of fruitive work; *śravaṇa*—hearing; *smaraṇa*—remembering; *arhāṇi*—worshiping; *kariṣyan*—may perform; *iti*—thus; *kecana*—others.

TRANSLATION

And yet others say that You appeared to rejuvenate the devotional service of hearing, remembering, worshiping and so on in order that the conditioned souls suffering from material pangs might take advantage and gain liberation.

PURPORT

In the *Śrīmad Bhagavad-gītā* the Lord asserts that He appears in every millennium just to reestablish the way of religion. The way of religion is made by the Supreme Lord. No one can manufacture a new path of religion, as is the fashion for certain ambitious persons. The factual way of religion is to accept the Lord as the supreme authority and thus render service unto Him in spontaneous love. A living being cannot help but render service because he is constitutionally made for that purpose. The only function of the living being is to render service to the Lord. The Lord is great, and living beings are subordinate to Him. Therefore, the duty of the living being is just to serve Him only. Unfortunately the illusioned living beings, out of misunderstanding only, become servants of the senses by material desire. This desire is called *avidyā,* or nescience. And out of such desire the living being makes different plans for material enjoyment centered about a perverted sex life. He therefore becomes entangled in the chain of birth and death by transmigrating into different bodies on different planets under the direction of the Supreme Lord. Unless, therefore, one is beyond the boundary of this nescience, one cannot get free from the threefold miseries of material life. That is the law of nature.

The Lord, however, out of His causeless mercy, because He is more merciful to the suffering living beings than they can expect, appears before them and renovates the principles of devotional service comprised of hearing, chanting, remembering, serving, worshiping, praying, cooperating and surrendering unto Him. Adoption of all the above-mentioned items, or any one of them, can help a conditioned soul get out of the tangle of nescience and thus become liberated from all material sufferings created by the living being illusioned by the external energy. This particular type of mercy is bestowed upon the living being by the Lord in the form of Lord Śrī Caitanya Mahāprabhu.

TEXT 36

शृण्वन्ति गायन्ति गृणन्त्यभीक्ष्णशः
स्मरन्ति नन्दन्ति तवेहितं जनाः ।
त एव पश्यन्त्यचिरेण तावकं
भवप्रवाहोपरमं पदाम्बुजम् ॥३६॥

śṛṇvanti gāyanti gṛṇanty abhīkṣṇaśaḥ
smaranti nandanti tavehitaṁ janāḥ
ta eva paśyanty acireṇa tāvakaṁ
bhava-pravāhoparamaṁ padāmbujam

śṛṇvanti—hear; *gāyanti*—chant; *gṛṇanti*—take; *abhīkṣṇaśaḥ*—continuously; *smaranti*—remember; *nandanti*—take pleasure; *tava*—Your; *īhitam*—activities; *janāḥ*—people in general; *te*—they; *eva*—certainly; *paśyanti*—can see; *acireṇa*—very soon; *tāvakam*—Your; *bhava-pravāha*—the current of rebirth; *uparamam*—cessation; *pada-ambujam*—lotus feet.

TRANSLATION

O Kṛṣṇa, those who continuously hear, chant and repeat Your transcendental activities, or take pleasure in others' doing so, certainly see Your lotus feet, which alone can stop the repetition of birth and death.

PURPORT

The Supreme Lord Śrī Kṛṣṇa cannot be seen by our present conditional vision. In order to see Him, one has to change his present vision by developing a different condition of life full of spontaneous love of Godhead. When Śrī Kṛṣṇa was personally present on the face of the globe, not everyone could see Him as the Supreme Personality of Godhead. Materialists like Rāvaṇa, Hiraṇyakaśipu, Kaṁsa, Jarāsandha and Śiśupāla were highly qualified personalities by acquisition of material assets, but they were unable to appreciate the presence of the Lord. Therefore, even though the Lord may be present before our eyes, it is not possible to see Him unless we have the necessary vision. This necessary qualification is developed by the process of devotional service only, beginning with hearing about the Lord from the right sources. The *Bhagavad-gītā* is one of the popular literatures which are generally heard, chanted, repeated, etc., by the people in general, but in spite of such hearing, etc., sometimes it is experienced that the performer of such devotional service does not see the Lord eye to eye. The reason is that the first item, *śravaṇa,* is very important. If hearing is from the right sources, it acts very quickly. Generally people hear from unauthorized persons. Such unauthorized persons may be very learned by academic qualifications, but because they do not follow the principles of devotional service, hearing from them becomes a sheer waste of time. Sometimes the texts are interpreted fashionably to suit their own purposes. Therefore, first one should select a competent and bona fide speaker and then hear from him. When the hearing process is perfect and complete, the other processes become automatically perfect in their own way.

There are different transcendental activities of the Lord, and each and every one of them is competent to bestow the desired result, provided the hearing process is perfect. In the *Bhāgavatam* the activities of the Lord begin from His dealings with the Pāṇḍavas. There are many other pastimes of the Lord in connection with His dealings with the *asuras* and others. And in the Tenth Canto the sublime dealings with His conjugal associates, the *gopīs,* as well as with His married wives at Dvārakā are mentioned. Since the Lord is absolute, there is no difference in the transcendental nature of each and every dealing of the Lord. But sometimes people, in an unauthorized hearing process, take more interest in hearing about His dealings with the *gopīs.* Such an inclination indicates the lusty feelings of the hearer, so a bona fide speaker of the dealings of the Lord never indulges in such hearings. One must hear about the Lord from the very beginning, as in the *Śrīmad-Bhāgavatam* or any other scriptures, and that will help the hearer attain perfection by progressive development. One should not, therefore, consider that His dealings with the Pāṇḍavas are less important than His dealings with the *gopīs.* We must always remember that the Lord is always transcendental to all mundane attachment. In all the above mentioned dealings of the Lord, He is the hero in all circumstances, and hearing about Him or about His devotees or combatants is conducive to spiritual life. It is said that the *Vedas* and *Purāṇas,* etc., are all made to revive our lost relation with Him. Hearing of all these scriptures is essential.

TEXT 37

अप्यद्य नस्त्वं स्वकृतेहित प्रभो
जिहाससि स्वित्सुहृदोऽनुजीविनः ।
येषां न चान्यद्भवतः पदाम्बुजात्
परायणं राजसु योजितांहसाम् ॥३७॥

apy adya nas tvaṁ sva-kṛtehita prabho
jihāsasi svit suhṛdo 'nujīvinaḥ
yeṣāṁ na cānyad bhavataḥ padāmbujāt
parāyaṇaṁ rājasu yojitāṁhasām

api—if; *adya*—today; *naḥ*—us; *tvam*—You; *sva-kṛta*—self-executed; *īhita*—all duties; *prabho*—O my Lord; *jihāsasi*—giving up; *svit*—possibly; *suhṛdaḥ*—intimate friends; *anujīvinaḥ*—living at the mercy of; *yeṣām*—of whom; *na*—nor; *ca*—and; *anyat*—anyone else; *bhavataḥ*—Your; *pada-ambujāt*—from the lotus feet; *parāyaṇam*—dependent; *rājasu*—unto the kings; *yojita*—engaged in; *aṁhasām*—enmity.

TRANSLATION

O my Lord, You have executed all duties Yourself. Are you leaving us today, though we are completely dependent on Your mercy and have no one else to protect us, now when all kings are at enmity with us?

PURPORT

The Pāṇḍavas are most fortunate because with all good luck they were entirely dependent on the mercy of the Lord. In the material world, to be dependent on the mercy of someone else is the utmost sign of misfortune, but in the case of our transcendental relation with the Lord, it is the most fortunate case when we can live completely dependent on Him. The material disease is due to thinking of becoming independent of everything. But the cruel material nature does not allow us to become independent. The false attempt to become independent of the stringent laws of nature is known as material advancement of experimental knowledge. The whole material world is moving on this false attempt of becoming independent of the laws of nature. Beginning from Rāvaṇa, who wanted to prepare a direct staircase to the planets of heaven, down to the present age, they are trying to overcome the laws of nature. They are trying now to approach distant planetary systems by electronic mechanical power. But the highest goal of human civilization is to work hard under the guidance of the Lord and become completely dependent on Him. The highest achievement of perfect civilization is to work with valor but at the same time depend completely on the Lord. The Pāṇḍavas were the ideal executors of this standard of civilization. Undoubtedly they were completely dependent on the good will of Lord Śrī Kṛṣṇa, but they were not idle parasites of the Lord. They were all highly qualified both by personal character and by physical activities. Still they always looked for the mercy of the Lord because they knew that every living being is dependent by constitutional position. The perfection of life is, therefore, to become dependent on the will of the Lord, instead of becoming falsely independent in the material world. Those who try to become falsely independent of the Lord are called *anātha,* or without any guardian, whereas those who are completely dependent on the will of the Lord are called *sanātha,* or those having someone to protect them. Therefore we must try to be *sanātha* so that we can always be protected from the unfavorable condition of material existence. By the deluding power of the external material nature we forget that the material condition of life is the most undesirable perplexity. The *Bhagavad-gītā* therefore directs us (7.19) that after many, many births one fortunate person becomes aware of the fact that Vāsudeva is all in all and that the best way of leading one's life is to surrender unto Him completely. That is the sign of a *mahātmā.* All the members of the Pāṇḍava family were *mahātmās* in household life. Mahārāja Yudhiṣṭhira was the head of these *mahātmās,* and Queen Kuntīdevī was the mother. The lessons of the *Bhagavad-gītā* and all the *Purāṇas,* specifically the *Bhāgavata Purāṇa,* are therefore inevitably connected with the history of the Pāṇḍava *mahātmās.* For them, separation from the Lord was just like the separation of a fish from water. Śrīmatī Kuntīdevī, therefore, felt such separation like a thunderbolt, and the whole prayer of the Queen is to try to persuade the Lord to stay with them. After the Battle of Kurukṣetra, although the inimical kings were killed, their sons and grandsons were still there to deal with the Pāṇḍavas. It is not only the Pāṇḍavas who were put into the condition of enmity, but all of us are always in such a condition, and the best way of living is to become completely dependent on the will of the Lord and thereby overcome all difficulties of material existence.

TEXT 38

के वयं नामरूपाभ्यां यदुभिः सह पाण्डवाः ।
भवतोऽदर्शनं यर्हि हृषीकाणामिवेशितुः ॥३८॥

ke vayaṁ nāma-rūpābhyāṁ
yadubhiḥ saha pāṇḍavāḥ
bhavato 'darśanaṁ yarhi
hṛṣīkāṇām iveśituḥ

ke—who are; *vayam*—we; *nāma-rūpābhyām*—without fame and ability; *yadubhiḥ*—with the Yadus; *saha*—along with; *pāṇḍavāḥ*—and the Pāṇḍavas; *bhavataḥ*—Your; *adarśanam*—absence; *yarhi*—as if; *hṛṣīkāṇām*—of the senses; *iva*—like; *īśituḥ*—of the living being.

TRANSLATION

As the name and fame of a particular body is finished with the disappearance of the living spirit, similarly if You do not look upon us, all our fame and activities, along with the Pāṇḍavas and Yadus, will end at once.

PURPORT

Kuntīdevī is quite aware that the existence of the Pāṇḍavas is due to Śrī Kṛṣṇa only. The Pāṇḍavas are undoubtedly well established in name and fame and are guided by the great King Yudhiṣṭhira, who is morality personified, and the Yadus are undoubtedly great allies, but without the guidance of Lord Kṛṣṇa all of them are nonentities, as much as the senses of the body are useless without the guidance of consciousness. No one should be proud of his prestige, power and fame without being guided by the favor of the Supreme Lord. The living beings are always dependent, and the ultimate dependable object is the Lord Himself. We may, therefore, invent by our advancement of material knowledge all sorts of counteracting material resources, but without being guided by the Lord all such inventions end in fiasco, however strong and stout the reactionary elements may be.

TEXT 39

नेयं शोभिष्यते तत्र यथेदानीं गदाधर।
त्वत्पदैरङ्किता भाति स्वलक्षणविलक्षितैः ॥३९॥

neyaṁ śobhiṣyate tatra
yathedānīṁ gadādhara
tvat-padair aṅkitā bhāti
sva-lakṣaṇa-vilakṣitaiḥ

na—not; *iyam*—this land of our kingdom; *śobhiṣyate*—will appear beautiful; *tatra*—then; *yathā*—as it is now; *idānīm*—how; *gadādhara*—O Kṛṣṇa; *tvat*—Your; *padaiḥ*—by the feet; *aṅkitā*—marked; *bhāti*—is dazzling; *sva-lakṣaṇa*—Your own marks; *vilakṣitaiḥ*—by the impressions.

TRANSLATION

O Gadādhara [Kṛṣṇa], our kingdom is now being marked by the impressions of Your feet, and therefore it appears beautiful. But when You leave, it will no longer be so.

PURPORT

There are certain particular marks on the feet of the Lord which distinguish the Lord from others. The marks of a flag, thunderbolt, and instrument to drive an elephant, umbrella, lotus, disc, etc., are on the bottom of the Lord's feet. These marks are impressed upon the soft dust of the land where the Lord traverses. The land of Hastināpura was thus marked while Lord Śrī Kṛṣṇa was there with the Pāṇḍavas, and the kingdom of the Pāṇḍavas thus flourished by such auspicious signs. Kuntīdevī pointed out these distinguished features and was afraid of ill luck in the absence of the Lord.

TEXT 40

इमे जनपदाः स्वृद्धाः सुपक्वौषधिवीरुधः ।
वनाद्रिनद्युदन्वन्तो ह्येधन्ते तव वीक्षितैः ॥४०॥

ime jana-padāḥ svṛddhāḥ
supakvauṣadhi-vīrudhaḥ
vanādri-nady-udanvanto
hy edhante tava vīkṣitaiḥ

ime—all these; *jana-padāḥ*—cities and towns; *svṛddhāḥ*—flourished; *supakva*—mature; *auṣadhi*—herbs; *vīrudhaḥ*—vegetables; *vana*—forests; *adri*—hills; *nadī*—rivers; *udanvantaḥ*—seas; *hi*—certainly; *edhante*—increasing; *tava*—by You; *vīkṣitaiḥ*—seen.

TRANSLATION

All these cities and villages are flourishing in all respects because the herbs and grains are in abundance, the trees are full of fruits, the rivers are flowing, the hills are full of minerals and the oceans full of wealth. And this is all due to Your glancing over them.

PURPORT

Human prosperity flourishes by natural gifts and not by gigantic industrial enterprises. The gigantic industrial enterprises are products of a godless civilization, and they cause the destruction of the noble aims of human life. The more we go on increasing such troublesome industries to squeeze out the vital energy of the human being, the more there will be unrest and dissatisfaction of the people in general, although a few only can live lavishly by exploitation. The natural gifts such as grains and vegetables, fruits, rivers, the hills of jewels and minerals, and the seas full of pearls are supplied by the order of the Supreme, and as He desires, material nature produces them in abundance or restricts them at times. The natural law is that the human being may take advantage of these godly gifts by nature and satisfactorily flourish on them without being captivated by the exploitative motive of lording it over material nature. The more we attempt to exploit material nature according to our whims of enjoyment, the more we shall become entrapped by the reaction of such exploitative attempts. If we have sufficient grains, fruits, vegetables and herbs, then what is the necessity of running a slaughterhouse and killing poor animals? A man need not kill an animal if he has sufficient grains and vegetables to eat. The flow of river waters fertilizes the fields, and there is more than what we need. Minerals are produced in the hills, and the jewels in the ocean. If the human civilization has sufficient grains, minerals, jewels, water, milk, etc., then why should it hanker after terrible industrial enterprises at the cost of the labor of some unfortunate men? But all these natural gifts are dependent on the mercy of the Lord. What we need, therefore, is to be obedient to the laws of the Lord and achieve the perfection of human life by devotional service. The indications by Kuntīdevī are just to the point. She desires that God's mercy be bestowed upon them so that natural prosperity be maintained by His grace.

TEXT 41

अथ विश्वेश विश्वात्मन् विश्वमूर्ते स्वकेषु मे ।
स्नेहपाशमिमं छिन्धि दृढं पाण्डुषु वृष्णिषु ॥४१॥

atha viśveśa viśvātman
viśva-mūrte svakeṣu me
sneha-pāśam imaṁ chindhi
dṛḍhaṁ pāṇḍuṣu vṛṣṇiṣu

atha—therefore; *viśva-īśa*—O Lord of the universe; *viśva-ātman*—O soul of the universe; *viśva-mūrte*—O personality of the universal form; *svakeṣu*—unto my own kinsmen; *me*—my; *sneha-pāśam*—tie of affection; *imam*—this; *chindhi*—cut off; *dṛḍham*—deep; *pāṇḍuṣu*—for the Pāṇḍavas; *vṛṣṇiṣu*—for the Vṛṣṇis also.

TRANSLATION

O Lord of the universe, soul of the universe, O personality of the form of the universe, please, therefore, sever my tie of affection for my kinsmen, the Pāṇḍavas and the Vṛṣṇis.

PURPORT

A pure devotee of the Lord is ashamed to ask anything in self-interest from the Lord. But the householders are sometimes obliged to ask favors from the Lord, being bound by the tie of family affection. Śrīmatī Kuntīdevī was conscious of this fact, and therefore she prayed to the Lord to cut off the affectionate tie from her own kinsmen, the Pāṇḍavas and the Vṛṣṇis. The Pāṇḍavas are her own sons, and the Vṛṣṇis are the members of her paternal family. Kṛṣṇa was equally related to both the families. Both the families required the Lord's help because both were dependent devotees of the Lord. Śrīmatī Kuntīdevī wished Śrī Kṛṣṇa to remain with her sons the Pāṇḍavas, but by His doing so her paternal house would be bereft of the benefit. All these partialities troubled the mind of Kuntī, and therefore she desired to cut off the affectionate tie.

A pure devotee cuts off the limited ties of affection for his family and widens his activities of devotional service for all forgotten souls. The typical example is the band of six Gosvāmīs, who followed the path of Lord Caitanya. All of them belonged to the most enlightened and cultured rich families of the higher castes, but for the benefit of the mass of population they left their comfortable homes and became mendicants. To cut off all family affection means to broaden the field of activities. Without doing this, no one can be qualified as a *brāhmaṇa,* a king, a public leader or a devotee of the Lord. The Personality of Godhead, as an ideal king, showed this by example. Śrī

Rāmacandra cut off the tie of affection for His beloved wife to manifest the qualities of an ideal king.

Such personalities as a *brāhmaṇa,* a devotee, a king or a public leader must be very broad minded in discharging their respective duties. Śrīmatī Kuntīdevī was conscious of this fact, and being weak she prayed to be free from such bondage of family affection. The Lord is addressed as the Lord of the universe, or the Lord of the universal mind, indicating His all-powerful ability to cut the hard knot of family affection. Therefore, it is sometimes experienced that the Lord, out of His special affinity towards a weak devotee, breaks the family affection by force of circumstances arranged by His all-powerful energy. By doing so He causes the devotee to become completely dependent on Him and thus clears the path for his going back to Godhead.

TEXT 42

त्वयि मेऽनन्यविषया मतिर्मधुपतेऽसकृत्।
रतिमुद्वहतादद्धा गङ्गेवौघमुदन्वति ॥४२॥

tvayi me 'nanya-viṣayā
matir madhu-pate 'sakṛt
ratim udvahatād addhā
gaṅgevaugham udanvati

tvayi—unto You; *me*—my; *ananya-viṣayā*—unalloyed; *matiḥ*—attention; *madhu-pate*—O Lord of Madhu; *asakṛt*—continuously; *ratim*—attraction; *udvahatāt*—may overflow; *addhā*—directly; *gaṅgā*—the Ganges; *iva*—like; *ogham*—flows; *udanvati*—down to the sea.

TRANSLATION

O Lord of Madhu, as the Ganges forever flows to the sea without hindrance, let my attraction be constantly drawn unto You without being diverted to anyone else.

PURPORT

Perfection of pure devotional service is attained when all attention is diverted towards the transcendental loving service of the Lord. To cut off the tie of all other affections does not mean complete negation of the finer elements, like affection for someone else. This is not possible. A living being, whoever he may be, must have this feeling of affection for others because this is a symptom of life. The symptoms of life, such as desire, anger, hankerings, feelings of attraction, etc., cannot be annihilated. Only the objective has to be changed. Desire cannot be negated, but in devotional service the desire is changed only for the service of the Lord in place of desire for sense gratification. The so-called affection for family, society, country, etc., consists of different phases of sense gratification. When this desire is changed for the satisfaction of the Lord, it is called devotional service.

In the *Bhagavad-gītā* we can see that Arjuna desired not to fight with his brothers and relations just to satisfy his own personal desires. But when he heard the message of the Lord, *Śrīmad Bhagavad-gītā,* he changed his decision and served the Lord. And for his doing so, he became a famous devotee of the Lord, for it is declared in all the scriptures that Arjuna attained spiritual perfection by devotional service to the Lord in friendship. The fighting was there, the friendship was there, Arjuna was there, and Kṛṣṇa was there, but Arjuna became a different person by devotional service. Therefore, the prayers of Kuntī also indicate the same categorical changes in activities. Śrīmatī Kuntī wanted to serve the Lord without diversion, and that was her prayer. This unalloyed devotion is the ultimate goal of life. Our attention is usually diverted to the service of something which is nongodly or not in the program of the Lord. When the program is changed into the service of the Lord, that is to say when the senses are purified in relation with the service of the Lord, it is called pure unalloyed devotional service. Śrīmatī Kuntīdevī wanted that perfection and prayed for it from the Lord.

Her affection for the Pāṇḍavas and the Vṛṣṇis is not out of the range of devotional service because the service of the Lord and the service of the devotees are identical. Sometimes service to the devotee is more valuable than service to the Lord. But here the affection of Kuntīdevī for the Pāṇḍavas and the Vṛṣṇis was due to family relation. This tie of affection in terms of material relation is the relation of *māyā* because the relations of the body or the mind are due to the influence of the external energy. Relations of the soul, established in relation with the Supreme Soul, are factual relations. When Kuntīdevī wanted to cut off the family relation, she meant to cut off the relation of the skin. The skin relation is the cause of material bondage, but the relation of the soul is the cause of freedom. This relation of the soul to the soul can be established by the via medium of the relation with the Supersoul. Seeing in the darkness is not seeing. But seeing by the light of the sun means to see the sun and everything else which was unseen in the darkness. That is the way of devotional service.

TEXT 43

श्रीकृष्ण कृष्णसख वृष्ण्यृषभावनिध्रुग्
राजन्यवंशदहनानपवर्गवीर्य ।
गोविन्द गोद्विजसुरार्तिहरावतार
योगेश्वराखिलगुरो भगवन्नमस्ते ॥४३॥

śrī-kṛṣṇa kṛṣṇa-sakha vṛṣṇy-ṛṣabhāvani-dhrug-
rājanya-vaṁśa-dahanānapavarga-vīrya
govinda go-dvija-surārti-harāvatāra
yogeśvarākhila-guro bhagavan namas te

śrī-kṛṣṇa—O Śrī Kṛṣṇa; *kṛṣṇa-sakha*—O friend of Arjuna; *vṛṣṇi*—of descendants of Vṛṣṇi; *ṛṣabha*—O chief; *avani*—the earth; *dhruk*—rebellious; *rājanya-vaṁśa*—dynasties of the kings; *dahana*—O annihilator; *anapavarga*—without deterioration of; *vīrya*—prowess; *govinda*—O proprietor of Golokadhāma; *go*—of the cows; *dvija*—the *brāhmaṇas; sura*—the demigods; *arti-hara*—to relieve distress; *avatāra*—O Lord who descend; *yoga-īśvara*—O master of all mystic powers; *akhila*—universal; *guro*—O preceptor; *bhagavan* —O possessor of all opulences; *namaḥ te*—respectful obeisances unto You.

TRANSLATION

O Kṛṣṇa, O friend of Arjuna, O chief amongst the descendants of Vṛṣṇi, You are the destroyer of those political parties which are disturbing elements on this earth. Your prowess never deteriorates. You are the proprietor of the transcendental abode, and You descend to relieve the distresses of the cows, the brāhmaṇas and the devotees. You possess all mystic powers, and You are the preceptor of the entire universe. You are the almighty God, and I offer You my respectful obeisances.

PURPORT

A summary of the Supreme Lord Śrī Kṛṣṇa is made herein by Śrīmatī Kuntīdevī. The almighty Lord has His eternal transcendental abode where He is engaged in keeping *surabhi* cows. He is served by hundreds and thousands of goddesses of fortune. He descends on the material world to reclaim His devotees and to annihilate the disturbing elements in groups of political parties and kings who are supposed to be in charge of administration work. He creates, maintains and annihilates by His unlimited energies, and still He is always full with prowess and does not deteriorate in potency. The cows, the *brāhmaṇas* and the devotees of the Lord are all objects of His special attention because they are very important factors for the general welfare of living beings.

TEXT 44

सूत उवाच
पृथयेत्थं कलपदैः परिणूताखिलोदयः ।
मन्दं जहास वैकुण्ठो मोहयन्निव मायया ॥४४॥

sūta uvāca
pṛthayetthaṁ kala-padaiḥ
pariṇūtākhilodayaḥ
mandaṁ jahāsa vaikuṇṭho
mohayann iva māyayā

sūtaḥ uvāca—Sūta said; *pṛthayā*—by Pṛthā (Kuntī); *ittham*—this; *kala-padaiḥ*—by chosen words; *pariṇūta*—being worshiped; *akhila*—universal; *udayaḥ*—glories; *mandam*—mildly; *jahāsa*—smiled; *vaikuṇṭhaḥ*—the Lord; *mohayan*—captivating; *iva*—like; *māyayā*—His mystic power.

TRANSLATION

Sūta Gosvāmī said: The Lord, thus hearing the prayers of Kuntīdevī, composed in choice words for His glorification, mildly smiled. That smile was as enchanting as His mystic power.

PURPORT

Anything that is enchanting in the world is said to be a representation of the Lord. The conditioned souls, who are engaged in trying to lord it over the material world, are also enchanted by His mystic powers, but His devotees are enchanted in a different way by the glories of the Lord, and His merciful blessings are upon them. His energy is displayed in different ways, as electrical energy works in manifold capacities. Śrīmatī Kuntīdevī has prayed to the Lord just to enunciate a fragment of His glories. All His devotees worship Him in that way, by chosen words, and therefore the Lord is known as Uttamaśloka. No amount of chosen words is sufficient to enumerate the Lord's glory, and yet He is satisfied by such prayers as the father is satisfied even by the broken linguistic attempts of the growing child. The word *māyā* is used both in the sense of delusion and mercy. Herein the word *māyā* is used in the sense of the Lord's mercy upon Kuntīdevī.

TEXT 45

तां बाढमित्युपामन्त्र्य प्रविश्य गजसाह्वयम् ।
स्त्रियश्च स्वपुरं यास्यन् प्रेम्णा राज्ञा निवारितः ॥४५॥

tāṁ bāḍham ity upāmantrya
praviśya gajasāhvayam
striyaś ca sva-puraṁ yāsyan
premṇā rājñā nivāritaḥ

tām—all those; *bāḍham*—accepted; *iti*—thus; *upāmantrya*—subsequently informed; *praviśya*—entering; *gajasāhvayam*—the palace of Hastināpura; *striyaḥ ca*—other ladies; *sva-puram*—own residence; *yāsyan*—while starting for; *premṇā*—with love; *rājñā*—by the King; *nivāritaḥ*—stopped.

TRANSLATION

Thus accepting the prayers of Śrīmatī Kuntīdevī, the Lord subsequently informed other ladies of His departure by entering the palace of Hastināpura. But upon preparing to leave, He was stopped by King Yudhiṣṭhira, who implored Him lovingly.

PURPORT

No one could make Lord Kṛṣṇa stay at Hastināpura when He decided to start for Dvārakā, but the simple request of King Yudhiṣṭhira that the Lord remain there for a few days more was immediately effective. This signifies that the power of King Yudhiṣṭhira was loving affection, which the Lord could not deny. The almighty God is thus conquered only by loving service and nothing else. He is fully independent in all His dealings, but He voluntarily accepts obligations by the loving affection of His pure devotees.

TEXT 46

व्यासाद्यैरीश्वरेहाज्ञैः कृष्णेनाद्भुतकर्मणा ।
प्रबोधितोऽपीतिहासैर्नाबुध्यत शुचार्पितः ॥४६॥

vyāsādyair īśvarehājñaiḥ
kṛṣṇenādbhuta-karmaṇā

prabodhito 'pītihāsair
nābudhyata śucārpitaḥ

vyāsa-ādyaiḥ—by great sages headed by Vyāsa; *īśvara*—the almighty God; *īhā*—by the will of; *jñaiḥ*—by the learned; *kṛṣṇena*—by Kṛṣṇa Himself; *adbhuta-karmaṇā*—by one who performs all superhuman work; *prabodhitaḥ*—being solaced; *api*—although; *itihāsaiḥ*—by evidences from the histories; *na*—not; *abudhyata*—satisfied; *śucā arpitaḥ*—distressed.

TRANSLATION

King Yudhiṣṭhira, who was much aggrieved, could not be convinced, despite instructions by great sages headed by Vyāsa and the Lord Kṛṣṇa Himself, the performer of superhuman feats, and despite all historical evidence.

PURPORT

The pious King Yudhiṣṭhira was mortified because of the mass massacre of human beings in the Battle of Kurukṣetra, especially on his account. Duryodhana was there on the throne, and he was doing well in his administration, and in one sense there was no need of fighting. But on the principle of justice Yudhiṣṭhira was to replace him. The whole clique of politics centered around this point, and all the kings and residents of the whole world became involved in this fight between the rival brothers. Lord Kṛṣṇa was also there on the side of King Yudhiṣṭhira. It is said in the *Mahābhārata, Ādi-parva* (20) that 640,000,000 men were killed in the eighteen days of the Battle of Kurukṣetra, and some hundreds of thousands were missing. Practically this was the greatest battle in the world within five thousand years.

This mass killing simply to enthrone Mahārāja Yudhiṣṭhira was too mortifying, so he tried to be convinced with evidences from histories by great sages like Vyāsa and the Lord Himself that the fight was just because the cause was just. But Mahārāja Yudhiṣṭhira would not be satisfied, even though he was instructed by the greatest personalities of the time. Kṛṣṇa is designated herein as the performer of superhuman actions, but in this particular instance neither He nor Vyāsa could convince King Yudhiṣṭhira. Does it mean that He failed to be a superhuman actor? No, certainly not. The interpretation is that the Lord as *Īśvara*, or the Supersoul in the hearts of both King Yudhiṣṭhira and Vyāsa, performed still more superhuman action because the Lord desired it. As

Supersoul of King Yudhiṣṭhira, He did not allow the King to be convinced by the words of Vyāsa and others, including Himself, because He desired that the King hear instructions from the dying Bhīṣmadeva, who was another great devotee of the Lord. The Lord wanted that at the last stage of his material existence the great warrior Bhīṣmadeva see Him personally and see his beloved grandchildren, King Yudhiṣṭhira, etc., now situated on the throne, and thus pass away very peacefully. Bhīṣmadeva was not at all satisfied to fight against the Pāṇḍavas, who were his beloved fatherless grandchildren. But the *kṣatriyas* are also very stern people, and therefore he was obliged to take the side of Duryodhana because he was maintained at the expense of Duryodhana. Besides this, the Lord also desired that King Yudhiṣṭhira be pacified by the words of Bhīṣmadeva so that the world could see that Bhīṣmadeva excelled all in knowledge, including the Lord Himself.

TEXT 47

आह राजा धर्मसुतश्चिन्तयन् सुहृदां वधम् ।
प्राकृतेनात्मना विप्राः स्नेहमोहवशं गतः ॥४७॥

āha rājā dharma-sutaś
cintayan suhṛdāṁ vadham
prākṛtenātmanā viprāḥ
sneha-moha-vaśaṁ gataḥ

āha—said; *rājā*—King Yudhiṣṭhira; *dharma-sutaḥ*—the son of Dharma (Yamarāja); *cintayan*—thinking of; *suhṛdām*—of the friends; *vadham*—killing; *prākṛtena*—by material conception only; *ātmanā*—by the self; *viprāḥ*—O *brāhmaṇa; sneha*—affection; *moha*—delusion; *vaśam*—being carried away by; *gataḥ*—having gone.

TRANSLATION

King Yudhiṣṭhira, son of Dharma, overwhelmed by the death of his friends, was aggrieved just like a common, materialistic man. O sages, thus deluded by affection, he began to speak.

PURPORT

King Yudhiṣṭhira, though he was not expected to become aggrieved like a common man, became deluded by worldly affection by the will of the Lord (just as Arjuna was apparently deluded). A man who sees knows well that the living entity is neither the body nor the mind, but is transcendental to the material conception of life. The common man thinks of violence and nonviolence in terms of the body, but that is a kind of delusion. Everyone is duty-bound according to one's occupational duties. A *kṣatriya* is bound to fight for the right cause, regardless of the opposite party. In such discharge of duty, one should not be disturbed by annihilation of the material body, which is only an external dress of the living soul. All this was perfectly known to Mahārāja Yudhiṣṭhira, but by the will of the Lord he became just like a common man because there was another great idea behind this delusion: the King would be instructed by Bhīṣma as Arjuna was instructed by the Lord Himself.

TEXT 48

अहो मे पश्यताज्ञानं हृदि रूढं दुरात्मनः ।
पारक्यस्यैव देहस्य बह्व्यो मेऽक्षौहिणीर्हताः ॥४८॥

aho me paśyatājñānaṁ
hṛdi rūḍhaṁ durātmanaḥ
pārakyasyaiva dehasya
bahvyo me 'kṣauhiṇīr hatāḥ

aho—O; *me*—my; *paśyata*—just see; *ajñānam*—ignorance; *hṛdi*—in the heart; *rūḍham*—situated in; *durātmanaḥ*—of the sinful; *pārakyasya*—meant for others; *eva*—certainly; *dehasya*—of the body; *bahvyaḥ*—many, many; *me*—by me; *akṣauhiṇīḥ*—combination of military phalanxes; *hatāḥ*—killed.

TRANSLATION

King Yudhiṣṭhira said: O my lot! I am the most sinful man! Just see my heart, which is full of ignorance! This body, which is ultimately meant for others, has killed many, many phalanxes of men.

PURPORT

A solid phalanx of 21,870 chariots, 21,870 elephants, 109,650 infantry and 65,600 cavalry is called an *akṣauhiṇī*. And many *akṣauhiṇīs* were killed on the Battlefield of Kurukṣetra. Mahārāja Yudhiṣṭhira, as the most pious king of the world, takes for himself the responsibility for killing such a huge number of living beings because the battle was fought to reinstate him on the throne. This body is, after all, meant for others. While there is life in the body, it is meant for the service of others, and when it is dead it is meant to be eaten by dogs and jackals or maggots. He is sorry because for such a temporary body such a huge massacre was committed.

TEXT 49

बालद्विजसुहृन्मित्रपितृभ्रातृगुरुद्रुहः ।
न मे स्यान्निरयान्मोक्षो ह्यपि वर्षायुतायुतैः ॥४९॥

bāla-dvija-suhṛn-mitra-
pitṛ-bhrātṛ-guru-druhaḥ
na me syān nirayān mokṣo
hy api varṣāyutāyutaiḥ

bāla—boys; *dvi-ja*—the twice-born; *suhṛt*—well-wishers; *mitra*—friends; *pitṛ*—parents; *bhrātṛ*—brothers; *guru*—preceptors; *druhaḥ*—one who has killed; *na*—never; *me*—my; *syāt*—there shall be; *nirayāt*—from hell; *mokṣaḥ*—liberation; *hi*—certainly; *api*—although; *varṣa*—years; *ayuta*—millions; *āyutaiḥ*—being added.

TRANSLATION

I have killed many boys, brāhmaṇas, well-wishers, friends, parents, preceptors and brothers. Though I live millions of years, I will not be relieved from the hell that awaits me for all these sins.

PURPORT

Whenever there is a war, there is certainly a massacre of many innocent living beings, such as boys, *brāhmaṇas* and women, whose killing is considered to be the greatest of sins. They are all innocent creatures, and in all circumstances killing of them is forbidden in the scriptures. Mahārāja Yudhiṣṭhira was aware of these mass killings. Similarly, there were friends, parents and preceptors also on both sides, and all of them were killed. It was simply horrible for him to think of such killing, and therefore he was thinking of residing in hell for millions and billions of years.

TEXT 50

नैनो राज्ञः प्रजाभर्तुर्धर्मयुद्धे वधो द्विषाम् ।
इति मे न तु बोधाय कल्पते शासनं वचः ॥५०॥

naino rājñaḥ prajā-bhartur
dharma-yuddhe vadho dviṣām
iti me na tu bodhāya
kalpate śāsanaṁ vacaḥ

na—never; *enaḥ*—sins; *rājñaḥ*—of the king; *prajā-bhartuḥ*—of one who is engaged in the maintenance of the citizens; *dharma*—for the right cause; *yuddhe*—in the fight; *vadhaḥ*—killing; *dviṣām*—of the enemies; *iti*—all these; *me*—for me; *na*—never; *tu*—but; *bodhāya*—for satisfaction; *kalpate*—they are meant for administration; *śāsanam*—injunction; *vacaḥ*—words of.

TRANSLATION

There is no sin for a king who kills for the right cause, who is engaged in maintaining his citizens. But this injunction is not applicable to me.

PURPORT

Mahārāja Yudhiṣṭhira thought that although he was not actually involved in the administration of the kingdom, which was being carried on well by Duryodhana without harm to the citizens, he caused the killing of so many living beings only for his personal gain of the kingdom from the hands of Duryodhana. The killing was committed not in the course of administration but for the sake of self-aggrandizement, and as such he thought himself responsible for all the sins.

TEXT 51

स्त्रीणां मद्धतबन्धूनां द्रोहो योऽसाविहोत्थितः ।
कर्मभिर्गृहमेधीयैर्नाहं कल्पो व्यपोहितुम् ॥५१॥

strīṇāṁ mad-dhata-bandhūnāṁ
droho yo 'sāv ihotthitaḥ
karmabhir gṛhamedhīyair
nāhaṁ kalpo vyapohitum

strīṇām—of the women; *mat*—by me; *hata-bandhūnām*—of the friends who are killed; *drohaḥ*—enmity; *yaḥ*—that; *asau*—all those; *iha*—herewith; *utthitaḥ*—has accrued; *karmabhiḥ*—by dint of work; *gṛhamedhīyaiḥ*—by persons engaged in material welfare; *na*—never; *aham*—I; *kalpaḥ*—can expect; *vyapohitum*—undoing the same.

TRANSLATION

I have killed many friends of women, and I have thus caused enmity to such an extent that it is not possible to undo it by material welfare work.

PURPORT

The *gṛhamedhīs* are those whose only business is to perform welfare work for the sake of material prosperity. Such material prosperity is sometimes hampered by sinful activities, for the materialist is sure to commit sins, even unintentionally, in the course of discharging material duties. To get relief from such sinful reactions, the *Vedas* prescribe several kinds of sacrifices. It is said in the *Vedas* that by performing the *aśvamedha-yajña* (horse sacrifice) one can get relief from even *brahma-hatyā* (killing of a *brāhmaṇa*).

Yudhiṣṭhira Mahārāja performed this *aśvamedha-yajña*, but he thinks that even by performing such *yajñas* it is not possible to get relief from the great sins committed. In war either the husband or the brother or even the father or sons go to fight. And when they are killed, a fresh enmity is created, and thus a chain of actions and reactions increases which is not possible to be counteracted even by thousands of *aśvamedha-yajñas.*

The way of work (*karma*) is like that. It creates one action and another reaction simultaneously and thus increases the chain of material activities, binding the performer in material bondage. In the *Bhagavad-gītā* (9.27–28) the remedy is suggested that such actions and reactions of the path of work can be checked only when work is done on behalf of the Supreme Lord. The Battle of Kurukṣetra was actually fought by the will of the Supreme Lord Śrī Kṛṣṇa, as it is evident from His version, and only by His will was Yudhiṣṭhira placed on the throne of Hastināpura. Therefore, factually no sin whatsoever touched the Pāṇḍavas, who were only the order carriers of the Lord. For others, who declare war out of personal interest, the whole responsibility lies on them.

TEXT 52

यथा पङ्केन पङ्काम्भः सुरया वा सुराकृतम् ।
भूतहत्यां तथैवैकां न यज्ञैर्मार्ष्टुमर्हति ॥५२॥

yathā paṅkena paṅkāmbhaḥ
surayā vā surākṛtam
bhūta-hatyāṁ tathaivaikāṁ
na yajñair mārṣṭum arhati

yathā—as much as; *paṅkena*—by the mud; *paṅka-ambhaḥ*—water mixed with mud; *surayā*—by wine; *vā*—either; *surākṛtam*—impurity caused by the slight touch of wine; *bhūta-hatyām*—killing of animals; *tathā*—like that; *eva*—certainly; *ekām*—one; *na*—never; *yajñaiḥ*—by the prescribed sacrifices; *mārṣṭum*—to counteract; *arhati*—is worthwhile.

TRANSLATION

As it is not possible to filter muddy water through mud, or purify a wine-stained pot with wine, it is not possible to counteract the killing of men by sacrificing animals.

PURPORT

Aśvamedha-yajñas or *gomedha-yajñas,* sacrifices in which a horse or a bull is sacrificed, were not, of course, for the purpose of killing the animals. Lord Caitanya said that such animals sacrificed on the altar of *yajña* were rejuvenated and a new life was given to them. It was just to prove the efficacy of the hymns of the *Vedas.* By recitation of the hymns of the *Vedas* in the proper way, certainly the performer gets relief from the reactions of sins, but in case of such sacrifices improperly done under inexpert management, surely one has to become responsible for animal sacrifice. In this age of quarrel and hypocrisy there is no possibility of performing the *yajñas* perfectly for want of expert *brāhmaṇas* who are able to conduct such *yajñas.* Mahārāja Yudhiṣṭhira therefore gives a hint to performing sacrifices in the age of Kali. In the Kali-yuga the only sacrifice recommended is the performance of *hari-nāma-yajña* inaugurated by Lord Śrī Caitanya Mahāprabhu. But one should not indulge in animal killing and counteract it by performing the *hari-nāma-yajña.* Those who are devotees of the Lord never kill an animal for self-interest, and (as the Lord ordered Arjuna) they do not refrain from performing the duty of a *kṣatriya.* The whole purpose, therefore, is served when everything is done for the will of the Lord. This is possible only for the devotees.

Thus end the Bhaktivedanta purports of the First Canto, Eighth Chapter, of the Śrīmad-Bhāgavatam, *entitled "Prayers by Queen Kuntī and Parīkṣit Saved."*

CHAPTER NINE

The Passing Away of Bhīṣmadeva in the Presence of Lord Kṛṣṇa

TEXT 1

सूत उवाच
इति भीतः प्रजाद्रोहात्सर्वधर्मविवित्सया ।
ततो विनशनं प्रागाद् यत्र देवव्रतोऽपतत् ॥१॥

sūta uvāca
iti bhītaḥ prajā-drohāt
sarva-dharma-vivitsayā
tato vinaśanaṁ prāgād
yatra deva-vrato 'patat

sūtaḥ uvāca—Śrī Sūta Gosvāmī said; *iti*—thus; *bhītaḥ*—being afraid of; *prajā-drohāt*—because of killing the subjects; *sarva*—all; *dharma*—acts of religion; *vivitsayā*—for understanding; *tataḥ*—thereafter; *vinaśanam*—the place where the fight was held; *prāgāt*—he went; *yatra*—where; *deva-vrataḥ*—Bhīṣmadeva; *apatat*—lay down for passing away.

TRANSLATION

Sūta Gosvāmī said: Being afraid for having killed so many subjects on the Battlefield of Kurukṣetra, Mahārāja Yudhiṣṭhira went to the scene of the massacre. There, Bhīṣmadeva was lying on a bed of arrows, about to pass away.

PURPORT

In this Ninth Chapter, as it is willed by Lord Śrī Kṛṣṇa, Bhīṣmadeva will impart instructions to King Yudhiṣṭhira on the subject of occupational duties. Bhīṣmadeva will also offer his last prayer to the Lord on the verge of passing away from this mortal world and thus become liberated from the bondage of further material engagements. Bhīṣmadeva was endowed with the power of leaving his material body at will, and his lying down on the bed of arrows was his own choice. This passing away of the great warrior attracted the attention of all the contemporary elites, and all of them assembled there to show their feelings of love, respect and affection for the great soul.

TEXT 2

तदा ते भ्रातरः सर्वे सदश्वैः स्वर्णभूषितैः ।
अन्वगच्छन् रथैर्विप्रा व्यासधौम्यादयस्तथा ॥२॥

tadā te bhrātaraḥ sarve
sadaśvaiḥ svarṇa-bhūṣitaiḥ
anvagacchan rathair viprā
vyāsa-dhaumyādayas tathā

tadā—at that time; *te*—all of them; *bhrātaraḥ*—the brothers; *sarve*—all together; *sat-aśvaiḥ*—drawn by first-class horses; *svarṇa*—gold; *bhūṣitaiḥ*—being decorated with; *anvagacchan*—followed one after another; *rathaiḥ*—on the chariots; *viprāḥ*—O *brāhmaṇas; vyāsa*—the sage Vyāsa; *dhaumya*—Dhaumya; *ādayaḥ*—and others; *tathā*—also.

TRANSLATION

At that time all his brothers followed him on beautiful chariots drawn by first-class horses decorated with gold ornaments. With them were Vyāsa and ṛṣis like Dhaumya [the learned priest of the Pāṇḍavas] and others.

TEXT 3

भगवानपि विप्रर्षे रथेन सधनञ्जयः ।
स तैर्व्यरोचत नृपः कुवेर इव गुह्यकैः ॥३॥

bhagavān api viprarṣe
rathena sa-dhanañjayaḥ
sa tair vyarocata nṛpaḥ
kuvera iva guhyakaiḥ

bhagavān—the Personality of Godhead (Śrī Kṛṣṇa); *api*—also; *vipra-ṛṣe*—O sage among the *brāhmaṇas; rathena*—on the chariot; *sa-dhanañjayaḥ*—with Dhanañjaya (Arjuna); *saḥ*—He; *taiḥ*—by them; *vyarocata*—appeared to be highly aristocratic; *nṛpaḥ*—the King (Yudhiṣṭhira); *kuvera*

—Kuvera, the treasurer of the demigods; *iva*—as; *guhyakaiḥ*—companions known as Guhyakas.

TRANSLATION

O sage amongst the brāhmaṇas, Lord Śrī Kṛṣṇa, the Personality of Godhead, also followed, seated on a chariot with Arjuna. Thus King Yudhiṣṭhira appeared very aristocratic, like Kuvera surrounded by his companions [the Guhyakas].

PURPORT

Lord Śrī Kṛṣṇa wanted the Pāṇḍavas to be present before Bhīṣmadeva in the most aristocratic order so that he might be pleased to see them happy at the time of his death. Kuvera is the richest of all the demigods, and herein King Yudhiṣṭhira appeared like him (Kuvera), for the procession along with Śrī Kṛṣṇa was quite appropriate to the royalty of King Yudhiṣṭhira.

TEXT 4

दृष्ट्वा निपतितं भूमौ दिवश्च्युतमिवामरम्।
प्रणेमुः पाण्डवा भीष्मं सानुगाः सह चक्रिणा ॥४॥

dṛṣṭvā nipatitaṁ bhūmau
divaś cyutam ivāmaram
praṇemuḥ pāṇḍavā bhīṣmaṁ
sānugāḥ saha cakriṇā

dṛṣṭvā—thus seeing; *nipatitam*—lying down; *bhūmau*—on the ground; *divaḥ*—from the sky; *cyutam*—fallen; *iva*—like; *amaram*—demigod; *praṇemuḥ*—bowed down; *pāṇḍavāḥ*—the sons of Pāṇḍu; *bhīṣmam*—unto Bhīṣma; *sa-anugāḥ*—with the younger brothers; *saha*—also with; *cakriṇā*—the Lord (carrying the disc).

TRANSLATION

Seeing him [Bhīṣma] lying on the ground, like a demigod fallen from the sky, the Pāṇḍava King Yudhiṣṭhira, along with his younger brothers and Lord Kṛṣṇa, bowed down before him.

PURPORT

Lord Kṛṣṇa was also a younger cousin of Mahārāja Yudhiṣṭhira as well as the intimate friend of Arjuna. But all the family members of the Pāṇḍavas knew

Lord Kṛṣṇa as the Supreme Personality of Godhead. The Lord, although conscious of His supreme position, always behaved in a humanly custom, and so He also bowed down before the dying Bhīṣmadeva as if He were one of the younger brothers of King Yudhiṣṭhira.

TEXT 5

तत्र ब्रह्मर्षयः सर्वे देवर्षयश्च सत्तम।
राजर्षयश्च तत्रासन् द्रष्टुं भरतपुङ्गवम् ॥५॥

tatra brahmarṣayaḥ sarve
devarṣayaś ca sattama
rājarṣayaś ca tatrāsan
draṣṭuṁ bharata-puṅgavam

tatra—there; *brahma-ṛṣayaḥ*—*ṛṣis* among the *brāhmaṇas; sarve*—all; *deva-ṛṣayaḥ*—*ṛṣis* among the demigods; *ca*—and; *sattama*—situated in the quality of goodness; *rāja-ṛṣayaḥ*—*ṛṣis* among the kings; *ca*—and; *tatra*—in that place; *āsan*—were present; *draṣṭum*—just to see; *bharata*—the descendants of King Bharata; *puṅgavam*—the chief of.

TRANSLATION

Just to see the chief of the descendants of King Bharata [Bhīṣma], all the great souls in the universe, namely the ṛṣis amongst the demigods, brāhmaṇas and kings, all situated in the quality of goodness, were assembled there.

PURPORT

The *ṛṣis* are those who have attained perfection by spiritual achievements. Such spiritual achievements can be earned by all, whether one is a king or a mendicant. Bhīṣmadeva himself was also one of the *brahmarṣis* and the chief of the descendants of King Bharata. All *ṛṣis* are situated in the quality of goodness. All of them assembled there on hearing the news of the great warrior's impending death.

TEXTS 6–7

पर्वतो नारदो धौम्यो भगवान् बादरायणः।
बृहदश्वो भरद्वाजः सशिष्यो रेणुकासुतः ॥६॥

वसिष्ठ इन्द्रप्रमदस्त्रितो गृत्समदोऽसितः ।
कक्षीवान् गौतमोऽत्रिश्च कौशिकोऽथ सुदर्शनः ॥ ७ ॥

parvato nārado dhaumyo
bhagavān bādarāyaṇaḥ
bṛhadaśvo bharadvājaḥ
saśiṣyo reṇukā-sutaḥ

vasiṣṭha indrapramadas
trito gṛtsamado 'sitaḥ
kakṣīvān gautamo 'triś ca
kauśiko 'tha sudarśanaḥ

parvataḥ—Parvata Muni; *nāradaḥ*—Nārada Muni; *dhaumyaḥ*—Dhaumya; *bhagavān*—incarnation of Godhead; *bādarāyaṇaḥ*—Vyāsadeva; *bṛhadaśvaḥ*—Bṛhadaśva; *bharadvājaḥ*—Bharadvāja; *sa-śiṣyaḥ*—along with disciples; *reṇukā-sutaḥ*—Paraśurāma; *vasiṣṭhaḥ*—Vasiṣṭha; *indrapramadaḥ*—Indrapramada; *tritaḥ*—Trita; *gṛtsamadaḥ*—Gṛtsamada; *asitaḥ*—Asita; *kakṣīvān*—Kakṣīvān; *gautamaḥ*—Gautama; *atriḥ*—Atri; *ca*—and; *kauśikaḥ*—Kauśika; *atha*—as well as; *sudarśanaḥ*—Sudarśana.

TRANSLATION

All the sages like Parvata Muni, Nārada, Dhaumya, Vyāsa the incarnation of God, Bṛhadaśva, Bharadvāja and Paraśurāma and disciples, Vasiṣṭha, Indrapramada, Trita, Gṛtsamada, Asita, Kakṣīvān, Gautama, Atri, Kauśika and Sudarśana were present.

PURPORT

Parvata Muni is considered to be one of the oldest sages. He is almost always a constant companion of Nārada Muni. They are also spacemen competent to travel in the air without the help of any material vehicle. Parvata Muni is also a *devarṣi,* or a great sage amongst the demigods, like Nārada. He was present along with Nārada at the sacrificial ceremony of Mahārāja Janamejaya, son of Mahārāja Parīkṣit. In this sacrifice all the snakes of the world were to be killed. Parvata Muni and Nārada Muni are called Gandharvas also because they can travel in the air singing the glories of the Lord. Since they can travel in the air, they observed Draupadī's *svayaṁvara* ceremony (selecting of her own husband) from the air. Like Nārada Muni, Parvata Muni also used to visit the royal assembly in the heaven of King Indra. As a Gandharva, sometimes he visited the royal assembly of Kuvera, one of the important demigods. Both Nārada and Parvata were once in trouble with the daughter of Mahārāja Sṛñjaya. Mahārāja Sṛñjaya got the benediction of a son by Parvata Muni.

Nārada Muni is inevitably associated with the narrations of the *Purāṇas.* He is described in the *Bhāgavatam.* In his previous life he was the son of a maidservant, but by good association with pure devotees he became enlightened in devotional service, and in the next life he became a perfect man comparable with himself only. In the *Mahābhārata* his name is mentioned in many places. He is the principal *devarṣi,* or the chief sage among the demigods. He is the son and disciple of Brahmājī, and from him the disciplic succession in the line of Brahmā has been spread. He initiated Prahlāda Mahārāja, Dhruva Mahārāja and many celebrated devotees of the Lord. He initiated even Vyāsadeva, the author of the Vedic literatures, and from Vyāsadeva, Madhvācārya was initiated, and thus the Madhva-sampradāya, in which the Gauḍīya sampradāya is also included, has spread all over the universe. Śrī Caitanya Mahāprabhu belonged to this Madhva-sampradāya; therefore, Brahmājī, Nārada, Vyāsa, down to Madhva, Caitanya and the Gosvāmīs all belonged to the same line of disciplic succession. Nāradajī has instructed many kings from time immemorial. In the *Bhāgavatam* we can see that he instructed Prahlāda Mahārāja while he was in the womb of his mother, and he instructed Vasudeva, father of Kṛṣṇa, as well as Mahārāja Yudhiṣṭhira.

Dhaumya: A great sage who practiced severe penances at Utkocaka Tīrtha and was appointed royal priest of the Pāṇḍava kings. He acted as the priest in many religious functions of the Pāṇḍavas (*saṁskāra*), and also each of the Pāṇḍavas was attended by him at the betrothal of Draupadī. He was present even during the exile of the Pāṇḍavas and used to advise them in circumstances when they were perplexed. He instructed them how to live incognito for one year, and his instructions were strictly followed by the Pāṇḍavas during that time. His name is mentioned also when the general funeral ceremony was performed after the Battle of Kurukṣetra. In the *Anuṣāsana-parva* of *Mahābhārata* (127.15–16), he gave very elaborate religious instructions to Mahārāja Yudhiṣṭhira. He was actually the right type of priest of a householder, for he could guide the Pāṇḍavas on the right path of religion. A priest is meant for guiding the householder progressively in the right path of *āśrama-dharma,* or the occupational duty of a particular caste. There is practically no difference between the family priest and the spiritual master. The sages, saints and *brāhmaṇas* were especially meant for such functions.

Bādarāyaṇa (*Vyāsadeva*): He is known as Kṛṣṇa, Kṛṣṇa-dvaipāyana, Dvaipāyana, Satyavatī-suta, Pārāśarya, Parāśarātmaja, Bādarāyaṇa, Vedavyāsa, etc. He was the son of Mahāmuni Parāśara in the womb of Satyavatī prior to her betrothal with Mahārāja Śantanu, the father of the great general Grandfather Bhīṣmadeva. He is a powerful incarnation of Nārāyaṇa, and he broadcasts the Vedic wisdom to the world. As such, Vyāsadeva is offered respects before one chants the Vedic literature, especially the *Purāṇas.* Śukadeva Gosvāmī was his son, and *ṛṣis* like Vaiśampāyana were his disciples for different branches of the *Vedas.* He is the author of the great epic *Mahābhārata* and the great transcendental literature *Bhāgavatam.* The *Brahma-sūtras*—the *Vedānta-sūtras,* or *Bādarāyaṇa-sūtras*—were compiled by him. Amongst sages he is the most respected author by dint of severe penances. When he wanted to record the great epic *Mahābhārata* for the welfare of all people in the age of Kali, he was feeling the necessity of a powerful writer who could take up his dictation. By the order of Brahmājī, Śrī Gaṇeśajī took up the charge of noting down the dictation on the condition that Vyāsadeva would not stop dictation for a moment. The *Mahābhārata* was thus compiled by the joint endeavor of Vyāsa and Gaṇeśa.

By the order of his mother, Satyavatī, who was later married to Mahārāja Śantanu, and by the request of Bhīṣmadeva, the eldest son of Mahārāja Śantanu by his first wife, the Ganges, he begot three brilliant sons, whose names are Dhṛtarāṣṭra, Pāṇḍu and Vidura. The *Mahābhārata* was compiled by Vyāsadeva after the Battle of Kurukṣetra and after the death of all the heroes of *Mahābhārata.* It was first spoken in the royal assembly of Mahārāja Janamejaya, the son of Mahārāja Parīkṣit.

Bṛhadaśva: An ancient sage who used to meet Mahārāja Yudhiṣṭhira now and then. First of all he met Mahārāja Yudhiṣṭhira at Kāmyavana. This sage narrated the history of Mahārāja Nala. There is another Bṛhadaśva, who is the son of the Ikṣvāku dynasty (*Mahābhārata, Vana-parva* 209.4–5).

Bharadvāja: He is one of the seven great *ṛṣis* and was present at the time of the birth ceremony of Arjuna. The powerful *ṛṣi* sometimes undertook severe penances on the shore of the Ganges, and his *āśrama* is still celebrated at Prayāgadhāma. It is learned that this *ṛṣi,* while taking bath in the Ganges, happened to meet Ghṛtācī, one of the beautiful society girls of heaven, and thus he discharged semen, which was kept and preserved in an earthen pot and from which Droṇa was born. So Droṇācārya is the son of Bharadvāja Muni.

Others say that Bharadvāja the father of Droṇa is a different person from Maharṣi Bharadvāja. He was a great devotee of Brahmā. Once he approached Droṇācārya and requested him to stop the Battle of Kurukṣetra.

Paraśurāma, or *Reṇukāsuta:* He is the son of Maharṣi Jamadagni and Śrīmatī Reṇukā. Thus he is also known as Reṇukāsuta. He is one of the powerful incarnations of God, and he killed the *kṣatriya* community as a whole twenty-one times. With the blood of the *kṣatriyas* he pleased the souls of his forefathers. Later on he underwent severe penances at the Mahendra Parvata. After taking the whole earth from the *kṣatriyas,* he gave it in charity to Kaśyapa Muni. Paraśurāma instructed the *Dhanur-veda,* or the science of fighting, to Droṇācārya because he happened to be a *brāhmaṇa.* He was present during the coronation of Mahārāja Yudhiṣṭhira, and he celebrated the function along with other great *ṛṣis.*

Paraśurāma is so old that he met both Rāma and Kṛṣṇa at different times. He fought with Rāma, but he accepted Kṛṣṇa as the Supreme Personality of Godhead. He also praised Arjuna when he saw him with Kṛṣṇa. When Bhīṣma refused to marry Ambā, who wanted him to become her husband, Ambā met Paraśurāma, and by her request only, he asked Bhīṣmadeva to accept her as his wife. Bhīṣma refused to obey his order, although he was one of the spiritual masters of Bhīṣmadeva. Paraśurāma fought with Bhīṣmadeva when Bhīṣma neglected his warning. Both of them fought very severely, and at last Paraśurāma was pleased with Bhīṣma and gave him the benediction of becoming the greatest fighter in the world.

Vasiṣṭha: The great celebrated sage among the *brāhmaṇas,* well known as the Brahmarṣi Vasiṣṭhadeva. He is a prominent figure in both the *Rāmāyaṇa* and *Mahābhārata* periods. He celebrated the coronation ceremony of the Personality of Godhead Śrī Rāma. He was present also on the Battlefield of Kurukṣetra. He could approach all the higher and lower planets, and his name is also connected with the history of Hiraṇyakaśipu. There was a great tension between him and Viśvāmitra, who wanted his *kāmadhenu,* wish-fulfilling cow. Vasiṣṭha Muni refused to spare his *kāmadhenu,* and for this Viśvāmitra killed his one hundred sons. As a perfect *brāhmaṇa* he tolerated all the taunts of Viśvāmitra. Once he tried to commit suicide on account of Viśvāmitra's torture, but all his attempts were unsuccessful. He jumped from a hill, but the stones on which he fell became a stack of cotton, and thus he was saved. He jumped into the ocean, but the waves washed him ashore. He jumped into the river, but the river also washed him ashore. Thus all his suicide attempts were unsuccessful. He is also one of the seven *ṛṣis* and husband of Arundhatī, the famous star.

Indrapramada: Another celebrated *ṛṣi.*

Trita: One of the three sons of Prajāpati Gautama. He was the third son, and his other two brothers were known as Ekat and Dvita. All the brothers were great sages and strict followers of the principles of religion. By dint of severe penances they were promoted to Brahmaloka (the planet where Brahmājī lives). Once Trita Muni fell into a well. He was an organizing worker of many sacrifices, and as one of the great sages he also came to show respect to Bhīṣmajī at his deathbed. He was one of the seven sages in the Varuṇaloka. He hailed from the Western countries of the world. As such, most probably he belonged to the European countries. At that time the whole world was under one Vedic culture.

Gṛtsamada: One of the sages of the heavenly kingdom. He was a close friend of Indra, the King of heaven, and was as great as Bṛhaspati. He used to visit the royal assembly of Mahārāja Yudhiṣṭhira, and he also visited the place where Bhīṣmadeva breathed his last. Sometimes he explained the glories of Lord Śiva before Mahārāja Yudhiṣṭhira. He was the son of Vitahavya, and he resembled in features the body of Indra. Sometimes the enemies of Indra mistook him to be Indra and arrested him. He was a great scholar of the *Ṛg-veda,* and thus he was highly respected by the *brāhmaṇa* community. He lived a life of celibacy and was powerful in every respect.

Asita: There was a king of the same name, but herein the Asita mentioned is the Asita Devala Ṛṣi, a great powerful sage of the time. He explained to his father 1,500,000 verses from the *Mahābhārata.* He was one of the members in the snake sacrifice of Mahārāja Janamejaya. He was also present during the coronation ceremony of Mahārāja Yudhiṣṭhira along with other great *ṛṣis.* He also gave Mahārāja Yudhiṣṭhira instructions while he was on the Añjana Hill. He was also one of the devotees of Lord Śiva.

Kakṣīvān: One of the sons of Gautama Muni and the father of the great sage Candakausika. He was one of the members of Parliament of Mahārāja Yudhiṣṭhira.

Atri: Atri Muni was a great *brāhmaṇa* sage and was one of the mental sons of Brahmājī. Brahmājī is so powerful that simply by thinking of a son he can have it. These sons are known as *mānasa-putras.* Out of seven *mānasa-putras* of Brahmājī and out of the seven great *brāhmaṇa* sages, Atri was one. In his family the great Pracetās were also born. Atri Muni had two *kṣatriya* sons who became kings. King Arthama is one of them. He is counted as one of the twenty-one *prajāpatis.* His wife's name was Anasūyā, and he helped Mahārāja Parīkṣit in his great sacrifices.

Kauśika: One of the permanent *ṛṣi* members in the royal assembly of Mahārāja Yudhiṣṭhira. He sometimes met Lord Kṛṣṇa. There are several other sages of the same name.

Sudarśana: This wheel which is accepted by the Personality of Godhead (Viṣṇu or Kṛṣṇa) as His personal weapon is the most powerful weapon, greater than the *brahmāstras* or similar other disastrous weapons. In some of the Vedic literatures it is said that Agnideva, the fire god, presented this weapon to Lord Śrī Kṛṣṇa, but factually this weapon is eternally carried by the Lord. Agnideva presented this weapon to Kṛṣṇa in the same way that Rukmiṇī was given by Mahārāja Rukma to the Lord. The Lord accepts such presentations from His devotees, even though such presentations are eternally His property. There is an elaborate description of this weapon in the *Ādi-parva* of the *Mahābhārata.* Lord Śrī Kṛṣṇa used this weapon to kill Śiśupāla, a rival of the Lord. He also killed Śālva by this weapon, and sometimes He wanted His friend Arjuna to use it to kill his enemies (*Mahābhārata, Virāṭa-parva* 56.3).

TEXT 8

अन्ये च मुनयो ब्रह्मन् ब्रह्मरातादयोऽमलाः ।
शिष्यैरुपेता आजग्मुः कश्यपाङ्गिरसादयः ॥८॥

anye ca munayo brahman
brahmarātādayo 'malāḥ
śiṣyair upetā ājagmuḥ
kaśyapāṅgirasādayaḥ

anye—many others; *ca*—also; *munayaḥ*—sages; *brahman*—O *brāhmaṇas; brahmarāta*—Śukadeva Gosvāmī; *ādayaḥ*—and such others; *amalāḥ*—completely purified; *śiṣyaiḥ*—by the disciples; *upetāḥ*—accompanied; *ājagmuḥ*—arrived; *kaśyapa*—Kaśyapa; *āṅgirasa*—Āṅgirasa; *ādayaḥ*—others.

TRANSLATION

And many others like Śukadeva Gosvāmī and other purified souls, Kaśyapa and Āṅgirasa and others, all accompanied by their respective disciples, arrived there.

PURPORT

Śukadeva Gosvāmī (*Brahmarāta*): The famous son and disciple of Śrī Vyāsadeva, who taught him first the *Mahābhārata* and then *Śrīmad-*

Bhāgavatam. Śukadeva Gosvāmī recited 1,400,000 verses of the *Mahābhārata* in the councils of the Gandharvas, Yakṣas and Rākṣasas, and he recited *Śrīmad-Bhāgavatam* for the first time in the presence of Mahārāja Parīkṣit. He thoroughly studied all the Vedic literatures from his great father. Thus he was a completely purified soul by dint of his extensive knowledge in the principles of religion. From *Mahābhārata, Sabhā-parva* (4.11), it is understood that he was also present in the royal assembly of Mahārāja Yudhiṣṭhira and at the fasting of Mahārāja Parīkṣit. As a bona fide disciple of Śrī Vyāsadeva, he inquired from his father very extensively about religious principles and spiritual values, and his great father also satisfied him by teaching him the *yoga* system by which one can attain the spiritual kingdom, the difference between fruitive work and empiric knowledge, the ways and means of attaining spiritual realization, the four *āśramas* (namely the student life, the householder's life, the retired life and the renounced life), the sublime position of the Supreme Personality of Godhead, the process of seeing Him eye to eye, the bona fide candidate for receiving knowledge, the consideration of the five elements, the unique position of intelligence, the consciousness of the material nature and the living entity, the symptoms of the self-realized soul, the working principles of the material body, the symptoms of the influential modes of nature, the tree of perpetual desire, and psychic activities. Sometimes he went to the sun planet with the permission of his father and Nāradajī. Descriptions of his travel in space are given in the *Śānti-parva* of the *Mahābhārata* (332). At last he attained the transcendental realm. He is known by different names like Araṇeya, Aruṇisuta, Vaiyāsaki and Vyāsātmaja.

Kaśyapa: One of the *prajāpatis,* the son of Marīci and one of the sons-in-law of Prajāpati Dakṣa. He is the father of the gigantic bird Garuḍa, who was given elephants and tortoises as eatables. He married thirteen daughters of Prajāpati Dakṣa, and their names are Aditi, Diti, Danu, Kāṣṭhā, Ariṣṭā, Surasā, Ilā, Muni, Krodhavaśā, Tāmrā, Surabhi, Saramā and Timi. He begot many children, both demigods and demons, by those wives. From his first wife, Aditi, all the twelve Ādityas were born; one of them is Vāmana, the incarnation of Godhead. This great sage, Kaśyapa, was also present at the time of Arjuna's birth. He received a presentation of the whole world from Paraśurāma, and later on he asked Paraśurāma to go out of the world. His other name is Ariṣṭanemi. He lives on the northern side of the universe.

Āṅgirasa: He is the son of Maharṣi Aṅgirā and is known as Bṛhaspati, the priest of the demigods. It is said that Droṇācārya was his partial incarnation. Śukrācārya was the spiritual master of the demons, and Bṛhaspati challenged him. His son is Kaca, and he delivered the fire weapon first to Bharadvāja Muni. He begot six sons (like the fire-god) by his wife Candramāsī, one of the reputed stars. He could travel in space, and therefore he could present himself even in the planets of Brahmaloka and Indraloka. He advised the King of heaven, Indra, about conquering the demons. Once he cursed Indra, who thus had to become a hog on the earth and was unwilling to return to heaven. Such is the power of the attraction of the illusory energy. Even a hog does not wish to part with its earthly possessions in exchange for a heavenly kingdom. He was the religious preceptor of the natives of different planets.

TEXT 9

तान् समेतान् महाभागानुपलभ्य वसूत्तमः ।
पूजयामास धर्मज्ञो देशकालविभागवित् ॥९॥

tān sametān mahā-bhāgān
upalabhya vasūttamaḥ
pūjayām āsa dharma-jño
deśa-kāla-vibhāgavit

tān—all of them; *sametān*—assembled together; *mahā-bhāgān*—all greatly powerful; *upalabhya*—having received; *vasu-uttamaḥ*—the best among the Vasus (Bhīṣmadeva); *pūjayām āsa*—welcomed; *dharma-jñaḥ*—one who knows religious principles; *deśa*—place; *kāla*—time; *vibhāga-vit*—one who knows the adjustment of place and time.

TRANSLATION

Bhīṣmadeva, who was the best amongst the eight Vasus, received and welcomed all the great and powerful ṛṣis who were assembled there, for he knew perfectly all the religious principles according to time and place.

PURPORT

Expert religionists know perfectly well how to adjust religious principles in terms of time and place. All the great *ācāryas* or religious preachers or reformers of the world executed their mission by adjustment of religious principles in terms of time and place. There are different climates and situations in different parts of the world, and if one has to discharge his duties to preach the message of the Lord, he must be expert in adjusting things in terms of the time and place. Bhīṣmadeva was one of the twelve great authorities in preaching this cult of devotional service, and therefore he could receive and welcome all the powerful sages assembled there at his deathbed from all parts of the universe. He was certainly unable at that time to welcome and receive them physically because he was neither at his home nor in a normal healthy condition. But he was quite fit by the activities of his sound mind, and therefore he could utter sweet words with hearty expressions, and all of them were well received. One can perform one's duty by physical work, by mind and by words. And he knew well how to utilize them in the proper place, and therefore there was no difficulty for him to receive them, although physically unfit.

TEXT 10

कृष्णं च तत्प्रभावज्ञ आसीनं जगदीश्वरम्।
हृदिस्थं पूजयामास माययोपात्तविग्रहम् ॥१०॥

kṛṣṇaṁ ca tat-prabhāva-jña
āsīnaṁ jagad-īśvaram
hṛdi-sthaṁ pūjayām āsa
māyayopātta-vigraham

kṛṣṇam—unto Lord Śrī Kṛṣṇa; *ca*—also; *tat*—of Him; *prabhāva-jñaḥ*—the knower of the glories (Bhīṣma); *āsīnam*—sitting; *jagat-īśvaram*—the Lord of the universe; *hṛdi-stham*—situated in the heart; *pūjayām āsa*—worshiped; *māyayā*—by internal potency; *upātta*—manifested; *vigraham*—a form.

TRANSLATION

Lord Śrī Kṛṣṇa is situated in everyone's heart, yet He manifests His transcendental form by His internal potency. This very Lord was sitting before Bhīṣmadeva, and since Bhīṣmadeva knew of His glories, he worshiped Him duly.

PURPORT

The Lord's omnipotency is displayed by His simultaneous presence in every place. He is present always in His eternal abode Goloka Vṛndāvana, and still He is present in everyone's heart and even within every invisible atom. When He manifests His eternal transcendental form in the material world, He does so by His internal potency. The external potency, or the material energy, has nothing to do with His eternal form. All these truths were known to Śrī Bhīṣmadeva, who worshiped Him accordingly.

TEXT 11

पाण्डुपुत्रानुपासीनान् प्रश्रयप्रेमसङ्गतान् ।
अभ्याचष्टानुरागाश्रैरन्धीभूतेन चक्षुषा ॥११॥

pāṇḍu-putrān upāsīnān
praśraya-prema-saṅgatān
abhyācaṣṭānurāgāśrair
andhībhūtena cakṣuṣā

pāṇḍu—the late father of Mahārāja Yudhiṣṭhira and his brothers; *putrān*—the sons of; *upāsīnān*—sitting silently nearby; *praśraya*—being overtaken; *prema*—in feelings of love; *saṅgatān*—having gathered; *abhyācaṣṭa*—congratulated; *anurāga*—feelingly; *aśraiḥ*—by tears of ecstasy; *andhībhūtena*—overwhelmed; *cakṣuṣā*—with his eyes.

TRANSLATION

The sons of Mahārāja Pāṇḍu were sitting silently nearby, overtaken with affection for their dying grandfather. Seeing this, Bhīṣmadeva congratulated them with feeling. There were tears of ecstasy in his eyes, for he was overwhelmed by love and affection.

PURPORT

When Mahārāja Pāṇḍu died, his sons were all small children, and naturally they were brought up under the affection of elderly members of the royal family, specifically by Bhīṣmadeva. Later on, when the Pāṇḍavas were grown up, they were cheated by cunning Duryodhana and company, and Bhīṣmadeva, although he knew that the Pāṇḍavas were innocent and were unnecessarily put into trouble, could not take the side of the Pāṇḍavas for political reasons. At the last stage of his life, when Bhīṣmadeva saw his most exalted grandsons, headed by Mahārāja Yudhiṣṭhira, sitting very gently at his side, the great warrior-grandfather could not check his loving tears, which were automatically flowing from his eyes. He remembered the great tribulations suffered by his most pious grandsons. Certainly he was the most satisfied man because of Yudhiṣṭhira's being enthroned in place of Duryodhana, and thus he began to congratulate them.

TEXT 12

अहो कष्टमहोऽन्याय्यं यद्यूयं धर्मनन्दनाः ।
जीवितुं नार्हथ क्लिष्टं विप्रधर्माच्युताश्रयाः ॥१२॥

aho kaṣṭam aho 'nyāyyaṁ
yad yūyaṁ dharma-nandanāḥ
jīvituṁ nārhatha kliṣṭaṁ
vipra-dharmācyutāśrayāḥ

aho—oh; *kaṣṭam*—what terrible sufferings; *aho*—oh; *anyāyyam*—what terrible injustice; *yat*—because; *yūyam*—all of you good souls; *dharma-nandanāḥ*—sons of religion personified; *jīvitum*—to remain alive; *na*—never; *arhatha*—deserve; *kliṣṭam*—suffering; *vipra*—*brāhmaṇas; dharma*—piety; *acyuta*—God; *āśrayāḥ*—being protected by.

TRANSLATION

Bhīṣmadeva said: Oh, what terrible sufferings and what terrible injustices you good souls suffer for being the sons of religion personified. You did not deserve to remain alive under those tribulations, yet you were protected by the brāhmaṇas, God and religion.

PURPORT

Mahārāja Yudhiṣṭhira was disturbed due to the great massacre in the Battle of Kurukṣetra. Bhīṣmadeva could understand this, and therefore he spoke first of the terrible sufferings of Mahārāja Yudhiṣṭhira. He was put into difficulty by injustice only, and the Battle of Kurukṣetra was fought just to counteract this injustice. Therefore, he should not regret the great massacre. He wanted to point out particularly that they were always protected by the *brāhmaṇas,* the Lord and religious principles. As long as they were protected by these three important items, there was no cause of disappointment. Thus Bhīṣmadeva encouraged Mahārāja Yudhiṣṭhira to dissipate his despondency. As long as a person is fully in cooperation with the wishes of the Lord, guided by the bona fide *brāhmaṇas* and Vaiṣṇavas and strictly following religious principles, one has no cause for despondency, however trying the circumstances of life. Bhīṣmadeva, as one of the authorities in the line, wanted to impress this point upon the Pāṇḍavas.

TEXT 13

संस्थितेऽतिरथे पाण्डौ पृथा बालप्रजा वधूः ।
युष्मत्कृते बहून् क्लेशान् प्राप्ता तोकवती मुहुः ॥१३॥

saṁsthite 'tirathe pāṇḍau
pṛthā bāla-prajā vadhūḥ
yuṣmat-kṛte bahūn kleśān
prāptā tokavatī muhuḥ

saṁsthite—after the demise; *ati-rathe*—of the great general; *pāṇḍau*—Pāṇḍu; *pṛthā*—Kuntī; *bāla-prajā*—having young children; *vadhūḥ*—my daughter-in-law; *yuṣmat-kṛte*—on your account; *bahūn*—multifarious; *kleśān*—afflictions; *prāptā*—underwent; *toka-vatī*—in spite of having grown-up boys; *muhuḥ*—constantly.

TRANSLATION

As far as my daughter-in-law Kuntī is concerned, upon the great General Pāṇḍu's death, she became a widow with many children, and therefore she suffered greatly. And when you were grown up she suffered a great deal also because of your actions.

PURPORT

The sufferings of Kuntīdevī are doubly lamented. She suffered greatly because of early widowhood and to get her minor children brought up in the royal family. And when her children were grown up, she continued to suffer because of her sons' actions. So her sufferings continued. This means that she was destined to suffer by providence, and this one has to tolerate without being disturbed.

TEXT 14

सर्वं कालकृतं मन्ये भवतां च यदप्रियम् ।
सपालो यद्वशे लोको वायोरिव घनावलिः ॥१४॥

sarvaṁ kāla-kṛtaṁ manye
bhavatāṁ ca yad-apriyam
sapālo yad-vaśe loko
vāyor iva ghanāvaliḥ

sarvam—all this; *kāla-kṛtam*—done by inevitable time; *manye*—I think; *bhavatām ca*—for you also; *yat*—whatever; *apriyam*—detestable; *sa-pālaḥ*—with the rulers; *yat-vaśe*—under the control of that time; *lokaḥ*—everyone in every planet; *vāyoḥ*—the wind carries; *iva*—as; *ghana-āvaliḥ*—a line of clouds.

TRANSLATION

In my opinion, this is all due to inevitable time, under whose control everyone in every planet is carried, just as the clouds are carried by the wind.

PURPORT

There is control by time all over the space within the universe, as there is [illegible] the planets. All the big gigantic planets, including the [illegible] carried by the [illegible] *kāla,* a forceful representa[illegible] Yudhiṣṭhira should not be sorry for the inconceivable action of time. [illegible] has to bear the actions and reactions of time as long as one is within the conditions of the material world. Yudhiṣṭhira should not think that he had committed sins in his previous birth and is suffering the consequence. Even the most pious has to suffer the condition of material nature. But a pious man is faithful to the Lord, for he is guided by the bona fide *brāhmaṇa* and Vaiṣṇava following the religious principles. These three guiding principles should be the aim of life. One should not be disturbed by the tricks of eternal time. Even the great controller of the universe, Brahmājī, is also under the control of that time; therefore, one should not grudge being thus controlled by time despite being a true follower of religious principles.

TEXT 15

यत्र धर्मसुतो राजा गदापाणिर्वृकोदरः ।
कृष्णोऽस्त्री गाण्डिवं चापं सुहृत्कृष्णस्ततो विपत् ॥१५॥

yatra dharma-suto rājā
gadā-pāṇir vṛkodaraḥ
kṛṣṇo 'strī gāṇḍivaṁ cāpaṁ
suhṛt kṛṣṇas tato vipat

yatra—where there is; *dharma-sutaḥ*—the son of Dharmarāja; *rājā*—the King; *gadā-pāṇiḥ*—with his mighty club in hand; *vṛkodaraḥ*—Bhīma; *kṛṣṇaḥ*—Arjuna; *astrī*—carrier of the weapon; *gāṇḍivam*—Gāṇḍīva; *cāpam*—bow; *suhṛt*—well-wisher; *kṛṣṇaḥ*—Lord Kṛṣṇa, the Personality of Godhead; *tataḥ*—thereof; *vipat*—reverse.

TRANSLATION

O how wonderful is the influence of inevitable time. It is irreversible—otherwise, how can there be reverses in the presence of King Yudhiṣṭhira, the son of the demigod controlling religion; Bhīma, the great fighter with a club; the great bowman Arjuna with his mighty weapon Gāṇḍīva; and above all, the Lord, the direct well-wisher of the Pāṇḍavas?

PURPORT

As far as the material or spiritual resources were required, there was no scarcity in the case of the Pāṇḍavas. Materially they were well equipped because two great warriors, namely Bhīma and Arjuna, were there. Spiritually the King himself was the symbol of religion, and above all of them the Personality of Godhead, Lord Śrī Kṛṣṇa, was personally concerned with their affairs as the well-wisher. And yet there were so many reverses on the side of the Pāṇḍavas. Despite the power of pious acts, the power of personalities, the power of expert management and the power of weapons under the direct supervision of Lord Kṛṣṇa, the Pāṇḍavas suffered so many practical reverses, which can only be explained as due to the influence of *kāla,* inevitable time. *Kāla* is identical with the Lord Himself, and therefore the influence of *kāla* indicates the inexplicable wish of the Lord Himself. There is nothing to be lamented when a matter is beyond the control of any human being.

TEXT 16

न ह्यस्य कर्हिचिद्राजन् पुमान् वेद विधित्सितम् ।
यद्विजिज्ञासया युक्ता मुह्यन्ति कवयोऽपि हि ॥१६॥

na hy asya karhicid rājan
pumān veda vidhitsitam
yad vijijñāsayā yuktā
muhyanti kavayo 'pi hi

na—never; *hi*—certainly; *asya*—His; *karhicit*—whatsoever; *rājan*—O King; *pumān*—anyone; *veda*—knows; *vidhitsitam*—plan; *yat*—which; *vijijñāsayā*—with exhaustive inquiries; *yuktāḥ*—being engaged; *muhyanti*—bewildered; *kavayaḥ*—great philosophers; *api*—even; *hi*—certainly.

TRANSLATION

O King, no one can know the plan of the Lord [Śrī Kṛṣṇa]. Even though great philosophers inquire exhaustively, they are bewildered.

PURPORT

The bewilderment of Mahārāja Yudhiṣṭhira over his past sinful acts and the resultant sufferings, etc., is completely negated by the great authority Bhīṣma (one of the twelve authorized persons). Bhīṣma wanted to impress upon Mahārāja Yudhiṣṭhira that since time immemorial no one, including such demigods as Śiva and Brahmā, could ascertain the real plan of the Lord. So what [illegible] about it? It is useless also to inquire about it. Even the [illegible] own devotees su[illegible] in order to establish the conquest of virtue. Bhīṣmadeva was certainly satisfied by seeing the triumph of virtue, and he was glad to see King Yudhiṣṭhira on the throne, although he himself fought against him. Even a great fighter like Bhīṣma could not win the Battle of Kurukṣetra because the Lord wanted to show that vice cannot conquer virtue, regardless of who tries to execute it. Bhīṣmadeva was a great devotee of the Lord, but he chose to fight against the Pāṇḍavas by the will of the Lord because the Lord wanted to show that a fighter like Bhīṣma cannot win on the wrong side.

TEXT 17

तस्मादिदं दैवतन्त्रं व्यवस्य भरतर्षभ।
तस्यानुविहितोऽनाथा नाथ पाहि प्रजाः प्रभो ॥१७॥

tasmād idaṁ daiva-tantraṁ
vyavasya bharatarṣabha
tasyānuvihito 'nāthā
nātha pāhi prajāḥ prabho

tasmāt—therefore; *idam*—this; *daiva-tantram*—enchantment of providence only; *vyavasya*—ascertaining; *bharata-ṛṣabha*—O best among the descendants of Bharata; *tasya*—by Him; *anuvihitaḥ*—as desired; *anāthāḥ*—helpless; *nātha*—O master; *pāhi*—just take care of; *prajāḥ*—of the subjects; *prabho*—O Lord.

TRANSLATION

O best among the descendants of Bharata [Yudhiṣṭhira], I maintain, therefore, that all this is within the plan of the Lord. Accepting the inconceivable plan of the Lord, you must follow it. You are now the appointed administrative head, and, my lord, you should now take care of those subjects who are now rendered helpless.

PURPORT

The popular saying is that a housewife teaches the daughter-in-law by teaching the daughter. Similarly, the Lord teaches the world by teaching the devotee. The devotee does not have to learn anything new from the Lord because the Lord teaches the sincere devotee always from within. Whenever, therefore, a show is made to teach the devotee, as in the case of the teachings of *Bhagavad-gītā,* it is for teaching the less intelligent men. A devotee's duty, therefore, is to ungrudgingly accept tribulations from the Lord as a benediction. The Pāṇḍavas were advised by Bhīṣmadeva to accept the responsibility of administration without hesitation. The poor subjects were without protection due to the Battle of Kurukṣetra, and they were awaiting the assumption of power by Mahārāja Yudhiṣṭhira. A pure devotee of the Lord accepts tribulations as favors from the Lord. Since the Lord is absolute, there is no mundane difference between the two.

TEXT 18

एष वै भगवान्साक्षादाद्यो नारायणः पुमान्।
मोहयन्मायया लोकं गूढश्चरति वृष्णिषु ॥१८॥

eṣa vai bhagavān sākṣād
ādyo nārāyaṇaḥ pumān
mohayan māyayā lokaṁ
gūḍhaś carati vṛṣṇiṣu

eṣaḥ—this; *vai*—positively; *bhagavān*—the Personality of Godhead; *sākṣāt*—original; *ādyaḥ*—the first; *nārāyaṇaḥ*—the Supreme Lord (who lies down on the water); *pumān*—the supreme enjoyer; *mohayan*—bewildering; *māyayā*—by His self-created energy; *lokam*—the planets; *gūḍhaḥ*—who is inconceivable; *carati*—moves; *vṛṣṇiṣu*—among the Vṛṣṇi family.

TRANSLATION

This Śrī Kṛṣṇa is no other than the inconceivable, original Personality of Godhead. He is the first Nārāyaṇa, the supreme enjoyer. But He is moving amongst the descendants of King Vṛṣṇi just like one of us, and He is bewildering us with His self-created energy.

PURPORT

The Vedic system of acquiring knowledge is the deductive process. The Vedic knowledge is received perfectly by disciplic succession from authorities. Such knowledge is never dogmatic, as ill conceived by less intelligent persons. The mother is the authority to verify the identity of the father. She is the authority for such confidential knowledge. Therefore, authority is not dogmatic. In the *Bhagavad-gītā* this truth is confirmed in the Fourth Chapter (Bg. 4.2), and the perfect system of learning is to receive it from authority. The [illegible] system is accepted universally as truth, but only the false arguer [illegible]craft fly in the sky, and when [illegible] accep[illegible] direct perception of Vedic knowledge, but foolishly they deny it. [illegible] that the misguided man can believe one authority, the scientist, but will reject the authority of the *Vedas*. The result is that people have degenerated.

Here is an authority speaking about Śrī Kṛṣṇa as the original Personality of Godhead and the first Nārāyaṇa. Even such an impersonalist as Ācārya Śaṅkara has said in the beginning of his commentation on the *Bhagavad-gītā* that Nārāyaṇa, the Personality of Godhead, is beyond the material creation*. The universe is one of the material creations, but Nārāyaṇa is transcendental to such material paraphernalia.

---

*nārāyaṇaḥ paro 'vyaktād
aṇḍam avyakta-sambhavam
aṇḍasyāntas tv ime lokāḥ
sapta dvipā ca medinī

(Bg. *Bhāṣya* of Śaṅkara)

Bhīṣmadeva is one of the twelve *mahājanas* who know the principles of transcendental knowledge. His confirmation of Lord Śrī Kṛṣṇa's being the original Personality of Godhead is also corroborated by the impersonalist Śaṅkara. All other *ācāryas* have also confirmed this statement, and thus there is no chance of not accepting Lord Śrī Kṛṣṇa as the original Personality of Godhead. Bhīṣmadeva says that He is the first Nārāyaṇa. This is also confirmed by Brahmājī in the *Bhāgavatam* (10.14.14). Kṛṣṇa is the first Nārāyaṇa. In the spiritual world (Vaikuṇṭha) there are unlimited numbers of Nārāyaṇas, who are all the same Personality of Godhead and are considered to be the plenary expansions of the original Personality of Godhead, Śrī Kṛṣṇa. The first form of the Lord, Śrī Kṛṣṇa, first expands Himself as the form of Baladeva, and Baladeva expands in so many other forms, such as Saṅkarṣaṇa, Pradyumna, Aniruddha, Vāsudeva, Nārāyaṇa, Puruṣa, Rāma and Nṛsiṁha. All these expansions are one and the same *viṣṇu-tattva,* and Śrī Kṛṣṇa is the original source of all the plenary expansions. He is therefore the direct Personality of Godhead. He is the creator of the material world, and He is the predominating Deity known as Nārāyaṇa in all the Vaikuṇṭha planets. Therefore, His movements amongst human beings are another sort of bewilderment. The Lord therefore says in the *Bhagavad-gītā* that foolish persons consider Him to be one of the human beings without knowing the intricacies of His movements.

The bewilderment regarding Śrī Kṛṣṇa is due to the action of His twofold internal and external energies upon the third one, called marginal energy. The living entities are expansions of His marginal energy, and thus they are sometimes bewildered by the internal energy and sometimes by the external energy. By internal energetic bewilderment, Śrī Kṛṣṇa expands Himself into unlimited numbers of Nārāyaṇas and exchanges or accepts transcendental loving service from the living entities in the transcendental world. And by His external energetic expansions, He incarnates Himself in the material world amongst the men, animals or demigods to reestablish His forgotten relation with the living entities in different species of life. Great authorities like Bhīṣma, however, escape His bewilderment by the mercy of the Lord.

TEXT 19

अस्यानुभावं भगवान् वेद गुह्यतमं शिवः।
देवर्षिर्नारदः साक्षाद्भगवान् कपिलो नृप ॥१९॥

asyānubhāvaṁ bhagavān
veda guhyatamaṁ śivaḥ

devarṣir nāradaḥ sākṣād
bhagavān kapilo nṛpa

asya—of Him; *anubhāvam*—glories; *bhagavān*—the most powerful; *veda*—knows; *guhya-tamam*—very confidentially; *śivaḥ*—Lord Śiva; *deva-ṛṣiḥ*—the great sage among the demigods; *nāradaḥ*—Nārada; [illegible] —directly; *bhagavān*—the Personality of Godhead; *kapilaḥ*—Kapila; *nṛpa*—O King.

TRANSLATION

O King, Lord Śiva, Nārada the sage amongst the demigods, and Kapila, the incarnation of Godhead, all know very confidentially about His glories through direct contact.

PURPORT

Pure devotees of the Lord are all *bhāvas,* or persons who know the glories of the Lord in different transcendental loving services. As the Lord has innumerable expansions of His plenary form, there are innumerable pure devotees of the Lord, who are engaged in the exchange of service of different humors. Ordinarily there are twelve great devotees of the Lord, namely Brahmā, Nārada, Śiva, Kumāra, Kapila, Manu, Prahlāda, Bhīṣma, Janaka, Śukadeva Gosvāmī, Bali Mahārāja and Yamarāja. Bhīṣmadeva, although one of them, has mentioned only three important names of the twelve who know the glories of the Lord. Śrīla Viśvanātha Cakravartī Ṭhākura, one of the great *ācāryas* in the modern age, explains that *anubhāva,* or the glory of the Lord, is first appreciated by the devotee in ecstasy manifesting the symptoms of perspiring, trembling, weeping, bodily eruptions, etc., which are further enhanced by steady understanding of the glories of the Lord. Such different understandings of *bhāvas* are exchanged between Yaśodā and the Lord (binding the Lord by ropes) and in the chariot driving by the Lord in the exchange of love with Arjuna. These glories of the Lord are exhibited in His being subordinated before His devotees, and that is another feature of the glories of the Lord. Śukadeva Gosvāmī and the Kumāras, although situated in the transcendental position, became converted by another feature of *bhāva* and turned into pure devotees of the Lord. Tribulations imposed upon the devotees by the Lord constitute another exchange of transcendental *bhāva* between the Lord and the devotees. The Lord says, "I put My devotee into difficulty, and thus the devotee becomes more purified in exchanging transcendental *bhāva* with Me." Placing the devotee into material troubles necessitates delivering him from the illusory material relations. The material relations are based on reciprocation of material enjoyment, which depends mainly on material resources. Therefore, when material resources are withdrawn by the Lord, the devotee is cent percent attracted toward the transcendental loving service of the Lord. Thus the Lord snatches the fallen soul from the mire of material existence. Tribulations offered by the Lord to His devotee are different from the tribulations resulting from vicious action. All these glories of the Lord are especially known to the great *mahājanas* like Brahmā, Śiva, Nārada, Kapila, Kumāra and Bhīṣma, as mentioned above, and one is able to grasp it by their grace.

TEXT 20

यं मन्यसे मातुलेयं प्रियं मित्रं सुहृत्तमम्।
अकरोः सचिवं दूतं सौहृदादथ सारथिम् ॥२०॥

yaṁ manyase mātuleyaṁ
priyaṁ mitraṁ suhṛttamam
akaroḥ sacivaṁ dūtaṁ
sauhṛdād atha sārathim

yam—the person; *manyase*—you think; *mātuleyam*—maternal cousin; *priyam*—very dear; *mitram*—friend; *suhṛt-tamam*—ardent well-wisher; *akaroḥ*—executed; *sacivam*—counsel; *dūtam*—messenger; *sauhṛdāt*—by good will; *atha*—thereupon; *sārathim*—charioteer.

TRANSLATION

O King, that personality whom, out of ignorance only, you thought to be your maternal cousin, your very dear friend, well-wisher, counselor, messenger, benefactor, etc., is that very Personality of Godhead Śrī Kṛṣṇa.

PURPORT

Lord Śrī Kṛṣṇa, although acting as the cousin, brother, friend, well-wisher, counselor, messenger, benefactor, etc., of the Pāṇḍavas, was still the Supreme Personality of Godhead. Out of His causeless mercy and favor upon His unalloyed devotees, He performs all kinds of service, but that does not mean that He has changed His position as the Absolute Person. To think of Him as an ordinary man is the grossest type of ignorance.

TEXT 21

सर्वात्मनः समदृशो ह्यद्वयस्यानहङ्कृतेः ।
तत्कृतं मतिवैषम्यं निरवद्यस्य न क्वचित् ॥२१॥

sarvātmanaḥ sama-dṛśo
hy advayasyānahaṅkṛteḥ
tat-kṛtaṁ mati-vaiṣamyaṁ
niravadyasya na kvacit

sarva-ātmanaḥ—of one who is present in everyone's heart; *sama-dṛśaḥ*—of one who is equally kind to one and all; *hi*—certainly; *advayasya*—of the Absolute; *anahaṅkṛteḥ*—free from all material identity of false ego; *tat-kṛtam*—everything done by Him; *mati*—consciousness; *vaiṣamyam*—differentiation; *niravadyasya*—freed from all attachment; *na*—never; *kvacit*—at any stage.

TRANSLATION

Being the Absolute Personality of Godhead, He is present in everyone's heart. He is equally kind to everyone, and He is free from the false ego of differentiation. Therefore whatever He does is free from material inebriety. He is equibalanced.

PURPORT

Because He is absolute, there is nothing different from Him. He is *kaivalya;* there is nothing except Himself. Everything and everyone is the manifestation of His energy, and thus He is present everywhere by His energy, being nondifferent from it. The sun is identified with every inch of the sun rays and every molecular particle of the rays. Similarly, the Lord is distributed by His different energies. He is Paramātmā, or the Supersoul, present in everyone as the supreme guidance, and therefore He is already the chariot driver and counsel of all living beings. When He, therefore, exhibits Himself as chariot driver of Arjuna, there is no change in His exalted position. It is the power of devotional service only that demonstrates Him as the chariot driver or the messenger. Since He has nothing to do with the material conception of life because He is absolute spiritual identity, there is for Him no superior or inferior action. Being the Absolute Personality of Godhead, He has no false ego, and so He does not identify Himself with anything different from Him. The material conception of ego is equibalanced in Him. He does not feel, therefore, inferior by becoming the chariot driver of His pure devotee. It is the glory of the pure devotee that only he can bring about service from the affectionate Lord.

TEXT 22

तथाप्येकान्तभक्तेषु पश्य भूपानुकम्पितम् ।
यन्मेऽसूंस्त्यजतः साक्षात्कृष्णो दर्शनमागतः ॥२२॥

tathāpy ekānta-bhakteṣu
paśya bhūpānukampitam
yan me 'sūṁs tyajataḥ sākṣāt
kṛṣṇo darśanam āgataḥ

tathāpi—still; *ekānta*—unflinching; *bhakteṣu*—unto the devotees; *paśya*—see here; *bhū-pa*—O King; *anukampitam*—how sympathetic; *yat*—for which; *me*—my; *asūn*—life; *tyajataḥ*—ending; *sākṣāt*—directly; *kṛṣṇaḥ*—the Personality of Godhead; *darśanam*—in my view; *āgataḥ*—has kindly come.

TRANSLATION

Yet, despite His being equally kind to everyone, He has graciously come before me while I am ending my life, for I am His unflinching servitor.

PURPORT

The Supreme Lord, the Absolute Personality of Godhead, Śrī Kṛṣṇa, although equal to everyone, is still more inclined to His unflinching devotee who is completely surrendered and knows no one else as his protector and master. Having unflinching faith in the Supreme Lord as one's protector, friend and master is the natural condition of eternal life. A living entity is so made by the will of the Almighty that he is most happy when placing himself in a condition of absolute dependence.

The opposite tendency is the cause of falldown. The living entity has this tendency of falling down by dint of misidentifying himself as fully independent to lord it over the material world. The root cause of all troubles is there in false egotism. One must draw towards the Lord in all circumstances.

The appearance of Lord Kṛṣṇa at the deathbed of Bhīṣmajī is due to his being an unflinching devotee of the Lord. Arjuna had some bodily relation with Kṛṣṇa because the Lord happened to be his maternal cousin. But Bhīṣma had no such bodily relation. Therefore the cause of attraction was due to the intimate relation of the soul. Yet because the relation of the body is very pleasing and natural, the Lord is more pleased when He is addressed as the son of Mahārāja Nanda, the son of Yaśodā, the lover of Rādhārāṇī. This affinity by bodily relation with the Lord is another feature of reciprocating loving service with the Lord. Bhīṣmadeva is conscious of this sweetness of transcendental humor, and therefore he likes to address the Lord as Vijaya-sakhe, Pārtha-sakhe, etc., exactly like Nanda-nandana or Yaśodā-nandana. The best way to establish our relation in transcendental sweetness is to approach Him through His recognized devotees. One should not try to establish the relation directly; there must be a via medium which is transparent and competent to lead us to the right path.

TEXT 23

भक्त्यावेश्य मनो यस्मिन् वाचा यन्नाम कीर्तयन् ।
त्यजन् कलेवरं योगी मुच्यते कामकर्मभिः ॥२३॥

bhaktyāveśya mano yasmin
vācā yan-nāma kīrtayan
tyajan kalevaraṁ yogī
mucyate kāma-karmabhiḥ

bhaktyā—with devout attention; *āveśya*—meditating; *manaḥ*—mind; *yasmin*—in whose; *vācā*—by words; *yat*—Kṛṣṇa; *nāma*—holy name; *kīrtayan*—by chanting; *tyajan*—quitting; *kalevaram*—this material body; *yogī*—the devotee; *mucyate*—gets release; *kāma-karmabhiḥ*—from fruitive activities.

TRANSLATION

The Personality of Godhead, who appears in the mind of the devotee by attentive devotion and meditation and by chanting of the holy name, releases the devotee from the bondage of fruitive activities at the time of his quitting the material body.

PURPORT

Yoga means concentration of the mind detached from all other subject matter. And actually such concentration is *samādhi,* or cent-percent engagement in the service of the Lord. And one who concentrates his attention in that manner is called a *yogī.* Such a *yogī* devotee of the Lord engages himself twenty-four hours daily in the service of the Lord so that his whole attention is engrossed with the thoughts of the Lord in ninefold devotional service, namely hearing, chanting, remembering, worshiping, praying, becoming a voluntary servant, carrying out orders, establishing a friendly relationship, or offering all that one may possess in the service of the Lord. By such practice of *yoga,* or linking up in the service of the Lord, one is recognized by the Lord Himself, as it is explained in the *Bhagavad-gītā* concerning the highest perfectional stage of *samādhi.* The Lord calls such a rare devotee the best amongst all the *yogīs.* Such a perfect *yogī* is enabled by the divine grace of the Lord to concentrate his mind upon the Lord with a perfect sense of consciousness, and thus by chanting His holy name before quitting the body the *yogī* is at once transferred by the internal energy of the Lord to one of the eternal planets where there is no question of material life and its concomitant factors. In material existence a living being has to endure the material conditions of threefold miseries, life after life, according to his fruitive work. Such material life is produced by material desires only. Devotional service to the Lord does not kill the natural desires of the living being, but they are applied in the right cause of devotional service. This qualifies the desire to be transferred to the spiritual sky. General Bhīṣmadeva is referring to a particular type of *yoga* called *bhakti-yoga,* and he was fortunate enough to have the Lord directly in his presence before he quitted his material body. He therefore desired that the Lord stay before his view in the following verses.

TEXT 24

स देवदेवो भगवान् प्रतीक्षतां
कलेवरं यावदिदं हिनोम्यहम् ।
प्रसन्नहासारुणलोचनोल्लस-
न्मुखाम्बुजो ध्यानपथश्चतुर्भुजः ॥२४॥

sa deva-devo bhagavān pratīkṣatāṁ
kalevaraṁ yāvad idaṁ hinomy aham
prasanna-hāsāruṇa-locanollasan-
mukhāmbujo dhyāna-pathaś catur-bhujaḥ

saḥ—He; *deva-devaḥ*—the Supreme Lord of the lords; *bhagavān*—the Personality of Godhead; *pratīkṣatām*—may kindly wait; *kalevaram*—body; *yāvat*—as long as; *idam*—this (material body); *hinomi*—may quit; *aham*—I; *prasanna*—cheerful; *hāsa*—smiling; *aruṇa-locana*—eyes red like the morning sun; *ullasat*—beautifully decorated; *mukha-ambujaḥ*—the lotus flower of His face; *dhyāna-pathaḥ*—in the path of my meditation; *catur-bhujaḥ*—the four-handed form of Nārāyaṇa (the worshipable Deity of Bhīṣmadeva).

TRANSLATION

May my Lord, who is four-handed and whose beautifully decorated lotus face, with eyes as red as the rising sun, is smiling, kindly await me at that moment when I quit this material body.

PURPORT

Bhīṣmadeva knew well that Lord Kṛṣṇa is the original Nārāyaṇa. His worshipable Deity was four-handed Nārāyaṇa, but he knew that four-handed Nārāyaṇa is a plenary expansion of Lord Kṛṣṇa. Indirectly he desired Lord Śrī Kṛṣṇa to manifest Himself in His four-handed feature of Nārāyaṇa. A Vaiṣṇava is always humble in his behavior. Although it was cent percent certain that Bhīṣmadeva was approaching Vaikuṇṭha-dhāma just after leaving his material body, still as a humble Vaiṣṇava he desired to see the beautiful face of the Lord, for after quitting the present body he might not be in a position to see the Lord any more. A Vaiṣṇava is not puffed up, although the Lord guarantees His pure devotee entrance into His abode. Here Bhīṣmadeva says "as long as I do not quit this body." This means that the great general would quit the body by his own will; he was not being forced by the laws of nature. He was so powerful that he could stay in his body as long as he desired. He got this benediction from his father. He desired that the Lord stay before him in His four-handed Nārāyaṇa feature so that he might concentrate upon Him and thus be in trance in that meditation. Then his mind might be sanctified with thinking of the Lord. Thus he did not mind wherever he might go. A pure devotee is never very anxious to go back to the kingdom of God. He entirely depends on the good will of the Lord. He is equally satisfied even if the Lord desires him to go to hell. The only desire that a pure devotee entertains is that he may always be in rapt attention with thinking of the lotus feet of the Lord, regardless. Bhīṣmadeva wanted this much only: that his mind be absorbed in thinking of the Lord and that he pass away thus. That is the highest ambition of a pure devotee.

TEXT 25

सूत उवाच

युधिष्ठिरस्तदाकर्ण्य शयानं शरपञ्जरे ।
अपृच्छद्विविधान्धर्मानृषीणां चानुशृण्वताम् ॥२५॥

sūta uvāca
yudhiṣṭhiras tad ākarṇya
śayānaṁ śara-pañjare
apṛcchad vividhān dharmān
ṛṣīṇāṁ cānuśṛṇvatām

sūtaḥ uvāca—Śrī Sūta Gosvāmī said; *yudhiṣṭhiraḥ*—King Yudhiṣṭhira; *tat*—that; *ākarṇya*—hearing; *śayānam*—lying down; *śara-pañjare*—on the bed of arrows; *apṛcchat*—asked; *vividhān*—multifarious; *dharmān*—duties; *ṛṣīṇām*—of the *ṛṣis; ca*—and; *anuśṛṇvatām*—hearing after.

TRANSLATION

Sūta Gosvāmī said: Mahārāja Yudhiṣṭhira, after hearing Bhīṣmadeva speak in that appealing tone, asked him, in the presence of all the great ṛṣis, about the essential principles of various religious duties.

PURPORT

Bhīṣmadeva, speaking in that appealing tone, convinced Mahārāja Yudhiṣṭhira that he was very soon passing away. And Mahārāja Yudhiṣṭhira was inspired by Lord Śrī Kṛṣṇa to ask him of the principles of religion. Lord Śrī Kṛṣṇa inspired Mahārāja Yudhiṣṭhira to ask Bhīṣmadeva in the presence of many great sages, indicating thereby that the Lord's devotee like Bhīṣmadeva, although apparently living as a worldly man, is far superior to many great sages, even Vyāsadeva. Another point is that Bhīṣmadeva at that time was not only lying on a deathbed of arrows, but was greatly aggrieved because of that state. One should not have asked him any question at that time, but Lord Śrī Kṛṣṇa wanted to prove that His pure devotees are always sound in body and mind by dint of spiritual enlightenment, and thus in any circumstances a devotee of the Lord is in perfect order to speak of the right way of life. Yudhiṣṭhira also preferred to solve his problematic questions by asking Bhīṣmadeva rather than ask anyone else present there who was seemingly more learned than Bhīṣmadeva. This is all due to the arrangement of the great wheel-carrier Lord Śrī Kṛṣṇa, who establishes the glories of His devotee. The father likes to see the son become more famous than himself. The Lord declares very emphatically that worship of His devotee is more valuable than the worship of the Lord Himself.

TEXT 26

पुरुषस्वभावविहितान् यथावर्णं यथाश्रमम् ।
वैराग्यरागोपाधिभ्यामाम्नातोभयलक्षणान् ॥२६॥

puruṣa-sva-bhāva-vihitān
yathā-varṇaṁ yathāśramam
vairāgya-rāgopādhibhyām
āmnātobhaya-lakṣaṇān

puruṣa—the human being; *sva-bhāva*—by his own acquired qualities; *vihitān*—prescribed; *yathā*—according to; *varṇam*—classification of castes; *yathā*—according to; *āśramam*—orders of life; *vairāgya*—detachment; *rāga*—attachment; *upādhibhyām*—out of such designations; *āmnāta*—systematically; *ubhaya*—both; *lakṣaṇān*—symptoms.

TRANSLATION

At Mahārāja Yudhiṣṭhira's inquiry, Bhīṣmadeva first defined all the classifications of castes and orders of life in terms of the individual's qualifications. Then he systematically, in twofold divisions, described counteraction by detachment and interaction by attachment.

PURPORT

The conception of four castes and four orders of life, as planned by the Lord Himself (Bg. 4.13), is to accelerate transcendental qualities of the individual person so that he may gradually realize his spiritual identity and thus act accordingly to get free from material bondage, or conditional life. In almost all the *Purāṇas* the subject matter is described in the same spirit, and so also in the *Mahābhārata* it is more elaborately described by Bhīṣmadeva in the *Śānti-parva,* beginning from the sixtieth chapter.

The *varṇāśrama-dharma* is prescribed for the civilized human being just to train him to successfully terminate human life. Self-realization is distinguished from the life of the lower animals engaged in eating, sleeping, fearing and mating. Bhīṣmadeva advised for all human beings nine qualifications: (1) not to become angry, (2) not to lie, (3) to equally distribute wealth, (4) to forgive, (5) to beget children only by one's legitimate wife, (6) to be pure in mind and hygienic in body, (7) not to be inimical toward anyone, (8) to be simple, and (9) to support servants or subordinates. One cannot be called a civilized person without acquiring the above-mentioned preliminary qualities. Besides these, the *brāhmaṇas* (the intelligent men), the administrative men, the mercantile community and the laborer class must acquire special qualities in terms of occupational duties mentioned in all the Vedic scriptures. For the intelligent men, controlling the senses is the most essential qualification. It is the basis of morality. Sex indulgence even with a legitimate wife must also be controlled, and thereby family control will automatically follow. An intelligent man abuses his great qualifications if he does not follow the Vedic way of life. This means he must seriously make a study of the Vedic literatures, especially of the *Śrīmad-Bhāgavatam* and the *Bhagavad-gītā.* For learning Vedic knowledge, one must approach a person who is cent percent engaged in devotional service. He must not do things which are forbidden in the *śāstras.* A person cannot be a teacher if he drinks or smokes. In the modern system of education the teacher's academic qualification is taken into consideration without evaluation of his moral life. Therefore, the result of education is misuse of high intelligence in so many ways.

The *kṣatriya,* the member of the administrative class, is especially advised to give charity *and not to accept charity in any circumstances.* Modern administrators raise subscriptions for some political functions, but never give charity to the citizens in any state function. It is just the reverse in the injunctions of the *śāstras.* The administrative class must be well versed in the *śāstras,* but must not take to the profession of teachers. *The administrators should never pretend to become nonviolent* and thereby go to hell. When Arjuna wanted to become a nonviolent coward on the Battlefield of Kurukṣetra, he was severely chastised by Lord Kṛṣṇa. The Lord degraded Arjuna at that time to the status of an uncivilized man for his avowed acceptance of the cult of nonviolence. The administrative class must be personally trained in military education. Cowards should not be elevated to the presidential throne by dint of numerical votes only. The monarchs were all chivalrous personalities, and therefore monarchy should be maintained provided the monarch is regularly trained in the occupational duties of a king. *In fighting, the king or the president should never return home without being hurt by the enemy.* The so-called king of today never visits the warfield. He is very much expert in artificially encouraging the fighting strength in the hope of false national prestige. As soon as the administrative class is turned into a gang of mercantile and laborer men, the whole machinery of government becomes polluted.

The *vaiśyas,* the members of the mercantile communities, are especially advised to protect the cows. Cow protection means increasing the milk productions, namely curd and butter. Agriculture and distribution of the foodstuff are the primary duties of the mercantile community backed by education in Vedic knowledge and trained to give in charity. As the *kṣatriyas* were given charge of the protection of the citizens, *vaiśyas* were given the charge of the protection of animals. Animals are never meant to be killed. Killing of animals is a symptom of barbarian society. For a human being, agricultural produce, fruits and milk are sufficient and compatible foodstuffs. The human society should give more attention to animal protection. The productive energy of the laborer is misused when he is occupied by industrial enterprises. Industry of various types cannot produce the essential needs of man, namely rice, wheat, grains, milk, fruits and vegetables. The production of machines and machine tools increases the artificial living fashion of a class of vested interests and keeps thousands of men in starvation and unrest. This should not be the standard of civilization.

The *śūdra* class is less intelligent and should have no independence. They are meant for rendering sincere service to the three higher sections of the society. The *śūdra* class can attain all comforts of life simply by rendering service to the higher classes. It is especially enjoined that a *śūdra* should never bank money. As soon as the *śūdras* accumulate wealth, it will be misused for sinful activities in wine, women and gambling. *Wine, women and gambling indicate that the population is degraded to less than śūdra quality.* The higher castes should always look after the maintenance of the *śūdras,* and they should provide them with old and used garments. A *śūdra* should not leave his master when the master is old and invalid, and the master should keep the servants satisfied in all respects. The *śūdras* must first of all be satisfied by sumptuous food and clothing before any sacrifice is performed. In this age so many functions are held by spending millions, *but the poor laborer is not sumptuously fed or given charity, clothing, etc.* The laborers are thus dissatisfied, and so they make agitation.

The *varṇas* are, so to speak, classifications of different occupations, and *āśrama-dharma* is gradual progress on the path of self-realization. Both are interrelated, and one is dependent on the other. The main purpose of *āśrama-dharma* is to awaken knowledge and detachment. The *brahmacārī-āśrama* is the training ground for the prospective candidates. In this *āśrama* it is instructed that this material world is not actually the home of the living being. The conditioned souls under material bondage are prisoners of matter, and therefore self-realization is the ultimate aim of life. The whole system of *āśrama-dharma* is a means to detachment. One who fails to assimilate this spirit of detachment is allowed to enter into family life with the same spirit of detachment. Therefore, one who attains detachment may at once adopt the fourth order, namely, renounced, and thus live on charity only, not to accumulate wealth, but just to keep body and soul together for ultimate realization. Household life is for *one who is attached,* and the *vānaprastha* and *sannyāsa* orders of life are for *those who are detached* from material life. The *brahmacārī-āśrama* is especially meant for training both the attached and detached.

TEXT 27

दानधर्मान् राजधर्मान् मोक्षधर्मान् विभागशः ।
स्त्रीधर्मान् भगवद्धर्मान् समासव्यासयोगतः ॥२७॥

dāna-dharmān rāja-dharmān
mokṣa-dharmān vibhāgaśaḥ
strī-dharmān bhagavad-dharmān
samāsa-vyāsa-yogataḥ

dāna-dharmān—the acts of charity; *rāja-dharmān*—pragmatic activities of the kings; *mokṣa-dharmān*—the acts for salvation; *vibhāgaśaḥ*—by divisions; *strī-dharmān*—duties of women; *bhagavat-dharmān*—the acts of the devotees; *samāsa*—generally; *vyāsa*—explicitly; *yogataḥ*—by means of.

TRANSLATION

He then explained, by divisions, acts of charity, the pragmatic activities of a king and activities for salvation. Then he described the duties of women and devotees, both briefly and extensively.

PURPORT

To give charity is one of the householder's main functions, and he should be prepared to give in charity at least fifty percent of his hard-earned money. A *brahmacārī,* or student, should perform sacrifices, a householder should give charity, and a person in the retired life or in the renounced order should practice penances and austerities. Those are the general functions of all the *āśramas,* or orders of life on the path of self-realization. In the *brahmacārī* life the training is sufficiently imparted so that one may understand that the world as property belongs to the Supreme Lord, the Personality of Godhead. No one, therefore, can claim to be the proprietor of anything in the world. Therefore, in the life of a householder, which is a sort of license for sex enjoyment, one must give in charity for the service of the Lord. Everyone's energy is generated or borrowed from the reservoir of energy of the Lord; therefore, the resultant actions of such energy must be given to the Lord in the shape of transcendental loving service for Him. As the rivers draw water from the sea through the clouds and again go down to the sea, similarly our energy is borrowed from the supreme source, the Lord's energy, and it must return to the Lord. That is the perfection of our energy. The Lord, therefore, in the *Bhagavad-gītā* (9.27) says that whatever we do, whatever we undergo as penance, whatever we sacrifice, whatever we eat or whatever we give in charity must be offered to Him (the Lord). That is the way of utilizing our borrowed energy. When our energy is utilized in that way, our energy is purified from the contamination of material inebrieties, and thus we become fit for our original natural life of service to the Lord.

Rāja-dharma is a great science, unlike modern diplomacy for political supremacy. The kings were trained systematically to become munificent and not merely be tax collectors. They were trained to perform different sacrifices only for the prosperity of the subjects. To lead the *prajās* to the attainment of salvation was a great duty of the king. The father, the spiritual master and the king are not to become irresponsible in the matter of leading their subjects to the path of ultimate liberation from birth, death, diseases and old age. When these primary duties are properly discharged, there is no need of government of the people, by the people. In modern days the people in general occupy the administration by the strength of manipulated votes, but they are never trained in the primary duties of the king, and that is also not possible for everyone. Under the circumstances the untrained administrators play havoc to make the subjects happy in all respects. On the other hand, these untrained administrators gradually become rogues and thieves and increase the taxation to finance a top-heavy administration that is useless for all purposes. Actually the qualified *brāhmaṇas* are meant to give direction to the kings for proper administration in terms of the scriptures like the *Manu-saṁhitā* and *Dharma-śāstras* of Parāśara. A typical king is the ideal of the people in general, and if the king is pious, religious, chivalrous and munificent, the citizens generally follow him. Such a king is not a lazy sensuous person living at the cost of the subjects, but alert always to kill thieves and dacoits. The pious kings were not merciful to dacoits and thieves in the name of nonsensical *ahiṁsā* (nonviolence). The thieves and dacoits were punished in an exemplary way so that in the future no one would dare commit such nuisances in an organized form. Such thieves and dacoits were never meant for administration as they are now.

The taxation law was simple. There was no force, no encroachment. The king had a right to take one fourth of the production made by the subject. The king had a right to claim a fourth of one's allotted wealth. One would never grudge parting with it because due to the pious king and religious harmony there was enough natural wealth, namely grains, fruits, flowers, silk, cotton, milk, jewels, minerals, etc., and therefore no one was materially unhappy. The citizens were rich in agriculture and animal husbandry, and therefore they had enough grains, fruits and milk without any artificial needs of soaps and toilets, cinemas and bars.

The king had to see that the reserved energy of humanity was properly utilized. Human energy is meant not exactly for fulfilling animal propensities, but for self-realization. The whole government was specifically designed to fulfill this particular purpose. As such, the king had to select properly the cabinet ministers, but not on the strength of voting background. The ministers, the military commanders and even the ordinary soldiers were all selected by personal qualification, and the king had to supervise them properly before they were appointed to their respective posts. The king was especially vigilant to see that the *tapasvīs,* or persons who sacrificed everything for disseminating spiritual knowledge, were never disregarded. *The king knew well that the Supreme Personality of Godhead never tolerates any insult to His unalloyed devotees.* Such *tapasvīs* were trusted leaders even of the rogues and thieves, who would never disobey the orders of *tapasvīs.* The king would give special protection to illiterates, the helpless and widows of the state. Defense measures were arranged previous to any attack by the enemies. The taxing process was easy, and it was not meant for squandering, but was for strengthening the reserve fund. The soldiers were recruited from all parts of the world, and they were trained for special duties.

As far as salvation is concerned, one has to conquer the principles of lust, anger, unlawful desires, avarice and bewilderment. To get freedom from anger, one should learn how to forgive. To be free from unlawful desires one should not make plans. By spiritual culture one is able to conquer sleep. By tolerance only can one conquer desires and avarice. Disturbances from various diseases can be avoided by regulated diets. By self-control one can be free from false hopes, and money can be saved by avoiding undesirable association. By practice of *yoga* one can control hunger, and worldliness can be avoided by culturing the knowledge of impermanence. Dizziness can be conquered by rising up, and false arguments can be conquered by factual ascertainment. Talkativeness can be avoided by gravity and silence, and by prowess one can avoid fearfulness. Perfect knowledge can be obtained by self-cultivation. One must be free from lust, avarice, anger, dreaming, etc., to actually attain the path of salvation.

As far as the women class are concerned, they are accepted as a power of inspiration for men. As such, women are more powerful than men. Mighty Julius Caesar was controlled by a Cleopatra. Such powerful women are controlled by shyness. Therefore, shyness is important for women. Once this control valve is loosened, women can create havoc in society by adultery. Adultery means production of unwanted children known as *varṇa-saṅkara,* who disturb the world.

The last item taught by Bhīṣmadeva was the process of pleasing the Lord. We are all eternal servants of the Lord, and when we forget this essential part of our nature we are put into material conditions of life. The simple process of pleasing the Lord (for the householders especially) is to install the Deity of the Lord at home. By concentrating on the Deity, one may progressively go on with the daily routine work. Worshiping the Deity at home, serving the devotee, hearing the *Śrīmad-Bhāgavatam,* residing in a holy place and chanting the holy name of the Lord are all inexpensive items by which one can please the Lord. Thus the subject matter was explained by the grandfather to his grandchildren.

TEXT 28

धर्मार्थकाममोक्षांश्च सहोपायान् यथा मुने ।
नानाख्यानेतिहासेषु वर्णयामास तत्त्ववित् ॥२८॥

dharmārtha-kāma-mokṣāṁś ca
sahopāyān yathā mune
nānākhyānetihāseṣu
varṇayām āsa tattvavit

dharma—occupational duties; *artha*—economic development; *kāma*—fulfillment of desires; *mokṣān*—ultimate salvation; *ca*—and; *saha*—along with; *upāyān*—means; *yathā*—as it is; *mune*—O sage; *nānā*—various; *ākhyāna*—by recitation of historical narrations; *itihāseṣu*—in the histories; *varṇayām āsa*—described; *tattva-vit*—one who knows the truth.

TRANSLATION

Then he described the occupational duties of different orders and statuses of life, citing instances from history, for he was himself well acquainted with the truth.

PURPORT

Incidents mentioned in the Vedic literatures such as the *Purāṇas, Mahābhārata* and *Rāmāyaṇa* are factual historical narrations that took place sometime in the past, although not in any chronological order. Such historical facts, being instructive for ordinary men, were assorted without chronological reference. Besides that, they happen on different planets, nay, in different universes, and thus the description of the narrations is sometimes measured by three dimensions. We are simply concerned with the instructive lessons of such incidents, even though they are not in order by our limited range of understanding. Bhīṣmadeva described such narrations before Mahārāja Yudhiṣṭhira in reply to his different questions.

TEXT 29

धर्मं प्रवदतस्तस्य स कालः प्रत्युपस्थितः ।
यो योगिनश्छन्दमृत्योर्वाञ्छितस्तूत्तरायणः ॥२९॥

dharmaṁ pravadatas tasya
sa kālaḥ pratyupasthitaḥ
yo yoginaś chanda-mṛtyor
vāñchitas tūttarāyaṇaḥ

dharmam—occupational duties; *pravadataḥ*—while describing; *tasya*—his; *saḥ*—that; *kālaḥ*—time; *pratyupasthitaḥ*—exactly appeared; *yaḥ*—that is; *yoginaḥ*—for the mystics; *chanda-mṛtyoḥ*—of one who dies according to one's own selection of time; *vāñchitaḥ*—is desired by; *tu*—but; *uttarāyaṇaḥ*—the period when the sun runs on the northern horizon.

TRANSLATION

While Bhīṣmadeva was describing occupational duties, the sun's course ran into the northern hemisphere. This period is desired by mystics who die at their will.

PURPORT

The perfect *yogīs* or mystics can leave the material body at their own sweet will at a suitable time and go to a suitable planet desired by them. In the *Bhagavad-gītā* (8.24) it is said that self-realized souls who have exactly identified themselves with the interest of the Supreme Lord can generally leave the material body during the time of the fire-god's effulgence and when the sun is in the northern horizon, and thus achieve the transcendental sky. In the *Vedas* these times are considered auspicious for quitting the body, and they are taken advantage of by the expert mystics who have perfected the system. Perfection of *yoga* means attainment of such supermental states as to be able to leave the material body as desired. *Yogīs* can also reach any planet within no time without a material vehicle. The *yogīs* can reach the highest planetary system within a very short time, and this is impossible for the materialist. Even attempting to reach the highest planet will take millions of years at a speed of millions of miles per hour. This is a different science, and Bhīṣmadeva knew well how to utilize it. He was just waiting for the suitable moment to quit his material body, and the golden opportunity arrived when he was instructing his noble grandsons, the Pāṇḍavas. He thus prepared himself to quit his body before the exalted Lord Śrī Kṛṣṇa, the pious Pāṇḍavas and the great sages headed by Bhagavān Vyāsa, etc., all great souls.

TEXT 30

तदोपसंहृत्य गिरः सहस्रणी-
  र्विमुक्तसङ्गं मन आदिपूरुषे ।
कृष्णे लसत्पीतपटे चतुर्भुजे
  पुरःस्थितेऽमीलितदृग्व्यधारयत् ॥३०॥

tadopasaṁhṛtya giraḥ sahasraṇīr
  vimukta-saṅgaṁ mana ādi-pūruṣe
kṛṣṇe lasat-pīta-paṭe catur-bhuje
  puraḥ sthite 'mīlita-dṛg vyadhārayat

tadā—at that time; *upasaṁhṛtya*—withdrawing; *giraḥ*—speech; *sahasraṇīḥ*—Bhīṣmadeva (who was expert in thousands of sciences and arts); *vimukta-saṅgam*—completely freed from everything else; *manaḥ*—mind; *ādi-pūruṣe*—unto the original Personality of Godhead; *kṛṣṇe*—unto Kṛṣṇa; *lasat-pīta-paṭe*—decorated with yellow garments; *catur-bhuje*—unto the four-handed original Nārāyaṇa; *puraḥ*—just before; *sthite*—standing; *amīlita*—widespread; *dṛk*—vision; *vyadhārayat*—fixed.

TRANSLATION

Thereupon that man who spoke on different subjects with thousands of meanings, and who fought on thousands of battlefields and protected

thousands of men, stopped speaking and, being completely freed from all bondage, withdrew his mind from everything else and fixed his wide-open eyes upon the original Personality of Godhead, Śrī Kṛṣṇa, who stood before him, four-handed, dressed in yellow garments that glittered and shined.

PURPORT

In the momentous hour of leaving his material body, Bhīṣmadeva set the glorious example concerning the important function of the human form of life. *The subject matter which attracts the dying man becomes the beginning of his next life.* Therefore, if one is absorbed in thoughts of the Supreme Lord Śrī Kṛṣṇa, he is sure to go back to Godhead without any doubt. This is confirmed in the *Bhagavad-gītā* (8.5–15):

5: And whoever, at the time of death, quits his body remembering Me alone at once attains My nature. Of this there is no doubt.

6: Whatever state of being one remembers when he quits his body, that state he will attain without fail.

7: Therefore, Arjuna, you should always think of Me in the form of Kṛṣṇa and at the same time carry out your prescribed duty of fighting. With your activities dedicated to Me and your mind and intelligence fixed on Me, you will attain Me without doubt.

8: He who meditates on the Supreme Personality of Godhead, his mind constantly engaged in remembering Me, undeviated from the path, he, O Pārtha [Arjuna], is sure to reach Me.

9: One should meditate upon the Supreme Person as the one who knows everything, as He who is the oldest, who is the controller, who is smaller than the smallest, who is the maintainer of everything, who is beyond all material conception, who is inconceivable, and who is always a person. He is luminous like the sun and, being transcendental, is beyond this material nature.

10: One who, at the time of death, fixes his life air between the eyebrows and in full devotion engages himself in remembering the Supreme Lord will certainly attain to the Supreme Personality of Godhead.

11: Persons learned in the *Vedas,* who utter *oṁkāra* and who are great sages in the renounced order, enter into Brahman. Desiring such perfection, one practices celibacy. I shall now explain to you this process by which one may attain salvation.

12: The yogic situation is that of detachment from all sensual engagements. Closing all the doors of the senses and fixing the mind on the heart and the life air at the top of the head, one establishes himself in *yoga.*

13: After being situated in this *yoga* practice and vibrating the sacred syllable *oṁ*, the supreme combination of letters, if one thinks of the Supreme Personality of Godhead and quits his body, he will certainly reach the spiritual planets.

14: For one who remembers Me without deviation, I am easy to obtain, O son of Pṛthā, because of his constant engagement in devotional service.

15: After attaining Me, the great souls, who are *yogīs* in devotion, never return to this temporary world, which is full of miseries, because they have attained the highest perfection.

Śrī Bhīṣmadeva attained the perfection of quitting his body at will and was fortunate enough to have Lord Kṛṣṇa, the object of his attention, personally present at the time of death. He therefore fixed his open eyes upon Him. He wanted to see Śrī Kṛṣṇa for a long time out of his spontaneous love for Him. Because he was a pure devotee, he had very little to do with the detailed performance of yogic principles. Simple *bhakti-yoga* is enough to bring about perfection. Therefore, the ardent desire of Bhīṣmadeva was to see the *person* of Lord Kṛṣṇa, the most lovable object, and by the grace of the Lord, Śrī Bhīṣmadeva had this opportunity at the last stage of his breathing.

TEXT 31

विशुद्धया धारणया हताशुभ-
स्तदीक्षयैवाशु गतायुधश्रमः ।
निवृत्तसर्वेन्द्रियवृत्तिविभ्रम-
स्तुष्टाव जन्यं विसृजञ्जनार्दनम् ॥३१॥

viśuddhayā dhāraṇayā hatāśubhas
tad-īkṣayaivāśu gatā-yudha-śramaḥ
nivṛtta-sarvendriya-vṛtti-vibhramas
tuṣṭāva janyaṁ visṛjañ janārdanam

viśuddhayā—by purified; *dhāraṇayā*—meditation; *hata-aśubhaḥ*—one who has minimized the inauspicious qualities of material existence; *tat*—Him; *īkṣayā*—by looking on; *eva*—simply; *āśu*—immediately; *gatā*—having gone away; *yudha*—from the arrows; *śramaḥ*—fatigue; *nivṛtta*—being stopped; *sarva*—all; *indriya*—senses; *vṛtti*—activities; *vibhramaḥ*—being widely engaged; *tuṣṭāva*—he prayed; *janyam*—the material tabernacle; *visṛjan*—while quitting; *janārdanam*—to the controller of the living beings.

TRANSLATION

By pure meditation, looking at Lord Śrī Kṛṣṇa, he at once was freed from all material inauspiciousness and was relieved of all bodily pains caused by the arrow wounds. Thus all the external activities of his senses at once stopped, and he prayed transcendentally to the controller of all living beings while quitting his material body.

PURPORT

The material body is a gift of the material energy, technically called illusion. Identification with the material body is due to forgetfulness of our eternal relationship with the Lord. For a pure devotee of the Lord like Bhīṣmadeva, this illusion was at once removed as soon as the Lord arrived. Lord Kṛṣṇa is like the sun, and the illusory, external material energy is like darkness. In the presence of the sun there is no possibility that darkness can stand. Therefore, just on the arrival of Lord Kṛṣṇa, all material contamination was completely removed, and Bhīṣmadeva was thus able to be transcendentally situated by stopping the activities of the impure senses in collaboration with matter. The soul is originally pure and so also the senses. By material contamination the senses assume the role of imperfection and impurity. By revival of contact with the Supreme Pure, Lord Kṛṣṇa, the senses again become freed from material contaminations. Bhīṣmadeva attained all these transcendental conditions prior to his leaving the material body because of the Lord's presence. The Lord is the controller and benefactor of all living beings. That is the verdict of all *Vedas.* He is the supreme eternity and living entity amongst all the eternal living beings*. And He alone provides all the necessities for all kinds of living beings. Thus He provided all facilities to fulfill the transcendental desires of His great devotee Bhīṣmadeva, who prayed as follows.

TEXT 32

श्रीभीष्म उवाच

इति मतिरुपकल्पिता वितृष्णा
भगवति सात्वतपुङ्गवे विभूम्नि ।
स्वसुखमुपगते क्वचिद्विहर्तुं
प्रकृतिमुपेयुषि यद्भवप्रवाहः ॥३२॥

**nityo nityānāṁ cetanaś cetanānām*
eko bahūnāṁ yo vidadhāti kāmān
(*Kaṭha Upaniṣad*)

śrī-bhīṣma uvāca
iti matir upakalpitā vitṛṣṇā
bhagavati sātvata-puṅgave vibhūmni
sva-sukham upagate kvacid vihartuṁ
prakṛtim upeyuṣi yad-bhava-pravāhaḥ

śrī-bhīṣmaḥ uvāca—Śrī Bhīṣmadeva said; *iti*—thus; *matiḥ*—thinking, feeling and willing; *upakalpitā*—invested; *vitṛṣṇā*—freed from all sense desires; *bhagavati*—unto the Personality of Godhead; *sātvata-puṅgave*—unto the leader of the devotees; *vibhūmni*—unto the great; *sva-sukham*—self-satisfaction; *upagate*—unto He who has attained it; *kvacit*—sometimes; *vihartum*—out of transcendental pleasure; *prakṛtim*—in the material world; *upeyuṣi*—do accept it; *yat-bhava*—from whom the creation; *pravāhaḥ*—is made and annihilated.

TRANSLATION

Bhīṣmadeva said: Let me now invest my thinking, feeling and willing, which were so long engaged in different subjects and occupational duties, in the all-powerful Lord Śrī Kṛṣṇa. He is always self-satisfied, but sometimes, being the leader of the devotees, He enjoys transcendental pleasure by descending on the material world, although from Him only the material world is created.

PURPORT

Because Bhīṣmadeva was a statesman, the head of the Kuru dynasty, a great general and a leader of *kṣatriyas,* his mind was strewn over so many subjects, and his thinking, feeling and willing were engaged in different matters. Now, in order to achieve pure devotional service, he wanted to invest all powers of thinking, feeling and willing entirely in the Supreme Being, Lord Kṛṣṇa. He is described herein as the leader of the devotees and all-powerful. Although Lord Kṛṣṇa is the original Personality of Godhead, He Himself descends on earth to bestow upon His pure devotees the boon of devotional service. He descends sometimes as Lord Kṛṣṇa as He is, and sometimes as Lord Caitanya. Both are leaders of the pure devotees. Pure devotees of the Lord have no desire other than the service of the Lord, and therefore they are called *sātvata.* The Lord is the chief amongst such *sātvatas.* Bhīṣmadeva, therefore, had no other desires. Unless one is purified from all sorts of material desires, the Lord does not become one's leader. Desires cannot be wiped out, but they have only to be purified. It is confirmed in the *Bhagavad-gītā* by the Lord Himself that He gives His instruction from within the heart of a pure devotee who is constantly engaged in the service of the Lord. Such instruction is given not for any material purpose but only for going back home, back to Godhead(Bg.10.10). For the ordinary man who wants to lord it over material nature, the Lord not only sanctions and becomes a witness of activities, but He never gives the nondevotee instructions for going back to Godhead. That is the difference in dealings by the Lord with different living beings, both the devotee and the nondevotee. He is leader of all the living beings, as the king of the state rules both the prisoners and the free citizens. But His dealings are different in terms of devotee and nondevotee. Nondevotees never care to take any instruction from the Lord, and therefore the Lord is silent in their case, although He witnesses all their activities and awards them the necessary results, good or bad. The devotees are above this material goodness and badness. They are progressive on the path of transcendence, and therefore they have no desire for anything material. The devotee also knows Śrī Kṛṣṇa as the original Nārāyaṇa because Lord Śrī Kṛṣṇa, by His plenary portion, appears as the Kāraṇodakaśāyī Viṣṇu, the original source of all material creation. The Lord also desires the association of His pure devotees, and for them only the Lord descends to the earth and enlivens them. The Lord appears out of His own will. He is not forced by the conditions of material nature. He is therefore described here as the *vibhu,* or the almighty, for He is never conditioned by the laws of material nature.

TEXT 33

त्रिभुवनकमनं तमालवर्णं
रविकरगौरवराम्बरं दधाने।
वपुरलककुलावृताननाब्जं
विजयसखे रतिरस्तु मेऽनवद्या ॥३३॥

tri-bhuvana-kamanaṁ tamāla-varṇaṁ
ravi-kara-gaura-vara-ambaraṁ dadhāne
vapur alaka-kulāvṛtānanābjaṁ
vijaya-sakhe ratir astu me 'navadyā

tri-bhuvana—three statuses of planetary systems; *kamanam*—the most desirable; *tamāla-varṇam*—bluish like the *tamāla* tree; *ravi-kara*—sun rays; *gaura*—golden color; *varāmbaram*—glittering dress; *dadhāne*—one who wears; *vapuḥ*—body; *alaka-kula-āvṛta*—covered with paintings of sandalwood pulp; *anana-abjam*—face like a lotus; *vijaya-sakhe*—unto the friend of Arjuna; *ratiḥ astu*—may attraction be reposed upon Him; *me*—my; *anavadyā*—without desire for fruitive results.

TRANSLATION

Śrī Kṛṣṇa is the intimate friend of Arjuna. He has appeared on this earth in His transcendental body, which resembles the bluish color of the tamāla tree. His body attracts everyone in the three planetary systems [upper, middle and lower]. May His glittering yellow dress and His lotus face, covered with paintings of sandalwood pulp, be the object of my attraction, and may I not desire fruitive results.

PURPORT

When Śrī Kṛṣṇa by His own internal pleasure appears on earth, He does so by the agency of His internal potency. The attractive features of His transcendental body are desired in all the three worlds, namely the upper, middle and lower planetary systems. Nowhere in the universe are there such beautiful bodily features as those of Lord Kṛṣṇa. Therefore His transcendental body has nothing to do with anything materially created. Arjuna is described here as the conqueror, and Kṛṣṇa is described as his intimate friend. Bhīṣmadeva, on his bed of arrows after the Battle of Kurukṣetra, is remembering the particular dress of Lord Kṛṣṇa which He put on as the driver of Arjuna's chariot. While fighting was going on between Arjuna and Bhīṣma, Bhīṣma's attraction was drawn by the glittering dress of Kṛṣṇa, and indirectly he admired his so-called enemy Arjuna for possessing the Lord as his friend. Arjuna was always a conqueror because the Lord was his friend. Bhīṣmadeva takes this opportunity to address the Lord as *vijaya-sakhe* (friend of Arjuna) because the Lord is pleased when He is addressed conjointly with His devotees, who are related with Him in different transcendental humors. While Kṛṣṇa was the charioteer of Arjuna, sun rays glittered on the dress of the Lord, and the beautiful hue created by the reflection of such rays was never forgotten by Bhīṣmadeva. As a great fighter he was relishing the relation of Kṛṣṇa in the chivalrous humor. Transcendental relation with the Lord in any one of the different *rasas* (humors) is relishable by the respective devotees in the highest ecstasy. Less intelligent mundaners who want to make a show of being transcendentally related with the Lord artificially jump at once to the relation of conjugal love, imitating the damsels of Vrajadhāma. Such a cheap relation with the Lord exhibits only the base mentality of the mundaner because one who has relished conjugal humor with the Lord cannot be attached to worldly conjugal *rasa,* which is condemned even by mundane ethics. The eternal relation of a particular soul with the Lord is evolved. A genuine relation of the living being with the Supreme Lord can take any form out of the five principal *rasas,* and it does not make any difference in transcendental degree to the genuine devotee. Bhīṣmadeva is a concrete example of this, and it should be carefully observed how the great general is transcendentally related with the Lord.

TEXT 34

युधि तुरगरजोविधूम्रविष्वक्-
कचलुलितश्रमवार्यलङ्कृतास्ये ।
मम निशितशरैर्विभिद्यमान-
त्वचि विलसत्कवचेऽस्तु कृष्ण आत्मा ॥ ३४ ॥

yudhi turaga-rajo-vidhūmra-viṣvak-
kaca-lulita-śramavāry-alaṅkṛtāsye
mama niśita-śarair vibhidyamāna-
tvaci vilasat-kavace 'stu kṛṣṇa ātmā

yudhi—on the battlefield; *turaga*—horses; *rajaḥ*—dust; *vidhūmra*—turned an ashen color; *viṣvak*—waving; *kaca*—hair; *lulita*—scattered; *śramavāri*—perspiration; *alaṅkṛta*—decorated with; *āsye*—unto the face; *mama*—my; *niśita*—sharp; *śaraiḥ*—by the arrows; *vibhidyamāna*—pierced by; *tvaci*—in the skin; *vilasat*—enjoying pleasure; *kavace*—protecting armor; *astu*—let there be; *kṛṣṇe*—unto Śrī Kṛṣṇa; *ātmā*—mind.

TRANSLATION

On the battlefield [where Śrī Kṛṣṇa attended Arjuna out of friendship], the flowing hair of Lord Kṛṣṇa turned ashen due to the dust raised by the hoofs of the horses. And because of His labor, beads of sweat wetted His face. All these decorations, intensified by the wounds dealt by my sharp arrows, were enjoyed by Him. Let my mind thus go unto Śrī Kṛṣṇa.

PURPORT

The Lord is the absolute form of eternity, bliss and knowledge. As such, transcendental loving service to the Lord in one of the five principal relations, namely *śānta, dāsya, sakhya, vātsalya* and *mādhurya,* i.e., neutrality, servitorship, fraternity, filial affection and conjugal love, is graciously accepted by the Lord when offered to the Lord in genuine love and affection. Śrī Bhīṣmadeva is a great devotee of the Lord in the relation of servitorship. Thus his throwing of sharp arrows at the transcendental body of the Lord is as good as the worship of another devotee who throws soft roses upon Him.

It appears that Bhīṣmadeva is repenting the actions he committed against the person of the Lord. But factually the Lord's body was not at all pained, due to His transcendental existence. His body is not matter. Both He Himself and His body are complete spiritual identity. Spirit is never pierced, burnt, dried, moistened, etc. This is vividly explained in the *Bhagavad-gītā.* So also it is stated in the *Skanda Purāṇa.* It is said there that spirit is always uncontaminated and indestructible. It cannot be distressed, nor can it be dried up. When Lord Viṣṇu in His incarnation appears before us, He seems to be like one of the conditioned souls, materially encaged, just to bewilder the *asuras,* or the nonbelievers, who are always alert to kill the Lord, even from the very beginning of His appearance. Kaṁsa wanted to kill Kṛṣṇa, and Rāvaṇa wanted to kill Rāma, because foolishly they were unaware of the fact that the Lord is never killed, for the spirit is never annihilated.

Therefore Bhīṣmadeva's piercing of the body of Lord Kṛṣṇa is a sort of bewildering problem for the nondevotee atheist, but those who are devotees, or liberated souls, are not bewildered.

Bhīṣmadeva appreciated the all-merciful attitude of the Lord because He did not leave Arjuna alone, although He was disturbed by the sharpened arrows of Bhīṣmadeva, nor was He reluctant to come before Bhīṣma's deathbed, even though He was ill-treated by him on the battlefield. Bhīṣma's repentance and the Lord's merciful attitude are both unique in this picture.

Śrī Viśvanātha Cakravartī Ṭhākura, a great *ācārya* and devotee in the humor of conjugal love with the Lord, remarks very saliently in this regard. He says that the wounds created on the body of the Lord by the sharpened arrows of Bhīṣmadeva were as pleasing to the Lord as the biting of a fiancée who bites the Lord's body directed by a strong sense of sex desire. Such biting by the opposite sex is never taken as a sign of enmity, even if there is a wound on the body. Therefore, the fighting as an exchange of transcendental pleasure between the Lord and His pure devotee, Śrī Bhīṣmadeva, was not at all mundane. Besides that, since the Lord's body and the Lord are identical, there was no possibility of wounds in the absolute body. The apparent wounds caused by the sharpened arrows are misleading to the common man, but one who has a little absolute knowledge can understand the transcendental exchange in the chivalrous relation. The Lord was perfectly happy with the wounds caused by the sharpened arrows of Bhīṣmadeva. The word *vibhidyamāna* is significant because the Lord's skin is not different from the Lord. Because our skin is different from our soul, in our case the word *vibhidyamāna,* or being bruised and cut, would have been quite suitable. Transcendental bliss is of different varieties, and the variety of activities in the mundane world is but a perverted reflection of transcendental bliss. Because everything in the mundane world is qualitatively mundane, it is full of inebrieties, whereas in the absolute realm, because everything is of the same absolute nature, there are varieties of enjoyment without inebriety. The Lord enjoyed the wounds created by His great devotee Bhīṣmadeva, and because Bhīṣmadeva is a devotee in the chivalrous relation, he fixes up his mind on Kṛṣṇa in that wounded condition.

TEXT 35

सपदि सखिवचो निशम्य मध्ये
निजपरयोर्बलयो रथं निवेश्य ।
स्थितवति परसैनिकायुरक्ष्णा
हृतवति पार्थसखे रतिर्ममास्तु ॥३५॥

sapadi sakhi-vaco niśamya madhye
nija-parayor balayo rathaṁ niveśya
sthitavati para-sainikāyur akṣṇā
hṛtavati pārtha-sakhe ratir mamāstu

sapadi—on the battlefield; *sakhi-vacaḥ*—command of the friend; *niśamya*—after hearing; *madhye*—in the midst; *nija*—His own; *parayoḥ*—and the opposite party; *balayoḥ*—strength; *ratham*—chariot; *niveśya*—having entered; *sthitavati*—while staying there; *para-sainika*—of the soldiers on the opposite side; *āyuḥ*—duration of life; *akṣṇā*—by looking over; *hṛtavati*—act of diminishing; *pārtha*—of Arjuna, son of Pṛthā (Kuntī); *sakhe*—unto the friend; *ratiḥ*—intimate relation; *mama*—my; *astu*—let there be.

TRANSLATION

In obedience to the command of His friend, Lord Śrī Kṛṣṇa entered the arena of the Battlefield of Kurukṣetra between the soldiers of Arjuna and

Duryodhana, and while there He shortened the life spans of the opposite party by His merciful glance. This was done simply by His looking at the enemy. Let my mind be fixed upon that Kṛṣṇa.

PURPORT

In the *Bhagavad-gītā* (1.21–25) Arjuna ordered the infallible Lord Śrī Kṛṣṇa to place his chariot between the phalanxes of the soldiers. He asked Him to stay there until he had finished observing the enemies he had to face in the battle. When the Lord was so asked, He at once did so, just like an order carrier. And the Lord pointed out all the important men on the opposite side, saying, "Here is Bhīṣma, here is Droṇa," and so on. The Lord, being the supreme living being, is never the order supplier or order carrier of anyone, whoever he may be. But out of His causeless mercy and affection for His pure devotees, sometimes He carries out the order of the devotee like an awaiting servant. By executing the order of a devotee, the Lord becomes pleased, as a father is pleased to carry out the order of his small child. This is possible only out of pure transcendental love between the Lord and His devotees, and Bhīṣmadeva was quite aware of this fact. He therefore addressed the Lord as the friend of Arjuna.

The Lord diminished the duration of life of the opposite party by His merciful glance. It is said that all the fighters who assembled on the Battlefield of Kurukṣetra attained salvation by personally seeing the Lord at the time of death. Therefore, His diminishing the duration of life of Arjuna's enemy does not mean that He was partial to the cause of Arjuna. Factually He was merciful to the opposite party because they would not have attained salvation by dying at home in the ordinary course of life. Here was a chance to see the Lord at the time of death and thus attain salvation from material life. Therefore, the Lord is all good, and whatever He does is for everyone's good. Apparently it was for the victory of Arjuna, His intimate friend, but factually it was for the good of Arjuna's enemies. Such are the transcendental activities of the Lord, and whoever understands this also gets salvation after quitting this material body. The Lord does no wrong in any circumstance because He is absolute, all good at all times.

TEXT 36

व्यवहितपृतनामुखं निरीक्ष्य
स्वजनवधाद्विमुखस्य दोषबुद्ध्या ।
कुमतिमहरदात्मविद्यया य-
श्चरणरतिः परमस्य तस्य मेऽस्तु ॥३६॥

vyavahita-pṛtanā-mukhaṁ nirīkṣya
sva-jana-vadhād vimukhasya doṣa-buddhyā
kumatim aharad ātma-vidyayā yaś
caraṇa-ratiḥ paramasya tasya me 'stu

vyavahita—standing at a distance; *pṛtanā*—soldiers; *mukham*—faces; *nirīkṣya*—by looking upon; *sva-jana*—kinsmen; *vadhāt*—from the act of killing; *vimukhasya*—one who is reluctant; *doṣa-buddhyā*—by polluted intelligence; *kumatim*—poor fund of knowledge; *aharat*—eradicated; *ātma-vidyayā*—by transcendental knowledge; *yaḥ*—He who; *caraṇa*—to the feet; *ratiḥ*—attraction; *paramasya*—of the Supreme; *tasya*—for Him; *me*—my; *astu*—let there be.

TRANSLATION

When Arjuna was seemingly polluted by ignorance upon observing the soldiers and commanders before him on the battlefield, the Lord eradicated his ignorance by delivering transcendental knowledge. May His lotus feet always remain the object of my attraction.

PURPORT

The kings and the commanders were to stand in the front of the fighting soldiers. That was the system of actual fighting. The kings and commanders were not so-called presidents or ministers of defense as they are today. They would not stay home while the poor soldiers or mercenaries were fighting face to face. This may be the regulation of modern democracy, but when actual monarchy was prevailing, the monarchs were not cowards elected without consideration of qualification. As it was evident from the Battlefield of Kurukṣetra, all the executive heads of both parties, like Droṇa, Bhīṣma, Arjuna and Duryodhana, were not sleeping; all of them were actual participants in the fighting, which was selected to be executed at a place away from the civil residential quarters. This means that the innocent citizens were immune from all effects of fighting between the rival royal parties. The citizens had no business in seeing what was going to happen during such fighting. They were to pay one fourth of their income to the ruler, whether he be Arjuna or Duryodhana. All the commanders of the parties on the Battlefield of Kurukṣetra were standing face to face, and Arjuna saw them with great compassion and lamented that he was to kill his kinsmen on the battlefield for the sake of the empire. He was not at all afraid of the giant military phalanx presented by Duryodhana, but as a merciful devotee of the Lord, renunciation of worldly things was natural for him, and thus he decided not to fight for worldly possessions. But this was due to a poor fund of knowledge, and therefore it is said here that his intelligence became polluted. His intelligence could not be polluted at any time because he was a devotee and constant companion of the Lord, as is clear in the Fourth Chapter of the *Bhagavad-gītā.* Apparently Arjuna's intelligence became polluted because otherwise there would not have been a chance to deliver the teachings of *Bhagavad-gītā* for the good of all polluted conditioned souls engaged in material bondage by the conception of the false material body. The *Bhagavad-gītā* was delivered to the conditioned souls of the world to deliver them from the wrong conception of identifying the body with the soul and to reestablish the soul's eternal relation with the Supreme Lord. *Ātma-vidyā,* or transcendental knowledge of Himself, was primarily spoken by the Lord for the benefit of all concerned in all parts of the universe.

TEXT 37

स्वनिगममपहाय मत्प्रतिज्ञा-
मृतमधिकर्तुमवप्लुतो रथस्थः ।
धृतरथचरणोऽभ्ययाच्चलद्गु-
र्हरिरिव हन्तुमिभं गतोत्तरीयः ॥३७॥

sva-nigamam apahāya mat-pratijñām
ṛtam adhikartum avapluto rathasthaḥ
dhṛta-ratha-caraṇo 'bhyayāc caladgur
harir iva hantum ibhaṁ gatottarīyaḥ

sva-nigamam—own truthfulness; *apahāya*—for nullifying; *mat-pratijñām*—my own promise; *ṛtam*—factual; *adhi*—more; *kartum*—for doing it; *avaplutaḥ*—getting down; *ratha-sthaḥ*—from the chariot; *dhṛta*—taking up; *ratha*—chariot; *caraṇaḥ*—wheel; *abhyayāt*—went hurriedly; *caladguḥ*—trampling the earth; *hariḥ*—lion; *iva*—like; *hantum*—to kill; *ibham*—elephant; *gata*—leaving aside; *uttarīyaḥ*—covering cloth.

TRANSLATION

Fulfilling my desire and sacrificing His own promise, He got down from the chariot, took up its wheel, and ran towards me hurriedly, just as a lion goes to kill an elephant. He even dropped His outer garment on the way.

PURPORT

The Battle of Kurukṣetra was fought on military principles but at the same time in a sporting spirit, like a friend's fight with another friend. Duryodhana criticized Bhīṣmadeva, alleging that he was reluctant to kill Arjuna because of paternal affection. A *kṣatriya* cannot tolerate insults on the principle of fighting. Bhīṣmadeva therefore promised that the next day he would kill all five Pāṇḍavas with special weapons made for the purpose. Duryodhana was satisfied, and he kept the arrows with him to be delivered the next day during the fight. By tricks Arjuna took the arrows from Duryodhana, and Bhīṣmadeva could understand that this was the trick of Lord Kṛṣṇa. So he took a vow that the next day Kṛṣṇa would have to take up weapons Himself, otherwise His friend Arjuna would die. In the next day's fighting Bhīṣmadeva fought so violently that both Arjuna and Kṛṣṇa were in trouble. Arjuna was almost defeated; the situation was so tense that he was about to be killed by Bhīṣmadeva the very next moment. At that time Lord Kṛṣṇa wanted to please His devotee, Bhīṣma, by keeping Bhīṣma's promise, which was more important than His own. Seemingly He broke His own promise. He promised before the beginning of the Battle of Kurukṣetra that He would remain without weapons and would not use His strength for either of the parties. But to protect Arjuna He got down from the chariot, took up the wheel of the chariot and hurriedly rushed at Bhīṣmadeva in an angry mood, as a lion goes to kill an elephant. He dropped His covering cloth on the way, and out of great anger He did not know that He had dropped it. Bhīṣmadeva at once gave up his weapons and stood to be killed by Kṛṣṇa, his beloved Lord. The fighting of the day was thus ended at that very moment, and Arjuna was saved. Of course there was no possibility of Arjuna's death because the Lord Himself was on the chariot, but because Bhīṣmadeva wanted to see Lord Kṛṣṇa take up some weapon to save His friend, the Lord created this situation, making Arjuna's death imminent. He stood before Bhīṣmadeva to show him that his promise was fulfilled and that He had taken up the wheel.

TEXT 38

शितविशिखहतो विशीर्णदंशः
क्षतजपरिप्लुत आततायिनो मे।
प्रसभमभिससार मद्वधार्थं
स भवतु मे भगवान् गतिर्मुकुन्दः ॥३८॥

śita-viśikha-hato viśīrṇa-daṁśaḥ
kṣataja-paripluta ātatāyino me
prasabham abhisasāra mad-vadhārthaṁ
sa bhavatu me bhagavān gatir mukundaḥ

śita—sharp; *viśikha*—arrows; *hataḥ*—wounded by; *viśīrṇa-daṁśaḥ*—scattered shield; *kṣataja*—by wounds; *pariplutaḥ*—smeared with blood; *ātatāyinaḥ*—the great aggressor; *me*—my; *prasabham*—in an angry mood; *abhisasāra*—began to move on; *mat-vadha-artham*—for the purpose of killing me; *saḥ*—He; *bhavatu*—may become; *me*—my; *bhagavān*—the Personality of Godhead; *gatiḥ*—destination; *mukundaḥ*—who awards salvation.

TRANSLATION

May He, Lord Śrī Kṛṣṇa, the Personality of Godhead, who awards salvation, be my ultimate destination. On the battlefield He charged me, as if angry because of the wounds dealt by my sharp arrows. His shield was scattered, and His body was smeared with blood due to the wounds.

PURPORT

The dealings of Lord Kṛṣṇa and Bhīṣmadeva on the Battlefield of Kurukṣetra are interesting because the activities of Lord Śrī Kṛṣṇa appeared to be partial to Arjuna and at enmity with Bhīṣmadeva; but factually all this was especially meant to show special favor to Bhīṣmadeva, a great devotee of the Lord. *The astounding feature of such dealings is that a devotee can please the Lord by playing the part of an enemy.* The Lord, being absolute, can accept service from His pure devotee even in the garb of an enemy. The Supreme Lord cannot have any enemy, nor can a so-called enemy harm Him because He is *ajita,* or unconquerable. But still He takes pleasure when His pure devotee beats Him like an enemy or rebukes Him from a superior position, although no one can be superior to the Lord. These are some of the transcendental reciprocatory dealings of the devotee with the Lord. And those who have no information of pure devotional service cannot penetrate into the mystery of such dealings. Bhīṣmadeva played the part of a valiant warrior, and he purposely pierced the body of the Lord so that to the common eyes it appeared that the Lord was wounded, but factually all this was to bewilder the nondevotees. The all-spiritual body cannot be wounded, and a devotee cannot become the enemy of the Lord. Had it been so, Bhīṣmadeva would not have desired to have the very same Lord as the ultimate destination of his life. Had Bhīṣmadeva been an enemy of the Lord, Lord Kṛṣṇa could have annihilated him without even moving. There was no need to come before Bhīṣmadeva with blood and wounds. But He did so because the warrior devotee wanted to see the transcendental beauty of the Lord decorated with wounds created by a pure devotee. This is the way of exchanging transcendental *rasa,* or relations between the Lord and the servitor. By such dealings both the Lord and the devotee become glorified in their respective positions. The Lord was so angry that Arjuna checked Him when He was moving towards Bhīṣmadeva, but in spite of Arjuna's checking, He proceeded towards Bhīṣmadeva as a lover goes to a lover, without caring for hindrances. Apparently His determination was to kill Bhīṣmadeva, but factually it was to please him as a great devotee of the Lord. The Lord is undoubtedly the deliverer of all conditioned souls. The impersonalists desire salvation from Him, and He always awards them according to their aspiration, but here Bhīṣmadeva aspires to see the Lord in His personal feature. All pure devotees aspire for this.

TEXT 39

विजयरथकुटुम्ब आत्ततोत्रे
धृतहयरश्मिनि तच्छ्रियेक्षणीये ।
भगवति रतिरस्तु मे मुमूर्षो-
र्यमिह निरीक्ष्य हता गताः स्वरूपम् ॥३९॥

vijaya-ratha-kuṭumbha ātta-totre
dhṛta-haya-raśmini tac-chriyekṣaṇīye
bhagavati ratir astu me mumūrṣor
yam iha nirīkṣya hatā gatāḥ sva-rūpam

vijaya—Arjuna; *ratha*—chariot; *kuṭumbe*—the object of protection at all risk; *ātta-totre*—with a whip in the right hand; *dhṛta-haya*—controlling the horses; *raśmini*—ropes; *tat-śriyā*—beautifully standing; *īkṣaṇīye*—to look at; *bhagavati*—unto the Personality of Godhead; *ratiḥ astu*—let my attraction be; *mumūrṣoḥ*—one who is about to die; *yam*—upon whom; *iha*—in this world; *nirīkṣya*—by looking; *hatāḥ*—those who died; *gatāḥ*—attained; *sva-rūpam*—original form.

TRANSLATION

At the moment of death, let my ultimate attraction be to Śrī Kṛṣṇa, the Personality of Godhead. I concentrate my mind upon the chariot driver of

Arjuna who stood with a whip in His right hand and a bridle rope in His left, who was very careful to give protection to Arjuna's chariot by all means. Those who saw Him on the Battlefield of Kurukṣetra attained their original forms after death.

PURPORT

A pure devotee of the Lord constantly sees the presence of the Lord within himself because of being transcendentally related by loving service. Such a pure devotee cannot forget the Lord for a moment. This is called trance. The mystic (*yogī*) tries to concentrate upon the Supersoul by controlling the senses from all other engagements, and thus he ultimately attains *samādhi.* A devotee more easily attains *samādhi,* or trance, by constantly remembering the Lord's personal feature along with His holy name, fame, pastimes, etc. Therefore, the concentration of the mystic *yogī* and that of the devotee are not on the same level. The concentration of the mystic is mechanical, whereas that of the pure devotee is natural in pure love and spontaneous affection. Bhīṣmadeva was a pure devotee, and as a military marshal he constantly remembered the battlefield feature of the Lord as Pārtha-sārathi, the chariot driver of Arjuna. Therefore, the Lord's pastime as Pārtha-sārathi is also eternal. The pastimes of the Lord, beginning from His birth at the prison house of Kaṁsa up to the *mauśala-līlā* at the end, all move one after another in all the universes, just as the clock hand moves from one point to another. And in such pastimes His associates like the Pāṇḍavas and Bhīṣma are constant eternal companions. So Bhīṣmadeva never forgot the beautiful feature of the Lord as Pārtha-sārathi, which even Arjuna could not see. Arjuna was behind the beautiful Pārtha-sārathi while Bhīṣmadeva was just in front of the Lord. As far as the military feature of the Lord is concerned, Bhīṣmadeva observed this with more relish than Arjuna.

All the soldiers and persons on the Battlefield of Kurukṣetra attained their original spiritual form like the Lord after their death because by the causeless mercy of the Lord they were able to see Him face to face on that occasion. The conditioned souls rotating in the evolutionary cycle from the aquatics up to the form of Brahmā are all in the form of *māyā,* or the form obtained by one's own actions and awarded by material nature. The material forms of the conditioned souls are all foreign dresses, and when the conditioned soul becomes liberated from the clutches of material energy, he attains his original form. The impersonalist wants to attain the impersonal Brahman effulgence of the Lord, but that is not at all congenial to the living sparks, parts and parcels of the Lord. Therefore, the impersonalists again fall down and get material forms, which are all false to the spirit soul. A spiritual form like the Lord's, either two-handed or four-handed, is attained by the devotees of the Lord either in the Vaikuṇṭhas or in the Goloka planet, according to the original nature of the soul. This form, which is cent percent spiritual, is the *svarūpa* of the living being, and all the living beings who participated on the Battlefield of Kurukṣetra, on both sides, attained their *svarūpa,* as confirmed by Bhīṣmadeva. So Lord Śrī Kṛṣṇa was not merciful only to the Pāṇḍavas; He was also merciful to the other parties because all of them attained the same result. Bhīṣmadeva wanted the same facility also, and that was his prayer to the Lord, although his position as an associate of the Lord is assured in all circumstances. The conclusion is that whoever dies looking on the Personality of Godhead within or without attains his *svarūpa,* which is the highest perfection of life.

TEXT 40

ललितगतिविलासवल्गुहास-
प्रणयनिरीक्षणकल्पितोरुमानाः ।
कृतमनुकृतवत्य उन्मदान्धाः
प्रकृतिमगन् किल यस्य गोपवध्वः ॥४०॥

lalita-gati-vilāsa-valguhāsa-
praṇaya-nirīkṣaṇa-kalpitorumānāḥ
kṛta-manu-kṛta-vatya unmadāndhāḥ
prakṛtim agan kila yasya gopa-vadhvaḥ

lalita—attractive; *gati*—movements; *vilāsa*—fascinating acts; *valgu-hāsa*—sweet smiling; *praṇaya*—loving; *nirīkṣaṇa*—looking upon; *kalpita*—mentality; *urumānāḥ*—highly glorified; *kṛta-manu-kṛta vatyaḥ*—in the act of copying the movements; *unmada-andhāḥ*—gone mad in ecstasy; *prakṛtim*—characteristics; *agan*—underwent; *kila*—certainly; *yasya*—whose; *gopa-vadhvaḥ*—the cowherd damsels.

TRANSLATION

Let my mind be fixed upon Lord Śrī Kṛṣṇa, whose motions and smiles of love attracted the damsels of Vrajadhāma [the gopīs]. The damsels imitated the characteristic movements of the Lord [after His disappearance from the rāsa dance].

PURPORT

By intense ecstasy in loving service, the damsels of Vrajabhūmi attained qualitative oneness with the Lord by dancing with Him on an equal level, embracing Him in nuptial love, smiling at Him in joke, and looking at Him with a loving attitude. The relation of the Lord with Arjuna is undoubtedly praiseworthy for devotees like Bhīṣmadeva, but the relation of the *gopīs* with the Lord is still more praiseworthy because of their still more purified loving service. By the grace of the Lord, Arjuna was fortunate enough to have the fraternal service of the Lord as chariot driver, but the Lord did not award Arjuna with equal strength. The *gopīs,* however, practically became one with the Lord by attainment of equal footing with the Lord. Bhīṣma's aspiration to remember the *gopīs* is a prayer to have their mercy also at the last stage of his life. The Lord is satisfied more when His pure devotees are glorified, and therefore Bhīṣmadeva has not only glorified the acts of Arjuna, his immediate object of attraction, but has also remembered the *gopīs,* who were endowed with unrivalled opportunities by rendering loving service to the Lord. The *gopīs'* equality with the Lord should never be misunderstood to be like the *sāyujya* liberation of the impersonalist. The equality is one of perfect ecstasy where the differential conception is completely eradicated, for the interests of the lover and the beloved become identical.

TEXT 41

मुनिगणनृपवर्यसङ्कुलेऽन्तः
सदसि युधिष्ठिरराजसूय एषाम् ।
अर्हणमुपपेद ईक्षणीयो
मम दृशिगोचर एष आविरात्मा ॥४१॥

muni-gaṇa-nṛpa-varya-saṅkule 'ntaḥ-
sadasi yudhiṣṭhira-rājasūya eṣām
arhaṇam upapeda īkṣaṇīyo
mama dṛśi-gocara eṣa āvir ātmā

muni-gaṇa—the great learned sages; *nṛpa-varya*—the great ruling kings; *saṅkule*—in the great assembly of; *antaḥ-sadasi*—conference; *yudhiṣṭhira*—of Emperor Yudhiṣṭhira; *rāja-sūye*—a royal performance of sacrifice; *eṣām*—of all the great elites; *arhaṇam*—respectful worship; *upapeda*—received; *īkṣaṇīyaḥ*—the object of attraction; *mama*—my; *dṛśi*—sight; *gocaraḥ*—within the view of; *eṣaḥ āviḥ*—personally present; *ātmā*—the soul.

TRANSLATION

At the Rājasūya-yajña [sacrifice] performed by Mahārāja Yudhiṣṭhira, there was the greatest assembly of all the elite men of the world, the royal and learned orders, and in that great assembly Lord Śrī Kṛṣṇa was worshiped by one and all as the most exalted Personality of Godhead. This happened during my presence, and I remembered the incident in order to keep my mind upon the Lord.

PURPORT

After gaining victory in the Battle of Kurukṣetra, Mahārāja Yudhiṣṭhira, the Emperor of the world, performed the Rājasūya sacrificial ceremony. The emperor, in those days, upon his ascendance to the throne, would send a challenge horse all over the world to declare his supremacy, and any ruling prince or king was at liberty to accept the challenge and express his tacit willingness either to obey or to disobey the supremacy of the particular emperor. One who accepted the challenge had to fight with the emperor and establish his own supremacy by victory. The defeated challenger would have to sacrifice his life, making a place for another king or ruler. So Mahārāja Yudhiṣṭhira also dispatched such challenging horses all over the world, and every ruling prince and king all over the world accepted Mahārāja Yudhiṣṭhira's leadership as the Emperor of the world. After this, all rulers of the world under the regime of Mahārāja Yudhiṣṭhira were invited to participate in the great sacrificial ceremony of Rājasūya. Such performances required hundreds of millions of dollars, and it was not an easy job for a petty king. Such a sacrificial ceremony, being too expensive and also difficult to perform under present circumstances, is now impossible in this age of Kali. Nor can anyone secure the required expert priesthood to take charge of the ceremony.

So, after being invited, all the kings and great learned sages of the world assembled in the capital of Mahārāja Yudhiṣṭhira. The learned society, including the great philosophers, religionists, physicians, scientists and all great sages, was invited. That is to say, the *brāhmaṇas* and the *kṣatriyas* were the topmost leading men in society, and they were all invited to participate in the assembly. The *vaiśyas* and *śūdras* were unimportant elements in society, and they are not mentioned herein. Due to the change of social activities in the modern age, the importance of men has also changed in terms of occupational positions.

So in that great assembly, Lord Śrī Kṛṣṇa was the cynosure of neighboring eyes. Everyone wanted to see Lord Kṛṣṇa, and everyone wanted to pay his humble respects to the Lord. Bhīṣmadeva remembered all this and was glad that his worshipful Lord, the Personality of Godhead, was present before him in His actual formal presence. So to meditate on the Supreme Lord is to meditate on the activities, form, pastimes, name and fame of the Lord. That is easier than what is imagined as meditation on the impersonal feature of the Supreme. In the *Bhagavad-gītā* (12.5) it is clearly stated that to meditate upon the impersonal feature of the Supreme is very difficult. It is practically no meditation or simply a waste of time because very seldom is the desired result obtained. The devotees, however, meditate upon the Lord's factual form and pastimes, and therefore the Lord is easily approachable by the devotees. This is also stated in the *Bhagavad-gītā* (12.9). The Lord is nondifferent from His transcendental activities. It is indicated also in this *śloka* that Lord Śrī Kṛṣṇa, while actually present before human society, especially in connection with the Battle of Kurukṣetra, was accepted as the greatest personality of the time, although He might not have been recognized as the Supreme Personality of Godhead. The propaganda that a very great man is worshiped as God after his death is misleading because a man after his death cannot be made into God. Nor can the Personality of Godhead be a human being, even when He is personally present. Both ideas are misconceptions. The idea of anthropomorphism cannot be applicable in the case of Lord Kṛṣṇa.

TEXT 42

तमिममहमजं शरीरभाजां
हृदि हृदि धिष्ठितमात्मकल्पितानाम् ।
प्रतिदृशमिव नैकधार्कमेकं
समधिगतोऽस्मि विधूतभेदमोहः ॥४२॥

tam imam aham ajaṁ śarīra-bhājāṁ
hṛdi hṛdi dhiṣṭhitam ātma-kalpitānām
pratidṛśam iva naikadhārkam ekaṁ
samadhi-gato 'smi vidhūta-bheda-mohaḥ

tam—that Personality of Godhead; *imam*—now present before me; *aham*—I; *ajam*—the unborn; *śarīra-bhājām*—of the conditioned soul; *hṛdi*—in the heart; *hṛdi*—in the heart; *dhiṣṭhitam*—situated; *ātma*—the Supersoul; *kalpitānām*—of the speculators; *pratidṛśam*—in every direction;

iva—like; *na ekadhā*—not one; *arkam*—the sun; *ekam*—one only; *samadhi-gataḥ asmi*—I have undergone trance in meditation; *vidhūta*—being freed from; *bheda-mohaḥ*—misconception of duality.

TRANSLATION

Now I can meditate with full concentration upon that one Lord, Śrī Kṛṣṇa, now present before me because now I have transcended the misconceptions of duality in regard to His presence in everyone's heart, even in the hearts of the mental speculators. He is in everyone's heart. The sun may be perceived differently, but the sun is one.

PURPORT

Lord Śrī Kṛṣṇa is the one Absolute Supreme Personality of Godhead, but He has expanded Himself into His multiplenary portions by His inconceivable energy. The conception of duality is due to ignorance of His inconceivable energy. In the *Bhagavad-gītā* (9.11) the Lord says that only the foolish take Him to be a mere human being. Such foolish men are not aware of His inconceivable energies. By His inconceivable energy He is present in everyone's heart, as the sun is present before everyone all over the world. The Paramātmā feature of the Lord is an expansion of His plenary portions. He expands Himself as Paramātmā in everyone's heart by His inconceivable energy, and He also expands Himself as the glowing effulgence of *brahmajyoti* by expansion of His personal glow. It is stated in the *Brahma-saṁhitā* that the *brahmajyoti* is His personal glow. Therefore, there is no difference between Him and His personal glow, *brahmajyoti,* or His plenary portions as Paramātmā. Less intelligent persons who are not aware of this fact consider *brahmajyoti* and Paramātmā to be different from Śrī Kṛṣṇa. This misconception of duality is completely removed from the mind of Bhīṣmadeva, and he is now satisfied that it is Lord Śrī Kṛṣṇa only who is all in all in everything. This enlightenment is attained by the great *mahātmās* or devotees, as it is stated in *Bhagavad-gītā* (7.19) that Vāsudeva is all in all in everything and that there is no existence of anything without Vāsudeva. Vāsudeva, or Lord Śrī Kṛṣṇa, is the original Supreme Person, as now confirmed by a *mahājana,* and therefore both the neophytes and the pure devotees must try to follow in his footsteps. That is the way of the devotional line.

The worshipable object of Bhīṣmadeva is Lord Śrī Kṛṣṇa as Pārtha-sārathi, and that of the *gopīs* is the same Kṛṣṇa in Vṛndāvana as the most attractive

Śyāmasundara. Sometimes less intelligent scholars make a mistake and think that the Kṛṣṇa of Vṛndāvana and that of the Battle of Kurukṣetra are different personalities. But for Bhīṣmadeva this misconception is completely removed. Even the impersonalist's object of destination is Kṛṣṇa as the impersonal *jyoti,* and the *yogī's* destination of Paramātmā is also Kṛṣṇa. Kṛṣṇa is both *brahmajyoti* and localized Paramātmā, but in *brahmajyoti* or Paramātmā there is no Kṛṣṇa or sweet relations with Kṛṣṇa. In His personal feature Kṛṣṇa is both Pārtha-sārathi and Śyāmasundara of Vṛndāvana, but in His impersonal feature He is neither in the *brahmajyoti* nor in the Paramātmā. Great *mahātmās* like Bhīṣmadeva realize all these different features of Lord Śrī Kṛṣṇa, and therefore they worship Lord Kṛṣṇa, knowing Him as the origin of all features.

TEXT 43

सूत उवाच
कृष्ण एवं भगवति मनोवाग्दृष्टिवृत्तिभिः ।
आत्मन्यात्मानमावेश्य सोऽन्तःश्वास उपारमत् ॥४३॥

sūta uvāca
kṛṣṇa evaṁ bhagavati
mano-vāg-dṛṣṭi-vṛttibhiḥ
ātmany ātmānam āveśya
so 'ntaḥśvāsa upāramat

sūtaḥ uvāca—Sūta Gosvāmī said; *kṛṣṇe*—Lord Kṛṣṇa, the Supreme Personality of Godhead; *evam*—only; *bhagavati*—unto Him; *manaḥ*—with mind; *vāk*—speech; *dṛṣṭi*—sight; *vṛttibhiḥ*—activities; *ātmani*—unto the Supersoul; *ātmānam*—the living being; *āveśya*—having merged in; *saḥ*—he; *antaḥ-śvāsaḥ*—inhaling; *upāramat*—became silent.

TRANSLATION

Sūta Gosvāmī said: Thus Bhīṣmadeva merged himself in the Supersoul, Lord Śrī Kṛṣṇa, the Supreme Personality of Godhead, with his mind, speech, sight and actions, and thus he became silent, and his breathing stopped.

PURPORT

The stage attained by Bhīṣmadeva while quitting his material body is called *nirvikalpa-samādhi* because he merged his self into thinking of the Lord and his mind into remembering His different activities. He chanted the glories of the Lord, and by his sight he began to see the Lord personally present before him, and thus all his activities became concentrated upon the Lord without deviation. This is the highest stage of perfection, and it is possible for everyone to attain this stage by practice of devotional service. The devotional service of the Lord consists of nine principles of service activities, and they are (1) hearing, (2) chanting, (3) remembering, (4) serving the lotus feet, (5) worshiping, (6) praying, (7) executing the orders, (8) fraternizing, and (9) fully surrendering. Any one of them or all of them are equally competent to award the desired result, but they require to be practiced persistently under the guidance of an expert devotee of the Lord. The first item, hearing, is the most important item of all, and therefore hearing of the *Bhagavad-gītā* and, later on, *Śrīmad-Bhāgavatam* is essential for the serious candidate who wants to attain the stage of Bhīṣmadeva at the end. The unique situation at Bhīṣmadeva's time of death can be attained, even though Lord Kṛṣṇa may not be personally present. His words of the *Bhagavad-gītā* or those of *Śrīmad-Bhāgavatam* are identical with the Lord. They are sound incarnations of the Lord, and one can fully utilize them to be entitled to attain the stage of Śrī Bhīṣmadeva, who was one of the eight Vasus. Every man or animal must die at a certain stage of life, but one who dies like Bhīṣmadeva attains perfection, and one who dies forced by the laws of nature dies like an animal. That is the difference between a man and an animal. The human form of life is especially meant for dying like Bhīṣmadeva.

TEXT 44

सम्पद्यमानमाज्ञाय भीष्मं ब्रह्मणि निष्कले ।
सर्वे बभूवुस्ते तूष्णीं वयांसीव दिनात्यये ॥४४॥

sampadyamānam ājñāya
bhīṣmaṁ brahmaṇi niṣkale
sarve babhūvus te tūṣṇīṁ
vayāṁsīva dinātyaye

sampadyamānam—having merged into; *ājñāya*—after knowing this; *bhīṣmam*—about Śrī Bhīṣmadeva; *brahmaṇi*—into the Supreme Absolute; *niṣkale*—unlimited; *sarve*—all present; *babhūvuḥ te*—all of them became; *tūṣṇīm*—silent; *vayāṁsi iva*—like birds; *dina-atyaye*—at the end of the day.

TRANSLATION

Knowing that Bhīṣmadeva had merged into the unlimited eternity of the Supreme Absolute, all present there became silent like birds at the end of the day.

PURPORT

To enter into or to become merged into the unlimited eternity of the Supreme Absolute means to enter the original home of the living being. The living beings are all component parts and parcels of the Absolute Personality of Godhead, and therefore they are eternally related with Him as the servitor and the served. The Lord is served by all His parts and parcels, as the complete machine is served by its parts and parcels. Any part of the machine removed from the whole is no longer important. Similarly, any part and parcel of the Absolute detached from the service of the Lord is useless. The living beings who are in the material world are all disintegrated parts and parcels of the supreme whole, and they are no longer as important as the original parts and parcels. There are, however, more integrated living beings who are eternally liberated. The material energy of the Lord, called Durgā-śakti, or the superintendent of the prison house, takes charge of the disintegrated parts and parcels, and thus they undergo a conditioned life under the laws of material nature. When the living being becomes conscious of this fact, he tries to go back home, back to Godhead, and thus the spiritual urge of the living being begins. This spiritual urge is called *brahma-jijñāsā,* or inquiry about Brahman. Principally this *brahma-jijñāsā* is successful by knowledge, renunciation and devotional service to the Lord. *Jñāna,* or knowledge, means knowledge of everything of Brahman, the Supreme; renunciation means detachment of material affection, and devotional service is the revival by practice of the original position of the living being. The successful living beings who are eligible to enter into the realm of the Absolute are called the *jñānīs,* the *yogīs* and the *bhaktas.* The *jñānīs* and *yogīs* enter into the impersonal rays of the Supreme, but the *bhaktas* enter into the spiritual planets known as the Vaikuṇṭhas. In these spiritual planets the Supreme Lord as Nārāyaṇa predominates, and the healthy, unconditioned living beings live there by rendering loving service to the Lord in the capacity of servant, friend, parents and fiancee. There the unconditioned living beings enjoy life in full freedom with the Lord, whereas the impersonalist *jñānīs* and *yogīs* enter into the impersonal glowing effulgence of the Vaikuṇṭha planets. The Vaikuṇṭha planets are all self-illuminating like the sun, and the rays of the Vaikuṇṭha planets are called the *brahmajyoti.* The *brahmajyoti* is spread unlimitedly, and the material world is but a covered portion of an insignificant part of the same *brahmajyoti.* This covering is temporary, and therefore it is a sort of illusion.

Bhīṣmadeva, as a pure devotee of the Lord, entered the spiritual realm in one of the Vaikuṇṭha planets where the Lord in His eternal form of Pārtha-sārathi predominates over the unconditioned living beings who are constantly engaged in the service of the Lord. The love and affection which bind the Lord and devotee are exhibited in the case of Bhīṣmadeva. Bhīṣmadeva never forgot the Lord in His transcendental feature as the *pārtha-sārathi,* and the Lord was present personally before Bhīṣmadeva while he was passing to the transcendental world. That is the highest perfection of life.

TEXT 45

तत्र दुन्दुभयो नेदुर्देवमानववादिताः ।
शशंसुः साधवो राज्ञां खात्पेतुः पुष्पवृष्टयः ॥४५॥

tatra dundubhayo nedur
deva-mānava-vāditāḥ
śaśaṁsuḥ sādhavo rājñāṁ
khāt petuḥ puṣpa-vṛṣṭayaḥ

tatra—thereafter; *dundubhayaḥ*—drums; *neduḥ*—were sounded; *deva*—the demigods from other planets; *mānava*—men from all countries; *vāditāḥ*—beaten by; *śaśaṁsuḥ*—praised; *sādhavaḥ*—honest; *rājñām*—by the royal order; *khāt*—from the sky; *petuḥ*—began to fall; *puṣpa-vṛṣṭayaḥ*—showers of flowers.

TRANSLATION

Thereafter, both men and demigods sounded drums in honor, and the honest royal order commenced demonstrations of honor and respect. And from the sky fell showers of flowers.

PURPORT

Bhīṣmadeva was respected both by the human beings and by the demigods. The human beings live on earth and similar other planets in the Bhūr and Bhuvar group of planets, but the demigods live in the Svar, or heavenly planets, and all of them knew Bhīṣmadeva as a great warrior and devotee of the Lord. As a *mahājana* (or authority) he was on the level of Brahmā, Nārada and Śiva, although he was a human being. Qualification on a par with the great demigods is possible only on attainment of spiritual perfection. Thus Bhīṣmadeva was known all over the universes, and during his time interplanetary travel was effected by finer methods than the futile endeavors of mechanical spacecraft. When the distant planets were informed of the passing away of Bhīṣmadeva, all the inhabitants of the upper planets as well as of the earth dropped showers of flowers to show due respect to the departed great personality. This showering of flowers from heaven is a sign of recognition by great demigods, and it should never be compared to the decoration of a dead body. The body of Bhīṣmadeva lost its material effects due to being surcharged with spiritual realization, and thus the body was spiritualized as when iron becomes red-hot when in contact with fire. The body of a fully self-realized soul is not, therefore, accepted as material. Special ceremonies are observed for such spiritual bodies. The respect and recognition of Bhīṣmadeva are never to be imitated by artificial means, as it has become a fashion to observe the so-called *jayantī* ceremony for any and every common man. According to authorized *śāstras,* such a *jayantī* ceremony for an ordinary man, however exalted he may be materially, is an offense to the Lord because *jayantī* is reserved for the day when the Lord appears on the earth. Bhīṣmadeva was unique in his activities, and his passing away to the kingdom of God is also unique.

TEXT 46

तस्य निर्हरणादीनि सम्परेतस्य भार्गव।
युधिष्ठिरः कारयित्वा मुहूर्तं दुःखितोऽभवत् ॥४६॥

tasya nirharaṇādīni
samparetasya bhārgava
yudhiṣṭhiraḥ kārayitvā
muhūrtaṁ duḥkhito 'bhavat

tasya—his; *nirharaṇa-ādīni*—funeral ceremony; *samparetasya*—of the dead body; *bhārgava*—O descendant of Bhṛgu; *yudhiṣṭhiraḥ*—Mahārāja Yudhiṣṭhira; *kārayitvā*—having performed it; *muhūrtam*—for a moment; *duḥkhitaḥ*—sorry; *abhavat*—became.

TRANSLATION

O descendant of Bhṛgu [Śaunaka], after performing funeral rituals for the dead body of Bhīṣmadeva, Mahārāja Yudhiṣṭhira was momentarily overtaken with grief.

PURPORT

Bhīṣmadeva was not only a great family head of Mahārāja Yudhiṣṭhira, but also he was a great philosopher and friend to him, his brothers and his mother. Since Mahārāja Pāṇḍu, the father of the five brothers headed by Mahārāja Yudhiṣṭhira, had died, Bhīṣmadeva was the most affectionate grandfather of the Pāṇḍavas and caretaker of the widow daughter-in-law Kuntīdevī. Although Mahārāja Dhṛtarāṣṭra, the elder uncle of Mahārāja Yudhiṣṭhira, was there to look after them, his affection was more on the side of his hundred sons, headed by Duryodhana. Ultimately a colossal clique was fabricated to deprive the five fatherless brothers of the rightful claim of the kingdom of Hastināpura. There was great intrigue, common in imperial palaces, and the five brothers were exiled to the wilderness. But Bhīṣmadeva was always a sincerely sympathetic well-wisher, grandfather, friend and philosopher to Mahārāja Yudhiṣṭhira, even up to the last moment of his life. He died very happily by seeing Mahārāja Yudhiṣṭhira to the throne, otherwise he would have long ago quitted his material body, instead of suffering agony over the undue sufferings of the Pāṇḍavas. He was simply waiting for the opportune moment because he was sure and certain that the sons of Pāṇḍu would come out victorious in the Battlefield of Kurukṣetra, as His Lordship Śrī Kṛṣṇa was their protector. As a devotee of the Lord, he knew that the Lord's devotee cannot be vanquished at any time. Mahārāja Yudhiṣṭhira was quite aware of all these good wishes of Bhīṣmadeva, and therefore he must have been feeling the great separation. He was sorry for the separation of a great soul, and not for the material body which Bhīṣmadeva relinquished. The funeral ceremony was a necessary duty, although Bhīṣmadeva was a liberated soul. Since Bhīṣmadeva was without issue, the eldest grandson, namely Mahārāja Yudhiṣṭhira, was the rightful person to perform this ceremony. It was a great boon to Bhīṣmadeva that an equally great son of the family undertook the last rites of a great man.

TEXT 47

तुष्टुवुर्मुनयो हृष्टाः कृष्णं तद्गुह्यनामभिः ।
ततस्ते कृष्णहृदयाः स्वाश्रमान् प्रययुः पुनः ॥४७॥

tuṣṭuvur munayo hṛṣṭāḥ
kṛṣṇaṁ tad-guhya-nāmabhiḥ
tatas te kṛṣṇa-hṛdayāḥ
svāśramān prayayuḥ punaḥ

tuṣṭuvuḥ—satisfied; *munayaḥ*—the great sages, headed by Vyāsadeva, etc.; *hṛṣṭāḥ*—all in a happy mood; *kṛṣṇam*—unto Lord Kṛṣṇa, the Personality of Godhead; *tat*—His; *guhya*—confidential; *nāmabhiḥ*—by His holy name, etc.; *tataḥ*—thereafter; *te*—they; *kṛṣṇa-hṛdayāḥ*—persons who always bear Lord Kṛṣṇa in their hearts; *sva-āśramān*—to their respective hermitages; *prayayuḥ*—returned; *punaḥ*—again.

TRANSLATION

All the great sages then glorified Lord Śrī Kṛṣṇa, who was present there, by confidential Vedic hymns. Then all of them returned to their respective hermitages, bearing always Lord Kṛṣṇa within their hearts.

PURPORT

The devotees of the Lord are always in the heart of the Lord, and the Lord is always in the hearts of the devotees. That is the sweet relation between the Lord and His devotees. Due to unalloyed love and devotion for the Lord, the devotees always see Him within themselves, and the Lord also, although He has nothing to do and nothing to aspire to, is always busy in attending to the welfare of His devotees. For the ordinary living beings the law of nature is there for all actions and reactions, but He is always anxious to put His devotees on the right path. The devotees, therefore, are under the direct care of the Lord. And the Lord also voluntarily puts Himself under the care of His devotees only. So all the sages, headed by Vyāsadeva, were devotees of the Lord, and therefore they chanted the Vedic hymns after the funeral ceremony just to please the Lord, who was present there personally. All the Vedic hymns are chanted to please Lord Kṛṣṇa. This is confirmed in the *Bhagavad-gītā* (15.15). All the *Vedas, Upaniṣads, Vedānta,* etc., are seeking Him only, and all hymns are for glorifying Him only. The sages, therefore, performed the exact acts suitable for the purpose, and they happily departed for their respective hermitages.

TEXT 48

ततो युधिष्ठिरो गत्वा सहकृष्णो गजाह्वयम् ।
पितरं सान्त्वयामास गान्धारीं च तपस्विनीम् ॥४८॥

tato yudhiṣṭhiro gatvā
saha-kṛṣṇo gajāhvayam
pitaraṁ sāntvayām āsa
gāndhārīṁ ca tapasvinīm

tataḥ—thereafter; *yudhiṣṭhiraḥ*—Mahārāja Yudhiṣṭhira; *gatvā*—going there; *saha*—with; *kṛṣṇaḥ*—the Lord; *gajāhvayam*—in the capital named Gajāhvaya Hastināpura; *pitaram*—unto his uncle (Dhṛtarāṣṭra); *sāntvayām āsa*—consoled; *gāndhārīm*—the wife of Dhṛtarāṣṭra; *ca*—and; *tapasvinīm*—an ascetic lady.

TRANSLATION

Thereafter, Mahārāja Yudhiṣṭhira at once went to his capital, Hastināpura, accompanied by Lord Śrī Kṛṣṇa, and there he consoled his uncle and aunt Gāndhārī, who was an ascetic.

PURPORT

Dhṛtarāṣṭra and Gāndhārī, the father and the mother of Duryodhana and his brothers, were the elder uncle and aunt of Mahārāja Yudhiṣṭhira. After the Battle of Kurukṣetra, the celebrated couple, having lost all their sons and grandsons, were under the care of Mahārāja Yudhiṣṭhira. They were passing their days in great agony over such a heavy loss of life and were practically living the life of ascetics. The death news of Bhīṣmadeva, uncle of Dhṛtarāṣṭra, was another great shock for the King and the Queen, and therefore they required solace from Mahārāja Yudhiṣṭhira. Mahārāja Yudhiṣṭhira was conscious of his duty, and he at once hurried to the spot with Lord Kṛṣṇa and satisfied the bereaved Dhṛtarāṣṭra with kind words, from both himself and the Lord also.

Gāndhārī was a powerful ascetic, although she was living the life of a faithful wife and a kind mother. It is said that Gāndhārī also voluntarily closed her eyes because of the blindness of her husband. A wife's duty is to follow the husband cent percent. And Gāndhārī was so true to her husband that she followed him even in his perpetual blindness. Therefore in her actions she was a great ascetic. Besides that, the shock she suffered because of the wholesale killing of her one hundred sons and her grandsons also was certainly too much for a woman. But she suffered all this just like an ascetic. Gāndhārī, although a woman, is no less than Bhīṣmadeva in character. They are both remarkable personalities in the *Mahābhārata.*

TEXT 49

पित्रा चानुमतो राजा वासुदेवानुमोदितः ।
चकार राज्यं धर्मेण पितृपैतामहं विभुः ॥४९॥

pitrā cānumato rājā
vāsudevānumoditaḥ
cakāra rājyaṁ dharmeṇa
pitṛ-paitāmahaṁ vibhuḥ

pitrā—by his uncle, Dhṛtarāṣṭra; *ca*—and; *anumataḥ*—with his approval; *rājā*—King Yudhiṣṭhira; *vāsudeva-anumoditaḥ*—confirmed by Lord Śrī Kṛṣṇa; *cakāra*—executed; *rājyam*—the kingdom; *dharmeṇa*—in compliance with the codes of royal principles; *pitṛ*—father; *paitāmaham*—forefather; *vibhuḥ*—as great as.

TRANSLATION

After this, the great religious King, Mahārāja Yudhiṣṭhira, executed the royal power in the kingdom strictly according to the codes and royal principles approved by his uncle and confirmed by Lord Śrī Kṛṣṇa.

PURPORT

Mahārāja Yudhiṣṭhira was not a mere tax collector. He was always conscious of his duty as a king, which is no less than that of a father or spiritual master. The king is to see to the welfare of the citizens from all angles of social, political, economic and spiritual upliftment. The king must know that human life is meant for liberating the encaged soul from the bondage of material conditions, and therefore his duty is to see that the citizens are properly looked after to attain this highest stage of perfection.

Mahārāja Yudhiṣṭhira followed these principles strictly, as will be seen from the next chapter. Not only did he follow the principles, but he also got approval from his old uncle, who was experienced in political affairs, and that was also confirmed by Lord Kṛṣṇa, the speaker of the philosophy of *Bhagavad-gītā.*

Mahārāja Yudhiṣṭhira is the ideal monarch, and monarchy under a trained king like Mahārāja Yudhiṣṭhira is by far the most superior form of government, superior to modern republics or governments of the people, by the people. The mass of people, especially in this age of Kali, are all born *śūdras,* basically lowborn, ill-trained, unfortunate and badly associated. They themselves do not know the highest perfectional aim of life. Therefore, votes cast by them actually have no value, and thus persons elected by such irresponsible votes cannot be responsible representatives like Mahārāja Yudhiṣṭhira.

Thus end the Bhaktivedanta purports of the First Canto, Ninth Chapter, of the Śrīmad-Bhāgavatam, *entitled "The Passing Away of Bhīṣmadeva in the Presence of Lord Kṛṣṇa."*

CHAPTER TEN

Departure of Lord Kṛṣṇa for Dvārakā

TEXT 1

शौनक उवाच

हत्वा स्वरिक्थस्पृध आततायिनो
युधिष्ठिरो धर्मभृतां वरिष्ठः ।
सहानुजैः प्रत्यवरुद्धभोजनः
कथं प्रवृत्तः किमकारषीत्ततः ॥१॥

śaunaka uvāca
hatvā svariktha-spṛdha ātatāyino
yudhiṣṭhiro dharma-bhṛtāṁ variṣṭhaḥ
sahānujaiḥ pratyavaruddha-bhojanaḥ
kathaṁ pravṛttaḥ kim akāraṣīt tataḥ

śaunakaḥ uvāca—Śaunaka inquired; *hatvā*—after killing; *svariktha*—the legal inheritance; *spṛdhaḥ*—desiring to usurp; *ātatāyinaḥ*—the aggressor; *yudhiṣṭhiraḥ*—King Yudhiṣṭhira; *dharma-bhṛtām*—of those who strictly follow religious principles; *variṣṭhaḥ*—greatest; *saha-anujaiḥ*—with his younger brothers; *pratyavaruddha*—restricted; *bhojanaḥ*—acceptance of necessities; *katham*—how; *pravṛttaḥ*—engaged; *kim*—what; *akāraṣīt*—executed; *tataḥ*—thereafter.

TRANSLATION

Śaunaka Muni asked: After killing his enemies who desired to usurp his rightful inheritance, how did the greatest of all religious men, Mahārāja Yudhiṣṭhira, assisted by his brothers, rule his subjects? Surely he could not freely enjoy his kingdom with unrestricted consciousness.

PURPORT

Mahārāja Yudhiṣṭhira was the greatest of all men of religion. Thus he was not at all inclined to fight with his cousins for the sake of enjoying the kingdom; he fought for the right cause because the kingdom of Hastināpura was his rightful inheritance and his cousins wanted to usurp it for themselves. He fought, therefore, for the right cause under the guidance of Lord Śrī Kṛṣṇa, but he could not enjoy the results of his victory because his cousins were all killed in the fight. He therefore ruled over the kingdom as a matter of duty, assisted by his younger brothers. The inquiry was important for Śaunaka Ṛṣi, who wanted to know about the behavior of Mahārāja Yudhiṣṭhira when he was at ease to enjoy the kingdom.

TEXT 2

सूत उवाच

वंशं कुरोर्वंशदवाग्निनिर्हृतं
संरोहयित्वा भवभावनो हरिः ।
निवेशयित्वा निजराज्य ईश्वरो
युधिष्ठिरं प्रीतमना बभूव ह ॥२॥

sūta uvāca
vaṁśaṁ kuror vaṁśa-davāgni-nirhṛtaṁ
saṁrohayitvā bhava-bhāvano hariḥ
niveśayitvā nija-rājya īśvaro
yudhiṣṭhiraṁ prīta-manā babhūva ha

sūtaḥ uvāca—Sūta Gosvāmī replied; *vaṁśam*—dynasty; *kuroḥ*—of King Kuru; *vaṁśa-dava-agni*—a forest fire set by the bamboos; *nirhṛtam*—exhausted; *saṁrohayitvā*—seedling of the dynasty; *bhava-bhāvanaḥ*—the maintainer of creation; *hariḥ*—the Personality of Godhead Śrī Kṛṣṇa; *niveśayitvā*—having reestablished; *nija-rājye*—in his own kingdom; *īśvaraḥ*—the Supreme Lord; *yudhiṣṭhiram*—unto Mahārāja Yudhiṣṭhira; *prīta-manāḥ*—pleased in His mind; *babhūva ha*—became.

TRANSLATION

Sūta Gosvāmī said: Lord Śrī Kṛṣṇa, the Supreme Personality of Godhead, who is the maintainer of the world, became pleased after reestablishing Mahārāja Yudhiṣṭhira in his own kingdom and after restoring the Kuru dynasty, which had been exhausted by the bamboo fire of anger.

PURPORT

This world is compared to a forest fire caused by the cohesion of bamboo bushes. Such a forest fire takes place automatically, for bamboo cohesion occurs without external cause. Similarly, in the material world the wrath of those who want to lord it over material nature interacts, and the fire of war takes place, exhausting the unwanted population. Such fires or wars take place, and the Lord has nothing to do with them. But because He wants to maintain the creation, He desires the mass of people to follow the right path of self-realization, which enables the living beings to enter into the kingdom of God. The Lord wants the suffering human beings to come back home, back to Him, and cease to suffer the threefold material pangs. The whole plan of creation is made in that way, and one who does not come to his senses suffers in the material world by pangs inflicted by the illusory energy of the Lord. The Lord therefore wants His bona fide representative to rule the world. Lord Śrī Kṛṣṇa descended to establish this sort of regime and to kill the unwanted persons who have nothing to do with His plan. The Battle of Kurukṣetra was fought according to the plan of the Lord so that undesirable persons could get out of the world and a peaceful kingdom under His devotee could be established. The Lord was therefore fully satisfied when King Yudhiṣṭhira was on the throne and the seedling of the dynasty of Kuru, in the person of Mahārāja Parīkṣit, was saved.

TEXT 3

निशम्य भीष्मोक्तमथाच्युतोक्तं
प्रवृत्तविज्ञानविधूतविभ्रमः ।
शशास गामिन्द्र इवाजिताश्रयः
परिध्युपान्तामनुजानुवर्तितः ॥३॥

niśamya bhīṣmoktam athācyutoktaṁ
pravṛtta-vijñāna-vidhūta-vibhramaḥ
śaśāsa gām indra ivājitāśrayaḥ
paridhyupāntām anujānuvartitaḥ

niśamya—after listening; *bhīṣma-uktam*—what was spoken by Bhīṣmadeva; *atha*—as also; *acyuta-uktam*—what was spoken by the infallible Lord Kṛṣṇa; *pravṛtta*—being engaged in; *vijñāna*—perfect knowledge; *vidhūta*—completely washed; *vibhramaḥ*—all misgivings; *śaśāsa*—ruled over; *gām*—the earth; *indra*—the king of the heavenly planet; *iva*—like; *ajita-āśrayaḥ*—protected by the invincible Lord; *paridhi-upāntām*—including the seas; *anuja*—the younger brothers; *anuvartitaḥ*—being followed by them.

TRANSLATION

Mahārāja Yudhiṣṭhira, after being enlightened by what was spoken by Bhīṣmadeva and Lord Śrī Kṛṣṇa, the infallible, engaged himself in matters of perfect knowledge because all his misgivings were eradicated. Thus he ruled over the earth and seas and was followed by his younger brothers.

PURPORT

The modern English law of primogeniture, or the law of inheritance by the firstborn, was also prevalent in those days when Mahārāja Yudhiṣṭhira ruled the earth and seas. In those days the King of Hastināpura (now part of New Delhi) was the emperor of the world, including the seas, up to the time of Mahārāja Parīkṣit, the grandson of Mahārāja Yudhiṣṭhira. Mahārāja Yudhiṣṭhira's younger brothers were acting as his ministers and commanders of state, and there was full cooperation between the perfectly religious brothers of the King. Mahārāja Yudhiṣṭhira was the ideal king or representative of Lord Śrī Kṛṣṇa to rule over the kingdom of earth and was comparable to King Indra, the representative ruler of the heavenly planets. The demigods like Indra, Candra, Sūrya, Varuṇa and Vāyu are representative kings of different planets of the universe, and similarly Mahārāja Yudhiṣṭhira was also one of them, ruling over the kingdom of the earth. Mahārāja Yudhiṣṭhira was not a typically unenlightened political leader of modern democracy. Mahārāja Yudhiṣṭhira was instructed by Bhīṣmadeva and the infallible Lord also, and therefore he had full knowledge of everything in perfection.

The modern elected executive head of a state is just like a puppet because he has no kingly power. Even if he is enlightened like Mahārāja Yudhiṣṭhira, he cannot do anything out of his own good will due to his constitutional position. Therefore, there are so many states over the earth quarreling because of ideological differences or other selfish motives. But a king like Mahārāja Yudhiṣṭhira had no ideology of his own. He had but to follow the instructions of the infallible Lord and the Lord's representative and the authorized agent, Bhīṣmadeva. It is instructed in the *śāstras* that one should follow the great authority and the infallible Lord without any personal motive and manufactured ideology. Therefore, it was possible for Mahārāja Yudhiṣṭhira to rule the whole world, including the seas, because the principles were infallible and universally applicable to everyone. The conception of one world state can only be fulfilled if we can follow the infallible authority. An imperfect human being cannot create an ideology acceptable to everyone. Only the perfect and the infallible can create a program which is applicable at every place and can be followed by all in the world. It is the person who rules, and not the impersonal government. If the person is perfect, the government is perfect. If the person is a fool, the government is a fool's paradise. That is the law of nature. There are so many stories of imperfect kings or executive heads. Therefore, the executive head must be a trained person like Mahārāja Yudhiṣṭhira, and he must have the full autocratic power to rule over the world. The conception of a world state can take shape only under the regime of a perfect king like Mahārāja Yudhiṣṭhira. The world was happy in those days because there were kings like Mahārāja Yudhiṣṭhira to rule over the world.

TEXT 4

कामं ववर्ष पर्जन्यः सर्वकामदुघा मही।
सिषिचुः स्म व्रजान् गावः पयसोधस्वतीर्मुदा ॥४॥

kāmaṁ vavarṣa parjanyaḥ
sarva-kāma-dughā mahī
siṣicuḥ sma vrajān gāvaḥ
payasodhasvatīr mudā

kāmam—everything needed; *vavarṣa*—was showered; *parjanyaḥ*—rains; *sarva*—everything; *kāma*—necessities; *dughā*—producer; *mahī*—the land; *siṣicuḥ sma*—moisten; *vrajān*—pasturing grounds; *gāvaḥ*—the cow; *payasā udhasvatīḥ*—due to swollen milk bags; *mudā*—because of a joyful attitude.

TRANSLATION

During the reign of Mahārāja Yudhiṣṭhira, the clouds showered all the water that people needed, and the earth produced all the necessities of man in profusion. Due to its fatty milk bag and cheerful attitude, the cow used to moisten the grazing ground with milk.

PURPORT

The basic principle of economic development is centered on *land* and *cows.* The necessities of human society are food grains, fruits, milk, minerals, clothing, wood, etc. One requires all these items to fulfill the material needs of the body. Certainly one does not require flesh and fish or iron tools and machinery. During the regime of Mahārāja Yudhiṣṭhira, all over the world there were regulated rainfalls. Rainfalls are not in the control of the human being. The heavenly king Indradeva is the controller of rains, and he is the servant of the Lord. When the Lord is obeyed by the king and the people under the king's administration, there are regulated rains from the horizon, and these rains are the causes of all varieties of production on the land. Not only do regulated rains help ample production of grains and fruits, but when they combine with astronomical influences there is ample production of valuable stones and pearls. Grains and vegetables can sumptuously feed a man and animals, and a fatty cow delivers enough milk to supply a man sumptuously with vigor and vitality. If there is enough milk, enough grains, enough fruit, enough cotton, enough silk and enough jewels, then why do the people need cinemas, houses of prostitution, slaughterhouses, etc.? What is the need of an artificial luxurious life of cinema, cars, radio, flesh and hotels? Has this civilization produced anything but quarreling individually and nationally? Has this civilization enhanced the cause of equality and fraternity by sending thousands of men into a hellish factory and the war fields at the whims of a particular man?

It is said here that the cows used to moisten the pasturing land with milk because their milk bags were fatty and the animals were joyful. Do they not require, therefore, proper protection for a joyful life by being fed with a sufficient quantity of grass in the field? Why should men kill cows for their selfish purposes? Why should man not be satisfied with grains, fruits and milk, which, combined together, can produce hundreds and thousands of palatable dishes? Why are there slaughterhouses all over the world to kill innocent animals? Mahārāja Parīkṣit, grandson of Mahārāja Yudhiṣṭhira, while touring his vast kingdom, saw a black man attempting to kill a cow. The King at once arrested the butcher and chastised him sufficiently. Should not a king or executive head protect the lives of the poor animals who are unable to defend themselves? Is this humanity? Are not the animals of a country citizens also? Then why are they allowed to be butchered in organized slaughterhouses? Are these the signs of equality, fraternity and nonviolence?

Therefore, in contrast with the modern, advanced, civilized form of government, an autocracy like Mahārāja Yudhiṣṭhira's is by far superior to a so-called democracy in which animals are killed and a man less than an animal is allowed to cast votes for another less-than-animal man.

We are all creatures of material nature. In the *Bhagavad-gītā* it is said that the Lord Himself is the seed-giving father and material nature is the mother of *all living beings in all shapes.* Thus mother material nature has enough foodstuff both for animals and for men, by the grace of the father almighty, Śrī Kṛṣṇa. The human being is the elder brother of all other living beings. He is endowed with intelligence more powerful than animals' for realizing the course of nature and the indications of the almighty father. Human civilizations should depend on the production of material nature without artificially attempting economic development to turn the world into a chaos of artificial greed and power only for the purpose of artificial luxuries and sense gratification. This is but the life of dogs and hogs.

TEXT 5

नद्यः समुद्रा गिरयः सवनस्पतिवीरुधः ।
फलन्त्योषधयः सर्वाः काममन्वृतु तस्य वै ॥५॥

nadyaḥ samudrā girayaḥ
savanaspati-vīrudhaḥ
phalanty oṣadhayaḥ sarvāḥ
kāmam anvṛtu tasya vai

nadyaḥ—rivers; *samudrāḥ*—oceans; *girayaḥ*—hills and mountains; *savanaspati*—vegetables; *vīrudhaḥ*—creepers; *phalanti*—active; *oṣadhayaḥ*—drugs; *sarvāḥ*—all; *kāmam*—necessities; *anvṛtu*—seasonal; *tasya*—for the King; *vai*—certainly.

TRANSLATION

The rivers, oceans, hills, mountains, forests, creepers and active drugs, in every season, paid their tax quota to the King in profusion.

PURPORT

Since Mahārāja Yudhiṣṭhira was under the protection of the *ajita,* the infallible Lord, as above mentioned, the properties of the Lord, namely the rivers, oceans, hills, forests, etc., were all pleased, and they used to supply their respective quota of taxes to the King. The secret to success *is to take refuge under the protection of the Supreme Lord.* Without His sanction, nothing can be possible. To make economic development by our own endeavors on the strength of tools and machinery is not all. The sanction of the Supreme Lord must be there, otherwise despite all instrumental arrangements everything will be unsuccessful. The ultimate cause of success is the *daiva,* the Supreme. Kings like Mahārāja Yudhiṣṭhira knew perfectly well that the king is the agent of the Supreme Lord to look after the welfare of the mass of people. Actually the state belongs to the Supreme Lord. The rivers, oceans, forests, hills, drugs, etc., are not creations of man. They are all creations of the Supreme Lord, and the living being is allowed to make use of the property of the Lord for the service of the Lord. Today's slogan is that everything is for the people, and therefore the government is for the people and by the people. But to produce a new species of humanity at the present moment on the basis of God consciousness and perfection of human life, the ideology of godly communism, the world has to again follow in the footsteps of kings like Mahārāja Yudhiṣṭhira or Parīkṣit. There is enough of everything by the will of the Lord, and we can make proper use of things to live comfortably without enmity between men, or animal and man or nature. The control of the Lord is everywhere, and if the Lord is pleased, every part of nature will be pleased. The river will flow profusely to fertilize the land; the oceans will supply sufficient quantities of minerals, pearls and jewels; the forest will supply sufficient wood, drugs and vegetables, and the seasonal changes will effectively help produce fruits and flowers in profuse quantity. The artificial way of living depending on factories and tools can render so-called happiness only to a limited number at the cost of millions. Since the energy of the mass of people is engaged in factory production, the natural products are being hampered, and for this the mass is unhappy. Without being educated properly, the mass of people are following in the footsteps of the vested interests by exploiting natural reserves, and therefore there is acute competition between individual and individual and nation and nation. There is no control by the trained agent of the Lord. We must look into the defects of modern civilization by comparison here, and should follow in the footsteps of Mahārāja Yudhiṣṭhira to cleanse man and wipe out anachronisms.

TEXT 6

नाधयो व्याधयः क्लेशा दैवभूतात्महेतवः ।
अजातशत्रावभवन् जन्तूनां राज्ञि कर्हिचित् ॥६॥

nādhayo vyādhayaḥ kleśā
daiva-bhūtātma-hetavaḥ
ajāta-śatrāv abhavan
jantūnāṁ rājñi karhicit

na—never; *ādhayaḥ*—anxieties; *vyādhayaḥ*—diseases; *kleśāḥ*—trouble due to excessive heat and cold; *daiva-bhūta-ātma*—all due to the body, supernatural power and other living beings; *hetavaḥ*—due to the cause of; *ajāta-śatrau*—unto one who has no enemy; *abhavan*—happened; *jantūnām*—of the living beings; *rājñi*—unto the King; *karhicit*—at any time.

TRANSLATION

Because of the King's having no enemy, the living beings were not at any time disturbed by mental agonies, diseases, or excessive heat or cold.

PURPORT

To be nonviolent to human beings and to be a killer or enemy of the poor animals is Satan's philosophy. In this age there is enmity toward poor animals, and therefore the poor creatures are always anxious. The reaction of the poor animals is being forced on human society, and therefore there is always the strain of cold or hot war between men, individually, collectively or nationally. At the time of Mahārāja Yudhiṣṭhira, there were no different nations, although there were different subordinate states. The whole world was united, and the supreme head, being a trained king like Yudhiṣṭhira, kept all the inhabitants free from anxiety, diseases and excessive heat and cold. They were not only economically well-to-do, but also physically fit and undisturbed by supernatural power, by enmity from other living beings and by disturbance of bodily and mental agonies. There is a proverb in Bengali that a bad king spoils the kingdom and a bad housewife spoils the family. This truth is applicable here also. Because the King was pious and obedient to the Lord and sages, because he was no one's enemy and because he was a recognized agent of the Lord and therefore protected by Him, all the citizens under the King's protection were, so to speak, directly protected by the Lord and His authorized agents. Unless one is pious and recognized by the Lord, he cannot make others happy who are under his care. There is full cooperation between man and God and man and nature, and this conscious cooperation between man and God and man and nature, as exemplified by King Yudhiṣṭhira, can bring about happiness, peace and prosperity in the world. The attitude of exploiting one another, the custom of the day, will only bring misery.

TEXT 7

उषित्वा हास्तिनपुरे मासान् कतिपयान् हरिः ।
सुहृदां च विशोकाय स्वसुश्च प्रियकाम्यया ॥७॥

uṣitvā hāstinapure
māsān katipayān hariḥ
suhṛdāṁ ca viśokāya
svasuś ca priya-kāmyayā

uṣitvā—staying; *hāstinapure*—in the city of Hastināpura; *māsān*—months; *katipayān*—a few; *hariḥ*—Lord Śrī Kṛṣṇa; *suhṛdām*—relatives; *ca*—also; *viśokāya*—for pacifying them; *svasuḥ*—the sister; *ca*—and; *priya-kāmyayā*—for pleasing.

TRANSLATION

Śrī Hari, Lord Śrī Kṛṣṇa, resided at Hastināpura for a few months to pacify His relatives and please His own sister [Subhadrā].

PURPORT

Kṛṣṇa was to start for Dvārakā, His own kingdom, after the Battle of Kurukṣetra and Yudhiṣṭhira's being enthroned, but to oblige the request of Mahārāja Yudhiṣṭhira and to show special mercy to Bhīṣmadeva, Lord Kṛṣṇa stopped at Hastināpura, the capital of the Pāṇḍavas. The Lord decided to stay especially to pacify the aggrieved King as well as to please Subhadrā, sister of Lord Śrī Kṛṣṇa. Subhadrā was especially to be pacified because she lost her only son, Abhimanyu, who was just married. The boy left his wife, Uttarā, mother of Mahārāja Parīkṣit. The Lord is always pleased to satisfy His devotees in any capacity. Only His devotees can play the parts of His relatives. The Lord is absolute.

TEXT 8

आमन्त्र्य चाभ्यनुज्ञातः परिष्वज्याभिवाद्य तम् ।
आरुरोह रथं कैश्चित्परिष्वक्तोऽभिवादितः ॥८॥

āmantrya cābhyanujñātaḥ
pariṣvajyābhivādya tam
āruroha rathaṁ kaiścit
pariṣvakto 'bhivāditaḥ

āmantrya—taking permission; *ca*—and; *abhyanujñātaḥ*—being permitted; *pariṣvajya*—embracing; *abhivādya*—bowing down at the feet; *tam*—unto Mahārāja Yudhiṣṭhira; *āruroha*—ascended; *ratham*—the chariot;

kaiścit—by someone; *pariṣvaktaḥ*—being embraced; *abhivāditaḥ*—being offered obeisances.

TRANSLATION

Afterwards, when the Lord asked permission to depart and the King gave it, the Lord offered His respects to Mahārāja Yudhiṣṭhira by bowing down at his feet, and the King embraced Him. After this the Lord, being embraced by others and receiving their obeisances, got into His chariot.

PURPORT

Mahārāja Yudhiṣṭhira was the elder cousin of Lord Kṛṣṇa, and therefore while departing from him the Lord bowed down at the King's feet. The King embraced Him as a younger brother, although the King knew perfectly well that Kṛṣṇa is the Supreme Personality of Godhead. The Lord takes pleasure when some of His devotees accept Him as less important in terms of love. No one is greater than or equal to the Lord, but He takes pleasure in being treated as younger than His devotees. These are all transcendental pastimes of the Lord. The impersonalist cannot enter into the supernatural roles played by the devotee of the Lord. Thereafter Bhīma and Arjuna embraced the Lord because they were of the same age, but Nakula and Sahadeva bowed down before the Lord because they were younger than He.

TEXTS 9–10

सुभद्रा द्रौपदी कुन्ती विराटतनया तथा ।
गान्धारी धृतराष्ट्रश्च युयुत्सुर्गौतमो यमौ ॥९॥
वृकोदरश्च धौम्यश्च स्त्रियो मत्स्यसुतादयः ।
न सेहिरे विमुह्यन्तो विरहं शार्ङ्गधन्वनः ॥१०॥

subhadrā draupadī kuntī
virāṭa-tanayā tathā
gāndhārī dhṛtarāṣṭraś ca
yuyutsur gautamo yamau

vṛkodaraś ca dhaumyaś ca
striyo matsya-sutādayaḥ
na sehire vimuhyanto
virahaṁ śārṅga dhanvanaḥ

subhadrā—the sister of Kṛṣṇa; *draupadī*—the wife of the Pāṇḍavas; *kuntī*—the mother of the Pāṇḍavas; *virāṭa-tanayā*—the daughter of Virāṭa (Uttarā); *tathā*—also; *gāndhārī*—the mother of Duryodhana; *dhṛtarāṣṭraḥ*—the father of Duryodhana; *ca*—and; *yuyutsuḥ*—the son of Dhṛtarāṣṭra by his *vaiśya* wife; *gautamaḥ*—Kṛpācārya; *yamau*—the twin brothers Nakula and Sahadeva; *vṛkodaraḥ*—Bhīma; *ca*—and; *dhaumyaḥ*—Dhaumya; *ca*—and; *striyaḥ*—also other ladies of the palace; *matsya-sutā-ādayaḥ*—the daughter of a fisherman (Satyavatī, Bhīṣma's stepmother); *na*—could not; *sehire*—tolerate; *vimuhyantaḥ*—almost fainting; *viraham*—separation; *śārṅga-dhanvanaḥ*—of Śrī Kṛṣṇa, who bears a conch in His hand.

TRANSLATION

At that time Subhadrā, Draupadī, Kuntī, Uttarā, Gāndhārī, Dhṛtarāṣṭra, Yuyutsu, Kṛpācārya, Nakula, Sahadeva, Bhīmasena, Dhaumya and Satyavatī all nearly fainted because it was impossible for them to bear separation from Lord Kṛṣṇa.

PURPORT

Lord Śrī Kṛṣṇa is so attractive for the living beings, especially for the devotees, that it is impossible for them to tolerate separation. The conditioned soul under the spell of illusory energy forgets the Lord, otherwise he cannot. The feeling of such separation cannot be described, but it can simply be imagined by devotees only. After His separation from Vṛndāvana and the innocent rural cowherd boys, girls, ladies and others, they all felt shock throughout their lives, and the separation of Rādhārāṇī, the most beloved cowherd girl, is beyond expression. Once they met at Kurukṣetra during a solar eclipse, and the feeling which was expressed by them is heartrending. There is, of course, a difference in the qualities of the transcendental devotees of the Lord, but none of them who have ever contacted the Lord by direct communion or otherwise can leave Him for a moment. That is the attitude of the pure devotee.

TEXTS 11–12

सत्सङ्गान्मुक्तदुःसङ्गो हातुं नोत्सहते बुधः ।
कीर्त्यमानं यशो यस्य सकृदाकर्ण्य रोचनम् ॥११॥
तस्मिन्न्यस्तधियः पार्थाः सहेरन् विरहं कथम् ।
दर्शनस्पर्शसंलापशयनासनभोजनैः ॥१२॥

sat-saṅgān mukta-duḥsaṅgo
hātuṁ notsahate budhaḥ
kīrtyamānaṁ yaśo yasya
sakṛd ākarṇya rocanam

tasmin nyasta-dhiyaḥ pārthāḥ
saheran virahaṁ katham
darśana-sparśa-saṁlāpa-
śayanāsana-bhojanaiḥ

sat-saṅgāt—by the association of pure devotees; *mukta-duḥsaṅgaḥ*—freed from bad materialistic association; *hātum*—to give up; *na utsahate*—never attempts; *budhaḥ*—one who has understood the Lord; *kīrtyamānam*—glorifying; *yaśaḥ*—fame; *yasya*—whose; *sakṛt*—once only; *ākarṇya*—hearing only; *rocanam*—pleasing; *tasmin*—unto Him; *nyasta-dhiyaḥ*—one who has given his mind unto Him; *pārthāḥ*—the sons of Pṛthā; *saheran*—can tolerate; *viraham*—separation; *katham*—how; *darśana*—seeing face to face; *sparśa*—touching; *saṁlāpa*—conversing; *śayana*—sleeping; *āsana*—sitting; *bhojanaiḥ*—dining together.

TRANSLATION

The intelligent, who have understood the Supreme Lord in association with pure devotees and have become freed from bad materialistic association, can never avoid hearing the glories of the Lord, even though they have heard them only once. How, then, could the Pāṇḍavas tolerate His separation, for they had been intimately associated with His person, seeing Him face to face, touching Him, conversing with Him, and sleeping, sitting and dining with Him?

PURPORT

The living being's constitutional position is one of serving a superior. He is obliged to serve by force the dictates of illusory material energy in different phases of sense gratification. And in serving the senses he is never tired. Even though he may be tired, the illusory energy perpetually forces him to do so without being satisfied. There is no end to such sense gratificatory business, and the conditioned soul becomes entangled in such servitude without hope of release. The release is only effected by association with pure devotees. By such association one is gradually promoted to his transcendental consciousness. Thus he can know that his eternal position is to render service unto the Lord and not to the perverted senses in the capacity of lust, anger, desire to lord it over, etc. Material society, friendship and love are all different phases of lust. Home, country, family, society, wealth and all sorts of corollaries are all causes of bondage in the material world, where the threefold miseries of life are concomitant factors. By associating with pure devotees and by hearing them submissively, attachment for material enjoyment becomes slackened, and attraction for hearing about the transcendental activities of the Lord becomes prominent. Once they are, they will go on progressively without stoppage, like fire in gunpowder. It is said that Hari, the Personality of Godhead, is so transcendentally attractive that even those who are self-satisfied by self-realization and are factually liberated from all material bondage also become devotees of the Lord. Under the circumstances it is easily understood what must have been the position of the Pāṇḍavas, who were constant companions of the Lord. They could not even think of separation from Śrī Kṛṣṇa, since the attraction was more intense for them because of continuous personal contact. His remembrance by His form, quality, name, fame, pastimes, etc., is also attractive for the pure devotee, so much so that he forgets all forms, quality, name, fame and activities of the mundane world, and due to his mature association with pure devotees he is not out of contact with the Lord for a moment.

TEXT 13

सर्वे तेऽनिमिषैरक्षैस्तमनुद्रुतचेतसः ।
वीक्षन्तः स्नेहसम्बद्धा विचेलुस्तत्र तत्र ह ॥१३॥

sarve te 'nimiṣair akṣais
tam anu druta-cetasaḥ
vīkṣantaḥ sneha-sambaddhā
vicelus tatra tatra ha

sarve—all; *te*—they; *animiṣaiḥ*—without twinkling of the eyes; *akṣaiḥ*—by the eye; *tam anu*—after Him; *druta-cetasaḥ*—melted heart; *vīkṣantaḥ*—looking upon Him; *sneha-sambaddhāḥ*—bound by pure affection; *viceluḥ*—began to move; *tatra tatra*—here and there; *ha*—so they did.

TRANSLATION

All their hearts were melting for Him on the pot of attraction. They looked at Him without blinking their eyes, and they moved hither and thither in perplexity.

PURPORT

Kṛṣṇa is naturally attractive for all living beings because He is the chief eternal amongst all eternals. He alone is the maintainer of the many eternals. This is stated in the *Kaṭha Upaniṣad,* and thus one can obtain permanent peace and prosperity by revival of one's eternal relation with Him, now forgotten under the spell of *māyā,* the illusory energy of the Lord. Once this relation is slightly revived, the conditioned soul at once becomes freed from the illusion of material energy and becomes mad after the association of the Lord. This association is made possible not only by personal contact with the Lord, but also by association with His name, fame, form and quality. *Śrīmad-Bhāgavatam* trains the conditioned soul to this stage of perfection by submissive hearing from the pure devotee.

TEXT 14

न्यरुन्धन्नुद्गलद्बाष्पमौत्कण्ठ्याद्देवकीसुते ।
निर्यात्यगारान्नोऽभद्रमिति स्याद्बान्धवस्त्रियः ॥१४॥

nyarundhann udgalad bāṣpam
autkaṇṭhyād devakī-sute
niryāty agārān no 'bhadram
iti syād bāndhava-striyaḥ

nyarundhan—checking with great difficulty; *udgalat*—overflowing; *bāṣpam*—tears; *autkaṇṭhyāt*—because of great anxiety; *devakī-sute*—unto the son of Devakī; *niryāti*—having come out; *agārāt*—from the palace; *naḥ*—not; *abhadram*—inauspiciousness; *iti*—thus; *syāt*—may happen; *bāndhava*—relative; *striyaḥ*—ladies.

TRANSLATION

The female relatives, whose eyes were flooded with tears out of anxiety for Kṛṣṇa, came out of the palace. They could stop their tears only with great difficulty. They feared that tears would cause misfortune at the time of departure.

PURPORT

There were hundreds of ladies in the palace of Hastināpura. All of them were affectionate to Kṛṣṇa. All of them were relatives also. When they saw that Kṛṣṇa was going away from the palace for His native place, they were very anxious for Him, and as usual tears began to roll down their cheeks. They thought, at the same time, that tears at that moment might be a cause of misfortune for Kṛṣṇa; therefore they wanted to check them. This was very difficult for them because the tears could not be checked. Therefore, they smeared their tears in their eyes, and their hearts throbbed. Therefore ladies who were the wives and daughters-in-law of those who died in the battlefield never came in direct contact with Kṛṣṇa. But all of them heard of Him and His great activities, and thus they thought of Him, talked of Him, His name, fame, etc., and became affectionate also, like those who were in direct contact. Therefore directly or indirectly anyone who thinks of Kṛṣṇa, talks of Kṛṣṇa or worships Kṛṣṇa becomes attached to Him. Because Kṛṣṇa is absolute, there is no difference between His name, form, quality, etc. Our intimate relation with Kṛṣṇa can be confidentially revived by our talking of, hearing of, or remembering Him. It is so done due to spiritual potency.

TEXT 15

मृदङ्गशङ्खभेर्यश्च वीणापणवगोमुखाः ।
धुन्धुर्यानकघण्टाद्या नेदुर्दुन्दुभयस्तथा ॥१५॥

mṛdaṅga-śaṅkha-bheryaś ca
vīṇā-paṇava-gomukhāḥ
dhundhury-ānaka-ghaṇṭādyā
nedur dundubhayas tathā

mṛdaṅga—sweet-sounding drum; *śaṅkha*—conchshell; *bheryaḥ*—brass band; *ca*—and; *vīṇā*—string band; *paṇava*—a kind of flute; *gomukhāḥ*—another flute; *dhundhurī*—another drum; *ānaka*—kettle; *ghaṇṭā*—bell; *ādyāḥ*—others; *neduḥ*—sounded; *dundubhayaḥ*—other different types of drums; *tathā*—at that time.

TRANSLATION

While the Lord was departing from the palace of Hastināpura, different types of drums– like the mṛdaṅga, dhola, nagra, dhundhurī and dundubhi– and flutes of different types, the vīṇā, gomukha and bherī, all sounded together to show Him honor.

TEXT 16

प्रासादशिखरारूढाः कुरुनार्यो दिदृक्षया ।
ववृषुः कुसुमैः कृष्णं प्रेमव्रीडास्मितेक्षणाः ॥१६॥

prāsāda-śikharārūḍhāḥ
kuru-nāryo didṛkṣayā
vavṛṣuḥ kusumaiḥ kṛṣṇaṁ
prema-vrīḍā-smitekṣaṇāḥ

prāsāda—palace; *śikhara*—the roof; *ārūḍhāḥ*—ascending; *kuru-nāryaḥ*—the ladies of the Kuru royalty; *didṛkṣayā*—seeing; *vavṛṣuḥ*—showered; *kusumaiḥ*—by flowers; *kṛṣṇam*—upon Lord Kṛṣṇa; *prema*—out of affection and love; *vrīḍā-smita-īkṣaṇāḥ*—glancing with shy smiles.

TRANSLATION

Out of a loving desire to see the Lord, the royal ladies of the Kurus got up on top of the palace, and smiling with affection and shyness, they showered flowers upon the Lord.

PURPORT

Shyness is a particular extra-natural beauty of the fair sex, and it commands respect from the opposite sex. This custom was observed even during the days of the *Mahābhārata,* i.e., more than five thousand years ago. It is only the less intelligent persons not well versed in the history of the world who say that observance of separation of female from male is an introduction of the Mohammedan period in India. This incident from the *Mahābhārata* period proves definitely that the ladies of the palace observed strict *pardā* (restricted association with men), and instead of coming down in the open air where Lord Kṛṣṇa and others were assembled, the ladies of the palace went up on the top of the palace and from there paid their respects to Lord Kṛṣṇa by showers of flowers. It is definitely stated here that the ladies were smiling there on the top of the palace, checked by shyness. This shyness is a gift of nature to the fair sex, and it enhances their beauty and prestige, even if they are of a less important family or even if they are less attractive. We have practical experience of this fact. A sweeper woman commanded the respect of many respectable gentlemen simply by manifesting a lady's shyness. Half-naked ladies in the street do not command any respect, but a shy sweeper's wife commands respect from all.

Human civilization, as conceived of by the sages of India, is to help one free himself from the clutches of illusion. The material beauty of a woman is an illusion because actually the body is made of earth, water, fire, air, etc. But because there is the association of the living spark with matter, it appears to be beautiful. No one is attracted by an earthen doll, even if it is most perfectly prepared to attract the attention of others. The dead body has no beauty because no one will accept the dead body of a so-called beautiful woman. Therefore, the conclusion is that the spirit spark is beautiful, and because of the soul's beauty one is attracted by the beauty of the outward body. The Vedic wisdom, therefore, forbids us to be attracted by false beauty. But because we are now in the darkness of ignorance, the Vedic civilization allows very restricted mixing of woman and man. They say that the woman is considered to be the fire, and the man is considered to be the butter. The butter must melt in association with fire, and therefore they may be brought together only when it is necessary. And shyness is a check to the unrestricted mixing. It is nature's gift, and it must be utilized.

TEXT 17

सितातपत्रं जग्राह मुक्तादामविभूषितम् ।
रत्नदण्डं गुडाकेशः प्रियः प्रियतमस्य ह ॥१७॥

sitātapatraṁ jagrāha
muktādāma-vibhūṣitam
ratna-daṇḍaṁ guḍākeśaḥ
priyaḥ priyatamasya ha

sita-ātapatram—soothing umbrella; *jagrāha*—took up; *muktā-dāma*—decorated with laces and pearls; *vibhūṣitam*—embroidered; *ratna-daṇḍam*—with a handle of jewels; *guḍākeśaḥ*—Arjuna, the expert warrior, or one who has conquered sleep; *priyaḥ*—most beloved; *priyatamasya*—of the most beloved; *ha*—so he did.

TRANSLATION

At that time Arjuna, the great warrior and conqueror of sleep, who is the intimate friend of the most beloved Supreme Lord, took up an umbrella which had a handle of jewels and was embroidered with lace and pearls.

PURPORT

Gold, jewels, pearls and valuable stones were used in the luxurious royal ceremonies. They are all nature's gifts and are produced by the hills, oceans, etc., by the order of the Lord, when man does not waste his valuable time in producing unwanted things in the name of necessities. By so-called development of industrial enterprises, they are now using pots of gutta-percha instead of metals like gold, silver, brass and copper. They are using margarine instead of purified butter, and one fourth of the city population has no shelter.

TEXT 18

उद्धवः सात्यकिश्चैव व्यजने परमाद्भुते ।
विकीर्यमाणः कुसुमै रेजे मधुपतिः पथि ॥१८॥

uddhavaḥ sātyakiś caiva
vyajane paramādbhute
vikīryamāṇaḥ kusumai
reje madhu-patiḥ pathi

uddhavaḥ—a cousin-brother of Kṛṣṇa's; *sātyakiḥ*—His driver; *ca*—and; *eva*—certainly; *vyajane*—engaged in fanning; *parama-adbhute*—decorative; *vikīryamāṇaḥ*—seated on scattered; *kusumaiḥ*—flowers all around; *reje*—commanded; *madhu-patiḥ*—the master of Madhu (Kṛṣṇa); *pathi*—on the road.

TRANSLATION

Uddhava and Sātyaki began to fan the Lord with decorated fans, and the Lord, as the master of Madhu, seated on scattered flowers, commanded them along the road.

TEXT 19

अश्रूयन्ताशिषः सत्यास्तत्र तत्र द्विजेरिताः ।
नानुरूपानुरूपाश्च निर्गुणस्य गुणात्मनः ॥१९॥

aśrūyantāśiṣaḥ satyās
tatra tatra dvijeritāḥ
nānurūpānurūpāś ca
nirguṇasya guṇātmanaḥ

aśrūyanta—being heard; *āśiṣaḥ*—benediction; *satyāḥ*—all truths; *tatra*—here; *tatra*—there; *dvija-īritāḥ*—sounded by learned *brāhmaṇas; na*—not; *anurūpa*—befitting; *anurūpāḥ*—fitting; *ca*—also; *nirguṇasya*—of the Absolute; *guṇa-ātmanaḥ*—playing the role of a human being.

TRANSLATION

It was being heard here and there that the benedictions being paid to Kṛṣṇa were neither befitting nor unbefitting because they were all for the Absolute, who was now playing the part of a human being.

PURPORT

At places there were sounds of Vedic benediction aiming at the Personality of Godhead, Śrī Kṛṣṇa. The benedictions were fitting in the sense that the Lord was playing the part of a human being, as if a cousin of Mahārāja Yudhiṣṭhira, but they were also unfitting because the Lord is absolute and has nothing to do with any kind of material relativities. He is *nirguṇa,* or there are no material qualities in Him, but He is full of transcendental qualities. In the transcendental world there is nothing contradictory, whereas in the relative world everything has its opposite. In the relative world white is the opposite conception of black, but in the transcendental world there is no distinction between white and black. Therefore the sounds of benedictions uttered by the learned *brāhmaṇas* here and there appear to be contradictory in relation with the Absolute Person, but when they are applied to the Absolute Person they lose all contradiction and become transcendental. One example may clear this idea. Lord Śrī Kṛṣṇa is sometimes described as a thief. He is very famous amongst His pure devotees as the Mākhana-cora. He used to steal butter from the houses of neighbors at Vṛndāvana in His early age. Since then He is famous as a thief. But in spite of His being famous as a thief, He is worshiped as a thief, whereas in the mundane world a thief is punished and is never praised. Since He is the Absolute Personality of Godhead, everything is applicable to Him, and still in spite of all contradictions He is the Supreme Personality of Godhead.

TEXT 20

अन्योन्यमासीत्संजल्प उत्तमश्लोकचेतसाम् ।
कौरवेन्द्रपुरस्त्रीणां सर्वश्रुतिमनोहरः ॥२०॥

anyonyam āsīt sañjalpa
uttama-śloka-cetasām
kauravendra-pura-strīṇāṁ
sarva-śruti-mano-haraḥ

anyonyam—among each other; *āsīt*—there was; *sañjalpaḥ*—talking; *uttama-śloka*—the Supreme, who is praised by selected poetry; *cetasām*—

of those whose hearts are absorbed in that way; *kaurava-indra*—the king of the Kurus; *pura*—capital; *strīṇām*—all the ladies; *sarva*—all; *śruti*—the *Vedas; manaḥ-haraḥ*—attractive to the mind.

TRANSLATION

Absorbed in the thought of the transcendental qualities of the Lord, who is sung in select poetry, the ladies on the roofs of all the houses of Hastināpura began to talk of Him. This talk was more attractive than the hymns of the Vedas.

PURPORT

In the *Bhagavad-gītā* it is said that in all the Vedic literatures the goal is the Personality of Godhead, Śrī Kṛṣṇa. Factually the glories of the Lord are depicted in such literature as the *Vedas, Rāmāyaṇa* and *Mahābhārata.* And in the *Bhāgavatam* they are specifically mentioned in respect to the Supreme Lord. Therefore, while the ladies on the tops of the houses in the capital of the kings of the Kuru dynasty were talking about the Lord, their talk was more pleasing than the Vedic hymns. Anything sung in the praise of the Lord is *śruti-mantra.* There are songs of Ṭhākura Narottama dāsa, one of the *ācāryas* in the Gauḍīya *sampradāya,* composed in simple Bengali language. But Ṭhākura Viśvanātha Cakravartī, another very learned *ācārya* of the same *sampradāya,* has approved the songs by Ṭhākura Narottama dāsa to be as good as Vedic *mantras.* And this is so because of the subject matter. The language is immaterial, but the subject matter is important. The ladies, who were all absorbed in the thought and actions of the Lord, developed the consciousness of Vedic wisdom by the grace of the Lord. And therefore although such ladies might not have been very learned scholars in Sanskrit or otherwise, still whatever they spoke was more attractive than the Vedic hymns. The Vedic hymns in the *Upaniṣads* are sometimes indirectly directed to the Supreme Lord. But the talks of the ladies were directly spoken of the Lord, and thus they were more pleasing to the heart. The ladies' talks appeared to be more valuable than the learned *brāhmaṇas'* benedictions.

TEXT 21

स वै किलायं पुरुषः पुरातनो
य एक आसीदविशेष आत्मनि ।

अग्रे गुणेभ्यो जगदात्मनीश्वरे
निमीलितात्मन्निशि सुप्तशक्तिषु ॥२१॥

sa vai kilāyaṁ puruṣaḥ purātano
ya eka āsīd aviśeṣa ātmani
agre guṇebhyo jagad-ātmanīśvare
nimīlitātman niśi supta-śaktiṣu

saḥ—He (Kṛṣṇa); *vai*—as I remember; *kila*—definitely; *ayam*—this; *puruṣaḥ*—Personality of Godhead; *purātanaḥ*—the original; *yaḥ*—who; *ekaḥ*—only one; *āsīt*—existed; *aviśeṣaḥ*—materially unmanifested; *ātmani*—own self; *agre*—before creation; *guṇebhyaḥ*—of the modes of nature; *jagat-ātmani*—unto the Supersoul; *īśvare*—unto the Supreme Lord; *nimīlita*—merged into; *ātman*—the living entity; *niśi supta*—inactive at night; *śaktiṣu*—of the energies.

TRANSLATION

They said: Here He is, the original Personality of Godhead as we definitely remember Him. He alone existed before the manifested creation of the modes of nature, and in Him only, because He is the Supreme Lord, all living beings merge, as if sleeping at night, their energy suspended.

PURPORT

There are two types of dissolution of the manifested cosmos. At the end of every 4,320,000,000 solar years, when Brahmā, the lord of one particular universe, goes to sleep, there is one annihilation. And at the end of Lord Brahmā's life, which takes place at the end of Brahmā's one hundred years of age, in our calculation at the end of 8,640,000,000 x 30 x 12 x 100 solar years, there is complete annihilation of the entire universe, and in both the periods both the material energy called the *mahat-tattva* and the marginal energy called *jīva-tattva* merge in the person of the Supreme Lord. The living beings remain asleep within the body of the Lord until there is another creation of the material world, and that is the way of the creation, maintenance and annihilation of the material manifestation.

The material creation is effected by the interaction of the three modes of material nature set in action by the Lord, and therefore it is said here that the Lord existed before the modes of material nature were set in motion. In the *śruti-mantra* it is said that only Viṣṇu, the Supreme Lord, existed before the creation, and there was no Brahmā, Śiva or other demigods. Viṣṇu means the

Mahā-Viṣṇu, who is lying on the Causal Ocean. By His breathing only all the universes are generated in seeds and gradually develop into gigantic forms with innumerable planets within each and every universe. The seeds of universes develop into gigantic forms in the way seeds of a banyan tree develop into numberless banyan trees.

This Mahā-Viṣṇu is the plenary portion of the Lord Śrī Kṛṣṇa, who is mentioned in the *Brahma-saṁhitā* as follows:

"Let me offer my respectful obeisances unto the original Personality of Godhead, Govinda, whose plenary portion is the Mahā-Viṣṇu. All the Brahmās, the heads of the universes, live only for the period of His exhaling, after the universes are generated from the pores of His transcendental body." (*Brahma-saṁhitā* 5.58)

Thus Govinda, or Lord Kṛṣṇa, is the cause of Mahā-Viṣṇu also. The ladies talking about this Vedic truth must have heard it from authoritative sources. An authoritative source is the only means of knowing about transcendental subject matter definitely. There is no alternative.

The merging of the living beings into the body of Mahā-Viṣṇu takes place automatically at the end of Brahmā's one hundred years. But that does not mean that the individual living being loses his identity. The identity is there, and as soon as there is another creation by the supreme will of the Lord, all the sleeping, inactive living beings are again let loose to begin their activities in the continuation of past different spheres of life. It is called *suptotthita-nyāya,* or awakening from sleep and again engaging in one's respective continuous duty. When a man is asleep at night, he forgets himself, what he is, what his duty is and everything of his waking state. But as soon as he awakens from slumber, he remembers all that he has to do and thus engages himself again in his prescribed activities. The living beings also remain merged in the body of Mahā-Viṣṇu during the period of annihilation, but as soon as there is another creation they arise to take up their unfinished work. This is also confirmed in the *Bhagavad-gītā* (8.18–20).

The Lord existed before the creative energy was set in action. The Lord is not a product of the material energy. His body is completely spiritual, and there is no difference between His body and Himself. Before creation the Lord remained in His abode, which is absolute and one.

TEXT 22

स एव भूयो निजवीर्यचोदितां
स्वजीवमायां प्रकृतिं सिसृक्षताम् ।

अनामरूपात्मनि रूपनामनी
विधित्समानोऽनुससार शास्त्रकृत् ॥२२॥

sa eva bhūyo nija-vīrya-coditāṁ
sva-jīva-māyāṁ prakṛtiṁ sisṛkṣatīm
anāma-rūpātmani rūpa-nāmanī
vidhitsamāno 'nusasāra śāstra-kṛt

saḥ—He; *eva*—thus; *bhūyaḥ*—again; *nija*—own personal; *vīrya*—potency; *coditām*—performance of; *sva*—own; *jīva*—living being; *māyām*—external energy; *prakṛtim*—unto material nature; *sisṛkṣatīm*—while re-creating; *anāma*—without mundane designation; *rūpa-ātmani*—forms of the soul; *rūpa-nāmanī*—forms and names; *vidhitsamānaḥ*—desiring to award; *anusasāra*—entrusted; *śāstra-kṛt*—the compiler of revealed scripture.

TRANSLATION

The Personality of Godhead, again desiring to give names and forms to His parts and parcels, the living entities, placed them under the guidance of material nature. By His own potency, material nature is empowered to re-create.

PURPORT

The living entities are parts and parcels of the Lord. They are of two varieties, namely *nitya-mukta* and *nitya-baddha*. The *nitya-muktas* are eternally liberated souls, and they are eternally engaged in the reciprocation of transcendental loving service with the Lord in His eternal abode beyond the manifested mundane creations. But the *nitya-baddha,* or eternally conditioned souls, are entrusted to His external energy, *māyā,* for rectification of their rebellious attitude toward the supreme father. *Nitya-baddhas* are eternally forgetful of their relation with the Lord as parts and parcels. They are bewildered by the illusory energy as products of matter, and thus they are very busy in making plans in the material world for becoming happy. They go on merrily with plans, but by the will of the Lord both the plan-makers and the plans are annihilated at the end of a certain period, as above mentioned. This is confirmed in the *Bhagavad-gītā* as follows: "O son of Kuntī, at the end of the millennium all the living entities merge into My nature, and again when the time of creation is ripe, I begin creation by the agency of My external energy." (Bg. 9.7)

The word *bhūyaḥ* indicates "again and again," that is to say the process of creation,maintenance and annihilation is going on perpetually by the external energy of the Lord. He is the cause of everything. But the living beings, who are constitutionally the parts and parcels of the Lord and are forgetful of the sweet relation,are given a chance again to get rid of the clutches of the external energy. And to revive his (the living being's) consciousness, the revealed scriptures are also created by the Lord. Vedic literatures are the guiding directions for the conditioned souls so they can get free from the repetition of creation and annihilation of the material world and the material body.

The Lord says in the *Bhagavad-gītā,* "This created world and material energy are under My control. Under the influence of *prakṛti,* automatically they are created again and again, and this is done by Me through the agency of My external energy."

Actually the spiritual spark living entities have no material names or forms. But in order to fulfill their desire to lord it over the material energy of material forms and names, they are given a chance for such false enjoyment, and at the same time they are given a chance to understand the real position through the revealed scriptures. The foolish and forgetful living being is always busy with false forms and false names. Modern nationalism is the culmination of such false names and false forms. Men are mad after false name and form. The form of body obtained under certain conditions is taken up as factual, and the name also taken bewilders the conditioned soul into misusing the energy in the name of so many "isms." The scriptures, however, supply the clue for understanding the real position, but men are reluctant to take lessons from the scriptures created by the Lord for different places and times. For example, the *Bhagavad-gītā* is the guiding principle for all human beings, but by the spell of material energy they do not take care to carry out the programs of life in terms of the *Bhagavad-gītā. Śrīmad-Bhāgavatam* is the postgraduate study of knowledge for one who has thoroughly understood the principles of the *Bhagavad-gītā.* Unfortunately people have no taste for them, and therefore they are under the clutches of *māyā* for repetition of birth and death.

TEXT 23

स वा अयं यत्पदमत्र सूरयो
जितेन्द्रिया निर्जितमातरिश्वनः ।

पश्यन्ति भक्त्युत्कलितामलात्मना
नन्वेष सत्त्वं परिमार्ष्टुमर्हति ॥२३॥

sa vā ayaṁ yat padam atra sūrayo
jitendriyā nirjita-mātariśvanaḥ
paśyanti bhakty-utkalitāmalātmanā
nanv eṣa sattvaṁ parimārṣṭum arhati

saḥ—He; *vai*—by providence; *ayam*—this; *yat*—that which; *padam atra*—here is the same Personality of Godhead Śrī Kṛṣṇa; *sūrayaḥ*—great devotees; *jita-indriyāḥ*—who have overcome the influence of the senses; *nirjita*—thoroughly controlled; *mātariśvanaḥ*—life; *paśyanti*—can see; *bhakti*—by dint of devotional service; *utkalita*—developed; *amala-ātmanā*—those whose minds are thoroughly cleansed; *nanu eṣaḥ*—certainly by this only; *sattvam*—existence; *parimārṣṭum*—for purifying the mind completely; *arhati*—deserve.

TRANSLATION

Here is the same Supreme Personality of Godhead whose transcendental form is experienced by the great devotees who are completely cleansed of material consciousness by dint of rigid devotional service and full control of life and the senses. And that is the only way to purify existence.

PURPORT

As it is stated in *Bhagavad-gītā,* the Lord can be known in His real nature by dint of pure devotional service only. So it is stated here that only the great devotees of the Lord who are able to clear the mind of all material dust by rigid devotional service can experience the Lord as He is. *Jitendriya* means one who has full control over the senses. The senses are active parts of the body, and their activities cannot be stopped. The artificial means of the yogic processes to make the senses inactive has proved to be abject failure, even in the case of great *yogīs* like Viśvāmitra Muni. Viśvāmitra Muni controlled the senses by yogic trance, but when he happened to meet Menakā (a heavenly society woman), he became a victim of sex, and the artificial way of controlling the senses failed. But in the case of a pure devotee, the senses are not at all artificially stopped from doing anything, but they are given different good engagements. When the senses are engaged in more attractive activities, there is no chance of their being attracted by any inferior engagements. In the *Bhagavad-gītā* it is said that *the senses can be controlled only by better engagements.* Devotional service necessitates purifying the senses or engaging them in the activities of devotional service. Devotional service is not inaction. Anything done in the service of the Lord becomes at once purified of its material nature. The material conception is due to ignorance only. There is nothing beyond Vāsudeva. The Vāsudeva conception gradually develops in the heart of the learned after a prolonged acceleration of the receptive organs. But the process ends in the knowledge of accepting Vāsudeva as all in all. In the case of devotional service, this very same method is accepted from the very beginning, and by the grace of the Lord all factual knowledge becomes revealed in the heart of a devotee due to dictation by the Lord from within. Therefore controlling the senses by devotional service is the only and easiest means.

TEXT 24

स वा अयं सख्यनुगीतसत्कथो
वेदेषु गुह्येषु च गुह्यवादिभिः ।
य एक ईशो जगदात्मलीलया
सृजत्यवत्यत्ति न तत्र सज्जते ॥२४॥

sa vā ayaṁ sakhy anugīta-sat-katho
vedeṣu guhyeṣu ca guhya-vādibhiḥ
ya eka īśo jagad-ātma-līlayā
sṛjaty avaty atti na tatra sajjate

saḥ—He; *vai*—also; *ayam*—this; *sakhi*—O my friend; *anugīta*—described; *sat-kathaḥ*—the excellent pastimes; *vedeṣu*—in the Vedic literatures; *guhyeṣu*—confidentially; *ca*—as also; *guhya-vādibhiḥ*—by the confidential devotees; *yaḥ*—one who; *ekaḥ*—one only; *īśaḥ*—the supreme controller; *jagat*—of the complete creation; *ātma*—Supersoul; *līlayā*—by manifestation of pastimes; *sṛjati*—creates; *avati atti*—also maintains and annihilates; *na*—never; *tatra*—there; *sajjate*—becomes attached to it.

TRANSLATION

O dear friends, here is that very Personality of Godhead whose attractive and confidential pastimes are described in the confidential parts

of Vedic literature by His great devotees. It is He only who creates, maintains and annihilates the material world and yet remains unaffected.

PURPORT

As it is stated in the *Bhagavad-gītā,* all the Vedic literatures are glorifying the greatness of Lord Śrī Kṛṣṇa. Here it is confirmed in the *Bhāgavatam* also. The *Vedas* are expanded by many branches and subbranches by great devotees and empowered incarnations of the Lord like Vyāsa, Nārada, Śukadeva Gosvāmī, the Kumāras, Kapila, Prahlāda, Janaka, Bali and Yamarāja, but in the *Śrīmad-Bhāgavatam* especially, the confidential parts of His activities are described by the confidential devotee Śukadeva Gosvāmī. In the *Vedānta-sūtras* or *Upaniṣads* there is only a hint of the confidential parts of His pastimes. In such Vedic literatures as the *Upaniṣads,* the Lord has expressively been distinguished from the mundane conception of His existence. His identity being fully spiritual, His form, name, quality, and paraphernalia, etc., have been elaborately distinguished from matter, and therefore He is sometimes misunderstood by less intelligent persons as impersonal. But factually He is the Supreme Person, Bhagavān, and He is partially represented as Paramātmā or impersonal Brahman.

TEXT 25

यदा ह्यधर्मेण तमोधियो नृपा
जीवन्ति तत्रैष हि सत्त्वतः किल ।
धत्ते भगं सत्यमृतं दयां यशो
भवाय रूपाणि दधद्युगे युगे ॥२५॥

yadā hy adharmeṇa tamo-dhiyo nṛpā
jīvanti tatraiṣa hi sattvataḥ kila
dhatte bhagaṁ satyam ṛtaṁ dayāṁ yaśo
bhavāya rūpāṇi dadhad yuge yuge

yadā—whenever; *hi*—assuredly; *adharmeṇa*—against the principles of God's will; *tamaḥ-dhiyaḥ*—persons in the lowest material modes; *nṛpāḥ*—kings and administrators; *jīvanti*—live like animals; *tatra*—thereupon; *eṣaḥ*—He; *hi*—only; *sattvataḥ*—transcendental; *kila*—certainly; *dhatte*—is manifested; *bhagam*—supreme power; *satyam*—truth; *ṛtam*—positiveness; *dayām*—mercy; *yaśaḥ*—wonderful activities; *bhavāya*—for the maintenance; *rūpāṇi*—in various forms; *dadhat*—manifested; *yuge*—different periods; *yuge*—and ages.

TRANSLATION

Whenever there are kings and administrators living like animals in the lowest modes of existence, the Lord in His transcendental form manifests His supreme power, the Truth Positive, shows special mercy to the faithful, performs wonderful activities and manifests various transcendental forms as is necessary in different periods and ages.

PURPORT

As mentioned above, the cosmic creation is the property of the Supreme Lord. This is the basic philosophy of *Īśopaniṣad:* everything is the property of the Supreme Being. No one should encroach upon the property of the Supreme Lord. One should accept only what is kindly awarded by Him. Therefore, the earth or any other planet or universe is the absolute property of the Lord. The living beings are certainly His parts and parcels, or sons, and thus every one of them has a right to live at the mercy of the Lord to execute his prescribed work. No one, therefore, can encroach upon the right of another individual man or animal without being so sanctioned by the Lord. The king or the administrator is the representative of the Lord to look after the management of the Lord's will. He must therefore be a recognized person like Mahārāja Yudhiṣṭhira or Parīkṣit. Such kings have full responsibility and knowledge from authorities about the administration of the world. But at times, due to the influence of the ignorance mode of material nature (*tamo-guṇa*), the lowest of the material modes, kings and administrators come into power without knowledge and responsibility, and such foolish administrators live like animals for the sake of their own personal interest. The result is that the whole atmosphere becomes surcharged with anarchy and vicious elements. Nepotism, bribery, cheating, aggression and, therefore, famine, epidemic, war and similar other disturbing features become prominent in human society. And the devotees of the Lord or the faithful are persecuted by all means. All these symptoms indicate the time of an incarnation of the Lord to reestablish the principles of religion and to vanquish the maladministrators. This is also confirmed in the *Bhagavad-gītā.*

The Lord then appears in His transcendental form without any tinge of material qualities. He descends just to keep the state of His creation in a normal condition. The normal condition is that the Lord has provided each and every planet with all the needs of the native living beings. They can happily live and execute their predestined occupations to attain salvation at the end, following the rules and regulations mentioned in the revealed scriptures. The material world is created to satisfy the whims of the *nitya-baddha,* or everlasting conditioned souls, just as naughty boys are provided with playing cradles. Otherwise, there was no need of the material world. But when they become intoxicated with the power of material science to exploit the resources unlawfully without the sanction of the Lord, and that also only for sense gratification, there is necessity of the Lord's incarnation to chastise the rebellious and to protect the faithful.

When He descends, He exhibits superhuman acts just to prove His supreme right, and materialists like Rāvaṇa, Hiraṇyakaśipu and Kaṁsa are sufficiently punished. He acts in a manner which no one can imitate. For example, the Lord, when He appeared as Rāma, bridged the Indian Ocean. When He appeared as Kṛṣṇa, from His very childhood He showed superhuman activities by killing Pūtanā, Aghāsura, Śakaṭāsura, Kāliya, etc., and then His maternal uncle Kaṁsa. When He was at Dvārakā He married 16,108 queens, and all of them were blessed with a sufficient number of children. The sum total of His personal family members amounted to about 100,000, popularly known as the Yadu-vaṁśa. And again, during His lifetime, He managed to vanquish them all. He is famous as the Govardhana-dhārī Hari because He lifted at the age of only seven the hill known as Govardhana. The Lord killed many undesirable kings in His time, and as a *kṣatriya* He fought chivalrously. He is famous as *asamordhva,* unparalleled. No one is equal to or greater than Him.

TEXT 26

अहो अलं श्लाघ्यतमं यदोः कुल-
महो अलं पुण्यतमं मधोर्वनम् ।
यदेष पुंसामृषभः श्रियः पतिः
स्वजन्मना चङ्क्रमणेन चाञ्चति ॥२६॥

aho alaṁ ślāghyatamaṁ yadoḥ kulam
aho alaṁ puṇyatamaṁ madhor vanam
yad eṣa puṁsām ṛṣabhaḥ śriyaḥ patiḥ
sva-janmanā caṅkramaṇena cāñcati

aho—oh; *alam*—verily; *ślāghya-tamam*—supremely glorified; *yadoḥ*—of King Yadu; *kulam*—dynasty; *aho*—oh; *alam*—verily; *puṇya-tamam*—supremely virtuous; *madhoḥ vanam*—the land of Mathurā; *yat*—because; *eṣaḥ*—this; *puṁsām*—of all the living beings; *ṛṣabhaḥ*—supreme leader; *śriyaḥ*—of the goddess of fortune; *patiḥ*—husband; *sva-janmanā*—by His appearance; *caṅkramaṇena*—by crawling; *ca añcati*—glories.

TRANSLATION

Oh, how supremely glorified is the dynasty of King Yadu, and how virtuous is the land of Mathurā, where the supreme leader of all living beings, the husband of the goddess of fortune, has taken His birth and wandered in His childhood.

PURPORT

In the *Bhagavad-gītā* the Personality of Godhead, Śrī Kṛṣṇa, has expressively given a description of His transcendental appearance, disappearance and activities. The Lord appears in a particular family or place by His inconceivable potency. He does not take His birth as a conditioned soul quits his body and accepts another body. His birth is like the appearance and disappearance of the sun. The sun arises on the eastern horizon, but that does not mean that the eastern horizon is the parent of the sun. The sun is existent in every part of the solar system, but he becomes visible at a scheduled time and so also becomes invisible at another scheduled time. Similarly, the Lord appears in this universe like the sun and again leaves our sight at another time. He exists at all times and at every place, but by His causeless mercy when He appears before us we take it for granted that He has taken His birth. Anyone who can understand this truth, in terms of the statements of revealed scriptures, certainly becomes liberated just after quitting the present body. Liberation is obtainable after many births and after great endeavor in patience and perseverance, in knowledge and renunciation. But simply by knowing in truth about the Lord's transcendental births and activities, one can get liberation at once. That is the verdict of the *Bhagavad-gītā.* But those who are in the darkness of ignorance conclude that the Lord's birth and activities in the material world are similar to those of the ordinary living being. Such imperfect conclusions cannot give anyone liberation. His birth, therefore, in the family of King Yadu as the son of King Vasudeva and His transfer into the family of Nanda Mahārāja in the land of Mathurā are all transcendental arrangements made by the internal potency of the Lord. The fortunes of the Yadu dynasty and that of the inhabitants of the land of Mathurā cannot be materially estimated. If simply by knowing the transcendental nature of the birth and activities of the Lord one can get liberation easily, we can just imagine what is in store for those who actually enjoyed the company of the Lord in person as a family member or as a neighbor. All those who were fortunate enough to associate with the Lord, the husband of the goddess of fortune, certainly obtained something *more than what is known as liberation.* Therefore, rightly, the dynasty and the land are both ever glorious by the grace of the Lord.

TEXT 27

अहो बत स्वर्यशसस्तिरस्करी
कुशस्थली पुण्ययशस्करी भुवः ।
पश्यन्ति नित्यं यदनुग्रहेषितं
स्मितावलोकं स्वपतिं स्म यत्प्रजाः ॥२७॥

aho bata svar-yaśasas tiraskarī
kuśasthalī puṇya-yaśaskarī bhuvaḥ
paśyanti nityaṁ yad anugraheṣitaṁ
smitāvalokaṁ sva-patiṁ sma yat-prajāḥ

aho bata—how wonderful this is; *svaḥ-yaśasaḥ*—the glories of the heavenly planets; *tiraskarī*—that which defeats; *kuśasthalī*—Dvārakā; *puṇya*—virtue; *yaśaskarī*—famous; *bhuvaḥ*—the planet earth; *paśyanti*—see; *nityam*—constantly; *yat*—that which; *anugraha-iṣitam*—to bestow benediction; *smita-avalokam*—glance with the favor of sweet smiling; *sva-patim*—unto the soul of the living being (Kṛṣṇa); *sma*—used to; *yat-prajāḥ*—the inhabitants of the place.

TRANSLATION

Undoubtedly it is wonderful that Dvārakā has defeated the glories of the heavenly planets and has enhanced the celebrity of the earth. The inhabitants of Dvārakā are always seeing the soul of all living beings [Kṛṣṇa] in His loving feature. He glances at them and favors them with sweet smiles.

PURPORT

The heavenly planets are inhabited by demigods like Indra, Candra, Varuṇa and Vāyu, and the pious souls reach there after performance of many virtuous acts on earth. Modern scientists agree that the timing arrangement in higher planetary systems is different from that of the earth. Thus it is understood from the revealed scriptures that the duration of life there is ten thousand years (by our calculation). Six months on earth is equal to one day on the heavenly planets. Facilities of enjoyment are also similarly enhanced, and the beauty of the inhabitants is legendary. Common men on the earth are very much fond of reaching the heavenly planets because they have heard that comforts of life are far greater there than on the earth. They are now trying to reach the moon by spacecraft. Considering all this, the heavenly planets are more celebrated than the earth. But the celebrity of earth has defeated that of the heavenly planets because of Dvārakā, where Lord Śrī Kṛṣṇa reigned as King. Three places, namely Vṛndāvana, Mathurā and Dvārakā, are more important than the famous planets within the universe. These places are perpetually sanctified because whenever the Lord descends on earth He displays His transcendental activities particularly in these three places. They are perpetually the holy lands of the Lord, and the inhabitants still take advantage of the holy places, even though the Lord is now out of their sight. The Lord is the soul of all living beings, and He desires always to have all the living beings, in their *svarūpa,* in their constitutional position, to participate in transcendental life in His association. His attractive features and sweet smiles go deep into the heart of everyone, and once it is so done the living being is admitted into the kingdom of God, from which no one returns. This is confirmed in the *Bhagavad-gītā.*

The heavenly planets may be very famous for offering better facilities of material enjoyment, but as we learn from the *Bhagavad-gītā* (9.20–21), one has to come back again to the earth planet as soon as the acquired virtue is finished. Dvārakā is certainly more important than the heavenly planets because whoever has been favored with the smiling glance of the Lord shall never come back again to this rotten earth, which is certified by the Lord Himself as a place of misery. Not only this earth but also all the planets of the universes are places of misery because in none of the planets within the universe is there eternal life, eternal bliss and eternal knowledge. Any person engaged in the devotional service of the Lord is recommended to live in one of the above-mentioned three places, namely Dvārakā, Mathurā or Vṛndāvana. Because devotional service in these three places is magnified, those who go there to follow the principles in terms of instructions imparted in the revealed scriptures surely achieve the same result as obtained during the presence of Lord Śrī Kṛṣṇa. His abode and He Himself are identical, and a pure devotee under the guidance of another experienced devotee can obtain all the results, even at present.

TEXT 28

नूनं व्रतस्नानहुतादिनेश्वरः
समर्चितो ह्यस्य गृहीतपाणिभिः ।
पिबन्ति याः सख्यधरामृतं मुहु-
र्व्रजस्त्रियः सम्मुमुहुर्यदाशयाः ॥२८॥

nūnaṁ vrata-snāna-hutādineśvaraḥ
samarcito hy asya gṛhīta-pāṇibhiḥ
pibanti yāḥ sakhy adharāmṛtaṁ muhur
vraja-striyaḥ sammumuhur yad-āśayāḥ

nūnam—certainly in the previous birth; *vrata*—vow; *snāna*—bath; *huta*—sacrifice in the fire; *ādinā*—by all these; *īśvaraḥ*—the Personality of Godhead; *samarcitaḥ*—perfectly worshiped; *hi*—certainly; *asya*—His; *gṛhīta-pāṇibhiḥ*—by the married wives; *pibanti*—relishes; *yāḥ*—those who; *sakhi*—O friend; *adhara-amṛtam*—the nectar from His lips; *muhuḥ*—again and again; *vraja-striyaḥ*—the damsels of Vrajabhūmi; *sammumuhuḥ*—often fainted; *yat-āśayāḥ*—expecting to be favored in that way.

TRANSLATION

O friends, just think of His wives, whose hands He has accepted. How they must have undergone vows, baths, fire sacrifices and perfect worship of the Lord of the universe to constantly relish now the nectar from His lips [by kissing]. The damsels of Vrajabhūmi would often faint just by expecting such favors.

PURPORT

Religious rites prescribed in the scriptures are meant to purify the mundane qualities of the conditioned souls to enable them to be gradually promoted to the stage of rendering transcendental service unto the Supreme Lord. Attainment of this stage of pure spiritual life is the highest perfection, and this stage is called *svarūpa,* or the factual identity of the living being. Liberation means renovation of this stage of *svarūpa.* In that perfect stage of *svarūpa,* the living being is established in five phases of loving service, one of which is the stage of *mādhurya-rasa,* or the humor of conjugal love. The Lord is always perfect in Himself, and thus He has no hankering for Himself. He, however, becomes a master, a friend, a son or a husband to fulfill the intense love of the devotee concerned. Herein two classes of devotees of the Lord are mentioned in the stage of conjugal love. One is *svakīya,* and the other is *parakīya.* Both of them are in conjugal love with the Personality of Godhead, Kṛṣṇa. The queens at Dvārakā were *svakīya,* or duly married wives, but the damsels of Vraja were young friends of the Lord while He was unmarried. The Lord stayed at Vṛndāvana till the age of sixteen, and His friendly relations with the neighboring girls were in terms of *parakīya.* These girls, as well as the queens, underwent severe penances by taking vows, bathing and offering sacrifices in the fire, as prescribed in the scriptures. The rites, as they are, are not an end in themselves, nor are fruitive action, culture of knowledge or perfection in mystic powers ends in themselves. They are all means to attain to the highest stage of *svarūpa,* to render constitutional transcendental service to the Lord. Each and every living being has his individual position in one of the above-mentioned five different kinds of reciprocating means with the Lord, and in one's pure spiritual form of *svarūpa* the relation becomes manifest without mundane affinity. The kissing of the Lord, either by His wives or His young girl friends who aspired to have the Lord as their fiancé, is not of any mundane perverted quality. Had such things been mundane, a liberated soul like Śukadeva would not have taken the trouble to relish them, nor would Lord Śrī Caitanya Mahāprabhu have been inclined to participate in those subjects after renouncing worldly life. The stage is earned after many lives of penance.

TEXT 29

या वीर्यशुल्केन हृताः स्वयंवरे
प्रमथ्य चैद्यप्रमुखान् हि शुष्मिणः ।
प्रद्युम्नसाम्बाम्बसुतादयोऽपरा
याश्चाहृता भौमवधे सहस्रशः ॥२९॥

yā vīrya-śulkena hṛtāḥ svayaṁvare
pramathya caidya-pramukhān hi śuṣmiṇaḥ
pradyumna-sāmbāmba-sutādayo 'parā
yāś cāhṛtā bhauma-vadhe sahasraśaḥ

yā—the lady; *vīrya*—prowess; *śulkena*—by payment of the price; *hṛtāḥ*—taken away by force; *svayaṁvare*—in the open selection of the bridegroom;

pramathya—harassing; *caidya*—King Śiśupāla; *pramukhān*—headed by; *hi*—positively; *śuṣmiṇaḥ*—all very powerful; *pradyumna*—Pradyumna (Kṛṣṇa's son); *sāmba*—Sāmba; *amba*—Amba; *suta-ādayaḥ*—children; *aparāḥ*—other ladies; *yāḥ*—those; *ca*—also; *āhṛtāḥ*—similarly brought; *bhauma-vadhe*—after killing kings; *sahasraśaḥ*—by the thousands.

TRANSLATION

The children of these ladies are Pradyumna, Sāmba, Amba, etc. Ladies like Rukmiṇī, Satyabhāmā and Jāmbavatī were forcibly taken away by Him from their svayaṁvara ceremonies after He defeated many powerful kings, headed by Śiśupāla. And other ladies were also forcibly taken away by Him after He killed Bhaumāsura and thousands of his assistants. All of these ladies are glorious.

PURPORT

Exceptionally qualified daughters of powerful kings were allowed to make a choice of their own bridegrooms in open competition, and such ceremonies were called *svayaṁvara,* or selection of the bridegroom. Because the *svayaṁvara* was an open competition between the rival and valiant princes, such princes were invited by the father of the princess, and usually there were regular fights between the invited princely order in a sporting spirit. But it so happened that sometimes the belligerent princes were killed in such marriage-fighting, and the victorious prince was offered the trophy princess for whom so many princes died. Rukmiṇī, the principal queen of Lord Kṛṣṇa, was the daughter of the King of Vidarbha, who wished that his qualified and beautiful daughter be given away to Lord Kṛṣṇa. But her eldest brother wanted her to be given away to King Śiśupāla, who happened to be a cousin of Kṛṣṇa. So there was open competition, and as usual Lord Kṛṣṇa emerged successful, after harassing Śiśupāla and other princes by His unrivalled prowess. Rukmiṇī had ten sons, like Pradyumna. There were other queens also taken away by Lord Kṛṣṇa in a similar way. Full description of this beautiful booty of Lord Kṛṣṇa will be given in the Tenth Canto. There were 16,100 beautiful girls who were daughters of many kings and were forcibly stolen by Bhaumāsura, who kept them captive for his carnal desire. These girls prayed piteously to Lord Kṛṣṇa for their deliverance, and the merciful Lord, called by their fervent prayer, released them all by fighting and killing Bhaumāsura. All these captive princesses were then accepted by the Lord as His wives, although in the estimation of society they were all fallen girls. The all-powerful Lord Kṛṣṇa accepted the humble prayers of these girls and married them with the adoration of queens. So altogether Lord Kṛṣṇa had 16,108 queens at Dvārakā, and in each of them He begot ten children. All these children grew up, and each had as many children as the father. The aggregate of the family numbered in the millions.

TEXT 30

एताः परं स्त्रीत्वमपास्तपेशलं
निरस्तशौचं बत साधु कुर्वते।
यासां गृहात्पुष्करलोचनः पति-
र्न जात्वपैत्याहृतिभिर्हृदि स्पृशन् ॥३०॥

etāḥ paraṁ strītvam apāstapeśalaṁ
nirasta-śaucaṁ bata sādhu kurvate
yāsāṁ gṛhāt puṣkara-locanaḥ patir
na jātv apaity āhṛtibhir hṛdi spṛśan

etāḥ—all these women; *param*—highest; *strītvam*—womanhood; *apāstapeśalam*—without individuality; *nirasta*—without; *śaucam*—purity; *bata sādhu*—auspiciously glorified; *kurvate*—do they make; *yāsām*—from whose; *gṛhāt*—homes; *puṣkara-locanaḥ*—the lotus-eyed; *patiḥ*—husband; *na jātu*—never at any time; *apaiti*—goes away; *āhṛtibhiḥ*—by presentation; *hṛdi*—in the heart; *spṛśan*—endeared.

TRANSLATION

All these women auspiciously glorified their lives despite their being without individuality and without purity. Their husband, the lotus-eyed Personality of Godhead, never left them alone at home. He always pleased their hearts by making valuable presentations.

PURPORT

The devotees of the Lord are purified souls. As soon as the devotees surrender unto the lotus feet of the Lord sincerely, the Lord accepts them, and thus the devotees at once become free from all material contaminations. Such devotees are above the three modes of material nature. There is no bodily disqualification of a devotee, just as there is no qualitative difference between the Ganges water and the filthy drain water when they are amalgamated. Women, merchants and laborers are not very intelligent, and thus it is very difficult for them to understand the science of God or to be engaged in the devotional service of the Lord. They are more materialistic, and less than them are the Kirātas, Hūṇas, Āndhras, Pulindas, Pulkaśas, Ābhīras, Kaṅkas, Yavanas, Khasas, etc., but all of them can be delivered if they are properly engaged in the devotional service of the Lord. By engagement in the service of the Lord, the designative disqualifications are removed, and as pure souls they become eligible to enter into the kingdom of God.

The fallen girls under the clutches of Bhaumāsura sincerely prayed to Lord Śrī Kṛṣṇa for their deliverance, and their sincerity of purpose made them at once pure by virtue of devotion. The Lord therefore accepted them as His wives, and thus their lives became glorified. Such auspicious glorification was still more glorified when the Lord played with them as the most devoted husband.

The Lord used to live with His 16,108 wives constantly. He expanded Himself into 16,108 plenary portions, and each and every one of Them was the Lord Himself without deviation from the original personality. The *śruti-mantra* affirms that the Lord can expand Himself into many. As husband of so many wives, He pleased them all with presentations, even at a costly endeavor. He brought the *pārijāta* plant from heaven and implanted it at the palace of Satyabhāmā, one of the principal queens. If, therefore, anyone desires the Lord to become one's husband, the Lord fulfills such desires in full.

TEXT 31

एवंविधा गदन्तीनां स गिरः पुरयोषिताम् ।
निरीक्षणेनाभिनन्दन् सस्मितेन ययौ हरिः ॥३१॥

evaṁvidhā gadantīnām
sa giraḥ pura-yoṣitām
nirīkṣaṇenābhinandan
sasmitena yayau hariḥ

evaṁvidhāḥ—in this way; *gadantīnām*—thus praying and talking about Him; *saḥ*—He (the Lord); *giraḥ*—of words; *pura-yoṣitām*—of the ladies of the capital; *nirīkṣaṇena*—by His grace of glancing over them; *abhinandan*—and greeting them; *sa-smitena*—with a smiling face; *yayau*—departed; *hariḥ*—the Personality of Godhead.

TRANSLATION

While the ladies of the capital Hastināpura were greeting Him and talking in this way, the Lord, smiling, accepted their good greetings, and casting the grace of His glance over them, He departed from the city.

TEXT 32

अजातशत्रुः पृतनां गोपीथाय मधुद्विषः ।
परेभ्यः शङ्कितः स्नेहात्प्रायुङ्क्त चतुरङ्गिणीम् ॥३२॥

ajāta-śatruḥ pṛtanāṁ
gopīthāya madhu-dviṣaḥ
parebhyaḥ śaṅkitaḥ snehāt
prāyuṅkta catur-aṅgiṇīm

ajāta-śatruḥ—Mahārāja Yudhiṣṭhira, who was no one's enemy; *pṛtanām*—defensive forces; *gopīthāya*—for giving protection; *madhu-dviṣaḥ*—of the enemy of Madhu (Śrī Kṛṣṇa); *parebhyaḥ*—from others (enemies); *śaṅkitaḥ*—being afraid of; *snehāt*—out of affection; *prāyuṅkta*—engaged; *catuḥ-aṅginīm*—four defensive divisions.

TRANSLATION

Mahārāja Yudhiṣṭhira, although no one's enemy, engaged four divisions of defense [horse, elephant, chariot and army] to accompany Lord Kṛṣṇa, the enemy of the asuras [demons]. The Mahārāja did this because of the enemy, and also out of affection for the Lord.

PURPORT

Natural defensive measures are horses and elephants combined with chariots and men. Horses and elephants are trained to move to any part of the hills or forests and plains. The charioteers could fight with many horses and elephants by the strength of powerful arrows, even up to the standard of the *brahmāstra* (similar to modern atomic weapons). Mahārāja Yudhiṣṭhira knew well that Kṛṣṇa is everyone's friend and well-wisher, and yet there were *asuras* who were by nature envious of the Lord. So out of fear of attack from others and out of affection also, he engaged all varieties of defensive forces as bodyguards of Lord Kṛṣṇa. If required, Lord Kṛṣṇa Himself was sufficient to defend Himself from the attack of others who counted the Lord as their enemy.

but still He accepted all the arrangements made by Mahārāja Yudhiṣṭhira because He could not disobey the King, who was His elder cousin. The Lord plays the part of a subordinate in His transcendental sporting, and thus sometimes He puts Himself in the care of Yaśodāmātā for His protection in His so-called helplessness of childhood. That is the transcendental *līlā,* or pastime of the Lord. The basic principle for all transcendental exchanges between the Lord and His devotees is exhibited to enjoy a transcendental bliss for which there is no comparison, even up to the level of *brahmānanda.*

TEXT 33

अथ दूरागतान् शौरिः कौरवान् विरहातुरान्।
संनिवर्त्य दृढं स्निग्धान् प्रायात्स्वनगरीं प्रियैः ॥३३॥

atha dūrāgatān śauriḥ
kauravān virahāturān
sannivartya dṛḍhaṁ snigdhān
prāyāt sva-nagarīṁ priyaiḥ

atha—thus; *dūrāgatān*—having accompanied Him for a long distance; *śauriḥ*—Lord Kṛṣṇa; *kauravān*—the Pāṇḍavas; *virahāturān*—overwhelmed by a sense of separation; *sannivartya*—politely persuaded; *dṛḍham*—determined; *snigdhān*—full of affection; *prāyāt*—proceeded; *sva-nagarīm*—towards His own city (Dvārakā); *priyaiḥ*—with dear companions.

TRANSLATION

Out of profound affection for Lord Kṛṣṇa, the Pāṇḍavas, who were of the Kuru dynasty, accompanied Him a considerable distance to see Him off. They were overwhelmed with the thought of future separation. The Lord, however, persuaded them to return home, and He proceeded towards Dvārakā with His dear companions.

TEXTS 34–35

कुरुजाङ्गलपाञ्चालान् शूरसेनान् सयामुनान् ।
ब्रह्मावर्तं कुरुक्षेत्रं मत्स्यान् सारस्वतानथ ॥३४॥
मरुधन्वमतिक्रम्य सौवीराभीरयोः परान् ।
आनर्तान् भार्गवोपागाच्छ्रान्तवाहो मनाग्विभुः ॥३५॥

kuru-jāṅgala-pāñcālān
śūrasenān sayāmunān
brahmāvartaṁ kurukṣetraṁ
matsyān sārasvatān atha

maru-dhanvam atikramya
sauvīrābhīrayoḥ parān
ānartān bhārgavopāgāc
chrāntavāho manāg vibhuḥ

kuru-jāṅgala—the province of Delhi; *pāñcālān*—part of the province Pānjab; *śūrasenān*—part of the province of Uttar Pradesh; *sa*—with; *yāmunān*—the districts on the bank of the Yamunā; *brahmāvartam*—part of northern Uttar Pradesh; *kurukṣetram*—the place where the battle was fought; *matsyān*—the province Matsyā; *sārasvatān*—part of Punjab; *atha*—and so on; *maru*—Rajasthan, the land of deserts; *dhanvam*—Madhya Pradesh, where water is very scanty; *ati-kramya*—after passing; *sauvīra*—Saurastra; *ābhīrayoḥ*—part of Gujarat; *parān*—western side; *ānartān*—the province of Dvārakā; *bhārgava*—O Śaunaka; *upāgāt*—overtaken by; *śrānta*—fatigue; *vāhaḥ*—the horses; *manāk vibhuḥ*—slightly, because of the long journey.

TRANSLATION

O Śaunaka, the Lord then proceeded towards Kurujāṅgala, Pāñcālā, Śūrasenā, the land on the bank of the river Yamunā, Brahmāvarta, Kurukṣetra, Matsyā , Sārasvatā, the province of the desert and the land of scanty water. After crossing these provinces He gradually reached the Sauvīra and Ābhīra provinces, then, west of these, reached Dvārakā at last.

PURPORT

The provinces passed over by the Lord in those days were differently named, but the direction given is sufficient to indicate that He traveled through Delhi, Punjab, Rajasthan, Madhya Pradesh, Saurastra and Gujarat and at last reached His home province at Dvārakā. We do not gain any profit simply by researching the analogous provinces of those days up to now, but it appears that the desert of Rajasthan and the provinces of scanty water like Madhya Pradesh were present even five thousand years ago. The theory of soil experts that the desert developed in recent years is not supported by the statements of *Bhāgavatam.* We may leave the matter for expert geologists to research because the changing universe has different phases of geological development. We are satisfied that the Lord has now reached His own province, Dvārakā-dhāma, from the Kuru provinces. Kurukṣetra continues to exist since the Vedic age, and it is sheer foolishness when interpreters ignore or deny the existence of Kurukṣetra.

TEXT 36

तत्र तत्र ह तत्रत्यैर्हरिः प्रत्युद्यतार्हणः ।
सायं भेजे दिशं पश्चाद्गविष्ठो गां गतस्तदा ॥३६॥

tatra tatra ha tatratyair
hariḥ pratyudyatārhaṇaḥ
sāyaṁ bheje diśaṁ paścād
gaviṣṭho gāṁ gatas tadā

tatra tatra—at different places; *ha*—it so happened; *tatratyaiḥ*—by local inhabitants; *hariḥ*—the Personality of Godhead; *pratyudyata-arhaṇaḥ*—being offered presentations and worshipful regards; *sāyam*—the evening; *bheje*—having overtaken; *diśam*—direction; *paścāt*—western; *gaviṣṭhaḥ*—the sun in the sky; *gām*—to the ocean; *gataḥ*—having gone; *tadā*—at that time.

TRANSLATION

On His journey through these provinces He was welcomed, worshiped and given various presentations. In the evening, in all places, the Lord suspended His journey to perform evening rites. This was regularly observed after sunset.

PURPORT

It is said here that the Lord observed the religious principles regularly while He was on the journey. There are certain philosophical speculations that even the Lord is under the obligations of fruitive action. But actually this is not the case. He does not depend on the action of any good or bad work. *Since the Lord is absolute, everything done by Him is good for everyone.* But when He descends on earth, He acts for the protection of the devotees and for the annihilation of the impious nondevotees. Although He has no obligatory duty, still He does everything so that others may follow. That is the way of factual teaching; one must act properly himself and teach the same to others, otherwise no one will accept one's blind teaching. He is Himself the awarder of fruitive results. He is self-sufficient, and yet He acts according to the rulings of the revealed scripture in order to teach us the process. If He does not do so, the common man may go wrong. But in the advanced stage, when one can understand the transcendental nature of the Lord, one does not try to imitate Him. This is not possible.

The Lord in human society does what is the duty of everyone, but sometimes He does something extraordinary and not to be imitated by the living being. His acts of evening prayer as stated herein must be followed by the living being, but it is not possible to follow His mountain-lifting or dancing with the *gopīs.* One cannot imitate the sun, which can exhaust water even from a filthy place; the most powerful can do something which is all-good, but our imitation of such acts will put us into endless difficulty. Therefore, in all actions, the experienced guide, the spiritual master, who is the manifested mercy of the Lord, should always be consulted, and the path of progress will be assured.

Thus end the Bhaktivedanta purports of the First Canto, Tenth Chapter, of the Śrīmad-Bhāgavatam, *entitled "Departure of Lord Kṛṣṇa for Dvārakā."*

CHAPTER ELEVEN

Lord Kṛṣṇa's Entrance into Dvārakā

TEXT 1

सूत उवाच
आनर्तान् स उपव्रज्य स्वृद्धाञ्जनपदान् स्वकान् ।
दध्मौ दरवरं तेषां विषादं शमयन्निव ॥१॥

sūta uvāca
ānartān sa upavrajya
svṛddhāñ jana-padān svakān
dadhmau daravaraṁ teṣāṁ
viṣādaṁ śamayann iva

sūtaḥ uvāca—Sūta Gosvāmī said; *ānartān*—the country known as Ānartān (Dvārakā); *saḥ*—He; *upavrajya*—reaching the border of; *svṛddhān*—most prosperous; *jana-padān*—city; *svakān*—His own; *dadhmau*—sounded; *daravaram*—the auspicious conchshell (Pāñcajanya); *teṣām*—of them; *viṣādam*—dejection; *śamayan*—pacifying; *iva*—seemingly.

TRANSLATION

Sūta Gosvāmī said: Upon reaching the border of His most prosperous metropolis, known as the country of the Ānartas [Dvārakā], the Lord sounded His auspicious conchshell, heralding His arrival and apparently pacifying the dejection of the inhabitants.

PURPORT

The beloved Lord was away from His own prosperous metropolis of Dvārakā for a considerably long period because of the Battle of Kurukṣetra, and thus all the inhabitants were overcome with melancholia due to the separation. When the Lord descends on the earth, His eternal associates also come with Him, just as the entourage of a king accompanies him. Such associates of the Lord are eternally liberated souls, and they cannot bear the separation of the Lord even for a moment because of intense affection for the Lord. Thus the inhabitants of the city of Dvārakā were in a mood of dejection and expected the arrival of the Lord at any moment. So the heralding sound of the auspicious conchshell was very encouraging, and apparently the sound pacified their dejection. They were still more aspirant to see the Lord amongst themselves, and all of them became alert to receive Him in the befitting manner. These are the signs of spontaneous love of Godhead.

TEXT 2

स उच्चकाशे धवलोदरो दरो-
ऽप्युरुक्रमस्याधरशोणशोणिमा ।
दाध्मायमानः करकञ्जसम्पुटे
यथाब्जखण्डे कलहंस उत्स्वनः ॥२॥

sa uccakāśe dhavalodaro daro
'py urukramasyādharaśoṇa-śoṇimā
dādhmāyamānaḥ kara-kañja-sampuṭe
yathābja-khaṇḍe kala-haṁsa utsvanaḥ

saḥ—that; *uccakāśe*—became brilliant; *dhavala-udaraḥ*—white and fat-boweled; *daraḥ*—conchshell; *api*—although it is so; *urukramasya*—of the great adventurer; *adharaśoṇa*—by the transcendental quality of His lips; *śoṇimā*—reddened; *dādhmāyamānaḥ*—being sounded; *kara-kañja-sampuṭe*—being caught by the grip of the lotus hand; *yathā*—as it is; *abja-khaṇḍe*—by the stems of lotus flowers; *kala-haṁsaḥ*—ducking swan; *utsvanaḥ*—loudly sounding.

TRANSLATION

The white and fat-bowled conchshell, being gripped by the hand of Lord Kṛṣṇa and sounded by Him, appeared to be reddened by the touch of His transcendental lips. It seemed that a white swan was playing in the stems of red lotus flowers.

PURPORT

The redness of the white conchshell due to the lip-touch of the Lord is a symbol of spiritual significance. The Lord is all spirit, and matter is ignorance of this spiritual existence. Factually there is nothing like matter in spiritual enlightenment, and this spiritual enlightenment takes place at once by the contact of the Supreme Lord Śrī Kṛṣṇa. The Lord is present in every particle of all existence, and He can manifest His presence in anyone. By ardent love and devotional service to the Lord, or in other words by spiritual contact with the Lord, everything becomes spiritually reddened like the conchshell in the grip of the Lord, and the *paramahaṁsa,* or the supremely intelligent person, plays the part of the ducking swan in the water of spiritual bliss, eternally decorated by the lotus flower of the Lord's feet.

TEXT 3

तमुपश्रुत्य निनदं जगद्भयभयावहम् ।
प्रत्युद्ययुः प्रजाः सर्वा भर्तृदर्शनलालसाः ॥ ३ ॥

tam upaśrutya ninadaṁ
jagad-bhaya-bhayāvaham
pratyudyayuḥ prajāḥ sarvā
bhartṛ-darśana-lālasāḥ

tam—that; *upaśrutya*—having overheard; *ninadam*—sound; *jagat-bhaya*—the fear of material existence; *bhaya-āvaham*—the threatening principle; *prati*—towards; *udyayuḥ*—rapidly proceeded; *prajāḥ*—the citizens; *sarvāḥ*—all; *bhartṛ*—the protector; *darśana*—audience; *lālasāḥ*—having so desired.

TRANSLATION

The citizens of Dvārakā, having heard that sound which threatens fear personified in the material world, began to run towards Him fast, just to have a long desired audience with the Lord, who is the protector of all devotees.

PURPORT

As already explained, the citizens of Dvārakā who lived at the time of Lord Kṛṣṇa's presence there were all liberated souls who descended there along with the Lord as entourage. All were very anxious to have an audience with the Lord, although because of spiritual contact they were never separated from the Lord. Just as the *gopīs* at Vṛndāvana used to think of Kṛṣṇa while He was away from the village for cowherding engagements, the citizens of Dvārakā were all immersed in thought of the Lord while He was away from Dvārakā to attend the Battle of Kurukṣetra. Some distinguished fiction writer in Bengal concluded that the Kṛṣṇa of Vṛndāvana, that of Mathurā and that of Dvārakā were different personalities. Historically there is no truth in this conclusion. The Kṛṣṇa of Kurukṣetra and the Kṛṣṇa of Dvārakā are one and the same personality.

The citizens of Dvārakā were thus in a state of melancholy due to the Lord's absence from the transcendental city, as much as we are put in a state of melancholy at night because of the absence of the sun. The sound heralded by Lord Kṛṣṇa was something like the heralding of the sunrise in the morning. So all the citizens of Dvārakā awoke from a state of slumber because of the sunrise of Kṛṣṇa, and they all hastened towards Him just to have an audience. The devotees of the Lord know no one else as protector.

This sound of the Lord is identical with the Lord, as we have tried to explain by the nondual position of the Lord. The material existence of our present status is full of fear. Out of the four problems of material existence, namely the food problem, the shelter problem, the fear problem and the mating problem, the fear problem gives us more trouble than the others. We are always fearful due to our ignorance of the next problem. The whole material existence is full of problems, and thus the fear problem is always prominent. This is due to our association with the illusory energy of the Lord, known as *māyā* or external energy, yet all fear is vanished as soon as there is the sound of the Lord, represented by His holy name, as it was sounded by Lord Śrī Caitanya Mahāprabhu in the following sixteen words:

Hare Kṛṣṇa, Hare Kṛṣṇa, Kṛṣṇa Kṛṣṇa, Hare Hare
Hare Rāma, Hare Rāma, Rāma Rāma, Hare Hare

We can take advantage of these sounds and be free from all threatening problems of material existence.

TEXTS 4–5

तत्रोपनीतबलयो रवेर्दीपमिवादृताः ।
आत्मारामं पूर्णकामं निजलाभेन नित्यदा ॥ ४ ॥
प्रीत्युत्फुल्लमुखाः प्रोचुर्हर्षगद्गदया गिरा ।
पितरं सर्वसुहृदमवितारमिवार्भकाः ॥ ५ ॥

tatropanīta-balayo
raver dīpam ivādṛtāḥ
ātmārāmaṁ pūrṇa-kāmaṁ
nija-lābhena nityadā

prīty-utphulla-mukhāḥ procur
harṣa-gadgadayā girā
pitaraṁ sarva-suhṛdam
avitāram ivārbhakāḥ

tatra—thereupon; *upanīta*—having offered; *balayaḥ*—presentations; *raveḥ*—up to the sun; *dīpam*—lamp; *iva*—like; *ādṛtāḥ*—being evaluated; *ātma-ārāmam*—unto the self-sufficient; *pūrṇa-kāmam*—fully satisfied; *nija-lābhena*—by His own potencies; *nitya-dā*—one who supplies incessantly; *prīti*—affection; *utphulla-mukhāḥ*—cheerful faces; *procuḥ*—said; *harṣa*—gladdened; *gadgadayā*—ecstatic; *girā*—speeches; *pitaram*—unto the father; *sarva*—all; *suhṛdam*—friends; *avitāram*—the guardian; *iva*—like; *arbhakāḥ*—wards.

TRANSLATION

The citizens arrived before the Lord with their respective presentations, offering them to the fully satisfied and self-sufficient one, who, by His own potency, incessantly supplies others. These presentations were like the offering of a lamp to the sun. Yet the citizens began to speak in ecstatic language to receive the Lord, just as wards welcome their guardian and father.

PURPORT

The Supreme Lord Kṛṣṇa is described herein as *ātmārāma.* He is self-sufficient, and there is no need for Him to seek happiness from anything beyond Himself. He is self-sufficient because His very transcendental existence is total bliss. He is eternally existent; He is all-cognizant and all-blissful. Therefore, any presentation, however valuable it may be, is not needed by Him. But still, because He is the well-wisher for one and all, He accepts from everyone everything that is offered to Him in pure devotional service. It is not that He is in want for such things, because the things are themselves generated from His energy. The comparison is made herein that making offerings to the Lord is something like offering a lamp in the worship of the sun-god. Anything fiery and illuminating is but an emanation of the energy of the sun, and yet to worship the sun-god it is necessary to offer him a lamp. In the worship of the sun, there is some sort of demand made by the worshiper, but in the case of devotional service to the Lord, there is no question of demand from either side. It is all a sign of pure love and affection between the Lord and the devotee.

The Lord is the supreme father of all living beings, and therefore those who are conscious of this *vital* relation with God can make filial demands from the father, and the father is pleased to supply the demands of such obedient sons without bargaining. The Lord is just like the *desire tree,* and from Him everyone can have everything by the causeless mercy of the Lord. As the supreme father, the Lord, however, does not supply to a pure devotee what is considered to be a barrier to the discharge of devotional service. Those who are engaged in the devotional service of the Lord can rise to the position of unalloyed devotional service by His transcendental attraction.

TEXT 6

नताः स्म ते नाथ सदाङ्घ्रिपङ्कजं
विरिञ्चवैरिञ्च्यसुरेन्द्रवन्दितम् ।
परायणं क्षेममिहेच्छतां परं
न यत्र कालः प्रभवेत् परः प्रभुः ॥६॥

natāḥ sma te nātha sadāṅghri-paṅkajaṁ
viriñca-vairiñcya-surendra-vanditam
parāyaṇaṁ kṣemam ihecchatāṁ paraṁ
na yatra kālaḥ prabhavet paraḥ prabhuḥ

natāḥ—bowed down; *sma*—we had done so; *te*—unto You; *nātha*—O Lord; *sadā*—always; *aṅghri-paṅkajam*—the lotus feet; *viriñca*—Brahmā, the first living being; *vairiñcya*—sons of Brahmā like Sanaka and Sanātana; *sura-indra*—the King of heaven; *vanditam*—worshiped by; *parāyaṇam*—the supreme; *kṣemam*—welfare; *iha*—in this life; *icchatām*—one who so desires; *param*—the highest; *na*—never; *yatra*—wherein; *kālaḥ*—inevitable time; *prabhavet*—can exert its influence; *paraḥ*—transcendental; *prabhuḥ*—the Supreme Lord.

TRANSLATION

The citizens said: O Lord, You are worshiped by all demigods like Brahmā, the four Sanas and even the King of heaven. You are the ultimate rest for those who are really aspiring to achieve the highest benefit of life. You are the supreme transcendental Lord, and inevitable time cannot exert its influence upon You.

PURPORT

The Supreme Lord is Śrī Kṛṣṇa, as confirmed in *Bhagavad-gītā, Brahma-saṁhitā* and other authorized Vedic literatures. No one is equal to or greater than Him, and that is the verdict of all scriptures. The influence of time and space is exerted upon the dependent living entities, who are all parts and parcels of the Supreme Lord. The living entities are predominated *brahman,* whereas the Supreme Lord is the predominating Absolute. As soon as we forget this clear fact, we are at once in illusion, and thus we are put into threefold miseries, as one is put into dense darkness. The clear consciousness of the cognizant living being is God consciousness, in which one bows down unto Him in all circumstances.

TEXT 7

भवाय नस्त्वं भव विश्वभावन
त्वमेव माताथ सुहृत्पतिः पिता ।
त्वं सद्गुरुर्नः परमं च दैवतं
यस्यानुवृत्त्या कृतिनो बभूविम ॥७॥

bhavāya nas tvaṁ bhava viśva-bhāvana
tvam eva mātātha suhṛt-patiḥ pitā
tvaṁ sad-gurur naḥ paramaṁ ca daivataṁ
yasyānuvṛttyā kṛtino babhūvima

bhavāya—for welfare; *naḥ*—for us; *tvam*—Your Lordship; *bhava*—just become; *viśva-bhāvana*—the creator of the universe; *tvam*—Your Lordship; *eva*—certainly; *mātā*—mother; *atha*—as also; *suhṛt*—well-wisher; *patiḥ*—husband; *pitā*—father; *tvam*—Your Lordship; *sat-guruḥ*—spiritual master; *naḥ*—our; *paramam*—the supreme; *ca*—and; *daivatam*—worshipable Deity; *yasya*—whose; *anuvṛttyā*—following in the footsteps; *kṛtinaḥ*—successful; *babhūvima*—we have become.

TRANSLATION

O creator of the universe, You are our mother, well-wisher, Lord, father, spiritual master and worshipable Deity. By following in Your footsteps we have become successful in every respect. We pray, therefore, that You continue to bless us with Your mercy.

PURPORT

The all-good Personality of Godhead, being the creator of the universe, also plans for the good of all good living beings. The good living beings are advised by the Lord to follow His good advice, and by doing so they become successful in all spheres of life. There is no need to worship any deity but the Lord. The Lord is all-powerful, and if He is satisfied by our obedience unto His lotus feet, He is competent to bestow upon us all kinds of blessings for the successful execution of both our material and spiritual lives. For attaining spiritual existence, the human form is a chance for all to understand our eternal relation with God. Our relation with Him is eternal; it can neither be broken nor vanquished. It may be forgotten for the time being, but it can be revived also by the grace of the Lord, if we follow His injunctions, which are revealed in the scriptures of all times and all places.

TEXT 8

अहो सनाथा भवता स्म यद्वयं
त्रैविष्टपानामपि दूरदर्शनम् ।
प्रेमस्मितस्निग्धनिरीक्षणाननं
पश्येम रूपं तव सर्वसौभगम् ॥८॥

aho sanāthā bhavatā sma yad vayaṁ
traiviṣṭapānām api dūra-darśanam
prema-smita-snigdha-nirīkṣaṇānanaṁ
paśyema rūpaṁ tava sarva-saubhagam

aho—oh, it is our good luck; *sa-nāthāḥ*—to be under the protection of the master; *bhavatā*—by Your good self; *sma*—as we have become; *yat vayam*—as we are; *traiviṣṭa-pānām*—of the demigods; *api*—also; *dūra-darśanam*—very rarely seen; *prema-smita*—smiling with love; *snigdha*—affectionate; *nirīkṣaṇa-ānanam*—face looking in that mode; *paśyema*—let us look; *rūpam*—beauty; *tava*—Your; *sarva*—all; *saubhagam*—auspiciousness.

TRANSLATION

Oh, it is our good luck that we have come again today under Your protection by Your presence, for Your Lordship rarely visits even the

denizens of heaven. Now it is possible for us to look into Your smiling face, which is full of affectionate glances. We can now see Your transcendental form, full of all auspiciousness.

PURPORT

The Lord in His eternal personal form can be seen only by the pure devotees. The Lord is never impersonal, but He is the Supreme Absolute Personality of Godhead, possible to be visited by devotional service face to face, which is impossible to be done even by the denizens of higher planets. When Brahmājī and other demigods want to consult Lord Viṣṇu, the plenary portion of Lord Kṛṣṇa, they have to wait on the shore of the ocean of milk where Lord Viṣṇu is lying on White Land (Śvetadvīpa). This ocean of milk and the Śvetadvīpa planet are the replica of Vaikuṇṭhaloka within the universe. Neither Brahmājī nor the demigods like Indra can enter into this island of Śvetadvīpa, but they can stand on the shore of the ocean of milk and transmit their message to Lord Viṣṇu, known as Kṣīrodakaśāyī Viṣṇu. Therefore, the Lord is rarely seen by them, but the inhabitants of Dvārakā, because of their being pure devotees without any tinge of the material contamination of fruitive activities and empiric philosophical speculation, can see Him face to face by the grace of the Lord. This is the original state of the living entities and can be attained by reviving our natural and constitutional state of life, which is discovered by devotional service only.

TEXT 9

यर्ह्यम्बुजाक्षापससार भो भवान्
कुरून् मधून् वाथ सुहृद्दिदृक्षया ।
तत्राब्दकोटिप्रतिमः क्षणो भवेद्
रविं विनाक्ष्णोरिव नस्तवाच्युत ॥ ९ ॥

yarhy ambujākṣāpasasāra bho bhavān
kurūn madhūn vātha suhṛd-didṛkṣayā
tatrābda-koṭi-pratimaḥ kṣaṇo bhaved
raviṁ vinākṣṇor iva nas tavācyuta

yarhi—whenever; *ambuja-akṣa*—O lotus-eyed one; *apasasāra*—You go away; *bho*—oh; *bhavān*—Yourself; *kurūn*—the descendants of King Kuru; *madhūn*—the inhabitants of Mathurā (Vrajabhūmi); *vā*—either; *atha*—

therefore; *suhṛt-didṛkṣayā*—for meeting them; *tatra*—at that time; *abda-koṭi*—millions of years; *pratimaḥ*—like; *kṣaṇaḥ*—moments; *bhavet*—becomes; *ravim*—the sun; *vinā*—without; *akṣṇoḥ*—of the eyes; *iva*—like that; *naḥ*—ours; *tava*—Your; *acyuta*—O infallible one.

TRANSLATION

O lotus-eyed Lord, whenever You go away to Mathurā, Vṛndāvana or Hastināpura to meet Your friends and relatives, every moment of Your absence seems like a million years. O infallible one, at that time our eyes become useless, as if bereft of sun.

PURPORT

We are all proud of our material senses for making experiments to determine the existence of God. But we forget that our senses are not absolute by themselves. They can only act under certain conditions. For example, our eyes. As long as the sunshine is there, our eyes are useful to a certain extent. But in the absence of sunshine, the eyes are useless. Lord Śrī Kṛṣṇa, being the primeval Lord, the Supreme Truth, is compared to the sun. Without Him all our knowledge is either false or partial. The opposite of the sun is the darkness, and similarly the opposite of Kṛṣṇa is *māyā,* or illusion. The devotees of the Lord can see everything in true perspective due to the light disseminated by Lord Kṛṣṇa. By the grace of the Lord the pure devotee cannot be in the darkness of ignorance. Therefore, it is necessary that we must always be in the sight of Lord Kṛṣṇa so that we can see both ourselves and the Lord with His different energies. As we cannot see anything in the absence of the sun, so also we cannot see anything, including our own self, without the factual presence of the Lord. Without Him all our knowledge is covered by illusion.

TEXT 10

कथं वयं नाथ चिरोषिते त्वयि प्रसन्नदृष्ट्याखिलतापशोषणम् ।
जीवेम ते सुन्दरहासशोभितमपश्यमाना वदनं मनोहरम् ।
इति चोदीरिता वाचः प्रजानां भक्तवत्सलः ।
शृण्वानोऽनुग्रहं दृष्ट्या वितन्वन् प्राविशत् पुरम् ॥१०॥

kathaṁ vayaṁ nātha ciroṣite tvayi
prasanna-dṛṣṭyākhila-tāpa-śoṣaṇam

jīvema te sundara-hāsa-śobhitam
apaśyamānā vadanaṁ manoharam

iti codīritā vācaḥ
prajānāṁ bhakta-vatsalaḥ
śṛṇvāno 'nugrahaṁ dṛṣṭyā
vitanvan prāviśat puram

katham—how; *vayam*—we; *nātha*—O Lord; *ciroṣite*—being abroad almost always; *tvayi*—by You; *prasanna*—satisfaction; *dṛṣṭyā*—by the glance; *akhila*—universal; *tāpa*—miseries; *śoṣaṇam*—vanquishing; *jīvema*—shall be able to live; *te*—Your; *sundara*—beautiful; *hāsa*—smiling; *śobhitam*—decorated; *apaśyamānāḥ*—without seeing; *vadanam*—face; *manoharam*—attractive; *iti*—thus; *ca*—and; *udīritāḥ*—speaking; *vācaḥ*—words; *prajānām*—of the citizens; *bhakta-vatsalaḥ*—kind to the devotees; *śṛṇvānaḥ*—thus learning; *anugraham*—kindness; *dṛṣṭyā*—by glances; *vitanvan*—distributing; *prāviśat*—entered; *puram*—Dvārakāpurī.

TRANSLATION

O master, if You live abroad all the time, then we cannot look at Your attractive face, whose smiles vanquish all our sufferings. How can we exist without Your presence?

Upon hearing their speeches, the Lord, who is very kind to the citizens and the devotees, entered the city of Dvārakā and acknowledged all their greetings by casting His transcendental glance over them.

PURPORT

Lord Kṛṣṇa's attraction is so powerful that once being attracted by Him one cannot tolerate separation from Him. Why is this so? Because we are all eternally related with Him as the sun rays are eternally related with the sun disc. The sun rays are molecular parts of the solar radiation. Thus the sun rays and the sun cannot be separated. The separation by the cloud is temporary and artificial, and as soon as the cloud is cleared, the sun rays again display their natural effulgence in the presence of the sun. Similarly, the living entities, who are molecular parts of the whole spirit, are separated from the Lord by the artificial covering of *māyā,* illusory energy. This illusory energy, or the curtain of *māyā,* has to be removed, and when it is so done, the living entity can see the Lord face to face, and all his miseries are at once removed. Every one of us wants to remove the miseries of life, but we do not know how to do it. The solution is given here, and it rests on us to assimilate it or not.

TEXT 11

मधुभोजदशार्हार्हकुकुरान्धकवृष्णिभिः ।
आत्मतुल्यबलैर्गुप्तां नागैर्भोगवतीमिव ॥११॥

madhu-bhoja-daśārhārha-
kukurāndhaka-vṛṣṇibhiḥ
ātma-tulya-balair guptāṁ
nāgair bhogavatīm iva

madhu—Madhu; *bhoja*—Bhoja; *daśārha*—Daśārha; *arha*—Arha; *kukura*—Kukura; *andhaka*—Andhaka; *vṛṣṇibhiḥ*—by the descendants of Vṛṣṇi; *ātma-tulya*—as good as Himself; *balaiḥ*—by strength; *guptām*—protected; *nāgaiḥ*—by the Nāgas; *bhogavatīm*—the capital of Nāgaloka; *iva*—like.

TRANSLATION

As Bhogavatī, the capital of Nāgaloka, is protected by the Nāgas, so was Dvārakā protected by the descendants of Vṛṣṇi—Bhoja, Madhu, Daśārha, Arha, Kukura, Andhaka, etc.—who were as strong as Lord Kṛṣṇa.

PURPORT

The Nāgaloka planet is situated below the earth planet, and it is understood that the sun rays are hampered there. The darkness of the planet is, however, removed by the flashes of the jewels set on the heads of the Nāgas (celestial serpents), and it is said that there are beautiful gardens, rivulets, etc., for the enjoyment of the Nāgas. It is understood here also that the place is well protected by the inhabitants. So also the city of Dvārakā was well protected by the descendants of Vṛṣṇi, who were as powerful as the Lord, insofar as He manifested His strength upon this earth.

TEXT 12

सर्वर्तुसर्वविभवपुण्यवृक्षलताश्रमैः ।
उद्यानोपवनारामैर्वृतपद्माकरश्रियम् ॥१२॥

sarvartu-sarva-vibhava-
puṇya-vṛkṣa-latāśramaiḥ
udyānopavanārāmair
vṛta-padmākara-śriyam

sarva—all; *ṛtu*—seasons; *sarva*—all; *vibhava*—opulences; *puṇya*—pious; *vṛkṣa*—trees; *latā*—creepers; *āśramaiḥ*—with hermitages; *udyāna*—orchards; *upavana*—flower gardens; *ārāmaiḥ*—pleasure gardens and beautiful parks; *vṛta*—surrounded by; *padma-ākara*—the birthplaces of lotuses or nice reservoirs of water; *śriyam*—increasing the beauty.

TRANSLATION

The city of Dvārakāpurī was filled with the opulences of all seasons. There were hermitages, orchards, flower gardens, parks and reservoirs of water breeding lotus flowers all over.

PURPORT

Perfection of human civilization is made possible by utilizing the gifts of nature in their own way. As we find herewith in the description of its opulence, Dvārakā was surrounded by flower gardens and fruit orchards along with reservoirs of water and growing lotuses. There is no mention of mills and factories supported by slaughterhouses, which are the necessary paraphernalia of the modern metropolis. The propensity to utilize nature's own gifts is still there, even in the heart of modern civilized man. The leaders of modern civilization select their own residential quarters in a place where there are such naturally beautiful gardens and reservoirs of water, but they leave the common men to reside in congested areas without parks and gardens. Herein of course we find a different description of the city of Dvārakā. It is understood that the whole *dhāma,* or residential quarter, was surrounded by such gardens and parks with reservoirs of water where lotuses grew. It is understood that all the people depended on nature's gifts of fruits and flowers without industrial enterprises promoting filthy huts and slums for residential quarters. Advancement of civilization is estimated not on the growth of mills and factories to deteriorate the finer instincts of the human being, but on developing the potent spiritual instincts of human beings and giving them a chance to go back to Godhead. Development of factories and mills is called *ugra-karma,* or pungent activities, and such activities deteriorate the finer sentiments of the human being and society to form a dungeon of demons.

We find herein the mention of pious trees which produce seasonal flowers and fruits. The impious trees are useless jungles only, and they can only be used to supply fuels. In the modern civilization such impious trees are planted on the sides of roads. Human energy should be properly utilized in developing the finer senses for spiritual understanding, in which lies the solution of life. Fruits, flowers, beautiful gardens, parks and reservoirs of water with ducks and swans playing in the midst of lotus flowers, and cows giving sufficient milk and butter are essential for developing the finer tissues of the human body. As against this, the dungeons of mines, factories and workshops develop demoniac propensities in the working class. The vested interests flourish at the cost of the working class, and consequently there are severe clashes between them in so many ways. The description of Dvārakā-dhāma is the ideal of human civilization.

TEXT 13

गोपुरद्वारमार्गेषु कृतकौतुकतोरणाम् ।
चित्रध्वजपताकाग्रैरन्तः प्रतिहतातपाम् ॥१३॥

gopura-dvāra-mārgeṣu
kṛta-kautuka-toraṇām
citra-dhvaja-patākāgrair
antaḥ pratihatātapām

gopura—the gateway of the city; *dvāra*—door; *mārgeṣu*—on different roads; *kṛta*—undertaken; *kautuka*—because of the festival; *toraṇām*—decorated arch; *citra*—painted; *dhvaja*—flags; *patākā-agraiḥ*—by the foremost signs; *antaḥ*—within; *pratihata*—checked; *ātapām*—sunshine.

TRANSLATION

The city gateway, the household doors and festooned arches along the roads were all nicely decorated with festive signs like plantain trees and mango leaves, all to welcome the Lord. Flags, garlands and painted signs and slogans all combined to shade the sunshine.

PURPORT

Signs of decoration in special festivals were also collected from the gifts of nature, such as the plantain trees, the mango trees, fruits and flowers. Mango trees, coconut palms and plantain trees are still accepted as auspicious signs.

The flags mentioned above were all painted with the picture of either Garuḍa or Hanumān, the two great servitors of the Lord. For devotees, such paintings and decorations are still adored, and the servitor of the master is paid more respects for the satisfaction of the Lord.

TEXT 14

सम्मार्जितमहामार्गरथ्यापणकचत्वराम् ।
सिक्तां गन्धजलैरुप्तां फलपुष्पाक्षताङ्कुरैः ॥१४॥

sammārjita-mahā-mārga-
rathyāpaṇaka-catvarām
siktāṁ gandha-jalair uptāṁ
phala-puṣpākṣatāṅkuraiḥ

sammārjita—thoroughly cleansed; *mahā-mārga*—highways; *rathya*—lanes and subways; *āpaṇaka*—shopping marketplaces; *catvarām*—public meeting places; *siktām*—moistened with; *gandha-jalaiḥ*—scented water; *uptām*—was strewn with; *phala*—fruits; *puṣpa*—flowers; *akṣata*—unbroken; *aṅkuraiḥ*—seeds.

TRANSLATION

The highways, subways, lanes, markets and public meeting places were all thoroughly cleansed and then moistened with scented water. And to welcome the Lord, fruits, flowers and unbroken seeds were strewn everywhere.

PURPORT

Scented waters prepared by distilling flowers like rose and *keora* were requisitioned to wet the roads, streets and lanes of Dvārakā dhāma. Such places, along with the marketplace and public meeting places, were thoroughly cleansed. From the above description, it appears that the city of Dvārakā dhāma was considerably big, containing many highways, streets and public meeting places with parks, gardens and reservoirs of water, all very nicely decorated with flowers and fruits. And to welcome the Lord such flowers and fruits with unbroken seeds of grain were also strewn over the public places. Unbroken seeds of grain or fruits in the seedling stage were considered auspicious, and they are still so used by the Hindus in general on festival days.

TEXT 15

द्वारि द्वारि गृहाणां च दध्यक्षतफलेक्षुभिः ।
अलङ्कृतां पूर्णकुम्भैर्बलिभिर्धूपदीपकैः ॥१५॥

dvāri dvāri gṛhāṇāṁ ca
dadhy-akṣata-phalekṣubhiḥ
alaṅkṛtāṁ pūrṇa-kumbhair
balibhir dhūpa-dīpakaiḥ

dvāri dvāri—the door of each and every house; *gṛhāṇām*—of all the residential buildings; *ca*—and; *dadhi*—curd; *akṣata*—unbroken; *phala*—fruit; *ikṣubhiḥ*—sugarcane; *alaṇkṛtām*—decorated; *pūrṇa-kumbhaiḥ*—full waterpots; *balibhiḥ*—along with articles for worship; *dhūpa*—incense; *dīpakaiḥ*—with lamps and candles.

TRANSLATION

In each and every door of the residential houses, auspicious things like curd, unbroken fruits, sugarcane and full waterpots, and articles for worship, incense and candles were all displayed.

PURPORT

The process of reception according to Vedic rites is not at all dry. The reception was made not simply by decorating the roads and streets as above mentioned, but by worshiping the Lord with requisite ingredients like incense, lamps, flowers, sweets, fruits and other palatable eatables, according to one's capacity. All were offered to the Lord, and the remnants of the foodstuff were distributed amongst the gathering citizens. So it was not like a dry reception of these modern days. Each and every house was ready to receive the Lord in a similar way, and thus each and every house on the roads and streets distributed such remnants of food to the citizens, and therefore the festival was successful. Without distribution of food, no function is complete, and that is the way of Vedic culture.

TEXTS 16–17

निशम्य प्रेष्ठमायान्तं वसुदेवो महामनाः ।
अक्रूरश्चोग्रसेनश्च रामश्चाद्भुतविक्रमः ॥१६॥

प्रद्युम्नश्चारुदेष्णश्च साम्बो जाम्बवतीसुतः ।
प्रहर्षवेगोच्छशितशयनासनभोजनाः ॥१७॥

niśamya preṣṭham āyāntaṁ
vasudevo mahā-manāḥ
akrūraś cograsenaś ca
rāmaś cādbhuta-vikramaḥ

pradyumnaś cārudeṣṇaś ca
sāmbo jāmbavatī-sutaḥ
praharṣa-vegocchaśita-
śayanāsana-bhojanāḥ

niśamya—just hearing; *preṣṭham*—the dearmost; *āyāntam*—coming home; *vasudevaḥ*—Vasudeva (the father of Kṛṣṇa); *mahā-manāḥ*—the magnanimous; *akrūraḥ*—Akrūra; *ca*—and; *ugrasenaḥ*—Ugrasena; *ca*—and; *rāmaḥ*—Balarāma (the elder brother of Kṛṣṇa); *ca*—and; *adbhuta*—superhuman; *vikramaḥ*—prowess; *pradyumnaḥ*—Pradyumna; *cārudeṣṇaḥ*—Cārudeṣṇa; *ca*—and; *sāmbaḥ*—Sāmba; *jāmbavatī-sutaḥ*—the son of Jāmbavatī; *praharṣa*—extreme happiness; *vega*—force; *ucchaśita*—being influenced by; *śayana*—lying down; *āsana*—sitting on; *bhojanāḥ*—dining.

TRANSLATION

On hearing that the most dear Kṛṣṇa was approaching Dvārakā-dhāma, magnanimous Vasudeva, Akrūra, Ugrasena, Balarāma (the superhumanly powerful), Pradyumna, Cārudeṣṇa and Sāmba the son of Jāmbavatī, all extremely happy, abandoned resting, sitting and dining.

PURPORT

Vasudeva: Son of King Śūrasena, husband of Devakī and father of Lord Śrī Kṛṣṇa. He is the brother of Kuntī and father of Subhadrā. Subhadrā was married with her cousin Arjuna, and this system is still prevalent in some parts of India. Vasudeva was appointed minister of Ugrasena, and later on he married eight daughters of Ugrasena's brother Devaka. Devakī is only one of them. Kaṁsa was his brother-in-law, and Vasudeva accepted voluntary imprisonment by Kaṁsa on mutual agreement to deliver the eighth son of Devakī. This was foiled by the will of Kṛṣṇa. As maternal uncle of the Pāṇḍavas, he took active parts in the purificatory process of the Pāṇḍavas. He sent for the priest Kaśyapa at Śatasṛṅga Parvata, and he executed the functions. When Kṛṣṇa appeared within the bars of Kaṁsa's prison house, He was transferred by Vasudeva to the house of Nanda Mahārāja, the foster father of Kṛṣṇa, at Gokula. Kṛṣṇa disappeared along with Baladeva prior to the disappearance of Vasudeva, and Arjuna (Vasudeva's nephew) undertook the charge of the funeral ceremony after Vasudeva's disappearance.

Akrūra: The commander in chief of the Vṛṣṇi dynasty and a great devotee of Lord Kṛṣṇa. Akrūra attained success in devotional service to the Lord by the one single process of offering prayers. He was the husband of Sūtanī, daughter of Ahūka. He supported Arjuna when Arjuna took Subhadrā forcibly away by the will of Kṛṣṇa. Both Kṛṣṇa and Akrūra went to see Arjuna after his successful kidnapping of Subhadrā. Both of them presented dowries to Arjuna after this incident. Akrūra was present also when Abhimanyu, the son of Subhadrā, was married with Uttarā, mother of Mahārāja Parīkṣit. Ahūka, the father-in-law of Akrūra, was not on good terms with Akrūra. But both of them were devotees of the Lord.

Ugrasena: One of the powerful kings of the Vṛṣṇi dynasty and cousin of Mahārāja Kuntibhoja. His other name is Ahūka. His minister was Vasudeva, and his son was the powerful Kaṁsa. This Kaṁsa imprisoned his father and became the King of Mathurā. By the grace of Lord Kṛṣṇa and His brother, Lord Baladeva, Kaṁsa was killed, and Ugrasena was reinstalled on the throne. When Śālva attacked the city of Dvārakā, Ugrasena fought very valiantly and repulsed the enemy. Ugrasena inquired from Nāradajī about the divinity of Lord Kṛṣṇa. When the Yadu dynasty was to be vanquished, Ugrasena was entrusted with the iron lump produced from the womb of Sāmba. He cut the iron lump into pieces and then pasted it and mixed it up with the sea water on the coast of Dvārakā. After this, he ordered complete prohibition within the city of Dvārakā and the kingdom. He got salvation after his death.

Baladeva: He is the divine son of Vasudeva by his wife Rohiṇī. He is also known as Rohiṇī-nandana, the beloved son of Rohiṇī. He was also entrusted to Nanda Mahārāja along with His mother, Rohiṇī, when Vasudeva embraced imprisonment by mutual agreement with Kaṁsa. So Nanda Mahārāja is also the foster father of Baladeva along with Lord Kṛṣṇa. Lord Kṛṣṇa and Lord Baladeva were constant companions from Their very childhood, although They were stepbrothers. He is the plenary manifestation of the Supreme Personality of Godhead, and therefore He is as good and powerful as Lord Kṛṣṇa. He belongs to the *viṣṇu-tattva* (the principle of Godhead). He attended the *svayaṁvara* ceremony of Draupadī along with Śrī Kṛṣṇa. When Subhadrā was kidnapped by Arjuna by the organized plan of Śrī Kṛṣṇa, Baladeva was very angry with Arjuna and wanted to kill him at once. Śrī Kṛṣṇa, for the sake of His dear friend, fell at the feet of Lord Baladeva and implored Him not to be so angry. Śrī Baladeva was thus satisfied. Similarly, He was once very angry with the Kauravas, and He wanted to throw their whole city into the depths of the Yamunā. But the Kauravas satisfied Him by surrendering unto His divine lotus feet. He was actually the seventh son of Devakī prior to the birth of Lord Kṛṣṇa, but by the will of the Lord He was transferred to the womb of Rohiṇī to escape the wrath of Kaṁsa. His other name is therefore Saṅkarṣaṇa, who is also the plenary portion of Śrī Baladeva. Because He is as powerful as Lord Kṛṣṇa and can bestow spiritual power to the devotees, He is therefore known as Baladeva. In the *Vedas* also it is enjoined that no one can know the Supreme Lord without being favored by Baladeva. *Bala* means spiritual strength, not physical. Some less intelligent persons interpret *bala* as the strength of the body. But no one can have spiritual realization by physical strength. Physical strength ends with the end of the physical body, but spiritual strength follows the spirit soul to the next transmigration, and therefore the strength obtained by Baladeva is never wasted. The strength is eternal, and thus Baladeva is the original spiritual master of all devotees.

Śrī Baladeva was also a class friend of Lord Śrī Kṛṣṇa as a student of Sāndīpani Muni. In His childhood He killed many *asuras* along with Śrī Kṛṣṇa, and specifically He killed the Dhenukāsura at Tālavana. During the Kurukṣetra battle, He remained neutral, and He tried His best not to bring about the fight. He was in favor of Duryodhana, but still He remained neutral. When there was a club-fight between Duryodhana and Bhīmasena, He was present on the spot. He was angry at Bhīmasena when the latter struck Duryodhana on the thigh or below the belt, and He wanted to retaliate the unfair action. Lord Śrī Kṛṣṇa saved Bhīma from His wrath. But He left the place at once, being disgusted at Bhīmasena, and after His departure Duryodhana fell to the ground to meet his death. The funeral ceremony of Abhimanyu, the son of Arjuna, was performed by Him, as He was the maternal uncle. It was impossible to be performed by any one of the Pāṇḍavas, who were all overwhelmed with grief. At the last stage, He departed from this world by producing a great white snake from His mouth, and thus He was carried by Śeṣanāga in the shape of a serpent.

Pradyumna: Incarnation of Kāmadeva or, according to others, incarnation of Sanat-kumāra, born as the son of the Personality of Godhead Lord Śrī Kṛṣṇa and Lakṣmīdevī Śrīmatī Rukmiṇī, the principal queen at Dvārakā. He was one of those who went to congratulate Arjuna upon his marrying Subhadrā. He was one of the great generals who fought with Śālva, and while fighting with him he became unconscious on the battlefield. His charioteer brought him back to the camp from the battlefield, and for this action he was very sorry and rebuked his charioteer. However, he fought again with Śālva and was victorious. He heard all about the different demigods from Nāradajī. He is one of the four plenary expansions of Lord Śrī Kṛṣṇa. He is the third one. He inquired from his father, Śrī Kṛṣṇa, about the glories of the *brāhmaṇas.* During the fratricidal war amongst the descendants of Yadu, he died at the hand of Bhoja, another king of the Vṛṣṇis. After his death, he was installed in his original position.

Cārudeṣṇa: Another son of Lord Śrī Kṛṣṇa and Rukmiṇīdevī. He was also present during the *svayaṁvara* ceremony of Draupadī. He was a great warrior like his brothers and father. He fought with Vivinidhaka and killed him in the fight.

Sāmba: One of the great heroes of the Yadu dynasty and the son of Lord Śrī Kṛṣṇa by His wife Jāmbavatī. He learned the military art of throwing arrows from Arjuna, and he became a member of parliament during the time of Mahārāja Yudhiṣṭhira. He was present during the Rājasūya-yajña of Mahārāja Yudhiṣṭhira. When all the Vṛṣṇis were assembled during the time of Prabhāsa-yajña, his glorious activities were narrated by Sātyaki before Lord Baladeva. He was also present along with his father, Lord Śrī Kṛṣṇa, during the *aśvamedha-yajña* performed by Yudhiṣṭhira. He was presented before some *ṛṣis* falsely dressed as a pregnant woman by his brothers, and in fun he asked the *ṛṣis* what he was going to deliver. The *ṛṣis* replied that he would deliver a lump of iron, which would be the cause of fratricidal war in the family of Yadu. The next day, in the morning, Sāmba delivered a large lump of iron, which was entrusted with Ugrasena for necessary action. Actually later on there was the foretold fratricidal war, and Sāmba died in that war.

So all these sons of Lord Kṛṣṇa left their respective palaces and leaving aside all engagements, including lying down, sitting and dining, hastened toward their exalted father.

TEXT 18

वारणेन्द्रं पुरस्कृत्य ब्राह्मणैः ससुमङ्गलैः ।
शङ्खतूर्यनिनादेन ब्रह्मघोषेण चादृताः ।
प्रत्युज्जग्मू रथैर्हृष्टाः प्रणयागतसाध्वसाः ॥१८॥

vāraṇendraṁ puraskṛtya
brāhmaṇaiḥ sasumaṅgalaiḥ
śaṅkha-tūrya-ninādena
brahma-ghoṣeṇa cādṛtāḥ
pratyujjagmū rathair hṛṣṭāḥ
praṇayāgata-sādhvasāḥ

vāraṇa-indram—elephants on the auspicious mission; *puraskṛtya*—putting in the front; *brāhmaṇaiḥ*—by the *brāhmaṇas; sa-sumaṅgalaiḥ*—with all-auspicious signs; *śaṅkha*—conchshell; *tūrya*—bugle; *ninādena*—by the sound of; *brahma-ghoṣeṇa*—by chanting the hymns of the *Vedas; ca*—and; *ādṛtāḥ*—glorified; *prati*—towards; *ujjagmuḥ*—proceeded hurriedly; *rathaiḥ*—on the chariots; *hṛṣṭāḥ*—in cheerfulness; *praṇayāgata*—saturated with affection; *sādhvasāḥ*—all-respectful.

TRANSLATION

They hastened toward the Lord on chariots with brāhmaṇas bearing flowers. Before them were elephants, emblems of good fortune. Conchshells and bugles were sounded, and Vedic hymns were chanted. Thus they offered their respects, which were saturated with affection.

PURPORT

The Vedic way of receiving a great personality creates an atmosphere of respect, which is saturated with affection and veneration for the person received. The auspicious atmosphere of such a reception depends on the paraphernalia described above, including conchshells, flowers, incense, decorated elephants, and the qualified *brāhmaṇas* reciting verses from the Vedic literatures. Such a program of reception is full of sincerity, on the part of both the receiver and the received.

TEXT 19

वारमुख्याश्च शतशो यानैस्तद्दर्शनोत्सुकाः ।
लसत्कुण्डलनिर्भातकपोलवदनश्रियः ॥१९॥

vāramukhyāś ca śataśo
yānais tad-darśanotsukāḥ
lasat-kuṇḍala-nirbhāta-
kapola-vadana-śriyaḥ

vāramukhyāḥ—well-known prostitutes; *ca*—and; *śataśaḥ*—hundreds of; *yānaiḥ*—by vehicles; *tat-darśana*—for meeting Him (Lord Śrī Kṛṣṇa); *utsukāḥ*—very much anxious; *lasat*—hanging; *kuṇḍala*—earrings; *nirbhāta*—dazzling; *kapola*—forehead; *vadana*—face; *śriyaḥ*—beauty.

TRANSLATION

At the same time, many hundreds of well-known prostitutes began to proceed on various vehicles. They were all very eager to meet the Lord, and their beautiful faces were decorated with dazzling earrings, which enhanced the beauty of their foreheads.

PURPORT

We may not hate even the prostitutes if they are devotees of the Lord. Even to date there are many prostitutes in great cities of India who are sincere devotees of the Lord. By tricks of chance one may be obliged to adopt a profession which is not very adorable in society, but that does not hamper one in executing devotional service to the Lord. Devotional service to the Lord is uncheckable in all circumstances. It is understood herewith that even in those days, about five thousand years ago, there were prostitutes in a city like Dvārakā, where Lord Kṛṣṇa resided. This means that prostitutes are necessary citizens for the proper upkeep of society. The government opens wine shops, but this does not mean that the government encourages the drinking of wine. The idea is that there is a class of men who will drink at any cost, and it has been experienced that prohibition in great cities encouraged illicit smuggling of wine. Similarly, men who are not satisfied at home require such concessions, and if there is no prostitute, then such low men will induce others into prostitution. It is better that prostitutes be available in the marketplace so that the sanctity of society can be maintained. It is better to maintain a class of prostitutes than to encourage prostitutes within society. The real reformation is to enlighten all people to become devotees of the Lord, and that will check all kinds of deteriorating factors of life.

Śrī Bilvamaṅgala Ṭhākura, a great *ācārya* of the Viṣṇusvāmī Vaiṣṇava sect, in his householder life was overly attached to a prostitute who happened to be a devotee of the Lord. One night when the Ṭhākura came to Cintāmaṇi's house in torrents of rain and thunder, Cintāmaṇi was astonished to see how the Ṭhākura could come on such a dreadful night after crossing a foaming river which was full of waves. She said to Ṭhākura Bilvamaṅgala that his attraction for the flesh and bone of an insignificant woman like her would be properly utilized if it could be diverted to the devotional service of the Lord to achieve attraction for the transcendental beauty of the Lord. It was a momentous hour for the Ṭhākura, and he took a turn towards spiritual realization by the words of a prostitute. Later on the Ṭhākura accepted the prostitute as his spiritual master, and in several places of his literary works he has glorified the name of Cintāmaṇi, who showed him the right path.

In the *Bhagavad-gītā* (9.32) the Lord says, "O son of Pṛthā, even the low-born *caṇḍālas* and those who are born in a family of unbelievers, and even the prostitutes, shall attain perfection of life if they take shelter of unalloyed devotional service to Me, because in the path of devotional service there are no impediments due to degraded birth and occupation. The path is open for everyone who agrees to follow it."

It appears that the prostitutes of Dvārakā, who were so eager to meet the Lord, were all His unalloyed devotees, and thus they were all on the path of salvation according to the above version of the *Bhagavad-gītā*. Therefore, the only reformation that is necessary in society is to make an organized effort to turn the citizens into devotees of the Lord, and thus all good qualities of the denizens of heaven will overtake them in their own way. On the other hand, those who are nondevotees have no good qualifications whatsoever, however they may be materially advanced. The difference is that the devotees of the Lord are on the path of liberation, whereas the nondevotees are on the path of further entanglement in material bondage. The criterion of advancement of civilization is whether the people are educated and advanced on the path of salvation.

TEXT 20

नटनर्तकगन्धर्वाः सूतमागधवन्दिनः ।
गायन्ति चोत्तमश्लोकचरितान्यद्भुतानि च ॥२०॥

naṭa-nartaka-gandharvāḥ
sūta-māgadha-vandinaḥ
gāyanti cottamaśloka-
caritāny adbhutāni ca

naṭa—dramatists; *nartaka*—dancers; *gandharvāḥ*—celestial singers; *sūta*—professional historians; *māgadha*—professional genealogists; *vandinaḥ*—professional learned speakers; *gāyanti*—chant; *ca*—respectively;

uttamaśloka—the Supreme Lord; *caritāni*—activities; *adbhutāni*—all superhuman; *ca*—and.

TRANSLATION

Expert dramatists, artists, dancers, singers, historians, genealogists and learned speakers all gave their respective contributions, being inspired by the superhuman pastimes of the Lord. Thus they proceeded on and on.

PURPORT

It appears that five thousand years ago the society also needed the services of the dramatists, artists, dancers, singers, historians, genealogists, public speakers, etc. Dancers, singers and dramatic artists mostly hailed from the *śūdra* community, whereas the learned historians, genealogists and public speakers hailed from the *brāhmaṇa* community. All of them belonged to a particular caste, and they became so trained in their respective families. Such dramatists, dancers, singers, historians, genealogists and public speakers would dwell on the subject of the Lord's superhuman activities in different ages and millenniums, and not on ordinary events. Nor were they in chronological order. All the *Purāṇas* are historical facts described only in relation with the Supreme Lord in different ages and times as well as on different planets also. Therefore, we do not find any chronological order. The modern historians, therefore, cannot catch up the link, and thus they unauthoritatively remark that the *Purāṇas* are all imaginary stories only.

Even one hundred years ago in India, all dramatic performances were centered around the superhuman activities of the Supreme Lord. The common people would be verily entertained by the performances of dramas, and *yātrā* parties played wonderfully on the superhuman activities of the Lord, and thus even the illiterate agriculturist would be a participant in the knowledge of Vedic literature, despite a considerable lack of academic qualifications. Therefore, expert players in drama, dancers, singers, speakers, etc., are required for the spiritual enlightenment of the common man. The genealogists would give account completely of the descendants of a particular family. Even at the present moment the guides in the pilgrimage sites of India submit a complete account of genealogical tables before a newcomer. This wonderful act sometimes attracts more customers to receive such important information.

TEXT 21

भगवांस्तत्र बन्धूनां पौराणामनुवर्तिनाम् ।
यथाविध्युपसङ्गम्य सर्वेषां मानमादधे ॥२१॥

bhagavāṁs tatra bandhūnāṁ
paurāṇām anuvartinām
yathā-vidhy upasaṅgamya
sarveṣāṁ mānam ādadhe

bhagavān—Śrī Kṛṣṇa, the Personality of Godhead; *tatra*—in that place; *bandhūnām*—of the friends; *paurāṇām*—of the citizens; *anuvartinām*—those who approached Him to receive and welcome; *yathā-vidhi*—as it behooves; *upasaṅgamya*—going nearer; *sarveṣām*—for each and every one; *mānam*—honor and respects; *ādadhe*—offered.

TRANSLATION

Lord Kṛṣṇa, the Personality of Godhead, approached them and offered due honor and respect to each and every one of the friends, relatives, citizens and all others who came to receive and welcome Him.

PURPORT

The Supreme Lord Personality of Godhead is neither impersonal nor an inert object unable to reciprocate the feelings of His devotees. Here the word *yathā-vidhi,* or "just as it behooves," is significant. He reciprocates "just as it behooves" with His different types of admirers and devotees. Of course, the pure devotees are of one type only because they have no other object for service but the Lord, and therefore the Lord also reciprocates with such pure devotees just as it behooves, namely, He is always attentive to all the matters of His pure devotees. There are others who designate Him as impersonal, and so the Lord also does not take any personal interest. He satisfies everyone in terms of one's development of spiritual consciousness, and a sample of such reciprocation is exhibited here with His different welcomers.

TEXT 22

प्रह्वाभिवादनाश्लेषकरस्पर्शस्मितेक्षणैः ।
आश्वास्य चाश्वपाकेभ्यो वरैश्चाभिमतैर्विभुः ॥२२॥

prahvābhivādanāśleṣa-
kara-sparśa-smitekṣaṇaiḥ
āśvāsya cāśvapākebhyo
varaiś cābhimatair vibhuḥ

prahvā—by bowing His head; *abhivādana*—by greeting with words; *āśleṣa*—embracing; *kara-sparśa*—shaking hands; *smita-īkṣaṇaiḥ*—by a glancing smile; *āśvāsya*—by encouragement; *ca*—and; *āśvapākebhyaḥ*—down to the lowest rank of dog-eaters; *varaiḥ*—by benedictions; *ca*—also; *abhimataiḥ*—as desired by; *vibhuḥ*—the Almighty.

TRANSLATION

The almighty Lord greeted everyone present by bowing His head, exchanging greetings, embracing, shaking hands, looking and smiling, giving assurances and awarding benedictions, even to the lowest in rank.

PURPORT

To receive the Lord Śrī Kṛṣṇa there were all grades of population, beginning from Vasudeva, Ugrasena and Gargamuni—the father, grandfather and teacher—down to the prostitutes and *caṇḍālas,* who are accustomed to eat dogs. And every one of them was properly greeted by the Lord in terms of rank and position. As pure living entities, all are the separated parts and parcels of the Lord, and thus no one is alien by His eternal relation. Such pure living entities are graded differently in terms of contamination of the modes of material nature, but the Lord is equally affectionate to all His parts and parcels, despite material gradation. He descends only to recall these materialistic living beings back to His kingdom, and intelligent persons take advantage of this facility offered by the Personality of Godhead to all living beings. No one is rejected by the Lord from the kingdom of God, and it remains with the living being to accept this or not.

TEXT 23

स्वयं च गुरुभिर्विप्रैः सदारैः स्थविरैरपि ।
आशीर्भिर्युज्यमानोऽन्यैर्वन्दिभिश्चाविशत्पुरम् ॥२३॥

svayaṁ ca gurubhir vipraiḥ
sadāraiḥ sthavirair api

āśīrbhir yujyamāno 'nyair
vandibhiś cāviśat puram

svayam—Himself; *ca*—also; *gurubhiḥ*—by elderly relatives; *vipraiḥ*—by the *brāhmaṇas; sadāraiḥ*—with their wives; *sthaviraiḥ*—invalid; *api*—also; *āśīrbhiḥ*—by the blessing of; *yujyamānaḥ*—being praised by; *anyaiḥ*—by others; *vandibhiḥ*—admirers; *ca*—and; *aviśat*—entered; *puram*—the city.

TRANSLATION

Then the Lord personally entered the city accompanied by elderly relatives and invalid brāhmaṇas with their wives, all offering benedictions and singing the glories of the Lord. Others also praised the glories of the Lord.

PURPORT

The *brāhmaṇas* in society were never attentive to banking money for future retired life. When they were old invalids, they used to approach the assembly of the kings, and simply by praising the glorious deeds performed by the kings, along with their wives, they would be provided with all necessities of life. Such *brāhmaṇas* were not, so to speak, flatterers of the kings, but the kings were actually glorified by their actions, and they were sincerely still more encouraged in pious acts by such *brāhmaṇas* in a dignified way. Lord Śrī Kṛṣṇa is worthy of all glories, and the praying *brāhmaṇas* and others were glorified themselves by chanting the glories of the Lord.

TEXT 24

राजमार्गं गते कृष्णे द्वारकायाः कुलस्त्रियः ।
हर्म्याण्यारुरुहुर्विप्र तदीक्षणमहोत्सवाः ॥२४॥

rāja-mārgaṁ gate kṛṣṇe
dvārakāyāḥ kula-striyaḥ
harmyāṇy āruruhur vipra
tad-īkṣaṇa-mahotsavāḥ

rāja-mārgam—the public roads; *gate*—while passing over; *kṛṣṇe*—by Lord Kṛṣṇa; *dvārakāyāḥ*—of the city of Dvārakā; *kula-striyaḥ*—ladies of the respectable families; *harmyāṇi*—on the palaces; *āruruhuḥ*—got up; *vipra*—

O *brāhmaṇas; tat-īkṣaṇa*—just to look upon Him (Kṛṣṇa); *mahā-utsavāḥ*—accepted as the greatest festival.

TRANSLATION

When Lord Kṛṣṇa passed over the public roads, all the ladies from the respectable families of Dvārakā went up to the roofs of their palaces just to have a look at the Lord. They considered this to be the greatest festival.

PURPORT

To have a look at the Lord is a great festive occasion undoubtedly, as it was considered by the metropolitan ladies of Dvārakā. This is still followed by the devout ladies of India. Especially during the days of the Jhulana and Janmāṣṭamī ceremonies, the ladies of India still throng up in the greatest number at the temple of the Lord, where His transcendental eternal form is worshiped. The transcendental form of the Lord installed in a temple is not different from the Lord personally. Such a form of the Lord is called *arca-vigraha,* or *arcā* incarnation, and is expanded by the Lord by His internal potency just to facilitate the devotional service of His innumerable devotees who are in the material world. The material senses cannot perceive the spiritual nature of the Lord, and therefore the Lord accepts the *arca-vigraha,* which is apparently made of material elements like earth, wood and stone, but actually there is no material contamination. The Lord being *kaivalya* (one alone), there is no matter in Him. He is one without a second, and therefore the almighty Lord can appear in any form without being contaminated by the material conception. Therefore, festivities in the temple of the Lord, as held generally, are like festivals performed during the manifestive days of the Lord of Dvārakā, about five thousand years ago. The authorized *ācāryas,* who know the science perfectly, install such temples of the Lord under regulative principles just to offer facilities to the common man, but persons who are less intelligent, without being conversant with the science, mistake this great attempt to be *idol worship* and poke their nose into that to which they have no access. Therefore, the ladies or men who observe festivals in the temples of the Lord just to have a look at the transcendental form are a thousand times more glorious than those who are nonbelievers in the transcendental form of the Lord.

It appears from the verse that the inhabitants of Dvārakā were all owners of big palaces. This indicates the prosperity of the city. The ladies got up on the roofs just to have a look at the procession and the Lord. The ladies did not mix with the crowd on the street, and thus their respectability was perfectly observed. There was no artificial equality with the man. Female respectability is preserved more elegantly by keeping the woman separate from the man. The sexes should not mix unrestrictedly.

TEXT 25

नित्यं निरीक्षमाणानां यदपि द्वारकौकसाम् ।
न वितृप्यन्ति हि दृशः श्रियो धामाङ्गमच्युतम् ॥२५॥

nityaṁ nirīkṣamāṇānāṁ
yad api dvārakaukasām
na vitṛpyanti hi dṛśaḥ
śriyo dhāmāṅgam acyutam

nityam—regularly, always; *nirīkṣamāṇānām*—of those who look at Him; *yat*—although; *api*—in spite of; *dvārakā-okasām*—the inhabitants of Dvārakā; *na*—never; *vitṛpyanti*—satisfied; *hi*—exactly; *dṛśaḥ*—sight; *śriyaḥ*—beauties; *dhāma-aṅgam*—the bodily reservoir; *acyutam*—the infallible.

TRANSLATION

The inhabitants of Dvārakā were regularly accustomed to look upon the reservoir of all beauty, the infallible Lord, yet they were never satiated.

PURPORT

When the ladies of the city of Dvārakā got up on the roofs of their palaces, they never thought that they had previously many times seen the beautiful body of the infallible Lord. This indicates that they had no satiation in desiring to see the Lord. Anything material seen for a number of times ultimately becomes unattractive by the law of satiation. The law of satiation acts materially, but there is no scope for it in the spiritual realm. The word *infallible* is significant here, because although the Lord has mercifully descended on earth, He is still infallible. The living entities are fallible because when they come in contact with the material world they lack their spiritual identity, and thus the body materially obtained becomes subjected to birth, growth, transformation, situation, deterioration and annihilation under the laws of nature. The Lord's body is not like that. He descends as He is and is never under the laws of the material modes. His body is the source of everything that be, the reservoir of all beauties beyond our experience. No one, therefore, is satiated by seeing the transcendental body of the Lord because there are always manifestations of newer and newer beauties. The transcendental name, form, qualities, entourage, etc., are all spiritual manifestations, and there is no satiation in chanting the holy name of the Lord, there is no satiation in discussing the qualities of the Lord, and there is no limitation of the entourage of the Lord. He is the source of all and is limitless.

TEXT 26

श्रियो निवासो यस्योरः पानपात्रं मुखं दृशाम् ।
बाहवो लोकपालानां सारङ्गाणां पदाम्बुजम् ॥२६॥

śriyo nivāso yasyoraḥ
pāna-pātraṁ mukhaṁ dṛśām
bāhavo loka-pālānāṁ
sāraṅgāṇāṁ padāmbujam

śriyaḥ—of the goddess of fortune; *nivāsaḥ*—residential place; *yasya*—one whose; *uraḥ*—chest; *pāna-pātram*—the drinking pot; *mukham*—face; *dṛśām*—of eyes; *bāhavaḥ*—the arms; *loka-pālānām*—of the administrative demigods; *sāraṅgāṇām*—of the devotees who talk and sing of the essence or substance; *pada-ambujam*—the lotus feet.

TRANSLATION

The Lord's chest is the abode of the goddess of fortune. His moonlike face is the drinking vessel for eyes which hanker after all that is beautiful. His arms are the resting places for the administrative demigods. And His lotus feet are the refuge of pure devotees who never talk or sing of any subject except His Lordship.

PURPORT

There are different classes of human beings, all seeking different enjoyments from different objects. There are persons who are seeking after the favor of the goddess of fortune, and for them the Vedic literatures give information that the Lord is always served with all reverence by thousands and thousands of goddesses of fortune at the *cintāmaṇi-dhāma,** the

---

**cintāmaṇi-prakara-sadmasu kalpa-vṛkṣa-*
lakṣāvṛteṣu surabhīr abhipālayantam
lakṣmī-sahasra-śata-sambhrama-sevyamānaṁ
govindam ādi-puruṣaṁ tam ahaṁ bhajāmi (Bs. 5.29)

transcendental abode of the Lord where the trees are all desire trees and the buildings are made of touchstone. The Lord Govinda is engaged there in herding the *surabhi* cows as His natural occupation. These goddesses of fortune can be seen automatically if we are attracted by the bodily features of the Lord. The impersonalists cannot observe such goddesses of fortune because of their dry speculative habit. And those who are artists, overtaken by the beautiful creation, should better see to the beautiful face of the Lord for complete satisfaction. The face of the Lord is the embodiment of beauty. What they call beautiful nature is but His smile, and what they call the sweet songs of the birds are but specimens of the whispering voice of the Lord. There are administrative demigods in charge of departmental service of cosmic management, and there are tiny administrative gods in the state service. They are always afraid of other competitors, but if they take shelter of the arms of the Lord, the Lord can protect them always from the attacks of enemies. A faithful servant of the Lord engaged in the service of administration is the ideal executive head and can well protect the interest of the people in general. Other so-called administrators are symbols of anachronisms leading to the acute distress of the people who are governed by them. The administrators can remain safely under the protection of the arms of the Lord. The essence of everything is the Supreme Lord: He is called the *sāram.* And those who sing and talk about Him are called the *sāraṅgas,* or the pure devotees. The pure devotees are always hankering after the lotus feet of the Lord. The lotus has a kind of honey which is transcendentally relished by the devotees. They are like the bees who are always after the honey. Śrīla Rūpa Gosvāmī, the great devotee *ācārya* of the Gauḍīya-Vaiṣṇava-sampradāya, has sung a song about this lotus honey, comparing himself to the bee: "O my Lord Kṛṣṇa, I beg to offer my prayers unto You. My mind is like the bee, and it is after some honey. Kindly, therefore, give my bee-mind a place at Your lotus feet, which are the resources for all transcendental honey. I know that even big demigods like Brahmā do not see the rays of the nails of Your lotus feet, even though they are engaged in deep meditation for years together. Still, O infallible one, my ambition is such, for You are very merciful to your surrendered devotees. O Mādhava, I know also that I have no genuine devotion for the service of Your lotus feet, but because Your Lordship is inconceivably powerful, You can do what is impossible to be done. Your lotus feet can deride even the nectar of the heavenly kingdom, and therefore I am very much attracted by them. O supreme eternal, please, therefore, let my mind be fixed at Your lotus feet so that eternally I may be able to relish the taste of Your transcendental service."

The devotees are satisfied with being placed at the lotus feet of the Lord and have no ambition to see His all-beautiful face or aspire for the protection of the strong arms of the Lord. They are humble by nature, and the Lord is always leaning towards such humble devotees.

TEXT 27

सितातपत्रव्यजनैरुपस्कृतः
प्रसूनवर्षैरभिवर्षितः पथि ।
पिशङ्गवासा वनमालया बभौ
घनो यथार्कोडुपचापवैद्युतैः ॥२७॥

sitātapatra-vyajanair upaskṛtaḥ
prasūna-varṣair abhivarṣitaḥ pathi
piśaṅga-vāsā vana-mālayā babhau
ghano yathārkoḍupa-cāpa-vaidyutaiḥ

sita-ātapatra—white umbrella; *vyajanaiḥ*—with a *cāmara* fan; *upaskṛtaḥ*—being served by; *prasūna*—flowers; *varṣaiḥ*—by the showers; *abhivarṣitaḥ*—thus being covered; *pathi*—on the road; *piśaṅga-vāsāḥ*—by the yellow garments; *vana-mālayā*—by the flower garlands; *babhau*—thus it became; *ghanaḥ*—cloud; *yathā*—as if; *arka*—the sun; *uḍupa*—the moon; *cāpa*—the rainbow; *vaidyutaiḥ*—by the lightning.

TRANSLATION

As the Lord passed along the public road of Dvārakā, His head was protected from the sunshine by a white umbrella. White feathered fans moved in semicircles, and showers of flowers fell upon the road. His yellow garments and garlands of flowers made it appear as if a dark cloud were surrounded simultaneously by sun, moon, lightning and rainbows.

PURPORT

The sun, moon, rainbow and lightning do not appear in the sky simultaneously. When there is sun, the moonlight becomes insignificant, and if there are clouds and a rainbow, there is no manifestation of lightning. The Lord's bodily hue is just like a new monsoon cloud. He is compared herein to the cloud. The white umbrella over His head is compared to the sun. The movement of the bunch-hair fan of flukes is compared to the moon. The showers of flowers are compared to the stars. His yellow garments are compared to the rainbow. So all these activities of the firmament, being impossible simultaneous factors, cannot be adjusted by comparison. The adjustment is possible only when we think of the inconceivable potency of the Lord. The Lord is all-powerful, and in His presence anything impossible can be made possible by His inconceivable energy. But the situation created at the time of His passing on the roads of Dvārakā was beautiful and could not be compared to anything besides the description of natural phenomena.

TEXT 28

प्रविष्टस्तु गृहं पित्रोः परिष्वक्तः स्वमातृभिः ।
ववन्दे शिरसा सप्त देवकीप्रमुखा मुदा ॥२८॥

praviṣṭas tu gṛhaṁ pitroḥ
pariṣvaktaḥ sva-mātṛbhiḥ
vavande śirasā sapta
devakī-pramukhā mudā

praviṣṭaḥ—after entering; *tu*—but; *gṛham*—houses; *pitroḥ*—of the father; *pariṣvaktaḥ*—embraced; *sva-mātṛbhiḥ*—by His own mothers; *vavande*—offered obeisances; *śirasā*—His head; *sapta*—seven; *devakī*—Devakī; *pramukhā*—headed by; *mudā*—gladly.

TRANSLATION

After entering the house of His father, He was embraced by the mothers present, and the Lord offered His obeisances unto them by placing His head at their feet. The mothers were headed by Devakī [His real mother].

PURPORT

It appears that Vasudeva, the father of Lord Kṛṣṇa, had completely separate residential quarters where he lived with his eighteen wives, out of whom Śrīmatī Devakī is the real mother of Lord Kṛṣṇa. But in spite of this, all other stepmothers were equally affectionate to Him, as will be evident from the following verse. Lord Kṛṣṇa also did not distinguish His real mother from His stepmothers, and He equally offered His obeisances unto all the wives of Vasudeva present on the occasion. According to scriptures also, there are seven mothers: (1) the real mother, (2) the wife of the spiritual master, (3) the wife of a *brāhmaṇa,* (4) the wife of the king, (5) the cow, (6) the nurse, and (7) the earth. All of them are mothers. Even by this injunction of the *śāstras,* the stepmother, who is the wife of the father, is also as good as the mother because the father is also one of the spiritual masters. Lord Kṛṣṇa, the Lord of the universe, plays the part of an ideal son just to teach others how to treat their stepmothers.

TEXT 29

ताः पुत्रमङ्कमारोप्य स्नेहस्नुतपयोधराः ।
हर्षविह्वलितात्मानः सिषिचुर्नेत्रजैर्जलैः ॥२९॥

tāḥ putram aṅkam āropya
sneha-snuta-payodharāḥ
harṣa-vihvalitātmānaḥ
siṣicur netrajair jalaiḥ

tāḥ—all of them; *putram*—the son; *aṅkam*—the lap; *āropya*—having placed on; *sneha-snuta*—moistened by affection; *payodharāḥ*—breasts filled up; *harṣa*—delight; *vihvalita-ātmānaḥ*—overwhelmed by; *siṣicuḥ*—wet; *netrajaiḥ*—from the eyes; *jalaiḥ*—water.

TRANSLATION

The mothers, after embracing their son, sat Him on their laps. Due to pure affection, milk sprang from their breasts. They were overwhelmed with delight, and the tears from their eyes wetted the Lord.

PURPORT

When Lord Kṛṣṇa was at Vṛndāvana even the cows would become moistened by affection towards Him, and He would draw milk from the nipples of every affectionate living being, so what to speak of the stepmothers who were already as good as His own mother.

TEXT 30

अथाविशत् स्वभवनं सर्वकाममनुत्तमम् ।
प्रासादा यत्र पत्नीनां सहस्राणि च षोडश ॥३०॥

athāviśat sva-bhavanaṁ
sarva-kāmam anuttamam

prāsādā yatra patnīnāṁ
sahasrāṇi ca ṣoḍaśa

atha—thereafter; *aviśat*—entered; *sva-bhavanam*—personal palaces; *sarva*—all; *kāmam*—desires; *anuttamam*—perfect to the fullest extent; *prāsādāḥ*—palaces; *yatra*—where; *patnīnām*—of the wives numbering; *sahasrāṇi*—thousands; *ca*—over and above; *ṣoḍaśa*—sixteen.

TRANSLATION

Thereafter, the Lord entered His palaces, which were perfect to the fullest extent. His wives lived in them, and they numbered over sixteen thousand.

PURPORT

Lord Kṛṣṇa had 16,108 wives, and for each and every one of them there was a fully equipped palace complete with necessary compounds and gardens. Full description of these palaces is given in the Tenth Canto. All the palaces were made of the best marble stone. They were illuminated by jewels and decorated by curtains and carpets of velvet and silk, nicely bedecked and embroidered with gold lace. The Personality of Godhead means one who is full with all power, all energy, all opulences, all beauties, all knowledge and all renunciation. Therefore, in the palaces of the Lord there was nothing wanting for fulfilling all desires of the Lord. The Lord is unlimited, and therefore His desires are also unlimited, and the supply is also unlimited. Everything being unlimited, it is concisely described here as *sarva-kāmam,* or full with all desirable equipment.

TEXT 31

पत्न्यः पतिं प्रोष्य गृहानुपागतं
विलोक्य संजातमनोमहोत्सवाः ।
उत्तस्थुरारात् सहसासनाशयात्
साकं व्रतैर्व्रीडितलोचनाननाः ॥३१॥

patnyaḥ patiṁ proṣya gṛhānupāgataṁ
vilokya sañjāta-mano-mahotsavāḥ
uttasthur ārāt sahasāsanāśayāt
sākaṁ vratair vrīḍita-locanānanāḥ

patnyaḥ—the ladies (wives of Lord Śrī Kṛṣṇa); *patim*—husband; *proṣya*—who was away from home; *gṛha-anupāgatam*—now returned home; *vilokya*—thus seeing; *sañjāta*—having developed; *manaḥ-mahā-utsavāḥ*—a sense of joyful ceremony within the mind; *uttasthuḥ*—got up; *ārāt*—from a distance; *sahasā*—all of a sudden; *āsanā*—from the seats; *āśayāt*—from the state of meditation; *sākam*—along with; *vrataiḥ*—the vow; *vrīḍita*—looking coyly; *locana*—eyes; *ānanāḥ*—with such faces.

TRANSLATION

The queens of Lord Śrī Kṛṣṇa rejoiced within their minds to see their husband home after a long period abroad. The queens got up at once from their seats and meditations. As was socially customary, they covered their faces shyly and looked about coyly.

PURPORT

As mentioned above, the Lord entered His home palaces occupied by 16,108 queens. This means that the Lord at once expanded Himself in as many plenary expansions as there were queens and palaces and entered in each and every one of them simultaneously and separately. Here is another manifestation of the feature of His internal potency. He can expand Himself in as many forms of spiritual identity as He desires, even though He is one without a second. It is confirmed by the *Śruti-mantra* that the Absolute is one alone, and yet He becomes many as soon as He so desires. These manifold expansions of the Supreme Lord are manifested as plenary and separated portions. The separated portions are representations of His energy, and the plenary portions are manifestations of His Personality. Thus the Personality of Godhead manifested Himself in 16,108 plenary expansions and simultaneously entered into each and every one of the palaces of the queens. This is called *vaibhava,* or the transcendental potency of the Lord. And because He can do so, He is also known as Yogeśvara. Ordinarily, a *yogī* or mystic living being is able to expand himself at utmost to tenfold expansions of his body, but the Lord can do so to the extent of as many thousands or infinitely, as He likes. Unbelievers become astonished to learn that Lord Kṛṣṇa married more than 16,000 queens because they think of Lord Kṛṣṇa as one of them and measure the potency of the Lord by their own limited potency. One should know, therefore, that the Lord is never on the level of the living beings, who are but expansions of His marginal potency, and one should never equalize the potent and the potency, although there is very little difference of quality between the potent and the potency. The queens were also expansions of His internal potency, and thus the potent and potencies are perpetually exchanging transcendental pleasures, known as pastimes of the Lord. One should not, therefore, become astonished to learn that the Lord married so many wives. On the contrary, one should affirm that even if the Lord marries sixteen thousand million wives, He is not completely manifesting His unlimited and inexhaustible potency. He married *only* 16,000 wives and entered in each and every one of the different palaces just to impress in the history of the human beings on the surface of the earth that the Lord is never equal to or less than any human being, however powerful he may be. No one, therefore, is either equal to or greater than the Lord. The Lord is always great in all respects. "God is great" is eternal truth.

Therefore, as soon as the queens saw from a distance their husband, who was away from home for long periods due to the Battle of Kurukṣetra, they all arose from the slumber of meditation and prepared to receive their most beloved. According to Yājñavalkya's religious injunctions, a woman whose husband is away from home should not take part in any social functions, should not decorate her body, should not laugh and should not go to any relative's house in any circumstance. This is the vow of the ladies whose husbands are away from home. At the same time, it is also enjoined that a wife should never present herself before the husband in an unclean state. She must decorate herself with ornaments and good dress and should always be present before the husband in a happy and joyous mood. The queens of Lord Kṛṣṇa were all in meditation, thinking of the Lord's absence, and were always meditating upon Him. The Lord's devotees cannot live for a moment without meditating on the Lord, and what to speak of the queens, who were all goddesses of fortune incarnated as queens in the pastimes of the Lord at Dvārakā. They can never be separated from the Lord, either by presence or by trance. The *gopīs* at Vṛndāvana could not forget the Lord when the Lord was away in the forest cowherding. When the Lord boy Kṛṣṇa was absent from the village, the *gopīs* at home used to worry about Him traversing the rough ground with His soft lotus feet. By thinking thus, they were sometimes overwhelmed in trance and mortified in the heart. Such is the condition of the pure associates of the Lord. They are always in trance, and so the queens also were in trance during the absence of the Lord. Presently, having seen the Lord from a distance, they at once gave up all their engagements, including the vows of women as described above. According to Śrī Viśvanātha Carkavartī

Ṭhākura, there was a regular psychological reaction on the occasion. First of all, rising from their seats, although they wanted to see their husband, they were deterred because of feminine shyness. But due to strong ecstasy, they overcame that stage of weakness and became caught up with the idea of embracing the Lord, and this thought factually made them unconscious of their surrounding environment. This prime state of ecstasy annihilated all other formalities and social conventions, and thus they escaped all stumbling blocks on the path of meeting the Lord. And that is the perfect stage of meeting the Lord of the soul, Śrī Kṛṣṇa.

TEXT 32

तमात्मजैर्दृष्टिभिरन्तरात्मना
दुरन्तभावाः परिरेभिरे पतिम् ।
निरुद्धमप्यास्रवदम्बु नेत्रयो-
र्विलज्जतीनां भृगुवर्य वैक्लवात् ॥३२॥

tam ātmajair dṛṣṭibhir antarātmanā
duranta-bhāvāḥ parirebhire patim
niruddham apy āsravad ambu netrayor
vilajjatīnāṁ bhṛgu-varya vaiklavāt

tam—Him (the Lord); *ātma-jaiḥ*—by the sons; *dṛṣṭibhiḥ*—by the sight; *antara-ātmanā*—by the innermost part of the heart; *duranta-bhāvāḥ*—insuperable ecstasy; *parirebhire*—embraced; *patim*—husband; *niruddham*—choked up; *api*—in spite of; *āsravat*—tears; *ambu*—like drops of water; *netrayoḥ*—from the eyes; *vilajjatīnām*—of those situated in shyness; *bhṛgu-varya*—O chief of the Bhṛgus; *vaiklavāt*—inadvertently.

TRANSLATION

The insuperable ecstasy was so strong that the queens, who were shy, first embraced the Lord in the innermost recesses of their hearts. Then they embraced Him visually, and then they sent their sons to embrace Him [which is equal to personal embracing]. But, O chief amongst the Bhṛgus, though they tried to restrain their feelings, they inadvertently shed tears.

PURPORT

Although due to feminine shyness there were many hindrances to embracing the dear husband, Lord Śrī Kṛṣṇa, the queens performed that act by seeing Him, by putting Him in the cores of their hearts, and by sending their sons to embrace Him. Still, the act remained unfinished, and tears rolled down their cheeks despite all endeavors to check them. One indirectly embraces the husband by sending the son to embrace him because the son is developed as part of the mother's body. The embrace of the son is not exactly the embrace of husband and wife from the sexual point of view, but the embrace is satisfaction from the affectionate point of view. The embrace of the eyes is more effective in the conjugal relation, and thus according to Śrīla Jīva Gosvāmī there is nothing wrong in such an exchange of feeling between husband and wife.

TEXT 33

यद्यप्यसौ पार्श्वगतो रहोगत-
स्तथापि तस्याङ्घ्रियुगं नवं नवम् ।
पदे पदे का विरमेत तत्पदा-
च्चलापि यच्छ्रीर्न जहाति कर्हिचित् ॥३३॥

yadyapy asau pārśva-gato raho-gatas
tathāpi tasyāṅghri-yugaṁ navaṁ navam
pade pade kā virameta tat-padāc
calāpi yac chrīr na jahāti karhicit

yadi—although; *api*—certainly; *asau*—He (Lord Śrī Kṛṣṇa); *pārśva-gataḥ*—just by the side; *rahaḥ-gataḥ*—exclusively alone; *tathāpi*—still; *tasya*—His; *aṅghri-yugam*—the feet of the Lord; *navam navam*—newer and newer; *pade*—step; *pade*—in every step; *kā*—who; *virameta*—can be detached from; *tat-padāt*—from His feet; *calāpi*—moving; *yat*—whom; *śrīḥ*—the goddess of fortune; *na*—never; *jahāti*—quits; *karhicit*—at any time.

TRANSLATION

Although Lord Śrī Kṛṣṇa was constantly by their sides, as well as exclusively alone, His feet appeared to them to be newer and newer. The goddess of fortune, although by nature always restless and moving, could not quit the Lord's feet. So what woman can be detached from those feet, having once taken shelter of them?

PURPORT

Conditioned living beings are always after the favor of the goddess of fortune, although by nature she is moving from one place to another. In the material world no one is permanently fortunate, however clever one may be. There have been so many big empires in different parts of the world, there have been so many powerful kings all over the world, and there have been so many fortunate men, but all of them have been liquidated gradually. This is the law of material nature. But spiritually it is different. According to *Brahma-saṁhitā,* the Lord is served very respectfully by hundreds and thousands of goddesses of fortune. They are always in a lonely place also with the Lord. But still the association of the Lord is so inspiringly newer and newer that they cannot quit the Lord for a moment, even though they are by nature very restless and are moving about. The spiritual relation with the Lord is so enlivening and resourceful that no one can leave the company of the Lord, once having taken shelter of Him.

The living beings are by constitution feminine by nature. The male or enjoyer is the Lord, and all manifestations of His different potencies are feminine by nature. In the *Bhagavad-gītā,* the living beings are designated as *parā-prakṛti,* or the superior potency. The material elements are *aparā-prakṛti,* or inferior potency. Such potencies are always employed for the satisfaction of the employer, or the enjoyer. The supreme enjoyer is the Lord Himself, as stated in the *Bhagavad-gītā* (5.29). The potencies, therefore, when engaged directly in the service of the Lord, revive the natural color, and thus there is no disparity in the relation of the potent and potency.

Generally people engaged in service are always seeking some post under the government or the supreme enjoyer of the state. Since the Lord is the supreme enjoyer of everything in or outside the universe, it is happiness to be employed by Him. Once engaged in the supreme governmental service of the Lord, no living being wishes to be relieved from the engagement. The highest perfection of human life is to seek some employment under the Lord's supreme service. That will make one extremely happy. One need not seek the moving goddess of fortune without the relation of the Lord.

TEXT 34

एवं नृपाणां क्षितिभारजन्मना-
मक्षौहिणीभिः परिवृत्ततेजसाम् ।
विधाय वैरं श्वसनो यथानलं
मिथो वधेनोपरतो निरायुधः ॥३४॥

evaṁ nṛpāṇāṁ kṣiti-bhāra-janmanām
akṣauhiṇībhiḥ parivṛtta-tejasām

vidhāya vairaṁ śvasano yathānalaṁ
mitho vadhenoparato nirāyudhaḥ

evam—thus; *nṛpāṇām*—of the kings or administrators; *kṣiti-bhāra*—the burden of the earth; *janmanām*—born in that way; *akṣauhiṇībhiḥ*—empowered by a military strengOth of horses, elephants, chariots and infantry; *parivṛtta*—being puffed up by such surroundings; *tejasām*—prowess; *vidhāya*—having created; *vairam*—hostility; *śvasanaḥ*—interaction of the wind and the pipe plants; *yathā*—as it is; *analam*—fire; *mithaḥ*—with one another; *vadhena*—by killing them; *uparataḥ*—relieved; *nirāyudhaḥ*—by Himself without being a party to such fighting.

TRANSLATION

The Lord was pacified after killing those kings who were burdensome to the earth. They were puffed up with their military strength, their horses, elephants, chariots, infantry, etc. He Himself was not a party in the fight. He simply created hostility between the powerful administrators, and they fought amongst themselves. He was like the wind which causes friction between bamboos and so sparks a fire.

PURPORT

As stated above, the living beings are not factual enjoyers of things which are manifested as God's creation. The Lord is the genuine proprietor and enjoyer of everything manifested in His creation. Unfortunately, influenced by the deluding energy, the living being becomes *a false enjoyer* under the dictation of the modes of nature. Puffed up by such a false sense of becoming God, the deluded living being increases his material strength by so many activities and thus becomes the burden of the earth, so much so that the earth becomes completely uninhabitable by the sane. This state of affairs is called *dharmasya glāniḥ,* or misuse of the energy of the human being. When such misuse of human energy is prominent, the saner living beings become perturbed by the awkward situation created by the vicious administrators, who are simply burdens of the earth, and the Lord appears by His internal potency just to save the saner section of humanity and to alleviate the burden due to the earthly administrators in different parts of the world. He does not favor either of the unwanted administrators, but by His potential power He creates hostility between such unwanted administrators, as the air creates fire in the forest by the friction of the bamboos. The fire in the forest takes place automatically by the force of the air, and similarly the hostility between different groups of politicians takes place by the unseen design of the Lord. The unwanted administrators, puffed up by false power and military strength, thus become engaged in fighting amongst themselves over ideological conflicts and so exhaust themselves of all powers. The history of the world reflects this factual will of the Lord, and it will continue to be enacted until the living beings are attached to the service of the Lord. In the *Bhagavad-gītā* this fact is very vividly described(Bg. 7.14). It is said, "The deluding energy is My potency, and thus it is not possible for the dependent living beings to supersede the strength of the material modes. But those who take shelter in Me [the Personality of Godhead, Śrī Kṛṣṇa] can cross over the gigantic ocean of material energy." This means that no one can establish peace and prosperity in the world by fruitive activities or by speculative philosophy or ideology. The only way is to surrender unto the Supreme Lord and thus become free from the illusion of the deluding energy.

Unfortunately persons who are engaged in destructive work are unable to surrender to the Personality of Godhead. They are all fools of the first order; they are the lowest of the human species of life; they are robbed of their knowledge, although apparently they seem to be academically educated. They are all of the demoniac mentality, always challenging the supreme power of the Lord. Those who are very materialistic, always hankering after material power and strength, are undoubtedly fools of the first order because they have no information of the living energy, and being ignorant of that supreme spiritual science, they are absorbed in material science, which ends with the end of the material body. They are the lowest of human beings because the human life is especially meant for reestablishing the lost relation with the Lord, and they miss this opportunity by being engaged in material activities. They are robbed of their knowledge because even after prolonged speculation they cannot reach to the stage of knowing the Personality of Godhead, the *summum bonum* of everything. And all of them are men of demoniac principle, and they suffer the consequences, as did such materialistic heroes as Rāvaṇa, Hiraṇyakaśipu, Kaṁsa and others.

TEXT 35

स एष नरलोकेऽस्मिन्नवतीर्णः स्वमायया ।
रेमे स्त्रीरत्नकूटस्थो भगवान् प्राकृतो यथा ॥३५॥

sa eṣa nara-loke 'sminn
avatīrṇaḥ sva-māyayā
reme strī-ratna-kūṭastho
bhagavān prākṛto yathā

saḥ—He (the Supreme Personality of Godhead); *eṣaḥ*—all these; *nara-loke*—on this planet of human beings; *asmin*—on this; *avatīrṇaḥ*—having appeared; *sva*—personal, internal; *māyayā*—causeless mercy; *reme*—enjoyed; *strī-ratna*—woman who is competent to become a wife of the Lord; *kūṭasthaḥ*—among; *bhagavān*—the Personality of Godhead; *prākṛtaḥ*—mundane; *yathā*—as if it were.

TRANSLATION

That Supreme Personality of Godhead, Śrī Kṛṣṇa, out of His causeless mercy, appeared on this planet by His internal potency and enjoyed Himself amongst competent women as if He were engaging in mundane affairs.

PURPORT

The Lord married and lived like a householder. This is certainly like a mundane affair, but when we learn that He married 16,108 wives and *lived with them separately* in each and every palace, certainly it is not mundane. Therefore, the Lord, living as a householder amongst His competent wives, is never mundane, and His behavior with them is never to be understood as mundane sex relation. The women who became the wives of the Lord are certainly not ordinary women, because to get the Lord as one's husband is the result of many, many millions of births' *tapasya* (austerity). When the Lord appears on different *lokas,* or planets, or on this planet of human beings, He displays His transcendental pastimes just to attract the conditioned souls to become His eternal servitors, friends, parents and lovers respectively in the transcendental world, where the Lord eternally reciprocates such exchanges of service. Service is pervertedly represented in the material world and broken untimely, resulting in sad experience. The illusioned living being conditioned by material nature cannot understand out of ignorance that all our relations here in the mundane world are temporary and full of inebrieties. Such relations cannot help us be happy perpetually, but if the same relation is established with the Lord, then we are transferred to the transcendental world after leaving this material body and become eternally related with Him in the relation we desire. The women amongst whom He lived as their husband are not, therefore, women of this mundane world, but are eternally related with Him as transcendental wives, a position which they attained by perfection of devotional service. That is their competency. The Lord is *paraṁ brahma,* or the Supreme Personality of Godhead. Conditioned souls seek after perpetual happiness in all places—not only on this earth but also on other planets throughout the universe—because constitutionally a spiritual spark, as he is, can travel to any part of God's creation. But being conditioned by the material modes, he tries to travel in space by spacecraft and so fails to reach his destination. The law of gravitation is binding upon him like the shackles of a prisoner. By other processes he can reach anywhere, but even if he reaches the highest planet, he cannot attain that perpetual happiness for which he is searching life after life. When he comes to his senses, however, he seeks after Brahman happiness, knowing it for certain that unlimited happiness, which he is seeking, is never attainable in the material world. As such, the Supreme Being, Parabrahman, certainly does not seek His happiness anywhere in the material world. Nor can His paraphernalia of happiness be found in the material world. He is not impersonal. Because He is the leader and Supreme Being amongst innumerable living beings, He cannot be impersonal. He is exactly like us, and He has all the propensities of an individual living being in fullness. He marries exactly like us, but His marriage is neither mundane nor limited by our experience in the conditioned state. His wives, therefore, appear like mundane women, but factually they are all transcendental liberated souls, perfect manifestations of internal energy.

TEXT 36

उद्दामभावपिशुनामलवल्गुहास-
ब्रीडावलोकनिहतो मदनोऽपि यासाम् ।
सम्मुह्य चापमजहात्प्रमदोत्तमास्ता
यस्येन्द्रियं विमथितुं कुहकैर्न शेकुः ॥३६॥

uddāma-bhāva-piśunāmala-valgu-hāsa-
vrīḍāvaloka-nihato madano 'pi yāsām
sammuhya cāpam ajahāt pramadottamās tā
yasyendriyaṁ vimathituṁ kuhakair na śekuḥ

uddāma—very grave; *bhāva*—expression; *piśuna*—exciting; *amala*—spotless; *valgu-hāsa*—beautiful smiling; *vrīḍa*—corner of the eye; *avaloka*—looking; *nihataḥ*—conquered; *madanaḥ*—Cupid (or *amadana*—the greatly tolerant Śiva); *api*—also; *yāsām*—whose; *sammuhya*—being overpowered by; *cāpam*—bows; *ajahāt*—gave up; *pramada*—woman, who maddens; *uttamāḥ*—of high grade; *tā*—all; *yasya*—whose; *indriyam*—senses; *vimathitum*—to perturb; *kuhakaiḥ*—by magical feats; *na*—never; *śekuḥ*—was able.

TRANSLATION

Although the queens' beautiful smiles and furtive glances were all spotless and exciting, and although they could conquer Cupid himself by making him give up his bow in frustration, and although even the tolerant Śiva could fall victim to them, still, despite all their magical feats and attractions, they could not agitate the senses of the Lord.

PURPORT

The path of salvation or the path going back to Godhead always forbids the association of women, and the complete *sanātana-dharma* or *varṇāśrama-dharma* scheme forbids or restricts association with women. How, then, can one be accepted as the Supreme Personality of Godhead who is addicted to more than sixteen thousand wives? This question may be relevantly raised by inquisitive persons really anxious to know about the transcendental nature of the Supreme Lord. And to answer such questions, the sages at Naimiṣāraṇya have discussed the transcendental character of the Lord in this and in following verses. It is clear herein that the feminine attractive features which can conquer Cupid or even the supermost tolerant Lord Śiva could not conquer the senses of the Lord. Cupid's business is to invoke mundane lust. The whole universe is moving, being agitated by Cupid's arrow. The activities of the world are being carried on by the central attraction of male and female. A male is searching after a mate to his liking, and the female is looking after a suitable male. That is the way of material stimulus. And as soon as a male is combined with a female, the material bondage of the living being is at once tightly interlocked by sex relation, and as a result of this, both the male's and female's attraction for sweet home, motherland, bodily offspring, society and friendship and accumulation of wealth becomes the illusory field of activities, and thus a false but indefatigable attraction for the temporary material existence, which is full of miseries, is manifest. Those who are, therefore, on the path of salvation for going back home, back to Godhead, are especially advised by all scriptural instruction to become free from such paraphernalia of material attraction. And that is possible only by the association of the devotees of the Lord, who are called the *mahātmās.* Cupid throws his arrow upon the living beings to make them mad after the opposite sex, whether the party is actually beautiful or not. Cupid's provocations are going on, even among beastly societies who are all ugly-looking in the estimation of the civilized nations. Thus Cupid's influence is exerted even amongst the ugliest forms, and what to speak of the most perfect beauties. Lord Śiva, who is considered to be most tolerant, was also struck by Cupid's arrow because he also became mad after the Mohinī incarnation of the Lord and acknowledged himself to be defeated. Cupid, however, was himself captivated by the grave and exciting dealings of the goddesses of fortune, and he voluntarily gave up his bow and arrow in a spirit of frustration. Such was the beauty and attraction of the queens of Lord Kṛṣṇa. Yet they could not disturb the transcendental senses of the Lord. This is because the Lord is all-perfect *ātmārāma,* or self-sufficient. He does not require anyone's extraneous help for His personal satisfaction. Therefore, the queens could not satisfy the Lord by their feminine attractiveness, but *they satisfied Him by their sincere affection and service.* Only by unalloyed transcendental loving service could they satisfy the Lord, and the Lord was pleased to treat them as wives in reciprocation. Thus being satisfied by their unalloyed service only, the Lord reciprocated the service just like a devout husband. Otherwise He had no business becoming the husband of so many wives. He is the husband of everyone, but to one who accepts Him as such, He reciprocates. This unalloyed affection for the Lord is never to be compared to mundane lust. It is purely transcendental. And the grave dealings, which the queens displayed in natural feminine ways, were also transcendental because the feelings were expressed out of transcendental ecstasy. It is already explained in the previous verse that the Lord appeared like a mundane husband, but factually His relation with His wives was transcendental, pure and unconditioned by the modes of material nature.

TEXT 37

तमयं मन्यते लोको ह्यसङ्गमपि सङ्गिनम् ।
आत्मौपम्येन मनुजं व्यापृण्वानं यतोऽबुधः ॥३७॥

tam ayaṁ manyate loko
hy asaṅgam api saṅginam

ātmaupamyena manujaṁ
vyāpṛṇvānaṁ yato 'budhaḥ

tam—unto Lord Kṛṣṇa; *ayam*—all these (common men); *manyate*—do speculate within the mind; *lokaḥ*—the conditioned souls; *hi*—certainly; *asaṅgam*—unattached; *api*—in spite of; *saṅginam*—affected; *ātma*—self; *aupamyena*—by comparison with the self; *manujam*—ordinary man; *vyāpṛṇvānam*—being engaged in; *yataḥ*—because; *abudhaḥ*—foolish because of ignorance.

TRANSLATION

The common materialistic conditioned souls speculate that the Lord is one of them. Out of their ignorance they think that the Lord is affected by matter, although He is unattached.

PURPORT

The word *abudhaḥ* is significant here. Due to ignorance only, the foolish mundane wranglers misunderstand the Supreme Lord and spread their foolish imaginations amongst innocent persons by propaganda. The Supreme Lord Śrī Kṛṣṇa is the original primeval Personality of Godhead, and when He was personally present before the eyes of everyone, He displayed full-fledged divine potency in every field of activities. As we have already explained in the first verse of *Śrīmad-Bhāgavatam,* He is completely independent to act however He likes, but all His actions are full of bliss, knowledge and eternity. Only the foolish mundaners misunderstand Him, unaware of His eternal form of knowledge and bliss, which is confirmed in the *Bhagavad-gītā* and *Upaniṣads.* His different potencies work in a perfect plan of natural sequence, and doing everything by the agency of His different potencies, He remains eternally the supreme independent. When He descends on the material world by His causeless mercy to different living beings, He does so by His own potency. He is not subject to any condition of the material modes of nature, and He descends as He is originally. The mental speculators misunderstand Him as the Supreme Person, and they consider His impersonal features as inexplicable Brahman to be all. Such a conception is also the product of conditioned life because they cannot go beyond their own personal capacity. Therefore, one who considers the Lord on the level of one's limited potency is only a common man. Such a man cannot be convinced that the Personality of Godhead is always unaffected by the modes of material nature. He cannot understand that the sun is always unaffected by infectious matter. The mental speculators compare everything from the standpoint of experimental knowledge of their own selves. Thus when the Lord is found to act like an ordinary person in matrimonial bondage, they consider Him to be like one of them, without considering that the Lord can at once marry sixteen thousand wives or more. Due to a poor fund of knowledge they accept one side of the picture while disbelieving the other. This means that due to ignorance only they always think of Lord Kṛṣṇa as like themselves and make their own conclusions, which are absurd and unauthentic from the version of the *Śrīmad-Bhāgavatam.*

TEXT 38

एतदीशनमीशस्य प्रकृतिस्थोऽपि तद्गुणैः ।
न युज्यते सदात्मस्थैर्यथा बुद्धिस्तदाश्रया ॥३८॥

etad īśanam īśasya
prakṛti-stho 'pi tad-guṇaiḥ
na yujyate sadātma-sthair
yathā buddhis tad-āśrayā

etat—this; *īśanam*—divinity; *īśasya*—of the Personality of Godhead; *prakṛti-sthaḥ*—being in contact with material nature; *api*—in spite of; *tat-guṇaiḥ*—by the qualities; *na*—never; *yujyate*—is affected; *sadā ātma-sthaiḥ*—by those who are situated in eternity; *yathā*—as is; *buddhiḥ*—intelligence; *tat*—the Lord; *āśrayā*—those who are under the shelter of.

TRANSLATION

This is the divinity of the Personality of Godhead: He is not affected by the qualities of material nature, even though He is in contact with them. Similarly, the devotees who have taken shelter of the Lord do not become influenced by the material qualities.

PURPORT

In the *Vedas* and Vedic literatures (*Śruti* and *Smṛti*) it is affirmed that in the Divinity there is nothing material. He is transcendental (*nirguṇa*) only, the supreme cognizant. Hari, or the Personality of Godhead, is the supreme transcendental person situated beyond the range of material affection. These statements are also confirmed even by Ācārya Śaṅkara. One may argue that His relation with the goddesses of fortune may be transcendental, but what about His relation with the Yadu dynasty, being born in that family, or His killing the nonbelievers like Jarāsandha and other *asuras* directly in contact with the modes of material nature? The answer is that the divinity of the Personality of Godhead is never in contact with the qualities of material nature in any circumstances. Actually He is in contact with such qualities because He is the ultimate source of everything, yet He is above the actions of such qualities. He is known, therefore, as Yogeśvara, or the master of mystic power, or in other words the all-powerful. Even His learned devotees are not affected by the influence of the material modes. The great six Gosvāmīs of Vṛndāvana all came from greatly rich and aristocratic families, but when they adopted the life of mendicants at Vṛndāvana, superficially they appeared to be in wretched conditions of life, but factually they were the richest of all in spiritual values. Such *mahā-bhāgavatas,* or first-grade devotees, although moving amongst men, are not contaminated by honor or insult, hunger or satisfaction, sleep or wakefulness, which are all resultant actions of the three modes of material nature. Similarly, some of them are engaged in worldly dealings, yet are unaffected. Unless these neutralities of life are there, one cannot be considered situated in transcendence. The Divinity and His associates are on the same transcendental plane, and their glories are always sanctified by the action of *yoga māyā,* or the internal potency of the Lord. The devotees of the Lord are always transcendental, even if they are sometimes found to have fallen in their behavior. The Lord emphatically declares in the *Bhagavad-gītā* (9.30) that even if an unalloyed devotee is found to be fallen due to a previous material contamination, he is nevertheless to be accepted as fully transcendental because of his being engaged cent percent in the devotional service of the Lord. The Lord protects him always because of his rendering service unto Him, and the fallen conditions are to be considered accidental and temporary. They will vanish in no time.

TEXT 39

तं मेनिरेऽबला मूढाः स्त्रैणं चानुव्रतं रहः ।
अप्रमाणविदो भर्तुरीश्वरं मतयो यथा ॥३९॥

taṁ menire 'balā mūḍhāḥ
straiṇaṁ cānuvrataṁ rahaḥ

apramāṇa-vido bhartur
īśvaraṁ matayo yathā

tam—unto Lord Śrī Kṛṣṇa; *menire*—took it for granted; *abalāḥ*—delicate; *mūḍhāḥ*—because of simplicity; *straiṇam*—one who is dominated by his wife; *ca*—also; *anuvratam*—follower; *rahaḥ*—lonely place; *apramāṇa-vidaḥ*—unaware of the extent of glories; *bhartuḥ*—of their husband; *īśvaram*—the supreme controller; *matayaḥ*—thesis; *yathā*—as it is.

TRANSLATION

The simple and delicate women truly thought that Lord Śrī Kṛṣṇa, their beloved husband, followed them and was dominated by them. They were unaware of the extent of the glories of their husband, as the atheists are unaware of Him as the supreme controller.

PURPORT

Even the transcendental wives of Lord Śrī Kṛṣṇa did not know completely the unfathomable glories of the Lord. This ignorance is not mundane because there is some action of the internal potency of the Lord in the exchange of feelings between Him and His eternal associates. The Lord exchanges transcendental relations in five ways, as proprietor, master, friend, son and lover, and in each of these pastimes He plays fully by the potency of *yogamāyā,* the internal potency. He plays exactly like an equal friend with the cowherd boys or even with friends like Arjuna. He plays exactly like a son in the presence of Yaśodāmātā, He plays exactly like a lover in the presence of the cowherd damsels, and He plays exactly like a husband in the presence of the queens of Dvārakā. Such devotees of the Lord never think of the Lord as the Supreme, but think of Him exactly as a common friend, a pet son, or a lover or husband very much dear to heart and soul. That is the relation between the Lord and His transcendental devotees, who act as His associates in the spiritual sky, where there are innumerable Vaikuṇṭha planets. When the Lord descends, He does so along with His entourage to display a complete picture of the transcendental world, where pure love and devotion for the Lord prevail without any mundane tinge of lording it over the creation of the Lord. Such devotees of the Lord are all liberated souls, perfect representations of the marginal or internal potency in complete negation of the influence of the external potency. The wives of Lord Kṛṣṇa were made to forget the immeasurable glories of the Lord by the internal potency so that there might not be any flaw of exchange, and they took it for granted that the Lord was a henpecked husband, always following them in lonely places. In other words, even the personal associates of the Lord do not know Him perfectly well, so what do the thesis writers or mental speculators know about the transcendental glories of the Lord? The mental speculators present different theses as to His becoming the causes of the creation, the ingredients of the creation, or the material and efficient cause of the creation, etc., but all this is but partial knowledge about the Lord. Factually they are as ignorant as the common man. The Lord can be known by the mercy of the Lord only, and by no other means. But since the dealings of the Lord with His wives are based on pure transcendental love and devotion, the wives are all on the transcendental plane without material contamination.

Thus end the Bhaktivedanta purports of the First Canto, Eleventh Chapter, of the Śrīmad-Bhāgavatam, *entitled "Lord Kṛṣṇa's Entrance into Dvārakā."*

CHAPTER TWELVE

Birth of Emperor Parīkṣit

TEXT 1

शौनक उवाच
अश्वत्थाम्नोपसृष्टेन ब्रह्मशीर्ष्णोरुतेजसा ।
उत्तराया हतो गर्भ ईशेनाजीवितः पुनः ॥१॥

śaunaka uvāca
aśvatthāmnopasṛṣṭena
brahma-śīrṣṇoru-tejasā
uttarāyā hato garbha
īśenājīvitaḥ punaḥ

śaunakaḥ uvāca—the sage Śaunaka said; *aśvatthāmna*—of Aśvatthāmā (the son of Droṇa); *upasṛṣṭena*—by release of; *brahma-śīrṣṇā*—the invincible weapon, *brahmāstra; uru-tejasā*—by high temperature; *uttarāyāḥ*—of Uttarā (mother of Parīkṣit); *hataḥ*—being spoiled; *garbhaḥ*—womb; *īśena*—by the Supreme Lord; *ājīvitaḥ*—brought to life; *punaḥ*—again.

TRANSLATION

The sage Śaunaka said: The womb of Uttarā, mother of Mahārāja Parīkṣit, was spoiled by the dreadful and invincible brahmāstra weapon released by Aśvatthāmā. But Mahārāja Parīkṣit was saved by the Supreme Lord.

PURPORT

The sages assembled in the forest of Naimiṣāraṇya inquired from Sūta Gosvāmī about the birth of Mahārāja Parīkṣit, but in the course of the narration other topics like the release of the *brahmāstra* by the son of Droṇa, his punishment by Arjuna, Queen Kuntīdevī's prayers, the Pāṇḍavas' visit to the place where Bhīṣmadeva was lying, his prayers and thereafter the Lord's departure for Dvārakā were discussed. His arrival at Dvārakā and residing with the sixteen thousand queens, etc., were narrated. The sages were absorbed in hearing such descriptions, but now they wanted to turn to the original topic, and thus the inquiry was made by Śaunaka Ṛṣi. So the subject of the release of the *brahmāstra* weapon by Aśvatthāmā is renewed.

TEXT 2

तस्य जन्म महाबुद्धेः कर्माणि च महात्मनः ।
निधनं च यथैवासीत्स प्रेत्य गतवान् यथा ॥२॥

tasya janma mahā-buddheḥ
karmāṇi ca mahātmanaḥ
nidhanaṁ ca yathaivāsīt
sa pretya gatavān yathā

tasya—his (of Mahārāja Parīkṣit); *janma*—birth; *mahā-buddheḥ*—of great intelligence; *karmāṇi*—activities; *ca*—also; *mahā-ātmanaḥ*—of the great devotee; *nidhanam*—demise; *ca*—also; *yathā*—as it was; *eva*—of course; *āsīt*—happened; *saḥ*—he; *pretya*—destination after death; *gatavān*—achieved; *yathā*—as it were.

TRANSLATION

How was the great emperor Parīkṣit, who was a highly intelligent and great devotee, born in that womb? How did his death take place, and what did he achieve after his death?

PURPORT

The king of Hastināpura (now Delhi) used to be the emperor of the world, at least till the time of the son of Emperor Parīkṣit. Mahārāja Parīkṣit was saved by the Lord in the womb of his mother, so he could certainly be saved from an untimely death due to the ill will of the son of a *brāhmaṇa.* Because the age of Kali began to act just after the assumption of power by Mahārāja Parīkṣit, the first sign of misgivings was exhibited in the cursing of such a greatly intelligent and devoted king as Mahārāja Parīkṣit. The king is the protector of the helpless citizens, and their welfare, peace and prosperity depend on him. Unfortunately, by the instigation of the fallen age of Kali, an unfortunate *brāhmaṇa's* son was employed to condemn the innocent Mahārāja Parīkṣit, and so the King had to prepare himself for death within seven days. Mahārāja Parīkṣit is especially famous as one who is protected by Viṣṇu, and when he was unduly cursed by a *brāhmaṇa's* son, he could have invoked the mercy of the Lord to save him, but he did not want to because he was a pure devotee. A pure devotee never asks the Lord for any undue favor. Mahārāja Parīkṣit knew that the curse of the *brāhmaṇa's* son upon him was unjustified, as everyone else knew, but he did not want to counteract it because he knew also that the age of Kali had begun and that the first symptom of the age, namely degradation of the highly talented *brāhmaṇa* community, had also begun. He did not want to interfere with the current of the time, but he prepared himself to meet death very cheerfully and very properly. Being fortunate, he got at least seven days to prepare himself to meet death, and so he properly utilized the time in the association of Śukadeva Gosvāmī, the great saint and devotee of the Lord.

TEXT 3

तदिदं श्रोतुमिच्छामो गदितुं यदि मन्यसे ।
ब्रूहि नः श्रद्दधानानां यस्य ज्ञानमदाच्छुकः ॥३॥

tad idaṁ śrotum icchāmo
gadituṁ yadi manyase
brūhi naḥ śraddadhānānāṁ
yasya jñānam adāc chukaḥ

tat—all; *idam*—this; *śrotum*—to hear; *icchāmaḥ*—all willing; *gaditum*—to narrate; *yadi*—if; *manyase*—you think; *brūhi*—please speak; *naḥ*—we; *śraddadhānānām*—who are very much respectful; *yasya*—whose; *jñānam*—transcendental knowledge; *adāt*—delivered; *śukaḥ*—Śrī Śukadeva Gosvāmī.

TRANSLATION

We all respectfully want to hear about him [Mahārāja Parīkṣit] to whom Śukadeva Gosvāmī imparted transcendental knowledge. Please speak on this matter.

PURPORT

Śukadeva Gosvāmī imparted transcendental knowledge to Mahārāja Parīkṣit during the remaining seven days of his life, and Mahārāja Parīkṣit heard him properly, just like an ardent student. The effect of such a bona fide hearing and chanting of *Śrīmad-Bhāgavatam* was equally shared by both the hearer and the chanter. Both of them were benefited. Out of the nine different transcendental means of devotional service to the Lord prescribed in the *Bhāgavatam,* either all of them, or some of them or even one of them are equally beneficial if properly discharged. Mahārāja Parīkṣit and Śukadeva Gosvāmī were serious performers of the first two important items, namely the process of chanting and the process of hearing, and therefore both of them were successful in their laudable attempt. Transcendental realization is attained by such serious hearing and chanting and not otherwise. There is a type of spiritual master and disciple much advertised in this age of Kali. It is said that the master injects spiritual force into the disciple by an electrical current generated by the master, and the disciple begins to feel the shock. He becomes unconscious, and the master weeps for his exhausting his store of so-called spiritual assets. Such bogus advertisement is going on in this age, and the poor common man is becoming the victim of such advertisement. We do not find such folk tales in the dealings of Śukadeva Gosvāmī and his great disciple Mahārāja Parīkṣit. The sage recited *Śrīmad-Bhāgavatam* in devotion, and the great King heard him properly. The King did not feel any shock of electrical current from the master, nor did he become unconscious while receiving knowledge from the master. One should not, therefore, become a victim of these unauthorized advertisements made by some bogus representative of Vedic knowledge. The sages of Naimiṣāraṇya were very respectful in hearing about Mahārāja Parīkṣit because of his receiving knowledge from Śukadeva Gosvāmī by means of *ardent hearing.* Ardent hearing from the bona fide master is the only way to receive transcendental knowledge, and there is no need for medical performances or occult mysticism for miraculous effects. The process is simple, but only the sincere party can achieve the desired result.

TEXT 4

सूत उवाच

अपीपलद्धर्मराजः पितृवद् रञ्जयन् प्रजाः ।
निःस्पृहः सर्वकामेभ्यः कृष्णपादानुसेवया ॥४॥

sūta uvāca
apīpalad dharma-rājaḥ
pitṛvad rañjayan prajāḥ
niḥspṛhaḥ sarva-kāmebhyaḥ
kṛṣṇa-pādānusevayā

sūtaḥ uvāca—Śrī Sūta Gosvāmī said; *apīpalat*—administered prosperity; *dharma-rājaḥ*—King Yudhiṣṭhira; *pitṛ-vat*—exactly like his father; *rañjayan*—pleasing; *prajāḥ*—all those who took birth; *niḥspṛhaḥ*—without personal ambition; *sarva*—all; *kāmebhyaḥ*—from sense gratification; *kṛṣṇa-pāda*—the lotus feet of Lord Śrī Kṛṣṇa; *anusevayā*—by dint of rendering continuous service.

TRANSLATION

Śrī Sūta Gosvāmī said: Emperor Yudhiṣṭhira administered generously to everyone during his reign. He was exactly like his father. He had no personal ambition and was freed from all sorts of sense gratification because of his continuous service unto the lotus feet of the Lord Śrī Kṛṣṇa.

PURPORT

As mentioned in our introduction, "There is a need for the science of Kṛṣṇa in human society for all the suffering humanity of the world, and we simply request the leading personalities of all nations to take to the science of Kṛṣṇa for their own good, for the good of society, and for the good of all the people of the world." So it is confirmed herein by the example of Mahārāja Yudhiṣṭhira, the personality of goodness. In India the people hanker after *Rāma-rājya* because the Personality of Godhead was the ideal king and all other kings or emperors in India controlled the destiny of the world for the prosperity of every living being who took birth on the earth. Herein the word *prajāḥ* is significant. The etymological import of the word is "that which is born." On the earth there are many species of life, from the aquatics up to the perfect human beings, and all are known as *prajās.* Lord Brahmā, the creator of this particular universe, is known as the *prajāpati* because he is the grandfather of all who have taken birth. Thus *prajā* is used in a broader sense than it is now used. The king represents all living beings, the aquatics, plants, trees, reptiles, birds, animals and man. Every one of them is a part and parcel of the Supreme Lord (Bg. 14.4), and the king, being the representative of the Supreme Lord, is duty-bound to give proper protection to every one of them. This is not the case with the presidents and dictators of this demoralized system of administration, where the lower animals are given no protection while the higher animals are given so-called protection. But this is a great science which can be learned only by one who knows the *science of Kṛṣṇa.* By knowing the science of Kṛṣṇa, one can become the most perfect man in the world, and unless one has knowledge in this science, all qualifications and doctorate diplomas acquired by academic education are spoiled and useless. Mahārāja Yudhiṣṭhira knew this science of Kṛṣṇa very well, for it is stated here that by continuous cultivation of this science, or by continuous devotional service to Lord Kṛṣṇa, he acquired the qualification of administering the state. The father is sometimes seemingly cruel to the son, but that does not mean that the father has lost the qualification to be a father. A father is always a father because he always has the good of the son at heart. The father wants every one of his sons to become a better man than himself. Therefore, a king like Mahārāja Yudhiṣṭhira, who was the personality of goodness, wanted everyone under his administration, especially human beings who have better developed consciousness, to become devotees of Lord Kṛṣṇa so that everyone can become free from the trifles of material existence. His motto of administration was all good for the citizens, for as personified goodness he knew perfectly well what is actually good for them. He conducted the administration on that principle, and not on the *rākṣasī*, demonic, principle of sense gratification. As an ideal king, he had no personal ambition, and there was no place for sense gratification because all his senses at all times were engaged in the loving service of the Supreme Lord, which includes the partial service to the living beings, who form the parts and parcels of the complete whole. Those who are busy rendering service to the parts and parcels, leaving aside the whole, only spoil time and energy, as one does when watering the leaves of a tree without watering the root. If water is poured on the root, the leaves are enlivened perfectly and automatically, but if water is poured on the leaves only, the whole energy is spoiled. Mahārāja Yudhiṣṭhira, therefore, was constantly engaged in the service of the Lord, and thus the parts and parcels of the Lord, the living beings under his careful administration, were perfectly attended with all comforts in this life and all progress in the next. That is the way of perfect management of state administration.

TEXT 5

सम्पदः क्रतवो लोका महिषी भ्रातरो मही ।
जम्बूद्वीपाधिपत्यं च यशश्च त्रिदिवं गतम् ॥५॥

sampadaḥ kratavo lokā
mahiṣī bhrātaro mahī
jambudvīpādhipatyaṁ ca
yaśaś ca tri-divaṁ gatam

sampadaḥ—opulence; *kratavaḥ*—sacrifices; *lokāḥ*—future destination; *mahiṣī*—the queens; *bhrātaraḥ*—the brothers; *mahī*—the earth; *jambu-dvīpa*—the globe or planet of our residence; *ādhipatyam*—sovereignty; *ca*—also; *yaśaḥ*—fame; *ca*—and; *tri-divam*—celestial planets; *gatam*—spread over.

TRANSLATION

News even reached the celestial planets about Mahārāja Yudhiṣṭhira's worldly possessions, the sacrifices by which he would attain a better destination, his queen, his stalwart brothers, his extensive land, his sovereignty over the planet earth, and his fame, etc.

PURPORT

Only a rich and great man's name and fame are known all over the world, and the name and fame of Mahārāja Yudhiṣṭhira reached the higher planets because of his good administration, worldly possessions, glorious wife Draupadī, the strength of his brothers Bhīma and Arjuna, and his solid sovereign power over the world, known as Jambudvīpa. Here the word *lokāḥ* is significant. There are different *lokas* or higher planets scattered all over the sky, both material and spiritual. A person can reach them by dint of his work in the present life, as stated in *Bhagavad-gītā* (9.25). No forceful entrance is allowed there. The tiny material scientists and engineers who have discovered vehicles to travel over a few thousand miles in outer space will not be allowed entrance. That is not the way to reach the better planets. One must qualify himself to enter into such happy planets by sacrifice and service. Those who are sinful in every step of life can expect only to be degraded into animal life to suffer more and more the pangs of material existence, and this is also stated in *Bhagavad-gītā* (16.19). Mahārāja Yudhiṣṭhira's good sacrifices and qualifications were so lofty and virtuous that even the residents of the higher celestial planets were already prepared to receive him as one of them.

TEXT 6

किं ते कामाः सुरस्पार्हा मुकुन्दमनसो द्विजाः ।
अधिजह्रुर्मुदं राज्ञः क्षुधितस्य यथेतरे ॥६॥

kiṁ te kāmāḥ sura-spārhā
mukunda-manaso dvijāḥ

adhijahrur mudaṁ rājñaḥ
kṣudhitasya yathetare

kim—what for; *te*—all those; *kāmāḥ*—objects of sense enjoyment; *sura*—of the denizens of heaven; *spārhāḥ*—aspirations; *mukunda-manasaḥ*—of one who is already God conscious; *dvijāḥ*—O *brāhmaṇas; adhijahruḥ*—could satisfy; *mudam*—pleasure; *rājñaḥ*—of the king; *kṣudhitasya*—of the hungry; *yathā*—as it is; *itare*—in other things.

TRANSLATION

O brāhmaṇas, the opulence of the King was so enchanting that the denizens of heaven aspired for it. But because he was absorbed in the service of the Lord, nothing could satisfy him except the Lord's service.

PURPORT

There are two things in the world which can satisfy living beings. When one is materially engrossed, he is satisfied only by sense gratification, but when one is liberated from the conditions of the material modes, he is satisfied only by rendering loving service for the satisfaction of the Lord. This means that the living being is constitutionally a *servitor,* and not one who is *served.* Being illusioned by the conditions of the external energy, one falsely thinks himself to be the served, but actually he is not served; he is servant of the senses like lust, desire, anger, avarice, pride, madness and intolerance. When one is in his proper senses by attainment of spiritual knowledge, he realizes that he is not the master of the material world, but is only a servant of the senses. At that time he begs for the service of the Lord and thus becomes happy without being illusioned by so-called material happiness. Mahārāja Yudhiṣṭhira was one of the liberated souls, and therefore for him there was no pleasure in a vast kingdom, good wife, obedient brothers, happy subjects and prosperous world. These blessings automatically follow for a pure devotee, even though the devotee does not aspire for them. The example set herein is exactly suitable. It is said that one who is hungry is never satisfied by anything other than food.

The whole material world is full of hungry living beings. The hunger is not for good food, shelter or sense gratification. *The hunger is for the spiritual atmosphere.* Due to ignorance only they think that the world is dissatisfied because there is not sufficient food, shelter, defense and objects of sense gratification. This is called illusion. When the living being is hungry for spiritual satisfaction, he is misrepresented by material hunger. But the foolish leaders cannot see that even the people who are most sumptuously materially satisfied are still hungry. And what is their hunger and poverty? This hunger is actually for spiritual food, spiritual shelter, spiritual defense and spiritual sense gratification. These can be obtained in the association of the Supreme Spirit, Lord Śrī Kṛṣṇa, and therefore one who has them cannot be attracted by the so-called food, shelter, defense and sense gratification of the material world, even if they are relished by the denizens of the heavenly planets. Therefore, in the *Bhagavad-gītā* (8.16) it is said by the Lord that even in the topmost planet of the universe, namely the Brahmaloka, where the duration of life is multiplied by millions of years by earth calculation, one cannot satisfy his hunger. Such hunger can be satisfied only when the living being is situated in immortality, which is attained in the spiritual sky, far, far above the Brahmaloka, in the association of Lord Mukunda, the Lord who awards His devotees the transcendental pleasure of liberation.

TEXT 7

मातुर्गर्भगतो वीरः स तदा भृगुनन्दन ।
ददर्श पुरुषं कञ्चिद्दह्यमानोऽस्त्रतेजसा ॥७॥

mātur garbha-gato vīraḥ
sa tadā bhṛgu-nandana
dadarśa puruṣaṁ kañcid
dahyamāno 'stra-tejasā

mātuḥ—mother; *garbha*—womb; *gataḥ*—being situated there; *vīraḥ*—the great fighter; *saḥ*—child Parīkṣit; *tadā*—at that time; *bhṛgu-nandana*—O son of Bhṛgu; *dadarśa*—could see; *puruṣam*—the Supreme Lord; *kañcit*—as someone else; *dahyamānaḥ*—suffering from being burned; *astra*—the *brahmāstra; tejasā*—temperature.

TRANSLATION

O son of Bhṛgu [Śaunaka], when the child Parīkṣit, the great fighter, was in the womb of his mother, Uttarā, and was suffering from the burning heat of the brahmāstra [thrown by Aśvatthāmā], he could observe the Supreme Lord coming to him.

PURPORT

Death generally involves remaining in trance for seven months. A living being, according to his own action, is allowed to enter into the womb of a mother by the vehicle of a father's semen, and thus he develops his desired body. This is the law of birth in specific bodies according to one's past actions. When he is awake from trance, he feels the inconvenience of being confined within the womb, and thus he wants to come out of it and sometimes fortunately prays to the Lord for such liberation. Mahārāja Parīkṣit, while in the womb of his mother, was struck by the *brahmāstra* released by Aśvatthāmā, and he was feeling the burning heat. But because he was a devotee of the Lord, the Lord at once appeared Himself within the womb by His all-powerful energy, and the child could see that someone else had come to save him. Even in that helpless condition, the child Parīkṣit endured the unbearable temperature due to his being a great fighter by nature. And for this reason the word *vīraḥ* has been used.

TEXT 8

अङ्गुष्ठमात्रममलं स्फुरत्पुरटमौलिनम् ।
अपीव्यदर्शनं श्यामं तडिद्वाससमच्युतम् ॥८॥

aṅguṣṭha-mātram amalaṁ
sphurat-puraṭa-maulinam
apīvya-darśanaṁ śyāmaṁ
taḍid vāsasam acyutam

aṅguṣṭha—by the measure of a thumb; *mātram*—only; *amalam*—transcendental; *sphurat*—blazing; *puraṭa*—gold; *maulinam*—helmet; *apīvya*—very beautiful; *darśanam*—to look at; śyāmam—blackish; *taḍit*—lightning; *vāsasam*—clothing; *acyutam*—the Infallible (the Lord).

TRANSLATION

He [the Lord] was only thumb high, but He was all transcendental. He had a very beautiful, blackish, infallible body, and He wore a dress of lightning yellow and a helmet of blazing gold. Thus He was seen by the child.

TEXT 9

श्रीमद्दीर्घचतुर्बाहुं तप्तकाञ्चनकुण्डलम् ।
क्षतजाक्षं गदापाणिमात्मनः सर्वतोदिशम् ।
परिभ्रमन्तमुल्काभां भ्रामयन्तं गदां मुहुः ॥९॥

śrīmad-dīrgha-catur-bāhuṁ
tapta-kāñcana-kuṇḍalam
kṣatajākṣaṁ gadā-pāṇim
ātmanaḥ sarvato diśam
paribhramantam ulkābhāṁ
bhrāmayantaṁ gadāṁ muhuḥ

śrīmat—enriched; *dīrgha*—prolonged; *catuḥ-bāhum*—four-handed; *tapta-kāñcana*—molten gold; *kuṇḍalam*—earrings; *kṣataja-akṣam*—eyes with the redness of blood; *gadā-pāṇim*—hand with a club; *ātmanaḥ*—own; *sarvataḥ*—all; *diśam*—around; *paribhramantam*—loitering; *ulkābhām*—like shooting stars; *bhrāmayantam*—encircling; *gadām*—the club; *muhuḥ*—constantly.

TRANSLATION

The Lord was enriched with four hands, earrings of molten gold and eyes blood red with fury. As He loitered about, His club constantly encircled Him like a shooting star.

PURPORT

It is said in the *Brahma-saṁhitā* (Ch. 5) that the Supreme Lord Govinda, by His one plenary portion, enters into the halo of the universe and distributes Himself as Paramātmā, or the Supersoul, not only within the heart of every living being, but also within every atom of the material elements. Thus the Lord is all-pervading by His inconceivable potency, and thus He entered the womb of Uttarā to save His beloved devotee Mahārāja Parīkṣit. In the *Bhagavad-gītā* (9.31) the Lord assured everyone that His devotees are never to be vanquished. No one can kill a devotee of the Lord because he is protected by the Lord, and no one can save a person whom the Lord desires to kill. The Lord is all-powerful, and therefore He can both save and kill as He likes. He became visible to His devotee Mahārāja Parīkṣit even in that awkward position (in the womb of his mother) in a shape just suitable for his vision. The Lord can become bigger than thousands of universes and can become smaller than an atom at the same time. Merciful as He is, He becomes just suitable to the vision of the limited living being. He is unlimited. He is not limited by any measurement of our calculation. He can become bigger than what we can think of, and He can become smaller than what we can conceive. But in all circumstances He is the same all-powerful Lord. There is no difference between the thumblike Viṣṇu in the womb of Uttarā and the full-fledged Nārāyaṇa in the Vaikuṇṭha-dhāma, the kingdom of Godhead. He accepts the form of *arcā-vigraha* (worshipable Deity) just to accept service from His different incapable devotees. By the mercy of the *arcā-vigraha,* the form of the Lord in material elements, the devotees who are in the material world can easily approach the Lord, although He is not conceivable by the material senses. The *arcā-vigraha* is therefore an all-spiritual form of the Lord to be perceived by the material devotees; such an *arcā-vigraha* of the Lord is never to be considered material. There is no difference between matter and spirit for the Lord, although there is a gulf of difference between the two in the case of the conditioned living being. For the Lord there is nothing but spiritual existence, and similarly there is nothing except spiritual existence for the pure devotee of the Lord in his intimate relation with the Lord.

TEXT 10

अस्त्रतेजः स्वगदया नीहारमिव गोपतिः ।
विधमन्तं सन्निकर्षे पर्यैक्षत क इत्यसौ ॥१०॥

astra-tejaḥ sva-gadayā
nīhāram iva gopatiḥ
vidhamantaṁ sannikarṣe
paryaikṣata ka ity asau

astra-tejaḥ—radiation of the *brahmāstra; sva-gadayā*—by means of His own club; *nīhāram*—drops of dew; *iva*—like; *gopatiḥ*—the sun; *vidhamantam*—the act of vanishing; *sannikarṣe*—nearby; *paryaikṣata*—observing; *kaḥ*—who; *iti asau*—this body.

TRANSLATION

The Lord was thus engaged in vanquishing the radiation of the brahmāstra, just as the sun evaporates a drop of dew. He was observed by the child, who thought about who He was.

TEXT 11

विधूय तदमेयात्मा भगवान्धर्मगुब् विभुः ।
मिषतो दशमासस्य तत्रैवान्तर्दधे हरिः ॥११॥

vidhūya tad ameyātmā
bhagavān dharma-gub vibhuḥ
miṣato daśamāsasya
tatraivāntardadhe hariḥ

vidhūya—having completely washed off; *tat*—that; *ameyātmā*—the all-pervading Supersoul; *bhagavān*—the Personality of Godhead; *dharma-gup*—the protector of righteousness; *vibhuḥ*—the Supreme; *miṣataḥ*—while observing; *daśamāsasya*—of one who is dressed by all directions; *tatra eva*—then and there; *antaḥ*—out of sight; *dadhe*—became; *hariḥ*—the Lord.

TRANSLATION

While thus being observed by the child, the Supreme Lord Personality of Godhead, the Supersoul of everyone and the protector of the righteous, who stretches in all directions and who is unlimited by time and space, disappeared at once.

PURPORT

Child Parīkṣit was not observing a living being who is limited by time and space. There is a gulf of difference between the Lord and the individual living being. The Lord is mentioned herein as the supreme living being unlimited by time and space. Every living being is limited by time and space. Even though a living being is qualitatively one with the Lord, quantitatively there is a great difference between the Supreme Soul and the common individual soul. In the *Bhagavad-gītā* both the living beings and the Supreme Being are said to be all-pervading (*yena sarvam idaṁ tatam*), yet there is a difference between these two kinds of all-pervasiveness. A common living being or soul can be all-pervading within his own limited body, but the supreme living being is all-pervading in all space and all time. A common living being cannot extend its influence over another common living being by its all- pervasiveness, but the Supreme Supersoul, the Personality of Godhead, is unlimitedly able to exert His influence over all places and all times and over all living beings. And because He is all-pervasive, unlimited by time and space, He can appear even within the womb of the mother of child Parīkṣit. He is mentioned herein as the protector of the righteous. Anyone who is a surrendered soul unto the Supreme is righteous, and he is specifically protected by the Lord in all circumstances. The Lord is the indirect protector of the unrighteous also, for He rectifies their sins through His external potency. The Lord is mentioned herein as one who is dressed in the ten directions. This means dressed with garments on ten sides, up and down. He is present everywhere and can appear and disappear at His will from everywhere and anywhere. His disappearance from the sight of the child Parīkṣit does not mean that He appeared on the spot from any other place. He was present there, and even after His disappearance He was there, although invisible to the eyes of the child. This material covering of the effulgent firmament is also something like a womb of the mother nature, and we are all put into the womb by the Lord, the father of all living beings. He is present everywhere, even in this material womb of mother Durgā, and those who are deserving can see the Lord.

TEXT 12

ततः सर्वगुणोदर्के सानुकूलग्रहोदये ।
जज्ञे वंशधरः पाण्डोर्भूयः पाण्डुरिवौजसा ॥१२॥

tataḥ sarva-guṇodarke
sānukūla-grahodaye
jajñe vaṁśa-dharaḥ pāṇḍor
bhūyaḥ pāṇḍur ivaujasā

tataḥ—thereupon; *sarva*—all; *guṇa*—good signs; *udarke*—having gradually evolved; *sa-anukūla*—all favorable; *grahodaye*—constellation of stellar influence; *jajñe*—took birth; *vaṁśa-dharaḥ*—heir apparent; *pāṇḍoḥ*—of Pāṇḍu; *bhūyaḥ*—being; *pāṇḍuḥ iva*—exactly like Pāṇḍu; *ojasā*—by prowess.

TRANSLATION

Thereupon, when all the good signs of the zodiac gradually evolved, the heir apparent of Pāṇḍu, who would be exactly like him in prowess, took birth.

PURPORT

Astronomical calculations of stellar influences upon a living being are not suppositions, but are factual, as confirmed in *Śrīmad-Bhāgavatam.* Every living being is controlled by the laws of nature at every minute, just as a citizen is controlled by the influence of the state. The state laws are grossly observed, but the laws of material nature, being subtle to our gross understanding, cannot be experienced grossly. As stated in the *Bhagavad-gītā* (3.9), every action of life produces another reaction, which is binding upon us, and only those who are acting on behalf of Yajña (Viṣṇu) are not bound by reactions. Our actions are judged by the higher authorities, the agents of the Lord, and thus we are awarded bodies according to our activities. The law of nature is so subtle that every part of our body is influenced by the respective stars, and a living being obtains his working body to fulfill his terms of imprisonment by the manipulation of such astronomical influence. A man's destiny is therefore ascertained by the birthtime constellation of stars, and a factual horoscope is made by a learned astrologer. It is a great science, and misuse of a science does not make it useless. Mahārāja Parīkṣit or even the Personality of Godhead appear in certain constellations of good stars, and thus the influence is exerted upon the body thus born at an auspicious moment. The most auspicious constellation of stars takes place during the appearance of the Lord in this material world, and it is specifically called *jayantī,* a word not to be abused for any other purposes. Mahārāja Parīkṣit was not only a great *kṣatriya* emperor, but also a great devotee of the Lord. Thus he cannot take his birth at any inauspicious moment. As a proper place and time is selected to receive a respectable personage, so also to receive such a personality as Mahārāja Parīkṣit, who was especially cared for by the Supreme Lord, a suitable moment is chosen when all good stars assembled together to exert their influence upon the King. Thus he took his birth just to be known as the great hero of *Śrīmad-Bhāgavatam.* This suitable arrangement of astral influences is never a creation of man's will, but is the arrangement of the superior management of the agency of the Supreme Lord. Of course, the arrangement is made according to the good or bad deeds of the living being. Herein lies the importance of pious acts performed by the living being. Only by pious acts can one be allowed to get good wealth, good education and beautiful features. The *saṁskāras* of the school of *sanātana-dharma* (man's eternal engagement) are highly suitable for creating an atmosphere for taking advantage of good stellar influences, and therefore *garbhādhāna-saṁskāra,* or the first seedling purificatory process prescribed for the higher castes, is the beginning of all pious acts to receive a good pious and intelligent class of men in human society. There will be peace and prosperity in the world due to good and sane population only; there is hell and disturbance only because of the unwanted, insane populace addicted to sex indulgence.

TEXT 13

तस्य प्रीतमना राजा विप्रैर्धौम्यकृपादिभिः ।
जातकं कारयामास वाचयित्वा च मङ्गलम् ॥१३॥

tasya prīta-manā rājā
viprair dhaumya-kṛpādibhiḥ
jātakaṁ kārayām āsa
vācayitvā ca maṅgalam

tasya—his; *prīta-manāḥ*—satisfied; *rājā*—King Yudhiṣṭhira; *vipraiḥ*—by the learned *brāhmaṇas; dhaumya*—Dhaumya; *kṛpa*—Kṛpa; *ādibhiḥ*—and others also; *jātakam*—one of the purificatory processes performed just after the birth of a child; *kārayām āsa*—had them performed; *vācayitvā*—by recitation; *ca*—also; *maṅgalam*—auspicious.

TRANSLATION

King Yudhiṣṭhira, who was very satisfied with the birth of Mahārāja Parīkṣit, had the purificatory process of birth performed. Learned brāhmaṇas, headed by Dhaumya and Kṛpa, recited auspicious hymns.

PURPORT

There is a need for a good and intelligent class of *brāhmaṇas* who are expert in performing the purificatory processes prescribed in the system of *varṇāśrama-dharma.* Unless such purificatory processes are performed, there is no possibility of good population, and in the age of Kali the population all over the world is of *śūdra* quality or lower for want of this purificatory process. It is not possible, however, to revive the Vedic process of purification in this age, for want of proper facilities and good *brāhmaṇas,* but there is the *Pāñcarātrika* system also recommended for this age. The *Pāñcarātrika* system acts on the *śūdra* class of men, supposedly the population of the Kali-yuga, and it is the prescribed purificatory process suitable to the age and time. Such a purificatory process is allowed only for spiritual upliftment and not for any other purpose. Spiritual upliftment is never conditioned by higher or lower parentage.

After the *garbhādhāna* purificatory process, there are certain other *saṁskāras* like *sīmāntonnayana, sadha-bhakṣaṇam,* etc., during the period of pregnancy, and when the child is born the first purificatory process is *jāta-*

karma. This was performed duly by Mahārāja Yudhiṣṭhira with the help of good and learned *brāhmaṇas* like Dhaumya, the royal priest, and Kṛpācārya, who was not only a priest but also a great general. Both these learned and perfect priests, assisted by other good *brāhmaṇas,* were employed by Mahārāja Yudhiṣṭhira to perform the ceremony. Therefore all the *saṁskāras,* purificatory processes, are not mere formalities or social functions only, but they are all for practical purposes and can be successfully performed by expert *brāhmaṇas* like Dhaumya and Kṛpa. Such *brāhmaṇas* are not only rare, but also not available in this age, and therefore, for the purpose of spiritual upliftment in this fallen age, the Gosvāmīs prefer the purificatory processes under *Pāñcarātrika* formulas to the Vedic rites.

Kṛpācārya is the son of the great Ṛṣi Sardban and was born in the family of Gautama. The birth is said to be accidental. By chance, the great Ṛṣi Sardban met Janapadī, a famous society girl of heaven, and the Ṛṣi Sardban discharged semen in two parts. By one part immediately a male child and by the other part a female child were born as twins. The male child was later on known as Kṛpa, and the female child was known as Kṛpī. Mahārāja Śantanu, while engaged in chase in the jungle, picked up the children and brought them up to the brahminical status by the proper purificatory process. Kṛpācārya later became a great general like Droṇācārya, and his sister was married to Droṇācārya. Kṛpācārya later on took part in the Battle of Kurukṣetra and joined the party of Duryodhana. Kṛpācārya helped kill Abhimanyu, the father of Mahārāja Parīkṣit, but he was still held in esteem by the family of the Pāṇḍavas due to his being as great a *brāhmaṇa* as Droṇācārya. When the Pāṇḍavas were sent to the forest after being defeated in the gambling game with Duryodhana, Dhṛtarāṣṭra entrusted the Pāṇḍavas to Kṛpācārya for guidance. After the end of the battle, Kṛpācārya again became a member of the royal assembly, and he was called during the birth of Mahārāja Parīkṣit for recitation of auspicious Vedic hymns to make the ceremony successful. Mahārāja Yudhiṣṭhira, while quitting the palace for his great departure to the Himalayas, entrusted Kṛpācārya with Mahārāja Parīkṣit as his disciple, and he left home satisfied because of Kṛpācārya's taking charge of Mahārāja Parīkṣit. The great administrators, kings and emperors were always under the guidance of learned *brāhmaṇas* like Kṛpācārya and thus were able to act properly in the discharge of political responsibilities.

TEXT 14

हिरण्यं गां महीं ग्रामान् हस्त्यश्वान्नृपतिर्वरान् ।
प्रादात्स्वन्नं च विप्रेभ्यः प्रजातीर्थे स तीर्थवित् ॥१४॥

hiraṇyaṁ gāṁ mahīṁ grāmān
hasty-aśvān nṛpatir varān
prādāt svannaṁ ca viprebhyaḥ
prajā-tīrthe sa tīrthavit

hiraṇyam—gold; *gām*—cows; *mahīm*—land; *grāmān*—villages; *hasti*—elephants; *aśvān*—horses; *nṛpatiḥ*—the King; *varān*—rewards; *prādāt*—gave in charity; *su-annam*—good food grains; *ca*—and; *viprebhyaḥ*—unto the *brāhmaṇas; prajā-tīrthe*—on the occasion of giving in charity on the birthday of a son; *saḥ*—he; *tīrtha-vit*—one who knows how, when and where charity is to be given.

TRANSLATION

Upon the birth of a son, the King, who knew how, where and when charity should be given, gave gold, land, villages, elephants, horses and good food grains to the brāhmaṇas.

PURPORT

Only the *brāhmaṇas* and *sannyāsīs* are authorized to accept charity from the householders. In all the different occasions of *saṁskāras,* especially during the time of birth, marriage and death, wealth is distributed to the *brāhmaṇas* because the *brāhmaṇas* give the highest quality of service in regard to the prime necessity of humankind. The charity was substantial in the shape of gold, land, villages, horses, elephants and food grains, with other materials for cooking complete foodstuff. The *brāhmaṇas* were not, therefore, poor in the actual sense of the term. On the contrary, because they possessed gold, land, villages, horses, elephants and sufficient grains, they had nothing to earn for themselves. They would simply devote themselves to the well-being of the entire society.

The word *tīrthavit* is significant because the King knew well where and when charity has to be given. Charity is never unproductive or blind. In the *śāstras* charity was offered to persons who deserve to accept charity by dint of spiritual enlightenment. The so-called *daridra-nārāyaṇa,* a misconception of the Supreme Lord by unauthorized persons, is never to be found in the *śāstras* as the object of charity. Nor can a wretched poor man receive much munificent charity in the way of horses, elephants, land and villages. The conclusion is that the intelligent men, or the *brāhmaṇas* specifically engaged in the service of the Lord, were properly maintained without anxiety for the needs of the body, and the King and other householders gladly looked after all their comforts.

It is enjoined in the *śāstras* that as long as a child is joined with the mother by the navel pipe, the child is considered to be of one body with the mother, but as soon as the pipe is cut and the child is separated from the mother, the purificatory process of *jāta-karma* is performed. The administrative demigods and past forefathers of the family come to see a newly born child, and such an occasion is specifically accepted as the proper time for distributing wealth to the right persons productively for the spiritual advancement of society.

TEXT 15

तमूचुर्ब्राह्मणास्तुष्टा राजानं प्रश्रयान्वितम् ।
एष ह्यस्मिन् प्रजातन्तौ पुरूणां पौरवर्षभ ॥१५॥

tam ūcur brāhmaṇās tuṣṭā
rājānaṁ praśrayānvitam
eṣa hy asmin prajā-tantau
purūṇāṁ pauravarṣabha

tam—unto him; *ūcuḥ*—addressed; *brāhmaṇāḥ*—the learned *brāhmaṇas; tuṣṭāḥ*—very much satisfied; *rājānam*—unto the King; *praśraya-anvitam*—very much obliging; *eṣaḥ*—this; *hi*—certainly; *asmin*—in the chain of; *prajā-tantau*—descending line; *purūṇām*—of the Pūrus; *paurava-ṛṣabha*—the chief among the Pūrus.

TRANSLATION

The learned brāhmaṇas, who were very satisfied with the charities of the King, addressed him as the chief amongst the Pūrus and informed him that his son was certainly in the line of descent from the Pūrus.

TEXT 16

दैवेनाप्रतिघातेन शुक्ले संस्थामुपेयुषि ।
रातो वोऽनुग्रहार्थाय विष्णुना प्रभविष्णुना ॥१६॥

daivenāpratighātena
śukle saṁsthām upeyuṣi
rāto vo 'nugrahārthāya
viṣṇunā prabhaviṣṇunā

daivena—by supernatural power; *apratighātena*—by what is irresistible; *śukle*—unto the pure; *saṁsthām*—destruction; *upeyuṣi*—having been enforced; *rātaḥ*—restored; *vaḥ*—for you; *anugraha-arthāya*—for the sake of obliging; *viṣṇunā*—by the all-pervasive Lord; *prabhaviṣṇunā*—by the all-powerful.

TRANSLATION

The brāhmaṇas said: This spotless son has been restored by the all-powerful and all-pervasive Lord Viṣṇu, the Personality of Godhead, in order to oblige you. He was saved when he was doomed to be destroyed by an irresistible supernatural weapon.

PURPORT

The child Parīkṣit was saved by the all-powerful and all-pervasive Viṣṇu (Lord Kṛṣṇa) for two reasons. The first reason is that the child in the womb of his mother was spotless due to his being a pure devotee of the Lord. The second reason is that the child was the only surviving male descendant of Puru, the pious forefather of the virtuous King Yudhiṣṭhira. The Lord wants to continue the line of pious kings to rule over the earth as His representatives for the actual progress of a peaceful and prosperous life. After the Battle of Kurukṣetra, even up to the next generation of Mahārāja Yudhiṣṭhira was annihilated, and there were none who could generate another son in the great royal family. Mahārāja Parīkṣit, the son of Abhimanyu, was the only surviving heir apparent in the family, and by the irresistible supernatural *brahmāstra* weapon of Aśvatthāmā, he was forced to be annihilated. Lord Kṛṣṇa is described herein as Viṣṇu, and this is also significant. Lord Kṛṣṇa, the original Personality of Godhead, does the work of protection and annihilation in His capacity of Viṣṇu. Lord Viṣṇu is the plenary expansion of Lord Kṛṣṇa. The all-pervasive activities of the Lord are executed by Him in His Viṣṇu feature. Child Parīkṣit is described here as spotlessly white because he is an unalloyed devotee of the Lord. Such unalloyed devotees of the Lord appear on the earth just to execute the mission of the Lord. The Lord desires the conditioned souls hovering in the material creation to be reclaimed to go back home, back to Godhead, and thus He helps them by preparing the transcendental literatures like the *Vedas,* by sending missionaries of saints and sages and by deputing His representative, the spiritual master. Such transcendental literatures, missionaries and representatives of the Lord are spotlessly white because the contamination of the material qualities cannot even touch them. They are always protected by the Lord when they are threatened with annihilation. Such foolish threats are made by the gross materialists. The *brahmāstra,* which was thrown by Aśvatthāmā at the child Parīkṣit, was certainly supernaturally powerful, and nothing of the material world could resist its force of penetration. But the all-powerful Lord, who is present everywhere, within and without, could counteract it by His all-powerful potency just to save a bona fide servant of the Lord and descendant of another devotee, Mahārāja Yudhiṣṭhira, who was always obliged by the Lord by His causeless mercy.

TEXT 17

तस्मान्नाम्ना विष्णुरात इति लोके भविष्यति ।
न सन्देहो महाभाग महाभागवतो महान् ॥१७॥

tasmān nāmnā viṣṇu-rāta
iti loke bhaviṣyati
na sandeho mahā-bhāga
mahā-bhāgavato mahān

tasmāt—therefore; *nāmnā*—by the name; *viṣṇu-rātaḥ*—protected by Viṣṇu, the Personality of Godhead; *iti*—thus; *loke*—in all the planets; *bhaviṣyati*—shall become well known; *na*—no; *sandehaḥ*—doubts; *mahā-bhāga*—most fortunate; *mahā-bhāgavataḥ*—the first-class devotee of the Lord; *mahān*—qualified by all good qualities.

TRANSLATION

For this reason this child will be well known in the world as one who is protected by the Personality of Godhead. O most fortunate one, there is no doubt that this child will become a first-class devotee and will be qualified with all good qualities.

PURPORT

The Lord gives protection to all living beings because He is their supreme leader. The Vedic hymns confirm that the Lord is the Supreme Person amongst all personalities. The difference between the two living beings is that the one, the Personality of Godhead, provides for all other living beings, and by knowing

Him one can achieve eternal peace (*Kaṭha Upaniṣad*). Such protection is given by His different potencies to different grades of living beings. But as far as His unalloyed devotees are concerned, He gives the protection personally. Therefore, Mahārāja Parīkṣit is protected from the very beginning of his appearance in the womb of his mother. And because he is especially given protection by the Lord, the indication must be concluded that the child would be a first-grade devotee of the Lord with all good qualities. There are three grades of devotees, namely the *mahā-bhāgavata, madhyama-adhikārī* and the *kaniṣṭha-adhikārī.* Those who go to the temples of the Lord and offer worshipful respect to the Deity without sufficient knowledge in the theological science and therefore without any respect for the devotees of the Lord are called materialistic devotees, or *kaniṣṭha-adhikārī,* the third-grade devotees. Secondly, the devotees who have developed a mentality of genuine service to the Lord and who thus make friendships only with similar devotees, show favor to the neophytes and avoid the atheists are called the second-grade devotees. But those who see everything in the Lord or everything of the Lord and also see in everything an eternal relation of the Lord, so that there is nothing within their purview of sight except the Lord, are called the *mahā-bhāgavatas,* or the first-grade devotees of the Lord. Such first-grade devotees of the Lord are perfect in all respects. A devotee who may be in any of these categories is automatically qualified by all good qualities, and thus a *mahā-bhāgavata* devotee like Mahārāja Parīkṣit is certainly perfect in all respects. And because Mahārāja Parīkṣit took his birth in the family of Mahārāja Yudhiṣṭhira, he is addressed herein as the *mahā-bhāgavata,* or the greatest of the fortunates. The family in which a *mahā-bhāgavata* takes his birth is fortunate because due to the birth of a first-grade devotee the members of the family, past, present and future up to one hundred generations, become liberated by the grace of the Lord, out of respect for His beloved devotee. Therefore, the highest benefit is done to one's family simply by becoming an unalloyed devotee of the Lord.

TEXT 18

श्रीराजोवाच

अप्येष वंश्यान् राजर्षीन् पुण्यश्लोकान् महात्मनः ।
अनुवर्तिता स्विद्यशसा साधुवादेन सत्तमाः ॥१८॥

śrī-rājovāca
apy eṣa vaṁśyān rājarṣīn
puṇya-ślokān mahātmanaḥ

anuvartitā svid yaśasā
sādhu-vādena sattamāḥ

śrī-rājā—the all-good king (Mahārāja Yudhiṣṭhira); *uvāca*—said; *api*—whether; *eṣaḥ*—this; *vaṁśyān*—family; *rāja-ṛṣīn*—of saintly kings; *puṇya-ślokān*—pious by the very name; *mahā-ātmanaḥ*—all great souls; *anuvartitā*—follower; *svit*—will it be; *yaśasā*—by achievements; *sādhu-vādena*—by glorification; *sat-tamāḥ*—O great souls.

TRANSLATION

The good King [Yudhiṣṭhira] inquired: O great souls, will he become as saintly a king, as pious in his very name and as famous and glorified in his achievements, as others who appeared in this great royal family?

PURPORT

The forefathers of King Yudhiṣṭhira were all great saintly kings, pious and glorified by their great achievements. They were all saints on the royal throne. And therefore all the members of the state were happy, pious, well-behaved, prosperous and spiritually enlightened. Under strict guidance of the great souls and spiritual injunctions, such great saintly kings were trained up, and as a result the kingdom was full of saintly persons and was a happy land of spiritual life. Mahārāja Yudhiṣṭhira was himself a replica of his ancestors, and he desired that the next king after him become exactly like his great forefathers. He was happy to learn from the learned *brāhmaṇas* that by astrological calculations the child would be born a first-grade devotee of the Lord, and more confidentially he wanted to know whether the child was going to follow in the footsteps of his great forefathers. That is the way of the monarchical state. The reigning king should be a pious, chivalrous devotee of the Lord and fear personified for the upstarts. He must also leave an heir apparent equally qualified to rule over the innocent citizens. In the modern setup of the democratic states, the people themselves are fallen to the qualities of the *śūdras* or less, and the government is run by their representative, who is ignorant of the scriptural mode of administrative education. Thus the whole atmosphere is surcharged with *śūdra* qualities, manifested by lust and avarice. Such administrators quarrel every day among themselves. The cabinet of ministers changes often due to party and group selfishness. Everyone wants to exploit the state resources till he dies. No one retires from political life unless forced to do so. How can such low-grade men do good to the people? The result is corruption, intrigue and hypocrisy. They should learn from the *Śrīmad-Bhāgavatam* how ideal the administrators must be before they can be given charge of different posts.

TEXT 19

ब्राह्मणा ऊचुः

पार्थ प्रजाविता साक्षादिक्ष्वाकुरिव मानवः ।
ब्रह्मण्यः सत्यसन्धश्च रामो दाशरथिर्यथा ॥१९॥

brāhmaṇā ūcuḥ
pārtha prajāvitā sākṣād
ikṣvākur iva mānavaḥ
brahmaṇyaḥ satya-sandhaś ca
rāmo dāśarathir yathā

brāhmaṇāḥ—the good *brāhmaṇas; ūcuḥ*—said; *pārtha*—O son of Pṛthā (Kuntī); *prajā*—those who are born; *avitā*—maintainer; *sākṣāt*—directly; *ikṣvākuḥ iva*—exactly like King Ikṣvāku; *mānavaḥ*—son of Manu; *brahmaṇyaḥ*—followers and respectful to the *brāhmaṇas; satya-sandhaḥ*—truthful by promise; *ca*—also; *rāmaḥ*—the Personality of Godhead Rāma; *dāśarathiḥ*—the son of Mahārāja Daśaratha; *yathā*—like Him.

TRANSLATION

The learned brāhmaṇas said: O son of Pṛthā, this child shall be exactly like King Ikṣvāku, son of Manu, in maintaining all those who are born. And as for following the brahminical principles, especially in being true to his promise, he shall be exactly like Rāma, the Personality of Godhead, the son of Mahārāja Daśaratha.

PURPORT

Prajā means the living being who has taken his birth in the material world. Actually the living being has no birth and no death, but because of his separation from the service of the Lord and due to his desire to lord it over material nature, he is offered a suitable body to satisfy his material desires. In doing so, one becomes conditioned by the laws of material nature, *and the material body is changed in terms of his own work.* The living entity thus transmigrates from one body to another in 8,400,000 species of life. But due to his being the part and parcel of the Lord, he not only is maintained with all necessaries of life by the Lord, but also is protected by the Lord and His representatives, the saintly kings. These saintly kings give protection to all the *prajās,* or living beings, to live and to fulfill their terms of imprisonment. Mahārāja Parīkṣit was actually an ideal saintly king because while touring his kingdom he happened to see that a poor cow was about to be killed by the personified Kali, whom he at once took to task as a murderer. This means that even the animals were given protection by the saintly administrators, not from any sentimental point of view, but because those who have taken their birth in the material world have the right to live. All the saintly kings, beginning from the King of the sun globe down to the King of the earth, are so inclined by the influence of the Vedic literatures. The Vedic literatures are taught in higher planets also, as there is reference in the *Bhagavad-gītā* (4.1) about the teachings to the sun-god (Vivasvān) by the Lord, and such lessons are transferred by disciplic succession, as it was done by the sun-god to his son Manu, and from Manu to Mahārāja Ikṣvāku. There are fourteen Manus in one day of Brahmā, and the Manu referred to herein is the seventh Manu, who is one of the *prajāpatis* (those who create progeny), and he is the son of the sun-god. He is known as the Vaivasvata Manu. He had ten sons, and Mahārāja Ikṣvāku is one of them. Mahārāja Ikṣvāku also learned *bhakti-yoga* as taught in the *Bhagavad-gītā* from his father, Manu, who got it from his father, the sun-god. Later on the teaching of the *Bhagavad-gītā* came down by disciplic succession from Mahārāja Ikṣvāku, but in course of time the chain was broken by unscrupulous persons, and therefore it again had to be taught to Arjuna on the Battlefield of Kurukṣetra. So all the Vedic literatures are current from the very beginning of creation of the material world, and thus the Vedic literatures are known as *apauruṣeya* ("not made by man"). The Vedic knowledge was spoken by the Lord and first heard by Brahmā, the first created living being within the universe.

Mahārāja Ikṣvāku: One of the sons of Vaivasvata Manu. He had one hundred sons. He prohibited meat-eating. His son Śaśāda became the next king after his death.

Manu: The Manu mentioned in this verse as the father of Ikṣvāku is the seventh Manu, of the name Vaivasvata Manu, the son of sun-god Vivasvān, to whom Lord Kṛṣṇa instructed the teachings of *Bhagavad-gītā* prior to His teaching them to Arjuna. Mankind is the descendant of Manu. This Vaivasvata Manu had ten sons, named Ikṣvāku, Nabhaga, Dhṛṣṭa, Śaryāti, Nariṣyanta,

Nābhāga, Diṣṭa, Karūṣa, Pṛṣadhra and Vasumān. The Lord's incarnation Matsya (the gigantic fish) was advented during the beginning of Vaivasvata Manu's reign. He learned the principles of *Bhagavad-gītā* from his father, Vivasvān, the sun-god, and he reinstructed the same to his son Mahārāja Ikṣvāku. In the beginning of the Tretā-yuga the sun-god instructed devotional service to Manu, and Manu in his turn instructed it to Ikṣvāku for the welfare of the whole human society.

Lord Rāma: The Supreme Personality of Godhead incarnated Himself as Śrī Rāma, accepting the sonhood of His pure devotee Mahārāja Daśaratha, the King of Ayodhyā. Lord Rāma descended along with His plenary portions, and all of them appeared as His younger brothers. In the month of Caitra on the ninth day of the growing moon in the Tretā-yuga, the Lord appeared, as usual, to establish the principles of religion and to annihilate the disturbing elements. When He was just a young boy, He helped the great sage Viśvāmitra by killing Subāhu and striking Mārīcā, the she-demon,who was disturbing the sages in their daily discharge of duties. The *brāhmaṇas* and *kṣatriyas* are meant to cooperate for the welfare of the mass of people. The *brāhmaṇa* sages endeavor to enlighten the people by perfect knowledge, and the *kṣatriyas* are meant for their protection. Lord Rāmacandra is the ideal king for maintaining and protecting the highest culture of humanity, known as *brahmaṇya-dharma.* The Lord is specifically the protector of the cows and the *brāhmaṇas,* and hence He enhances the prosperity of the world. He rewarded the administrative demigods by effective weapons to conquer the demons through the agency of Viśvāmitra. He was present in the bow sacrifice of King Janaka, and by breaking the invincible bow of Śiva, He married Sītādevī, daughter of Mahārāja Janaka.

After His marriage He accepted exile in the forest for fourteen years by the order of His father, Mahārāja Daśaratha. To help the administration of the demigods, He killed fourteen thousand demons, and by the intrigues of the demons, His wife, Sītādevī, was kidnapped by Rāvaṇa. He made friendship with Sugrīva, who was helped by the Lord to kill Vali, brother of Sugrīva. By the help of Lord Rāma, Sugrīva became the king of the Vānaras (a race of gorillas). The Lord built a floating bridge of stones on the Indian Ocean and reached Laṅkā, the kingdom of Rāvaṇa, who had kidnapped Sītā. Later on Rāvaṇa was killed by Him and Rāvaṇa's brother Vibhīṣaṇa was installed on the throne of Laṅkā. Vibhīṣaṇa was one of the brothers of Rāvaṇa, a demon, but Lord Rāma made him immortal by His blessings. On the expiry of fourteen years, after settling the affairs at Laṅkā, the Lord came back to His kingdom, Ayodhyā, by flower plane. He instructed His brother Śatrughna to attack Lavaṇāsura, who reigned at Mathurā, and the demon was killed. He performed ten *aśvamedha* sacrifices, and later on He disappeared while taking a bath in the Śarayu River. The great epic *Rāmāyaṇa* is the history of Lord Rāma's activities in the world, and the authoritative *Rāmāyaṇa* was written by the great poet Vālmīki.

TEXT 20

एष दाता शरण्यश्च यथा ह्यौशीनरः शिबिः ।
यशो वितनिता स्वानां दौष्यन्तिरिव यज्वनाम् ॥२०॥

eṣa dātā śaraṇyaś ca
yathā hy auśīnaraḥ śibiḥ
yaśo vitanitā svānāṁ
dauṣyantir iva yajvanām

eṣaḥ—this child; *dātā*—donor in charity; *śaraṇyaḥ*—protector of the surrendered; *ca*—and; *yathā*—as; *hi*—certainly; *auśīnaraḥ*—the country named Uśīnara; *śibiḥ*—Śibi; *yaśaḥ*—fame; *vitanitā*—disseminator; *svānām*—of the kinsmen; *dauṣyantih iva*—like Bharata, the son of Duṣyanta; *yajvanām*—of those who have performed many sacrifices.

TRANSLATION

This child will be a munificent donor of charity and protector of the surrendered, like the famous King Śibi of the Uśīnara country. And he will expand the name and fame of his family like Bharata, the son of Mahārāja Duṣyanta.

PURPORT

A king becomes famous by his acts of charity, performances of *yajñas,* protection of the surrendered, etc. A *kṣatriya* king is proud to give protection to the surrendered souls. This attitude of a king is called *īśvara-bhāva,* or factual power to give protection in a righteous cause. In the *Bhagavad-gītā* the Lord instructs living beings to surrender unto Him, and He promises all protection. The Lord is all-powerful and true to His word, and therefore He never fails to give protection to His different devotees. The king, being the representative of the Lord, must possess this attitude of giving protection to the surrendered souls at all risk. Mahārāja Śibi, the King of Uśīnara, was an intimate friend of Mahārāja Yayāti, who was able to reach the heavenly planets along with Mahārāja Śibi. Mahārāja Śibi was aware of the heavenly planet where he was to be transferred after his death, and the description of this heavenly planet is given in the *Mahābhārata (Ādi-parva* 96.6–9*)*. Mahārāja Śibi was so charitably disposed that he wanted to give over his acquired position in the heavenly kingdom to Yayāti, but he did not accept it. Yayāti went to the heavenly planet along with great *ṛṣis* like Aṣṭaka and others. On inquiry from the *ṛṣis,* Yayāti gave an account of Śibi's pious acts when all of them were on the path to heaven. He has become a member of the assembly of Yamarāja, who has become his worshipful deity. As confirmed in the *Bhagavad-gītā,* the worshiper of the demigods goes to the planets of the demigods (*yānti deva-vratā devān);* so Mahārāja Śibi has become an associate of the great Vaiṣṇava authority Yamarāja on that particular planet. While he was on the earth he became very famous as a protector of surrendered souls and a donor of charities. The King of heaven once took the shape of a pigeon-hunter bird (eagle), and Agni, the fire-god, took the shape of a pigeon. The pigeon, while being chased by the eagle, took shelter on the lap of Mahārāja Śibi, and the hunter eagle wanted the pigeon back from the King. The King wanted to give it some other meat to eat and requested the bird not to kill the pigeon. The hunter bird refused to accept the King's offer, but it was settled later on that the eagle would accept flesh from the body of the King of the pigeon's equivalent weight. The King began to cut flesh from his body to weigh in the balance equivalent to the weight of the pigeon, but the mystic pigeon always remained heavier. The King then put himself on the balance to equate with the pigeon, and the demigods were pleased with him. The King of heaven and the fire-god disclosed their identity, and the King was blessed by them. Devarṣi Nārada also glorified Mahārāja Śibi for his great achievements, specifically in charity and protection. Mahārāja Śibi sacrificed his own son for the satisfaction of human beings in his kingdom. And thus child Parīkṣit was to become a second Śibi in charity and protection.

Dauṣyanti Bharata: There are many Bharatas in history, of which Bharata the brother of Lord Rāma, Bharata the son of King Ṛṣabha, and Bharata the son of Mahārāja Duṣyanta are very famous. And all these Bharatas are historically known to the universe. This earth planet is known as Bhārata, or Bhārata-varṣa, due to King Bharata the son of Ṛṣabha, but according to some this land is known as Bhārata due to the reign of the son of Duṣyanta. So far as we are convinced, this land's name Bhārata-varṣa was established from the reign of

Bharata the son of King Ṛṣabha. Before him the land was known as Ilāvṛta-varṣa, but just after the coronation of Bharata, the son of Ṛṣabha, this land became famous as Bhārata-varṣa.

But despite all this, Bharata the son of Mahārāja Duṣyanta was not less important. He is the son of the famous beauty Śakuntalā. Mahārāja Duṣyanta fell in love with Śakuntalā in the forest, and Bharata was conceived. After that, Mahārāja forgot his wife Śakuntalā by the curse of Kaṇva Muni, and the child Bharata was brought up in the forest by his mother. Even in his childhood he was so powerful that he challenged the lions and elephants in the forest and would fight with them as little children play with cats and dogs. Because of the boy's becoming so strong, more than the so-called modern Tarzan, the *ṛṣis* in the forest called him Sarvadamana, or one who is able to control everyone. A full description of Mahārāja Bharata is given in the *Mahābhārata, Ādi-parva.* The Pāṇḍavas, or the Kurus, are sometimes addressed as Bhārata due to being born in the dynasty of the famous Mahārāja Bharata, the son of King Duṣyanta.

TEXT 21

धन्विनामग्रणीरेष तुल्यश्चार्जुनयोर्द्वयोः ।
हुताश इव दुर्धर्षः समुद्र इव दुस्तरः ॥२१॥

dhanvinām agraṇīr eṣa
tulyaś cārjunayor dvayoḥ
hutāśa iva durdharṣaḥ
samudra iva dustaraḥ

dhanvinām—of the great bowmen; *agraṇīḥ*—the foreman; *eṣaḥ*—this child; *tulyaḥ*—equally good; *ca*—and; *arjunayoḥ*—of the Arjunas; *dvayoḥ*—of the two; *hutāśaḥ*—fire; *iva*—like; *durdharṣaḥ*—irresistible; *samudraḥ*—ocean; *iva*—like; *dustaraḥ*—unsurpassable.

TRANSLATION

Amongst great bowmen, this child will be as good as Arjuna. He will be as irresistible as fire and as unsurpassable as the ocean.

PURPORT

In history there are two Arjunas. One is Kārtavīrya Arjuna, the King of Haihaya, and the other is the grandfather of the child. Both the Arjunas are famous for their bowmanship, and the child Parīkṣit is foretold to be equal to both of them, particularly in fighting. A short description of the Pāṇḍava Arjuna is given below:

Pāṇḍava Arjuna: The great hero of the *Bhagavad-gītā.* He is the *kṣatriya* son of Mahārāja Pāṇḍu. Queen Kuntīdevī could call for any one of the demigods, and thus she called Indra, and Arjuna was born by him. Arjuna is therefore a plenary part of the heavenly king Indra. He was born in the month of Phālguna (February–March), and therefore he is also called Phālguni. When he appeared as the son of Kuntī, his future greatness was proclaimed by air messages, and all the important personalities from different parts of the universe, such as the demigods, the Gandharvas, the Ādityas (from the sun globe), the Rudras, the Vasus, the Nāgas, the different *ṛṣis* (sages) of importance, and the Apsarās (the society girls of heaven), all attended the ceremony. The Apsarās pleased everyone by their heavenly dances and songs. Vasudeva, the father of Lord Kṛṣṇa and the maternal uncle of Arjuna, sent his priest representative Kaśyapa to purify Arjuna by all the prescribed *saṁskāras,* or reformatory processes. His *saṁskāra* of being given a name was performed in the presence of the *ṛṣis,* residents of Śataśṛṅga. He married four wives, Draupadī, Subhadrā, Citrāṅgadā and Ulūpī, from whom he got four sons of the names Śrutakīrti, Abhimanyu, Babhruvāhana and Irāvān respectively.

During his student life he was entrusted to study under the great professor Droṇācārya, along with other Pāṇḍavas and the Kurus. But he excelled everyone by his studious intensity, and Droṇācārya was especially attracted by his disciplinary affection. Droṇācārya accepted him as a first-grade scholar and loved heartily to bestow upon him all the blessings of military science. He was so ardent a student that he used to practice bowmanship even at night, and for all these reasons Professor Droṇācārya was determined to make him the topmost bowman of the world. He passed very brilliantly the examination in piercing the target, and Droṇācārya was very pleased. Royal families at Maṇipura and Tripura are descendants of Arjuna's son Babhruvāhana. Arjuna saved Droṇācārya from the attack of a crocodile, and the Ācārya, being pleased with him, rewarded him with a weapon of the name *brahmaśiras.* Mahārāja Drupada was inimical toward Droṇācārya, and thus when he attacked the Ācārya, Arjuna got him arrested and brought him before Droṇācārya. He besieged a city of the name Ahicchatra, belonging to Mahārāja Drupada, and after taking it over he gave it to Droṇācārya. The confidential treatment of the weapon *brahmaśiras* was explained to Arjuna, and Droṇācārya was promised by Arjuna that he would use the weapon if necessary when he (Droṇācārya) personally became an enemy of Arjuna. By this, the *ācārya* forecasted the future Battle of Kurukṣetra, in which Droṇācārya was on the opposite side. Mahārāja Drupada, although defeated by Arjuna on behalf of his professor Droṇācārya, decided to hand over his daughter Draupadī to his young combatant, but he was disappointed when he heard the false news of Arjuna's death in the fire of a shellac house intrigued by Duryodhana. He therefore arranged for Draupadī's personal selection of a groom who could pierce the eye of a fish hanging on the ceiling. This trick was especially made because only Arjuna could do it, and he was successful in his desire to hand over his equally worthy daughter to Arjuna. Arjuna's brothers were at that time living incognito under agreement with Duryodhana, and Arjuna and his brothers attended the meeting of Draupadī's selection in the dress of *brāhmaṇas.* When all the *kṣatriya* kings assembled saw that a poor *brāhmaṇa* had been garlanded by Draupadī for her lord, Śrī Kṛṣṇa disclosed his identity to Balarāma.

He met Ulūpī at Haridvāra (Hardwar), and he was attracted by a girl belonging to Nāgaloka, and thus Iravān was born. Similarly, he met Citrāṅgadā, a daughter of the King of Maṇipura, and thus Babhruvāhana was born. Lord Śrī Kṛṣṇa made a plan to help Arjuna to kidnap Subhadrā, sister of Śrī Kṛṣṇa, because Baladeva was inclined to hand her over to Duryodhana. Yudhiṣṭhira also agreed with Śrī Kṛṣṇa, and thus Subhadrā was taken by force by Arjuna and then married to him. Subhadrā's son is Abhimanyu, the father of Parīkṣit Mahārāja, the posthumous child. Arjuna satisfied the fire-god by setting fire to the Khāṇḍava Forest, and thus the fire-god gave him one weapon. Indra was angry when the fire was set in the Khāṇḍava Forest, and thus Indra, assisted by all other demigods, began fighting with Arjuna for his great challenge. They were defeated by Arjuna, and Indradeva returned to his heavenly kingdom. Arjuna also promised all protection to one Mayāsura, and the latter presented him one valuable conchshell celebrated as the Devadatta. Similarly, he received many other valuable weapons from Indradeva when he was satisfied to see his chivalry.

When Mahārāja Yudhiṣṭhira was disappointed in defeating the King of Magadha, Jarāsandha, it was Arjuna only who gave King Yudhiṣṭhira all kinds of assurances, and thus Arjuna, Bhīma and Lord Kṛṣṇa started for Magadha to kill Jarāsandha. When he went out to bring all other kings of the world under the subjection of the Pāṇḍavas, as was usual after the coronation of every emperor, he conquered the country named Kelinda and brought in subjugation King Bhagadatta. Then he traveled through countries like Antagiri, Ulūkapura and Modāpura and brought under subjugation all the rulers.

Sometimes he underwent severe types of penances, and later on he was rewarded by Indradeva. Lord Śiva also wanted to try the strength of Arjuna, and in the form of an aborigine, Lord Śiva met him. There was a great fight between the two, and at last Lord Śiva was satisfied with him and disclosed his identity. Arjuna prayed to the lord in all humbleness, and the lord, being pleased with him, presented him the *pāśupata* weapon. He acquired many other important weapons from different demigods. He received *daṇḍāstra* from Yamarāja, *pāśāstra* from Varuṇa, and *antardhānāstra* from Kuvera, the treasurer of the heavenly kingdom. Indra wanted him to come to the heavenly kingdom, the Indraloka planet beyond the moon planet. In that planet he was cordially received by the local residents, and he was awarded reception in the heavenly parliament of Indradeva. Then he met Indradeva, who not only presented him with his *vajra* weapon, but also taught him the military and musical science as used in the heavenly planet. In one sense, Indra is the real father of Arjuna, and therefore indirectly he wanted to entertain Arjuna with the famous society girl of heaven, Urvaśī, the celebrated beauty. The society girls of heaven are lusty, and Urvaśī was very eager to contact Arjuna, the strongest human being. She met him in his room and expressed her desires, but Arjuna sustained his unimpeachable character by closing his eyes before Urvaśī, addressing her as mother of the Kuru dynasty and placing her in the category of his mothers Kuntī, Mādrī and Śacīdevī, wife of Indradeva. Disappointed, Urvaśī cursed Arjuna and left. In the heavenly planet he also met the great celebrated ascetic Lomaśa and prayed to him for the protection of Mahārāja Yudhiṣṭhira.

When his inimical cousin Duryodhana was under the clutches of the Gandharvas, he wanted to save him and requested the Gandharvas to release Duryodhana, but the Gandharvas refused, and thus he fought with them and got Duryodhana released. When all the Pāṇḍavas lived incognito, he presented himself in the court of King Virāṭa as a eunuch and was employed as the musical teacher of Uttarā, his future daughter-in-law, and was known in the Virāṭa court as the Bṛhannala. As Bṛhannala, he fought on behalf of Uttarā, the son of King Virāṭa, and thus defeated the Kurus in the fight incognito. His secret weapons were safely kept in the custody of a *somi* tree, and he ordered Uttarā to get them back. His identity and his brothers' identity were later on disclosed to Uttarā. Droṇācārya was informed of Arjuna's presence in the fight of the Kurus and the Virāṭas. Later, on the Battlefield of Kurukṣetra, Arjuna killed many great generals like Karṇa and others. After the Battle of Kurukṣetra, he punished Aśvatthāmā, who had killed all the five sons of Draupadī. Then all the brothers went to Bhīṣmadeva.

It is due to Arjuna only that the great philosophical discourses of the *Bhagavad-gītā* were again spoken by the Lord on the Battlefield of Kurukṣetra. His wonderful acts on the Battlefield of Kurukṣetra are vividly described in the *Mahābhārata.* Arjuna was defeated, however, by his son Babhruvāhana at Maṇipura and fell unconscious when Ulūpī saved him. After the disappearance of Lord Kṛṣṇa, the message was brought by Arjuna to Mahārāja Yudhiṣṭhira. Again, Arjuna visited Dvārakā, and all the widow wives of Lord Kṛṣṇa lamented before him. He took them all in the presence of Vasudeva and pacified all of them. Later on, when Vasudeva passed away, he performed his funeral ceremony in the absence of Kṛṣṇa. While Arjuna was taking all the wives of Kṛṣṇa to Indraprastha, he was attacked on the way, and he could not protect the ladies in his custody. At last, advised by Vyāsadeva, all the brothers headed for Mahāprasthāna. On the way, at the request of his brother, he gave up all important weapons as useless, and he dropped them all in the water.

TEXT 22

मृगेन्द्र इव विक्रान्तो निषेव्यो हिमवानिव ।
तितिक्षुर्वसुधेवासौ सहिष्णुः पितराविव ॥२२॥

mṛgendra iva vikrānto
niṣevyo himavān iva
titikṣur vasudhevāsau
sahiṣṇuḥ pitarāv iva

mṛgendraḥ—the lion; *iva*—like; *vikrāntaḥ*—powerful; *niṣevyaḥ*—worthy of taking shelter; *himavān*—the Himalaya Mountains; *iva*—like; *titikṣuḥ*—forbearance; *vasudhā iva*—like the earth; *asau*—the child; *sahiṣṇuḥ*—tolerant; *pitarau*—parents; *iva*—like.

TRANSLATION

This child will be as strong as a lion, and as worthy a shelter as the Himalaya Mountains. He will be forbearing like the earth, and as tolerant as his parents.

PURPORT

One is compared to the lion when one is very strong in chasing an enemy. One should be a lamb at home and a lion in the chase. The lion never fails in the chase of an animal; similarly, the head of the state should never fail in chasing an enemy. The Himalaya Mountains are famous for all richness. There are innumerable caves to live in, numberless trees of good fruits to eat, good springs to drink water from and profuse drugs and minerals to cure diseases. Any man who is not materially prosperous can take shelter of these great mountains, and he will be provided with everything required. Both the materialist and the spiritualist can take advantage of the great shelter of the Himalayas. On the surface of the earth there are so many disturbances caused by the inhabitants. In the modern age the people have begun to detonate atomic weapons on the surface of the earth, and still the earth is forbearing to the inhabitants, like a mother who excuses a little child. Parents are always tolerant to children for all sorts of mischievous acts. An ideal king may be possessed of all these good qualities, and the child Parīkṣit is foretold to have all these qualities in perfection.

TEXT 23

पितामहसमः साम्ये प्रसादे गिरिशोपमः ।
आश्रयः सर्वभूतानां यथा देवो रमाश्रयः ॥२३॥

pitāmaha-samaḥ sāmye
prasāde giriśopamaḥ
āśrayaḥ sarva-bhūtānāṁ
yathā devo ramāśrayaḥ

pitāmaha—the grandfather, or Brahmā; *samaḥ*—equally good; *sāmye*—in the matter; *prasāde*—in charity or in munificence; *giriśa*—Lord Śiva; *upamaḥ*—comparison of equilibrium; *āśrayaḥ*—resort; *sarva*—all; *bhūtānām*—of the living beings; *yathā*—as; *devaḥ*—the Supreme Lord; *ramā-āśrayaḥ*—the Personality of Godhead.

TRANSLATION

This child will be like his grandfather Yudhiṣṭhira or Brahmā in equanimity of mind. He will be munificent like the lord of the Kailāsa Hill, Śiva. And he will be the resort of everyone, like the Supreme Personality of Godhead, Nārāyaṇa, who is even the shelter of the goddess of fortune.

PURPORT

Mental equanimity refers both to Mahārāja Yudhiṣṭhira and to Brahmā, the grandfather of all living beings. According to Śrīdhara Svāmī, the grandfather referred to is Brahmā, but according to Viśvanātha Cakravartī, the grandfather is Mahārāja Yudhiṣṭhira himself. But in both cases the comparison is equally good because both of them are recognized representatives of the Supreme Lord, and thus both of them have to maintain mental equanimity, being engaged in welfare work for the living being. Any responsible executive agent at the top of administration has to tolerate different types of onslaughts from the very persons for whom he works. Brahmājī was criticized even by the *gopīs,* the highest perfectional devotees of the Lord. The *gopīs* were dissatisfied with the work of Brahmājī because Lord Brahmā, as creator of this particular universe, created eyelids which obstructed their seeing Lord Kṛṣṇa. They could not tolerate a moment's blinking of the eyes, for it kept them from seeing their beloved Lord Kṛṣṇa. So what to speak of others, who are naturally very critical of every action of a responsible man? Similarly, Mahārāja Yudhiṣṭhira had to cross over many difficult situations created by his enemies, and he proved to be the most perfect maintainer of mental equanimity in all critical circumstances. Therefore the example of both grandfathers for maintaining equanimity of mind is quite fitting.

Lord Śiva is a celebrated demigod who awards gifts to beggars. His name is therefore Āśutoṣa, or one who is pleased very easily. He is also called the Bhūtanātha, or the lord of the common folk, who are mainly attached to him because of his munificent gifts, even without consideration of the aftereffects. Rāvaṇa was very attached to Lord Śiva, and by easily pleasing him, Rāvaṇa became so powerful that he wanted to challenge the authority of Lord Rāma. Of course, Rāvaṇa was never helped by Lord Śiva when he fought with Rāma, the Supreme Personality of Godhead and the Lord of Lord Śiva. To Vṛkāsura, Lord Śiva awarded a benediction which was not only awkward, but also disturbing. Vṛkāsura became empowered, by the grace of Lord Śiva, to vanish anyone's head simply by touching it. Although this was awarded by Lord Śiva, the cunning fellow wanted to make an experiment of the power by touching the head of Lord Śiva. Thus the lord had to take shelter of Viṣṇu to save himself from trouble, and the Lord Viṣṇu, by His illusory potency, asked Vṛkāsura to make an experiment with his own head. The fellow did it and was finished himself, and so the world was saved from all sorts of trouble by such a cunning beggar of the demigods. The excellent point is that Lord Śiva never denies anyone any sort of gift. He is therefore the most generous, although sometimes some kind of a mistake is made.

Ramā means the goddess of fortune. And her shelter is Lord Viṣṇu. Lord Viṣṇu is the maintainer of all living beings. There are innumerable living beings, not only on the surface of this planet but also in all other hundreds of thousands of planets. All of them are provided with all necessities of life for the progressive march towards the end of self-realization, but on the path of sense gratification they are put into difficulty by the agency of *māyā,* the illusory energy, and so travel the path of a false plan of economic development. Such economic development is never successful because it is illusory. These men are always after the mercy of the illusory goddess of fortune, but they do not know that the goddess of fortune can live only under the protection of Viṣṇu. Without Viṣṇu, the goddess of fortune is an illusion. We should therefore seek the protection of Viṣṇu instead of directly seeking the protection of the goddess of fortune. Only Viṣṇu and the devotees of Viṣṇu can give protection to all, and because Mahārāja Parīkṣit was himself protected by Viṣṇu, it was quite possible for him to give complete protection to all who wanted to live under his rule.

TEXT 24

सर्वसद्‌गुणमाहात्म्ये एष कृष्णमनुव्रतः ।
रन्तिदेव इवोदारो ययातिरिव धार्मिकः ॥२४॥

sarva-sad-guṇa-māhātmye
eṣa kṛṣṇam anuvrataḥ
rantideva ivodāro
yayātir iva dhārmikaḥ

sarva-sat-guṇa-māhātmye—glorified by all godly attributes; *eṣaḥ*—this child; *kṛṣṇam*—like Lord Kṛṣṇa; *anuvrataḥ*—a follower in His footsteps; *rantidevaḥ*—Rantideva; *iva*—like; *udāraḥ*—in the matter of magnanimity; *yayātiḥ*—Yayāti; *iva*—like; *dhārmikaḥ*—concerning religion.

TRANSLATION

This child will be almost as good as Lord Śrī Kṛṣṇa by following in His footsteps. In magnanimity he will become as great as King Rantideva. And in religion he will be like Mahārāja Yayāti.

PURPORT

The last instruction of Lord Śrī Kṛṣṇa in the *Bhagavad-gītā* is that one should give up everything and should follow in the footsteps of the Lord alone. Less intelligent persons do not agree to this great instruction of the Lord, as ill luck would have it, but one who is actually intelligent catches up this sublime instruction and is immensely benefited. Foolish people do not know that association is the cause of acquiring qualities. Association with fire makes an object hot, even in the material sense. Therefore, association with the Supreme Personality of Godhead makes one qualified like the Lord. As we have discussed previously, one can achieve seventy-eight percent of the godly qualities by the Lord's intimate association. To follow the instructions of the Lord is to associate with the Lord. *The Lord is not a material object whose presence one has to feel for such association.* The Lord is present everywhere and at all times. It is quite possible to have His association simply by following His instruction because the Lord and His instruction and the Lord and His name, fame, attributes and paraphernalia are all identical with Him, being absolute knowledge. Mahārāja Parīkṣit associated with the Lord even from the womb of his mother up to the last day of his valuable life, and thus he acquired all the essential good qualities of the Lord in all perfection.

Rantideva: An ancient king prior to the *Mahābhārata* period, referred to by Nārada Muni while instructing Sañjaya, as mentioned in *Mahābhārata* (*Droṇa-parva* 67). He was a great king, liberal for hospitality and distribution of foodstuff. Even Lord Śrī Kṛṣṇa praised his acts of charity and hospitality. He was blessed by the great Vasiṣṭha Muni for supplying him cold water, and thus he achieved the heavenly planet. He used to supply fruits, roots and leaves to the *ṛṣis,* and thus he was blessed by them with fulfillment of his desires. *Although a kṣatriya by birth, he never ate flesh in his life.* He was especially hospitable to Vasiṣṭha Muni, and by his blessings only he attained the higher planetary residence. He is one of those pious kings whose names are remembered in the morning and evening.

Yayāti: The great emperor of the world and the original forefather of all great nations of the world who belong to the Āryan and Indo-European stock. He is the son of Mahārāja Nahuṣa, and he became the emperor of the world due to his elder brother's becoming a great and liberated saintly mystic. He ruled over the world for several thousands of years and performed many sacrifices and pious activities recorded in history, although his early youth was very lustful and full of romantic stories. He fell in love with Devayānī, the most beloved daughter of Śukrācārya. Devayānī wished to marry him, but at first he refused to accept her because of her being a daughter of a *brāhmaṇa.* According to *śāstras,* a *brāhmaṇa* could marry the daughter of a *brāhmaṇa.* They were very much cautious about *varṇa-saṅkara* population in the world.

Śukrācārya amended this law of forbidden marriage and induced Emperor Yayāti to accept Devayānī. Devayānī had a girlfriend named Śarmiṣṭhā, who also fell in love with the emperor and thus went with her friend Devayānī. Śukrācārya forbade Emperor Yayāti to call Śarmiṣṭhā into his bedroom, but Yayāti could not strictly follow his instruction. He secretly married Śarmiṣṭhā also and begot sons by her. When this was known by Devayānī, she went to her father and lodged a complaint. Yayāti was much attached to Devayānī, and when he went to his father-in-law's place to call her, Śukrācārya was angry with him and cursed him to become impotent. Yayāti begged his father-in-law to withdraw his curse, but the sage asked Yayāti to ask youthfulness from his sons and let them become old as the condition of his becoming potent. He had five sons, two from Devayānī and three from Śarmiṣṭhā. From his five sons, namely (1) Yadu, (2) Turvasu, (3) Druhyu, (4) Anu and (5) Pūru, five famous dynasties, namely (1) the Yadu dynasty, (2) the Yavana (Turk) dynasty, (3) the Bhoja dynasty, (4) the Mleccha dynasty (Greek) and (5) the Paurava dynasty, all emanated to spread all over the world. He reached the heavenly planets by dint of his pious acts, but he fell down from there because of his self-advertisement and criticizing other great souls. After his fall, his daughter and grandson bestowed upon him their accumulated virtues, and by the help of his grandson and friend Śibi, he was again promoted to the heavenly kingdom, becoming one of the assembly members of Yamarāja, with whom he is staying as a devotee. He performed more than one thousand different sacrifices, gave in charity very liberally and was a very influential king. His majestic power was felt all over the world. His youngest son agreed to award him his youthfulness when he was troubled with lustful desires, even for one thousand years. Finally he became detached from worldly life and returned the youthfulness again to his son Pūru. He wanted to hand over the kingdom to Pūru, but his noblemen and the subjects did not agree. But when he explained to his subjects the greatness of Pūru, they agreed to accept Pūru as the King, and thus Emperor Yayāti retired from family life and left home for the forest.

TEXT 25

धृत्या बलिसमः कृष्णे प्रह्लाद इव सद्ग्रहः ।
आहर्तैषोऽश्वमेधानां वृद्धानां पर्युपासकः ॥२५॥

dhṛtyā bali-samaḥ kṛṣṇe
prahrāda iva sad-grahaḥ

āhartaiṣo 'śvamedhānāṁ
vṛddhānāṁ paryupāsakaḥ

dhṛtyā—by patience; *bali-samaḥ*—like Bali Mahārāja; *kṛṣṇe*—unto Lord Śrī Kṛṣṇa; *prahrāda*—Prahlāda Mahārāja; *iva*—like; *sat-grahaḥ*—devotee of; *āhartā*—performer; *eṣaḥ*—this child; *aśvamedhānām*—of Aśvamedha sacrifices; *vṛddhānām*—of the old and experienced men; *paryupāsakaḥ*—follower.

TRANSLATION

This child will be like Bali Mahārāja in patience, a staunch devotee of Lord Kṛṣṇa like Prahlāda Mahārāja, a performer of many aśvamedha [horse] sacrifices and a follower of the old and experienced men.

PURPORT

Bali Mahārāja: One of the twelve authorities in the devotional service of the Lord. Bali Mahārāja is a great authority in devotional service because he sacrificed everything to please the Lord and relinquished the connection of his so-called spiritual master who obstructed him on the path of risking everything for the service of the Lord. The highest perfection of religious life is to attain to the stage of unqualified devotional service of the Lord without any cause or without being obstructed by any kind of worldly obligation. Bali Mahārāja was determined to give up everything for the satisfaction of the Lord, and he did not care for any obstruction whatsoever. He is the grandson of Prahlāda Mahārāja, another authority in the devotional service of the Lord. Bali Mahārāja and the history of his dealings with Viṣṇu Vāmanadeva are described in the Eighth Canto of *Śrīmad-Bhāgavatam* (Chapter 11–24).

Prahlāda Mahārāja: A perfect devotee of Lord Kṛṣṇa (Viṣṇu). His father, Hiraṇyakaśipu, chastised him severely when he was only five years old for his becoming an unalloyed devotee of the Lord. He was the first son of Hiraṇyakaśipu, and his mother's name was Kayādhu. Prahlāda Mahārāja was an authority in the devotional service of the Lord because he had his father killed by Lord Nṛsiṁhadeva, setting the example that even a father should be removed from the path of devotional service if such a father happens to be an obstacle. He had four sons, and the eldest son, Virocana, is the father of Bali Mahārāja, mentioned above. The history of Prahlāda Mahārāja's activities is described in the Seventh Canto of *Śrīmad-Bhāgavatam.*

TEXT 26

राजर्षीणां जनयिता शास्ता चोत्पथगामिनाम् ।
निग्रहीता कलेरेष भुवो धर्मस्य कारणात् ॥२६॥

rājarṣīṇāṁ janayitā
śāstā cotpatha-gāminām
nigrahītā kaler eṣa
bhuvo dharmasya kāraṇāt

rāja-ṛṣīṇām—of kings as good as sages; *janayitā*—producer; *śāstā*—chastiser; *ca*—and; *utpatha-gāminām*—of the upstarts; *nigrahītā*—molester; *kaleḥ*—of the quarrelsome; *eṣaḥ*—this; *bhuvaḥ*—of the world; *dharmasya*—of religion; *kāraṇāt*—on account of.

TRANSLATION

This child will be the father of kings who will be like sages. For world peace and for the sake of religion, he will be the chastiser of the upstarts and the quarrelsome.

PURPORT

The wisest man in the world is a devotee of the Lord. The sages are called wise men, and there are different types of wise men for different branches of knowledge. Unless, therefore, the king or the head of the state is the wisest man, he cannot control all types of wise men in the state. In the line of royal succession in the family of Mahārāja Yudhiṣṭhira, all the kings, without exception, were the wisest men of their times, and so also it is foretold about Mahārāja Parīkṣit and his son Mahārāja Janamejaya, who was yet to be born. Such wise kings can become chastisers of upstarts and uprooters of Kali, or quarrelsome elements. As will be clear in the chapters ahead, Mahārāja Parīkṣit wanted to kill the personified Kali, who was attempting to kill a cow, the emblem of peace and religion. The symptoms of Kali are (1) wine, (2) women, (3) gambling and (4) slaughterhouses. Wise rulers of all states should take lessons from Mahārāja Parīkṣit in how to maintain peace and morality by subduing the upstarts and quarrelsome people who indulge in wine, illicit connection with women, gambling and meat-eating supplied by regularly maintained slaughterhouses. In this age of Kali, regular license is issued for maintaining all of these different departments of quarrel. So how can they expect peace and morality in the state? The state fathers, therefore, must follow the principles of becoming wiser by devotion to the Lord, by chastising the breaker of discipline and by uprooting the symptoms of quarrel, as mentioned above. If we want blazing fire, we must use dry fuel. Blazing fire and moist fuel go ill together. Peace and morality can prosper only by the principles of Mahārāja Parīkṣit and his followers.

TEXT 27

तक्षकादात्मनो मृत्युं द्विजपुत्रोपसर्जितात् ।
प्रपत्स्यत उपश्रुत्य मुक्तसङ्गः पदं हरेः ॥२७॥

takṣakād ātmano mṛtyuṁ
dvija-putropasarjitāt
prapatsyata upaśrutya
mukta-saṅgaḥ padaṁ hareḥ

takṣakāt—by the snakebird; *ātmanaḥ*—of his personal self; *mṛtyum*—death; *dvija-putra*—the son of a *brāhmaṇa; upasarjitāt*—being sent by; *prapatsyate*—having taken shelter of; *upaśrutya*—after hearing; *mukta-saṅgaḥ*—freed from all attachment; *padam*—position; *hareḥ*—of the Lord.

TRANSLATION

After hearing about his death, which will be caused by the bite of a snakebird sent by a son of a brāhmaṇa, he will get himself freed from all material attachment and surrender unto the Personality of Godhead, taking shelter of Him.

PURPORT

Material attachment and taking shelter of the lotus feet of the Lord go ill together. Material attachment means ignorance of transcendental happiness under the shelter of the Lord. Devotional service to the Lord, while existing in the material world, is a way to practice one's transcendental relation with the Lord, and when it is matured, one gets completely free from all material attachment and becomes competent to go back home, back to Godhead. Mahārāja Parīkṣit, being especially attached to the Lord from the beginning of his body in the womb of his mother, was continuously under the shelter of the Lord, and the so-called warning of his death within seven days from the date of the curse by the *brāhmaṇa's* son was a boon to him to enable him to prepare himself to go back home, back to Godhead. Since he was always protected by the Lord, he could have avoided the effect of such a curse by the grace of the Lord, but he did not take such undue advantage for nothing. Rather, he made the best use of a bad bargain. For seven days continuously he heard *Śrīmad-Bhāgavatam* from the right source, and thus he got shelter at the lotus feet of the Lord by that opportunity.

TEXT 28

जिज्ञासितात्मयाथार्थ्यो मुनेर्व्याससुतादसौ ।
हित्वेदं नृप गङ्गायां यास्यत्यद्धाकुतोभयम् ॥२८॥

jijñāsitātma-yāthārthyo
muner vyāsa-sutād asau
hitvedaṁ nṛpa gaṅgāyāṁ
yāsyaty addhākutobhayam

jijñāsita—having inquired of; *ātma-yāthārthyaḥ*—right knowledge of one's own self; *muneḥ*—from the learned philosopher; *vyāsa-sutāt*—the son of Vyāsa; *asau*—he; *hitvā*—quitting; *idam*—this material attachment; *nṛpa*—O King; *gaṅgāyām*—on the bank of the Ganges; *yāsyati*—will go; *addhā*—directly; *akutaḥ-bhayam*—the life of fearlessness.

TRANSLATION

After inquiring about proper self-knowledge from the son of Vyāsadeva, who will be a great philosopher, he will renounce all material attachment and achieve a life of fearlessness.

PURPORT

Material knowledge means ignorance of the knowledge of one's own self. Philosophy means to seek after the right knowledge of one's own self, or the knowledge of self-realization. Without self-realization, philosophy is dry speculation or a waste of time and energy. *Śrīmad-Bhāgavatam* gives the right knowledge of one's own self, and by hearing *Śrīmad-Bhāgavatam* one can get free from material attachment and enter into the kingdom of fearlessness. This material world is fearfulness. Its prisoners are always fearful as within a prison house. In the prison house no one can violate the jail rules and regulations, and violating the rules means another term for extension of prison life. Similarly, we in this material existence are always fearful. This fearfulness is called anxiety. Everyone in the material life, in all species and varieties of life, is full of anxieties, either by breaking or without breaking the laws of nature. Liberation, or *mukti,* means getting relief from these constant anxieties. This is possible only when the anxiety is changed to the devotional service of the Lord. *Śrīmad-Bhāgavatam* gives us the chance to change the quality of anxiety from matter to spirit. This is done in the association of a learned philosopher like the self-realized Śukadeva Gosvāmī, the great son of Śrī Vyāsadeva. Mahārāja Parīkṣit, after receiving warning of his death, took advantage of this opportunity by association with Śukadeva Gosvāmī and achieved the desired result.

There is a sort of imitation of this reciting and hearing of *Śrīmad-Bhāgavatam* by professional men, and their foolish audience thinks that they will get free from the clutches of material attachment and attain the life of fearlessness. Such imitative hearing of *Śrīmad-Bhāgavatam* is a caricature only, and one should not be misled by such a performance of *bhāgavatam saptāha* undertaken by ridiculous greedy fellows to maintain an establishment of material enjoyment.

TEXT 29

इति राज्ञ उपादिश्य विप्रा जातककोविदाः ।
लब्धापचितयः सर्वे प्रतिजग्मुः स्वकान् गृहान् ॥२९॥

iti rājña upādiśya
viprā jātaka-kovidāḥ
labdhāpacitayaḥ sarve
pratijagmuḥ svakān gṛhān

iti—thus; *rājñe*—unto the King; *upādiśya*—having advised; *viprāḥ*—persons well versed in the *Vedas; jātaka-kovidāḥ*—persons expert in astrology and in the performance of birth ceremonies; *labdha-apacitayaḥ*—those who had received sumptuously as remuneration; *sarve*—all of them; *pratijagmuḥ*—went back; *svakān*—their own; *gṛhān*—houses.

TRANSLATION

Thus those who were expert in astrological knowledge and in performance of the birth ceremony instructed King Yudhiṣṭhira about the future history of his child. Then, being sumptuously remunerated, they all returned to their respective homes.

PURPORT

The *Vedas* are the storehouse of knowledge, both material and spiritual. But such knowledge aims at perfection of self-realization. In other words, the *Vedas* are the guides for the civilized man in every respect. Since human life is the opportunity to get free from all material miseries, it is properly guided by the knowledge of the *Vedas,* in the matters of both material needs and spiritual salvation. The specific intelligent class of men who were devoted particularly to the knowledge of the *Vedas* were called the *vipras,* or the graduates of the Vedic knowledge. There are different branches of knowledge in the *Vedas,* of which astrology and pathology are two important branches necessary for the common man. So the intelligent men, generally known as the *brāhmaṇas,* took up all the different branches of Vedic knowledge to guide society. Even the department of military education (*Dhanur-veda*) was also taken up by such intelligent men, and the *vipras* were also teachers of this section of knowledge, as were Droṇācārya, Kṛpācārya, etc.

The word *vipra* mentioned herein is significant. There is a little difference between the *vipras* and the *brāhmaṇas.* The *vipras* are those who are expert in *karma-kāṇḍa,* or fruitive activities, guiding the society towards fulfilling the material necessities of life, whereas the *brāhmaṇas* are expert in spiritual knowledge of transcendence. This department of knowledge is called *jñāna-kāṇḍa,* and above this there is the *upāsanā-kāṇḍa.* The culmination of *upāsanā-kāṇḍa* is the devotional service of the Lord Viṣṇu, and when the *brāhmaṇas* achieve perfection, they are called Vaiṣṇavas. Viṣṇu worship is the highest of the modes of worship. Elevated *brāhmaṇas* are Vaiṣṇavas engaged in the transcendental loving service of the Lord, and thus *Śrīmad-Bhāgavatam,* which is the science of devotional service, is very dear to the Vaiṣṇavas. And as explained in the beginning of the *Śrīmad-Bhāgavatam,* it is the mature fruit of Vedic knowledge and is superior subject matter, above the three *kāṇḍas,* namely *karma, jñāna* and *upāsanā.*

Amongst the *karma-kāṇḍa* experts, the *jātaka* expert *vipras* were good astrologers who could tell all the future history of a born child simply by the astral calculations of the time (*lagna*). Such expert *jātaka-vipras* were present during the birth of Mahārāja Parīkṣit, and his grandfather, Mahārāja Yudhiṣṭhira, awarded the *vipras* sufficiently with gold, land, villages, grains and other valuable necessaries of life, which also include cows. There is a need of such *vipras* in the social structure, and it is the duty of the state to maintain them comfortably, as designed in the Vedic procedure. Such expert *vipras,* being sufficiently paid by the state, could give free service to the people in general, and thus this department of Vedic knowledge could be available for all.

TEXT 30

स एष लोके विख्यातः परीक्षिदिति यत्प्रभुः ।
पूर्वं दृष्टमनुध्यायन् परीक्षेत नरेष्विह ॥३०॥

sa eṣa loke vikhyātaḥ
parīkṣid iti yat prabhuḥ
pūrvaṁ dṛṣṭam anudhyāyan
parīkṣeta nareṣv iha

saḥ—he; *eṣaḥ*—in this; *loke*—world; *vikhyātaḥ*—famous; *parīkṣit*—one who examines; *iti*—thus; *yat*—what; *prabhuḥ*—O my King; *pūrvam*—before; *dṛṣṭam*—seen; *anudhyāyan*—constantly contemplating; *parīkṣeta*—shall examine; *nareṣu*—unto every man; *iha*—here.

TRANSLATION

So his son would become famous in the world as Parīkṣit [examiner] because he would come to examine all human beings in his search after that personality whom he saw before his birth. Thus he would come to constantly contemplate Him.

PURPORT

Mahārāja Parīkṣit, fortunate as he was, got the impression of the Lord even in the womb of his mother, and thus his contemplation on the Lord was constantly with him. Once the impression of the transcendental form of the Lord is fixed in one's mind, one can never forget Him in any circumstance. Child Parīkṣit, after coming out of the womb, was in the habit of examining everyone to see whether he was the same personality whom he first saw in the womb. But no one could be equal to or more attractive than the Lord, and therefore he never accepted anyone. But the Lord was constantly with him by such examination, and thus Mahārāja Parīkṣit was always engaged in the devotional service of the Lord by remembrance.

Śrīla Jīva Gosvāmī remarks in this connection that every child, if given an impression of the Lord from his very childhood, certainly becomes a great devotee of the Lord like Mahārāja Parīkṣit. One may not be as fortunate as Mahārāja Parīkṣit to have the opportunity to see the Lord in the womb of his mother, but even if he is not so fortunate, he can be made so if the parents of the child desire him to be so. There is a practical example in my personal life in this connection. My father was a pure devotee of the Lord, and when I was only four or five years old, my father gave me a couple of forms of Rādhā and Kṛṣṇa. In a playful manner, I used to worship these Deities along with my sister, and I used to imitate the performances of a neighboring temple of Rādhā-Govinda. By constantly visiting this neighboring temple and copying the ceremonies in connection with my own Deities of play, I developed a natural affinity for the Lord. My father used to observe all the ceremonies befitting my position. Later on, these activities were suspended due to my association in the schools and colleges, and I became completely out of practice. But in my youthful days, when I met my spiritual master, Śrī Śrīmad Bhaktisiddhānta Sarasvatī Gosvāmī Mahārāja, again I revived my old habit, and the same playful Deities became my worshipful Deities in proper regulation. This was followed up until I left the family connection, and I am pleased that my generous father gave the first impression which was developed later into regulative devotional service by His Divine Grace. Mahārāja Prahlāda also advised that such impressions of a godly relation must be impregnated from the beginning of childhood; otherwise one may miss the opportunity of the human form of life, which is very valuable although it is temporary like others.

TEXT 31

स राजपुत्रो ववृधे आशु शुक्ल इवोडुपः ।
आपूर्यमाणः पितृभिः काष्ठाभिरिव सोऽन्वहम् ॥३१॥

sa rāja-putro vavṛdhe
āśu śukla ivoḍupaḥ
āpūryamāṇaḥ pitṛbhiḥ
kāṣṭhābhir iva so 'nvaham

saḥ—that; *rāja-putraḥ*—the royal prince; *vavṛdhe*—grew up; *āśu*—very soon; *śukle*—waxing moon; *iva*—like; *uḍupaḥ*—the moon; *āpūryamāṇaḥ*—luxuriantly; *pitṛbhiḥ*—by the parental guardians; *kāṣṭhābhiḥ*—plenary development; *iva*—like; *saḥ*—he; *anvaham*—day after day.

TRANSLATION

As the moon, in its waxing fortnight, develops day after day, so the royal prince [Parīkṣit] very soon developed luxuriantly under the care and full facilities of his guardian grandfathers.

TEXT 32

यक्ष्यमाणोऽश्वमेधेन ज्ञातिद्रोहजिहासया ।
राजा लब्धधनो दध्यौ नान्यत्र करदण्डयोः ॥३२॥

yakṣyamāṇo 'śvamedhena
jñāti-droha-jihāsayā
rājā labdha-dhano dadhyau
nānyatra kara-daṇḍayoḥ

yakṣyamāṇaḥ—desiring to perform; *aśvamedhena*—by the horse sacrifice ceremony; *jñāti-droha*—fighting with kinsmen; *jihāsayā*—for getting free; *rājā*—King Yudhiṣṭhira; *labdha-dhanaḥ*—for getting some wealth; *dadhyau*—thought about it; *na anyatra*—not otherwise; *kara-daṇḍayoḥ*—taxes and fines.

TRANSLATION

Just at this time, King Yudhiṣṭhira was considering performing a horse sacrifice to get freed from sins incurred from fighting with kinsmen. But he became anxious to get some wealth, for there were no surplus funds outside of fines and tax collection.

PURPORT

As the *brāhmaṇas* and *vipras* had a right to be subsidized by the state, the state executive head had the right to collect taxes and fines from the citizens. After the Battle of Kurukṣetra the state treasury was exhausted, and therefore there was no surplus fund except the fund from tax collection and fines. Such funds were sufficient only for the state budget, and having no excess fund, the King was anxious to get more wealth in some other way in order to perform the horse sacrifice. Mahārāja Yudhiṣṭhira wanted to perform this sacrifice under the instruction of Bhīṣmadeva.

TEXT 33

तदभिप्रेतमालक्ष्य भ्रातरोऽच्युतचोदिताः ।
धनं प्रहीणमाजह्रुरुदीच्यां दिशि भूरिशः ॥३३॥

tad abhipretam ālakṣya
bhrātaro 'cyuta-coditāḥ

dhanaṁ prahīṇam ājahrur
udīcyāṁ diśi bhūriśaḥ

tat—his; *abhipretam*—wishes of the mind; *ālakṣya*—observing; *bhrātaraḥ*—his brothers; *acyuta*—the infallible (Lord Śrī Kṛṣṇa); *coditāḥ*—being advised by; *dhanam*—riches; *prahīṇam*—to collect; *ājahruḥ*—brought about; *udīcyām*—northern; *diśi*—direction; *bhūriśaḥ*—sufficient.

TRANSLATION

Understanding the hearty wishes of the King, his brothers, as advised by the infallible Lord Kṛṣṇa, collected sufficient riches from the north [left by King Marutta].

PURPORT

Mahārāja Marutta: one of the great emperors of the world. He reigned over the world long before the reign of Mahārāja Yudhiṣṭhira. He was the son of Mahārāja Avikṣit and was a great devotee of the son of the sun-god, known as Yamarāja. His brother Samvarta was a rival priest of the great Bṛhaspati, the learned priest of the demigods. He conducted one sacrifice called Saṅkara-yajña by which the Lord was so satisfied that He was pleased to hand over to him the charge of a mountain peak of gold. This peak of gold is somewhere in the Himalaya Mountains, and modern adventurers may try to find it there. He was so powerful an emperor that at the day's end of sacrifice, the demigods from the other planets like Indra, Candra and Bṛhaspati used to visit his palace. And because he had the gold peak at his disposal, he had sufficient gold in his possession. The canopy of the sacrificial altar was completely made of gold. In his daily performances of the sacrificial ceremonies, some of the inhabitants of the Vāyuloka (airy planets) were invited to expedite the cooking work of the ceremony. And the assembly of the demigods in the ceremony was led by Viśvadeva.

By his constant pious work he was able to drive out all kinds of diseases from the jurisdiction of his kingdom. All the inhabitants of higher planets like Devaloka and Pitṛloka were pleased with him for his great sacrificial ceremonies. Every day he used to give in charity to the learned *brāhmaṇas* such things as beddings, seats, conveyances and sufficient quantities of gold. Because of munificent charities and performances of innumerable sacrifices, the King of heaven, Indradeva, was fully satisfied with him and always wished for his welfare. Due to his pious activities, he remained a young man throughout his life and reigned over the world for one thousand years, surrounded by his satisfied subjects, ministers, legitimate wife, sons and brothers. Even Lord Śrī Kṛṣṇa praised his spirit of pious activities. He handed over his only daughter to Maharṣi Aṅgirā, and by his good blessings, he was elevated to the kingdom of heaven. First of all, he wanted to offer the priesthood of his sacrifices to learned Bṛhaspati, but the demigod refused to accept the post because of the King's being a human being, a man of this earth. He was very sorry for this, but on the advice of Nārada Muni he appointed Samvarta to the post, and he was successful in his mission.

The success of a particular type of sacrifice completely depends on the priest in charge. In this age, all kinds of sacrifice are forbidden because there is no learned priest amongst the so-called *brāhmaṇas,* who go by the false notion of becoming sons of *brāhmaṇas* without brahminical qualifications. In this age of Kali, therefore, only one kind of sacrifice is recommended, *saṅkīrtana-yajña,* as inaugurated by Lord Śrī Caitanya Mahāprabhu.

TEXT 34

तेन सम्भृतसम्भारो धर्मपुत्रो युधिष्ठिरः ।
वाजिमेधैस्त्रिभिर्भीतो यज्ञैः समयजद्धरिम् ॥३४॥

tena sambhṛta-sambhāro
dharma-putro yudhiṣṭhiraḥ
vājimedhais tribhir bhīto
yajñaiḥ samayajad dharim

tena—with that wealth; *sambhṛta*—collected; *sambhāraḥ*—ingredients; *dharma-putraḥ*—the pious king; *yudhiṣṭhiraḥ*—Yudhiṣṭhira; *vājimedhaiḥ*—by horse sacrifices; *tribhiḥ*—three times; *bhītaḥ*—being greatly afraid after the Battle of Kurukṣetra; *yajñaiḥ*—sacrifices; *samayajat*—perfectly worshiped; *harim*—the Personality of Godhead.

TRANSLATION

By those riches, the King could procure the ingredients for three horse sacrifices. Thus the pious King Yudhiṣṭhira, who was very fearful after the Battle of Kurukṣetra, pleased Lord Hari, the Personality of Godhead.

PURPORT

Mahārāja Yudhiṣṭhira was the ideal and celebrated pious King of the world, and still he was greatly afraid after the execution of the Battle of

Kurukṣetra because of the mass killing in the fight, all of which was done only to install him on the throne. He therefore took all the responsibility for sins committed in the warfare, and to get rid of all these sins, he wanted to perform three sacrifices in which horses are offered at the altar. Such a sacrifice is very costly. Even Mahārāja Yudhiṣṭhira had to collect the necessary heaps of gold left by Mahārāja Marutta and the *brāhmaṇas* who were given gold in charity by King Marutta. The learned *brāhmaṇas* could not take away all the loads of gold given by Mahārāja Marutta, and therefore they left behind the major portion of the gift. And Mahārāja Marutta also did not again collect such heaps of gold given away in charity. Besides that, all the golden plates and utensils which were used in the sacrifice were also thrown in the dustbins, and all such heaps of gold remained unclaimed property for a long time, till Mahārāja Yudhiṣṭhira collected them for his own purposes. Lord Śrī Kṛṣṇa advised the brothers of Mahārāja Yudhiṣṭhira to collect the unclaimed property because it belonged to the King. The more astonishing thing is that no subject of the state also collected such unclaimed gold for industrial enterprise or anything like that. This means that the state citizens were completely satisfied with all necessities of life and therefore not inclined to accept unnecessary productive enterprises for sense gratification. Mahārāja Yudhiṣṭhira also requisitioned the heaps of gold for performing sacrifices and for pleasing the Supreme Hari Personality of Godhead. Otherwise he had no desire to collect them for the state treasury.

One should take lessons from the acts of Mahārāja Yudhiṣṭhira. He was afraid of sins committed on the battlefield, and therefore he wanted to satisfy the supreme authority. This indicates that unintentional sins are also committed in our daily occupational discharge of duties, and to counteract even such unintentional crimes, one must perform sacrifices as they are recommended in the revealed scriptures. The Lord says in *Bhagavad-gītā* (*yajñārthāt karmaṇo 'nyatra loko 'yaṁ karma-bandhanaḥ*) that one must perform sacrifices recommended in the scriptures in order to get rid of commitments of all unauthorized work, or even unintentional crimes which we are apt to commit. By doing so, one shall be freed from all kinds of sins. And those who do not do so but work for self-interest or sense gratification have to undergo all tribulations accrued from committed sins. Therefore, the main purpose of performing sacrifices is to satisfy the Supreme Personality Hari. The process of performing sacrifices may be different in terms of different times, places and persons, but the aim of such sacrifices is one and the same at all times and in all circumstances, viz., satisfaction of the Supreme

Lord Hari. That is the way of pious life, and that is the way of peace and prosperity in the world at large. Mahārāja Yudhiṣṭhira did all these as the ideal pious king in the world.

If Mahārāja Yudhiṣṭhira is a sinner in his daily discharge of duties, in royal administration of state affairs, wherein killing of man and animals is a recognized art, then we can just imagine the amount of sins committed consciously or unconsciously by the untrained population of the Kali-yuga who have no way to perform sacrifice to please the Supreme Lord. The *Bhāgavatam* says, therefore, that the prime duty of the human being is to satisfy the Supreme Lord by the performance of one's occupational duty (*Bhāg.* 1.2.13).

Let any man of any place or community, caste or creed be engaged in any sort of occupational duty, but he must agree to perform sacrifices as it is recommended in the scriptures for the particular place, time and person. In the Vedic literatures it is recommended that in Kali-yuga people engage in glorifying the Lord by chanting the holy name of Kṛṣṇa (*kīrtanād eva kṛṣṇasya mukta-saṅgaḥ paraṁ vrajet*) without offense. By doing so one can be freed from all sins and thus can attain the highest perfection of life by returning home, back to Godhead. We have already discussed this more than once in this great literature in different places, especially in the introductory portion by sketching the life of Lord Śrī Caitanya Mahāprabhu, and still we are repeating the same with a view to bring about peace and prosperity in society.

The Lord has declared openly in *Bhagavad-gītā* how He becomes pleased with us, and the same process is practically demonstrated in the life and preaching work of Lord Śrī Caitanya Mahāprabhu. The perfect process of performing *yajñas,* or sacrifice, to please the Supreme Lord Hari (the Personality of Godhead, who gets us free from all miseries of existence) is to follow the ways of Lord Śrī Caitanya Mahāprabhu in this dark age of quarrel and dissension.

Mahārāja Yudhiṣṭhira had to collect heaps of gold to secure the paraphernalia for the horse sacrifice *yajñas* in days of sufficiency, so we can hardly think of such performance of *yajñas* in these days of insufficiency and complete scarcity of gold. At the present moment we have heaps of papers and promises of their being converted into gold by economic development of modern civilization, and still there is no possibility of spending riches like Mahārāja Yudhiṣṭhira, either individually or collectively or by state patronization. Just suitable, therefore, for the age is the method recommended by Lord Śrī Caitanya Mahāprabhu in terms of the *śāstra.* Such a method requires no expenditure at all and yet can award more benefit than other expensive methods of *yajña* performances.

The horse sacrifice *yajña* or cow sacrifice *yajña* performed by the Vedic regulations shouldn't be misunderstood as a process of killing animals. On the contrary, animals offered for the *yajña* were rejuvenated to a new span of life by the transcendental power of chanting the Vedic hymns, which, if properly chanted, are different from what is understood by the common layman. The *Veda-mantras* are all practical, and the proof is rejuvenation of the sacrificed animal.

There is no possibility of such methodical chanting of the Vedic hymns by the so-called *brāhmaṇas* or priests of the present age. The untrained descendants of the twice-born families are no more like their forefathers, and thus they are counted amongst the *śūdras,* or once-born men. The once-born man is unfit to chant the Vedic hymns, and therefore there is no practical utility of chanting the original hymns.

And to save them all, Lord Śrī Caitanya Mahāprabhu propounded the *saṅkīrtana* movement or *yajña* for all practical purposes, and the people of the present age are strongly recommended to follow this sure and recognized path.

TEXT 35

आहूतो भगवान् राज्ञा याजयित्वा द्विजैर्नृपम् ।
उवास कतिचिन्मासान् सुहृदां प्रियकाम्यया ॥३५॥

āhūto bhagavān rājñā
yājayitvā dvijair nṛpam
uvāsa katicin māsān
suhṛdāṁ priya-kāmyayā

āhūtaḥ—being called by; *bhagavān*—Lord Kṛṣṇa, the Personality of Godhead; *rājñā*—by the King; *yājayitvā*—causing to be performed; *dvijaiḥ*—by the learned *brāhmaṇas; nṛpam*—on behalf of the King; *uvāsa*—resided; *katicit*—a few; *māsān*—months; *suhṛdām*—for the sake of the relatives; *priya-kāmyayā*—for the pleasure.

TRANSLATION

Lord Śrī Kṛṣṇa, the Personality of Godhead, being invited to the sacrifices by Mahārāja Yudhiṣṭhira, saw to it that they were performed by qualified [twice-born] brāhmaṇas. After that, for the pleasure of the relatives, the Lord remained a few months.

PURPORT

Lord Śrī Kṛṣṇa was invited by Mahārāja Yudhiṣṭhira to look into the supervision of the performances of *yajña,* and the Lord, to abide by the orders of His elderly cousin, caused the performance of *yajñas* by learned twice-born *brāhmaṇas.* Simply taking birth in the family of a *brāhmaṇa* does not make one qualified to perform *yajñas.* One must be twice-born by proper training and initiation from the bona fide *ācārya.* The once-born scions of *brāhmaṇa* families are equal with the once-born *śūdras,* and such *brahma-bandhus,* or unqualified once-born scions, must be rejected for any purpose of religious or Vedic function. Lord Śrī Kṛṣṇa was entrusted to look after this arrangement, and perfect as He is, He caused the *yajñas* to be performed by the bona fide twice-born *brāhmaṇas* for successful execution.

TEXT 36

ततो राज्ञाभ्यनुज्ञातः कृष्णया सह बन्धुभिः ।
ययौ द्वारवतीं ब्रह्मन् सार्जुनो यदुभिर्वृतः ॥३६॥

tato rājñābhyanujñātaḥ
kṛṣṇayā saha-bandhubhiḥ
yayau dvāravatīṁ brahman
sārjuno yadubhir vṛtaḥ

tataḥ—thereafter; *rājñā*—by the King; *abhyanujñātaḥ*—being permitted; *kṛṣṇayā*—as well as by Draupadī; *saha*—along with; *bandhubhiḥ*—other relatives; *yayau*—went to; *dvāravatīm*—Dvārakā-dhāma; *brahman*—O *brāhmaṇas; sa-arjunaḥ*—along with Arjuna; *yadubhiḥ*—by the members of the Yadu dynasty; *vṛtaḥ*—surrounded.

TRANSLATION

O Śaunaka, thereafter the Lord, having bade farewell to King Yudhiṣṭhira, Draupadī and other relatives, started for the city of Dvārakā, accompanied by Arjuna and other members of the Yadu dynasty.

Thus end the Bhaktivedanta purports of the First Canto, Twelfth Chapter, of the Śrīmad-Bhāgavatam, *entitled "Birth of Emperor Parīkṣit."*

CHAPTER THIRTEEN

Dhṛtarāṣṭra Quits Home

TEXT 1

सूत उवाच
विदुरस्तीर्थयात्रायां मैत्रेयादात्मनो गतिम् ।
ज्ञात्वागाद्धास्तिनपुरं तयावाप्तविवित्सितः ॥१॥

sūta uvāca
viduras tīrtha-yātrāyāṁ
maitreyād ātmano gatim
jñātvāgād dhāstinapuraṁ
tayāvāpta-vivitsitaḥ

sūtaḥ uvāca—Śrī Sūta Gosvāmī said; *viduraḥ*—Vidura; *tīrtha-yātrāyām*—while traveling to different places of pilgrimage; *maitreyāt*—from the great sage Maitreya; *ātmanaḥ*—of the self; *gatim*—destination; *jñātvā*—by knowing it; *āgāt*—went back; *hāstinapuram*—the city of Hastināpura; *tayā*—by that knowledge; *avāpta*—sufficiently a gainer; *vivitsitaḥ*—being well versed in everything knowable.

TRANSLATION

Śrī Sūta Gosvāmī said: While traveling on a pilgrimage, Vidura received knowledge of the destination of the self from the great sage Maitreya and then returned to Hastināpura. He became as well versed in the subject as he desired.

PURPORT

Vidura: One of the prominent figures in the history of the *Mahābhārata.* He was conceived by Vyāsadeva in the womb of the maidservant of Ambikā, mother of Mahārāja Pāṇḍu. He is the incarnation of Yamarāja. Being cursed by Maṇḍūka Muni, he was to become a *śūdra.* The story is narrated as follows. Once upon a time the state police caught some thieves who had concealed themselves in the hermitage of Maṇḍūka Muni. The police constables, as usual, arrested all the thieves and Maṇḍūka Muni along with them. The magistrate specifically punished the *muni* to death by being pierced with a lance. When he was just to be pierced, the news reached the king, and he at once stopped the act on consideration of his being a great *muni.* The king personally begged the *muni's* pardon for the mistake of his men, and the saint at once went to Yamarāja, who prescribes the destiny of the living beings. Yamarāja, being questioned by the *muni,* replied that the *muni* in his childhood pierced an ant with a sharpened straw, and for that reason he was put into difficulty. The *muni* thought it unwise on the part of Yamarāja that he was punished for his childish innocence, and thus the *muni* cursed Yamarāja to become a *śūdra,* and this *śūdra* incarnation of Yamarāja was known as Vidura, the *śūdra* brother of Dhṛtarāṣṭra and Mahārāja Pāṇḍu. But this *śūdra* son of the Kuru dynasty was equally treated by Bhīṣmadeva, along with his other nephews, and in due course Vidura was married with a girl who was also born in the womb of a *śūdrāṇī* by a *brāhmaṇa.* Although Vidura did not inherit the property of his father (the brother of Bhīṣmadeva), still he was given sufficient state property by Dhṛtarāṣṭra, the elder brother of Vidura. Vidura was very much attached to his elder brother, and all along he tried to guide him on the right path. During the fratricidal war of Kurukṣetra, Vidura repeatedly implored his elder brother to do justice to the sons of Pāṇḍu, but Duryodhana did not like such interference by his uncle, and thus he practically insulted Vidura. This resulted in Vidura's leaving home for pilgrimage and taking instructions from Maitreya.

TEXT 2

यावतः कृतवान् प्रश्नान् क्षत्ता कौषारवाग्रतः ।
जातैकभक्तिर्गोविन्दे तेभ्यश्चोपरराम ह ॥२॥

yāvataḥ kṛtavān praśnān
kṣattā kauṣāravāgrataḥ
jātaika-bhaktir govinde
tebhyaś copararāma ha

yāvataḥ—all that; *kṛtavān*—did he put; *praśnān*—questions; *kṣattā*—a name of Vidura; *kauṣārava*—a name of Maitreya; *agrataḥ*—in the presence of; *jāta*—having grown up; *eka*—one; *bhaktiḥ*—transcendental loving service; *govinde*—unto Lord Kṛṣṇa; *tebhyaḥ*—regarding further questions; *ca*—and; *uparарāma*—retired from; *ha*—in the past.

TRANSLATION

After asking various questions and becoming established in the transcendental loving service of Lord Kṛṣṇa, Vidura retired from putting questions to Maitreya Muni.

PURPORT

Vidura retired from putting questions before Maitreya Muni when he was convinced by Maitreya Ṛṣi that the *summum bonum* of life is to be finally situated in the transcendental loving service of Lord Śrī Kṛṣṇa, who is Govinda, or one who satisfies His devotees in all respects. The conditioned soul, the living being in material existence, seeks happiness by employing his senses in the modes of materialism, but that cannot give him satisfaction. He then searches after the Supreme Truth by the empiric philosophic speculative method and intellectual feats. But if he does not find the ultimate goal, he again goes down to material activities and engages himself in various philanthropic and altruistic works, which all fail to give him satisfaction. So neither fruitive activities nor dry philosophical speculation can give one satisfaction because by nature a living being is the eternal servitor of the Supreme Lord Śrī Kṛṣṇa, and all the Vedic literatures give him direction towards that ultimate end. The *Bhagavad-gītā* (15.15) confirms this statement.

Like Vidura, an inquisitive conditioned soul must approach a bona fide spiritual master like Maitreya and by intelligent inquiries must try to know everything about *karma* (fruitive activities), *jñāna* (philosophical research for the Supreme Truth) and *yoga* (the linking process of spiritual realization). One who is not seriously inclined to put questions before a spiritual master need not accommodate a show-bottle spiritual master, nor should a person who may be a spiritual master for others pose to be so if he is unable to engage his disciple ultimately in the transcendental loving service of Lord Śrī Kṛṣṇa. Vidura was successful in approaching such a spiritual master like Maitreya, and he got the ultimate goal of life: *bhakti* unto Govinda. Thus there was nothing to be known further about spiritual progress.

TEXTS 3–4

तं बन्धुमागतं दृष्ट्वा धर्मपुत्रः सहानुजः ।
धृतराष्ट्रो युयुत्सुश्च सूतः शारद्वतः पृथा ॥३॥

गान्धारी द्रौपदी ब्रह्मन् सुभद्रा चोत्तरा कृपी ।
अन्याश्च जामयः पाण्डोर्ज्ञातयः ससुताः स्त्रियः ॥४॥

taṁ bandhum āgataṁ dṛṣṭvā
dharma-putraḥ sahānujaḥ
dhṛtarāṣṭro yuyutsuś ca
sūtaḥ śāradvataḥ pṛthā

gāndhārī draupadī brahman
subhadrā cottarā kṛpī
anyāś ca jāmayaḥ pāṇḍor
jñātayaḥ sasutāḥ striyaḥ

tam—him; *bandhum*—relative; *āgatam*—having arrived there; *dṛṣṭvā*—by seeing it; *dharma-putraḥ*—Yudhiṣṭhira; *saha-anujaḥ*—along with his younger brothers; *dhṛtarāṣṭraḥ*—Dhṛtarāṣṭra; *yuyutsuḥ*—Sātyaki; *ca*—and; *sūtaḥ*—Sañjaya; *śāradvataḥ*—Kṛpācārya; *pṛthā*—Kuntī; *gāndhārī*—Gāndhārī; *draupadī*—Draupadī; *brahman*—O *brāhmaṇas; subhadrā*—Subhadrā; *ca*—and; *uttarā*—Uttarā; *kṛpī*—Kṛpī; *anyāḥ*—others; *ca*—and; *jāmayaḥ*—wives of other family members; *pāṇḍoḥ*—of the Pāṇḍavas; *jñātayaḥ*—family members; *sa-sutāḥ*—along with their sons; *striyaḥ*—the ladies.

TRANSLATION

When they saw Vidura return to the palace, all the inhabitants—Mahārāja Yudhiṣṭhira, his younger brothers, Dhṛtarāṣṭra, Sātyaki, Sañjaya, Kṛpācārya, Kuntī, Gāndhārī, Draupadī, Subhadrā, Uttarā, Kṛpī, many other wives of the Kauravas, and other ladies with children—all hurried to him in great delight. It so appeared that they had regained their consciousness after a long period.

PURPORT

Gāndhārī: The ideal chaste lady in the history of the world. She was the daughter of Mahārāja Subala, the King of Gāndhāra (now Kandahar in Kabul), and in her maiden state she worshiped Lord Śiva. Lord Śiva is generally worshiped by Hindu maidens to get a good husband. Gāndhārī satisfied Lord Śiva, and by his benediction to obtain one hundred sons, she was betrothed to Dhṛtarāṣṭra, despite his being blind forever. When Gāndhārī came to know that her would-be husband was a blind man, to follow her life companion she decided to become voluntarily blind. So she wrapped up her eyes with many silk linens, and she was married to Dhṛtarāṣṭra under the guidance of her elder brother Śakuni. She was the most beautiful girl of her time, and she was equally qualified by her womanly qualities, which endeared every member of the Kaurava court. But despite all her good qualities, she had the natural frailties of a woman, and she was envious of Kuntī when the latter gave birth to a male child. Both the queens were pregnant, but Kuntī first gave birth to a male child. Thus Gāndhārī became angry and gave a blow to her own abdomen. As a result, she gave birth to a lump of flesh only, but since she was a devotee of Vyāsadeva, by the instruction of Vyāsadeva the lump was divided into one hundred parts, and each part gradually developed to become a male child. Thus her ambition to become the mother of one hundred sons was fulfilled, and she began to nourish all the children according to her exalted position. When the intrigue of the Battle of Kurukṣetra was going on, she was not in favor of fighting with the Pāṇḍavas; rather, she blamed Dhṛtarāṣṭra, her husband, for such a fratricidal war. She desired that the state be divided into two parts, for the sons of Pāṇḍu and her own. She was very affected when all her sons died in the Battle of Kurukṣetra, and she wanted to curse Bhīmasena and Yudhiṣṭhira, but she was checked by Vyāsadeva. Her mourning over the death of Duryodhana and Duḥśāsana before Lord Kṛṣṇa was very pitiful, and Lord Kṛṣṇa pacified her by transcendental messages. She was equally aggrieved on the death of Karṇa, and she described to Lord Kṛṣṇa the lamentation of Karṇa's wife. She was pacified by Śrīla Vyāsadeva when he showed her dead sons, then promoted to the heavenly kingdoms. She died along with her husband in the jungles of the Himalayas near the mouth of the Ganges; she burned in a forest fire. Mahārāja Yudhiṣṭhira performed the death ceremony of his uncle and aunt.

Pṛthā: Daughter of Mahārāja Śūrasena and sister of Vasudeva, Lord Kṛṣṇa's father. Later she was adopted by Mahārāja Kuntibhoja, and hence she is known as Kuntī. She is the incarnation of the success potency of the Personality of Godhead. The heavenly denizens from the upper planets used to visit the palace of King Kuntibhoja, and Kuntī was engaged for their reception. She also served the great mystic sage Durvāsā, and being satisfied by her faithful service, Durvāsā Muni gave her a *mantra* by which it was possible for her to call for any demigod she pleased. As a matter of inquisitiveness, she at once called for the sun-god, who desired couplement with her, but she declined. But the sun-god assured her immunity from virgin adulteration, and so she agreed to his proposal. As a result of this couplement, she became pregnant, and Karṇa was born by her. By the grace of the sun, she again turned into a virgin girl, but being afraid of her parents, she quitted the newly born child, Karṇa. After that, when she actually selected her own husband, she preferred Pāṇḍu to be her husband. Mahārāja Pāṇḍu later wanted to retire from family life and adopt the renounced order of life. Kuntī refused to allow her husband to adopt such life, but at last Mahārāja Pāṇḍu gave her permission to become a mother of sons by calling some other suitable personalities. Kuntī did not accept this proposal at first, but when vivid examples were set by Pāṇḍu she agreed. Thus by dint of the *mantra* awarded by Durvāsā Muni she called for Dharmarāja, and thus Yudhiṣṭhira was born. She called for the demigod Vāyu (air), and thus Bhīma was born. She called for Indra, the King of heaven, and thus Arjuna was born. The other two sons, namely Nakula and Sahadeva, were begotten by Pāṇḍu himself in the womb of Mādrī. Later on, Mahārāja Pāṇḍu died at an early age, for which Kuntī was so aggrieved that she fainted. Two co-wives, namely Kuntī and Mādrī, decided that Kuntī should live for the maintenance of the five minor children, the Pāṇḍavas, and Mādrī should accept the *satī* rituals by meeting voluntary death along with her husband. This agreement was endorsed by great sages like Śatasṛṅga and others present on the occasion.

Later on, when the Pāṇḍavas were banished from the kingdom by the intrigues of Duryodhana, Kuntī followed her sons, and she equally faced all sorts of difficulties during those days. During the forest life one demon girl, Hiḍimbā, wanted Bhīma as her husband. Bhīma refused, but when the girl approached Kuntī and Yudhiṣṭhira, they ordered Bhīma to accept her proposal and give her a son. As a result of this combination, Ghaṭotkaca was born, and he fought very valiantly with his father against the Kauravas. In their forest life they lived with a *brāhmaṇa* family that was in trouble because of one Bakāsura demon, and Kuntī ordered Bhīma to kill the Bakāsura to protect the *brāhmaṇa* family against troubles created by the demon. She advised Yudhiṣṭhira to start for the Pāñcāladeśa. Draupadī was gained in this Pāñcāladeśa by Arjuna, but by order of Kuntī all five of the Pāṇḍava brothers became equally the husbands of Pāñcālī, or Draupadī. She was married with five Pāṇḍavas in the presence of Vyāsadeva. Kuntīdevī never forgot her first child, Karṇa, and after Karṇa's death in the Battle of Kurukṣetra she lamented and admitted before her other sons that Karṇa was her eldest son prior to her marriage with Mahārāja Pāṇḍu. Her prayers for the Lord after the Battle of Kurukṣetra, when Lord Kṛṣṇa was going back home, are excellently explained. Later she went to the forest with

Gāndhārī for severe penance. She used to take meals after each thirty days. She finally sat down in profound meditation and later burned to ashes in a forest fire.

Draupadī: The most chaste daughter of Mahārāja Drupada and partly an incarnation of goddess Śacī, the wife of Indra. Mahārāja Drupada performed a great sacrifice under the superintendence of the sage Yaja. By his first offering, Dhṛṣṭadyumna was born, and by the second offering, Draupadī was born. She is therefore the sister of Dhṛṣṭadyumna, and she is also named Pāñcālī. The five Pāṇḍavas married her as a common wife, and each of them begot a son in her. Mahārāja Yudhiṣṭhira begot a son named Pratibhit, Bhīmasena begot a son named Sutasoma, Arjuna begot Śrutakīrti, Nakula begot Śatānīka, and Sahadeva begot Śrutakarmā. She is described as a most beautiful lady, equal to her mother-in-law, Kuntī. During her birth there was an aeromessage that she should be called Kṛṣṇā. The same message also declared that she was born to kill many a *kṣatriya.* By dint of her blessings from Śaṅkara, she was awarded five husbands, equally qualified. When she preferred to select her own husband, princes and kings were invited from all the countries of the world. She was married with the Pāṇḍavas during their exile in the forest, but when they went back home Mahārāja Drupada gave them immense wealth as a dowry. She was well received by all the daughters-in-law of Dhṛtarāṣṭra. When she was lost in a gambling game, she was forcibly dragged into the assembly hall, and an attempt was made by Duḥśāsana to see her naked beauty, even though there were elderly persons like Bhīṣma and Droṇa present. She was a great devotee of Lord Kṛṣṇa, and by her praying, the Lord Himself became an unlimited garment to save her from the insult. A demon of the name Jaṭāsura kidnapped her, but her second husband, Bhīmasena, killed the demon and saved her. She saved the Pāṇḍavas from the curse of Maharṣi Durvāsā by the grace of Lord Kṛṣṇa. When the Pāṇḍavas lived incognito in the palace of Virāṭa, Kīcaka was attracted by her exquisite beauty, and by arrangement with Bhīma the devil was killed and she was saved. She was very much aggrieved when her five sons were killed by Aśvatthāmā. At the last stage, she accompanied her husband Yudhiṣṭhira and others and fell on the way. The cause of her falling was explained by Yudhiṣṭhira, but when Yudhiṣṭhira entered the heavenly planet he saw Draupadī gloriously present there as the goddess of fortune in the heavenly planet.

Subhadrā: Daughter of Vasudeva and sister of Lord Śrī Kṛṣṇa. She was not only a very dear daughter of Vasudeva, but also a very dear sister to both Kṛṣṇa and Baladeva. The two brothers and sister are represented in the famous

Jagannātha temple of Purī, and the temple is still visited by thousands of pilgrims daily. This temple is in remembrance of the Lord's visit at Kurukṣetra during an occasion of solar eclipse and His subsequent meeting with the residents of Vṛndāvana. The meeting of Rādhā and Kṛṣṇa during this occasion is a very pathetic story, and Lord Śrī Caitanya, in the ecstasy of Rādhārāṇī, always pined for Lord Śrī Kṛṣṇa at Jagannātha Purī. While Arjuna was at Dvārakā, he wanted to have Subhadrā as his queen, and he expressed his desire to Lord Kṛṣṇa. Śrī Kṛṣṇa knew that His elder brother, Lord Baladeva, was arranging her marriage elsewhere, and since He did not dare to go against the arrangement of Baladeva, He advised Arjuna to kidnap Subhadrā. So when all of them were on a pleasure trip on the Raivata Hill, Arjuna managed to kidnap Subhadrā according to the plan of Śrī Kṛṣṇa. Śrī Baladeva was very angry at Arjuna, and He wanted to kill him, but Lord Kṛṣṇa implored His brother to excuse Arjuna. Then Subhadrā was duly married with Arjuna, and Abhimanyu was born of Subhadrā. At the premature death of Abhimanyu, Subhadrā was very mortified, but on the birth of Parīkṣit she was happy and solaced.

TEXT 5

प्रत्युज्जग्मुः प्रहर्षेण प्राणं तन्व इवागतम् ।
अभिसङ्गम्य विधिवत् परिष्वङ्गाभिवादनैः ॥५॥

pratyujjagmuḥ praharṣeṇa
prāṇaṁ tanva ivāgatam
abhisaṅgamya vidhivat
pariṣvaṅgābhivādanaiḥ

prati—towards; *ujjagmuḥ*—went; *praharṣeṇa*—with great delight; *prāṇam*—life; *tanvaḥ*—of the body; *iva*—like; *āgatam*—returned; *abhisaṅgamya*—approaching; *vidhi-vat*—in due form; *pariṣvaṅga*—embracing; *abhivādanaiḥ*—by obeisances.

TRANSLATION

With great delight they all approached him, as if life had returned to their bodies. They exchanged obeisances and welcomed each other with embraces.

PURPORT

In the absence of consciousness, the limbs of the body remain inactive. But when consciousness returns, the limbs and senses become active, and existence itself becomes delightful. Vidura was so dear to the members of the Kaurava family that his long absence from the palace was comparable to inactivity. All of them were feeling acute separation from Vidura, and therefore his return to the palace was joyful for all.

TEXT 6

मुमुचुः प्रेमबाष्पौघं विरहौत्कण्ठ्यकातराः ।
राजा तमर्हयाञ्चक्रे कृतासनपरिग्रहम् ॥६॥

mumucuḥ prema-bāṣpaughaṁ
virahautkaṇṭhya-kātarāḥ
rājā tam arhayāṁ cakre
kṛtāsana-parigraham

mumucuḥ—emanated; *prema*—affectionate; *bāṣpa-ogham*—emotional tears; *viraha*—separation; *autkaṇṭhya*—anxiousness; *kātarāḥ*—being aggrieved; *rājā*—King Yudhiṣṭhira; *tam*—unto him (Vidura); *arhayām cakre*—offered; *kṛta*—performance of; *āsana*—sitting accommodations; *parigraham*—arrangement of.

TRANSLATION

Due to anxieties and long separation, they all cried out of affection. King Yudhiṣṭhira then arranged to offer sitting accommodations and a reception.

TEXT 7

तं भुक्तवन्तं विश्रान्तमासीनं सुखमासने ।
प्रश्रयावनतो राजा प्राह तेषां च शृण्वताम् ॥७॥

taṁ bhuktavantaṁ viśrāntam
āsīnaṁ sukham āsane
praśrayāvanato rājā
prāha teṣāṁ ca śṛṇvatām

tam—him (Vidura); *bhuktavantam*—after feeding him sumptuously; *viśrāntam*—and having taken rest; *āsīnam*—being seated; *sukham āsane*—on a comfortable seat; *praśraya-avanataḥ*—naturally very gentle and meek; *rājā*—King Yudhiṣṭhira; *prāha*—began to speak; *teṣām ca*—and by them; *śṛṇvatām*—being heard.

TRANSLATION

After Vidura ate sumptuously and took sufficient rest, he was comfortably seated. Then the King began to speak to him, and all who were present there listened.

PURPORT

King Yudhiṣṭhira was expert in reception also, even in the case of his family members. Vidura was well received by all the family members by exchange of embraces and obeisances. After that, bathing and arrangements for a sumptuous dinner were made, and then he was given sufficient rest. After finishing his rest, he was offered a comfortable place to sit, and then the King began to talk about all happenings, both family and otherwise. That is the proper way to receive a beloved friend, or even an enemy. According to Indian moral codes, even an enemy received at home should be so well received that he will not feel any fearful situation. An enemy is always afraid of his enemy, but this should not be so when he is received at home by his enemy. This means that a person, when received at home, should be treated as a relative, so what to speak of a family member like Vidura, who was a well-wisher for all the members of the family. Thus Yudhiṣṭhira Mahārāja began to speak in the presence of all the other members.

TEXT 8

युधिष्ठिर उवाच

अपि स्मरथ नो युष्मत्पक्षच्छायासमेधितान् ।
विपद्गणाद्विषाग्न्यादेर्मोचिता यत्समातृकाः ॥८॥

yudhiṣṭhira uvāca
api smaratha no yuṣmat-
pakṣa-cchāyā-samedhitān
vipad-gaṇād viṣāgnyāder
mocitā yat samātṛkāḥ

yudhiṣṭhiraḥ uvāca—Mahārāja Yudhiṣṭhira said; *api*—whether; *smaratha*—you remember; *naḥ*—us; *yuṣmat*—from you; *pakṣa*—partiality towards us like the wings of a bird; *chāyā*—protection; *samedhitān*—we who were brought up by you; *vipat-gaṇāt*—from various types of calamities; *viṣa*—by administration of poison; *agni-ādeḥ*—by setting on fire; *mocitāḥ*—

released from; *yat*—what you have done; *sa*—along with; *mātṛkāḥ*—our mother.

TRANSLATION

Mahārāja Yudhiṣṭhira said: My uncle, do you remember how you always protected us, along with our mother, from all sorts of calamities? Your partiality, like the wings of a bird, saved us from poisoning and arson.

PURPORT

Due to Pāṇḍu's death at an early age, his minor children and widow were the object of special care by all the elderly members of the family, especially Bhīṣmadeva and Mahātmā Vidura. Vidura was more or less partial to the Pāṇḍavas due to their political position. Although Dhṛtarāṣṭra was equally careful for the minor children of Mahārāja Pāṇḍu, he was one of the intriguing parties who wanted to wash away the descendants of Pāṇḍu and replace them by raising his own sons to become the rulers of the kingdom. Mahātmā Vidura could follow this intrigue of Dhṛtarāṣṭra and company, and therefore, even though he was a faithful servitor of his eldest brother, Dhṛtarāṣṭra, he did not like his political ambition for the sake of his own sons. He was therefore very careful about the protection of the Pāṇḍavas and their widow mother. Thus he was, so to speak, partial to the Pāṇḍavas, preferring them to the sons of Dhṛtarāṣṭra, although both of them were equally affectionate in his ordinary eyes. He was equally affectionate to both the camps of nephews in the sense that he always chastised Duryodhana for his intriguing policy against his cousins. He always criticized his elder brother for his policy of encouragement to his sons, and at the same time he was always alert in giving special protection to the Pāṇḍavas. All these different activities of Vidura within the palace politics made him well known as partial to the Pāṇḍavas. Mahārāja Yudhiṣṭhira has referred to the past history of Vidura before his going away from home for a prolonged pilgrim's journey. Mahārāja Yudhiṣṭhira reminded him that he was equally kind and partial to his grown-up nephews, even after the Battle of Kurukṣetra, a great family disaster.

Before the Battle of Kurukṣetra, Dhṛtarāṣṭra's policy was peaceful annihilation of his nephews, and therefore he ordered Purocana to build a house at Vāraṇāvata, and when the building was finished Dhṛtarāṣṭra desired that his brother's family live there for some time. When the Pāṇḍavas were going there in the presence of all the members of the royal family, Vidura tactfully gave instructions to the Pāṇḍavas about the future plan of Dhṛtarāṣṭra. This is specifically described in the *Mahābhārata* (*Ādi-parva* 114). He indirectly hinted, "A weapon not made of steel or any other material element can be more than sharp to kill an enemy, and he who knows this is never killed." That is to say, he hinted that the party of the Pāṇḍavas was being sent to Vāraṇāvata to be killed, and thus he warned Yudhiṣṭhira to be very careful in their new residential palace. He also gave indications of fire and said that fire cannot extinguish the soul but can annihilate the material body. But one who protects the soul can live. Kuntī could not follow such indirect conversations between Mahārāja Yudhiṣṭhira and Vidura, and thus when she inquired from her son about the purport of the conversation, Yudhiṣṭhira replied that from the talks of Vidura it was understood that there was a hint of fire in the house where they were proceeding. Later on, Vidura came in disguise to the Pāṇḍavas and informed them that the housekeeper was going to set fire to the house on the fourteenth night of the waning moon. It was an intrigue of Dhṛtarāṣṭra that the Pāṇḍavas might die all together with their mother. And by his warning the Pāṇḍavas escaped through a tunnel underneath the earth so that their escape was also unknown to Dhṛtarāṣṭra, so much so that after setting the fire, the Kauravas were so certain of the death of the Pāṇḍavas that Dhṛtarāṣṭra performed the last rites of death with great cheerfulness. And during the mourning period all the members of the palace became overwhelmed with lamentation, but Vidura did not become so, because of his knowledge that the Pāṇḍavas were alive somewhere. There are many such instances of calamities, and in each of them Vidura gave protection to the Pāṇḍavas on one hand, and on the other he tried to restrain his brother Dhṛtarāṣṭra from such intriguing policies. Therefore, he was always partial to the Pāṇḍavas, just as a bird protects its eggs by its wing.

TEXT 9

कया वृत्त्या वर्तितं वश्चरद्भिः क्षितिमण्डलम् ।
तीर्थानि क्षेत्रमुख्यानि सेवितानीह भूतले ॥९॥

kayā vṛttyā vartitaṁ vaś
caradbhiḥ kṣiti-maṇḍalam
tīrthāni kṣetra-mukhyāni
sevitānīha bhūtale

kayā—by which; *vṛttyā*—means; *vartitam*—maintained your livelihood; *vaḥ*—your good self; *caradbhiḥ*—while traveling; *kṣiti-maṇḍalam*—on the surface of the earth; *tīrthāni*—places of pilgrimage; *kṣetra-mukhyāni*—the principal holy places; *sevitāni*—served by you; *iha*—in this world; *bhūtale*—on this planet.

TRANSLATION

While traveling on the surface of the earth, how did you maintain your livelihood? At which holy places and pilgrimage sites did you render service?

PURPORT

Vidura went out from the palace to detach himself from household affairs, especially political intrigues. As referred to hereinbefore, he was practically insulted by Duryodhana's calling him a son of a *śūdrāṇī,* although it was not out of place to talk loosely in the case of one's grandmother. Vidura's mother, although a *śūdrāṇī,* was the grandmother of Duryodhana, and funny talks are sometimes allowed between grandmother and grandchildren. But because the remark was an actual fact, it was unpalatable talk to Vidura, and it was accepted as a direct insult. He therefore decided to quit his paternal house and prepare for the renounced order of life. This preparatory stage is called *vānaprastha-āśrama,* or retired life for traveling and visiting the holy places on the surface of the earth. In the holy places of India, like Vṛndāvana, Hardwar, Jagannātha Purī, and Prayāga, there are many great devotees, and there are still free kitchen houses for persons who desire to advance spiritually. Mahārāja Yudhiṣṭhira was inquisitive to learn whether Vidura maintained himself by the mercy of the free kitchen houses (*chatras*).

TEXT 10

भवद्विधा भागवतास्तीर्थभूताः स्वयं विभो ।
तीर्थीकुर्वन्ति तीर्थानि स्वान्तःस्थेन गदाभृता ॥१०॥

bhavad-vidhā bhāgavatās
tīrtha-bhūtāḥ svayaṁ vibho
tīrthī-kurvanti tīrthāni
svāntaḥ-sthena gadābhṛtā

bhavat—your good self; *vidhāḥ*—like, *bhāgavatāḥ*—devotees; *tīrtha*—the holy places of pilgrimage; *bhūtāḥ*—converted into; *svayam*—personally; *vibho*—O powerful one; *tīrthī-kurvanti*—make into a holy place of pilgrimage; *tīrthāni*—the holy places; *sva-antaḥ-sthena*—having been situated in the heart; *gadā-bhṛtā*—the Personality of Godhead.

TRANSLATION

My Lord, devotees like your good self are verily holy places personified. Because you carry the Personality of Godhead within your heart, you turn all places into places of pilgrimage.

PURPORT

The Personality of Godhead is omnipresent by His diverse potencies everywhere, just as the power of electricity is distributed everywhere within space. Similarly, the Lord's omnipresence is perceived and manifested by His unalloyed devotees like Vidura, just as electricity is manifested in an electric bulb. A pure devotee like Vidura always feels the presence of the Lord everywhere. He sees everything in the potency of the Lord and the Lord in everything. The holy places all over the earth are meant for purifying the polluted consciousness of the human being by an atmosphere surcharged with the presence of the Lord's unalloyed devotees. If anyone visits a holy place, he must search out the pure devotees residing in such holy places, take lessons from them, try to apply such instructions in practical life and thus gradually prepare oneself for the ultimate salvation, going back to Godhead. To go to some holy place of pilgrimage does not mean only to take a bath in the Ganges or Yamunā or to visit the temples situated in those places. One should also find representatives of Vidura who have no desire in life save and except to serve the Personality of Godhead. The Personality of Godhead is always with such pure devotees because of their unalloyed service, which is without any tinge of fruitive action or utopian speculation. They are in the actual service of the Lord, specifically by the process of hearing and chanting. The pure devotees hear from the authorities and chant, sing and write of the glories of the Lord. Mahāmuni Vyāsadeva heard from Nārada, and then he chanted in writing; Śukadeva Gosvāmī studied from his father, and he described it to Parīkṣit; that is the way of *Śrīmad-Bhāgavatam*. So by their actions the pure devotees of the Lord can render any place into a place of pilgrimage, and the holy places are worth the name only on their account. Such pure devotees are able to rectify the polluted atmosphere of any place, and what to speak of a holy place rendered unholy by the questionable actions of interested persons who try to adopt a professional life at the cost of the reputation of a holy place.

TEXT 11

अपि नः सुहृदस्तात बान्धवाः कृष्णदेवताः ।
दृष्टाः श्रुता वा यदवः स्वपुर्यां सुखमासते ॥११॥

api naḥ suhṛdas tāta
bāndhavāḥ kṛṣṇa-devatāḥ
dṛṣṭāḥ śrutā vā yadavaḥ
sva-puryāṁ sukham āsate

api—whether; *naḥ*—our; *suhṛdaḥ*—well-wishers; *tāta*—O my uncle; *bāndhavāḥ*—friends; *kṛṣṇa-devatāḥ*—those who are always rapt in the service of Lord Śrī Kṛṣṇa; *dṛṣṭāḥ*—by seeing them; *śrutāḥ*—or by hearing about them; *vā*—either; *yadavaḥ*—the descendants of Yadu; *sva-puryām*—along with their residential place; *sukham āsate*—if they are all happy.

TRANSLATION

My uncle, you must have visited Dvārakā. In that holy place are our friends and well-wishers, the descendants of Yadu, who are always rapt in the service of the Lord Śrī Kṛṣṇa. You might have seen them or heard about them. Are they all living happily in their abodes?

PURPORT

The particular word *kṛṣṇa-devatāḥ,* i.e., those who are always rapt in the service of Lord Kṛṣṇa, is significant. The Yādavas and the Pāṇḍavas, who were always rapt in the thought of the Lord Kṛṣṇa and His different transcendental activities, were all pure devotees of the Lord like Vidura. Vidura left home in order to devote himself completely to the service of the Lord, but the Pāṇḍavas and the Yādavas were always rapt in the thought of Lord Kṛṣṇa. Thus there is no difference in their pure devotional qualities. Either remaining at home or leaving home, the real qualification of a pure devotee is to become rapt in the thought of Kṛṣṇa favorably, i.e., knowing well that Lord Kṛṣṇa is the Absolute Personality of Godhead. Kaṁsa, Jarāsandha, Śiśupāla and other demons like them were also always rapt in the thought of Lord Kṛṣṇa, but they were absorbed in a different way, namely unfavorably, or thinking Him to be a powerful man only. Therefore, Kaṁsa and Śiśupāla are not on the same level as pure devotees like Vidura, the Pāṇḍavas and the Yādavas.

Mahārāja Yudhiṣṭhira was also always rapt in the thought of Lord Kṛṣṇa and His associates at Dvārakā. Otherwise he could not have asked all about them from Vidura. Mahārāja Yudhiṣṭhira was therefore on the same level of devotion as Vidura, although engaged in the state affairs of the kingdom of the world.

TEXT 12

इत्युक्तो धर्मराजेन सर्वं तत् समवर्णयत् ।
यथानुभूतं क्रमशो विना यदुकुलक्षयम् ॥१२॥

ity ukto dharma-rājena
sarvaṁ tat samavarṇayat
yathānubhūtaṁ kramaśo
vinā yadu-kula-kṣayam

iti—thus; *uktaḥ*—being asked; *dharma-rājena*—by King Yudhiṣṭhira; *sarvam*—all; *tat*—that; *samavarṇayat*—properly described; *yathā-anubhūtam*—as he experienced; *kramaśaḥ*—one after another; *vinā*—without; *yadu-kula-kṣayam*—annihilation of the Yadu dynasty.

TRANSLATION

Thus being questioned by Mahārāja Yudhiṣṭhira, Mahātmā Vidura gradually described everything he had personally experienced, except news of the annihilation of the Yadu dynasty.

TEXT 13

नन्वप्रियं दुर्विषहं नृणां स्वयमुपस्थितम् ।
नावेदयत् सकरुणो दुःखितान् द्रष्टुमक्षमः ॥१३॥

nanv apriyaṁ durviṣahaṁ
nṛṇāṁ svayam upasthitam
nāvedayat sakaruṇo
duḥkhitān draṣṭum akṣamaḥ

nanu—as a matter of fact; *apriyam*—unpalatable; *durviṣaham*—unbearable; *nṛṇām*—of humankind; *svayam*—in its own way; *upasthitam*—appearance; *na*—did not; *āvedayat*—expressed; *sakaruṇaḥ*—compassionate; *duḥkhitān*—distressed; *draṣṭum*—to see; *akṣamaḥ*—unable.

TRANSLATION

Compassionate Mahātmā Vidura could not stand to see the Pāṇḍavas distressed at any time. Therefore he did not disclose this unpalatable and unbearable incident because calamities come of their own accord.

PURPORT

According to *Nīti-śāstra* (civic laws) one should not speak an unpalatable truth to cause distress to others. Distress comes upon us in its own way by the laws of nature, so one should not aggravate it by propaganda. For a compassionate soul like Vidura, especially in his dealings with the beloved Pāṇḍavas, it was almost impossible to disclose an unpalatable piece of news like the annihilation of the Yadu dynasty. Therefore he purposely refrained from it.

TEXT 14

कञ्चित्कालमथावात्सीत्सत्कृतो देववत्सुखम् ।
भ्रातुर्ज्येष्ठस्य श्रेयस्कृत्सर्वेषां सुखमावहन् ॥१४॥

kañcit kālam athāvātsīt
sat-kṛto devavat sukham
bhrātur jyeṣṭhasya śreyas-kṛt
sarveṣāṁ sukham āvahan

kañcit—for a few days; *kālam*—time; *atha*—thus; *avātsīt*—resided; *sat-kṛtaḥ*—being well treated; *deva-vat*—just like a godly personality; *sukham*—amenities; *bhrātuḥ*—of the brother; *jyeṣṭhasya*—of the elder; *śreyaḥ-kṛt*—for doing good to him; *sarveṣām*—all others; *sukham*—happiness; *āvahan*—made it possible.

TRANSLATION

Thus Mahātmā Vidura, being treated just like a godly person by his kinsmen, remained there for a certain period just to rectify the mentality of his eldest brother and in this way bring happiness to all the others.

PURPORT

Saintly persons like Vidura must be treated as well as a denizen from heaven. In those days denizens of heavenly planets used to visit homes like that of Mahārāja Yudhiṣṭhira, and sometimes persons like Arjuna and others used to visit higher planets. Nārada is a spaceman who can travel unrestrictedly, not only within the material universes but also in the spiritual universes. Even Nārada used to visit the palace of Mahārāja Yudhiṣṭhira and what to speak of other celestial demigods. It is only the spiritual culture of the people concerned that makes interplanetary travel possible, even in the present body. Mahārāja Yudhiṣṭhira therefore received Vidura in the manner of reception offered to the demigods.

Mahātmā Vidura had already adopted the renounced order of life, and therefore he did not return to his paternal palace to enjoy some material comforts. He accepted out of his own mercy what was offered to him by Mahārāja Yudhiṣṭhira, but the purpose of living in the palace was to deliver his elder brother, Dhṛtarāṣṭra, who was too much materially attached. Dhṛtarāṣṭra lost all his state and descendants in the fight with Mahārāja Yudhiṣṭhira, and still, due to his sense of helplessness, he did not feel ashamed to accept the charity and hospitality of Mahārāja Yudhiṣṭhira. On the part of Mahārāja Yudhiṣṭhira, it was quite in order to maintain his uncle in a befitting manner, but acceptance of such magnanimous hospitality by Dhṛtarāṣṭra was not at all desirable. He accepted it because he thought that there was no alternative. Vidura particularly came to enlighten Dhṛtarāṣṭra and to give him a lift to the higher status of spiritual cognition. It is the duty of enlightened souls to deliver the fallen ones, and Vidura came for that reason. But talks of spiritual enlightenment are so refreshing that while instructing Dhṛtarāṣṭra, Vidura attracted the attention of all the members of the family, and all of them took pleasure in hearing him patiently. This is the way of spiritual realization. The message should be heard attentively, and if spoken by a realized soul, it will act on the dormant heart of the conditioned soul. And by continuously hearing, one can attain the perfect stage of self-realization.

TEXT 15

अबिभ्रदर्यमा दण्डं यथावदघकारिषु ।
यावद्दधार शूद्रत्वं शापाद्वर्षशतं यमः ॥१५॥

abibhrad aryamā daṇḍaṁ
yathāvad agha-kāriṣu
yāvad dadhāra śūdratvaṁ
śāpād varṣa-śataṁ yamaḥ

-dministered; *aryamā*—Aryamā; *daṇḍam*—punishment; -uitable; *agha-kāriṣu*—unto persons who had committed sins; *yāvat*—as long as; *dadhāra*—accepted; *śūdratvam*—the tabernacle of a *śūdra; śāpāt*—as the result of a curse; *varṣa-śatam*—for one hundred years; *yamaḥ*—Yamarāja.

TRANSLATION

As long as Vidura played the part of a śūdra, being cursed by Maṇḍūka Muni, Aryamā officiated at the post of Yamarāja to punish those who committed sinful acts.

PURPORT

Vidura, born in the womb of a *śūdra* woman, was forbidden even to be a party of royal heritage along with his brothers Dhṛtarāṣṭra and Pāṇḍu. Then how could he occupy the post of a preacher to instruct such learned kings and *kṣatriyas* as Dhṛtarāṣṭra and Mahārāja Yudhiṣṭhira? The first answer is that even though it is accepted that he was a *śūdra* by birth, because he renounced the world for spiritual enlightenment by the authority of Ṛṣi Maitreya and was thoroughly educated by him in transcendental knowledge, he was quite competent to occupy the post of an *ācārya,* or spiritual preceptor. According to Śrī Caitanya Mahāprabhu, anyone who is conversant in the transcendental knowledge, or the science of Godhead, be he a *brāhmaṇa* or a *śūdra,* a householder or a *sannyāsī,* is eligible to become a spiritual master. Even in the ordinary moral codes (maintained by Cāṇakya Paṇḍita, the great politician and moralist) there is no harm in taking lessons from a person who may be by birth less than a *śūdra.* This is one part of the answer. The other is that Vidura was not actually a *śūdra.* He was to play the part of a so-called *śūdra* for one hundred years, being cursed by Maṇḍūka Muni. He was the incarnation of Yamarāja, one of the twelve *mahājanas,* on the level with such exalted personalities as Brahmā, Nārada, Śiva, Kapila, Bhīṣma, Prahlāda, etc. Being a *mahājana,* it is the duty of Yamarāja to preach the cult of devotion to the people of the world, as Nārada, Brahmā, and other *mahājanas* do. But Yamarāja is always busy in his plutonic kingdom punishing the doers of sinful acts. Yamarāja is deputed by the Lord to a particular planet, some hundreds of thousands of miles away from the planet of earth, to take away the corrupt souls after death and convict them in accordance with their respective sinful activities. Thus Yamarāja has very little time to take leave from his responsible office of punishing the wrongdoers. There are more wrongdoers than righteous men. Therefore Yamarāja has to do more work than other demigods who are also authorized agents of the Supreme Lord. But he wanted to preach the glories of the Lord, and therefore by the will of the Lord he was cursed by Maṇḍūka Muni to come into the world in the incarnation of Vidura and work very hard as a great devotee. Such a devotee is neither a *śūdra* nor a *brāhmaṇa.* He is transcendental to such divisions of mundane society, just as the Personality of Godhead assumes His incarnation as a hog, but He is neither a hog nor a Brahmā. He is above all mundane creatures. The Lord and His different authorized devotees sometimes have to play the role of many lower creatures to claim the conditioned souls, but both the Lord and His pure devotees are always in the transcendental position. When Yamarāja thus incarnated himself as Vidura, his post was officiated by Aryamā, one of the many sons of Kaśyapa and Aditi. The Ādityas are sons of Aditi, and there are twelve Ādityas. Aryamā is one of the twelve Ādityas, and therefore it was quite possible for him to take charge of the office of Yamarāja during his one hundred years' absence in the form of Vidura. The conclusion is that Vidura was never a *śūdra,* but was greater than the purest type of *brāhmaṇa.*

TEXT 16

युधिष्ठिरो लब्धराज्यो दृष्ट्वा पौत्रं कुलन्धरम् ।
भ्रातृभिर्लोकपालाभैर्मुमुदे परया श्रिया ॥१६॥

yudhiṣṭhiro labdha-rājyo
dṛṣṭvā pautraṁ kulan-dharam
bhrātṛbhir loka-pālābhair
mumude parayā śriyā

yudhiṣṭhiraḥ—Yudhiṣṭhira; *labdha-rājyaḥ*—possessing his paternal kingdom; *dṛṣṭvā*—by seeing; *pautram*—the grandson; *kulam-dharam*—just suitable for the dynasty; *bhrātṛbhiḥ*—by the brothers; *loka-pālābhaiḥ*—who were all expert administrators; *mumude*—enjoyed life; *parayā*—uncommon; *śriyā*—opulence.

TRANSLATION

Having won his kingdom and observed the birth of one grandson competent to continue the noble tradition of his family, Mahārāja Yudhiṣṭhira reigned peacefully and enjoyed uncommon opulence in cooperation with his younger brothers, who were all expert administrators to the common people.

PURPORT

Both Mahārāja Yudhiṣṭhira and Arjuna were unhappy from the beginning of the Battle of Kurukṣetra, but even though they were unwilling to kill their own men in the fight, it had to be done as a matter of duty, for it was planned by the supreme will of Lord Śrī Kṛṣṇa. After the battle, Mahārāja Yudhiṣṭhira was unhappy over such mass killings. Practically there was none to continue the Kuru dynasty after them, the Pāṇḍavas. The only remaining hope was the child in the womb of his daughter-in-law, Uttarā, and he was also attacked by Aśvatthāmā, but by the grace of the Lord the child was saved. So after the settlement of all disturbing conditions and reestablishment of the peaceful order of the state, and after seeing the surviving child, Parīkṣit, well satisfied, Mahārāja Yudhiṣṭhira felt some relief as a human being, although he had very little attraction for material happiness, which is always illusory and temporary.

TEXT 17

एवं गृहेषु सक्तानां प्रमत्तानां तदीहया ।
अत्यक्रामदविज्ञातः कालः परमदुस्तरः ॥१७॥

evaṁ gṛheṣu saktānāṁ
pramattānāṁ tad-īhayā
atyakrāmad avijñātaḥ
kālaḥ parama-dustaraḥ

evam—thus; *gṛheṣu*—in the family affairs; *saktānām*—of persons who are too attached; *pramattānām*—insanely attached; *tat-īhayā*—engrossed in such thoughts; *atyakrāmat*—surpassed; *avijñātaḥ*—imperceptibly; *kālaḥ*—eternal time; *parama*—supremely; *dustaraḥ*—insurmountable.

TRANSLATION

Insurmountable, eternal time imperceptibly overcomes those who are too much attached to family affairs and are always engrossed in their thought.

PURPORT

"I am now happy; I have everything in order; my bank balance is quite enough; I can now give my children enough estate; I am now successful; the poor beggar *sannyāsīs* depend on God, but they come to beg from me; therefore I am more than the Supreme God." These are some of the thoughts which engross the insanely attached householder who is blind to the passing of eternal time. Our duration of life is measured, and no one is able to enhance it even by a second against the scheduled time ordained by the supreme will. Such valuable time, especially for the human being, should be cautiously spent because even a second passed away imperceptibly cannot be replaced, even in exchange for thousands of golden coins amassed by hard labor. Every second of human life is meant for making an ultimate solution to the problems of life, i.e., repetition of birth and death and revolving in the cycle of 8,400,000 different species of life. The material body, which is subject to birth and death, diseases and old age, is the cause of all sufferings of the living being, otherwise the living being is eternal; he is never born, nor does he ever die. Foolish persons forget this problem. They do not know at all how to solve the problems of life, but become engrossed in temporary family affairs not knowing that eternal time is passing away imperceptibly and that their measured duration of life is diminishing every second, without any solution to the big problem, namely repetition of birth and death, disease and old age. This is called illusion.

But such illusion cannot work on one who is awake in the devotional service of the Lord. Yudhiṣṭhira Mahārāja and his brothers the Pāṇḍavas were all engaged in the service of the Lord Śrī Kṛṣṇa, and they had very little attraction for the illusory happiness of this material world. As we have discussed previously, Mahārāja Yudhiṣṭhira was fixed in the service of the Lord Mukunda (the Lord, who can award salvation), and therefore he had no attraction even for such comforts of life as are available in the kingdom of heaven, because even the happiness obtained on the planet Brahmaloka is also temporary and illusory. Because the living being is eternal, he can be happy only in the eternal abode of the kingdom of God (*paravyoma*), from which no one returns to this region of repeated birth and death, disease and old age. Therefore, any comfort of life or any material happiness which does not warrant an eternal life is but illusion for the eternal living being. One who understands this factually is learned and such a learned person can sacrifice any amount of material happiness to achieve the desired goal known as *brahma-sukham,* or absolute happiness. Real transcendentalists are hungry for this happiness, and as a hungry man cannot be made happy by all comforts of life minus foodstuff, so the man hungry for eternal absolute happiness cannot be satisfied by any amount of material happiness. Therefore, the instruction described in this verse cannot be applied to Mahārāja Yudhiṣṭhira or his brothers and mother.

It was meant for persons like Dhṛtarāṣṭra, for whom Vidura came especially to impart lessons.

TEXT 18

विदुरस्तदभिप्रेत्य धृतराष्ट्रमभाषत ।
राजन्निर्गम्यतां शीघ्रं पश्येदं भयमागतम् ॥१८॥

viduras tad abhipretya
dhṛtarāṣṭram abhāṣata
rājan nirgamyatāṁ śīghraṁ
paśyedaṁ bhayam āgatam

viduraḥ—Mahātmā Vidura; *tat*—that; *abhipretya*—knowing it well; *dhṛtarāṣṭram*—unto Dhṛtarāṣṭra; *abhāṣata*—said; *rājan*—O King; *nirgamyatām*—please get out immediately; *śīghram*—without the least delay; *paśya*—just see; *idam*—this; *bhayam*—fear; *āgatam*—already arrived.

TRANSLATION

Mahātmā Vidura knew all this, and therefore he addressed Dhṛtarāṣṭra, saying: My dear King, please get out of here immediately. Do not delay. Just see how fear has overtaken you.

PURPORT

Cruel death cares for none, be he Dhṛtarāṣṭra or even Mahārāja Yudhiṣṭhira; therefore spiritual instruction, as was given to old Dhṛtarāṣṭra, was equally applicable to younger Mahārāja Yudhiṣṭhira. As a matter of fact, everyone in the royal palace, including the King and his brothers and mother, was raptly attending the lectures. But it was known to Vidura that his instructions were especially meant for Dhṛtarāṣṭra, who was too materialistic. The word *rājan* is especially addressed to Dhṛtarāṣṭra significantly. Dhṛtarāṣṭra was the eldest son of his father, and therefore according to law he was to be installed on the throne of Hastināpura. But because he was blind from birth, he was disqualified from his rightful claim. But he could not forget the bereavement, and his disappointment was somewhat compensated after the death of Pāṇḍu, his younger brother. His younger brother left behind him some minor children, and Dhṛtarāṣṭra became the natural guardian of them, but at heart he wanted to become the factual king and hand the kingdom over to his own sons, headed by Duryodhana. With all these imperial ambitions, Dhṛtarāṣṭra wanted to become a king, and he contrived all sorts of intrigues in consultation with his brother-in-law Śakuni. But everything failed by the will of the Lord, and at the last stage, even after losing everything, men and money, he wanted to remain as king, being the eldest uncle of Mahārāja Yudhiṣṭhira. Mahārāja Yudhiṣṭhira, as a matter of duty, maintained Dhṛtarāṣṭra in royal honor, and Dhṛtarāṣṭra was happily passing away his numbered days in the illusion of being a king or the royal uncle of King Yudhiṣṭhira. Vidura, as a saint and as the duty-bound affectionate youngest brother of Dhṛtarāṣṭra, wanted to awaken Dhṛtarāṣṭra from his slumber of disease and old age. Vidura therefore sarcastically addressed Dhṛtarāṣṭra as the "King," which he was actually not. Everyone is the servant of eternal time, and therefore no one can be king in this material world. King means the person who can order. The celebrated English king wanted to order time and tide, but the time and tide refused to obey his order. Therefore one is a false king in the material world, and Dhṛtarāṣṭra was particularly reminded of this false position and of the factual fearful happenings which had already approached him at that time. Vidura asked him to get out immediately, if he wanted to be saved from the fearful situation which was approaching him fast. He did not ask Mahārāja Yudhiṣṭhira in that way because he knew that a king like Mahārāja Yudhiṣṭhira is aware of all the fearful situations of this flimsy world and would take care of himself, in due course, even though Vidura might not be present at that time.

TEXT 19

प्रतिक्रिया न यस्येह कुतश्चित्कर्हिचित्प्रभो ।
स एष भगवान् कालः सर्वेषां नः समागतः ॥१९॥

pratikriyā na yasyeha
kutaścit karhicit prabho
sa eṣa bhagavān kālaḥ
sarveṣāṁ naḥ samāgataḥ

pratikriyā—remedial measure; *na*—there is none; *yasya*—of which; *iha*—in this material world; *kutaścit*—by any means; *karhicit*—or by anyone; *prabho*—O my lord; *saḥ*—that; *eṣaḥ*—positively; *bhagavān*—the Personality of Godhead; *kālaḥ*—eternal time; *sarveṣām*—of all; *naḥ*—of us; *samāgataḥ*—arrived.

TRANSLATION

This frightful situation cannot be remedied by any person in this material world. My lord, it is the Supreme Personality of Godhead as eternal time [kāla] that has approached us all.

PURPORT

There is no superior power which can check the cruel hands of death. No one wants to die, however acute the source of bodily sufferings may be. Even in the days of so-called scientific advancement of knowledge, there is no remedial measure either for old age or for death. Old age is the notice of the arrival of death served by cruel time, and no one can refuse to accept either summon calls or the supreme judgment of eternal time. This is explained before Dhṛtarāṣṭra because he might ask Vidura to find out some remedial measure for the imminent fearful situation, as he had ordered many times before. Before ordering, however, Vidura informed Dhṛtarāṣṭra that there was no remedial measure by anyone or from any source in this material world. And because there is no such thing in the material world, death is identical with the Supreme Personality of Godhead, as it is said by the Lord Himself in the *Bhagavad-gītā* (10.34).

Death cannot be checked by anyone or from any source within this material world. Hiraṇyakaśipu wanted to be immortal and underwent a severe type of penance by which the whole universe trembled, and Brahmā himself approached him to dissuade Hiraṇyakaśipu from such a severe type of penance. Hiraṇyakaśipu asked Brahmā to award him the blessings of immortality, but Brahmā said that he himself was subject to death, even in the topmost planet, so how could he award him the benediction of immortality? So there is death even in the topmost planet of this universe, and what to speak of other planets, which are far, far inferior in quality to Brahmaloka, the residing planet of Brahmā. Wherever there is the influence of eternal time, there is this set of tribulations, namely birth, disease, old age and death, and all of them are invincible.

TEXT 20

येन चैवाभिपन्नोऽयं प्राणैः प्रियतमैरपि ।
जनः सद्यो वियुज्येत किमुतान्यैर्धनादिभिः ॥२०॥

yena caivābhipanno 'yaṁ
prāṇaiḥ priyatamair api

janaḥ sadyo viyujyeta
kim utānyair dhanādibhiḥ

yena—pulled by such time; *ca*—and; *eva*—certainly; *abhipannaḥ*—overtaken; *ayam*—this; *prāṇaiḥ*—with life; *priya-tamaiḥ*—which is most dear to everyone; *api*—even though; *janaḥ*—person; *sadyaḥ*—forthwith; *viyujyeta*—do give up; *kim uta anyaiḥ*—what to speak of any other thing; *dhana-ādibhiḥ*—such as wealth, honor, children, land and house.

TRANSLATION

Whoever is under the influence of supreme kāla [eternal time] must surrender his most dear life, and what to speak of other things, such as wealth, honor, children, land and home.

PURPORT

A great Indian scientist, busy in the plan-making business, was suddenly called by invincible eternal time while going to attend a very important meeting of the planning commission, and he had to surrender his life, wife, children, house, land, wealth, etc. During the political upsurge in India and its division into Pakistan and Hindustan, so many rich and influential Indians had to surrender life, property and honor due to the influence of time, and there are hundreds and thousands of examples like that all over the world, all over the universe, which are all effects of the influence of time. Therefore, the conclusion is that there is no powerful living being within the universe who can overcome the influence of time. Many poets have written verses lamenting the influence of time. Many devastations have taken place over the universes due to the influence of time, and no one could check them by any means. Even in our daily life, so many things come and go in which we have no hand, but we have to suffer or tolerate them without remedial measure. That is the result of time.

TEXT 21

पितृभ्रातृसुहृत्पुत्रा हतास्ते विगतं वयम् ।
आत्मा च जरया ग्रस्तः परगेहमुपाससे ॥२१॥

pitṛ-bhrātṛ-suhṛt-putrā
hatās te vigataṁ vayam

ātmā ca jarayā grastaḥ
para-geham upāsase

pitṛ—father; *bhrātṛ*—brother; *suhṛt*—well-wishers; *putrāḥ*—sons; *hatāḥ* —all dead; *te*—yours; *vigatam*—expended; *vayam*—age; *ātmā*—the body; *ca*—also; *jarayā*—by invalidity; *grastaḥ*—overcome; *para-geham*—another's home; *upāsase*—you do live.

TRANSLATION

Your father, brother, well-wishers and sons are all dead and passed away. You yourself have expended the major portion of your life, your body is now overtaken by invalidity, and you are living in the home of another.

PURPORT

The King is reminded of his precarious condition, influenced by cruel time, and by his past experience he should have been more intelligent to see what was going to happen to his own life. His father, Vicitravīrya, died long ago, when he and his younger brothers were all little children, and it was due to the care and kindness of Bhīṣmadeva that they were properly brought up. Then again his brother Pāṇḍu died also. Then in the Battlefield of Kurukṣetra his one hundred sons and his grandsons all died, along with all other well-wishers like Bhīṣmadeva, Droṇācārya, Karṇa and many other kings and friends. So he had lost all men and money, and now he was living at the mercy of his nephew, whom he had put into troubles of various types. And despite all these reverses, he thought that he would prolong his life more and more. Vidura wanted to point out to Dhṛtarāṣṭra that everyone has to protect himself by his action and the grace of the Lord. One has to execute his duty faithfully, depending for the result on the supreme authority. No friend, no children, no father, no brother, no state and no one else can protect a person who is not protected by the Supreme Lord. One should, therefore, seek the protection of the Supreme Lord, for the human form of life is meant for seeking that protection. He was warned of his precarious conditions more and more by the following words.

TEXT 22

अन्धः पुरैव वधिरो मन्दप्रज्ञाश्च साम्प्रतम् ।
विशीर्णदन्तो मन्दाग्निः सरागः कफमुद्वहन् ॥२२॥

andhaḥ puraiva vadhiro
manda-prajñāś ca sāmpratam
viśīrṇa-danto mandāgniḥ
sarāgaḥ kapham udvahan

andhaḥ—blind; *purā*—from the beginning; *eva*—certainly; *vadhiraḥ*—hard of hearing; *manda-prajñāḥ*—memory shortened; *ca*—and; *sāmpratam*—recently; *viśīrṇa*—loosened; *dantaḥ*—teeth; *manda-agniḥ*—liver action decreased; *sa-rāgaḥ*—with sound; *kapham*—coughing much mucus; *udvahan*—coming out.

TRANSLATION

You have been blind from your very birth, and recently you have become hard of hearing. Your memory is shortened, and your intelligence is disturbed. Your teeth are loose, your liver is defective, and you are coughing up mucus.

PURPORT

The symptoms of old age, which had already developed in Dhṛtarāṣṭra, were all one after another pointed out to him as warning that death was nearing very quickly, and still he was foolishly carefree about his future. The signs pointed out by Vidura in the body of Dhṛtarāṣṭra were signs of *apakṣaya,* or dwindling of the material body before the last stroke of death. The body is born, it develops, stays, creates other bodies, dwindles and then vanishes. But foolish men want to make a permanent settlement of the perishable body and think that their estate, children, society, country, etc., will give them protection. With such foolish ideas, they become overtaken by such temporary engagements and forget altogether that they must give up this temporary body and take a new one, again to arrange for another term of society, friendship and love, again to perish ultimately. They forget their permanent identity and become foolishly active for impermanent occupations, forgetting altogether their prime duty. Saints and sages like Vidura approach such foolish men to awaken them to the real situation, but they take such *sādhus* and saints as parasites of society, and almost all of them refuse to hear the words of such *sādhus* and saints, although they welcome show-bottle *sādhus* and so-called saints who can satisfy their senses. Vidura was not a *sādhu* to satisfy the ill-gotten sentiment of Dhṛtarāṣṭra. He was correctly pointing out the real situation of life, and how one can save oneself from such catastrophies.

TEXT 23

अहो महीयसी जन्तोर्जीविताशा यथा भवान् ।
भीमापवर्जितं पिण्डमादत्ते गृहपालवत् ॥२३॥

aho mahīyasī jantor
jīvitāśā yathā bhavān
bhīmāpavarjitaṁ piṇḍam
ādatte gṛha-pālavat

aho—alas; *mahīyasī*—powerful; *jantoḥ*—of the living beings; *jīvita-āśā*—hope for life; *yathā*—as much as; *bhavān*—you are; *bhīma*—of Bhīmasena (a brother of Yudhiṣṭhira's); *apavarjitam*—remnants; *piṇḍam*—foodstuff; *ādatte*—eaten by; *gṛha-pāla-vat*—like a household dog.

TRANSLATION

Alas, how powerful are the hopes of a living being to continue his life. Verily, you are living just like a household dog and are eating remnants of food given by Bhīma.

PURPORT

A *sādhu* should never flatter kings or rich men to live comfortably at their cost. A *sādhu* is to speak to the householders about the naked truth of life so that they may come to their senses about the precarious life in material existence. Dhṛtarāṣṭra is a typical example of an attached old man in household life. He had become a pauper in the true sense, yet he wanted to live comfortably in the house of the Pāṇḍavas, of whom Bhīma especially is mentioned because personally he killed two prominent sons of Dhṛtarāṣṭra, namely Duryodhana and Duḥśāsana. These two sons were very much dear to him for their notorious and nefarious activities, and Bhīma is particularly pointed out because he killed these two pet sons. Why was Dhṛtarāṣṭra living there at the house of the Pāṇḍavas? Because he wanted to continue his life comfortably, even at the risk of all humiliation. Vidura, therefore, was astonished how powerful is the urge to continue life. This sense of continuing one's life indicates that a living being is eternally a living entity and does not want to change his bodily habitation. The foolish man does not know that a particular term of bodily existence is awarded to him to undergo a term of imprisonment, and the human body is awarded, after many, many births and deaths, as a chance for self-realization to go back home, back to Godhead. But persons like Dhṛtarāṣṭra try to make plans to live there in a comfortable position with profit and interest, for they do not see things as they are. Dhṛtarāṣṭra is blind and continues to hope to live comfortably in the midst of all kinds of reverses of life. A *sādhu* like Vidura is meant to awaken such blind persons and thus help them go back to Godhead, where life is eternal. Once going there, no one wants to come back to this material world of miseries. We can just imagine how responsible a task is entrusted to a *sādhu* like Mahātmā Vidura.

TEXT 24

अग्निर्निसृष्टो दत्तश्च गरो दाराश्च दूषिताः ।
हृतं क्षेत्रं धनं येषां तद्दत्तैरसुभिः कियत् ॥२४॥

agnir nisṛṣṭo dattaś ca
garo dārāś ca dūṣitāḥ
hṛtaṁ kṣetraṁ dhanaṁ yeṣāṁ
tad-dattair asubhiḥ kiyat

agniḥ—fire; *nisṛṣṭaḥ*—set; *dattaḥ*—given; *ca*—and; *garaḥ*—poison; *dārāḥ*—married wife; *ca*—and; *dūṣitāḥ*—insulted; *hṛtam*—usurped; *kṣetram*—kingdom; *dhanam*—wealth; *yeṣām*—of those; *tat*—their; *dattaiḥ*—given by; *asubhiḥ*—subsisting; *kiyat*—is unnecessary.

TRANSLATION

There is no need to live a degraded life and subsist on the charity of those whom you tried to kill by arson and poisoning. You also insulted one of their wives and usurped their kingdom and wealth.

PURPORT

The system of *varṇāśrama* religion sets aside a part of one's life completely for the purpose of self-realization and attainment of salvation in the human form of life. That is a routine division of life, but persons like Dhṛtarāṣṭra, even at their weary ripened age, want to stay home, even in a degraded condition of accepting charity from enemies. Vidura wanted to point this out and impressed upon him that it was better to die like his sons than accept such humiliating charity. Five thousand years ago there was one Dhṛtarāṣṭra, but at the present moment there are Dhṛtarāṣṭras in every home. Politicians especially do not retire from political activities unless they are dragged by the cruel hand of death or killed by some opposing element. To stick to family life to the end of one's human life is the grossest type of degradation and there is an absolute need for the Viduras to educate such Dhṛtarāṣṭras, even at the present moment.

TEXT 25

तस्यापि तव देहोऽयं कृपणस्य जिजीविषोः ।
परैत्यनिच्छतो जीर्णो जरया वाससी इव ॥२५॥

tasyāpi tava deho 'yaṁ
kṛpaṇasya jijīviṣoḥ
paraity anicchato jīrṇo
jarayā vāsasī iva

tasya—of this; *api*—in spite of; *tava*—your; *dehaḥ*—body; *ayam*—this; *kṛpaṇasya*—of one who is miserly; *jijīviṣoḥ*—of you who desire life; *paraiti*—will dwindle; *anicchataḥ*—even unwilling; *jīrṇaḥ*—deteriorated; *jarayā*—old; *vāsasī*—garments; *iva*—like.

TRANSLATION

Despite your unwillingness to die and your desire to live even at the cost of honor and prestige, your miserly body will certainly dwindle and deteriorate like an old garment.

PURPORT

The words *kṛpaṇasya jijīviṣoḥ* are significant. There are two classes of men. One is called the *kṛpaṇa,* and the other is called the *brāhmaṇa.* The *kṛpaṇa,* or the miserly man, has no estimation of his material body, but the *brāhmaṇa* has a true estimation of himself and the material body. The *kṛpaṇa,* having a wrong estimation of his material body, wants to enjoy sense gratification with his utmost strength, and even in old age he wants to become a young man by medical treatment or otherwise. Dhṛtarāṣṭra is addressed herein as a *kṛpaṇa* because without any estimation of his material body he wants to live at any cost. Vidura is trying to open his eyes to see that he cannot live more than his term and that he must prepare for death. Since death is inevitable, why should he accept such a humiliating position for living? It is better to take the right path, even at the risk of death. Human life is meant for finishing all kinds of miseries of material existence, and life should be so regulated that one can achieve the desired goal. Dhṛtarāṣṭra, due to his wrong conception of life, had already spoiled eighty percent of his achieved energy, so it behooved him to utilize the remaining days of his miserly life for the ultimate good. Such a life is called miserly because one cannot properly utilize the assets of the human form of life. Only by good luck does such a miserly man meet a self-realized soul like Vidura and by his instruction gets rid of the nescience of material existence.

TEXT 26

गतस्वार्थमिमं देहं विरक्तो मुक्तबन्धनः ।
अविज्ञातगतिर्जह्यात् स वै धीर उदाहृतः ॥२६॥

gata-svārtham imaṁ dehaṁ
virakto mukta-bandhanaḥ
avijñāta-gatir jahyāt
sa vai dhīra udāhṛtaḥ

gata-sva-artham—without being properly utilized; *imam*—this; *deham*—material body; *viraktaḥ*—indifferently; *mukta*—being freed; *bandhanaḥ*—from all obligations; *avijñāta-gatiḥ*—unknown destination; *jahyāt*—one should give up this body; *saḥ*—such a person; *vai*—certainly; *dhīraḥ*—undisturbed; *udāhṛtaḥ*—is said to be so.

TRANSLATION

He is called undisturbed who goes to an unknown, remote place and, freed from all obligations, quits his material body when it has become useless.

PURPORT

Narottama dāsa Ṭhākura, a great devotee and *ācārya* of the Gauḍīya Vaiṣṇava sect, has sung, "My Lord, I have simply wasted my life. Having obtained the human body, I have neglected to worship Your Lordship, and therefore I have willingly drunk poison." In other words, the human body is especially meant for cultivating knowledge of devotional service to the Lord, without which life becomes full of anxieties and miserable conditions. Therefore, one who has spoiled his life without such cultural activities is advised to leave home without knowledge of friends and relatives and, being thus freed from all obligations of family, society, country, etc., give up the body at some unknown destination so that others may not know where and how he has met his death. *Dhīra* means one who is not disturbed, even when there is sufficient provocation. One cannot give up a comfortable family life due to his affectionate relation with wife and children. Self-realization is obstructed by such undue affection for family, and if anyone is at all able to forget such a relation, he is called undisturbed, or *dhīra.* This is, however, the path of renunciation based on a frustrated life, but stabilization of such renunciation is possible only by association with bona fide saints and self-realized souls by which one can be engaged in the loving devotional service of the Lord. Sincere surrender unto the lotus feet of the Lord is possible by awakening the transcendental sense of service. This is made possible by association with pure devotees of the Lord. Dhṛtarāṣṭra was lucky enough to have a brother whose very association was a source of liberation for this frustrated life.

TEXT 27

यः स्वकात्परतो वेह जातनिर्वेद आत्मवान् ।
हृदि कृत्वा हरिं गेहात्प्रव्रजेत्स नरोत्तमः ॥२७॥

yaḥ svakāt parato veha
jāta-nirveda ātmavān
hṛdi kṛtvā hariṁ gehāt
pravrajet sa narottamaḥ

yaḥ—anyone who; *svakāt*—by his own awakening; *parataḥ vā*—or by hearing from another; *iha*—here in this world; *jāta*—becomes; *nirvedaḥ*—indifferent to material attachment; *ātmavān*—consciousness; *hṛdi*—within the heart; *kṛtvā*—having been taken by; *harim*—the Personality of Godhead; *gehāt*—from home; *pravrajet*—goes away; *saḥ*—he is; *nara-uttamaḥ*—the first-class human being.

TRANSLATION

He is certainly a first-class man who awakens and understands, either by himself or from others, the falsity and misery of this material world and thus leaves home and depends fully on the Personality of Godhead residing within his heart.

PURPORT

There are three classes of transcendentalists, namely, (1) the *dhīra,* or the one who is not disturbed by being away from family association, (2) one in the renounced order of life, a *sannyāsī* by frustrated sentiment, and (3) a sincere devotee of the Lord, who awakens God consciousness by hearing and chanting and leaves home depending completely on the Personality of Godhead, who resides in his heart. The idea is that the renounced order of life, after a frustrated life of sentiment in the material world, may be the stepping stone on the path of self-realization, *but real perfection of the path of liberation is attained when one is practiced to depend fully on the Supreme Personality of Godhead,* who lives in everyone's heart as Paramātmā. One may live in the darkest jungle alone out of home, but a steadfast devotee knows very well that he is not alone. The Supreme Personality of Godhead is with him, and He can protect His sincere devotee in any awkward circumstance. One should therefore practice devotional service at home, hearing and chanting the holy name, quality, form, pastimes, entourage, etc., in association with pure devotees, and this practice will help one awaken God consciousness in proportion to one's sincerity of purpose. One who desires material benefit by such devotional activities can never depend on the Supreme Personality of Godhead, although He sits in everyone's heart. Nor does the Lord give any direction to persons who worship Him for material gain. Such materialistic devotees may be blessed by the Lord with material benefits, but they cannot reach the stage of the first-class human being, as above mentioned. There are many examples of such sincere devotees in the history of the world, especially in India, and they are our guides on the path of self-realization. Mahātmā Vidura is one such great devotee of the Lord, and we should all try to follow in his lotus footsteps for self-realization.

TEXT 28

अथोदीचीं दिशं यातु स्वैरज्ञातगतिर्भवान् ।
इतोऽर्वाक्प्रायशः कालः पुंसां गुणविकर्षणः ॥२८॥

athodīcīṁ diśaṁ yātu
svair ajñāta-gatir bhavān
ito 'rvāk prāyaśaḥ kālaḥ
puṁsāṁ guṇa-vikarṣaṇaḥ

atha—therefore; *udīcīm*—northern side; *diśam*—direction; *yātu*—please go away; *svaiḥ*—by your relatives; *ajñāta*—without knowledge; *gatiḥ*—movements; *bhavān*—of yourself; *itaḥ*—after this; *arvāk*—will usher in; *prāyaśaḥ*—generally; *kālaḥ*—time; *puṁsām*—of men; *guṇa*—qualities; *vikarṣaṇaḥ*—diminishing.

TRANSLATION

Please, therefore, leave for the North immediately, without letting your relatives know, for soon that time will approach which will diminish the good qualities of men.

PURPORT

One can compensate for a life of frustration by becoming a *dhīra,* or leaving home for good without communicating with relatives, and Vidura advised his eldest brother to adopt this way without delay because very quickly the age of Kali was approaching. A conditioned soul is already degraded by the material association, and still in the Kali-yuga the good qualities of a man will deteriorate to the lowest standard. He was advised to leave home before Kali-yuga approached because the atmosphere which was created by Vidura, his valuable instructions on the facts of life, would fade away due to the influence of the age which was fast approaching. To become *narottama,* or a first-class human being depending completely on the Supreme Lord Śrī Kṛṣṇa, is not possible for any ordinary man. It is stated in *Bhagavad-gītā* (7.28) that a person who is completely relieved of all taints of sinful acts can alone depend on the Supreme Lord Śrī Kṛṣṇa, the Personality of Godhead. Dhṛtarāṣṭra was advised by Vidura at least to become a *dhīra* in the beginning if it were impossible for him to become a *sannyāsī* or a *narottama.* Persistently endeavoring on the line of self-realization helps a person to rise to the conditions of a *narottama* from the stage of a *dhīra.* The *dhīra* stage is attained after prolonged practice of the *yoga* system, but by the grace of Vidura one can attain the stage immediately simply by willing to adopt the means of the *dhīra* stage, which is the preparatory stage for *sannyāsa.* The *sannyāsa* stage is the preparatory stage of *paramahaṁsa,* or the first-grade devotee of the Lord.

TEXT 29

एवं राजा विदुरेणानुजेन
प्रज्ञाचक्षुर्बोधित आजमीढः ।
छित्त्वा स्वेषु स्नेहपाशान्द्रढिम्नो
निश्चक्राम भ्रातृसन्दर्शिताध्वा ॥२९॥

evaṁ rājā vidureṇānujena
prajñā-cakṣur bodhita ājamīḍhaḥ

chittvā sveṣu sneha-pāśān draḍhimno
niścakrāma bhrātṛ-sandarśitādhvā

evam—thus; *rājā*—King Dhṛtarāṣṭra; *vidureṇa anujena*—by his younger brother Vidura; *prajñā*—introspective knowledge; *cakṣuḥ*—eyes; *bodhitaḥ*—being understood; *ājamīḍhaḥ*—Dhṛtarāṣṭra, scion of the family of Ajamīḍha; *chittvā*—by breaking; *sveṣu*—regarding kinsmen; *sneha-pāśān*—strong network of affection; *draḍhimnaḥ*—because of steadfastness; *niścakrāma*—got out; *bhrātṛ*—by his brother; *sandarśita*—direction to; *adhvā*—the path of liberation.

TRANSLATION

Thus Mahārāja Dhṛtarāṣṭra, the scion of the family of Ajamīḍha, firmly convinced by introspective knowledge [prajñā], broke at once the strong network of familial affection by his resolute determination. Thus he immediately left home to set out on the path of liberation, as directed by his younger brother Vidura.

PURPORT

Lord Śrī Caitanya Mahāprabhu, the great preacher of the principles of *Śrīmad-Bhāgavatam,* has stressed the importance of association with *sādhus,* pure devotees of the Lord. He said that even by a moment's association with a pure devotee, one can achieve all perfection. We are not ashamed to admit that this fact was experienced in our practical life. Were we not favored by His Divine Grace Śrīmad Bhaktisiddhānta Sarasvatī Gosvāmī Mahārāja, by our first meeting for a few minutes only, it would have been impossible for us to accept this mighty task of describing *Śrīmad-Bhāgavatam* in English. Without seeing him at that opportune moment, we could have become a very great business magnate, but never would we have been able to walk the path of liberation and be engaged in the factual service of the Lord under instructions of His Divine Grace. And here is another practical example by the action of Vidura's association with Dhṛtarāṣṭra. Mahārāja Dhṛtarāṣṭra was tightly bound in a network of material affinities related to politics, economy and family attachment, and he did everything in his power to achieve so-called success in his planned projects, but he was frustrated from the beginning to the end so far as his material activities were concerned. And yet, despite his life of failure, he achieved the greatest of all success in self-realization by the forceful instructions of a pure devotee of the Lord, who is the typical emblem of a *sādhu.* The scriptures enjoin, therefore, that one should associate with *sādhus* only, rejecting all other kinds of association, and by doing so one will have ample opportunity to hear the *sādhus,* who can cut to pieces the bonds of illusory affection in the material world. It is a fact that the material world is a great illusion because everything appears to be a tangible reality but at the next moment evaporates like the dashing foam of the sea or a cloud in the sky. A cloud in the sky undoubtedly appears to be a reality because it rains, and due to rains so many temporary green things appear, but in the ultimate issue, everything disappears, namely the cloud, rain and green vegetation, all in due course. But the sky remains, and the varieties of sky or luminaries also remain forever. Similarly, the Absolute Truth, which is compared to the sky, remains eternally, and the temporary cloudlike illusion comes and goes away. Foolish living beings are attracted by the temporary cloud, but intelligent men are more concerned with the eternal sky with all its variegatedness.

TEXT 30

पतिं प्रयान्तं सुबलस्य पुत्री
पतिव्रता चानुजगाम साध्वी ।
हिमालयं न्यस्तदण्डप्रहर्षं
मनस्विनामिव सत्सम्प्रहारः ॥३०॥

patiṁ prayāntaṁ subalasya putrī
pati-vratā cānujagāma sādhvī
himālayaṁ nyasta-daṇḍa-praharṣaṁ
manasvinām iva satsaṃprahāraḥ

patim—her husband; *prayāntam*—while leaving home; *subalasya*—of King Subala; *putrī*—the worthy daughter; *pati-vratā*—devoted to her husband; *ca*—also; *anujagāma*—followed; *sādhvī*—the chaste; *himālayam*—towards the Himalaya Mountains; *nyasta-daṇḍa*—one who has accepted the rod of the renounced order; *praharṣam*—object of delight; *manasvinām*—of the great fighters; *iva*—like; *sat*—legitimate; *samprahāraḥ*—good lashing.

TRANSLATION

The gentle and chaste Gāndhārī, who was the daughter of King Subala of Kandahar [or Gāndhāra], followed her husband, seeing that he was going to the Himalaya Mountains, which are the delight of those who have

accepted the staff of the renounced order like fighters who have accepted a good lashing from the enemy.

PURPORT

Saubalinī, or Gāndhārī, daughter of King Subala and wife of King Dhṛtarāṣṭra, was ideal as a wife devoted to her husband. The Vedic civilization especially prepares chaste and devoted wives, of whom Gāndhārī is one amongst many mentioned in history. Lakṣmījī Sītādevī was also a daughter of a great king, but she followed her husband, Lord Rāmacandra, into the forest. Similarly, as a woman Gāndhārī could have remained at home or at her father's house, but as a chaste and gentle lady she followed her husband without consideration. Instructions for the renounced order of life were imparted to Dhṛtarāṣṭra by Vidura, and Gāndhārī was by the side of her husband. But he did not ask her to follow him because he was at that time fully determined, like a great warrior who faces all kinds of dangers in the battlefield. He was no longer attracted to so-called wife or relatives, and he decided to start alone, but as a chaste lady Gāndhārī decided to follow her husband till the last moment. Mahārāja Dhṛtarāṣṭra accepted the order of *vānaprastha,* and at this stage the wife is allowed to remain as a voluntary servitor, but in the *sannyāsa* stage no wife can stay with her former husband. A *sannyāsī* is considered to be a dead man civilly, and therefore the wife becomes a civil widow without connection with her former husband. Mahārāja Dhṛtarāṣṭra did not deny his faithful wife, and she followed her husband at her own risk.

The *sannyāsīs* accept a rod as the sign of the renounced order of life. There are two types of *sannyāsīs.* Those who follow the Māyāvādī philosophy, headed by Śrīpāda Śaṅkarācārya, accept only one rod (*eka-daṇḍa*), but those who follow the Vaiṣṇavite philosophy accept three combined rods (*tri-daṇḍa*). The Māyāvādī *sannyāsīs* are *ekadaṇḍi-svāmīs,* whereas the Vaiṣṇava *sannyāsīs* are known as *tridaṇḍi-svāmīs,* or more distinctly, *tridaṇḍi-gosvāmīs,* in order to be distinguished from the Māyāvādī philosophers. The *ekadaṇḍi-svāmīs* are mostly fond of the Himalayas, but the Vaiṣṇava *sannyāsīs* are fond of Vṛndāvana and Purī. The Vaiṣṇava *sannyāsīs* are *narottamas,* whereas the Māyāvādī *sannyāsīs* are *dhīras.* Mahārāja Dhṛtarāṣṭra was advised to follow the *dhīras* because at that stage it was difficult for him to become a *narottama.*

TEXT 31

अजातशत्रुः कृतमैत्रो हुताग्नि-
विप्रान्नत्वा तिलगोभूमिरुक्मैः ।

गृहं प्रविष्टो गुरुवन्दनाय
न चापश्यत्पितरौ सौबलीं च ॥३१॥

ajāta-śatruḥ kṛta-maitro hutāgnir
viprān natvā tila-go-bhūmi-rukmaiḥ
gṛhaṁ praviṣṭo guru-vandanāya
na cāpaśyat pitarau saubalīṁ ca

ajāta—never born; *śatruḥ*—enemy; *kṛta*—having performed; *maitraḥ*—worshiping the demigods; *huta-agniḥ*—and offering fuel in the fire; *viprān*—the *brāhmaṇas; natvā*—offering obeisances; *tila-go-bhūmi-rukmaiḥ*—along with grains, cows, land and gold; *gṛham*—within the palace; *praviṣṭaḥ*—having entered into; *guru-vandanāya*—for offering respect to the elderly members; *na*—did not; *ca*—also; *apaśyat*—see; *pitarau*—his uncles; *saubalīm*—Gāndhārī; *ca*—also.

TRANSLATION

Mahārāja Yudhiṣṭhira, whose enemy was never born, performed his daily morning duties by praying, offering fire sacrifice to the sun-god, and offering obeisances, grains, cows, land and gold to the brāhmaṇas. He then entered the palace to pay respects to the elderly. However, he could not find his uncles or aunt, the daughter of King Subala.

PURPORT

Mahārāja Yudhiṣṭhira was the most pious king because he personally practiced daily the pious duties for the householders. The householders are required to rise early in the morning, and after bathing they should offer respects to the Deities at home by prayers, by offering fuel in the sacred fire, by giving the *brāhmaṇas* in charity land, cows, grains, gold, etc., and at last offering to the elderly members due respects and obeisances. One who is not prepared to practice injunctions prescribed in the *śāstras* cannot be a good man simply by book knowledge. Modern householders are practiced to different modes of life, namely to rise late and then take bed tea without any sort of cleanliness and without any purificatory practices as mentioned above. The household children are taken to practice what the parents practice, and therefore the whole generation glides towards hell. Nothing good can be expected from them unless they associate with *sādhus.* Like Dhṛtarāṣṭra, the materialistic person may take lessons from a *sādhu* like Vidura and thus be cleansed of the effects of modern life.

Mahārāja Yudhiṣṭhira, however, could not find in the palace his two uncles, namely Dhṛtarāṣṭra and Vidura, along with Gāndhārī, the daughter of King Subala. He was anxious to see them and therefore asked Sañjaya, the private secretary of Dhṛtarāṣṭra.

TEXT 32

तत्र सञ्जयमासीनं पप्रच्छोद्विग्नमानसः ।
गावल्गणे क्व नस्तातो वृद्धो हीनश्च नेत्रयोः ॥३२॥

tatra sañjayam āsīnaṁ
papracchodvigna-mānasaḥ
gāvalgaṇe kva nas tāto
vṛddho hīnaś ca netrayoḥ

tatra—there; *sañjayam*—unto Sañjaya; *āsīnam*—seated; *papraccha*—he inquired from; *udvigna-mānasaḥ*—filled with anxiety; *gāvalgaṇe*—the son of Gavalgaṇa, Sañjaya; *kva*—where is; *naḥ*—our; *tātaḥ*—uncle; *vṛddhaḥ*—old; *hīnaḥ ca*—and bereft of; *netrayoḥ*—the eyes.

TRANSLATION

Mahārāja Yudhiṣṭhira, full of anxiety, turned to Sañjaya, who was sitting there, and said: O Sañjaya, where is our uncle, who is old and blind?

TEXT 33

अम्बा च हतपुत्रार्ता पितृव्यः क्व गतः सुहृत् ।
अपि मय्यकृतप्रज्ञे हतबन्धुः स भार्यया ।
आशंसमानः शमलं गङ्गायां दुःखितोऽपतत् ॥३३॥

ambā ca hata-putrārtā
pitṛvyaḥ kva gataḥ suhṛt
api mayy akṛta-prajñe
hata-bandhuḥ sa bhāryayā
āśaṁsamānaḥ śamalaṁ
gaṅgāyāṁ duḥkhito 'patat

ambā—mother-aunt; *ca*—and; *hata-putrā*—who had lost all her sons; *ārtā*—in a sorry plight; *pitṛvyaḥ*—uncle Vidura; *kva*—where; *gataḥ*—gone;

suhṛt—well-wisher; *api*—whether; *mayi*—unto me; *akṛta-prajñe*—ungrateful; *hata-bandhuḥ*—one who has lost all his sons; *saḥ*—Dhṛtarāṣṭra; *bhāryayā*—with his wife; *āśaṁsamānaḥ*—in doubtful mind; *śamalam*—offenses; *gaṅgāyām*—in the Ganges water; *duḥkhitaḥ*—in distressed mind; *apatat*—fell down.

TRANSLATION

Where is my well-wisher, uncle Vidura, and Mother Gāndhārī, who is very afflicted due to all her sons' demise? My uncle Dhṛtarāṣṭra was also very mortified due to the death of all his sons and grandsons. Undoubtedly I am very ungrateful. Did he, therefore, take my offenses very seriously and, along with his wife, drown himself in the Ganges?

PURPORT

The Pāṇḍavas, especially Mahārāja Yudhiṣṭhira and Arjuna, anticipated the aftereffects of the Battle of Kurukṣetra, and therefore Arjuna declined to execute the fighting. The fight was executed by the will of the Lord, but the effects of family aggrievement, as they had thought of it before, had come to be true. Mahārāja Yudhiṣṭhira was always conscious of the great plight of his uncle Dhṛtarāṣṭra and aunt Gāndhārī, and therefore he took all possible care of them in their old age and aggrieved conditions. When, therefore, he could not find his uncle and aunt in the palace, naturally his doubts arose, and he conjectured that they had gone down to the water of the Ganges. He thought himself ungrateful because when the Pāṇḍavas were fatherless, Mahārāja Dhṛtarāṣṭra had given them all royal facilities to live, and in return he had killed all Dhṛtarāṣṭra's sons in the Battle of Kurukṣetra. As a pious man, Mahārāja Yudhiṣṭhira took into account all his unavoidable misdeeds, and he never thought of the misdeeds of his uncle and company. Dhṛtarāṣṭra had suffered the effects of his own misdeeds by the will of the Lord, but Mahārāja Yudhiṣṭhira was thinking only of his own unavoidable misdeeds. That is the nature of a good man and devotee of the Lord. A devotee never finds fault with others, but tries to find his own and thus rectify them as far as possible.

TEXT 34

पितर्युपरते पाण्डौ सर्वान्नः सुहृदः शिशून् ।
अरक्षतां व्यसनतः पितृव्यौ क्व गतावितः ॥३४॥

pitary uparate pāṇḍau
sarvān naḥ suhṛdaḥ śiśūn
arakṣatāṁ vyasanataḥ
pitṛvyau kva gatāv itaḥ

pitari—upon my father; *uparate*—falling down; *pāṇḍau*—Mahārāja Pāṇḍu; *sarvān*—all; *naḥ*—of us; *suhṛdaḥ*—well-wishers; *śiśūn*—small children; *arakṣatām*—protected; *vyasanataḥ*—from all kinds of dangers; *pitṛvyau*—uncles; *kva*—where; *gatau*—have departed; *itaḥ*—from this place.

TRANSLATION

When my father, Pāṇḍu, fell down and we were all small children, these two uncles gave us protection from all kinds of calamities. They were always our good well-wishers. Alas, where have they gone from here?

TEXT 35

सूत उवाच
कृपया स्नेहवैक्लव्यात्सूतो विरहकर्शितः ।
आत्मेश्वरमचक्षाणो न प्रत्याहातिपीडितः ॥३५॥

sūta uvāca
kṛpayā sneha-vaiklavyāt
sūto viraha-karśitaḥ
ātmeśvaram acakṣāṇo
na pratyāhātipīḍitaḥ

sūtaḥ uvāca—Sūta Gosvāmī said; *kṛpayā*—out of full compassion; *sneha-vaiklavyāt*—mental derangement due to profound affection; *sūtaḥ*—Sañjaya; *viraha-karśitaḥ*—distressed by separation; *ātma-īśvaram*—his master; *acakṣāṇaḥ*—having not seen; *na*—did not; *pratyāha*—replied; *ati-pīḍitaḥ*—being too aggrieved.

TRANSLATION

Sūta Gosvāmī said: Because of compassion and mental agitation, Sañjaya, not having seen his own master, Dhṛtarāṣṭra, was aggrieved and could not properly reply to Mahārāja Yudhiṣṭhira.

PURPORT

Sañjaya was the personal assistant of Mahārāja Dhṛtarāṣṭra for a very long time, and thus he had the opportunity to study the life of Dhṛtarāṣṭra. And when he saw at last that Dhṛtarāṣṭra had left home without his knowledge, his sorrows had no bound. He was fully compassionate toward Dhṛtarāṣṭra because in the game of the Battle of Kurukṣetra, King Dhṛtarāṣṭra had lost everything, men and money, and at last the King and the Queen had to leave home in utter frustration. He studied the situation in his own way because he did not know that the inner vision of Dhṛtarāṣṭra has been awakened by Vidura and that therefore he had left home in enthusiastic cheerfulness for a better life after departure from the dark well of home. Unless one is convinced of a better life after renunciation of the present life, one cannot stick to the renounced order of life simply by artificial dress or staying out of the home.

TEXT 36

विमृज्याश्रूणि पाणिभ्यां विष्टभ्यात्मानमात्मना ।
अजातशत्रुं प्रत्यूचे प्रभोः पादावनुस्मरन् ॥३६॥

vimṛjyāśrūṇi pāṇibhyāṁ
viṣṭabhyātmānam ātmanā
ajāta-śatruṁ pratyūce
prabhoḥ pādāv anusmaran

vimṛjya—smearing; *aśrūṇi*—tears of the eyes; *pāṇibhyām*—with his hands; *viṣṭabhya*—situated; *ātmānam*—the mind; *ātmanā*—by intelligence; *ajāta-śatrum*—unto Mahārāja Yudhiṣṭhira; *pratyūce*—began to reply; *prabhoḥ*—of his master; *pādau*—feet; *anusmaran*—thinking after.

TRANSLATION

First he slowly pacified his mind by intelligence, and wiping away his tears and thinking of the feet of his master, Dhṛtarāṣṭra, he began to reply to Mahārāja Yudhiṣṭhira.

TEXT 37

संजय उवाच

नाहं वेद व्यवसितं पित्रोर्वः कुलनन्दन ।
गान्धार्या वा महाबाहो मुषितोऽस्मि महात्मभिः ॥३७॥

sañjaya uvāca
nāhaṁ veda vyavasitaṁ
pitror vaḥ kula-nandana
gāndhāryā vā mahā-bāho
muṣito 'smi mahātmabhiḥ

sañjayaḥ uvāca—Sañjaya said; *na*—not; *aham*—I; *veda*—know; *vyavasitam*—determination; *pitroḥ*—of your uncles; *vaḥ*—your; *kula-nandana*—O descendant of the Kuru dynasty; *gāndhāryāḥ*—of Gāndhārī; *vā*—or; *mahā-bāho*—O great King; *muṣitaḥ*—cheated; *asmi*—I have been; *mahā-ātmabhiḥ*—by those great souls.

TRANSLATION

Sañjaya said: My dear descendant of the Kuru dynasty, I have no information of the determination of your two uncles and Gāndhārī. O King, I have been cheated by those great souls.

PURPORT

That great souls cheat others may be astonishing to know, but it is a fact that great souls cheat others for a great cause. It is said that Lord Kṛṣṇa also advised Yudhiṣṭhira to tell a lie before Droṇācārya, and it was also for a great cause. The Lord wanted it, and therefore it was a great cause. Satisfaction of the Lord is the criterion of one who is bona fide, and the highest perfection of life is to satisfy the Lord by one's occupational duty. That is the verdict of *Gītā* and *Bhāgavatam.** Dhṛtarāṣṭra and Vidura, followed by Gāndhārī, did not disclose their determination to Sañjaya, although he was constantly with Dhṛtarāṣṭra as his personal assistant. Sañjaya never thought that Dhṛtarāṣṭra could perform any act without consulting him. But Dhṛtarāṣṭra's going away from home was so confidential that it could not be disclosed even to Sañjaya. Sanātana Gosvāmī also cheated the keeper of the prison house while going away to see Śrī Caitanya Mahāprabhu, and similarly Raghunātha dāsa Gosvāmī also cheated his priest and left home for good to satisfy the Lord. To satisfy the Lord, anything is good, for it is in relation with the Absolute

---

**yataḥ pravṛttir bhūtānāṁ/ yena sarvam idaṁ tatam*
sva-karmaṇā tam abhyarcya/ siddhiṁ vindati mānavaḥ (Bg.18.46)

ataḥ pumbhir dvija-śreṣṭhā/ varṇāśrama-vibhāgaśaḥ
svanuṣṭhitasya dharmasya/ saṁsiddhir hari-toṣaṇam (*Bhāg.*1.2.13)

Truth. We also had the same opportunity to cheat the family members and leave home to engage in the service of *Śrīmad-Bhāgavatam.* Such cheating was necessary for a great cause, and there is no loss for any party in such transcendental fraud.

TEXT 38

अथाजगाम भगवान् नारदः सहतुम्बुरुः ।
प्रत्युत्थायाभिवाद्याह सानुजोऽभ्यर्चयन्मुनिम् ॥३८॥

athājagāma bhagavān
nāradaḥ saha-tumburuḥ
pratyutthāyābhivādyāha
sānujo 'bhyarcayan munim

atha—thereafter; *ājagāma*—arrived; *bhagavān*—the godly personality; *nāradaḥ*—Nārada; *saha-tumburuḥ*—along with his *tumburu* (musical instrument); *pratyutthāya*—having gotten up from their seats; *abhivādya*—offering their due obeisances; *āha*—said; *sa-anujaḥ*—along with younger brothers; *abhyarcayan*—thus while receiving in a proper mood; *munim*—the sage.

TRANSLATION

While Sañjaya was thus speaking, Śrī Nārada, the powerful devotee of the Lord, appeared on the scene carrying his tumburu. Mahārāja Yudhiṣṭhira and his brothers received him properly by getting up from their seats and offering obeisances.

PURPORT

Devarṣi Nārada is described herein as *bhagavān* due to his being the most confidential devotee of the Lord. The Lord and His very confidential devotees are treated on the same level by those who are actually engaged in the loving service of the Lord. Such confidential devotees of the Lord are very much dear to the Lord because they travel everywhere to preach the glories of the Lord in different capacities and try their utmost to convert the nondevotees of the Lord into devotees in order to bring them to the platform of sanity. Actually a living being cannot be a nondevotee of the Lord because of his constitutional position, but when one becomes a nondevotee or nonbeliever, it is to be understood that the person concerned is not in a sound condition of life. The confidential devotees of the Lord treat such illusioned living beings, and therefore they are most pleasing in the eyes of the Lord. The Lord says in the *Bhagavad-gītā* that no one is dearer to Him than one who actually preaches the glories of the Lord to convert the nonbelievers and nondevotees. Such personalities as Nārada must be offered all due respects, like those offered to the Personality of Godhead Himself, and Mahārāja Yudhiṣṭhira, along with his noble brothers, were examples for others in receiving a pure devotee of the Lord like Nārada, who had no other business save and except singing the glories of the Lord along with his *vīṇā,* a musical stringed instrument.

TEXT 39

युधिष्ठिर उवाच

नाहं वेद गतिं पित्रोर्भगवन् क्व गतावितः ।
अम्बा वा हतपुत्रार्ता क्व गता च तपस्विनी ॥३९॥

yudhiṣṭhira uvāca
nāhaṁ veda gatiṁ pitror
bhagavan kva gatāv itaḥ
ambā vā hata-putrārtā
kva gatā ca tapasvinī

yudhiṣṭhiraḥ uvāca—Mahārāja Yudhiṣṭhira said; *na*—do not; *aham*—myself; *veda*—know it; *gatim*—departure; *pitroḥ*—of the uncles; *bhagavan*—O godly personality; *kva*—where; *gatau*—gone; *itaḥ*—from this place; *ambā*—mother-aunt; *vā*—either; *hata-putrā*—bereft of her sons; *ārtā*—aggrieved; *kva*—where; *gatā*—gone; *ca*—also; *tapasvinī*—ascetic.

TRANSLATION

Mahārāja Yudhiṣṭhira said: O godly personality, I do not know where my two uncles have gone. Nor can I find my ascetic aunt who is griefstricken by the loss of all her sons.

PURPORT

Mahārāja Yudhiṣṭhira, as a good soul and devotee of the Lord, was always conscious of the great loss of his aunt and her sufferings as an ascetic. An ascetic is never disturbed by all kinds of sufferings, and that makes him strong and determined on the path of spiritual progress. Queen Gāndhārī is a typical example of an ascetic because of her marvelous character in many trying situations. She was an ideal woman as mother, wife and ascetic, and in the history of the world such character in a woman is rarely found.

TEXT 40

कर्णधार इवापारे भगवान् पारदर्शकः ।
अथाबभाषे भगवान् नारदो मुनिसत्तमः ॥४०॥

karṇadhāra ivāpāre
bhagavān pāra-darśakaḥ
athābabhāṣe bhagavān
nārado muni-sattamaḥ

karṇa-dhāraḥ—captain of the ship; *iva*—like; *apāre*—in the extensive oceans; *bhagavān*—representative of the Lord; *pāra-darśakaḥ*—one who can give directions to the other side; *atha*—thus; *ābabhāṣe*—began to say; *bhagavān*—the godly personality; *nāradaḥ*—the great sage Nārada; *muni-sat-tamaḥ*—the greatest among the devotee philosophers.

TRANSLATION

You are like a captain of a ship in a great ocean and you can direct us to our destination. Thus addressed, the godly personality, Devarṣi Nārada, greatest of the philosopher devotees, began to speak.

PURPORT

There are different types of philosophers, and the greatest of all of them are those who have seen the Personality of Godhead and have surrendered themselves in the transcendental loving service of the Lord. Among all such pure devotees of the Lord, Devarṣi Nārada is the chief, and therefore he has been described herein as the greatest of all philosopher devotees. Unless one has become a sufficiently learned philosopher by hearing the Vedānta philosophy from a bona fide spiritual master, one cannot be a learned philosopher devotee. One must be very faithful, learned and renounced, otherwise one cannot be a pure devotee. A pure devotee of the Lord can give us direction towards the other end of nescience. Devarṣi Nārada used to visit the palace of Mahārāja Yudhiṣṭhira because the Pāṇḍavas were all pure devotees of the Lord, and the Devarṣi was always ready to give them good counsel whenever needed.

TEXT 41

नारद उवाच
मा कंचन शुचो राजन् यदीश्वरवशं जगत् ।
लोकाः सपाला यस्येमे वहन्ति बलिमीशितुः ।
स संयुनक्ति भूतानि स एव वियुनक्ति च ॥४१॥

nārada uvāca
mā kañcana śuco rājan
yad īśvara-vaśaṁ jagat
lokāḥ sapālā yasyeme
vahanti balim īśituḥ
sa saṁyunakti bhūtāni
sa eva viyunakti ca

nāradaḥ uvāca—Nārada said; *mā*—never; *kañcana*—by all means; *śucaḥ*—do you lament; *rājan*—O King; *yat*—because; *īśvara-vaśam*—under the control of the Supreme Lord; *jagat*—world; *lokāḥ*—all living beings; *sa-pālāḥ*—including their leaders; *yasya*—whose; *ime*—all these; *vahanti*—do bear; *balim*—means of worship; *īśituḥ*—for being protected; *saḥ*—He; *saṁyunakti*—gets together; *bhūtāni*—all living beings; *saḥ*—He; *eva*—also; *viyunakti*—disperses; *ca*—and.

TRANSLATION

Śrī Nārada said: O pious King, do not lament for anyone, for everyone is under the control of the Supreme Lord. Therefore all living beings and their leaders carry on worship to be well protected. It is He only who brings them together and disperses them.

PURPORT

Every living being, either in this material world or in the spiritual world, is under the control of the Supreme Lord, the Personality of Godhead. Beginning from Brahmājī, the leader of this universe, down to the insignificant ant, all are abiding by the order of the Supreme Lord. Thus the constitutional position of the living being is subordination under the control of the Lord. The foolish living being, especially man, artificially rebels against the law of the Supreme and thus becomes chastised as an *asura,* or lawbreaker. A living being is placed in a particular position by the order of the Supreme Lord, and he is again shifted from that place by the order of the Supreme Lord or His authorized agents. Brahmā, Śiva, Indra, Candra, Mahārāja Yudhiṣṭhira or, in modern history, Napoleon, Akbar, Alexander, Gandhi, Shubhash and Nehru all are servants of the Lord, and they are placed in and removed from their respective positions by the supreme will of the Lord. None of them is independent. Even though such men or leaders rebel so as not to recognize the supremacy of the Lord, they are put under still more rigorous laws of the material world by different miseries. Only the foolish man, therefore, says that there is no God. Mahārāja Yudhiṣṭhira was being convinced of this naked truth because he was greatly overwhelmed by the sudden departure of his old uncles and aunt. Mahārāja Dhṛtarāṣṭra was placed in that position according to his past deeds; he had already suffered or enjoyed the benefits accrued to him in the past, but due to his good luck, somehow or other he had a good younger brother, Vidura, and by his instruction he left to achieve salvation by closing all accounts in the material world.

Ordinarily one cannot change the course of one's due happiness and distress by plan. Everyone has to accept them as they come under the subtle arrangement of *kāla,* or invincible time. There is no use trying to counteract them. The best thing is, therefore, that one should endeavor to achieve salvation, and this prerogative is given only to man because of his developed condition of mental activities and intelligence. Only for man are there different Vedic instructions for attainment of salvation during the human form of existence. One who misuses this opportunity of advanced intelligence is verily condemned and put into different types of miseries, either in this present life or in the future. That is the way the Supreme controls everyone.

TEXT 42

यथा गावो नसि प्रोतास्तन्त्यां बद्धाश्च दामभिः ।
वाक्तन्त्यां नामभिर्बद्धा वहन्ति बलिमीशितुः ॥४२॥

yathā gāvo nasi protās
tantyāṁ baddhāś ca dāmabhiḥ
vāk-tantyāṁ nāmabhir baddhā
vahanti balim īśituḥ

yathā—as much as; *gāvaḥ*—cow; *nasi*—by the nose; *protāḥ*—strung; *tantyām*—by the thread; *baddhāḥ*—bound by; *ca*—also; *dāmabhiḥ*—by ropes; *vāk-tantyām*—in the network of Vedic hymns; *nāmabhiḥ*—by nomenclatures; *baddhāḥ*—conditioned; *vahanti*—carry on; *balim*—orders; *īśituḥ*—for being controlled by the Supreme Lord.

TRANSLATION

As a cow, bound through the nose by a long rope, is conditioned, so also human beings are bound by different Vedic injunctions and are conditioned to obey the orders of the Supreme.

PURPORT

Every living being, whether a man or an animal or a bird, thinks that he is free by himself, but actually no one is free from the severe laws of the Lord. The laws of the Lord are severe because they cannot be disobeyed in any circumstance. The man-made laws may be evaded by cunning outlaws, but in the codes of the supreme lawmaker there is not the slightest possibility of neglecting the laws. A slight change in the course of God-made law can bring about a massive danger to be faced by the lawbreaker. Such laws of the Supreme are generally known as the codes of religion, under different conditions, but the principle of religion everywhere is one and the same, namely, obey the orders of the Supreme God, the codes of religion. That is the condition of material existence. All living beings in the material world have taken up the risk of conditioned life by their own selection and are thus entrapped by the laws of material nature. The only way to get out of the entanglement is to agree to obey the Supreme. But instead of becoming free from the clutches of *māyā,* or illusion, foolish human beings become bound up by different nomenclatures, being designated as *brāhmaṇas, kṣatriyas, vaiśyas, śūdras,* Hindus, Mohammedans, Indians, Europeans, Americans, Chinese, and many others, and thus they carry out the orders of the Supreme Lord under the influence of respective scriptural or legislative injunctions. The statutory laws of the state are imperfect imitation replicas of religious codes. The secular state, or the godless state, allows the citizens to break the laws of God, but restricts them from disobeying the laws of the state; the result is that the people in general suffer more by breaking the laws of God than by obeying the imperfect laws made by man. Every man is imperfect by constitution under conditions of material existence, and there is not the least possibility that even the most materially advanced man can enact perfect legislation. On the other hand, there is no such imperfection in the laws of God. If leaders are educated in the laws of God, there is no necessity of a makeshift legislative council of aimless men. There is necessity of change in the makeshift laws of man, but there is no change in the God-made laws because they are made perfect by the all-perfect Personality of Godhead. The codes of religion, scriptural injunctions, are made by liberated representatives of God in consideration of different conditions of living, and by carrying out the orders of the Lord, the conditioned living beings gradually become free from the clutches of material existence. The factual position of the living being is, however, that he is the eternal servitor of the Supreme Lord. In his liberated state he renders service to the Lord in transcendental love and thus enjoys a life of full freedom, even sometimes on an equal level with the Lord or sometimes more than the Lord. But in the conditioned material world, every living being wants to be the Lord of other living beings, and thus by the illusion of *māyā* this mentality of lording it over becomes a cause of further extension of conditional life. So in the material world the living being is still more conditioned, until he surrenders unto the Lord by reviving his original state of eternal servitorship. That is the last instruction of the *Bhagavad-gītā* and all other recognized scriptures of the world.

TEXT 43

यथा क्रीडोपस्करणां संयोगविगमाविह ।
इच्छया क्रीडितुः स्यातां तथैवेशेच्छया नृणाम् ॥४३॥

yathā krīḍopaskarāṇāṁ
saṁyoga-vigamāv iha
icchayā krīḍituḥ syātāṁ
tathaiveśecchayā nṛṇām

yathā—as much as; *krīḍa-upaskarāṇām*—playthings; *saṁyoga*—union; *vigamau*—disunion; *iha*—in this world; *icchayā*—by the will of; *krīḍituḥ*—just to play a part; *syātām*—takes place; *tathā*—so also; *eva*—certainly; *īśa*—the Supreme Lord; *icchayā*—by the will of; *nṛṇām*—of the human beings.

TRANSLATION

As a player sets up and disperses his playthings according to his own sweet will, so the supreme will of the Lord brings men together and separates them.

PURPORT

We must know for certain that the particular position in which we are now set up is an arrangement of the supreme will in terms of our own acts in the past. The Supreme Lord is present as the localized Paramātmā in the heart of every living being, as it is said in the *Bhagavad-gītā* (13.23), and therefore he knows everything of our activities in every stage of our lives. He rewards the reactions of our actions by placing us in some particular place. A rich man gets his son born with a silver spoon in his mouth, but the child who came as the rich man's son deserved such a place, and therefore he is placed there by the will of the Lord. And at a particular moment when the child has to be removed from that place, he is also carried by the will of the Supreme, even if the child or the father does not wish to be separated from the happy relation. The same thing happens in the case of a poor man also. Neither rich man nor poor man has any control over such meetings or separations of living beings. The example of a player and his playthings should not be misunderstood. One may argue that since the Lord is bound to award the reactionary results of our own actions, the example of a player cannot be applied. But it is not so. We must always remember that the Lord is the supreme will, and He is not bound by any law. Generally the law of *karma* is that one is awarded the result of one's own actions, but in special cases, by the will of the Lord, such resultant actions are changed also. But this change can be affected by the will of the Lord only, and no other. Therefore, the example of the player cited in this verse is quite appropriate, for the Supreme Will is absolutely free to do whatever He likes, and because He is all-perfect, there is no mistake in any of His actions or reactions. These changes of resultant actions are especially rendered by the Lord when a pure devotee is involved. It is assured in the *Bhagavad-gītā* (9.30–31) that the Lord saves a pure devotee who has surrendered unto Him without reservation from all sorts of reactions of sins, and there is no doubt about this. There are hundreds of examples of reactions changed by the Lord in the history of the world. If the Lord is able to change the reactions of one's past deeds, then certainly He is not Himself bound by any action or reaction of His own deeds. He is perfect and transcendental to all laws.

TEXT 44

यन्मन्यसे ध्रुवं लोकमध्रुवं वा न चोभयम् ।
सर्वथा न हि शोच्यास्ते स्नेहादन्यत्र मोहजात् ॥४४॥

yan manyase dhruvaṁ lokam
adhruvaṁ vā na cobhayam
sarvathā na hi śocyās te
snehād anyatra mohajāt

yat—even though; *manyase*—you think; *dhruvam*—Absolute Truth; *lokam*—persons; *adhruvam*—nonreality; *vā*—either; *na*—or not; *ca*—also; *ubhayam*—or bothwise; *sarvathā*—in all circumstances; *na*—never; *hi*—certainly; *śocyāḥ*—subject for lamentation; *te*—they; *snehāt*—due to affection; *anyatra*—or otherwise; *moha-jāt*—due to bewilderment.

TRANSLATION

O King, in all circumstances, whether you consider the soul to be an eternal principle, or the material body to be perishable, or everything to exist in the impersonal Absolute Truth, or everything to be an inexplicable combination of matter and spirit, feelings of separation are due only to illusory affection and nothing more.

PURPORT

The actual fact is that every living being is an individual part and parcel of the Supreme Being, and his constitutional position is subordinate cooperative service. Either in his conditional material existence or in his liberated position of full knowledge and eternity, the living entity is eternally under the control of the Supreme Lord. But those who are not conversant with factual knowledge put forward many speculative propositions about the real position of the living entity. It is admitted, however, by all schools of philosophy that the living being is eternal and that the covering body of the five material elements is perishable and temporary. The eternal living entity transmigrates from one material body to another by the law of *karma,* and material bodies are perishable by their fundamental structures. Therefore there is nothing to be lamented in the case of the soul's being transferred into another body, or the material body's perishing at a certain stage. There are others also who believe in the merging of the spirit soul in the Supreme Spirit when it is uncovered by the material encagement, and there are others also who do not believe in the existence of spirit or soul, but believe in tangible matter. In our daily experience we find so many transformations of matter from one form to another, but we do not lament such changing features. In either of the above cases, the force of divine energy is uncheckable; no one has any hand in it, and thus there is no cause of grief.

TEXT 45

तस्माज्जह्यङ्ग वैक्लव्यमज्ञानकृतमात्मनः ।
कथं त्वनाथाः कृपणा वर्तेरंस्ते च मां विना ॥४५॥

tasmāj jahy aṅga vaiklavyam
ajñāna-kṛtam ātmanaḥ
kathaṁ tv anāthāḥ kṛpaṇā
varteraṁs te ca māṁ vinā

tasmāt—therefore; *jahi*—give up; *aṅga*—O King; *vaiklavyam*—mental disparity; *ajñāna*—ignorance; *kṛtam*—due to; *ātmanaḥ*—of yourself; *katham*—how; *tu*—but; *anāthāḥ*—helpless; *kṛpaṇāḥ*—poor creatures; *varteran*—be able to survive; *te*—they; *ca*—also; *mām*—me; *vinā*—without.

TRANSLATION

Therefore give up your anxiety due to ignorance of the self. You are now thinking of how they, who are helpless poor creatures, will exist without you.

PURPORT

When we think of our kith and kin as being helpless and dependent on us, it is all due to ignorance. Every living creature is allowed all protection by the order of the Supreme Lord in terms of each one's acquired position in the world. The Lord is known as *bhūta-bhṛt,* one who gives protection to all living beings. One should discharge his duties only, for no one but the Supreme Lord can give protection to anyone else. This is explained more clearly in the following verse.

TEXT 46

कालकर्मगुणाधीनो देहोऽयं पाञ्चभौतिकः ।
कथमन्यांस्तु गोपायेत्सर्पग्रस्तो यथा परम् ॥४६॥

kāla-karma-guṇādhīno
deho 'yaṁ pāñca-bhautikaḥ
katham anyāṁs tu gopāyet
sarpa-grasto yathā param

kāla—eternal time; *karma*—action; *guṇa*—modes of nature; *adhīnaḥ*—under the control of; *dehaḥ*—material body and mind; *ayam*—this; *pāñca-bhautikaḥ*—made of the five elements; *katham*—how; *anyān*—others; *tu*—but; *gopāyet*—give protection; *sarpa-grastaḥ*—one who is bitten by the snake; *yathā*—as much as; *param*—others.

TRANSLATION

This gross material body made of five elements is already under the control of eternal time [kāla], action [karma] and the modes of material nature [guṇa]. How, then, can it, being already in the jaws of the serpent, protect others?

PURPORT

The world's movements for freedom through political, economic, social, and cultural propaganda can do no benefit to anyone, for they are controlled by superior power. A conditioned living being is under the full control of material nature, represented by eternal time and activities under the dictation of different modes of nature. There are three material modes of nature, namely goodness, passion and ignorance. Unless one is situated in the mode of goodness, one cannot see things as they are. The passionate and the ignorant cannot even see things as they are. Therefore a person who is passionate and ignorant cannot direct his activities on the right path. Only the man in the quality of goodness can help to a certain extent. Most persons are passionate and ignorant, and therefore their plans and projects can hardly do any good to others. Above the modes of nature is eternal time, which is called *kāla* because it changes the shape of everything in the material world. Even if we are able to do something temporarily beneficial, time will see that the good project is frustrated in course of time. The only thing possible to be done is to get rid of eternal time, *kāla,* which is compared to *kāla-sarpa,* or the cobra snake, whose bite is always lethal. No one can be saved from the bite of a cobra. The best remedy for getting out of the clutches of the cobralike *kāla* or its integrity, the modes of nature, is *bhakti-yoga,* as it is recommended in the *Bhagavad-gītā* (14.26). The highest perfectional project of philanthropic activities is to engage everyone in the act of preaching *bhakti-yoga* all over the world because that alone can save the people from the control of *māyā,* or the material nature represented by *kāla, karma* and *guṇa,* as described above. The *Bhagavad-gītā* (14.26) confirms this definitely.

TEXT 47

अहस्तानि सहस्तानामपदानि चतुष्पदाम् ।
फल्गूनि तत्र महतां जीवो जीवस्य जीवनम् ॥४७॥

ahastāni sahastānām
apadāni catuṣ-padām

phalgūni tatra mahatāṁ
jīvo jīvasya jīvanam

ahastāni—those who are devoid of hands; *sa-hastānām*—of those who are endowed with hands; *apadāni*—those who are devoid of legs; *catuḥ-padām*—of those who have four legs; *phalgūni*—those who are weak; *tatra*—there; *mahatām*—of the powerful; *jīvaḥ*—the living being; *jīvasya*—of the living being; *jīvanam*—subsistence.

TRANSLATION

Those who are devoid of hands are prey for those who have hands; those devoid of legs are prey for the four-legged. The weak are the subsistence of the strong, and the general rule holds that one living being is food for another.

PURPORT

A systematic law of subsistence in the struggle for existence is there by the supreme will, and there is no escape for anyone by any amount of planning. The living beings who have come to the material world against the will of the Supreme Being are under the control of a supreme power called *māyā-śakti,* the deputed agent of the Lord, and this *daivī māyā* is meant to pinch the conditioned souls by threefold miseries, one of which is explained here in this verse: *the weak are the subsistence of the strong.* No one is strong enough to protect himself from the onslaught of a stronger, and by the will of the Lord there are systematic categories of the weak, the stronger and the strongest. There is nothing to be lamented if a tiger eats a weaker animal, including a man, because that is the law of the Supreme Lord. But although the law states that a human being must subsist on another living being, there is the law of good sense also, for the human being is meant to obey the laws of the scriptures. This is impossible for other animals. The human being is meant for self-realization, and for that purpose he is not to eat anything which is not first offered to the Lord. The Lord accepts from His devotee all kinds of food preparations made of vegetables, fruits, leaves and grains. Fruits, leaves and milk in different varieties can be offered to the Lord, and after the Lord accepts the foodstuff, the devotee can partake of the *prasāda,* by which all suffering in the struggle for existence will be gradually mitigated. This is confirmed in the *Bhagavad-gītā* (9.26). Even those who are accustomed to eat animals can offer foodstuff, not to the Lord directly, but to an agent of the Lord, under certain conditions of religious rites. Injunctions of the scriptures are meant not to encourage the eaters of animals, but to restrict them by regulative principles.

The living being is the source of subsistence for other, stronger living beings. No one should be very anxious for his subsistence in any circumstances because there are living beings everywhere, and no living being starves for want of food at any place. Mahārāja Yudhiṣṭhira is advised by Nārada not to worry about his uncles' suffering for want of food, for they could live on vegetables available in the jungles as *prasāda* of the Supreme Lord and thus realize the path of salvation.

Exploitation of the weaker living being by the stronger is the natural law of existence; there is always an attempt to devour the weak in different kingdoms of living beings. There is no possibility of checking this tendency by any artificial means under material conditions; it can be checked only by awakening the spiritual sense of the human being by practice of spiritual regulations. The spiritual regulative principles, however, do not allow a man to slaughter weaker animals on one side and teach others peaceful coexistence. If man does not allow the animals peaceful coexistence, how can he expect peaceful existence in human society? The blind leaders must therefore understand the Supreme Being and then try to implement the kingdom of God. The kingdom of God, or Rāma-rājya, is impossible without the awakening of God consciousness in the mass mind of the people of the world.

TEXT 48

तदिदं भगवान् राजन्नेक आत्मात्मनां स्वदृक् ।
अन्तरोऽनन्तरो भाति पश्य तं माययोरुधा ॥४८॥

tad idaṁ bhagavān rājann
eka ātmātmanāṁ sva-dṛk
antaro 'nantaro bhāti
paśya taṁ māyayorudhā

tat—therefore; *idam*—this manifestation; *bhagavān*—the Personality of Godhead; *rājan*—O King; *ekaḥ*—one without a second; *ātmā*—the Supersoul; *ātmanām*—by His energies; *sva-dṛk*—qualitatively like Him; *antaraḥ*—without; *anantaraḥ*—within and by Himself; *bhāti*—so manifests; *paśya*—look; *tam*—unto Him only; *māyayā*—by manifestations of different energies; *urudhā*—appears to be many.

TRANSLATION

Therefore, O King, you should look to the Supreme Lord only, who is one without a second and who manifests Himself by different energies and is both within and without.

PURPORT

The Supreme Lord Personality of Godhead is one without a second, but He manifests Himself by different energies because He is by nature blissful. The living beings are also manifestations of His marginal energy, qualitatively one with the Lord, and there are innumerable living beings both within and without the external and internal energies of the Lord. Since the spiritual world is a manifestation of the Lord's internal energy, the living beings within that internal potency are qualitatively one with the Lord without contamination from the external potency. Although qualitatively one with the Lord, the living being, due to contamination of the material world, is pervertedly manifested, and therefore he experiences so-called happiness and distress in the material world. Such experiences are all ephemeral and do not affect the spirit soul. The perception of such ephemeral happiness and distress is due only to the forgetfulness of his qualities, which are equal to the Lord's. There is, however, a regular current from the Lord Himself, from within and without, by which to rectify the fallen condition of the living being. From within He corrects the desiring living beings as localized Paramātmā, and from without He corrects by His manifestations, the spiritual master and the revealed scriptures. One should look unto the Lord; one should not be disturbed by the so-called manifestations of happiness or distress, but he should try to cooperate with the Lord in His outward activities for correcting the fallen souls. By His order only, one should become a spiritual master and cooperate with the Lord. One should not become a spiritual master for one's personal benefit, for some material gain or as an avenue of business or occupation for earning livelihood. Bona fide spiritual masters who look unto the Supreme Lord to cooperate with Him are actually qualitatively one with the Lord, and the forgetful ones are perverted reflections only. Yudhiṣṭhira Mahārāja is advised by Nārada, therefore, not to be disturbed by the affairs of so-called happiness and distress, but to look only unto the Lord to execute the mission for which the Lord has descended. That was his prime duty.

TEXT 49

सोऽयमद्य महाराज भगवान् भूतभावनः ।
कालरूपोऽवतीर्णोऽस्यामभावाय सुरद्विषाम् ॥४९॥

so 'yam adya mahārāja
bhagavān bhūta-bhāvanaḥ
kāla-rūpo 'vatīrṇo 'syām
abhāvāya sura-dviṣām

saḥ—that Supreme Lord; *ayam*—the Lord Śrī Kṛṣṇa; *adya*—at present; *mahārāja*—O King; *bhagavān*—the Personality of Godhead; *bhūta-bhāvanaḥ*—the creator or the father of everything created; *kāla-rūpaḥ*—in the disguise of all-devouring time; *avatīrṇaḥ*—descended; *asyām*—upon the world; *abhāvāya*—for eliminating; *sura-dviṣām*—those who are against the will of the Lord.

TRANSLATION

That Supreme Personality of Godhead, Lord Śrī Kṛṣṇa, in the guise of all-devouring time [kāla-rūpa] has now descended on earth to eliminate the envious from the world.

PURPORT

There are two classes of human beings, namely the envious and the obedient. Since the Supreme Lord is one and the father of all living beings, the envious living beings are also His sons, but they are known as the *asuras.* But the living beings who are obedient to the supreme father are called *devatās,* or demigods, because they are not contaminated by the material conception of life. Not only are the *asuras* envious of the Lord in even denying the existence of the Lord, but they are also envious of all other living beings. The predominance of *asuras* in the world is occasionally rectified by the Lord when He eliminates them from the world and establishes a rule of *devatās* like the Pāṇḍavas. His designation as *kāla* in disguise is significant. He is not at all dangerous, but He is the transcendental form of eternity, knowledge and bliss. For the devotees His factual form is disclosed, and for the nondevotees He appears like *kāla rūpa,* which is causal form. This causal form of the Lord is not at all pleasing to the *asuras,* and therefore they think of the Lord as formless in order to feel secure that they will not be vanquished by the Lord.

TEXT 50

निष्पादितं देवकृत्यमवशेषं प्रतीक्षते ।
तावद् यूयमवेक्षध्वं भवेद् यावदिहेश्वरः ॥५०॥

niṣpāditaṁ deva-kṛtyam
avaśeṣaṁ pratīkṣate
tāvad yūyam avekṣadhvaṁ
bhaved yāvad iheśvaraḥ

niṣpāditam—performed; *deva-kṛtyam*—what was to be done on behalf of the demigods; *avaśeṣam*—the rest; *pratīkṣate*—being awaited; *tāvat*—up to that time; *yūyam*—all of you Pāṇḍavas; *avekṣadhvam*—observe and wait; *bhavet*—may; *yāvat*—as long as; *iha*—in this world; *īśvaraḥ*—the Supreme Lord.

TRANSLATION

The Lord has already performed His duties to help the demigods, and He is awaiting the rest. You Pāṇḍavas may wait as long as the Lord is here on earth.

PURPORT

The Lord descends from His abode (Kṛṣṇaloka), the topmost planet in the spiritual sky, in order to help the demigod administrators of this material world when they are greatly vexed by the *asuras,* who are envious not only of the Lord but also of His devotees. As referred to above, the conditioned living beings contact material association by their own choice, dictated by a strong desire to lord it over the resources of the material world and become imitation lords of all they survey. Everyone is trying to become an imitation God; there is keen competition amongst such imitation gods, and such competitors are generally known as *asuras.* When there are too many *asuras* in the world, then it becomes a hell for those who are devotees of the Lord. Due to the growth of the *asuras,* the mass of people who are generally devoted to the Lord by nature and the pure devotees of the Lord, including the demigods in higher planets, pray to the Lord for relief, and the Lord either descends personally from His abode or deputes some of His devotees to remodel the fallen condition of human society, or even animal society. Such disruptions take place not only in human society but also among animals, birds or other living beings, including the demigods in the higher planets. Lord Śrī Kṛṣṇa descended personally to vanquish *asuras* like Kaṁsa, Jarāsandha and Śiśupāla, and during the reign of Mahārāja Yudhiṣṭhira almost all these *asuras* were killed by the Lord. Now he was awaiting the annihilation of His own dynasty, called the Yadu-vaṁśa, who appeared by His will in this world. He wanted to take them away before His own departure to His eternal abode. Nārada, like Vidura, did not disclose the imminent annihilation of the Yadu dynasty, but indirectly gave a hint to the King and his brothers to wait till the incident happened and the Lord departed.

TEXT 51

धृतराष्ट्रः सह भ्रात्रा गान्धार्या च स्वभार्यया ।
दक्षिणेन हिमवत ऋषीणामाश्रमं गतः ॥५१॥

dhṛtarāṣṭraḥ saha bhrātrā
gāndhāryā ca sva-bhāryayā
dakṣiṇena himavata
ṛṣīṇām āśramaṁ gataḥ

dhṛtarāṣṭraḥ—Dhṛtarāṣṭra; *saha*—along with; *bhrātrā*—his brother Vidura; *gāndhāryā*—Gāndhārī also; *ca*—and; *sva-bhāryayā*—his own wife; *dakṣiṇena*—by the southern side; *himavataḥ*—of the Himalaya Mountains; *ṛṣīṇām*—of the *ṛṣis; āśramam*—in shelter; *gataḥ*—he has gone.

TRANSLATION

O King, your uncle Dhṛtarāṣṭra, his brother Vidura and his wife Gāndhārī have gone to the southern side of the Himalaya Mountains, where there are shelters of the great sages.

PURPORT

To pacify the mourning Mahārāja Yudhiṣṭhira, Nārada first of all spoke from the philosophical point of view, and then he began to describe the future movements of his uncle, which he could see by his foreseeing powers, and thus began to describe as follows.

TEXT 52

स्रोतोभिः सप्तभिर्या वै स्वर्धुनी सप्तधा व्यधात् ।
सप्तानां प्रीतये नाना सप्तस्रोतः प्रचक्षते ॥५२॥

srotobhiḥ saptabhir yā vai
svardhunī saptadhā vyadhāt
saptānāṁ prītaye nānā
sapta-srotaḥ pracakṣate

srotobhiḥ—by currents; *saptabhiḥ*—by seven (divisions); *yā*—the river; *vai*—certainly; *svardhunī*—the sacred Ganges; *saptadhā*—seven branches; *vyadhāt*—created; *saptānām*—of the seven; *prītaye*—for the satisfaction of; *nānā*—various; *sapta-srotaḥ*—seven sources; *pracakṣate*—known by name.

TRANSLATION

The place is called Saptasrota ["divided by seven"] because there the waters of the sacred Ganges were divided into seven branches. This was done for the satisfaction of the seven great ṛṣis.

TEXT 53

स्नात्वानुसवनं तस्मिन्हुत्वा चाग्नीन्यथाविधि ।
अब्भक्ष उपशान्तात्मा स आस्ते विगतैषणः ॥५३॥

snātvānusavanaṁ tasmin
hutvā cāgnīn yathā-vidhi
ab-bhakṣa upaśāntātmā
sa āste vigataiṣaṇaḥ

snātvā—by taking bath; *anusavanam*—regularly three times (morning, noon and evening); *tasmin*—in that Ganges divided into seven; *hutvā*—by performing the Agni-hotra sacrifice; *ca*—also; *agnīn*—in the fire; *yathā-vidhi*—just according to the tenets of the scripture; *ap-bhakṣaḥ*—fasting by drinking only water; *upaśānta*—completely controlled; *ātmā*—the gross senses and the subtle mind; *saḥ*—Dhṛtarāṣṭra; *āste*—would be situated; *vigata*—devoid of; *eṣaṇaḥ*—thoughts in relation with family welfare.

TRANSLATION

On the banks at Saptasrota, Dhṛtarāṣṭra is now engaged in beginning aṣṭāṅga-yoga by bathing three times daily, in the morning, noon and evening, by performing the Agni-hotra sacrifice with fire and by drinking only water. This helps one control the mind and the senses and frees one completely from thoughts of familial affection.

PURPORT

The *yoga* system is a mechanical way to control the senses and the mind and divert them from matter to spirit. The preliminary processes are the sitting posture, meditation, spiritual thoughts, manipulation of air passing within the body, and gradual situation in trance, facing the Absolute Person, Paramātmā. Such mechanical ways of rising to the spiritual platform prescribe some regulative principles of taking bath daily three times, fasting as far as possible, sitting and concentrating the mind on spiritual matters and thus gradually becoming free from *viṣaya,* or material objectives. Material existence means to be absorbed in the material objective, which is simply illusory. House, country, family, society, children, property and business are some of the material coverings of the spirit, *ātmā,* and the *yoga* system helps one to become free from all these illusory thoughts and gradually turn towards the Absolute Person, Paramātmā. By material association and education, we learn simply to concentrate on flimsy things, but *yoga* is the process of forgetting them altogether. Modern so-called *yogīs* and *yoga* systems manifest some magical feats, and ignorant persons are attracted by such false things, or they accept the *yoga* system as a cheap healing process for diseases of the gross body. But factually the *yoga* system is the process of learning to forget what we have acquired throughout the struggle for existence. Dhṛtarāṣṭra was all along engaged in improving family affairs by raising the standard of living of his sons or by usurping the property of the Pāṇḍavas for the sake of his own sons. These are common affairs for a man grossly materialistic and without knowledge of the spiritual force. He does not see how this can drag one from heaven to hell. By the grace of his younger brother Vidura, Dhṛtarāṣṭra was enlightened and could see his grossly illusory engagements, and by such enlightenment he was able to leave home for spiritual realization. Śrī Nāradadeva was just foretelling the way of his spiritual progress in a place which was sanctified by the flow of the celestial Ganges. Drinking water only, without solid food, is also considered fasting. This is necessary for advancement of spiritual knowledge. A foolish man wants to be a cheap *yogī* without observing the regulative principles. A man who has no control over the tongue at first can hardly become a *yogī. Yogī* and *bhogī* are two opposite terms. The *bhogī,* or the merry man who eats and drinks, cannot be a *yogī,* for a *yogī* is never allowed to eat and drink unrestrictedly. We may note with profit how Dhṛtarāṣṭra began his *yoga* system by drinking water only and sitting calmly in a place with a spiritual atmosphere, deeply absorbed in the thoughts of the Lord Hari, the Personality of Godhead.

TEXT 54

जितासनो जितश्वासः प्रत्याहृतषडिन्द्रियः ।
हरिभावनया ध्वस्तरजःसत्त्वतमोमलः ॥५४॥

jitāsano jita-śvāsaḥ
pratyāhṛta-ṣaḍ-indriyaḥ
hari-bhāvanayā dhvasta-
rajaḥ-sattva-tamo-malaḥ

jita-āsanaḥ—one who has controlled the sitting posture; *jita-śvāsaḥ*—one who has controlled the breathing process; *pratyāhṛta*—turning back; *ṣaṭ*—six; *indriyaḥ*—senses; *hari*—the Absolute Personality of Godhead; *bhāvanayā*—absorbed in; *dhvasta*—conquered; *rajaḥ*—passion; *sattva*—goodness; *tamaḥ*—ignorance; *malaḥ*—contaminations.

TRANSLATION

One who has controlled the sitting postures [the yogic āsanas] and the breathing process can turn the senses toward the Absolute Personality of Godhead and thus become immune to the contaminations of the modes of material nature, namely mundane goodness, passion and ignorance.

PURPORT

The preliminary activities of the way of *yoga* are *āsana, prāṇāyāma, pratyāhāra, dhyāna, dhāraṇā,* etc. Mahārāja Dhṛtarāṣṭra was to attain success in those preliminary actions because he was seated in a sanctified place and was concentrating upon one objective, namely the Supreme Personality of Godhead (Hari). Thus all his senses were being engaged in the service of the Lord. This process directly helps the devotee to get freedom from the contaminations of the three material modes of nature. Even the highest mode, the material mode of goodness, is also a cause of material bondage, and what to speak of the other qualities, namely passion and ignorance. Passion and ignorance increase the material propensities of hankering for material enjoyment, and a strong sense of lust provokes the accumulation of wealth and power. One who has conquered these two base mentalities and has raised himself to the platform of goodness, which is full of knowledge and morality, cannot also control the senses, namely the eyes, the tongue, the nose, the ear and touch. But one who has surrendered himself unto the lotus feet of Lord Hari, as above mentioned, can transcend all influences of the modes of material nature and be fixed in the service of the Lord. The *bhakti-yoga* process, therefore, directly applies the senses to the loving service of the Lord. This prohibits the performer from engaging in material activities. This process of turning the senses from material attachment to the loving transcendental service of the Lord is called *pratyāhāra,* and the very process is called *prāṇāyāma,* ultimately ending in *samādhi,* or absorption in pleasing the Supreme Lord Hari by all means.

TEXT 55

विज्ञानात्मनि संयोज्य क्षेत्रज्ञे प्रविलाप्य तम् ।
ब्रह्मण्यात्मानमाधारे घटाम्बरमिवाम्बरे ॥५५॥

vijñānātmani saṁyojya
kṣetrajñe pravilāpya tam
brahmaṇy ātmānam ādhāre
ghaṭāmbaram ivāmbare

vijñāna—purified identity; *ātmani*—in intelligence; *saṁyojya*—perfectly fixing; *kṣetra-jñe*—in the matter of the living being; *pravilāpya*—merging; *tam*—him; *brahmaṇi*—in the Supreme; *ātmānam*—pure living being; *ādhāre*—in the reservoir; *ghaṭa-ambaram*—sky within the block; *iva*—like; *ambare*—in the supreme sky.

TRANSLATION

Dhṛtarāṣṭra will have to amalgamate his pure identity with intelligence and then merge into the Supreme Being with knowledge of his qualitative oneness, as a living entity, with the Supreme Brahman. Being freed from the blocked sky, he will have to rise to the spiritual sky.

PURPORT

The living being, by his desiring to lord it over the material world and declining to cooperate with the Supreme Lord, contacts the sum total of the material world, namely the *mahat-tattva,* and from the *mahat-tattva* his false identity with the material world, intelligence, mind and senses is developed. This covers his pure spiritual identity. By the yogic process, when his pure identity is realized in self-realization, one has to revert to the original position by amalgamating the five gross elements and the subtle elements, mind and intelligence, into the *mahat-tattva* again. Thus getting freed from the clutches of the *mahat-tattva,* he has to merge in the existence of the Supersoul. In other words, he has to realize that qualitatively he is nondifferent from the Supersoul, and thus he transcends the material sky by his pure identical intelligence and thus becomes engaged in the transcendental loving service of the Lord. This is the highest perfectional development of spiritual identity, which was attained by Dhṛtarāṣṭra by the grace of Vidura and the Lord. The Lord's mercy was bestowed upon him by his personal contact with Vidura, and when he was actually practicing the instructions of Vidura, the Lord helped him to attain the highest perfectional stage.

A pure devotee of the Lord does not live on any planet of the material sky, nor does he feel any contact with material elements. His so-called material body does not exist, being surcharged with the spiritual current of the Lord's identical interest, and thus he is permanently freed from all contaminations of the sum total of the *mahat-tattva.* He is always in the spiritual sky, which he attains by being transcendental to the sevenfold material coverings by the effect of his devotional service. The conditioned souls are within the coverings, whereas the liberated soul is far beyond the cover.

TEXT 56

ध्वस्तमायागुणोदर्को निरुद्धकरणाशयः ।
निवर्तिताखिलाहार आस्ते स्थाणुरिवाचलः ।
तस्यान्तरायो मैवाभूः सन्न्यस्ताखिलकर्मणः ॥ ५६ ॥

dhvasta-māyā-guṇodarko
niruddha-karaṇāśayaḥ
nivartitākhilāhāra
āste sthāṇur ivācalaḥ
tasyāntarāyo maivābhūḥ
sannyastākhila-karmaṇaḥ

dhvasta—being destroyed; *māyā-guṇa*—the modes of material nature; *udarkaḥ*—aftereffects; *niruddha*—being suspended; *karaṇa-āśayaḥ*—the senses and the mind; *nivartita*—stopped; *akhila*—all; *āhāraḥ*—food for the senses; *āste*—is sitting; *sthāṇuḥ*—immovable; *iva*—like; *acalaḥ*—fixed; *tasya*—his; *antarāyaḥ*—hindrances; *mā eva*—never like that; *abhūḥ*—be; *sannyasta*—renounced; *akhila*—all sorts; *karmaṇaḥ*—material duties.

TRANSLATION

He will have to suspend all the actions of the senses, even from the outside, and will have to be impervious to interactions of the senses, which are influenced by the modes of material nature. After renouncing all material duties, he must become immovably established, beyond all sources of hindrances on the path.

PURPORT

Dhṛtarāṣṭra had attained, by the yogic process, the stage of negation of all sorts of material reaction. The effects of the material modes of nature draw the victim to indefatigable desires of enjoying matter, but one can escape such false enjoyment by the yogic process. Every sense is always busy in searching for its food, and thus the conditioned soul is assaulted from all sides and has no chance to become steady in any pursuit. Mahārāja Yudhiṣṭhira was advised by Nārada not to disturb his uncle by attempting to bring him back home. He was now beyond the attraction of anything material. The material modes of nature (the *guṇas*) have their different modes of activities, but above the material modes of nature is a spiritual mode, which is absolute. *Nirguṇa* means without reaction. The spiritual mode and its effect are identical; therefore the spiritual quality is distinguished from its material counterpart by the word *nirguṇa.* After complete suspension of the material modes of nature, one is admitted to the spiritual sphere, and action dictated by the spiritual modes is called devotional service, or *bhakti. Bhakti* is therefore *nirguṇa* attained by direct contact with the Absolute.

TEXT 57

स वा अद्यतनाद् राजन् परतः पञ्चमेऽहनि ।
कलेवरं हास्यति स्वं तच्च भस्मीभविष्यति ॥५७॥

sa vā adyatanād rājan
parataḥ pañcame 'hani
kalevaraṁ hāsyati svaṁ
tac ca bhasmī-bhaviṣyati

saḥ—he; *vā*—in all probability; *adya*—today; *tanāt*—from; *rājan*—O King; *parataḥ*—ahead; *pañcame*—on the fifth; *ahani*—day; *kalevaram*—body; *hāsyati*—shall quit; *svam*—his own; *tat*—that; *ca*—also; *bhasmī*—ashes; *bhaviṣyati*—will turn into.

TRANSLATION

O King, he will quit his body, most probably on the fifth day from today. And his body will turn to ashes.

PURPORT

Nārada Muni's prophecy prohibited Yudhiṣṭhira Mahārāja from going to the place where his uncle was staying because even after quitting the body by his own mystic power, Dhṛtarāṣṭra would not be in need of any funeral ceremony; Nārada Muni indicated that his body by itself would burn to ashes. The perfection of the *yoga* system is attained by such mystic power. The *yogī* is able to quit his body by his own choice of time and can attain any planet he desires by turning the present body into ashes by self-made fire.

TEXT 58

दह्यमानेऽग्निभिर्देहे पत्युः पत्नी सहोटजे ।
बहिः स्थिता पतिं साध्वी तमग्निमनु वेक्ष्यति ॥५८॥

dahyamāne 'gnibhir dehe
patyuḥ patnī sahoṭaje
bahiḥ sthitā patiṁ sādhvī
tam agnim anu vekṣyati

dahyamāne—while it is burning; *agnibhiḥ*—by the fire; *dehe*—the body; *patyuḥ*—of the husband; *patnī*—the wife; *saha-uṭaje*—along with the thatched cottage; *bahiḥ*—outside; *sthitā*—situated; *patim*—unto the husband; *sādhvī*—the chaste lady; *tam*—that; *agnim*—fire; *anu vekṣyati*—looking with great attention will enter the fire.

TRANSLATION

While outside observing her husband, who will burn in the fire of mystic power along with his thatched cottage, his chaste wife will enter the fire with rapt attention.

PURPORT

Gāndhārī was an ideal chaste lady, a life companion of her husband, and therefore when she saw her husband burning in the fire of mystic *yoga* along with his cottage of leaves, she despaired. She left home after losing her one hundred sons, and in the forest she saw that her most beloved husband was also burning. Now she actually felt alone, and therefore she entered the fire of her husband and followed her husband to death. This entering of a chaste lady into the fire of her dead husband is called the *satī* rite, and the action is considered to be most perfect for a woman. In a later age, this *satī* rite became an obnoxious criminal affair because the ceremony was forced upon even an unwilling woman. In this fallen age it is not possible for any lady to follow the *satī* rite as chastely as it was done by Gāndhārī and others in past ages. A chaste wife like Gāndhārī would feel the separation of her husband to be more burning than actual fire. Such a lady can observe the *satī* rite voluntarily, and there is no criminal force by anyone. When the rite became a formality only and force was applied upon a lady to follow the principle, actually it became criminal, and therefore the ceremony was to be stopped by state law. This prophecy of Nārada Muni to Mahārāja Yudhiṣṭhira forbade him to go to his widowed aunt.

TEXT 59

विदुरस्तु तदाश्चर्यं निशाम्य कुरुनन्दन ।
हर्षशोकयुतस्तस्माद् गन्ता तीर्थनिषेवकः ॥५९॥

viduras tu tad āścaryaṁ
niśāmya kuru-nandana
harṣa-śoka-yutas tasmād
gantā tīrtha-niṣevakaḥ

viduraḥ—Vidura also; *tu*—but; *tat*—that incident; *āścaryam*—wonderful; *niśāmya*—seeing; *kuru-nandana*—O son of the Kuru dynasty; *harṣa*—delight; *śoka*—grief; *yutaḥ*—affected by; *tasmāt*—from that place; *gantā*—will go away; *tīrtha*—place of pilgrimage; *niṣevakaḥ*—for being enlivened.

TRANSLATION

Vidura, being affected with delight and grief, will then leave that place of sacred pilgrimage.

PURPORT

Vidura was astonished to see the marvelous departure of his brother Dhṛtarāṣṭra as a liberated *yogī,* for in his past life he was much attached to materialism. Of course it was only due to Vidura that his brother attained the desirable goal of life. Vidura was therefore glad to learn about it. But he was sorry that he could not make his brother turn into a pure devotee. This was not done by Vidura because of Dhṛtarāṣṭra's being inimical to the Pāṇḍavas, who were all devotees of the Lord. An offense at the feet of a Vaiṣṇava is more dangerous than an offense at the lotus feet of the Lord. Vidura was certainly very liberal to bestow mercy upon his brother Dhṛtarāṣṭra, whose past life was very materialistic. But ultimately the result of such mercy certainly depended on the will of the Supreme Lord in the present life; therefore Dhṛtarāṣṭra attained liberation only, and after many such liberated states of life one can attain to the stage of devotional service. Vidura was certainly very mortified by the death of his brother and sister-in-law, and the only remedy to mitigate such lamentation was to go out to pilgrimage. Thus Mahārāja Yudhiṣṭhira had no chance to call back Vidura, his surviving uncle.

TEXT 60

इत्युक्त्वाथारुहत् स्वर्गं नारदः सहतुम्बुरुः ।
युधिष्ठिरो वचस्तस्य हृदि कृत्वाजहाच्छुचः ॥६०॥

ity uktvāthāruhat svargaṁ
nāradaḥ saha-tumburuḥ
yudhiṣṭhiro vacas tasya
hṛdi kṛtvājahāc chucaḥ

iti—thus; *uktvā*—having addressed; *atha*—thereafter; *āruhat*—ascended; *svargam*—into outer space; *nāradaḥ*—the great sage Nārada; *saha*—along with; *tumburuḥ*—his stringed instrument; *yudhiṣṭhiraḥ*—Mahārāja Yudhiṣṭhira; *vacaḥ*—instructions; *tasya*—of his; *hṛdi kṛtvā*—keeping in the heart; *ajahāt*—gave up; *śucaḥ*—all lamentations.

TRANSLATION

Having spoken thus, the great sage Nārada, along with his vīṇā, ascended into outer space. Yudhiṣṭhira kept his instruction in his heart and so was able to get rid of all lamentations.

PURPORT

Śrī Nāradajī is an eternal spaceman, having been endowed with a spiritual body by the grace of the Lord. He can travel in the outer spaces of both the material and spiritual worlds without restriction and can approach any planet in unlimited space within no time. We have already discussed his previous life as the son of a maidservant. Because of his association with pure devotees, he was elevated to the position of an eternal spaceman and thus had freedom of movement. One should therefore try to follow in the footsteps of Nārada Muni and not make a futile effort to reach other planets by mechanical means. Mahārāja Yudhiṣṭhira was a pious king, and therefore he could see Nārada Muni occasionally; anyone who desires to see Nārada Muni must first be pious and follow in the footsteps of Nārada Muni.

Thus end the Bhaktivedanta purports of the First Canto, Thirteenth Chapter, of the Śrīmad-Bhāgavatam, *entitled "Dhṛtarāṣṭra Quits Home."*

CHAPTER FOURTEEN

The Disappearance of Lord Kṛṣṇa

TEXT 1

सूत उवाच
सम्प्रस्थिते द्वारकायां जिष्णौ बन्धुदिदृक्षया ।
ज्ञातुं च पुण्यश्लोकस्य कृष्णस्य च विचेष्टितम् ॥१॥

sūta uvāca
samprasthite dvārakāyāṁ
jiṣṇau bandhu-didṛkṣayā
jñātuṁ ca puṇya-ślokasya
kṛṣṇasya ca viceṣṭitam

sūtaḥ uvāca—Śrī Sūta Gosvāmī said; *samprasthite*—having gone to; *dvārakāyām*—the city of Dvārakā; *jiṣṇau*—Arjuna; *bandhu*—friends and relatives; *didṛkṣayā*—for meeting them; *jñātum*—to know; *ca*—also; *puṇya-ślokasya*—of one whose glories are sung by Vedic hymns; *kṛṣṇasya*—of Lord Kṛṣṇa; *ca*—and; *viceṣṭitam*—further programs of work.

TRANSLATION

Śrī Sūta Gosvāmī said: Arjuna went to Dvārakā to see Lord Śrī Kṛṣṇa and other friends and also to learn from the Lord of His next activities.

PURPORT

As stated in *Bhagavad-gītā,* the Lord descended to earth for the protection of the faithful and annihilation of the impious, so after the Battle of Kurukṣetra and establishment of Mahārāja Yudhiṣṭhira, the mission of the Lord was complete. The Pāṇḍavas, especially Śrī Arjuna, were eternal companions of the Lord, and therefore Arjuna went to Dvārakā to hear from the Lord of His next program of work.

TEXT 2

व्यतीताः कतिचिन्मासास्तदा नायात्ततोऽर्जुनः ।
ददर्श घोररूपाणि निमित्तानि कुरूद्वहः ॥२॥

vyatītāḥ katicin māsās
tadā nāyāt tato 'rjunaḥ
dadarśa ghora-rūpāṇi
nimittāni kurūdvahaḥ

vyatītāḥ—after passing; *katicit*—a few; *māsāḥ*—months; *tadā*—at that time; *na āyāt*—did not return; *tataḥ*—from there; *arjunaḥ*—Arjuna; *dadarśa*—observed; *ghora*—fearful; *rūpāṇi*—appearances; *nimittāni*—various causes; *kuru-udvahaḥ*—Mahārāja Yudhiṣṭhira.

TRANSLATION

A few months passed, and Arjuna did not return. Mahārāja Yudhiṣṭhira then began to observe some inauspicious omens, which were fearful in themselves.

PURPORT

Lord Śrī Kṛṣṇa the Supreme Personality of Godhead is *ad infinitum,* more powerful than the most powerful sun of our experience. Millions and billions of suns are created by Him and annihilated by Him within His one breathing period. In the material world the sun is considered to be the source of all productivity and material energy, and only due to the sun can we have the necessities of life. Therefore, during the personal presence of the Lord on the earth, all paraphernalia for our peace and prosperity, especially religion and knowledge, were in full display because of the Lord's presence, just as there is a full flood of light in the presence of the glowing sun. Mahārāja Yudhiṣṭhira observed some discrepancies in his kingdom, and therefore he became very anxious about Arjuna, who was long absent, and there was also no news about Dvārakā's well-being. He suspected the disappearance of Lord Kṛṣṇa, otherwise there would have been no possibility of fearful omens.

TEXT 3

कालस्य च गतिं रौद्रां विपर्यस्तर्तुधर्मिणः ।
पापीयसीं नृणां वार्तां क्रोधलोभानृतात्मनाम् ॥३॥

kālasya ca gatiṁ raudrāṁ
viparyastartu-dharmiṇaḥ
pāpīyasīṁ nṛṇāṁ vārtāṁ
krodha-lobhānṛtātmanām

kālasya—of eternal time; *ca*—also; *gatim*—direction; *raudrām*—fearful; *viparyasta*—reversed; *ṛtu*—seasonal; *dharmiṇaḥ*—regularities; *pāpīyasīm*—sinful; *nṛṇām*—of the human being; *vārtām*—means of livelihood; *krodha*—anger; *lobha*—greed; *anṛta*—falsehood; *ātmanām*—of the people.

TRANSLATION

He saw that the direction of eternal time had changed, and this was very fearful. There were disruptions in the seasonal regularities. The people in general had become very greedy, angry and deceitful. And he saw that they were adopting foul means of livelihood.

PURPORT

When civilization is disconnected from the loving relation of the Supreme Personality of Godhead, symptoms like changes of seasonal regulations, foul means of livelihood, greed, anger and fraudulence become rampant. The change of seasonal regulations refers to one season's atmosphere becoming manifest in another season—for example the rainy season's being transferred to autumn, or the fructification of fruits and flowers from one season in another season. A godless man is invariably greedy, angry and fraudulent. Such a man can earn his livelihood by any means, black or white. During the reign of Mahārāja Yudhiṣṭhira, all the above symptoms were conspicuous by their absence. But Mahārāja Yudhiṣṭhira was astonished to experience even a slight change in the godly atmosphere of his kingdom, and at once he suspected the disappearance of the Lord. Foul means of livelihood implies deviation from one's occupational duty. There are prescribed duties for everyone, such as the *brāhmaṇa, kṣatriya, vaiśya* and *śūdra,* but anyone who deviates from his prescribed duty and declares another's duty to be his own is following a foul and improper duty. A man becomes too greedy for wealth and power when he has no higher objective in life and when he thinks that this earthly life of a few years is all in all. Ignorance is the cause for all these anomalies in human society, and to remove this ignorance, especially in this age of degradation, the powerful sun is there to distribute light in the shape of *Śrīmad-Bhāgavatam.*

TEXT 4

जिह्मप्रायं व्यवहृतं शाठ्यमिश्रं च सौहृदम् ।
पितृमातृसुहृद्भ्रातृदम्पतीनां च कल्कनम् ॥४॥

jihma-prāyaṁ vyavahṛtaṁ
śāṭhya-miśraṁ ca sauhṛdam
pitṛ-mātṛ-suhṛd-bhrātṛ-
dam-patīnāṁ ca kalkanam

jihma-prāyam—cheating; *vyavahṛtam*—in all ordinary transactions; *śāṭhya*—duplicity; *miśram*—adulterated in; *ca*—and; *sauhṛdam*—regarding friendly well-wishers; *pitṛ*—father; *mātṛ*—regarding the mother; *suhṛt*—well-wishers; *bhrātṛ*—one's own brother; *dam-patīnām*—regarding husband and wife; *ca*—also; *kalkanam*—mutual quarrel.

TRANSLATION

All ordinary transactions and dealings became polluted with cheating, even between friends. And in familial affairs, there was always misunderstanding between fathers, mothers and sons, between well-wishers, and between brothers. Even between husband and wife there was always strain and quarrel.

PURPORT

A conditioned living being is endowed with four principles of malpractice, namely errors, insanity, inability and cheating. These are signs of imperfection, and out of the four the propensity to cheat others is most prominent. And this cheating practice is there in the conditioned souls because the conditioned souls are primarily in the material world imbued with an unnatural desire to lord it over the material world. A living being in his pure state is not conditioned by the laws because in his pure state he is conscious that a living being is eternally subservient to the Supreme Being, and thus it is always good for him to remain subservient, instead of falsely trying to lord it over the property of the Supreme Lord. In the conditioned state the living being is not satisfied even if he actually becomes the lord of all that he surveys, which he never becomes, and therefore he becomes the victim of all kinds of cheating, even with his nearest and most intimate relations. In such an unsatisfactory state of affairs, there is no harmony, even between father and sons or between husband and wife. But all these contending difficulties can be mitigated by one process, and that is the devotional service of the Lord. The world of hypocrisy can be checked only by counteraction through devotional service to the Lord and nothing else. Mahārāja Yudhiṣṭhira, having observed the disparities, conjectured the disappearance of the Lord from the earth.

TEXT 5

निमित्तान्यत्यरिष्टानि काले त्वनुगते नृणाम् ।
लोभाद्यधर्मप्रकृतिं दृष्ट्वोवाचानुजं नृपः ॥५॥

nimittāny atyariṣṭāni
kāle tv anugate nṛṇām
lobhādy-adharma-prakṛtiṁ
dṛṣṭvovācānujaṁ nṛpaḥ

nimittāni—causes; *ati*—very serious; *ariṣṭāni*—bad omens; *kāle*—in course of time; *tu*—but; *anugate*—passing away; *nṛṇām*—of humanity at large; *lobha-ādi*—such as greed; *adharma*—irreligious; *prakṛtim*—habits; *dṛṣṭvā*—having observed; *uvāca*—said; *anujam*—younger brother; *nṛpaḥ*—the King.

TRANSLATION

In course of time it came to pass that people in general became accustomed to greed, anger, pride, etc. Mahārāja Yudhiṣṭhira, observing all these omens, spoke to his younger brother.

PURPORT

Such a pious king as Mahārāja Yudhiṣṭhira at once became perturbed when there were such inhuman symptoms as greed, anger, irreligiosity and hypocrisy rampant in society. It appears from this statement that all these symptoms of degraded society were unknown to the people of the time, and it was astonishing for them to have experienced them with the advent of the Kali-yuga, or the age of quarrel.

TEXT 6

युधिष्ठिर उवाच
सम्प्रेषितो द्वारकायां जिष्णुर्बन्धुदिदृक्षया ।
ज्ञातुं च पुण्यश्लोकस्य कृष्णस्य च विचेष्टितम् ॥६॥

yudhiṣṭhira uvāca
sampreṣito dvārakāyāṁ
jiṣṇur bandhu-didṛkṣayā
jñātuṁ ca puṇya-ślokasya
kṛṣṇasya ca viceṣṭitam

yudhiṣṭhiraḥ uvāca—Mahārāja Yudhiṣṭhira said; *sampreṣitaḥ*—has gone to; *dvārakāyām*—Dvārakā; *jiṣṇuḥ*—Arjuna; *bandhu*—friends; *didṛkṣayā*—for the sake of meeting; *jñātum*—to know; *ca*—also; *puṇya-ślokasya*—of the Personality of Godhead; *kṛṣṇasya*—of Lord Śrī Kṛṣṇa; *ca*—and; *viceṣṭitam*—program of work.

TRANSLATION

Mahārāja Yudhiṣṭhira said to his younger brother Bhīmasena: I sent Arjuna to Dvārakā to meet his friends and to learn from the Personality of Godhead, Kṛṣṇa, of His program of work.

TEXT 7

गताः सप्ताधुना मासा भीमसेन तवानुजः ।
नायाति कस्य वा हेतोर्नाहं वेदेदमञ्जसा ॥७॥

gatāḥ saptādhunā māsā
bhīmasena tavānujaḥ
nāyāti kasya vā hetor
nāhaṁ vededam añjasā

gatāḥ—has gone; *sapta*—seven; *adhunā*—to date; *māsāḥ*—months; *bhīmasena*—O Bhīmasena; *tava*—your; *anujaḥ*—younger brother; *na*—does not; *āyāti*—come back; *kasya*—for what; *vā*—or; *hetoḥ*—reason; *na*—not; *aham*—I; *veda*—know; *idam*—this; *añjasā*—factually.

TRANSLATION

Since he departed, seven months have passed, yet he has not returned. I do not know factually how things are going there.

TEXT 8

अपि देवर्षिणादिष्टः स कालोऽयमुपस्थितः ।
यदात्मनोऽङ्गमाक्रीडं भगवानुत्सिसृक्षति ॥८॥

api devarṣiṇādiṣṭaḥ
sa kālo 'yam upasthitaḥ
yadātmano 'ṅgam ākrīḍaṁ
bhagavān utsisṛkṣati

api—whether; *deva-ṛṣiṇā*—by the demigod-saint (Nārada); *ādiṣṭaḥ*—instructed; *saḥ*—that; *kālaḥ*—eternal time; *ayam*—this; *upasthitaḥ*—arrived; *yadā*—when; *ātmanaḥ*—of His own self; *aṅgam*—plenary portion; *ākrīḍam*—manifestation; *bhagavān*—the Personality of Godhead; *utsisṛkṣati*—is going to quit.

TRANSLATION

Is He going to quit His earthly pastimes, as Devarṣi Nārada indicated? Has that time already arrived?

PURPORT

As we have discussed many times, the Supreme Personality of Godhead, Lord Śrī Kṛṣṇa, has many plenary expansions, and each and every one of them, although equally powerful, executes different functions. In *Bhagavad-gītā* there are different statements by the Lord, and each of these statements is meant for different plenary portions or portions of the plenary portions. For example, Śrī Kṛṣṇa, the Lord, says in *Bhagavad-gītā:*

"Whenever and wherever there is a decline in religious practice, O descendant of Bharata, and a predominant rise of irreligion—at that time I descend Myself." (Bg. 4.7)

"To deliver the faithful, to annihilate the miscreants and also to reestablish the principles of occupational duty, I appear in every age." (Bg. 4.8)

"If I should cease to work, then all humanity would be misdirected. I would also be the cause of creating unwanted population, and I would thereby destroy the peace of all sentient beings." (Bg. 3.24)

"Whatever action a great man performs, common men will follow. And whatever standards he sets by exemplary acts, all the world pursues." (Bg. 3.21)

All the above statements by the Lord apply to different plenary portions of the Lord, namely His expansions such as Saṅkarṣaṇa, Vāsudeva, Pradyumna, Aniruddha and Nārāyaṇa. These are all He Himself in different transcendental expansions, and still the Lord as Śrī Kṛṣṇa functions in a different sphere of transcendental exchange with different grades of devotees. And yet Lord Kṛṣṇa as He is appears once every twenty-four hours of Brahmā's time (or after a lapse of 8,640,000,000 solar years) in each and every universe, and all His transcendental pastimes are displayed in each and every universe in a routine spool. But in that routine spool the functions of Lord Kṛṣṇa, Lord Vāsudeva, etc., are complex problems for the layman. There is no difference between the Lord's Self and the Lord's transcendental body. The expansions execute differential activities. When the Lord, however, appears in His person as Lord Śrī Kṛṣṇa, His other plenary portions also join in Him by His inconceivable potency called *yogamāyā,* and thus the Lord Kṛṣṇa of Vṛndāvana is different from the Lord Kṛṣṇa of Mathurā or the Lord Kṛṣṇa of Dvārakā. The *virāṭ-rūpa* of Lord Kṛṣṇa is also different from Him, by His inconceivable potency. The *virāṭ-rūpa* exhibited on the Battlefield of Kurukṣetra is the material conception of His form. Therefore it should be understood that when Lord Kṛṣṇa was apparently killed by the bow and arrow of the hunter, the Lord left His so-called material body in the material world. The Lord is *kaivalya,* and for Him there is no difference between matter and spirit because everything is created from Him. Therefore His quitting one sort of body or accepting another body does not mean that He is like the ordinary living being. All such activities are simultaneously one and different by His inconceivable potency. When Mahārāja Yudhiṣṭhira was lamenting the possibility of His disappearance, it was just in pursuance of a custom of lamenting the disappearance of a great friend, but factually the Lord never quits His transcendental body, as is misconceived by less intelligent persons. Such less intelligent persons have been condemned by the Lord Himself in *Bhagavad-gītā,* and they are known as the *mūḍhas.* That the Lord left His body means that He left again His plenary portions in the respective *dhāmas* (transcendental abodes), as He left His *virāṭ-rūpa* in the material world.

TEXT 9

यस्मान्नः सम्पदो राज्यं दाराः प्राणाः कुलं प्रजाः ।
आसन्सपत्नविजयो लोकाश्च यदनुग्रहात् ॥९॥

yasmān naḥ sampado rājyaṁ
dārāḥ prāṇāḥ kulaṁ prajāḥ
āsan sapatna-vijayo
lokāś ca yad-anugrahāt

yasmāt—from whom; *naḥ*—our; *sampadaḥ*—opulence; *rājyam*—kingdom; *dārāḥ*—good wives; *prāṇāḥ*—existence of life; *kulam*—dynasty; *prajāḥ*—subjects; *āsan*—have become possible; *sapatna*—competitors; *vijayaḥ*—conquering; *lokāḥ*—future accommodation in higher planets; *ca*—and; *yat*—by whose; *anugrahāt*—by the mercy of.

TRANSLATION

From Him only, all our kingly opulence, good wives, lives, progeny, control over our subjects, victory over our enemies, and future accommodations in higher planets have become possible. All this is due to His causeless mercy upon us.

PURPORT

Material prosperity consists of a good wife, good home, sufficient land, good children, aristocratic family relations, victory over competitors and, by pious work, attainment of accommodations in the higher celestial planets for better facilities of material amenities. These facilities are earned not only by one's hard manual labor or by unfair means, but by the mercy of the Supreme Lord. Prosperity earned by one's personal endeavor also depends on the mercy of the Lord. Personal labor must be there in addition to the Lord's benediction, but without the Lord's benediction no one is successful simply by personal labor. The modernized man of Kali-yuga believes in personal endeavor and denies the benediction of the Supreme Lord. Even a great *sannyāsī* of India delivered speeches in Chicago protesting the benedictions of the Supreme Lord. But as far as Vedic *śāstras* are concerned, as we find in the pages of *Śrīmad-Bhāgavatam,* the ultimate sanction for all success rests in the hands of the Supreme Lord. Mahārāja Yudhiṣṭhira admits this truth in his personal success, and it behooves one to follow in the footsteps of a great king and devotee of the Lord to make life a full success. If one could achieve success without the sanction of the Lord then no medical practitioner would fail to cure a patient. Despite the most advanced treatment of a suffering patient by the most up-to-date medical practitioner, there is death, and even in the most hopeless case, without medical treatment, a patient is cured astonishingly. Therefore the conclusion is that God's sanction is the immediate cause for all happenings, good or bad. Any successful man should feel grateful to the Lord for all he has achieved.

TEXT 10

पश्योत्पातान्नरव्याघ्र दिव्यान् भौमान् सदैहिकान् ।
दारुणान् शंसतोऽदूराद्भयं नो बुद्धिमोहनम् ॥१०॥

paśyotpātān nara-vyāghra
divyān bhaumān sadaihikān

dāruṇān śaṁsato 'dūrād
bhayaṁ no buddhi-mohanam

paśya—just see; *utpātān*—disturbances; *nara-vyāghra*—O man of tigerlike strength; *divyān*—happenings in the sky or by planetary influence; *bhaumān*—happenings on the earth; *sa-daihikān*—happenings of the body and the mind; *dāruṇān*—awfully dangerous; *śaṁsataḥ*—indicating; *adūrāt*—in the near future; *bhayam*—danger; *naḥ*—our; *buddhi*—intelligence; *mohanam*—deluding.

TRANSLATION

Just see, O man with a tiger's strength, how many miseries due to celestial influences, earthly reactions and bodily pains—all very dangerous in themselves—are foreboding danger in the near future by deluding our intelligence.

PURPORT

Material advancement of civilization means advancement of the reactions of the threefold miseries due to celestial influence, earthly reactions and bodily or mental pains. By the celestial influence of the stars there are many calamities like excessive heat, cold, rains or no rains, and the aftereffects are famine, disease and epidemic. The aggregate result is agony of the body and the mind. Man-made material science cannot do anything to counteract these threefold miseries. They are all punishments from the superior energy of *māyā* under the direction of the Supreme Lord. Therefore our constant touch with the Lord by devotional service can give us relief without our being disturbed in the discharge of our human duties. The *asuras,* however, who do not believe in the existence of God, make their own plans to counteract all these threefold miseries, and so they meet with failures every time. The *Bhagavad-gītā* (7.14) clearly states that the reaction of material energy is never to be conquered, because of the binding effects of the three modes. They can simply be overcome by one who surrenders fully in devotion under the lotus feet of the Lord.

TEXT 11

ऊर्वक्षिबाहवो मह्यं स्फुरन्त्यङ्ग पुनः पुनः ।
वेपथुश्चापि हृदये आराद्दास्यन्ति विप्रियम् ॥११॥

ūrv-akṣi-bāhavo mahyaṁ
sphuranty aṅga punaḥ punaḥ
vepathuś cāpi hṛdaye
ārād dāsyanti vipriyam

ūru—thighs; *akṣi*—eyes; *bāhavaḥ*—the arms; *mahyam*—in my; *sphuranti*—quivering; *aṅga*—left side of the body; *punaḥ punaḥ*—again and again; *vepathuḥ*—palpitations; *ca*—also; *api*—certainly; *hṛdaye*—in the heart; *ārāt*—due to fear; *dāsyanti*—indicating; *vipriyam*—undesirables.

TRANSLATION

The left side of my body, my thighs, arms and eyes are all quivering again and again. I am having heart palpitations due to fear. All this indicates undesirable happenings.

PURPORT

Material existence is full of undesirables. Things we do not want are forced upon us by some superior energy, and we do not see that these undesirables are under the grip of the three modes of material nature. When a man's eyes, arms and thighs quiver constantly, one must know that something is going to happen which is undesirable. These undesirables are compared to fire in a forest. No one goes into the forest to set fires, but fires automatically take place in the forest, creating inconceivable calamities for the living beings of the forest. Such a fire cannot be extinguished by any human efforts. The fire can be extinguished only by the mercy of the Lord, who sends clouds to pour water on the forest. Similarly, undesirable happenings in life cannot be checked by any number of plans. Such miseries can be removed only by the mercy of the Lord, who sends His bona fide representatives to enlighten human beings and thus save them from all calamities.

TEXT 12

शिवैषोद्यन्तमादित्यमभिरौत्यनलानना ।
मामङ्ग सारमेयोऽयमभिरेभत्यभीरुवत् ॥१२॥

śivaiṣodyantam ādityam
abhirauty analānanā
mām aṅga sārameyo 'yam
abhirebhaty abhīruvat

śivā—jackal; *eṣā*—this; *udyantam*—rising; *ādityam*—unto the sun; *abhi*—towards; *rauti*—crying; *anala*—fire; *ānanā*—face; *mām*—unto me; *aṅga*—O Bhīma; *sārameyaḥ*—dog; *ayam*—this; *abhirebhati*—barks towards; *abhīru-vat*—without fear.

TRANSLATION

Just see, O Bhīma, how the she-jackal cries at the rising sun and vomits fire, and how the dog barks at me fearlessly.

PURPORT

These are some bad omens indicating something undesirable in the near future.

TEXT 13

शस्ताः कुर्वन्ति मां सव्यं दक्षिणं पशवोऽपरे ।
वाहांश्च पुरुषव्याघ्र लक्षये रुदतो मम ॥१३॥

śastāḥ kurvanti māṁ savyaṁ
dakṣiṇaṁ paśavo 'pare
vāhāṁś ca puruṣa-vyāghra
lakṣaye rudato mama

śastāḥ—useful animals like the cow; *kurvanti*—are keeping; *mām*—me; *savyam*—on the left; *dakṣiṇam*—circumambulating; *paśavaḥ apare*—other lower animals like asses; *vāhān*—the horses (carriers); *ca*—also; *puruṣa-vyāghra*—O tiger among men; *lakṣaye*—I see; *rudataḥ*—weeping; *mama*—of mine.

TRANSLATION

O Bhīmasena, tiger amongst men, now useful animals like cows are passing me on my left side, and lower animals like the asses are circumambulating me. My horses appear to weep upon seeing me.

TEXT 14

मृत्युदूतः कपोतोऽयमुलूकः कम्पयन् मनः ।
प्रत्युलूकश्च कुह्वानैर्विश्वं वै शून्यमिच्छतः ॥१४॥

mṛtyu-dūtaḥ kapoto 'yam
ulūkaḥ kampayan manaḥ
pratyulūkaś ca kuhvānair
viśvaṁ vai śūnyam icchataḥ

mṛtyu—death; *dūtaḥ*—messenger of; *kapotaḥ*—pigeon; *ayam*—this; *ulūkaḥ*—owl; *kampayan*—trembling; *manaḥ*—mind; *pratyulūkaḥ*—the rivals of owls (crows); *ca*—and; *kuhvānaiḥ*—shrieking scream; *viśvam*—the cosmos; *vai*—either; *śūnyam*—void; *icchataḥ*—wishing.

TRANSLATION

Just see! This pigeon is like a messenger of death. The shrieks of the owls and their rival crows make my heart tremble. It appears that they want to make a void of the whole universe.

TEXT 15

धूम्रा दिशः परिधयः कम्पते भूः सहाद्रिभिः ।
निर्घातश्च महांस्तात साकं च स्तनयित्नुभिः ॥१५॥

dhūmrā diśaḥ paridhayaḥ
kampate bhūḥ sahādribhiḥ
nirghātaś ca mahāṁs tāta
sākaṁ ca stanayitnubhiḥ

dhūmrāḥ—smoky; *diśaḥ*—all directions; *paridhayaḥ*—encirclement; *kampate*—throbbing; *bhūḥ*—the earth; *saha adribhiḥ*—along with the hills and mountains; *nirghātaḥ*—bolt from the blue; *ca*—also; *mahān*—very great; *tāta*—O Bhīma; *sākam*—with; *ca*—also; *stanayitnubhiḥ*—thundering sound without any cloud.

TRANSLATION

Just see how the smoke encircles the sky. It appears that the earth and mountains are throbbing. Just hear the cloudless thunder and see the bolts from the blue.

TEXT 16

वायुर्वाति खरस्पर्शो रजसा विसृजंस्तमः ।
असृग् वर्षन्ति जलदा बीभत्समिव सर्वतः ॥१६॥

vāyur vāti khara-sparśo
rajasā visṛjaṁs tamaḥ
asṛg varṣanti jaladā
bībhatsam iva sarvataḥ

vāyuḥ—wind; *vāti*—blowing; *khara-sparśaḥ*—sharply; *rajasā*—by the dust; *visṛjan*—creating; *tamaḥ*—darkness; *asṛk*—blood; *varṣanti*—are raining; *jaladāḥ*—the clouds; *bībhatsam*—disastrous; *iva*—like; *sarvataḥ*—everywhere.

TRANSLATION

The wind blows violently, blasting dust everywhere and creating darkness. Clouds are raining everywhere with bloody disasters.

TEXT 17

सूर्यं हतप्रभं पश्य ग्रहमर्दं मिथो दिवि ।
ससङ्कुलैर्भूतगणैर्ज्वलिते इव रोदसी ॥१७॥

sūryaṁ hata-prabhaṁ paśya
graha-mardaṁ mitho divi
sasaṅkulair bhūta-gaṇair
jvalite iva rodasī

sūryam—the sun; *hata-prabham*—its rays declining; *paśya*—just see; *graha-mardam*—clashes of the stars; *mithaḥ*—among one another; *divi*—in the sky; *sa-saṅkulaiḥ*—being mixed with; *bhūta-gaṇaiḥ*—by the living entities; *jvalite*—being ignited; *iva*—as if; *rodasī*—crying.

TRANSLATION

The rays of the sun are declining, and the stars appear to be fighting amongst themselves. Confused living entities appear to be ablaze and weeping.

TEXT 18

नद्यो नदाश्च क्षुभिताः सरांसि च मनांसि च ।
न ज्वलत्यग्निराज्येन कालोऽयं किं विधास्यति ॥१८॥

nadyo nadāś ca kṣubhitāḥ
sarāṁsi ca manāṁsi ca

na jvalaty agnir ājyena
kālo 'yaṁ kiṁ vidhāsyati

nadyaḥ—rivers; *nadāḥ ca*—and the tributaries; *kṣubhitāḥ*—all perturbed; *sarāṁsi*—reservoirs of water; *ca*—and; *manāṁsi*—the mind; *ca*—also; *na*—does not; *jvalati*—ignite; *agniḥ*—fire; *ājyena*—with the help of butter; *kālaḥ*—the time; *ayam*—extraordinary it is; *kim*—what; *vidhāsyati*—going to happen.

TRANSLATION

Rivers, tributaries, ponds, reservoirs and the mind are all perturbed. Butter no longer ignites fire. What is this extraordinary time? What is going to happen?

TEXT 19

न पिबन्ति स्तनं वत्सा न दुह्यन्ति च मातरः ।
रुदन्त्यश्रुमुखा गावो न हृष्यन्त्यृषभा व्रजे ॥१९॥

na pibanti stanaṁ vatsā
na duhyanti ca mātaraḥ
rudanty aśru-mukhā gāvo
na hṛṣyanty ṛṣabhā vraje

na—does not; *pibanti*—suck; *stanam*—breast; *vatsāḥ*—the calves; *na*—do not; *duhyanti*—allow milking; *ca*—also; *mātaraḥ*—the cows; *rudanti*—crying; *aśru-mukhāḥ*—with a tearful face; *gāvaḥ*—the cows; *na*—do not; *hṛṣyanti*—take pleasure; *ṛṣabhāḥ*—the bulls; *vraje*—in the pasturing ground.

TRANSLATION

The calves do not suck the teats of the cows, nor do the cows give milk. They are standing, crying, tears in their eyes, and the bulls take no pleasure in the pasturing grounds.

TEXT 20

दैवतानि रुदन्तीव स्विद्यन्ति ह्युच्चलन्ति च ।
इमे जनपदा ग्रामाः पुरोद्यानाकराश्रमाः ।
भ्रष्टश्रियो निरानन्दाः किमघं दर्शयन्ति नः ॥२०॥

daivatāni rudantīva
svidyanti hy uccalanti ca
ime jana-padā grāmāḥ
purodyānākarāśramāḥ
bhraṣṭa-śriyo nirānandāḥ
kim aghaṁ darśayanti naḥ

daivatāni—the Deities in the temples; *rudanti*—seem to be crying; *iva*—like that; *svidyanti*—perspiring; *hi*—certainly; *uccalanti*—as if going out; *ca*—also; *ime*—these; *jana-padāḥ*—cities; *grāmāḥ*—villages; *pura*—towns; *udyāna*—gardens; *ākara*—mines; *āśramāḥ*—hermitages, etc.; *bhraṣṭa*—devoid of; *śriyaḥ*—beauty; *nirānandāḥ*—bereft of all happiness; *kim*—what sort of; *agham*—calamities; *darśayanti*—shall manifest; *naḥ*—to us.

TRANSLATION

The Deities seem to be crying in the temple, lamenting and perspiring. They seem about to leave. All the cities, villages, towns, gardens, mines and hermitages are now devoid of beauty and bereft of all happiness. I do not know what sort of calamities are now awaiting us.

TEXT 21

मन्य एतैर्महोत्पातैर्नूनं भगवतः पदैः ।
अनन्यपुरुषश्रीभिर्हीना भूर्हतसौभगा ॥२१॥

manya etair mahotpātair
nūnaṁ bhagavataḥ padaiḥ
ananya-puruṣa-śrībhir
hīnā bhūr hata-saubhagā

manye—I take it for granted; *etaiḥ*—by all these; *mahā*—great; *utpātaiḥ*—upsurges; *nūnam*—for want of; *bhagavataḥ*—of the Personality of Godhead; *padaiḥ*—the marks on the sole of the foot; *ananya*—extraordinary; *puruṣa*—of the Supreme Personality; *śrībhiḥ*—by the auspicious signs; *hīnā*—dispossessed; *bhūḥ*—the earth; *hata-saubhagā*—without the fortune.

TRANSLATION

I think that all these earthly disturbances indicate some greater loss to the good fortune of the world. The world was fortunate to have been

marked with the footprints of the lotus feet of the Lord. These signs indicate that this will no longer be.

TEXT 22

इति चिन्तयतस्तस्य दृष्टारिष्टेन चेतसा ।
राज्ञः प्रत्यागमद् ब्रह्मन् यदुपुर्याः कपिध्वजः ॥२२॥

iti cintayatas tasya
dṛṣṭāriṣṭena cetasā
rājñaḥ pratyāgamad brahman
yadu-puryāḥ kapi-dhvajaḥ

iti—thus; *cintayataḥ*—while thinking to himself; *tasya*—he; *dṛṣṭā*—by observing; *ariṣṭena*—bad omens; *cetasā*—by the mind; *rājñaḥ*—the King; *prati*—back; *āgamat*—came; *brahman*—O *brāhmaṇa; yadu-puryāḥ*—from the kingdom of the Yadus; *kapi-dhvajaḥ*—Arjuna.

TRANSLATION

O Brāhmaṇa Śaunaka, while Mahārāja Yudhiṣṭhira, observing the inauspicious signs on the earth at that time, was thus thinking to himself, Arjuna came back from the city of the Yadus [Dvārakā].

TEXT 23

तं पादयोर्निपतितमयथापूर्वमातुरम् ।
अधोवदनमब्बिन्दून् सृजन्तं नयनाब्जयोः ॥२३॥

taṁ pādayor nipatitam
ayathā-pūrvam āturam
adho-vadanam ab-bindūn
sṛjantaṁ nayanābjayoḥ

tam—him (Arjuna); *pādayoḥ*—at the feet; *nipatitam*—bowing down; *ayathā-pūrvam*—unprecedented; *āturam*—dejected; *adhaḥ-vadanam*—downward face; *ap-bindūn*—drops of water; *sṛjantam*—creating; *nayana-abjayoḥ*—from the lotuslike eyes.

TRANSLATION

When he bowed at his feet, the King saw that his dejection was unprecedented. His head was down, and tears glided from his lotus eyes.

TEXT 24

विलोक्योद्विग्नहृदयो विच्छायमनुजं नृपः ।
पृच्छति स्म सुहृन्मध्ये संस्मरन्नारदेरितम् ॥२४॥

vilokyodvigna-hṛdayo
vicchāyam anujaṁ nṛpaḥ
pṛcchati sma suhṛn madhye
saṁsmaran nāraderitam

vilokya—by seeing; *udvigna*—anxious; *hṛdayaḥ*—heart; *vicchāyam*—pale appearance; *anujam*—Arjuna; *nṛpaḥ*—the King; *pṛcchati sma*—asked; *suhṛt*—friends; *madhye*—amongst; *saṁsmaran*—remembering; *nārada*—Sage Nārada; *īritam*—indicated by.

TRANSLATION

Seeing Arjuna pale due to heartfelt anxieties, the King, remembering the indications of the sage Nārada, questioned him in the midst of friends.

TEXT 25

युधिष्ठिर उवाच
कच्चिदानर्तपुर्यां नः स्वजनाः सुखमासते ।
मधुभोजदशार्हार्हसात्वतान्धकवृष्णयः ॥२५॥

yudhiṣṭhira uvāca
kaccid ānarta-puryāṁ naḥ
sva-janāḥ sukham āsate
madhu-bhoja-daśārhārha-
sātvatāndhaka-vṛṣṇayaḥ

yudhiṣṭhiraḥ uvāca—Yudhiṣṭhira said; *kaccit*—whether; *ānarta-puryām*—of Dvārakā; *naḥ*—our; *sva-janāḥ*—relatives; *sukham*—happily; *āsate*—are passing their days; *madhu*—Madhu; *bhoja*—Bhoja; *daśārha*—Daśārha; *ārha*—Ārha; *sātvata*—Sātvata; *andhaka*—Andhaka; *vṛṣṇayaḥ*—of the family of Vṛṣṇi.

TRANSLATION

Mahārāja Yudhiṣṭhira said: My dear brother, please tell me whether our friends and relatives, such as Madhu, Bhoja, Daśārha, Ārha, Sātvata,

Andhaka and the members of the Yadu family are all passing their days in happiness.

TEXT 26

शूरो मातामहः कच्चित्स्वस्त्यास्ते वाथ मारिषः ।
मातुलः सानुजः कच्चित्कुशल्यानकदुन्दुभिः ॥२६॥

śūro mātāmahaḥ kaccit
svasty āste vātha māriṣaḥ
mātulaḥ sānujaḥ kaccit
kuśaly ānakadundubhiḥ

śūraḥ—Śūrasena; *mātāmahaḥ*—maternal grandfather; *kaccit*—whether; *svasti*—all good; *āste*—passing his days; *vā*—or; *atha*—therefore; *māriṣaḥ*—respectful; *mātulaḥ*—maternal uncle; *sa-anujaḥ*—with his younger brothers; *kaccit*—whether; *kuśalī*—all well; *ānaka-dundubhiḥ*—Vasudeva.

TRANSLATION

Is my respectable grandfather Śūrasena in a happy mood? And are my maternal uncle Vasudeva and his younger brothers all doing well?

TEXT 27

सप्त स्वसारस्तत्पत्न्यो मातुलान्यः सहात्मजाः ।
आसते सस्नुषाः क्षेमं देवकीप्रमुखाः स्वयम् ॥२७॥

sapta sva-sāras tat-patnyo
mātulānyaḥ sahātmajāḥ
āsate sasnuṣāḥ kṣemaṁ
devakī-pramukhāḥ svayam

sapta—seven; *sva-sāraḥ*—own sisters; *tat-patnyaḥ*—his wives; *mātulānyaḥ*—maternal aunts; *saha*—along with; *ātma-jāḥ*—sons and grandsons; *āsate*—are all; *sasnuṣāḥ*—with their daughters-in-law; *kṣemam*—happiness; *devakī*—Devakī; *pramukhāḥ*—headed by; *svayam*—personally.

TRANSLATION

His seven wives, headed by Devakī, are all sisters. Are they and their sons and daughters-in-law all happy?

TEXTS 28–29

कच्चिद्राजाहुको जीवत्यसत्पुत्रोऽस्य चानुजः ।
हृदीकः ससुतोऽक्रूरो जयन्तगदसारणाः ॥२८॥
आसते कुशलं कच्चिद्ये च शत्रुजिदादयः ।
कच्चिदास्ते सुखं रामो भगवान् सात्वतां प्रभुः ॥२९॥

kaccid rājāhuko jīvaty
asat-putro 'sya cānujaḥ
hṛdīkaḥ sasuto 'krūro
jayanta-gada-sāraṇāḥ

āsate kuśalaṁ kaccid
ye ca śatrujid-ādayaḥ
kaccid āste sukhaṁ rāmo
bhagavān sātvatāṁ prabhuḥ

kaccit—whether; *rājā*—the King; *āhukaḥ*—another name of Ugrasena; *jīvati*—still living; *asat*—mischievous; *putraḥ*—son; *asya*—his; *ca*—also; *anujaḥ*—younger brother; *hṛdīkaḥ*—Hṛdīka; *sa-sutaḥ*—along with son, Kṛtavarmā; *akrūraḥ*—Akrūra; *jayanta*—Jayanta; *gada*—Gada; *sāraṇāḥ*—Sāraṇa; *āsate*—are they all; *kuśalam*—in happiness; *kaccit*—whether; *ye*—they; *ca*—also; *śatrujit*—Śatrujit; *ādayaḥ*—headed by; *kaccit*—whether; *āste*—are they; *sukham*—all right; *rāmaḥ*—Balarāma; *bhagavān*—the Personality of Godhead; *sātvatām*—of the devotees; *prabhuḥ*—protector.

TRANSLATION

Are Ugrasena, whose son was the mischievous Kaṁsa, and his younger brother still living? Are Hṛdīka and his son Kṛtavarmā happy? Are Akrūra, Jayanta, Gada, Sāraṇa and Śatrujit all happy? How is Balarāma, the Personality of Godhead and the protector of devotees?

PURPORT

Hastināpura, the capital of the Pāṇḍavas, was situated somewhere near present New Delhi, and the kingdom of Ugrasena was situated in Mathurā. While returning to Delhi from Dvārakā, Arjuna must have visited the city of Mathurā, and therefore the inquiry about the King of Mathurā is valid. Amongst various names of the relatives, the name of Rāma or Balarāma, eldest brother of Lord Kṛṣṇa, is added with the words "the Personality of Godhead" because Lord Balarāma is the immediate expansion of *viṣṇu-tattva* as *prakāśa-vigraha* of Lord Kṛṣṇa. The Supreme Lord, although one without a second, expands Himself as many other living beings. The *viṣṇu-tattva* living beings are expansions of the Supreme Lord, and all of them are qualitatively and quantitatively equal with the Lord. But expansions of the *jīva-śakti,* the category of the ordinary living beings, are not at all equal with the Lord. One who considers the *jīva-śakti* and the *viṣṇu-tattva* to be on an equal level is considered a condemned soul of the world. Śrī Rāma, or Balarāma, is the protector of the devotees of the Lord. Baladeva acts as the spiritual master of all devotees, and by His causeless mercy the fallen souls are delivered. Śrī Baladeva appeared as Śrī Nityānanda Prabhu during the advent of Lord Caitanya, and the great Lord Nityānanda Prabhu exhibited His causeless mercy by delivering a pair of extremely fallen souls, namely Jagāi and Mādhāi. Therefore it is particularly mentioned herein that Balarāma is the protector of the devotees of the Lord. By His divine grace only one can approach the Supreme Lord Śrī Kṛṣṇa, and thus Śrī Balarāma is the mercy incarnation of the Lord, manifested as the spiritual master, the savior of the pure devotees.

TEXT 30

प्रद्युम्नः सर्ववृष्णीनां सुखमास्ते महारथः ।
गम्भीररयोऽनिरुद्धो वर्धते भगवानुत ॥३०॥

pradyumnaḥ sarva-vṛṣṇīnāṁ
sukham āste mahā-rathaḥ
gambhīra-rayo 'niruddho
vardhate bhagavān uta

pradyumnaḥ—Pradyumna (a son of Lord Kṛṣṇa); *sarva*—all; *vṛṣṇīnām*—of the members of the Vṛṣṇi family; *sukham*—happiness; *āste*—are in; *mahā-rathaḥ*—the great general; *gambhīra*—deeply; *rayaḥ*—dexterity; *aniruddhaḥ*—Aniruddha (a grandson of Lord Kṛṣṇa); *vardhate*—flourishing; *bhagavān*—the Personality of Godhead; *uta*—must.

TRANSLATION

How is Pradyumna, the great general of the Vṛṣṇi family? Is He happy? And is Aniruddha, the plenary expansion of the Personality of Godhead, faring well?

PURPORT

Pradyumna and Aniruddha are also expansions of the Personality of Godhead, and thus They are also *viṣṇu-tattva.* At Dvārakā, Lord Vāsudeva is engaged in His transcendental pastimes along with His plenary expansions, namely Saṅkarṣaṇa, Pradyumna and Aniruddha, and therefore each and every one of Them can be addressed as the Personality of Godhead, as it is mentioned in connection with the name Aniruddha.

TEXT 31

सुषेणश्चारुदेष्णश्च साम्बो जाम्बवतीसुतः ।
अन्ये च कार्ष्णिप्रवराः सपुत्रा ऋषभादयः ॥३१॥

suṣeṇaś cārudeṣṇaś ca
sāmbo jāmbavatī-sutaḥ
anye ca kārṣṇi-pravarāḥ
saputrā ṛṣabhādayaḥ

suṣeṇaḥ—Suṣeṇa; *cārudeṣṇaḥ*—Cārudeṣṇa; *ca*—and; *sāmbaḥ*—Sāmba; *jāmbavatī-sutaḥ*—the son of Jāmbavatī; *anye*—others; *ca*—also; *kārṣṇi*—the sons of Lord Kṛṣṇa; *pravarāḥ*—all chieftains; *sa-putrāḥ*—along with their sons; *ṛṣabha*—Ṛṣabha; *ādayaḥ*—etc.

TRANSLATION

Are all the chieftain sons of Lord Kṛṣṇa, such as Suṣeṇa, Cārudeṣṇa, Sāmba the son of Jāmbavatī, and Ṛṣabha, along with their sons, all doing well?

PURPORT

As already mentioned, Lord Kṛṣṇa married 16,108 wives, and each of them had ten sons. Therefore 16,108 x 10 = 161,080 sons. They all grew up, and each of them had as many sons as their father, and the whole aggregate was something near 1,610,800 family members of the Lord. The Lord is the father of all living beings, who are countless in number; therefore only a few of them are called to associate with the Lord in His transcendental pastimes as the Lord of Dvārakā on this earth. It is not astonishing that the Lord maintained a visible family consisting of so many members. It is better to refrain from comparing the Lord's position to ours, and it becomes a simple truth as soon as we understand at least a partial calculation of the Lord's transcendental position. King Yudhiṣṭhira, while inquiring about the Lord's sons and grandsons at Dvārakā, mentioned only the chieftains amongst them, for it was impossible for him to remember all the names of the Lord's family members.

TEXTS 32–33

तथैवानुचराः शौरेः श्रुतदेवोद्धवादयः ।
सुनन्दनन्दशीर्षण्या ये चान्ये सात्वतर्षभाः ॥३२॥
अपि स्वस्त्यासते सर्वे रामकृष्णभुजाश्रयाः ।
अपि स्मरन्ति कुशलमस्माकं बद्धसौहृदाः ॥३३॥

tathaivānucarāḥ śaureḥ
śrutadevoddhavādayaḥ
sunanda-nanda-śīrṣaṇyā
ye cānye sātvatarṣabhāḥ

api svasty āsate sarve
rāma-kṛṣṇa-bhujāśrayāḥ
api smaranti kuśalam
asmākaṁ baddha-sauhṛdāḥ

tathā eva—similarly; *anucarāḥ*—constant companions; *śaureḥ*—of Lord Śrī Kṛṣṇa such as; *śrutadeva*—Śrutadeva; *uddhava-ādayaḥ*—Uddhava and others; *sunanda*—Sunanda; *nanda*—Nanda; *śīrṣaṇyāḥ*—other leaders; *ye*—all of them; *ca*—and; *anye*—others; *sātvata*—liberated souls; *ṛṣabhāḥ*—the best men; *api*—if; *svasti*—doing well; *āsate*—are; *sarve*—all of them; *rāma*—Balarāma; *kṛṣṇa*—Lord Kṛṣṇa; *bhuja-āśrayāḥ*—under the protection of; *api*—if also; *smaranti*—do remember; *kuśalam*—welfare; *asmākam*—about ourselves; *baddha-sauhṛdāḥ*—bound by eternal friendship.

TRANSLATION

Also, Śrutadeva, Uddhava and others, Nanda, Sunanda and other leaders of liberated souls who are constant companions of the Lord are protected by Lord Balarāma and Kṛṣṇa. Are they all doing well in their respective functions? Do they, who are all eternally bound in friendship with us, remember our welfare?

PURPORT

The constant companions of Lord Kṛṣṇa, such as Uddhava, are all liberated souls, and they descended along with Lord Kṛṣṇa to this material world to fulfill the mission of the Lord. The Pāṇḍavas are also liberated souls who descended along with Lord Kṛṣṇa to serve Him in His transcendental pastimes on this earth. As stated in the *Bhagavad-gītā* (4.8), the Lord and His eternal associates, who are also liberated souls like the Lord, come down on this earth at certain intervals. The Lord remembers them all, but His associates, although liberated souls, forget due to their being *taṭasthā śakti,* or marginal potency of the Lord. That is the difference between the *viṣṇu-tattva* and *jīva-tattva.* The *jīva-tattvas* are infinitesimal potential particles of the Lord, and therefore they require the protection of the Lord at all times. And to the eternal servitors of the Lord, the Lord is pleased to give all protection at all times. The liberated souls never, therefore, think themselves as free as the Lord or as powerful as the Lord, but they always seek the protection of the Lord in all circumstances, both in the material world and in the spiritual world. This dependence of the liberated soul is constitutional, for the liberated souls are like sparks of a fire that are able to exhibit the glow of fire along with the fire and not independently. Independently the glow of the sparks is extinguished, although the quality of fire or the glowing is there. Thus those who give up the protection of the Lord and become so-called lords themselves, out of spiritual ignorance, come back again to this material world, even after prolonged *tapasya* of the severest type. That is the verdict of all Vedic literature.

TEXT 34

भगवानपि गोविन्दो ब्रह्मण्यो भक्तवत्सलः ।
कच्चित्पुरे सुधर्मायां सुखमास्ते सुहृद्वृतः ॥३४॥

bhagavān api govindo
brahmaṇyo bhakta-vatsalaḥ
kaccit pure sudharmāyāṁ
sukham āste suhṛd-vṛtaḥ

bhagavān—the Personality of Godhead, Kṛṣṇa; *api*—also; *govindaḥ*—one who enlivens the cows and the senses; *brahmaṇyaḥ*—devoted to the devotees or the *brāhmaṇas; bhakta-vatsalaḥ*—affectionate to the devotees; *kaccit*—whether; *pure*—in Dvārakā Purī; *sudharmāyām*—pious assembly; *sukham*—happiness; *āste*—does enjoy; *suhṛt-vṛtaḥ*—surrounded by friends.

TRANSLATION

Is Lord Kṛṣṇa, the Supreme Personality of Godhead, who gives pleasure to the cows, the senses and the brāhmaṇas, who is very affectionate towards His devotees, enjoying the pious assembly at Dvārakā Purī surrounded by friends?

PURPORT

Here in this particular verse the Lord is described as *bhagavān, govinda, brahmaṇya* and *bhakta-vatsala.* He is *bhagavān svayam,* or the original Supreme Personality of Godhead, full with all opulences, all power, all knowledge, all beauty, all fame and all renunciation. No one is equal to or greater than Him. He is Govinda because He is the pleasure of the cows and the senses. Those who have purified their senses by the devotional service of the Lord can render unto Him real service and thereby derive transcendental pleasure out of such purified senses. Only the impure conditioned living being cannot derive any pleasure from the senses, but being illusioned by false pleasures of the senses, he becomes servant of the senses. Therefore, we need His protection for our own interest. The Lord is the protector of cows and the brahminical culture. A society devoid of cow protection and brahminical culture is not under the direct protection of the Lord, just as the prisoners in the jails are not under the protection of the king but under the protection of a severe agent of the king. Without cow protection and cultivation of the brahminical qualities in human society, at least for a section of the members of society, no human civilization can prosper at any length. By brahminical culture, the development of the dormant qualities of goodness, namely truthfulness, equanimity, sense control, forbearance, simplicity, general knowledge, transcendental knowledge and firm faith in the Vedic wisdom, one can become a *brāhmaṇa* and thus see the Lord as He is. And after surpassing the brahminical perfection, one has to become a devotee of the Lord so that His loving affection in the form of proprietor, master, friend, son and lover can be transcendentally achieved. The stage of a devotee, which attracts the transcendental affection of the Lord, does not develop unless one has developed the qualities of a *brāhmaṇa* as above mentioned. The Lord is inclined to a *brāhmaṇa* of quality and not of false prestige. Those who are less than a *brāhmaṇa* by qualification cannot establish any relation with the Lord, just as fire cannot be kindled from the raw earth unless there is wood, although there is a relation between wood and the earth. Since the Lord is all-perfect in

Himself, there could not be any question of His welfare, and Mahārāja Yudhiṣṭhira refrained from asking this question. He simply inquired about His residential place, Dvārakā Purī, where pious men assemble. The Lord stays only where pious men assemble and takes pleasure in their glorifying the Supreme Truth. Mahārāja Yudhiṣṭhira was anxious to know about the pious men and their pious acts in the city of Dvārakā.

TEXTS 35–36

मङ्गलाय च लोकानां क्षेमाय च भवाय च ।
आस्ते यदुकुलाम्भोधावाद्योऽनन्तसखः पुमान् ॥३५॥
यद्बाहुदण्डगुप्तायां स्वपुर्यां यदवोऽर्चिताः ।
क्रीडन्ति परमानन्दं महापौरुषिका इव ॥३६॥

maṅgalāya ca lokānāṁ
kṣemāya ca bhavāya ca
āste yadu-kulāmbhodhāv
ādyo 'nanta-sakhaḥ pumān

yad bāhu-daṇḍa-guptāyāṁ
sva-puryāṁ yadavo 'rcitāḥ
krīḍanti paramānandaṁ
mahā-pauruṣikā iva

maṅgalāya—for all good; *ca*—also; *lokānām*—of all the planets; *kṣemāya*—for protection; *ca*—and; *bhavāya*—for elevation; *ca*—also; *āste*—is there; *yadu-kula-ambhodhau*—in the ocean of the Yadu dynasty; *ādyaḥ*—the original; *ananta-sakhaḥ*—in the company of Ananta (Balarāma); *pumān*—the supreme enjoyer; *yat*—whose; *bāhu-daṇḍa-guptāyām*—being protected by His arms; *sva-puryām*—in His own city; *yadavaḥ*—the members of the Yadu family; *arcitāḥ*—as they deserve; *krīḍanti*—are relishing; *parama-ānandam*—transcendental pleasure; *mahā-pauruṣikāḥ*—the residents of the spiritual sky; *iva*—like.

TRANSLATION

The original Personality of Godhead, the enjoyer, and Balarāma, the primeval Lord Ananta, are staying in the ocean of the Yadu dynasty for the welfare, protection and general progress of the entire universe. And the

members of the Yadu dynasty, being protected by the arms of the Lord, are enjoying life like the residents of the spiritual sky.

PURPORT

As we have discussed many times, the Personality of Godhead, Viṣṇu, resides within each and every universe in two capacities, namely as the Garbhodakaśāyī Viṣṇu and the Kṣīrodakaśāyī Viṣṇu. The Kṣīrodakaśāyī Viṣṇu has His own planet on the northern top of the universe, and there is a great ocean of milk where the Lord resides on the bed of the Ananta incarnation of Baladeva. Thus Mahārāja Yudhiṣṭhira has compared the Yadu dynasty to the ocean of milk and Śrī Balarāma to the Ananta where Lord Kṛṣṇa resides. He has compared the citizens of Dvārakā to the liberated inhabitants of the Vaikuṇṭhalokas. Beyond the material sky, further than we can see with our eyes and beyond the sevenfold coverings of the universe, there is the Causal Ocean in which all the universes are floating like footballs, and beyond the Causal Ocean there is an unlimited span of spiritual sky generally known as the effulgence of Brahman. Within this effulgence there are innumerable spiritual planets, and they are known as the Vaikuṇṭha planets. Each and every Vaikuṇṭha planet is many, many times bigger than the biggest universe within the material world, and in each of them there are innumerable inhabitants who look exactly like Lord Viṣṇu. These inhabitants are known as the Mahā-pauruṣikas, or persons directly engaged in the service of the Lord. They are happy in those planets and are without any kind of misery, and they live perpetually in full youthfulness, enjoying life in full bliss and knowledge without fear of birth, death, old age or disease, and without the influence of *kāla,* eternal time. Mahārāja Yudhiṣṭhira has compared the inhabitants of Dvārakā to the Mahā-pauruṣikas of Vaikuṇṭhaloka because they are so happy with the Lord. In the *Bhagavad-gītā* there are many references to the Vaikuṇṭhalokas, and they are mentioned there as *mad-dhāma,* or the kingdom of the Lord.

TEXT 37

यत्पादशुश्रूषणमुख्यकर्मणा
सत्यादयो द्व्यष्टसहस्रयोषितः ।
निर्जित्य सङ्ख्ये त्रिदशांस्तदाशिषो
हरन्ति वज्रायुधवल्लभोचिताः ॥३७॥

yat-pāda-śuśrūṣaṇa-mukhya-karmaṇā
satyādayo dvy-aṣṭa-sahasra-yoṣitaḥ

nirjitya saṅkhye tri-daśāṁs tad-āśiṣo
haranti vajrāyudha-vallabhocitāḥ

yat—whose; *pāda*—feet; *śuśrūṣaṇa*—administration of comforts; *mukhya*—the most important; *karmaṇā*—by the acts of; *satya-ādayaḥ*—queens headed by Satyabhāmā; *dvi-aṣṭa*—twice eight; *sahasra*—thousand; *yoṣitaḥ*—the fair sex; *nirjitya*—by subduing; *saṅkhye*—in the battle; *tri-daśān*—of the denizens of heaven; *tat-āśiṣaḥ*—what is enjoyed by the demigods; *haranti*—do take away; *vajra-āyudha-vallabhā*—the wives of the personality who controls the thunderbolt; *ucitāḥ*—deserving.

TRANSLATION

Simply by administering comforts at the lotus feet of the Lord, which is the most important of all services, the queens at Dvārakā, headed by Satyabhāmā, induced the Lord to conquer the demigods. Thus the queens enjoy things which are prerogatives of the wives of the controller of thunderbolts.

PURPORT

Satyabhāmā: One of the principal queens of Lord Śrī Kṛṣṇa at Dvārakā. After killing Narakāsura, Lord Kṛṣṇa visited the palace of Narakāsura accompanied by Satyabhāmā. He went to Indraloka also with Satyabhāmā, and she was received by Śacīdevī, who introduced her to the mother of the demigods, Aditi. Aditi was very much pleased with Satyabhāmā, and she blessed her with the benediction of permanent youth as long as Lord Kṛṣṇa remained on the earth. Aditi also took her with her to show her the special prerogatives of the demigods in the heavenly planets. When Satyabhāmā saw the *pārijāta* flower, she desired to have it in her palace at Dvārakā. After that, she came back to Dvārakā along with her husband and expressed her willingness to have the *pārijāta* flower at her palace. Satyabhāmā's palace was especially bedecked with valuable jewels, and even in the hottest season of summer the inside of the palace remained cool, as if air-conditioned. She decorated her palace with various flags, heralding the news of her great husband's presence there. Once, along with her husband, she met Draupadī, and she was anxious to be instructed by Draupadī in the ways and means of pleasing her husband. Draupadī was expert in this affair because she kept five husbands, the Pāṇḍavas, and all were very much pleased with her. On receipt of Draupadī's instructions, she was very much pleased and offered her good wishes and returned to Dvārakā. She was the daughter of Satrājit. After the departure of Lord Kṛṣṇa, when Arjuna visited Dvārakā, all the queens, including Satyabhāmā and Rukmiṇī, lamented for the Lord with great feeling. At the last stage of her life, she left for the forest to undergo severe penance.

Satyabhāmā instigated her husband to get the *pārijāta* flower from the heavenly planets, and the Lord got it even by force from the demigods, as a common husband secures things to please his wife. As already explained, the Lord had very little to do with so many wives to carry out their orders like an ordinary man. But because the queens accepted the high quality of devotional service, namely administering the Lord all comforts, the Lord played the part of a faithful and complete husband. No earthly creature can expect to have things from the heavenly kingdom, especially the *pārijāta* flowers, which are simply to be used by the demigods. But due to their becoming the Lord's faithful wives, all of them enjoyed the special prerogatives of the great wives of the denizens of heaven. In other words, since the Lord is the proprietor of everything within His creation, it is not very astonishing for the queens of Dvārakā to have any rare thing from any part of the universe.

TEXT 38

यद्बाहुदण्डाभ्युदयानुजीविनो
यदुप्रवीरा ह्यकुतोभया मुहुः ।
अधिक्रमन्त्यङ्घ्रिभिराहृतां बलात्
सभां सुधर्मां सुरसत्तमोचिताम् ॥३८॥

yad bāhu-daṇḍābhyudayānujīvino
yadu-pravīrā hy akutobhayā muhuḥ
adhikramanty aṅghribhir āhṛtāṁ balāt
sabhāṁ sudharmāṁ sura-sattamocitām

yat—whose; *bāhu-daṇḍa*—arms; *abhyudaya*—influenced by; *anujīvinaḥ*—always living; *yadu*—the members of the Yadu dynasty; *pravīrāḥ*—great heroes; *hi akutobhayāḥ*—fearless in every respect; *muhuḥ*—constantly; *adhikramanti*—traversing; *aṅghribhiḥ*—by foot; *āhṛtām*—brought about; *balāt*—by force; *sabhām*—assembly house; *sudharmām*—Sudharmā; *sura-sat-tama*—the best among the demigods; *ucitām*—deserving.

TRANSLATION

The great heroes of the Yadu dynasty, being protected by the arms of Lord Śrī Kṛṣṇa, always remain fearless in every respect. And therefore their feet trample over the Sudharmā assembly house, which the best demigods deserved but which was taken away from them.

PURPORT

Those who are directly servitors of the Lord are protected by the Lord from all fearfulness, and they also enjoy the best of things, even if they are forcibly accumulated. The Lord is equal in behavior to all living beings, but He is partial to His pure devotees, being very affectionate toward them. The city of Dvārakā was flourishing, being enriched with the best of things in the material world. The state assembly house is constructed according to the dignity of the particular state. In the heavenly planets, the state assembly house called Sudharmā was deserving of the dignity of the best of the demigods. Such an assembly house is never meant for any state on the globe because the human being on the earth is unable to construct it, however far a particular state may be materially advanced. But during the time of Lord Kṛṣṇa's presence on the earth, the members of the Yadu family forcibly brought the celestial assembly house to earth and placed it at Dvārakā. They were able to use such force because they were certain of the indulgence and protection of the Supreme Lord Kṛṣṇa. In other words, the Lord is provided with the best things in the universe by His pure devotees. Lord Kṛṣṇa was provided with all kinds of comforts and facilities available within the universe by the members of the Yadu dynasty, and in return such servitors of the Lord were protected and fearless.

A forgetful, conditioned soul is fearful. But a liberated soul is never fearful, just as a small child completely dependent on the mercy of his father is never fearful of anyone. Fearfulness is a sort of illusion for the living being when he is in slumber and forgetting his eternal relation with the Lord. Since the living being is never to die by his constitution, as stated in *Bhagavad-gītā* (2.20), then what is the cause of fearfulness? A person may be fearful of a tiger in a dream, but another man who is awake by his side sees no tiger there. The tiger is a myth for both of them, namely the person dreaming and the person awake, because actually there is no tiger; but the man forgetful of his awakened life is fearful, whereas the man who has not forgotten his position is not at all fearful. Thus the members of the Yadu dynasty were fully awake in their service to the Lord, and therefore there was no tiger for them to be afraid of at any time. Even if there were a real tiger, the Lord was there to protect them.

TEXT 39

कच्चित्तेऽनामयं तात भ्रष्टतेजा विभासि में ।
अलब्धमानोऽवज्ञातः किं वा तात चिरोषितः ॥३९॥

kaccit te 'nāmayaṁ tāta
bhraṣṭa-tejā vibhāsi me
alabdha-māno 'vajñātaḥ
kiṁ vā tāta ciroṣitaḥ

kaccit—whether; *te*—your; *anāmayam*—health is all right; *tāta*—my dear brother; *bhraṣṭa*—bereft; *tejāḥ*—luster; *vibhāsi*—appear; *me*—to me; *alabdha-mānaḥ*—without respect; *avajñātaḥ*—neglected; *kim*—whether; *vā*—or; *tāta*—my dear brother; *ciroṣitaḥ*—because of long residence.

TRANSLATION

My brother Arjuna, please tell me whether your health is all right. You appear to have lost your bodily luster. Is this due to others disrespecting and neglecting you because of your long stay at Dvārakā?

PURPORT

From all angles of vision, the Mahārāja inquired from Arjuna about the welfare of Dvārakā, but he concluded at last that as long as Lord Śrī Kṛṣṇa Himself was there, nothing inauspicious could happen. But at the same time, Arjuna appeared to be bereft of his bodily luster, and thus the King inquired of his personal welfare and asked so many vital questions.

TEXT 40

कच्चिन्नाभिहतोऽभावैः शब्दादिभिरमङ्गलैः ।
न दत्तमुक्तमर्थिभ्य आशया यत्प्रतिश्रुतम् ॥४०॥

kaccin nābhihato 'bhāvaiḥ
śabdādibhir amaṅgalaiḥ
na dattam uktam arthibhya
āśayā yat pratiśrutam

kaccit—whether; *na*—could not; *abhihataḥ*—addressed by; *abhāvaiḥ*—unfriendly; *śabda-ādibhiḥ*—by sounds; *amaṅgalaiḥ*—inauspicious; *na*—did not; *dattam*—give in charity; *uktam*—is said; *arthibhyaḥ*—unto one who asked; *āśayā*—with hope; *yat*—what; *pratiśrutam*—promised to be paid.

TRANSLATION

Has someone addressed you with unfriendly words or threatened you? Could you not give charity to one who asked, or could you not keep your promise to someone?

PURPORT

A *kṣatriya* or a rich man is sometimes visited by persons who are in need of money. When they are asked for a donation, it is the duty of the possessor of wealth to give in charity in consideration of the person, place and time. If a *kṣatriya* or a rich man fails to comply with this obligation, he must be very sorry for this discrepancy. Similarly, one should not fail to keep his promise to give in charity. These discrepancies are sometimes causes of despondency, and thus failing, a person becomes subjected to criticism, which might also be the cause of Arjuna's plight.

TEXT 41

कच्चित्त्वं ब्राह्मणं बालं गां वृद्धं रोगिणं स्त्रियम् ।
शरणोपसृतं सत्त्वं नात्याक्षीः शरणप्रदः ॥४१॥

kaccit tvaṁ brāhmaṇaṁ bālaṁ
gāṁ vṛddhaṁ rogiṇaṁ striyam
śaraṇopasṛtaṁ sattvaṁ
nātyākṣīḥ śaraṇa-pradaḥ

kaccit—whether; *tvam*—yourself; *brāhmaṇam*—the *brāhmaṇas; bālam*—the child; *gām*—the cow; *vṛddham*—old; *rogiṇam*—the diseased; *striyam*—the woman; *śaraṇa-upasṛtam*—having approached for protection; *sattvam*—any living being; *na*—whether; *atyākṣīḥ*—not given shelter; *śaraṇa-pradaḥ*—deserving protection.

TRANSLATION

You are always the protector of the deserving living beings, such as brāhmaṇas, children, cows, women and the diseased. Could you not give them protection when they approached you for shelter?

PURPORT

The *brāhmaṇas,* who are always engaged in researching knowledge for the society's welfare work, both materially and spiritually, deserve the protection of the king in all respects. Similarly, the children of the state, the cow, the diseased person, the woman and the old man specifically require the protection of the state or a *kṣatriya* king. If such living beings do not get protection by the *kṣatriya,* or the royal order, or by the state, it is certainly shameful for the *kṣatriya* or the state. If such things had actually happened to Arjuna, Mahārāja Yudhiṣṭhira was anxious to know about these discrepancies.

TEXT 42

कच्चित्त्वं नागमोऽगम्यां गम्यां वासत्कृतां स्त्रियम् ।
पराजितो वाथ भवान्नोत्तमैर्नासमैः पथि ॥४२॥

kaccit tvaṁ nāgamo 'gamyāṁ
gamyāṁ vāsat-kṛtāṁ striyam
parājito vātha bhavān
nottamair nāsamaiḥ pathi

kaccit—whether; *tvam*—yourself; *na*—not; *agamaḥ*—did contact; *agamyām*—impeachable; *gamyām*—acceptable; *vā*—either; *asat-kṛtām*—improperly treated; *striyam*—a woman; *parājitaḥ*—defeated by; *vā*—either; *atha*—after all; *bhavān*—your good self; *na*—nor; *uttamaiḥ*—by superior power; *na*—not; *asamaiḥ*—by equals; *pathi*—on the road.

TRANSLATION

Have you contacted a woman of impeachable character, or have you not properly treated a deserving woman? Or have you been defeated on the way by someone who is inferior or equal to you?

PURPORT

It appears from this verse that during the time of the Pāṇḍavas free contact between man and woman was allowed in certain conditions only. The higher-caste men, namely the *brāhmaṇas* and *kṣatriyas,* could accept a woman of the *vaiśya* or the *śūdra* community, but a man from the lower castes could not contact a woman of the higher caste. Even a *kṣatriya* could not contact a woman of the *brāhmaṇa* caste. The wife of a *brāhmaṇa* is considered one of the seven mothers (namely one's own mother, the wife of the spiritual master or teacher, the wife of a *brāhmaṇa,* the wife of a king, the cow, the nurse and the earth). Such contact between man and woman was known as *uttama* and *adhama.* Contact of a *brāhmaṇa* with a *kṣatriya* woman is *uttama,* but the contact of a *kṣatriya* with a *brāhmaṇa* woman is *adhama* and therefore condemned. A woman approaching a man for contact should never be refused, but at the same time the discretion as above mentioned may also be considered. Bhīma was approached by Hiḍimbī from a community lower than the *śūdras,* and Yayāti refused to marry the daughter of Śukrācārya because of Śukrācārya's being a *brāhmaṇa.* Vyāsadeva, a *brāhmaṇa,* was called to beget Pāṇḍu and Dhṛtarāṣṭra. Satyavatī belonged to a family of fishermen, but Parāśara, a great *brāhmaṇa,* begot in her Vyāsadeva. So there are so many examples of contacts with woman, but in all cases the contacts were not abominable nor were the results of such contacts bad. Contact between man and woman is natural, but that also must be carried out under regulative principles so that social consecration may not be disturbed or unwanted worthless population be increased for the unrest of the world.

It is abominable for a *kṣatriya* to be defeated by one who is inferior in strength or equal in strength. If one is defeated at all, he should be defeated by some superior power. Arjuna was defeated by Bhīṣmadeva, and Lord Kṛṣṇa saved him from the danger. This was not an insult for Arjuna because Bhīṣmadeva was far superior to Arjuna in all ways, namely age, respect and strength. But Karṇa was equal to Arjuna, and therefore Arjuna was in crisis when fighting with Karṇa. It was felt by Arjuna, and therefore Karṇa was killed even by crooked means. Such are the engagements of the *kṣatriyas,* and Mahārāja Yudhiṣṭhira inquired from his brother whether anything undesirable happened on the way home from Dvārakā.

TEXT 43

अपि स्वित्पर्यभुङ्क्थास्त्वं सम्भोज्यान् वृद्धबालकान् ।
जुगुप्सितं कर्म किंचित्कृतवान्न यदक्षमम् ॥४३॥

api svit parya-bhuṅkthās tvaṁ
sambhojyān vṛddha-bālakān
jugupsitaṁ karma kiñcit
kṛtavān na yad akṣamam

api svit—if it were so that; *parya*—by leaving aside; *bhuṅkthāḥ*—have dined; *tvam*—yourself; *sambhojyān*—deserving to dine together; *vṛddha*—the old men; *bālakān*—boys; *jugupsitam*—abominable; *karma*—action; *kiñcit*—something; *kṛtavān*—you must have done; *na*—not; *yat*—that which; *akṣamam*—unpardonable.

TRANSLATION

Have you not taken care of old men and boys who deserve to dine with you? Have you left them and taken your meals alone? Have you committed some unpardonable mistake which is considered to be abominable?

PURPORT

It is the duty of a householder to feed first of all the children, the old members of the family, the *brāhmaṇas* and the invalids. Besides that, an ideal householder is required to call for any unknown hungry man to come and dine before he himself goes to take his meals. He is required to call for such a hungry man thrice on the road. The neglect of this prescribed duty of a householder, especially in the matter of the old men and children, is unpardonable.

TEXT 44

कच्चित् प्रेष्ठतमेनाथ हृदयेनात्मबन्धुना ।
शून्योऽस्मि रहितो नित्यं मन्यसे तेऽन्यथा न रुक् ॥४४॥

kaccit preṣṭhatamenātha
hṛdayenātma-bandhunā
śūnyo 'smi rahito nityaṁ
manyase te 'nyathā na ruk

kaccit—whether; *preṣṭha-tamena*—unto the most dear one; *atha*—my brother Arjuna; *hṛdayena*—most intimate; *ātma-bandhunā*—own friend Lord Kṛṣṇa; *śūnyaḥ*—void; *asmi*—I am; *rahitaḥ*—having lost; *nityam*—for all time; *manyase*—you think; *te*—your; *anyathā*—otherwise; *na*—never; *ruk*—mental distress.

TRANSLATION

Or is it that you are feeling empty for all time because you might have lost your most intimate friend, Lord Kṛṣṇa? O my brother Arjuna, I can think of no other reason for your becoming so dejected.

PURPORT

All the inquisitiveness of Mahārāja Yudhiṣṭhira about the world situation was already conjectured by Mahārāja Yudhiṣṭhira on the basis of Lord Kṛṣṇa's disappearance from the vision of the world, and this was now disclosed by him because of the acute dejection of Arjuna, which could not have been possible otherwise. So even though he was doubtful about it, he was obliged to inquire frankly from Arjuna on the basis of Śrī Nārada's indication.

Thus end the Bhaktivedanta purports of the First Canto, Fourteenth Chapter, of the Śrīmad-Bhāgavatam, *entitled "The Disappearance of Lord Kṛṣṇa."*

CHAPTER FIFTEEN

The Pāṇḍavas Retire Timely

TEXT 1

सूत उवाच
एवं कृष्णसखः कृष्णो भ्रात्रा राज्ञा विकल्पितः ।
नानाशङ्कास्पदं रूपं कृष्णविश्लेषकर्शितः ॥१॥

sūta uvāca
evaṁ kṛṣṇa-sakhaḥ kṛṣṇo
bhrātrā rājñā vikalpitaḥ
nānā-śaṅkāspadaṁ rūpaṁ
kṛṣṇa-viśleṣa-karśitaḥ

sūtaḥ uvāca—Sūta Gosvāmī said; *evam*—thus; *kṛṣṇa-sakhaḥ*—the celebrated friend of Kṛṣṇa; *kṛṣṇaḥ*—Arjuna; *bhrātrā*—by his elder brother; *rājñā*—King Yudhiṣṭhira; *vikalpitaḥ*—speculated; *nānā*—various; *śaṅka-āspadam*—based on many doubts; *rūpam*—forms; *kṛṣṇa*—Lord Śrī Kṛṣṇa; *viśleṣa*—feelings of separation; *karśitaḥ*—became greatly bereaved.

TRANSLATION

Sūta Gosvāmī said: Arjuna, the celebrated friend of Lord Kṛṣṇa, was griefstricken because of his strong feeling of separation from Kṛṣṇa, over and above all Mahārāja Yudhiṣṭhira's speculative inquiries.

PURPORT

Being too much aggrieved, Arjuna practically became choked up, and therefore it was not possible for him to reply properly to the various speculative inquiries of Mahārāja Yudhiṣṭhira.

TEXT 2

शोकेन शुष्यद्वदनहृत्सरोजो हतप्रभः ।
विभुं तमेवानुस्मरन्नाशक्नोत्प्रतिभाषितुम् ॥२॥

śokena śuṣyad-vadana-
hṛt-sarojo hata-prabhaḥ
vibhuṁ tam evānusmaran
nāśaknot pratibhāṣitum

śokena—due to bereavement; *śuṣyat-vadana*—drying up of the mouth; *hṛt-sarojaḥ*—lotuslike heart; *hata*—lost; *prabhaḥ*—bodily luster; *vibhum*—the Supreme; *tam*—unto Lord Kṛṣṇa; *eva*—certainly; *anusmaran*—thinking within; *na*—could not; *aśaknot*—be able; *pratibhāṣitum*—properly replying.

TRANSLATION

Due to grief, Arjuna's mouth and lotuslike heart had dried up. Therefore his body lost all luster. Now, remembering the Supreme Lord, he could hardly utter a word in reply.

TEXT 3

कृच्छ्रेण संस्तभ्य शुचः पाणिनामृज्य नेत्रयोः ।
परोक्षेण समुन्नद्धप्रणयौत्कण्ठ्यकातरः ॥३॥

kṛcchreṇa saṁstabhya śucaḥ
pāṇināmṛjya netrayoḥ
parokṣeṇa samunnaddha-
praṇayautkaṇṭhya-kātaraḥ

kṛcchreṇa—with great difficulty; *saṁstabhya*—by checking the force; *śucaḥ*—of bereavement; *pāṇinā*—with his hands; *āmṛjya*—smearing; *netrayoḥ*—the eyes; *parokṣeṇa*—due to being out of sight; *samunnaddha*—increasingly; *praṇaya-autkaṇṭhya*—eagerly thinking of the affection; *kātaraḥ*—distressed.

TRANSLATION

With great difficulty he checked the tears of grief that smeared his eyes. He was very distressed because Lord Kṛṣṇa was out of his sight, and he increasingly felt affection for Him.

TEXT 4

सख्यं मैत्रीं सौहृदं च सारथ्यादिषु संस्मरन् ।
नृपमग्रजमित्याह बाष्पगद्गदया गिरा ॥४॥

sakhyaṁ maitrīṁ sauhṛdaṁ ca
sārathyādiṣu saṁsmaran
nṛpam agrajam ity āha
bāṣpa-gadgadayā girā

sakhyam—well-wishing; *maitrīm*—benediction; *sauhṛdam*—intimately related; *ca*—also; *sārathya-ādiṣu*—in becoming the chariot driver; *saṁsmaran*—remembering all these; *nṛpam*—unto the King; *agrajam*—the eldest brother; *iti*—thus; *āha*—said; *bāṣpa*—heavily breathing; *gadgadayā*—overwhelmingly; *girā*—by speeches.

TRANSLATION

Remembering Lord Kṛṣṇa and His well wishes, benefactions, intimate familial relations and His chariot driving, Arjuna, overwhelmed and breathing very heavily, began to speak.

PURPORT

The supreme living being is perfect in all relations with His pure devotee. Śrī Arjuna is one of the typical pure devotees of the Lord reciprocating in the fraternal relationship, and the Lord's dealings with Arjuna are displays of friendship of the highest perfect order. He was not only a well-wisher of Arjuna but actually a benefactor, and to make it still more perfect the Lord tied him into a family relationship by arranging Subhadrā's marriage with him. And above all, the Lord agreed to become a chariot driver of Arjuna in order to protect His friend from warfare risks, and the Lord became actually happy when He established the Pāṇḍavas to rule over the world. Arjuna remembered all these one after another, and thus he became overwhelmed with such thoughts.

TEXT 5

अर्जुन उवाच
वञ्चितोऽहं महाराज हरिणा बन्धुरूपिणा ।
येन मेऽपहृतं तेजो देवविस्मापनं महत् ॥५॥

arjuna uvāca
vañcito 'haṁ mahā-rāja
hariṇā bandhu-rūpiṇā

yena me 'pahṛtaṁ tejo
deva-vismāpanaṁ mahat

arjunaḥ uvāca—Arjuna said; *vañcitaḥ*—left by Him; *aham*—myself; *mahā-rāja*—O King; *hariṇā*—by the Personality of Godhead; *bandhu-rūpiṇā*—as if an intimate friend; *yena*—by whom; *me*—my; *apahṛtam*—I have been bereft; *tejaḥ*—power; *deva*—the demigods; *vismāpanam*—astonishing; *mahat*—astounding.

TRANSLATION

Arjuna said: O King! The Supreme Personality of Godhead, Hari, who treated me exactly like an intimate friend, has left me alone. Thus my astounding power, which astonished even the demigods, is no longer with me.

PURPORT

In the *Bhagavad-gītā* (10.41) the Lord says, "Anyone specifically powerful and opulent in wealth, strength, beauty, knowledge and all that is materially desirable is to be considered but a product of an insignificant portion of the complete whole of My energy." No one, therefore, can be independently powerful in any measure without being endowed by the Lord. When the Lord descends on the earth along with His eternal ever-liberated associates, He not only displays the divine energy possessed by Himself, but also empowers His associate devotees with the required energy to execute His mission of incarnation. It is also stated in the *Bhagavad-gītā* (4.5) that the Lord and His eternal associates descend on the earth many times, but the Lord remembers all the different roles of incarnations, whereas the associates, by His supreme will, forget them. Similarly, the Lord takes away with Him all His associates when He disappears from the earth. The power and energy which were bestowed upon Arjuna were required for fulfillment of the mission of the Lord, but when His mission was fulfilled, the emergency powers were withdrawn from Arjuna because the astounding powers of Arjuna, which were astonishing even to the denizens of heaven, were no longer required, and they were not meant for going back home, back to Godhead. If endowment of powers and withdrawal of powers by the Lord are possible even for a great devotee like Arjuna, or even the demigods in heaven, then what to speak of the ordinary living beings who are but figs compared to such great souls. The lesson is, therefore, that no one should be puffed up for his powers borrowed from the Lord. The sane man should rather feel obliged to the Lord for such benefactions and must utilize such power for the service of the Lord. Such power can be withdrawn at any time by the Lord, so the best use of such power and opulence is to engage them in the service of the Lord.

TEXT 6

यस्य क्षणवियोगेन लोको ह्यप्रियदर्शनः ।
उक्थेन रहितो ह्येष मृतकः प्रोच्यते यथा ॥६॥

yasya kṣaṇa-viyogena
loko hy apriya-darśanaḥ
ukthena rahito hy eṣa
mṛtakaḥ procyate yathā

yasya—whose; *kṣaṇa*—a moment; *viyogena*—by separation; *lokaḥ*—all the universes; *hi*—certainly; *apriya-darśanaḥ*—everything appears unfavorable; *ukthena*—by life; *rahitaḥ*—being devoid of; *hi*—certainly; *eṣaḥ*—all these bodies; *mṛtakaḥ*—dead bodies; *procyate*—are designated; *yathā*—as it were.

TRANSLATION

I have just lost Him whose separation for a moment would render all the universes unfavorable and void, like bodies without life.

PURPORT

Factually for a living being there is no one dearer than the Lord. The Lord expands Himself by innumerable parts and parcels as *svāṁśa* and *vibhinnāṁśa.* Paramātmā is the *svāṁśa* part of the Lord, whereas the *vibhinnāṁśa* parts are the living beings. As the living being is the important factor in the material body, for without the living being the material body has no value, similarly without Paramātmā the living being has no status quo. Similarly, Brahman or Paramātmā has no *locus standi* without the Supreme Lord Kṛṣṇa. This is thoroughly explained in the *Bhagavad-gītā.* They are all interlinked with one another, or interdependent factors; thus in the ultimate issue the Lord is the *summum bonum* and therefore the vital principle of everything.

TEXT 7

यत्संश्रयाद् द्रुपदगेहमुपागतानां
राज्ञां स्वयंवरमुखे स्मरदुर्मदानाम् ।
तेजो हृतं खलु मयाभिहतश्च मत्स्यः
सज्जीकृतेन धनुषाधिगता च कृष्णा ॥ ७ ॥

yat-saṁśrayād drupada-geham upāgatānāṁ
rājñāṁ svayaṁvara-mukhe smara-durmadānām
tejo hṛtaṁ khalu mayābhihataś ca matsyaḥ
sajjīkṛtena dhanuṣādhigatā ca kṛṣṇā

yat—by whose merciful; *saṁśrayāt*—by strength; *drupada-geham*—in the palace of King Drupada; *upāgatānām*—all those assembled; *rājñām*—of the princes; *svayaṁvara-mukhe*—on the occasion of the selection of the bridegroom; *smara-durmadānām*—all lusty in thought; *tejaḥ*—power; *hṛtam*—vanquished; *khalu*—as it were; *mayā*—by me; *abhihataḥ*—pierced; *ca*—also; *matsyaḥ*—the fish target; *sajjī-kṛtena*—by equipping the bow; *dhanuṣā*—by that bow also; *adhigatā*—gained; *ca*—also; *kṛṣṇā*—Draupadī.

TRANSLATION

Only by His merciful strength was I able to vanquish all the lusty princes assembled at the palace of King Drupada for the selection of the bridegroom. With my bow and arrow I could pierce the fish target and thereby gain the hand of Draupadī.

PURPORT

Draupadī was the most beautiful daughter of King Drupada, and when she was a young girl almost all the princes desired her hand. But Drupada Mahārāja decided to hand over his daughter to Arjuna only and therefore contrived a peculiar way. There was a fish hanging on the inner roof of the house under the protection of a wheel. The condition was that out of the princely order, one must be able to pierce the fish's eyes through the wheel of protection, and no one would be allowed to look up at the target. On the ground there was a waterpot in which the target and wheel were reflected, and one had to fix his aim towards the target by looking at the trembling water in the pot. Mahārāja Drupada well knew that only Arjuna or alternately Karṇa could successfully carry out the plan. But still he wanted to hand his daughter to Arjuna. And in the assembly of the princely order, when Dhṛṣṭadyumna, the brother of Draupadī, introduced all the princes to his grown-up sister, Karṇa was also present in the game. But Draupadī tactfully avoided Karṇa as the rival of Arjuna, and she expressed her desires through her brother Dhṛṣṭadyumna that she was unable to accept anyone who was less than a *kṣatriya.* The *vaiśyas* and the *śūdras* are less important than the *kṣatriyas.* Karṇa was known as the son of a carpenter, a *śūdra.* So Draupadī avoided Karṇa by this plea. When Arjuna, in the dress of a poor *brāhmaṇa,* pierced the difficult target, everyone was astonished, and all of them, especially Karṇa, offered a stiff fight to Arjuna, but as usual by the grace of Lord Kṛṣṇa he was able to emerge very successful in the princely fight and thus gain the valuable hand of Kṛṣṇā, or Draupadī. Arjuna was lamentingly remembering the incident in the absence of the Lord, by whose strength only he was so powerful.

TEXT 8

यत्सन्निधावहमु खाण्डवमग्नयेऽदा-
मिन्द्रं च सामरगणं तरसा विजित्य ।
लब्धा सभा मयकृताद्भुतशिल्पमाया
दिग्भ्योऽहरन्नृपतयो बलिमध्वरे ते ॥८॥

yat-sannidhāv aham u khāṇḍavam agnaye 'dām
indraṁ ca sāmara-gaṇaṁ tarasā vijitya
labdhā sabhā maya-kṛtādbhuta-śilpa-māyā
digbhyo 'haran nṛpatayo balim adhvare te

yat—whose; *sannidhau*—being nearby; *aham*—myself; *u*—note of astonishment; *khāṇḍavam*—the protected forest of Indra, King of heaven; *agnaye*—unto the fire-god; *adām*—delivered; *indram*—Indra; *ca*—also; *sa*—along with; *amara-gaṇam*—the demigods; *tarasā*—with all dexterity; *vijitya*—having conquered; *labdhā*—having obtained; *sabhā*—assembly house; *maya-kṛtā*—built by Maya; *adbhuta*—very wonderful; *śilpa*—art and workmanship; *māyā*—potency; *digbhyaḥ*—from all directions; *aharan*—collected; *nṛpatayaḥ*—all princes; *balim*—presentations; *adhvare*—brought; *te*—your.

TRANSLATION

Because He was near me, it was possible for me to conquer with great dexterity the powerful King of heaven, Indradeva, along with his demigod

associates and thus enable the fire-god to devastate the Khāṇḍava Forest. And only by His grace was the demon named Maya saved from the blazing Khāṇḍava Forest, and thus we could build our assembly house of wonderful architectural workmanship, where all the princes assembled during the performance of Rājasūya-yajña and paid you tributes.

PURPORT

The demon Maya Dānava was an inhabitant of the forest Khāṇḍava, and when the Khāṇḍava Forest was set on fire, he asked protection from Arjuna. Arjuna saved his life, and as a result of this the demon felt obliged. He reciprocated by building a wonderful assembly house for the Pāṇḍavas, which attracted the extraordinary attention of all state princes. They felt the supernatural power of the Pāṇḍavas, and thus without grudge all of them submitted and paid tributes to the Emperor. The demons possess wonderful and supernatural powers to create material wonders. But they are always disturbing elements of the society. The modern demons are the harmful material scientists who create some material wonders for disturbance in the society. For example, the creation of nuclear weapons has caused some panic in human society. Maya was also a materialist like that, and he knew the art of creating such wonderful things. And yet Lord Kṛṣṇa wanted to kill him. When he was chased both by the fire and by the wheel of Lord Kṛṣṇa, he took shelter of such a devotee as Arjuna, who saved him from the wrath of the fire of Lord Śrī Kṛṣṇa. Devotees are therefore more merciful than the Lord, and in devotional service the mercy of a devotee is more valuable than the mercy of the Lord. Both the fire and the Lord ceased from chasing the demon as soon as both of them saw that the demon was given shelter by such a devotee as Arjuna. This demon, feeling obliged to Arjuna, wanted to do him some service to show his gratefulness, but Arjuna declined to accept anything from him in exchange. Lord Śrī Kṛṣṇa, however, being pleased with Maya for his taking shelter of a devotee, asked him to render service unto King Yudhiṣṭhira by building a wonderful assembly house. The process is that by the grace of the devotee the mercy of the Lord is obtained, and by the mercy of the Lord a chance to serve the Lord's devotee is obtained. The club of Bhīmasena was also a gift of Maya Dānava.

TEXT 9

यत्तेजसा नृपशिरोऽङ्घ्रिमहन्मखार्थम्
आर्योऽनुजस्तव गजायुतसत्त्ववीर्यः ।

तेनाहृताः प्रमथनाथमखाय भूपा
यन्मोचितास्तदनयन्बलिमध्वरे ते ॥९॥

yat-tejasā nṛpa-śiro-'ṅghrim ahan makhārtham
āryo 'nujas tava gajāyuta-sattva-vīryaḥ
tenāhṛtāḥ pramatha-nātha-makhāya bhūpā
yan-mocitās tad-anayan balim adhvare te

yat—whose; *tejasā*—by influence; *nṛpa-śiraḥ-aṅghrim*—one whose feet are adored by the heads of kings; *ahan*—killed; *makha-artham*—for the sacrifice; *āryaḥ*—respectable; *anujaḥ*—younger brother; *tava*—your; *gaja-ayuta*—ten thousand elephants; *sattva-vīryaḥ*—powerful existence; *tena*—by him; *āhṛtāḥ*—collected; *pramatha-nātha*—the lord of the ghosts (Mahābhairava); *makhāya*—for sacrifice; *bhūpāḥ*—kings; *yat-mocitāḥ*—by whom they were released; *tat-anayan*—all of them brought; *balim*—taxes; *adhvare*—presented; *te*—your.

TRANSLATION

Your respectable younger brother, who possesses the strength of ten thousand elephants, killed, by His grace, Jarāsandha, whose feet were worshiped by many kings. These kings had been brought for sacrifice in Jarāsandha's Mahābhairava-yajña, but they were thus released. Later they paid tribute to Your Majesty.

PURPORT

Jarāsandha was a very powerful king of Magadha, and the history of his birth and activities is also very interesting. His father, King Bṛhadratha, was also a very prosperous and powerful king of Magadha, but he had no son, although he married two daughters of the King of Kāśī. Being disappointed in not getting a son from either of the two queens, the King, along with his wives, left home to live in the forest for austerities, but in the forest he was benedicted by one great *ṛṣi* to have a son, and he gave him one mango to be eaten by the queens. The queens did so and were very soon pregnant. The King was very happy to see the queens bearing children, but when the ripe time approached, the queens delivered one child in two parts, one from each of the queens' wombs. The two parts were thrown in the forest, where a great she-demon used to live, and she was glad to have some delicate flesh and blood from the newly born child. Out of curiosity she joined the two parts, and the child became complete and regained life. The she-demon was known as Jarā, and being compassionate on the childless King, she went to the King and presented him with the nice child. The King was very pleased with the she-demon and wanted to reward her according to her desire. The she-demon expressed her desire that the child be named after her, and thus the child was surnamed Jarāsandha, or one who was joined by Jarā, the she-demon. In fact, this Jarāsandha was born as one of the parts and parcels of the demon Vipracitti. The saint by whose benedictions the queens bore the child was called Candra Kauśika, who foretold of the child before his father Bṛhadratha.

Since Jarāsandha possessed demoniac qualities from birth, naturally he became a great devotee of Lord Śiva, the lord of all ghostly and demoniac men. Rāvaṇa was a great devotee of Śiva, and so also Jarāsandha. He used to sacrifice all arrested kings before Lord Mahābhairava (Śiva), and by his military power he defeated many small kings and arrested them to butcher before Mahābhairava. There are many devotees of Lord Mahābhairava, or Kālabhairava, in the province of Bihar, formerly called Magadha. Jarāsandha was a relative of Kaṁsa, the maternal uncle of Kṛṣṇa, and therefore after Kaṁsa's death King Jarāsandha became a great enemy of Kṛṣṇa, and there were many fights between Jarāsandha and Kṛṣṇa. Lord Kṛṣṇa wanted to kill him, but He also wanted that those who served as military men for Jarāsandha might not be killed. Therefore a plan was adopted to kill him. Kṛṣṇa, Bhīma and Arjuna together went to Jarāsandha in the dress of poor *brāhmaṇas* and begged charity from King Jarāsandha. Jarāsandha never refused charity to any *brāhmaṇa,* and he performed many sacrifices also, yet he was not on a par with devotional service. Lord Kṛṣṇa, Bhīma and Arjuna asked Jarāsandha for the facility of fighting him, and it was settled that Jarāsandha would fight with Bhīma only. So all of them were both guests and combatants of Jarāsandha, and Bhīma and Jarāsandha fought every day for several days. Bhīma became disappointed, but Kṛṣṇa gave him hints about Jarāsandha's being joined together as an infant, and thus Bhīma dissected him again and so killed him. All the kings who were detained in the concentration camp to be killed before Mahābhairava were thus released by Bhīma. Feeling thus obliged to the Pāṇḍavas, they paid tribute to King Yudhiṣṭhira.

TEXT 10

पत्न्यास्तवाधिमखक्लृप्तमहाभिषेक-
श्लाघिष्ठचारुकबरं कितवैः सभायाम् ।

स्पृष्टं विकीर्य पदयोः पतिताश्रुमुख्या
यस्तत्स्त्रियोऽकृतहतेशविमुक्तकेशाः ॥१०॥

patnyās tavādhimakha-kḷpta-mahābhiṣeka-
ślāghiṣṭha-cāru-kabaraṁ kitavaiḥ sabhāyām
spṛṣṭaṁ vikīrya padayoḥ patitāśru-mukhyā
yas tat-striyo 'kṛta-hateśa-vimukta-keśāḥ

patnyāḥ—of the wife; *tava*—your; *adhimakha*—during the great sacrificial ceremony; *kḷpta*—dressed; *mahā-abhiṣeka*—greatly sanctified; *ślāghiṣṭha*—thus glorified; *cāru*—beautiful; *kabaram*—clustered hair; *kitavaiḥ*—by the miscreants; *sabhāyām*—in the great assembly; *spṛṣṭam*—being caught; *vikīrya*—being loosened; *padayoḥ*—on the feet; *patita-aśru-mukhyāḥ*—of the one who fell down with tears in the eyes; *yaḥ*—He; *tat*—their; *striyaḥ*—wives; *akṛta*—became; *hata-īśa*—bereft of husbands; *vimukta-keśāḥ*—loosened hair.

TRANSLATION

It was He only who loosened the hair of all the wives of the miscreants who dared open the cluster of your Queen's hair, which had been nicely dressed and sanctified for the great Rājasūya sacrificial ceremony. At that time she fell down at the feet of Lord Kṛṣṇa with tears in her eyes.

PURPORT

Queen Draupadī had a beautiful bunch of hair which was sanctified in the ceremonial function of Rājasūya-yajña. But when she was lost in a bet, Duḥśāsana touched her glorified hair to insult her. Draupadī then fell down at the lotus feet of Lord Kṛṣṇa, and Lord Kṛṣṇa decided that all the wives of Duḥśāsana and company should have their hair loosened as a result of the Battle of Kurukṣetra. Thus after the Battle of Kurukṣetra, after all the sons and grandsons of Dhṛtarāṣṭra died in battle, all the wives of the family were obliged to loosen their hair as widows. In other words, all the wives of the Kuru family became widows because of Duḥśāsana's insulting a great devotee of the Lord. The Lord can tolerate insults upon Himself by any miscreant because the father tolerates even insults from the son. But He never tolerates insults upon His devotees. By insulting a great soul, one has to forego all the results of pious acts and benedictions also.

TEXT 11

यो नो जुगोप वन एत्य दुरन्तकृच्छ्राद्
दुर्वाससोऽरिरचितादयुताग्रभुग् यः ।
शाकान्नशिष्टमुपयुज्य यतस्त्रिलोकीं
तृप्ताममंस्त सलिले विनिमग्नसङ्घः ॥११॥

yo no jugopa vana etya duranta-kṛcchrād
durvāsaso 'ri-racitād ayutāgra-bhug yaḥ
śākānna-śiṣṭam upayujya yatas tri-lokīṁ
tṛptām amaṁsta salile vinimagna-saṅghaḥ

yaḥ—one who; *naḥ*—us; *jugopa*—gave protection; *vane*—forest; *etya*—getting in; *duranta*—dangerously; *kṛcchrāt*—trouble; *durvāsasaḥ*—of Durvāsā Muni; *ari*—enemy; *racitāt*—fabricated by; *ayuta*—ten thousand; *agra-bhuk*—one who eats before; *yaḥ*—that person; *śāka-anna-śiṣṭam*—remnants of foodstuff; *upayujya*—having accepted; *yataḥ*—because; *tri-lokīm*—all the three worlds; *tṛptām*—satisfied; *amaṁsta*—thought within the mind; *salile*—while in the water; *vinimagna-saṅghaḥ*—all merged into the water.

TRANSLATION

During our exile, Durvāsā Muni, who eats with his ten thousand disciples, intrigued with our enemies to put us in dangerous trouble. At that time He [Lord Kṛṣṇa], simply by accepting the remnants of food, saved us. By His accepting food thus, the assembly of munis, while bathing in the river, felt sumptuously fed. And all the three worlds were also satisfied.

PURPORT

Durvāsā Muni: A powerful mystic *brāhmaṇa* determined to observe the principles of religion with great vows and under strict austerities. His name is associated with many historical events, and it appears that the great mystic could be both easily satisfied and easily annoyed, like Lord Śiva. When he was satisfied, he could do tremendous good to the servitor, but if he was dissatisfied he could bring about the greatest calamity. Kumārī Kuntī, at her father's house, used to minister all kinds of services to all great *brāhmaṇas,* and being satisfied with her good reception Durvāsā Muni benedicted her with a power to call any demigod she desired. It is understood that he was a plenary incarnation of Lord Śiva, and thus he could be either easily satisfied or annoyed. He was a great devotee of Lord Śiva, and by Lord Śiva's order he accepted the priesthood of King Śvetaketu because of the King's performance of sacrifice for one hundred years. Sometimes he used to visit the parliamentary assembly of the heavenly kingdom of Indradeva. He could travel in space by his great mystic powers, and it is understood that he traveled a great distance through space, even up to the Vaikuṇṭha planets beyond material space. He traveled all these long distances within one year, during his quarrel with King Ambarīṣa, the great devotee and Emperor of the world.

He had about ten thousand disciples, and wherever he visited and became a guest of the great *kṣatriya* kings, he used to be accompanied by a number of followers. Once he visited the house of Duryodhana, the enemy cousin of Mahārāja Yudhiṣṭhira. Duryodhana was intelligent enough to satisfy the *brāhmaṇa* by all means, and the great *ṛṣi* wanted to give some benediction to Duryodhana. Duryodhana knew his mystic powers, and he knew also that the mystic *brāhmaṇa,* if dissatisfied, could cause some havoc, and thus he designed to engage the *brāhmaṇa* to show his wrath upon his enemy cousins, the Pāṇḍavas. When the *ṛṣi* wanted to award some benediction to Duryodhana, the latter wished that he should visit the house of Mahārāja Yudhiṣṭhira, who was the eldest and chief among all his cousins. But by his request he would go to him after he had finished his meals with his Queen, Draupadī. Duryodhana knew that after Draupadī's dinner it would be impossible for Mahārāja Yudhiṣṭhira to receive such a large number of *brāhmaṇa* guests, and thus the *ṛṣi* would be annoyed and would create some trouble for his cousin Mahārāja Yudhiṣṭhira. That was the plan of Duryodhana. Durvāsā Muni agreed to this proposal, and he approached the King in exile, according to the plan of Duryodhana, after the King and Draupadī had finished their meals.

On his arrival at the door of Mahārāja Yudhiṣṭhira, he was at once well received, and the King requested him to finish his noontime religious rites in the river, for by that time the foodstuff would be prepared. Durvāsā Muni, along with his large number of disciples, went to take a bath in the river, and Mahārāja Yudhiṣṭhira was in great anxiety about the guests. As long as Draupadī had not taken her meals, food could be served to any number of guests, but the *ṛṣi,* by the plan of Duryodhana, reached there after Draupadī had finished her meals.

When the devotees are put into difficulty, they have an opportunity to recollect the Lord with rapt attention. So Draupadī was thinking of Lord Kṛṣṇa in that dangerous position, and the all-pervading Lord could at once know the dangerous position of His devotees. He therefore came there on the scene and asked Draupadī to give whatever food she might have in her stock. On her being so requested by the Lord, Draupadī was sorrowful because the Supreme Lord asked her for some food and she was unable to supply it at that time. She said to the Lord that the mysterious dish which she had received from the sun-god could supply any amount of food if she herself had not eaten. But on that day she had already taken her meals, and thus they were in danger. By expressing her difficulties she began to cry before the Lord as only a woman would do in such a position. The Lord, however, asked Draupadī to bring up the cooking pots to see if there was any particle of foodstuff left, and on Draupadī's doing so, the Lord found some particle of vegetable sticking to the pot. The Lord at once picked it up and ate it. After doing so, the Lord asked Draupadī to call for her guests, the company of Durvāsā.

Bhīma was sent to call them from the river. Bhīma said, "Why are you delaying, sirs? Come on, the food is ready for you." But the *brāhmaṇas,* because of Lord Kṛṣṇa's accepting a little particle of food, felt sumptuously fed, even while they were in the water. They thought that since Mahārāja Yudhiṣṭhira must have prepared many valuable dishes for them and since they were not hungry and could not eat, the King would feel very sorry, so it was better not to go there. Thus they decided to go away.

This incident proves that the Lord is the greatest mystic, and therefore He is known as Yogeśvara. Another instruction is that every householder must offer food to the Lord, and the result will be that everyone, even a company of guests numbering ten thousand, will be satisfied because of the Lord's being satisfied. That is the way of devotional service.

TEXT 12

यत्तेजसाथ भगवान् युधि शूलपाणि-
विस्मापितः सगिरिजोऽस्त्रमदान्निजं मे ।
अन्येऽपि चाहममुनैव कलेवरेण
प्राप्तो महेन्द्रभवने महदासनार्धम् ॥१२॥

yat-tejasātha bhagavān yudhi śūla-pāṇir
vismāpitaḥ sagirijo 'stram adān nijaṁ me
anye 'pi cāham amunaiva kalevareṇa
prāpto mahendra-bhavane mahad-āsanārdham

yat—by whose; *tejasā*—by influence; *atha*—at one time; *bhagavān*—the personality of god (Lord Śiva); *yudhi*—in the battle; *śūla-pāṇiḥ*—one who has a trident in his hand; *vismāpitaḥ*—astonished; *sa-girijaḥ*—along with the daughter of the Himalaya Mountains; *astram*—weapon; *adāt*—awarded; *nijam*—of his own; *me*—unto me; *anye api*—so also others; *ca*—and; *aham*—myself; *amunā*—by this; *eva*—definitely; *kalevareṇa*—by the body; *prāptaḥ*—obtained; *mahā-indra-bhavane*—in the house of Indradeva; *mahat*—great; *āsana-ardham*—half-elevated seat.

TRANSLATION

It was by His influence only that in a fight I was able to astonish the personality of god Lord Śiva and his wife, the daughter of Mount Himalaya. Thus he [Lord Śiva] became pleased with me and awarded me his own weapon. Other demigods also delivered their respective weapons to me, and in addition I was able to reach the heavenly planets in this present body and was allowed a half-elevated seat.

PURPORT

By the grace of the Supreme Personality of Godhead Śrī Kṛṣṇa, all the demigods, including Lord Śiva, were pleased with Arjuna. The idea is that one who is favored by Lord Śiva or any other demigod may not necessarily be favored by the Supreme Lord Śrī Kṛṣṇa. Rāvaṇa was certainly a great devotee of Lord Śiva, but he could not be saved from the wrath of the Supreme Personality of Godhead Lord Rāmacandra. And there are many instances like that in the histories of the *Purāṇas.* But here is an instance where we can see that Lord Śiva became pleased even in the fight with Arjuna. The devotees of the Supreme Lord know how to respect the demigods, but the devotees of the demigods sometimes foolishly think that the Supreme Personality of Godhead is no greater than the demigods. By such a conception, one becomes an offender and ultimately meets with the same end as Rāvaṇa and others. The instances described by Arjuna during his friendly dealings with Lord Śrī Kṛṣṇa are instructive for all who may be convinced by the lessons that one can achieve all favors simply by pleasing the Supreme Lord Śrī Kṛṣṇa, whereas the devotees or worshipers of the demigods may achieve only partial benefits, which are also perishable, just as the demigods themselves are.

Another significance of the present verse is that Arjuna, by the grace of Lord Śrī Kṛṣṇa, was able to reach the heavenly planet even with the selfsame body and was honored by the heavenly demigod Indradeva, being seated with him half elevated. One can reach the heavenly planets by the pious acts recommended in the *śāstras* in the category of fruitive activities. And as stated in the *Bhagavad-gītā* (9.21), when the reactions of such pious acts are spent, the enjoyer is again degraded to this earthly planet. The moon is also on the level with the heavenly planets, and only persons who have performed virtues only—performing sacrifices, giving charity and undergoing severe austerities—can be allowed to enter into the heavenly planets after the duration of life of the body. Arjuna was allowed to enter into the heavenly planets in the selfsame body simply by the grace of the Lord, otherwise it is not possible to do so. The present attempts to enter into the heavenly planets by the modern scientists will certainly prove futile because such scientists are not on the level of Arjuna. They are ordinary human beings, without any assets of sacrifice, charity or austerities. The material body is influenced by the three modes of material nature, namely goodness, passion and ignorance. The present population is more or less influenced by the modes of passion and ignorance, and the symptoms for such influence are exhibited in their becoming very lusty and greedy. Such degraded fellows can hardly approach the higher planetary systems. Above the heavenly planets there are many other planets also, which only those who are influenced by goodness can reach. In heavenly and other planets within the universe, the inhabitants are all highly intelligent, many more times than the human beings, and they are all pious in the higher and highest mode of goodness. They are all devotees of the Lord, and although their goodness is not unadulterated, still they are known as demigods possessing the maximum amount of good qualities possible within the material world.

TEXT 13

तत्रैव मे विहरतो भुजदण्डयुग्मं
गाण्डीवलक्षणमरातिवधाय देवाः ।
सेन्द्राः श्रिता यदनुभावितमाजमीढ
तेनाहमद्य मुषितः पुरुषेण भूम्ना ॥१३॥

tatraiva me viharato bhuja-daṇḍa-yugmaṁ
gāṇḍīva-lakṣaṇam arāti-vadhāya devāḥ
sendrāḥ śritā yad-anubhāvitam ājamīḍha
tenāham adya muṣitaḥ puruṣeṇa bhūmnā

tatra—in that heavenly planet; *eva*—certainly; *me*—myself; *viharataḥ*—while staying as a guest; *bhuja-daṇḍa-yugmam*—both of my arms; *gāṇḍīva*—the bow named Gāṇḍīva; *lakṣaṇam*—mark; *arāti*—a demon named Nivātakavaca; *vadhāya*—for killing; *devāḥ*—all the demigods; *sa*—along with; *indrāḥ*—the heavenly King, Indra; *śritāḥ*—taken shelter of; *yat*—by whose; *anubhāvitam*—made it possible to be powerful; *ājamīḍha*—O descendant of King Ajamīḍha; *tena*—by Him; *aham*—myself; *adya*—at the present moment; *muṣitaḥ*—bereft of; *puruṣeṇa*—the personality; *bhūmnā*—supreme.

TRANSLATION

When I stayed for some days as a guest in the heavenly planets, all the heavenly demigods, including King Indradeva, took shelter of my arms, which were marked with the Gāṇḍīva bow, to kill the demon named Nivātakavaca. O King, descendant of Ajamīḍha, at the present moment I am bereft of the Supreme Personality of Godhead, by whose influence I was so powerful.

PURPORT

The heavenly demigods are certainly more intelligent, powerful and beautiful, and yet they had to take help from Arjuna because of his Gāṇḍīva bow, which was empowered by the grace of Lord Śrī Kṛṣṇa. The Lord is all-powerful, and by His grace His pure devotee can be as powerful as He may desire, and there is no limit to it. And when the Lord withdraws His power from anyone, he is powerless by the will of the Lord.

TEXT 14

यद्बान्धवः कुरुबलाब्धिमनन्तपार-
मेको रथेन ततरेऽहमतीर्यसत्त्वम् ।
प्रत्याहृतं बहु धनं च मया परेषां
तेजास्पदं मणिमयं च हृतं शिरोभ्यः ॥१४॥

yad-bāndhavaḥ kuru-balābdhim ananta-pāram
eko rathena tatare 'ham atīrya-sattvam
pratyāhṛtaṁ bahu dhanaṁ ca mayā pareṣāṁ
tejās-padaṁ maṇimayaṁ ca hṛtaṁ śirobhyaḥ

yat-bāndhavaḥ—by whose friendship only; *kuru-bala-abdhim*—the ocean of the military strength of the Kurus; *ananta-pāram*—which was insurmountable; *ekaḥ*—alone; *rathena*—being seated on the chariot; *tatare* —was able to cross over; *aham*—myself; *atīrya*—invincible; *sattvam*—existence; *pratyāhṛtam*—drew back; *bahu*—very large quantity; *dhanam* —wealth; *ca*—also; *mayā*—by my; *pareṣām*—of the enemy; *tejāḥ-padam*—source of brilliance; *maṇi-mayam*—bedecked with jewels; *ca*—also; *hṛtam* —taken by force; *śirobhyaḥ*—from their heads.

TRANSLATION

The military strength of the Kauravas was like an ocean in which there dwelled many invincible existences, and thus it was insurmountable. But because of His friendship, I, seated on the chariot, was able to cross over it. And only by His grace was I able to regain the cows and also collect by force many helmets of the kings which were bedecked with jewels that were sources of all brilliance.

PURPORT

On the Kaurava side there were many stalwart commanders like Bhīṣma, Droṇa, Kṛpa and Karṇa, and their military strength was as insurmountable as the great ocean. And yet it was due to Lord Kṛṣṇa's grace that Arjuna alone, sitting on the chariot, could manage to vanquish them one after another without difficulty. There were many changes of commanders on the other side, but on the Pāṇḍavas' side Arjuna alone on the chariot driven by Lord Kṛṣṇa could manage the whole responsibility of the great war. Similarly, when the Pāṇḍavas were living at the palace of Virāṭa incognito, the Kauravas picked a quarrel with King Virāṭa and decided to take away his large number of cows. While they were taking away the cows, Arjuna fought with them incognito and was able to regain the cows along with some booty taken by force—the jewels set on the turbans of the royal order. Arjuna remembered that all this was possible by the grace of the Lord.

TEXT 15

यो भीष्मकर्णगुरुशल्यचमूष्वदभ्र-
राजन्यवर्यरथमण्डलमण्डितासु ।
अग्रेचरो मम विभो रथयूथपाना-
मायुर्मनांसि च दृशा सह ओज आर्च्छत् ॥१५॥

yo bhīṣma-karṇa-guru-śalya-camūṣv adabhra-
rājanya-varya-ratha-maṇḍala-maṇḍitāsu
agrecaro mama vibho ratha-yūthapānām
āyur manāṁsi ca dṛśā saha oja ārcchat

yaḥ—it is He only; *bhīṣma*—Bhīṣma; *karṇa*—Karṇa; *guru*—Droṇācārya; *śalya*—Śalya; *camūṣu*—in the midst of the military phalanx; *adabhra*—immense; *rājanya-varya*—great royal princes; *ratha-maṇḍala*—chain of chariots; *maṇḍitāsu*—being decorated with; *agecaraḥ*—going forward; *mama*—of mine; *vibho*—O great King; *ratha-yūtha-pānām*—all the charioteers; *āyuḥ*—duration of life or fruitive activities; *manāṁsi*—mental upsurges; *ca*—also; *dṛśā*—by glance; *sahaḥ*—power; *ojaḥ*—strength; *ārcchat*—withdrew.

TRANSLATION

It was He only who withdrew the duration of life from everyone and who, in the battlefield, withdrew the speculative power and strength of enthusiasm from the great military phalanx made by the Kauravas, headed by Bhīṣma, Karṇa, Droṇa, Śalya, etc. Their arrangement was expert and more than adequate, but He [Lord Śrī Kṛṣṇa], while going forward, did all this.

PURPORT

The Absolute Personality of Godhead, Lord Śrī Kṛṣṇa, expands Himself by His plenary Paramātmā portion in everyone's heart, and thus He directs everyone in the matter of recollection, forgetfulness, knowledge, the absence of intelligence and all psychological activities (Bg. 15.15). As the Supreme Lord, He can increase or decrease the duration of life of a living being. Thus the Lord conducted the Battle of Kurukṣetra according to His own plan. He wanted that battle to establish Yudhiṣṭhira as the Emperor of this planet, and to facilitate this transcendental business He killed all who were on the opposite party by His omnipotent will. The other party was equipped with all military strength supported by big generals like Bhīṣma, Droṇa and Śalya, and it would have been physically impossible for Arjuna to win the battle had the Lord not helped him by every kind of tactic. Such tactics are generally followed by every statesman, even in modern warfare, but they are all done materially by powerful espionages, military tactics and diplomatic maneuvers. But because

Arjuna was the Lord's affectionate devotee, the Lord did all this Himself without personal anxiety by Arjuna. That is the way of the devotional service to the Lord.

TEXT 16

यद्दोःषु मा प्रणिहितं गुरुभीष्मकर्ण-
नप्तृत्रिगर्तशल्यसैन्धवबाह्लिकाद्यैः ।
अस्त्राण्यमोघमहिमानि निरूपितानि
नोपस्पृशुर्नृहरिदासमिवासुराणि ॥१६॥

yad-doḥṣu mā praṇihitaṁ guru-bhīṣma-karṇa-
naptṛ-trigarta-śalya-saindhava-bāhlikādyaiḥ
astrāṇy amogha-mahimāni nirūpitāni
nopaspṛśur nṛhari-dāsam ivāsurāṇi

yat—under whose; *doḥṣu*—protection of arms; *mā praṇihitam*—myself being situated; *guru*—Droṇācārya; *bhīṣma*—Bhīṣma; *karṇa*—Karṇa; *naptṛ*—Bhūriśravā; *trigarta*—King Suśarmā; *śalya*—Śalya; *saindhava*—King Jayadratha; *bāhlika*—brother of Mahārāja Śāntanu (Bhīṣma's father); *ādyaiḥ*—etc.; *astrāṇi*—weapons; *amogha*—invincible; *mahimāni*—very powerful; *nirūpitāni*—applied; *na*—not; *upaspṛśuḥ*—touched; *nṛhari-dāsam*—servitor of Nṛsiṁhadeva (Prahlāda); *iva*—like; *asurāṇi*—weapons employed by the demons.

TRANSLATION

Great generals like Bhīṣma, Droṇa, Karṇa, Bhūriśravā, Suśarmā, Śalya, Jayadratha, and Bāhlika all directed their invincible weapons against me. But by His [Lord Kṛṣṇa's] grace they could not even touch a hair on my head. Similarly, Prahlāda Mahārāja, the supreme devotee of Lord Nṛsiṁhadeva, was unaffected by the weapons the demons used against him.

PURPORT

The history of Prahlāda Mahārāja, the great devotee of Nṛsiṁhadeva, is narrated in the Seventh Canto of *Śrīmad-Bhāgavatam.* Prahlāda Mahārāja, a small child of only five years, became the object of envy for his great father, Hiraṇyakaśipu, only because of his becoming a pure devotee of the Lord. The demon father employed all his weapons to kill the devotee son, Prahlāda, but by the grace of the Lord he was saved from all sorts of dangerous actions by his father. He was thrown in a fire, in boiling oil, from the top of a hill, underneath the legs of an elephant, and he was administered poison. At last the father himself took up a chopper to kill his son, and thus Nṛsiṁhadeva appeared and killed the heinous father in the presence of the son. Thus no one can kill the devotee of the Lord. Similarly, Arjuna was also saved by the Lord, although all dangerous weapons were employed by his great opponents like Bhīṣma.

Karṇa: Born of Kuntī by the sun- god prior to her marriage with Mahārāja Pāṇḍu, Karṇa took his birth with bangles and earrings, extraordinary signs for an undaunted hero. In the beginning his name was Vasusena, but when he grew up he presented his natural bangles and earrings to Indradeva, and thenceforward he became known as Vaikartana. After his birth from the maiden Kuntī, he was thrown in the Ganges. Later he was picked up by Adhiratha, and he and his wife Rādhā brought him up as their own offspring. Karṇa was very charitable, especially toward the *brāhmaṇas.* There was nothing he could not spare for a *brāhmaṇa.* In the same charitable spirit he gave in charity his natural bangles and earrings to Indradeva, who, being very much satisfied with him, gave him in return a great weapon called Śakti. He was admitted as one of the students of Droṇācārya, and from the very beginning there was some rivalry between him and Arjuna. Seeing his constant rivalry with Arjuna, Duryodhana picked him up as his companion, and this gradually grew into greater intimacy. He was also present in the great assembly of Draupadī's *svayaṁvara* function, and when he attempted to exhibit his talent in that meeting, Draupadī's brother declared that Karṇa could not take part in the competition because of his being the son of a *śūdra* carpenter. Although he was refused in the competition, still when Arjuna was successful in piercing the fish target on the ceiling and Draupadī bestowed her garland upon Arjuna, Karṇa and the other disappointed princes offered an unusual stumbling block to Arjuna while he was leaving with Draupadī. Specifically, Karṇa fought with him very valiantly, but all of them were defeated by Arjuna. Duryodhana was very much pleased with Karṇa because of his constant rivalry with Arjuna, and when he was in power he enthroned Karṇa in the state of Aṅga. Being baffled in his attempt to win Draupadī, Karṇa advised Duryodhana to attack King Drupada, for after defeating him both Arjuna and Draupadī could be arrested. But Droṇācārya rebuked them for this conspiracy, and they refrained from the action. Karṇa was defeated many times, not only by Arjuna but also by Bhīmasena. He was the king of the kingdom of Bengal, Orissa and Madras combined. Later on he took an active part in the Rājasūya sacrifice of Mahārāja Yudhiṣṭhira, and when there was gambling between the rival brothers, designed by Śakuni Karṇa took part in the game, and he was very pleased when Draupadī was offered as a bet in the gambling. This fed his old grudge. When Draupadī was in the game he was very enthusiastic to declare the news, and it is he who ordered Duḥśāsana to take away the garments of both the Pāṇḍavas and Draupadī. He asked Draupadī to select another husband because, being lost by the Pāṇḍavas, she was rendered a slave of the Kurus. He was always an enemy of the Pāṇḍavas, and whenever there was an opportunity, he tried to curb them by all means. During the Battle of Kurukṣetra, he foresaw the conclusive result, and he expressed his opinion that due to Lord Kṛṣṇa's being the chariot driver of Arjuna, the battle should be won by Arjuna. He always differed with Bhīṣma, and sometimes he was proud enough to say that within five days he could finish up the Pāṇḍavas, if Bhīṣma would not interfere with his plan of action. But he was much mortified when Bhīṣma died. He killed Ghaṭotkaca with the Śakti weapon obtained from Indradeva. His son, Vṛṣasena, was killed by Arjuna. He killed the largest number of Pāṇḍava soldiers. At last there was a severe fight with Arjuna, and it was he only who was able to knock off the helmet of Arjuna. But it so happened that the wheel of his chariot stuck in the battlefield mud, and when he got down to set the wheel right, Arjuna took the opportunity and killed him, although he requested Arjuna not to do so.

Naptā, or *Bhūriśravā:* Bhūriśravā was the son of Somadatta, a member of the Kuru family. His other brother was Śalya. Both the brothers and the father attended the *svayaṁvara* ceremony of Draupadī. All of them appreciated the wonderful strength of Arjuna due to his being the devotee friend of the Lord, and thus Bhūriśravā advised the sons of Dhṛtarāṣṭra not to pick any quarrel or fight with them. All of them also attended the Rājasūya yajña of Mahārāja Yudhiṣṭhira. He possessed one *akṣauhiṇī* regiment of army, cavalry, elephants and chariots, and all these were employed in the Battle of Kurukṣetra on behalf of Duryodhana's party. He was counted by Bhīma as one of the *yūtha-patis.* In the Battle of Kurukṣetra he was especially engaged in a fight with Sātyaki, and he killed ten sons of Sātyaki. Later on, Arjuna cut off his hands, and he was ultimately killed by Sātyaki. After his death he merged into the existence of Viśvadeva.

Trigarta, or *Suśarmā:* Son of Mahārāja Vṛddhakṣetra, he was the King of Trigartadeśa, and he was also present in the *svayaṁvara* ceremony of Draupadī. He was one of the allies of Duryodhana, and he advised Duryodhana to attack the Matsyadeśa (Darbhaṅga). During the time of cow-stealing in

Virāṭa-nagara, he was able to arrest Mahārāja Virāṭa, but later Mahārāja Virāṭa was released by Bhīma. In the Battle of Kurukṣetra he also fought very valiantly, but at the end he was killed by Arjuna.

Jayadratha: Another son of Mahārāja Vṛddhakṣetra. He was the King of Sindhudeśa (modern Sind Pakistan). His wife's name was Duḥśalā. He was also present in the *svayaṁvara* ceremony of Draupadī, and he desired very strongly to have her hand, but he failed in the competition. But since then he always sought the opportunity to get in touch with Draupadī. When he was going to marry in the Śalyadeśa, on the way to Kāmyavana he happened to see Draupadī again and was too much attracted to her. The Pāṇḍavas and Draupadī were then in exile, after losing their empire in gambling, and Jayadratha thought it wise to send news to Draupadī in an illicit manner through Koṭiśaṣya, one of his associates. Draupadī at once refused vehemently the proposal of Jayadratha, but being so much attracted by the beauty of Draupadī, he tried again and again. Every time he was refused by Draupadī. He tried to take her away forcibly on his chariot, and at first Draupadī gave him a good dashing, and he fell like a cut-root tree. But he was not discouraged, and he was able to force Draupadī to sit on the chariot. This incident was seen by Dhaumya Muni, and he strongly protested the action of Jayadratha. He also followed the chariot, and through Dhātreyikā the matter was brought to the notice of Mahārāja Yudhiṣṭhira. The Pāṇḍavas then attacked the soldiers of Jayadratha and killed them all, and at last Bhīma caught hold of Jayadratha and beat him very severely, almost dead. Then all but five hairs were cut off his head and he was taken to all the kings and introduced as the slave of Mahārāja Yudhiṣṭhira. He was forced to admit himself to be the slave of Mahārāja Yudhiṣṭhira before all the princely order, and in the same condition he was brought before Mahārāja Yudhiṣṭhira. Mahārāja Yudhiṣṭhira was kind enough to order him released, and when he admitted to being a tributary prince under Mahārāja Yudhiṣṭhira, Queen Draupadī also desired his release. After this incident, he was allowed to return to his country. Being so insulted, he went to Gaṅgotri in the Himalayas and undertook a severe type of penance to please Lord Śiva. He asked his benediction to defeat all the Pāṇḍavas, at least one at a time. Then the Battle of Kurukṣetra began, and he took sides with Duryodhana. In the first day's fight he was engaged with Mahārāja Drupada, then with Virāṭa and then with Abhimanyu. While Abhimanyu was being killed, mercilessly surrounded by seven great generals, the Pāṇḍavas came to his help, but Jayadratha, by the mercy of Lord Śiva, repulsed them with great ability. At this, Arjuna took a vow to kill him, and on hearing this, Jayadratha wanted to leave the warfield and asked permission from the Kauravas for this cowardly action. But he was not allowed to do so. On the contrary, he was obliged to fight with Arjuna, and while the fight was going on Lord Kṛṣṇa reminded Arjuna that the benediction of Śiva upon Jayadratha was that whoever would cause his head to fall on the ground would die at once. He therefore advised Arjuna to throw the head of Jayadratha directly onto the lap of his father, who was engaged in penances at the Samanta-pañcaka pilgrimage. This was actually done by Arjuna. Jayadratha's father was surprised to see a severed head on his lap, and he at once threw it to the ground. The father immediately died, his forehead being cracked in seven pieces.

TEXT 17

सौत्ये वृतः कुमतिनात्मद ईश्वरो मे
यत्पादपद्ममभवाय भजन्ति भव्याः ।
मां श्रान्तवाहमरयो रथिनो भुविष्ठं
न प्राहरन् यदनुभावनिरस्तचित्ताः ॥१७॥

sautye vṛtaḥ kumatinātmada īśvaro me
yat-pāda-padmam abhavāya bhajanti bhavyāḥ
māṁ śrānta-vāham arayo rathino bhuvi-ṣṭhaṁ
na prāharan yad-anubhāva-nirasta-cittāḥ

sautye—regarding a chariot driver; *vṛtaḥ*—engaged; *kumatinā*—by bad consciousness; *ātma-daḥ*—one who delivers; *īśvaraḥ*—the Supreme Lord; *me*—my; *yat*—whose; *pāda-padmam*—lotus feet; *abhavāya*—in the matter of salvation; *bhajanti*—do render service; *bhavyāḥ*—the intelligent class of men; *mām*—unto me; *śrānta*—thirsty; *vāham*—my horses; *arayaḥ*—the enemies; *rathinaḥ*—a great general; *bhuvi-ṣṭham*—while standing on the ground; *na*—did not; *prāharan*—attack; *yat*—whose; *anubhāva*—mercy; *nirasta*—being absent; *cittāḥ*—mind.

TRANSLATION

It was by His mercy only that my enemies neglected to kill me when I descended from my chariot to get water for my thirsty horses. And it was due to my lack of esteem for my Lord that I dared engage Him as my chariot driver, for He is worshiped and offered services by the best men to attain salvation.

PURPORT

The Supreme Lord, the Personality of Godhead Śrī Kṛṣṇa, is the object of worship both by impersonalists and by the devotees of the Lord. The impersonalists worship His glowing effulgence, emanating from His transcendental body of eternal form, bliss and knowledge, and the devotees worship Him as the Supreme Personality of Godhead. Those who are below even the impersonalists consider Him to be one of the great historical personalities. The Lord, however, descends to attract all by His specific transcendental pastimes, and thus He plays the part of the most perfect master, friend, son and lover. His transcendental relation with Arjuna was in friendship, and the Lord therefore played the part perfectly, as He did with His parents, lovers and wives. While playing in such a perfect transcendental relation, the devotee forgets, by the internal potency of the Lord, that his friend or son is the Supreme Personality of Godhead, although sometimes the devotee is bewildered by the acts of the Lord. After the departure of the Lord, Arjuna was conscious of his great friend, but there was no mistake on the part of Arjuna, nor any ill estimation of the Lord. Intelligent men are attracted by the transcendental acting of the Lord with a pure, unalloyed devotee like Arjuna.

In the war field, scarcity of water is a well-known fact. Water is very rare there, and both the animals and men, working strenuously on the warfield, constantly require water to quench their thirst. Especially wounded soldiers and generals feel very thirsty at the time of death, and it sometimes so happens that simply for want of water one has to die unavoidably. But such scarcity of water was solved in the Battle of Kurukṣetra by means of boring the ground. By God's grace, water can be easily obtained from any place if there is facility for boring the ground. The modern system works on the same principle of boring the ground, but modern engineers are still unable to dig immediately wherever necessary. It appears, however, from the history as far back as the days of the Pāṇḍavas, that big generals like Arjuna could at once supply water even to the horses, and what to speak of men, by drawing water from underneath the hard ground simply by penetrating the stratum with a sharp arrow, a method still unknown to the modern scientists.

TEXT 18

नर्माण्युदाररुचिरस्मितशोभितानि
हे पार्थ हेऽर्जुन सखे कुरुनन्दनेति ।

संजल्पितानि नरदेव हृदिस्पृशानि
स्मर्तुर्लुठन्ति हृदयं मम माधवस्य ॥१८॥

narmāṇy udāra-rucira-smita-śobhitāni
he pārtha he 'rjuna sakhe kuru-nandaneti
sañjalpitāni nara-deva hṛdi-spṛśāni
smartur luṭhanti hṛdayaṁ mama mādhavasya

narmāṇi—conversation in jokes; *udāra*—talked very frankly; *rucira*—pleasing; *smita-śobhitāni*—decorated with a smiling face; *he*—note of address; *pārtha*—O son of Pṛthā; *he*—note of address; *arjuna*—Arjuna; *sakhe*—friend; *kuru-nandana*—son of the Kuru dynasty; *iti*—and so on; *sañjalpitāni*—such conversation; *nara-deva*—O King; *hṛdi*—heart; *spṛśāni*—touching; *smartuḥ*—by remembering them; *luṭhanti*—overwhelms; *hṛdayam*—heart and soul; *mama*—my; *mādhavasya*—of Mādhava (Kṛṣṇa).

TRANSLATION

O King! His jokings and frank talks were pleasing and beautifully decorated with smiles. His addresses unto me as "O son of Pṛthā, O friend, O son of the Kuru dynasty," and all such heartiness are now remembered by me, and thus I am overwhelmed.

TEXT 19

शय्यासनाटनविकत्थनभोजनादि-
ष्वैक्याद्वयस्य ऋतवानिति विप्रलब्धः ।
सख्युः सखेव पितृवत्तनयस्य सर्वं
सेहे महान्महितया कुमतेरघं में ॥१९॥

śayyāsanāṭana-vikatthana-bhojanādiṣv
aikyād vayasya ṛtavān iti vipralabdhaḥ
sakhyuḥ sakheva pitṛvat tanayasya sarvaṁ
sehe mahān mahitayā kumater aghaṁ me

śayya—sleeping on one bed; *āsana*—sitting on one seat; *aṭana*—walking together; *vikatthana*—self-adoration; *bhojana*—dining together; *ādiṣu*—and in all such dealings; *aikyāt*—because of oneness; *vayasya*—O my friend; *ṛtavān*—truthful; *iti*—thus; *vipralabdhaḥ*—misbehaved; *sakhyuḥ*

—unto a friend; *sakhā iva*—just like a friend; *pitṛvat*—just like the father; *tanayasya*—of a child; *sarvam*—all; *sehe*—tolerated; *mahān*—great; *mahitayā*—by glories; *kumateḥ*—of one who is of low mentality; *agham*—offense; *me*—mine.

TRANSLATION

Generally both of us used to live together and sleep, sit and loiter together. And at the time of advertising oneself for acts of chivalry, sometimes, if there were any irregularity, I used to reproach Him by saying, "My friend, You are very truthful." Even in those hours when His value was minimized, He, being the Supreme Soul, used to tolerate all those utterings of mine, excusing me exactly as a true friend excuses his true friend, or a father excuses his son.

PURPORT

Since the Supreme Lord Śrī Kṛṣṇa is all-perfect, His transcendental pastimes with His pure devotees never lack anything in any respect, either as a friend, son or lover. The Lord relishes the reproaches of friends, parents or fiancées more than the Vedic hymns offered to Him by great learned scholars and religionists in an official fashion.

TEXT 20

सोऽहं नृपेन्द्र रहितः पुरुषोत्तमेन
सख्या प्रियेण सुहृदा हृदयेन शून्यः ।
अध्वन्युरुक्रमपरिग्रहमङ्ग रक्षन्
गोपैरसद्भिरबलेव विनिर्जितोऽस्मि ॥२०॥

so 'haṁ nṛpendra rahitaḥ puruṣottamena
sakhyā priyeṇa suhṛdā hṛdayena śūnyaḥ
adhvany urukrama-parigraham aṅga rakṣan
gopair asadbhir abaleva vinirjito 'smi

saḥ—that; *aham*—myself; *nṛpa-indra*—O Emperor; *rahitaḥ*—bereft of; *puruṣa-uttamena*—by the Supreme Lord; *sakhyā*—by my friend; *priyeṇa*—by my dearmost; *suhṛdā*—by the well-wisher; *hṛdayena*—by the heart and soul; *śūnyaḥ*—vacant; *adhvani*—recently; *urukrama-parigraham*—the wives of the all-powerful; *aṅga*—bodies; *rakṣan*—while protecting; *gopaiḥ*—by the cowherds; *asadbhiḥ*—by the infidels; *abalā iva*—like a weak woman; *vinirjitaḥ asmi*—I have been defeated.

TRANSLATION

O Emperor, now I am separated from my friend and dearmost well-wisher, the Supreme Personality of Godhead, and therefore my heart appears to be void of everything. In His absence I have been defeated by a number of infidel cowherd men while I was guarding the bodies of all the wives of Kṛṣṇa.

PURPORT

The important point in this verse is how it was possible that Arjuna could be defeated by a gang of ignoble cowherd men and how such mundane cowherd men could touch the bodies of the wives of Lord Kṛṣṇa, who were under the protection of Arjuna. Śrīla Viśvanātha Cakravartī Ṭhākura has justified the contradiction by research in the *Viṣṇu Purāṇa* and *Brahma Purāṇa.* In these *Purāṇas* it is said that once the fair denizens of heaven pleased Aṣṭāvakra Muni by their service and were blessed by the *muni* to have the Supreme Lord as their husband. Aṣṭāvakra Muni was curved in eight joints of his body, and thus he used to move in a peculiar curved manner. The daughters of the demigods could not check their laughter upon seeing the movements of the *muni,* and the *muni,* being angry at them, cursed them that they would be kidnapped by rogues, even if they would get the Lord as their husband. Later on, the girls again satisfied the *muni* by their prayers, and the *muni* blessed them that they would regain their husband even after being robbed by the rogues. So, in order to keep the words of the great *muni,* the Lord Himself kidnapped His wives from the protection of Arjuna, otherwise they would have at once vanished from the scene as soon as they were touched by the rogues. Besides that, some of the *gopīs* who prayed to become wives of the Lord returned to their respective positions after their desire was fulfilled. After the departure of Lord Kṛṣṇa, He wanted all His entourage back to Godhead, and they were called back under different conditions only.

TEXT 21

तद्वै धनुस्त इषवः स रथो हयास्ते
सोऽहं रथी नृपतयो यत आनमन्ति ।

सर्वं क्षणेन तदभूदसदीशरिक्तं
भस्मन्हुतं कुहकराद्धमिवोप्तमूष्याम् ॥२१॥

tad vai dhanus ta iṣavaḥ sa ratho hayās te
so 'haṁ rathī nṛpatayo yata ānamanti
sarvaṁ kṣaṇena tad abhūd asad īśa-riktaṁ
bhasman hutaṁ kuhaka-rāddham ivoptam ūṣyām

tat—the same; *vai*—certainly; *dhanuḥ te*—the same bow; *iṣavaḥ*—arrows; *saḥ*—the very same; *rathaḥ*—chariot; *hayāḥ te*—the very same horses; *saḥ aham*—I am the same Arjuna; *rathī*—the chariot-fighter; *nṛpatayaḥ*—all the kings; *yataḥ*—whom; *ānamanti*—offered their respects; *sarvam*—all; *kṣaṇena*—at a moment's notice; *tat*—all those; *abhūt*—became; *asat*—useless; *īśa*—because of the Lord; *riktam*—being void; *bhasman*—ashes; *hutam*—offering butter; *kuhaka-rāddham*—money created by magical feats; *iva*—like that; *uptam*—sown; *ūṣyām*—in barren land.

TRANSLATION

I have the very same Gāṇḍīva bow, the same arrows, the same chariot drawn by the same horses, and I use them as the same Arjuna to whom all the kings offered their due respects. But in the absence of Lord Kṛṣṇa, all of them, at a moment's notice, have become null and void. It is exactly like offering clarified butter on ashes, accumulating money with a magic wand or sowing seeds on barren land.

PURPORT

As we have discussed more than once, one should not be puffed up by borrowed plumes. All energies and powers are derived from the supreme source, Lord Kṛṣṇa, and they act as long as He desires and cease to function as soon as He withdraws. All electrical energies are received from the powerhouse, and as soon as the powerhouse stops supplying energy, the bulbs are of no use. In a moment's time such energies can be generated or withdrawn by the supreme will of the Lord. Material civilization without the blessing of the Lord is child's play only. As long as the parents allow the child to play, it is all right. As soon as the parents withdraw, the child has to stop. Human civilization and all activities thereof must be dovetailed with the supreme blessing of the Lord, and without this blessing all advancement of human civilization is like decoration on a dead body. It is said here that a dead civilization and its activities are something like clarified butter on ashes, the accumulation of money by a magic wand and the sowing of seeds in a barren land.

TEXTS 22–23

राजंस्त्वयानुपृष्टानां सुहृदां नः सुहृत्पुरे ।
विप्रशापविमूढानां निघ्नतां मुष्टिभिर्मिथः ॥२२॥
वारुणीं मदिरां पीत्वा मदोन्मथितचेतसाम् ।
अजानतामिवान्योन्यं चतुःपञ्चावशेषिताः ॥२३॥

rājaṁs tvayānupṛṣṭānāṁ
suhṛdāṁ naḥ suhṛt-pure
vipra-śāpa-vimūḍhānāṁ
nighnatāṁ muṣṭibhir mithaḥ

vāruṇīṁ madirāṁ pītvā
madonmathita-cetasām
ajānatām ivānyonyaṁ
catuḥ-pañcāvaśeṣitāḥ

rājan—O King; *tvayā*—by you; *anupṛṣṭānām*—as you inquired; *suhṛdām*—of friends and relatives; *naḥ*—our; *suhṛt-pure*—in the city of Dvārakā; *vipra*—the *brāhmaṇas; śāpa*—by the curse of; *vimūḍhānām*—of the befooled; *nighnatām*—of the killed; *muṣṭibhiḥ*—with bunches of sticks; *mithaḥ*—among themselves; *vāruṇīm*—fermented rice; *madirām*—wine; *pītvā*—having drunk; *mada-unmathita*—being intoxicated; *cetasām*—of that mental situation; *ajānatām*—of the unrecognized; *iva*—like; *anyonyam*—one another; *catuḥ*—four; *pañca*—five; *avaśeṣitāḥ*—now remaining.

TRANSLATION

O King, since you have asked me about our friends and relatives in the city of Dvārakā, I will inform you that all of them were cursed by the brāhmaṇas, and as a result they all became intoxicated with wine made of putrefied rice and fought among themselves with sticks, not even recognizing one another. Now all but four or five of them are dead and gone.

TEXT 24

प्रायेणैतद् भगवत ईश्वरस्य विचेष्टितम् ।
मिथो निघ्नन्ति भूतानि भावयन्ति च यन्मिथः ॥२४॥

prāyeṇaitad bhagavata
īśvarasya viceṣṭitam
mitho nighnanti bhūtāni
bhāvayanti ca yan mithaḥ

prāyeṇa etat—it is almost by; *bhagavataḥ*—of the Personality of Godhead; *īśvarasya*—of the Lord; *viceṣṭitam*—by the will of; *mithaḥ*—one another; *nighnanti*—do kill; *bhūtāni*—the living beings; *bhāvayanti*—as also protect; *ca*—also; *yat*—of whom; *mithaḥ*—one another.

TRANSLATION

Factually this is all due to the supreme will of the Lord, the Personality of Godhead. Sometimes people kill one another, and at other times they protect one another.

PURPORT

According to the anthropologists, there is nature's law of struggle for existence and survival of the fittest. But they do not know that behind the law of nature is the supreme direction of the Supreme Personality of Godhead. In the *Bhagavad-gītā* it is confirmed that the law of nature is executed under the direction of the Lord. Whenever, therefore, there is peace in the world, it must be known that it is due to the good will of the Lord. And whenever there is upheaval in the world, it is also due to the supreme will of the Lord. Not a blade of grass moves without the will of the Lord. Whenever, therefore, there is disobedience of the established rules enacted by the Lord, there is war between men and nations. The surest way to the path of peace, therefore, is dovetailing everything to the established rule of the Lord. The established rule is that whatever we do, whatever we eat, whatever we sacrifice or whatever we give in charity must be done to the full satisfaction of the Lord. No one should do anything, eat anything, sacrifice anything or give anything in charity against the will of the Lord. Discretion is the better part of valor, and one must learn how to discriminate between actions which may be pleasing to the Lord and those which may not be pleasing to the Lord. An action is thus judged by the Lord's pleasure or displeasure. There is no room for personal whims; we must always be guided by the pleasure of the Lord. Such action is called *yogaḥ karmasu kauśalam,* or actions performed which are linked with the Supreme Lord. That is the art of doing a thing perfectly.

TEXTS 25–26

जलौकसां जले यद्वन्महान्तोऽदन्त्यणीयसः ।
दुर्बलान्बलिनो राजन्महान्तो बलिनो मिथः ॥२५॥
एवं बलिष्ठैर्यदुभिर्महद्भिरितरान् विभुः ।
यदून्यदुभिरन्योन्यं भूभारान् संजहार ह ॥२६॥

jalaukasāṁ jale yadvan
mahānto 'danty aṇīyasaḥ
durbalān balino rājan
mahānto balino mithaḥ

evaṁ baliṣṭhair yadubhir
mahadbhir itarān vibhuḥ
yadūn yadubhir anyonyaṁ
bhū-bhārān sañjahāra ha

jalaukasām—of the aquatics; *jale*—in the water; *yadvat*—as it is; *mahāntaḥ*—the larger one; *adanti*—swallows; *aṇīyasaḥ*—smaller ones; *durbalān*—the weak; *balinaḥ*—the stronger; *rājan*—O King; *mahāntaḥ*—the strongest; *balinaḥ*—less strong; *mithaḥ*—in a duel; *evam*—thus; *baliṣṭhaiḥ*—by the strongest; *yadubhiḥ*—by the descendants of Yadu; *mahadbhiḥ*—one who has greater strength; *itarān*—the common ones; *vibhuḥ*—the Supreme Personality of Godhead; *yadūn*—all the Yadus; *yadubhiḥ*—by the Yadus; *anyonyam*—among one another; *bhū-bhārān*—the burden of the world; *sañjahāra*—has unloaded; *ha*—in the past.

TRANSLATION

O King, as in the ocean the bigger and stronger aquatics swallow up the smaller and weaker ones, so also the Supreme Personality of Godhead, to lighten the burden of the earth, has engaged the stronger Yadu to kill the weaker, and the bigger Yadu to kill the smaller.

PURPORT

In the material world the struggle for existence and survival of the fittest are laws because in the material world there is disparity between conditioned souls due to everyone's desire to lord it over the material resources. This very mentality of lording it over the material nature is the root cause of conditioned life. And to give facility to such imitation lords, the illusory energy of the Lord has created a disparity between conditioned living beings by creating the stronger and the weaker in every species of life. The mentality of lording it over the material nature and the creation has naturally created a disparity and therefore the law of struggle for existence. In the spiritual world there is no such disparity, nor is there such a struggle for existence. In the spiritual world there is no struggle for existence because everyone there exists eternally. There is no disparity because everyone wants to render service to the Supreme Lord, and no one wants to imitate the Lord in becoming the beneficiary. The Lord, being creator of everything, including the living beings, factually is the proprietor and enjoyer of everything that be, but in the material world, by the spell of *māyā,* or illusion, this eternal relation with the Supreme Personality of Godhead is forgotten, and so the living being is conditioned under the law of struggle for existence and survival of the fittest.

TEXT 27

देशकालार्थयुक्तानि हृत्तापोपशमानि च ।
हरन्ति स्मरतश्चित्तं गोविन्दाभिहितानि मे ॥२७॥

deśa-kālārtha-yuktāni
hṛt-tāpopaśamāni ca
haranti smarataś cittaṁ
govindābhihitāni me

deśa—space; *kāla*—time; *artha*—importance; *yuktāni*—impregnated with; *hṛt*—the heart; *tāpa*—burning; *upaśamāni*—extinguishing; *ca*—and; *haranti*—are attracting; *smarataḥ*—by remembering; *cittam*—mind; *govinda*—the Supreme Personality of pleasure; *abhihitāni*—narrated by; *me* —unto me.

TRANSLATION

Now I am attracted to those instructions imparted to me by the Personality of Godhead [Govinda] because they are impregnated with

instructions for relieving the burning heart in all circumstances of time and space.

PURPORT

Herein Arjuna refers to the instruction of the *Bhagavad-gītā,* which was imparted to him by the Lord on the Battlefield of Kurukṣetra. The Lord left behind Him the instructions of the *Bhagavad-gītā* not for the benefit of Arjuna alone, but also for all time and in all lands. The *Bhagavad-gītā,* being spoken by the Supreme Personality of Godhead, is the essence of all Vedic wisdom. It is nicely presented by the Lord Himself for all who have very little time to go through the vast Vedic literatures like the *Upaniṣads, Purāṇas* and *Vedānta-sūtras.* It is put within the study of the great historical epic *Mahābhārata,* which was especially prepared for the less intelligent class, namely the women, the laborers and those who are worthless descendants of the *brāhmaṇas, kṣatriyas* and higher sections of the *vaiśyas.* The problem which arose in the heart of Arjuna on the Battlefield of Kurukṣetra was solved by the teachings of the *Bhagavad-gītā.* Again, after the departure of the Lord from the vision of earthly people, when Arjuna was face to face with being vanquished in his acquired power and prominence, he wanted again to remember the great teachings of the *Bhagavad-gītā* just to teach all concerned that the *Bhagavad-gītā* can be consulted in all critical times, not only for solace from all kinds of mental agonies, but also for the way out of great entanglements which may embarrass one in some critical hour.

The merciful Lord left behind Him the great teachings of the *Bhagavad-gītā* so that one can take the instructions of the Lord even when He is not visible to material eyesight. Material senses cannot have any estimation of the Supreme Lord, but by His inconceivable power the Lord can incarnate Himself to the sense perception of the conditioned souls in a suitable manner through the agency of matter, which is also another form of the Lord's manifested energy. Thus the *Bhagavad-gītā,* or any authentic scriptural sound representation of the Lord, is also the incarnation of the Lord. There is no difference between the sound representation of the Lord and the Lord Himself. One can derive the same benefit from the *Bhagavad-gītā* as Arjuna did in the personal presence of the Lord.

The faithful human being who is desirous of being liberated from the clutches of material existence can very easily take advantage of the *Bhagavad-gītā,* and with this in view, the Lord instructed Arjuna as if Arjuna were in need of it. In the *Bhagavad-gītā,* five important factors of knowledge have been delineated pertaining to (1) the Supreme Lord, (2) the living being, (3) nature,

(4) time and space and (5) the process of activity. Out of these, the Supreme Lord and the living being are qualitatively one. The difference between the two has been analyzed as the difference between the whole and the part and parcel. Nature is inert matter displaying the interaction of three different modes, and eternal time and unlimited space are considered to be beyond the existence of the material nature. Activities of the living being are different varieties of aptitudes which can entrap or liberate the living being within and without material nature. All these subject matters are concisely discussed in the *Bhagavad-gītā,* and later the subject matters are elaborated in the *Śrīmad-Bhāgavatam* for further enlightenment. Out of the five subjects, the Supreme Lord, the living entity, nature, and time and space are eternal, but the living entity, nature and time are under the direction of the Supreme Lord, who is absolute and completely independent of any other control. The Supreme Lord is the supreme controller. The material activity of the living being is beginningless, but it can be rectified by transferal into the spiritual quality. Thus it can cease its material qualitative reactions. Both the Lord and the living entity are cognizant, and both have the sense of identification, of being conscious as a living force. But the living being under the condition of material nature, called *mahat-tattva,* misidentifies himself as being different from the Lord. The whole scheme of Vedic wisdom is targeted to the aim of eradicating such a misconception and thus liberating the living being from the illusion of material identification. When such an illusion is eradicated by knowledge and renunciation, the living beings are responsible actors and enjoyers also. The sense of enjoyment in the Lord is real, but such a sense in the living being is a sort of wishful desire only. This difference in consciousness is the distinction of the two identities, namely the Lord and the living being. Otherwise there is no difference between the Lord and the living being. The living being is therefore eternally one and different simultaneously. The whole instruction of the *Bhagavad-gītā* stands on this principle.

In the *Bhagavad-gītā* the Lord and the living beings are both described as *sanātana,* or eternal, and the Lord's abode, far beyond the material sky, is also described as *sanātana.* The living being is invited to live in the *sanātana* existence of the Lord, and the process which can help a living being to approach the Lord's abode, where the liberated activity of the soul is exhibited, is called *sanātana dharma.* One cannot, however, reach the eternal abode of the Lord without being free from the misconception of material identification, and the *Bhagavad-gītā* gives us the clue how to achieve this stage of perfection. The process of being liberated from the misconception of material identification is called, in different stages, fruitive activity, empiric philosophy and devotional service, up to transcendental realization. Such transcendental realization is made possible by dovetailing all the above items in relation with the Lord. Prescribed duties of the human being, as directed in the *Vedas,* can gradually purify the sinful mind of the conditioned soul and raise him to the stage of knowledge. The purified stage of acquiring knowledge becomes the basis of devotional service to the Lord. As long as one is engaged in researching the solution of the problems of life, his knowledge is called *jñāna,* or purified knowledge, but on realizing the actual solution of life, one becomes situated in the devotional service of the Lord. The *Bhagavad-gītā* begins with the problems of life by discriminating the soul from the elements of matter and proves by all reason and argument that the soul is indestructible in all circumstances and that the outer covering of matter, the body and the mind, change for another term of material existence which is full of miseries. The *Bhagavad-gītā* is therefore meant for terminating all different types of miseries, and Arjuna took shelter of this great knowledge, which had been imparted to him during the Kurukṣetra battle.

TEXT 28

सूत उवाच
एवं चिन्तयतो जिष्णोः कृष्णपादसरोरुहम् ।
सौहार्देनातिगाढेन शान्तासीद्विमला मतिः ॥२८॥

sūta uvāca
evaṁ cintayato jiṣṇoḥ
kṛṣṇa-pāda-saroruham
sauhārdenātigāḍhena
śāntāsīd vimalā matiḥ

sūtaḥ uvāca—Sūta Gosvāmī said; *evam*—thus; *cintayataḥ*—while thinking of the instructions; *jiṣṇoḥ*—of the Supreme Personality of Godhead; *kṛṣṇa-pāda*—the feet of Kṛṣṇa; *saroruham*—resembling lotuses; *sauhārdena*—by deep friendship; *ati-gāḍhena*—in great intimacy; *śāntā*—pacified; *āsīt*—it so became; *vimalā*—without any tinge of material contamination; *matiḥ*—mind.

TRANSLATION

Sūta Gosvāmī said: Thus being deeply absorbed in thinking of the instructions of the Lord, which were imparted in the great intimacy of

friendship, and in thinking of His lotus feet, Arjuna's mind became pacified and free from all material contamination.

PURPORT

Since the Lord is absolute, deep meditation upon Him is as good as yogic trance. The Lord is nondifferent from His name, form, quality, pastimes, entourage and specific actions. Arjuna began to think of the Lord's instructions to him on the Battlefield of Kurukṣetra. Only those instructions began to eliminate the tinges of material contamination in the mind of Arjuna. The Lord is like the sun; the sun's appearance means immediate dissipation of darkness, or ignorance, and the Lord's appearance within the mind of the devotee can at once drive away the miserable material effects. Lord Caitanya has therefore recommended constant chanting of the name of the Lord for protection from all contamination of the material world. The feeling of separation from the Lord is undoubtedly painful to the devotee, but because it is in connection with the Lord, it has a specific transcendental effect which pacifies the heart. Feelings of separation are also sources of transcendental bliss, and they are never comparable to contaminated material feelings of separation.

TEXT 29

वासुदेवाङ्घ्र्यनुध्यानपरिबृंहितरंहसा ।
भक्त्या निर्मथिताशेषकषायधिषणोऽर्जुनः ॥२९॥

vāsudevāṅghry-anudhyāna-
paribṛṁhita-raṁhasā
bhaktyā nirmathitāśeṣa-
kaṣāya-dhiṣaṇo 'rjunaḥ

vāsudeva-aṅghri—the lotus feet of the Lord; *anudhyāna*—by constant remembrance; *paribṛṁhita*—expanded; *raṁhasā*—with great velocity; *bhaktyā*—in devotion; *nirmathita*—subsided; *aśeṣa*—unlimited; *kaṣāya*—dint; *dhiṣaṇaḥ*—conception; *arjunaḥ*—Arjuna.

TRANSLATION

Arjuna's constant remembrance of the lotus feet of Lord Śrī Kṛṣṇa rapidly increased his devotion, and as a result all the trash in his thoughts subsided.

PURPORT

Material desires in the mind are the trash of material contamination. By such contamination, the living being is faced with so many compatible and incompatible things that discourage the very existence of spiritual identity. Birth after birth the conditioned soul is entrapped with so many pleasing and displeasing elements, which are all false and temporary. They accumulate due to our reactions to material desires, but when we get in touch with the transcendental Lord in His variegated energies by devotional service, the naked forms of all material desires become manifest, and the intelligence of the living being is pacified in its true color. As soon as Arjuna turned his attention towards the instructions of the Lord, as they are inculcated in the *Bhagavad-gītā,* his true color of eternal association with the Lord became manifest, and thus he felt freed from all material contaminations.

TEXT 30

गीतं भगवता ज्ञानं यत् तत् सङ्ग्राममूर्धनि ।
कालकर्मतमोरुद्धं पुनरध्यगमत् प्रभुः ॥३०॥

gītaṁ bhagavatā jñānaṁ
yat tat saṅgrāma-mūrdhani
kāla-karma-tamo-ruddhaṁ
punar adhyagamat prabhuḥ

gītam—instructed; *bhagavatā*—by the Personality of Godhead; *jñānam* —transcendental knowledge; *yat*—which; *tat*—that; *saṅgrāma-mūrdhani*—in the midst of battle; *kāla-karma*—time and actions; *tamaḥ-ruddham* —enwrapped by such darkness; *punaḥ adhyagamat*—revived them again; *prabhuḥ*—the lord of his senses.

TRANSLATION

Because of the Lord's pastimes and activities and because of His absence, it appeared that Arjuna forgot the instructions left by the Personality of Godhead. But factually this was not the case, and again he became lord of his senses.

PURPORT

A conditioned soul is enwrapped in his fruitive activities by the force of eternal time. But the Supreme Lord, when He incarnates on the earth, is not influenced by *kāla,* or the material conception of past, present and future. The activities of the Lord are eternal, and they are manifestations of His *ātma-māyā,* or internal potency. All pastimes or activities of the Lord are spiritual in nature, but to the laymen they appear to be on the same level with material activities. It so appeared that Arjuna and the Lord were engaged in the Battle of Kurukṣetra as the other party was also engaged, but factually the Lord was executing His mission of incarnation and association with His eternal friend Arjuna. Therefore such apparently material activities of Arjuna did not drive him away from his transcendental position, but on the contrary revived his consciousness of the songs of the Lord, as He sang them personally. This revival of consciousness is assured by the Lord in the *Bhagavad-gītā* (18.65) as follows:

man-manā bhava mad-bhakto
mad-yājī māṁ namaskuru
mām evaiṣyasi satyaṁ te
pratijāne priyo 'si me

One should think of the Lord always; the mind should not forget Him. One should become a devotee of the Lord and offer obeisances unto Him. One who lives in that fashion becomes undoubtedly endowed with the blessing of the Lord by achieving the shelter of His lotus feet. There is nothing to doubt about this eternal truth. Because Arjuna was His confidential friend, the secret was disclosed to him.

Arjuna had no desire to fight with his relatives, but he fought for the mission of the Lord. He was always engaged in the execution of His mission only, and therefore after the Lord's departure he remained in the same transcendental position, even though it appeared that he forgot all the instructions of the *Bhagavad-gītā.* One should, therefore, adjust the activities of life in pace with the mission of the Lord, and by doing this one is sure to return back home, back to Godhead. This is the highest perfection of life.

TEXT 31

विशोको ब्रह्मसम्पत्त्या संछिन्नद्वैतसंशयः ।
लीनप्रकृतिनैर्गुण्यादलिङ्गत्वादसम्भवः ॥ ३१ ॥

viśoko brahma-sampattyā
sañchinna-dvaita-saṁśayaḥ

līna-prakṛti-nairguṇyād
aliṅgatvād asambhavaḥ

viśokaḥ—free from bereavement; *brahma-sampattyā*—by possession of spiritual assets; *sañchinna*—being completely cut off; *dvaita-saṁśayaḥ*—from the doubts of relativity; *līna*—merged in; *prakṛti*—material nature; *nairguṇyāt*—due to being in transcendence; *aliṅgatvāt*—because of being devoid of a material body; *asambhavaḥ*—free from birth and death.

TRANSLATION

Because of his possessing spiritual assets, the doubts of duality were completely cut off. Thus he was freed from the three modes of material nature and placed in transcendence. There was no longer any chance of his becoming entangled in birth and death, for he was freed from material form.

PURPORT

Doubts of duality begin from the misconception of the material body, which is accepted as the self by less intelligent persons. The most foolish part of our ignorance is our identifying this material body with the self. Everything in relation with the body is ignorantly accepted as our own. Doubts due to misconceptions of "myself" and "mine"—in other words, "my body," "my relatives," "my property," "my wife," "my children," "my wealth," "my country," "my community" and hundreds and thousands of similar illusory contemplations—cause bewilderment for the conditioned soul. By assimilating the instructions of the *Bhagavad-gītā,* one is sure to be released from such bewilderment because real knowledge is knowledge that the Supreme Personality of Godhead, Vāsudeva, Lord Kṛṣṇa, is everything, including one's self. Everything is a manifestation of His potency as part and parcel. The potency and the potent are nondifferent, so the conception of duality is at once mitigated by attainment of perfect knowledge. As soon as Arjuna took up the instructions of the *Bhagavad-gītā,* expert as he was, he could at once eradicate the material conception of Lord Kṛṣṇa, his eternal friend. He could realize that the Lord was still present before him by His instruction, by His form, by His pastimes, by His qualities and everything else related to Him. He could realize that Lord Kṛṣṇa, his friend, was still present before him by His transcendental presence in different nondual energies, and there was no question of attainment of the association of the Lord by another change of body under the influence of time and space. By attainment of absolute knowledge, one can be in association with the Lord constantly, even in this present life, simply by hearing, chanting, thinking of and worshiping the Supreme Lord. One can see Him, one can feel His presence even in this present life simply by understanding the *advaya jñāna* Lord, or the Absolute Lord, through the process of devotional service, which begins with hearing about Him. Lord Caitanya says that simply by chanting the holy name of the Lord one can at once wash off the dust on the mirror of pure consciousness, and as soon as the dust is removed, one is at once freed from all material conditions. To become free from material conditions means to liberate the soul. As soon as one is, therefore, situated in absolute knowledge, his material conception of life is removed, or he emerges from a false conception of life. Thus the function of the pure soul is revived in spiritual realization. This practical realization of the living being is made possible due to his becoming free from the reaction of the three modes of material nature, namely goodness, passion and ignorance. By the grace of the Lord, a pure devotee is at once raised to the place of the Absolute, and there is no chance of the devotee's becoming materially entangled again in conditioned life. One is not able to feel the presence of the Lord in all circumstances until one is endowed with the required transcendental vision made possible by devotional service prescribed in the revealed scriptures. Arjuna had attained this stage long before on the Battlefield of Kurukṣetra, and when he apparently felt the absence of the Lord, he at once took shelter of the instructions of the *Bhagavad-gītā,* and thus again he was placed in his original position. This is the position of *viśoka,* or the stage of being freed from all grief and anxieties.

TEXT 32

निशम्य भगवन्मार्गं संस्थां यदुकुलस्य च ।
स्वःपथाय मतिं चक्रे निभृतात्मा युधिष्ठिरः ॥३२॥

niśamya bhagavan-mārgaṁ
saṁsthāṁ yadu-kulasya ca
svaḥ-pathāya matiṁ cakre
nibhṛtātmā yudhiṣṭhiraḥ

niśamya—deliberating; *bhagavat*—regarding the Lord; *mārgam*—the ways of His appearance and disappearance; *saṁsthām*—end; *yadu-kulasya*

—of the dynasty of King Yadu; *ca*—also; *svaḥ*—the abode of the Lord; *pathāya* —on the way of; *matim*—desire; *cakre*—gave attention; *nibhṛta-ātmā*—lonely and alone; *yudhiṣṭhiraḥ*—King Yudhiṣṭhira.

TRANSLATION

Upon hearing of Lord Kṛṣṇa's returning to His abode, and upon understanding the end of the Yadu dynasty's earthly manifestation, Mahārāja Yudhiṣṭhira decided to go back home, back to Godhead.

PURPORT

Mahārāja Yudhiṣṭhira also turned his attention to the instructions of the *Bhagavad-gītā* after hearing about the Lord's departure from the vision of earthly people. He began to deliberate on the Lord's way of appearance and departure. The mission of the Lord's appearance and disappearance in the mortal universe is completely dependent on His supreme will. He is not forced to appear or disappear by any superior energy, as the living beings appear and disappear, being forced by the laws of nature. Whenever the Lord likes, He can appear Himself from anywhere and everywhere without disturbing His appearance and disappearance in any other place. He is like the sun. The sun appears and disappears on its own accord at any place without disturbing its presence in other places. The sun appears in the morning in India without disappearing from the Western Hemisphere. The sun is present everywhere and anywhere all over the solar system, but it so appears that in a particular place the sun appears in the morning and also disappears at some fixed time in the evening. The time limitation even of the sun is of no concern, and so what to speak of the Supreme Lord who is the creator and controller of the sun. Therefore, in the *Bhagavad-gītā* it is stated that anyone who factually understands the transcendental appearance and disappearance of the Lord by His inconceivable energy becomes liberated from the laws of birth and death and is placed in the eternal spiritual sky where the Vaikuṇṭha planets are. There such liberated persons can eternally live without the pangs of birth, death, old age and disease. In the spiritual sky the Lord and those who are eternally engaged in the transcendental loving service of the Lord are all eternally young because there is no old age and disease and there is no death. Because there is no death there is no birth. It is concluded, therefore, that simply by understanding the Lord's appearance and disappearance in truth, one can attain the perfectional stage of eternal life. Therefore, Mahārāja Yudhiṣṭhira also began to consider going back to Godhead. The Lord appears on the earth or any other mortal planet along with His associates who live with Him eternally, and the members of the Yadu family who were engaged in supplementing the pastimes of the Lord are no other than His eternal associates, and so also Mahārāja Yudhiṣṭhira and his brothers and mother, etc. Since the appearance and disappearance of the Lord and His eternal associates are transcendental, one should not be bewildered by the external features of appearance and disappearance.

TEXT 33

पृथाप्यनुश्रुत्य धनञ्जयोदितं
नाशं यदूनां भगवद्गतिं च ताम् ।
एकान्तभक्त्या भगवत्यधोक्षजे
निवेशितात्मोपरराम संसृतेः ॥३३॥

pṛthāpy anuśrutya dhanañjayoditaṁ
nāśaṁ yadūnāṁ bhagavad-gatiṁ ca tām
ekānta-bhaktyā bhagavaty adhokṣaje
niveśitātmopararāma saṁsṛteḥ

pṛthā—Kuntī; *api*—also; *anuśrutya*—overhearing; *dhanañjaya*—Arjuna; *uditam*—uttered by; *nāśam*—end; *yadūnām*—of the Yadu dynasty; *bhagavat*—of the Personality of Godhead; *gatim*—disappearance; *ca*—also; *tām*—all those; *eka-anta*—unalloyed; *bhaktyā*—devotion; *bhagavati*—unto the Supreme Lord, Śrī Kṛṣṇa; *adhokṣaje*—transcendence; *niveśita-ātmā*—with full attention; *uparарāma*—became released from; *saṁsṛteḥ*—material existence.

TRANSLATION

Kuntī, after overhearing Arjuna's telling of the end of the Yadu dynasty and disappearance of Lord Kṛṣṇa, engaged in the devotional service of the transcendental Personality of Godhead with full attention and thus gained release from the course of material existence.

PURPORT

The setting of the sun does not mean the end of the sun. It means that the sun is out of our sight. Similarly, the end of the mission of the Lord on a particular planet or universe only means that He is out of our sight. The end of the Yadu dynasty also does not mean that it is annihilated. It disappears, along with the Lord, out of our sight. As Mahārāja Yudhiṣṭhira decided to prepare to go back to Godhead, so also Kuntī decided, and thus she fully engaged herself in the transcendental devotional service of the Lord which guarantees one a passport for going back to Godhead after quitting this present material body. The beginning of devotional service to the Lord is the beginning of spiritualizing the present body, and thus an unalloyed devotee of the Lord loses all material contact in the present body. The abode of the Lord is not a myth, as is thought by the unbelievers or ignorant people, but one cannot reach there by any material means like a sputnik or space capsule. But one can certainly reach there after leaving this present body, and one must prepare himself to go back to Godhead by practicing devotional service. That guarantees a passport for going back to Godhead, and Kuntī adopted it.

TEXT 34

ययाहरद् भुवो भारं तां तनुं विजहावजः ।
कण्टकं कण्टकेनेव द्वयं चापीशितुः समम् ॥३४॥

yayāharad bhuvo bhāraṁ
tāṁ tanuṁ vijahāv ajaḥ
kaṇṭakaṁ kaṇṭakeneva
dvayaṁ cāpīśituḥ samam

yayā—that by which; *aharat*—took away; *bhuvaḥ*—of the world; *bhāram*—burden; *tām*—that; *tanum*—body; *vijahau*—relinquished; *ajaḥ*—the unborn; *kaṇṭakam*—thorn; *kaṇṭakena*—by the thorn; *iva*—like that; *dvayam*—both; *ca*—also; *api*—although; *īśituḥ*—controlling; *samam*—equal.

TRANSLATION

The supreme unborn, Lord Śrī Kṛṣṇa, caused the members of the Yadu dynasty to relinquish their bodies, and thus He relieved the burden of the world. This action was like picking out a thorn with a thorn, though both are the same to the controller.

PURPORT

Śrīla Viśvanātha Cakravartī Ṭhākura suggests that the *ṛṣis* like Śaunaka and others who were hearing *Śrīmad-Bhāgavatam* from Sūta Gosvāmī at Naimiṣāraṇya were not happy to hear about the Yadus' dying in the madness of intoxication. To give them relief from this mental agony, Sūta Gosvāmī assured them that the Lord caused the members of the Yadu dynasty to relinquish their bodies by which they had to take away the burden of the world. The Lord and His eternal associates appeared on earth to help the administrative demigods in eradicating the burden of the world. He therefore called for some of the confidential demigods to appear in the Yadu family and serve Him in His great mission. After the mission was fulfilled, the demigods, by the will of the Lord, relinquished their corporeal bodies by fighting amongst themselves in the madness of intoxication. The demigods are accustomed to drinking the *soma-rasa* beverage, and therefore the drinking of wine and intoxication are not unknown to them. Sometimes they were put into trouble for indulging in intoxication. Once the sons of Kuvera fell in the wrath of Nārada for being intoxicated, but afterwards they regained their original forms by the grace of the Lord Śrī Kṛṣṇa. We shall find this story in the Tenth Canto. For the Supreme Lord, both the *asuras* and the demigods are equal, but the demigods are obedient to the Lord, whereas the *asuras* are not. Therefore, the example of picking out a thorn by another thorn is quite befitting. One thorn, which causes pinpricks on the leg of the Lord, is certainly disturbing to the Lord, and the other thorn, which takes out the disturbing elements, certainly gives service to the Lord. So although every living being is a part and parcel of the Lord, still one who is a pinprick to the Lord is called an *asura,* and one who is a voluntary servitor of the Lord is called a *devatā,* or demigod. In the material world the *devatās* and *asuras* are always contending, and the *devatās* are always saved from the hands of the *asuras* by the Lord. Both of them are under the control of the Lord. The world is full of two kinds of living beings, and the Lord's mission is always to protect the *devatās* and destroy the *asuras,* whenever there is such a need in the world, and to do good to both of them.

TEXT 35

यथा मत्स्यादिरूपाणि धत्ते जह्याद् यथा नटः ।
भूभारः क्षपितो येन जहौ तच्च कलेवरम् ॥३५॥

yathā matsyādi-rūpāṇi
dhatte jahyād yathā naṭaḥ
bhū-bhāraḥ kṣapito yena
jahau tac ca kalevaram

yathā—as much as; *matsya-ādi*—incarnation as a fish, etc.; *rūpāṇi*—forms; *dhatte*—eternally accepts; *jahyāt*—apparently relinquishes; *yathā*

—exactly like; *naṭaḥ*—magician; *bhū-bhāraḥ*—burden of the world; *kṣapitaḥ*—relieved; *yena*—by which; *jahau*—let go; *tat*—that; *ca*—also; *kalevaram*—body.

TRANSLATION

The Supreme Lord relinquished the body which He manifested to diminish the burden of the earth. Just like a magician, He relinquishes one body to accept different ones, like the fish incarnation and others.

PURPORT

The Supreme Lord Personality of Godhead is neither impersonal nor formless, but His body is nondifferent from Him, and therefore He is known as the embodiment of eternity, knowledge and bliss. In the *Bṛhad-vaiṣṇava Tantra* it is clearly mentioned that anyone who considers the form of Lord Kṛṣṇa to be made of material energy must be ostracized by all means. And if by chance the face of such an infidel is seen, one must clean himself by jumping in the river with his clothing. The Lord is described as *amṛta,* or deathless, because He has no material body. Under the circumstances, the Lord's dying or quitting His body is like the jugglery of a magician. The magician shows by his tricks that he is cut to pieces, burnt to ashes or made unconscious by hypnotic influences, but all are false shows only. Factually the magician himself is neither burnt to ashes nor cut to pieces, nor is he dead or unconscious at any stage of his magical demonstration. Similarly, the Lord has His eternal forms of unlimited variety, of which the fish incarnation, as was exhibited within this universe, is also one. Because there are innumerable universes, somewhere or other the fish incarnation must be manifesting His pastimes without cessation. In this verse, the particular word *dhatte* ("eternally accepted," and not the word *dhitvā,* "accepted for the occasion") is used. The idea is that the Lord does not create the fish incarnation; He eternally has such a form, and the appearance and disappearance of such an incarnation serves particular purposes. In the *Bhagavad-gītā* (7.24–25) the Lord says, "The impersonalists think that I have no form, that I am formless, but that at present I have accepted a form to serve a purpose, and now I am manifested. But such speculators are factually without sharp intelligence. Though they may be good scholars in the Vedic literatures, they are practically ignorant of My inconceivable energies and My eternal forms of personality. The reason is that I reserve the power of not being exposed to the nondevotees by My mystic curtain. The less intelligent fools are therefore unaware of My eternal form, which is never to be vanquished and is unborn." In the *Padma Purāṇa* it is said that those who are envious and always angry at the Lord are unfit to know the actual and eternal form of the Lord. In the *Bhāgavatam* also it is said that the Lord appeared like a thunderbolt to those who were wrestlers. Śiśupāla, at the time of being killed by the Lord, could not see Him as Kṛṣṇa, being dazzled by the glare of the *brahmajyoti.* Therefore, the temporary manifestation of the Lord as a thunderbolt to the wrestlers appointed by Kaṁsa, or the glaring appearance of the Lord before Śiśupāla, was relinquished by the Lord, but the Lord as a magician is eternally existent and is never vanquished in any circumstance. Such forms are temporarily shown to the *asuras* only, and when such exhibitions are withdrawn, the *asuras* think that the Lord is no more existent, just as the foolish audience thinks the magician to be burnt to ashes or cut to pieces. The conclusion is that the Lord has no material body, and therefore He is never to be killed or changed by His transcendental body.

TEXT 36

यदा मुकुन्दो भगवानिमां महीं
जहौ स्वतन्वा श्रवणीयसत्कथः ।
तदाहरेवाप्रतिबुद्धचेतसा-
मभद्रहेतुः कलिरन्ववर्तत ॥३६॥

yadā mukundo bhagavān imāṁ mahīṁ
jahau sva-tanvā śravaṇīya-sat-kathaḥ
tadāhar evāpratibuddha-cetasām
abhadra-hetuḥ kalir anvavartata

yadā—when; *mukundaḥ*—Lord Kṛṣṇa; *bhagavān*—the Personality of Godhead; *imām*—this; *mahīm*—earth; *jahau*—left; *sva-tanvā*—with His selfsame body; *śravaṇīya-sat-kathaḥ*—hearing about Him is worthwhile; *tadā*—at that time; *ahaḥ eva*—from the very day; *aprati-buddha-cetasām*—of those whose minds are not sufficiently developed; *abhadra-hetuḥ*—cause of all ill fortune; *kaliḥ anvavartata*—Kali fully manifested.

TRANSLATION

When the Personality of Godhead, Lord Kṛṣṇa, left this earthly planet in His selfsame form, from that very day Kali, who had already partially

appeared, became fully manifest to create inauspicious conditions for those who are endowed with a poor fund of knowledge.

PURPORT

The influence of Kali can be enforced only upon those who are not fully developed in God consciousness. One can neutralize the effects of Kali by keeping oneself fully under the supreme care of the Personality of Godhead. The age of Kali ensued just after the Battle of Kurukṣetra, but it could not exert its influence because of the presence of the Lord. The Lord, however, left this earthly planet in His own transcendental body, and as soon as He left, the symptoms of the Kali-yuga, as were envisioned by Mahārāja Yudhiṣṭhira prior to Arjuna's arrival from Dvārakā, began to manifest, and Mahārāja Yudhiṣṭhira rightly conjectured on the departure of the Lord from the earth. As we have already explained, the Lord left our sight just as when the sun sets it is out of our sight.

TEXT 37

युधिष्ठिरस्तत्परिसर्पणं बुधः
पुरे च राष्ट्रे च गृहे तथात्मनि ।
विभाव्य लोभानृतजिह्महिंसना-
द्यधर्मचक्रं गमनाय पर्यधात् ॥३७॥

yudhiṣṭhiras tat parisarpaṇaṁ budhaḥ
pure ca rāṣṭre ca gṛhe tathātmani
vibhāvya lobhānṛta-jihma-hiṁsanādy-
adharma-cakraṁ gamanāya paryadhāt

yudhiṣṭhiraḥ—Mahārāja Yudhiṣṭhira; *tat*—that; *parisarpaṇam*—expansion; *budhaḥ*—thoroughly experienced; *pure*—in the capital; *ca*—as also; *rāṣṭre*—in the state; *ca*—and; *gṛhe*—at home; *tathā*—as also; *ātmani*—in person; *vibhāvya*—observing; *lobha*—avarice; *anṛta*—untruth; *jihma*—diplomacy; *hiṁsana-ādi*—violence, envy; *adharma*—irreligion; *cakram*—a vicious circle; *gamanāya*—for departure; *paryadhāt*—dressed himself accordingly.

TRANSLATION

Mahārāja Yudhiṣṭhira was intelligent enough to understand the influence of the age of Kali, characterized by increasing avarice, falsehood,

cheating and violence throughout the capital, state, home and among individuals. So he wisely prepared himself to leave home, and he dressed accordingly.

PURPORT

The present age is influenced by the specific qualities of Kali. Since the days of the Battle of Kurukṣetra, about five thousand years ago, the influence of the age of Kali began manifesting, and from authentic scriptures it is learned that the age of Kali is still to run on for 427,000 years. The symptoms of the Kali-yuga, as mentioned above, namely avarice, falsehood, diplomacy, cheating, nepotism, violence and all such things, are already in vogue, and no one can imagine what is going to happen gradually with further increase of the influence of Kali till the day of annihilation. We have already come to know that the influence of the age of Kali is meant for godless so-called civilized man; those who are under the protection of the Lord have nothing to fear from this horrible age. Mahārāja Yudhiṣṭhira was a great devotee of the Lord, and there was no necessity of his being afraid of the age of Kali, but he preferred to retire from active household life and prepare himself to go back home, back to Godhead. The Pāṇḍavas are eternal companions of the Lord, and therefore they are more interested in the company of the Lord than anything else. Besides that, being an ideal king, Mahārāja Yudhiṣṭhira wanted to retire just to set an example for others. As soon as there is some young fellow to look after the household affairs, one should at once retire from family life to uplift oneself to spiritual realization. One should not rot in the dark well of household life till one is dragged out by the will of Yamarāja. Modern politicians should take lessons from Mahārāja Yudhiṣṭhira about voluntary retirement from active life and should make room for the younger generation. Also retired old gentlemen should take lessons from him and leave home for spiritual realization before forcefully dragged away to meet death.

TEXT 38

स्वराट् पौत्रं विनयिनमात्मनः सुसमं गुणैः ।
तोयनीव्याः पतिं भूमेरभ्यषिञ्चद्गजाह्वये ॥३८॥

sva-rāṭ pautraṁ vinayinam
ātmanaḥ susamaṁ guṇaiḥ
toya-nīvyāḥ patiṁ bhūmer
abhyaṣiñcad gajāhvaye

sva-rāṭ—the emperor; *pautram*—unto the grandson; *vinayinam*—properly trained; *ātmanaḥ*—his own self; *su-samam*—equal in all respects; *guṇaiḥ*—by the qualities; *toya-nīvyāḥ*—bordered by the seas; *patim*—master; *bhūmeḥ*—of the land; *abhyaṣiñcat*—enthroned; *gajāhvaye*—in the capital of Hastināpura.

TRANSLATION

Thereafter, in the capital of Hastināpura, he enthroned his grandson, who was trained and equally qualified, as the emperor and master of all land bordered by the seas.

PURPORT

The total land on the earth bordered by the seas was under the subjugation of the King of Hastināpura. Mahārāja Yudhiṣṭhira trained his grandson, Mahārāja Parīkṣit, who was equally qualified, in state administration in terms of the king's obligation to the citizens. Thus Parīkṣit was enthroned on the seat of Mahārāja Yudhiṣṭhira prior to his departure back to Godhead. Concerning Mahārāja Parīkṣit, the specific word used, *vinayinam,* is significant. Why was the King of Hastināpura, at least till the time of Mahārāja Parīkṣit, accepted as the Emperor of the world? The only reason is that the people of the world were happy because of the good administration of the emperor. The happiness of the citizens was due to the ample production of natural produce such as grains, fruits, milk, herbs, valuable stones, minerals and everything that the people needed. They were even free from all bodily miseries, anxieties of mind, and disturbances caused by natural phenomena and other living beings. Because everyone was happy in all respects, there was no resentment, although there were sometimes battles between the state kings for political reasons and supremacy. Everyone was trained to attain the highest goal of life, and therefore the people were also enlightened enough not to quarrel over trivialities. The influence of the age of Kali gradually infiltrated the good qualities of both the kings and the citizens, and therefore a tense situation developed between the ruler and the ruled, but still even in this age of disparity between the ruler and the ruled, there can be spiritual emolument and God consciousness. That is a special prerogative.

TEXT 39

मथुरायां तथा वज्रं शूरसेनपतिं ततः ।
प्राजापत्यां निरूप्येष्टिमग्नीनपिबदीश्वरः ॥३९॥

mathurāyāṁ tathā vajraṁ
śūrasena-patiṁ tataḥ
prājāpatyāṁ nirūpyeṣṭim
agnīn apibad īśvaraḥ

mathurāyām—at Mathurā; *tathā*—also; *vajram*—Vajra; *śūrasena-patim*—King of the Śūrasenas; *tataḥ*—thereafter; *prājāpatyām*—Prājāpatya sacrifice; *nirūpya*—having performed; *iṣṭim*—goal; *agnīn*—fire; *apibat*—placed in himself; *īśvaraḥ*—capable.

TRANSLATION

Then he posted Vajra, the son of Aniruddha [grandson of Lord Kṛṣṇa], at Mathurā as the King of Śūrasena. Afterwards Mahārāja Yudhiṣṭhira performed a Prājāpatya sacrifice and placed in himself the fire for quitting household life.

PURPORT

Mahārāja Yudhiṣṭhira, after placing Mahārāja Parīkṣit on the imperial throne of Hastināpura, and after posting Vajra, the great-grandson of Lord Kṛṣṇa, as the King of Mathurā, accepted the renounced order of life. The system of four orders of life and four castes in terms of quality and work, known as *varṇāśrama-dharma,* is the beginning of real human life, and Mahārāja Yudhiṣṭhira, as the protector of this system of human activities, timely retired from active life as a *sannyāsī,* handing over the charge of the administration to a trained prince, Mahārāja Parīkṣit. The scientific system of *varṇāśrama-dharma* divides the human life into four divisions of occupation and four orders of life. The four orders of life as *brahmacārī, gṛhastha, vānaprastha* and *sannyāsī* are to be followed by all, irrespective of the occupational division. Modern politicians do not wish to retire from active life, even if they are old enough, but Yudhiṣṭhira Mahārāja, as an ideal king, voluntarily retired from active administrative life to prepare himself for the next life. Everyone's life must be so arranged that the last stage of life, say at least the last fifteen to twenty years prior to death, can be absolutely devoted to the devotional service of the Lord to attain the highest perfection of life. It is really foolishness to engage oneself all the days of one's life in material enjoyment and fruitive activities, because as long as the mind remains absorbed in fruitive work for material enjoyment, there is no chance of getting out from conditioned life, or material bondage. No one should follow the suicidal policy of neglecting one's supreme task of attaining the highest perfection of life, namely going back home, back to Godhead.

TEXT 40

विसृज्य तत्र तत् सर्वं दुकूलवलयादिकम् ।
निर्ममो निरहङ्कारः संछिन्नाशेषबन्धनः ॥४०॥

visṛjya tatra tat sarvaṁ
dukūla-valayādikam
nirmamo nirahaṅkāraḥ
sañchinnāśeṣa-bandhanaḥ

visṛjya—relinquishing; *tatra*—all those; *tat*—that; *sarvam*—everything; *dukūla*—belt; *valaya-ādikam*—and bangles; *nirmamaḥ*—uninterested; *nirahaṅkāraḥ*—unattached; *sañchinna*—perfectly cut off; *aśeṣa-bandhanaḥ*—unlimited attachment.

TRANSLATION

Mahārāja Yudhiṣṭhira at once relinquished all his garments, belt and ornaments of the royal order and became completely disinterested and unattached to everything.

PURPORT

To become purified of material contamination is the necessary qualification for becoming one of the associates of the Lord. No one can become an associate of the Lord or can go back to Godhead without such purification. Mahārāja Yudhiṣṭhira, therefore, to become spiritually pure, at once gave up his royal opulence, relinquishing his royal dress and garments. The *kaṣāya,* or saffron loincloth of a *sannyāsī,* indicates freedom from all attractive material garments, and thus he changed his dress accordingly. He became disinterested in his kingdom and family and thus became free from all material contamination, or material designation. People are generally attached to various kinds of designations—the designations of family, society, country, occupation, wealth, position and many others. As long as one is attached to such designations, he is considered materially impure. The so-called leaders of men in the modern age are attached by national consciousness, but they do not know that such false consciousness is also another designation of the materially conditioned soul; one has to relinquish such designations before one can become eligible to go back to Godhead. Foolish people adore such men who die in national consciousness, but here is an example of Mahārāja Yudhiṣṭhira, a royal king who prepared himself to leave this world without such national consciousness. And yet he is remembered even today because he was a great pious king, almost on the same level with the Personality of Godhead Śrī Rāma. And because people of the world were dominated by such pious kings, they were happy in all respects, and it was quite possible for such great emperors to rule the world.

TEXT 41

वाचं जुहाव मनसि तत्प्राण इतरे च तम् ।
मृत्यावपानं सोत्सर्गं तं पञ्चत्वे ह्यजोहवीत् ॥४१॥

vācaṁ juhāva manasi
tat prāṇa itare ca tam
mṛtyāv apānaṁ sotsargaṁ
taṁ pañcatve hy ajohavīt

vācam—speeches; *juhāva*—relinquished; *manasi*—into the mind; *tat prāṇe*—mind into breathing; *itare ca*—other senses also; *tam*—into that; *mṛtyau*—into death; *apānam*—breathing; *sa-utsargam*—with all dedication; *tam*—that; *pañcatve*—into the body made of five elements; *hi*—certainly; *ajohavīt*—amalgamated it.

TRANSLATION

Then he amalgamated all the sense organs into the mind, then the mind into life, life into breathing, his total existence into the embodiment of the five elements, and his body into death. Then, as pure self, he became free from the material conception of life.

PURPORT

Mahārāja Yudhiṣṭhira, like his brother Arjuna, began to concentrate and gradually became freed from all material bondage. First he concentrated all the actions of the senses and amalgamated them into the mind, or in other words he turned his mind toward the transcendental service of the Lord. He prayed that since all material activities are performed by the mind in terms of actions and reactions of the material senses, and since he was going back to Godhead, the mind would wind up its material activities and be turned towards the transcendental service to the Lord. There was no longer a need for material activities. Actually the activities of the mind cannot be stopped, for they are the reflection of the eternal soul, but the quality of the activities can be changed from matter to the transcendental service of the Lord. The material color of the mind is changed when one washes it from contaminations of life-breathing and thereby frees it from the contamination of repeated births and deaths and situates it in pure spiritual life. All is manifested by the temporary embodiment of the material body, which is a production of the mind at the time of death, and if the mind is purified by practice of transcendental loving service to the Lord and is constantly engaged in the service of the lotus feet of the Lord, there is no more chance of the mind's producing another material body after death. It will be freed from absorption in material contamination. The pure soul will be able to return home, back to Godhead.

TEXT 42

त्रित्वे हुत्वा च पञ्चत्वं तच्चैकत्वेऽजुहोन्मुनिः ।
सर्वमात्मन्यजुहवीद्ब्रह्मण्यात्मानमव्यये ॥४२॥

tritve hutvā ca pañcatvaṁ
tac caikatve 'juhon muniḥ
sarvam ātmany ajuhavīd
brahmaṇy ātmānam avyaye

tritve—into the three qualities; *hutvā*—having offered; *ca*—also; *pañcatvam*—five elements; *tat*—that; *ca*—also; *ekatve*—in one nescience; *ajuhot*—amalgamated; *muniḥ*—the thoughtful; *sarvam*—the sum total; *ātmani*—in the soul; *ajuhavīt*—fixed; *brahmaṇi*—unto the spirit; *ātmānam*—the soul; *avyaye*—unto the inexhaustible.

TRANSLATION

Thus annihilating the gross body of five elements into the three qualitative modes of material nature, he merged them in one nescience and then absorbed that nescience in the self, Brahman, which is inexhaustible in all circumstances.

PURPORT

All that is manifested in the material world is the product of the *mahat-tattva-avyakta,* and things that are visible in our material vision are nothing but combinations and permutations of such variegated material products. But the living entity is different from such material products. It is due to the living entity's forgetfulness of his eternal nature as eternal servitor of the Lord, and his false conception of being a so-called lord of the material nature, that he is obliged to enter into the existence of false sense enjoyment. Thus a concomitant generation of material energies is the principal cause of the mind's being materially affected. Thus the gross body of five elements is produced. Mahārāja Yudhiṣṭhira reversed the action and merged the five elements of the body in the three modes of material nature. The qualitative distinction of the body as being good, bad or mediocre is extinguished, and again the qualitative manifestations become merged in the material energy, which is produced from a false sense of the pure living being. When one is thus inclined to become an associate of the Supreme Lord, the Personality of Godhead, in one of the innumerable planets of the spiritual sky, especially in Goloka Vṛndāvana, one has to think always that he is different from the material energy; he has nothing to do with it, and he has to realize himself as pure spirit, Brahman, qualitatively equal with the Supreme Brahman (Parameśvara). Mahārāja Yudhiṣṭhira, after distributing his kingdom to Parīkṣit and Vajra, did not think himself Emperor of the world or head of the Kuru dynasty. This sense of freedom from material relations, as well as freedom from the material encagement of the gross and subtle encirclement, makes one free to act as the servitor of the Lord, even though one is in the material world. This stage is called the *jīvan-mukta* stage, or the liberated stage, even in the material world. That is the process of ending material existence. One must not only think that he is Brahman, but must act like Brahman. One who only thinks himself Brahman is an impersonalist. And one who acts like Brahman is the pure devotee.

TEXT 43

चीरवासा निराहारो बद्धवाङ्मुक्तमूर्धजः ।
दर्शयन्नात्मनो रूपं जडोन्मत्तपिशाचवत् ।
अनवेक्षमाणो निरगादशृण्वन्बधिरो यथा ॥४३॥

cīra-vāsā nirāhāro
baddha-vāṅ mukta-mūrdhajaḥ

darśayann ātmano rūpaṁ
jaḍonmatta-piśācavat
anavekṣamāṇo niragād
aśṛṇvan badhiro yathā

cīra-vāsāḥ—accepted torn clothing; *nirāhāraḥ*—gave up all solid foodstuff; *baddha-vāk*—stopped talking; *mukta-mūrdhajaḥ*—untied his hair; *darśayan*—began to show; *ātmanaḥ*—of himself; *rūpam*—bodily features; *jaḍa*—inert; *unmatta*—mad; *piśāca-vat*—just like an urchin; *anavekṣamāṇaḥ*—without waiting for; *niragāt*—was situated; *aśṛṇvan*—without hearing; *badhiraḥ*—just like a deaf man; *yathā*—as if.

TRANSLATION

After that, Mahārāja Yudhiṣṭhira dressed himself in torn clothing, gave up eating all solid foods, voluntarily became dumb and let his hair hang loose. All this combined to make him look like an urchin or madman with no occupation. He did not depend on his brothers for anything. And, just like a deaf man, he heard nothing.

PURPORT

Thus being freed from all external affairs, he had nothing to do with imperial life or family prestige, and for all practical purposes he posed himself exactly like an inert mad urchin and did not speak of material affairs. He had no dependence on his brothers, who had all along been helping him. This stage of complete independence from everything is also called the purified stage of fearlessness.

TEXT 44

उदीचीं प्रविवेशाशां गतपूर्वां महात्मभिः ।
हृदि ब्रह्म परं ध्यायन्नावर्तेत यतो गतः ॥४४॥

udīcīṁ praviveśāśāṁ
gata-pūrvāṁ mahātmabhiḥ
hṛdi brahma paraṁ dhyāyan
nāvarteta yato gataḥ

udīcīm—the northern side; *praviveśa-āśām*—those who wanted to enter there; *gata-pūrvām*—the path accepted by his forefathers; *mahā-ātmabhiḥ*

—by the broad-minded; *hṛdi*—within the heart; *brahma*—the Supreme; *param*—Godhead; *dhyāyan*—constantly thinking of; *na āvarteta*—passed his days; *yataḥ*—wherever; *gataḥ*—went.

TRANSLATION

He then started towards the north, treading the path accepted by his forefathers and great men, to devote himself completely to the thought of the Supreme Personality of Godhead. And he lived in that way wherever he went.

PURPORT

It is understood from this verse that Mahārāja Yudhiṣṭhira followed in the footsteps of his forefathers and the great devotees of the Lord. We have discussed many times before that the system of *varṇāśrama-dharma,* as it was strictly followed by the inhabitants of the world, specifically by those who inhabited the Āryāvarta province of the world, emphasizes the importance of leaving all household connections at a certain stage of life. The training and education was so imparted, and thus a respectable person like Mahārāja Yudhiṣṭhira had to leave all family connection for self-realization and going back to Godhead. No king or respectable gentleman would continue family life till the end, because that was considered suicidal and against the interest of the perfection of human life. In order to be free from all family encumbrances and devote oneself cent percent in the devotional service of Lord Kṛṣṇa, this system is always recommended for everyone because it is the path of authority. The Lord instructs in the *Bhagavad-gītā* (18.62) that one must become a devotee of the Lord at least at the last stage of one's life. A sincere soul of the Lord like Mahārāja Yudhiṣṭhira must abide by this instruction of the Lord for his own interest.

The specific words *brahma param* indicate Lord Śrī Kṛṣṇa. This is corroborated in the *Bhagavad-gītā* (10.13) by Arjuna with reference to great authorities like Asita, Devala, Nārada and Vyāsa. Thus Mahārāja Yudhiṣṭhira, while leaving home for the north, constantly remembered Lord Śrī Kṛṣṇa within himself, following in the footsteps of his forefathers as well as the great devotees of all times.

TEXT 45

सर्वे तमनुनिर्जग्मुर्भ्रातरः कृतनिश्चयाः ।
कलिनाधर्ममित्रेण दृष्ट्वा स्पृष्टाः प्रजा भुवि ॥४५॥

sarve tam anunirjagmur
bhrātaraḥ kṛta-niścayāḥ
kalinādharma-mitreṇa
dṛṣṭvā spṛṣṭāḥ prajā bhuvi

sarve—all his younger brothers; *tam*—him; *anunirjagmuḥ*—left home by following the elder; *bhrātaraḥ*—brothers; *kṛta-niścayāḥ*—decidedly; *kalinā*—by the age of Kali; *adharma*—principle of irreligion; *mitreṇa*—by the friend; *dṛṣṭvā*—observing; *spṛṣṭāḥ*—having overtaken; *prajāḥ*—all citizens; *bhuvi*—on the earth.

TRANSLATION

The younger brothers of Mahārāja Yudhiṣṭhira observed that the age of Kali had already arrived throughout the world and that the citizens of the kingdom were already affected by irreligious practice. Therefore they decided to follow in the footsteps of their elder brother.

PURPORT

The younger brothers of Mahārāja Yudhiṣṭhira were already obedient followers of the great Emperor, and they had sufficiently been trained to know the ultimate goal of life. They therefore decidedly followed their eldest brother in rendering devotional service to Lord Śrī Kṛṣṇa. According to the principles of *sanātana-dharma,* one must retire from family life after half the duration of life is finished and must engage himself in self-realization. But the question of engaging oneself is not always decided. Sometimes retired men are bewildered about how to engage themselves for the last days of life. Here is a decision by authorities like the Pāṇḍavas. All of them engaged themselves in favorably culturing the devotional service of the Lord Śrī Kṛṣṇa, the Supreme Personality of Godhead. According to Svāmī Śrīdhara, *dharma, artha, kāma* and *mokṣa,* or fruitive activities, philosophical speculations and salvation, as conceived by several persons, are not the ultimate goal of life. They are more or less practiced by persons who have no information of the ultimate goal of life. The ultimate goal of life is already indicated by the Lord Himself in the *Bhagavad-gītā* (18.64), and the Pāṇḍavas were intelligent enough to follow it without hesitation.

TEXT 46

ते साधुकृतसर्वार्था ज्ञात्वात्यन्तिकमात्मनः ।
मनसा धारयामासुर्वैकुण्ठचरणाम्बुजम् ॥४६॥

te sādhu-kṛta-sarvārthā
jñātvātyantikam ātmanaḥ
manasā dhārayām āsur
vaikuṇṭha-caraṇāmbujam

te—all of them; *sādhu-kṛta*—having performed everything worthy of a saint; *sarva-arthāḥ*—that which includes everything worthy; *jñātvā*—knowing it well; *ātyantikam*—the ultimate; *ātmanaḥ*—of the living being; *manasā*—within the mind; *dhārayām āsuḥ*—sustained; *vaikuṇṭha*—the Lord of the spiritual sky; *caraṇa-ambujam*—the lotus feet.

TRANSLATION

They all had performed all the principles of religion and as a result rightly decided that the lotus feet of the Lord Śrī Kṛṣṇa are the supreme goal of all. Therefore they meditated upon His feet without interruption.

PURPORT

In the *Bhagavad-gītā* (7.28) the Lord says that only those who have done pious deeds in previous lives and have become freed from the results of all impious acts can concentrate upon the lotus feet of the Supreme Lord Śrī Kṛṣṇa. The Pāṇḍavas, not only in this life but also in their previous lives, had always performed the supreme pious work, and thus they are ever free from all the reactions of impious work. It is quite reasonable, therefore, that they concentrated their minds upon the lotus feet of the Supreme Lord Śrī Kṛṣṇa. According to Śrī Viśvanātha Cakravartī, *dharma, artha, kāma* and *mokṣa* principles are accepted by persons who are not free from the results of impious action. Such persons affected with the contaminations of the above four principles cannot at once accept the lotus feet of the Lord in the spiritual sky. The Vaikuṇṭha world is situated far beyond the material sky. The material sky is under the management of Durgā Devī, or the material energy of the Lord, but the Vaikuṇṭha world is managed by the personal energy of the Lord.

TEXTS 47–48

तद्ध्यानोद्रिक्तया भक्त्या विशुद्धधिषणाः परे ।
तस्मिन् नारायणपदे एकान्तमतयो गतिम् ॥४७॥
अवापुर्दुरवापां ते असद्भिर्विषयात्मभिः ।
विधूतकल्मषा स्थानं विरजेनात्मनैव हि ॥४८॥

tad-dhyānodriktayā bhaktyā
viśuddha-dhiṣaṇāḥ pare
tasmin nārāyaṇa-pade
ekānta-matayo gatim

avāpur duravāpāṁ te
asadbhir viṣayātmabhiḥ
vidhūta-kalmaṣā sthānaṁ
virajenātmanaiva hi

tat—that; *dhyāna*—positive meditation; *utriktayā*—being freed from; *bhaktyā*—by a devotional attitude; *viśuddha*—purified; *dhiṣaṇāḥ*—by intelligence; *pare*—unto the Transcendence; *tasmin*—in that; *nārāyaṇa*—the Personality of Godhead Śrī Kṛṣṇa; *pade*—unto the lotus feet; *ekānta-matayaḥ*—of those who are fixed in the Supreme, who is one; *gatim*—destination; *avāpuḥ*—attained; *duravāpām*—very difficult to obtain; *te*—by them; *asadbhiḥ*—by the materialists; *viṣaya-ātmabhiḥ*—absorbed in material needs; *vidhūta*—washed off; *kalmaṣāḥ*—material contaminations; *sthānam*—abode; *virajena*—without material passion; *ātmanā eva*—by the selfsame body; *hi*—certainly.

TRANSLATION

Thus by pure consciousness due to constant devotional remembrance, they attained the spiritual sky, which is ruled over by the Supreme Nārāyaṇa, Lord Kṛṣṇa. This is attained only by those who meditate upon the one Supreme Lord without deviation. This abode of the Lord Śrī Kṛṣṇa, known as Goloka Vṛndāvana, cannot be attained by persons who are absorbed in the material conception of life. But the Pāṇḍavas, being completely washed of all material contamination, attained that abode in their very same bodies.

PURPORT

According to Śrīla Jīva Gosvāmī, a person freed from the three modes of material qualities, namely goodness, passion and ignorance, and situated in transcendence can reach the highest perfection of life without change of body. Śrīla Sanātana Gosvāmī in his *Hari-bhakti-vilāsa* says that a person, whatever he may be, can attain the perfection of a twice-born *brāhmaṇa* by undergoing the spiritual disciplinary actions under the guidance of a bona fide spiritual master, exactly as a chemist can turn gun metal into gold by chemical manipulation. It is therefore the actual guidance that matters in the process of becoming a *brāhmaṇa,* even without change of body, or in going back to Godhead without change of body. Śrīla Jīva Gosvāmī remarks that the word *hi* used in this connection positively affirms this truth, and there is no doubt about this factual position. The *Bhagavad-gītā* (14.26) also affirms this statement of Śrīla Jīva Gosvāmī when the Lord says that anyone who executes devotional service systematically without deviation can attain the perfection of Brahman by surpassing the contamination of the three modes of material nature, and when the Brahman perfection is still more advanced by the selfsame execution of devotional service, there is no doubt at all that one can attain the supreme spiritual planet, Goloka Vṛndāvana, without change of body, as we have already discussed in connection with the Lord's returning to His abode without a change of body.

TEXT 49

विदुरोऽपि परित्यज्य प्रभासे देहमात्मनः ।
कृष्णावेशेन तच्चित्तः पितृभिः स्वक्षयं ययौ ॥४९॥

viduro 'pi parityajya
prabhāse deham ātmanaḥ
kṛṣṇāveśena tac-cittaḥ
pitṛbhiḥ sva-kṣayaṁ yayau

viduraḥ—Vidura (the uncle of Mahārāja Yudhiṣṭhira); *api*—also; *parityajya*—after quitting the body; *prabhāse*—in the place of pilgrimage at Prabhāsa; *deham ātmanaḥ*—his body; *kṛṣṇa*—the Personality of Godhead; *āveśena*—being absorbed in that thought; *tat*—his; *cittaḥ*—thoughts and actions; *pitṛbhiḥ*—along with the residents of Pitṛloka; *sva-kṣayam*—his own abode; *yayau*—departed.

TRANSLATION

Vidura, while on pilgrimage, left his body at Prabhāsa. Because he was absorbed in thought of Kṛṣṇa, he was received by the denizens of the Pitṛloka planet, where he returned to his original post.

PURPORT

The difference between the Pāṇḍavas and Vidura is that the Pāṇḍavas are eternal associates of the Lord, the Personality of Godhead, whereas Vidura is one of the administrative demigods in charge of the Pitṛloka planet and is known as Yamarāja. Men are afraid of Yamarāja because it is he only who awards punishment to the miscreants of the material world, but those who are devotees of the Lord have nothing to fear from him. To the devotees he is a cordial friend, but to the nondevotees he is fear personified. As we have already discussed, it is understood that Yamarāja was cursed by Maṇḍūka Muni to be degraded as a *śūdra,* and therefore Vidura was an incarnation of Yamarāja. As an eternal servitor of the Lord, he displayed his devotional activities very ardently and lived a life of a pious man, so much so that a materialistic man like Dhṛtarāṣṭra also got salvation by his instruction. So by his pious activities in the devotional service of the Lord he was able to always remember the lotus feet of the Lord, and thus he became washed of all contamination of a *śūdra*-born life. At the end he was again received by the denizens of Pitṛloka and posted in his original position. The demigods are also associates of the Lord without personal touch, whereas the direct associates of the Lord are in constant personal touch with Him. The Lord and His personal associates incarnate in many universes without cessation. The Lord remembers them all, whereas the associates forget due to their being very minute parts and parcels of the Lord; they are apt to forget such incidents due to being infinitesimal. This is corroborated in the *Bhagavad-gītā* (4.5).

TEXT 50

द्रौपदी च तदाज्ञाय पतीनामनपेक्षताम् ।
वासुदेवे भगवति ह्येकान्तमतिराप तम् ॥५०॥

draupadī ca tadājñāya
patīnām anapekṣatām
vāsudeve bhagavati
hy ekānta-matir āpa tam

draupadī—Draupadī (the wife of the Pāṇḍavas); *ca*—and; *tadā*—at that time; *ājñāya*—knowing Lord Kṛṣṇa fully well; *patīnām*—of the husbands; *anapekṣatām*—who did not care for her; *vāsudeve*—unto Lord Vāsudeva (Kṛṣṇa); *bhagavati*—the Personality of Godhead; *hi*—exactly; *eka-anta*—absolutely; *matiḥ*—concentration; *āpa*—got; *tam*—Him (the Lord).

TRANSLATION

Draupadī also saw that her husbands, without caring for her, were leaving home. She knew well about Lord Vāsudeva, Kṛṣṇa, the Personality

of Godhead. Both she and Subhadrā became absorbed in thoughts of Kṛṣṇa and attained the same results as their husbands.

PURPORT

When flying an airplane, one cannot take care of other planes. Everyone has to take care of his own plane, and if there is any danger, no other plane can help another in that condition. Similarly, at the end of life, when one has to go back home, back to Godhead, everyone has to take care of himself without help rendered by another. The help is, however, offered on the ground before flying in space. Similarly, the spiritual master, the father, the mother, the relatives, the husband and others can all render help during one's lifetime, but while crossing the sea one has to take care of himself and utilize the instructions formerly received. Draupadī had five husbands, and no one asked Draupadī to come; Draupadī had to take care of herself without waiting for her great husbands. And because she was already trained, she at once took to concentration upon the lotus feet of Lord Vāsudeva, Kṛṣṇa, the Personality of Godhead. The wives also got the same result as their husbands, in the same manner; that is to say, without changing their bodies they reached the destination of Godhead. Śrīla Viśvanātha Cakravartī Ṭhākura suggests that both Draupadī and Subhadrā, although her name is not mentioned herein, got the same result. None of them had to quit the body.

TEXT 51

यः श्रद्धयैतद् भगवत्प्रियाणां
पाण्डोः सुतानामिति सम्प्रयाणम् ।
शृणोत्यलं स्वस्त्ययनं पवित्रं
लब्ध्वा हरौ भक्तिमुपैति सिद्धिम् ॥५१॥

yaḥ śraddhayaitad bhagavat-priyāṇāṁ
pāṇḍoḥ sutānām iti samprayāṇam
śṛṇoty alaṁ svastyayanaṁ pavitraṁ
labdhvā harau bhaktim upaiti siddhim

yaḥ—anyone who; *śraddhayā*—with devotion; *etat*—this; *bhagavat-priyāṇām*—of those who are very dear to the Personality of Godhead; *pāṇḍoḥ*—of Pāṇḍu; *sutānām*—of the sons; *iti*—thus; *samprayāṇam*—departure for the ultimate goal; *śṛṇoti*—hears; *alam*—only; *svastyayanam*—good fortune; *pavitram*—perfectly pure; *labdhvā*—by obtaining; *harau*

—unto the Supreme Lord; *bhaktim*—devotional service; *upaiti*—gains; *siddhim*—perfection.

TRANSLATION

The subject of the departure of the sons of Pāṇḍu for the ultimate goal of life, back to Godhead, is fully auspicious and is perfectly pure. Therefore anyone who hears this narration with devotional faith certainly gains the devotional service of the Lord, the highest perfection of life.

PURPORT

Śrīmad-Bhāgavatam is a narration about the Personality of Godhead and the devotees of the Lord like the Pāṇḍavas. The narration of the Personality of Godhead and His devotees is absolute in itself, and thus to hear it with a devotional attitude is to associate with the Lord and constant companions of the Lord. By the process of hearing *Śrīmad-Bhāgavatam* one can attain the highest perfection of life, namely going back home, back to Godhead, without failure.

Thus end the Bhaktivedanta purports of the First Canto, Fifteenth Chapter, of the Śrīmad-Bhāgavatam, *entitled "The Pāṇḍavas Retire Timely."*

CHAPTER SIXTEEN

How Parīkṣit Received the Age of Kali

TEXT 1

सूत उवाच
ततः परीक्षिद् द्विजवर्यशिक्षया
 महीं महाभागवतः शशास ह ।
यथा हि सूत्यामभिजातकोविदाः
 समादिशन् विप्र महद्गुणस्तथा ॥१॥

sūta uvāca
tataḥ parīkṣid dvija-varya-śikṣayā
mahīṁ mahā-bhāgavataḥ śaśāsa ha
yathā hi sūtyām abhijāta-kovidāḥ
samādiśan vipra mahad-guṇas tathā

sūtaḥ uvāca—Sūta Gosvāmī said; *tataḥ*—thereafter; *parīkṣit*—Mahārāja Parīkṣit; *dvija-varya*—the great twice-born *brāhmaṇas; śikṣayā*—by their instructions; *mahīm*—the earth; *mahā-bhāgavataḥ*—the great devotee; *śaśāsa*—ruled; *ha*—in the past; *yathā*—as they told it; *hi*—certainly; *sūtyām*—at the time of his birth; *abhijāta-kovidāḥ*—expert astrologers at the time of birth; *samādiśan*—gave their opinions; *vipra*—O *brāhmaṇas; mahat-guṇaḥ*—great qualities; *tathā*—true to that.

TRANSLATION

Sūta Gosvāmī said: O learned brāhmaṇas, Mahārāja Parīkṣit then began to rule over the world as a great devotee of the Lord under the instructions of the best of the twice-born brāhmaṇas. He ruled by those great qualities which were foretold by expert astrologers at the time of his birth.

PURPORT

At the time of Mahārāja Parīkṣit's birth, the expert astrologer-*brāhmaṇas* foretold some of his qualities. Mahārāja Parīkṣit developed all those qualities, being a great devotee of the Lord. The real qualification is to become a devotee of the Lord, and gradually all the good qualities worthy of possession develop. Mahārāja Parīkṣit was a *mahā-bhāgavata,* or a first-class devotee, who was not only well versed in the science of devotion but also able to convert others to become devotees by his transcendental instructions. Mahārāja Parīkṣit was, therefore, a devotee of the first order, and thus he used to consult great sages and learned *brāhmaṇas,* who could advise him by the *śāstras* how to execute the state administration. Such great kings were more responsible than modern elected executive heads because they obliged the great authorities by following their instructions left in Vedic literatures. There was no need for impractical fools to enact daily a new legislative bill and to conveniently alter it again and again to serve some purpose. The rules and regulations were already set forth by great sages like Manu, Yājñavalkya, Parāśara and other liberated sages, and the enactments were all suitable for all ages in all places. Therefore the rules and regulations were standard and without flaw or defect. Kings like Mahārāja Parīkṣit had their council of advisers, and all the members of that council were either great sages or *brāhmaṇas* of the first order. They did not accept any salary, nor had they any necessity for such salaries. *The state would get the best advice without expenditure.* They were themselves *sama-darśī,* equal to everyone, both man and animal. They would not advise the king to give protection to man and instruct him to kill the poor animals. Such council members were not fools or representatives to compose a fool's paradise. They were all self-realized souls, and they knew perfectly well how all living beings in the state would be happy, both in this life and in the next. They were not concerned with the hedonistic philosophy of eat, drink, be merry and enjoy. They were philosophers in the real sense, and they knew well what is the mission of human life. Under all these obligations, the advisory council of the king would give correct directions, and the king or executive head, being himself a qualified devotee of the Lord, would scrutinizingly follow them for the welfare of the state. The state in the days of Mahārāja Yudhiṣṭhira or Mahārāja Parīkṣit was a welfare state in the real sense of the term because no one was unhappy in that state, be he man or animal. Mahārāja Parīkṣit was an ideal king for a welfare state of the world.

TEXT 2

स उत्तरस्य तनयामुपयेम इरावतीम् ।
जनमेजयादींश्चतुरस्तस्यामुत्पादयत् सुतान् ॥२॥

sa uttarasya tanayām
upayema irāvatīm
janamejayādīṁś caturas
tasyām utpādayat sutān

saḥ—he; *uttarasya*—of King Uttara; *tanayām*—daughter; *upayeme*—married; *irāvatīm*—Irāvatī; *janamejaya-ādīn*—headed by Mahārāja Janamejaya; *caturaḥ*—four; *tasyām*—in her; *utpādayat*—begot; *sutān*—sons.

TRANSLATION

King Parīkṣit married the daughter of King Uttara and begot four sons, headed by Mahārāja Janamejaya.

PURPORT

Mahārāja Uttara was the son of Virāṭa and maternal uncle of Mahārāja Parīkṣit. Irāvatī, being the daughter of Mahārāja Uttara, was the cousin-sister of Mahārāja Parīkṣit, but cousin-brothers and sisters were allowed to get married if they did not belong to the same *gotra,* or family. In the Vedic system of marriage, the importance of the *gotra,* or family, was stressed. Arjuna also married Subhadrā, although she was his maternal cousin-sister.

Janamejaya: One of the *rājarṣi* kings and the famous son of Mahārāja Parīkṣit. His mother's name was Irāvatī, or according to some, Mādravatī. Mahārāja Janamejaya begot two sons of the names Jñātānīka and Śaṅkukarṇa. He celebrated several sacrifices in the Kurukṣetra pilgrimage site, and he had three younger brothers named Śrutasena, Ugrasena and Bhīmasena II. He invaded Takṣalā (Ajanta), and he decided to avenge the unlawful curse upon his great father, Mahārāja Parīkṣit. He performed a great sacrifice called Sarpa-yajña, to kill the race of serpents, including the *takṣaka,* which had bitten his father to death. On request from many influential demigods and sages, he had to change his decision to kill the race of snakes, but despite stopping the sacrifice, he satisfied everyone concerned in the sacrifice by rewarding them properly. In the ceremony, Mahāmuni Vyāsadeva also was present, and he personally narrated the history of the Battle of Kurukṣetra before the King. Later on by the order of Vyāsadeva, his disciple Vaiśampāyana narrated before the King the subject matter of *Mahābhārata.* He was much affected by his great father's untimely death and was very anxious to see him again, and he expressed his desire before the great sage Vyāsadeva. Vyāsadeva also fulfilled his desire. His father was present before him, and he worshiped both his father and Vyāsadeva with great respect and pomp. Being fully satisfied, he most munificently gave charity to the *brāhmaṇas* present at the sacrifice.

TEXT 3

आजहाराश्वमेधांस्त्रीन् गङ्गायां भूरिदक्षिणान् ।
शारद्वतं गुरुं कृत्वा देवा यत्राक्षिगोचराः ॥ ३ ॥

ājahārāśva-medhāṁs trīn
gaṅgāyāṁ bhūri-dakṣiṇān
śāradvataṁ guruṁ kṛtvā
devā yatrākṣi-gocarāḥ

ājahāra—performed; *aśva-medhān*—horse sacrifices; *trīn*—three; *gaṅgāyām*—the bank of the Ganges; *bhūri*—sufficiently; *dakṣiṇān*—rewards; *śāradvatam*—unto Kṛpācārya; *gurum*—spiritual master; *kṛtvā*—having selected; *devāḥ*—the demigods; *yatra*—wherein; *akṣi*—eyes; *gocarāḥ*—within the purview.

TRANSLATION

Mahārāja Parīkṣit, after having selected Kṛpācārya for guidance as his spiritual master, performed three horse sacrifices on the banks of the Ganges. These were executed with sufficient rewards for the attendants. And at these sacrifices, even the common man could see demigods.

PURPORT

It appears from this verse that interplanetary travel by the denizens of higher planets is easy. In many statements in *Bhāgavatam,* we have observed that the demigods from heaven used to visit this earth to attend sacrifices performed by influential kings and emperors. Herein also we find that during the time of the horse sacrifice ceremony of Mahārāja Parīkṣit, the demigods from other planets were visible even to the common man, due to the sacrificial ceremony. The demigods are not generally visible to common men, as the Lord is not visible. But as the Lord, by His causeless mercy, descends to be visible to the common man, similarly the demigods also become visible to the common man by their own grace. Although celestial beings are not visible to the naked eyes of the inhabitants of this earth, it was due to the influence of Mahārāja Parīkṣit that the demigods also agreed to be visible. The kings used to spend lavishly during such sacrifices, as a cloud distributes rains. A cloud is nothing but another form of water, or, in other words, the waters of the earth transform into clouds. Similarly, the charity made by the kings in such sacrifices are but another form of the taxes collected from the citizens. But, as the rains fall down very lavishly and appear to be more than necessary, the charity made by such kings also seems to be more than what the citizen needs. Satisfied citizens will never organize agitation against the king, and thus there was no need in changing the monarchial state.

Even for a king like Mahārāja Parīkṣit there was need of a spiritual master for guidance. Without such guidance one cannot make progress in spiritual life. The spiritual master must be bona fide, and one who wants to have self-realization must approach and take shelter of a bona fide spiritual master to achieve real success.

TEXT 4

निजग्राहौजसा वीरः कलिं दिग्विजये क्वचित् ।
नृपलिङ्गधरं शूद्रं घ्नन्तं गोमिथुनं पदा ॥४॥

nijagrāhaujasā vīraḥ
kaliṁ digvijaye kvacit
nṛpa-liṅga-dharaṁ śūdraṁ
ghnantaṁ go-mithunaṁ padā

nijagrāha—sufficiently punished; *ojasā*—by prowess; *vīraḥ*—valiant hero; *kalim*—unto Kali, the master of the age; *digvijaye*—on his way to conquer the world; *kvacit*—once upon a time; *nṛpa-liṅga-dharam*—one who passes in the dress of a king; *śūdram*—the lower class; *ghnantam*—hurting; *go-mithunam*—a cow and bull; *padā*—on the leg.

TRANSLATION

Once, when Mahārāja Parīkṣit was on his way to conquer the world, he saw the master of Kali-yuga, who was lower than a śūdra, disguised as a king and hurting the legs of a cow and bull. The King at once caught hold of him to deal sufficient punishment.

PURPORT

The purpose of a king's going out to conquer the world is not for self-aggrandizement. Mahārāja Parīkṣit went out to conquer the world after his ascendance to the throne, but this was not for the purpose of aggression on other states. He was the Emperor of the world, and all small states were already under his regime. His purpose in going out was to see how things were going on in terms of the godly state. The king, being the representative of the Lord, has to execute the will of the Lord duly. There is no question of self-aggrandizement. Thus as soon as Mahārāja Parīkṣit saw that a lower-class man in the dress of a king was hurting the legs of a cow and a bull, at once he arrested and punished him. The king cannot tolerate insults to the most important animal, the cow, nor can he tolerate disrespect for the most important man, the *brāhmaṇa.* Human civilization means to advance the cause of brahminical culture, and to maintain it, cow protection is essential. There is a miracle in milk, for it contains all the necessary vitamins to sustain human physiological conditions for higher achievements. Brahminical culture can advance only when man is educated to develop the quality of goodness, and for this there is a prime necessity of food prepared with milk, fruits and grains. Mahārāja Parīkṣit was astonished to see that a black *śūdra,* dressed like a ruler, was mistreating a cow, the most important animal in human society.

The age of Kali means mismanagement and quarrel. And the root cause of all mismanagement and quarrel is that worthless men with the modes of lower-class men, who have no higher ambition in life, come to the helm of the state management. Such men at the post of a king are sure to first hurt the cow and the brahminical culture, thereby pushing all society towards hell. Mahārāja Parīkṣit, trained as he was, got the scent of this root cause of all quarrel in the world. Thus he wanted to stop it in the very beginning.

TEXT 5

शौनक उवाच
कस्य हेतोर्निजग्राह कलिं दिग्विजये नृपः ।
नृदेवचिह्नधृक्शूद्रकोऽसौ गां यः पदाहनत् ।
तत्कथ्यतां महाभाग यदि कृष्णकथाश्रयम् ॥५॥

śaunaka uvāca
kasya hetor nijagrāha
kaliṁ digvijaye nṛpaḥ
nṛdeva-cihna-dhṛk śūdra-
ko 'sau gāṁ yaḥ padāhanat
tat kathyatāṁ mahā-bhāga
yadi kṛṣṇa-kathāśrayam

śaunakaḥ uvāca—Śaunaka Ṛṣi said; *kasya*—for what; *hetoḥ*—reason; *nijagrāha*—sufficiently punished; *kalim*—the master of the age of Kali; *digvijaye*—during the time of his world tour; *nṛpaḥ*—the King; *nṛ-deva*—royal person; *cihna-dhṛk*—decorated like; *śūdrakaḥ*—lowest of the *śūdras; asau*—he; *gām*—cow; *yaḥ*—one who; *padā ahanat*—struck with his leg; *tat*—all that; *kathyatām*—please describe; *mahā-bhāga*—O greatly fortunate one; *yadi*—if, however; *kṛṣṇa*—about Kṛṣṇa; *kathā-āśrayam*—related with His topics.

TRANSLATION

Śaunaka Ṛṣi inquired: Why did Mahārāja Parīkṣit simply punish him, since he was the lowest of the śūdras, having dressed as a king and having struck a cow on the leg? Please describe all these incidents if they relate to the topics of Lord Kṛṣṇa.

PURPORT

Śaunaka and the *ṛṣis* were astonished to hear that the pious Mahārāja Parīkṣit simply punished the culprit and did not kill him. This suggests that a pious king like Mahārāja Parīkṣit should have at once killed an offender who wanted to cheat the public by dressing like a king and at the same time daring to insult the purest of the animals, a cow. The *ṛṣis* in those days, however, could not even imagine that in the advanced days of the age of Kali the lowest of the *śūdras* will be elected as administrators and will open organized slaughterhouses for killing cows. Anyway, although hearing about a *śūdraka* who was a cheat and insulter of a cow was not very interesting to the great *ṛṣis,* they nevertheless wanted to hear about it to see if the event had any connection with Lord Kṛṣṇa. They were simply interested in the topics of Lord Kṛṣṇa, for anything that is dovetailed with the narration of Kṛṣṇa is worth hearing. There are many topics in the *Bhāgavatam* about sociology, politics, economics, cultural affairs, etc., but all of them are in relation with Kṛṣṇa, and therefore all of them are worth hearing. Kṛṣṇa is the purifying ingredient in all matters, regardless of what they are. In the mundane world, everything is impure due to its being a product of the three mundane qualities. The purifying agent, however, is Kṛṣṇa.

TEXT 6

अथवास्य पदाम्भोजमकरन्दलिहां सताम् ।
किमन्यैरसदालापैरायुषो यदसद्व्ययः ॥ ६ ॥

athavāsya padāmbhoja-
makaranda-lihāṁ satām
kim anyair asad-ālāpair
āyuṣo yad asad-vyayaḥ

athavā—otherwise; *asya*—of His (Lord Kṛṣṇa's); *pada-ambhoja*—lotus feet; *makaranda-lihām*—of those who lick the honey from such a lotus flower; *satām*—of those who are to exist eternally; *kim anyaiḥ*—what is the use of anything else; *asat*—illusory; *ālāpaiḥ*—topics; *āyuṣaḥ*—of the duration of life; *yat*—that which is; *asat-vyayaḥ*—unnecessary waste of life.

TRANSLATION

The devotees of the Lord are accustomed to licking up the honey available from the lotus feet of the Lord. What is the use of topics which simply waste one's valuable life?

PURPORT

Lord Kṛṣṇa and His devotees are both on the transcendental plane; therefore the topics of Lord Kṛṣṇa and of His pure devotees are equally good. The Battle of Kurukṣetra is full of politics and diplomacy, but because the topics are related with Lord Kṛṣṇa, the *Bhagavad-gītā* is therefore adored all over the world. There is no need to eradicate politics, economics, sociology, etc., which are mundane to the mundaners. To a pure devotee, who is actually related with the Lord, such mundane things are transcendental if dovetailed with the Lord or with His pure devotees. We have heard and talked about the activities of the Pāṇḍavas, and we now are dealing with the topics of Mahārāja Parīkṣit, but because all these topics are related to the Lord Śrī Kṛṣṇa, they are all transcendental, and pure devotees have great interest in hearing them. We have already discussed this matter in connection with the prayers of Bhīṣmadeva.

Our duration of life is not very long, and there is no certainty of when we shall be ordered to leave everything for the next stage. Thus it is our duty to see that not a moment of our life is wasted in topics which are not related with Lord Kṛṣṇa. Any topic, however pleasant, is not worth hearing if it is devoid of its relation to Kṛṣṇa.

The spiritual planet, Goloka Vṛndāvana, the eternal abode of Lord Kṛṣṇa, is shaped like the whorl of a lotus flower. Even when the Lord descends to any one of the mundane planets, He does so by manifesting His own abode as it is. Thus His feet remain always on the same big whorl of the lotus flower. His feet are also as beautiful as the lotus flower. Therefore it is said that Lord Kṛṣṇa has lotus feet.

A living being is eternal by constitution. He is, so to speak, in the whirlpool of birth and death due to his contact with material energy. Freed from such material energy, a living entity is liberated and is eligible to return home, back to Godhead. Those who want to live forever without changing their material bodies should not waste valuable time with topics other than those relating to Lord Kṛṣṇa and His devotees.

TEXT 7

क्षुद्रायुषां नृणामङ्ग मर्त्यानामृतमिच्छताम् ।
इहोपहूतो भगवान्मृत्युः शामित्रकर्मणि ॥७॥

kṣudrāyuṣāṁ nṛṇām aṅga
martyānām ṛtam icchatām
ihopahūto bhagavān
mṛtyuḥ śāmitra-karmaṇi

kṣudra—very small; *āyuṣām*—of the duration of life; *nṛṇām*—of the human beings; *aṅga*—O Sūta Gosvāmī; *martyānām*—of those who are sure to meet death; *ṛtam*—eternal life; *icchatām*—of those who desire it; *iha*—herein; *upahūtaḥ*—called for being present; *bhagavān*—representing the Lord; *mṛtyuḥ*—the controller of death, Yamarāja; *śāmitra*—suppressing; *karmaṇi*—performances.

TRANSLATION

O Sūta Gosvāmī, there are those amongst men who desire freedom from death and get eternal life. They escape the slaughtering process by calling the controller of death, Yamarāja.

PURPORT

The living entity, as he develops from lower animal life to a higher human being and gradually to higher intelligence, becomes anxious to get free from the clutches of death. Modern scientists try to avoid death by physiochemical advancement of knowledge, but alas, the controller of death, Yamarāja, is so cruel that he does not spare even the very life of the scientist himself. The scientist, who puts forward the theory of stopping death by advancement of scientific knowledge, becomes himself a victim of death when he is called by Yamarāja. What to speak of stopping death, no one can enhance the short period of life even by a fraction of a moment. The only hope of suspending the cruel slaughtering process of Yamarāja is to call him to hear and chant the holy name of the Lord. Yamarāja is a great devotee of the Lord, and he likes to be invited to *kīrtanas* and sacrifices by the pure devotees, who are constantly engaged in the devotional service of the Lord. Thus the great sages, headed by Śaunaka and others, invited Yamarāja to attend the sacrifice performed at Naimiṣāraṇya. This was good for those who did not want to die.

TEXT 8

न कश्चिन्म्रियते तावद् यावदास्त इहान्तकः ।
एतदर्थं हि भगवानाहूतः परमर्षिभिः ।
अहो नृलोके पीयेत हरिलीलामृतं वचः ॥८॥

na kaścin mriyate tāvad
yāvad āsta ihāntakaḥ
etad-arthaṁ hi bhagavān
āhūtaḥ paramarṣibhiḥ
aho nṛ-loke pīyeta
hari-līlāmṛtaṁ vacaḥ

na—not; *kaścit*—anyone; *mriyate*—will die; *tāvat*—so long; *yāvat*—as long as; *āste*—is present; *iha*—herein; *antakaḥ*—one who causes the end of life; *etat*—this; *artham*—reason; *hi*—certainly; *bhagavān*—the representative of the Lord; *āhūtaḥ*—invited; *parama-ṛṣibhiḥ*—by the great sages; *aho*—alas; *nṛ-loke*—in human society; *pīyeta*—let them drink; *hari-līlā*—transcendental pastimes of the Lord; *amṛtam*—nectar for eternal life; *vacaḥ*—narrations.

TRANSLATION

As long as Yamarāja, who causes everyone's death, is present here, no one shall meet with death. The great sages have invited the controller of death, Yamarāja, who is the representative of the Lord. Living beings who are under his grip should take advantage by hearing the deathless nectar in the form of this narration of the transcendental pastimes of the Lord.

PURPORT

Every human being dislikes meeting death, but he does not know how to get rid of death. The surest remedy for avoiding death is to accustom oneself to hearing the nectarean pastimes of the Lord as they are systematically narrated in the text of *Śrīmad-Bhāgavatam.* It is advised herein, therefore, that any human being who desires freedom from death should take to this course of life as recommended by the *ṛṣis* headed by Śaunaka.

TEXT 9

मन्दस्य मन्दप्रज्ञस्य वयो मन्दायुषश्च वै ।
निद्रया ह्रियते नक्तं दिवा च व्यर्थकर्मभिः ॥९॥

mandasya manda-prajñasya
vayo mandāyuṣaś ca vai
nidrayā hriyate naktaṁ
divā ca vyartha-karmabhiḥ

mandasya—of the lazy; *manda*—paltry; *prajñasya*—of intelligence; *vayaḥ*—age; *manda*—short; *āyuṣaḥ*—of duration of life; *ca*—and; *vai*—exactly; *nidrayā*—by sleeping; *hriyate*—passes away; *naktam*—night; *divā*—daytime; *ca*—also; *vyartha*—for nothing; *karmabhiḥ*—by activities.

TRANSLATION

Lazy human beings with paltry intelligence and a short duration of life pass the night sleeping and the day performing activities that are for naught.

PURPORT

The less intelligent do not know the real value of the human form of life. The human form is a special gift of material nature in the course of her enforcing stringent laws of miseries upon the living being. It is a chance to achieve the highest boon of life, namely to get out of the entanglement of repeated birth and death. The intelligent take care of this important gift by strenuously endeavoring to get out of the entanglement. But the less intelligent are lazy and unable to evaluate the gift of the human body to achieve liberation from the material bondage; they become more interested in so-called economic development and work very hard throughout life simply for the sense enjoyment of the temporary body. Sense enjoyment is also allowed to the lower animals by the law of nature, and thus a human being is also destined to a certain amount of sense enjoyment according to his past or present life. But one should definitely try to understand that sense enjoyment is not the ultimate goal of human life. Herein it is said that during the daytime one works "for nothing" because the aim is nothing but sense enjoyment. We can particularly observe how the human being is engaged for nothing in the great cities and industrial towns. There are so many things manufactured by human energy, but they are all meant for sense enjoyment, and not for getting out of material bondage. And after working hard during the daytime, a tired man either sleeps or engages in sex habits at night. That is the program of materialistic civilized life for the less intelligent. Therefore they are designated herein as lazy, unfortunate and short-lived.

TEXT 10

सूत उवाच

यदा परीक्षित् कुरुजाङ्गलेऽवसत्
कलिं प्रविष्टं निजचक्रवर्तिते ।
निशम्य वार्तामनतिप्रियां ततः
शरासनं संयुगशौण्डिरादद े ॥१०॥

sūta uvāca
yadā parīkṣit kuru-jāṅgale 'vasat
kaliṁ praviṣṭaṁ nija-cakravartite
niśamya vārtām anatipriyāṁ tataḥ
śarāsanaṁ saṁyuga-śauṇḍir ādade

sūtaḥ uvāca—Sūta Gosvāmī said; *yadā*—when; *parīkṣit*—Mahārāja Parīkṣit; *kuru-jāṅgale*—in the capital of Kuru's empire; *avasat*—was residing; *kalim*—the symptoms of the age of Kali; *praviṣṭam*—entered; *nija-cakravartite*—within his jurisdiction; *niśamya*—thus hearing; *vārtām*—news; *anati-priyām*—not very palatable; *tataḥ*—thereafter; *śarāsanam*—arrows and bow; *saṁyuga*—having gotten a chance for; *śauṇḍiḥ*—martial activities; *ādade*—took up.

TRANSLATION

Sūta Gosvāmī said: While Mahārāja Parīkṣit was residing in the capital of the Kuru empire, the symptoms of the age of Kali began to infiltrate

within the jurisdiction of his state. When he learned about this, he did not think the matter very palatable. This did, however, give him a chance to fight. He took up his bow and arrows and prepared himself for military activities.

PURPORT

The state administration of Mahārāja Parīkṣit was so perfect that he was sitting in his capital peacefully. But he got the news that the symptoms of the age of Kali had already infiltrated into the jurisdiction of his state, and he did not like this news. What are the symptoms of the age of Kali? They are (1) illicit connection with women, (2) indulgence in meat-eating, (3) intoxication and (4) taking pleasure in gambling. The age of Kali literally means the age of quarrel, and the above-mentioned four symptoms in human society are the root causes for all kinds of quarrel. Mahārāja Parīkṣit heard that some of the people of the state had already taken to those symptoms, and he wanted to take immediate steps against such causes of unrest. This means that at least up to the regime of Mahārāja Parīkṣit, such symptoms of public life were practically unknown, and as soon as they were slightly detected, he wanted to root them out. The news was not palatable for him, but in a way it was, because Mahārāja Parīkṣit got a chance to fight. There was no need to fight with small states because everyone was peacefully under his subordination, but the Kali-yuga miscreants gave his fighting spirit a chance for exhibition. A perfect *kṣatriya* king is always jubilant as soon as he gets a chance to fight, just as a sportsman is eager when there is a chance for a sporting match. It is no argument that in the age of Kali such symptoms are predestined. If so, then why was there preparation for fighting out such symptoms? Such arguments are offered by lazy and unfortunate men. In the rainy season, rain is predestined, and yet people take precautions to protect themselves. Similarly, in the age of Kali the symptoms as above mentioned are sure to infiltrate into social life, but it is the duty of the state to save the citizens from the association of the agents of the age of Kali. Mahārāja Parīkṣit wanted to punish the miscreants indulging in the symptoms of Kali, and thus save the innocent citizens who were pure in habit by culture of religion. It is the duty of the king to give such protection, and Mahārāja Parīkṣit was perfectly right when he prepared himself to fight.

TEXT 11

स्वलङ्कृतं श्यामतुरङ्गयोजितं
रथं मृगेन्द्रध्वजमाश्रितः पुरात् ।

वृतो रथाश्वद्विपपत्तियुक्तया
स्वसेनया दिग्विजयाय निर्गतः ॥११॥

svalaṅkṛtaṁ śyāma-turaṅga-yojitaṁ
rathaṁ mṛgendra-dhvajam āśritaḥ purāt
vṛto rathāśva-dvipapatti-yuktayā
sva-senayā digvijayāya nirgataḥ

su-alaṅkṛtam—very well decorated; *śyāma*—black; *turaṅga*—horses; *yojitam*—tackled; *ratham*—chariot; *mṛga-indra*—lion; *dhvajam*—flagged; *āśritaḥ*—under the protection; *purāt*—from the capital; *vṛtaḥ*—surrounded by; *ratha*—charioteers; *aśva*—cavalry; *dvipapatti*—elephants; *yuktayā*—thus being equipped; *sva-senayā*—along with infantry; *digvijayāya*—for the purpose of conquering; *nirgataḥ*—went out.

TRANSLATION

Mahārāja Parīkṣit sat on a chariot drawn by black horses. His flag was marked with the sign of a lion. Being so decorated and surrounded by charioteers, cavalry, elephants and infantry soldiers, he left the capital to conquer in all directions.

PURPORT

Mahārāja Parīkṣit is distinguished from his grandfather Arjuna, for black horses pulled his chariot instead of white horses. He marked his flag with the mark of a lion, and his grandfather marked his with the mark of Hanumānjī. A royal procession like that of Mahārāja Parīkṣit surrounded by well-decorated chariots, cavalry, elephants, infantry and band not only is pleasing to the eyes, but also is a sign of a civilization that is aesthetic even on the fighting front.

TEXT 12

भद्राश्वं केतुमालं च भारतं चोत्तरान् कुरून् ।
किम्पुरुषादीनि वर्षाणि विजित्य जगृहे बलिम् ॥१२॥

bhadrāśvaṁ ketumālaṁ ca
bhāratam cottarān kurūn
kimpuruṣādīni varṣāṇi
vijitya jagṛhe balim

bhadrāśvam—Bhadrāśva; *ketumālam*—Ketumāla; *ca*—also; *bhāratam*—Bhārata; *ca*—and; *uttarān*—the northern countries; *kurūn*—the kingdom of the Kuru dynasty; *kimpuruṣa-ādīni*—a country beyond the northern side of the Himalayas; *varṣāṇi*—parts of the earth planet; *vijitya*—conquering; *jagṛhe*—exacted; *balim*—strength.

TRANSLATION

Mahārāja Parīkṣit then conquered all parts of the earthly planet—Bhadrāśva, Ketumāla, Bhārata, the northern Kuru, Kimpuruṣa, etc.—and exacted tributes from their respective rulers.

PURPORT

Bhadrāśva: It is a tract of land near Meru Parvata, and it extends from Gandha-mādana Parvata to the saltwater ocean. There is a description of this *varṣa* in the *Mahābhārata* (*Bhīṣma-parva* 7.14–18). The description was narrated by Sañjaya to Dhṛtarāṣṭra.

Mahārāja Yudhiṣṭhira also conquered this *varṣa,* and thus the province was included within the jurisdiction of his empire. Mahārāja Parīkṣit was formerly declared to be the emperor of all lands ruled by his grandfather, but still he had to establish his supremacy while he was out of his capital to exact tribute from such states.

Ketumāla: This earth planet is divided into seven *dvīpas* by seven oceans, and the central *dvīpa,* called Jambūdvīpa, is divided into nine *varṣas,* or parts, by eight huge mountains. Bhārata-varṣa is one of the above-mentioned nine *varṣas,* and Ketumāla is also described as one of the above *varṣas.* It is said that in Ketumāla *varṣa,* women are the most beautiful. This *varṣa* was conquered by Arjuna also. A description of this part of the world is available in the *Mahābhārata* (*Sabhā* 28.6).

It is said that this part of the world is situated on the western side of the Meru Parvata, and inhabitants of this province used to live up to ten thousand years (*Bhīṣma-parva* 6.31). Human beings living in this part of the globe are of golden color, and the women resemble the angels of heaven. The inhabitants are free from all kinds of diseases and grief.

Bhārata-varṣa: This part of the world is also one of the nine *varṣas* of the Jambūdvīpa. A description of Bhārata-varṣa is given in the *Mahābhārata* (*Bhīṣma-parva,* Chapters 9 and 10).

In the center of Jambūdvīpa is Ilāvṛta-varṣa, and south of Ilāvṛta-varṣa is Hari-varṣa. The description of these *varṣas* is given in the *Mahābhārata* (*Sabhā-parva* 28.7–8) as follows:

nagarāṁś ca vanāṁś caiva
nadīś ca vimalodakāḥ
puruṣān deva-kalpāṁś ca
nārīś ca priya-darśanāḥ

adṛṣṭa-pūrvān subhagān
sa dadarśa dhanañjayaḥ
sadanāni ca śubhrāṇi
nārīś cāpsarasāṁ nibhāḥ

It is mentioned here that the women in both these *varṣas* are beautiful, and some of them are equal to the Apsarās, or heavenly women.

Uttarakuru: According to Vedic geography the northernmost portion of Jambūdvīpa is called Uttarakuru-varṣa. It is surrounded by the saltwater ocean from three sides and divided by Śṛṅgavān Mountain from the Hiraṇmaya-varṣa.

Kimpuruṣa-varṣa: It is stated to be situated north of the great Himalaya Mountain, which is eighty thousand miles in length and height and which covers sixteen thousand miles in width. These parts of the world were also conquered by Arjuna (*Sabhā* 28.1–2). The Kimpuruṣas are descendants of a daughter of Dakṣa. When Mahārāja Yudhiṣṭhira performed a horse sacrifice *yajña,* the inhabitants of these countries were also present to take part in the festival, and they paid tributes to the Emperor. This part of the world is called Kimpuruṣa-varṣa, or sometimes the Himalayan provinces (Himavatī). It is said that Śukadeva Gosvāmī was born in these Himalayan provinces and that he came to Bhārata-varṣa after crossing the Himalayan countries.

In other words, Mahārāja Parīkṣit conquered all the world. He conquered all the continents adjoining all the seas and oceans in all directions, namely the eastern, western, northern and southern parts of the world.

TEXTS 13–15

तत्र तत्रोपशृण्वानः स्वपूर्वेषां महात्मनाम् ।
प्रगीयमाणं च यशः कृष्णमाहात्म्यसूचकम् ॥१३॥
आत्मानं च परित्रातमश्वत्थाम्नोऽस्त्रतेजसः ।
स्नेहं च वृष्णिपार्थानां तेषां भक्तिं च केशवे ॥१४॥
तेभ्यः परमसन्तुष्टः प्रीत्युज्जृम्भितलोचनः ।
महाधनानि वासांसि ददौ हारान् महामनाः ॥१५॥

tatra tatropaśṛṇvānaḥ
sva-pūrveṣāṁ mahātmanām
pragīyamāṇaṁ ca yaśaḥ
kṛṣṇa-māhātmya-sūcakam

ātmānaṁ ca paritrātam
aśvatthāmno 'stra-tejasaḥ
snehaṁ ca vṛṣṇi-pārthānāṁ
teṣāṁ bhaktiṁ ca keśave

tebhyaḥ parama-santuṣṭaḥ
prīty-ujjṛmbhita-locanaḥ
mahā-dhanāni vāsāṁsi
dadau hārān mahā-manāḥ

tatra tatra—everywhere the King visited; *upaśṛṇvānaḥ*—continuously he heard; *sva-pūrveṣām*—about his own forefathers; *mahā-ātmanām*—who were all great devotees of the Lord; *pragīyamāṇam*—unto those who were thus addressing; *ca*—also; *yaśaḥ*—glories; *kṛṣṇa*—Lord Kṛṣṇa; *māhātmya*—glorious acts; *sūcakam*—indicating; *ātmānam*—his personal self; *ca*—also; *paritrātam*—delivered; *aśvatthāmnaḥ*—of Aśvatthāmā; *astra*—weapon; *tejasaḥ*—powerful rays; *sneham*—affection; *ca*—also; *vṛṣṇi-pārthānām*—between descendants of Vṛṣṇi and those of Pṛthā; *teṣām*—of all of them; *bhaktim*—devotion; *ca*—also; *keśave*—unto Lord Kṛṣṇa; *tebhyaḥ*—unto them; *parama*—extremely; *santuṣṭaḥ*—pleased; *prīti*—attraction; *ujjṛmbhita*—pleasingly open; *locanaḥ*—one who has such eyes; *mahā-dhanāni*—valuable riches; *vāsāṁsi*—clothing; *dadau*—gave in charity; *hārān*—necklace; *mahā-manāḥ*—one who has a broader outlook.

TRANSLATION

Wherever the King visited, he continuously heard the glories of his great forefathers, who were all devotees of the Lord, and also of the glorious acts of Lord Kṛṣṇa. He also heard how he himself had been protected by the Lord from the powerful heat of the weapon of Aśvatthāmā. People also mentioned the great affection between the descendants of Vṛṣṇi and Pṛthā due to the latter's great devotion to Lord Keśava. The King, being very pleased with the singers of such glories, opened his eyes in great satisfaction. Out of magnanimity he was pleased to award them very valuable necklaces and clothing.

PURPORT

Kings and great personalities of the state are presented with welcome addresses. This is a system from time immemorial, and Mahārāja Parīkṣit, since he was one of the well-known emperors of the world, was also presented with addresses of welcome in all parts of the world as he visited those places. The subject matter of those welcome addresses was Kṛṣṇa. Kṛṣṇa means Kṛṣṇa and His eternal devotees, as the king means the king and his confidential associates.

Kṛṣṇa and His unalloyed devotees cannot be separated, and therefore glorifying the devotee means glorifying the Lord and vice versa. Mahārāja Parīkṣit would not have been glad to hear about the glories of his forefathers like Mahārāja Yudhiṣṭhira and Arjuna had they not been connected with the acts of Lord Kṛṣṇa. The Lord descends specifically to deliver His devotees (*paritrāṇāya sādhūnām*). The devotees are glorified by the presence of the Lord because they cannot live for a moment without the presence of the Lord and His different energies. The Lord is present for the devotee by His acts and glories, and therefore Mahārāja Parīkṣit felt the presence of the Lord when He was glorified by His acts, especially when he was saved by the Lord in the womb of his mother. The devotees of the Lord are never in danger, but in the material world which is full of dangers at every step, the devotees are apparently placed into dangerous positions, and when they are saved by the Lord, the Lord is glorified. Lord Kṛṣṇa would not have been glorified as the speaker of the *Bhagavad-gītā* had His devotees like the Pāṇḍavas not been entangled in the Battlefield of Kurukṣetra. All such acts of the Lord were mentioned in the addresses of welcome, and Mahārāja Parīkṣit, in full satisfaction, rewarded those who presented such addresses. The difference between the presentation of welcome addresses today and in those days is that formerly the welcome addresses were presented to a person like Mahārāja Parīkṣit. The welcome addresses were full of facts and figures, and those who presented such addresses were sufficiently rewarded, whereas in the present days the welcome addresses are presented not always with factual statements but to please the post holder, and often they are full of flattering lies. And rarely are those who present such welcome addresses rewarded by the poor receiver.

TEXT 16

सारथ्यपारषदसेवनसख्यदौत्य-
वीरासनानुगमनस्तवनप्रणामान् ।

स्निग्धेषु पाण्डुषु जगत्प्रणतिं च विष्णो-
र्भक्तिं करोति नृपतिश्चरणारविन्दे ॥१६॥

sārathya-pāraṣada-sevana-sakhya-dautya-
vīrāsanānugamana-stavana-praṇāmān
snigdheṣu pāṇḍuṣu jagat-praṇatiṁ ca viṣṇor
bhaktiṁ karoti nṛ-patiś caraṇāravinde

sārathya—acceptance of the post of a chariot driver; *pāraṣada*—acceptance of the presidency in the assembly of the Rājasūya sacrifice; *sevana*—engaging the mind constantly in the service of the Lord; *sakhya*—to think of the Lord as a friend; *dautya*—acceptance of the post of a messenger; *vīra-āsana*—acceptance of the post of a watchman with a drawn sword at night; *anugamana*—following in the footsteps; *stavana*—offering of prayers; *praṇāmān*—offering obeisances; *snigdheṣu*—unto them who are malleable to the will of the Lord; *pāṇḍuṣu*—unto the sons of Pāṇḍu; *jagat*—the universal; *praṇatim*—one who is obeyed; *ca*—and; *viṣṇoḥ*—of Viṣṇu; *bhaktim*—devotion; *karoti*—does; *nṛ-patiḥ*—the King; *caraṇa-aravinde*—unto His lotus feet.

TRANSLATION

Mahārāja Parīkṣit heard that out of His causeless mercy Lord Kṛṣṇa [Viṣṇu], who is universally obeyed, rendered all kinds of service to the malleable sons of Pāṇḍu by accepting posts ranging from chariot driver to president to messenger, friend, night watchman, etc., according to the will of the Pāṇḍavas, obeying them like a servant and offering obeisances like one younger in years. When he heard this, Mahārāja Parīkṣit became overwhelmed with devotion to the lotus feet of the Lord.

PURPORT

Lord Kṛṣṇa is everything to the unalloyed devotees like the Pāṇḍavas. The Lord was for them the Supreme Lord, the spiritual master, the worshipable Deity, the guide, the chariot driver, the friend, the servant, the messenger and everything they could conceive of. And thus the Lord also reciprocated the feelings of the Pāṇḍavas. Mahārāja Parīkṣit, as a pure devotee of the Lord, could appreciate the Lord's transcendental reciprocation of the feelings of His devotees, and thus he himself also was overwhelmed with the dealings of the Lord. Simply by appreciating the dealings of the Lord with His pure devotees, one can attain salvation. The Lord's dealings with His devotees appear to be ordinary human dealings, but one who knows them in truth becomes at once eligible to go back home, back to Godhead. The Pāṇḍavas were so malleable to the will of the Lord that they could sacrifice any amount of energy for the service of the Lord, and by such unalloyed determination they could secure the Lord's mercy in any shape they desired.

TEXT 17

तस्यैवं वर्तमानस्य पूर्वेषां वृत्तिमन्वहम् ।
नातिदूरे किलाश्चर्यं यदासीत् तन्निबोध में ॥१७॥

tasyaivaṁ vartamānasya
pūrveṣāṁ vṛttim anvaham
nātidūre kilāścaryaṁ
yad āsīt tan nibodha me

tasya—of Mahārāja Parīkṣit; *evam*—thus; *vartamānasya*—remaining absorbed in such thought; *pūrveṣām*—of his forefathers; *vṛttim*—good engagement; *anvaham*—day after day; *na*—not; *ati-dūre*—far off; *kila*—verily; *āścaryam*—astonishing; *yat*—that; *āsīt*—was; *tat*—which; *nibodha*—know it; *me*—from me.

TRANSLATION

Now you may hear from me of what happened while Mahārāja Parīkṣit was passing his days hearing of the good occupations of his forefathers and being absorbed in thought of them.

TEXT 18

धर्मः पदैकेन चरन् विच्छायामुपलभ्य गाम् ।
पृच्छति स्माश्रुवदनां विवत्सामिव मातरम् ॥१८॥

dharmaḥ padaikena caran
vicchāyām upalabhya gām
pṛcchati smāśru-vadanāṁ
vivatsām iva mātaram

dharmaḥ—the personality of religious principles; *padā*—leg; *ekena*—on one only; *caran*—wandering; *vicchāyām*—overtaken by the shadow of grief;

upalabhya—having met; *gām*—the cow; *pṛcchati sma*—asked; *aśru-vadanām*—with tears on the face; *vivatsām*—one who has lost her offspring; *iva*—like; *mātaram*—the mother.

TRANSLATION

The personality of religious principles, Dharma, was wandering about in the form of a bull. And he met the personality of earth in the form of a cow who appeared to grieve like a mother who had lost her child. She had tears in her eyes, and the beauty of her body was lost. Thus Dharma questioned the earth as follows.

PURPORT

The bull is the emblem of the moral principle, and the cow is the representative of the earth. When the bull and the cow are in a joyful mood, it is to be understood that the people of the world are also in a joyful mood. The reason is that the bull helps production of grains in the agricultural field, and the cow delivers milk, the miracle of aggregate food values. The human society, therefore, maintains these two important animals very carefully so that they can wander everywhere in cheerfulness. But at the present moment in this age of Kali both the bull and the cow are now being slaughtered and eaten up as foodstuff by a class of men who do not know the brahminical culture. The bull and the cow can be protected for the good of all human society simply by the spreading of brahminical culture as the topmost perfection of all cultural affairs. By advancement of such culture, the morale of society is properly maintained, and so peace and prosperity are also attained without extraneous effort. When brahminical culture deteriorates, the cow and bull are mistreated, and the resultant actions are prominent by the following symptoms.

TEXT 19

धर्म उवाच

कच्चिद्भद्रेऽनामयमात्मनस्ते
विच्छायासि म्लायतेषन्मुखेन ।
आलक्षये भवतीमन्तराधिं
दूरे बन्धुं शोचसि कञ्चनाम्ब ॥१९॥

dharma uvāca
kaccid bhadre 'nāmayam ātmanas te
vicchāyāsi mlāyateṣan mukhena
ālakṣaye bhavatīm antarādhiṁ
dūre bandhuṁ śocasi kañcanāmba

dharmaḥ uvāca—Dharma inquired; *kaccit*—whether; *bhadre*—madam; *anāmayam*—quite hale and hearty; *ātmanaḥ*—self; *te*—unto you; *vicchāyā asi*—appear to be covered with the shadow of grief; *mlāyatā*—which darkens; *īṣat*—slightly; *mukhena*—by the face; *ālakṣaye*—you look; *bhavatīm*—unto yourself; *antarādhim*—some disease within; *dūre*—long distant; *bandhum*—friend; *śocasi*—thinking of; *kañcana*—someone; *amba*—O Mother.

TRANSLATION

Dharma [in the form of a bull] asked: Madam, are you not hale and hearty? Why are you covered with the shadow of grief? It appears by your face that you have become black. Are you suffering from some internal disease, or are you thinking of some relative who is away in a distant place?

PURPORT

The people of the world in this age of Kali are always full of anxieties. Everyone is diseased with some kind of ailment. From the very faces of the people of this age, one can find out the index of the mind. Everyone feels the absence of his relative who is away from home. The particular symptom of the age of Kali is that no family is now blessed to live together. To earn a livelihood, the father lives at a place far away from the son, or the wife lives far away from the husband and so on. There are sufferings from internal diseases, separation from those near and dear, and anxieties for maintaining the status quo. These are but some important factors which make the people of this age always unhappy.

TEXT 20

पादैर्न्यूनं शोचसि मैकपाद-
मात्मानं वा वृषलैर्भोक्ष्यमाणम् ।
आहो सुरादीन् हृतयज्ञभागान्
प्रजा उत स्विन्मघवत्यवर्षति ॥२०॥

pādair nyūnaṁ śocasi maika-pādam
ātmānaṁ vā vṛṣalair bhokṣyamāṇam
āho surādīn hṛta-yajña-bhāgān
prajā uta svin maghavaty avarṣati

pādaiḥ—by three legs; *nyūnam*—diminished; *śocasi*—if you are lamenting for that; *mā*—my; *eka-pādam*—only one leg; *ātmānam*—own body; *vā*—or; *vṛṣalaiḥ*—by the unlawful meat-eaters; *bhokṣyamāṇam*—to be exploited; *āhoḥ*—in sacrifice; *sura-ādīn*—the authorized demigods; *hṛta-yajña*—devoid of sacrificial; *bhāgān*—share; *prajāḥ*—the living beings; *uta*—increasing; *svit*—whether; *maghavati*—in famine and scarcity; *avarṣati*—because of rainlessness.

TRANSLATION

I have lost my three legs and am now standing on one only. Are you lamenting for my state of existence? Or are you in great anxiety because henceforward the unlawful meat-eaters will exploit you? Or are you in a sorry plight because the demigods are now bereft of their share of sacrificial offerings because no sacrifices are being performed at present? Or are you grieving for living beings because of their sufferings due to famine and drought?

PURPORT

With the progress of the age of Kali, four things particularly, namely the duration of life, mercy, the power of recollection, and moral or religious principles will gradually diminish. Since Dharma, or the principles of religion, would be lost in the proportion of three out of four, the symbolic bull was standing on one leg only. When three fourths of the population of the whole world become irreligious, the situation is converted into hell for the animals. In the age of Kali, godless civilizations will create so many so-called religious societies in which the Personality of Godhead will be directly or indirectly defied. And thus faithless societies of men will make the world uninhabitable for the saner section of people. There are gradations of human beings in terms of proportionate faith in the Supreme Personality of Godhead. The first-class faithful men are the Vaiṣṇavas and the *brāhmaṇas,* then the *kṣatriyas,* then the *vaiśyas,* then the *śūdras,* then the *mlecchas,* the *yavanas* and at last the *caṇḍālas.* The degradation of the human instinct begins from the *mlecchas,* and the *caṇḍāla* state of life is the last word in human degradation. All the above terms mentioned in the Vedic literatures are never meant for any particular community or birth. They are different qualifications of human beings in general. There is no question of birthright or community. One can acquire the respective qualifications by one's own efforts, and thus the son of a Vaiṣṇava can become a *mleccha,* or the son of a *caṇḍāla* can become more than a *brāhmaṇa,* all in terms of their association and intimate relation with the Supreme Lord.

The meat-eaters are generally called *mlecchas.* But all meat-eaters are not *mlecchas.* Those who accept meat in terms of scriptural injunctions are not *mlecchas,* but those who accept meat without restriction are called *mlecchas.* Beef is forbidden in the scriptures, and the bulls and cows are offered special protection by followers of the *Vedas.* But in this age of Kali, people will exploit the body of the bull and the cow as they like, and thus they will invite sufferings of various types.

The people of this age will not perform any sacrifice. The *mleccha* population will care very little for performances of sacrifices, although performance of sacrifice is essential for persons who are materially engaged in sense enjoyment. In the *Bhagavad-gītā* performance of sacrifices is strongly recommended. (Bg.3.14–16)

The living beings are created by the creator Brahmā, and just to maintain the created living being progressively towards the path back to Godhead, the system of performing sacrifice is also created by him. The system is that living beings live on the produce of grains and vegetables, and by eating such foodstuff they get vital power of the body in the shape of blood and semen, and from blood and semen one living being is able to create other living beings. But the production of grains, grass, etc., becomes possible by rain, and this rain is made to shower properly by performance of recommended sacrifices. Such sacrifices are directed by the rites of the *Vedas,* namely *Sāma, Yajur, Ṛg* and *Atharva.* In the *Manu-smṛti* it is recommended that by offerings of sacrifice on the altar of the fire, the sun-god is pleased. When the sun-god is pleased, he properly collects water from the sea, and thus sufficient clouds collect on the horizon and rains fall. After sufficient rains fall, there is sufficient production of grains for men and all animals, and thus there is energy in the living being for progressive activity. The *mlecchas,* however, make plans to install slaughterhouses for killing bulls and cows along with other animals, thinking that they will prosper by increasing the number of factories and live on animal food without caring for performance of sacrifices and production of grains. But they must know that even for the animals they must produce grass and vegetables, otherwise the animals cannot live. And to produce grass for the animals, they require sufficient rains. Therefore they have to depend ultimately on the mercy of the demigods like the sun-god, Indra and Candra, and such demigods must be satisfied by performances of sacrifice.

This material world is a sort of prison house, as we have several times mentioned. The demigods are the servants of the Lord who see to the proper upkeep of the prison house. These demigods want to see that the rebel living beings, who want to survive faithlessly, are gradually turned towards the supreme power of the Lord. Therefore, the system of offering sacrifice is recommended in the scriptures.

The materialistic men want to work hard and enjoy fruitive results for sense enjoyment. Thus they are committing many types of sins at every step of life. Those, however, who are consciously engaged in the devotional service of the Lord are transcendental to all varieties of sin and virtue. Their activities are free from the contamination of the three modes of material nature. For the devotees there is no need for performance of prescribed sacrifices because the very life of the devotee is a symbol of sacrifice. But persons who are engaged in fruitive activities for sense enjoyment must perform the prescribed sacrifices because that is the only means to get free from the reaction of all sins committed by fruitive workers. Sacrifice is the means for counteracting such accumulated sins. The demigods are pleased when such sacrifices are performed, just as prison officers are satisfied when the prisoners are turned into obedient subjects. Lord Caitanya, however, has recommended only one *yajña,* or sacrifice, called the *saṅkīrtana-yajña,* the chanting of Hare Kṛṣṇa, in which everyone can take part. Thus both devotees and fruitive workers can derive equal benefit from the performances of *saṅkīrtana-yajña.*

TEXT 21

अरक्ष्यमाणाः स्त्रिय उर्वि बालान्
शोचस्यथो पुरुषादैरिवार्तान् ।
वाचं देवीं ब्रह्मकुले कुकर्म-
ण्यब्रह्मण्ये राजकुले कुलाग्र्यान् ॥२१॥

arakṣyamāṇāḥ striya urvi bālān
śocasy atho puruṣādair ivārtān
vācaṁ devīṁ brahma-kule kukarmaṇy
abrahmaṇye rāja-kule kulāgryān

arakṣyamāṇāḥ—unprotected; *striyaḥ*—women; *urvi*—on the earth; *bālān*—children; *śocasi*—you are feeling compassion; *atho*—as such; *puruṣa-ādaiḥ*—by men; *iva*—like that; *ārtān*—those who are unhappy; *vācam*—vocabulary; *devīm*—the goddess; *brahma-kule*—in the family of the *brāhmaṇa; kukarmaṇi*—acts against the principles of religion; *abrahmaṇye*—persons against the brahminical culture; *rāja-kule*—in the administrative family; *kula-agryān*—most of all the families (the *brāhmaṇas*).

TRANSLATION

Are you feeling compunction for the unhappy women and children who are left forlorn by unscrupulous persons? Or are you unhappy because the goddess of learning is being handled by brāhmaṇas addicted to acts against the principles of religion? Or are you sorry to see that the brāhmaṇas have taken shelter of administrative families that do not respect brahminical culture?

PURPORT

In the age of Kali, the women and the children, along with *brāhmaṇas* and cows, will be grossly neglected and left unprotected. In this age illicit connection with women will render many women and children uncared for. Circumstantially, the women will try to become independent of the protection of men, and marriage will be performed as a matter of formal agreement between man and woman. In most cases, the children will not be taken care of properly. The *brāhmaṇas* are traditionally intelligent men, and thus they will be able to pick up modern education to the topmost rank, but as far as moral and religious principles are concerned, they shall be the most fallen. Education and bad character go ill together, but such things will run parallel. The administrative heads as a class will condemn the tenets of Vedic wisdom and will prefer to conduct a so-called secular state, and the so-called educated *brāhmaṇas* will be purchased by such unscrupulous administrators. Even a philosopher and writer of many books on religious principles may also accept an exalted post in a government which denies all the moral codes of the *śāstras.* The *brāhmaṇas* are specifically restricted from accepting such service. But in this age they will not only accept service, but they will do so even if it is of the meanest quality. These are some of the symptoms of the Kali age which are harmful to the general welfare of human society.

TEXT 22

किं क्षत्रबन्धून् कलिनोपसृष्टान्
राष्ट्राणि वा तैरवरोपितानि ।
इतस्ततो वाशनपानवासः
स्नानव्यवायोन्मुखजीवलोकम् ॥२२॥

kiṁ kṣatra-bandhūn kalinopasṛṣṭān
rāṣṭrāṇi vā tair avaropitāni
itas tato vāśana-pāna-vāsaḥ-
snāna-vyavāyonmukha-jīva-lokam

kim—whether; *kṣatra-bandhūn*—the unworthy administrators; *kalinā*—by the influence of the age of Kali; *upasṛṣṭān*—bewildered; *rāṣṭrāṇi*—state affairs; *vā*—or; *taiḥ*—by them; *avaropitāni*—put into disorder; *itaḥ*—here; *tataḥ*—there; *vā*—or; *aśana*—accepting foodstuff; *pāna*—drink; *vāsaḥ*—residence; *snāna*—bath; *vyavāya*—sexual intercourse; *unmukha*—inclined; *jīva-lokam*—human society.

TRANSLATION

The so-called administrators are now bewildered by the influence of this age of Kali, and thus they have put all state affairs into disorder. Are you now lamenting this disorder? Now the general populace does not follow the rules and regulations for eating, sleeping, drinking, mating, etc., and they are inclined to perform such anywhere and everywhere. Are you unhappy because of this?

PURPORT

There are some necessities of life on a par with those of the lower animals, and they are eating, sleeping, fearing and mating. These bodily demands are for both the human beings and the animals. But the human being has to fulfill such desires not like animals, but like a human being. A dog can mate with a bitch before the public eyes without hesitation, but if a human being does so the act will be considered a public nuisance, and the person will be criminally prosecuted. Therefore for the human being there are some rules and regulations, even for fulfilling common demands. The human society avoids such rules and regulations when it is bewildered by the influence of the age of Kali. In this age, people are indulging in such necessities of life without following the rules and regulations, and this deterioration of social and moral rules is certainly lamentable because of the harmful effects of such beastly behavior. In this age, the fathers and the guardians are not happy with the behavior of their wards. They should know that so many innocent children are victims of bad association awarded by the influence of this age of Kali. We know from *Śrīmad-Bhāgavatam* that Ajāmila, an innocent son of a *brāhmaṇa*, was walking down a road and saw a *śūdra* pair sexually embracing. This attracted the boy, and later on the boy became a victim of all debaucheries. From a pure *brāhmaṇa*, he fell down to the position of a wretched urchin, and it was all due to bad association. There was but one victim like Ajāmila in those days, but in this age of Kali the poor innocent students are daily victims of cinemas which attract men only for sex indulgence. The so-called administrators are all untrained in the affairs of a *kṣatriya*. The *kṣatriyas* are meant for administration, as the *brāhmaṇas* are meant for knowledge and guidance. The word *kṣatra-bandhu* refers to the so-called administrators or persons promoted to the post of the administrator without proper training by culture and tradition. Nowadays they are promoted to such exalted posts by the votes of the people who are themselves fallen in the rules and regulations of life. How can such people select a proper man when they are themselves fallen in the standard of life? Therefore, by the influence of the age of Kali, everywhere, politically, socially or religiously, everything is topsy-turvy, and therefore for the sane man it is all regrettable.

TEXT 23

यद्वाम्ब ते भूरिभरावतार
कृतावतारस्य हरेर्धरित्रि ।
अन्तर्हितस्य स्मरती विसृष्टा
कर्माणि निर्वाणविलम्बितानि ॥२३॥

yadvāmba te bhūri-bharāvatāra-
kṛtāvatārasya harer dharitri
antarhitasya smaratī visṛṣṭā
karmāṇi nirvāṇa-vilambitāni

yadvā—that may be; *amba*—O mother; *te*—your; *bhūri*—heavy; *bhara*—load; *avatāra*—decreasing the load; *kṛta*—done; *avatārasya*—one who incarnated; *hareḥ*—of Lord Śrī Kṛṣṇa; *dharitri*—O earth; *antarhitasya*—of

Him who is now out of sight; *smaratī*—while thinking of; *visṛṣṭā*—all that were performed; *karmāṇi*—activities; *nirvāṇa*—salvation; *vilambitāni*—that which entails.

TRANSLATION

O mother earth, the Supreme Personality of Godhead, Hari, incarnated Himself as Lord Śrī Kṛṣṇa just to unload your heavy burden. All His activities here are transcendental, and they cement the path of liberation. You are now bereft of His presence. You are probably now thinking of those activities and feeling sorry in their absence.

PURPORT

The activities of the Lord include liberation, but they are more relishable than the pleasure derived from *nirvāṇa,* or liberation. According to Śrīla Jīva Gosvāmī and Viśvanātha Cakravartī Ṭhākura, the word used here is *nirvāṇa-vilambitāni,* "that which minimizes the value of liberation." To attain *nirvāṇa,* liberation, one has to undergo a severe type of *tapasya,* austerity, but the Lord is so merciful that He incarnates to diminish the burden of the earth. Simply by remembering such activities, one can defy the pleasure derived from *nirvāṇa* and reach the transcendental abode of the Lord to associate with Him, eternally engaged in His blissful loving service.

TEXT 24

इदं ममाचक्ष्व तवाधिमूलं
वसुन्धरे येन विकर्शितासि ।
कालेन वा ते बलिनां बलीयसा
सुरार्चितं किं हृतमम्ब सौभगम् ॥२४॥

idaṁ mamācakṣva tavādhi-mūlaṁ
vasundhare yena vikarśitāsi
kālena vā te balināṁ balīyasā
surārcitaṁ kiṁ hṛtam amba saubhagam

idam—this; *mama*—unto me; *ācakṣva*—kindly inform; *tava*—your; *ādhimūlam*—the root cause of your tribulations; *vasundhare*—O reservoir of all riches; *yena*—by which; *vikarśitā asi*—reduced to much weakness; *kālena*—by the influence of time; *vā*—or; *te*—your; *balinām*—very powerful;

balīyasā—more powerful; *sura-arcitam*—adored by the demigods; *kim*—whether; *hṛtam*—taken away; *amba*—mother; *saubhagam*—fortune.

TRANSLATION

Mother, you are the reservoir of all riches. Please inform me of the root cause of your tribulations by which you have been reduced to such a weak state. I think that the powerful influence of time, which conquers the most powerful, might have forcibly taken away all your fortune, which was adored even by the demigods.

PURPORT

By the grace of the Lord, each and every planet is created fully equipped. So not only is this earth fully equipped with all the riches for the maintenance of its inhabitants, but also, when the Lord descends on the earth the whole earth becomes so enriched with all kinds of opulences that even the denizens of heaven worship it with all affection. But by the will of the Lord, the whole earth can at once be changed. He can do and undo a thing by His sweet will. Therefore no one should consider himself to be self-sufficient or independent of the Lord.

TEXT 25

धरण्युवाच
भवान् हि वेद तत्सर्वं यन्मां धर्मानुपृच्छसि ।
चतुर्भिर्वर्तसे येनपादैर्लोकसुखावहैः ॥२५॥

dharaṇy uvāca
bhavān hi veda tat sarvaṁ
yan māṁ dharmānupṛcchasi
caturbhir vartase yena
pādair loka-sukhāvahaiḥ

dharaṇī uvāca—mother earth replied; *bhavān*—your good self; *hi*—certainly; *veda*—know; *tat sarvam*—all that you have inquired from me; *yat*—that; *mām*—from me; *dharma*—O personality of religious principles; *anupṛcchasi*—you have inquired one after another; *caturbhiḥ*—by four; *vartase*—you exist; *yena*—by which; *pādaiḥ*—by the legs; *loka*—in each and every planet; *sukha-āvahaiḥ*—increasing the happiness.

TRANSLATION

The earthly deity [in the form of a cow] thus replied to the personality of religious principles [in the form of a bull]: O Dharma, whatever you have inquired from me shall be known to you. I shall try to reply to all those questions. Once you too were maintained by your four legs, and you increased happiness all over the universe by the mercy of the Lord.

PURPORT

The principles of religion are laid down by the Lord Himself, and the executor of such laws is Dharmarāja, or Yamarāja. Such principles work fully in the age of Satya-yuga; in the Tretā-yuga they are reduced by a fraction of one fourth; in the Dvāpara-yuga they are reduced to one half, and in the Kali-yuga they are reduced to one fourth, gradually diminishing to the zero point, and then devastation takes place. Happiness in the world depends proportionately on the maintenance of the religious principles, individually or collectively. The best part of valor is to maintain the principles despite all kinds of odds. Thus one can be happy during the span of life and ultimately return to Godhead.

TEXTS 26–30

सत्यं शौचं दया क्षान्तिस्त्यागः सन्तोष आर्जवम् ।
शमो दमस्तपः साम्यं तितिक्षोपरतिः श्रुतम् ॥२६॥
ज्ञानं विरक्तिरैश्वर्यं शौर्यं तेजो बलं स्मृतिः ।
स्वातन्त्र्यं कौशलं कान्तिर्धैर्यं मार्दवमेव च ॥२७॥
प्रागल्भ्यं प्रश्रयः शीलं सह ओजो बलं भगः ।
गाम्भीर्यं स्थैर्यमास्तिक्यं कीर्तिर्मानोऽनहङ्कृतिः ॥२८॥
एते चान्ये च भगवन्नित्या यत्र महागुणाः ।
प्रार्थ्या महत्त्वमिच्छद्भिर्न वियन्ति स्म कर्हिचित् ॥२९॥
तेनाहं गुणपात्रेण श्रीनिवासेन साम्प्रतम् ।
शोचामि रहितं लोकं पाप्मना कलिनेक्षितम् ॥३०॥

satyaṁ śaucaṁ dayā kṣāntis
tyāgaḥ santoṣa ārjavam
śamo damas tapaḥ sāmyaṁ
titikṣoparatiḥ śrutam

jñānaṁ viraktir aiśvaryaṁ
śauryaṁ tejo balaṁ smṛtiḥ
svātantryaṁ kauśalaṁ kāntir
dhairyaṁ mārdavam eva ca

prāgalbhyaṁ praśrayaḥ śīlaṁ
saha ojo balaṁ bhagaḥ
gāmbhīryaṁ sthairyam āstikyaṁ
kīrtir māno 'nahaṅkṛtiḥ

ete cānye ca bhagavan
nityā yatra mahā-guṇāḥ
prārthyā mahattvam icchadbhir
na viyanti sma karhicit

tenāhaṁ guṇa-pātreṇa
śrī-nivāsena sāmpratam
śocāmi rahitaṁ lokaṁ
pāpmanā kalinekṣitam

satyam—truthfulness; *śaucam*—cleanliness; *dayā*—intolerance of others' unhappiness; *kṣāntiḥ*—self-control even if there is cause of anger; *tyāgaḥ*—magnanimity; *santoṣaḥ*—self-satisfaction; *ārjavam*—straightforwardness; *śamaḥ*—fixing of the mind; *damaḥ*—control of the sense organs; *tapaḥ*—trueness to one's responsibility; *sāmyam*—indiscrimination between friend and foe; *titikṣā*—tolerance of the offenses of others; *uparatiḥ*—indifference to loss and gain; *śrutam*—following scriptural injunctions; *jñānam*—knowledge (self-realization); *viraktiḥ*—detachment from sense enjoyment; *aiśvaryam*—leadership; *śauryam*—chivalry; *tejaḥ*—influence; *balam*—to render possible that which is impossible; *smṛtiḥ*—to find one's proper duty; *svātantryam*—not to depend on others; *kauśalam*—dexterity in all activities; *kāntiḥ*—beauty; *dhairyam*—freedom from disturbance; *mārdavam*—kindheartedness; *eva*—thus; *ca*—also; *prāgalbhyam*—ingenuity; *praśrayaḥ*—gentility; *śīlam*—mannerliness; *sahaḥ*—determination; *ojaḥ*—perfect knowledge; *balam*—proper execution; *bhagaḥ*—object of enjoyment; *gāmbhīryam*—joyfulness; *sthairyam*—immovability; *āstikyam*—faithfulness; *kīrtiḥ*—fame; *mānaḥ*—worthy of being worshiped; *anahaṅkṛtiḥ*—pridelessness; *ete*—all these; *ca anye*—also many others; *ca*—and; *bhagavan*—the Personality of Godhead; *nityāḥ*—

everlasting; *yatra*—where; *mahā-guṇāḥ*—great qualities; *prārthyāḥ*—worthy to possess; *mahattvam*—greatness; *icchadbhiḥ*—those who desire so; *na*—never; *viyanti*—deteriorates; *sma*—ever; *karhicit*—at any time; *tena*—by Him; *aham*—myself; *guṇa-pātreṇa*—the reservoir of all qualities; *śrī*—the goddess of fortune; *nivāsena*—by the resting place; *sāmpratam*—very recently; *śocāmi*—I am thinking of; *rahitam*—bereft of; *lokam*—planets; *pāpmanā*—by the store of all sins; *kalinā*—by Kali; *īkṣitam*—is seen.

TRANSLATION

In Him reside (1) truthfulness, (2) cleanliness, (3) intolerance of another's unhappiness, (4) the power to control anger, (5) self-satisfaction, (6) straightforwardness, (7) steadiness of mind, (8) control of the sense organs, (9) responsibility, (10) equality, (11) tolerance, (12) equanimity, (13) faithfulness, (14) knowledge, (15) absence of sense enjoyment, (16) leadership, (17) chivalry, (18) influence, (19) the power to make everything possible, (20) the discharge of proper duty, (21) complete independence, (22) dexterity, (23) fullness of all beauty, (24) serenity, (25) kindheartedness, (26) ingenuity, (27) gentility, (28) magnanimity, (29) determination, (30) perfection in all knowledge, (31) proper execution, (32) possession of all objects of enjoyment, (33) joyfulness, (34) immovability, (35) fidelity, (36) fame, (37) worship, (38) pridelessness, (39) being (as the Personality of Godhead), (40) eternity, and many other transcendental qualities which are eternally present and never to be separated from Him. That Personality of Godhead, the reservoir of all goodness and beauty, Lord Śrī Kṛṣṇa, has now closed His transcendental pastimes on the face of the earth. In His absence the age of Kali has spread its influence everywhere, so I am sorry to see this condition of existence.

PURPORT

Even if it were possible to count the atoms after smashing the earth into powder, still it would not be possible to estimate the unfathomable transcendental qualities of the Lord. It is said that Lord Anantadeva has tried to expound the transcendental qualities of the Supreme Lord with His numberless tongues, and that for numberless years together it has been impossible to estimate the qualities of the Lord. The above statement of the qualities of the Lord is just to estimate His qualities as far as a human being is able to see Him. But even if it is so, the above qualities can be divided into many subheadings. According to Śrīla Jīva Gosvāmī, the third quality, intolerance of another's unhappiness, can be subdivided into (1) protection of the surrendered souls and (2) well wishes for the devotees. In the *Bhagavad-gītā* the Lord states that He wants every soul to surrender unto Him only, and He assures everyone that if one does so He will give protection from the reactions of all sins. Unsurrendered souls are not devotees of the Lord, and thus there is no particular protection for everyone in general. For the devotees He has all good wishes, and for those who are actually engaged in loving transcendental service of the Lord, He gives particular attention. He gives direction to such pure devotees to help them discharge their responsibilities on the path back to Godhead. By equality (10), the Lord is equally kind to everyone, as the sun is equal in distributing its rays over everyone. Yet there are many who are unable to take advantage of the sun's rays. Similarly, the Lord says that surrendering unto Him is the guarantee for all protection from Him, but unfortunate persons are unable to accept this proposition, and therefore they suffer from all material miseries. So even though the Lord is equally well-wishing to everyone, the unfortunate living being, due to bad association only, is unable to accept His instructions *in toto,* and for this the Lord is never to be blamed. He is called the well-wisher for the devotees only. He appears to be partial to His devotees, but factually the matter rests on the living being to accept or reject equal treatment by the Lord.

The Lord never deviates from His word of honor. When He gives assurance for protection, the promise is executed in all circumstances. It is the duty of the pure devotee to be fixed in the discharge of the duty entrusted to him by the Lord or the Lord's bona fide representative, the spiritual master. The rest is carried on by the Lord without a break.

The responsibility of the Lord is also unique. The Lord has no responsibility because all His work is done by His different appointed energies. But still He accepts voluntary responsibilities in displaying different roles in His transcendental pastimes. As a boy, He was playing the part of a cowboy. As the son of Nanda Mahārāja, He discharged responsibility perfectly. Similarly, when He was playing the part of a *kṣatriya* as the son of Mahārāja Vasudeva, He displayed all the skill of a martially spirited *kṣatriya.* In almost all cases, the *kṣatriya* king has to secure a wife by fighting or kidnapping. This sort of behavior for a *kṣatriya* is praiseworthy in the sense that a *kṣatriya* must show his power of chivalry to his would-be wife so that the daughter of a *kṣatriya* can see the valor of her would-be husband. Even the Personality of Godhead

Śrī Rāma displayed such a spirit of chivalry during His marriage. He broke the strongest bow, called Haradhanur, and achieved the hand of Sītādevī, the mother of all opulence. The *kṣatriya* spirit is displayed during marriage festivals, and there is nothing wrong in such fighting. Lord Śrī Kṛṣṇa discharged such responsibility fully because although He had more than sixteen thousand wives, in each and every case He fought like a chivalrous *kṣatriya* and thus secured a wife. To fight sixteen thousand times to secure sixteen thousand wives is certainly possible only for the Supreme Personality of Godhead. Similarly, He displayed full responsibility in every action of His different transcendental pastimes.

The fourteenth quality, knowledge, can be further extended into five subheadings, namely (1) intelligence, (2) gratefulness, (3) power of understanding the circumstantial environments of place, object and time, (4) perfect knowledge of everything, and (5) knowledge of the self. Only fools are ungrateful to their benefactors. The Lord, however, does not require benefit from anyone besides Himself because He is full in Himself; still He feels benefited by the unalloyed services of His devotees. The Lord feels grateful to His devotees for such unsophisticated, unconditional service and tries to reciprocate it by rendering service, although the devotee also has no such desire in his heart. The transcendental service of the Lord is itself a transcendental benefit for the devotee, and therefore the devotee has nothing to expect from the Lord. On the assertion of the Vedic aphorism *sarvaṁ khalv idaṁ brahma,* we can understand that the Lord, by the omnipresent rays of His effulgence, called *brahmajyoti,* is all-pervading inside or outside of everything, like the omnipresent material sky, and thus He is also omniscient.

As far as the beauty of the Lord is concerned, He has some special features that distinguish Him from all other living beings, and over and above that He has some special attractive beautiful features by which He attracts the mind of even Rādhārāṇī, the supermost beautiful creation of the Lord. He is known, therefore, as Madana-mohana, or one who attracts the mind of even Cupid. Śrīla Jīva Gosvāmī Prabhu has scrutinizingly analyzed other transcendental qualities of the Lord and affirms that Lord Śrī Kṛṣṇa is the Absolute Supreme Personality of Godhead (Parabrahman). He is omnipotent by His inconceivable energies, and therefore He is the Yogeśvara, or the supreme master of all mystic powers. Being the Yogeśvara, His eternal form is spiritual, a combination of eternity, bliss and knowledge. The nondevotee class cannot understand the dynamic nature of His knowledge because they are satisfied to reach up to His eternal form of knowledge. All great souls aspire to be equal in knowledge with Him. This means that all other knowledge is ever insufficient, flexible and measurable, whereas the knowledge of the Lord is ever fixed and unfathomable. Śrīla Sūta Gosvāmī affirms in the *Bhāgavatam* that although He was observed by the citizens of Dvārakā every day, they were ever increasingly anxious to see Him again and again. The living beings can appreciate the qualities of the Lord as the ultimate goal, but they cannot attain the status quo of such equality. This material world is a product of the *mahat-tattva,* which is a state of the Lord's dreaming condition in His *yoga-nidrā* mystic slumber in the Causal Ocean, and yet the whole creation appears to be a factual presentation of His creation. This means that the Lord's dreaming conditions are also factual manifestations. He can therefore bring everything under His transcendental control, and thus whenever and wherever He does appear, He does so in His fullness.

The Lord, being all that is described above, maintains the affairs of the creation, and by His so doing He gives salvation even to His enemies who are killed by Him. He is attractive even to the topmost liberated soul, and thus He is worshipable even by Brahmā and Śiva, the greatest of all demigods. Even in His incarnation of *puruṣa-avatāra* He is the Lord of the creative energy. The creative material energy is working under His direction, as confirmed in the *Bhagavad-gītā* (9.10). He is the control switch of the material energy, and to control the material energy in the innumerable universes, He is the root cause of innumerable incarnations in all the universes. There are more than five hundred thousand incarnations of Manu in only one universe, besides other incarnations in different universes. In the spiritual world, however, beyond the *mahat-tattva,* there is no question of incarnations, but there are plenary expansions of the Lord in different Vaikuṇṭhas. The planets in the spiritual sky are at least three times the number of those within the innumerable universes in the *mahat-tattva.* And all the Nārāyaṇa forms of the Lord are but expansions of His Vāsudeva feature, and thus He is Vāsudeva, Nārāyaṇa and Kṛṣṇa simultaneously. He is *śrī-kṛṣṇa govinda hare murāre he nātha nārāyaṇa vāsudeva,* all in one. His qualities, therefore, cannot be counted by anyone, however great one may be.

TEXT 31

आत्मानं चानुशोचामि भवन्तं चामरोत्तमम् ।
देवान् पितॄनृषीन् साधून् सर्वान् वर्णांस्तथाश्रमान् ॥३१॥

ātmānaṁ cānuśocāmi
bhavantaṁ cāmarottamam

devān pitṝn ṛṣīn sādhūn
sarvān varṇāṁs tathāśramān

ātmānam—myself; *ca*—also; *anuśocāmi*—lamenting; *bhavantam*—yourself; *ca*—as well as; *amara-uttamam*—the best amongst the demigods; *devān*—about the demigods; *pitṝn*—about the denizens of the Pitṛloka planet; *ṛṣīn*—about the sages; *sādhūn*—about the devotees; *sarvān*—all of them; *varṇān*—sections; *tathā*—as also; *āśramān*—orders of human society.

TRANSLATION

I am thinking about myself and also, O best amongst the demigods, about you, as well as about all the demigods, sages, denizens of Pitṛloka, devotees of the Lord and all men obedient to the system of varṇa and āśrama in human society.

PURPORT

To effect the perfection of human life there is cooperation between men and demigods, sages, denizens of the Pitṛloka, devotees of the Lord and the scientific system of *varṇa* and *āśrama* orders of life. The distinction between human life and animal life therefore begins with the scientific system of *varṇa* and *āśrama,* guided by the experience of the sages in relation with the demigods, gradually rising to the summit of reestablishing our eternal relation with the Supreme Absolute Truth, the Personality of Godhead, Lord Śrī Kṛṣṇa. When God-made *varṇāśrama-dharma,* which is strictly meant for developing animal consciousness into human consciousness and human consciousness into godly consciousness, is broken by advancement of foolishness, the whole system of peaceful and progressive life is at once disturbed. In the age of Kali, the first attack of the venomous snake strikes against the God-made *varṇāśrama-dharma,* and thus a person properly qualified as a *brāhmaṇa* is called a *śūdra,* and a *śūdra* by qualification is passing as a *brāhmaṇa,* all on a false birthright claim. To become a *brāhmaṇa* by a birthright claim is not at all bona fide, although it may be a fulfillment of one of the conditions. But the real qualification of a *brāhmaṇa* is to control the mind and the senses, and to cultivate tolerance, simplicity, cleanliness, knowledge, truthfulness, devotion and faith in the Vedic wisdom. In the present age, consideration of the necessary qualification is being neglected, and the false birthright claim is being supported even by a popular, sophisticated poet, the author of *Rāma-carita-mānasa.*

This is all due to the influence of the age of Kali. Thus mother earth, represented as a cow, was lamenting the regrettable condition.

TEXTS 32–33

ब्रह्मादयो बहुतिथं यदपाङ्गमोक्ष-
कामास्तपः समचरन् भगवत्प्रपन्नाः ।
सा श्रीः स्ववासमरविन्दवनं विहाय
यत्पादसौभगमलं भजतेऽनुरक्ता ॥३२॥
तस्याहमब्जकुलिशाङ्कुशकेतुकेतैः
श्रीमत्पदैर्भगवतः समलङ्कृताङ्गी ।
त्रीनत्यरोच उपलभ्य ततो विभूतिं
लोकान् स मां व्यसृजदुत्स्मयतीं तदन्ते ॥ ३३ ॥

brahmādayo bahu-titham yad-apāṅga-mokṣa-
kāmās tapaḥ samacaran bhagavat-prapannāḥ
sā śrīḥ sva-vāsam aravinda-vanaṁ vihāya
yat-pāda-saubhagam alaṁ bhajate 'nuraktā

tasyāham abja-kuliśāṅkuśa-ketu-ketaiḥ
śrīmat-padair bhagavataḥ samalaṅkṛtāṅgī
trīn atyaroca upalabhya tato vibhūtiṁ
lokān sa māṁ vyasṛjad utsmayatīṁ tad-ante

brahma-ādayaḥ—demigods such as Brahmā; *bahu-titham*—for many days; *yat*—of Lakṣmī, the goddess of fortune; *apāṅga-mokṣa*—glance of grace; *kāmāḥ*—being desirous of; *tapaḥ*—penances; *samacaran*—executing; *bhagavat*—unto the Personality of Godhead; *prapannāḥ*—surrendered; *sā*—she (the goddess of fortune); *śrīḥ*—Lakṣmījī; *sva-vāsam*—her own abode; *aravinda-vanam*—the forest of lotus flowers; *vihāya*—leaving aside; *yat*—whose; *pāda*—feet; *saubhagam*—all-blissful; *alam*—without hesitation; *bhajate*—worships; *anuraktā*—being attached; *tasya*—His; *aham*—myself; *abja*—lotus flower; *kuliśa*—thunderbolt; *aṅkuśa*—rod for driving elephants; *ketu*—flag; *ketaiḥ*—impressions; *śrīmat*—the owner of all opulence; *padaiḥ* —by the soles of the feet; *bhagavataḥ*—of the Personality of Godhead; *samalaṅkṛta-aṅgī*—one whose body is so decorated; *trīn*—three; *ati*—superseding; *aroce*—beautifully decorated; *upalabhya*—having obtained; *tataḥ*—thereafter; *vibhūtim*—specific powers; *lokān*—planetary systems;

saḥ—He; *mām*—me; *vyasṛjat*—gave up; *utsmayatīm*—while feeling proud; *tat-ante*—at the end.

TRANSLATION

Lakṣmījī, the goddess of fortune, whose glance of grace was sought by demigods like Brahmā and for whom they surrendered many a day unto the Personality of Godhead, gave up her own abode in the forest of lotus flowers and engaged herself in the service of the lotus feet of the Lord. I was endowed with specific powers to supersede the fortune of all the three planetary systems by being decorated with the impressions of the flag, thunderbolt, elephant-driving rod and lotus flower, which are signs of the lotus feet of the Lord. But at the end, when I felt I was so fortunate, the Lord left me.

PURPORT

The beauty and opulence of the world can be enhanced by the grace of the Lord and not by any man-made planning. When the Lord Śrī Kṛṣṇa was present on this earth, the impressions of the special signs of His lotus feet were stamped on the dust, and as a result of this specific grace, the whole earth was made as perfect as possible. In other words, the rivers, the seas, the forests, the hills and the mines, which are the supplying agents for the necessities of men and animals, were fully discharging their respective duties. Therefore the riches of the world surpassed all the riches of all other planets in the three planetary systems of the universe. One should, therefore, ask that the grace of the Lord always be present on earth so that we may be favored with His causeless mercy and be happy, having all necessities of life. One may ask how we can detain the Supreme Lord on this earth after His mission is fulfilled and He has left this earth for His own abode. The answer is that there is no need to detain the Lord. The Lord, being omnipresent, can be present with us if we want Him at all. By His omnipresence, He can always be with us if we are attached to His devotional service by hearing, chanting, remembering, etc.

There is nothing in the world with which the Lord is disconnected. The only thing we must learn is to excavate the source of connection and thus be linked with Him by offenseless service. We can be connected with Him by the transcendental sound representation of the Lord. The holy name of the Lord and the Lord Himself are identical, and one who chants the holy name of the Lord in an offenseless manner can at once realize that the Lord is present before him. Even by the vibration of radio sound, we can partially realize sound relativity, and by resounding the sound of transcendence we can verily feel the presence of the Lord. In this age, when everything is polluted by the contamination of Kali, it is instructed in the scriptures and preached by Lord Śrī Caitanya Mahāprabhu that by chanting the holy name of the Lord, we can at once be free from contamination and gradually rise to the status of transcendence and go back to Godhead. The offenseless chanter of the holy name of the Lord is as auspicious as the Lord Himself, and the movement of pure devotees of the Lord all over the world can at once change the troublesome face of the world. Only by the propagation of the chanting of the holy name of the Lord can we be immune from all effects of the age of Kali.

TEXT 34

योवै ममातिभरमासुरवंशराज्ञा-
मक्षौहिणीशतमपानुददात्मतन्त्रः ।
त्वां दुःस्थमूनपदमात्मनि पौरुषेण
सम्पादयन् यदुषु रम्यमबिभ्रदङ्गम् ॥३४॥

yo vai mamātibharam āsura-vaṁśa-rājñām
akṣauhiṇī-śatam apānudad ātma-tantraḥ
tvāṁ duḥstham ūna-padam ātmani pauruṣeṇa
sampādayan yaduṣu ramyam abibhrad aṅgam

yaḥ—He who; *vai*—certainly; *mama*—mine; *ati-bharam*—too burdensome; *āsura-vaṁśa*—unbelievers; *rājñām*—of the kings; *akṣauhiṇī*—one military division;* *śatam*—hundreds of such divisions; *apānudat*—extirpated; *ātma-tantraḥ*—self-sufficient; *tvām*—unto you; *duḥstham*—put into difficulty; *ūna-padam*—devoid of strength to stand; *ātmani*—internal; *pauruṣeṇa*—by dint of energy; *sampādayan*—for executing; *yaduṣu*—in the Yadu dynasty; *ramyam*—transcendentally beautiful; *abibhrat*—accepted; *aṅgam*—body.

TRANSLATION

O personality of religion, I was greatly overburdened by the undue military phalanxes arranged by atheistic kings, and I was relieved by the grace of the Personality of Godhead. Similarly you were also in a distressed condition, weakened in your standing strength, and thus

*An *akṣauhiṇī* phalanx consists of 21,870 chariots, 21,870 elephants, 109,350 infantry-men and 65,610 horses.

He also incarnated by His internal energy in the family of the Yadus to relieve you.

PURPORT

The *asuras* want to enjoy a life of sense gratification, even at the cost of others' happiness. In order to fulfill this ambition, the *asuras,* especially atheistic kings or state executive heads, try to equip themselves with all kinds of deadly weapons to bring about a war in a peaceful society. They have no ambition other than personal aggrandizement, and thus mother earth feels overburdened by such undue increases of military strength. By increase of the asuric population, those who follow the principles of religion become unhappy, especially the devotees, or *devas.*

In such a situation, the Personality of Godhead incarnates to vanquish the unwanted *asuras* and to reestablish the true principles of religion. This was the mission of Lord Śrī Kṛṣṇa, and He fulfilled it.

TEXT 35

का वा सहेत विरहं पुरुषोत्तमस्य
प्रेमावलोकरुचिरस्मितवल्गुजल्पैः ।
स्थैर्यं समानमहरन्मधुमानिनीनां
रोमोत्सवो मम यदङ्घ्रिविटङ्किताया: ॥ ३५ ॥

kā vā saheta virahaṁ puruṣottamasya
premāvaloka-rucira-smita-valgu-jalpaiḥ
sthairyaṁ samānam aharan madhu-mānininīnāṁ
romotsavo mama yad-aṅghri-viṭaṅkitāyāḥ

kā—who; *vā*—either; *saheta*—can tolerate; *viraham*—separation; *puruṣa-uttamasya*—of the Supreme Personality of Godhead; *prema*—loving; *avaloka*—glancing; *rucira-smita*—pleasing smile; *valgu-jalpaiḥ*—hearty appeals; *sthairyam*—gravity; *sa-mānam*—along with passionate wrath; *aharat*—conquered; *madhu*—sweethearts; *māninīnām*—women such as Satyabhāmā; *roma-utsavaḥ*—hair standing on end out of pleasure; *mama*—mine; *yat*—whose; *aṅghri*—feet; *viṭaṅkitāyāḥ*—imprinted with.

TRANSLATION

Who, therefore, can tolerate the pangs of separation from that Supreme Personality of Godhead? He could conquer the gravity and passionate

wrath of His sweethearts like Satyabhāmā by His sweet smile of love, pleasing glance and hearty appeals. When He traversed my [earth's] surface, I would be immersed in the dust of His lotus feet and thus would be sumptuously covered with grass which appeared like hairs standing on me out of pleasure.

PURPORT

There were chances of separation between the Lord and His thousands of queens because of the Lord's being absent from home, but as far as His connection with earth was concerned, the Lord would traverse the earth with His lotus feet, and therefore there was no chance of separation. When the Lord left the surface of the earth to return to His spiritual abode, the earth's feelings of separation were therefore more acute.

TEXT 36

तयोरेवं कथयतोः पृथिवीधर्मयोस्तदा ।
परीक्षिन्नाम राजर्षिः प्राप्तः प्राचीं सरस्वतीम् ॥३६॥

tayor evaṁ kathayatoḥ
pṛthivī-dharmayos tadā
parīkṣin nāma rājarṣiḥ
prāptaḥ prācīṁ sarasvatīm

tayoḥ—between them; *evam*—thus; *kathayatoḥ*—engaged in conversation; *pṛthivī*—earth; *dharmayoḥ*—and the personality of religion; *tadā*—at that time; *parīkṣit*—King Parīkṣit; *nāma*—of the name; *rāja-ṛṣiḥ*—a saint amongst kings; *prāptaḥ*—arrived; *prācīm*—flowing towards the east; *sarasvatīm*—river Sarasvatī.

TRANSLATION

While the earth and the personality of religion were thus engaged in conversation, the saintly King Parīkṣit reached the shore of the Sarasvatī River, which flowed towards the east.

Thus end the Bhaktivedanta purports of the First Canto, Sixteenth Chapter, of the Śrīmad-Bhāgavatam, *entitled "How Parīkṣit Received the Age of Kali."*

CHAPTER SEVENTEEN

Punishment and Reward of Kali

TEXT 1

सूत उवाच
तत्र गोमिथुनं राजा हन्यमानमनाथवत् ।
दण्डहस्तं च वृषलं ददृशे नृपलाञ्छनम् ॥१॥

sūta uvāca
tatra go-mithunaṁ rājā
hanyamānam anāthavat
daṇḍa-hastaṁ ca vṛṣalaṁ
dadṛśe nṛpa-lāñchanam

sūtaḥ uvāca—Śrī Sūta Gosvāmī said; *tatra*—thereupon; *go-mithunam*—a cow and a bull; *rājā*—the King; *hanyamānam*—being beaten; *anātha-vat*—appearing to be bereft of their owner; *daṇḍa-hastam*—with a club in hand; *ca*—also; *vṛṣalam*—lower-caste *śūdra; dadṛśe*—observed; *nṛpa*—a king; *lāñchanam*—dressed like.

TRANSLATION

Sūta Gosvāmī said: After reaching that place, Mahārāja Parīkṣit observed that a lower-caste śūdra, dressed like a king, was beating a cow and a bull with a club, as if they had no owner.

PURPORT

The principal sign of the age of Kali is that lower-caste *śūdras,* i.e., men without brahminical culture and spiritual initiation, will be dressed like administrators or kings, and the principal business of such non-*kṣatriya* rulers will be to kill the innocent animals, especially the cows and the bulls, who shall be unprotected by their masters, the bona fide *vaiśyas,* the mercantile community. In the *Bhagavad-gītā* (18.44) it is said that the *vaiśyas* are meant to deal in agriculture, cow protection and trade. In the age of Kali, the degraded *vaiśyas,* the mercantile men, are engaged in supplying cows to slaughterhouses. The *kṣatriyas* are meant to protect the citizens of the state, whereas the *vaiśyas* are meant to protect the cows and bulls and utilize them to produce grains and milk. The cow is meant to deliver milk, and the bull is meant to produce grains. But in the age of Kali, the *śūdra* class of men are in the posts of administrators, and the cows and bulls, or the mothers and the fathers, unprotected by the *vaiśyas,* are subjected to the slaughterhouses organized by the *śūdra* administrators.

TEXT 2

वृषं मृणालधवलं मेहन्तमिव बिभ्यतम् ।
वेपमानं पदैकेन सीदन्तं शूद्रताडितम् ॥२॥

vṛṣaṁ mṛṇāla-dhavalaṁ
mehantam iva bibhyatam
vepamānaṁ padaikena
sīdantaṁ śūdra-tāḍitam

vṛṣam—the bull; *mṛṇāla-dhavalam*—as white as a white lotus; *mehantam*—urinating; *iva*—as if; *bibhyatam*—being too afraid; *vepamānam*—trembling; *padā ekena*—standing on only one leg; *sīdantam*—terrified; *śūdra-tāḍitam*—being beaten by a *śūdra.*

TRANSLATION

The bull was as white as a white lotus flower. He was terrified of the śūdra who was beating him, and he was so afraid that he was standing on one leg, trembling and urinating.

PURPORT

The next symptom of the age of Kali is that principles of religion, which are all spotlessly white, like the white lotus flower, will be attacked by the uncultured *śūdra* population of the age. They may be descendants of *brāhmaṇa* or *kṣatriya* forefathers, but in the age of Kali, for want of sufficient education and culture of Vedic wisdom, such a *śūdra*-like population will defy the principles of religion, and persons who are religiously endowed will be terrified by such men. They will declare themselves as adherents of no religious principles, and many "isms" and cults will spring up in Kali-yuga only to kill the spotless bull of religion. The state will be declared to be secular, or without any particular principle of religion, and as a result there will be total indifference to the principles of religion. The citizens will be free to act as they like, without respect for *sādhu, śāstra* and *guru.* The bull standing on one leg indicates that the principles of religion are gradually diminishing. Even the fragmental existence of religious principles will be embarrassed by so many obstacles as if in the trembling condition of falling down at any time.

TEXT 3

गां च धर्मदुघां दीनां भृशं शूद्रपदाहताम् ।
विवत्सामाश्रुवदनां क्षामां यवसमिच्छतीम् ॥३॥

gāṁ ca dharma-dughāṁ dīnāṁ
bhṛśaṁ śūdra-padāhatām
vivatsām āśru-vadanāṁ
kṣāmāṁ yavasam icchatīm

gām—the cow; *ca*—also; *dharma-dughām*—beneficial because one can draw religion from her; *dīnām*—now rendered poor; *bhṛśam*—distressed; *śūdra*—the lower caste; *pada-āhatām*—beaten on the legs; *vivatsām*—without any calf; *āśru-vadanām*—with tears in her eyes; *kṣāmām*—very weak; *yavasam*—grass; *icchatīm*—as if desiring to have some grass to eat.

TRANSLATION

Although the cow is beneficial because one can draw religious principles from her, she was now rendered poor and calfless. Her legs were being beaten by a śūdra. There were tears in her eyes, and she was distressed and weak. She was hankering after some grass in the field.

PURPORT

The next symptom of the age of Kali is the distressed condition of the cow. Milking the cow means drawing the principles of religion in a liquid form. The great *ṛṣis* and *munis* would live only on milk. Śrīla Śukadeva Gosvāmī would go to a householder while he was milking a cow, and he would simply take a little quantity of it for subsistence. Even fifty years ago, no one would deprive a *sadhu* of a quart or two of milk, and every householder would give milk like water. For a Sanātanist (a follower of Vedic principles) it is the duty of every householder to have cows and bulls as household paraphernalia, not only for drinking milk, but also for deriving religious principles. The Sanātanist worships cows on religious principles and respects *brāhmaṇas.* The cow's milk is required for the sacrificial fire, and by performing sacrifices the householder can be happy. The cow's calf not only is beautiful to look at, but also gives satisfaction to the cow, and so she delivers as much milk as possible. But in the Kali-yuga, the calves are separated from the cows as early as possible for purposes which may not be mentioned in these pages of *Śrīmad-Bhāgavatam.* The cow stands with tears in her eyes, the *śūdra* milkman draws milk from the cow artificially, and when there is no milk the cow is sent to be slaughtered. These greatly sinful acts are responsible for all the troubles in present society. People do not know what they are doing in the name of economic development. The influence of Kali will keep them in the darkness of ignorance. Despite all endeavors for peace and prosperity, they must try to see the cows and the bulls happy in all respects. Foolish people do not know how one earns happiness by making the cows and bulls happy, but it is a fact by the law of nature. Let us take it from the authority of *Śrīmad-Bhāgavatam* and adopt the principles for the total happiness of humanity.

TEXT 4

पप्रच्छ रथमारूढः कार्तस्वरपरिच्छदम् ।
मेघगम्भीरया वाचा समारोपितकार्मुकः ॥४॥

papraccha ratham ārūḍhaḥ
kārtasvara-paricchadam
megha-gambhīrayā vācā
samāropita-kārmukaḥ

papraccha—inquired; *ratham*—chariot; *ārūḍhaḥ*—seated on; *kārtasvara*—gold; *paricchadam*—embossed with; *megha*—cloud; *gambhīrayā*—exonerating; *vācā*—sound; *samāropita*—well equipped; *kārmukaḥ*—arrows and bow.

TRANSLATION

Mahārāja Parīkṣit, well equipped with arrows and bow and seated on a gold-embossed chariot, spoke to him [the śūdra] with a deep voice sounding like thunder.

PURPORT

An administrative head or king like Mahārāja Parīkṣit, with full majestic authority, well equipped with weapons to chastise miscreants, can challenge the agents of the age of Kali. Then only will it be possible to counteract the degraded age. And in the absence of such strong executive heads, there is always disruption of tranquillity. The elected show-bottle executive head, as representative of a degraded public, cannot be equal with a strong king like Mahārāja Parīkṣit. The dress or style of royal order does not count. It is one's actions which are counted.

TEXT 5

कस्त्वं मच्छरणे लोके बलाद्धंस्यबलान् बली ।
नरदेवोऽसि वेषेण नटवत्कर्मणाद्विजः ॥५॥

kas tvaṁ mac-charaṇe loke
balād dhaṁsy abalān balī
nara-devo 'si veṣeṇa
naṭavat karmaṇā 'dvijaḥ

kaḥ—who are; *tvam*—you; *mat*—my; *śaraṇe*—under protection; *loke*—in this world; *balāt*—by force; *haṁsi*—killing; *abalān*—those who are helpless; *balī*—although full of strength; *nara-devaḥ*—man-god; *asi*—appear to be; *veṣeṇa*—by your dress; *naṭa-vat*—like a theatrical player; *karmaṇā*—by deeds; *advi-jaḥ*—a man not twice-born by culture.

TRANSLATION

Oh, who are you? You appear to be strong and yet you dare kill, within my protection, those who are helpless! By your dress you pose yourself to be a godly man [king], but by your deeds you are opposing the principles of the twice-born kṣatriyas.

PURPORT

The *brāhmaṇas, kṣatriyas* and *vaiśyas* are called twice-born because for these higher classes of men there is one birth by parental conjugation and there is another birth of cultural rejuvenation by spiritual initiation from the bona fide *ācārya,* or spiritual master. So a *kṣatriya* is also twice-born like a *brāhmaṇa,* and his duty is to give protection to the helpless. The *kṣatriya* king is considered to be the representative of God to give protection to the helpless and chastise the miscreants. Whenever there are anomalies in this routine work by the administrators, there is an incarnation of the Lord to reestablish the principles of a godly kingdom. In the age of Kali, the poor helpless animals, especially the cows, which are meant to receive all sorts of protection from the administrative heads, are killed without restriction. Thus the administrative heads under whose noses such things happen are representatives of God in name only. Such powerful administrators are rulers of the poor citizens by dress or office, but factually they are worthless, lower-class men without the cultural assets of the twice-born. No one can expect justice or equality of treatment from once-born (spiritually uncultured) lower-class men. Therefore in the age of Kali everyone is unhappy due to the maladministration of the state. The modern human society is not twice-born by spiritual culture. Therefore the people's government, by the people who are not twice-born, must be a government of Kali in which everyone is unhappy.

TEXT 6

यस्त्वं कृष्णे गते दूरं सहगाण्डीवधन्वना ।
शोच्योऽस्यशोच्यान् रहसि प्रहरन् वधमर्हसि ॥६॥

yas tvaṁ kṛṣṇe gate dūraṁ
saha-gāṇḍīva-dhanvanā
śocyo 'sy aśocyān rahasi
praharan vadham arhasi

yaḥ—on account of; *tvam*—you rogue; *kṛṣṇe*—Lord Kṛṣṇa; *gate*—having gone away; *dūram*—out of sight; *saha*—along with; *gāṇḍīva*—the bow named Gāṇḍīva; *dhanvanā*—the carrier, Arjuna; *śocyaḥ*—culprit; *asi*—you are considered; *aśocyān*—innocent; *rahasi*—in a secluded place; *praharan*—beating; *vadham*—to be killed; *arhasi*—deserve.

TRANSLATION

You rogue, do you dare beat an innocent cow because Lord Kṛṣṇa and Arjuna, the carrier of the Gāṇḍīva bow, are out of sight? Since you are beating the innocent in a secluded place, you are considered a culprit and therefore deserve to be killed.

PURPORT

In a civilization where God is conspicuously banished, and there is no devotee warrior like Arjuna, the associates of the age of Kali take advantage of this lawless kingdom and arrange to kill innocent animals like the cow in secluded slaughterhouses. Such murderers of animals stand to be condemned to death by the order of a pious king like Mahārāja Parīkṣit. For a pious king, the culprit who kills an animal in a secluded place is punishable by the death penalty, exactly like a murderer who kills an innocent child in a secluded place.

TEXT 7

त्वं वा मृणालधवलः पादैर्न्यूनः पदा चरन् ।
वृषरूपेण किं कश्चिद् देवो नः परिखेदयन् ॥७॥

tvaṁ vā mṛṇāla-dhavalaḥ
pādair nyūnaḥ padā caran
vṛṣa-rūpeṇa kiṁ kaścid
devo naḥ parikhedayan

tvam—you; *vā*—either; *mṛṇāla-dhavalaḥ*—as white as a lotus; *pādaiḥ*—of three legs; *nyūnaḥ*—being deprived; *padā*—on one leg; *caran*—moving; *vṛṣa*—bull; *rūpeṇa*—in the form of; *kim*—whether; *kaścit*—someone; *devaḥ*—demigod; *naḥ*—us; *parikhedayan*—causing grief.

TRANSLATION

Then he [Mahārāja Parīkṣit] asked the bull: Oh, who are you? Are you a bull as white as a white lotus, or are you a demigod? You have lost three of your legs and are moving on only one. Are you some demigod causing us grief in the form of a bull?

PURPORT

At least up to the time of Mahārāja Parīkṣit, no one could imagine the wretched conditions of the cow and the bull. Mahārāja Parīkṣit, therefore, was astonished to see such a horrible scene. He inquired whether the bull was not a demigod assuming such a wretched condition to indicate the future of the cow and the bull.

TEXT 8

न जातु कौरवेन्द्राणां दोर्दण्डपरिरम्भिते ।
भूतलेऽनुपतन्त्यस्मिन् विना ते प्राणिनां शुचः ॥८॥

na jātu kauravendrāṇāṁ
dordaṇḍa-parirambhite

bhū-tale 'nupatanty asmin
vinā te prāṇināṁ śucaḥ

na—not; *jātu*—at any time; *kaurava-indrāṇām*—of the kings in the Kuru dynasty; *dordaṇḍa*—strength of arms; *parirambhite*—protected by; *bhū-tale*—on the surface of the earth; *anupatanti*—grieving; *asmin*—up till now; *vinā*—save and except; *te*—you; *prāṇinām*—of the living being; *śucaḥ*—tears in the eyes.

TRANSLATION

Now for the first time in a kingdom well protected by the arms of the kings of the Kuru dynasty, I see you grieving with tears in your eyes. Up till now no one on earth has ever shed tears because of royal negligence.

PURPORT

The protection of the lives of both the human beings and the animals is the first and foremost duty of a government. A government must not discriminate in such principles. It is simply horrible for a purehearted soul to see organized animal killing by the state in this age of Kali. Mahārāja Parīkṣit was lamenting for the tears in the eyes of the bull, and he was astonished to see such an unprecedented thing in his good kingdom. Men and animals were equally protected as far as life was concerned. That is the way in God's kingdom.

TEXT 9

मा सौरभेयात्र शुचो व्येतु ते वृषलाद् भयम् ।
मा रोदीरम्ब भद्रं ते खलानां मयि शास्तरि ॥९॥

mā saurabheyātra śuco
vyetu te vṛṣalād bhayam
mā rodīr amba bhadraṁ te
khalānāṁ mayi śāstari

mā—do not; *saurabheya*—O son of Surabhi; *atra*—in my kingdom; *śucaḥ*—lamentation; *vyetu*—let there be; *te*—your; *vṛṣalāt*—by the *śūdra; bhayam*—cause of fear; *mā*—do not; *rodīḥ*—cry; *amba*—mother cow; *bhadram*—all good; *te*—unto you; *khalānām*—of the envious; *mayi*—while I am living; *śāstari*—the ruler or subduer.

TRANSLATION

O son of Surabhi, you need lament no longer now. There is no need to fear this low-class śūdra. And, O mother cow, as long as I am living as the ruler and subduer of all envious men, there is no cause for you to cry. Everything will be good for you.

PURPORT

Protection of bulls and cows and all other animals can be possible only when there is a state ruled by an executive head like Mahārāja Parīkṣit. Mahārāja Parīkṣit addresses the cow as mother, for he is a cultured, twice-born, *kṣatriya* king. *Surabhi* is the name of the cows which exist in the spiritual planets and are especially reared by Lord Śrī Kṛṣṇa Himself. As men are made after the form and features of the Supreme Lord, so also the cows are made after the form and features of the *surabhi* cows in the spiritual kingdom. In the material world the human society gives all protection to the human being, but there is no law to protect the descendants of Surabhi, who can give all protection to men by supplying the miracle food, milk. But Mahārāja Parīkṣit and the Pāṇḍavas were fully conscious of the importance of the cow and bull, and they were prepared to punish the cow killer with all chastisement, including death. There has sometimes been agitation for the protection of the cow, but for want of pious executive heads and suitable laws, the cow and the bull are not given protection. The human society should recognize the importance of the cow and the bull and thus give all protection to these important animals, following in the footsteps of Mahārāja Parīkṣit. For protecting the cows and brahminical culture, the Lord, who is very kind to the cow and the *brāhmaṇas* (*go-brāhmaṇa-hitāya*), will be pleased with us and will bestow upon us real peace.

TEXTS 10–11

यस्य राष्ट्रे प्रजाः सर्वास्त्रस्यन्ते साध्व्यसाधुभिः ।
तस्य मत्तस्य नश्यन्ति कीर्तिरायुर्भगो गतिः ॥१०॥
एष राज्ञां परो धर्मो ह्यार्तानामार्तिनिग्रहः ।
अत एनं वधिष्यामि भूतद्रुहमसत्तमम् ॥११॥

yasya rāṣṭre prajāḥ sarvās
trasyante sādhvy asādhubhiḥ
tasya mattasya naśyanti
kīrtir āyur bhago gatiḥ

eṣa rājñāṁ paro dharmo
hy ārtānām ārti-nigrahaḥ
ata enaṁ vadhiṣyāmi
bhūta-druham asattamam

yasya—one whose; *rāṣṭre*—in the state; *prajāḥ*—living beings; *sarvāḥ*—one and all; *trasyante*—are terrified; *sādhvi*—O chaste one; *asādhubhiḥ*—by the miscreants; *tasya*—his; *mattasya*—of the illusioned; *naśyanti*—vanishes; *kīrtiḥ*—fame; *āyuḥ*—duration of life; *bhagaḥ*—fortune; *gatiḥ*—good rebirth; *eṣaḥ*—these are; *rājñām*—of the kings; *paraḥ*—superior; *dharmaḥ*—occupation; *hi*—certainly; *ārtānām*—of the sufferers; *ārti*—sufferings; *nigrahaḥ*—subduing; *ataḥ*—therefore; *enam*—this man; *vadhiṣyāmi*—I shall kill; *bhūta-druham*—revolter against other living beings; *asat-tamam*—the most wretched.

TRANSLATION

O chaste one, the king's good name, duration of life and good rebirth vanish when all kinds of living beings are terrified by miscreants in his kingdom. It is certainly the prime duty of the king to subdue first the sufferings of those who suffer. Therefore I must kill this most wretched man because he is violent against other living beings.

PURPORT

When there is some disturbance caused by wild animals in a village or town, the police or others take action to kill them. Similarly, it is the duty of the government to kill at once all bad social elements such as thieves, dacoits and murderers. The same punishment is also due to animal killers because the animals of the state are also the *prajā. Prajā* means one who has taken birth in the state, and this includes both men and animals. Any living being who takes birth in a state has the primary right to live under the protection of the king. The jungle animals are also subject to the king, and they also have a right to live. So what to speak of domestic animals like the cows and bulls.

Any living being, if he terrifies other living beings, is a most wretched subject, and the king should at once kill such a disturbing element. As the wild animal is killed when it creates disturbances, similarly any man who unnecessarily kills or terrifies the jungle animals or other animals must be punished at once. By the law of the Supreme Lord, all living beings, in whatever shape they may be, are the sons of the Lord, and no one has any right to kill another animal, unless it is so ordered by the codes of natural law. The tiger can kill a lower animal for his subsistence, but a man cannot kill an animal for his subsistence. That is the law of God, who has created the law that a living being subsists by eating another living being. Thus the vegetarians are also living by eating other living beings. Therefore, the law is that one should live only by eating specific living beings, as ordained by the law of God. The *Īśopaniṣad* directs that one should live by the direction of the Lord and not at one's sweet will. A man can subsist on varieties of grains, fruits and milk ordained by God, and there is no need of animal food, save and except in particular cases.

The illusioned king or executive head, even though sometimes advertised as a great philosopher and learned scholar, will allow slaughterhouses in the state without knowing that torturing poor animals clears the way to hell for such foolish kings or executive heads. The executive head must always be alert to the safety of the *prajās,* both man and animal, and inquire whether a particular living being is harassed at any place by another living being. The harassing living being must at once be caught and put to death, as shown by Mahārāja Parīkṣit.

The people's government, or government by the people, should not allow killing of innocent animals by the sweet will of foolish government men. They must know the codes of God, as mentioned in the revealed scriptures. Mahārāja Parīkṣit quotes here that according to the codes of God the irresponsible king or state executive jeopardizes his good name, duration of life, power and strength and ultimately his progressive march towards a better life and salvation after death. Such foolish men do not even believe in the existence of a next life.

While commenting on this particular verse, we have in our presence the statement of a great modern politician who has recently died and left his will, which discloses his poor fund of knowledge of the codes of God mentioned by Mahārāja Parīkṣit. The politician was so ignorant of the codes of God that he writes: "I do not believe in any such ceremonies, and to submit to them, even as a matter of form, would be hypocrisy and an attempt to delude ourselves and others.... I have no religious sentiment in the matter."

Contrasting these statements of a great politician in the modern age with those of Mahārāja Parīkṣit, we find a vast difference. Mahārāja Parīkṣit was pious according to the scriptural codes, whereas the modern politician goes by his personal belief and sentiments. Any great man of the material world is, after all, a conditioned soul. He is bound by his hands and feet by the ropes of material nature, and still the foolish conditioned soul thinks of himself as free to act by his whimsical sentiments. The conclusion is that people in the time of Mahārāja Parīkṣit were happy, and the animals were given proper protection because the executive head was not whimsical or ignorant of God's law. Foolish, faithless creatures try to avoid the existence of the Lord and proclaim themselves secular at the cost of valuable human life. The human life is especially meant for knowing the science of God, but foolish creatures, especially in this age of Kali, instead of knowing God scientifically, make propaganda against religious belief as well as the existence of God, even though they are always bound by the laws of God by the symptoms of birth, death, old age and disease.

TEXT 12

कोऽवृश्चत् तव पादांस्त्रीन् सौरभेय चतुष्पद ।
मा भूवंस्त्वादृशा राष्ट्रे राज्ञां कृष्णानुवर्तिनाम् ॥१२॥

ko 'vṛścat tava pādāṁs trīn
saurabheya catuṣ-pada
mā bhūvaṁs tvādṛśā rāṣṭre
rājñāṁ kṛṣṇānuvartinām

kaḥ—who is he; *avṛścat*—cut off; *tava*—your; *pādān*—legs; *trīn*—three; *saurabheya*—O son of Surabhi; *catuḥ-pada*—you are four-legged; *mā*—never to be; *bhūvan*—it so happened; *tvādṛśāḥ*—as yourself; *rāṣṭre*—in the state; *rājñām*—of the kings; *kṛṣṇa-anuvartinām*—those who follow the codes of Kṛṣṇa, the Supreme Personality of Godhead.

TRANSLATION

He [Mahārāja Parīkṣit] repeatedly addressed and questioned the bull thus: O son of Surabhi, who has cut off your three legs? In the state of the kings who are obedient to the laws of the Supreme Personality of Godhead, Kṛṣṇa, there is no one as unhappy as you.

PURPORT

The kings or the executive heads of all states must know the codes of Lord Kṛṣṇa (generally *Bhagavad-gītā* and *Śrīmad-Bhāgavatam*) and must act accordingly in order to fulfill the mission of human life, which is to make an end to all miseries of material conditions. One who knows the codes of Lord Kṛṣṇa can achieve this end without any difficulty. In the *Bhagavad-gītā,* in a synopsis, we can understand the codes of Godhead, and in the *Śrīmad-Bhāgavatam* the same codes are explained further.

In a state where the codes of Kṛṣṇa are followed, no one is unhappy. Where such codes are not followed, the first sign is that three legs of the representative of religion are cut off, and thereby all miseries follow. When Kṛṣṇa was personally present, the codes of Kṛṣṇa were being followed without question, but in His absence such codes are presented in the pages of *Śrīmad-Bhāgavatam* for the guidance of the blind persons who happen to be at the helm of all affairs.

TEXT 13

आख्याहि वृष भद्रं वः साधूनामकृतागसाम् ।
आत्मवैरूप्यकर्तारं पार्थानां कीर्तिदूषणम् ॥१३॥

ākhyāhi vṛṣa bhadraṁ vaḥ
sādhūnām akṛtāgasām
ātma-vairūpya-kartāraṁ
pārthānāṁ kīrti-dūṣaṇam

ākhyāhi—just let me know; *vṛṣa*—O bull; *bhadram*—good; *vaḥ*—for you; *sādhūnām*—of the honest; *akṛta-āgasām*—of those who are offenseless; *ātma-vairūpya*—deformation of the self; *kartāram*—the doer; *pārthānām*—of the sons of Pṛthā; *kīrti-dūṣaṇam*—blackmailing the reputation.

TRANSLATION

O bull, you are offenseless and thoroughly honest; therefore I wish all good to you. Please tell me of the perpetrator of these mutilations, which blackmail the reputation of the sons of Pṛthā.

PURPORT

The reputation of the reign of Mahārāja Rāmacandra and that of the kings who followed in the footsteps of Mahārāja Rāmacandra, like the Pāṇḍavas and their descendants, are never to be forgotten because in their kingdom offenseless and honest living beings were never in trouble. The bull and the cow are the symbols of the most offenseless living beings because even the stool and urine of these animals are utilized to benefit human society. The descendants of the sons of Pṛthā, like Mahārāja Parīkṣit, were afraid of losing their reputations, but in the modern days the leaders are not even afraid of killing such offenseless animals. Herein lies the difference between the reign of those pious kings and the modern states ruled by irresponsible executive heads without knowledge of the codes of God.

TEXT 14

जनेऽनागस्यघं युञ्जन् सर्वतोऽस्य च मद्भयम् ।
साधूनां भद्रमेव स्यादसाधुदमने कृते ॥१४॥

jane 'nāgasy aghaṁ yuñjan
sarvato 'sya ca mad-bhayam
sādhūnāṁ bhadram eva syād
asādhu-damane kṛte

jane—to the living beings; *anāgasi*—those who are offenseless; *agham*—sufferings; *yuñjan*—by applying; *sarvataḥ*—anywhere and everywhere; *asya*—of such offenders; *ca*—and; *mat-bhayam*—fear me; *sādhūnām*—of the honest persons; *bhadram*—good fortune; *eva*—certainly; *syāt*—will take place; *asādhu*—dishonest miscreants; *damane*—curbed; *kṛte*—being so done.

TRANSLATION

Whoever causes offenseless living beings to suffer must fear me anywhere and everywhere in the world. By curbing dishonest miscreants, one automatically benefits the offenseless.

PURPORT

Dishonest miscreants flourish because of cowardly and impotent executive heads of state. But when the executive heads are strong enough to curb all sorts of dishonest miscreants, in any part of the state, certainly they cannot flourish. When the miscreants are punished in an exemplary manner, automatically all good fortune follows. As said before, it is the prime duty of the king or the executive head to give protection in all respects to the peaceful, offenseless citizens of the state. The devotees of the Lord are by nature peaceful and offenseless, and therefore it is the prime duty of the state to arrange to convert everyone to become a devotee of the Lord. Thus automatically there will be peaceful, offenseless citizens. Then the only duty of the king will be to curb the dishonest miscreants. That will bring about peace and harmony all over human society.

TEXT 15

अनागःस्विह भूतेषु य आगस्कृन्निरङ्कुशः ।
आहर्तास्मि भुजं साक्षादमर्त्यस्यापि साङ्गदम् ॥१५॥

anāgaḥsv iha bhūteṣu
ya āgas-kṛn niraṅkuśaḥ
āhartāsmi bhujaṁ sākṣād
amartyasyāpi sāṅgadam

anāgaḥsu iha—to the offenseless; *bhūteṣu*—living beings; *yaḥ*—the person; *āgaḥ-kṛt*—commits offense; *niraṅkuśaḥ*—upstart; *āhartā asmi*—I shall bring forth; *bhujam*—arms; *sākṣāt*—directly; *amartyasya api*—even one who is a demigod; *sa-aṅgadam*—with decorations and armor.

TRANSLATION

An upstart living being who commits offenses by torturing those who are offenseless shall be directly uprooted by me, even though he be a denizen of heaven with armor and decorations.

PURPORT

The denizens of the heavenly kingdom are called *amara,* or deathless, due to their possessing a long span of life, far greater than that of the human beings. For a human being, who has only a maximum one-hundred-year duration of life, a span of life spreading over millions of years is certainly considered to be deathless. For example, from the *Bhagavad-gītā* we learn that on the Brahmaloka planet the duration of one day is calculated to be 4,300,000 x 1,000 solar years. Similarly, in other heavenly planets one day is calculated to be six months of this planet, and the inhabitants get a life of ten million of their years. Therefore, in all higher planets, since the span of life is far greater than that of the human being, the denizens are called deathless by imagination, although actually no one within the material universe is deathless.

Mahārāja Parīkṣit challenges even such denizens of heaven if they torture the offenseless. This means that the state executive head must be as strong as Mahārāja Parīkṣit so that he may be determined to punish the strongest offenders. It should be the principle of a state executive head that the offender of the codes of God is always punished.

TEXT 16

राज्ञो हि परमो धर्मः स्वधर्मस्थानुपालनम् ।
शासतोऽन्यान् यथाशास्त्रमनापद्युत्पथानिह ॥१६॥

rājño hi paramo dharmaḥ
sva-dharma-sthānupālanam
śāsato 'nyān yathā-śāstram
anāpady utpathān iha

rājñaḥ—of the king or the executive head; *hi*—certainly; *paramaḥ*—supreme; *dharmaḥ*—occupational duty; *sva-dharma-stha*—one who is faithful to his prescribed duty; *anupālanam*—giving protection always; *śāsataḥ*—while ruling; *anyān*—others; *yathā*—according to; *śāstram*—rulings of scriptures; *anāpadi*—without danger; *utpathān*—persons going astray; *iha*—as a matter of fact.

TRANSLATION

The supreme duty of the ruling king is to give all protection to law-abiding persons and to chastise those who stray from the ordinances of the scriptures in ordinary times, when there is no emergency.

PURPORT

In the scriptures there is mention of *āpad-dharma,* or occupational duty at times of extraordinary happenings. It is said that sometimes the great sage Viśvāmitra had to live on the flesh of dogs in some extraordinary dangerous position. In cases of emergency, one may be allowed to live on the flesh of animals of all description, but that does not mean that there should be regular slaughterhouses to feed the animal-eaters and that this system should be encouraged by the state. No one should try to live on flesh in ordinary times simply for the sake of the palate. If anyone does so, the king or the executive head should punish him for gross enjoyment.

There are regular scriptural injunctions for different persons engaged in different occupational duties, and one who follows them is called *sva-dharma-stha,* or faithful in one's prescribed duties. In the *Bhagavad-gītā* (18.48) it is advised that one should not give up his occupational prescribed duties, even if they are not always flawless. Such *sva-dharma* might be violated in cases of emergency, if one is forced by circumstances, but they cannot be violated in ordinary times. The state executive head is to see that such *sva-dharma* is not changed by the follower, whatever it may be, and he should give all protection to the follower of *sva-dharma.* The violator is subject to punishment in terms of the *śāstra,* and the duty of the king is to see that everyone strictly follows his occupational duty, as prescribed in the scripture.

TEXT 17

धर्म उवाच
एतद् वः पाण्डवेयानां युक्तमार्ताभयं वचः ।
येषां गुणगणैः कृष्णो दौत्यादौ भगवान् कृतः ॥१७॥

dharma uvāca
etad vaḥ pāṇḍaveyānāṁ
yuktam ārtābhayaṁ vacaḥ
yeṣāṁ guṇa-gaṇaiḥ kṛṣṇo
dautyādau bhagavān kṛtaḥ

dharmaḥ uvāca—the personality of religion said; *etat*—all these; *vaḥ*—by you; *pāṇḍaveyānām*—of those who are in the Pāṇḍava dynasty; *yuktam*—just befitting; *ārta*—the sufferer; *abhayam*—freedom from all fears; *vacaḥ*—speeches; *yeṣām*—those; *guṇa-gaṇaiḥ*—by the qualifications; *kṛṣṇaḥ*—even Lord Kṛṣṇa; *dautya-ādau*—the duty of a messenger, etc.; *bhagavān*—the Personality of Godhead; *kṛtaḥ*—performed.

TRANSLATION

The personality of religion said: These words just spoken by you befit a person of the Pāṇḍava dynasty. Captivated by the devotional qualities of the Pāṇḍavas, even Lord Kṛṣṇa, the Personality of Godhead, performed duties as a messenger.

PURPORT

The assurances and challenges made by Mahārāja Parīkṣit are never exaggerations of his real power. The Mahārāja said that even the denizens of heaven could not escape his stringent government if they were violators of religious principles. He was not falsely proud, for a devotee of the Lord is equally as powerful as the Lord or sometimes more powerful by His grace, and any promise made by a devotee, though it may be ordinarily very difficult to fulfill, is properly executed by the grace of the Lord. The Pāṇḍavas, by their unalloyed devotional service and full surrender unto the Lord, made it possible for the Lord to become a chariot driver or sometimes their letter messenger. Such duties executed by the Lord for His devotee are always very pleasing to the Lord because the Lord wants to render service to His unalloyed devotee, whose life has no other engagement than to serve the Lord with full love and devotion. Mahārāja Parīkṣit, grandson of Arjuna, the celebrated friendly servitor of the Lord, was a pure devotee of the Lord like his grandfather, and therefore the Lord was always with him, even from the time when he was helplessly lying in the womb of his mother and was attacked by the blazing *brahmāstra* weapon of Aśvatthāmā. A devotee is always under the protection of the Lord, and therefore the assurance of protection by Mahārāja Parīkṣit could never be without meaning. The personality of religion accepted this fact and thus thanked the King for his being true to his exalted position.

TEXT 18

न वयं क्लेशबीजानि यतः स्युः पुरुषर्षभ ।
पुरुषं तं विजानीमो वाक्यभेदविमोहिताः ॥१८॥

na vayaṁ kleśa-bījāni
yataḥ syuḥ puruṣarṣabha
puruṣaṁ taṁ vijānīmo
vākya-bheda-vimohitāḥ

na—not; *vayam*—we; *kleśa-bījāni*—the root cause of sufferings; *yataḥ*—wherefrom; *syuḥ*—it so happens; *puruṣa-ṛṣabha*—O greatest of all human beings; *puruṣam*—the person; *tam*—that; *vijānīmaḥ*—know; *vākya-bheda*—difference of opinion; *vimohitāḥ*—bewildered by.

TRANSLATION

O greatest among human beings, it is very difficult to ascertain the particular miscreant who has caused our sufferings, because we are bewildered by all the different opinions of theoretical philosophers.

PURPORT

There are many theoretical philosophers in the world who put forward their own theories of cause and effect especially about the cause of suffering and its effect on different living beings. Generally there are six great philosophers: Kaṇāda, the author of Vaiśeṣika philosophy; Gautama, the author of logic; Patañjali, the author of mystic *yoga;* Kapila, the author of Sāṅkhya philosophy; Jaimini, the author of Karma-mīmāṁsā; and Vyāsadeva, the author of Vedānta-darśana.

Although the bull, or the personality of religion, and the cow, the personality of the earth, knew perfectly well that the personality of Kali was the direct cause of their sufferings, still, as devotees of the Lord, they knew well also that without the sanction of the Lord no one could inflict trouble upon them. According to the *Padma Purāṇa,* our present trouble is due to the fructifying of seedling sins, but even those seedling sins also gradually fade away by execution of pure devotional service. Thus even if the devotees see the mischief-mongers, they do not accuse them for the sufferings inflicted. They take it for granted that the mischief-monger is made to act by some indirect cause, and therefore they tolerate the sufferings, thinking them to be God-given in small doses, for otherwise the sufferings should have been greater.

Mahārāja Parīkṣit wanted to get a statement of accusation against the direct mischief-monger, but they declined to give it on the above-mentioned grounds. Speculative philosophers, however, do not recognize the sanction of the Lord; they try to find out the cause of sufferings in their own way, as will be described in the following verses. According to Śrīla Jīva Gosvāmī, such speculators are themselves bewildered, and thus they cannot know that the ultimate cause of all causes is the Supreme Lord, the Personality of Godhead.

TEXT 19

केचिद् विकल्पवसना आहुरात्मानमात्मनः ।
दैवमन्येऽपरे कर्म स्वभावमपरे प्रभुम् ॥१९॥

kecid vikalpa-vasanā
āhur ātmānam ātmanaḥ
daivam anye 'pare karma
svabhāvam apare prabhum

kecit—some of them; *vikalpa-vasanāḥ*—those who deny all kinds of duality; *āhuḥ*—declare; *ātmānam*—own self; *ātmanaḥ*—of the self; *daivam*—superhuman; *anye*—others; *apare*—someone else; *karma*—activity; *svabhāvam*—material nature; *apare*—many other; *prabhum*—authorities.

TRANSLATION

Some of the philosophers, who deny all sorts of duality, declare that one's own self is responsible for his personal happiness and distress. Others say that superhuman powers are responsible, while yet others say that activity is responsible, and the gross materialists maintain that nature is the ultimate cause.

PURPORT

As referred to above, philosophers like Jaimini and his followers establish that fruitive activity is the root cause of all distress and happiness, and that even if there is a superior authority, some superhuman powerful God or gods, He or they are also under the influence of fruitive activity because they reward result according to one's action. They say that action is not independent because action is performed by some performer; therefore, the performer himself is the cause of his own happiness or distress. In the *Bhagavad-gītā* (6.5) also it is confirmed that by one's mind, freed from material affection, one can deliver himself from the sufferings of material pangs. So one should not entangle oneself in matter by the mind's material affections. Thus one's own mind is one's friend or enemy in one's material happiness and distress.

Atheistic, materialistic Sāṅkhyaites conclude that material nature is the cause of all causes. According to them, combinations of material elements are the causes of material happiness and distress, and disintegration of matter is the cause of freedom from all material pangs. Gautama and Kaṇāda find that atomic combination is the cause of everything, and impersonalists like Aṣṭāvakra discover that the spiritual effulgence of Brahman is the cause of all causes. But in the *Bhagavad-gītā* the Lord Himself declares that He is the source of impersonal Brahman, and therefore He, the Personality of Godhead, is the ultimate cause of all causes. It is also confirmed in the *Brahma-saṁhitā* that Lord Kṛṣṇa is the ultimate cause of all causes.

TEXT 20

अप्रतर्क्यादनिर्देश्यादिति केष्वपि निश्चयः ।
अत्रानुरूपं राजर्षे विमृश स्वमनीषया ॥२०॥

apratarkyād anirdeśyād
iti keṣv api niścayaḥ
atrānurūpaṁ rājarṣe
vimṛśa sva-manīṣayā

apratarkyāt—beyond the power of reasoning; *anirdeśyāt*—beyond the power of thinking; *iti*—thus; *keṣu*—someone; *api*—also; *niścayaḥ*—definitely concluded; *atra*—herein; *anurūpam*—which of them is right; *rāja-ṛṣe*—O sage amongst the kings; *vimṛśa*—judge yourself; *sva*—by your own; *manīṣayā*—power of intelligence.

TRANSLATION

There are also some thinkers who believe that no one can ascertain the cause of distress by argumentation, nor know it by imagination, nor express it by words. O sage amongst kings, judge for yourself by thinking over all this with your own intelligence.

PURPORT

The Vaiṣṇavites, the devotees of the Lord, do believe, as above explained, that nothing can take place without the sanction of the Supreme Lord. He is the supreme director, for He confirms in the *Bhagavad-gītā* (15.15) that He, as all-pervading Paramātmā, stays in everyone's heart and keeps vigilance over all actions and witnesses all activities. The argument of the atheist that one cannot be punished for one's misdeeds unless proved before a qualified justice is refuted herein, for we accept the perpetual witness and constant companion of the living being. A living being may forget all that he might have done in his past or present life, but one must know that in the same tree of the material body, the individual soul and the Supreme Soul as Paramātmā are sitting like two birds. One of them, the living being, is enjoying the fruits of the tree, whereas the Supreme Being is there to witness the activities. Therefore the Paramātmā feature, the Supreme Soul, is actually the witness of all activities of the living being, and only by His direction can the living being remember or forget what he might have done in the past. He is, therefore, both the all-pervading impersonal Brahman and the localized Paramātmā in everyone's heart. He is the knower of all past, present and future, and nothing can be concealed from Him. The devotees know this truth, and therefore they discharge their duties sincerely, without being overly anxious for rewards. Besides that, one cannot estimate the Lord's reactions, either by speculation or by scholarship. Why does He put some into difficulty and not others? He is the supreme knower of the Vedic knowledge, and thus He is the factual Vedāntist. At the same time He is the compiler of the *Vedānta*. No one is independent of Him, and everyone is engaged in His service in different ways. In the conditioned state, such services are rendered by the living being under force of the material nature, whereas in the liberated state the living being is helped by the spiritual nature in the voluntary loving service of the Lord. There is no incongruity or inebriety in His actions. All are on the path of Absolute Truth. Bhīṣmadeva correctly estimated the inconceivable actions of the Lord. The conclusion is, therefore, that the sufferings of the representative of religion and the representative of the earth, as present before Mahārāja Parīkṣit, were planned to prove that Mahārāja Parīkṣit was the ideal executive head because he knew well how to give protection to the cows (the earth) and the *brāhmaṇas* (religious principles), the two pillars of spiritual advancement. Everyone is under the full control of the Lord. He is quite correct in His action when He desires something to be done by someone, irrespective of the consideration of the particular case. Mahārāja Parīkṣit was thus put to test for his greatness. Now let us see how he solves it by his sagacious mind.

TEXT 21

सूत उवाच

एवं धर्मे प्रवदति स सम्राड् द्विजसत्तमाः ।
समाहितेन मनसा विखेदः पर्यचष्ट तम् ॥२१॥

sūta uvāca
evaṁ dharme pravadati
sa samrāḍ dvija-sattamāḥ
samāhitena manasā
vikhedaḥ paryacaṣṭa tam

sūtaḥ uvāca—Sūta Gosvāmī said; *evam*—so; *dharme*—the personality of religion; *pravadati*—thus having spoken; *saḥ*—he; *samrāṭ*—the Emperor; *dvija-sattamāḥ*—O best among the *brāhmaṇas; samāhitena*—with proper attention; *manasā*—by the mind; *vikhedaḥ*—without any mistake; *paryacaṣṭa*—counterreplied; *tam*—unto him.

TRANSLATION

Sūta Gosvāmī said: O best among the brāhmaṇas, the Emperor Parīkṣit, thus hearing the personality of religion speak, was fully satisfied, and without mistake or regret he gave his reply.

PURPORT

The statement of the bull, the personality of religion, was full of philosophy and knowledge, and the King was satisfied, since he could understand that the suffering bull was not an ordinary one. Unless one is perfectly conversant with the law of the Supreme Lord, one cannot speak such things touching philosophical truths. The Emperor, being also on an equal level of sagacity, replied to the point, without doubts or mistakes.

TEXT 22

राजोवाच
धर्मं ब्रवीषि धर्मज्ञ धर्मोऽसि वृषरूपधृक् ।
यदधर्मकृतः स्थानं सूचकस्यापि तद्भवेत् ॥२२॥

rājovāca
dharmaṁ bravīṣi dharma-jña
dharmo 'si vṛṣa-rūpa-dhṛk
yad adharma-kṛtaḥ sthānaṁ
sūcakasyāpi tad bhavet

rājā uvāca—the King said; *dharmam*—religion; *bravīṣi*—as you speak; *dharma-jña*—O one who knows the codes of religion; *dharmaḥ*—the personality of religion; *asi*—you are; *vṛṣa-rūpa-dhṛk*—in the disguise of a bull; *yat*—whatever; *adharma-kṛtaḥ*—one who acts irreligiously; *sthānam*—place; *sūcakasya*—of the identifier; *api*—also; *tat*—that; *bhavet*—becomes.

TRANSLATION

The King said: O you, who are in the form of a bull! You know the truth of religion, and you are speaking according to the principle that the destination intended for the perpetrator of irreligious acts is also intended for one who identifies the perpetrator. You are no other than the personality of religion.

PURPORT

A devotee's conclusion is that no one is directly responsible for being a benefactor or mischief-monger without the sanction of the Lord; therefore he does not consider anyone to be directly responsible for such action. But in both the cases he takes it for granted that either benefit or loss is God-sent, and thus it is His grace. In case of benefit, no one will deny that it is God-sent, but in case of loss or reverses one becomes doubtful about how the Lord could be so unkind to His devotee as to put him in great difficulty. Jesus Christ was seemingly put into such great difficulty, being crucified by the ignorant, but he was never angry at the mischief-mongers. That is the way of accepting a thing, either favorable or unfavorable. Thus for a devotee the identifier is equally a sinner, like the mischief-monger. By God's grace, the devotee tolerates all reverses. Mahārāja Parīkṣit observed this, and therefore he could understand that the bull was no other than the personality of religion himself. In other words, a devotee has no suffering at all because so-called suffering is also God's grace for a devotee who sees God in everything. The cow and bull never placed any complaint before the King for being tortured by the personality of Kali, although everyone lodges such complaints before the state authorities. The extraordinary behavior of the bull made the King conclude that the bull was certainly the personality of religion, for no one else could understand the finer intricacies of the codes of religion.

TEXT 23

अथवा देवमायाया नूनं गतिरगोचरा ।
चेतसो वचसश्चापि भूतानामिति निश्चयः ॥२३॥

athavā deva-māyāyā
nūnaṁ gatir agocarā
cetaso vacasaś cāpi
bhūtānām iti niścayaḥ

athavā—alternatively; *deva*—the Lord; *māyāyāḥ*—energies; *nūnam*—very little; *gatiḥ*—movement; *agocarā*—inconceivable; *cetasaḥ*—either by the mind; *vacasaḥ*—by words; *ca*—or; *api*—also; *bhūtānām*—of all living beings; *iti*—thus; *niścayaḥ*—concluded.

TRANSLATION

Thus it is concluded that the Lord's energies are inconceivable. No one can estimate them by mental speculation or by word jugglery.

PURPORT

A question may be raised as to why a devotee should refrain from identifying an actor, although he knows definitely that the Lord is the ultimate doer of everything. Knowing the ultimate doer, one should not pose himself as ignorant of the actual performer. To answer this doubt, the reply is that the Lord is also not directly responsible, for everything is done by His deputed *māyā-śakti,* or material energy. The material energy is always provoking doubts about the supreme authority of the Lord. The personality of religion knew perfectly well that nothing can take place without the sanction of the Supreme Lord, and still he was put into doubts by the deluding energy, and thus he refrained from mentioning the supreme cause. This doubtfulness was due to the contamination of both Kali and the material energy. The whole atmosphere of the age of Kali is magnified by the deluding energy, and the proportion of measurement is inexplicable.

TEXT 24

तपः शौचं दया सत्यमिति पादाः कृते कृताः ।
अधर्मांशैस्त्रयो भग्नाः स्मयसङ्गमदैस्तव ॥२४॥

tapaḥ śaucaṁ dayā satyam
iti pādāḥ kṛte kṛtāḥ
adharmāṁśais trayo bhagnāḥ
smaya-saṅga-madais tava

tapaḥ—austerity; *śaucam*—cleanliness; *dayā*—mercy; *satyam*—truthfulness; *iti*—thus; *pādāḥ*—legs; *kṛte*—in the age of Satya; *kṛtāḥ*—established; *adharma*—irreligiosity; *aṁśaiḥ*—by the parts; *trayaḥ*—three combined; *bhagnāḥ*—broken; *smaya*—pride; *saṅga*—too much association with women; *madaiḥ*—intoxication; *tava*—your.

TRANSLATION

In the age of Satya [truthfulness] your four legs were established by the four principles of austerity, cleanliness, mercy and truthfulness. But it appears that three of your legs are broken due to rampant irreligion in the form of pride, lust for women, and intoxication.

PURPORT

The deluding energy, or material nature, can act upon the living beings proportionately in terms of the living beings' falling prey to the deluding attraction of *māyā.* Moths are captivated by the glaring brightness of light, and thus they become prey to the fire. Similarly, the deluding energy is always captivating the conditioned souls to become prey to the fire of delusion, and the Vedic scriptures warn the conditioned souls not to become prey to delusion but to get rid of it. The *Vedas* warn us to go not to the darkness of ignorance but to the progressive path of light. The Lord Himself also warns that the deluding power of material energy is too powerful to overcome, but one who completely surrenders unto the Lord can easily do so. But to surrender unto the lotus feet of the Lord is also not very easy. Such surrender is possible by persons of austerity, cleanliness, mercy and truthfulness. These four principles of advanced civilization were remarkable features in the age of Satya. In that age, every human being was practically a qualified *brāhmaṇa* of the highest order, and in the social orders of life they were all *paramahaṁsas,* or the topmost in the renounced order. By cultural standing, the human beings were not at all subjected to the deluding energy. Such strong men of character were competent enough to get away from the clutches of *māyā.* But gradually, as the basic principles of brahminical culture, namely austerity, cleanliness, mercy and truthfulness, became curtailed by proportionate development of pride, attachment for women and intoxication, the path of salvation or the path of transcendental bliss retreated far, far away from human society. With the progression of the age of Kali, people are becoming very proud, and attached to women and intoxication. By the influence of the age of Kali, even a pauper is proud of his penny, the women are always dressed in an overly attractive fashion to victimize the minds of men, and the man is addicted to drinking wine, smoking, drinking tea and chewing tobacco, etc. All these habits, or so-called advancement of civilization, are the root causes of all irreligiosities, and therefore it is not possible to check corruption, bribery and nepotism. Man cannot check all these evils simply by statutory acts and police vigilance, but he can cure the disease of the mind by the proper medicine, namely advocating the principles of brahminical culture or the principles of austerity, cleanliness, mercy and truthfulness. Modern civilization and economic development are creating a new situation of poverty and scarcity with the result of blackmailing the consumer's commodities. If the leaders and the rich men of the society spend fifty percent of their accumulated wealth mercifully for the misled mass of people and educate them in God consciousness, the knowledge of *Bhāgavatam,* certainly the age of Kali will be defeated in its attempt to entrap the conditioned souls. We must always remember that false pride, or too high an estimation of one's own values of life, undue attachment to women or association with them, and intoxication will divert human civilization from the path of peace, however much the people clamor for peace in the world. The preaching of the *Bhāgavatam* principles will automatically render all men austere, clean both inside and outside, merciful to the suffering, and truthful in daily behavior. That is the way of correcting the flaws of human society, which are very prominently exhibited at the present moment.

TEXT 25

इदानीं धर्म पादस्ते सत्यं निर्वर्तयेद्यतः ।
तं जिघृक्षत्यधर्मोऽयमनृतेनैधितः कलिः ॥२५॥

idānīṁ dharma pādas te
satyaṁ nirvartayed yataḥ
taṁ jighṛkṣaty adharmo 'yam
anṛtenaidhitaḥ kaliḥ

idānīm—at the present moment; *dharma*—O personality of religion; *pādaḥ*—leg; *te*—of you; *satyam*—truthfulness; *nirvartayet*—hobbling along somehow or other; *yataḥ*—whereby; *tam*—that; *jighṛkṣati*—trying to destroy; *adharmaḥ*—the personality of irreligion; *ayam*—this; *anṛtena*—by deceit; *edhitaḥ*—flourishing; *kaliḥ*—quarrel personified.

TRANSLATION

You are now standing on one leg only, which is your truthfulness, and you are somehow or other hobbling along. But quarrel personified [Kali], flourishing by deceit, is also trying to destroy that leg.

PURPORT

The principles of religion do not stand on some dogmas or man-made formulas, but they stand on four primary regulative observances, namely austerity, cleanliness, mercy and truthfulness. The mass of people must be taught to practice these principles from childhood. Austerity means to accept voluntarily things which may not be very comfortable for the body but are conducive for spiritual realization, for example, fasting. Fasting twice or four times a month is a sort of austerity which may be voluntarily accepted for spiritual realization only, and not for any other purposes, political or otherwise. Fastings which are meant not for self-realization but for some other purposes are condemned in the *Bhagavad-gītā* (17.5–6). Similarly, cleanliness is necessary both for the mind and for the body. Simply bodily cleanliness may help to some extent, but cleanliness of the mind is necessary, and it is effected by glorifying the Supreme Lord. No one can cleanse the accumulated mental dust without glorifying the Supreme Lord. A godless civilization cannot cleanse the mind because it has no idea of God, and for this simple reason people under such a civilization cannot have good qualifications, however they may be materially equipped. We have to see things by their resultant action. The resultant action of human civilization in the age of Kali is dissatisfaction, so everyone is anxious to get peace of mind. This peace of mind was complete in the Satya age because of the existence of the above-mentioned attributes of the human beings. Gradually these attributes have diminished in the Tretā-yuga to three fourths, in the Dvāpara to half, and in this age of Kali to one fourth, which is also gradually diminishing on account of prevailing untruthfulness. By pride, either artificial or real, the resultant action of austerity is spoiled; by too much affection for female association, cleanliness is spoiled; by too much addiction to intoxication, mercy is spoiled; and by too much lying propaganda, truthfulness is spoiled. The revival of *bhāgavata-dharma* can save human civilization from falling prey to evils of all description.

TEXT 26

इयं च भूमिर्भगवता न्यासितोरुभरा सती ।
श्रीमद्भिस्तत्पदन्यासैः सर्वतः कृतकौतुका ॥२६॥

iyaṁ ca bhūmir bhagavatā
nyāsitoru-bharā satī
śrīmadbhis tat-pada-nyāsaiḥ
sarvataḥ kṛta-kautukā

iyam—this; *ca*—and; *bhūmiḥ*—surface of the earth; *bhagavatā*—by the Personality of Godhead; *nyāsita*—being performed personally as well as by others; *uru*—great; *bharā*—burden; *satī*—being so done; *śrīmadbhiḥ*—by the all-auspicious; *tat*—that; *pada-nyāsaiḥ*—footprints; *sarvataḥ*—all around; *kṛta*—done; *kautukā*—good fortune.

TRANSLATION

The burden of the earth was certainly diminished by the Personality of Godhead and by others as well. When He was present as an incarnation, all good was performed because of His auspicious footprints.

TEXT 27

शोचत्यश्रुकला साध्वी दुर्भगेवोज्झिता सती ।
अब्रह्मण्या नृपव्याजाः शूद्रा भोक्ष्यन्ति मामिति ॥२७॥

śocaty aśru-kalā sādhvī
durbhagevojjhitā satī
abrahmaṇyā nṛpa-vyājāḥ
śūdrā bhokṣyanti mām iti

śocati—lamenting; *aśru-kalā*—with tears in the eyes; *sādhvī*—the chaste; *durbhagā*—as if the most unfortunate; *iva*—like; *ujjhitā*—forlorn; *satī*—being so done; *abrahmaṇyāḥ*—devoid of brahminical culture; *nṛpa-vyājāḥ*—posed as the ruler; *śūdrāḥ*—lower class; *bhokṣyanti*—would enjoy; *mām*—me; *iti*—thus.

TRANSLATION

Now she, the chaste one, being unfortunately forsaken by the Personality of Godhead, laments her future with tears in her eyes, for now she is being ruled and enjoyed by lower-class men who pose as rulers.

PURPORT

The *kṣatriya,* or the man who is qualified to protect the sufferers, is meant to rule the state. Untrained lower-class men, or men without ambition to protect the sufferers, cannot be placed on the seat of an administrator. Unfortunately, in the age of Kali the lower-class men, without training, occupy the post of a ruler by strength of popular votes, and instead of protecting the sufferers, such men create a situation quite intolerable for everyone. Such rulers illegally gratify themselves at the cost of all comforts of the citizens, and thus the chaste mother earth cries to see the pitiable condition of her sons, both men and animals. That is the future of the world in the age of Kali, when irreligiosity prevails most prominently. And in the absence of a suitable king to curb irreligious tendencies, educating the people systematically in the teaching of *Śrīmad-Bhāgavatam* will clear up the hazy atmosphere of corruption, bribery, blackmail, etc.

TEXT 28

इति धर्मं महीं चैव सान्त्वयित्वा महारथः ।
निशातमाददे खड्गं कलयेऽधर्महेतवे ॥२८॥

iti dharmaṁ mahīṁ caiva
sāntvayitvā mahā-rathaḥ
niśātam ādade khaḍgaṁ
kalaye 'dharma-hetave

iti—thus; *dharmam*—the personality of religion; *mahīm*—the earth; *ca*—also; *eva*—as; *sāntvayitvā*—after pacifying; *mahā-rathaḥ*—the general who could fight alone with thousands of enemies; *niśātam*—sharp; *ādade*—took up; *khaḍgam*—sword; *kalaye*—to kill the personified Kali; *adharma*—irreligion; *hetave*—the root cause.

TRANSLATION

Mahārāja Parīkṣit, who could fight one thousand enemies single-handedly, thus pacified the personality of religion and the earth. Then he took up his sharp sword to kill the personality of Kali, who is the cause of all irreligion.

PURPORT

As described above, the personality of Kali is he who deliberately commits all kinds of sinful acts which are forbidden in the revealed scriptures. This age of Kali will certainly be full of all activities of Kali, but this does not mean that the leaders of society, the executive heads, the learned and intelligent men or, above all, the devotees of the Lord should sit down tightly and become callous to the reactions of the age of Kali. In the rainy season certainly there will be profuse rainfalls, but that does not mean that men should not take means to protect themselves from the rains. It is the duty of the executive heads of state and others to take all necessary actions against the activities of Kali or the persons influenced by the age of Kali; and Mahārāja Parīkṣit is the ideal executive head of the state, for at once he was ready to kill the personality of Kali with his sharp sword. The administrators should not simply pass resolutions for anticorruptional steps, but they must be ready with sharp swords to kill the persons creating corruptions from the angle of vision of the recognized *śāstras.* The administrators cannot prevent corrupt activities by allowing wine shops. They must at once close all shops of intoxicating drugs and wine and force punishment even by death for those who indulge in habits of intoxication of all description. That is the way of stopping the activities of Kali, as exhibited herein by Mahārāja Parīkṣit, the *mahā-ratha.*

TEXT 29

तं जिघांसुमभिप्रेत्य विहाय नृपलाञ्छनम् ।
तत्पादमूलं शिरसा समगाद् भयविह्वलः ॥२९॥

taṁ jighāṁsum abhipretya
vihāya nṛpa-lāñchanam
tat-pāda-mūlaṁ śirasā
samagād bhaya-vihvalaḥ

tam—him; *jighāṁsum*—willing to kill; *abhipretya*—knowing it well; *vihāya*—leaving aside; *nṛpa-lāñchanam*—the dress of a king; *tat-pāda-mūlam*—at his feet; *śirasā*—by the head; *samagāt*—fully surrendered; *bhaya-vihvalaḥ*—under pressure of fearfulness.

TRANSLATION

When the personality of Kali understood that the King was willing to kill him, he at once abandoned the dress of a king and, under pressure of fear, completely surrendered to him, bowing his head.

PURPORT

The royal dress of the personality of Kali is artificial. The royal dress is suitable for a king or *kṣatriya,* but when a lower-class man artificially dresses himself as a king, his real identity is disclosed by the challenge of a bona fide *kṣatriya* like Mahārāja Parīkṣit. A real *kṣatriya* never surrenders. He accepts the challenge of his rival *kṣatriya,* and he fights either to die or to win. Surrender is unknown to a real *kṣatriya.* In the age of Kali there are so many pretenders dressed and posed like administrators or executive heads, but their real identity is disclosed when they are challenged by a real *kṣatriya.* Therefore when the artificially dressed personality of Kali saw that to fight Mahārāja Parīkṣit was beyond his ability, he bowed down his head like a subordinate and gave up his royal dress.

TEXT 30

पतितं पादयोर्वीरः कृपया दीनवत्सलः ।
शरण्यो नावधीच्छ्लोक्य आह चेदं हसन्निव ॥३०॥

patitaṁ pādayor vīraḥ
kṛpayā dīna-vatsalaḥ

śaraṇyo nāvadhīc chlokya
āha cedaṁ hasann iva

patitam—fallen; *pādayoḥ*—at the feet; *vīraḥ*—the hero; *kṛpayā*—out of compassion; *dīna-vatsalaḥ*—kind to the poor; *śaraṇyaḥ*—one who is qualified to accept surrender; *na*—not; *avadhīt*—did kill; *ślokyaḥ*—one who is worthy of being sung; *āha*—said; *ca*—also; *idam*—this; *hasan*—smiling; *iva*—like.

TRANSLATION

Mahārāja Parīkṣit, who was qualified to accept surrender and worthy of being sung in history, did not kill the poor surrendered and fallen Kali, but smiled compassionately, for he was kind to the poor.

PURPORT

Even an ordinary *kṣatriya* does not kill a surrendered person, and what to speak of Mahārāja Parīkṣit, who was by nature compassionate and kind to the poor. He was smiling because the artificially dressed Kali had disclosed his identity as a lower-class man, and he was thinking how ironic it was that although no one was saved from his sharp sword when he desired to kill, the poor lower-class Kali was spared by his timely surrender. Mahārāja Parīkṣit's glory and kindness are therefore sung in history. He was a kind and compassionate emperor, fully worthy of accepting surrender even from his enemy. Thus the personality of Kali was saved by the will of providence.

TEXT 31

राजोवाच
न ते गुडाकेशयशोधराणां
बद्धाञ्जलेर्वै भयमस्ति किंचित् ।
न वर्तितव्यं भवता कथंचन
क्षेत्रे मदीये त्वमधर्मबन्धुः ॥३१॥

rājovāca
na te guḍākeśa-yaśo-dharāṇāṁ
baddhāñjaler vai bhayam asti kiñcit
na vartitavyaṁ bhavatā kathañcana
kṣetre madīye tvam adharma-bandhuḥ

rājā uvāca—the King said; *na*—not; *te*—your; *guḍākeśa*—Arjuna; *yaśaḥ-dharāṇām*—of us who inherited the fame; *baddha-añjaleḥ*—one with folded hands; *vai*—certainly; *bhayam*—fear; *asti*—there is; *kiñcit*—even a slight; *na*—neither; *vartitavyam*—can be allowed to live; *bhavatā*—by you; *kathañcana*—by all means; *kṣetre*—in the land; *madīye*—in my kingdom; *tvam*—you; *adharma-bandhuḥ*—the friend of irreligion.

TRANSLATION

The King thus said: We have inherited the fame of Arjuna; therefore since you have surrendered yourself with folded hands you need not fear for your life. But you cannot remain in my kingdom, for you are the friend of irreligion.

PURPORT

The personality of Kali, who is the friend of all kinds of irreligiosities, may be excused if he surrenders, but in all circumstances he cannot be allowed to live as a citizen in any part of a welfare state. The Pāṇḍavas were entrusted representatives of the Personality of Godhead, Lord Kṛṣṇa, who practically brought into being the Battle of Kurukṣetra, but not for any personal interest. He wanted an ideal king like Mahārāja Yudhiṣṭhira and his descendants like Mahārāja Parīkṣit to rule the world, and therefore a responsible king like Mahārāja Parīkṣit could not allow the friend of irreligiosity to flourish in his kingdom at the cost of the good fame of the Pāṇḍavas. That is the way of wiping out corruption in the state, and not otherwise. The friends of irreligiosity should be banished from the state, and that will save the state from corruption.

TEXT 32

त्वां वर्तमानं नरदेवदेहे-
ष्वनुप्रवृत्तोऽयमधर्मपूगः ।
लोभोऽनृतं चौर्यमनार्यमंहो
ज्येष्ठा च माया कलहश्च दम्भः ॥३२॥

tvāṁ vartamānaṁ nara-deva-deheṣv
anupravṛtto 'yam adharma-pūgaḥ
lobho 'nṛtaṁ cauryam anāryam aṁho
jyeṣṭhā ca māyā kalahaś ca dambhaḥ

tvām—you; *vartamānam*—while present; *nara-deva*—a man-god, or a king; *deheṣu*—in the body; *anupravṛttaḥ*—taking place everywhere; *ayam*—all these; *adharma*—irreligious principles; *pūgaḥ*—in the masses; *lobhaḥ*—greed; *anṛtam*—falsity; *cauryam*—robbery; *anāryam*—incivility; *aṁhaḥ*—treachery; *jyeṣṭhā*—misfortune; *ca*—and; *māyā*—cheating; *kalahaḥ*—quarrel; *ca*—and; *dambhaḥ*—vanity.

TRANSLATION

If the personality of Kali, irreligion, is allowed to act as a man-god or an executive head, certainly irreligious principles like greed, falsehood, robbery, incivility, treachery, misfortune, cheating, quarrel and vanity will abound.

PURPORT

The principles of religion, namely *austerity, cleanliness, mercy and truthfulness,* as we have already discussed, may be followed by the follower of any faith. There is no need to turn from Hindu to Mohammedan to Christian or some other faith and thus become a renegade and not follow the principles of religion. The *Bhāgavatam religion* urges following the *principles of religion.* The principles of religion are not the dogmas or regulative principles of a certain faith. Such regulative principles may be different in terms of the time and place concerned. One has to see whether the aims of religion have been achieved. Sticking to the dogmas and formulas without attaining the real principles is not good. A secular state may be impartial to any particular type of faith, but the state cannot be indifferent to the principles of religion as above mentioned. But in the age of Kali, the executive heads of state will be indifferent to such religious principles, and therefore under their patronage the opponents of religious principles, such as greed, falsehood, cheating and pilfery, will naturally follow, and so there will be no meaning to propaganda crying to stop corruption in the state.

TEXT 33

न वर्तितव्यं तदधर्मबन्धो
धर्मेण सत्येन च वर्तितव्ये ।
ब्रह्मावर्ते यत्र यजन्ति यज्ञै-
र्यज्ञेश्वरं यज्ञवितानविज्ञाः ॥३३॥

na vartitavyaṁ tad adharma-bandho
dharmeṇa satyena ca vartitavye
brahmāvarte yatra yajanti yajñair
yajñeśvaraṁ yajña-vitāna-vijñāḥ

na—not; *vartitavyam*—deserve to remain; *tat*—therefore; *adharma*—irreligiosity; *bandho*—friend; *dharmeṇa*—with religion; *satyena*—with truth; *ca*—also; *vartitavye*—being situated in; *brahma-āvarte*—place where sacrifice is performed; *yatra*—where; *yajanti*—duly perform; *yajñaiḥ*—by sacrifices or devotional services; *yajña-īśvaram*—unto the Supreme Lord, the Personality of Godhead; *yajña*—sacrifice; *vitāna*—spreading; *vijñāḥ*—experts.

TRANSLATION

Therefore, O friend of irreligion, you do not deserve to remain in a place where experts perform sacrifices according to truth and religious principles for the satisfaction of the Supreme Personality of Godhead.

PURPORT

Yajñeśvara, or the Supreme Personality of Godhead, is the beneficiary of all kinds of sacrificial ceremonies. Such sacrificial ceremonies are prescribed differently in the scriptures for different ages. In other words, sacrifice means to accept the supremacy of the Lord and thereby perform acts by which the Lord may be satisfied in all respects. The atheists do not believe in the existence of God, and they do not perform any sacrifice for the satisfaction of the Lord. Any place or country where the supremacy of the Lord is accepted and thus sacrifice is performed is called *brahmāvarta.* There are different countries in different parts of the world, and each and every country may have different types of sacrifice to please the Supreme Lord, but the central point in pleasing Him is ascertained in the *Bhāgavatam,* and it is truthfulness. The basic principle of religion is truthfulness, and the ultimate goal of all religions is to satisfy the Lord. In this age of Kali, the greatest common formula of sacrifice is the *saṅkīrtana-yajña.* That is the opinion of the experts who know how to propagate the process of *yajña.* Lord Caitanya preached this method of *yajña,* and it is understood from this verse that the sacrificial method of *saṅkīrtana-yajña* may be performed anywhere and everywhere in order to drive away the personality of Kali and save human society from falling prey to the influence of the age.

TEXT 34

यस्मिन् हरिर्भगवानिज्यमान
इज्यात्ममूर्तिर्यजतां शं तनोति ।
कामानमोघान् स्थिरजङ्गमाना-
मन्तर्बहिर्वायुरिवैष आत्मा ॥३४॥

yasmin harir bhagavān ijyamāna
ijyātma-mūrtir yajatāṁ śaṁ tanoti
kāmān amoghān sthira-jaṅgamānām
antar bahir vāyur ivaiṣa ātmā

yasmin—in such sacrificial ceremonies; *hariḥ*—the Supreme Lord; *bhagavān*—the Personality of Godhead; *ijyamānaḥ*—being worshiped; *ijya-ātma*—the soul of all worshipable deities; *mūrtiḥ*—in the forms; *yajatām*—those who worship; *śam*—welfare; *tanoti*—spreads; *kāmān*—desires; *amoghān*—inviolable; *sthira-jaṅgamānām*—of all the moving and nonmoving; *antaḥ*—within; *bahiḥ*—outside; *vāyuḥ*—air; *iva*—like; *eṣaḥ*—of all of them; *ātmā*—spirit soul.

TRANSLATION

In all sacrificial ceremonies, although sometimes a demigod is worshiped, the Supreme Lord Personality of Godhead is worshiped because He is the Supersoul of everyone, and exists both inside and outside like the air. Thus it is He only who awards all welfare to the worshiper.

PURPORT

It is even sometimes seen that demigods like Indra and Candra are worshiped and offered sacrificial awards, yet the rewards of all such sacrifices are awarded to the worshiper by the Supreme Lord, and it is the Lord only who can offer all welfare to the worshiper. The demigods, although worshiped, cannot do anything without the sanction of the Lord because the Lord is the Supersoul of everyone, both moving and nonmoving.

In *Bhagavad-gītā* (9.23) the Lord Himself confirms this in the following *śloka:*

ye 'py anya-devatā-bhaktā
yajante śraddhayānvitāḥ

te 'pi mām eva kaunteya
yajanty avidhi-pūrvakam

"Whatever a man may sacrifice to other gods, O son of Kuntī, is really meant for Me alone, but it is offered without true understanding."

The fact is that the Supreme Lord is one without a second. There is no God other than the Lord Himself. Thus the Supreme Lord is eternally transcendental to the material creation. But there are many who worship the demigods like the sun, the moon and Indra, who are only material representatives of the Supreme Lord. These demigods are indirect, qualitative representations of the Supreme Lord. A learned scholar or devotee, however, knows who is who. Therefore he directly worships the Supreme Lord and is not diverted by the material, qualitative representations. Those who are not so learned worship such qualitative, material representations, but their worship is unceremonious because it is irregular.

TEXT 35

सूत उवाच
परीक्षितैवमादिष्टः स कलिर्जातवेपथुः ।
तमुद्यतासिमाहेदं दण्डपाणिमिवोद्यतम् ॥३५॥

sūta uvāca
parīkṣitaivam ādiṣṭaḥ
sa kalir jāta-vepathuḥ
tam udyatāsim āhedaṁ
daṇḍa-pāṇim ivodyatam

sūtaḥ uvāca—Śrī Sūta Gosvāmī said; *parīkṣitā*—by Mahārāja Parīkṣit; *evam*—thus; *ādiṣṭaḥ*—being ordered; *saḥ*—he; *kaliḥ*—the personality of Kali; *jāta*—there was; *vepathuḥ*—trembling; *tam*—him; *udyata*—raised; *asim*—sword; *āha*—said; *idam*—thus; *daṇḍa-pāṇim*—Yamarāja, the personality of death; *iva*—like; *udyatam*—almost ready.

TRANSLATION

Śrī Sūta Gosvāmī said: The personality of Kali, thus being ordered by Mahārāja Parīkṣit, began to tremble in fear. Seeing the King before him like Yamarāja, ready to kill him, Kali spoke to the King as follows.

PURPORT

The King was ready to kill the personality of Kali at once, as soon as he disobeyed his order. Otherwise the King had no objection to allowing him to prolong his life. The personality of Kali also, after attempting to get rid of the punishment in various ways, decided that he must surrender unto him, and thus he began to tremble in fear of his life. The king, or the executive head, must be so strong as to stand before the personality of Kali like the personality of death, Yamarāja. The King's order must be obeyed, otherwise the culprit's life is in risk. That is the way to rule the personalities of Kali who create disturbance in the normal life of the state citizens.

TEXT 36

कलिरुवाच
यत्र क्व वाथ वत्स्यामि सार्वभौम तवाज्ञया ।
लक्षये तत्र तत्रापि त्वामात्तेषुशरासनम् ॥३६॥

kalir uvāca
yatra kva vātha vatsyāmi
sārva-bhauma tavājñayā
lakṣaye tatra tatrāpi
tvām ātteṣu-śarāsanam

kaliḥ uvāca—the personality of Kali said; *yatra*—anywhere; *kva*—and everywhere; *vā*—either; *atha*—thereof; *vatsyāmi*—I shall reside; *sārva-bhauma*—O lord (or emperor) of the earth; *tava*—your; *ājñayā*—by the order; *lakṣaye*—I see; *tatra tatra*—anywhere and everywhere; *api*—also; *tvām*—Your Majesty; *ātta*—taken over; *iṣu*—arrows; *śarāsanam*—bows.

TRANSLATION

O Your Majesty, though I may live anywhere and everywhere under your order, I shall but see you with bow and arrows wherever I look.

PURPORT

The personality of Kali could see that Mahārāja Parīkṣit was the emperor of all lands all over the world, and thus anywhere he might live he would have to meet with the same mood of the King. The personality of Kali was meant for mischief, and Mahārāja Parīkṣit was meant for subduing all kinds of mischief-mongers, especially the personality of Kali. It was better, therefore, for the personality of Kali to have been killed by the King then and there instead of being killed elsewhere. He was, after all, a surrendered soul before the King, and it was for the King to do what was required.

TEXT 37

तन्मे धर्मभृतां श्रेष्ठ स्थानं निर्देष्टुमर्हसि ।
यत्रैव नियतो वत्स्य आतिष्ठंस्तेऽनुशासनम् ॥३७॥

tan me dharma-bhṛtāṁ śreṣṭha
sthānaṁ nirdeṣṭum arhasi
yatraiva niyato vatsya
ātiṣṭhaṁs te 'nuśāsanam

tat—therefore; *me*—me; *dharma-bhṛtām*—of all the protectors of religion; *śreṣṭha*—O chief; *sthānam*—place; *nirdeṣṭum*—fix; *arhasi*—may you do so; *yatra*—where; *eva*—certainly; *niyataḥ*—always; *vatsye*—can reside; *ātiṣṭhan*—permanently situated; *te*—your; *anuśāsanam*—under your rule.

TRANSLATION

Therefore, O chief amongst the protectors of religion, please fix some place for me where I can live permanently under the protection of your government.

PURPORT

The personality of Kali addressed Mahārāja Parīkṣit as the chief amongst the protectors of religiosity because the King refrained from killing a person who surrendered unto him. A surrendered soul should be given all protection, even though he may be an enemy. That is the principle of religion. And we can just imagine what sort of protection is given by the Personality of Godhead to the person who surrenders unto Him, not as an enemy but as a devoted servitor. The Lord protects the surrendered soul from all sins and all resultant reactions of sinful acts (Bg. 18.66).

TEXT 38

सूत उवाच
अभ्यर्थितस्तदा तस्मै स्थानानि कलये ददौ ।
द्यूतं पानं स्त्रियः सूना यत्राधर्मश्चतुर्विधः ॥३८॥

sūta uvāca
abhyarthitas tadā tasmai
sthānāni kalaye dadau
dyūtaṁ pānaṁ striyaḥ sūnā
yatrādharmaś catur-vidhaḥ

sūtaḥ uvāca—Sūta Gosvāmī said; *abhyarthitaḥ*—thus being petitioned; *tadā*—at that time; *tasmai*—unto him; *sthānāni*—places; *kalaye*—to the personality of Kali; *dadau*—gave him permission; *dyūtam*—gambling; *pānam*—drinking; *striyaḥ*—illicit association with women; *sūnā*—animal slaughter; *yatra*—wherever; *adharmaḥ*—sinful activities; *catuḥ-vidhaḥ*—four kinds of.

TRANSLATION

Sūta Gosvāmī said: Mahārāja Parīkṣit, thus being petitioned by the personality of Kali, gave him permission to reside in places where gambling, drinking, prostitution and animal slaughter were performed.

PURPORT

The basic principles of irreligiosity, such as pride, prostitution, intoxication and falsehood, counteract the four principles of religion, namely austerity, cleanliness, mercy and truthfulness. The personality of Kali was given permission to live in four places particularly mentioned by the King, namely the place of gambling, the place of prostitution, the place of drinking and the place of animal slaughter.

Śrīla Jīva Gosvāmī directs that drinking against the principles of scriptures, such as the *sautrāmaṇī-yajña,* association with women outside marriage, and killing animals against the injunctions of scriptures are irreligious. In the *Vedas* two different types of injunctions are there for the *pravṛttas,* or those who are engaged in material enjoyment, and for the *nivṛttas,* or those who are liberated from material bondage. The Vedic injunction for the *pravṛttas* is to gradually regulate their activities towards the path of liberation. Therefore, for those who are in the lowest stage of ignorance and who indulge in wine, women and flesh, drinking by performing *sautrāmaṇī-yajña,* association of women by marriage, and flesh-eating by sacrifices are sometimes recommended. Such recommendations in the Vedic literature are meant for a particular class of men, and not for all. But because they are injunctions of the *Vedas* for particular types of persons, such activities by the *pravṛttas* are not considered *adharma.* One man's food may be poison for others; similarly, what is recommended for those in the mode of ignorance may be poison for those in the mode of goodness. Śrīla Jīva Gosvāmī Prabhu, therefore, affirms that recommendations in the scriptures for a certain class of men are never to be considered *adharma,* or irreligious. But such activities are factually *adharma,* and they are never to be encouraged. The recommendations in the scriptures are not meant for the encouragement of such *adharma,* but for regulating the necessary *adharma* gradually toward the path of *dharma.*

Following in the footsteps of Mahārāja Parīkṣit, it is the duty of all executive heads of states to see that the principles of religion, namely austerity, cleanliness, mercy and truthfulness, are established in the state, and that the principles of irreligion, namely pride, illicit female association or prostitution, intoxication and falsity, are checked by all means. And to make the best use of a bad bargain, the personality of Kali may be transferred to places of gambling, drinking, prostitution and slaughterhouses, if there are any places like that. Those who are addicted to these irreligious habits may be regulated by the injunctions of the scripture. In no circumstances should they be encouraged by any state. In other words, the state should categorically stop all sorts of gambling, drinking, prostitution and falsity. The state which wants to eradicate corruption by majority may introduce the principles of religion in the following manner:

1. Two compulsory fasting days in a month, if not more (austerity). Even from the economic point of view, such two fasting days in a month in the state will save tons of food, and the system will also act very favorably on the general health of the citizens.

2. There must be compulsory marriage of young boys and girls attaining twenty-four years of age and sixteen years of age respectively. There is no harm in coeducation in the schools and colleges, provided the boys and girls are duly married, and in case there is any intimate connection between a male and female student, they should be married properly without illicit relation. The divorce act is encouraging prostitution, and this should be abolished.

3. The citizens of the state must give in charity up to fifty percent of their income for the purpose of creating a spiritual atmosphere in the state or in human society, both individually and collectively. They should preach the principles of *Bhāgavatam* by (a) *karma-yoga,* or doing everything for the satisfaction of the Lord, (b) regular hearing of the *Śrīmad-Bhāgavatam* from authorized persons or realized souls, (c) chanting of the glories of the Lord congregationally at home or at places of worship, (d) rendering all kinds of service to *bhāgavatas* engaged in preaching *Śrīmad-Bhāgavatam* and (e)

residing in a place where the atmosphere is saturated with God consciousness. If the state is regulated by the above process, naturally there will be God consciousness everywhere.

Gambling of all description, even speculative business enterprise, is considered to be degrading, and when gambling is encouraged in the state, there is a complete disappearance of truthfulness. Allowing young boys and girls to remain unmarried more than the above-mentioned ages and licensing animal slaughterhouses of all description should be at once prohibited. The flesh-eaters may be allowed to take flesh as mentioned in the scriptures, and not otherwise. Intoxication of all description—even smoking cigarettes, chewing tobacco or the drinking of tea—must be prohibited.

TEXT 39

पुनश्च याचमानाय जातरूपमदात्प्रभुः ।
ततोऽनृतं मदं कामं रजो वैरं च पञ्चमम् ॥३९॥

punaś ca yācamānāya
jāta-rūpam adāt prabhuḥ
tato 'nṛtaṁ madaṁ kāmaṁ
rajo vairaṁ ca pañcamam

punaḥ—again; *ca*—also; *yācamānāya*—to the beggar; *jāta-rūpam*—gold; *adāt*—gave away; *prabhuḥ*—the King; *tataḥ*—whereby; *anṛtam*—falsehood; *madam*—intoxication; *kāmam*—lust; *rajaḥ*—on account of a passionate mood; *vairam*—enmity; *ca*—also; *pañcamam*—the fifth one.

TRANSLATION

The personality of Kali asked for something more, and because of his begging, the King gave him permission to live where there is gold because wherever there is gold there is also falsity, intoxication, lust, envy and enmity.

PURPORT

Although Mahārāja Parīkṣit gave Kali permission to live in four places, it was very difficult for him to find the places because during the reign of Mahārāja Parīkṣit there were no such places. Therefore Kali asked the King to give him something practical which could be utilized for his nefarious purposes. Mahārāja Parīkṣit thus gave him permission to live in a place where there is gold, because wherever there is gold there are all the above-mentioned four things, and over and above them there is enmity also. So the personality of Kali became gold-standardized. According to *Śrīmad-Bhāgavatam,* gold encourages falsity, intoxication, prostitution, envy and enmity. Even a gold-standard exchange and currency is bad. Gold-standard currency is based on falsehood because the currency is not on a par with the reserved gold. The basic principle is falsity because currency notes are issued in value beyond that of the actual reserved gold. This artificial inflation of currency by the authorities encourages prostitution of the state economy. The price of commodities becomes artificially inflated because of bad money, or artificial currency notes. Bad money drives away good money. Instead of paper currency, actual gold coins should be used for exchange, and this will stop prostitution of gold. Gold ornaments for women may be allowed by control, not by quality, but by quantity. This will discourage lust, envy and enmity. When there is actual gold currency in the form of coins, the influence of gold in producing falsity, prostitution, etc., will automatically cease. There will be no need of an anticorruption ministry for another term of prostitution and falsity of purpose.

TEXT 40

अमूनि पञ्च स्थानानि ह्यधर्मप्रभवः कलिः ।
औत्तरेयेण दत्तानि न्यवसत् तन्निदेशकृत् ॥४०॥

amūni pañca sthānāni
hy adharma-prabhavaḥ kaliḥ
auttareyeṇa dattāni
nyavasat tan-nideśa-kṛt

amūni—all those; *pañca*—five; *sthānāni*—places; *hi*—certainly; *adharma*—irreligious principles; *prabhavaḥ*—encouraging; *kaliḥ*—the age of Kali; *auttareyeṇa*—by the son of Uttarā; *dattāni*—delivered; *nyavasat*—dwelt; *tat*—by him; *nideśa-kṛt*—directed.

TRANSLATION

Thus the personality of Kali, by the directions of Mahārāja Parīkṣit, the son of Uttarā, was allowed to live in those five places.

PURPORT

Thus the age of Kali began with gold standardization, and therefore falsity, intoxication, animal slaughter and prostitution are rampant all over the world, and the saner section is eager to drive out corruption. The counteracting process is suggested above, and everyone can take advantage of this suggestion.

TEXT 41

अथैतानि न सेवेत बुभूषुः पुरुषः क्वचित् ।
विशेषतो धर्मशीलो राजा लोकपतिर्गुरुः ॥४१॥

athaitāni na seveta
bubhūṣuḥ puruṣaḥ kvacit
viśeṣato dharma-śīlo
rājā loka-patir guruḥ

atha—therefore; *etāni*—all these; *na*—never; *seveta*—come in contact; *bubhūṣuḥ*—those who desire well-being; *puruṣaḥ*—person; *kvacit*—in any circumstances; *viśeṣataḥ*—specifically; *dharma-śīlaḥ*—those who are on the progressive path of liberation; *rājā*—the king; *loka-patiḥ*—public leader; *guruḥ*—the *brāhmaṇas* and the *sannyāsīs.*

TRANSLATION

Therefore, whoever desires progressive well-being, especially kings, religionists, public leaders, brāhmaṇas and sannyāsīs, should never come in contact with the four above-mentioned irreligious principles.

PURPORT

The *brāhmaṇas* are the religious preceptors for all other castes, and the *sannyāsīs* are the spiritual masters for all the castes and orders of society. So also are the king and the public leaders who are responsible for the material welfare of all people. The progressive religionists and those who are responsible human beings or those who do not want to spoil their valuable human lives should refrain from all the principles of irreligiosity, especially illicit connection with women. If a *brāhmaṇa* is not truthful, all his claims as a *brāhmaṇa* at once become null and void. If a *sannyāsī* is illicitly connected with women, all his claims as a *sannyāsī* at once become false. Similarly, if the king and the public leader are unnecessarily proud or habituated to drinking and smoking, certainly they become disqualified to discharge public welfare activities. Truthfulness is the basic principle for all religions. The four leaders of the human society, namely the *sannyāsīs,* the *brāhmaṇa,* the king and the public leader, must be tested crucially by their character and qualification. Before one can be accepted as a spiritual or material master of society, he must be tested by the above-mentioned criteria of character. Such public leaders may be less qualified in academic qualifications, but it is necessary primarily that they be free from the contamination of the four disqualifications, namely gambling, drinking, prostitution and animal slaughter.

TEXT 42

वृषस्य नष्टांस्त्रीन् पादान् तपः शौचं दयामिति ।
प्रतिसन्दध आश्वास्य महीं च समवर्धयत् ॥४२॥

vṛṣasya naṣṭāṁs trīn pādān
tapaḥ śaucaṁ dayām iti
pratisandadha āśvāsya
mahīṁ ca samavardhayat

vṛṣasya—of the bull (the personality of religion); *naṣṭān*—lost; *trīn*—three; *pādān*—legs; *tapaḥ*—austerity; *śaucam*—cleanliness; *dayām*—mercy; *iti*—thus; *pratisandadhe*—reestablished; *āśvāsya*—by encouraging activities; *mahīm*—the earth; *ca*—and; *samavardhayat*—perfectly improved.

TRANSLATION

Thereafter the King reestablished the lost legs of the personality of religion [the bull], and by encouraging activities he sufficiently improved the condition of the earth.

PURPORT

By designating particular places for the personality of Kali, Mahārāja Parīkṣit practically cheated Kali. In the presence of Kali, Dharma (in the shape of a bull), and the earth (in the shape of a cow), he could actually estimate the general condition of his kingdom, and therefore he at once took proper steps to reestablish the legs of the bull, namely austerity, cleanliness and mercy. And for the general benefit of the people of the world, he saw that the gold stock might be employed for stabilization. Gold is certainly a generator of falsity, intoxication, prostitution, enmity and violence, but under the guidance of a proper king or public leader, or a *brāhmaṇa* or *sannyāsī*, the same gold can be properly utilized to reestablish the lost legs of the bull, the personality of religion.

Mahārāja Parīkṣit, therefore, like his grandfather Arjuna, collected all illicit gold kept for the propensities of Kali and employed it in the *saṅkīrtana-yajña,* as per instruction of the *Śrīmad-Bhāgavatam.* As we have suggested before, one's accumulated wealth may be divided into three parts for distribution, namely fifty percent for the service of the Lord, twenty-five percent for the family members and twenty-five percent for personal necessities. Spending fifty percent for the service of the Lord or for propagation of spiritual knowledge in society by way of the *saṅkīrtana-yajña* is the maximum display of human mercy. People of the world are generally in darkness regarding spiritual knowledge, especially in regard to the devotional service of the Lord, and therefore to propagate the systematic transcendental knowledge of devotional service is the greatest mercy that one can show in this world. When everyone is taught to sacrifice fifty percent of his accumulated gold for the Lord's service, certainly austerity, cleanliness and mercy automatically ensue, and thus the lost three legs of the personality of religion are automatically established. When there is sufficient austerity, cleanliness, mercy and truthfulness, naturally mother earth is completely satisfied, and there is very little chance for Kali to infiltrate the structure of human society.

TEXTS 43–44

स एष एतर्ह्यध्यास्त आसनं पार्थिवोचितम् ।
पितामहेनोपन्यस्तं राज्ञारण्यं विविक्षता ॥४३॥
आस्तेऽधुना स राजर्षिः कौरवेन्द्रश्रियोल्लसन् ।
गजाह्वये महाभागश्चक्रवर्ती बृहच्छ्रवाः ॥४४॥

sa eṣa etarhy adhyāsta
āsanaṁ pārthivocitam
pitāmahenopanyastaṁ
rājñāraṇyaṁ vivikṣatā

āste 'dhunā sa rājarṣiḥ
kauravendra-śriyollasan
gajāhvaye mahā-bhāgaś
cakravartī bṛhac-chravāḥ

saḥ—he; *eṣaḥ*—this; *etarhi*—at the present; *adhyāste*—is ruling over; *āsanam*—the throne; *pārthiva-ucitam*—just befitting a king; *pitāmahena*—by the grandfather; *upanyastam*—being handed over; *rājñā*—by the King;

araṇyam—forest; *vivikṣatā*—desiring; *āste*—is there; *adhunā*—at present; *saḥ*—that; *rāja-ṛṣiḥ*—the sage amongst the kings; *kaurava-indra*—the chief amongst the Kuru kings; *śriyā*—glories; *ullasan*—spreading; *gajāhvaye*—in Hastināpura; *mahā-bhāgaḥ*—the most fortunate; *cakravartī*—the Emperor; *bṛhat-śravāḥ*—highly famous.

TRANSLATION

The most fortunate emperor Mahārāja Parīkṣit, who was entrusted with the kingdom of Hastināpura by Mahārāja Yudhiṣṭhira when he desired to retire to the forest, is now ruling the world with great success due to his being glorified by the deeds of the kings of the Kuru dynasty.

PURPORT

The prolonged sacrificial ceremonies undertaken by the sages of Naimiṣāraṇya were begun shortly after the demise of Mahārāja Parīkṣit. The sacrifice was to continue for one thousand years, and it is understood that in the beginning some of the contemporaries of Baladeva, the elder brother of Lord Kṛṣṇa, also visited the sacrificial place. According to some authorities, the present tense is also used to indicate the nearest margin of time from the past. In that sense, the present tense is applied to the reign of Mahārāja Parīkṣit here. For a continuous fact, also, present tense can be used. The principles of Mahārāja Parīkṣit can be still continued, and human society can still be improved if there is determination by the authorities. We can still purge out from the state all the activities of immorality introduced by the personality of Kali if we are determined to take action like Mahārāja Parīkṣit. He allotted some place for Kali, but in fact Kali could not find such places in the world at all because Mahārāja Parīkṣit was strictly vigilant to see that there were no places for gambling, drinking, prostitution and animal slaughter. Modern administrators want to banish corruption from the state, but fools as they are, they do not know how to do it. They want to issue licenses for gambling houses, wine and other intoxicating drug houses, brothels, hotel prostitution and cinema houses, and falsity in every dealing, even in their own, and they want at the same time to drive out corruption from the state. They want the kingdom of God without God consciousness. How can it be possible to adjust two contradictory matters? If we want to drive out corruption from the state, we must first of all organize society to accept the principles of religion, namely austerity, cleanliness, mercy and truthfulness, and to make the condition favorable we must close all places of gambling, drinking, prostitution and falsity. These are some of the practical lessons from the pages of *Śrīmad-Bhāgavatam.*

TEXT 45

इत्थम्भूतानुभावोऽयमभिमन्युसुतो नृपः ।
यस्य पालयतः क्षौणीं यूयं सत्राय दीक्षिताः ॥४५॥

ittham-bhūtānubhāvo 'yam
abhimanyu-suto nṛpaḥ
yasya pālayataḥ kṣauṇīṁ
yūyaṁ satrāya dīkṣitāḥ

ittham-bhūta—being thus; *anubhāvaḥ*—experience; *ayam*—of this; *abhimanyu-sutaḥ*—son of Abhimanyu; *nṛpaḥ*—the king; *yasya*—whose; *pālayataḥ*—on account of his ruling; *kṣauṇīm*—on the earth; *yūyam*—you all; *satrāya*—in performing sacrifices; *dīkṣitāḥ*—initiated.

TRANSLATION

Mahārāja Parīkṣit, the son of Abhimanyu, is so experienced that by dint of his expert administration and patronage, it has been possible for you to perform a sacrifice such as this.

PURPORT

The *brāhmaṇas* and the *sannyāsīs* are expert in the spiritual advancement of society, whereas the *kṣatriyas* or the administrators are expert in the material peace and prosperity of human society. Both of them are the pillars of all happiness, and therefore they are meant for full cooperation for common welfare. Mahārāja Parīkṣit was experienced enough to drive away Kali from his field of activities and thereby make the state receptive to spiritual enlightenment. If the common people are not receptive, it is very difficult to impress upon them the necessity of spiritual enlightenment. Austerity, cleanliness, mercy and truthfulness, the basic principles of religion, prepare the ground for the reception of advancement in spiritual knowledge, and Mahārāja Parīkṣit made this favorable condition possible. Thus the *ṛṣis* of Naimiṣāraṇya were able to perform the sacrifices for a thousand years. In other words, without state support, no doctrines of philosophy or religious principles can progressively advance. There should be complete cooperation between the *brāhmaṇas* and the *kṣatriyas* for this common good. Even up to Mahārāja Aśoka, the same spirit was prevailing. Lord Buddha was sufficiently supported by King Aśoka, and thus his particular cult of knowledge was spread all over the world.

Thus end the Bhaktivedanta purports of the First Canto, Seventeenth Chapter, of the Śrīmad-Bhāgavatam, *entitled "Punishment and Reward of Kali."*

CHAPTER EIGHTEEN

Mahārāja Parīkṣit Cursed by a Brāhmaṇa Boy

TEXT 1

सूत उवाच
योो वै द्रौण्यस्त्रविप्लुष्टो न मातुरुदरे मृतः ।
अनुग्रहाद् भगवतः कृष्णस्याद्भुतकर्मणः ॥१॥

sūta uvāca
yo vai drauṇy-astra-vipluṣṭo
na mātur udare mṛtaḥ
anugrahād bhagavataḥ
kṛṣṇasyādbhuta-karmaṇaḥ

sūtaḥ uvāca—Śrī Sūta Gosvāmī said; *yaḥ*—one who; *vai*—certainly; *drauṇi-astra*—by the weapon of the son of Droṇa; *vipluṣṭaḥ*—burned by; *na*—never; *mātuḥ*—of the mother; *udare*—in the womb; *mṛtaḥ*—met his death; *anugrahāt*—by the mercy; *bhagavataḥ*—of the Personality of Godhead; *kṛṣṇasya*—Kṛṣṇa; *adbhuta-karmaṇaḥ*—who acts wonderfully.

TRANSLATION

Śrī Sūta Gosvāmī said: Due to the mercy of the Personality of Godhead, Śrī Kṛṣṇa, who acts wonderfully, Mahārāja Parīkṣit, though struck by the weapon of the son of Droṇa in his mother's womb, could not be burned.

PURPORT

The sages of Naimiṣāraṇya became struck with wonder after hearing about the wonderful administration of Mahārāja Parīkṣit, especially in reference to his punishing the personality of Kali and making him completely unable to do any harm within the kingdom. Sūta Gosvāmī was equally anxious to describe Mahārāja Parīkṣit's wonderful birth and death, and this verse is stated by Sūta Gosvāmī to increase the interest of the sages of Naimiṣāraṇya.

TEXT 2

ब्रह्मकोपोत्थिताद् यस्तु तक्षकात्प्राणविप्लवात् ।
न सम्मुमोहोरुभयाद् भगवत्यर्पिताशयः ॥२॥

brahma-kopotthitād yas tu
takṣakāt prāṇa-viplavāt
na sammumohorubhayād
bhagavaty arpitāśayaḥ

brahma-kopa—fury of a *brāhmaṇa; utthitāt*—caused by; *yaḥ*—what was; *tu*—but; *takṣakāt*—by the snake-bird; *prāṇa-viplavāt*—from dissolution of life; *na*—never; *sammumoha*—was overwhelmed; *uru-bhayāt*—great fear; *bhagavati*—unto the Personality of Godhead; *arpita*—surrendered; *āśayaḥ*—consciousness.

TRANSLATION

Furthermore, Mahārāja Parīkṣit was always consciously surrendered to the Personality of Godhead, and therefore he was neither afraid nor overwhelmed by fear due to a snake-bird which was to bite him because of the fury of a brāhmaṇa boy.

PURPORT

A self-surrendered devotee of the Lord is called *nārāyaṇa-parāyaṇa.* Such a person is never afraid of any place or person, not even of death. For him nothing is as important as the Supreme Lord, and thus he gives equal importance to heaven and hell. He knows well that both heaven and hell are creations of the Lord, and similarly life and death are different conditions of existence created by the Lord. But in all conditions and in all circumstances, remembrance of Nārāyaṇa is essential. The *nārāyaṇa-parāyaṇa* practices this constantly. Mahārāja Parīkṣit was such a pure devotee. He was wrongfully cursed by an inexperienced son of a *brāhmaṇa,* who was under the influence of Kali, and Mahārāja Parīkṣit took this to be sent by Nārāyaṇa. He knew that Nārāyaṇa (Lord Kṛṣṇa) had saved him when he was burned in the womb of his mother, and if he were to be killed by a snake bite, it would also take place by the will of the Lord. The devotee never goes against the will of the Lord; anything sent by God is a blessing for the devotee. Therefore Mahārāja Parīkṣit was neither afraid of nor bewildered by such things. That is the sign of a pure devotee of the Lord.

TEXT 3

उत्सृज्य सर्वतः सङ्गं विज्ञाताजितसंस्थितिः ।
वैयासकेर्जहौ शिष्यो गङ्गायां स्वं कलेवरम् ॥३॥

utsṛjya sarvataḥ saṅgaṁ
vijñātājita-saṁsthitiḥ
vaiyāsaker jahau śiṣyo
gaṅgāyāṁ svaṁ kalevaram

utsṛjya—after leaving aside; *sarvataḥ*—all around; *saṅgam*—association; *vijñāta*—being understood; *ajita*—one who is never conquered (the Personality of Godhead); *saṁsthitiḥ*—actual position; *vaiyāsakeḥ*—unto the son of Vyāsa; *jahau*—gave up; *śiṣyaḥ*—as a disciple; *gaṅgāyām*—on the bank of the Ganges; *svam*—his own; *kalevaram*—material body.

TRANSLATION

Furthermore, after leaving all his associates, the King surrendered himself as a disciple to the son of Vyāsa [Śukadeva Gosvāmī], and thus he was able to understand the actual position of the Personality of Godhead.

PURPORT

The word *ajita* is significant here. The Personality of Godhead, Śrī Kṛṣṇa, is known as Ajita, or unconquerable, and He is so in every respect. No one can know His actual position. He is unconquerable by knowledge also. We have heard about His *dhāma,* or place, eternal Goloka Vṛndāvana, but there are many scholars who interpret this abode in different ways. But by the grace of a spiritual master like Śukadeva Gosvāmī, unto whom the King gave himself up as a most humble disciple, one is able to understand the actual position of the Lord, His eternal abode, and His transcendental paraphernalia in that *dhāma,* or abode. Knowing the transcendental position of the Lord and the transcendental method by which one can approach that transcendental *dhāma,* the King was confident about his ultimate destination, and by knowing this he could leave aside everything material, even his own body, without any difficulty of attachment. In the *Bhagavad-gītā,* it is stated, *paraṁ dṛṣṭvā nivartate:* one can give up all connection with material attachment when one is able to see the *param,* or the superior quality of things. From *Bhagavad-gītā* we understand the quality of the Lord's energy that is superior to the material quality of energy, and by the grace of a bona fide spiritual master like Śukadeva Gosvāmī, it is quite possible to know everything of the superior energy of the Lord by which the Lord manifests His eternal name, quality, pastimes, paraphernalia and variegatedness. Unless one thoroughly understands this superior or eternal energy of the Lord, it is not possible to leave the material energy, however one may theoretically speculate on the true nature of the Absolute Truth. By the grace of Lord Kṛṣṇa, Mahārāja Parīkṣit was able to receive the mercy of such a personality as Śukadeva Gosvāmī, and thus he was able to know the actual position of the unconquerable Lord. It is very difficult to find the Lord from the Vedic literatures, but it is very easy to know Him by the mercy of a liberated devotee like Śukadeva Gosvāmī.

TEXT 4

नोत्तमश्लोकवार्तानां जुषतां तत्कथामृतम् ।
स्यात्सम्भ्रमोऽन्तकालेऽपि स्मरतां तत्पदाम्बुजम् ॥४॥

nottamaśloka-vārtānāṁ
juṣatāṁ tat-kathāmṛtam
syāt sambhramo 'nta-kāle 'pi
smaratāṁ tat-padāmbujam

na—never; *uttama-śloka*—the Personality of Godhead, of whom the Vedic hymns sing; *vārtānām*—of those who live on them; *juṣatām*—of those who are engaged in; *tat*—His; *kathā-amṛtam*—transcendental topics about Him; *syāt*—it so happens; *sambhramaḥ*—misconception; *anta*—at the end; *kāle*—in time; *api*—also; *smaratām*—remembering; *tat*—His; *pada-ambujam*—lotus feet.

TRANSLATION

This was so because those who have dedicated their lives to the transcendental topics of the Personality of Godhead, of whom the Vedic hymns sing, and who are constantly engaged in remembering the lotus feet of the Lord, do not run the risk of having misconceptions even at the last moment of their lives.

PURPORT

The highest perfection of life is attained by remembering the transcendental nature of the Lord at the last moment of one's life. This perfection of life is made possible by one who has learned the actual transcendental nature of the Lord from the Vedic hymns sung by a liberated soul like Śukadeva Gosvāmī or someone in that line of disciplic succession. There is no gain in hearing the Vedic hymns from some mental speculator. When the same is heard from an actual self-realized soul and is properly understood by service and submission, everything becomes transparently clear. Thus a submissive disciple is able to live transcendentally and continue to the end of life. By scientific adaptation, one is able to remember the Lord even at the end of life, when the power of remembrance is slackened due to derangement of bodily membranes. For a common man, it is very difficult to remember things as they are at the time of death, but by the grace of the Lord and His bona fide devotees, the spiritual masters, one can get this opportunity without difficulty. And it was done in the case of Mahārāja Parīkṣit.

TEXT 5

तावत्कलिर्न प्रभवेत् प्रविष्टोऽपीह सर्वतः ।
यावदीशो महानुर्व्यामाभिमन्यव एकराट् ॥५॥

tāvat kalir na prabhavet
praviṣṭo 'pīha sarvataḥ
yāvad īśo mahān urvyām
ābhimanyava eka-rāṭ

tāvat—so long; *kaliḥ*—the personality of Kali; *na*—cannot; *prabhavet*—flourish; *praviṣṭaḥ*—entered in; *api*—even though; *iha*—here; *sarvataḥ*—everywhere; *yāvat*—as long as; *īśaḥ*—the lord; *mahān*—great; *urvyām*—powerful; *ābhimanyavaḥ*—the son of Abhimanyu; *eka-rāṭ*—the one emperor.

TRANSLATION

As long as the great, powerful son of Abhimanyu remains the Emperor of the world, there is no chance that the personality of Kali will flourish.

PURPORT

As we have already explained, the personality of Kali had entered the jurisdiction of this earth long ago, and he was looking for an opportunity to spread his influence all over the world. But he could not do so satisfactorily due to the presence of Mahārāja Parīkṣit. That is the way of good government.

The disturbing elements like the personality of Kali will always try to extend their nefarious activities, but it is the duty of the able state to check them by all means. Although Mahārāja Parīkṣit allotted places for the personality of Kali, at the same time he gave no chance for the citizens to be swayed by the personality of Kali.

TEXT 6

यस्मिन्नहनि यर्ह्येव भगवानुत्ससर्ज गाम् ।
तदैवेहानुवृत्तोऽसावधर्मप्रभवः कलिः ॥६॥

yasminn ahani yarhy eva
bhagavān utsasarja gām
tadaivehānuvṛtto 'sāv
adharma-prabhavaḥ kaliḥ

yasmin—on that; *ahani*—very day; *yarhi eva*—in the very moment; *bhagavān*—the Personality of Godhead; *utsasarja*—left aside; *gām*—the earth; *tadā*—at that time; *eva*—certainly; *iha*—in this world; *anuvṛttaḥ*—followed; *asau*—he; *adharma*—irreligion; *prabhavaḥ*—accelerating; *kaliḥ*—the personality of quarrel.

TRANSLATION

The very day and moment the Personality of Godhead, Lord Śrī Kṛṣṇa, left this earth, the personality of Kali, who promotes all kinds of irreligious activities, came into this world.

PURPORT

The Personality of Godhead and His holy name, qualities, etc., are all identical. The personality of Kali was not able to enter the jurisdiction of the earth due to the presence of the Personality of Godhead. And similarly, if there is an arrangement for the constant chanting of the holy names, qualities, etc., of the Supreme Personality of Godhead, there is no chance at all for the personality of Kali to enter. That is the technique of driving away the personality of Kali from the world. In modernized human society there are great advancements of material science, and they have invented the radio to distribute sound in the air. So instead of vibrating some nuisance sound for sense enjoyment, if the state arranges to distribute transcendental sound by resounding the holy name, fame and activities of the Lord, as they are authorized in the *Bhagavad-gītā* or *Śrīmad-Bhāgavatam,* then a favorable condition will be created, the principles of religion in the world will be reestablished, and thus the executive heads, who are so anxious to drive away corruption from the world, will be successful. Nothing is bad if properly used for the service of the Lord.

TEXT 7

नानुद्वेष्टि कलिं सम्राट् सारङ्ग इव सारभुक् ।
कुशलान्याशु सिद्ध्यन्ति नेतराणि कृतानि यत् ॥७॥

nānudveṣṭi kaliṁ samrāṭ
sāraṅga iva sāra-bhuk
kuśalāny āśu siddhyanti
netarāṇi kṛtāni yat

na—never; *anudveṣṭi*—envious; *kalim*—unto the personality of Kali; *samrāṭ*—the Emperor; *sāram-ga*—realist, like the bees; *iva*—like; *sāra-bhuk*—one who accepts the substance; *kuśalāni*—auspicious objects; *āśu*—immediately; *siddhyanti*—become successful; *na*—never; *itarāṇi*—which are inauspicious; *kṛtāni*—being performed; *yat*—as much as.

TRANSLATION

Mahārāja Parīkṣit was a realist, like the bees who only accept the essence [of a flower]. He knew perfectly well that in this age of Kali, auspicious things produce good effects immediately, whereas inauspicious acts must be actually performed [to render effects]. So he was never envious of the personality of Kali.

PURPORT

The age of Kali is called the fallen age. In this fallen age, because the living beings are in an awkward position, the Supreme Lord has given some special facilities to them. So by the will of the Lord, a living being does not become a victim of a sinful act until the act is actually performed. In other ages, simply by thinking of performing a sinful act, one used to become a victim of the act. On the contrary, a living being in this age is awarded with the results of pious acts simply by thinking of them. Mahārāja Parīkṣit, being the most learned and experienced king by the grace of the Lord, was not unnecessarily envious of the personality of Kali because he did not intend to give him any chance to perform any sinful act. He protected his subjects from falling prey to the sinful acts of the age of Kali, and at the same time he gave full facility to the age of Kali by allotting him some particular places. At the end of the *Śrīmad-Bhāgavatam* it is said that even though all nefarious activities of the personality of Kali are present, there is a great advantage in the age of Kali. One can attain salvation simply by chanting the holy name of the Lord. Thus Mahārāja Parīkṣit made an organized effort to propagate the chanting of the Lord's holy name, and thus he saved the citizens from the clutches of Kali. It is for this advantage only that great sages sometimes wish all good for the age of Kali. In the *Vedas* also it is said that by discourse on Lord Kṛṣṇa's activities, one can get rid of all the disadvantages of the age of Kali. In the beginning of the *Śrīmad-Bhāgavatam* it is also said that by the recitation of *Śrīmad-Bhāgavatam,* the Supreme Lord becomes at once arrested within one's heart. These are some of the great advantages of the age of Kali, and Mahārāja Parīkṣit took all the advantages and did not think any ill of the age of Kali, true to his Vaiṣṇavite cult.

TEXT 8

किं नु बालेषु शूरेण कलिना धीरभीरुणा ।
अप्रमत्तः प्रमत्तेषु यो वृको नृषु वर्तते ॥८॥

kiṁ nu bāleṣu śūreṇa
kalinā dhīra-bhīruṇā
apramattaḥ pramatteṣu
yo vṛko nṛṣu vartate

kim—what; *nu*—may be; *bāleṣu*—among the less intelligent persons; *śūreṇa*—by the powerful; *kalinā*—by the personality of Kali; *dhīra*—self-controlled; *bhīruṇā*—by one who is afraid of; *apramattaḥ*—one who is careful; *pramatteṣu*—among the careless; *yaḥ*—one who; *vṛkaḥ*—tiger; *nṛṣu*—among men; *vartate*—exists.

TRANSLATION

Mahārāja Parīkṣit considered that less intelligent men might find the personality of Kali to be very powerful, but that those who are self-controlled would have nothing to fear. The King was powerful like a tiger and took care for the foolish, careless persons.

PURPORT

Those who are not devotees of the Lord are careless and unintelligent. Unless one is thoroughly intelligent, one cannot be a devotee of the Lord. Those who are not devotees of the Lord fall prey to the actions of Kali. It will not be possible to bring about a saner condition in society unless we are prepared to accept the modes of action adopted by Mahārāja Parīkṣit, i.e., propagation of the devotional service of the Lord to the common man.

TEXT 9

उपवर्णितमेतद्वः पुण्यं पारीक्षितं मया ।
वासुदेवकथोपेतमाख्यानं यदपृच्छत ॥९॥

upavarṇitam etad vaḥ
puṇyaṁ pārīkṣitaṁ mayā
vāsudeva-kathopetam
ākhyānaṁ yad apṛcchata

upavarṇitam—almost everything described; *etat*—all these; *vaḥ*—unto you; *puṇyam*—pious; *pārīkṣitam*—about Mahārāja Parīkṣit; *mayā*—by me; *vāsudeva*—of Lord Kṛṣṇa; *kathā*—narrations; *upetam*—in connection with; *ākhyānam*—statements; *yat*—what; *apṛcchata*—you asked from me.

TRANSLATION

O sages, as you did ask me, now I have described almost everything regarding the narrations about Lord Kṛṣṇa in connection with the history of the pious Mahārāja Parīkṣit.

PURPORT

Śrīmad-Bhāgavatam is the history of the activities of the Lord. And the activities of the Lord are performed in relation with the devotees of the Lord. Therefore, the history of the devotees is not different from the history of Lord Kṛṣṇa's activities. A devotee of the Lord regards both the activities of the Lord and those of His pure devotees on an equal level, for they are all transcendental.

TEXT 10

या याः कथा भगवतः कथनीयोरुकर्मणः ।
गुणकर्माश्रयाः पुम्भिः संसेव्यास्ता बुभूषुभिः ॥१०॥

yā yāḥ kathā bhagavataḥ
kathanīyoru-karmaṇaḥ
guṇa-karmāśrayāḥ pumbhiḥ
saṁsevyās tā bubhūṣubhiḥ

yāḥ—whatever; *yāḥ*—and whatsoever; *kathāḥ*—topics; *bhagavataḥ*—about the Personality of Godhead; *kathanīya*—were to be spoken by me; *uru-karmaṇaḥ*—of Him who acts wonderfully; *guṇa*—transcendental qualities; *karma*—uncommon deeds; *āśrayāḥ*—involving; *pumbhiḥ*—by persons; *saṁsevyāḥ*—ought to be heard; *tāḥ*—all of them; *bubhūṣubhiḥ*—by those who want their own welfare.

TRANSLATION

Those who are desirous of achieving complete perfection in life must submissively hear all topics that are connected with the transcendental activities and qualities of the Personality of Godhead, who acts wonderfully.

PURPORT

The systematic hearing of the transcendental activities, qualities and names of Lord Śrī Kṛṣṇa pushes one towards eternal life. Systematic hearing means knowing Him gradually in truth and fact, and this knowing Him in truth and fact means attaining eternal life, as stated in the *Bhagavad-gītā.* Such transcendental, glorified activities of Lord Śrī Kṛṣṇa are the prescribed remedy for counteracting the process of birth, death, old age and disease, which are considered to be material awards for the conditioned living being. The culmination of such a perfectional stage of life is the goal of human life and the attainment of transcendental bliss.

TEXT 11

ऋषय ऊचुः
सूत जीव समाः सौम्य शाश्वतीर्विशदं यशः ।
यस्त्वं शंससि कृष्णस्य मर्त्यानाममृतं हि नः ॥११॥

ṛṣaya ūcuḥ
sūta jīva samāḥ saumya
śāśvatīr viśadaṁ yaśaḥ

yas tvaṁ śaṁsasi kṛṣṇasya
martyānām amṛtaṁ hi naḥ

ṛṣayaḥ ūcuḥ—the good sages said; *sūta*—O Sūta Gosvāmī; *jīva*—we wish you life for; *samāḥ*—many years; *saumya*—grave; *śāśvatīḥ*—eternal; *viśadam*—particularly; *yaśaḥ*—in fame; *yaḥ tvam*—because you; *śaṁsasi*—speaking nicely; *kṛṣṇasya*—of Lord Śrī Kṛṣṇa; *martyānām*—of those who die; *amṛtam*—eternity of life; *hi*—certainly; *naḥ*—our.

TRANSLATION

The good sages said: O grave Sūta Gosvāmī ! May you live many years and have eternal fame, for you are speaking very nicely about the activities of Lord Kṛṣṇa, the Personality of Godhead. This is just like nectar for mortal beings like us.

PURPORT

When we hear about the transcendental qualities and activities of the Personality of Godhead, we may always remember what has been spoken by the Lord Himself in the *Bhagavad-gītā* (4.9). His acts, even when He acts in human society, are all transcendental, for they are all accentuated by the spiritual energy of the Lord, which is distinguished from His material energy. As stated in the *Bhagavad-gītā,* such acts are called *divyam.* This means that He does not act or take His birth like an ordinary living being under the custody of material energy. Nor is His body material or changeable like that of ordinary living beings. And one who understands this fact, either from the Lord or from authorized sources, is not reborn after leaving the present material body. Such an enlightened soul is admitted into the spiritual realm of the Lord and engages in the transcendental loving service of the Lord. Therefore, the more we hear about the transcendental activities of the Lord, as they are stated in the *Bhagavad-gītā* and *Śrīmad-Bhāgavatam,* the more we can know about His transcendental nature and thus make definite progress on the path back to Godhead.

TEXT 12

कर्मण्यस्मिन्ननाश्वासे धूमधूम्रात्मनां भवान् ।
आपाययति गोविन्दपादपद्मासवं मधु ॥१२॥

karmaṇy asminn anāśvāse
dhūma-dhūmrātmanāṁ bhavān
āpāyayati govinda-
pāda-padmāsavaṁ madhu

karmaṇi—performance of; *asmin*—in this; *anāśvāse*—without certainty; *dhūma*—smoke; *dhūmra-ātmanām*—tinged body and mind; *bhavān*—your good self; *āpāyayati*—very much pleasing; *govinda*—the Personality of Godhead; *pāda*—feet; *padma-āsavam*—nectar of the lotus flower; *madhu*—honey.

TRANSLATION

We have just begun the performance of this fruitive activity, a sacrificial fire, without certainty of its result due to the many imperfections in our action. Our bodies have become black from the smoke, but we are factually pleased by the nectar of the lotus feet of the Personality of Godhead, Govinda, which you are distributing.

PURPORT

The sacrificial fire kindled by the sages of Naimiṣāraṇya was certainly full of smoke and doubts because of so many flaws. The first flaw is that there is an acute scarcity of expert *brāhmaṇas* able to carry out such performances successfully in this age of Kali. Any discrepancy in such sacrifices spoils the whole show, and the result is uncertain, like agricultural enterprises. The good result of tilling the paddy field depends on providential rain, and therefore the result is uncertain. Similarly, performance of any kind of sacrifice in this age of Kali is also uncertain. Unscrupulous greedy *brāhmaṇas* of the age of Kali induce the innocent public to such uncertain sacrificial shows without disclosing the scriptural injunction that in the age of Kali there is no fruitful sacrificial performance but the sacrifice of the congregational chanting of the holy name of the Lord. Sūta Gosvāmī was narrating the transcendental activities of the Lord before the congregation of sages, and they were factually perceiving the result of hearing these transcendental activities. One can feel this practically, as one can feel the result of eating food. Spiritual realization acts in that way.

The sages of Naimiṣāraṇya were practically sufferers from the smoke of a sacrificial fire and were doubtful about the result, but by hearing from a realized person like Sūta Gosvāmī, they were fully satisfied. In the *Brahma-vaivarta Purāṇa,* Viṣṇu tells Śiva that in the age of Kali, men full of anxieties of various kinds can vainly labor in fruitive activity and philosophical speculations, but when they are engaged in devotional service, the result is sure and certain, and there is no loss of energy. In other words, nothing performed for spiritual realization or for material benefit can be successful without the devotional service to the Lord.

TEXT 13

तुलयाम लवेनापि न स्वर्गं नापुनर्भवम् ।
भगवत्सङ्गिसङ्गस्य मर्त्यानां किमुताशिषः ॥१३॥

tulayāma lavenāpi
na svargaṁ nāpunar-bhavam
bhagavat-saṅgi-saṅgasya
martyānāṁ kim utāśiṣaḥ

tulayāma—to be balanced with; *lavena*—by a moment; *api*—even; *na*—never; *svargam*—heavenly planets; *na*—nor; *apunaḥ-bhavam*—liberation from matter; *bhagavat-saṅgi*—devotee of the Lord; *saṅgasya*—of the association; *martyānām*—those who are meant for death; *kim*—what is there; *uta*—to speak of; *āśiṣaḥ*—worldly benediction.

TRANSLATION

The value of a moment's association with the devotee of the Lord cannot even be compared to the attainment of heavenly planets or liberation from matter, and what to speak of worldly benedictions in the form of material prosperity, which are for those who are meant for death.

PURPORT

When there are some similar points, it is possible to compare one thing to another. One cannot compare the association of a pure devotee to anything material. Men who are addicted to material happiness aspire to reach the heavenly planets like the moon, Venus and Indraloka, and those who are advanced in material philosophical speculations aspire after liberation from all material bondage. When one becomes frustrated with all kinds of material advancement, one desires the opposite type of liberation, which is called *apunar-bhava,* or no rebirth. But the pure devotees of the Lord do not aspire after the happiness obtained in the heavenly kingdom, nor do they aspire after liberation from material bondage. In other words, for the pure devotees of the Lord the material pleasures obtainable in the heavenly planets are like phantasmagoria, and because they are already liberated from all material conceptions of pleasure and distress, they are factually liberated even in the material world. This means that the pure devotees of the Lord are engaged in a transcendental existence, namely in the loving service of the Lord, both in the material world and in the spiritual world. As a government servant is always the same, either in the office or at home or at any place, so a devotee has nothing to do with anything material, for he is exclusively engaged in the transcendental service of the Lord. Since he has nothing to do with anything material, what pleasure can he derive from material benedictions like kingship or other overlordships, which are finished quickly with the end of the body? Devotional service is eternal; it has no end, because it is spiritual. Therefore, since the assets of a pure devotee are completely different from material assets, there is no comparison between the two. Sūta Gosvāmī was a pure devotee of the Lord, and therefore his association with the *ṛṣis* in Naimiṣāraṇya is unique. In the material world, association with gross materialists is veritably condemned. The materialist is called *yoṣit-saṅgī,* or one who is much attached to material entanglement (women and other paraphernalia). Such attachment is conditioned because it drives away the benedictions of life and prosperity. And just the opposite is *bhāgavata-saṅgī,* or one who is always in the association with the Lord's name, form, qualities, etc. Such association is always desirable; it is worshipable, it is praiseworthy, and one may accept it as the highest goal of life.

TEXT 14

को नाम तृप्येद् रसवित्कथायां
महत्तमैकान्तपरायणस्य ।
नान्तं गुणानामगुणस्य जग्मु-
र्योगेश्वरा ये भवपाद्मुख्याः ॥१४॥

ko nāma tṛpyed rasavit kathāyāṁ
mahattamaikānta-parāyaṇasya
nāntaṁ guṇānām aguṇasya jagmur
yogeśvarā ye bhava-pādma-mukhyāḥ

kaḥ—who is he; *nāma*—specifically; *tṛpyet*—get full satisfaction; *rasa-vit*—expert in relishing mellow nectar; *kathāyām*—in the topics of; *mahat-tama*—the greatest amongst the living beings; *ekānta*—exclusively; *parāyaṇasya*—of one who is the shelter of; *na*—never; *antam*—end; *guṇānām*—of attributes; *aguṇasya*—of the Transcendence; *jagmuḥ*—could ascertain; *yoga-īśvarāḥ*—the lords of mystic power; *ye*—all they; *bhava*—Lord Śiva; *pādma*—Lord Brahmā; *mukhyāḥ*—heads.

TRANSLATION

The Personality of Godhead, Lord Kṛṣṇa [Govinda], is the exclusive shelter for all great living beings, and His transcendental attributes cannot even be measured by such masters of mystic powers as Lord Śiva and Lord Brahmā. Can anyone who is expert in relishing nectar [rasa] ever be fully satiated by hearing topics about Him?

PURPORT

Lord Śiva and Lord Brahmā are two chiefs of the demigods. They are full of mystic powers. For example, Lord Śiva drank an ocean of poison of which one drop was sufficient to kill an ordinary living being. Similarly, Brahmā could create many powerful demigods, including Lord Śiva. So they are *īśvaras,* or lords of the universe. But they are not the supreme powerful. The supreme powerful is Govinda, Lord Kṛṣṇa. He is the Transcendence, and His transcendental attributes cannot be measured even by such powerful *īśvaras* as Śiva and Brahmā. Therefore Lord Kṛṣṇa is the exclusive shelter of the greatest of all living beings. Brahmā is counted amongst the living beings, but he is the greatest of all of us. And why is the greatest of all the living beings so much attached to the transcendental topics of Lord Kṛṣṇa? Because He is the reservoir of all enjoyment. Everyone wants to relish some kind of taste in everything, but one who is engaged in the transcendental loving service of the Lord can derive unlimited pleasure from such engagement. The Lord is unlimited, and His name, attributes, pastimes, entourage, variegatedness, etc., are unlimited, and those who relish them can do so unlimitedly and still not feel satiated. This fact is confirmed in the *Padma Purāṇa:*

ramante yogino 'nante satyānanda-cid-ātmani
iti rāma-padenāsau paraṁ brahmābhidhīyate

"The mystics derive unlimited transcendental pleasures from the Absolute Truth, and therefore the Supreme Absolute Truth, the Personality of Godhead, is also known as Rāma."

There is no end to such transcendental discourses. In mundane affairs there is the law of satiation, but in transcendence there is no such satiation. Sūta Gosvāmī desired to continue the topics of Lord Kṛṣṇa before the sages of Naimiṣāraṇya, and the sages also expressed their readiness to hear from him continuously. Since the Lord is transcendence and His attributes are transcendental, such discourses increase the receptive mood of the purified audience.

TEXT 15

तन्नो भवान् वै भगवत्प्रधानो
महत्तमैकान्तपरायणस्य ।
हरेरुदारं चरितं विशुद्धं
शुश्रूषतां नो वितनोतु विद्वन् ॥१५॥

tan no bhavān vai bhagavat-pradhāno
mahattamaikānta-parāyaṇasya
harer udāraṁ caritaṁ viśuddhaṁ
śuśrūṣatāṁ no vitanotu vidvan

tat—therefore; *naḥ*—of us; *bhavān*—your good self; *vai*—certainly; *bhagavat*—in relation with the Personality of Godhead; *pradhānaḥ*—chiefly; *mahat-tama*—the greatest of all greats; *ekānta*—exclusively; *parāyaṇasya*—of the shelter; *hareḥ*—of the Lord; *udāram*—impartial; *caritam*—activities; *viśuddham*—transcendental; *śuśrūṣatām*—those who are receptive; *naḥ*—ourselves; *vitanotu*—kindly describe; *vidvan*—O learned one.

TRANSLATION

O Sūta Gosvāmī, you are a learned and pure devotee of the Lord because the Personality of Godhead is your chief object of service. Therefore please describe to us the pastimes of the Lord, which are above all material conception, for we are anxious to receive such messages.

PURPORT

The speaker on the transcendental activities of the Lord should have only one object of worship and service, Lord Kṛṣṇa, the Supreme Personality of Godhead. And the audience for such topics should be anxious to hear about Him. When such a combination is possible, namely a qualified speaker and a qualified audience, it is then and there very much congenial to continue discourses on the Transcendence. Professional speakers and a materially absorbed audience cannot derive real benefit from such discourses. Professional speakers make a show of *Bhāgavata-saptāha* for the sake of family maintenance, and the materially disposed audience hears such discourses of *Bhāgavata-saptāha* for some material benefit, namely religiosity, wealth, gratification of the senses, or liberation. Such *Bhāgavatam* discourses are not purified from the contamination of the material qualities. But the discourses between the saints of Naimiṣāraṇya and Śrī Sūta Gosvāmī are on the transcendental level. There is no motive for material gain. In such discourses, unlimited transcendental pleasure is relished both by the audience and by the speaker, and therefore they can continue the topics for many thousands of years. Now *Bhāgavata-saptāhas* are held for seven days only, and after finishing the show, both the audience and the speaker become engaged in material activities as usual. They can do so because the speaker is not *bhagavat-pradhāna* and the audience is not *śuśrūṣatām,* as explained above.

TEXT 16

स वै महाभागवतः परीक्षिद्
येनापवर्गाख्यमदभ्रबुद्धिः ।
ज्ञानेन वैयासकिशब्दितेन
भेजे खगेन्द्रध्वजपादमूलम् ॥१६॥

sa vai mahā-bhāgavataḥ parīkṣid
yenāpavargākhyam adabhra-buddhiḥ
jñānena vaiyāsaki-śabditena
bheje khagendra-dhvaja-pāda-mūlam

saḥ—he; *vai*—certainly; *mahā-bhāgavataḥ*—first-class devotee; *parīkṣit*—the King; *yena*—by which; *apavarga-ākhyam*—by the name of liberation; *adabhra*—fixed; *buddhiḥ*—intelligence; *jñānena*—by knowledge; *vaiyāsaki*—the son of Vyāsa; *śabditena*—vibrated by; *bheje*—taken to; *khaga-indra*—Garuḍa, the king of the birds; *dhvaja*—flag; *pāda-mūlam*—soles of the feet.

TRANSLATION

O Sūta Gosvāmī, please describe those topics of the Lord by which Mahārāja Parīkṣit, whose intelligence was fixed on liberation, attained the

lotus feet of the Lord, who is the shelter of Garuḍa, the king of birds. Those topics were vibrated by the son of Vyāsa [Śrīla Śukadeva].

PURPORT

There is some controversy amongst the students on the path of liberation. Such transcendental students are known as impersonalists and devotees of the Lord. The devotee of the Lord worships the transcendental form of the Lord, whereas the impersonalist meditates upon the glaring effulgence, or the bodily rays of the Lord, known as the *brahmajyoti.* Here in this verse it is said that Mahārāja Parīkṣit attained the lotus feet of the Lord by instructions in knowledge delivered by the son of Vyāsadeva, Śrīla Śukadeva Gosvāmī. Śukadeva Gosvāmī was also an impersonalist in the beginning, as he himself has admitted in the *Bhāgavatam* (2.1.9), but later on he was attracted by the transcendental pastimes of the Lord and thus became a devotee. Such devotees with perfect knowledge are called *mahā-bhāgavatas,* or first-class devotees. There are three classes of devotees, namely the *prākṛta, madhyama* and *mahā-bhāgavata.* The *prākṛta,* or third-class devotees, are temple worshipers without specific knowledge of the Lord and the Lord's devotees. The *madhyama,* or the second-class devotee, knows well the Lord, the Lord's devotees, the neophytes and the nondevotees also. But the *mahā-bhāgavata,* or the first-class devotee, sees everything in relation with the Lord and the Lord present in everyone's relation. The *mahā-bhāgavata,* therefore, does not make any distinction, particularly between a devotee and nondevotee. Mahārāja Parīkṣit was such a *mahā-bhāgavata* devotee because he was initiated by a *mahā-bhāgavata* devotee, Śukadeva Gosvāmī. He was equally kind, even to the personality of Kali, and what to speak of others.

So there are many instances in the transcendental histories of the world of an impersonalist who has later become a devotee. But a devotee has never become an impersonalist. This very fact proves that on the transcendental steps, the step occupied by a devotee is higher than the step occupied by an impersonalist. It is also stated in the *Bhagavad-gītā* (12.5) that persons stuck on the impersonal step undergo more sufferings than achievement of reality. Therefore knowledge imparted by Śukadeva Gosvāmī unto Mahārāja Parīkṣit helped him attain the service of the Lord. And this stage of perfection is called *apavarga,* or the perfect stage of liberation. Simple knowledge of liberation is material knowledge. Actual freedom from material bondage is called liberation, but attainment of the transcendental service of the Lord is called the perfect stage of liberation. Such a stage is attained by knowledge and renunciation, as we have already explained (*Bhāg.* 1.2.12), and perfect knowledge, as delivered by Śrīla Śukadeva Gosvāmī, results in the attainment of the transcendental service of the Lord.

TEXT 17

तन्नः परं पुण्यमसंवृतार्थ-
माख्यानमत्यद्भुतयोगनिष्ठम् ।
आख्याह्यनन्ताचरितोपपन्नं
पारीक्षितं भागवताभिरामम् ॥१७॥

tan naḥ paraṁ puṇyam asaṁvṛtārtham
ākhyānam atyadbhuta-yoga-niṣṭham
ākhyāhy anantācaritopapannaṁ
pārīkṣitaṁ bhāgavatābhirāmam

tat—therefore; *naḥ*—unto us; *param*—supreme; *puṇyaṁ*—purifying; *asaṁvṛta-artham*—as it is; *ākhyānam*—narration; *ati*—very; *adbhuta*—wonderful; *yoga-niṣṭham*—compact in *bhakti-yoga; ākhyāhi*—describe; *ananta*—the Unlimited; *ācarita*—activities; *upapannam*—full of; *pārīkṣitam*—spoken to Mahārāja Parīkṣit; *bhāgavata*—of the pure devotees; *abhirāmam*—particularly very dear.

TRANSLATION

Thus please narrate to us the narrations of the Unlimited, for they are purifying and supreme. They were spoken to Mahārāja Parīkṣit, and they are very dear to the pure devotees, being full of bhakti-yoga.

PURPORT

What was spoken to Mahārāja Parīkṣit and what is very dear to the pure devotees is *Śrīmad-Bhāgavatam. Śrīmad-Bhāgavatam* is mainly full of the narrations of the activities of the Supreme Unlimited, and therefore it is the science of *bhakti-yoga,* or the devotional service of the Lord. Thus it is *para,* or supreme, because although it is enriched with all knowledge and religion, it is specifically enriched with the devotional service of the Lord.

TEXT 18

सूत उवाच
अहो वयं जन्मभृतोऽद्य हास्म
वृद्धानुवृत्त्यापि विलोमजाताः ।
दौष्कुल्यमाधिं विधुनोति शीघ्रं
महत्तमानामभिधानयोगः ॥१८॥

sūta uvāca
aho vayaṁ janma-bhṛto 'dya hāsma
vṛddhānuvṛttyāpi viloma-jātāḥ
dauṣkulyam ādhiṁ vidhunoti śīghraṁ
mahattamānām abhidhāna-yogaḥ

sūtaḥ uvāca—Sūta Gosvāmī said; *aho*—how; *vayam*—we; *janma-bhṛtaḥ*—promoted in birth; *adya*—today; *ha*—clearly; *āsma*—have become; *vṛddha-anuvṛttyā*—by serving those who are advanced in knowledge; *api*—although; *viloma-jātāḥ*—born in a mixed caste; *dauṣkulyam*—disqualification of birth; *ādhim*—sufferings; *vidhunoti*—purifies; *śīghram*—very soon; *mahat-tamānām*—of those who are great; *abhidhāna*—conversation; *yogaḥ*—connection.

TRANSLATION

Śrī Sūta Gosvāmī said: O God, although we are born in a mixed caste, we are still promoted in birthright simply by serving and following the great who are advanced in knowledge. Even by conversing with such great souls, one can without delay cleanse oneself of all disqualifications resulting from lower births.

PURPORT

Sūta Gosvāmī did not take his birth in a *brāhmaṇa* family. He was born in a family of mixed caste, or an uncultured low family. But because of higher association, like Śrī Śukadeva Gosvāmī and the great *ṛṣis* of Naimiṣāraṇya, certainly the disqualification of inferior birth was washed off. Lord Śrī Caitanya Mahāprabhu followed this principle in pursuance of the Vedic usages, and by His transcendental association He elevated many lowborn, or those disqualified by birth or action, to the status of devotional service and established them in the position of *ācāryas,* or authorities. He clearly stated that any man, whatever he may be, whether a *brāhmaṇa* or *śūdra* by birth, or a householder or mendicant in the order of society, if he is conversant with the science of Kṛṣṇa, he can be accepted as an *ācārya* or *guru,* a spiritual master.

Sūta Gosvāmī learned the science of Kṛṣṇa from great *ṛṣis* and authorities like Śukadeva and Vyāsadeva and he was so qualified that even the sages of Naimiṣāraṇya eagerly wanted to hear from him the science of Kṛṣṇa in the form of *Śrīmad-Bhāgavatam.* So he had the double association of great souls by hearing and preaching. Transcendental science, or the science of Kṛṣṇa, has to be learned from the authorities, and when one preaches the science, he becomes still more qualified. So Sūta Gosvāmī had both the advantages, and thus undoubtedly he was completely freed from all disqualifications of low birth and mental agonies. This verse definitely proves that Śrīla Śukadeva Gosvāmī did not refuse to teach Sūta Gosvāmī about the transcendental science nor did the sages of Naimiṣāraṇya refuse to hear lessons from him because of his inferior birth. This means that thousands of years ago there was no bar to learning or preaching the transcendental science because of inferior birth. The rigidity of the so-called caste system in Hindu society became prominent within only one hundred years or so when the number of *dvija-bandhus,* or disqualified men in the families of higher castes, increased. Lord Śrī Caitanya revived the original Vedic system, and He elevated Ṭhākura Haridāsa to the position of *nāmācārya,* or the authority in preaching the glories of the holy name of the Lord, although His Holiness Śrīla Haridāsa Ṭhākura was pleased to appear in a family of Mohammedans.

Such is the power of pure devotees of the Lord. The Ganges water is accepted as pure, and one can become purified after taking a bath in the waters of the Ganges. But as far as the great devotees of the Lord are concerned, they can purify a degraded soul even by being seen by the lowborn, and what to speak of association. Lord Śrī Caitanya Mahāprabhu wanted to purify the whole atmosphere of the polluted world by sending qualified preachers all over the world, and it remains with the Indians to take up this task scientifically and thus do the best kind of humanitarian work. The mental diseases of the present generation are more acute than bodily diseases; it is quite fit and proper to take up the preaching of *Śrīmad-Bhāgavatam* all over the world without delay. *Mahattamānam abhidhāna* also means dictionary of great devotees, or a book full of the words of great devotees. Such a dictionary of the words of great devotees and those of the Lord are in the *Vedas* and allied literatures, specifically the *Śrīmad-Bhāgavatam.*

TEXT 19

कुतः पुनर्गृणतो नाम तस्य
महत्तमैकान्तपरायणस्य ।
योऽनन्तशक्तिर्भगवाननन्तो
महद्गुणत्वाद् यमनन्तमाहुः ॥१९॥

kutaḥ punar gṛṇato nāma tasya
mahattamaikānta-parāyaṇasya
yo 'nanta-śaktir bhagavān ananto
mahad-guṇatvād yam anantam āhuḥ

kutaḥ—what to say; *punaḥ*—again; *gṛṇataḥ*—one who chants; *nāma*—holy name; *tasya*—His; *mahat-tama*—great devotees; *ekānta*—exclusive; *parāyaṇasya*—of one who takes shelter of; *yaḥ*—He who; *ananta*—is the Unlimited; *śaktiḥ*—potency; *bhagavān*—the Personality of Godhead; *anantaḥ*—immeasurable; *mahat*—great; *guṇatvāt*—on account of such attributes; *yam*—whom; *anantam*—by the name *ananta; āhuḥ*—is called.

TRANSLATION

And what to speak of those who are under the direction of the great devotees, chanting the holy name of the Unlimited, who has unlimited potency? The Personality of Godhead, unlimited in potency and transcendental by attributes, is called the ananta [the Unlimited].

PURPORT

The *dvija-bandhu,* or the less intelligent, uncultured men born of higher castes, put forward many arguments against the lower-caste men becoming *brāhmaṇas* in this life. They argue that birth in a family of *śūdras* or less than *śūdras* is made possible by one's previous sinful acts and that one therefore has to complete the terms of disadvantages due to lower birth. And to answer these false logicians, *Śrīmad-Bhāgavatam* asserts that one who chants the holy name of the Lord under the direction of a pure devotee can at once get free from the disadvantages due to a lower-caste birth. A pure devotee of the Lord does not commit any offense while chanting the holy name of the Lord. There are ten different offenses in the chanting of the holy name of the Lord. To chant the holy name under the direction of a pure devotee is offenseless chanting. Offenseless chanting of the holy name of the Lord is transcendental, and, therefore, such chanting can at once purify one from the effects of all kinds of previous sins. This offenseless chanting indicates that one has fully understood the transcendental nature of the holy name and has thus surrendered unto the Lord. Transcendentally the holy name of the Lord and the Lord Himself are identical, being absolute. The holy name of the Lord is as powerful as the Lord. The Lord is the all-powerful Personality of Godhead, and He has innumerable names, which are all nondifferent from Him and are equally powerful also. In the last word of the *Bhagavad-gītā* the Lord asserts that one who surrenders fully unto Him is protected from all sins by the grace of the Lord. Since His name and He Himself are identical, the holy name of the Lord can protect the devotee from all effects of sins. The chanting of the holy name of the Lord can undoubtedly deliver one from the disadvantages of a lower-caste birth. The Lord's unlimited power is extended on and on by the unlimited expansion of the devotees and incarnations, and thus every devotee of the Lord and incarnations also can be equally surcharged with the potency of the Lord. Since the devotee is surcharged with the potency of the Lord, even fractionally, the disqualification due to lower birth cannot stand in the way.

TEXT 20

एतावतालं ननु सूचितेन
गुणैरसाम्यानतिशायनस्य ।
हित्वेतरान् प्रार्थयतो विभूति-
र्यस्याङ्घ्रिरेणुं जुषतेऽनभीप्सोः ॥२०॥

etāvatālaṁ nanu sūcitena
guṇair asāmyānatiśāyanasya
hitvetarān prārthayato vibhūtir
yasyāṅghri-reṇuṁ juṣate 'nabhīpsoḥ

etāvatā—so far; *alam*—unnecessary; *nanu*—if at all; *sūcitena*—by description; *guṇaiḥ*—by attributes; *asāmya*—immeasurable; *anati-śāyanasya*—of one who is unexcelled; *hitvā*—leaving aside; *itarān*—others; *prārthayataḥ*—of those who ask for; *vibhūtiḥ*—favor of the goddess of fortune; *yasya*—one whose; *aṅghri*—feet; *reṇum*—dust; *juṣate*—serves; *anabhīpsoḥ*—of one who is unwilling.

TRANSLATION

It is now ascertained that He [the Personality of Godhead] is unlimited and there is none equal to Him. Consequently no one can speak of Him adequately. Great demigods cannot obtain the favor of the goddess of fortune even by prayers, but this very goddess renders service unto the Lord, although He is unwilling to have such service.

PURPORT

The Personality of Godhead, or the Parameśvara Parabrahman, according to the *śrutis,* has nothing to do. He has no equal. Nor does anyone excel Him. He has unlimited potencies, and His every action is carried out systematically in His natural and perfect ways. Thus the Supreme Personality of Godhead is full in Himself, and He has nothing to accept from anyone else, including the great demigods like Brahmā. Others ask for the favor of the goddess of fortune, and despite such prayers she declines to award such favors. But still she renders service unto the Supreme Personality of Godhead, although He has nothing to accept from her. The Personality of Godhead in His Garbhodakaśāyī Viṣṇu feature begets Brahmā, the first created person in the material world, from His navel lotus stem and not in the womb of the goddess of fortune, who is eternally engaged in His service. These are some of the instances of His complete independence and perfection. That He has nothing to do does not mean that He is impersonal. He is transcendentally so full of inconceivable potencies that simply by His willing, everything is done without physical or personal endeavor. He is called, therefore, Yogeśvara, or the Lord of all mystic powers.

TEXT 21

अथापि यत्पादनखावसृष्टं
जगद्विरिञ्चोपहृतार्हणाम्भः ।
सेशं पुनात्यन्यतमो मुकुन्दात्
को नाम लोके भगवत्पदार्थः ॥२१॥

athāpi yat-pāda-nakhāvasṛṣṭaṁ
jagad viriñcopahṛtārhaṇāmbhaḥ
seśaṁ punāty anyatamo mukundāt
ko nāma loke bhagavat-padārthaḥ

atha—therefore; *api*—certainly; *yat*—whose; *pāda-nakha*—nails of the feet; *avasṛṣṭam*—emanating; *jagat*—the whole universe; *viriñca*—Brahmājī; *upahṛta*—collected; *arhaṇa*—worship; *ambhaḥ*—water; *sa*—along with; *īśam* —Lord Śiva; *punāti*—purifies; *anyatamaḥ*—who else; *mukundāt*—besides the Personality of Godhead Śrī Kṛṣṇa; *kaḥ*—who; *nāma*—name; *loke*—within the world; *bhagavat*—Supreme Lord; *pada*—position; *arthaḥ*—worth.

TRANSLATION

Who can be worthy of the name of the Supreme Lord but the Personality of Godhead Śrī Kṛṣṇa? Brahmājī collected the water emanating from the nails of His feet in order to award it to Lord Śiva as a worshipful welcome. This very water [the Ganges] is purifying the whole universe, including Lord Śiva.

PURPORT

The conception of many gods in the Vedic literatures by the ignorant is completely wrong. The Lord is one without a second, but He expands Himself in many ways, and this is confirmed in the *Vedas.* Such expansions of the Lord are limitless, but some of them are the living entities. The living entities are not as powerful as the Lord's plenary expansions, and therefore there are two different types of expansions. Lord Brahmā is generally one of the living entities, and Lord Śiva is the via medium between the Lord and the living entities. In other words, even demigods like Lord Brahmā and Lord Śiva, who are the chief amongst all demigods, are never equal to or greater than Lord Viṣṇu, the Supreme Personality of Godhead. The goddess of fortune, Lakṣmī, and all-powerful demigods like Brahmā and Śiva are engaged in the worship of Viṣṇu or Lord Kṛṣṇa; therefore who can be more powerful than Mukunda (Lord Kṛṣṇa) to be factually called the Supreme Personality of Godhead? The goddess of fortune, Lakṣmījī, Lord Brahmā and Lord Śiva are not independently powerful; they are powerful as expansions of the Supreme Lord, and all of them are engaged in the transcendental loving service of the Lord, and so also are the living entities. There are four sects of worshipful devotees of the Lord, and the chief amongst them are the Brahma-sampradāya, Rudra-sampradāya and Śrī-sampradāya, descending directly from Lord Brahmā, Lord Śiva and the goddess of fortune, Lakṣmī, respectively. Besides the above-mentioned three *sampradāyas,* there is the Kumāra-sampradāya, descending from Sanat-kumāra. All of the four original *sampradāyas* are still scrupulously engaged in the transcendental service of the Lord up to date, and they all declare that Lord Kṛṣṇa, Mukunda, is the Supreme Personality of Godhead, and no other personality is equal to Him or greater than Him.

TEXT 22

यत्रानुरक्ताः सहसैव धीरा
व्यपोह्य देहादिषु सङ्गमूढम् ।
व्रजन्ति तत्पारमहंस्यमन्त्यं
यस्मिन्नहिंसोपशमः स्वधर्मः ॥२२॥

yatrānuraktāḥ sahasaiva dhīrā
vyapohya dehādiṣu saṅgam ūḍham
vrajanti tat pārama-haṁsyam antyaṁ
yasminn ahiṁsopaśamaḥ sva-dharmaḥ

yatra—unto whom; *anuraktāḥ*—firmly attached; *sahasā*—all of a sudden; *eva*—certainly; *dhīrāḥ*—self-controlled; *vyapohya*—leaving aside; *deha*—the gross body and subtle mind; *ādiṣu*—relating to; *saṅgam*—attachment; *ūḍham*—taken to; *vrajanti*—go away; *tat*—that; *pārama-haṁsyam*—the highest stage of perfection; *antyam*—and beyond that; *yasmin*—in which; *ahiṁsā*—nonviolence; *upaśamaḥ*—and renunciation; *sva-dharmaḥ*—consequential occupation.

TRANSLATION

Self-controlled persons who are attached to the Supreme Lord Śrī Kṛṣṇa can all of a sudden give up the world of material attachment, including the gross body and subtle mind, and go away to attain the highest perfection of the renounced order of life, by which nonviolence and renunciation are consequential.

PURPORT

Only the self-controlled can gradually be attached to the Supreme Personality of Godhead. Self-controlled means not indulging in sense enjoyment more than is necessary. And those who are not self-controlled are given over to sense enjoyment. Dry philosophical speculation is a subtle sense enjoyment of the mind. Sense enjoyment leads one to the path of darkness. Those who are self-controlled can make progress on the path of liberation from the conditional life of material existence. The *Vedas*, therefore, enjoin that one should not go on the path of darkness but should make a progressive march towards the path of light or liberation. Self-control is actually achieved not by artificially stopping the senses from material enjoyment, but by becoming factually attached to the Supreme Lord by engaging one's unalloyed senses in the transcendental service of the Lord. The senses cannot be forcibly curbed, but they can be given proper engagement. Purified senses, therefore, are always engaged in the transcendental service of the Lord. This perfectional stage of sense engagement is called *bhakti-yoga.* So those who are attached to the means of *bhakti-yoga* are factually self-controlled and can all of a sudden give up their homely or bodily attachment for the service of the Lord. This is called the *paramahaṁsa* stage. *Haṁsas,* or swans, accept only milk out of a mixture of milk and water. Similarly, those who accept the service of the Lord instead of *māyā's* service are called the *paramahaṁsas.* They are naturally qualified with all the good attributes, such as pridelessness, freedom from vanity, nonviolence, tolerance, simplicity, respectability, worship, devotion and sincerity. All these godly qualities exist in the devotee of the Lord spontaneously. Such *paramahaṁsas,* who are completely given up to the service of the Lord, are very rare. They are very rare even amongst the liberated souls. Real nonviolence means freedom from envy. In this world everyone is envious of his fellow being. But a perfect *paramahaṁsa,* being completely given up to the service of the Lord, is perfectly nonenvious. He loves every living being in relation with the Supreme Lord. Real renunciation means perfect dependence on God. Every living being is dependent on someone else because he is so made. Actually everyone is dependent on the mercy of the Supreme Lord, but when one forgets his relation with the Lord, he becomes dependent on the conditions of material nature. Renunciation means renouncing one's dependence on the conditions of material nature and thus becoming completely dependent on the mercy of the Lord. Real independence means complete faith in the mercy of the Lord without dependence on the conditions of matter. This *paramahaṁsa* stage is the highest perfectional stage in *bhakti-yoga,* the process of devotional service to the Supreme Lord.

TEXT 23

अहं हि पृष्टोऽर्यमणो भवद्भि-
राचक्ष आत्मावगमोऽत्र यावान् ।
नभः पतन्त्यात्मसमं पतत्त्रिण-
स्तथा समं विष्णुगतिं विपश्चितः ॥२३॥

ahaṁ hi pṛṣṭo 'ryamaṇo bhavadbhir
ācakṣa ātmāvagamo 'tra yāvān
nabhaḥ patanty ātma-samaṁ patattriṇas
tathā samaṁ viṣṇu-gatiṁ vipaścitaḥ

aham—my humble self; *hi*—certainly; *pṛṣṭaḥ*—asked by you; *aryamaṇaḥ*—as powerful as the sun; *bhavadbhiḥ*—by you; *ācakṣe*—may describe; *ātma-avagamaḥ*—as far as my knowledge is concerned; *atra*—herein; *yāvān*—so far; *nabhaḥ*—sky; *patanti*—fly; *ātma-samam*—as far as it can; *patattriṇaḥ*—the birds; *tathā*—thus; *samam*—similarly; *viṣṇu-gatim*—knowledge of Viṣṇu; *vipaścitaḥ*—even though learned.

TRANSLATION

O ṛṣis, who are as powerfully pure as the sun, I shall try to describe to you the transcendental pastimes of Viṣṇu as far as my knowledge is concerned. As the birds fly in the sky as far as their capacity allows, so do the learned devotees describe the Lord as far as their realization allows.

PURPORT

The Supreme Absolute Truth is unlimited. No living being can know about the unlimited by his limited capacity. The Lord is impersonal, personal and localized. By His impersonal feature He is all-pervading Brahman, by His localized feature He is present in everyone's heart as the Supreme Soul, and by His ultimate personal feature He is the object of transcendental loving service by His fortunate associates the pure devotees. The pastimes of the Lord in different features can only be estimated partly by the great learned devotees. So Śrīla Sūta Gosvāmī has rightly taken this position in describing the pastimes of the Lord as far as he has realized. Factually only the Lord Himself can describe Himself, and His learned devotee also can describe Him as far as the Lord gives him the power of description.

TEXTS 24–25

एकदा धनुरुद्यम्य विचरन् मृगयां वने ।
मृगाननुगतः श्रान्तः क्षुधितस्तृषितो भृशम् ॥२४॥
जलाशयमचक्षाणः प्रविवेश तमाश्रमम् ।
ददर्श मुनिमासीनं शान्तं मीलितलोचनम् ॥२५॥

ekadā dhanur udyamya
vicaran mṛgayāṁ vane
mṛgān anugataḥ śrāntaḥ
kṣudhitas tṛṣito bhṛśam

jalāśayam acakṣāṇaḥ
praviveśa tam āśramam
dadarśa munim āsīnaṁ
śāntaṁ mīlita-locanam

ekadā—once upon a time; *dhanuḥ*—arrows and bow; *udyamya*—taking firmly; *vicaran*—following; *mṛgayām*—hunting excursion; *vane*—in the forest; *mṛgān*—stags; *anugataḥ*—while following; *śrāntaḥ*—fatigued; *kṣudhitaḥ*—hungry; *tṛṣitaḥ*—being thirsty; *bhṛśam*—extremely; *jala-āśayam*—reservoir of water; *acakṣāṇaḥ*—while searching for; *praviveśa*—entered into; *tam*—that famous; *āśramam*—hermitage of Śamīka Ṛṣi; *dadarśa*—saw; *munim*—the sage; *āsīnam*—seated; *śāntam*—all silent; *mīlita*—closed; *locanam*—eyes.

TRANSLATION

Once upon a time Mahārāja Parīkṣit, while engaged in hunting in the forest with bow and arrows, became extremely fatigued, hungry and thirsty while following the stags. While searching for a reservoir of water, he entered the hermitage of the well-known Śamīka Ṛṣi and saw the sage sitting silently with closed eyes.

PURPORT

The Supreme Lord is so kind to His pure devotees that in proper time He calls such devotees up to Him and thus creates an auspicious circumstance for the devotee. Mahārāja Parīkṣit was a pure devotee of the Lord, and there was no reason for him to become extremely fatigued, hungry and thirsty because a devotee of the Lord never becomes perturbed by such bodily demands. But by the desire of the Lord, even such a devotee can become apparently fatigued and thirsty just to create a situation favorable for his renunciation of worldly activities. One has to give up all attachment for worldly relations before one is able to go back to Godhead, and thus when a devotee is too much absorbed in worldly affairs, the Lord creates a situation to cause indifference. The Supreme Lord never forgets His pure devotee, even though he may be engaged in so-called worldly affairs. Sometimes He creates an awkward situation, and the devotee becomes obliged to renounce all worldly affairs. The devotee can understand by the signal of the Lord, but others take it to be unfavorable and frustrating. Mahārāja Parīkṣit was to become the medium for the revelation of *Śrīmad-Bhāgavatam* by Lord Śrī Kṛṣṇa, as his grandfather Arjuna was the medium for the *Bhagavad-gītā.* Had Arjuna not been taken up with an illusion of family affection by the will of the Lord, the *Bhagavad-gītā* would not have been spoken by the Lord Himself for the good of all concerned. Similarly, had Mahārāja Parīkṣit not been fatigued, hungry and thirsty at this time, *Śrīmad-Bhāgavatam* would not have been spoken by Śrīla Śukadeva Gosvāmī, the prime authority of *Śrīmad-Bhāgavatam.* So this is a prelude to the circumstances under which *Śrīmad-Bhāgavatam* was spoken for the benefit of all concerned. The prelude, therefore, begins with the words "once upon a time."

TEXT 26

प्रतिरुद्धेन्द्रियप्राणमनोबुद्धिमुपारतम् ।
स्थानत्रयात्परं प्राप्तं ब्रह्मभूतमविक्रियम् ॥२६॥

pratiruddhendriya-prāṇa-
mano-buddhim upāratam
sthāna-trayāt paraṁ prāptaṁ
brahma-bhūtam avikriyam

pratiruddha—restrained; *indriya*—the sense organs; *prāṇa*—air of respiration; *manaḥ*—the mind; *buddhim*—intelligence; *upāratam*—inactive; *sthāna*—places; *trayāt*—from the three; *param*—transcendental; *prāptam*—achieved; *brahma-bhūtam*—qualitatively equal with the Supreme Absolute; *avikriyam*—unaffected.

TRANSLATION

The muni's sense organs, breath, mind and intelligence were all restrained from material activities, and he was situated in a trance apart from the three [wakefulness, dream and unconsciousness], having achieved a transcendental position qualitatively equal with the Supreme Absolute.

PURPORT

It appears that the *muni,* in whose hermitage the King entered, was in yogic trance. The transcendental position is attained by three processes, namely the process of *jñāna,* or theoretical knowledge of transcendence, the process of *yoga,* or factual realization of trance by manipulation of the physiological and psychological functions of the body, and the most approved process of *bhakti-yoga,* or the engagement of senses in the devotional service of the Lord. In the *Bhagavad-gītā* also we have the information of the gradual development of perception from matter to a living entity. Our material mind and body develop from the living entity, the soul, and being influenced by the three qualities of matter, we forget our real identity. The *jñāna* process theoretically speculates about the reality of the soul. But *bhakti-yoga* factually engages the spirit soul in activities. The perception of matter is transcended to still subtler states of the senses. The senses are transcended to the subtler mind, and then to breathing activities and gradually to intelligence. Beyond the intelligence, the living soul is realized by the mechanical activities of the *yoga* system, or practice of meditation restraining the senses, regulating the breathing system and applying intelligence to rise to the transcendental position. This trance stops all material activities of the body. The King saw the *muni* in that position. He also saw the *muni* as follows.

TEXT 27

विप्रकीर्णजटाच्छन्नं रौरवेणाजिनेन च ।
विशुष्यत्तालुरुदकं तथाभूतमयाचत ॥२७॥

viprakīrṇa-jaṭācchannaṁ
rauraveṇājinena ca
viśuṣyat-tālur udakaṁ
tathā-bhūtam ayācata

viprakīrṇa—all scattered; *jaṭa-ācchannam*—covered with compressed, long hair; *rauraveṇa*—by the skin of a stag; *ajinena*—by the skin; *ca*—also; *viśuṣyat*—dried up; *tāluḥ*—palate; *udakam*—water; *tathā-bhūtam*—in that state; *ayācata*—asked for.

TRANSLATION

The sage, in meditation, was covered by the skin of a stag, and long, compressed hair was scattered all over him. The King, whose palate was dry from thirst, asked him for water.

PURPORT

The King, being thirsty, asked the sage for water. That such a great devotee and king asked for water from a sage absorbed in trance was certainly providential. Otherwise there was no chance of such a unique happening. Mahārāja Parīkṣit was thus placed in an awkward position so that gradually *Śrīmad-Bhāgavatam* could be revealed.

TEXT 28

अलब्धतृणभूम्यादिरसम्प्राप्तार्घ्यसूनृतः ।
अवज्ञातमिवात्मानं मन्यमानश्चुकोप ह ॥२८॥

alabdha-tṛṇa-bhūmy-ādir
asamprāptārghya-sūnṛtaḥ
avajñātam ivātmānaṁ
manyamānaś cukopa ha

alabdha—having not received; *tṛṇa*—seat of straw; *bhūmi*—place; *ādiḥ*—and so on; *asamprāpta*—not properly received; *arghya*—water for reception; *sūnṛtaḥ*—sweet words; *avajñātam*—thus being neglected; *iva*—like that; *ātmānam*—personally; *manyamānaḥ*—thinking like that; *cukopa*—became angry; *ha*—in that way.

TRANSLATION

The King, not received by any formal welcome by means of being offered a seat, place, water and sweet addresses, considered himself neglected, and so thinking he became angry.

PURPORT

The law of reception in the codes of the Vedic principles states that even if an enemy is received at home, he must be received with all respects. He should not be given a chance to understand that he has come into the house of an enemy. When Lord Kṛṣṇa, accompanied by Arjuna and Bhīma, approached Jarāsandha in Magadha, the respectable enemies were given a royal reception by King Jarāsandha. The guest enemy, namely Bhīma, was to fight with Jarāsandha, and yet they were given a grand reception. At night they used to sit down together as friends and guests, and in the day they used to fight, risking life and death. That was the law of reception. The reception law enjoins that a poor man, who has nothing to offer his guest, should be good enough to offer a straw mat for sitting, a glass of water for drinking and some sweet words. Therefore, to receive a guest, either friend or foe, there is no expense. It is only a question of good manners.

When Mahārāja Parīkṣit entered the door of Śamīka Ṛṣi, he did not expect a royal reception by the *ṛṣi* because he knew that saints and *ṛṣis* are not materially rich men. But he never expected that a seat of straw, a glass of water and some sweet words would be denied to him. He was not an ordinary guest, nor was he an enemy of the *ṛṣi,* and therefore the cold reception by the *ṛṣi* astonished the King greatly. As a matter of fact, the King was right to get angry with the *ṛṣi* when he needed a glass of water very badly. To become angry in such a grave situation was not unnatural for the King, but because the King himself was not less than a great saint, his becoming angry and taking action were astonishing. So it must be accepted that it was so ordained by the supreme will of the Lord. The King was a great devotee of the Lord, and the saint was also as good as the King. But by the will of the Lord, the circumstances were so created that they became ways to the King's becoming unattached to family connection and governmental activities and thus becoming a completely surrendered soul unto the lotus feet of Lord Kṛṣṇa. The merciful Lord sometimes creates such awkward positions for his pure devotees in order to drag them towards Himself from the mire of material existence. But outwardly the situations appear to be frustrating to the devotees. The devotees of the Lord are always under the protection of the Lord, and in any condition, frustration or success, the Lord is the supreme guide for the devotees. The pure devotees, therefore, accept all conditions of frustration as blessings from the Lord.

TEXT 29

अभूतपूर्वः सहसा क्षुत्तृड्भ्यामर्दितात्मनः ।
ब्राह्मणं प्रत्यभूद् ब्रह्मन् मत्सरो मन्युरेव च ॥२९॥

abhūta-pūrvaḥ sahasā
kṣut-tṛḍbhyām arditātmanaḥ
brāhmaṇaṁ praty abhūd brahman
matsaro manyur eva ca

abhūta-pūrvaḥ—unprecedented; *sahasā*—circumstantially; *kṣut*—hunger; *tṛḍbhyām*—as well as by thirst; *ardita*—being distressed; *ātmanaḥ*

—of his self; *brāhmaṇam*—unto a *brāhmaṇa; prati*—against; *abhūt*—became; *brahman*—O *brāhmaṇas; matsaraḥ*—envious; *manyuḥ*—angry; *eva*—thus; *ca*—and.

TRANSLATION

O brāhmaṇas, the King's anger and envy, directed toward the brāhmaṇa sage, were unprecedented, being that circumstances had made him hungry and thirsty.

PURPORT

For a king like Mahārāja Parīkṣit to become angry and envious, especially at a sage and *brāhmaṇa,* was undoubtedly unprecedented. The King knew well that *brāhmaṇas,* sages, children, women and old men are always beyond the jurisdiction of punishment. Similarly, the king, even though he commits a great mistake, is never to be considered a wrongdoer. But in this case, Mahārāja Parīkṣit became angry and envious at the sage due to his thirst and hunger, by the will of the Lord. The King was right to punish his subject for coldly receiving him or neglecting him, but because the culprit was a sage and a *brāhmaṇa,* it was unprecedented. As the Lord is never envious of anyone, so also the Lord's devotee is never envious of anyone. The only justification for Mahārāja Parīkṣit's behavior is that it was ordained by the Lord.

TEXT 30

स तु ब्रह्मऋषेरंसे गतासुमुरगं रुषा ।
विनिर्गच्छन्धनुष्कोट्या निधाय पुरमागतः ॥३०॥

sa tu brahma-ṛṣer aṁse
gatāsum uragaṁ ruṣā
vinirgacchan dhanuṣ-koṭyā
nidhāya puram āgataḥ

saḥ—the King; *tu*—however; *brahma-ṛṣeḥ*—of the *brāhmaṇa* sage; *aṁse*—on the shoulder; *gata-asum*—lifeless; *uragam*—snake; *ruṣā*—in anger; *vinirgacchan*—while leaving; *dhanuḥ-koṭyā*—with the front of the bow; *nidhāya*—by placing it; *puram*—palace; *āgataḥ*—returned.

TRANSLATION

While leaving, the King, being so insulted, picked up a lifeless snake with his bow and angrily placed it on the shoulder of the sage. Then he returned to his palace.

PURPORT

The King thus treated the sage tit for tat, although he was never accustomed to such silly actions. By the will of the Lord, the King, while going away, found a dead snake in front of him, and he thought that the sage, who had coldly received him, thus might be coldly rewarded by being offered a garland of a dead snake. In the ordinary course of dealing, this was not very unnatural, but in the case of Mahārāja Parīkṣit's dealing with a *brāhmaṇa* sage, this was certainly unprecedented. It so happened by the will of the Lord.

TEXT 31

एष किं निभृताशेषकरणो मीलितेक्षणः ।
मृषासमाधिराहोस्वित्किं नु स्यात्क्षत्रबन्धुभिः ॥३१॥

eṣa kiṁ nibhṛtāśeṣa-
karaṇo mīlitekṣaṇaḥ
mṛṣā-samādhir āhosvit
kiṁ nu syāt kṣatra-bandhubhiḥ

eṣaḥ—this; *kim*—whether; *nibhṛta-aśeṣa*—meditative mood; *karaṇaḥ*—senses; *mīlita*—closed; *īkṣaṇaḥ*—eyes; *mṛṣā*—false; *samādhiḥ*—trance; *āho*—remains; *svit*—if it is so; *kim*—either; *nu*—but; *syāt*—may be; *kṣatra-bandhubhiḥ*—by the lower *kṣatriya.*

TRANSLATION

Upon returning, he began to contemplate and argue within himself whether the sage had actually been in meditation, with senses concentrated and eyes closed, or whether he had just been feigning trance just to avoid receiving a lower kṣatriya.

PURPORT

The King, being a devotee of the Lord, did not approve of his own action, and thus he began to wonder whether the sage was really in a trance or was just pretending in order to avoid receiving the King, who was a *kṣatriya* and therefore lower in rank. Repentance comes in the mind of a good soul as soon as he commits something wrong. Śrīla Viśvanātha Cakravartī Ṭhākura and Śrīla Jīva Gosvāmī do not believe that the King's action was due to his past misdeeds. The arrangement was so made by the Lord just to call the King back home, back to Godhead.

According to Śrīla Viśvanātha Cakravartī, the plan was made by the will of the Lord, and by the will of the Lord the situation of frustration was created. The plan was that for his so-called misdeed the King could be cursed by an inexperienced *brāhmaṇa* boy infected by the influence of Kali, and thus the King would leave his hearth and home for good. His connections with Śrīla Śukadeva Gosvāmī would enable the presentation of the great *Śrīmad-Bhāgavatam,* which is considered to be the book incarnation of the Lord. This book incarnation of the Lord gives much fascinating information of the transcendental pastimes of the Lord, like His *rāsa-līlā* with the spiritual cowherd damsels of Vrajabhūmi. This specific pastime of the Lord has a special significance because anyone who properly learns about this particular pastime of the Lord will certainly be dissuaded from mundane sex desire and be placed on the path of sublime devotional service to the Lord. The pure devotee's mundane frustration is meant to elevate the devotee to a higher transcendental position. By placing Arjuna and the Pāṇḍavas in frustration due to the intrigue of their cousin-brothers, the prelude of the Battle of Kurukṣetra was created by the Lord. This was to incarnate the sound representative of the Lord, *Bhagavad-gītā.* So by placing King Parīkṣit in an awkward position, the incarnation of *Śrīmad-Bhāgavatam* was created by the will of the Lord. Being distressed by hunger and thirst was only a show, because the King endured much, even in the womb of his mother. He was never disturbed by the glaring heat of the *brahmāstra* released by Aśvatthāmā. The King's distressed condition was certainly unprecedented. The devotees like Mahārāja Parīkṣit are powerful enough to forbear such distresses, by the will of the Lord, and they are never disturbed. The situation, in this case, was therefore all planned by the Lord.

TEXT 32

तस्य पुत्रोऽतितेजस्वी विहरन् बालकोऽर्भकैः ।
राज्ञाघं प्रापितं तातं श्रुत्वा तत्रेदमब्रवीत् ॥३२॥

tasya putro 'titejasvī
viharan bālako 'rbhakaiḥ

rājñāghaṁ prāpitaṁ tātaṁ
śrutvā tatredam abravīt

tasya—his (the sage's); *putraḥ*—son; *ati*—extremely; *tejasvī*—powerful; *viharan*—while playing; *bālakaḥ*—with boys; *arbhakaiḥ*—who were all childish; *rājñā*—by the King; *agham*—distress; *prāpitam*—made to have; *tātam*—the father; *śrutvā*—by hearing; *tatra*—then and there; *idam*—this; *abravīt*—spoke.

TRANSLATION

The sage had a son who was very powerful, being a brāhmaṇa's son. While he was playing with inexperienced boys, he heard of his father's distress, which was occasioned by the King. Then and there the boy spoke as follows.

PURPORT

Due to Mahārāja Parīkṣit's good government, even a boy of tender age, who was playing with other inexperienced boys, could become as powerful as a qualified *brāhmaṇa.* This boy was known as Śṛṅgi, and he achieved good training in *brahmacarya* by his father so that he could be as powerful as a *brāhmaṇa,* even at that age. But because the age of Kali was seeking an opportunity to spoil the cultural heritage of the four orders of life, the inexperienced boy gave a chance for the age of Kali to enter into the field of Vedic culture. Hatred of the lower orders of life began from this *brāhmaṇa* boy, under the influence of Kali, and thus cultural life began to dwindle day after day. The first victim of brahminical injustice was Mahārāja Parīkṣit, and thus the protection given by the King against the onslaught of Kali was slackened.

TEXT 33

अहो अधर्मः पालानां पीव्नां बलिभुजामिव ।
स्वामिन्यघं यद् दासानां द्वारपानां शुनामिव ॥३३॥

aho adharmaḥ pālānāṁ
pīvnāṁ bali-bhujām iva
svāminy aghaṁ yad dāsānāṁ
dvāra-pānāṁ śunāṁ iva

aho—just look at; *adharmaḥ*—irreligion; *pālānām*—of the rulers; *pīvnām*—of one who is brought up; *bali-bhujām*—like the crows; *iva*—like;

svāmini—unto the master; *agham*—sin; *yat*—what is; *dāsānām*—of the servants; *dvāra-pānām*—keeping watch at the door; *śunām*—of the dogs; *iva*—like.

TRANSLATION

[The brāhmaṇa's son, Śṛṅgi, said:] O just look at the sins of the rulers who, like crows and watchdogs at the door, perpetrate sins against their masters, contrary to the principles governing servants.

PURPORT

The *brāhmaṇas* are considered to be the head and brains of the social body, and the *kṣatriyas* are considered to be the arms of the social body. The arms are required to protect the body from all harm, but the arms must act according to the directions of the head and brain. That is a natural arrangement made by the supreme order, for it is confirmed in the *Bhagavad-gītā* that four social orders or castes, namely the *brāhmaṇas,* the *kṣatriyas,* the *vaiśyas* and the *śūdras,* are set up according to quality and work done by them. Naturally the son of a *brāhmaṇa* has a good chance to become a *brāhmaṇa* by the direction of his qualified father, as a son of a medical practitioner has a very good chance to become a qualified medical practitioner. So the caste system is quite scientific. The son must take advantage of the father's qualification and thus become a *brāhmaṇa* or medical practitioner, and not otherwise. Without being qualified, one cannot become a *brāhmaṇa* or medical practitioner, and that is the verdict of all scriptures and social orders. Herein Śṛṅgi, a qualified son of a great *brāhmaṇa,* attained the required brahminical power both by birth and by training, but he was lacking in culture because he was an inexperienced boy. By the influence of Kali, the son of a *brāhmaṇa* became puffed up with brahminical power and thus wrongly compared Mahārāja Parīkṣit to crows and watchdogs. The King is certainly the watchdog of the state in the sense that he keeps vigilant eyes over the border of the state for its protection and defense, but to address him as a watchdog is the sign of a less-cultured boy. Thus the downfall of the brahminical powers began as they gave importance to birthright without culture. The downfall of the *brāhmaṇa* caste began in the age of Kali. And since *brāhmaṇas* are the heads of the social order, all other orders of society also began to deteriorate. This beginning of brahminical deterioration was highly deplored by the father of Śṛṅgi, as we will find.

TEXT 34

ब्राह्मणैः क्षत्रबन्धुर्हि गृहपालो निरूपितः ।
स कथं तद्गृहे द्वाःस्थः सभाण्डं भोक्तुमर्हति ॥३४॥

brāhmaṇaiḥ kṣatra-bandhur hi
gṛha-pālo nirūpitaḥ
sa kathaṁ tad-gṛhe dvāḥ-sthaḥ
sabhāṇḍaṁ bhoktum arhati

brāhmaṇaiḥ—by the brahminical order; *kṣatra-bandhuḥ*—the sons of the *kṣatriyas; hi*—certainly; *gṛha-pālaḥ*—the watchdog; *nirūpitaḥ*—designated; *saḥ*—he; *katham*—on what grounds; *tat-gṛhe*—in the home of him (the master); *dvāḥ-sthaḥ*—keeping at the door; *sa-bhāṇḍam*—in the same pot; *bhoktum*—to eat; *arhati*—deserves.

TRANSLATION

The descendants of the kingly orders are definitely designated as watchdogs, and they must keep themselves at the door. On what grounds can dogs enter the house and claim to dine with the master on the same plate?

PURPORT

The inexperienced *brāhmaṇa* boy certainly knew that the King asked for water from his father and the father did not respond. He tried to explain away his father's inhospitality in an impertinent manner befitting an uncultured boy. He was not at all sorry for the King's not being well received. On the contrary, he justified the wrong act in a way characteristic of the *brāhmaṇas* of Kali-yuga. He compared the King to a watchdog, and so it was wrong for the King to enter the home of a *brāhmaṇa* and ask for water from the same pot. The dog is certainly reared by its master, but that does not mean that the dog shall claim to dine and drink from the same pot. This mentality of false prestige is the cause of downfall of the perfect social order, and we can see that in the beginning it was started by the inexperienced son of a *brāhmaṇa*. As the dog is never allowed to enter within the room and hearth, although it is reared by the master, similarly, according to Śṛṅgī, the King had no right to enter the house of Śamīka Ṛṣi. According to the boy's opinion, the King was on the wrong side and not his father, and thus he justified his silent father.

TEXT 35

कृष्णे गते भगवति शास्तर्युत्पथगामिनाम् ।
तद्भिन्नसेतूनद्याहं शास्मि पश्यत मे बलम् ॥३५॥

kṛṣṇe gate bhagavati
śāstary utpatha-gāminām
tad bhinna-setūn adyāhaṁ
śāsmi paśyata me balam

kṛṣṇe—Lord Kṛṣṇa; *gate*—having departed from this world; *bhagavati*—the Personality of Godhead; *śāstari*—the supreme ruler; *utpatha-gāminām*—of those who are upstarts; *tat bhinna*—being separated; *setūn*—the protector; *adya*—today; *aham*—myself; *śāsmi*—shall punish; *paśyata*—just see; *me*—my; *balam*—prowess.

TRANSLATION

After the departure of Lord Śrī Kṛṣṇa, the Personality of Godhead and supreme ruler of everyone, these upstarts have flourished, our protector being gone. Therefore I myself shall take up this matter and punish them. Just witness my power.

PURPORT

The inexperienced *brāhmaṇa,* puffed up by a little *brahma-tejas,* became influenced by the spell of Kali-yuga. Mahārāja Parīkṣit gave license to Kali to live in four places as mentioned hereinbefore, but by his very expert government the personality of Kali could hardly find the places allotted him. The personality of Kali-yuga, therefore, was seeking the opportunity to establish authority, and by the grace of the Lord he found a hole in the puffed-up, inexperienced son of a *brāhmaṇa.* The little *brāhmaṇa* wanted to show his prowess in destruction, and he had the audacity to punish such a great king as Mahārāja Parīkṣit. He wanted to take the place of Lord Kṛṣṇa after His departure. These are the principal signs of upstarts who want to take the place of Śrī Kṛṣṇa under the influence of the age of Kali. An upstart with a little power wants to become an incarnation of the Lord. There are many false incarnations after the departure of Lord Kṛṣṇa from the face of the globe, and they are misleading the innocent public by accepting the spiritual obedience of the general mass of people to maintain false prestige. In other words, the personality of Kali got the opportunity to reign through this son of a *brāhmaṇa,* Śṛṅgi.

TEXT 36

इत्युक्त्वा रोषताम्राक्षो वयस्यानृषिबालकः ।
कौशिक्याप उपस्पृश्य वाग्वज्रं विससर्ज ह ॥३६॥

ity uktvā roṣa-tāmrākṣo
vayasyān ṛṣi-bālakaḥ
kauśiky-āpa upaspṛśya
vāg-vajraṁ visasarja ha

iti—thus; *uktvā*—saying; *roṣa-tāmra-akṣaḥ*—with red-hot eyes due to being angry; *vayasyān*—unto the playmates; *ṛṣi-bālakaḥ*—the son of a *ṛṣi;* *kauśikī*—the River Kauśikā; *āpaḥ*—water; *upaspṛśya*—by touching; *vāk*—words; *vajram*—thunderbolt; *visasarja*—threw; *ha*—in the past.

TRANSLATION

The son of the ṛṣi, his eyes red-hot with anger, touched the water of the River Kauśika while speaking to his playmates and discharged the following thunderbolt of words.

PURPORT

The circumstances under which Mahārāja Parīkṣit was cursed were simply childish, as it appears from this verse. Śṛṅgi was showing his impudency amongst his playmates, who were innocent. Any sane man would have prevented him from doing such great harm to all human society. By killing a king like Mahārāja Parīkṣit, just to make a show of acquired brahminical power, the inexperienced son of a *brāhmaṇa* committed a great mistake.

TEXT 37

इति लङ्घितमर्यादं तक्षकः सप्तमेऽहनि ।
दङ्क्ष्यति स्म कुलाङ्गारं चोदितो मे ततद्रुहम् ॥३७॥

iti laṅghita-maryādaṁ
takṣakaḥ saptame 'hani
daṅkṣyati sma kulāṅgāraṁ
codito me tata-druham

iti—thus; *laṅghita*—surpassing; *maryādam*—etiquette; *takṣakaḥ*—snake-bird; *saptame*—on the seventh; *ahani*—day; *daṅkṣyati*—will bite; *sma*

—certainly; *kula-aṅgāram*—the wretched of the dynasty; *coditaḥ*—having done; *me*—my; *tata-druham*—enmity towards the father.

TRANSLATION

The brāhmaṇa's son cursed the King thus: On the seventh day from today a snake-bird will bite the most wretched one of that dynasty [Mahārāja Parīkṣit] because of his having broken the laws of etiquette by insulting my father.

PURPORT

Thus the beginning of the misuse of brahminical power began, and gradually the *brāhmaṇas* in the age of Kali became devoid of both brahminical powers and culture. The *brāhmaṇa* boy considered Mahārāja Parīkṣit to be *kulāṅgāra,* or the wretched of the dynasty, but factually the *brāhmaṇa* boy himself was so because only from him did the *brāhmaṇa* caste become powerless, like the snake whose poisoned teeth are broken. The snake is fearful as long as his poison teeth are there, otherwise he is fearful only to children. The personality of Kali conquered the *brāhmaṇa* boy first, and gradually the other castes. Thus the whole scientific system of the orders of society in this age has assumed the form of a vitiated caste system, which is now being uprooted by another class of men similarly influenced by the age of Kali. One should see to the root cause of vitiation and not try to condemn the system as it is, without knowledge of its scientific value.

TEXT 38

ततोऽभ्येत्याश्रमं बालो गले सर्पकलेवरम् ।
पितरं वीक्ष्य दुःखार्तो मुक्तकण्ठो रुरोद ह ॥३८॥

tato 'bhyetyāśramaṁ bālo
gale sarpa-kalevaram
pitaraṁ vīkṣya duḥkhārto
mukta-kaṇṭho ruroda ha

tataḥ—thereafter; *abhyetya*—after entering into; *āśramam*—the hermitage; *bālaḥ*—boy; *gale sarpa*—the snake on the shoulder; *kalevaram*—body; *pitaram*—unto the father; *vīkṣya*—having seen; *duḥkha-ārtaḥ*—in a sorry plight; *mukta-kaṇṭhaḥ*—loudly; *ruroda*—cried; *ha*—in the past.

TRANSLATION

Thereafter, when the boy returned to the hermitage, he saw a snake on his father's shoulder, and out of his grief he cried very loudly.

PURPORT

The boy was not happy because he committed a great mistake, and he wanted to be relieved of the burden on his heart by crying. So after entering the hermitage and seeing his father in that condition, he cried loudly so that he might be relieved. But it was too late. The father regretted the whole incident.

TEXT 39

स वा आङ्गिरसो ब्रह्मन् श्रुत्वा सुतविलापनम् ।
उन्मील्य शनकैर्नेत्रे दृष्ट्वा चांसे मृतोरगम् ॥३९॥

sa vā āṅgiraso brahman
śrutvā suta-vilāpanam
unmīlya śanakair netre
dṛṣṭvā cāṁse mṛtoragam

saḥ—he; *vai*—also; *āṅgirasaḥ*—the *ṛṣi* born in the family of Aṅgirā; *brahman*—O Śaunaka; *śrutvā*—on hearing; *suta*—his son; *vilāpanam*—crying in distress; *unmīlya*—opening; *śanakaiḥ*—gradually; *netre*—by the eyes; *dṛṣṭvā*—by seeing; *ca*—also; *aṁse*—on the shoulder; *mṛta*—dead; *uragam*—snake.

TRANSLATION

O brāhmaṇas, the ṛṣi, who was born in the family of Aṅgirā Muni, hearing his son crying, gradually opened his eyes and saw the dead snake around his neck.

TEXT 40

विसृज्य तं च पप्रच्छ वत्स कस्माद्धि रोदिषि ।
केन वा तेऽपकृतमित्युक्तः स न्यवेदयत् ॥४०॥

visṛjya taṁ ca papraccha
vatsa kasmād dhi rodiṣi
kena vā te 'pakṛtam
ity uktaḥ sa nyavedayat

visṛjya—throwing aside; *tam*—that; *ca*—also; *papraccha*—asked; *vatsa*—my dear son; *kasmāt*—what for; *hi*—certainly; *rodiṣi*—crying; *kena*—by whom; *vā*—otherwise; *te*—they; *apakṛtam*—misbehaved; *iti*—thus; *uktaḥ*—being asked; *saḥ*—the boy; *nyavedayat*—informed of everything.

TRANSLATION

He threw the dead snake aside and asked his son why he was crying, whether anyone had done him harm. On hearing this, the son explained to him what had happened.

PURPORT

The father did not take the dead snake on his neck very seriously. He simply threw it away. Actually there was nothing seriously wrong in Mahārāja Parīkṣit's act, but the foolish son took it very seriously, and being influenced by Kali he cursed the King and thus ended a chapter of happy history.

TEXT 41

निशम्य शप्तमतदर्हं नरेन्द्रं
स ब्राह्मणो नात्मजमभ्यनन्दत् ।
अहो बतांहो महदद्य ते कृत-
मल्पीयसि द्रोह उरुर्दमो धृतः ॥४१॥

niśamya śaptam atad-arhaṁ narendraṁ
sa brāhmaṇo nātmajam abhyanandat
aho batāṁho mahad adya te kṛtam
alpīyasi droha urur damo dhṛtaḥ

niśamya—after hearing; *śaptam*—cursed; *atat-arham*—never to be condemned; *nara-indram*—unto the King, best of humankind; *saḥ*—that; *brāhmaṇaḥ*—*brāhmaṇa-ṛṣi; na*—not; *ātma-jam*—his own son; *abhyanandat*—congratulated; *aho*—alas; *bata*—distressing; *aṁhaḥ*—sins; *mahat*—great; *adya*—today; *te*—yourself; *kṛtam*—performed; *alpīyasi*—insignificant; *drohe*—offense; *uruḥ*—very great; *damaḥ*—punishment; *dhṛtaḥ*—awarded.

TRANSLATION

The father heard from his son that the King had been cursed, although he should never have been condemned, for he was the best amongst all

human beings. The ṛṣi did not congratulate his son, but, on the contrary, began to repent, saying: Alas! What a great sinful act was performed by my son. He has awarded heavy punishment for an insignificant offense.

PURPORT

The king is the best of all human beings. He is the representative of God, and he is never to be condemned for any of his actions. In other words, the king can do no wrong. The king may order hanging of a culprit son of a *brāhmaṇa,* but he does not become sinful for killing a *brāhmaṇa.* Even if there is something wrong with the king, he is never to be condemned. A medical practitioner may kill a patient by mistaken treatment, but such a killer is never condemned to death. So what to speak of a good and pious king like Mahārāja Parīkṣit? In the Vedic way of life, the king is trained to become a *rājarṣi,* or a great saint, although he is ruling as king. It is the king only by whose good government the citizens can live peacefully and without any fear. The *rājarṣis* would manage their kingdoms so nicely and piously that their subjects would respect them as if they were the Lord. That is the instruction of the *Vedas.* The king is called *narendra,* or the best amongst the human beings. How then could a king like Mahārāja Parīkṣit be condemned by an inexperienced, puffed-up son of a *brāhmaṇa,* even though he had attained the powers of a qualified *brāhmaṇa?*

Since Śamīka Ṛṣi was an experienced, good *brāhmaṇa,* he did not approve of the actions of his condemned son. He began to lament for all that his son had done. The king was beyond the jurisdiction of curses as a general rule, and what to speak of a good king like Mahārāja Parīkṣit. The offense of the King was most insignificant, and his being condemned to death was certainly a very great sin for Śṛṅgi. Therefore Ṛṣi Śamīka regretted the whole incident.

TEXT 42

न वै नृभिर्नरदेवं पराख्यं
सम्मातुमर्हस्यविपक्वबुद्धे ।
यत्तेजसा दुर्विषहेण गुप्ता
विन्दन्ति भद्राण्यकुतोभयाः प्रजाः ॥४२॥

na vai nṛbhir nara-devaṁ parākhyaṁ
sammātum arhasy avipakva-buddhe
yat-tejasā durviṣaheṇa guptā
vindanti bhadrāṇy akutobhayāḥ prajāḥ

na—never; *vai*—as a matter of fact; *nṛbhiḥ*—by any man; *nara-devam*—unto a man-god; *para-ākhyam*—who is transcendental; *sammātum*—place on equal footing; *arhasi*—by the prowess; *avipakva*—unripe or immature; *buddhe*—intelligence; *yat*—of whom; *tejasā*—by the prowess; *durviṣaheṇa*—unsurpassable; *guptāḥ*—protected; *vindanti*—enjoys; *bhadrāṇi*—all prosperity; *akutaḥ-bhayāḥ*—completely defended; *prajāḥ*—the subjects.

TRANSLATION

O my boy, your intelligence is immature, and therefore you have no knowledge that the king, who is the best amongst human beings, is as good as the Personality of Godhead. He is never to be placed on an equal footing with common men. The citizens of the state live in prosperity, being protected by his unsurpassable prowess.

TEXT 43

अलक्ष्यमाणे नरदेवनाम्नि
रथाङ्गपाणावयमङ्ग लोकः ।
तदा हि चौरप्रचुरो विनङ्क्ष्य-
त्यरक्ष्यमाणोऽविवरूथवत् क्षणात् ॥४३॥

alakṣyamāṇe nara-deva-nāmni
rathāṅga-pāṇāv ayam aṅga lokaḥ
tadā hi caura-pracuro vinaṅkṣyaty
arakṣyamāṇo 'vivarūthavat kṣaṇāt

alakṣyamāṇe—being abolished; *nara-deva*—monarchical; *nāmni*—of the name; *ratha-aṅga-pāṇau*—the representative of the Lord; *ayam*—this; *aṅga*—O my boy; *lokaḥ*—this world; *tadā hi*—at once; *caura*—thieves; *pracuraḥ*—too much; *vinaṅkṣyati*—vanquishes; *arakṣyamāṇaḥ*—being not protected; *avivarūtha-vat*—like lambs; *kṣaṇāt*—at once.

TRANSLATION

My dear boy, the Lord, who carries the wheel of a chariot, is represented by the monarchical regime, and when this regime is abolished the whole world becomes filled with thieves, who then at once vanquish the unprotected subjects like scattered lambs.

PURPORT

According to *Śrīmad-Bhāgavatam* the monarchical regime represents the Supreme Lord, the Personality of Godhead. The king is said to be the representative of the Absolute Personality of Godhead because he is trained to acquire the qualities of God to protect the living beings. The Battle of Kurukṣetra was planned by the Lord to establish the real representative of the Lord, Mahārāja Yudhiṣṭhira. An ideal king thoroughly trained by culture and devotional service with the martial spirit makes a perfect king. Such a personal monarchy is far better than the so-called democracy of no training and responsibility. The thieves and rogues of modern democracy seek election by misrepresentation of votes, and the successful rogues and thieves devour the mass of population. One trained monarch is far better than hundreds of useless ministerial rogues, and it is hinted herein that by abolition of a monarchical regime like that of Mahārāja Parīkṣit, the mass of people become open to many attacks of the age of Kali. They are never happy in an overly advertised form of democracy. The result of such a kingless administration is described in the following verses.

TEXT 44

तदद्य नः पापमुपैत्यनन्वयं
यन्नष्टनाथस्य वसोर्विलुम्पकात् ।
परस्परं घ्नन्ति शपन्ति वृञ्जते
पशून् स्त्रियोऽर्थान् पुरुदस्यवो जनाः ॥४४॥

tad adya naḥ pāpam upaity ananvayaṁ
yan naṣṭa-nāthasya vasor vilumpakāt
parasparaṁ ghnanti śapanti vṛñjate
paśūn striyo 'rthān puru-dasyavo janāḥ

tat—for this reason; *adya*—from this day; *naḥ*—upon us; *pāpam*—reaction of sin; *upaiti*—will overtake; *ananvayam*—disruption; *yat*—because; *naṣṭa*—abolished; *nāthasya*—of the monarch; *vasoḥ*—of wealth; *vilumpakāt*—being plundered; *parasparam*—between one another; *ghnanti*—will kill; *śapanti*—will do harm; *vṛñjate*—will steal; *paśūn*—animals; *striyaḥ*—women; *arthān*—riches; *puru*—greatly; *dasyavaḥ*—thieves; *janāḥ*—the mass of people.

TRANSLATION

Due to the termination of the monarchical regimes and the plundering of the people's wealth by rogues and thieves, there will be great social disruptions. People will be killed and injured, and animals and women will be stolen. And for all these sins we shall be responsible.

PURPORT

The word *naḥ* (we) is very significant in this verse. The sage rightly takes the responsibility of the *brāhmaṇas* as a community for killing monarchical government and thus giving an opportunity to the so-called democrats, who are generally plunderers of the wealth of the state subjects. The so-called democrats capture the administrative machine without assuming responsibility for the prosperous condition of the citizens. Everyone captures the post for personal gratification, and thus instead of one king, a number of irresponsible kings grow up to tax the citizens. It is foretold herein that in the absence of good monarchical government, everyone will be the cause of disturbance for others by plundering riches, animals, women, etc.

TEXT 45

तदार्यधर्मः प्रविलीयते नृणां
वर्णाश्रमाचारयुतस्त्रयीमयः ।
ततोऽर्थकामाभिनिवेशितात्मनां
शुनां कपीनामिव वर्णसङ्करः ॥४५॥

tadārya-dharmaḥ pravilīyate nṛṇāṁ
varṇāśramācāra-yutas trayīmayaḥ
tato 'rtha-kāmābhiniveśitātmanāṁ
śunāṁ kapīnām iva varṇa-saṅkaraḥ

tadā—at that time; *ārya*—progressive civilization; *dharmaḥ*—engagement; *pravilīyate*—is systematically vanquished; *nṛṇām*—of humankind; *varṇa*—caste; *āśrama*—orders of society; *ācāra-yutaḥ*—composed in a good manner; *trayī-mayaḥ*—in terms of the Vedic injunction; *tataḥ*—thereafter; *artha*—economic development; *kāma-abhiniveśita*—fully absorbed in sense gratification; *ātmanām*—of men; *śunām*—like dogs; *kapīnām*—like monkeys; *iva*—thus; *varṇa-saṅkaraḥ*—unwanted population.

TRANSLATION

At that time the people in general will fall systematically from the path of a progressive civilization in respect to the qualitative engagements of the castes and the orders of society and the Vedic injunctions. Thus they will be more attracted to economic development for sense gratification, and as a result there will be an unwanted population on the level of dogs and monkeys.

PURPORT

It is foretold herein that in the absence of a monarchical regime, the general mass of people will be an unwanted population like dogs and monkeys. As the monkeys are too sexually inclined and dogs are shameless in sexual intercourse, the general mass of population born of illegitimate connection will systematically go astray from the Vedic way of good manners and qualitative engagements in the castes and orders of life.

The Vedic way of life is the progressive march of the civilization of the Āryans. The Āryans are progressive in Vedic civilization. The Vedic civilization's destination is to go back to Godhead, back home, where there is no birth, no death, no old age and no disease. The *Vedas* direct everyone not to remain in the darkness of the material world but to go towards the light of the spiritual kingdom far beyond the material sky. The qualitative caste system and the orders of life are scientifically planned by the Lord and His representatives, the great *ṛṣis.* The perfect way of life gives all sorts of instruction in things both material and spiritual. The Vedic way of life does not allow any man to be like the monkeys and dogs. A degraded civilization of sense gratification and economic development is the by-product of a godless or kingless government of the people, by the people, and for the people. The people should not, therefore, begrudge the poor administrations they themselves elect.

TEXT 46

धर्मपालो नरपतिः स तु सम्राड् बृहच्छ्रवाः ।
साक्षान्महाभागवतो राजर्षिर्हयमेधयाट् ।
क्षुत्तृट्श्रमयुतो दीनो नैवास्मच्छापमर्हति ॥४६॥

dharma-pālo nara-patiḥ
sa tu samrāḍ bṛhac-chravāḥ
sākṣān mahā-bhāgavato
rājarṣir haya-medhayāṭ

kṣut-tṛṭ-śrama-yuto dīno
naivāsmac chāpam arhati

dharma-pālaḥ—the protector of religion; *nara-patiḥ*—the King; *saḥ*—he; *tu*—but; *samrāṭ*—Emperor; *bṛhat*—highly; *śravāḥ*—celebrated; *sākṣāt*—directly; *mahā-bhāgavataḥ*—the first-class devotee of the Lord; *rāja-ṛṣiḥ*—saint amongst the royal order; *haya-medhayāṭ*—great performer of horse sacrifices; *kṣut*—hunger; *tṛṭ*—thirst; *śrama-yutaḥ*—tired and fatigued; *dīnaḥ*—stricken; *na*—never; *eva*—thus; *asmat*—by us; *śāpam*—curse; *arhati*—deserves.

TRANSLATION

The Emperor Parīkṣit is a pious king. He is highly celebrated and is a first-class devotee of the Personality of Godhead. He is a saint amongst royalty, and he has performed many horse sacrifices. When such a king is tired and fatigued, being stricken with hunger and thirst, he does not at all deserve to be cursed.

PURPORT

After explaining the general codes relating to the royal position and asserting that the king can do no wrong and therefore is never to be condemned, the sage Śamīka wanted to say something about Emperor Parīkṣit specifically. The specific qualification of Mahārāja Parīkṣit is summarized herein. The King, even calculated as a king only, was most celebrated as a ruler who administered the religious principles of the royal order. In the *śāstras* the duties of all castes and orders of society are prescribed. All the qualities of a *kṣatriya* mentioned in the *Bhagavad-gītā* (18.43) were present in the person of the Emperor. He was also a great devotee of the Lord and a self-realized soul. Cursing such a king, when he was tired and fatigued with hunger and thirst, was not at all proper. Śamīka Ṛṣi thus admitted from all sides that Mahārāja Parīkṣit was cursed most unjustly. Although all the *brāhmaṇas* were aloof from the incident, still for the childish action of a *brāhmaṇa* boy the whole world situation was changed. Thus Ṛṣi Śamīka, a *brāhmaṇa,* took responsibility for all deterioration of the good orders of the world.

TEXT 47

अपापेषु स्वभृत्येषु बालेनापक्वबुद्धिना ।
पापं कृतं तद्भगवान् सर्वात्मा क्षन्तुमर्हति ॥४७॥

apāpeṣu sva-bhṛtyeṣu
bālenāpakva-buddhinā
pāpaṁ kṛtaṁ tad bhagavān
sarvātmā kṣantum arhati

apāpeṣu—unto one who is completely free from all sins; *sva-bhṛtyeṣu*—unto one who is subordinate and deserves to be protected; *bālena*—by a child; *apakva*—who is immature; *buddhinā*—by intelligence; *pāpam*—sinful act; *kṛtam*—has been done; *tat bhagavān*—therefore the Personality of Godhead; *sarva-ātmā*—who is all-pervading; *kṣantum*—just to pardon; *arhati*—deserve.

TRANSLATION

Then the ṛṣi prayed to the all-pervading Personality of Godhead to pardon his immature boy, who had no intelligence and who committed the great sin of cursing a person who was completely free from all sins, who was subordinate and who deserved to be protected.

PURPORT

Everyone is responsible for his own action, either pious or sinful. Ṛṣi Śamīka could foresee that his son had committed a great sin by cursing Mahārāja Parīkṣit, who deserved to be protected by the *brāhmaṇas,* for he was a pious ruler and completely free from all sins because of his being a first-class devotee of the Lord. When an offense is done unto the devotee of the Lord, it is very difficult to overcome the reaction. The *brāhmaṇas,* being at the head of the social orders, are meant to give protection to their subordinates and not to curse them. There are occasions when a *brāhmaṇa* may furiously curse a subordinate *kṣatriya* or *vaiśya,* etc., but in the case of Mahārāja Parīkṣit there were no grounds, as already explained. The foolish boy had done it out of sheer vanity in being a *brāhmaṇa's* son, and thus he became liable to be punished by the law of God. The Lord never forgives a person who condemns His pure devotee. Therefore, by cursing a king the foolish Śṛṅgi had committed not only a sin but also the greatest offense. Therefore the *ṛṣi* could foresee that only the Supreme Personality of Godhead could save his boy from his sinful act. He therefore directly prayed for pardon from the Supreme Lord, who alone can undo a thing which is impossible to change. The appeal was made in the name of a foolish boy who had developed no intelligence at all.

A question may be raised herein that since it was the desire of the Lord that Parīkṣit Mahārāja be put into that awkward position so that he might be delivered from material existence, then why was a *brāhmaṇa's* son made responsible for this offensive act? The answer is that the offensive act was performed by a child only so that he could be excused very easily, and thus the prayer of the father was accepted. But if the question is raised why the *brāhmaṇa* community as a whole was made responsible for allowing Kali into the world affairs, the answer is given in the *Varāha Purāṇa* that the demons who acted inimically toward the Personality of Godhead but were not killed by the Lord were allowed to take birth in the families of *brāhmaṇas* to take advantage of the age of Kali. The all-merciful Lord gave them a chance to have their births in the families of pious *brāhmaṇas* so that they could progress toward salvation. But the demons, instead of utilizing the good opportunity, misused the brahminical culture due to being puffed up by vanity in becoming *brāhmaṇas.* The typical example is the son of Śamīka Ṛṣi, and all the foolish sons of *brāhmaṇas* are warned hereby not to become as foolish as Śṛṅgi and to be always on guard against the demoniac qualities which they had in their previous births. The foolish boy was, of course, excused by the Lord, but others, who may not have a father like Śamīka Ṛṣi, will be put into great difficulty if they misuse the advantages obtained by birth in a *brāhmaṇa* family.

TEXT 48

तिरस्कृता विप्रलब्धाः शप्ताः क्षिप्ता हता अपि ।
नास्य तत् प्रतिकुर्वन्ति तद्भक्ताः प्रभवोऽपि हि ॥४८॥

tiraskṛtā vipralabdhāḥ
śaptāḥ kṣiptā hatā api
nāsya tat pratikurvanti
tad-bhaktāḥ prabhavo 'pi hi

tiraḥ-kṛtāḥ—being defamed; *vipralabdhāḥ*—being cheated; *śaptāḥ*—being cursed; *kṣiptāḥ*—disturbed by negligence; *hatāḥ*—or even being killed; *api*—also; *na*—never; *asya*—for all these acts; *tat*—them; *pratikurvanti*—counteract; *tat*—the Lord's; *bhaktāḥ*—devotees; *prabhavaḥ*—powerful; *api*—although; *hi*—certainly.

TRANSLATION

The devotees of the Lord are so forbearing that even though they are defamed, cheated, cursed, disturbed, neglected or even killed, they are never inclined to avenge themselves.

PURPORT

Ṛṣi Śamīka also knew that the Lord does not forgive a person who has committed an offense at the feet of a devotee. The Lord can only give direction to take shelter of the devotee. He thought within himself that if Mahārāja Parīkṣit would countercurse the boy, he might be saved. But he knew also that a pure devotee is callous about worldly advantages or reverses. As such, the devotees are never inclined to counteract personal defamation, curses, negligence, etc. As far as such things are concerned, in personal affairs the devotees do not care for them. But in the case of their being performed against the Lord and His devotees, then the devotees take very strong action. It was a personal affair, and therefore Śamīka Ṛṣi knew that the King would not take counteraction. Thus there was no alternative than to place an appeal to the Lord for the immature boy.

It is not that only the *brāhmaṇas* are powerful enough to award curses or blessings upon the subordinates; the devotee of the Lord, even though he may not be a *brāhmaṇa,* is more powerful than a *brāhmaṇa.* But a powerful devotee never misuses the power for personal benefit. Whatever power the devotee may have is always utilized in service towards the Lord and His devotees only.

TEXT 49

इति पुत्रकृताघेन सोऽनुतप्तो महामुनिः ।
स्वयं विप्रकृतो राज्ञा नैवाघं तदचिन्तयत् ॥४९॥

iti putra-kṛtāghena
so 'nutapto mahā-muniḥ
svayaṁ viprakṛto rājñā
naivāghaṁ tad acintayat

iti—thus; *putra*—son; *kṛta*—done by; *aghena*—by the sin; *saḥ*—he (the *muni*); *anutaptaḥ*—regretting; *mahā-muniḥ*—the sage; *svayam*—personally; *viprakṛtaḥ*—being so insulted; *rājñā*—by the King; *na*—not; *eva*—certainly; *agham*—the sin; *tat*—that; *acintayat*—thought of it.

TRANSLATION

The sage thus regretted the sin committed by his own son. He did not take the insult paid by the King very seriously.

PURPORT

The whole incident is now cleared up. Mahārāja Parīkṣit's garlanding the sage with a dead snake was not at all a very serious offense, but Śṛṅgi's cursing the King was a serious offense. The serious offense was committed by a foolish child only; therefore he deserved to be pardoned by the Supreme Lord, although it was not possible to get free from the sinful reaction. Mahārāja Parīkṣit also did not mind the curse offered to him by a foolish *brāhmaṇa.* On the contrary, he took full advantage of the awkward situation, and by the great will of the Lord, Mahārāja Parīkṣit achieved the highest perfection of life through the grace of Śrīla Śukadeva Gosvāmī. Actually it was the desire of the Lord, and Mahārāja Parīkṣit, Ṛṣi Śamīka and his son Śṛṅgi were all instrumental in fulfilling the desire of the Lord. So none of them were put into difficulty because everything was done in relation with the Supreme Person.

TEXT 50

प्रायशः साधवो लोके परैर्द्वन्द्वेषु योजिताः ।
न व्यथन्ति न हृष्यन्ति यत आत्माऽगुणाश्रयः ॥५०॥

prāyaśaḥ sādhavo loke
parair dvandveṣu yojitāḥ
na vyathanti na hṛṣyanti
yata ātmā 'guṇāśrayaḥ

prāyaśaḥ—generally; *sādhavaḥ*—saints; *loke*—in this world; *paraiḥ*—by others; *dvandveṣu*—in duality; *yojitāḥ*—being engaged; *na*—never; *vyathanti*—distressed; *na*—nor; *hṛṣyanti*—takes pleasure; *yataḥ*—because; *ātmā*—self; *aguṇa-āśrayaḥ*—transcendental.

TRANSLATION

Generally the transcendentalists, even though engaged by others in the dualities of the material world, are not distressed. Nor do they take pleasure [in worldly things], for they are transcendentally engaged.

PURPORT

The transcendentalists are the empiric philosophers, the mystics and the devotees of the Lord. Empiric philosophers aim at the perfection of merging into the being of the Absolute, mystics aim at perceiving the all-pervading

Supersoul, and the devotees of the Lord are engaged in the transcendental loving service of the Personality of Godhead. Since Brahman, Paramātmā and Bhagavān are different phases of the same Transcendence, all these transcendentalists are beyond the three modes of material nature. Material distresses and happinesses are products of the three modes, and therefore the causes of such material distress and happiness have nothing to do with the transcendentalists. The King was a devotee, and the *ṛṣi* was a mystic. Therefore both of them were unattached to the accidental incident created by the supreme will. The playful child was an instrument in fulfilling the Lord's will.

Thus end the Bhaktivedanta purports of the First Canto, Eighteenth Chapter, of the Śrīmad-Bhāgavatam, *entitled "Mahārāja Parīkṣit Cursed by a Brāhmaṇa Boy."*

CHAPTER NINETEEN

The Appearance of Śukadeva Gosvāmī

TEXT 1

सूत उवाच
महीपतिस्त्वथ तत्कर्म गर्ह्यं
विचिन्तयन्नात्मकृतं सुदुर्मनाः ।
अहो मया नीचमनार्यवत्कृतं
निरागसि ब्रह्मणि गूढतेजसि ॥१॥

sūta uvāca
mahī-patis tv atha tat-karma garhyaṁ
vicintayann ātma-kṛtaṁ sudurmanāḥ
aho mayā nīcam anārya-vat kṛtaṁ
nirāgasi brahmaṇi gūḍha-tejasi

sūtaḥ uvāca—Sūta Gosvāmī said; *mahī-patiḥ*—the King; *tu*—but; *atha*—thus (while coming back home); *tat*—that; *karma*—act; *garhyam*—abominable; *vicintayan*—thus thinking; *ātma-kṛtam*—done by himself; *su-durmanāḥ*—very much depressed; *aho*—alas; *mayā*—by me; *nīcam*—heinous; *anārya*—uncivilized; *vat*—like; *kṛtam*—done; *nirāgasi*—unto one who is faultless; *brahmaṇi*—unto a *brāhmaṇa; gūḍha*—grave; *tejasi*—unto the powerful.

TRANSLATION

Śrī Sūta Gosvāmī said: While returning home, the King [Mahārāja Parīkṣit] felt that the act he had committed against the faultless and powerful brāhmaṇa was heinous and uncivilized. Consequently he was distressed.

PURPORT

The pious King regretted his accidental improper treatment of the powerful *brāhmaṇa,* who was faultless. Such repentance is natural for a good man like the King, and such repentance delivers a devotee from all kinds of sins accidentally committed. The devotees are naturally faultless. Accidental sins committed by a devotee are sincerely regretted, and by the grace of the Lord all sins unwillingly committed by a devotee are burnt in the fire of repentance.

TEXT 2

ध्रुवं ततो मे कृतदेवहेलनाद्
दुरत्ययं व्यसनं नातिदीर्घात् ।
तदस्तु कामं ह्यघनिष्कृताय मे
यथा न कुर्यां पुनरेवमद्धा ॥२॥

dhruvaṁ tato me kṛta-deva-helanād
duratyayaṁ vyasanaṁ nāti-dīrghāt
tad astu kāmaṁ hy agha-niṣkṛtāya me
yathā na kuryāṁ punar evam addhā

dhruvam—sure and certain; *tataḥ*—therefore; *me*—my; *kṛta-deva-helanāt*—because of disobeying the orders of the Lord; *duratyayam*—very difficult; *vyasanam*—calamity; *na*—not; *ati*—greatly; *dīrghāt*—far off; *tat*—that; *astu*—let it be; *kāmam*—desire without reservations; *hi*—certainly; *agha*—sins; *niṣkṛtāya*—for getting free; *me*—my; *yathā*—so that; *na*—never; *kuryām*—shall I do it; *punaḥ*—again; *evam*—as I have done; *addhā*—directly.

TRANSLATION

[King Parīkṣit thought:] Due to my neglecting the injunctions of the Supreme Lord I must certainly expect some difficulty to overcome me in the near future. I now desire without reservation that the calamity come now, for in this way I may be freed of the sinful action and not commit such an offense again.

PURPORT

The Supreme Lord enjoins that *brāhmaṇas* and cows must be given all protection. The Lord is Himself very much inclined to do good to *brāhmaṇas* and cows (*go-brāhmaṇa-hitāya ca*). Mahārāja Parīkṣit knew all this, and thus he concluded that his insulting a powerful *brāhmaṇa* was certainly to be punished by the laws of the Lord, and he was expecting something very difficult in the very near future. He therefore desired the imminent calamity to fall on him and not on his family members. A man's personal misconduct affects all his family members. Therefore Mahārāja Parīkṣit desired the calamity to fall on him alone. By suffering personally he would be restrained from future sins, and at the same time the sin which he had committed would be counteracted so that his descendants would not suffer. That is the way a responsible devotee thinks. The family members of a devotee also share the effects of a devotee's service unto the Lord. Mahārāja Prahlāda saved his demon father by his personal devotional service. A devotee son in the family is the greatest boon or blessing of the Lord.

TEXT 3

अद्यैव राज्यं बलमृद्धकोशं
प्रकोपितब्रह्मकुलानलो मे ।
दहत्वभद्रस्य पुनर्न मेऽभूत्
पापीयसी धीर्द्विजदेवगोभ्यः ॥३॥

adyaiva rājyaṁ balam ṛddha-kośaṁ
prakopita-brahma-kulānalo me
dahatv abhadrasya punar na me 'bhūt
pāpīyasī dhīr dvija-deva-gobhyaḥ

adya—this day; *eva*—on the very; *rājyam*—kingdom; *balam ṛddha*—strength and riches; *kośam*—treasury; *prakopita*—ignited by; *brahma-kula*—by the *brāhmaṇa* community; *analaḥ*—fire; *me dahatu*—let it burn me; *abhadrasya*—inauspiciousness; *punaḥ*—again; *na*—not; *me*—unto me; *abhūt*—may occur; *pāpīyasī*—sinful; *dhīḥ*—intelligence; *dvija*—*brāhmaṇas; deva*—the Supreme Lord; *gobhyaḥ*—and the cows.

TRANSLATION

I am uncivilized and sinful due to my neglect of brahminical culture, God consciousness and cow protection. Therefore I wish that my kingdom, strength and riches burn up immediately by the fire of the brāhmaṇa's wrath so that in the future I may not be guided by such inauspicious attitudes.

PURPORT

Progressive human civilization is based on brahminical culture, God consciousness and protection of cows. All economic development of the state by trade, commerce, agriculture and industries must be fully utilized in relation to the above principles, otherwise all so-called economic development becomes a source of degradation. Cow protection means feeding the brahminical culture, which leads towards God consciousness, and thus perfection of human civilization is achieved. The age of Kali aims at killing the higher principles of life, and although Mahārāja Parīkṣit strongly resisted the domination of the personality of Kali within the world, the influence of the age of Kali came at an opportune moment, and even a strong king like Mahārāja Parīkṣit was induced to disregard the brahminical culture due to a slight provocation of hunger and thirst. Mahārāja Parīkṣit lamented the accidental incident, and he desired that all his kingdom, strength and accumulation of wealth would be burned up for not being engaged in brahminical culture, etc.

Where wealth and strength are not engaged in the advancement of brahminical culture, God consciousness and cow protection, the state and home are surely doomed by providence. If we want peace and prosperity in the world, we should take lessons from this verse; every state and every home must endeavor to advance the cause of brahminical culture for self-purification, God consciousness for self-realization and cow protection for getting sufficient milk and the best food to continue a perfect civilization.

TEXT 4

स चिन्तयन्नित्थमथाशृणोद् यथा
मुनेःसुतोक्तो निर्ऋतिस्तक्षकाख्यः ।
स साधु मेने नचिरेण तक्षका-
नलं प्रसक्तस्य विरक्तिकारणम् ॥४॥

sa cintayann ittham athāśṛṇod yathā
muneḥ sutokto nirṛtis takṣakākhyaḥ
sa sādhu mene na cireṇa takṣakā-
nalaṁ prasaktasya virakti-kāraṇam

saḥ—he, the King; *cintayan*—thinking; *ittham*—like this; *atha*—now; *aśṛṇot*—heard; *yathā*—as; *muneḥ*—of the sage; *suta-uktaḥ*—uttered by the son; *nirṛtiḥ*—death; *takṣaka-ākhyaḥ*—in relation with the snake-bird; *saḥ*—he (the King); *sādhu*—well and good; *mene*—accepted; *na*—not; *cireṇa*—very long time; *takṣaka*—snake-bird; *analam*—fire; *prasaktasya*—for one who is too attached; *virakti*—indifference; *kāraṇam*—cause.

TRANSLATION

While the King was thus repenting, he received news of his imminent death, which would be due to the bite of a snake-bird, occasioned by the curse spoken by the sage's son. The King accepted this as good news, for it would be the cause of his indifference toward worldly things.

PURPORT

Real happiness is achieved by spiritual existence or by cessation of the repetition of birth and death. One can stop the repetition of birth and death only by going back to Godhead. In the material world, even by attaining the topmost planet (Brahmaloka), one cannot get rid of the conditions of repeated birth and death, but still we do not accept the path of attaining perfection. The path of perfection frees one from all material attachments, and thus one becomes fit to enter into the spiritual kingdom. Therefore, those who are materially poverty-stricken are better candidates than those who are materially prosperous. Mahārāja Parīkṣit was a great devotee of the Lord and a bona fide candidate for entering into the kingdom of God, but even though he was so, his material assets as the Emperor of the world were setbacks to perfect attainment of his rightful status as one of the associates of the Lord in the spiritual sky. As a devotee of the Lord, he could understand that the cursing of the *brāhmaṇa* boy, although unwise, was a blessing upon him, being the cause of detachment from worldly affairs, both political and social. Śamīka Muni also, after regretting the incident, conveyed the news to the King as a matter of duty so that the King would be able to prepare himself to go back to Godhead. Śamīka Muni sent news to the King that foolish Śṛṅgi, his son, although a powerful *brāhmaṇa* boy, unfortunately had misused his spiritual power by cursing the King unwarrantedly. The incident of the King's garlanding the *muni* was not sufficient cause for being cursed to death, but since there was no way to retract the curse, the King was informed to prepare for death within a week. Both Śamīka Muni and the King were self-realized souls. Śamīka Muni was a mystic, and Mahārāja Parīkṣit was a devotee. Therefore there was no difference between them in self-realization. Neither of them was afraid of meeting death. Mahārāja Parīkṣit could have gone to the *muni* to beg his pardon, but the news of imminent death was conveyed to the King with so much regret by the *muni* that the King did not want to shame the *muni* further by his presence there. He decided to prepare himself for his imminent death and find out the way to go back to Godhead.

The life of a human being is a chance to prepare oneself to go back to Godhead, or to get rid of the material existence, the repetition of birth and death. Thus in the system of *varṇāśrama-dharma* every man and woman is trained for this purpose. In other words, the system of *varṇāśrama-dharma* is known also as *sanātana-dharma,* or the eternal occupation. The system of *varṇāśrama-dharma* prepares a man for going back to Godhead, and thus a householder is ordered to go to the forest as a *vānaprastha* to acquire complete knowledge and then to take *sannyāsa* prior to his inevitable death. Parīkṣit Mahārāja was fortunate to get a seven-day notice to meet his inevitable death. But for the common man there is no definite notice, although death is inevitable for all. Foolish men forget this sure fact of death and neglect the duty of preparing themselves for going back to Godhead. They spoil their lives in animal propensities to eat, drink, be merry and enjoy. Such an irresponsible life is adopted by the people in the age of Kali because of a sinful desire to condemn brahminical culture, God consciousness and cow protection, for which the state is responsible. The state must employ revenue to advance these three items and thus educate the populace to prepare for death. The state which does so is the real welfare state. The state of India should better follow the examples of Mahārāja Parīkṣit, the ideal executive head, than to imitate other materialistic states which have no idea of the kingdom of Godhead, the ultimate goal of human life. Deterioration of the ideals of Indian civilization has brought about the deterioration of civic life, not only in India but also abroad.

TEXT 5

अथो विहायेममुं च लोकं
विमर्शितौ हेयतया पुरस्तात् ।
कृष्णाङ्घ्रिसेवामधिमन्यमान
उपाविशत् प्रायममर्त्यनद्याम् ॥५॥

atho vihāyemam amuṁ ca lokaṁ
vimarśitau heyatayā purastāt
kṛṣṇāṅghri-sevām adhimanyamāna
upāviśat prāyam amartya-nadyām

atho—thus; *vihāya*—giving up; *imam*—this; *amum*—and the next; *ca*—also; *lokam*—planets; *vimarśitau*—all of them being judged; *heyatayā*—because of inferiority; *purastāt*—hereinbefore; *kṛṣṇa-aṅghri*—the lotus feet of the Lord, Śrī Kṛṣṇa; *sevām*—transcendental loving service; *adhimanyamānaḥ*—one who thinks of the greatest of all achievements; *upāviśat*—sat down firmly; *prāyam*—for fasting; *amartya-nadyām*—on the bank of the transcendental river (the Ganges or the Yamunā).

TRANSLATION

Mahārāja Parīkṣit sat down firmly on the banks of the Ganges to concentrate his mind in Kṛṣṇa consciousness, rejecting all other practices of self-realization, because transcendental loving service to Kṛṣṇa is the greatest achievement, superseding all other methods.

PURPORT

For a devotee like Mahārāja Parīkṣit, none of the material planets, even the topmost Brahmaloka, is as desirable as Goloka Vṛndāvana, the abode of Lord Śrī Kṛṣṇa, the primeval Lord and original Personality of Godhead. This earth is one of the innumerable material planets within the universe, and there are innumerable universes also within the compass of the *mahat-tattva.* The devotees are told by the Lord and His representatives, the spiritual masters or *ācāryas,* that not one of the planets within all the innumerable universes is suitable for the residential purposes of a devotee. The devotee always desires to go back home, back to Godhead, just to become one of the associates of the Lord in the capacity of servitor, friend, parent or conjugal lover of the Lord, either in one of the innumerable Vaikuṇṭha planets or in Goloka Vṛndāvana, the planet of Lord Śrī Kṛṣṇa. All these planets are eternally situated in the spiritual sky, the *paravyoma,* which is on the other side of the Causal Ocean within the *mahat-tattva.* Mahārāja Parīkṣit was already aware of all this information due to his accumulated piety and birth in a high family of devotees, Vaiṣṇavas, and thus he was not at all interested in the material planets. Modern scientists are very eager to reach the moon by material arrangements, but they cannot conceive of the highest planet of this universe. But a devotee like Mahārāja Parīkṣit does not care a fig for the moon or, for that matter, any of the material planets. So when he was assured of his death on a fixed date, he became more determined in the transcendental loving service of Lord Kṛṣṇa by complete fasting on the bank of the transcendental river Yamunā, which flows down by the capital of Hastināpura (in the Delhi state). Both the Ganges and the Yamunā are *amartyā* (transcendental) rivers, and the Yamunā is still more sanctified for the following reasons.

TEXT 6

या वै लसच्छ्रीतुलसीविमिश्र-
कृष्णाङ्घ्रिरेण्वभ्यधिकाम्बुनेत्री ।
पुनाति लोकानुभयत्र सेशान्
कस्तां न सेवेत मरिष्यमाणः ॥६॥

yā vai lasac-chrī-tulasī-vimiśra-
kṛṣṇāṅghri-reṇv-abhyadhikāmbu-netrī
punāti lokān ubhayatra seśān
kas tāṁ na seveta mariṣyamāṇaḥ

yā—the river which; *vai*—always; *lasat*—floating with; *śrī-tulasī—tulasī* leaves; *vimiśra*—mixed; *kṛṣṇa-aṅghri*—the lotus feet of the Lord, Śrī Kṛṣṇa; *reṇu*—dust; *abhyadhika*—auspicious; *ambu*—water; *netrī*—that which is carrying; *punāti*—sanctifies; *lokān*—planets; *ubhayatra*—both the upper and lower or inside and outside; *sa-īśān*—along with Lord Śiva; *kaḥ*—who else; *tām*—that river; *na*—does not; *seveta*—worship; *mariṣyamāṇaḥ*—one who is to die at any moment.

TRANSLATION

The river [Ganges , by which the King sat to fast] carries the most auspicious water, which is mixed with the dust of the lotus feet of the Lord and tulasī leaves. Therefore that water sanctifies the three worlds inside and outside and even sanctifies Lord Śiva and other demigods. Consequently everyone who is destined to die must take shelter of this river.

PURPORT

Mahārāja Parīkṣit, just after receiving the news of his death within seven days, at once retired from family life and shifted himself to the sacred bank of the Yamunā River. Generally it is said that the King took shelter on the bank of the Ganges, but according to Śrīla Jīva Gosvāmī, the King took shelter on the bank of the Yamunā. Śrīla Jīva Gosvāmī's statement appears to be more accurate because of the geographical situation. Mahārāja Parīkṣit resided in his capital Hastināpura, situated near present Delhi, and the river Yamunā flows down past the city. Naturally the King would take shelter of the river Yamunā because she was flowing past his palace door. And as far as sanctity is concerned, the river Yamunā is more directly connected with Lord Kṛṣṇa than the Ganges. The Lord sanctified the river Yamunā from the beginning of His transcendental pastimes in the world. While His father Vasudeva was crossing the Yamunā with the baby Lord Kṛṣṇa for a safe place at Gokula on the other bank of the river from Mathurā, the Lord fell down in the river, and by the dust of His lotus feet the river at once became sanctified. It is especially mentioned herein that Mahārāja Parīkṣit took shelter of that particular river which is beautifully flowing, carrying the dust of the lotus feet of Lord Kṛṣṇa, mixed with *tulasī* leaves. Lord Kṛṣṇa's lotus feet are always besmeared with the *tulasī* leaves, and thus as soon as His lotus feet contact the water of the Ganges and the Yamunā, the rivers become at once sanctified. The Lord, however, contacted the river Yamunā more than the Ganges. According to the *Varāha Purāṇa,* as quoted by Śrīla Jīva Gosvāmī, there is no difference between the water of the Ganges and the Yamunā, *but when the water of the Ganges is sanctified one hundred times, it is called the Yamunā.* Similarly, it is said in the scriptures that one thousand names of Viṣṇu are equal to one name of Rāma, and three names of Lord Rāma are equal to one name of Kṛṣṇa.

TEXT 7

इति व्यवच्छिद्य स पाण्डवेयः
प्रायोपवेशं प्रति विष्णुपद्याम् ।
दधौ मुकुन्दाङ्घ्रिमनन्यभावो
मुनिव्रतो मुक्तसमस्तसङ्गः ॥ ७ ॥

iti vyavacchidya sa pāṇḍaveyaḥ
prāyopaveśaṁ prati viṣṇu-padyām
dadhau mukundāṅghrim ananya-bhāvo
muni-vrato mukta-samasta-saṅgaḥ

iti—thus; *vyavacchidya*—having decided; *saḥ*—the King; *pāṇḍaveyaḥ*—worthy descendant of the Pāṇḍavas; *prāya-upaveśam*—for fasting until death; *prati*—toward; *viṣṇu-padyām*—on the bank of the Ganges (emanating from the lotus feet of Lord Viṣṇu); *dadhau*—gave himself up; *mukunda-aṅghrim*—unto the lotus feet of Lord Kṛṣṇa; *ananya*—without deviation; *bhāvaḥ*—spirit; *muni-vrataḥ*—with the vows of a sage; *mukta*—liberated from; *samasta*—all kinds of; *saṅgaḥ*—association.

TRANSLATION

Thus the King, the worthy descendant of the Pāṇḍavas, decided once and for all and sat on the Ganges' bank to fast until death and give himself up to the lotus feet of Lord Kṛṣṇa, who alone is able to award liberation. So, freeing himself from all kinds of associations and attachments, he accepted the vows of a sage.

PURPORT

The water of the Ganges sanctifies all the three worlds, including the gods and the demigods, because it emanates from the lotus feet of the Personality of Godhead Viṣṇu. Lord Kṛṣṇa is the fountainhead of the principle of *viṣṇu-tattva,* and therefore shelter of His lotus feet can deliver one from all sins, including an offense committed by a king unto a *brāhmaṇa.* Mahārāja Parīkṣit, therefore, decided to meditate upon the lotus feet of Lord Śrī Kṛṣṇa, who is Mukunda, or the giver of liberations of all description. The banks of the Ganges or the Yamunā give one a chance to remember the Lord continuously. Mahārāja Parīkṣit freed himself from all sorts of material association and meditated upon the lotus feet of Lord Kṛṣṇa, and that is the way of liberation. To be free from all material association means to cease completely from committing any further sins. To meditate upon the lotus feet of the Lord means to become free from the effects of all previous sins. The conditions of the material world are so made that one has to commit sins willingly or unwillingly, and the best example is Mahārāja Parīkṣit himself, who was a recognized sinless, pious king. But he also became a victim of an offense, even though he was ever unwilling to commit such a mistake. He was cursed also, but because he was a great devotee of the Lord, even such reverses of life became favorable. The principle is that one should not willingly commit any sin in his life and should constantly remember the lotus feet of the Lord without deviation. Only in such a mood will the Lord help the devotee make regular progress toward the path of liberation and thus attain the lotus feet of the Lord. Even if there are accidental sins committed by the devotee, the Lord saves the surrendered soul from all sins, as confirmed in all scriptures.

sva-pāda-mūlaṁ bhajataḥ priyasya
tyaktāny abhāvasya hariḥ pareśaḥ
vikarma yac cotpatitaṁ kathañcid
dhunoti sarvaṁ hṛdi sanniviṣṭaḥ

(*Bhāg.* 11.5.42)

TEXT 8

तत्रोपजग्मुर्भुवनं पुनाना
महानुभावा मुनयः सशिष्याः ।
प्रायेण तीर्थाभिगमापदेशैः
स्वयं हि तीर्थानि पुनन्ति सन्तः ॥८॥

tatropajagmur bhuvanaṁ punānā
mahānubhāvā munayaḥ sa-śiṣyāḥ
prāyeṇa tīrthābhigamāpadeśaiḥ
svayaṁ hi tīrthāni punanti santaḥ

tatra—there; *upajagmuḥ*—arrived; *bhuvanam*—the universe; *punānāḥ*—those who can sanctify; *mahā-anubhāvāḥ*—great minds; *munayaḥ*—thinkers; *sa-śiṣyāḥ*—along with their disciples; *prāyeṇa*—almost; *tīrtha*—place of pilgrimage; *abhigama*—journey; *apadeśaiḥ*—on the plea of; *svayam*—personally; *hi*—certainly; *tīrthāni*—all the places of pilgrimage; *punanti*—sanctify; *santaḥ*—sages.

TRANSLATION

At that time all the great minds and thinkers, accompanied by their disciples, and sages who could verily sanctify a place of pilgrimage just by their presence, arrived there on the plea of making a pilgrim's journey.

PURPORT

When Mahārāja Parīkṣit sat down on the bank of the Ganges, the news spread in all directions of the universe, and the great-minded sages, who could follow the importance of the occasion, all arrived there on the plea of pilgrimage. Actually they came to meet Mahārāja Parīkṣit and not to take a bath of pilgrimage because all of them were competent enough to sanctify the places of pilgrimage. Common men go to pilgrimage sites to get themselves purified of all sins. Thus the places of pilgrimage become overburdened with the sins of others. But when such sages visit overburdened places of pilgrimage, they sanctify the places by their presence. Therefore the sages who came to meet Mahārāja Parīkṣit were not very much interested in getting themselves purified like common men, but on the plea of taking a bath in that place they came to meet Mahārāja Parīkṣit because they could foresee that *Śrīmad-Bhāgavatam* would be spoken by Śukadeva Gosvāmī. All of them wanted to take advantage of the great occasion.

TEXTS 9–10

अत्रिर्वसिष्ठश्च्यवनः शरद्वा-
नरिष्टनेमिर्भृगुरङ्गिराश्च ।
पराशरो गाधिसुतोऽथ राम
उतथ्य इन्द्रप्रमदेध्मवाहौ ॥९॥
मेधातिथिर्देवल आर्ष्टिषेणो
भारद्वाजो गौतमः पिप्पलादः ।
मैत्रेय और्वः कवषः कुम्भयोनि-
र्द्वैपायनो भगवान्नारदश्च ॥१०॥

atrir vasiṣṭhaś cyavanaḥ śaradvān
ariṣṭanemir bhṛgur aṅgirāś ca
parāśaro gādhi-suto 'tha rāma
utathya indrapramadedhmavāhau

medhātithir devala ārṣṭiṣeṇo
bhāradvājo gautamaḥ pippalādaḥ
maitreya aurvaḥ kavaṣaḥ kumbhayonir
dvaipāyano bhagavān nāradaś ca

atriḥ to *nāradaḥ*—all names of the different saintly personalities who arrived there from different parts of the universe.

TRANSLATION

From different parts of the universe there arrived great sages like Atri, Cyavana, Śaradvān, Ariṣṭanemi, Bhṛgu, Vasiṣṭha, Parāśara, Viśvāmitra, Aṅgirā, Paraśurāma, Utathya, Indrapramada, Idhmavāhu, Medhātithi, Devala, Ārṣṭiṣeṇa, Bhāradvāja, Gautama, Pippalāda, Maitreya, Aurva, Kavaṣa, Kumbhayoni, Dvaipāyana and the great personality Nārada.

PURPORT

Cyavana: A great sage and one of the sons of Bhṛgu Muni. He was born prematurely when his pregnant mother was kidnapped. Cyavana is one of the six sons of his father.

Bhṛgu: When Brahmājī was performing a great sacrifice on behalf of Varuṇa, Maharṣi Bhṛgu was born from the sacrificial fire. He was a great sage, and his very dear wife was Pulomā. He could travel in space like Durvāsā, Nārada and others, and he used to visit all the planets of the universe. Before the Battle of Kurukṣetra, he tried to stop the battle. Sometimes he instructed Bhāradvāja Muni about astronomical evolution, and he is the author of the great *Bhṛgu-saṁhitā,* the great astrological calculation. He explained how air, fire, water and earth are generated from ether. He explained how the air in the stomach works and regulates the intestines. As a great philosopher, he logically established the eternity of the living entity (*Mahābhārata*). He was also a great anthropologist, and the theory of evolution was long ago explained by him. He was a scientific propounder of the four divisions and orders of human society known as the *varṇāśrama* institution. He converted the *kṣatriya* king Vītahavya into a *brāhmaṇa.*

Vasiṣṭha: See *Śrīmad-Bhāgavatam* 1.9.6.

Parāśara: He is the grandson of Vasiṣṭha Muni and father of Vyāsadeva. He is the son of Maharṣi Śakti, and his mother's name was Adṛśyatī. He was in the womb of his mother when she was only twelve years old. And from within the womb of his mother he learned the *Vedas.* His father was killed by a demon, Kalmāṣapāda, and to avenge this he wanted to annihilate the whole world. He was restrained, however, by his grandfather Vasiṣṭha. He then performed a Rākṣasa-killing *yajña,* but Maharṣi Pulastya restrained him. He begot Vyāsadeva, being attracted by Satyavatī, who was to become the wife of Mahārāja Śāntanu. By the blessings of Parāśara, Satyavatī became fragrant for miles. He was present also during the time of Bhīṣma's death. He was the spiritual master of Mahārāja Janaka and a great devotee of Lord Śiva. He is the author of many Vedic scriptures and sociological directions.

Gādhi-suta, or *Viśvāmitra:* A great sage of austerity and mystic power. He is famous as Gādhi-suta because his father was Gādhi, a powerful king of the province of Kanyākubja (part of Uttara Pradesh). Although he was a *kṣatriya* by birth, he became a *brāhmaṇa* in the very same body by the power of his spiritual achievements. He picked a quarrel with Vasiṣṭha Muni when he was a *kṣatriya* king and performed a great sacrifice in cooperation with Magaṅga Muni and thus was able to vanquish the sons of Vasiṣṭha. He became a great *yogī,* and yet he failed to check his senses and thus was obliged to become the father of Śakuntalā, the beauty queen of world history. Once, when he was a *kṣatriya* king, he visited the hermitage of Vasiṣṭha Muni, and he was given a royal reception. Viśvāmitra wanted from Vasiṣṭha a cow named Nandinī, and the Muni refused to deliver it. Viśvāmitra stole the cow, and thus there was a quarrel between the sage and the King. Viśvāmitra was defeated by the spiritual strength of Vasiṣṭha, and thus the King decided to become a *brāhmaṇa.* Before becoming a *brāhmaṇa* he underwent severe austerity on the bank of the Kauśika. He was also one who tried to stop the Kurukṣetra war.

Aṅgirā: He is one of the six mental sons of Brahmā and the father of Bṛhaspati, the great learned priest of the demigods in the heavenly planets. He was born of the semen of Brahmājī given to a cinder of fire. Utathya and Saṁvarta are his sons. It is said that he is still performing austerity and chanting the holy name of the Lord at a place known as Alokānanda on the banks of the Ganges.

Paraśurāma: See *Śrīmad-Bhāgavatam* 1.9.6.

Utathya: One of the three sons of Maharṣi Aṅgirā. He was the spiritual master of Mahārāja Mandhātā. He married Bhadrā, the daughter of Soma (moon). Varuṇa kidnapped his wife Bhadrā, and to retaliate the offense of the god of water, he drank all the water of the world.

Medhātithi: An old sage of yore. An assembly member of the heavenly King Indradeva. His son was Kaṇva Muni, who brought up Śakuntalā in the forest. He was promoted to the heavenly planet by strictly following the principles of retired life (*vānaprastha*).

Devala: A great authority like Nārada Muni and Vyāsadeva. His good name is on the list of authorities mentioned in the *Bhagavad-gītā* when Arjuna acknowledged Lord Kṛṣṇa as the Supreme Personality of Godhead. He met Mahārāja Yudhiṣṭhira after the Battle of Kurukṣetra, and he was the elder brother of Dhaumya, the priest of the Pāṇḍava family. Like the *kṣatriyas,* he also allowed his daughter to select her own husband in a *svayaṁvara* meeting, and at that ceremony all the bachelor sons of the *ṛṣis* were invited. According to some, he is not Asita Devala.

Bhāradvāja: See *Śrīmad-Bhāgavatam* 1.9.6.

Gautama: One of the seven great sages of the universe. Śaradvān Gautama was one of his sons. Persons in the Gautama-gotra (dynasty) today are either his family descendants or in his disciplic succession. The *brāhmaṇas* who profess Gautama-gotra are generally family descendants, and the *kṣatriyas* and *vaiśyas* who profess Gautama-gotra are all in the line of his disciplic succession. He was the husband of the famous Ahalyā who turned into stone when Indradeva, the King of the heaven, molested her. Ahalyā was delivered by Lord Rāmacandra. Gautama was the grandfather of Kṛpācārya, one of the heroes of the Battle of Kurukṣetra.

Maitreya: A great *ṛṣi* of yore. He was the spiritual master of Vidura and a great religious authority. He advised Dhṛtarāṣṭra to keep good relations with the Pāṇḍavas. Duryodhana disagreed and thus was cursed by him. He met Vyāsadeva and had religious discourses with him.

TEXT 11

अन्ये च देवर्षिब्रह्मर्षिवर्या
राजर्षिवर्या अरुणादयश्च ।
नानार्षेयप्रवरान् समेता-
नभ्यर्च्य राजा शिरसा ववन्दे ॥११॥

anye ca devarṣi-brahmarṣi-varyā
rājarṣi-varyā aruṇādayaś ca
nānārṣeya-pravarān sametān
abhyarcya rājā śirasā vavande

anye—many others; *ca*—also; *devarṣi*—saintly demigods; *brahmarṣi*—saintly *brāhmaṇas; varyāḥ*—topmost; *rājarṣi-varyāḥ*—topmost saintly kings; *aruṇa-ādayaḥ*—a special rank of *rājarṣis; ca*—and; *nānā*—many others; *ārṣeya-pravarān*—chief amongst the dynasties of the sages; *sametān*—assembled together; *abhyarcya*—by worshiping; *rājā*—the Emperor; *śirasā*—bowed his head to the ground; *vavande*—welcomed.

TRANSLATION

There were also many other saintly demigods, kings and special royal orders called aruṇādayas [a special rank of rājarṣis] from different dynasties of sages. When they all assembled together to meet the Emperor [Parīkṣit], he received them properly and bowed his head to the ground.

PURPORT

The system of bowing the head to the ground to show respect to superiors is an excellent etiquette which obliges the honored guest deep into the heart. Even the first-grade offender is excused simply by this process, and Mahārāja Parīkṣit, although honored by all the *ṛṣis* and kings, welcomed all the big men in that humble etiquette in order to be excused from any offenses. Generally at the last stage of one's life this humble method is adopted by every sensible man in order to be excused before departure. In this way Mahārāja Parīkṣit implored everyone's good will for going back home, back to Godhead.

TEXT 12

सुखोपविष्टेष्वथ तेषु भूयः
कृतप्रणामः स्वचिकीर्षितं यत् ।
विज्ञापयामास विविक्तचेता
उपस्थितोऽग्रेऽभिगृहीतपाणिः ॥१२॥

sukhopaviṣṭeṣv atha teṣu bhūyaḥ
kṛta-praṇāmaḥ sva-cikīrṣitaṁ yat
vijñāpayām āsa vivikta-cetā
upasthito 'gre 'bhigṛhīta-pāṇiḥ

sukha—happily; *upaviṣṭeṣu*—all sitting down; *atha*—thereupon; *teṣu*—unto them (the visitors); *bhūyaḥ*—again; *kṛta-praṇāmaḥ*—having offered obeisances; *sva*—his own; *cikīrṣitam*—decision of fasting; *yat*—who; *vijñāpayām āsa*—submitted; *vivikta-cetāḥ*—one whose mind is detached from worldly affairs; *upasthitaḥ*—being present; *agre*—before them; *abhigṛhīta-pāṇiḥ*—humbly with folded hands.

TRANSLATION

After all the ṛṣis and others had seated themselves comfortably, the King, humbly standing before them with folded hands, told them of his decision to fast until death.

PURPORT

Although the King had already decided to fast until death on the bank of the Ganges, he humbly expressed his decision to elicit the opinions of the great authorities present there. Any decision, however important, should be confirmed by some authority. That makes the matter perfect. This means that the monarchs who ruled the earth in those days were not irresponsible dictators. They scrupulously followed the authoritative decisions of the saints and sages in terms of Vedic injunction. Mahārāja Parīkṣit, as a perfect king, followed the principles by consulting the authorities, even up to the last days of his life.

TEXT 13

राजोवाच
अहो वयं धन्यतमा नृपाणां
महत्तमानुग्रहणीयशीलाः ।
राज्ञां कुलं ब्राह्मणपादशौचाद्
दूराद् विसृष्टं बत गर्ह्यकर्म ॥१३॥

rājovāca
aho vayaṁ dhanyatamā nṛpāṇāṁ
mahattamānugrahaṇīya-śīlāḥ
rājñāṁ kulaṁ brāhmaṇa-pāda-śaucād
dūrād visṛṣṭaṁ bata garhya-karma

rājā uvāca—the fortunate King said; *aho*—ah; *vayam*—we; *dhanya-tamāḥ*—most thankful; *nṛpāṇām*—of all the kings; *mahat-tama*—of the great souls; *anugrahaṇīya-śīlāḥ*—trained to get favors; *rājñām*—of the royal; *kulam*—orders; *brāhmaṇa-pāda*—feet of the *brāhmaṇas; śaucāt*—refuse after cleaning; *dūrāt*—at a distance; *visṛṣṭam*—always left out; *bata*—on account of; *garhya*—condemnable; *karma*—activities.

TRANSLATION

The fortunate King said: Indeed, we are the most grateful of all the kings who are trained to get favors from the great souls. Generally you [sages] consider royalty as refuse to be rejected and left in a distant place.

PURPORT

According to religious principles, stool, urine, wash water, etc., must be left at a long distance. Attached bathrooms, urinals, etc., may be very convenient amenities of modern civilization, but they are ordered to be situated at a distance from residential quarters. That very example is cited herein in relation to the kingly order for those who are progressively marching back to Godhead. Lord Śrī Caitanya Mahāprabhu said that to be in intimate touch with dollars-and-cents men, or the kingly order, is worse than suicide for one who desires to go back to Godhead. In other words, the transcendentalists do not generally associate with men who are too enamored by the external beauty of God's creation. By advanced knowledge in spiritual realization, the transcendentalist knows that this beautiful material world is nothing but a shadowy reflection of the reality, the kingdom of God. They are not, therefore, very much captivated by royal opulence or anything like that. But in the case of Mahārāja Parīkṣit, the situation was different. Apparently the King was condemned to death by an inexperienced *brāhmaṇa* boy, but factually he was called by the Lord to return to Him. Other transcendentalists, the great sages and mystics who assembled together because of Mahārāja Parīkṣit's fasting unto death, were quite anxious to see him, for he was going back to Godhead. Mahārāja Parīkṣit also could understand that the great sages who assembled there were all kind to his forefathers, the Pāṇḍavas, because of their devotional service to the Lord. He therefore felt grateful to the sages for being present there at the last stage of his life, and he felt that it was all due to the greatness of his late forefathers or grandfathers. He felt proud, therefore, that he happened to be the descendant of such great devotees. Such pride for the devotees of the Lord is certainly not equal to the puffed-up sense of vanity for material prosperity. The first is reality, whereas the other is false and vain.

TEXT 14

तस्यैव मेऽघस्य परावरेशो
व्यासक्तचित्तस्य गृहेष्वभीक्ष्णम् ।
निर्वेदमूलो द्विजशापरूपो
यत्र प्रसक्तो भयमाशु धत्ते ॥१४॥

tasyaiva me 'ghasya parāvareśo
vyāsakta-cittasya gṛheṣv abhīkṣṇam
nirveda-mūlo dvija-śāpa-rūpo
yatra prasakto bhayam āśu dhatte

tasya—his; *eva*—certainly; *me*—mine; *aghasya*—of the sinful; *parā*—transcendental; *avara*—mundane; *īśaḥ*—controller, the Supreme Lord; *vyāsakta*—overly attached; *cittasya*—of the mind; *gṛheṣu*—to family affairs; *abhīkṣṇam*—always; *nirveda-mūlaḥ*—the source of detachment; *dvija-śāpa*—cursing by the *brāhmaṇa; rūpaḥ*—form of; *yatra*—whereupon; *prasaktaḥ*—one who is affected; *bhayam*—fearfulness; *āśu*—very soon; *dhatte*—take place.

TRANSLATION

The Supreme Personality of Godhead, the controller of both the transcendental and mundane worlds, has graciously overtaken me in the

form of a brāhmaṇa's curse. Due to my being too much attached to family life, the Lord, in order to save me, has appeared before me in such a way that only out of fear I will detach myself from the world.

PURPORT

Mahārāja Parīkṣit, although born in a family of great devotees, the Pāṇḍavas, and although securely trained in transcendental attachment for the association of the Lord, still found the allurement of mundane family life so strong that he had to be detached by a plan of the Lord. Such direct action is taken by the Lord in the case of a special devotee. Mahārāja Parīkṣit could understand this by the presence of the topmost transcendentalists in the universe. The Lord resides with His devotees, and therefore the presence of the great saints indicated the presence of the Lord. The King therefore welcomed the presence of the great *ṛṣis* as a mark of favor of the Supreme Lord.

TEXT 15

तं मोपयातं प्रतियन्तु विप्रा
गङ्गा च देवी धृतचित्तमीशे ।
द्विजोपसृष्टः कुहकस्तक्षको वा
दशत्वलं गायत विष्णुगाथाः ॥१५॥

taṁ mopayātaṁ pratiyantu viprā
gaṅgā ca devī dhṛta-cittam īśe
dvijopasṛṣṭaḥ kuhakas takṣako vā
daśatv alaṁ gāyata viṣṇu-gāthāḥ

tam—for that reason; *mā*—me; *upayātam*—taken shelter of; *pratiyantu*—just accept me; *viprāḥ*—O *brāhmaṇas; gaṅgā*—Mother Ganges; *ca*—also; *devī*—direct representative of the Lord; *dhṛta*—taken into; *cittam*—heart; *īśe*—unto the Lord; *dvija-upasṛṣṭaḥ*—created by the *brāhmaṇa; kuhakaḥ*—something magical; *takṣakaḥ*—the snake-bird; *vā*—either; *daśatu*—let it bite; *alam*—without further delay; *gāyata*—please go on singing; *viṣṇu-gāthāḥ*—narration of the deeds of Viṣṇu.

TRANSLATION

O brāhmaṇas, just accept me as a completely surrendered soul, and let Mother Ganges, the representative of the Lord, also accept me in that

way, for I have already taken the lotus feet of the Lord into my heart. Let the snake-bird—or whatever magical thing the brāhmaṇa created—bite me at once. I only desire that you all continue singing the deeds of Lord Viṣṇu.

PURPORT

As soon as one is given up completely unto the lotus feet of the Supreme Lord, he is not at all afraid of death. The atmosphere created by the presence of great devotees of the Lord on the bank of the Ganges and Mahārāja Parīkṣit's complete acceptance of the Lord's lotus feet were sufficient guarantee to the King for going back to Godhead. He thus became absolutely free from all fear of death.

TEXT 16

पुनश्च भूयाद्भगवत्यनन्ते
रतिः प्रसङ्गश्च तदाश्रयेषु ।
महत्सु यां यामुपयामि सृष्टिं
मैत्र्यस्तु सर्वत्र नमो द्विजेभ्यः ॥ १६ ॥

punaś ca bhūyād bhagavaty anante
ratiḥ prasaṅgaś ca tad-āśrayeṣu
mahatsu yāṁ yām upayāmi sṛṣṭiṁ
maitry astu sarvatra namo dvijebhyaḥ

punaḥ—again; *ca*—and; *bhūyāt*—let it be; *bhagavati*—unto Lord Śrī Kṛṣṇa; *anante*—who has unlimited potency; *ratiḥ*—attracting; *prasaṅgaḥ*—association; *ca*—also; *tat*—His; *āśrayeṣu*—with those who are His devotees; *mahatsu*—within the material creation; *yām yām*—wherever; *upayāmi*—I may take; *sṛṣṭim*—my birth; *maitrī*—friendly relation; *astu*—let it be; *sarvatra*—everywhere; *namaḥ*—my obeisances; *dvijebhyaḥ*—unto the *brāhmaṇas.*

TRANSLATION

Again, offering obeisances unto all you brāhmaṇas, I pray that if I should again take my birth in the material world I will have complete attachment to the unlimited Lord Kṛṣṇa, association with His devotees and friendly relations with all living beings.

PURPORT

That a devotee of the Lord is the only perfect living being is explained herein by Mahārāja Parīkṣit. A devotee of the Lord is no one's enemy, although there may be many enemies of a devotee. A devotee of the Lord does not like to associate with nondevotees, although he has no enmity with them. He desires association with the devotees of the Lord. This is perfectly natural because birds of the same feather mix together. And the most important function of a devotee is to have complete attachment for Lord Śrī Kṛṣṇa, the father of all living beings. As a good son of the father behaves in a friendly way with all his other brothers, so also the devotee of the Lord, being a good son of the supreme father, Lord Kṛṣṇa, sees all other living beings in relation with the supreme father. He tries to bring back the upstart sons of the father to a saner stage and to get them to accept the supreme fatherhood of God. Mahārāja Parīkṣit was certainly going back to Godhead, but even if he were not to go back, he prayed for a pattern of life which is the most perfect way in the material world. A pure devotee does not desire the company of a personality as great as Brahmā, but he prefers the association of a petty living being, provided he is a devotee of the Lord.

TEXT 17

इति स्म राजाध्यवसाययुक्तः
प्राचीनमूलेषु कुशेषु धीरः ।
उदङ्मुखो दक्षिणकूल आस्ते
समुद्रपत्न्याः स्वसुतन्यस्तभारः ॥१७॥

iti sma rājādhyavasāya-yuktaḥ
prācīna-mūleṣu kuśeṣu dhīraḥ
udaṅ-mukho dakṣiṇa-kūla āste
samudra-patnyāḥ sva-suta-nyasta-bhāraḥ

iti—thus; *sma*—as in the past; *rājā*—the King; *adhyavasāya*—perseverance; *yuktaḥ*—being engaged; *prācīna*—eastern; *mūleṣu*—with the root; *kuśeṣu*—on a seat made of *kuśa* straw; *dhīraḥ*—self-controlled; *udaṅ-mukhaḥ*—facing the northern side; *dakṣiṇa*—on the southern; *kūle*—bank; *āste*—situated; *samudra*—the sea; *patnyāḥ*—wife of (the Ganges); *sva*—own; *suta*—son; *nyasta*—given over; *bhāraḥ*—the charge of administration.

TRANSLATION

In perfect self-control, Mahārāja Parīkṣit sat down on a seat of straw, with straw-roots facing the east, placed on the southern bank of the Ganges, and he himself faced the north. Just previously he had given charge of his kingdom over to his son.

PURPORT

The River Ganges is celebrated as the wife of the sea. The seat of *kuśa* straw is considered to be sanctified if the straw is taken out of the earth complete with root, and if the root is pointed toward the east it is considered to be auspicious. Facing the north is still more favorable for attaining spiritual success. Mahārāja Parīkṣit handed over the charge of administration to his son before leaving home. He was thus fully equipped for all favorable conditions.

TEXT 18

एवं च तस्मिन्नरदेवदेवे
प्रायोपविष्टे दिवि देवसङ्घाः ।
प्रशस्य भूमौ व्यकिरन् प्रसूनै-
र्मुदा मुहुर्दुन्दुभयश्च नेदुः ॥१८॥

evaṁ ca tasmin nara-deva-deve
prāyopaviṣṭe divi deva-saṅghāḥ
praśasya bhūmau vyakiran prasūnair
mudā muhur dundubhayaś ca neduḥ

evam—thus; *ca*—and; *tasmin*—in that; *nara-deva-deve*—upon the King's; *prāya-upaviṣṭe*—being engaged in fasting to death; *divi*—in the sky; *deva*—demigods; *saṅghāḥ*—all of them; *praśasya*—having praised the action; *bhūmau*—on the earth; *vyakiran*—scattered; *prasūnaiḥ*—with flowers; *mudā*—in pleasure; *muhuḥ*—continually; *dundubhayaḥ*—celestial drums; *ca*—also; *neduḥ*—beaten.

TRANSLATION

Thus the King, Mahārāja Parīkṣit, sat to fast until death. All the demigods of the higher planets praised the King's actions and in pleasure continually scattered flowers over the earth and beat celestial drums.

PURPORT

Even up to the time of Mahārāja Parīkṣit there were interplanetary communications, and the news of Mahārāja Parīkṣit's fasting unto death to attain salvation reached the higher planets in the sky where the intelligent demigods live. The demigods are more luxurious than human beings, but all of them are obedient to the orders of the Supreme Lord. There is no one in the heavenly planets who is an atheist or nonbeliever. Thus any devotee of the Lord on the surface of the earth is always praised by them, and in the case of Mahārāja Parīkṣit they were greatly delighted and thus gave tokens of honor by scattering flowers over the earth and by beating celestial drums. A demigod takes pleasure in seeing someone go back to Godhead. He is always pleased with a devotee of the Lord, so much so that by his adhidaivic powers he may help the devotees in all respects. And by their actions, the Lord is pleased with them. There is an invisible chain of complete cooperation between the Lord, the demigods and the devotee of the Lord on earth.

TEXT 19

महर्षयो वै समुपागता ये
प्रशस्य साध्वित्यनुमोदमानाः ।
ऊचुः प्रजानुग्रहशीलसारा
यदुत्तमश्लोकगुणाभिरूपम् ॥१९॥

maharṣayo vai samupāgatā ye
praśasya sādhv ity anumodamānāḥ
ūcuḥ prajānugraha-śīla-sārā
yad uttama-śloka-guṇābhirūpam

maharṣayaḥ—the great sages; *vai*—as a matter of course; *samupāgatāḥ*—assembled there; *ye*—those who; *praśasya*—by praising; *sādhu*—quite all right; *iti*—thus; *anumodamānāḥ*—all approving; *ūcuḥ*—said; *prajā-anugraha*—doing good to the living being; *śīla-sārāḥ*—qualitatively powerful; *yat*—because; *uttama-śloka*—one who is praised by selected poems; *guṇa-abhirupam*—as beautiful as godly qualities.

TRANSLATION

All the great sages who were assembled there also praised the decision of Mahārāja Parīkṣit, and they expressed their approval by saying "Very

good." Naturally the sages are inclined to do good to common men, for they have all the qualitative powers of the Supreme Lord. Therefore they were very much pleased to see Mahārāja Parīkṣit, a devotee of the Lord, and they spoke as follows.

PURPORT

The natural beauty of a living being is enhanced by his rising up to the platform of devotional service. Mahārāja Parīkṣit was absorbed in attachment for Lord Kṛṣṇa. Seeing this, the great sages assembled were very pleased, and they expressed their approval by saying "Very good." Such sages are naturally inclined to do good to the common man, and when they see a personality like Mahārāja Parīkṣit advance in devotional service, their pleasure knows no bounds, and they offer all blessings in their power. The devotional service of the Lord is so auspicious that all demigods and sages, up to the Lord Himself, become pleased with the devotee, and therefore the devotee finds everything auspicious. All inauspicious matters are removed from the path of a progressive devotee. Meeting all the great sages at the time of death was certainly auspicious for Mahārāja Parīkṣit, and thus he was blessed by the so-called curse of a *brāhmaṇa's* boy.

TEXT 20

न वा इदं राजर्षिवर्य चित्रं
भवत्सु कृष्णं समनुव्रतेषु ।
येऽध्यासनं राजकिरीटजुष्टं
सद्यो जहुर्भगवत्पार्श्वकामाः ॥२०॥

na vā idaṁ rājarṣi-varya citraṁ
bhavatsu kṛṣṇaṁ samanuvrateṣu
ye 'dhyāsanaṁ rāja-kirīṭa-juṣṭaṁ
sadyo jahur bhagavat-pārśva-kāmāḥ

na—neither; *vā*—like this; *idam*—this; *rājarṣi*—saintly king; *varya*—the chief; *citram*—astonishing; *bhavatsu*—unto all of you; *kṛṣṇam*—Lord Kṛṣṇa; *samanuvrateṣu*—unto those who are strictly in the line of; *ye*—who; *adhyāsanam*—seated on the throne; *rāja-kirīṭa*—helmets of kings; *juṣṭam*—decorated; *sadyaḥ*—immediately; *jahuḥ*—gave up; *bhagavat*—the Personality of Godhead; *pārśva-kāmāḥ*—desiring to achieve association.

TRANSLATION

[The sages said:] O chief of all the saintly kings of the Pāṇḍu dynasty who are strictly in the line of Lord Śrī Kṛṣṇa! It is not at all astonishing that you give up your throne, which is decorated with the helmets of many kings, to achieve eternal association with the Personality of Godhead.

PURPORT

Foolish politicians who hold political administrative posts think that the temporary posts they occupy are the highest material gain of life, and therefore they stick to those posts even up to the last moment of life, without knowing that achievement of liberation as one of the associates of the Lord in His eternal abode is the highest gain of life. The human life is meant for achieving this end. The Lord has assured us in the *Bhagavad-gītā* many times that going back to Godhead, His eternal abode, is the highest achievement. Prahlāda Mahārāja, while praying to Lord Nṛsiṁha, said, "O my Lord, I am very much afraid of the materialistic way of life, and I am not the least afraid of Your present ghastly ferocious feature as Nṛsiṁhadeva. This materialistic way of life is something like a grinding stone, and we are being crushed by it. We have fallen into this horrible whirlpool of the tossing waves of life, and thus, my Lord, I pray at Your lotus feet to call me back to Your eternal abode as one of Your servitors. This is the summit liberation of this materialistic way of life. I have very bitter experience of the materialistic way of life. In whichever species of life I have taken birth, compelled by the force of my own activities, I have very painfully experienced two things, namely separation from my beloved and meeting with what is not wanted. And to counteract them, the remedies which I undertook were more dangerous than the disease itself. So I drift from one point to another, birth after birth, and I pray to You therefore to give me a shelter at Your lotus feet."

The Pāṇḍava kings, who are more than many saints of the world, knew the bitter results of the materialistic way of life. They were never captivated by the glare of the imperial throne they occupied, and they sought always the opportunity of being called by the Lord to associate with Him eternally. Mahārāja Parīkṣit was the worthy grandson of Mahārāja Yudhiṣṭhira. Mahārāja Yudhiṣṭhira gave up the imperial throne to his grandson, and similarly Mahārāja Parīkṣit, the grandson of Mahārāja Yudhiṣṭhira, gave up the imperial throne to his son Janamejaya. That is the way of all the kings in the dynasty because they are all strictly in the line of Lord Kṛṣṇa. Thus the devotees of the Lord are never enchanted by the glare of materialistic life, and they live impartially, unattached to the objects of the false, illusory materialistic way of life.

TEXT 21

सर्वे वयं तावदिहास्महेऽथ
कलेवरं यावदसौ विहाय ।
लोकं परं विरजस्कं विशोकं
यास्यत्ययं भागवतप्रधानः ॥२१॥

sarve vayaṁ tāvad ihāsmahe 'tha
kalevaraṁ yāvad asau vihāya
lokaṁ paraṁ virajaskaṁ viśokaṁ
yāsyaty ayaṁ bhāgavata-pradhānaḥ

sarve—all; *vayam*—of us; *tāvat*—as long as; *iha*—at this place; *āsmahe*—shall stay; *atha*—hereafter; *kalevaram*—the body; *yāvat*—so long; *asau*—the King; *vihāya*—giving up; *lokam*—the planet; *param*—the supreme; *virajaskam*—completely free from mundane contamination; *viśokam*—completely freed from all kinds of lamentation; *yāsyati*—returns; *ayam*—this; *bhāgavata*—devotee; *pradhānaḥ*—the foremost.

TRANSLATION

We shall all wait here until the foremost devotee of the Lord, Mahārāja Parīkṣit, returns to the supreme planet, which is completely free from all mundane contamination and all kinds of lamentation.

PURPORT

Beyond the limitation of the material creation, which is compared to the cloud in the sky, there is the *paravyoma,* or the spiritual sky, full of planets called Vaikuṇṭhas. Such Vaikuṇṭha planets are also differently known as the Puruṣottamaloka, Acyutaloka, Trivikramaloka, Hṛṣīkeśaloka, Keśavaloka, Aniruddhaloka, Mādhavaloka, Pradyumnaloka, Saṅkarṣaṇaloka, Śrīdharaloka, Vāsudevaloka, Ayodhyāloka, Dvārakāloka and many other millions of spiritual *lokas* wherein the Personality of Godhead predominates; all the living entities there are liberated souls with spiritual bodies as good as that of the Lord. There is no material contamination; everything there is spiritual, and therefore there is nothing objectively lamentable. They are full of transcendental bliss, and are without birth, death, old age and disease. And amongst all the above-mentioned Vaikuṇṭhalokas, there is one supreme *loka* called Goloka Vṛndāvana, which is the abode of the Lord Śrī Kṛṣṇa and His specific associates. Mahārāja Parīkṣit was destined to achieve this particular *loka,* and the great *ṛṣis* assembled there could foresee this. All of them consulted among themselves about the great departure of the great King, and they wanted to see him up to the last moment because they would no more be able to see such a great devotee of the Lord. When a great devotee of the Lord passes away, there is nothing to be lamented because the devotee is destined to enter into the kingdom of God. But the sorry plight is that such great devotees leave our sight, and therefore there is every reason to be sorry. As the Lord is rarely to be seen by our present eyes, so also are the great devotees. The great *ṛṣis,* therefore, correctly decided to remain on the spot till the last moment.

TEXT 22

आश्रुत्य तदृषिगणवचः परीक्षित्
समं मधुच्युद् गुरु चाव्यलीकम् ।
आभाषतैनानभिनन्द्य युक्तान्
शुश्रूषमाणश्चरितानि विष्णोः ॥२२॥

āśrutya tad ṛṣi-gaṇa-vacaḥ parīkṣit
samaṁ madhu-cyud guru cāvyalīkam
ābhāṣatainān abhinandya yuktān
śuśrūṣamāṇaś caritāni viṣṇoḥ

āśrutya—just after hearing; *tat*—that; *ṛṣi-gaṇa*—the sages assembled; *vacaḥ*—speaking; *parīkṣit*—Mahārāja Parīkṣit; *samam*—impartial; *madhu-cyut*—sweet to hear; *guru*—grave; *ca*—also; *avyalīkam*—perfectly true; *ābhāṣata*—said; *enān*—all of them; *abhinandya*—congratulated; *yuktān*—appropriately presented; *śuśrūṣamāṇaḥ*—being desirous to hear; *caritāni*—activities of; *viṣṇoḥ*—the Personality of Godhead.

TRANSLATION

All that was spoken by the great sages was very sweet to hear, full of meaning and appropriately presented as perfectly true. So after hearing them, Mahārāja Parīkṣit, desiring to hear of the activities of Lord Śrī Kṛṣṇa, the Personality of Godhead, congratulated the great sages.

TEXT 23

समागताः सर्वत एव सर्वे
वेदा यथा मूर्तिधरास्त्रिपृष्ठे ।
नेहाथ नामुत्र च कश्चनार्थ
ऋते परानुग्रहमात्मशीलम् ॥२३॥

samāgatāḥ sarvata eva sarve
vedā yathā mūrti-dharās tri-pṛṣṭhe
nehātha nāmutra ca kaścanārtha
ṛte parānugraham ātma-śīlam

samāgatāḥ—assembled; *sarvataḥ*—from all directions; *eva*—certainly; *sarve*—all of you; *vedāḥ*—supreme knowledge; *yathā*—as; *mūrti-dharāḥ*—personified; *tri-pṛṣṭhe*—on the planet of Brahmā (which is situated above the three planetary systems, namely the upper, intermediate and lower worlds); *na*—not; *iha*—in this world; *atha*—thereafter; *na*—nor; *amutra*—in the other world; *ca*—also; *kaścana*—any other; *arthaḥ*—interest; *ṛte*—save and except; *para*—others; *anugraham*—doing good to; *ātma-śīlam*—own nature.

TRANSLATION

The King said: O great sages, you have all very kindly assembled here, having come from all parts of the universe. You are all as good as supreme knowledge personified, who resides in the planet above the three worlds [Satyaloka]. Consequently you are naturally inclined to do good to others, and but for this you have no interest, either in this life or in the next.

PURPORT

Six kinds of opulences, namely wealth, strength, fame, beauty, knowledge and renunciation, are all originally the different attributes pertaining to the Absolute Personality of Godhead. The living beings, who are part-and-parcel entities of the Supreme Being, have all these attributes partially, up to the full strength of seventy-eight percent. In the material world these attributes (up to seventy-eight percent of the Lord's attributes) are covered by the material energy, as the sun is covered by a cloud. The covered strength of the sun is very dim, compared to the original glare, and similarly the original color of the living beings with such attributes becomes almost extinct. There are three planetary systems, namely the lower worlds, the intermediate worlds and the upper worlds. The human beings on earth are situated at the beginning of the intermediate worlds, but living beings like Brahmā and his contemporaries live in the upper worlds, of which the topmost is Satyaloka. In Satyaloka the inhabitants are fully cognizant of Vedic wisdom, and thus the mystic cloud of material energy is cleared. Therefore they are known as the *Vedas* personified. Such persons, being fully aware of knowledge both mundane and transcendental, have no interest in either the mundane or transcendental worlds. They are practically desireless devotees. In the mundane world they have nothing to achieve, and in the transcendental world they are full in themselves. Then why do they come to the mundane world? They descend to different planets as messiahs by the order of the Lord to deliver the fallen souls. On the earth they come down and do good to the people of the world in different circumstances under different climatic influences. They have nothing to do in this world save and except reclaim the fallen souls rotting in material existence, deluded by material energy.

TEXT 24

ततश्च वः पृच्छ्यमिमं विपृच्छे
विश्रभ्य विप्रा इति कृत्यतायाम् ।
सर्वात्मना म्रियमाणैश्च कृत्यं
शुद्धं च तत्रामृशताभियुक्ताः ॥२४॥

tataś ca vaḥ pṛcchyam imaṁ vipṛcche
viśrabhya viprā iti kṛtyatāyām
sarvātmanā mriyamāṇaiś ca kṛtyaṁ
śuddhaṁ ca tatrāmṛśatābhiyuktāḥ

tataḥ—as such; *ca*—and; *vaḥ*—unto you; *pṛcchyam*—that which is to be asked; *imam*—this; *vipṛcche*—beg to ask you; *viśrabhya*—trustworthy; *viprāḥ*—*brāhmaṇas; iti*—thus; *kṛtyatāyām*—out of all different duties; *sarva-ātmanā*—by everyone; *mriyamāṇaiḥ*—especially those who are just about to die; *ca*—and; *kṛtyam*—dutiful; *śuddham*—perfectly correct; *ca*—and; *tatra*—therein; *āmṛśata*—by complete deliberation; *abhiyuktāḥ*—just befitting.

TRANSLATION

O trustworthy brāhmaṇas, I now ask you about my immediate duty. Please, after proper deliberation, tell me of the unalloyed duty of everyone in all circumstances, and specifically of those who are just about to die.

PURPORT

In this verse the King has placed two questions before the learned sages. The first question is what is the duty of everyone in all circumstances, and the second question is what is the specific duty of one who is to die very shortly. Out of the two, the question relating to the dying man is most important because everyone is a dying man, either very shortly or after one hundred years. The duration of life is immaterial, but the duty of a dying man is very important. Mahārāja Parīkṣit placed these two questions before Śukadeva Gosvāmī also on his arrival, and practically the whole of the *Śrīmad-Bhāgavatam,* beginning from the Second Canto up to the last, the Twelfth Canto, deals with these two questions. The conclusion arrived at thereof is that devotional service of the Lord Śrī Kṛṣṇa, as it is confirmed by the Lord Himself in the last phases of the *Bhagavad-gītā,* is the last word in relation to everyone's permanent duty in life. Mahārāja Parīkṣit was already aware of this fact, but he wanted the great sages assembled there to unanimously give their verdict on his conviction so that he might be able to go on with his confirmed duty without controversy. He has especially mentioned the word *śuddha,* or perfectly correct. For transcendental realization or self-realization, many processes are recommended by various classes of philosophers. Some of them are first-class methods, and some of them are second- or third-class methods. The first-class method demands that one give up all other methods and surrender unto the lotus feet of the Lord and thus be saved from all sins and their reactions.

TEXT 25

तत्राभवद्भगवान् व्यासपुत्रो
यदृच्छया गामटमानोऽनपेक्षः ।
अलक्ष्यलिङ्गो निजलाभतुष्टो
वृतश्च बालैरवधूतवेषः ॥२५॥

tatrābhavad bhagavān vyāsa-putro
yadṛcchayā gām aṭamāno 'napekṣaḥ
alakṣya-liṅgo nija-lābha-tuṣṭo
vṛtaś ca bālair avadhūta-veṣaḥ

tatra—there; *abhavat*—appeared; *bhagavān*—powerful; *vyāsa-putraḥ*—son of Vyāsadeva; *yadṛcchayā*—as one desires; *gām*—the earth; *aṭamānaḥ*—while traveling; *anapekṣaḥ*—disinterested; *alakṣya*—unmanifested; *liṅgaḥ*

—symptoms; *nija-lābha*—self-realized; *tuṣṭaḥ*—satisfied; *vṛtaḥ*—surrounded; *ca*—and; *bālaiḥ*—by children; *avadhūta*—neglected by others; *veṣaḥ*—dressed.

TRANSLATION

At that moment there appeared the powerful son of Vyāsadeva, who traveled over the earth disinterested and satisfied with himself. He did not manifest any symptoms of belonging to any social order or status of life. He was surrounded with women and children, and he dressed as if others had neglected him.

PURPORT

The word *bhagavān* is sometimes used in relation with some of the great devotees of the Lord, like Śukadeva Gosvāmī. Such liberated souls are disinterested in the affairs of this material world because they are self-satisfied by the great achievements of devotional service. As explained before, Śukadeva Gosvāmī never accepted any formal spiritual master, nor did he undergo any formal reformatory performances. His father, Vyāsadeva, was his natural spiritual master because Śukadeva Gosvāmī heard *Śrīmad-Bhāgavatam* from him. After this, he became completely self-satisfied. Thus he was not dependent on any formal process. The formal processes are necessary for those who are expected to reach the stage of complete liberation, but Śrī Śukadeva Gosvāmī was already in that status by the grace of his father. As a young boy he was expected to be properly dressed, but he went about naked and was uninterested in social customs. He was neglected by the general populace, and inquisitive boys and women surrounded him as if he were a madman. He thus appears on the scene while traveling on the earth of his own accord. It appears that upon the inquiry of Mahārāja Parīkṣit, the great sages were not unanimous in their decision as to what was to be done. For spiritual salvation there were many prescriptions according to the different modes of different persons. But the ultimate aim of life is to attain the highest perfectional stage of devotional service to the Lord. As doctors differ, so also sages differ in their different prescriptions. While such things were going on, the great and powerful son of Vyāsadeva appeared on the scene.

TEXT 26

तं द्व्यष्टवर्षं सुकुमारपाद-
करोरुबाह्वंसकपोलगात्रम् ।

चार्वायताक्षोन्नसतुल्यकर्ण-
सुभ्र्वाननं कम्बुसुजातकण्ठम् ॥२६॥

taṁ dvyaṣṭa-varṣaṁ su-kumāra-pāda-
karoru-bāhv-aṁsa-kapola-gātram
cārv-āyatākṣonnasa-tulya-karṇa-
subhrv-ānanaṁ kambu-sujāta-kaṇṭham

tam—him; *dvi-aṣṭa*—sixteen; *varṣam*—years; *su-kumāra*—delicate; *pāda*—legs; *kara*—hands; *ūru*—thighs; *bāhu*—arms; *aṁsa*—shoulders; *kapola*—forehead; *gātram*—body; *cāru*—beautiful; *āyata*—broad; *akṣa*—eyes; *unnasa*—high nose; *tulya*—similar; *karṇa*—ears; *subhru*—nice brows; *ānanam*—face; *kambu*—conchshell; *sujāta*—nicely built; *kaṇṭham*—neck.

TRANSLATION

This son of Vyāsadeva was only sixteen years old. His legs, hands, thighs, arms, shoulders, forehead and the other parts of his body were all delicately formed. His eyes were beautifully wide, and his nose and ears were highly raised. He had a very attractive face, and his neck was well formed and beautiful like a conchshell.

PURPORT

A respectable personality is described beginning with the legs, and this honored system is observed here with Śukadeva Gosvāmī. He was only sixteen years of age. A person is honored for his achievements and not for advanced age. A person can be older by experience and not by age. Śrī Śukadeva Gosvāmī, who is described herein as the son of Vyāsadeva, was by his knowledge more experienced than all the sages present there, although he was only sixteen years old.

TEXT 27

निगूढजत्रुं पृथुतुङ्गवक्षस-
मावर्तनाभिं वलिवल्गूदरं च ।
दिगम्बरं वक्त्रविकीर्णकेशं
प्रलम्बबाहुं स्वमरोत्तमाभम् ॥२७॥

nigūḍha-jatruṁ pṛthu-tuṅga-vakṣasam
āvarta-nābhiṁ vali-valgūdaraṁ ca

dig-ambaraṁ vaktra-vikīrṇa-keśaṁ
pralamba-bāhuṁ svamarottamābham

nigūḍha—covered; *jatrum*—collarbone; *pṛthu*—broad; *tuṅga*—swollen; *vakṣasam*—chest; *āvarta*—whirled; *nābhim*—navel; *vali-valgu*—striped; *udaram*—abdomen; *ca*—also; *dik-ambaram*—dressed by all directions (naked); *vaktra*—curled; *vikīrṇa*—scattered; *keśam*—hair; *pralamba*—elongated; *bāhum*—hands; *su-amara-uttama*—the best among the gods (Kṛṣṇa); *ābham*—hue.

TRANSLATION

His collarbone was fleshy, his chest broad and thick, his navel deep and his abdomen beautifully striped. His arms were long, and curly hair was strewn over his beautiful face. He was naked, and the hue of his body reflected that of Lord Kṛṣṇa.

PURPORT

His bodily features indicate him to be different from common men. All the signs described in connection with the bodily features of Śukadeva Gosvāmī are uncommon symptoms, typical of great personalities, according to physiognomical calculations. His bodily hue resembled that of Lord Kṛṣṇa, who is the supreme among the gods, demigods and all living beings.

TEXT 28

श्यामं सदापीव्यवयोऽङ्गलक्ष्म्या
स्त्रीणां मनोज्ञं रुचिरस्मितेन ।
प्रत्युत्थितास्ते मुनयः स्वासनेभ्य-
स्तल्लक्षणज्ञा अपि गूढवर्चसम् ॥२८॥

śyāmaṁ sadāpīvya-vayo-'ṅga-lakṣmyā
strīṇāṁ mano-jñaṁ rucira-smitena
pratyutthitās te munayaḥ svāsanebhyas
tal-lakṣaṇa-jñā api gūḍha-varcasam

śyāmam—blackish; *sadā*—always; *apīvya*—excessively; *vayaḥ*—age; *aṅga*—symptoms; *lakṣmyā*—by the opulence of; *strīṇām*—of the fair sex; *manaḥ-jñam*—attractive; *rucira*—beautiful; *smitena*—smiling; *pratyutthitāḥ*

—stood up; *te*—all of them; *munayaḥ*—the great sages; *sva*—own; *āsanebhyaḥ*—from the seats; *tat*—those; *lakṣaṇa-jñāḥ*—expert in the art of physiognomy; *api*—even; *gūḍha-varcasam*—covered glories.

TRANSLATION

He was blackish and very beautiful due to his youth. Because of the glamor of his body and his attractive smiles, he was pleasing to women. Though he tried to cover his natural glories, the great sages present there were all expert in the art of physiognomy, and so they honored him by rising from their seats.

TEXT 29

स विष्णुरातोऽतिथय आगताय
तस्मै सपर्यां शिरसाजहार ।
ततो निवृत्ता ह्यबुधाः स्त्रियोऽर्भका
महासने सोपविवेश पूजितः ॥२९॥

sa viṣṇu-rāto 'tithaya āgatāya
tasmai saparyāṁ śirasājahāra
tato nivṛttā hy abudhāḥ striyo 'rbhakā
mahāsane sopaviveśa pūjitaḥ

saḥ—he; *viṣṇu-rātaḥ*—Mahārāja Parīkṣit (who is always protected by Lord Viṣṇu); *atithaye*—to become a guest; *āgatāya*—one who arrived there; *tasmai*—unto him; *saparyām*—with the whole body; *śirasā*—with bowed head; *ājahāra*—offered obeisances; *tataḥ*—thereafter; *nivṛttāḥ*—ceased; *hi*—certainly; *abudhāḥ*—less intelligent; *striyaḥ*—women; *arbhakāḥ*—boys; *mahā-āsane*—exalted seat; *sa*—he; *upaviveśa*—sat down; *pūjitaḥ*—being respected.

TRANSLATION

Mahārāja Parīkṣit, who is also known as Viṣṇurāta [one who is always protected by Viṣṇu], bowed his head to receive the chief guest, Śukadeva Gosvāmī. At that time all the ignorant women and boys ceased following Śrīla Śukadeva. Receiving respect from all, Śukadeva Gosvāmī took his exalted seat.

PURPORT

On Śukadeva Gosvāmī's arrival at the meeting, everyone, except Śrīla Vyāsadeva, Nārada and a few others, stood up, and Mahārāja Parīkṣit, who was glad to receive a great devotee of the Lord, bowed down before him with all the limbs of his body. Śukadeva Gosvāmī also exchanged the greetings and reception by embrace, shaking of hands, nodding and bowing down, especially before his father and Nārada Muni. Thus he was offered the presidential seat at the meeting. When he was so received by the king and sages, the street boys and less intelligent women who followed him were struck with wonder and fear. So they retired from their frivolous activities, and everything was full of gravity and calm.

TEXT 30

स संवृतस्तत्र महान् महीयसां
ब्रह्मर्षिराजर्षिदेवर्षिसङ्घैः ।
व्यरोचतालं भगवान् यथेन्दु-
र्ग्रहर्क्षतारानिकरैः परीतः ॥३०॥

sa saṁvṛtas tatra mahān mahīyasāṁ
brahmarṣi-rājarṣi-devarṣi-saṅghaiḥ
vyarocatālaṁ bhagavān yathendur
graharkṣa-tārā-nikaraiḥ parītaḥ

saḥ—Śrī Śukadeva Gosvāmī; *saṁvṛtaḥ*—surrounded by; *tatra*—there; *mahān*—great; *mahīyasām*—of the greatest; *brahmarṣi*—saint among the *brāhmaṇas; rājarṣi*—saint among the kings; *devarṣi*—saint among the demigods; *saṅghaiḥ*—by the assembly of; *vyarocata*—well deserved; *alam*—able; *bhagavān*—powerful; *yathā*—as; *induḥ*—the moon; *graha*—planets; *ṛkṣa*—heavenly bodies; *tārā*—stars; *nikaraiḥ*—by the assembly of; *parītaḥ*—surrounded by.

TRANSLATION

Śukadeva Gosvāmī was then surrounded by saintly sages and demigods just as the moon is surrounded by stars, planets and other heavenly bodies. His presence was gorgeous, and he was respected by all.

PURPORT

In the great assembly of saintly personalities, there was Vyāsadeva the *brahmarṣi,* Nārada the *devarṣi,* Paraśurāma the great ruler of the *kṣatriya* kings, etc. Some of them were powerful incarnations of the Lord. Śukadeva Gosvāmī was not known as *brahmarṣi, rājarṣi* or *devarṣi,* nor was he an incarnation like Nārada, Vyāsa or Paraśurāma. And yet he excelled them in respects paid. This means that the devotee of the Lord is more honored in the world than the Lord Himself. One should therefore never minimize the importance of a devotee like Śukadeva Gosvāmī.

TEXT 31

प्रशान्तमासीनमकुण्ठमेधसं
मुनिं नृपो भागवतोऽभ्युपेत्य ।
प्रणम्य मूर्ध्नावहितः कृताञ्जलि-
र्नत्वा गिरा सूनृतयान्वपृच्छत् ॥३१॥

praśāntam āsīnam akuṇṭha-medhasaṁ
muniṁ nṛpo bhāgavato 'bhyupetya
praṇamya mūrdhnāvahitaḥ kṛtāñjalir
natvā girā sūnṛtayānvapṛcchat

praśāntam—perfectly pacified; *āsīnam*—sitting; *akuṇṭha*—without hesitation; *medhasam*—one who has sufficient intelligence; *munim*—unto the great sage; *nṛpaḥ*—the King (Mahārāja Parīkṣit); *bhāgavataḥ*—the great devotee; *abhyupetya*—approaching him; *praṇamya*—bowing down; *mūrdhnā*—his head; *avahitaḥ*—properly; *kṛta-añjaliḥ*—with folded hands; *natvā*—politely; *girā*—by words; *sūnṛtayā*—in sweet voices; *anvapṛcchat*—inquired.

TRANSLATION

The sage Śrī Śukadeva Gosvāmī sat perfectly pacified, intelligent and ready to answer any question without hesitation. The great devotee, Mahārāja Parīkṣit, approached him, offered his respects by bowing before him, and politely inquired with sweet words and folded hands.

PURPORT

The gesture now adopted by Mahārāja Parīkṣit of questioning a master is quite befitting in terms of scriptural injunctions. The scriptural injunction is that one should humbly approach a spiritual master to understand the transcendental science. Mahārāja Parīkṣit was now prepared for meeting his death, and within the very short time of seven days he was to know the process of entering the kingdom of God. In such important cases, one is required to approach a spiritual master. There is no necessity of approaching a spiritual master unless one is in need of solving the problems of life. One who does not know how to put questions before the spiritual master has no business seeing him. And the qualification of the spiritual master is perfectly manifested in the person of Śukadeva Gosvāmī. Both the spiritual master and the disciple, namely Śrī Śukadeva Gosvāmī and Mahārāja Parīkṣit, attained perfection through the medium of *Śrīmad-Bhāgavatam.* Śukadeva Gosvāmī learned *Śrīmad-Bhāgavatam* from his father, Vyāsadeva, but he had no chance to recite it. Before Mahārāja Parīkṣit he recited *Śrīmad-Bhāgavatam* and answered the questions of Mahārāja Parīkṣit unhesitatingly, and thus both the master and the disciple got salvation.

TEXT 32

परीक्षिदुवाच

अहो अद्य वयं ब्रह्मन् सत्सेव्याः क्षत्रबन्धवः ।
कृपयातिथिरूपेण भवद्भिस्तीर्थकाः कृताः ॥३२॥

parīkṣid uvāca
aho adya vayaṁ brahman
sat-sevyāḥ kṣatra-bandhavaḥ
kṛpayātithi-rūpeṇa
bhavadbhis tīrthakāḥ kṛtāḥ

parīkṣit uvāca—the fortunate Mahārāja Parīkṣit said; *aho*—ah; *adya*—today; *vayam*—we; *brahman*—O *brāhmaṇa; sat-sevyāḥ*—eligible to serve the devotee; *kṣatra*—the ruling class; *bandhavaḥ*—friends; *kṛpayā*—by your mercy; *atithi-rūpeṇa*—in the manner of a guest; *bhavadbhiḥ*—by your good self; *tīrthakāḥ*—qualified for being places of pilgrimage; *kṛtāḥ*—done by you.

TRANSLATION

The fortunate King Parīkṣit said: O brāhmaṇa, by your mercy only, you have sanctified us, making us like unto places of pilgrimage, all by your presence here as my guest. By your mercy, we, who are but unworthy royalty, become eligible to serve the devotee.

PURPORT

Saintly devotees like Śukadeva Gosvāmī generally do not approach worldly enjoyers, especially those in royal orders. Mahārāja Pratāparudra was a follower of Lord Caitanya, but when he wanted to see the Lord, the Lord refused to see him because he was a king. For a devotee who desires to go back to Godhead, two things are strictly prohibited: worldly enjoyers and women. Therefore, devotees of the standard of Śukadeva Gosvāmī are never interested in seeing kings. Mahārāja Parīkṣit was, of course, a different case. He was a great devotee, although a king, and therefore Śukadeva Gosvāmī came to see him in his last stage of life. Mahārāja Parīkṣit, out of his devotional humility, felt himself an unworthy descendant of his great *kṣatriya* forefathers, although he was as great as his predecessors. The unworthy sons of the royal orders are called *kṣatra-bandhavas,* as the unworthy sons of the *brāhmaṇas* are called *dvija-bandhus* or *brahma-bandhus.* Mahārāja Parīkṣit was greatly encouraged by the presence of Śukadeva Gosvāmī. He felt himself sanctified by the presence of the great saint whose presence turns any place into a place of pilgrimage.

TEXT 33

येषां संस्मरणात्पुंसां सद्यः शुद्ध्यन्ति वै गृहाः ।
किं पुनर्दर्शनस्पर्शपादशौचासनादिभिः ॥३३॥

yeṣāṁ saṁsmaraṇāt puṁsāṁ
sadyaḥ śuddhyanti vai gṛhāḥ
kiṁ punar darśana-sparśa-
pāda-śaucāsanādibhiḥ

yeṣām—of whom; *saṁsmaraṇāt*—by remembrance; *puṁsām*—of a person; *sadyaḥ*—instantly; *śuddhyanti*—cleanses; *vai*—certainly; *gṛhāḥ*—all houses; *kim*—what; *punaḥ*—then; *darśana*—meeting; *sparśa*—touching; *pāda*—the feet; *śauca*—washing; *āsana-ādibhiḥ*—by offering a seat, etc.

TRANSLATION

Simply by our remembering you, our houses become instantly sanctified. And what to speak of seeing you, touching you, washing your holy feet and offering you a seat in our home?

PURPORT

The importance of holy places of pilgrimage is due to the presence of great sages and saints. It is said that sinful persons go to the holy places and leave their sins there to accumulate. But the presence of the great saints disinfects the accumulated sins, and thus the holy places continue to remain sanctified by the grace of the devotees and saints present there. If such saints appear in the homes of worldly people, certainly the accumulated sins of such worldly enjoyers become neutralized. Therefore, the holy saints actually have no self-interest with the householders. The only aim of such saints is to sanctify the houses of the householders, and the householders therefore should feel grateful when such saints and sages appear at their doors. A householder who dishonors such holy orders is a great offender. It is enjoined, therefore, that a householder who does not bow down before a saint at once must undergo fasting for the day in order to neutralize the great offense.

TEXT 34

सान्निध्यात्ते महायोगिन्पातकानि महान्त्यपि ।
सद्यो नश्यन्ति वै पुंसां विष्णोरिव सुरेतराः ॥३४॥

sānnidhyāt te mahā-yogin
pātakāni mahānty api
sadyo naśyanti vai puṁsāṁ
viṣṇor iva suretarāḥ

sānnidhyāt—on account of the presence; *te*—your; *mahā-yogin*—O great mystic; *pātakāni*—sins; *mahānti*—invulnerable; *api*—in spite of; *sadyaḥ*—immediately; *naśyanti*—vanquished; *vai*—certainly; *puṁsām*—of a person; *viṣṇoḥ*—like the presence of the Personality of Godhead; *iva*—like; *sura-itarāḥ*—other than the demigods.

TRANSLATION

Just as the atheist cannot remain in the presence of the Personality of Godhead, so also the invulnerable sins of a man are immediately vanquished in your presence, O saint! O great mystic!

PURPORT

There are two classes of human beings, namely the atheist and the devotee of the Lord. The devotee of the Lord, because of manifesting godly qualities, is called a demigod, whereas the atheist is called a demon. The demon cannot stand the presence of Viṣṇu, the Personality of Godhead. The demons are always busy in trying to vanquish the Personality of Godhead, but factually as soon as the Personality of Godhead appears, by either His transcendental name, form, attributes, pastimes, paraphernalia or variegatedness, the demon is at once vanquished. It is said that a ghost cannot remain as soon as the holy name of the Lord is chanted. The great saints and devotees of the Lord are in the list of His paraphernalia, and thus as soon as a saintly devotee is present, the ghostly sins are at once vanquished. That is the verdict of all Vedic literatures. One is recommended, therefore, to associate only with saintly devotees so that worldly demons and ghosts cannot exert their sinister influence.

TEXT 35

अपि मे भगवान् प्रीतः कृष्णः पाण्डुसुतप्रियः ।
पैतृष्वसेयप्रीत्यर्थं तद्गोत्रस्यात्तबान्धवः ॥३५॥

api me bhagavān prītaḥ
kṛṣṇaḥ pāṇḍu-suta-priyaḥ
paitṛ-ṣvaseya-prīty-arthaṁ
tad-gotrasyātta-bāndhavaḥ

api—definitely; *me*—unto me; *bhagavān*—the Personality of Godhead; *prītaḥ*—pleased; *kṛṣṇaḥ*—the Lord; *pāṇḍu-suta*—the sons of King Pāṇḍu; *priyaḥ*—dear; *paitṛ*—in relation with the father; *svaseya*—the sons of the sister; *prīti*—satisfaction; *artham*—in the matter of; *tat*—their; *gotrasya*—of the descendant; *ātta*—accepted; *bāndhavaḥ*—as a friend.

TRANSLATION

Lord Kṛṣṇa, the Personality of Godhead, who is very dear to the sons of King Pāṇḍu, has accepted me as one of those relatives just to please His great cousins and brothers.

PURPORT

A pure and exclusive devotee of the Lord serves his family interest more dexterously than others, who are attached to illusory family affairs. Generally people are attached to family matters, and the whole economic impetus of human society is moving under the influence of family affection. Such deluded persons have no information that one can render better service to the family by becoming a devotee of the Lord. The Lord gives special protection to the family members and descendants of a devotee, even though such members are themselves nondevotees! Mahārāja Prahlāda was a great devotee of the Lord, but his father, Hiraṇyakaśipu, was a great atheist and declared enemy of the Lord. But despite all this, Hiraṇyakaśipu was awarded salvation due to his being the father of Mahārāja Prahlāda. The Lord is so kind that he gives all protection to the family members of His devotee, and thus the devotee has no need to bother about his family members, even if one leaves such family members aside to discharge devotional service. Mahārāja Yudhiṣṭhira and his brothers were the sons of Kuntī, the paternal aunt of Lord Kṛṣṇa, and Mahārāja Parīkṣit admits the patronage of Lord Kṛṣṇa because of his being the only grandson of the great Pāṇḍavas.

TEXT 36

अन्यथा तेऽव्यक्तगतेर्दर्शनं नः कथं नृणाम् ।
नितरां म्रियमाणानां संसिद्धस्य वनीयसः ॥३६॥

anyathā te 'vyakta-gater
darśanaṁ naḥ kathaṁ nṛṇām
nitarāṁ mriyamāṇānāṁ
saṁsiddhasya vanīyasaḥ

anyathā—otherwise; *te*—your; *avyakta-gateḥ*—of one whose movements are invisible; *darśanam*—meeting; *naḥ*—for us; *katham*—how; *nṛṇām*—of the people; *nitarām*—specifically; *mriyamāṇānām*—of those who are about to die; *saṁsiddhasya*—of one who is all-perfect; *vanīyasaḥ*—voluntary appearance.

TRANSLATION

Otherwise [without being inspired by Lord Kṛṣṇa] how is it that you have voluntarily appeared here, though you are moving incognito to the common man and are not visible to us who are on the verge of death?

PURPORT

The great sage Śukadeva Gosvāmī was certainly inspired by Lord Kṛṣṇa to appear voluntarily before Mahārāja Parīkṣit, the great devotee of the Lord, just to give him the teachings of *Śrīmad-Bhāgavatam.* One can achieve the nucleus of the devotional service of the Lord by the mercy of the spiritual master and the Personality of Godhead. The spiritual master is the manifested representative of the Lord to help one achieve ultimate success. One who is not authorized by the Lord cannot become a spiritual master. Śrīla Śukadeva Gosvāmī is an authorized spiritual master, and thus he was inspired by the Lord to appear before Mahārāja Parīkṣit and instruct him in the teachings of *Śrīmad-Bhāgavatam.* One can achieve the ultimate success of going back to Godhead if he is favored by the Lord's sending His true representative. As soon as a true representative of the Lord is met by a devotee of the Lord, the devotee is assured a guarantee for going back to Godhead just after leaving the present body. This, however, depends on the sincerity of the devotee himself. The Lord is seated in the heart of all living beings, and thus he knows very well the movements of all individual persons. As soon as the Lord finds that a particular soul is very eager to go back to Godhead, the Lord at once sends His bona fide representative. The sincere devotee is thus assured by the Lord of going back to Godhead. The conclusion is that to get the assistance and help of a bona fide spiritual master means *to receive the direct help of the Lord Himself.*

TEXT 37

अतः पृच्छामि संसिद्धिं योगिनां परमं गुरुम् ।
पुरुषस्येह यत्कार्यं म्रियमाणस्य सर्वथा ॥३७॥

ataḥ pṛcchāmi saṁsiddhiṁ
yogināṁ paramaṁ gurum
puruṣasyeha yat kāryaṁ
mriyamāṇasya sarvathā

ataḥ—therefore; *pṛcchāmi*—beg to inquire; *saṁsiddhim*—the way of perfection; *yoginām*—of the saints; *paramam*—the supreme; *gurum*—the spiritual master; *puruṣasya*—of a person; *iha*—in this life; *yat*—whatever; *kāryam*—duty; *mriyamāṇasya*—of one who is going to die; *sarvathā*—in every way.

TRANSLATION

You are the spiritual master of great saints and devotees. I am therefore begging you to show the way of perfection for all persons, and especially for one who is about to die.

PURPORT

Unless one is perfectly anxious to inquire about the way of perfection, there is no necessity of approaching a spiritual master. A spiritual master is not a kind of decoration for a householder. Generally a fashionable materialist engages a so-called spiritual master without any profit. The pseudo spiritual master flatters the so-called disciple, and thereby both the master and his ward go to hell without a doubt. Mahārāja Parīkṣit is the right type of disciple because he puts forward questions vital to the interest of all men, particularly for the dying men. The question put forward by Mahārāja Parīkṣit is the basic principle of the complete thesis of *Śrīmad-Bhāgavatam.* Now let us see how intelligently the great master replies.

TEXT 38

यच्छ्रोतव्यमथो जप्यं यत्कर्तव्यं नृभिः प्रभो ।
स्मर्तव्यं भजनीयं वा ब्रूहि यद्वा विपर्ययम् ॥३८॥

yac chrotavyam atho japyaṁ
yat kartavyaṁ nṛbhiḥ prabho
smartavyaṁ bhajanīyaṁ vā
brūhi yad vā viparyayam

yat—whatever; *śrotavyam*—worth hearing; *atho*—thereof; *japyam*—chanted; *yat*—what also; *kartavyam*—executed; *nṛbhiḥ*—by the people in general; *prabho*—O master; *smartavyam*—that which is remembered; *bhajanīyam*—worshipable; *vā*—either; *brūhi*—please explain; *yad vā*—what it may be; *viparyayam*—against the principle.

TRANSLATION

Please let me know what a man should hear, chant, remember and worship, and also what he should not do. Please explain all this to me.

TEXT 39

नूनं भगवतो ब्रह्मन् गृहेषु गृहमेधिनाम् ।
न लक्ष्यते ह्यवस्थानमपि गोदोहनं क्वचित् ॥३९॥

nūnaṁ bhagavato brahman
gṛheṣu gṛha-medhinām

na lakṣyate hy avasthānam
api go-dohanaṁ kvacit

nūnam—because; *bhagavataḥ*—of you, who are powerful; *brahman*—O *brāhmaṇa; gṛheṣu*—in the houses; *gṛha-medhinām*—of the householders; *na*—not; *lakṣyate*—are seen; *hi*—exactly; *avasthānam*—staying in; *api*—even; *go-dohanam*—milking the cow; *kvacit*—rarely.

TRANSLATION

O powerful brāhmaṇa, it is said that you hardly stay in the houses of men long enough to milk a cow.

PURPORT

Saints and sages in the renounced order of life go to the houses of the householders at the time they milk the cows, early in the morning, and ask some quantity of milk for subsistence. A pound of milk fresh from the milk bag of a cow is sufficient to feed an adult with all vitamin values, and therefore saints and sages live only on milk. Even the poorest of the householders keep at least ten cows, each delivering twelve to twenty quarts of milk, and therefore no one hesitates to spare a few pounds of milk for the mendicants. It is the duty of householders to maintain the saints and sages, like the children. So a saint like Śukadeva Gosvāmī would hardly stay at the house of a householder for more than five minutes in the morning. In other words, such saints are very rarely seen in the houses of householders, and Mahārāja Parīkṣit therefore prayed to him to instruct him as soon as possible. The householders also should be intelligent enough to get some transcendental information from visiting sages. The householder should not foolishly ask a saint to deliver what is available in the market. That should be the reciprocal relation between the saints and the householders.

TEXT 40

सूत उवाच
एवमाभाषितः पृष्टः स राज्ञा श्लक्ष्णया गिरा ।
प्रत्यभाषत धर्मज्ञो भगवान् बादरायणिः ॥४०॥

sūta uvāca
evam ābhāṣitaḥ pṛṣṭaḥ
sa rājñā ślakṣṇayā girā

pratyabhāṣata dharma-jño
bhagavān bādarāyaṇiḥ

sūtaḥ uvāca—Śrī Sūta Gosvāmī said; *evam*—thus; *ābhāṣitaḥ*—being spoken; *pṛṣṭaḥ* —and asked for; *saḥ*—he; *rājñā*—by the King; *ślakṣṇayā*—by sweet; *girā*—language; *pratyabhāṣata*—began to reply; *dharma-jñaḥ*—one who knows the principles of religion; *bhagavān*—the powerful personality; *bādarāyaṇiḥ*—son of Vyāsadeva.

TRANSLATION

Śrī Sūta Gosvāmī said: The King thus spoke and questioned the sage, using sweet language. Then the great and powerful personality, the son of Vyāsadeva, who knew the principles of religion, began his reply.

Thus end the Bhaktivedanta purports of the First Canto, Nineteenth Chapter, of the Śrīmad-Bhāgavatam, *entitled "The Appearance of Śukadeva Gosvāmī."*

END OF THE FIRST CANTO

Appendixes

About the Author

His Divine Grace A.C. Bhaktivedanta Swami Prabhupāda appeared in this world in 1896 in Calcutta, India. He first met his spiritual master, Śrīla Bhaktisiddhānta Sarasvatī Gosvāmi, in Calcutta in 1922. Śrīla Bhaktisiddhānta Sarasvatī, a prominent religious scholar and the founder of sixty-four Gauḍīya Maṭhas (Vedic institutes) in India, liked this educated young man and convinced him to dedicate his life to teaching Vedic knowledge. Śrīla Prabhupāda became his student and, in 1933, his formally initiated disciple.

At their first meeting, Śrīla Bhaktisiddhānta Sarasvatī requested Śrīla Prabhupāda to broadcast Vedic knowledge in English. In the years that followed, Śrīla Prabhupāda wrote a commentary on the *Bhagavad-gītā,* assisted the Gauḍīya Maṭha in its work, and, in 1944, started *Back to Godhead,* an English fortnightly magazine. Single-handedly, Śrīla Prabhupāda edited it, typed the manuscripts, checked the galley proofs, and even distributed the individual copies. The magazine is now being continued by his disciples all over the world.

In 1950 Śrīla Prabhupāda retired from married life, adopting the *vānaprastha* (retired) order to devote more time to his studies and writing. He traveled to the holy city of Vṛndāvana, where he lived in humble circumstances in the historic temple of Rādhā-Dāmodara. There he engaged for several years in deep study and writing. He accepted the renounced order of life (*sannyāsa*) in 1959. At Rādhā-Dāmodara, Śrīla Prabhupāda began work on his life's masterpiece: a multivolume commentated translation of the eighteen-thousand-verse *Śrīmad-Bhāgavatam* (*Bhāgavata Purāṇa*). He also wrote *Easy Journey to Other Planets.*

After publishing three volumes of the *Bhāgavatam,* Śrīla Prabhupāda came to the United States, in September 1965, to fulfill the mission of his spiritual master. Subsequently, His Divine Grace wrote more than sixty volumes of authoritative commentated translations and summary studies of the philosophical and religious classics of India.

When he first arrived by freighter in New York City, Śrīla Prabhupāda was practically penniless. It was after almost a year of great difficulty that he established the International Society for Krishna Consciousness in July of 1966. Before he passed away on November 14, 1977, he had guided the Society and seen it grow to a worldwide confederation of more than one hundred *ashrams*, schools, temples, institutes, and farm communities.

In 1972 His Divine Grace introduced the Vedic system of primary and secondary education in the West by founding the *gurukula* school in Dallas, Texas. Since then his disciples have established similar schools throughout the United States and the rest of the world.

Śrīla Prabhupāda also inspired the construction of several large international cultural centers in India. The center at Śrīdhāma Māyāpur is the site for a planned spiritual city, an ambitious project for which construction will extend over many years to come. In Vṛndāvana are the magnificent Kṛṣṇa-Balarāma Temple and International Guesthouse, *gurukula* school, and Śrīla Prabhupāda Memorial and Museum. There is also a major cultural and educational center in Mumbai. There are beautiful temples in Delhi, Bangalore, Ahmedabad and Vadodara besides many other centers throughout India.

Śrīla Prabhupāda's most significant contribution, however, is his books. Highly respected by scholars for their authority, depth, and clarity, they are used as textbooks in numerous college courses. His writings have been translated into over fifty languages. The Bhaktivedanta Book Trust, established in 1972 exclusively to publish the works of His Divine Grace, has thus become the world's largest publisher of books in the field of Indian religion and philosophy.

In just twelve years, despite his advanced age, Śrīla Prabhupāda circled the globe fourteen times on lecture tours that took him to six continents. In spite of such a vigorous schedule, Śrīla Prabhupāda continued to write prolifically. His writings constitute a veritable library of Vedic philosophy, religion, literature, and culture.

References

The purports of *Śrīmad-Bhāgavatam* are all confirmed by standard Vedic authorities. The following authentic scriptures are cited in this volume. For specific page references, consult the general index.

Amarakośa dictionary

Bhagavad-gītā

Brahmāṇḍa Purāṇa

Brahma Purāṇa

Brahma-saṁhitā

Brahma-sūtra. See: Vedānta-sūtra

Brahma-vaivarta Purāṇa

Bṛhad-vaiṣṇava Tantra

Bṛhan-nāradīya Purāṇa

Chāndogya Upaniṣad

Hari-bhakti-sudhodaya

Hari-bhakti-vilāsa

Hari-nāmāmṛta-vyākaraṇa

Īśopaniṣad

Kaṭha Upaniṣad

Kaumudī dictionary

Mādhyandina-śruti

Mahābhārata

Manu-smṛti

Matsya Purāṇa

Narasiṁha Purāṇa

Nīti-śāstra

Padma Purāṇa

Rāmāyaṇa

Śabda-kośa dictionary

Sāma-veda Upaniṣad

Skanda Purāṇa

Śrīmad-Bhāgavatam

Upaniṣads

Vāmana Purāṇa

Varāha Purāṇa

Vāyavīya Tantra

Vedas

Viṣṇu Purāṇa

Glossary

A

Ācārya—a spiritual master who teaches by his own example, and who sets the proper religious example for all human beings.

Adhidaivic powers—the administrative functions delegated by the Lord to demigods, such as control over rain, wind and sun.

Ahiṁsā—nonviolence.

Akṣauhiṇī—a military division consisting of 21,870 chariots, 21,870 elephants, 109,350 infantrymen and 65,610 horsemen.

Anna-prāśana—the ceremony of offering a child his first food grains; one of the ten purificatory *saṁskāras*.

Ārati—a ceremony in which one greets and worships the Lord in His form of a Deity by offerings such as incense, a flame, water, a fine cloth, a fragrant flower, a peacock-feather, and yak-tail wisk, accompanied by ringing of a bell and chanting of *mantras*.

Arcana—the procedures followed for worshiping the *arcā-vigraha*, the Deity in the temple; engaging all the senses in the service of the Lord.

Artha—economic development.

Āsana—seat or throne; a sitting posture in *yoga* practice.

Āśrama—a spiritual order of life in the Vedic varṇāśrama system. The four āśramas are *brahmacārī* or student life, *gṛhastha* or married life, *vānaprastha* or retired life, and *sannyāsa* or the renounced order of life; the home of the spiritual master, a place where spiritual practices are executed.

Asura—a demon, one who does not follow the principles of scripture, an atheist, a gross materialist. One who is envious of God, and is averse to the supremacy and service of the Supreme Lord Viṣṇu.

Aśvamedha-yajña—a Vedic horse sacrifice. It was performed by kings who desired to expand their rule over other rulers and kings. The king performing the sacrifice would let the sacrificial horse wander over other kingdoms. The king who would challenge the sacrificial horse had to fight the king performing the yajña.

Avatāra—literally "one who descends." A partially or fully empowered incarnation of Lord Kṛṣṇa who descends from the spiritual sky to the material universe with a particular mission described in the scriptures. Lord

Śrī Kṛṣṇa is the original Personality of Godhead from whom all *avatāras* originate. There are two broad categories of *avatāras*. Some, like Śrī Kṛṣṇa, Śrī Rāma and Śrī Nṛsiṁha, are Viṣṇu-tattva, i.e. direct forms of God Himself, the source of all power. Others are ordinary souls (jīva-tattva) who are called *śaktyāveśa avatāras*, and are empowered by the Lord to execute a certain purpose.

B

Bhagavad-gītā—a seven-hundred verse record of a conversation between Lord Kṛṣṇa and His disciple, Arjuna, from the *Bhīṣma Parva* of the *Mahābhārata* of Vedavyāsa. The conversation took place between two armies minutes before the start of an immense fratricidal battle. Kṛṣṇa teaches the science of the Absolute Truth and the importance of devotional service to the despondent Arjuna, and it contains the essence of all Vedic wisdom. Śrīla Prabhupāda's annotated English translation is called *Bhagavad-gītā As It Is*; This most essential text of spiritual knowledge, The Song of the Lord, contains Kṛṣṇa's instructions to Arjuna at Kurukṣetra. It is found in the *Mahābhārata*. The *Mahābhārata* is classified as smṛti-śāstra, a supplement of the *śruti-śāstra*. *Śruti*, the core Vedic literature, includes the four Vedas (*Ṛg, Sāma, Yajur* and *Atharva*) and the *Upaniṣads*. *Śruti* advances the understanding of the absolute. *Bhagavad-gītā* is also known as *Gītopaniṣad*, or a *śruti* text spoken by the Supreme Personality of Godhead Himself. Therefore, Śrīla Prabhupāda wrote in a letter, the Gītā should be taken as *śruti*. But they take it as *smṛti* because it is part of the *smṛti* (*Mahābhārata*). In one sense it is both *śruti* and *smṛti*. In only 700 verses, the *Bhagavad-gītā* summarizes all Vedic knowledge about the soul, God, *sanātana-dharma*, sacrifice, *yoga*, *karma*, reincarnation, the modes of material nature, *Vedānta* and pure devotion.

Bhāgavata—anything related to Bhagavān, the Supreme Lord, especially the devotee of the Lord and the scripture *Śrīmad-Bhāgavatam*.

Bhāgavata-dharma—the science of devotional service to the Supreme Lord; the religious principles enunciated by the Lord; the eternal function of the living being.

Bhāgavata-saptāha—a seven-day series of lectures on *Śrīmad-Bhāgavatam*, quite often given by professional reciters to a paying audience.

Bhakta—a devotee of the Lord; one who performs devotional service *(bhakti)*.

Bhakti—devotional service to the Supreme Lord; purified service of the senses of the Lord by one's own senses; love and devotion to the Supreme

Personality of Godhead, Lord Kṛṣṇa. The formal systematization of devotion is called *bhakti-yoga*.

Bhaktivedāntas—advanced transcendentalists who have realized the conclusion of the *Vedas* through devotional service.

Bhakti-yoga—the system of cultivation of pure devotional service to the Supreme Personality of Godhead, Lord Kṛṣṇa, which is not tinged by sense gratification or philosophical speculation. It consists of nine *aṅgas* or parts: (1) *śravaṇaṁ*–hearing about the transcendental holy name, form, and other qualities of the Lord (2) *kīrtanaṁ*– chanting about these qualities, (3) *viṣṇoḥ smaraṇaṁ*–remembering them, (4) *pāda-sevanam*–serving the lotus feet of the Lord, (5) *arcanaṁ*–worshipping the Deity of the Lord, (6) *vandanaṁ*–offering prayers to the Lord, (7) *dāsyaṁ* –serving His mission, (8) *sakhyam*–making friends with the Lord, and (9) *ātma-nivedanam*–surrendering everything unto Him.

Bhāva—preliminary stage of ecstatic love of God, the stage experienced after transcendental affection; manifestation of ecstatic symptoms in the body of a devotee.

Brahmacarya—celibate student life, the first order of Vedic spiritual life; the vow of strict abstinence from sex indulgence.

Brahma-tejas—the potency of a *brāhmaṇa*.

Brahmajyoti—the impersonal bodily effulgence emanating from the transcendental body of the Supreme Lord Kṛṣṇa, which constitutes the brilliant illumination of the spiritual sky; From Kṛṣṇa's transcendental personal form of eternity, knowledge and bliss emanates a shining effulgence called the brahmajyoti (light of Brahman). The material *prakṛti*, the souls or *jīvas* who desire to enjoy matter, and *kāla* (time), are situated within this *brahmajyoti*, which is pure existence devoid of difference and activity. It is the impersonal Brahman of the Mayavādīs, and the Clear Light of some Buddhist sects. For many mystics and philosophers the world over, the *brahmajyoti* is the indefinable One from which all things emerge in the beginning and merge into at the end. The *brahmajyoti* is Kṛṣṇa's feature of *sat* (eternality) separated from *cit* (knowledge) and *ānanda* (bliss).

Brahman—(1) the infinitesimal spiritual individual soul, (2) the impersonal, all-pervasive aspect of the Supreme, (3) the Supreme Personality of Godhead and (4) the *mahat-tattva*, or total material substance; This Sanskrit term comes from the root *bṛh*, which means to grow or to evolve. The *Cāndogya Upaniṣad* describes Brahman as *tajjalān*, as that (*tat*) from which the world arises (*ja*), into which it returns (*la*), and by which is supported and lives (*an*). Impersonalists equate Brahman with the *brahmajyoti.* But in its fullest sense, Brahman is the *vastu,* the actual substance of the world: (1) Viṣṇu as the Supreme Soul (*paraṁ brahman*), (2) the individual self as the subordinate soul (*jīva-brahman*), and (3) matter as creative nature (*mahad-brahman*). Viṣṇu is accepted by all schools of Vaiṣṇava *Vedānta* as the transcendental, unlimited *Puruṣottama* (Supreme Person), while the individual souls and matter are His conscious and unconscious energies (cid-acid-śakti).

Brāhmaṇa—a member of the intellectual, priestly class; a person wise in Vedic knowledge, fixed in goodness and knowledge of Brahman, the Absolute Truth; one of the four orders of Vedic society. Their occupation consists of learning and teaching Vedic literature, learning and teaching Deity worship, and receiving and giving charity.

Brahmānanda—the spiritual bliss derived from impersonal Brahman realization.

Brahmarṣi—a title meaning "sage among the *brāhmaṇas.*"

Brahmāstra—a nuclear weapon produced by chanting a *mantra,* and more powerful than many atomic bombs. It could be used only on a person of equal or superior strength. This weapon was given by Droṇa to Arjuna.

C

Caṇḍāla—an outcaste or untouchable; dog-eater, the lowest class of human beings.

D

Daridra-nārāyaṇa—"poor Nārāyaṇa," an offensive term used by Māyāvādīs to equate poor men with the Supreme Lord.

Devarṣi—a title meaning "sage among the demigods"; usually refers to Nārada Muni.

Dharma—religious principles; one's natural occupation; the quality of rendering service, which is the essential, eternal quality of the soul, regarded as inseparable from it. The Sanskrit term *dharma* is variously translated as duty, virtue, morality, righteousness, or religion, but no single English word conveys the actual import of dharma. *Dharma* ultimately means to surrender to the Supreme Lord, as Lord Kṛṣṇa commands Arjuna in the Gītā.

Dhyāna—meditational *yoga.*

E

Ekādaśī—Directly presided over by Lord Hari, Ekādaśī is a holy day for Vaiṣṇavas. It falls on the eleventh day after both the full and new moon days. Abstinence from grains and beans is prescribed. One should utilize this day for fasting and increasing one's devotion to Lord Kṛṣṇa by intensifying the chanting of the Hare Kṛṣṇa *mantra* and other devotional activities.

G

Gandharvas—the celestial demigod singers, musicians and dancers of the heavenly planets.

Garbhādhāna-saṁskāra—the Vedic ceremony of purification to be performed by parents before conceiving a child.

Goloka Vṛndāvana (Kṛṣṇaloka)—the highest spiritual planet in the kingdom of God, Lord Kṛṣṇa's personal abode.

Gopīs—the cowherd girls of Vraja, who are generally the counterparts of Śrī Kṛṣṇa's *hlādini-sākti*, Śrīmatī Rādhārāṇī, and His most surrendered and confidential devotees. They assist Her as maidservants in her conjugal pastimes with the Supreme Personality of Godhead.

Gosvāmī—a person who has his senses under full control: the title of a *sannyāsi*, a person in the renounced order of life.

Gṛhastha—regulated householder life. One who leads a God conscious married life and raises a family in Kṛṣṇa consciousness according to the Vedic social system; the second order of Vedic spiritual life.

Guṇa-avatāras—the presiding deities of the three modes of nature: Viṣṇu, Brahmā and Śiva. They control the modes of goodness, passion and ignorance respectively.

Guru—spiritual master; one of the three spiritual authorities for a Vaiṣṇava. Literally, this term means heavy. The spiritual master is heavy with knowledge.

H

Hare Kṛṣṇa mantra—a sixteen-word prayer composed of the names Hare, Kṛṣṇa, and Rāma: Hare Kṛṣṇa, Hare Kṛṣṇa, Kṛṣṇa Kṛṣṇa, Hare Hare, Hare Rāma, Hare Rāma, Rāma Rāma, Hare Hare. Hare is an address to Harā, another name for His eternal consort, Śrīmatī Rādhārāṇī. Kṛṣṇa, "the all attractive one," and Rāma, "the all-pleasing one," are names of God. The chanting of this *mantra* is the most recommended means for spiritual progress in this age of Kali, as it cleanses the mind of all impurities, and helps to understand one's true identity as an eternal spiritual being. Lord Caitanya personally designated it as the *mahā-mantra* and practically demonstrated the effects of the chanting.

Harināma-yajña—congregational chanting of the holy names of the Supreme Lord, the recommended sacrifice for this age.

Haṭha-yoga—the practice of postures and breathing exercises for achieving purification and sense control.

I

Itihāsa—a historical account.

J

Jīva-tattva—the living entities, atomic parts of the Supreme Lord.

Jñāna—knowledge. Material jñāna is limited to the material body and its expansions. Transcendental jñāna discriminates between matter and spirit. Perfect jñāna is knowledge of the body, the soul and the Supreme Lord.

Jñāna-kāṇḍa—One of the three divisions of the *Vedas*, which deals with empirical speculation in pursuit of truth; also such speculation itself; the portions of the *Vedas* containing knowledge of Brahman or spirit.

K

Kaivalya—the impersonal liberation of merging into the spiritual effulgence of Brahman emanating from the Lord.

Kali-yuga—the present age, the Age of Kalī, the Age of Quarrel and Hypocrisy. The fourth and last age in the cycle of a *mahā-yuga*. It began 5,000 years ago, and lasts for a total of 432,000 years. It is characterized by irreligious practice and stringent material miseries.

Kalpa—Brahmā's daytime which lasts 4,320,000,000 years.

Kāma—lust; the desire to gratify one's own senses; desire—especially material desire and sexual desire; lust, as opposed to prema, or love of God.

Kāmadhenu—spiritual cows of the spiritual world which yield unlimited quantities of milk. Also known as Surabhi cows.

Karatālas—hand cymbals used in *kīrtana*.

Karma—1. Material action performed according to scriptural regulations; 2. Action pertaining to the development of the material body; 3. Any material action which will incur a subsequent reaction and 4. The material reaction one incurs due to fruitive activities. The soul receives due reaction to work by taking his next birth in a lower species, or the human species, or a higher species. Or the soul may be liberated from birth and death altogether. All this depends upon whether the *karma* performed within this lifetime is ignorant, passionate, good or transcendental.

Karmī—a fruitive laborer, one who is attached to the fruits of work, a materialist who works hard to enjoy material life.

Kīrtana—glorification of the Supreme Lord; narrating or singing the glories of the Supreme Personality of Godhead and His Holy Names; the devotional process of chanting the names and glories of the Supreme Lord.

Kṛṣṇaloka—See: Goloka Vṛndāvana

Kṣatriya—second of the four social orders of the *varṇāśrama* system; a warrior who is inclined to fight and lead others; the administrative or protective occupation.

L

Lakṣmī—the goddess of fortune and the eternal consort of the Supreme Lord as Lord Nārayaṇa, who resides in the unlimited spiritual realm of Vaikuṇṭha.

Līlā-avatāras—innumerable incarnations, like Matsya, Kurma, Rāma and Nṛsiṁha, who descend to display the spiritual pastimes of the Personality of Godhead in the material world.

Loka—planet.

M

Mahāmantra—See: Hare Kṛṣṇa *mantra*

Mahā-ratha—a powerful warrior who can single-handedly fight against ten thousand others.

Mahājana—one of the twelve great self-realized souls, an authority in the science of Kṛṣṇa consciousness, who preaches the path of devotional service to the people in general; one who understands the Absolute Truth.

Mahat-tattva—the original, undifferentiated form of the total material energy, from which the material world is manifested when the three modes of material nature are activated by the glance of Mahā-Viṣṇu.

Mahātmā—a "great soul," an exalted devotee of Lord Kṛṣṇa, free from material contamination. He factually understands that Kṛṣṇa is everything, and therefore surrenders unto Him.

Mantra—A transcendental sound or Vedic hymn, a prayer or chant, a pure sound vibration when repeated over and over can deliver the mind from its material inclinations and illusion. The Vedic scriptures are composed of many thousands of *mantras*.

Mathurā—Lord Kṛṣṇa's abode, and birth place, surrounding Vṛndāvana. Lord Krsṇa displayed many of His pastimes here after leaving Vṛndāvana. At the end of Lord Kṛṣṇa's manifest *līlā*, Vajranābha, His grandson, was put in charge of this sacred city.

Māyā—Māyāvāda philosophy. Māyāvāda in Sanskrit means doctrine of illusion. In India, the philosophies of the Buddha and of Śaṅkarācārya are called Māyāvāda. The second grew out of the first. The fundamental principles accepted by both are the following: (1) name, form, individuality, thoughts, desires and words arise from *māyā* or illusion, not God; (2) *māyā* cannot be rationally explained, since the very idea that anything needs explaining is itself *māyā*; (3) the individual self or soul is not eternal, because upon liberation it ceases to exist; (4) like *māyā*, the state of liberation is beyond all explanation. The main difference between the two is that Śaṅkarācārya's Māyāvāda asserts that beyond *māyā* is an eternal impersonal monistic reality, Brahman, the nature of which is the self. Buddhism, however, aims at extinction (*nirodha*) as the final goal. Of the two, Śaṅkarācārya's Māyāvāda is more dangerous, as it apparently derives its authority from the *Vedas*. Much word-jugglery is employed to defend the Vedic origins of Śaṅkarācārya's Māyāvāda. But ultimately Māyāvādīs dispense with Vedic authority by concluding that the Supreme cannot be known through *śabda*, that the name of Kṛṣṇa is a material vibration, that the form of Kṛṣṇa is illusion, and so on. The Śaṅkarites agree with the Buddhists that *nāma-rūpa* (name and form) must always be *māyā*. Therefore Vaiṣṇavas reject both kinds of Māyāvāda as atheism. Buddhists generally do not deny that they are atheists, whereas the Śaṅkarite Māyāvādīs claim to be theists. But actually they are monists and pantheists. Their claim to theism is refuted by their belief that the Supreme Self is overcome by *māyā* and becomes the bound soul. Śaṅkarācārya's Māyāvāda is similar in significant ways to the Western doctrine of solipsism. Like solipsism, it arrives at a philosophical dead end. The questions that remain unanswered are: If my consciousness is the only reality, why can't I change the universe at will, simply by thought? And if my own self is the only reality, why am I dependent for my life, learning and happiness upon a world full of living entities that refuse to acknowledge this reality?

Māyā—illusion; an energy of Krṣna's which deludes the living entity into forgetfulness of the Supreme Lord. That which is not, unreality, deception, forgetfulness, material illusion. Under illusion a man thinks he can be happy in this temporary material world. The nature of the material world is that the more a man tries to exploit the material situation, the more he is bound by *māyā's* complexities; This is a Sanskrit term of many meanings. It may mean energy; *yoga-māyā* is the spiritual energy sustaining the transcendental manifestation of the spiritual Vaikuṇṭha world, while the reflection, *mahā-māyā*, is the energy of the material world. The Lord's twofold *māyā* bewilders the jīva, hence *māyā* also means bewilderment or illusion. Transcendental bewilderment is in love, by which the devotee sees God as his master, friend, dependent or amorous beloved. The material bewilderment of the living entity begins with his attraction to the glare of the brahmajyoti. That attraction leads to his entanglement in the modes of material nature. According to Bhaktisiddhānta Sarasvatī Ṭhākura, māyā also means that which can be measured. This is the feature of Lord Kṛṣṇa's *prakṛti* that captures the minds of scientific materialists. The Vaiṣṇava and Māyāvāda explanations of *māyā* are not the same.

Māyāvāda—the impersonal philosophy propounded by Śaṅkarācārya, which proposes the unqualified oneness of God and the living entities (who are both conceived of as being ultimately formless) and the non-reality of manifest nature; the philosophy that everything is one and that the Absolute Truth is not a person.

Mayāvādī—one who propounds the impersonal philosophy of Māyāvāda.

Mokṣa—liberation from material bondage.

Mṛdaṅga—a two-headed clay drum used for *kīrtana* performances and congregational chanting.

Muni—a sage or self-realized soul.

N

Nirguṇa—without material qualities; uncontaminated by the three modes of material nature.

Nivṛtti-mārga—the path of renunciation, which leads to liberation; directions for giving up the material world for higher spiritual understanding.

P

Pañcarātra—Vedic literatures such as *Nārada-pañcarātra* which describe the process of Deity worship.

Paṇḍita—a scholar learned in Vedic literature, not only academically but also by dint of spiritual realization. The term is also loosely applied to any scholar.

Parakīya—the relationship between a married woman and her paramour; particularly the relationship between the damsels of Vṛndāvana and Kṛṣṇa.

Paramahaṁsa—a topmost, God-realized, swanlike devotee of the Supreme Lord; the highest stage of *sannyāsa.*

Parameśvara—the supreme controller, Lord Kṛṣṇa.

Paramparā—the disciplic succession, beginning with Kṛṣṇa, through which spiritual knowledge is transmitted by bonafide spiritual masters; literally, one after the other.

Prāṇāyāma—breath control used in *yoga* practice, especially *aṣṭāṅga-yoga,* one of the eight parts of the *aṣṭanga-yoga* system.

Prasāda, prasādam—"the mercy of Lord Kṛṣṇa." Food spiritualized by being prepared for the pleasure of Kṛṣṇa, and by offering to Him with love and devotion. Ordinary food subjects one to karmic reactions, one of the reasons being the many living entities that gave up their lives during the preparation. But food offered to Kṛṣṇa is freed of sin and invokes an attraction to Him.

Pravṛtti-mārga—the path of sense enjoyment in accordance with Vedic regulations.

Purāṇas— Literally, very old; the eighteen major and eighteen minor ancient Vedic literatures compiled about five thousand years ago in India by Śrīla Vyāsadeva that are histories of this and other planets; literatures supplementary to the *Vedas,* discussing such topics as the creation of the universe, incarnations of the Supreme Lord and demigods, and the history of dynasties of saintly kings. The eighteen principal *Purāṇas* discuss ten primary subject matters: (1) the primary creation, (2) the secondary creation, (3) the planetary systems, (4) protection and maintenance by the avatāras, (5) the Manus. (6) dynasties of great kings, (7) noble character and activities of great kings, (8) dissolution of the universe and liberation of the living entity, (9) the jīva (the spirit soul), (10) the Supreme Lord.

Puruṣa-avatāras—the primary expansions of Lord Viṣṇu who effect the creation, maintenance and destruction of the material universes.

R

Rājarṣi—a great saintly king.

Rājasūya-yajña—an elaborate sacrifice that establishes who is the emperor of the world. It was performed by Mahārāja Yudhiṣṭhira before the Battle of Kurukṣetra and attended by Lord Kṛṣṇa.

Rāma-rājya—a perfect Vedic kingdom following the example of Lord

Rāmacandra, the incarnation of the Supreme Lord appearing as the perfect king.

Rāsa dance—Lord Kṛṣṇa's pleasure dance with the cowherd maidens of Vṛndāvana, Vrajabhūmi. It is a pure exchange of spiritual love between the Lord and His most advanced, confidential servitors.

Rāsa-līlā—See: Rāsa dance.

Ṛṣi—a sage who performs austerities.

S

Sac-cid-ānanda-vigraha—the Lord's transcendental form, which is eternal and full of knowledge and bliss; the eternal transcendental form of the living entity.

Sādhu—a saint or Krishna conscious devotee, a Vaiṣṇava. A wandering holy man; a saintly person, one of the three authorities for a Vaiṣṇava. See: *Guru*, *Śāstra*.

Śālagrāma-śilā—the worshipable Deity of the Lord Nārāyaṇa in the form of a round stone. It is described in detail in the final canto of the Padma Purāṇa.

Sampradāya—a disciplic succession of spiritual masters, along with the followers in that tradition, through which spiritual knowledge is transmitted; school of thought.

Saṁskāra—Vedic reformatory rituals performed one by one from the time of conception until death for purifying a human being.

Sanātana-dharma—literally, the "eternal activity of the soul", or the eternal religion of the living being, which is to render devotional service to the Supreme Lord; executed in this age chiefly by chanting the Hare Kṛṣṇa *mahā-mantra*.

Saṅkīrtana— congregational or public glorification of the Supreme Lord Kṛṣṇa through chanting of His holy names, and glorification of His fame and pastimes.

Sannyāsa—the renounced order, the fourth stage of Vedic spiritual life in the Vedic system of *varṇāsrama-dharma*, which is free from family relationships, and in which all activities are completely dedicated to Kṛṣṇa. It is the order of ascetics who travel and constantly preach the message of Godhead for the benefit of all. It is usually accepted at age fifty, after a man has fulfilled his household responsibilities.

Śāstra—the revealed scriptures, obeyed by all those who follow the Vedic teachings. Śās means "to regulate and direct" and tra means "an instrument"; Vedic literature; The Vedic scriptures; one of the three authorities for a Vaiṣṇava. In his purport to Cc., *Ādi-līlā* 17.157, Śrīla Prabhupāda writes: The word *śāstra* is derived from the dhātu, or verbal root, śas. *Sas-dhātu* pertains to controlling or ruling. A government's ruling through force or weapons is called *śastra*. Thus whenever there is ruling, either by weapons or by injunctions, the *śas-dhātu* is the basic principle. Between *śastra* (ruling through weapons) and *śāstra* (ruling through the injunctions of the scriptures), the better is *śāstra*. Our Vedic scriptures are not ordinary law books of human common sense; they are the statements of factually liberated persons unaffected by the imperfectness of the senses. *Śāstra* must be correct always, not sometimes correct and sometimes incorrect. In the Vedic scriptures, the cow is described as a mother. Therefore she is a mother for all time; it is not, as some rascals say, that in the Vedic age she was a mother but she is not in this age. If *śāstra* is an authority, the cow is a mother always; she was a mother in the Vedic age, and she is a mother in this age also. If one acts according to the injunctions of *śāstra*, he is freed from the reactions of sinful activity. For example, the propensities for eating flesh, drinking wine and enjoying sex life are all natural to the conditioned soul. The path of such enjoyment is called *pravṛtti-mārga*. The *śāstra* says, *pravṛttir eṣāṁ bhūtānāṁ nivṛttis tu mahā-phalā*: one should not be carried away by the propensities of defective conditioned life; one should be guided by the principles of the *śāstras*. A child's propensity is to play all day long, but it is the injunction of the *śāstras* that the parents should take care to educate him. The *śāstras* are there just to guide the activities of human society. But because people do not refer to the instructions of *śāstras*, which are free from defects and imperfections, they are therefore misguided by so-called educated teachers and leaders who are full of the deficiencies of conditioned life.

Sāyujya-mukti—the liberation of merging into the Brahman effulgence of the Lord.

Smṛti—remembrance, a vyabhicāri-bhāva; revealed scriptures supplementary to the *śruti,* or original Vedic scriptures, which are the *Vedas* and *Upaniṣads*; scriptures compiled by living entities under transcendental direction; the corollaries of the *Vedas*; one of the five functions of buddhi.

Soma-rasa—a life-extending heavenly beverage available on the moon to demigods on the higher planets.

Sravaṇam kīrtanaṁ viṣṇoḥ—the devotional process of hearing and chanting about Lord Viṣṇu, or Kṛṣṇa.

Śruti—knowledge via hearing; the original Vedic scriptures (the *Vedas* and

Upaniṣads), given directly by the Supreme Lord.

Śūdra—a member of the fourth social order, laborer class, in the traditional Vedic social system. They render service to the three higher classes, namely the *brāhmaṇas*, the *kṣatriyas*, and the *vaiśyas*.

Śūdrāṇī—the wife of a *śūdra*.

Surabhi cows—See: Kāmadhenu

Svāmī—See: Gosvāmī.

Svargaloka—the heavenly planets or abodes of the demigods in the material world.

Svayaṁvara—the ceremony in which a princess is allowed to choose her husband.

T

Tapasya—the voluntary acceptance of hardships for spiritual realization, such as rising early in the morning and taking a bath, fasting on certain days of the month etc.

Tilaka—sacred clay markings placed on the forehead and other parts of the body which designate one as a follower of Viṣṇu, Rāma, Śiva etc.

Tulasī—a pure devotee of Kṛṣṇa in the form of a basil plant, worshipped by Vaiṣṇavas and other followers of Vedic culture, and very dear to Lord Kṛṣṇa. Its leaves and mañjarīs (buds) are always offered to His lotus feet.

V

Vaikuṇṭha—the eternal planets of the spiritual world, the abode of Lord Nārāyaṇa, which lies beyond the coverings of the material universe. Literally, "the place with no anxiety."

Vaiṣṇava—a devotee of the Supreme Lord, Viṣṇu, or Kṛṣṇa.

Vaiśya—member of the mercantile or agricultural class, according to the system of four social orders and four spiritual orders.

Vānaprastha—A retired householder, a member of the third Vedic spiritual order or *āśrama*, who quits home to cultivate renunciation and travels to holy places, in preparation for the renounced order of life.

Varṇa—the four socio-occupational divisions of Vedic society. Contrary to popular misconception, *varṇas* are not fixed by birth, but are determined by a person's inclination toward different types of work and his psychological qualities. The four *varṇas* are *brāhmaṇas*, *kṣatriyas*, *vaiśyas* and *śūdras*. See: *Brāhmaṇa*, *Kṣatriya*, *Vaiśya* and *Śūdra*.

Varṇa-śaṅkara—children conceived without regard for Vedic religious principles; thus unwanted population.

Varṇāśrama-dharma—the system of four social and four spiritual orders of Vedic society, based on the individual's psycho-physical qualities and tendencies toward particular types of work.

Vedānta—Literally, the end of all knowledge, it is based on the philosophy of the *Vedānta Sūtra.* It is the conclusion of Vedic philosophy, and shows Kṛṣṇa as the goal of all philosophy. It is one the six systems of Vedic philosophy, and traditionally reserved for the *sannyāsīs* (renunciates).

Vedas—the original *Veda* was divided into four by Śrīla Vyāsadeva. The four original Vedic scriptures, *Saṁhitās* (*Ṛg, Sāma, Atharva* and *Yajur*) and the 108 *Upaniṣads, Mahābhārata, Vedānta-sūtra,* etc. The system of eternal wisdom compiled by Śrīla Vyāsadeva, the literary incarnation of the Supreme Lord, for the gradual upliftment of all mankind from the state of bondage to the state of liberation. The word *veda* literally means "knowledge", and thus in a wider sense it refers to the whole body of Indian Sanskrit religious literature that is in harmony with the philosophical conclusions found in the original four Vedic *Saṁhitās* and *Upaniṣads.* The message of the transcendental realm that has come down to this phenomenal world through the medium of sound is known as the *Veda.* Being the very words of Godhead Himself, the *Vedas* have existed from eternity. Lord Kṛṣṇa originally revealed the *Vedas* to Brahmā, the first soul to appear in the realm of physical nature, and by him they were subsequently made available to other souls through the channel of spiritual disciplic succession; *Veda, Vedas,* Vedic knowledge. The Sanskrit root of the word Veda is vid, knowledge. This root is widespread even in modern Western language: e.g. *video* (from the Latin word to see) and idea (Gr. *ida*). The term Vedic refers to the teachings of the Vedic literatures. From these literatures we learn that this universe, along with countless others, was produced from the breath of Mahā-Viṣṇu some 155,250,000,000,000 years ago. The Lord's divine breath simultaneously transmitted all the knowledge mankind requires to meet his material needs and revive his dormant God consciousness. This knowledge is called *Veda.* Caturmukha (four-faced) Brahmā, the first created being within this universe, received *Veda* from Viṣṇu. Brahmā, acting as an obedient servant of the Supreme Lord, populated the planetary systems with all species of life. He spoke four *Vedas,* one from each of his mouths, to guide human beings in their spiritual and material progress. The *Vedas* are thus traced to the very beginning of the cosmos. Some of the most basic Vedic teachings are: (1)

every living creature is an eternal soul covered by a material body; (2) as long as the souls are bewildered by *māyā* (the illusion of identifying the self with the body) they must reincarnate from body to body, life after life; (3) to accept a material body means to suffer the four-fold pangs of birth, old age, disease and death; (4) depending upon the quality of work (*karma*) in the human form, a soul may take its next birth in a subhuman species, or the human species, or a superhuman species, or it may be freed from birth and death altogether; (5) *karma* dedicated in sacrifice to Viṣṇu as directed by Vedic injunctions elevates and liberates the soul.

Virāṭ-rupa—the universal form of the Supreme Lord conceived as containing the totality of the entire material manifestation.

Viṣṇu—literally, the all-pervading God; the Supreme Personality of Godhead in His four-armed expansion in Vaikuṇṭha. A plenary expansion of the original Supreme Personality of Godhead, Śrī Kṛṣṇa, He supervises the maintenance of the created universe, and enters into the material universe before creation. He is worshiped by all the demigods and sages, and described throughout the *Vedas* as the summum bonum of all knowledge.

Viṣṇu tattva—a primary expansion of Kṛṣṇa having full status as Godhead. The term also applies to primary expansions of the Supreme Lord such as Rāma, Nṛsiṁha etc.

Vṛndāvana—Kṛṣṇa's eternal abode, where He fully manifests His quality of sweetness; the village on this earth in which He enacted His childhood pastimes five thousand years ago; the topmost transcendental abode of the Supreme Lord. It is His personal spiritual abode descended to the earthly plane. It is situated on the western bank of the river Yamunā.

Vyāsadeva—the literary incarnation of God, and the greatest philosopher of ancient times. The son of Parāśara Muni and Satyavatī-devī, he rendered the *Vedas* into written texts some 5000 years ago. He divided the *Veda* into four parts, the *Ṛg*, *Yajur*, *Sāma* and *Atharva Veda*, and also compiled the supplementary Vedic literature such as the eighteen *Purāṇas*, *Vedānta-sūtra*, and the *Mahābhārata*. He played a very important part in guiding the Pāṇḍavas during crucial times. He gave the vision of the battle of Kurukṣetra to Sañjaya so that he could relate it to Dhṛtarāṣṭra. He is still living in this world; he is also known as Vedavyāsa, Bādarāyaṇa and Dvaipāyana Vyāsa.

Y

Yajña—a Vedic sacrifice; also a name for the Supreme Lord meaning "the personification of sacrifice"; the goal and enjoyer of all sacrifices.

Yātrā—a journey.

Yoga-nidrā—mystic slumber of Mahā Viṣṇu during which the countless material universes emanate from Him, and are again absorbed into Him. The universes exist for one breath of the Lord.

Yogī—a transcendentalist who practices one of the many authorized forms of *yoga* or processes of spiritual purification; one who practices the eightfold mystic *yoga* process to gain mystic *siddhis* (powers), or to achieve Paramātmā realization.

Yuga-avatāra—an incarnation of the Lord in each millennium who prescribes the appropriate process of self-realization for that age.

Yuga—one of the four ages of the universe; they differ in length and rotate like calendar months.

Z

Zamindār—a wealthy landowner.

Sanskrit Pronunciation Guide

Throughout the centuries, the Sanskrit language has been written in a variety of alphabets. The mode of writing most widely used throughout India, however, is called *devanāgarī*, which means, literally, the writing used in "the cities of the demigods." The *devanāgarī* alphabet consists of forty-eight characters: thirteen vowels and thirty-five consonants. Ancient Sanskrit grammarians arranged this alphabet according to practical linguistic principles, and this order has been accepted by all Western scholars. The system of transliteration used in this book conforms to a system that scholars have accepted to indicate the pronunciation of each Sanskrit sound.

Vowels

अ a आ ā इ i ई ī उ u ऊ ū ऋ ṛ ॠ ṝ ऌ ḷ

ए e ऐ ai ओ o औ au

Consonants

Guttarals:	क ka	ख kha	ग ga	घ gha	ङ ṅa
Palatals:	च ca	छ cha	ज ja	झ jha	ञ ña
Cerebrals:	ट ṭa	ठ ṭha	ड ḍa	ढ ḍha	ण ṇa
Dentals:	त ta	थ tha	द da	ध dha	न na
Labials:	प pa	फ pha	ब ba	भ bha	म ma
Semivowels:	य ya	र ra	ल la	व va	
Sibilants:	श śa	ष ṣa	स sa		
Aspirate :	ह ha	Anusvāra : ं ṁ	Visarga : ः ḥ		

Numerals

०–0 १–1 २–2 ३–3 ४–4 ५–5 ६–6 ७–7 ८–8 ९–9

The vowels are written as follows after a consonant:

ा ā ि i ी ī ु u ू ū ृ ṛ ॄ ṝ े e ै ai ो o ौ au

For example : क ka का kā कि ki की kī कु ku कू kū
कृ kṛ कॄ kṝ के ke कै kai को ko कौ kau

Generally two or more consonants in conjunction are written together in a special form, as for example: **क्ष kṣa त्र tra**

The vowel "a" is implied after a consonant with no vowel symbol.

The symbol virāma (्) indicates that there is no final vowel: क्

The vowels are pronounced as follows:.

a — as in b**u**t
ā — as in f**a**r but held twice as long as **a**
ai — as in **ai**sle
au — as in h**ow**
e — as in th**ey**
i — as in p**i**n
ī — as in pique but held twice as long as **i**
ḷ — as in **lree**
o — as in **go**
ṛ — as in **ri**m
ṝ — as in **ree**d but held twice as long as **ṛ**
u — as in p**u**sh
ū — as in r**u**le but held twice as long as **u**

The consonants are pronounced as follows:

Gutterals
(pronounced from the throat)
k — as in **k**ite
kh — as in Ec**kh**art
g — as in **g**ive
gh — as in di**g-h**ard
ṅ — as in si**ng**

Cerebrals
(pronounced with the tip of the tongue against the roof of the mouth)
ṭ — as in **t**ub
ṭh — as in ligh**t-h**eart
ḍ — as in **d**ove
ḍh — as in re**d-h**ot
ṇ — as in si**ng**

Labials
(pronounced with the lips)
p — as in **p**ine
ph — as in u**p-h**ill
b — as in **b**ird
bh — as in ru**b-h**ard
m — as in **m**other

Palatals
(pronounced with the middle of the tongue against the palate)
c — as in **ch**air
ch — as in staun**ch-h**eart
j — as in **j**oy
jh — as in he**dgeh**og
ñ — as in ca**ny**on

Dentals
(pronounced like the cerebrals but with the tongue against the teeth)

t	—	as in **t**ub
th	—	as in ligh**t-h**eart
d	—	as in **d**ove
dh	—	as in re**d-h**ot
n	—	as in **n**ut

Semivowels

y	—	as in **y**es
r	—	as in **r**un
l	—	as in **l**ight
v	—	as in **v**ine, except when preceded in the same syllable by a consonant, then like in s**w**an

Sibilants

ś	—	as in the German word *sprechen*
ṣ	—	as in **sh**ine
s	—	as in **s**un

Aspirate

h	—	as in **h**ome

Anusvāra

ṁ	—	a resonant nasal sound as in the French word *bon*

Visarga

ḥ	—	a final **h**-sound: **aḥ** is pronounced like **aha**; **iḥ** like **ihi.**

There is no strong accentuation of syllables in Sanskrit, or pausing between words in a line, only a flowing of short and long syllables (the long twice as long as the short). A long syllable is one whose vowel is long (**ā, ai, au, e , ī, o, ṝ, ū**) or whose short vowel is followed by more than one consonant (including **ḥ** and **ṁ**). Aspirated consonants (consonants followed by an **h**) count as single consonants.

Index of Sanskrit Verses

This index constitutes a complete listing of the first and third lines of each of the Sanskrit poetry verses of this volume of *Śrīmad-Bhāgavatam,* arranged in English alphabetical order. The first column gives the Sanskrit transliteration; the second, the chapter-verse reference. Apostrophes are alphabetized as a's.

A

B

E

G

O

P

R

S

Y

Index Of Verses Quoted

This index lists the verses quoted in the purports of this volume of *Śrīmad-Bhāgavatam*. Numerals in boldface type refer to the first or third lines of verses quoted in full; numerals in roman type refer to partially quoted verses.

General Index

The references to the translations and purports of the verses of *Śrīmad-Bhāgavatam* are presented in the following format: "xx.yy (para n)", where 'xx' is the chapter number, 'yy' is the verse number (text number) and 'n' is the paragraph number in the purport. Numerals in the boldface type indicate the translations and those in regular type indicate the purports. Numerals in the mixed type indicate both translation and purports. While counting the paragraphs in the purports, please remember that, the new paragraph begins (in the purport) only where the first word is indented.

A

Abhijñaḥ, Lord as, 1.1 (para 9)
Abhimanyu
- Kurus killed, 15.16 (para 5)
- son of, **17.45**, **18.5**
- as Subhadrā's son, 10.7
- as Uttarā's husband, 8.10

Absolute Truth
- access to, devotion to Lord as, 2.12 (para 1)
- as aim of life, 1.10 (para 2), 2.13 (para 1), 2.14
- as all-knowing, (Intro, pg 2)
- aspects of
  - as qualitatively one, 2.11 (para 1)
  - three, **2.11**, 2.12 (para 1)
- as basis of reality, (Intro, pg 1)
- *Bhāgavatam* reveals, **1.1**, 1.2 (para 4, 6), 2.3 (para 3)
- "body" of, as everything, 1.1 (para 8)
- "cheating" in service of, 13.37
- defined, (Intro, pg 1)
- demons reject, 8.19
- dependency of all on, 1.1 (para 9)
- duality as absent in, **2.11**, 2.11 (para 2)
- energies of, 2.11 (para 2)
  - *See also:* Energies of Supreme Lord
- features of, three, 9.42 (para 2)
- as full of opulences, (Intro, pg 21)
- as goal
  - of all works, **2.10**
  - of *varṇāśrama*, 2.13 (para 1)
  - of Vedic literature, (Intro, pg 20)
- goodness as needed to know, **2.1**
- hearing about, proper conditions for, 1.13
- highest concept about, (Intro, pg 28-29), 5.8 (para 1)

Absolute Truth (*continued*)
- impersonal aspect of, 1.2 (para 4), 2.12 (para 1), 7.4
- impersonal conception about, (Intro, pg 20-21)
- knower & known identical in, 2.11 (para 2)
- Kṛṣṇa as, (Intro, 20, 31), 2.5 (para 1), 2.12 (para 1), 9.42 (para 1), 15.6, 16.31 (para 1), 17.20
- oneness & separateness of, with all, 1.1 (para 7)
- as *paraṁ satyam,* (Intro, pg 1)
- personal aspect of, (Intro, pg 2, 20), 1.1 (para 13), 1.2 (para 4), **2.11**, 2.12 (para 1), 5.8 (para 1), 7.4
- realization of, imperfect & perfect, 2.12 (para 1), 7.4
- relativity absent in, 2.11 (para 2)
- as reservoir of everything, (Intro, pg 2)
- sexual nature in, 1.1 (para 13)
- as skylike, 13.29
- as source of everything, (Intro, pg 1, 2)
- as substance of categories, 1.2 (para 4)
- as *summum bonum,* (Intro, pg 1)
- as ultimate source, (Intro, pg 1)
- as *varṇāśrama's* goal, 2.13 (para 1)
- *See also:* Kṛṣṇa; Supreme Lord

Ācārya(s). See: Spiritual master(s)
Ācārya Śaṅkara. *See:* Śaṅkara
Activities
- absolute, compared with mundane, 9.34 (para 5)
- birth & death caused via, 10.20 (para 1)
- body given according to, 12.12
- devotional service transforms, 8.42 (para 2)
- failure of, 13.2 (para 1)

Arjuna (*continued*)
- heavenly planets visited by, **15.12**, **15.13**
- historical accounts of, 12.21
- in "illusion," , **9.36**
- as indebted to Droṇācārya, 7.49
- Indra
  - conquered by, **15.8**
  - honored, 15.12 (para 2)
  - protected by, **15.13**
- Jarāsandha with, 18.28 (para 1)
- Jayadratha beheaded by, 15.16 (para 5)
- Karṇa killed by, 14.42 (para 2), 15.16 (para 2)
- as Karṇa's rival, 15.16 (para 2)
- Kṛṣṇa
  - charioteer of, 9.19, 9.33, 9.35 (para 1), **9.39**, 15.4, 15.14, **15.17**
  - chastised, 9.26 (para 3)
  - "defeated" by, **15.20**
  - friend of, **15.4**, 15.14, **15.18–20**, **15.28**, 15.30 (para 1)
  - illusioned, 18.24–25
  - in-law of, 15.4
  - instructed, 15.27 (para 1), **15.28–31**
  - as power source for, **15.5**, **15.7**, **15.13–15**, **15.21**
  - protected, 15.4, **15.16**, **15.17**
  - saved, **8.24**, 9.37, 14.42 (para 2)
- as Kṛṣṇa's friend, 7.41, 9.33, **9.34**, 11.39, **15.4**, 15.14, **15.18–20**, **15.28**, **15.30**
- as Kṛṣṇa's in-law, 15.4
- Kuntī mother of, 12.21 (para 2)
- Kurukṣetra war grieved, 13.16, 13.33
- as Lord's eternal companion, 14.1
- Lord's mercy on, 15.7, **15.12–16**, **15.17**
- Lord's mission executed by, 15.30 (para 2)
- Maya demon saved by, **15.8**
- military conquests by, 12.21 (para 3 to 7)
- military conquests of, 16.11
- Nivātakavaca killed by, **15.13**
- Pāṇḍu father of, 12.21 (para 2)
- parents of, 13.3–4 (para 2)
- Parīkṣit compared with, 16.11
- as protector, 14.41
- as pure devotee, 15.4, 15.17 (para 1)
- quoted. *See:* Arjuna quoted
- Śiva pleased by, **15.12**
- sons of, 12.21 (para 2)
- as Subhadrā's husband, 13.3–4 (para 5), 16.2 (para 1)
- Suśarmā killed by, **15.16**
- tested by Kṛṣṇa, 7.40 (para 2)
- as transcendental, **15.28–31**
- weapons awarded to, **15.12**
- weapons of, **9.15**, 12.21 (para 6)
- wives of, 12.21 (para 2)
  - *See also:* Draupadī; Subhadrā
- Yudhiṣṭhira questioned, **14.24–34**, **14.39–44**

Arjuna, Kārtavīrya, 12.21 (para 1)

Arjuna quoted
- on Kṛṣṇa, **15.5**, **15.6–8**, **15.9**, **15.10**, **15.12**, **15.13–16**, **15.17–20**, **15.21**, **15.24**, **15.27**
- on Lord's instructions, **15.27**
- on Lord's will, **15.24**
- on Yadu dynasty's death, **15.22–23**, **15.24–26**

Arka, 7.18

Arrow(s)
- Arjuna takes Duryodhana's, 9.37
- Bhīṣma's bed of, **9.1**, **9.25**
- as water drill, 15.17 (para 2)

Art, 5.22 (para 2)

Artha
- life beyond, 15.45
- *See also:* Economic development; Fruitive activity

Arthama, 9.6–7 (para 16)

Aryamā
- parents of, 13.15
- as Yamarāja's substitute, **13.15**

Āryan(s), 12.24 (para 3)
- as progressive people, 18.45 (para 2)

Āryāvarta, 15.44 (para 1)

Asamordhva, Lord as, 1.1 (para 10)

Āsana, 2.28–29 (para 2)
- as yogic process, 13.54

Ascetic(s)
- Gāndhāri as, **13.39**
- qualification for, **13.39**

Asita, 1.17 (para 1), 15.44 (para 2)
- historical accounts on, 9.6–7 (para 14)

Asita Devala, 19.9–10 (para 10)

Aśoka Mahārāja, 17.45

B

C

D

H

I

K

Karma-yoga, 2.15 (para 2), 5.34 (para 1)
See also: Devotional service
Karmī(s), 1.17 (para 1), 7.9
See also: Fruitive worker(s); Materialist(s)
Karṇa
Arjuna killed, 14.42 (para 2)
heritage of, 15.7, 15.16 (para 2)
historical accounts on, 15.16 (para 2)
as Kuntī's son, 13.3–4 (para 2)
as Kuru commander, 15.14, **15.15**
Kārtavīrya Arjuna, 12.21 (para 1)
Kaṣāya defined, 15.40
Kāśī (Vārāṇasī), 7.18
Kāśī, king of, 15.9 (para 1)
Kāśī Miśra, (Intro, pg 17)
Kaṣyapa Muni, 13.15
at Arjuna's birth ceremony, 12.21 (para 2)
at Bhīṣma's deathbed, **9.8**
Earth given to, 9.6–7 (para 8)
historical accounts on, 9.8 (para 2)
Kaṭha Upaniṣad cited on Kṛṣṇa, 10.13, 12.17
Kaṭha Upaniṣad quoted on Kṛṣṇa, 9.31
Kaumudī dictionary cited on Kṛṣṇa, 7.7 (para 3)
Kauśika, 9.6–7 (para 17)
Kauśika River, 18.36, 19.9–10 (para 5)
Kavi-karṇapūra, (Intro, pg 5)
Kayādhu, 12.25 (para 2)
Kazi, Maulana Chand, (Intro, pg 9-10)
Kelinda, 12.21 (para 5)
Keṇa Upaniṣad cited on demigods, 7.5 (para 2)
Keśava Bhāratī, (Intro, pg 14)
Keśava Kāśmīri, (Intro, pg 8-9)
Ketumāla, **16.12**, 16.12 (para 3)
Khāṇḍava forest, 12.21 (para 4)
destruction of, **15.8**
Killing. *See:* Animal(s), sacrifice of; Animal slaughter; Murder
Kimpuruṣa, **16.12**, 16.12 (para 8)
King(s)
association with, dangerous, 19.13
authorities followed by, 19.12
brāhmaṇas direct, 3.14, 3.20
capital punishment by, **7.37**
charity by, 16.3 (para 1)
defined, 13.18
duty of, 3.14, 4.12, 9.40 (para 1), 10.6, 10.26 (para 1), 12.4, 12.18, **17.10–11**, 17.14, **17.16**, 17.16 (para 2)
King(s) (*continued*)
fame of, 12.20 (para 1)
function of, 12.2, 12.4
of heaven. *See:* Indra
as human being number one, **18.41**, **18.42**
Kali dressed as, **16.4**
in Kali-yuga degraded, 15.38, 17.1
killing by, rules for, **7.36**
as Lord's representative, 16.4 (para 1), 18.41 (para 1), 18.43
must not offend *brāhmaṇas,* **7.48**
pious & impious, 8.32
prisoners freed by, analogy of, 7.5 (para 1)
prison visited by, analogy of, 2.28–29 (para 5)
prosperity under, 4.12
protection by, 9.27 (para 4), 10.6, 10.6, 12.20 (para 1), 14.41, 16.10, 17.10–11 (para 2)
qualification for, 8.41 (para 2), 9.26 (para 3), 9.27 (para 2), 9.36
qualities of, 18.41 (para 1), **18.42**, 18.43, **18.46**, 18.46
represent God, 4.12
sages avoid, 19.13, 19.32
society under, 15.38, 15.40, **18.41–44**
Śṛṅgi slandered, **18.34**, 18.34
time as, 13.18
true & false, 13.18
under Jarāsandha freed, **15.9**
Vedic, compared with modern, 16.1, 16.4 (para1), 16.4 (para 2), 17.13
viṣṇu-tattva worshiped by, 2.26 (para 4)
See also: Government(s), leader(s); *Kṣatriya(s); specific kings*
Kingdom of God. *See:* Goloka Vṛndāvana; Spiritual world
Kīrtana, 1.6
See also: Chanting holy name(s) of Lord; Glorification of Supreme Lord; *Saṅkīrtana*
Knowledge
absolute, Kṛṣṇa as, (Intro, pg 4)
age determined via, 19.26
all, in *Vedas,* 1.3 (para 2)
basis of, in serving Lord, 2.15 (para 2), **5.12**, 5.12, **5.35**, 7.8
Brahmā received, from Lord, **1.1**, 1.1 (para 9)

N

O

P

Parīkṣit Mahārāja (*continued*)
Samīka's meeting with, 18.24–25, 18.28 (para 2), 18.29, **18.30**, 18.31 (para 2), 18.50, 18.50
saṅkīrtana propagated by, 17.42 (para 2)
Śibi compared with, **12.20**
Śiva compared with, **12.23**
sons of, **16.2**
spiritual destination of, **19.21**
as *Śrīmad-Bhāgavatam* medium, 18.24–25
as *Śrīmad-Bhāgavatam's* hero, 12.12, 12.27
Subhadrā gladdened by, 13.3 (para 5)
Śukadeva honored by, **19.29**, **19.31**
as Śukadeva's disciple, **18.3**, 18.16 (para 1)
as surrendered soul, **18.2**, 18.28 (para 2), **19.15**, 19.15
as Viṣṇurāta, 19.29
wife of, 16.2 (para 1)
as world emperor, **16.4**, **16.12**, 16.12 (para 9), 17.36, **17.43–44**, **18.5**, 18.46
world peace under, **12.26**
at Yamunā River, 19.6
Yayāti compared with, **12.24**
Yudhiṣṭhira
compared with, **12.23**
enthroned, 15.38, 19.20 (para 2)
grandfather of, 19.20 (para 2)
Parīkṣit Mahārāja quoted
on animal beater, **17.4–6**
on bull of religion, **17.7**, **17.12**
on Kalī personified, **17.31**
on kings & sages, **19.13**
on religion personified, **17.22**
on sages, **19.23**
on sinful reaction, **19.2**
on Śukadeva, **19.32–40**
Parivrājakācāryas, 3.13, 4.13 (para 1), 6.13
See also: Devotee(s), as preachers; *Sannyāsa* order
Parvata Muni, historical accounts on, 9.6–7 (para 1)
Pārvatī, (Intro, pg 8)
Pāṣaṇḍī(s), 2.26 (para 2)
Passion, mode of
bondage to, 13.54
Brahmā as deity of, 2.23
compared to coal (firewood), **2.24**
devotion to Lord vs., **2.19**
Passion, mode of (*continued*)
elevation from, 2.24 (para 1)
human society in, 2.20 (para 1), 2.24 (para 3)
present population in, 15.12 (para 2)
Vedas unknowable in, 4.24
worship in, **2.27**
Passion. *See:* Lust; Passion, mode of
Pastime(s) of Kṛṣṇa. *See:* Kṛṣṇa, pastime(s) of
Pastime(s) of Supreme Lord. *See:* Supreme Lord, pastime(s) of
Patañjali, 1.7, 17.18 (para 1)
Pathans, (Intro, pg 34)
Patient's being restricted, analogy of, 5.15 (para 4)
Peace
via brahminical culture, 17.9
via cow protection, 17.9
formula for, 17.24, 19.3 (para 2)
glorification of God for, (Intro, pg 27), **1.16**
via Kṛṣṇa consciousness, 15.24
as lacking in this age, 1.4 (para 6), 1.16, 5.11 (para 1), 5.13 (para 2), 7.7 (para 3)
via pleasing Viṣṇu & devotees, 1.4 (para 3)
via saintly kings, 18.41 (para 1)
saṅkīrtana for, (Intro, pg 29)
in society, 17.14
via *Śrīmad-Bhāgavatam,* 17.24
Śrīmad-Bhāgavatam brings, 1.16, 5.39, 5.40 (para 3)
surrender to Lord for, 5.20 (para 3)
via working for Lord, 5.32
world
Parīkṣit's reign brought, **12.26**
via pious population, 12.12
via sacrifice, 12.34 (para 2)
via surrender to Kṛṣṇa, 11.34 (para 1)
Penance
by Hiraṇyakaśipu, 13.19 (para 2)
by Jayadratha, 15.16 (para 5)
by Kuntī, 13.3–4 (para 3)
by Satyabhāmā, 14.37 (para 1)
See also: Austerity; Repentance
People
great, bodily features of, 19.27
ominous signs in, **14.3–5**
See also: Human being(s); Living entities; Soul(s); *specific persons*

S

- Society, human (*continued*)
  - love of god hampered in, 7.7 (para 3)
  - marriage compulsory in, 17.38 (para 5)
  - materialistic, as child's play, 15.21
  - materialistic, as prison society, 14.34
  - modern, 10.4 (para 3), 11.12 (para 2), 11.12 (para 2)
    - as monkeys & dogs, **18.45**, 18.45 (para 2)
    - unclean, 19.13
  - necessities of, **10.4**, 10.4 (para 1), 11.12 (para 2), 11.12 (para 1)
  - ominous signs in, **14.5**, **14.19**
  - orders of
    - compared to body, 18.33
    - *See also: Varṇāśrama-dharma*
  - peace for, 17.14
  - perfection in, 5.22 (para 1)
  - perfection of, 8.37
  - pious population for, 12.12
  - prejudice in, 18.32
  - prosperity in, 8.21, 8.40, 8.40 (para), 15.38
  - prostitutes in, 11.19 (para 1)
  - protection in, 8.5 (para 7)
  - purpose of, 10.16 (para 2)
  - quarrel's causes in, 16.10
  - reformation of, 11.19 (para 4)
  - saintly kings ruled, 12.18
  - socialist, as artificial, 1.2 (para 3)
  - spiritualization of, 5.36 (para 3)
  - spiritual masters in, **1.4**, 1.4 (para 4), 1.9
  - spiritual remedy for, 17.38 (para 3), 17.42 (para 2)
  - *Śrīmad-Bhāgavatam* for, (Intro, pg 25-27), 1.16, 5.13 (para 2), 17.38 (para 6), 17.43–44
  - status changes in, 9.41 (para 2)
  - suffering in, 13.42, 14.10
  - transcendental sound reforms, 18.6
  - *varṇāśrama-dharma*
    - in, 19.9–10 (para 2)
    - needed in, 2.13 (para 1)
    - *See also: Varṇāśrama-dharma*
  - Vedic compared with modern, 10.5, 10.6, 12.18
  - Vedic knowledge in, 12.29 (para 1)
  - *vipras* in, 12.29 (para 2)
  - welfare of, 8.43
  - *See also:* Kali-yuga; *Varṇāśrama-dharma*
- Somadatta, 15.16 (para 3)
- Soma, Lord, 19.9–10 (para 8)
- *Soma-rasa,* 5.18
  - demigods drink, 15.34
- Soul(s)
  - activity of, adulterated by matter, 2.19 (para 2)
  - as antimaterial, 15.42
  - as basis of mind & body, 2.8 (para 2), 3.32 (para 1)
  - as beauty's basis, 10.16 (para 2)
  - beyond gross & subtle forms, **3.32**
  - blissful normally, 2.19 (para 1)
  - body covers, 8.26
  - as Brahman, 15.42
  - Caitanya's criterion based on, (Intro, pg 25)
  - compared
    - to bird in cage, 2.8 (para 2)
    - to bird in tree, 2.31
    - with Supersoul, 2.31
  - conditioned. *See:* Conditioned soul(s)
  - covered by body & mind, 2.8 (para 2), 3.33 (para 2)
  - equal to Lord at no time, 2.26 (para 2)
  - expanded from Lord, 2.28–29 (para 5), 5.8 (para 1)
  - forgetfulness of, in material condition, 2.31, 3.33 (para 2)
  - form of Lord goal of, 6.18 (para 2)
  - freedom for, 2.8 (para 3), 2.19 (para 1), 2.21 (para 1), 2.21 (para 3), 6.37, 8.41 (para 2), 15.31, 15.41
  - ignorance concerning, 2.8 (para 2), 2.21 (para 1)
  - as invisible, 3.31
  - knowledge of, as stage of God realization, 5.34 (para 2)
  - as master, 2.21 (para 1)
  - material elements cover, 15.27 (para 4), **15.42**
  - mind reflects, 15.41
  - misconceptions concerning, 2.8 (para 1), 2.21 (para 1)
  - as one with & different from Lord, 1.1 (para 7), 2.21 (para 1)
  - purification of, 15.31
  - *rasas* of, 1.3 (para 4)
    - *See also: Rasa(s)*

Śūdra(s), (*continued*)
- kings in Kali-yuga as, 17.1
- *kṣatriyas* above, 15.7
- marriage for, 14.42 (para 1)
- occupations among, 11.20 (para 1)
- *Pāñcarātrika* for, 12.13 (para 1)
- protection of, 9.26 (para 5)
- qualities of, 9.26 (para 5)
- Vidura as, 13.1, 15.49
- Yamarāja as, 13.1, **13.15**
- *See also: Varṇāśrama-dharma*

Suffering
- automatically comes, 5.18
- basis of, **7.5**
- *Bhagavad-gītā* relieves, 15.27 (para 4)
- birth as, 13.19 (para 2)
- body as, 13.17 (para 1), 13.23
- cause(s) of, 13.48, 13.53
  - ignorance as, 8.35 (para 1)
  - illusion as, 11.6
  - impious king as, 8.32
  - Kali-yuga government as, 17.5
- of devotees, 17.18 (para 2), 17.22, 18.31 (para 2)
- devotion to Lord relieves, **7.6**, **7.7**
- of Dharma bull, 17.18 (para 2), 17.22
- of Dhṛtarāṣṭra, 13.33
- as firelike, 14.11
- freedom from, 1.2 (para 6), **3.29**, 3.29, 5.32, **6.38**
- as God-given, 17.18 (para 2), 17.22
- of human beings, 10.2
- human life meant for ending, 1.10 (para 2)
- inescapable in this world, 5.18
- kinds of, three, 1.2 (para 6)
- king relieves, 17.10–11 (para 3)
- of Kuntī, **9.13**
- of living entities, 8.28, 8.28, 13.17 (para 1), 13.23
- Lord's mercy relieves, 14.11
- material life as, 13.23, 14.11, 19.20 (para 1)
- material nature as, 9.14
- material world as, 8.25 (para 3), 12.6 (para 2), 13.18, 13.19 (para 1), 13.23, 13.27
- modes of nature'produce, 14.11, 18.50
- by nature's law, 13.13
- nondivinity evidenced by, 7.5 (para 2)

Suffering (*continued*)
- old age as, 13.19 (para 1)
- of Pāṇḍavas, 9.16
- philosophies on, 17.18 (para 1), **17.18**, 17.19 (para 2), **17.20**
- *prasāda* relieves, 13.47 (para 1)
- as purification, 9.19
- relieved via Vedic literature, 5.13 (para 2)
- of religion personified, 17.18 (para 2)
- in society, 13.42, 14.10
- *Śrīmad-Bhāgavatam* mitigates, **1.2**, **5.40**, **7.6**, **7.7**, 7.7 (para 1), 7.8
- via time, 13.19 (para 1), 13.41 (para 2)
- in womb, 12.7

Sugar candy & jaundice, analogy of, 5.11 (para 2)

Sugriva, 12.19 (para 5)

Śukadeva Gosvāmī
- as alert against illusion, 4.4
- as *ātmārāma*, 7.9
- attracted to *Bhāgavatam*, 1.3 (para 8), **7.11**, 7.11 (para 2)
- attracted to Lord, 7.10 (para 12), 7.11 (para 2)
- beauty of, **19.26**
- as *Bhāgavatam* reciter, **1.3**, 1.3 (para 9), 3.41 (para 2), **3.44**, 4.7
- Brahman realization of, 7.11 (para 3)
- brahminism included in, 2.2 (para 3)
- chanting perfected by, 12.3
- compared to parrot, 1.3 (para 10)
- as devotee of Lord, 2.2 (para 3), 7.10 (para 12), **7.11**, 7.11 (para 3)
- devotees of Lord represent, 2.12 (para 2)
- in disciplic line for *Bhāgavatam*, 1.3 (para 11 & 12), 1.5 (para 1), 3.41 (para 2), **3.42**
- equal vision of, **4.5**
- as example to renounced order, 4.8
- hearing was seeing him, 4.6
- historical accounts on, **9.8**, 19.25
- householders visited by, 19.39
- as impersonalist turned devotee, 7.11 (para 3), 18.16 (para 1)
- innocence of, **4.5**
- inquiries on, by Śaunaka, **4.4**
- leaves home, **2.2**
- as liberated from birth, 2.2 (para 1), 7.11 (para 1)

T

U

W

Y